CRITICAL SURVEY
OF
LONG FICTION

CRITICAL SURVEY

OF

LONG FICTION

Second Revised Edition

Volume 7

Jesse Stuart - Émile Zola

Editor, Second Revised Edition
Carl Rollyson
Baruch College, City University of New York

Editor, First Edition, English and Foreign Language Series
Frank N. Magill

SALEM PRESS, INC.
Pasadena, California   Hackensack, New Jersey

Managing Editor: Christina J. Moose
Research Supervisor: Jeffry Jensen
Acquisitions Editor: Mark Rehn
Photograph Editor: Karrie Hyatt
Manuscript Editors: Lauren M. D'Andrea, Doug Long
Research Assistant: Jun Ohnuki
Production Editor: Cynthia Beres
Layout: William Zimmerman
Graphics: Yasmine Cordoba

Some of the essays in this work, which have been updated, originally appeared in the following Salem Press publications: *Critical Survey of Long Fiction, English Language Series, Revised Edition* (1991), *Critical Survey of Long Fiction, Foreign Language Series* (1984).

Library of Congress Cataloging-in-Publication Data

Critical survey of long fiction / editor, Carl Rollyson ; editor, English and foreign language series, Frank N. Magill.—2nd rev. ed.

p. cm.

"The current reference work both updates and substantially adds to the previous editions of the Critical sur- vey from which it is partially drawn: the Critical survey of long fiction. English language series, revised edition (1991) and the Critical survey of long fiction. Foreign language series (1984)"—Publisher's note.

Includes bibliographical references and index.

ISBN 0-89356-889-9 (v. 7 : alk. paper) — ISBN 0-89356-882-1 (set : alk. paper)

1. Fiction—History and criticism. 2. Fiction—Bio-bibliography—Dictionaries. I. Rollyson, Carl E. (Carl Edmund) II. Magill, Frank Northen, 1907-1997.

PN3451.C75 2000
809.3—dc21   00-020195

First Printing

CONTENTS

CRITICAL SURVEY
OF
LONG FICTION

JESSE STUART

Born: W-Hollow, Riverton, Kentucky; August 8, 1907
Died: Ironton, Ohio; February 17, 1984

PRINCIPAL LONG FICTION

Trees of Heaven, 1940
Taps for Private Tussie, 1943
Foretaste of Glory, 1946
Hie to the Hunters, 1950
The Good Spirit of Laurel Ridge, 1953
Daughter of the Legend, 1965
Mr. Gallion's School, 1967
The Land Beyond the River, 1973
Cradle of the Copperheads, 1988

OTHER LITERARY FORMS

Jesse Stuart initially gained prominence as a poet. His first collection, *Harvest of Youth* (1930), contained eighty-one poems, which are considered largely juvenilia. His second collection, *Man with a Bull-Tongue Plow* (1934), was composed of 703 poems written in sonnetlike forms (Stuart did not always hold strictly to the sonnet structure). The book was a popular and critical success and brought Stuart his first recognition. His next volume of poetry, *Album of Destiny* (1944), was less well received, although Stuart considered it his best. Subsequently, he published three other books of verse: *Kentucky Is My Land* (1952), *Hold April* (1962), and *The World of Jesse Stuart: Selected Poems* (1975).

Stuart was also a prolific short-story writer. From his more than three hundred published short stories, Stuart gathered several collections, including *Head o' W-Hollow* (1936), *Men of the Mountains* (1941), *Tales from the Plum Grove Hills* (1946), *Clearing in the Sky and Other Stories* (1950), *Plowshare in Heaven: Tales True and Tall from the Kentucky Hills* (1958), *Save Every Lamb* (1964), *My Land Has a Voice* (1966), and *The Best-Loved Short Stories of Jesse Stuart* (1982). "Huey the Engineer," a story first published in *Esquire* (August, 1937), was later printed in an anthology, *The Best Short Stories of*

1938. It is generally agreed that Stuart's best work has been in the short story.

Stuart's biographical and autobiographical writings, which are among his most important, include *Beyond Dark Hills* (1938), *The Thread That Runs So True* (1949), *The Year of My Rebirth* (1956), and *God's Oddling* (1960). In addition, he has written several books for children, including *The Beatinest Boy* (1953), *A Penny's Worth of Character* (1954), *Red Mule* (1955), *The Rightful Owner* (1960), and *Andy Finds a Way* (1961).

ACHIEVEMENTS

As a writer, Stuart was both a spokesman for and a popularizer of Appalachia, a region and people that have long bewildered and fascinated the rest of the nation. In some ways, Stuart was responsible for, if

(Library of Congress)

not creating, then strengthening and prolonging a number of the myths and stereotypes which have beleaguered this area, although Stuart insisted that he rarely exaggerated the truth. Stuart himself seems larger than life, and since so much of his fiction is heavily dependent on his own life, it is difficult to determine where the actual leaves off and the imaginative begins. There was Stuart as the mountain boy from a large, poor family, who worked his way through school fired by a need for knowledge; then, as an educator who returned to his region and almost single-handedly (and sometimes two-fistedly) brought learning into a backward land; and finally as an extremely successful writer who scribbled poems by the bushel while plowing fields, who produced novels in a few weeks' time, and who gained a reputation as a true primitive, a writer who created as a force of nature. Still, there is no denying the impressive scope of Stuart's achievements. A man of boundless energy and enthusiasm, he established himself as perhaps the foremost American regionalist writer of the twentieth century.

Stuart was labeled as an original from the time of his first important work, *Man with a Bull-Tongue Plow*, in 1934. He claimed to have written these poems primarily for his own pleasure, as reflections and observations on the world of nature in which he lived; but when they were published, their vitality, apparent artlessness, and obvious sincerity captivated a large section of the literary establishment and the reading public. Stuart, the writing mountain man, was called "a modern Robert Burns," the kind of easy pigeonholing which reveals a misunderstanding of both men. When Stuart followed the poems with a collection of stories (*Head o' W-Hollow*), a book of autobiography (*Beyond Dark Hills*), and an impressive novel (*Trees of Heaven*), he had declared himself a writer to be reckoned with. The recognition and awards came quickly. In 1934, he received the Jeannette Sewal Davis poetry prize of one hundred dollars for *Man with a Bull-Tongue Plow* (beating out such other contenders as Ezra Pound and William Carlos Williams). In 1937, he was awarded the John Simon Guggenheim Literary Award for his poetry and short stories. In 1941, he was given the Academy of Arts and Sciences Award for *Men of the Mountains*, his second short-story collection. In 1943, his second novel, *Taps for Private Tussie*, was chosen for the Thomas Jefferson Southern Award of $2500 as the best Southern novel of the year. *The Thread That Runs So True*, which detailed Stuart's experiences as a young teacher in a one-room schoolhouse, was selected by the National Educational Association as the "most important book of 1949" written on the subject of education (the president of the NEA, Jay Elmer Morgan, called it "the best book on education written in the last fifty years"). In 1954, Stuart was named poet laureate of Kentucky; in 1955, he was given the Centennial Award for Literature by Berea College. The recognition which meant the most to Stuart came in 1961, when the 1960 Fellowship of the Academy of American Poets was bestowed on him for "distinguished service to American poetry."

BIOGRAPHY

Hilton Jesse Stuart was born on August 8, 1907, in W-Hollow in Greenup County, a very mountainous and, at the time, relatively isolated section of Kentucky which Stuart would use as the locale for most of his writings. He was the first child of Mitchell and Martha Hilton Stuart; six other children followed, but two died in infancy from pneumonia. Stuart's father's family had lived in Kentucky for generations. They were a clannish people—"Tall Figures of the Earth," in Stuart's own words. His grandfather, Mitchell Stuart, had fought in the Civil War, and Stuart honored this individualistic and often cantankerous old man in one of his first poems, "Elegy for Mitch Stuart," published by H. L. Mencken in *The American Mercury* in 1934. Stuart's father was a quieter man than "Mitch" Stuart; he worked as a coal miner, railroad man, and farmer, and his influence on his son was immense. Stuart used him as the prototype for some of his most impressive characters, and described his relationship with his father in his autobiographical *Beyond Dark Hills* and in *God's Oddling*, a biography of his father. His mother's family came to Kentucky from North Carolina and were apparently more "cultured"; it was she who encouraged her son to read and first supported him in his continuing quest for education.

The Stuarts moved from farm to farm throughout W-Hollow when Jesse was a boy, a way of life which gave him a sympathy for the plight of the landless. When he was seventeen, Stuart's enthusiasm for learning earned him the position of teacher in a one-room school, two years before he was graduated from Greenup High School. Following graduation in 1926, Stuart left the mountains, working for a short time in a carnival; then undergoing military training at Camp Knox, Kentucky; and finally spending an unhappy period in the Ashland, Kentucky, steel mills. Later in 1926, he was accepted at Lincoln Memorial University (Harrogate, Tennessee), where he studied under Professor Harry Harrison Kroll, a published writer and one of Stuart's greatest influences. While at Lincoln Memorial, with Kroll's encouragement, Stuart began writing poems, some of which were published in the school newspaper. After being graduated in 1929, Stuart returned to the mountains and served a year as principal and teacher of Warnock High School. In 1930, his first book, *Harvest of Youth*, was privately published; Stuart dedicated it to Harry Harrison Kroll.

In September of 1931, Stuart entered Vanderbilt University to undertake a master's degree in English. There he met such beginning writers as Robert Penn Warren and John Crowe Ransom, and he studied under his most important mentor, Donald Davidson. Stuart's year at Vanderbilt was a time of trial. He was working part-time to support his studies, he was homesick for the mountains, and he was uncertain of his future. When he was assigned by Professor Edwin Mims to write an autobiographical paper, Stuart complied with a work of more than three hundred pages, which, when revised several years later, became *Beyond Dark Hills*. Mims was impressed by Stuart's talents, rough though they were, and further encouraged him to continue his writing. Still, the year was largely one of frustration, capped by a dormitory fire which destroyed most of Stuart's possessions and his nearly finished thesis on the writings of John Fox, Jr. Thus, Stuart left Vanderbilt without a degree, but with experience, inspiration, connections, and material which he would use in his later work.

In September of 1932, Stuart became superintendent of Greenup County schools, but after a year spent embroiled in political turmoil, resigned to become principal of McKell High School, where he incorporated many of his then-radical educational theories. While serving as principal of McKell, from 1933 to 1937, he published *Man with a Bull-Tongue Plow* and *Head o' W-Hollow*. He also began to lecture throughout the country on matters of education and literature. In 1937, Stuart received a Guggenheim Fellowship and traveled to Scotland after obtaining a year's leave of absence from McKell, but when he returned in April of 1938, he found that a new administration had reneged on the agreement. Following another year's teaching in Ohio (just across the state line), while continuing his fight with the Kentucky school authorities (during which time his life was threatened and he was once actually beaten by an assailant), Stuart quit teaching in disgust and returned to farming. On October 14, 1939, he married Naomi Deane Norris; their only child, Jessica Jane, was born in 1942.

Stuart wrote about many of these experiences in two of his major books, *Beyond Dark Hills* and *The Thread That Runs So True*. After his retirement from teaching, he devoted a greater part of his time to his career as a writer and lecturer. His first novel, *Trees of Heaven*, appeared in 1940; his second, *Taps for Private Tussie*, in 1943, proved his greatest success, financially and critically, and was a main selection of the Book of the Month Club. From 1944 to 1945, Stuart served in the United States Naval Reserves, but continued to write. In 1954, he suffered a near-fatal heart attack after one of his many lectures and was left practically helpless for a year. Stuart described the experience in his "journal," *The Year of My Rebirth*. In 1956, he again returned to the field of education, serving as principal once more at McKell High School for the year, a time he discussed in a late novel, *Mr. Gallion's School*. In 1960-1961, he taught at the American University in Cairo, Egypt, in part because of his desire to challenge the spread of communism in this region. In 1962-1963, he undertook a seven-month lecture tour overseas for the State Department for the same reasons. In 1966, Stuart became writer-in-residence at Eastern Kentucky University. Stuart spent his last years in W-Hollow. He died in Ironton, Ohio, in February, 1984.

ANALYSIS

Jesse Stuart's works are a part of the rich literary heritage drawn from the people and traditions of the Appalachian Mountains. He is grouped with such writers as George Washington Harris, Mary Noailles Murfree, John Fox, Jr., Elizabeth Madox Roberts, James Still, Wilma Dykeman, and Harriette Arnow as creators (and sometimes debunkers) of one of America's most lasting stereotypes, the Southern "hillbilly." Of these writers, Stuart surely stands at the head, for he has captured the imagination and sympathy of the reading public as has none of the rest.

There are several reasons for Stuart's abiding popularity. His writings are, for the most part, easily accessible. His main interest is in telling a story or relating an emotion, and he does so with simplicity of style and directness of approach. Indeed, Stuart's works are rarely overtly analytical; his characters are not introspective, which has led to charges of an anti-intellectual strain in his writings. Certainly, Stuart does tend to answer complex problems with easy solutions: if a person is determined, brave, and honest, Stuart suggests, the greatest challenge will be overcome. His autobiographical works especially emphasize this idea, and, in truth, such solutions seem to have been borne out in Stuart's own life.

Stuart also has proven popular because of the uniqueness and inherent romance of his material. As Stuart presents them, his characters are a primitive people, in some ways unspoiled by the corruptions of the outside society, but often in need of the civilizing influences that such a society can offer through education. Thus, some of these people, such as Theopolis Akers in *The Good Spirit of Laurel Ridge*, glory in their separation from the rest of the world, while others, like so many of the Tussie clan, are desperately in need of some edifying influence. Because these characters are drawn in broad strokes and are easily labeled as "good" or "bad" (perhaps "worthy" or "worthless" would be more appropriate terms), they exist more as character types, clothed in the charm of dialect and locale, than as real, breathing people. Still, Stuart is capable of surprising subtlety in his work, a quality often overlooked by some of his critics. He can force his readers to question their initial judgments of such characters as Anse Bushman in *Trees of Heaven*, Grandpa Tussie in *Taps for Private Tussie*, and even Theopolis Akers in *The Good Spirit of Laurel Ridge*.

The land plays an all-important role in Stuart's works. He attended Vanderbilt University at the time of the Agrarian-Fugitive Movement (*I'll Take My Stand* was published by Twelve Southerners in 1930, the year before Stuart arrived), and he came into contact with a number of its leaders, but Stuart never became a disciple himself. Although he agreed with many of the ideas of the movement, Stuart felt that "their farming was on paper," whereas he had farmed in order to eat. His writings, however, always reflect the importance of place in a person's life, and *Man with a Bull-Tongue Plow* is essentially a celebration of the land and one's relationship with it. He clearly admired characters such as Theopolis Akers, Deutsia Huntoon in *Daughter of the Legend*, and Tarvin Bushman in *Trees of Heaven*, who live in harmony with nature and draw their strength and their morality from the world-spirit. In Stuart's work, nature can be dangerous to the unwary, but it offers peace and wisdom to those who approach it with respect.

Perhaps Stuart's greatest strength as a writer is his fine sense of the comic. He has been linked to such humorists as A. B. Longstreet, G. W. Harris, Mark Twain, Erskine Caldwell, and William Faulkner, and rightfully so. His most serious books, such as *Mr. Gallion's School*, are among his weakest, while *Taps for Private Tussie*, his comic masterpiece, continues to delight. Stuart's humor is basically good-natured. He laughs at people's foibles, enjoys their foolishness, and shakes his head at absurdities. He rarely condemns. Even in a satirical work such as Foretaste of Glory, in which he recounts the many hypocrisies to which people are given, Stuart deals gently with his characters. His comedy derives from the tall-tale tradition and is at its best when it ventures into that region wherein the absurd and the tragic coexist.

Although Stuart achieved honor and success in almost every form of literature, he was most effective in the short story. Despite his early fame as a poet, his verse has never received the attention it warrants. His novels generally are loosely structured; they tend to be episodic and uneven as he moves from one event to the next. His plots also rely heavily on convention or cliché. Still, in his large body of writing, Stuart created a unique fictional world, peopled with characters recognizably his own. It is a world that is likely to last.

TREES OF HEAVEN

Stuart wrote *Trees of Heaven* in 1939 after returning from Europe. He married Naomi Deane Norris while writing the book, and their romance is reflected in the love story of Tarvin Bushman and Subrinea Tussie. *Trees of Heaven* is a big, rambling book, less a well-constructed novel than a conglomeration of facts, observations, tales, and characterizations built around a very simple plot. Anse Bushman is a prominent landowner and farmer, one who takes great pride in the quality of his work and the number of his possessions. Boliver Tussie is a squatter who lives on the land that Anse owns. The two men are antithetical to each other. Anse works—and drives others to work— to such a degree that labor and ownership have become obsessions to him. Boliver opts for a more relaxed, indeed, indolent approach to life, unburdened by responsibility. The conflict arises when Tarvin Bushman, the only child still living with Anse, falls in love with Subrinea Tussie, Boliver's beautiful daughter. Through Tarvin's intervention, Anse agrees to take on the Tussies as sharecroppers, although he first compels Boliver to sign a contract specifying what he can and cannot do while living on Anse's land. The contract is an attempt to control not only the Tussies' work habits but their moral and social behavior as well. Although Boliver is offended by some of these demands, he is in no position to argue with Anse; thus, he agrees to stop drinking, to avoid dancing, and to abstain from fathering any more children until the harvest is over. Two such differing lifestyles cannot coexist peacefully, and when Anse becomes suspicious of his son's relationship with Subrinea and becomes convinced that the Tussies are taking advantage of his generosity, he evicts the family and takes their crops. After an accident, however—Anse is almost killed by a falling tree limb— he becomes a wiser, more tolerant man. Tarvin and Subrinea (who is already pregnant) marry, and, as the book ends, they are going to bring back the Tussies to work the land once again.

Although Anse Bushman is the central character of this novel and the one for whom the reader has the most sympathy and respect, he is by no means an entirely admirable character. His emphasis on work has driven away his other children, and his wife, Fronnie, has succumbed to premature aging. Indeed, toward the end of the book, she is clearly teetering on the edge of madness, haunted by nightmares of Anse's spiritual damnation and fearful that Tarvin will be caught up by his father's obsessions. Anse is a dictatorial old man who cannot balance his love of family with his greed for land. Still, Stuart does not present him as a villain; the reader can understand Anse and generally sides with him in his struggle against the Tussies. At the same time, the Tussies are more likable than one might expect. Their shiftlessness is a relief from Anse's discipline, but they are quite capable of hard work when the occasion demands and show a true love of the land on which they have lived for generations. In fact, Boliver Tussie is a farmer equal to Anse Bushman, although he is usually careless and negligent. The Tussies are a convincing thorn in Anse's side, but he is wrong in his attempt to impose his lifestyle on them.

It is difficult to label *Trees of Heaven* as either a Romantic or realistic novel, for it contains elements of each. The love story between Tarvin and Subrinea is idyllic and is the weakest part of the novel, while Stuart's detailed and factual discussions of farming and sheep raising interfere with the progress of the plot. The description of the Tussies and their kind— families that have become inbred over the years and that are capable of viciousness and violence— is sometimes at odds with their basically comic role in the book. The threat of bloodshed runs throughout the story, but it is generally averted through the author's manipulations.

Trees of Heaven is narrated in the present tense and is structured around the change of the seasons.

Both devices give it a sense of timelessness, as if the characters, the place, and the actions were occurring in the present in their own world. The use of present tense sometimes leads to repetition and oversimplification, however, and its effectiveness is not sustained throughout the book. Still, *Trees of Heaven* is an impressive first novel, a work of considerable art and scope.

TAPS FOR PRIVATE TUSSIE

Stuart's second novel, *Taps for Private Tussie*, is generally considered to be his best. Certainly it is his most successful comic work, although the tale it tells is marked by numerous tragic events. Indeed, Stuart claimed that he wrote the story as a "sad thing" and was surprised that others laughed at the antics it described. The book is more carefully constructed than *Trees of Heaven* and is effectively held together through the use of a first-person narrator, a young boy who tells the story with an appealing mixture of naïveté and native wisdom.

Private Kim Tussie is reported killed in action during World War II, and his family sets about burying the returned body. Like the Tussies in *Trees of Heaven*, this branch of the family is also made up of squatters. At the beginning of the book, they are living in a schoolhouse abandoned for the summer. The immediate family is composed of Kim's parents, Grandpa and Grandma Tussie, his wife, Vittie, his unmarried brother, Mott, and the boy-narrator, Sid. When Vittie collects Kim's ten-thousand-dollar insurance policy, the Tussies are able to fulfill their long-held dreams, First, they move from the schoolhouse (from which they are being evicted) to a "mansion," a fourteen-room house on the outskirts of town. Then they buy furniture for each of the rooms to replace that which has been destroyed on leaving the schoolhouse. Soon, as Grandma has predicted, other Tussies begin to arrive, hoping to benefit from Grandpa's "good fortune." The first of these is Uncle George, Grandpa's brother, who has been married five times. Others follow until finally there are forty-six Tussies living in the house. George and Mott have, by this time, begun vying for the attentions of Aunt Vittie, and as George grows more successful, Mott turns increasingly to drink.

After a period of communal living, the Tussies are again turned out of their home, which they have destroyed through their careless behavior, because Grandpa has lost his relief benefits, upon which they had depended. With the last of the insurance money, Grandpa buys a small piece of land, and the family moves into a run-down shack for the winter. Uncle George marries Vittie; Sid is forced to begin school; and Mott sinks into dissipation. Grandpa learns the pride of ownership and plans to farm the following spring, while Sid discovers the joy of education and begins to consider his future, but these plans are upset when Mott kills two of his cousins while drunk and is himself killed by Uncle George. Grandpa then prepares for his own approaching death and confines himself to bed, awaiting the end. At this point, hope returns with the appearance of Kim himself, who was not killed after all, and who stands ready to take Grandpa's place as the head of the remaining group. Uncle George is tracked down by a posse, Sid learns that Vittie is his mother, and the novel ends with a mixture of death and regeneration.

Taps for Private Tussie is an extremely enjoyable book. Grandpa Tussie is one of Stuart's most successful and memorable characters, a good and loving man despite his weaknesses. Sid Tussie comes from a long line of boy-narrators in American literature, including, most obviously, Huckleberry Finn, but also those boys in the works of Sherwood Anderson, William Faulkner, and Erskine Caldwell. Once again Stuart displays his sympathies for a basically unsympathetic group of people. Stuart distinguishes Sid from the Tussies through the revelation that he does not have Tussie blood and is therefore "superior" (he is smarter and more ambitious than the average Tussie). The book acts as a satire on the welfare system: Grandpa Tussie has so long depended on his relief check that he has forgotten the satisfaction of self-sufficiency; when he rediscovers it in the land, it is too late. Stuart often shows people at their worst—fawning, lying, killing—but *Taps for Private Tussie* finally offers hope of renewal. The Kim who left for war was, as Sid remembers, a vicious and hateful man; the one who returns has been reborn and shows the boy kindness and understanding. Grandpa must die, but Sid will begin to live with a new sense of self.

FORETASTE OF GLORY

Foretaste of Glory was begun while Stuart served in the Navy during World War II and was developed from stories he remembered and told about his home. It was not published until 1946, and it was poorly received by the people in Greenup County, Kentucky, who took the book as an affront. It recounts the events of one night—September 18, 1941—in Blakesburg, Kentucky, when the night sky is set ablaze by the uncommon appearance of the aurora borealis. Most of the townspeople are convinced that the display prefigures the end of the world, the Second Coming. Stuart examines the reactions of selected characters when faced with their apparent Day of Judgment. The book is constructed in an episodic manner, although some characters do appear in more than one episode, and certain ideas are repeated as Stuart mocks social distinctions, political alliances (as in *Taps for Private Tussie*), and basic hypocrisies. Stuart was attempting in this work to capture an overall sense of the community, in much the same manner as Sherwood Anderson did in *Winesburg, Ohio* (1919). The book is a satire, for most of the characters reveal their deceits and admit their sins as they await the arrival of the Lord, but the tone is not malicious. The author is more understanding and amused than cruel or vindictive. Although the book has been highly praised by some readers, its very concept finally limits its effectiveness. The narratives become redundant, the episodes are uneven, and the excitement is simply not sustained.

THE GOOD SPIRIT OF LAUREL RIDGE

Although Stuart considered *The Good Spirit of Laurel Ridge* the best novel he had written, it is a flawed work. Its plot and too many of its characters are unconvincing, although many readers have been charmed by its view of natural people in the natural world. The story is insubstantial. Theopolis Akers has lived all of his life on Laurel Ridge. His wife is dead; his daughter, Lucretia, was taken away from him when she was a child because of his drinking; and his simpleminded son, Jack, roams the land and appears only in the spring to see the butterflies. As the book begins, Op has undergone a cataract operation, and Lucretia has come to live with him as he regains his sight. Although the operation is successful, she decides to stay in the mountains with her father. A pretty girl, she is soon being courted by a local mountain swain, Hootbird Hammertight, but she is more interested in a mysterious stranger who is hiding out in the hills, a figure Op declares to be the ghost of Ted Newsome, a young man murdered for love many years ago. Op is convinced that spirits—both good and bad—inhabit this area of the mountains, and in his tales and memories he insists on the otherworldliness of Laurel Ridge.

Op's way of life has been disturbed by Lucretia's arrival, although her father comes to accept her. When, however, in a completely unrealistic plot contrivance, two other relatives—Alfred and Julia Pruitt, Lucretia's city cousins—arrive, Op finds himself pushed to the limits. Alf Pruitt is set up as a foil to Op, his city ways and suburban dread placed in stark contrast to Op's natural acceptance of life. Alf most fears the atom bomb, but modern civilization in general has driven him to distraction. Through Op's influence and in a series of mildly comic adventures, Alf learns the importance of nature, but he remains a nervous, essentially unhappy man. Finally, it is revealed that the ghost "Ted Newsome" is really a soldier Lucretia had known in the city. He is AWOL because he mistakenly believes that he has killed a man in a fight, and both he and Lucretia have come to Laurel Ridge to escape. When the military police track him down, just as he is about to be hanged by a group of angry mountaineers, the officer explains that the soldier has killed no one and that he can make amends with a brief prison sentence. Thus, he and Lucretia return to the city. Alfred and Julia also return, having benefited from their stay in the hills, although ultimately unable to adapt to such a rough way of life. Op is again left alone, a man at peace with himself.

The Good Spirit of Laurel Ridge is filled with the folklore of the hills, and Op Akers is a good storyteller and describer of these tales and customs. The plot, however, is so conventional and the ending such a cliché that the book's potential charm is never fully realized. Stuart's satire on the modern world, exemplified in Alf Pruitt, is much too heavy-handed and obvious to work for long. Despite its popularity, *The Good Spirit of Laurel Ridge* is not one of Stuart's better works.

DAUGHTER OF THE LEGEND

Generally considered Stuart's weakest novel, *Daughter of the Legend* in fact contains some of his best writing. Again, the plot of the novel is slight. The narrator, Dave Stoneking, a lumberjack, tells of his tragic love for Deutsia Huntoon, a Melungeon living in the mountains of eastern Tennessee. After a courtship in which Deutsia introduces Dave to a finer appreciation of nature than he has so far held, they are married and enjoy an idyllic winter together. In the spring, however, Deutsia dies in childbirth, and Dave leaves the land of the Melungeons a rather bitter man. The book is notable for two reasons. First, in his discussion of the Melungeon people, Stuart calls for racial compassion and understanding. The Melungeons are people of mixed heritage, and when Dave marries into their race, he suffers the discriminations they have long felt. His attempts to rectify these injustices give the book a contemporary social awareness missing from many other works by Stuart. In addition, *Daughter of the Legend* includes one of Stuart's finest comic episodes in the chapter dealing with the death and burial of Sylvania, a six-hundred-pound seller of moonshine. Although Stuart had written this tale as a short story years before, it fits smoothly into the novel and presents an ironic counterpoint to the more sentimental death of Deutsia.

MR. GALLION'S SCHOOL

Mr. Gallion's School is a semifictional account of Stuart's experiences as principal of McKell High School, to which he returned in 1956 following his heart attack. George Gallion is a thinly disguised version of Stuart himself. Against great odds, Mr. Gallion attempts to restore order and a sense of worth to the school. He must fight not only the defeatist attitudes of the students and teachers but also a corrupt and ineffectual political system which uses the schools as pawns in its power game. That Mr. Gallion succeeds so completely in his fight illustrates the weaknesses of the book. On a strictly realistic level, Stuart oversimplifies both the problems and the solutions. Indeed, the book often becomes a treatise on the author's theories of education. While *Mr. Gallion's School* holds the reader's attention, it is by no means one of Stuart's best novels.

Although Jesse Stuart has been the subject of numerous studies, he has never been accorded the kind of intensive scholarly study one might expect. This is caused, no doubt, by his reputation as a "popular" writer. His often romantic and sentimental picture of the Appalachian Mountains has come under attack in the past few decades, especially by many of the younger writers and critics from the area, who see Stuart as having helped to create the misleading and often condescending image of the mountaineer. Stuart's skills as a writer were considerable, however, and among his many publications are works which will continue to be read and admired.

Edwin T. Arnold III

OTHER MAJOR WORKS

SHORT FICTION: *Head o' W-Hollow*, 1936; *Men of the Mountains*, 1941; *Tales from the Plum Grove Hills*, 1946; *Clearing in the Sky and Other Stories*, 1950; *Plowshare in Heaven: Tales True and Tall from the Kentucky Hills*, 1958; *Save Every Lamb*, 1964; *My Land Has a Voice*, 1966; *Come Gentle Spring*, 1969; *Come Back to the Farm*, 1971; *Votes Before Breakfast*, 1974; *The Best-Loved Short Stories of Jesse Stuart*, 1982.

POETRY: *Harvest of Youth*, 1930; *Man with a Bull-Tongue Plow*, 1934; *Album of Destiny*, 1944; *Kentucky Is My Land*, 1952; *Hold April*, 1962; *The World of Jesse Stuart: Selected Poems*, 1975.

NONFICTION: *Beyond Dark Hills*, 1938; *The Thread That Runs So True*, 1949; *The Year of My Rebirth*, 1956; *God's Oddling*, 1960; *To Teach, To Love*, 1970; *My World*, 1975; *The Kingdom Within: A Spiritual Autobiography*, 1979; *Lost Sandstones and Lonely Skies and Other Essays*, 1979; *If I Were Seventeen Again and Other Essays*, 1980.

CHILDREN'S LITERATURE: *Mongrel Mettle: The Autobiography of a Dog*, 1944; *The Beatinest Boy*, 1953; *A Penny's Worth of Character*, 1954; *Red Mule*, 1955; *The Rightful Owner*, 1960; *Andy Finds a Way*, 1961.

BIBLIOGRAPHY

Blair, Everetta Love. *Jesse Stuart: His Life and Works*. Columbia: University of South Carolina Press, 1967. An early, full-length study of Stuart's work, somewhat limited in discussing his poetry but more satisfying in dealing with his fiction and autobiography, both of which have had larger audiences in the years since World War II. Contains a helpful index and a selected bibliography, both of value to high school and college students.

Bogart, Max. *A Jesse Stuart Reader*. New York: McGraw-Hill, 1963. Offers a good sample of Stuart's major work: stories, biography, and poetry. Aimed at the young person who might want help in reading Stuart, containing a foreword as well as commentary and study questions at the end, designed to stimulate thought and suggest writing topics. Although an older text, it is still readable and relevant.

Foster, Ruel E. *Jesse Stuart*. New York: Twayne, 1968. This excellent volume concentrates on Stuart as an imaginative writer who has created a "fictional place," as William Faulkner did. Puts into perspective both Stuart's primitivism and his anti-intellectualism and attempts to assess his place in American letters. Calls him a poet of a "vanished way of life" and genuinely folkloric, but not "synthetically folksy." Stuart emerges as a figure in the tradition of Walt Whitman and Edgar Lee Masters: energetic, democratic, and committed to his art.

LeMaster, J. R. *Jesse Stuart: Kentucky's Chronicler-Poet*. Memphis, Tenn.: Memphis State University Press, 1980. This full-length book concentrates on Stuart as a poet, although he has more often been admired as a popular writer for his prose. LeMaster's definition of poet is an inclusive one, however, meaning more nearly a *Dichter* (a writer of fiction) than a versifier. Stuart has an ear for sounds and an eye for images, and ballads and stories are an essential ingredient of his art. Helpful index is provided.

Richardson, H. Edward. *Jesse: The Biography of an American Writer*. New York: McGraw-Hill, 1984. While this study is chiefly a full-length portrait of an American regionalist and educator, it is objective, as well as appreciative and tolerant. More than five hundred pages long, containing sixteen pages of photographs, a bibliography of Stuart's sixty-one published works, and a select bibliography of secondary sources.

Thompson, Edgar H. "A Cure for the Malaise of the Dislocated Southerner: The Writing of Jesse Stuart." *Journal of the Appalachian Studies Association* 3 (1991): 146-151. A good survey of Stuart emphasizing his regional heritage.

THEODORE STURGEON
Edward Hamilton Waldo

Born: Staten Island, New York; February 26, 1918
Died: Eugene, Oregon; May 8, 1985

PRINCIPAL LONG FICTION

The Dreaming Jewels, 1950 (also known as *The Synthetic Man*, 1957)
More Than Human, 1953
I, Libertine, 1956 (as Frederick R. Ewing, with Jean Shepherd)
The Cosmic Rape, 1958
Venus Plus X, 1960
Some of Your Blood, 1961
Voyage to the Bottom of the Sea, 1961
Alien Cargo, 1984
Godbody, 1986

OTHER LITERARY FORMS

While Theodore Sturgeon was not as prolific as some of the science-fiction fraternity, he wrote more than 190 short stories, 130 articles, and a number of radio and television scripts. His short fiction was assembled in many collections, ranging from *Without Sorcery* (1948) to *The Golden Helix* (1980).

ACHIEVEMENTS

Theodore Sturgeon's work was once called "the single most important body of science fiction by an American to date." A founder of modern American science fiction, he contributed to the genre's transition from underground to mainstream literature. He was the recipient of Argosy (1947), International Fantasy (1954), Nebula (1970), and Hugo (1971) awards.

BIOGRAPHY

Theodore Sturgeon was born Edward Hamilton Waldo, on February 26, 1918, on Staten Island, New York. His parents were divorced, and, after his mother remarried in 1929, his name was legally changed when he was adopted by his stepfather. After he was graduated from high school, where his career as a gymnast was ended by rheumatic fever, he finished a term at Penn State Nautical School and then spent three years at sea. During that time he began to write, producing some forty conventional short stories for McClure's Syndicate before turning to science fiction, which he began to publish in John W. Campbell, Jr.'s *Astounding Science Fiction* in 1939.

Sturgeon recalled that science fiction was "the pornography of its day" and recounted how his stepfather discovered and destroyed his 1935 issues of *Amazing*. When he took up science fiction, Sturgeon was making a commitment to a literary form which promised little prestige and very modest financial returns. He married in the same year he launched his science-fiction career and contributed regularly to *Unknown* and *Astounding Science Fiction* in order to support his family. Although he produced highly regarded stories, such as "It" (1940) and "Microcosmic God" (1941), he had to seek employment outside of writing to earn a living.

After operating a hotel in the British West Indies in 1940, Sturgeon worked as a door-to-door salesman, as assistant chief steward at Fort Simonds, and as a bulldozer operator. In 1942, he pursued the latter occupation in Puerto Rico. Except for *Killdozer*, a novelette about a machine possessed by a malignant force, his literary output declined sharply between 1942 and 1944, when he returned to the United States and became a copy editor. These were difficult years for Sturgeon, financially and emotionally. Not until 1946, after his marriage ended in divorce, did he

fully resume his career under the encouragement of John Campbell.

While continuing to write, Sturgeon tried his hand at running a literary agency and producing advertising copy. The first substantial public recognition for his work came in 1947 when he won a thousand-dollar prize for "Bianca's Hands." (The runner-up in the contest, sponsored by the British magazine *Argosy*, was Graham Greene.) "Bianca's Hands" had been written on Sturgeon's honeymoon years earlier but had found no market because of its bizarre treatment of a "passionate human attachment." Its acceptance marked a turning point for Sturgeon, which was closely followed by the publication of the first of his many anthologies, *Without Sorcery*, with an introduction by Ray Bradbury.

As he entered the period of his greatest creativity, Sturgeon's personal life again underwent change, with a second marriage in 1949 and a third in 1951. His output of fiction was unabated, however, with *The Dreaming Jewels*, his first novel, appearing in 1950, and *More Than Human*, published in 1953, winning the 1954 International Fantasy Award, a confirmation of his rank as one of America's foremost writers of science fiction. His stories continued to be anthologized in his own collections and those of others, and he engaged in a broad range of literary activity, from a hoax with Jean Shepherd, *I, Libertine*, published under the name Frederick R. Ewing, to a fictional case history of vampirism, *Some of Your Blood*, and a novel depicting an androgynous utopia, *Venus Plus X*.

As a major author of speculative fiction, he helped to create a climate of acceptance for the genre among the general public. In his book reviews for the *National Review* (1961-1973), for example, he explained and defended his art while introducing some of contemporary science fiction's finest authors to an audience who might otherwise not have learned of them. He was involved in science fiction's growth in other media also, in 1966 moving to Los Angeles to write for the television series *Star Trek*. Late in his life, he published little new fiction, but he continued to compile anthologies of his previous work for new audiences. He married for the fourth time in 1969. Sturgeon was living in Eugene, Oregon, at the time of his death in 1985.

Though Sturgeon deplored the "inexcusable invasions into . . . authors' most intimate motivations" by academic critics, there are nevertheless certain definite biographical influences on his work. Beverly Friend called him "a highly personal writer drawing from his own suffering for his craft." She cites his parents' divorce, his estrangement from his stepfather, his illness in adolescence, and his marital and professional problems as sources for his art.

ANALYSIS

Theodore Sturgeon once said, "All great literature is great because it is fable—because it creates typical and archetypical characters and situations which can be applied outside the work to illuminate the human condition." He repeatedly insisted that he did not undervalue the science of science fiction, but he clearly inclined toward minimizing technology as a focus for his work; rather, he concentrated upon fable, often premising his work on occult matters upon which science has had little to say. He said that "in teaching, reviewing, and enjoying science fiction, my emphasis is always on the fiction." This is, he explained, "because I like writers to be read and remembered and (when they can) to move people and shake them; to ignite, to increase their ability to share their visions and their joy and their terror, as well as their knowledge." Sturgeon's criteria for art were more affective than cognitive, and he generally concentrated upon rites of passage rather than technological extrapolation.

Whatever Sturgeon's premise for a story, scientific, psychological, or occult, he wished the work to reflect essential human experiences: "love, and pain, and greed, and laughter, and hope, and above all loneliness." Loneliness is most significant, since he asserted that "what I have been trying to do all these years is to investigate this matter of love, sexual and asexual," and his major fictions are fables of growth toward community and maturity.

The four science-fiction novels which are the heart of Sturgeon's work (*The Dreaming Jewels, More Than Human, The Cosmic Rape,* and *Venus Plus X*) de-

velop the idea that "our strange species has two prime-motivating forces: sex, of course, and worship." Throughout his writing, the latter is the more important, and Sturgeon was unwilling to see the highest self-sacrificial and altruistic acts as having any foundation in sexuality. Sturgeon's center of worship, however, is not to be found outside man but in humanity.

Sturgeon's first novel, *The Dreaming Jewels,* is an exploration of what it means to be human. Its premise is the creation of a "synthetic man" by the action of alien crystals which have a deep collective life of their own, apparently unrelated to the affairs of people. These crystals, seemingly without purpose, "dream" objects into existence, sometimes imperfectly, creating freaks and monsters, and sometimes— when they are mating—perfectly, creating creatures with the power of self-transformation. Such materials are better suited to psychological symbolism than scientific discussion. This is precisely the direction of Sturgeon's art; since he found "more room in inner space than in outer space," his fables are essentially paradigms of psychological growth which begin with the frustrations and alienation of youth and end in maturation and integration. On a number of occasions, he defined science fiction in terms of the derivation of the word "science" from the Latin "to know." "Science fiction is knowledge fiction," he wrote, adding that "by far most of the knowledge is psychological."

In *More Than Human,* Sturgeon makes significant use of syzygy, a concept of nonreproductive union signified by a strange word. A collective identity is formed by a group of persons who retain their individuality while contributing to a gestalt which has the ultimate promise of a god. The collective person remains distinctly human, however, and the worship due it is finally worship of humanity. Here the components of the human being, conscience being the highest, are integrated and raised to the highest power. So, too, in a novel which deals directly with sexuality, *Venus Plus X,* the integration of the human personality and worship become paramount, with Sturgeon using androgyny as a symbol of wholeness and providing his utopia's inhabitants with a religion which worships the promise of man.

The form of Sturgeon's novels can present the critical reader with problems. Sturgeon is perhaps most at home as a writer of short stories, and his techniques of composition reflect at times an incomplete transition to the novel's demands. He seemingly pieces together sections which finally form the whole. This is not to say that the structuring of his books is unskillful, for he does finally bring to focus elements which run through them in parallel directions. Also, such a method can be seen as organic to Sturgeon's themes of integration, with loosely related parts finally encompassed in a total vision. Whatever a reader's verdict on form, however, his principal response will probably be to Sturgeon's handling of theme.

Sturgeon's work takes seriously his claim that "the best of science fiction is as good as the best of any modern literature—articulate, poetic, philosophical, provocative, searching, courageous, insightful." He once complained that though the finest science-fiction writers "open their veins into their typewriters, taking their craft and their readers seriously, they seem to be categorically disqualified from the serious attention of mainstream critics and readers." Fortunately, this is no longer the case, in part because of Sturgeon's fables of human nature.

THE DREAMING JEWELS

The reprinted title of *The Dreaming Jewels* is *The Synthetic Man*, a title which more clearly reflects the subject matter of Sturgeon's first novel but which loses some of the symbolic suggestiveness of the original. Paul Williams has commented that the work is in part based on Sturgeon's resentment of his stepfather and has pointed out the significance of the dream to the creative act of writing science fiction. To this might be added the importance of jewel symbolism in the light of Sturgeon's view of science fiction as "knowledge fiction."

Jewels often symbolize arcane knowledge and spiritual transformation; here they are connected with an unconscious dream-power that can be brought to light for good or ill, and in which reside keys to transformation and regeneration. Contesting for this power are Horty, the "synthetic man"—created by alien crystals that can bring objects, or people, into existence—and

Pierre Monetre, a most thoroughgoing misanthrope who would delight in the destruction of humankind. Horty's victory over Monetre (called "maneater" by his subordinates) comes about through his capacity to tap the power of the unconscious, and through the willing sacrifice of Zena, whose education of Horty to human values keeps him from becoming like the alienated Monetre.

Horty's potential alienation comes from abuse by a cruel stepfather, Armand Bluett, a figure Sturgeon has himself identified with "a lot of bitterness and hostility that I wanted to get out." Bluett's viciousness results in the accidental loss of three of Horty's fingers, and the young boy flees after bidding farewell to Kay Hallowell, a girl whose love balances Bluett's hatred. In his flight, Horty is befriended by carnival people, especially Zena, a midget, who notices the boy's sympathetic connection with his only possession, a jack-in-the-box with strange jewels for eyes. These gems prove to have had their effect on the child, gradually transforming him into a creature capable both of communicating with the inner life of the jewels and of transforming himself at will.

Horty's identity is hidden from Monetre, who owns the carnival. Zena disguises him as a girl and warns him never to reveal that he has regenerated his three lost fingers, which Monetre had treated upon his arrival. During his years with the carnival, Horty fails to grow and is only forced to leave when the owner discloses some curiosity about his hand. After leaving, he discovers his gift of transformation, which is useful when he encounters Armand Bluett, now a judge, victimizing Kay Hallowell. Horty cools off the sexually aggressive Bluett by taking Kay's place and slicing off his regenerated fingers, at which sight Bluett passes out. Horty thus becomes the woman who represents love for him so that he might perform a sacrificial mutilation which is both saving and vengeful.

In a series of improbable events, Kay comes under the power of Bluett and Monetre, who is clearly contrasted with Horty. While both are brilliantly gifted, Horty's mind, under Zena's guidance, has been shaped by "humanity and the extensions of humanity," as against Monetre's, which has been twisted by hatred and desire for power. In the confrontation between Horty and Monetre in a psychic duel, Zena sacrifices herself, instructing Horty to use his power to destroy jewel-created creatures. Since Monetre's character is so inhuman, he is assumed to be one. Ironically, Monetre is biologically human, without possessing any spirit of humanity, while Zena, a synthetic creature, sacrifices herself. In the end, however, Horty kills his adversary, resurrects Zena, who becomes his wife, and assumes Monetre's identity while traveling about trying to undo some of the harm he has done.

Sturgeon has assessed *The Dreaming Jewels* as "a rotten novel." Its chief faults are a contrived plot and a style which lacks the energy of the best of his stories of the 1940's. The use of psychological materials is compelling, however, making it one of Sturgeon's most popular works. Horty's series of transformations are representative of his possession of the secret of the unconscious, the capacity to convert revenge into sacrificial love, whose highest exemplar is Zena. The novel moves from mutilation to regeneration, from revenge to love, with Horty progressing toward wholeness by overcoming alienation and linking the transforming power of the unconscious to positive human values.

MORE THAN HUMAN

More Than Human, Sturgeon's second and best novel, has at the center of its three-part structure a section entitled "Baby Is Three," which was published separately a year before the novel appeared. According to Sam Moskowitz, Sturgeon wrote a prologue and epilogue to this section to compose the novel. Like *The Dreaming Jewels*, "Baby Is Three" is about an alienated superman, fifteen-year-old Gerry Thompson, who in a strong first-person narration relates his visit to a psychiatrist, to whom he reveals his murder of his guardian, Miss Alicia Kew. Gerry also explains that he is part of a composite being, *homo gestalt*, a uniting of persons with extraordinary telepathic and telekinetic powers. Gerry has the capacity to probe the minds of others—he does this with the psychiatrist to make sure that he will not remember his visit—but he lacks human sympathy and moral awareness.

Sturgeon once said that "you cannot write stories about ideas—which is why so much hard-core, nuts-and-bolts science fiction fails as literature." In *More Than Human*, however, he is fortunate in combining a powerful idea with a sure grasp of style and an effective structure. The first section of the novel, "The Fabulous Idiot," focuses on Lone (a shortened form of *alone*), who is an idiot in the root sense of the word. He is aware of himself alone. He gradually becomes aware of others, first through Miss Kew's sister, Evelyn, who along with Alicia had been the victim of a demonically sexually repressive father, and then through the Prodds, a pathetic couple who take him in, and whose retarded child, "Baby," becomes the center of the gestalt being.

Lone becomes aware of a human community to which he has at least rudimentary obligations and of a more specialized group, composed of abandoned or runaway children, to which Gerry belongs, and which is destined to become a new being. By the end of the novel, this group has become a potential god, "not an exterior force, not an awesome Watcher in the sky, but a laughing thing with a human heart and reverence for its origins." In the book's last section, "Morality," Hip Barrows, the being's final component, its conscience, confronts and converts the ruthless Gerry; Hip sees himself as "an atom and his gestalt as a molecule. He saw these others as cells among cells, and he saw the whole design of what, with joy, humanity would become." His response is a "sense of worship." He participates in a vision not unlike that shared by many Romantic writers of the nineteenth century, what Walt Whitman's follower R. M. Bucke called "Cosmic Consciousness." Sturgeon said that the willingness of science-fiction writers to treat religious themes, "to invent and extrapolate and regroup ideas and concepts in this as in all other areas of human growth and change delights me and is a source of my true love for the mad breed." *More Than Human* is Sturgeon's best illustration that such themes can be explored profitably.

More Than Human, like *The Dreaming Jewels*, traces the progress of the growth and integration of the person. In each novel, characters move from alienation to wholeness, but in *More Than Human*, the key conflict between misanthropy and humanity is handled with greater dramatic skill. In general a more sophisticated work in conception and structure, *More Than Human* manages to present the idea of a collective entity without losing sight of individual characters or the dynamics of personality. As a speculative fiction, it deserves the praise and popularity it has enjoyed.

THE COSMIC RAPE

The Cosmic Rape also employs the gestalt theme of *More Than Human*, extending the union to all of humankind, which in turn is joined to Medusa, an intergalactic composite creature. While the underlying theme of the book is essentially the same as that of *More Than Human*, it is by no means as successful. Its premises are extrapolated in far less believable fashion, and its structure is not dramatically engaging. Intercut scenes, which range from the United States to Rome to Africa, are skillfully coordinated, but character development suffers in the effort to show individuals becoming a part of the whole.

In *The Cosmic Rape*, Sturgeon attempts to put love into the largest terms, but, ironically, he employs a character most unlikely to initiate cosmic harmony. One Dan Gurlick, a loathsome bum, has become an atom in Medusa by ingesting a sort of seed concealed in a fragment of hamburger. Through him, Medusa seeks to take over the earth telepathically. Medusa is at first thwarted, having dealt only with collective minds elsewhere in the universe. This lack in humanity is repaired, however, as psychic unity among people appears as they cooperate in the destruction of invading machines created by Medusa. In the course of attaining collective consciousness, a variety of characters emerge from sexual repression and exploitation or social alienation to sacrifice themselves. Notable is the metamorphosis of Guido, a misfit who has turned to anarchism because his musical genius has been suppressed by a wicked stepfather.

Ultimately, Medusa is joined to the human collective mind. This connection occurs when Gurlick, himself excluded from the universal intelligence, is permitted to act out the sexual fantasies which Medusa has used to control him. What Gurlick intends as rape is welcomed by a woman now sexually liberated as a part of a larger design; likewise, the joining of humanity to Medusa is transformed from rape to consent. Medusa is in fact possessed by humanity rather than possessing it.

The Cosmic Rape extends the ideas of *More Than Human* as far as they can go. Unfortunately, the extrapolation is ultimately too fanciful and the dramatic power of Sturgeon's myth of human integration is diffused. There is a sense of his recognition of this in his next book, which he calls "a tract"; the social criticism of *Venus Plus X* gives ballast to an imagination which had overextended itself.

VENUS PLUS X

Sturgeon responded to the charge that "science fiction is characteristically asexual and unaware of love in its larger and largest senses." He believed that this impression had sometimes arisen because writers of science fiction often "work in geological or astronomical time rather than in biographical or historical perspective." Sturgeon had dealt with themes of love in both cosmic and personal perspectives in his earlier novels, but in *Venus Plus X* he turned to utopian fiction to keep the action on a more human scale.

Though Sturgeon had written stories on sex before—"The World Well Lost" (1953) deals with homosexuality, for example—*Venus Plus X* is his most extended statement on sexism and sexual taboos. While the book has been praised for its pioneering study of sex roles, preceding Ursula K. Le Guin's much discussed *The Left Hand of Darkness* (1969) by nine years, *Venus Plus X* is also notable for its skillfuly ironic employment of science-fiction conventions and for its handling of the symbolism of androgyny.

The novel is structured in alternating chapters of action which are connected only by theme. The first set of chapters deals with suburban life and the questions of sexual identity posed to America in the 1950's. Along with standard problems of sex-role definition for children and general sexism, there are hints of change; Herb Raile comes to realize how Western culture has degraded women and catches glimpses of the significance of androgyny in the style of a rock singer. Contrasted with suburban America is Ledom (*model* inverted), a utopia founded upon the fact that its inhabitants are biologically hermaphrodites. Here, sex-role definition is no problem, and the wholeness of the human being in assuming all social duties is stressed. Against the predatory capitalism and commercialized worship of the suburbs are posed charitable religion and universal sharing.

Androgyny is used by Sturgeon as a symbol of wholeness. Like the universal man of *More Than Human*, androgyny can be found in mystical thought as signifying the primordial unity of humankind. In order to stress this aspect of his work, Sturgeon provides the Ledomites with a religion that is an ecstatic celebration of the child. "We keep before us," says the guide to this utopia, "the image of that which is malleable and growing—of that which we have the power to improve. We worship that very power in ourselves, and the sense of responsibility which lives with it." Here again is Sturgeon's drive toward totality, a worship of human potential, yet in order to present this theme, he undercuts a number of science-fiction conventions to make his readers more aware of the symbolic nature of his statement.

The reader discovers that the book's nominal hero, Charlie Johns, is not a time-traveler as he first believes. Ledom does not exist in the distant future as it first appears; rather, it is a society hidden from the eyes of men. The Ledomites wish to test the reaction of the outside world to their culture, and they use Charlie Johns's responses as a gauge. After overcoming his initial bewilderment, Charlie embarks on a course of education, learning that Ledom's technical superiority consists in a machine that can inscribe thought patterns and has revolutionized learning, and a power supply that makes the community self-sufficient. Charlie's approval of technology comes to a screeching halt, however, when he discovers that the hermaphroditism of Ledomites is biologically engineered. His reaction convinces utopian planners that the world is not ready for the revelation of Ledom.

Charlie now regards Ledom as a den of perversion and indicates that it ought to be destroyed. His education, however, has been limited: He has not detected the hints throughout that the whole culture is symbolic, that its essence is "transition." It has been designed to preserve human values while the outside world destroys itself. The novel's disquisition on religion, in fact, suggests that if one human generation could adopt the religion of Ledom, it would be saved. No hermaphroditism would be necessary for a sense of human wholeness.

The final emphasis given Ledom's symbolic nature is the revelation that Charlie Johns is not actually Charlie Johns at all, but merely a collection of his memories, obtained when he was dying after a plane crash and inscribed on the previously blank mind of a biological control. The plot, however, first permits Johns to attempt the standard escape from a dystopia. He finds the one girl who has not been biologically altered, and he tries to leave in what he thinks is a time machine. When he does so, the Ledomites are forced to tell him the truth. He and his girl therefore take up life somewhere between the two worlds, trying to sort out their identities, presumably overcoming the sexism of the man Charlie was, and learning from the wisdom of Ledom. At the same time, on the other side, Herb Raile is working his way slowly and painfully to gain some of Ledom's values.

In spite of some dated writing in the sections on suburbia in the 1950's, this is a book which powerfully anticipates many of the themes taken up by feminists in the 1960's and 1970's. Sturgeon also made fine use of the conventions of utopian fiction only to undercut them, which is most appropriate to his major points about the nature of dynamic evolutionary change throughout his fiction. Utopia, he wrote, "must be life-oriented and recognize that life is change, which is why utopias, be they by Plato or Sir Thomas More, or Joanna Russ, have hidden in them the characteristics of the necropolis." He avoided this by permitting his own utopia to self-destruct, leaving behind the impact of its symbols, and providing in *Venus Plus X* what Sturgeon saw in William Golding's *Lord of the Flies* (1954), "a fable of cultural structures, with a meaning—a 'moral' if you like—far greater than the narrative itself."

Henry J. Lindborg

OTHER MAJOR WORKS

SHORT FICTION: *Without Sorcery*, 1948; *E Pluribus Unicorn*, 1953; *A Way Home*, 1955; *Caviar*, 1955; *A*

Touch of Strange, 1958; *Aliens 4*, 1959; *Beyond*, 1960; *Sturgeon in Orbit*, 1964; . . . *And My Fear Is Great/Baby Is Three*, 1965; *The Joyous Invasions*, 1965; *Starshine*, 1966; *Sturgeon Is Alive and Well*, 1971; *The Worlds of Theodore Sturgeon*, 1972; *To Here and the Easel*, 1973; *Sturgeon's West*, 1973 (with Don Ward); *Case and the Dreamer*, 1974; *Visions and Venturers*, 1978; *The Stars Are the Styx*, 1979; *The Golden Helix*, 1980.

BIBLIOGRAPHY

Friend, Beverly. "The Sturgeon Connection." In *Voices for the Future: Essays on Major Science Fiction Writers*, edited by Thomas D. Clareson. Vol. 1. Bowling Green, Ohio: Bowling Green University Popular Press, 1977. A stimulating discussion of the themes and formal structures of Sturgeon's fiction.

Gordon, Joan, and Veronica Hollinger, eds. *Blood Read: The Vampire as Metaphor in Contemporary Culture*. Philadelphia: University of Pennsylvania Press, 1997. Treats *Some of Your Blood* as a harbinger of the more recent sympathetic vampire novels. Includes a bibliography.

Hassler, Donald M. "Images for an Ethos, Images for Change and Style." *Extrapolation* 20 (Summer, 1979): 176-188. An analysis of Sturgeon's themes of love, loneliness, newness, and the nature of change in relation to his ethics and versatile technique. The works discussed include "Microcosmic God," "Slow Sculpture," *More Than Human*, and *The Cosmic Rape*.

Lawler, Donald L. "Theodore Sturgeon." In *Twentieth-Century American Science Fiction Writers*, edited by David Cowart and Thomas L. Wymer. Vol. 8 in *Dictionary of Literary Biography*. Detroit: Gale Research, 1981. An interesting and informative biography and critical analysis of Sturgeon's fiction. Includes photographs and selected primary and secondary bibliographies.

Moskowitz, Sam. "Theodore Sturgeon." In *Seekers of Tomorrow: Masters of Modern Science Fiction*. New York: Harper & Row, 1966. A discussion of Sturgeon's early fiction through *More Than Human*, with emphasis on his virtuoso style and in-

ventiveness. Includes brief summaries of many Sturgeon plots.

Sackmary, Regina. "An Ideal of Three: The Art of Theodore Sturgeon." In *Critical Encounters: Writers and Themes in Science Fiction*, edited by Dick Riley. New York: Frederick Ungar, 1978. A discussion of Sturgeon's frequent use in his fiction of groupings of threes to develop his themes of isolation, loneliness, love, wholeness, and unity. Includes notes for the essay.

WILLIAM STYRON

Born: Newport News, Virginia; June 11, 1925

PRINCIPAL LONG FICTION

Lie Down in Darkness, 1951
The Long March, 1952 (serial), 1956 (book)
Set This House on Fire, 1960
The Confessions of Nat Turner, 1967
Sophie's Choice, 1979

OTHER LITERARY FORMS

Until 1990, William Styron was among the few major modern literary figures who bear discussion in only a single genre—in his case, the novel. Except for a slight and rather odd play, *In the Clap Shack* (1972), and a collection of essays, *This Quiet Dust* (1982), Styron mainly concentrated on novels. In 1990, however, the publication of *Darkness Visible: A Memoir of Madness* was widely hailed. A candid and insightful recounting of Styron's personal battle with severe clinical depression, *Darkness Visible* was an immediate popular success. *A Tidewater Morning: Three Tales from Youth* is a collection of short stories published in 1993.

ACHIEVEMENTS

Until the publication of *The Confessions of Nat Turner* in 1967, Styron was well known in literary circles as a young novelist of great talent but largely unrealized potential. *The Confessions of Nat Turner,* riding the crest of a wave of social activism in the late 1960's and capitalizing on a national interest in black literature and history, gave Styron a major popular reputation as well as making him the center of a vitriolic controversy between academic and literary critics on one side, who tended to see the novel as an honest attempt to come to terms with history, and a small group of strident black critics on the other hand, who questioned, often abusively, the ability of any white writer to deal with the black experience, and who called Styron's portrait of Nat Turner unflattering and inaccurate. The book and the debate it engendered made Styron a major voice in twentieth century fiction, as well as a rich man.

Despite the twelve-year hiatus between the publication of *The Confessions of Nat Turner* and that of *Sophie's Choice*, Styron's reputation grew, particularly in terms of his role as an interpreter of the South. *Lie Down in Darkness* was recognized as one of the finest presentations in fiction of the modern southern family, haunted by memory, guilt, and time, and *The Confessions of Nat Turner* came to be seen as representative of the concern of southern writers with the burden of history. *The Confessions of Nat Turner* was accepted as a rhetorically beautiful evocation of the past, whatever its historical inaccuracies.

The publication of *Sophie's Choice* in 1979 cemented Styron's position as one of the major figures of contemporary literature. Although several major critics had reservations about the novel, its ambitious confrontation of a moral theme of enormous implication—the Holocaust—and Styron's compelling, lyrical prose made the novel the literary event of the year. With *Sophie's Choice*, some of Styron's lifelong concerns as a novelist become clearer: the unanswerable problem of pain and suffering, the elusive nature of memory, and the ambiguous legacy of history.

BIOGRAPHY

William Styron was born June 11, 1925, in Newport News, Virginia, which he later called "a very

(Peter Simon)

Southern part of the world." His mother, Pauline Margaret Abraham Styron, was from the North, but his father, William Clark Styron, a shipyard engineer, came from an old, if not aristocratic, land-poor Virginia family, and Styron remembers his grandmother telling him as a little boy of the days when the family owned slaves, a memory he was to incorporate years later into *Sophie's Choice*. Styron's father was a "Jeffersonian gentleman," liberal in his views for a southerner, who implanted in his son much of the philosophical curiosity which characterized the young Styron's novels. His mother, a gentling influence, died when Styron was twelve after a long, painful siege with cancer, an experience which was also to leave a mark on his fiction in the form of an almost obsessive concern with physical pain and suffering and the vulnerability of the flesh. After his mother's death, Styron began "going wild," and his father sent him to an Episcopal boys' school in Middlesex County, where he was an indifferent student but a voracious reader. Graduating, he enrolled in Davidson College during World War II but soon dropped out to enlist in the marines.

Styron's stint in Officers Candidate School marked the beginning of his writing career, for while there, he enrolled in a creative writing course at Duke University under William Blackburn, whom Styron acknowledges as the most powerful formative influence on his work. One of his stories, about a Southern lynching, similar in tone and execution to William Faulkner's "Dry September," appeared in a student anthology, Styron's first published fiction. At the tail end of the war, Styron was commissioned and was stationed on a troop ship in the San Francisco Bay, but the Japanese surrendered before he ever left port. Styron was to speak later of his sense of guilt at not having seen action, as well as his feeling of horror at the waste and destruction of the war and the terrible, almost casual way in which life could be lost. Styron condemned the absurdity of Marine Corps life, but he praised the tough training that transformed him physically and mentally. Styron resumed his program at Duke and was graduated in 1947. He took a job in New York as an associate editor in the book division at McGraw-Hill. His senior editor and immediate superior was Edward C. Aswell, the august second editor of Thomas Wolfe and an *éminence grise* to rival editor Maxwell Perkins; Aswell was to appear grotesquely as "The Weasel" in an autobiographical passage in *Sophie's Choice* nearly thirty years later. The callow young Styron found McGraw-Hill humorless and confining, and after six months he was fired.

Living in a Brooklyn boardinghouse on a tiny legacy from his grandmother, Styron took another creative writing course, this time from Hiram Haydn at the New School for Social Research. He began work on his first novel, *Lie Down in Darkness*, the story of a star-crossed upper-middle-class southern family whose failure to find love and meaning in life drives the sensitive daughter, Peyton Loftis, to insanity and suicide. The complex treatment of time in the novel and its high Southern rhetoric showed the influence of William Faulkner, whom Styron had been reading intensely, but *Lie Down in Darkness* was manifestly

the work of a powerful and original talent. At first, Styron found the writing of the book slow and difficult. Two years after leaving McGraw-Hill, he had written only a few pages that were usable. After Styron made drastic changes to the novel, dropping the original title ("Inheritance of Night"), eliminating the character Marcus Bonner, shifting the point of view to an omniscient narrator, and withholding the reader's knowledge of Peyton Loftis, Styron found the writing went surprisingly fast—he finished the book and saw it accepted for publication by Bobbs-Merrill before he was recalled by the Marine Corps for service in the Korean War. The novel was published in 1951. Styron was then on active reserve duty, from which he was eventually discharged for an eye problem, but which became the basis for his second novel, *The Long March*.

Lie Down in Darkness was an immediate critical success and a moderate popular one, winning the prestigious Prix de Rome in 1952. At that time, Styron had decamped to Paris and fallen in with a young crowd of American expatriate intellectuals, many of whom would later make names for themselves in literature. George Plimpton and Peter Matthiessen were at the center of a moiling, motley, talented crowd that included Harold Humes, John P. C. Train, Donald Hall, and, on the fringe, writers such as James Baldwin, James Jones, and Irwin Shaw. In 1952 and 1953, the group began compiling a literary magazine, *The Paris Review*, which was to become one of the most influential literary periodicals of the postwar period. Plimpton became the first editor and Matthiessen the fiction editor, and Styron wrote the statement of purpose for the first issue. He also gave the periodical one of the first of its famous "Writers at Work" interviews. It was recorded by Matthiessen and Plimpton at Patrick's, the *Paris Review* crowd's favorite bar, and in it Styron claimed that "this generation . . . will produce literature equal to that of any other generation" and that "a great writer . . . will give substance to and perhaps even explain all the problems of the world." From the start, his ambitions were large.

Although he later said he drank enough brandy in bistros to develop a *crise de foie*, and spent months in the summer of 1952 on a sybaritic "Ovidian idyll" on the Riviera with Humes, Styron was also writing at top speed during this period. In just six weeks, he wrote a novella based on his Marine Corps training-camp experience, *The Long March*, and it was accepted for publication in the fall by *discovery*, a literary magazine (Knopf would publish it as a book four years later). In 1953, he used the money from his Prix de Rome to travel in Italy, an experience that laid the groundwork for his 1960 novel of expatriates, *Set This House on Fire*, and during this time he met Rose Burgunder, a Jewish poet with some family money from Baltimore, whom he soon married. They returned to America, to Roxbury, Connecticut, which would remain Styron's home, and where he began work on the "big novel" that he planned to follow up the success of *Lie Down in Darkness*.

This was *Set This House on Fire*, a sprawling account of American intellectuals living a life of self-indulgence and self-destruction in postwar Italy. The book contained fine lyrical passages of description, particularly of the physical beauty of Italy and the horrifying squalor and suffering of its people, but as Styron later admitted, the novel was seriously flawed—undisciplined and melodramatic. The reviews were very mixed, and some of them savage. Styron's former friend Norman Mailer called *Set This House on Fire* "a bad, maggoty novel," suggesting that Styron could "write like an angel about landscape, but like an adolescent about people." The novel was better received by Styron's European critics—it is still highly regarded in France—but Styron was wounded by his first really bad press, and he retreated to Roxbury to work on his next book, a novel he resolved to make so thoroughly a work of craftsmanship as to defy criticism.

The Confessions of Nat Turner took years to research and write, and true to Styron's expectations, it was immediately acclaimed as a masterpiece. For years, Styron had had his mind on Nat Turner's 1831 slave rebellion as a subject for fiction. It had taken place close to his own Tidewater Virginia home, and Styron saw the suffering, the violence, and the misunderstanding of the revolt as emblematic both of the South's guilt and pain and of his personal concerns as a writer. Styron claimed that reading Albert Camus's

L'Étranger (1942; *The Stranger*, 1946) furnished him with the technique he was to use in presenting Nat Turner's story—the narrative persona reflecting from jail—and there is no doubt that much of the novel's perspective on black people and black problems was derived from Styron's friend, the black writer James Baldwin, who was a guest of Styron for months while he was writing *Another Country* (1962), Baldwin's first major novel about black/white relations. Styron called *The Confessions of Nat Turner* "less a `historical novel' than a meditation on history," but despite critical accolades, including the praise of Baldwin, who suggested that the novel might be considered the beginning of a black/white "mutual history," Styron became the target of a group of critics who protested vehemently Styron's depiction of Nat Turner. These critics assaulted Styron in print, accused him of racism and of attempting to demean the reputation of a great hero of black history, and hounded him at meetings, readings, and lectures. Ironically, Nat Turner, as Styron presented him, was a strong and sensitive character, unquestionably the hero of the novel, but so volatile was the political climate of America in the late 1960's that for some critics, any black character who was not a warrior saint was unacceptable as a fictional creation.

The critical assaults provoked by *The Confessions of Nat Turner* left Styron bruised, but he was encouraged by the praise for the novel's powerful rhetoric and masterly structure, not to mention its enormous financial success. Of the controversy, he said, "It really had very little effect on me . . . largely because of the fact that I knew that it was politically motivated and hysterical, and that I had not violated any truth that a novelist is capable of doing." He turned to new work, first to a lengthy projected novel, tentatively titled "The Way of the Warrior," a novel that explored the psyche of a career army officer, then to *Sophie's Choice*. While on Martha's Vineyard, Styron dreamed of Sophie, a Polish Catholic survivor of Auschwitz whom he had met in Brooklyn in 1949. He woke with a vision, seeing her name on a door; he decided that the book would focus on a mother who is forced to send her child to death. The book began as an autobiographical reminiscence of his aimless days as a junior editor at McGraw-Hill, when he found himself frustrated artistically, philosophically, and sexually. As he worked through his memories in the character of his narrator, Stingo, whose fictional background is almost identical to Styron's own, he found his real theme: the life and eventual death by suicide of a woman who survived the Nazi concentration camps but emerged terribly scarred emotionally. This woman, the Sophie of the title, becomes the vehicle through which Stingo confronts the potential horror of life, and through her he matures.

Sophie's Choice was five years in the writing, but Styron was richly rewarded when it was finally published in 1979. A few critics, notably John Gardner, raised questions about its structure, and about the sometimes jejune intrusions of the shallow Stingo, but for the most part the novel was accepted as a fine and satisfying offering by a major writer. "It has the feel of permanence," Peter Prescott wrote. The gratifyingly large sales were capped by a spectacular sale of the film rights. In 1983, Meryl Streep won an Academy Award for Best Actress for her portrayal of Sophie in that film.

In 1985, Styron was hospitalized with acute clinical depression. His struggle to overcome his suicidal feelings and to return to health are recounted in his memoir *Darkness Visible*, published five years later. Styron credited the peaceful seclusion of his hospital stay and the loving patience of his wife and grown children (three daughters and a son) as the principal factors in his recovery. After his hospitalization, Styron immediately wrote "A Tidewater Morning," a long short story that fictionalized the death of his mother. After writing *Darkness Visible*, he returned to his work on a novel set during World War II.

ANALYSIS

The informing patterns of William Styron's fiction are by no means self-evident, and they may not yield themselves readily to the casual critic. Unlike William Faulkner, whom he often resembles in style and technique, his subjects are radically diverse—a doomed Southern family, the intellectual jet set of American expatriates, a historical slave revolt, the horror of the Holocaust. He can shift stylistically from the direct "plain style" of *The Long March* to the purple rhetoric of sections in *Set This House on Fire*, and he moves easily from romantic abstraction to concrete objectivity.

Styron is preeminently, almost self-consciously, a writer of "big" novels of weighty moral significance—a fictional *homme sérieux*, as the French say (which may account for some of Styron's great popularity with French critics). The eternal verities embody themselves relentlessly in Styron's writing. Death, suffering, the silence of God—grave truths lumber ponderously and insistently at the reader in each novel, mercifully relieved by flashes of humor and lyrical passages of poetic beauty, which spare Styron the gray fate of being a sort of American Thomas Mann. Still, the metaphysical predominates in Styron's books.

Strongly underlying all of his novels is a concern with the past, not so much in the form of the passage of time, but rather an awareness that it is either lost or potentially reclaimable. Each of the major novels moves from the present to the past in an attempt to explain or understand how things came to be as they are. *Lie Down in Darkness*, with its relentless burrowing in the Loftis family past, looks backward to explain Peyton's death. In *Set This House on Fire*, Peter Leverett moves very deliberately into the past in pursuit of a piece of himself that is missing, and his whole purpose in dredging up the Italian incidents that form the body of the novel is to reveal the past so that he may deal with the present. Both *The Confessions of Nat Turner* and *Sophie's Choice* are historical novels concerned with the actual past and with what Robert Penn Warren has called "the awful burden of history."

Styron's fiction is historical, but in an intensely personal and psychological way. Each exploration of the past is filtered through the consciousness of a protagonist—Milton Loftis, Cass Kinsolving, Nat Turner, Sophie—and strongly colored by the neuroses of those characters. The alcoholism of Milton and Cass, Nat's brooding rage, and Sophie's aching guilt over her murdered child—at the core of each novel is psychological exploration rather than historical exposition. Historical process is only the context within which individual psychologies grope for resolution. Each of Styron's characters lives on the verge of apocalyptic catastrophe, always on the edge of mental breakdown. Each of his protagonists is close to outright insanity. Two actually commit suicide (Peyton and Sophie); Nat Turner essentially does; and Cass Kinsolving of *Set This House on Fire* is only saved from it by the thinnest of margins. His people may be constantly close to madness, yet Styron makes the reader feel that the madness is legitimate, for his characters search for meaning in a mad world, and only when they fail to find it do they become deranged. Peyton Loftis's loveless family, Nat Turner's unjust world, and the horrors of the concentration camp for Sophie are atmospheres in which genuine sanity is difficult, if not impossible. Perhaps the most representative Styron "hero," though, is Cass Kinsolving of *Set This House on Fire*, the only protagonist who is a philosopher as well as a sufferer. Cass's madness derives from his contemplation of the horror of human life and misery, and he staggers drunkenly around postwar Italy demanding a teleological answer for the chaos of existence in which God is silent; "you can shake the whole universe and just get a snicker up there."

Perhaps it is this tendency to project the struggles of his characters beyond the ordinary world and to magnify them to the borders of melodrama that gives all of Styron's novels powerful religious overtones. Some of this tendency derives from Styron's own Episcopalian background, which is strongly echoed in the style of *Lie Down in Darkness* and *Set This House on Fire* and is particularly evident in the rhetoric of Nat Turner, who is stylistically more Anglican than Baptist. The central problem in these novels is the conspicuous absence of God from human life. Styron's world is one in which, as Cass says in *Set This House on Fire*, "God has locked the door and gone away to leave us write letters to Him." They are unanswered. By the time Styron comes to reflecting on the horror of the Holocaust in his last book, it seems no answer is possible.

This is Styron's theme—the absence of God and the meaninglessness of life. Consistently, he approaches it through a single technique, the presentation and contemplation of pain and suffering. Styron's novels are a catalog of the slings and arrows of outrageous fortune, some physical, some mental, and some simply the result of an empathic identification with the suffering state of humankind.

On its most elemental level, Styron's depiction of suffering is as pure physical pain. Peyton Loftis is tortured by the ache in her womb, the soldiers of *The Long March* by the agony of their exhausted bodies, Nat Turner by the cold of his cell and the torments of his imprisonment, and Sophie by the tortures of the concentration camp. In *Set This House on Fire*, physical suffering is Styron's primary metaphor for the pain of humankind's empty relationship with the universe, and the novel is shot through with characters in various stages of suffering from "abuse of the carnal envelope."

Vivid as the physical suffering of Styron's characters is, it is nothing compared to their mental and emotional anguish. Often, this mental anguish derives from their acute sense of alienation—from one another and from God. Milton Loftis, Peyton, Cass Kinsolving, Nat Turner, and Sophie writhe painfully and actively, aware of a pervasive emptiness in their lives.

LIE DOWN IN DARKNESS

The structural complexities of *Lie Down in Darkness*, combined with the florid rhetoric of the novel, obscure for many readers the essentially simple causality which underlies the book. It is the story of how and why Peyton Loftis becomes insane and kills herself, tracing the roots of her tortured madness to her father's weakness and her mother's inability to love. Peyton's father, Milton, showers her with an excessive adoration that is one facet of his alcoholic self-indulgence; he smothers his daughter with a sloppy, undemanding adulation that counterpoints his wife Helen's psychotic frigidity. Helen is only able to show love in terms of compulsive formal discharge of parental obligations, bitterly resentful of the martyr role she has chosen to play. Eventually, Peyton instinctively rejects both her father's almost unnatural affection and her mother's unnatural lack of it. By the time Peyton cuts herself loose, however, she has been emotionally crippled, unable to accept any genuine love from a series of lovers, including the Jewish artist she marries and who might have brought her peace. She retreats deeper and deeper inside herself, watching first other people and finally the real world recede before her disintegrating mind. The last major section of the novel is her tormented, insane monologue, a brilliant tour de force reminiscent of the Benjy sections of Faulkner's *The Sound and the Fury* (1929).

When *Lie Down in Darkness* was published in 1951, it was widely hailed as a significant addition to the "southern" school of writing led by Faulkner, Ellen Glasgow, Flannery O'Connor, and Thomas Wolfe. Thematically, *Lie Down in Darkness* is not a markedly "southern" novel. Although the Loftis family is from Tidewater, Virginia, and there are mannerisms described in the book that are definitively southern, Milton Loftis's weakness, his wife's cold rage, and their daughter's breakdown are in no way regional. The story could as easily be that of a New England family, such as Eugene O'Neill's Manions. What is actually distinctive about the tragedy of the Loftises is how much it is exclusively their own, rather than a product of the dictates of fate or society. In this respect, the novel differs from Styron's later works, in which he increasingly attributes humanity's sufferings to forces beyond the individual. While the novel is a tragedy of a single family, Styron is condemning an entire generation that lost its children. In describing her parents' generation as lost, Peyton Loftis says, "They thought they were lost. They were crazy. They weren't lost. What they were doing was losing us."

If Styron traces a source of the Loftis family's deterioration, it is perhaps in their lifestyle. On one level, *Lie Down in Darkness* is almost a novel of manners, for in keeping with the Loftises' "country club" lives, much of the novel delineates social activity—parties, dances, dinners. Emblematic of this are three scenes in which Milton, Helen, and Peyton go through the motions of conventional social rituals while they are torn by violent emotions lying beneath the facade of meaningless behavior. The first of these is a dance at the country club at which Peyton tries to play the role of belle-of-the-ball while her father

makes drunken love to his mistress in a cloakroom and Helen seethes at both father and daughter in a jealous rage. Later, a Christmas dinner turns into a grotesque, painful fiasco, as Helen screams insults at her daughter while Milton slobbers drunkenly. Finally, Peyton's wedding becomes a nightmare when Milton again gets drunk and sloppy, and Helen, as always thinly concealing a bitter resentment of Peyton, finally cracks, screaming "Whore!" at her daughter. In a rage, Peyton claws her mother's face with her nails and flees the family forever.

The loss of love, or rather the failure to find it, informs the entire book. The three Loftises grope at one another in despair, reaching out to one another in their separate, psychologically crippled ways for an understanding and affection that will bring them some sort of emotional peace. That peace, though, is impossible because their psychic natures are flawed beyond redemption. Sigmund Freud spins the plot: Milton loves Peyton not wisely, but too well, as she uncomfortably senses, so his love of her must always seem unrequited, and he is destined to be deserted by her at the last; Helen suffers a patent jealous hatred for Peyton, who has a capacity for love that Helen lacks, and who is stranded between the two poles of her parents' emotional inadequacy. The result is endless pain and ultimately annihilation. As Milton wails, "It was awful not to be able to love. It was hell."

It is not hell, though, but obliteration—nothingness—that truly underlies this novel. In the opening scene, Milton meets the train that brings Peyton's body home for burial. The final scene is her throwing herself to her death from a New York City rooftop. Everything between, the whole body of the novel, is an explanation of that death, and the knowledge of Peyton's unavoidable extinction hangs heavily during the entire book. The title is taken from Sir Thomas Browne's gloomy *Hydriotaphia: Or, Urn Burial* (1658), a seventeenth century meditation on the inevitability of death, and the "darkness" of the title is that of the grave. Images of death haunt the dreams of the tortured characters, and the reader is never allowed to forget the ultimate negation implicit in the agony of life.

THE LONG MARCH

The agony of life, more than the nullity of death, became the focus of Styron's fiction following *Lie Down in Darkness*. His short novel *The Long March* serves almost as a précis for the motif of pain that came to dominate Styron's writing. Not much longer than a substantial short story, *The Long March* stands between the turgid psychological weight of *Lie Down in Darkness* and the ponderous solemnity of *Set This House on Fire* like a breath of fresh air. Short, clean, concise, and plotted without a wasted word, this unpretentious novella contains some of Styron's most disciplined and readable prose. He trimmed away all the heavy rhetorical and philosophical baggage of his "big" novels, leaving before the reader only his lean and awful central subject—pain and suffering. Appropriately, the pain here is of the most basic and primitive sort—pure physical agony. Stylistically, Styron's writing of the book in 1952 was anomalous in the development of his career, for it was at this period that he was gearing up to write *Set This House on Fire*, and the stylistic and structural complexities of *Lie Down in Darkness* were being inflated to match the ambitious range of the novel to come.

Like the best of Ernest Hemingway, *The Long March* is deceptively simple—a step-by-step account of a thirty-six-mile forced march inflicted on some Marine reserves by their mindless officers and endured by the men with varying degrees of courage or cowardice, acceptance or rejection, but mainly endured with pain. The march itself is relentlessly real for the reader on page after page, the physical pain of the characters becoming a kind of rhythmic pattern in the book. If the novel has a "message," it is embodied in the final lines, in which Captain Mannix, who has undergone the march protesting its sadistic insanity, swollen and aching, confronts a sympathetic barracks maid who asks if it hurts: "His words [were] uttered . . . not with self-pity, but only with the tone of a man who, having endured and lasted, was too weary to tell her anything but what was true. 'Deed it does,' he said."

SET THIS HOUSE ON FIRE

After the critical success of *Lie Down in Darkness* and the artistic success of *The Long March*, there fol-lowed the better part of a decade before the 1960 publication of *Set This House on Fire*. Comfortably ensconced in Roxbury, Connecticut, prosperous, rearing a family, and moving into the center of the New York literary world, Styron's reputation grew steadily, although his literary output did not. His house, along with George Plimpton's New York City apartment, became one of the new camping grounds for the old *Paris Review* crowd, and Peter Matthiessen, James Jones, and James Baldwin were frequent visitors. Throughout the late 1950's, word of his forthcoming "big" novel spread as Styron gave private readings from it, and the publication of *Set This House on Fire* was eagerly awaited.

The novel was indeed big; actually, it sprawled embarrassingly. In place of the personal, family tragedy of *Lie Down in Darkness*, Styron broadened his scope by giving the suffering in this novel a universal dimension and by exploring the metaphysical bases of it. It is not a family that suffers, but the world. The reader sees this world through the eyes of Peter Leverett, a Styron surrogate, but the real protagonist is Cass Kinsolving, a sensitive, drunken American artist in Italy in the 1950's who is aghast by the suffering of humanity. Much of the story is told to Leverett (and the reader) by Cass, who looks for the ultimate implications of every grain of sand. Looking back, he tells Leverett that he remembers Italy as "an infinity of remembered pain," and he finds divine aspects even in his drunkenness: "God surely had clever ways of tormenting a man, putting in his way a substance whereby He might briefly be reached, but which in the end . . . sent Him packing over the horizon trailing clouds of terror." To achieve this broadened projection, Styron enlarges his cast of characters, heightens his rhetoric, and throws the whole show on an enormous stage. A vast parade of people moves through *Set This House on Fire*, many of them poor, sick, or abused, the rest venal and contemptible. The action is lifted from the commonplace to the melodramatic; rape, murder, and mystery dominate. The characters, except for Leverett and Cass's wife, Poppy, are exotic. Mason Flagg is a monstrous idiot typifying Victor Hugo's Quasimodo of *The Hunchback of Notre Dame* (1831). He is the "super bastard" aesthete rich boy, whose cultivated corruption is nauseating but still rich and strange. Cass deteriorates theatrically, staggering about and raving lines from Greek tragedy, a far cry from the humdrum drunkard Milton Loftis.

Heightened rhetoric is Styron's principal method of extending the scope of *Set This House on Fire*. Much of the novel reads like gothic Thomas Wolfe, from Mason's mother's description of "the horror" of her son's expulsion from prep school to Leverett's account of one of the book's several nightmares: "an abomination made of the interlocking black wings of ravens crawling and loathsome with parasites . . . a country in cataclysm and upheaval." Cass spends much of the book in deliberate blasphemy, "raving at that black, baleful, and depraved Deity who seemed coolly-minded to annihilate His creatures," when he is not suffering from delirium tremens and seeing visions of a boiling sea, or giant spiders on Mt. Vesuvius.

This rhetoric not only complements, but makes possible, the projection of much of the novel on a dream level. Styron had done this before, in a Freudian fantasy of Helen Loftis's, in one of Peyton's lover's dreams of babies burning in hell, and in Peyton's entire closing soliloquy. In *Set This House on Fire*, though, the use of dream, vision, and hallucination is so pervasive that much of the novel approaches phantasmagoria. Leverett dreams of a malevolent fiend for several pages, and has recurrent, elaborately described nightmares; Cass is repeatedly haunted, and his drunken ordeal ends with an extended vision of disaster, a passage drawing heavily on Dante and the Book of Revelation. So extensive is Styron's use of dramatic and fantastic imagery that it is often difficult to tell whether he is presenting the reader with a metaphor or a dream, and at one point, when Cass describes himself first making love to a beautiful girl, then suddenly "groping for an answer on some foul black shore," it is impossible to tell whether he is just thinking or hallucinating again. Cass himself probably does not know.

Although they differ in scope and ambition, *Lie Down in Darkness* and *Set This House on Fire* are essentially the same kind of novel. Both are studies in personal alienation and deterioration. Both work through an elevated rhetoric and through psychological revelation. Although *Set This House on Fire* reaches self-consciously for transcendence and philosophical universality, the novel centers on the psychological aberrations of two characters, Cass Kinsolving and Mason Flagg. Similar to the tragedy of the Loftis family in *Lie Down in Darkness*, theirs are individual, not universal, tragedies. In *Lie Down in Darkness*, the tragedies are individual, but they represent the failings of a self-indulgent generation. In *Set This House on Fire*, the tragedies are also individual, yet they represent the tragedies of a hedonistic generation, a generation that was decadent and destructive.

THE CONFESSIONS OF NAT TURNER

Styron called *The Confessions of Nat Turner* "a meditation on history." Its subject is not only the character of Nat, but also the meaning of slavery itself—what it does to people, and to society. Like Styron's previous novels, the book is a contemplation of horror, with a protagonist who becomes a victim of that horror, but in this case, the horror is not a purely personal one. Significantly, unlike the Loftises and Cass Kinsolving, Nat does not deteriorate, but grows through the course of the book as his comprehension of society and life grows. Nat Turner is the richest and most psychologically complex of Styron's characters, and the historical subject matter of the work is filtered through his sensitive consciousness to produce a visionary "meditation" on the world of slavery, dreamlike in quality and poetic in execution. Southern Virginia of the 1830's, the novel's world, is very much a projection of Nat's mind—a mind produced by that world, and savaged by it.

To develop the subtlety of Nat's mind, Styron drew on all his technical and rhetorical resources. His mastery of time-shifts and dream sequences, already amply demonstrated, was enhanced in this novel, and he explored a variety of rhetorical styles, varying from rural black dialect to a high Anglican style echoing Joan Didion's *A Book of Common Prayer* (1977) for Nat's more poetic utterances. Nat's mind ranges with astonishing virtuosity over his universe—the natural world, the complexities of human relations, the elusive mysteries of God, and the bitterness of mortality. An enormously sophisticated narrative persona, Nat moves fluidly across time, contemplating the painful mystery of the past, represented by his long-dead African grandmother, and of the future, represented by his own forthcoming death. Nat tells the entire novel in flashback, remembering his abortive slave rebellion and the personal and historical events leading up to it, constantly trying to cipher out the meaning of those events. The novel is a study of the growth of knowledge and of the growth of Nat's mind. In the introspective isolation of his anguished imprisonment, he reconstructs his lifelong struggle to understand the meaning of existence. He recalls his progression from childhood, when he had no comprehension of what slavery meant, to an early adult period when he accepted his condition either bitterly or philosophically, to a final understanding of slavery in personal, societal, and moral terms. Ironically, as Nat becomes more morally and aesthetically sensitive, he becomes more insensitive in human terms, gravitating toward an acceptance of the violence that finally characterizes his revolt. Only a sudden, visionary conversion to a God of love at the end of the novel saves him from closing the book as an unrepentant apostle of retributory cruelty.

In the process of expanding his knowledge and developing his terrible vision of deliverance from slavery by violence, Nat becomes the spokesman for two familiar Styron themes—the complexity of human psychology and the mystery of human suffering. The most self-searching of Styron's characters, Nat exhaustively explores the ambivalence and ambiguity of his feelings about race, sex, religion, and violence. Although he casts himself convincingly as a Christian prophet, Nat is no simplistic fundamentalist, for he recognizes in his own emotional turmoil personal depths that he can plumb with only partial understanding. His psychology is the battleground of conflicting feelings, symbolized by his powerful attraction to his master's gentle daughter and his vitriolic hatred for all she represents. When he eventually kills her, neither he nor the reader can discriminate

his motives. She dies imploring, "Oh, Nat, it hurts so!" and his realization of her pain is the climax of his apprehension of the myriad pains of all humankind, particularly those of his own people. In this concern, he is representative of all Styron's protagonists.

It is almost impossible to deal with *The Confessions of Nat Turner* without mentioning the storm of controversy that followed its publication and success. A number of critics maintained that the novel was historically inaccurate (for example, it portrayed Nat as having homosexual tendencies, but never mentioned that there are records indicating that the real Nat Turner had a wife). Styron was also accused of demeaning a black hero, in that his Nat has reservations about his mission and is squeamish about wholesale slaughter. The real complaint against Styron, though, most thoroughly summarized in a casebook edited by John Henrik Clarke, *William Styron's Nat Turner: Ten Black Writers Respond* (1968), was that he was a white man attempting a theme that should be the province of black writers. In answer to the historical criticism, Styron and his defenders point out that *The Confessions of Nat Turner* is a work of fiction which does not pretend to be straight history, and that it violates no factual information known to Styron at the time of writing. The second complaint, that it degrades a black hero, is more difficult to understand. Unquestionably, Styron, like any true artist, presents his hero with his neuroses, self-doubts, and weaknesses. In the main, however, Nat is without doubt a positive and even heroic character, arguably the most admirable in all Styron's fiction. Only a critic in search of a black plaster saint *sans peur et sans reproche* could consider the creation of as rich and sensitive a character as Nat a slur. While Styron was researching *The Confessions of Nat Turner*, James Baldwin lived in Styron's cottage, and Baldwin encouraged Styron to write the book. Although Styron never acknowledged Baldwin as the model for his Nat Turner, there are similarities in thinking and speech, and Turner's sexual ambivalence may be based on Baldwin. In any case, Styron's Turner is as much a modern intellectual who ponders the effects of slavery as a historical figure.

Sophie's Choice

Styron's novel *Sophie's Choice* was some twelve years in the works, if somewhat less in the writing, and is in every way as ambitious a novel as *The Confessions of Nat Turner*, although its rank in the Styron canon is still in question. Having dealt in earlier novels with suicide, physical agony, existential despair, and slavery, Styron chose the Holocaust as the logical next state of human misery suitable for artistic contemplation. For a long time, Styron had been moving his narrative personae closer toward the subjects of his novels, introducing clearly autobiographical narrators in *The Long March* and *Set This House on Fire*, and making *The Confessions of Nat Turner* an intensely personal first-person narrative. For *Sophie's Choice*, Styron turned to the confessional form plied by novelists as various as Saul Bellow and Norman Mailer and poets such as Robert Lowell. The narrator of *Sophie's Choice*, a young southerner named Stingo, is, for all intents and purposes, indistinguishable from the young Styron. A young artist *manqué* in New York, Stingo meets and is fascinated by a beautiful survivor of a Nazi concentration camp, Sophie, who is permanently psychologically scarred by the horror she has undergone, the most ghastly aspect of which was being forced to decide which of her two children would live and which would die. Stingo is the ultimate naïf: sexually, emotionally, morally, and artistically immature. As he comes to know Sophie, he comes to know himself. Stingo is an artist in search of a subject, as Styron evidently felt that he himself had been. Styron's problems with finding subject matter commensurate with his talents as a technician have been pointed out by William Van O'Conner in "John Updike and William Styron: The Burden of Talent" (1964) and by other critics. Styron himself acknowledged his concern with finding a fit subject for his early fiction, but he also felt that a concern with pain had been central to his earlier work. In 1970, he said, "Consciousness of pain and suffering has informed my work. . . . I hope my present work will not be so preoccupied." At that time, he was working on his military novel "The Way of the Warrior," which he eventually abandoned to write a book that returned to the pain

motif with a vengeance, along with the other leitmotif of *Sophie's Choice*, that of the artist's finding of himself.

The emotional pain of Peyton Loftis is alienation from family and love. Cass Kinsolving suffers from guilt brought on by self-hatred and contemplation of human suffering. Nat Turner's ultimate pain derives from his isolation from all humankind and God. Sophie and Stingo suffer the pain of guilt. Stingo, the apotheosis of Styron's autobiographical WASP characters, feels he has not "paid his dues," suffered as others have suffered, and he learns of Sophie's anguished life with a guilty voyeurism. Sophie's guilt has a specific origin in her hideous choice to doom one of her children. She also feels ashamed that in Auschwitz she somehow "suffered less" since she was the commandant's mistress and finally survived when others died. Constantly and compulsively her mind plays over the fates of those dead—her little girl, her tortured friends, and the gassed millions whom she never knew. Even memories of her murdered husband and of her father, both of whom she despised, bring her reproach and grief. The knowledge that she did what she had to gives no relief. She says, "I see that it was—beyond my control, but it is still so terrible to wake up these many mornings with the memory of that, having to live with it . . . it makes everything unbearable. Just unbearable." Soon, she will kill herself to stop the pain.

After Sophie's death, the shattered Stingo, who had just become her lover, walks on the beach trying to find some sort of personal resolution and acceptance of a world in which horror and anguish such as Sophie's exist. Her message, though, has been clear: There is no resolution. Madness and suffering of the magnitude represented by the Holocaust can be neither accepted nor understood. Sophie, like Herman Melville's Ishmael, realizes that "there is a wisdom that is woe, and there is a woe that is madness." Stingo has come to know it, too.

With the death of Sophie, Styron seems to have come full circle in his exploration of human suffering and his search for meaning in a flawed and painful world. Both Sophie and Peyton Loftis find death to be the only release from lives so agonizing and painful as to be unbearable. In both his first novel and this one, Styron leads the reader to the edge of the grave and points to it as the goal of life—"therefore it cannot be long before we lie down in darkness, and have our light in ashes." The crucial difference between *Sophie's Choice* and *Lie Down in Darkness*, however, is the character of Stingo, who like Ishmael escapes to tell the tale. The earlier novel leaves the reader in desolation, but the latter, through Stingo, holds forth the possibility of an alternative existence, one not horribly haunted by the knowledge of pain. Stingo's life is hardly one of euphoria, but it is a tenable existence compared to Sophie's untenable one. To some degree, Stingo has paid his dues through her; he has come to know pain and evil through her sacrifice, and therefore he is sadder and wiser, but not destroyed as she is. His survival counterpoints her destruction; the novel that Stingo will write grows out of her ashes and becomes her immortality.

Sophie's Choice is not a cheerful novel, or even an affirmative one, but it is not nihilistic. Perhaps Stingo's optimism at the close is unjustified. A number of critics feel that when Stingo walks on the beach after Sophie's death and finds the morning "excellent and fair," anticipating his own promising career, Styron is simply tacking on an upbeat ending hardly defensible in view of the horror explored by the novel. Similarly, Cass Kinsolving in *Set This House on Fire* never satisfies his thirst for metaphysical answers to terrible questions, but simply decides to stop thirsting and take up fishing. In each of Styron's novels, characters suffer, and some suffer unto death. These tragedies reveal an unjust world, not a nihilistic one—Styron's tragedies are moral pronouncements. As moral pronouncements, the novels point to the possibility of a better way.

John L. Cobbs,
updated by Roark Mulligan

OTHER MAJOR WORKS

SHORT FICTION: *A Tidewater Morning: Three Tales from Youth*, 1993.

PLAY: *In the Clap Shack*, pr. 1972.

NONFICTION: *This Quiet Dust*, 1982; *Darkness Visible: A Memoir of Madness*, 1990.

BIBLIOGRAPHY

Casciato, Arthur D., and James L. W. West III, eds. *Critical Essays on William Styron*. Boston: G. K. Hall, 1982. A collection of critical essays that covers all of Styron's major novels and that includes bibliographical references.

Coale, Samuel. *William Styron Revisited*. Boston: Twayne, 1991. A brief biography and an analysis of Styron's novels. Coale devotes a chapter to each major work, including a selected bibliography.

Cologne-Brookes, Gavin. *The Novels of William Styron: From Harmony to History*. Baton Rouge: Louisiana State University Press, 1995. This work traces the influence of the modernist movement on Styron, explores Styron's psychological themes, and analyzes his shifting patterns of discourse. Includes analysis of Styron's later work.

Hadaller, David. *Gynicide: Women in the Novels of William Styron*. Madison, N.J.: Fairleigh Dickinson University Press, 1996. Explores women in Styron's fiction. In particular, Hadaller examines the deaths of women and the meaning of these deaths, arguing that Styron's depictions force the reader to question a society that victimizes women.

Morris, Robert K., and Irving Malin, eds. *The Achievement of William Styron*. Athens: University of Georgia Press, 1975. Provides essays by various critics on Styron's fiction up to *Sophie's Choice*. The essay by Morris and Malin on Styron's career as a visionary novelist is a good introduction to his work.

West, James L. W., III, ed. *Conversations with William Styron*. Jackson: University Press of Mississippi, 1985. A collection of interviews with William Styron in which Styron attempts to "restore a little balance," giving his side to the many controversies that his books have caused.

_____. *William Styron: A Life*. New York: Random House, 1998. The first comprehensive biography of Styron, West's extraordinary work lucidly and cogently connects events in Styron's life to his fiction. This is an essential work for anyone who wishes to understand Styron and his writing.

JONATHAN SWIFT

Born: Dublin, Ireland; November 30, 1667
Died: Dublin, Ireland; October 19, 1745

PRINCIPAL LONG FICTION

A Tale of a Tub, 1704
Gulliver's Travels, 1726 (originally entitled *Travels into Several Remote Nations of the World, in Four Parts, by Lemuel Gulliver, First a Surgeon, and Then a Captain of Several Ships*)

OTHER LITERARY FORMS

Jonathan Swift's oeuvre includes a large and important body of verse, best assembled in *The Poems of Jonathan Swift* (1937, 1958), edited by Harold Williams. His letters may be found in *The Correspondence of Jonathan Swift* (1963-1965), also edited by Williams. Outstanding among a variety of political writings are Swift's contributions to *The Examiner* (1710-1711), the treatise called *The Conduct of the Allies and of the Late Ministry, in Beginning and Carrying on the Present War* (1711), and the important *The Drapier's Letters to the People of Ireland* (1735). His prose, collected in *The Prose Works of Jonathan Swift* (1939-1968), is a fourteen-volume collection edited by Herbert Davis.

ACHIEVEMENTS

It is generally conceded that Swift is the greatest English satirist, possibly the most brilliant ironist and acerb wit in any language. Yet the force of his satiric barbs has rendered him controversial, and many critics have retaliated against his potent quill by claiming that Swift is wreckless, uncontrolled, spiteful, insensate, heathenish, and insane. Such rash responses merely demonstrate the powerful effect his writing instigates.

Swift is not an overt lampooner, diatribe-monger, or name-caller. Curiously, he never utilizes the direct approach: he almost always speaks through a defective mouthpiece, a flawed, self-incriminating persona who forges a case against himself. Indeed, Swift is to be remembered as a grand satiric mimic, finely shaping and generating the voices of knaves and fools alike (the "modern" hack writer in *A Tale of a Tub*, the ignorant serving-woman Frances Harris, the idiot astrologer Isaac Bickerstaff, the callous and mathematical Modest Proposer, the proud but demented simpleton Lemuel Gulliver).

Swift's ear for clichés and inflections of dullness is almost perfect, and an author such as Herbert Read (in *English Prose Style*, 1928) hails Swift as the inevitable and clear master of "pure prose" style. Swift is, without doubt, the major satirist in prose, yet he is also a first-rate light poet (in the manner of Horace and the coarser Samuel "Hudibras" Butler), and, if anything, his reputation as a poet is rising. Furthermore, Swift wrote political pamphlets with ruthless force, and his prose in sermons, letters, and treatises is virile and direct. Finally, Swift should not be forgotten as wit and jester. He invented a child-language when corresponding with Stella, wrote mock-Latin sayings, devised wicked epigrams, created paraphrases of Vergil and Ovid, and could even toy with versifying when devising invitations to dinner. In a word, Swift is the all-around English expert in straightforward exposition—especially when it is bent to provoke savage mockery and the *jeu d'esprit*.

BIOGRAPHY

Jonathan Swift was born in Dublin on November 30, 1667, after the death of his father, a lower-middle class Anglo-Irishman. His grandfather, the Reverend Thomas Swift, had been a vicar in Herefordshire. His father, Jonathan, had settled in Ireland to work as a steward of the King's Inns in Dublin. His mother was Abigail Erick, the daughter of a Leicestershire clergyman. Swift's mother had entrusted her young son to a nurse; the nurse had spirited the infant Swift away from Ireland for several years, and although he was eventually returned, Jonathan was peculiarly linked with Ireland throughout his life. In any case, it was his fancy to picture himself a lonely outcast amid barbarians. He attended Kilkenny School in his youth and Trinity College, Dublin, obtaining a Bachelor's degree in 1686. He spent most of the following decade at Moor Park, Surrey, in the household of Sir William Temple, the distinguished

Whig statesman. It was at Moor Park that Swift met, in 1689, the child of Esther Johnson (whom Swift later immortalized as "Stella"), the daughter of Temple's widowed housekeeper. Swift helped in supervising her education and inaugurated a lifelong (and little understood) relationship, for Stella later immigrated to Dublin and spent her life near the Anglican Dean Swift. Naturally, under Temple's aegis, Swift hoped for introductions and advancement, but little came of promises and possibilities; and in 1694, he returned to Dublin long enough to be ordained an Anglican priest (in 1695). He subsequently was reunited with Temple until the latter's death in 1699. Thereafter, he returned to Ireland as chaplain to the Earl of Berkeley. His reputation for talent and wit was rapidly growing.

Swift's great political period took place in London from 1708 to 1714. He became the chief spokesman, apologist, and pamphleteer for the powerful Tory leaders then in power, Robert Harley and Henry St. John Bolingbroke. Their fall and disgrace ushered in a lengthy era of Whig dominance that permanently drove Swift back to what he must have considered exile in Ireland. Swift had been finally rewarded (although he would have perceived it as a paltry recognition) with the Deanery of St. Patrick's Cathedral in Dublin, where he served for the remainder of his life. His powerful satires had earned him powerful enemies, and significant advancement in the Church or in England was never permitted to him.

In any event, Swift served with precision, justness, and rectitude as a clergyman, and continued throughout his career to be an admirable satirist and wit. He even elected to champion the rights of the maltreated Irish, and he came to be admired as their avatar and protector, a "Hibernian Patriot." In his last years, Swift suffered increasingly from deafness and vertigo (the results of a lifelong affliction by Ménière's Syndrome, a disease of the inner ear), which resulted in senility, and most likely a stroke. Guardians were appointed in his last years, and he died in 1745, shortly before his seventy-eighth birthday.

Swift's last ironic jest was played upon humankind in his will, which committed the bulk of his estate to the founding of a "hospital" for fools and madmen, just as he had pronounced the plan in his *Verses on the Death of Dr. Swift* (1731):

> He gave the little Wealth he had,
> To build a House for Fools and Mad;
> And shew'd by one satyric Touch,
> No Nation wanted it so much

ANALYSIS

Initially, it must be noted that Jonathan Swift's "fictions" are nothing like conventional novels. They seldom detail the "adventures" of a hero or even a protagonist and never conclude with his Romantic achievement of goals or fulfillment of desires. Indeed, Swift is the great master of fictionalizing nonfiction. His satires always purport to be something factual, humdrum, diurnal, unimaginative: a treatise, a travel diary, an annotated edition, a laborious oration, a tendentious allegory, a puffed-out "letter-to-a-

(Library of Congress)

friend." Extremist Protestant sects condemned fiction, and "projectors" and would-be investigators in the dawning Age of Science extolled the prosaic, the plodding, the scholarly, the methodical, and the factual. At the same time, urban population growth and the rise of the middle class created a growing new audience, and printing presses multiplied in accordance with demand. Many "popular" and best-seller art forms flourished: sermons, true confessions, retellings (and Second Parts) of hot-selling tales and political harangues, news items, hearsay gossip, and science all became jumbled together for public consumption, much of which led to spates of yellow journalism. Throughout his life Swift rebelled against such indelicacies and depravities, and his satiric procedure included the extremist parody of tasteless forms—*reductio ad absurdum*. It was by such means that Swift secured his fame as an author.

A TALE OF A TUB

Doubtless his most dazzling prose performance of this kind was his earliest, *A Tale of a Tub*, which appeared anonymously in 1704. (Swift, in fact, published most of his satires anonymously, although his work was usually instantly recognized and acclaimed.) *A Tale of a Tub* is actually a "medley" of pieces imitating the penchant for an author's combining fiction, essays, letters, verse, fragments, or anything to enable him to amass a booklength manuscript. It contained "The Battle of the Books," a wooden allegorical piece in the manner of Aesop's Fables, detailing the "quarrel of ancients versus moderns" and a fragmentary treatise upon "The Mechanical Operation of the Spirit," trussed up in the inept form of a casual letter to a friend.

The treatise mocked the new "scientific" trend of reducing all things to some species of Cartesian (or Newtonian) materialism. Rather comically, it deploys in a blasé manner the language of ancient Greek and Roman atomists—Democritus and Epicurus—as if they were contemporary modernists. Indeed, one pervasive theme throughout this volume is the ridiculousness of the modernist position of "independence"—although they might be ignorant of the past, the ideas and genres of classical antiquity keep recurring in their works, a fact which belies the Moderns'

supposed originality (even while demonstrating that, as a result of solipsism, their form and control disintegrate into chaos).

Clearly, the titular piece, "A Tale of a Tub," is Swift's early masterpiece, and one of the great (and most difficult) satires in any language. In its pages, an avowed fanatic "modern" aspires to "get off" an edition, to tout and sell himself, to make money, to demonstrate his uniqueness and, however evanescently, tyrannically to be "the latest modern." He seeks to reedit an old tale of three brothers and their adventures. Naturally, he decorates and updates such a version to give it the latest cut and fashion, the style and wit and jargon of the moment. (It is perhaps an accident that this tale of the dissensions of Peter, Martin, and Jack parallels the vicissitudes of the history of Christianity, as it splinters into differing and quarreling religious sects. The Modern appears ignorant of historical sense.)

The new version of the old story, however, is fragmented: Every time the Modern's imagination or his fancy supplies him with a spark, he promptly follows his rather meandering Muse and travels into an elaboration, an annotation, or a digression. In fact, the opening fifty pages of the work is cluttered with the paraphernalia of "modern" publishing: dedications, publisher's comments, introductions, apologies, and gratulations, notes to the second edition, acknowledgements, prefaces, and forewords. Thereafter, when such a cloud of ephemeral formalities would seem to have been dispensed with, the author still manages to interject a plethora of digressions—afterthoughts, asides, cute remarks *à propos* of nothing, commentary, snipings at critics, obsequious snivelings for the reader, canting pseudophilosophy for the learned, and pity and adoration for himself. In no time at all, the entire tale is awash in detours, perambulations, and divagations.

This modern storyteller is nothing if not effervescent, boorish, and chronically self-indulgent. He claims that his pipe dreams and diversions are in essence planned excursions and in fact deliberately philosophic meditations, rich with allegorical meanings. The opposite is also true, and the Modern's Tub is like an empty cart—rattling around most furiously in its vacuity, making the most noise. Furthermore, the digressions become unwieldy. The tale is disrupted more and more frequently and the digressions become longer and longer. The Modern is his most penetrating in the trenchant Section IX—a digression in praise of madness—as he coyly confesses that his reason has been overturned, his intellectuals rattled, and that he has been but recently confined. The continued multiplication of digressions (until they subvert sections of the tale) and the finale when the Modern loses his notes and his ramblings give out entirely are easily understood as the wanderings of a madman—a Modern who suppresses the past, memory, reason, and self-control.

If Swift's warning about the growing taste for newness, modernity, and things-of-the-moment appears madcap and farcical, it is nevertheless a painfully close nightmare preview of future fashions, fantasms, and fallacies that subsequently came to be real.

A Tale of a Tub clearly demonstrates several of Swift's most common fictional ploys and motifs. Some representative of the depraved "moderns" is usually present, always crass, irreligious, ignorant, arrogant, proud, self-adulatory, concerned with the events of the moment. Indeed, Swift was fond of scrupulously celebrating every April 1 as All Fool's Day, but he also recognized April 2: All Knave's Day. He doubtless felt that both halves of humankind deserved some token of official recognition. Yet Swift also favored mixing the two: He frequently shows readers that a man who is manipulator, con man, and knave in one set of circumstances is himself conned, befooled, and gulled in another. As such, the Modern reveals an unexpected complexity in his makeup; he also illustrates the era (as Swift imagines it) that he inhabits; a period overfull of bad taste and poor writing which are the broad marks of cultural decadence.

In the work of a satirist, the world is regularly depicted as cyclic in historic periods, and usually in decline. Swift and Sir William Temple both stressed some trend toward decay in the modern era, and spoke often of barbarians and invasions; it was a type of satiric myth suitable to the disruptive fictions that

the satirist envisions. In Section IX of *A Tale of a Tub*, the Modern vacillates between viewing all humankind as being "curious" or "credulous," as busy probers, analysts, and excavators, and the superficial and the inert: knaves versus fools. As is typical of Swift, the fool and knave personas are infused with enough familiar traits to suggest that all people partake of either. Further, Swift entraps his reader by implying that there are no other categories: One is either fool or knave or both. His irony is corrosive and inclusive, capturing the reader in its toils. In that sense, Swift is deliberately disruptive; he seeks to startle and to embroil the reader in his fictions about stupidity and depravity. To such an end, he tampers with logic to make his case appear substantial and manipulates paradox to keep his readers off balance. Such techniques lend Swift his volatile force.

These strategies are to be found in Swift's best verse; the same may be said for his two great, ironic short-prose pieces: *An Argument to Prove That the Abolishing of Christianity in England May, as Things Now Stand, Be Attended with Some Inconveniences, and Perhaps Not Produce Those Many Good Effects Proposed Thereby* (1708) and *A Modest Proposal for Preventing the Children of Poor People of Ireland from Being a Burden to Their Parents or the Country, and for Making Them Beneficial to the Public* (1729). Both of these works seek to shock the reader and to propose the discomforting, the alarming, the untenable.

GULLIVER'S TRAVELS

Swift's undisputed masterpiece is *Gulliver's Travels*, originally entitled *Travels into Several Remote Nations of the World, in Four Parts, by Lemuel Gulliver, First a Surgeon, and Then a Captain of Several Ships*. This fictional work accommodates all of Swift's perennial themes and does so effectually. First, the work is perhaps the definitive study of new middle-class values, specifically the preoccupation with slang, cash, smug self-righteousness, self-assertion, and self-gratulation. Second, it might not be considered a "novel" in the conventional sense of the term, but it is a delightfully fact-filled simulation of adventure fiction, and it stems assuredly from the satiric picaresque tradition (in Spain and France) that greatly contributed to the formulation of modern novelistic techniques and themes.

Swift's Lemuel Gulliver (a mulish gull) is a model representative of the fool and the knave: He aspires to befool others but nevertheless befuddles himself. His medium is the very popular literary genre of the travelogue or record of a "voyage of discovery." The genre grew popular through its Cartesian emphasis upon an inductive observer-self and the Romantic subject of adventures in far-off lands. Such a travelogue format allows the narrator to take his readers on a vicarious journey of adventure and concludes by suggesting that the traveler has fulfilled the pattern of the *Bildungsroman* and has attained education, growth, experience, and Aristotelian *cognitio* (insight, maturation, the acquisition of new knowledge). As might be expected in an exemplary case manipulated by Swift, Gulliver is anything but the apt learner. He is a crass materialist for whom experiences consist of precise measurements of objects observed, a tedious cataloging of dress, diet, and customs, and an infinite variety of pains in note-taking, recording, transcribing, and translating. He is superficiality and rank objectivity incarnate. Naturally, therefore, his everyday mean density prevents his acquisition of any true understanding.

Gulliver is a minor physician, the mediocre little man, anxious, like Daniel Defoe's Robinson Crusoe, to make sight-seeing tours and to acquire cash. His first of four voyages carries him to the land of six-inch mites, the Lilliputians, and his Second Voyage to the land of gargantuan giants, the Brobdingnagians. Gulliver remains myopic in either location, for he can hardly consider that little midgets can (and do) perpetuate monstrous deeds; and, once he perceives that the giants are rather tame, he leaps to the conclusion that they are infinitely superior to other human types (even though their political and social institutions are no better than they should be, given the quirks and flaws of human nature).

In sum, the tour from very small to very large merely stimulates in Gulliver a sense of wondrous contrast: He expects in these different worlds wondrous differences. Amusingly, what the reader finds is much the same, that is the uneven and imperfect human nature. Equally amusing, Gulliver behaves much the same himself in his attempts to ingratiate himself with his "superiors": He aspires to become a successful competitor in all worlds as a "titled" nobleman, a Nardac, a "courtier" with "connections" at court. Like many middle-class people, he is a man in the middle, aspiring above all for upward mobility, mouthing the commonplaces of the day, utterly incapable of judging people and events. He is also the worst sort of traveler; he is a man who sees no farther than his own predilections and preconceptions and who imitates all the manners that he sees around him. Actually, the realms of big and little are merely distortions of the real world. Here, one of the work's central ironies is found in the fact that Gulliver could have learned as much, or as little, if he had stayed at home.

The world of sizes is replaced in the Third Voyage by the world of concepts: The muddled peoples he visits are victims of mathomania and abstraction-worship. At the same time, it is revealed that the world of the past, like the world of the present, has been tainted and corrupt. Even the potentially ideal Struldbruggs—immortals who live forever—are exposed as being far from lucky. They are, rather, especially accursed by the afflictions of impotence, depression, and senility. Swift has, with cartoon facility, carted Gulliver all around the world, showing him the corrosive face of fallen humanity, even among the various robbers, cowards, pirates, and mutineers that had beset him as he traveled in European ships; but Gulliver does not see.

The stage is properly set for the Fourth Voyage. Utilizing his favorite ploys of reversal and entrapment, Swift puts Gulliver into a land of learned and rational horses (the Houyhnhnms) and debauched hairy monkeylike beasts (the Yahoos). Once again, there is no middle ground: All in this world is rational horse or wolfish (and oafish) bestiality. Obviously, Gulliver chooses the equestrian gentlemen as his leaders and masters. (Indeed, throughout all the voyages, Gulliver the conformist has been in quest of a staid position and "masters" who will tell him what to do and grant him praise and sustenance for his slavish adulation.)

Slowly it is revealed, however, the Yahoos are men: Gulliver *is* a debased, gross, and deformed member of the Yahoo tribe; as Swift sweetly and confoundingly phrases it, Gulliver is a "perfect yahoo." The horses themselves rebuff this upstart, and Gulliver, who has undergone every other sort of ignominy in the course of his travels, is finally evicted as an undersirable alien from the horsey paradise. At last, Gulliver thinks he has learned a lesson; he aspires to be a horse, and, back in Europe, he shuns the human species and favors the environs of straw and stables. He has hardly acquired the rationality of his leaders and appears quite mad. Swift's ultimate paradox seems to imply that people can "know" about reason and ideals but can never master or practice them. Yet, even here, Swift cruelly twists the knife at the last moment, for the fond Gulliver, several years later, is revealed as slowly forgetting his intense (and irrational) devotion to the Houyhnhnms and is slowly beginning to be able to tolerate and accept the lowly human race that he had earlier so intransigently spurned. Gulliver cannot even stick to a lesson painfully and rudely learned during many years; he has neither the brains, drive, ambition, nor consistency to keep him on any course. Gulliver's travels eventually get him nowhere.

In sum, *Gulliver's Travels* makes a huge tragicomical case for the absurdity of pretentious man. Gulliver is fool enough to believe that he is progressing and knave enough to boast about it, and to hope to gain some position and affluence from the event. Yet, at his proudest moments, he is little more than a driveller, a gibbering idiot who is raveningly insane. Gulliver's painful experiences and the brute instruction his readers acquire are a caustic finale to much of the heady and bold idealism of the Renaissance, and a cautionary plea for restraint in an era launched on celebrating reason, science, optimism, and enlightenment. Time has shown that Swift was largely right; blithe superconfidence in people, their sciences, and their so-called "progress" is very likely to come enormously to grief. *Gulliver's Travels* speaks to everyone because it addresses crucial issues about the human condition itself.

John R. Clark

OTHER MAJOR WORKS

POETRY: *Cadenus and Vanessa*, 1726; *Verses on the Death of Dr. Swift*, 1731; *On Poetry: A Rapsody*, 1733; *The Poems of Jonathan Swift*, 1937, 1958 (3 volumes; Harold Williams, editor).

NONFICTION: *A Discourse of the Contests and Dissensions Between the Nobles and the Commons in Athens and Rome*, 1701; *The Battle of the Books*, 1704; *An Argument to Prove That the Abolishing of Christianity in England May, as Things Now Stand, Be Attended with Some Inconveniences, and Perhaps Not Produce Those Many Good Effects Proposed Thereby*, 1708; *A Project for the Advancement of Religion, and the Reformation of Manners By a Person of Quality*, 1709; *The Conduct of the Allies and of the Late Ministry, in Beginning and Carrying on the Present War*, 1711; *A Proposal for Correcting, Improving and Ascertaining the English Tongue, in a Letter to the Most Honourable Robert Earl of Oxford and Mortimer, Lord High Treasurer of Great Britain*, 1712; *The Public Spirit of the Whigs, Set Forth in Their Generous Encouragement of the Author of the Crisis*, 1714; *A Letter from a Lay-Patron to a Gentleman, Designing for Holy Orders*, 1720; *A Modest Proposal for Preventing the Children of Poor People of Ireland from Being a Burden to Their Parents or the Country, and for Making Them Beneficial to the Public*, 1729; *The Drapier's Letters to the People of Ireland*, 1735; *A Complete Collection of Genteel and Ingenious Conversation, According to the Most Polite Mode and Method Now Used at Court, and in the Best Companies of England, in Three Dialogues, by Simon Wagstaff Esq.*, 1738; *Directions to Servants in General . . .*, 1745; *The History of the Four Last Years of the Queen, by the Late Jonathan Swift DD, DSPD*, 1758; *Journal to Stella*, 1766, 1768; *Letter to a Very Young Lady on Her Marriage*, 1797; *The Correspondence of Jonathan Swift*, 1963-1965 (5 volumes; Harold Williams, editor).

MISCELLANEOUS: *Miscellanies in Prose and Verse*, 1711; *Miscellanies*, 1727-1733 (4 volumes; with Alexander Pope and other members of the Scriblerus Club); *The Prose Works of Jonathan Swift*, 1939-1968 (14 volumes; Herbert Davis, editor).

BIBLIOGRAPHY

Ehrenpreis, Irvin. *Swift: The Man, His Works, and the Age.* 3 vols. Cambridge, Mass.: Harvard University Press, 1962-1983. A monumental biography that rejects long-held myths, provides much new information about Swift and his works, and relates him to the intellectual and political currents of his age.

Fox, Christopher, and Brenda Tooley, eds. *Walking Naboth's Vineyard: New Studies of Swift.* Notre Dame: University of Notre Dame Press, 1995. The introduction discusses Swift and Irish studies, and the subsequent essays all consider aspects of Swift as an Irish writer. Individual essays have notes, but there is no bibliography.

Hunting, Robert. *Jonathan Swift.* Rev. ed. Boston: Twayne, 1989. In this revision of his earlier book on Swift, Hunting incorporates recent scholarship to provide an overview of Swift's life and his major works. Includes a chronology and a selective, annotated secondary bibliography.

Nokes, David. *Jonathan Swift, A Hypocrite Reversed: A Critical Biography.* Oxford, England: Oxford University Press, 1985. Draws heavily on Swift's own writings, offering a good introduction for the general reader seeking information about his life and works. Nokes views Swift as a conservative humanist.

Palmieri, Frank, ed. *Critical Essays on Jonathan Swift.* New York: G. K. Hall, 1993. Divided into sections on Swift's life and writings, *Gulliver's Travels*, *A Tale of a Tub* and eighteenth century literature, and his poetry and nonfiction prose. Includes index but no bibliography.

Quintana, Ricardo. *The Mind and Art of Jonathan Swift.* 1936. Reprint. London: Oxford University Press, 1953. One of the standards of Swift criticism, concentrating on the public Swift. Examines his political activities and writings, tracing the intellectual sources of his thought. Includes synopses of his major works and provides a useful historical background. The 1953 edition contains additional notes and an updated bibliography.

Rawson, Claude. *The Character of Swift's Satire: A Revised Focus.* Newark: University of Delaware Press, 1983. Presents eleven essays by Swift scholars, including John Traugatt's excellent reading of *A Tale of a Tub*, Irvin Ehrenpreis on Swift as a letter writer, and F. P. Lock on Swift's role in the political affairs of Queen Anne's reign.

Real, Hermann J., and Heinz J. Vienken, eds. *Proceedings of the First Münster Symposium on Jonathan Swift.* Munich: Wilhelm Fink, 1985. Includes twenty-four essays on all aspects of Swift's work, each preceded by an abstract. Indexed for cross-referencing.

T

AMY TAN

Born: Oakland, California; February 19, 1952

PRINCIPAL LONG FICTION
The Joy Luck Club, 1989
The Kitchen God's Wife, 1991
The Hundred Secret Senses, 1995

OTHER LITERARY FORMS

She is best known for her novels, but Amy Tan's work also includes short essays, short stories, and two children's books—*The Moon Lady* (1992) and *The Chinese Siamese Cat* (1994). In addition, Tan wrote the screenplay for the 1993 film version of *The Joy Luck Club*.

ACHIEVEMENTS

Amy Tan is one of the best-known and most popular Asian American writers and, like Maxine Hong Kingston, is considered a guide to the landscape of the Asian American experience. Gracing the best-seller lists, Tan's novels have earned critical and popular acclaim, and *The Joy Luck Club* was made into a major motion picture. Tan won the Commonwealth Gold Award and the Bay Area Book Reviewers Award for *The Joy Luck Club*, which was also nominated for the National Book Award and the National Book Critics Circle Award.

Tan's novels contribute to the dialogue about the meanings of "Asian" and "American" by portraying the intercultural conflict threatening many Asian American immigrant families. Her strong storytelling ability ensures the accessibility of her fiction to general readers; moreover, her work appeals to feminist readers and critics because, as Sau-ling Cynthia Wong points out, Tan's novels belong to significant "discursive traditions" including "mainstream feminist writing; Asian American matrilineal literature;

quasi ethnography about the Orient; Chinese American 'tour-guiding' works."

BIOGRAPHY

Amy Tan was born to Daisy and John Tan, both of whom had emigrated from China; they met and married in the United States. As a child, Tan was acutely conscious that she was different from her classmates. She remembers wearing a clothespin on her nose in an effort to reshape that appendage to look more Caucasian. Like most Asian American young people, Tan was American at school and Chinese at home. Although her mother spoke to her in Chinese, Tan answered in English. The tensions in her dual heritage eventually found their way into her novels in her portrayal of the generational conflicts in immigrant families.

At fifteen, Tan lost both her father and her older brother: They died of brain tumors within months of each other. Her mother reacted by leaving California with the remaining children, moving first to the East Coast and then to Europe, where Tan finished high school in Switzerland.

Tan attended three colleges before earning her degree in English and linguistics from San Jose State University. Marrying Louis DeMattei, a tax lawyer, after graduation, Tan began work toward a doctorate in linguistics, but she abandoned her studies for a career before earning her degree. After years as a business writer, Tan realized that, despite a lucrative career, she was unsatisfied, and she decided to attempt a different kind of writing. When she was eight years old, she had won an essay contest, and she cherished dreams of someday writing fiction. Tan set out to fulfill those dreams. Joining a writer's group led by author Molly Giles, she commenced work on the short stories that became the nucleus of her first book.

Tan's first novel, *The Joy Luck Club*, published in 1989, was a critical and popular success, catapulting the author into the ranks of significant American novelists. *The Kitchen God's Wife* followed two years later, garnering high praise and another berth on the best-seller lists. In 1995, Tan published her third novel, *The Hundred Secret Senses*, an exploration of the nature of memory and love.

(Archive Photos/Lee)

ANALYSIS

Like the works of many late twentieth century writers, Amy Tan's books are difficult to classify into a single fictional genre. Although Tan's works are indisputably novels, readers and critics agree that her fiction fuses several narrative genres: memoir and autobiography, mythology and folktale, history and biography. Moreover, like Maxine Hong Kingston, Tan appropriates Chinese talk story—a combination of narrative genres from Chinese oral tradition expressed in a local vernacular—to give shape and a distinctive voice to her novels.

Tan's fictional landscape is both geographically vast and spatially confined. The American spaces embrace San Francisco and the Bay Area, while the Chinese locations include a large territory from Guilin to Shanghai and encompass time from feudal China to the twentieth century. Between her protagonists' ancestral homeland and their adopted country lies the Pacific Ocean, symbolically crossed by the

woman and the swan in the tale that begins *The Joy Luck Club.* Nonetheless, the crucial events in Tan's novels are contained within definitive boundaries: a circumscribed Chinatown neighborhood, the tiny village of Changmian, one-room accommodations for Chinese pilots and their wives, a stuffy apartment crammed with elderly mah-jongg enthusiasts.

Enclosed by framing narratives set in the late twentieth century, the embedded stories in Tan's novels are set in earlier eras, transporting readers to nineteenth century rural China, war-ravaged Nanking during World War II, or cosmopolitan Shanghai between the wars. Juxtaposing events separated by decades, Tan parallels the dislocations experienced by emigrants from a familiar culture into an alien one with their daughters' painful journeys from cultural confusion to acceptance of their dual heritage.

Tan's protagonists—members of that diaspora community called Asian Americans—represent two groups: Chinese-born immigrants, imperfectly acculturated despite decades of life in America, and American-born women of Chinese ancestry, uncomfortably straddling the border between their ethnic heritage and the American milieu that is their home. Enmeshed by their shared histories in California's ethnic neighborhoods, the women in Tan's novels struggle to create personal identities that reflect their lives, needs, and desires.

Through her fiction, Tan examines identity—its construction, boundaries, and contexts. Indelibly branded by their visible ethnicity, Tan's characters daily negotiate the minefields of cultural disjunction and tensions between Chinese tradition and Americanization, family connections and individual desires. These tensions inevitably surface, causing intergenerational conflict and the disintegration of family relationships as members of the older generation look back to China while their daughters remain firmly connected to California.

THE JOY LUCK CLUB

The Joy Luck Club tells the stories of four mother-daughter pairs: Suyuan and Jing-mei Woo, An-Mei and Rose Hsu Jordan, Lindo and Waverly Jong, and Ying-ying and Lena St. Clair. Implicit in the generational conflicts that erupt between the women is the bicultural angst separating the Chinese-born mothers from their American-born, assimilated daughters. Initially unable to discover common ground, the two groups of women speak different languages, embrace different values, aspire to different ambitions, and lead divergent lives.

The social club of the title binds together the lives of these eight women. As the novel opens, Jing-mei Woo prepares to take her dead mother's place at the mah-jongg table that anchors the club's activities. During Jing-mei's first game, the older women beg her to go to China on her mother's behalf, and their pleas trigger in Jing-mei painful memories of her Chinatown childhood. Jing-mei's first narrative introduces the other narrators, and except for Suyuan, whose story emerges through Jing-mei's, each woman tells her own story.

Representing the immigrant generation that fled China after World War II, the mothers have had difficult early lives: Suyuan Woo is driven to abandon twins to give them a chance to survive, An-Mei Hsu's mother commits suicide to force her husband to acknowledge An-Mei as his child; Lindo Jong endures an arranged marriage at twelve to an even younger child; and Ying-ying St. Clair, deserted by her first husband, experiences a decade of poverty. In the United States, the mothers must negotiate the traumas of leaving a war-ravaged homeland, starting over in an alien country, and trying to learn a strange language. Through their vicissitudes, they cling to memories of China and to fading traces of their ancestral culture, and they eventually establish stable new lives for themselves.

In contrast with their mothers, the daughters have had good lives—with plenty to eat, comfortable homes, intact families, music lessons, and college educations. Nevertheless, the daughters are discontented and unhappy: Jing-mei is single and aimless, Rose is separated from her husband, Waverly is already divorced, and Lena has summoned up the courage to examine her dysfunctional marriage. Each daughter feels detached from herself, her family, and her community; none of them knows how to reconnect.

The novel traces the evolution of understanding between the mothers and daughters, who are, at the end, finally able to articulate the depth of their caring for each other. The novel concludes when Jing-mei travels to China to meet her two half sisters—the women who were the infants that Suyuan lost in wartime China.

THE KITCHEN GOD'S WIFE

The Kitchen God's Wife also explores dynamics of the mother-daughter relationship in the context of cultural and ethnic disjunctions, albeit in less detail than does *The Joy Luck Club*. Instead, *The Kitchen God's Wife* focuses on a woman's journey to wholeness after an eventful life that replicates the Chinese immigrant experience in microcosm. The novel's title refers to Winnie Louie's version of the story of the Kitchen God who achieves deity status when he proves to be capable of shame upon discovering that the wife he has mistreated still cares about his welfare. Unfortunately, according to Winnie, the Kitchen God's wife is denied membership in the Chinese pantheon of deities despite her fidelity.

The novel tells two stories: the sketchy framing narrative that involves the widening rift between Winnie and her daughter, Pearl; and the fully developed chronicle of Winnie's life in China. Through her story, Pearl contextualizes Winnie's reminiscences, describing a series of events and revelations that ultimately changes their relationship. Required by family obligations to attend the funeral of an ancient "aunt" and the engagement party of a "cousin," Pearl spends more time with Winnie than she has in many months, and the enforced companionship prompts the younger woman to examine the roots of their estrangement. Winnie, goaded to action by a letter from China that closes a painful chapter in her past, decides to tell Pearl about her life in China.

Save for the early chapters in which Pearl speaks, and the epilogue in which Winnie and Pearl deify the Kitchen God's wife as Lady Sorrowfree, the novel chronicles the eventful life of Jiang Weili—Winnie's Chinese name—as she negotiates the difficult journey from a privileged childhood through an abusive marriage and the tragedy of war, and ultimately to a secure life in the United States.

The daughter of a wealthy Shanghai merchant, Jiang Weili marries the dashing Wen Fu, only to discover after the wedding that he has misrepresented his family's wealth and status. Worse yet, he turns out to be an adulterer, abuser, and pathological liar. Forced to follow her pilot husband as he is posted to different cities during the war, Weili tries to be a good wife and mother, laboring to establish a home wherever they happen to be assigned. She must spend her dowry for family expenses when Wen Fu gambles away his pay or squanders it on a mistress. After silently enduring her miserable existence and the deaths of her two children, Winnie finally escapes to America and a new life with Jimmy Louie.

THE HUNDRED SECRET SENSES

Unlike Tan's first two novels, which examine the dynamics of the mother-daughter dyad, *The Hundred Secret Senses* explores the psychological and emotional bonds between sisters. Still, the novel displays several characteristics common to Tan's fiction: conflict between generations in immigrant families; multiple points of view; a strong grounding in Chinese culture and history; and compelling narratives.

Although *The Hundred Secret Senses* is Olivia's story, Kwan is central to every narrative in the novel. One of Tan's most stunningly original creations, Kwan is an energetic woman who is Chinese at the core despite having adopted Western dress and American slang. Kwan claims to have *yin* eyes, which she describes as an ability to see and converse with the dead, whom she calls "*yin* people."

Central to the novel is the uncomfortable relationship between American-born Olivia and her Chinese sister, Kwan, who arrived in San Francisco at eighteen. Although sharing a father, the two women are markedly different: Olivia, whose mother is American, is completely Westernized; Kwan, born to a Chinese first wife, never completely assimilates, remaining predominantly Chinese. Embarrassed by Kwan's exuberant Chineseness, Olivia resists her sister's attempts to form a close relationship. She declines invitations, evades contact, and refuses all overtures of friendship. Despite Olivia's coolness, Kwan continues her friendly attempts to be a real sister to Olivia, whose unhappiness is palpable. Maneuvering Olivia and Olivia's estranged husband, Simon, into a trip to the hills beyond Guilin in China, Kwan engineers a

situation that forces Olivia and Simon to reassess their relationship and take tentative steps toward reconciliation.

Paralleling Olivia's story and embedded in the novel are Kwan's narratives about a previous life when she was Nunumu, a Chinese servant to a group of missionaries. In that household, Nunumu was befriended by Nelly Banner, a young American woman whose passion for a deceitful adventurer imperils the group, and whose love for a half-breed leads to death for herself and Nunumu. The story of Nunumu and Nelly Banner is set against the backdrop of the nineteenth century Taiping Rebellion, led by a charismatic leader who claimed to be Jesus's younger brother.

As in her first two novels, Amy Tan establishes clear parallels between past and present, between historical events and contemporary problems. Constantly relaying messages from her *yin* friends, who seem inordinately interested in Olivia's marital problems, Kwan brings Olivia to the brink of believing that she, Olivia, has somehow participated in Nunumu's life, has experienced fear of approaching rebel soldiers, has faced death on a rainy hillside. Whether Olivia truly once was Nelly Banner is never certain—what is certain at the end of the novel is Olivia's understanding of the unbreakable ties of love that exist between sisters, friends, and lovers.

E. D. Huntley

OTHER MAJOR WORKS

NONFICTION: "The Language of Discretion," 1990 (in *The State of the Language*, Christopher Ricks and Leonard Michaels, editors).

CHILDREN'S LITERATURE: *The Moon Lady*, 1992; *The Chinese Siamese Cat*, 1994.

BIBLIOGRAPHY

Cheung, King-Kok. *An Interethnic Companion to Asian American Literature.* Cambridge, England: Cambridge University Press, 1997. An essay collection with a critical overview of Asian American literary studies. Most interesting to readers of Tan's novels are essays by Sau-ling Cynthia Wong, Shirley Geok-lin Lim, Jinqi Ling, and Donald Geollnicht.

Huntley, E. D. *Amy Tan: A Critical Companion.* Westport, Conn.: Greenwood Press, 1998. Writing for general readers and students, Huntley introduces and discusses Tan's novels in the context of Asian American fiction. A feature of the book is the incorporation of several critical approaches to the novels.

Lim, Elaine. *Asian American Literature: An Introduction to the Writings and Their Social Context.* Philadelphia: Temple University Press, 1982. The first critical guide to Asian American literature, Lim's book is an essential introduction to the historical and literary contexts of Tan's work.

Ling, Amy. *Between Worlds: Women Writers of Chinese Ancestry.* New York: Pergamon, 1990. A chronological and thematic introduction to prose narratives in English by American women of Chinese or partial Chinese ancestry. Includes an extensive annotated bibliography of prose by Chinese American women.

Pearlman, Mickey, and Katherine Usher Henderson. "Amy Tan." *Inter/View: Talks with America's Writing Women.* Lexington: University Press of Kentucky, 1990. Provides biographical information on Tan, revealing the sources of some of the stories in *The Joy Luck Club.*

Somogyi, Barbara, and David Stanton. "Amy Tan." *Poets & Writers* 19, no. 5 (September 1, 1991): 24-32. One of the best interviews with Tan. Tan speaks about her childhood and her early career as a business writer, her decision to write fiction, and her success with *The Joy Luck Club.*

JUN'ICHIRŌ TANIZAKI

Born: Tokyo, Japan; July 24, 1886
Died: Yugawara, Japan; July 30, 1965

PRINCIPAL LONG FICTION

Chijin no ai, 1924-1925 (serial), 1925 (book; *Naomi*, 1985)
Manji, 1928-1930

Tade kuu mushi, 1928-1929 (serial), 1936 (book; *Some Prefer Nettles*, 1955)
Bushūkō hiwa, 1931-1932 (serial), 1935 (book; *The Secret History of the Lord of Musashi*, 1982)
Sasameyuki, 1943-1948 (serial), 1949 (book; *The Makioka Sisters*, 1957)
Shōshō Shigemoto no haha, 1950 (*The Mother of Captain Shigemoto*, 1956)
Kagi, 1956 (*The Key*, 1960)
Fūten rōjin nikki, 1961-1962 (serial), 1962 (book; *Diary of a Mad Old Man*, 1965)

OTHER LITERARY FORMS

The history of the "novel" in Japan is quite different from its history in the West, and the distinctions normally observed between the short story and the novel do not apply there. If, arbitrarily, one refers to Japanese works of fewer than one hundred pages of prose fiction as "short stories," Jun'ichirō Tanizaki is as famous for his short stories as for his longer works. Typical of his early period, "Shisei" (1910; "The Tattooer," 1963) indicates his early interest in sexual symbolism. "Akuma" (1912; Satan) deals with male masochism, and "Otsuya goroshi" (1913; a springtime case) deals with murder and amorality in Tokyo. Later, Tanizaki wrote such remarkable stories as "Ashikari" (1932; English translation, 1936), "Shunkinshō" (1933; "A Portrait of Shunkin," 1936), "Mōmoku monogatari" (1931; "A Blind Man's Tale," 1963), and the exquisite "Yume no ukihashi" (1959; "The Bridge of Dreams," 1963). Tanizaki also wrote a number of plays, including *Aisureba koso* (1921; all because of love), *Okumi to Gohei* (1922), and *Shiro-gitsune no yu* (1923; *The White Fox*, 1930). In 1932, he began translating Murasaki Shikibu's *Genji monogatari* (c. 1004; *The Tale of Genji*, 1936-4941, 1951-1954) into modern Japanese; over the years, he produced several revisions of it. *Bunsho no dukohon* (1934; a manual of style), in which he outlined his craftsmanlike attitude toward composing fiction, is often called a minor masterpiece of criticism. Although he published several highly accomplished reviews and essays, he seldom was persuaded to undertake them, believing that he ought to concentrate on his fiction.

ACHIEVEMENTS

Tanizaki was recognized as a remarkable talent even in his twenties and continued to be so recognized throughout a long and prolific career, which outlasted several publications of his complete works. At first, he was considered shockingly Western by his contemporaries; during the 1920's, however, he gradually began to incorporate more conservative Japanese literary elements, implicitly warning his readers of the dangers of being overly Westernized. Late in his career, his characters are not endangered by Western culture, enjoying, for example, Western clothes and houses as everyday realities in modern Japan.

Tanizaki's mastery of a carefully composed style and his insight into the psychology of his characters place him among the great writers of twentieth century world literature. A slow, careful writer, Tanizaki argued that one of the most important elements of Japanese is its "vagueness" in comparison to other languages, a vagueness that allows the Japanese author to suggest motives, feelings, and details in delicate strokes rather than in precise exposition. Considering the imagination crucial, Tanizaki often dealt with sensational material and abnormal states of mind; by controlling his style, he did not allow his intensity to become hysterical. Despite their bizarre aberrations, his characters rarely become unbelievable as human beings, because of the objective manner in which he treats them. Like many great writers, Tanizaki was also able to assimilate opposing elements such as tradition and innovation, imagination and realism, and the influences of West and East.

BIOGRAPHY

Jun'ichirō Tanizaki was born in the heart of downtown Tokyo. For generations, his ancestors had lived there as members of the merchant class engaged in rice-brokering and printing and had little of the traditional samurai-class interest in affairs of state. Despite the traditional male-dominated culture of Japan, Tanizaki's grandfather and father were allegedly feminists, his father nearly worshiping Tanizaki's mother. The boy, as a result, was drawn to his mother very strongly, thus establishing the reverential attitude toward women seen in so many of his works. Tanizaki

was also a handsome boy, but not a strong one, and, consequently, was often bullied by older classmates, perhaps encouraging a masochistic streak.

During Tanizaki's primary education, a young teacher noticed the boy's talents and gave him special instruction in Japanese and Chinese classics. It is often reported that Tanizaki became known as the brightest student ever to graduate from the First Municipal Secondary School of Tokyo. He entered Tokyo Imperial University in 1908, where he studied Japanese classical literature. He helped found the literary magazine of the university, *Shinshicho*, in which he published several short stories which received praise from older writers such as Mori Ogai and Nagai Kafu. After only a year, however, because he did not pay his fees, he left the university without finishing his degree.

Tanizaki's unfinished education did not hinder him unduly, because he was becoming known as a writer. A notorious frequenter of the "Bluff" or foreign sections of Yokohama, he wore checked suits and gaudy ties and was strongly under the influence of Decadent Western writers such as Edgar Allan Poe, Charles Baudelaire, and Oscar Wilde; Tanizaki translated Wilde's *Lady Windermere's Fan* (1892) in 1919. This lifestyle changed when he moved to Okamoto in 1923 after the Great Earthquake. In the Hakone mountains south of Yokohama, during the disaster, he first was delighted that all he despised of the old Japan had been destroyed. He predicted a new, modern Tokyo with wide boulevards, film theaters, and citizens wearing comfortable Western clothing. Yet, as time passed, he began to seek the traditional roots of Japanese literature and went, as is often asserted, from being merely a good author to being a great one.

By 1930, Tanizaki was so famous that his complete works were published. His personal life was almost as sensational as his fiction. After encouraging his wife Chiyoko to have an affair with his friend Sato Haruo, they were divorced in 1930 after fifteen years of marriage. In 1931, he married Furukawa Tomiko, a literary student whom he divorced in 1934. In 1935, he married his last wife, Morita Matzuko, the divorced wife of an Osaka millionaire and patroness of several artists and writers, including Tanizaki himself.

With the rise of militarism in Japan, Tanizaki's work—with its interest in aestheticism and sexuality—was considered improper, and he was forced to suppress the amorous passages of his translation of *The Tale of Genji*, which he had begun in 1935. His longest novel, *The Makioka Sisters*, was not published during the war because of the amorous content, but when it was finally released, it, along with his earlier works, established Tanizaki as possibly the most significant twentieth century Japanese author. In 1949, he received Japan's Imperial Prize for Literature.

During the 1950's and 1960's, Tanizaki returned to some of the themes of his earlier career. The publication of the first episode of *The Key* in the magazine *Chuo koron* in 1956 created a sensation in Japan as customers snatched up copies, at least partly because of its sexual content. It also became well known in the United States, as did "The Bridge of Dreams" and *Diary of a Mad Old Man*, as a result of a new Western interest in Japanese films (such as Akira Kurosawa's 1951 film of Ryunosuke Akutagawa's "Rashomon") and literature (notably the works of Yasunari Kawabata and Yukio Mishima). In 1960, a film version of *The Key* was released in the United States as *Odd Obsession*. In 1964, Tanizaki was elected honorary member of the American Academy of Arts and Letters and the National Institute of Arts and Letters. He spent his last few years struggling with various illnesses and living in a Western-style house on the Izu Coast. At the time of his death, Tanizaki was one of the leading candidates for the Nobel Prize.

ANALYSIS

Jun'ichirō Tanizaki's early literary career was characterized by a deep interest in Western literature. Although as a student he studied Japanese literature and had a nostalgia for classical Japanese works, he once commented that about 1918, "I had come to detest Japan, even though I was obviously a Japanese." Assiduously reading Baudelaire, Wilde, and especially Poe, he asserted the supremacy of the imagination in literature, as opposed to the naturalism

of many of his contemporaries, arguing that even Gustave Flaubert and Émile Zola could not have produced their naturalistic works without being highly imaginative. Once using Wilde's aphorism "Nature imitates art" as an epigraph to a story, Tanizaki believed that the representation of reality was not the primary function of literature; it was rather the presentation of truth. "The artist," he wrote, "justifies his existence only when he can transform his imagination into truth." This truth, in Tanizaki's view, was primarily psychological. Imagination allowed the author to see the subconscious depths of humanity. The writer perceived what people were, not what they could be. There was no need for a writer to justify his works for social or moral reasons, and Tanizaki was seen as an exponent of aestheticism.

As might be expected, the early influence of the Decadent authors led to intense, macabre works. They are, by turn, gothic, grotesque, hedonistic, diabolic, and erotic. Tanizaki's first important work, "The Tattooer," is typical. Seikichi is a master tattooer who has become so great he only tattoos according to his vision of his client's character. Further, he delights in the suffering his needles cause his clients. His obsession becomes the creation of a masterwork on the skin of a woman who meets his requirements of character as well as beauty. After four years, he sees the foot of a woman disappear into a palanquin, knows instantly that she is the one he has been searching for, but loses the palanquin in the crowd. The next spring, she appears at his house, and after he reveals her true, vampirish nature, he creates an exquisite tattoo of a black widow spider on her back and finds himself the slave of his own creation.

There are several elements characteristic of Tanizaki's work in this story. In most of his works, a man delights in his utter servitude to the woman he adores. Seikichi goes from sadist to masochist as the result of finding his perfect woman, and although Tanizaki devotes this work to the psychological and artistic obsessions of the tattooer, he was generally more interested in his women characters, because they expressed an ideal before which his men groveled. This subservient role has been frequently associated with Tanizaki's attitude toward his mother, who died in

1917. One will also note the foot fetishism implicit in Seikichi's first noticing the young girl. Throughout Tanizaki's career, women's feet play a large role in the sexual relationships between his characters. This is obvious in such works as "Fumiko no ashi" in which an old man is infatuated with the feet of his mistress and dies in ecstasy as Fumiko presses his forehead under her foot, but it reveals itself in other ways as well: Frequently, Tanizaki devotes more detail to his description of a woman's feet than he does to his description of her face.

Despite Tanizaki's interest in Western writers, many elements of his early work were derived from traditional Japanese literature. Throughout his career, he felt no hesitation in setting his stories in the Japanese past; "The Tattooer," for example, occurs in the Tokugawa period of the 1600's. In 1919, in the midst of his Decadent interests, the same year as "Fumiko no ashi" and his translation of *Lady Windermere's Fan*, he published a volume of erotic stories in the style of the Japanese 1830's and two novellas in the Chinese style. As they are depicted in works by Tanizaki, women are often portrayed as treacherous, cruel creatures in classical Japanese literature. The seventeenth century novelist Ihara Saikaku wrote many risqué stories, in some of which the heroine's insatiable sexual appetite exhausts the hero. Finally, grotesque and diabolic motifs are very common in classical Japanese literature, and it is perhaps too easy to overemphasize the influence of Poe's and Wilde's content upon Tanizaki, when he was more interested in adapting their conception of art in his reaction against naturalism.

There is no doubt, however, that Tanizaki's work changed at the beginning of the 1920's, particularly after he moved from Tokyo to the more conservative Kansai (Kyoto, Osaka, and Kobe) region after the Great Earthquake. Although in his later work he retained his masochistic heroes, characters for whom there are few precedents in traditional Japanese literature, he began to acknowledge more strongly the values and practices of his culture.

CHIJIN NO AI

Chijin no ai marks the division between Tanizaki's "Westernized" period and his more tradition-oriented works from the 1920's through the 1940's. Although, like so many of his works, *Chijin no ai* tells of a man's quest for the ideal woman, there is much implied criticism of Japanese worship of the West, despite the fact that the novel seems to have been based on W. Somerset Maugham's *Of Human Bondage* (1915). Joji, the narrator, is attracted to a European-looking waitress named Naomi. Her features make him think of Mary Pickford, and he asks her if she would like to go to a film. Instead of the usual polite evasions, she says (like Mildred in *Of Human Bondage*), "I don't mind if I do." Eventually, he takes her home with the intention of remaking her into his ideal of beauty—a woman he will not be ashamed of in front of blond foreigners—and marrying her within a few years. Naomi is given Western clothes, practices playing the piano, speaking English, and dancing. All of this merely encourages her decadent tendencies. He learns she has been unfaithful and attempts to leave her. He discovers he cannot, however, and gives in completely to her. She can do as she wishes, have whatever lover she wishes, as long as she remains his wife.

Joji is a fool as much in his obsessive love of Western things as in his love of the girl. He is ashamed of his racial identity. His shortness, his protruding teeth, his dark complexion, and other typically Japanese features embarrass him, but he is proud of his European-style Yokohama house. He is degraded by his sense of both cultural and sexual inferiority. Often offended by Naomi's crudity, he excuses it because of his fascination with her; to be humiliated by her is an honor. Even when she dresses and behaves like a prostitute, he is filled with masochistic pride that she is his.

SOME PREFER NETTLES

Tanizaki's next major novel, *Some Prefer Nettles*, deals with similar themes. This work tells of a character, Kaname, whose superficial Western tastes are gradually replaced by an appreciation of traditional Japanese culture. Kaname is unhappily married to Misako. He has lost sexual interest in her but is tormented by uncertainty over what to do about it. He encourages her to have an affair while he finds sexual satisfaction with a Eurasian prostitute. There is a superficial resemblance between this plot and certain events in Tanizaki's own life. Bored with his first wife, Chiyoko, one night at dinner he calmly asked Sato Haruo, poet and friend, if he would like to marry her. In 1930, after encouraging the affair, Tanizaki divorced Chiyoko, and she married Sato. Obviously, this arrangement was on his mind during the writing of *Some Prefer Nettles*, and his ambivalence is perhaps reflected by the book itself.

Far more important, however, in assessing the book, is the struggle in Kaname between his appreciation of Western culture and his appreciation of the merchants' culture of old Japan surviving in Osaka, particularly represented in this novel by the *Bunraku*, or puppet theater. At the end of the novel, Kaname confuses a puppet with the Osaka beauty O-hisa, showing perhaps that the old way of life is a fantasy which cannot be recaptured. Edward G. Seidensticker, who translated the novel, argues that Kaname (and Tanizaki) is attempting to return to the peace of childhood, although the adult knows the new world is here to stay. In his essay *In'ei raisan* (1934; *In Praise of Shadows*, 1955), Tanizaki wrote "I know as well as anyone that I am dreaming, and that, having come this far, we cannot turn back." It should also be noted that whatever ambivalence or vagueness readers might find in *Some Prefer Nettles* and other Tanizaki novels is as much a reflection of his aesthetic as of any personal feelings. He always insisted upon exploiting the "vagueness" of Japanese and objected to writers who were too clear. One cannot, for example, know exactly what will happen to Kaname the day after the novel closes. Primary among Tanizaki's goals in writing was to achieve poetic suggestiveness, which the last scene certainly does.

THE MAKIOKA SISTERS

During the late 1930's, Tanizaki continued his rediscovery of traditional Japanese culture by beginning his translation of *The Tale of Genji*, a work which, in many ways, influenced the composition of *The Makioka Sisters*, his longest and, many argue, his greatest novel. Although Tanizaki was always a slow, very careful writer, wartime circumstances forced him to work even more slowly than usual. He spent many years on *The Makioka Sisters*, and censor-ship prevented complete publication of the work until 1948. Before he began, he delineated a precise plan and followed it nearly to the conclusion. Despite this detailed planning, *The Makioka Sisters*—unlike his usual lean, straightforward novels—is a sprawling, indirect novel in the episodic form often favored by Japanese authors. Complex characterization and diverse social forces create many layers of action and emotion to give the book a texture quite different from that of Tanizaki's typical works, which focus on a single character.

In the novel, the four Makioka sisters represent various aspects of Japanese culture during the 1930's. Once a rich Osaka merchant family, the Makiokas have declined. Tsuruko, the eldest, is the most conservative, trying to hang on to a way of life they have outlived. Taeko, the youngest, seems the brightest, the most talented, and the most corrupted by the Tokyo-style intelligentsia with its Western fads. Sachiko, with her husband Teinosuke, holds the family together by mediating between the impulses that tear at it. Yukiko, despite her traditional beauty, is too shy to deal effectively with her sisters or the world about her.

Most of the novel concerns the attempt to find the aging Yukiko a husband; the Japanese title *Sasame-yuki* (thin snow) refers to the number of *miai* (marriage arrangements) that fail. Tsuruko generally insists upon going through the slow traditional investigation of potential husbands, while Sachiko recognizes the diminishing value of Yukiko as a bride and tries to carry the arrangements out in a reasonable, though not hurried, time. Taeko, who intends to marry a Westernized playboy, must wait for her elder sister's marriage before marrying on her own. Yukiko is so introverted that she often seems indifferent to the whole struggle, except when she rejects another candidate.

This plot, however, is not Tanizaki's main concern. Using details from his wife Tomiko's family history, he re-creates Osaka as it was before the war, revealing foreign influences that would inevitably destroy that way of life—the clothing, the foreign films, the German neighbors, the visit to the White Russians, Taeko's desire to go to Paris to learn dress-making—and the traditional Japanese customs as they were then practiced. Attention is devoted to the cherry blossom festival, Taeko's dollmaking, Kabuki, Japanese dance, and the old house of the Makiokas. The elegant Osaka dialect is spoken by the main characters and the Tokyo dialect is portrayed as being corrupted. Despite these contrasts, *The Makioka Sisters* is not a didactic work that preaches the superiority of the old ways over the new. It captures a particular way of life at a certain period in a certain place. Free of the grotesqueness that characterizes his early works and of the obsessive characters that populate most of his works, *The Makioka Sisters* is a panoramic view of diverse characters with complex motivations, a work unusual in Tanizaki's oeuvre but indisputably a masterpiece.

Unlike many writers, who, once they have achieved an integrated work such as *The Makioka Sisters*, run out of things to say, Tanizaki remained as creative in the final decades of his life as he had earlier. Entering the third phase of his career, he returned to many of the themes that had occupied him in his youth; with a more detached and sometimes ironic point of view, he dealt with the obsessions of sex in old age. Composed of the parallel diaries of a fifty-six-year-old professor and his forty-five-year-old wife, *The Key* progresses through the former's attempt to expand the sexual abilities of the latter, a woman whom he loves madly but who no longer satisfies him. Once again, one might note the autobiographical resonance of the professor's gradually directing his wife into the young Kimura's arms. One might also note the return of the devouring woman as the wife encourages the eating of beef and incite his jealousy, in spite of her knowledge of her husband's rising blood pressure, which eventually kills him.

THE KEY

The Key created a sensation on its publication, no doubt largely because of its frank treatment of sex; like other works of literature—Gustave Flaubert's *Madame Bovary* (1857) and D. H. Lawrence's *Lady Chatterley's Lover* (1928)—which achieved notoriety before their literary merits were admitted, *The Key*'s craftsmanship can now be assessed more objectively. Presenting one diary in the *katakana* script and the other in the *hiragana* script, Tanizaki exploits

the differences between the two characters' perceptions of the situation. Further, he complicates the ostensibly sincere presentations of the diaries by having each character aware that the other may be reading what is written. This complex treatment of point of view turns an apparently simple, short work into a multilayered psychological study.

DIARY OF A MAD OLD MAN

Tanizaki's last novel, *Diary of a Mad Old Man*, also consists mainly of a diary, but by a man even older than the protagonist of *The Key*. Also suffering from high blood pressure, he is sexually impotent as well. Nevertheless, he is attracted to his daughter-in-law Satsuko, estranged from her husband and having an affair with another man. As in many of Tanizaki's works, the narrator devotes much attention to Satsuko's feet as sexual objects, and he thinks often of his mother. He compares Satsuko's feet many times with his mother's, and he delights in kissing Satsuko's feet and biting her toes when she comes from the shower. Her feet also become associated with the Buddhist Goddess of Mercy, and the old man plans for his daughter-in-law's footprints to be carved on his tombstone.

Objectively treated, *Diary of a Mad Old Man* is a great deal less sensational than it would appear from a plot summary. The artistic coolness which Tanizaki worked so hard to achieve saves the work from any pornographic content. Further, the novel is comic in its attitude toward the main character, satirizing the high intensity of Tanizaki's early works. Several of his works have comic elements—he was fond of cats and often wrote of them in a lighthearted vein—and Tanizaki seems to have ended his career looking back on his extraordinary achievements with a whimsical detachment.

J. Madison Davis

OTHER MAJOR WORKS

SHORT FICTION: "Kirin," 1910; "Shisei," 1910 ("The Tattooer," 1963); "Shōnen," 1910; "Hōkan," 1911; "Akuma," 1912; "Kyōfu," 1913 ("Terror," 1963); "Otsuya goroshi," 1913; "Watakushi," 1921 ("The Thief," 1963); "Aoi Hano," 1922 ("Aguri," 1963); "Mōmoku monogatari," 1931 ("A Blind Man's

Tale," 1963); "Ashikari," 1932 (English translation, 1936); "Shunkinshō," 1933 ("A Portrait of Shunkin," 1936); *Hyofu*, 1950; "Yume no ukihashi," 1959 ("The Bridge of Dreams," 1963); *Yume no ukihashi*, 1960; *Kokumin no bungaku*, 1964; *Tanizaki Jun'ichirō shu*, 1970; *Seven Japanese Tales*, 1981.

PLAYS: *Aisureba koso*, pb. 1921; *Okumi to Gohei*, pb. 1922; *Shirogitsune no yu*, pb. 1923 (*The White Fox*, 1930); *Shinzei*, pb. 1949.

NONFICTION: *Bunsho no dukohon*, 1934; "In'ei raisan," 1934 ("In Praise of Shadows," 1955); *Kyōno yume, Ōsaka no yume*, 1950; *Yōshō-jidai*, 1957 (*Childhood Years: A Memoir*, 1988).

TRANSLATION: *Genji monogatari*, 1936-1941, 1951-1954 (of Murasaki Shikibu's medieval *Genji monogatari*).

MISCELLANEOUS: *Tanizaki Jun'ichirō zenshu*, 1930 (12 volumes); *Tanizaki Jun'ichirō zenshu*, 1966-1970 (28 volumes).

BIBLIOGRAPHY

Chambers, Anthony Hood. *The Secret Window: Ideal Worlds in Tanizaki's Fiction*. Cambridge, Mass.: Harvard University Press, 1994. Chapters on "ideal worlds," *The Secret History of the Lord of Musahi*, "A Portrait of Shunkin," *The Makioka Sisters, The Mother of Captain Shigemoto*, "The Bridge of Dreams." Includes notes and bibliography.

Gessel, Van C. *Three Modern Novelists: Soseki, Tanizaki, Kawabata*. New York: Kodansha International, 1993. Concentrates on Tanizaki's handling of the theme of modernism. With detailed notes but no bibliography.

Ito, Ken K. *Visions of Desire: Tanizaki's Fictional Worlds*. Stanford, Calif.: Stanford University Prcss, 1991. Chapters on his handling of the "Orient" and the "West," on his treatment of the past, "The Vision of the Blind," "Fair Dreams of Hanshin," "Writing as Power," and "A Mad Old Man's World." Includes notes, bibliography, and a section on names and sources.

Peterson, Gwenn Boardman. *The Moon in the Water: Understanding Tanizaki, Kawabata, and Mishima*. Honolulu: University of Hawaii Press, 1979. The section on Tanizaki includes discussions of "Fifty Years of Meiji Man," "Reality and Illusion: Dream and Shadow," "The Ambiguities of Love and Marriage," "Chronicles of Modern Japan," works available in English, and a partial chronology.

Suzuki, Tomi. *Narrating the Self: Fictions of Japanese Modernity*. Stanford, Calif.: Stanford University Press, 1996. See especially the epilogue, "Tanizaki's Speaking Subject and the Creation of Tradition." Includes notes and bibliography.

Ueda, Makota. *Modern Japanese Writers and the Nature of Literature*. Stanford, Calif.: Stanford University Press, 1976. Contains a chapter with an excellent overview of Tanizaki's career.

BOOTH TARKINGTON

Born: July 29, 1869; Indianapolis, Indiana
Died: May 19, 1946; Indianapolis, Indiana

PRINCIPAL LONG FICTION
The Gentleman from Indiana, 1899
Monsieur Beaucaire, 1900
Cherry, 1903
The Beautiful Lady, 1905
The Conquest of Canaan, 1905
His Own People, 1907
Beasley's Christmas Party, 1909
Beauty and the Jacobin, 1912
The Flirt, 1913
Penrod, 1914
The Turmoil, 1915
Penrod and Sam, 1916
Seventeen, 1916
The Magnificent Ambersons, 1918
Ramsey Milholland, 1919
Alice Adams, 1921
Gentle Julia, 1922
The Midlander, 1923
Growth, 1923 (includes *The Turmoil, The Magnificent Ambersons*, and *The Midlander*, the last here renamed *National Avenue*)

Penrod Jashber, 1929
Young Mrs. Greeley, 1929
Presenting Lily Mars, 1933
Little Orvie, 1934
The Lorenzo Bunch, 1936
The Heritage of Hatcher Ide, 1941
The Fighting Littles, 1941
Kate Fennigate, 1943
Image of Josephine, 1945

OTHER LITERARY FORMS

Although best known as a novelist, Booth Tarkington also enjoyed some success as a playwright, with such works as stage versions of his novels *Monsieur Beaucaire* (1901) and *The Gentleman from Indiana (1905)*, as well as *The Man from Home (1907)*. Tarkington also enjoyed considerable success as a writer of short stories. Two of his stories, "The One-Hundred Dollar Bill" and "Stella Crozier," were honored with the O. Henry Award in 1923 and 1926, respectively. In addition, Tarkington's short-story collection *Mr. White, the Red Barn, Hell, and Bridewater* (1935) is one of his most respected. Tarkington also published many magazine pieces in the genres of reminiscences and literary criticism. Chief among these are "As I Seem to Me," "Mr. Howells," and "The World Does Move."

(Library of Congress)

ACHIEVEMENTS

Few authors have enjoyed such critical and popular esteem as Booth Tarkington experienced during his lifetime. Tarkington won two Pulitzer Prizes, the first in 1918 for *The Magnificent Ambersons* and the second in 1921 for *Alice Adams*. Tarkington's short stories "The One-Hundred Dollar Bill" and "Stella Crozier" were honored with the O. Henry Awards for 1923 and 1926, respectively. In 1933, Tarkington received the National Institute of Arts and Letters Gold Medal, and in 1945 he received the American Academy of Arts William Dean Howells Medal. Tarkington was awarded so many honorary doctorates that he began refusing them. He did, however, accept an honorary degree in 1940 from Purdue University, which he attended for one year. Tarkington did not explore new modes of fiction, but he excelled at sub-

tle depictions of character in the realistic mode established by William Dean Howells and Henry James, both of whom he greatly admired.

BIOGRAPHY

Newton Booth Tarkington was born in Indianapolis, Indiana, on July 29, 1869, lived most of his life there, and passed away in his hometown on May 19, 1946. He took for his material the characters and concerns of his home city and home state, using the region to highlight the eternal concerns of humanity.

Tarkington was raised in an upper-middle-class family and received a superior education, particularly at Phillips Exeter Academy. A year spent at Purdue University in 1890-1891 brought him into contact with another Hoosier writer, George Ade, and with the illustrator John T. McCutcheon. Tarkington spent the years of 1891-1893 at Princeton University, although he did not take a degree. Although his education did not follow the usual pattern, it did energize him and afford him the opportunity to explore his literary talents.

After leaving Princeton, Tarkington played the part of the struggling writer for five years; however, with the publication of *The Gentleman from Indiana* in 1899, Tarkington was recognized as a major new writer. The novel became a best-seller, and Tarkington, a prolific writer throughout his career, followed it with short stories, novels, and plays. Established as a major young writer, Tarkington married Louisa Fletcher in 1902. That same year, Tarkington was elected to the Indiana House of Representatives. He served in that capacity for only two sessions before resigning due to ill health—he had contracted typhoid in a southern Indiana resort. Tarkington's bout with typhoid initiated what was to become a lifelong practice of spending the summers in Kennebunkport, Maine. Tarkington's only child, Laurel, was born in 1906. The Tarkingtons divorced in 1911. The rift between the two was due in part to Tarkington's heavy drinking; he eventually realized he was an alcoholic.

Tarkington soon recovered from depression and divorce, gave up alcohol, and married Susanah Robinson in 1912. The next decade witnessed the burst of creativity that produced his masterworks *Penrod*, *The Magnificent Ambersons*, and *Alice Adams*. The last two works won Pulitzer Prizes, and Tarkington found himself occupying the very pinnacle of American letters. Following this great success, however, was yet another dark period. Tarkington's father, with whom the writer had enjoyed a close relationship, died in January, 1923. This bereavement was followed by the harder blow that came in April: the death of his daughter, Laurel.

With the Great Depression, Tarkington's preoccupation with social concerns increased, but his popularity and success rested mainly on his earlier achievements. Tarkington became more socially active and lobbied for the adoption of the United Nations Charter. He died on May 19, 1946.

ANALYSIS

A realist in the mode of his mentor, writer William Dean Howells, Booth Tarkington excelled at characterization and the integration of moral dilemma with character and plot. In his most successful novels, Tarkington focused on regular people facing complex situations. The people Tarkington selected for his subjects were most often Hoosiers, and the setting was nearly always Indiana. Typically, the dilemmas faced by his characters highlight flaws marring otherwise sympathetic individuals. Always charming, Tarkington's characters are never entirely lost souls; there exists always the possibility of ethical growth and development.

THE GENTLEMAN FROM INDIANA

Tarkington's first success, *The Gentleman from Indiana*, won for him a national readership and propelled him to a place of prominence in American letters. This novel contains the themes and characters typical of Tarkington's later works, but with far less attention to psychological insight and a greater reliance on romance. The protagonist, John Harkless, is drawn in rather stereotypical fashion as a crusading newspaperman fighting racism and mob violence. The novel is compelling, but it lacks the kind of substantive, complex development of character typical of Tarkington's more mature work. The heroes and villains are clearly drawn, and readers view the action rather than participate in it. In later works, such as *Alice Adams*, Tarkington replicates the dilemmas of his characters within the minds of his readers. Still, the rudiments of Tarkington's concern for characterization and moral dilemma are fleshed out in *The Gentleman from Indiana*.

PENROD

The first volume of a trilogy, *Penrod* was followed by *Penrod and Sam* and *Penrod Jashber*. The title character and protagonist is a young boy who bears a striking resemblance to Mark Twain's Tom Sawyer. Like Tom, Penrod tells lies, often with hilarious results. Caught daydreaming in class, Penrod tells his teacher he has been distracted by his uncle's alcoholism. The yarn spins out beyond the boy's ability to control it, and trouble ensues. Similarly, when cast as an unwilling Launcelot in an amateur theatrical,

Penrod is mortified that the tights he has to wear are made from his father's long underwear. At the last minute, he dons the janitor's capacious overalls, ruining the serious tone the director had attempted to instill. Although *Penrod* is often compared to Twain's *The Adventures of Huckleberry Finn* (1884), it bears greater similarity to the earlier *The Adventures of Tom Sawyer* (1876). Tarkington's book is related from an omniscient point of view, like Twain's earlier work, and Penrod occupies a position within society, as does Tom. The point of view is particularly appropriate and fits the nostalgic air pervading the novel. *Penrod* was wildly popular during Tarkington's life, and it marks an important development of his artistry. With *Penrod*, Tarkington perfected his notable ability to connect plot and character; Tarkington himself observed that "Tom and Huck are realistic only in character. He Tarkington gave 'em what boys don't get, when it came to 'plot.'" Tarkington's protagonist is no more "real" than Twain's Tom or Huck, but the incidents Penrod participates in are arguably more typical than what Twain relates. As Tarkington approached his more mature work, he still insisted on the accurate depiction of character and plot.

THE MAGNIFICENT AMBERSONS

Tarkington had achieved commercial success with his earlier work, but it was with *The Magnificent Ambersons* that he achieved true critical success. It was for this novel that Tarkington received his first Pulitzer Prize. Critics recognized that the story of the Amberson family was at once a story about one midwestern family, but at the same time it was as universal a story as that of Aeschylus's tragic house of Atreus or of Leo Tolstoy's *Anna Karenina* (1875-1877). Tarkington's novel chronicles the fall of the Amberson family in the post-Civil War years. Major Amberson had managed to establish himself as a rich and powerful man through hard work in manufacturing, but the third generation scion of the family, George Amberson, wishes only to live the life of a gentleman. He rejects any suggestion that he should work, for he believes work is beneath a gentleman. The privilege enjoyed by the younger Ambersons born into wealth exerts a negative influence on character that militates against the preservation of wealth.

Spoiled, George suffers financial losses that derive from his character; he is described as "reckless" financially and is also "arrogant and conceited and bad-tempered."

The story of the Amberson family, then, is the American success story rewritten. Tarkington explores the Horatio Alger myth of rags to riches and finds it wanting in a family that finds itself unable to sustain the success of its founder. After seeing that even the name of Amberson Boulevard has been changed to Tenth Street, George realizes how low the family has fallen. "The city," readers are told, "had rolled over the Ambersons and buried them under to the last vestige." The novel does not conclude on such a somber note, however, and George seems to muster some inner resources left over from the old major. When he finally does go to work, he does so vigorously. In a somewhat sentimental vein more typical of Tarkington's earlier work, the novel ends with George's reunion with his true love, Lucy, in a hospital room. George had been struck by a car, just as the family as a whole had been "rolled over" by the city.

ALICE ADAMS

With *Alice Adams*, Tarkington returned to the theme of the American success story. This novel won for Tarkington his second Pulitzer Prize, and it is also widely regarded as Tarkington's greatest achievement. His heroine reminds the reader of other characters in literature who test the American myth of success expressed best by the Horatio Alger stories. For like Alger's Ragged Dick, Alice Adams strives to lift herself up into another social realm from the one in which she was born. As Tarkington's novel begins, Alice's family occupies a tenuous position in the midlevel manufacturing class of post-World War I Indiana. Their position affords them a modicum of respect, but they have slowly felt the pinch of declining fortune. They just manage to keep a cook, for example, but they can only afford to hire the surly specimens no other, more respectable families will employ.

Intent on improving the family fortunes, Mrs. Adams browbeats her husband Virgil into leaving his position with Lamb & Company, where he is respected for his work ethic, honesty, and loyalty. She insists he leave the "old hole," as she calls it, to start his own manufacturing company. Virgil's ethical dilemma revolves around his knowledge of a secret glue formula, whose rights are owned by Mr. Lamb. However, since Mr. Lamb has done nothing with the formula for years, Virgil allows himself to be convinced by his wife to steal it, quit his position, and open his own glue factory.

Mr. Adams's ethical dilemma and subsequent fall parallel his daughter's attempt to lift herself up socially, also through unethical means. Alice's head is filled with romance, and she begins lying in a futile attempt to deny the grim reality of the family's declining stature. In this pursuit, she is encouraged by her mother, whose mending of old dresses so they will appear to be new is a benign example of how Alice begins by shading the truth and ends by lying outright. Tarkington masterfully illustrates the process whereby economic emulation gradually becomes pernicious dishonesty. In a famous scene, Alice meets Mr. Arthur Russell and tries to impress him by lying that she has been to the tobacconist to procure cigars for her father, who never, she assures him, smokes a pipe; this petty lie grows into a larger claim that her father occupies an almost aristocratic position of wealth and power. The lies grow as Alice and Mr. Russell fall in love, but the lies are ultimately unable to sustain the fiction of the upper-class life she has created.

Three strands of the narrative come together when Mr. Russell comes to dinner at the Adamses' home. The behavior of Alice's family clearly demarcates their social class, undercutting all the things Alice said about them to her beau. Moreover, her brother Walter's embezzlement from the Lamb Company comes to light, even as the glue factory established by Mr. Adams fails. Alice knows when Arthur Russell leaves her house that she will never see him again.

Alice Adams is Tarkington at his most brilliant. Selecting the coming of age of an adolescent girl as his ostensible subject, Tarkington establishes the novel's main theme as the much larger issue of America's coming of age in the years after the Great War, World War I. The central themes are all developed around Alice's search for her own identity in a culture that seeks to impose identity based on class and economic position. Tarkington also includes some pointed jabs at romance as both an aesthetic movement and as a philosophical outlook. Alice has believed the romantic fictions she has been told, and she tells a few more of her own to Mr. Russell. Only at the end does she give up her romantic illusions and become realistic. As she approaches Frincke's Business College, Alice recalls "a French romance" she had once read and begins to grow sentimental over her own "destiny." Then, as if shaking off the idea, she mounts the stairs, turning her back on the romantic fictions that had led her astray.

Joe B. Fulton

OTHER MAJOR WORKS

SHORT FICTION: *In the Arena*, 1905; *The Fascinating Stranger and Other Stories*, 1923; *Mr. White, the Red Barn, Hell, and Bridewater*, 1935.

PLAYS: *Monsieur Beaucaire*, pr. 1901; *The Gentleman from Indiana*, pr. 1905; *The Man from Home*, pr. 1907; *The Guardian*, pb. 1907 (with Harry Leon Wilson); *Mister Antonio*, pr. 1916; *The Gibson Upright*, pb. 1919 (with Wilson); *Clarence*, pr. 1919.

NONFICTION: *The World Does Move*, 1928 (reminiscence).

BIBLIOGRAPHY

Fennimore, Keith J. *Booth Tarkington*. New York: Twayne, 1974. A volume in the Twayne United States Authors Series, this book is an excellent introduction to the author's life and work.

LeGates, Charlotte. "The Family in Booth Tarkington's Growth Trilogy." *Midamerica: The Yearbook of the Society for the Study of Midwestern Literature* 6 (1979): 88-99. The family occupies the center of Tarkington's world, and LeGates's discussion of it is exemplary.

Mayberry, Susanah. *My Amiable Uncle: Recollections about Booth Tarkington*. West Lafayette, Indiana: Purdue University Press, 1983. An important contribution to the biography of Tarkington.

Noverr, Douglass A. "Change, Growth, and the Human Dilemma in Booth Tarkington's *The Magnificent Ambersons." *Society for the Study of Mid-western Literature Newsletter* 11 (1981): 14-32. This article treats primarily one novel, but it has value for anyone seeking to understand the major themes of Tarkington's work.

Woodress, James. *Booth Tarkington, Gentleman from Indiana.* Philadelphia: Lippincott, 1955. An important biography of Tarkington, this volume offers some analysis of the novels. Considered the standard biography by most critics.

Wyatt, Edith F. "Booth Tarkington: The Seven Ages of Man." *North American Review* CCXVI (1922): 499-512. Wyatt provides a fine analysis of Tarkington's entire writing career.

WILLIAM MAKEPEACE THACKERAY

Born: Calcutta, India; July 18, 1811
Died: London, England; December 24, 1863

PRINCIPAL LONG FICTION

Catherine: A Story, 1839-1840 (as Ikey Solomons, Jr.)

The History of Samuel Titmarsh and the Great Hoggarty Diamond, 1841 (later as *The Great Hoggarty Diamond*, 1848)

The Luck of Barry Lyndon: A Romance of the Last Century, 1844

Vanity Fair: A Novel Without a Hero, 1847-1848

The History of Pendennis: His Fortunes and Misfortunes, His Friends and His Greatest Enemy, 1848-1850

Rebecca and Rowena: A Romance upon Romance, 1850 (as M. A. Titmarsh)

The History of Henry Esmond, Esquire, a Colonel in the Service of Her Majesty Q. Anne, 1852 (3 volumes)

The Newcomes: Memoirs of a Most Respectable Family, 1853-1855

The Virginians: A Tale of the Last Century, 1857-1859

Lovel the Widower, 1860

The Adventures of Philip on His Way Through the World, Shewing Who Robbed Him, Who Helped Him, and Who Passed Him By, 1861-1862

Denis Duval, 1864

OTHER LITERARY FORMS

William Makepeace Thackeray's career as a satirist and journalist contributed to his novelistic style. His works appeared in a number of periodicals, including *The National Standard*, which he owned, *The Constitutional*, for which he was Paris correspondent, and *The New Monthly Magazine*. More important, however, the bulk of his writing appeared in *Fraser's Magazine* and in *Punch*, until, in 1860, he became editor of the *Cornhill Magazine*. In many of his reviews, short stories, burlesques, and travel writings, he adopts facetious pen names that reveal the snobbish preconceptions of his personae. "The Yellowplush Correspondence" appeared in *Fraser's Magazine* in 1837-1838 as the supposed diary of Charles James Yellowplush, an illiterate footman who betrays all of the social prejudices of his employers. The story was later published as *Memoirs of Mr. Charles J. Yellowplush* in 1856. Thackeray assumed two pseudonyms for some of his comic pieces. As Michael Angelo Titmarsh, Thackeray published *A Legend of the Rhine* (1845), *Mrs. Perkin's Ball* (1847), and *The Rose and the Ring: Or, The History of Prince Giglio and Prince Bulbo* (1855) among others, in addition to some nonfiction works such as *The Paris Sketch Book* (1840), *The Irish Sketch Book* (1843), and *Notes of a Journey from Cornhill to Grand Cairo . . .* (1846); as George Savage Fitz-Boodle, an aging and susceptible bachelor, Thackeray wrote *The Fitz-Boodle Papers* (1852), *The Confessions of George Fitz-Boodle, and Some Passages in the Life of Major Gahagan* (1841-1842), and *Men's Wives* (1843). "Punch's Prize Novelists," which appeared in *Punch* magazine, was a series of parodies of popular novelists of the day, such as Benjamin Disraeli and James Fenimore Cooper, and was perhaps even more effective than the burlesque *Catherine* (which he wrote as Ikey Solomons, Jr.). Thackeray's other achievements include *The English Humourists of the Eighteenth Century* (1853) and *The Four Georges: Sketches of Manners, Morals, Court and Town Life* (1860); a number of tales and short stories, including *A Shabby Genteel Story and Other Tales* (1857), and a series of ballads and verses, such as the nostalgic "The Ballad of Bouillabaisse" (1849).

ACHIEVEMENTS

Long remembered as a social satirist *par excellence*, Thackeray wrote more in the manner of Henry Fielding than of Samuel Richardson and more in the realistic vein than in the style of the "novel of sensibility," that production of the early nineteenth century that sought to achieve heightened emotional effects at the expense of believable plot and characterization. Both in his miscellaneous writings and in his first great novel, *Vanity Fair*, Thackeray sought to counter the kind of melodramatic and pretentious entertainment provided by such authors as Edward Bulwer-Lytton, William Harrison Ainsworth, and even the early Charles Dickens. He attempted, instead, to make his readers see through the social and literary hypocrisy that, as he believed, characterized the age. To this end, he adopted a number of pseudonyms in his early essay writing, pseudonyms that can be said to foreshadow the personae he used in his fiction.

In reviewing both art and literature for such magazines as *Fraser's Magazine* and *The New Monthly Magazine*, Thackeray adopted the Yellowplush and Titmarsh signatures; he was thus able to ridicule in a lively way what he found false. His reviews were no less devastating to the current trend of idolizing criminals and rogues, as seen in the series of popular "Newgate Novels." As Ikey Solomons, Jr., he produced *Catherine*, the tale of a murderess, but even here, his attempt to deglamorize the account was mitigated by his growing sympathy for his created characters. Again, *A Shabby Genteel Story* attempted to deal with the middle class in unvarnished terms. His first sustained narrative, *The Luck of Barry Lyndon*, features an Irish adventurer recounting his own life; the novel follows the rise and fall of its picaresque hero to illustrate the specious nature of worldly success. Perhaps most telling in his ten-year preparation for fiction writing were two series that appeared in *Punch*. "The Snobs of England" was a series of ver-

(Library of Congress)

bal portraits of social types, most drawn for their pretension; "Punch's Prize Novelists" was a collection of parodic rewritings of popular novelists' works.

In his sustained works, however, Thackeray leaves his readers not with a collection of isolated vignettes but with a panoramic study of humankind under the guidance of a witty persona whose satirical bent is tempered by the realization that he himself partakes of the foibles of his own characters. Thackeray's characteristic persona derives not only from Fielding and his prefaces to the various books of *The History of Tom Jones, a Foundling* (1749), but also from Samuel Johnson, who ends *Rasselas, Prince of Abyssinia* (1759) by suggesting that since an ideal world is impossible, a wise individual will stoically accept the one that exists. Certainly, Thackeray's experimentations with the persona in *The History of Henry Esmond, Esquire*, for example, a novel written in the memoir form, laid the groundwork for such masters of psychological realism and irony as Henry James and James Joyce. In addition, Thackeray's experimentations with the generational form, in which several novels are melded together through the familial relationships of their characters, look forward to such productions as John Galsworthy's *The Forsyte Saga* (1922). In presenting the affairs of Henry Esmond's grandsons and the development of the beautiful Beatrix Esmond into a worldly old woman in *The Virginians*, he was also implicitly exploring the kind of genetic and environmental influence that the naturalists defined as determinism.

While many modern readers are perhaps not as comfortable as their nineteenth century forebears with the conception of the authorial voice as a constant, even necessary factor in the plot, Thackeray nevertheless remains noteworthy, especially in his early novels, both for the realistic renderings of individuals in all social walks and for his moral standpoint, best expressed in the preface to *Vanity Fair* as a charitable outlook on human foibles.

BIOGRAPHY

William Makepeace Thackeray was born on July 18, 1811, in Calcutta, India. His father, Richmond Thackeray, pursued a family career in the East India Company; his mother, Anne Becher, traced her ancestry back to a sixteenth century sheriff of London. The senior William Makepeace Thackeray and John Harman Becher had extensive interests in India. After his father's death in 1815, Thackeray's mother married Major Henry Carmichael-Smith, a former suitor. As was the custom, Thackeray was sent to England at the age of five for reasons of health and education. His unhappy, early experiences at the Arthurs' school and at Chiswick were later rendered in "Dr. Birch and his Young Friends" (1849). At Cambridge, as a member of a privileged class, he was trained in the standards and preconceptions that he later pilloried in his *The Book of Snobs* (1848, 1852) and in many other works. He was left with a distaste for bullying and with a distrust of his own intellectual abilities. After two years at Cambridge, Thackeray abandoned the pursuit of academic honors. Although he believed that his education had, on the whole, served him ill, it nevertheless had given him a background in history and culture, a double appreciation that is well evidenced in *The History of Henry Esmond, Esquire*;

it also convinced him of his social status, although his expensive aristocratic habits were to prove difficult to control.

The gentle satire evident in *Vanity Fair's* Pumpernickel chapters reflect Thackeray's happy six-month tour of Germany before he undertook to study law in London. While the discipline soon proved not to his taste, his life as a gentleman of fashion (a life that included large gambling debts) was congenial, at least until the collapse of many of the Indian commercial houses reversed his inheritance prospects. Almost relieved to be forced to make his own way, Thackeray decided to develop his talent for drawing, making friends with Daniel Maclise and being tutored by George Cruikshank. While in Paris studying art, he met and married Isabella Shawe, the daughter of a Colonel in the Indian army. He endeavored to support his family through journalistic activities, even offering to illustrate Charles Dickens's *Pickwick Papers* (1836-1837). His friendship with Daniel Maginn made his "Yellowplush Papers" welcome in the columns of *Fraser's Magazine*, whose readers were regaled with the malapropisms of a rascally footman. In addition, he wrote for the London *Times* and for a number of obscure journals. His first long attempt at fiction was *Catherine*, a parody of the "Newgate Novel"; in quick succession he produced *A Shabby Genteel Story* and *The Paris Sketch Book*.

In 1840, Thackeray was visited by domestic calamity; upon the birth of their third daughter, his wife, Isabella, went insane and required institutionalization. The child-rearing was assumed by Thackeray's parents, leaving him to recoup his writing career, initially with *The History of Samuel Titmarsh and the Great Hoggarty Diamond* and soon with contributions to *Punch* and the *Morning Chronicle*. During these middle years, Thackeray solaced himself for the want of domestic connections with a series of friendships with old Cambridge acquaintances such as Alfred, Lord Tennyson and W. H. Brookfield, as well as with journalistic brethren such as Francis Sylvester Mahoney (the "Father Prout" of *Fraser's Magazine* fame) and with Dickens himself, whom Thackeray could, however, never accept as a "gentleman." His travel literature was published at this time.

His connection with *Punch*, begun in 1842, was an important one. From contributing fillers, he went on to write a number of series; moreover, Thackeray's rivalry with the other principal writer, Douglass Jerrold, was to affect the course of *Punch*'s publishing history, turning the tide from radicalism and democracy to a Whiggish conservatism of which Dickens himself much disapproved.

The year 1847 was crucial for Thackeray. He began to parody novels for *Punch* in the "Punch's Prize Novelists" series, he began a long platonic affair with Jane Brookfield, and he published *Vanity Fair*, the novel that has achieved abiding interest for its panoramic social view and its narrator's satircal viewpoint. His four-year relationship with Jane Brookfield certainly affected his writing; much of the nostalgia and agonizing provoked by the affair are reproduced in *The History of Henry Esmond, Esquire*. Just as important was his entreé into aristocratic circles, for he, along with his daughters Anny and Minnie, with whom he had set up an establishment in Kensington, were welcome not only at Holland House but also in the demirep world of Lady Blessington. Leaving his daughters was the only blight on his first American tour in 1852, when he lectured about "English Humorists of the Eighteenth Century" and marveled at the way in which the *nouveau riche* mingled with the best society.

Upon his return, Thackeray entered the height of the London social season and visited his daughters in Paris. He began *The Newcomes*, a novel much interrupted by illness but, even as its title suggests, much influenced by his social experiences. His work on the "Four Georges," an indictment of the House of Hanover as well as of the monarchy and the upper classes, indicated his changed attitudes. After his second American tour (undertaken, like the first, to provide stipends for his daughters), Thackeray not only published *The Virginians*, but also became editor of *Cornhill Magazine*, a project that allowed him to move "out of novel-spinning back into the world" of the essay. The periodical was an immediate success, publishing such authors as Anthony Trollope and George Henry Lewes. Although Thackeray retired as editor in 1862, he continued to publish his

"Roundabout Papers" there until the year after. Indeed, his last unfinished novel, *Denis Duval*, appeared in *Cornhill Magazine* posthumously in 1864, after Thackeray had died on December 24, 1863, in London.

ANALYSIS

While William Makepeace Thackeray may indeed be best known as the author of *Vanity Fair*, to examine all of his novels is to understand why his contribution to the history of the novel is singular. His use of the intrusive narrator, although presaged by Henry Fielding, was developed so carefully that it became a new form of fiction, a "genuine creation of narrative experiment," as critic Alexander Welsh calls it. In addition, his panoramic realism—although creating that anathema of Henry James, the novel that is "a loose and baggy monster"—explored, both seriously and satirically, a number of topics from which other Victorian writers shied away, such as married life and the development of the middle-class gentleman.

Quite aside from the interest generated by the story line, many of Thackeray's novels offer explanations of the art of creating fiction as well as criticism of some of his contemporaries' inadequacies. When Amelia in *Vanity Fair*, for example, tries to visualize George's barracks, the doors are closed to her, for the romantic imagination is in all respects inadequate to the exigencies of real life. In *The Newcomes*, Thackeray compares his method of character-building to the work of the paleontologist who discovers a series of bones and who must construct the habits, behavior, and appearance of his subject from a mere skeleton. He thereby suggests that any such "reality" is merely an illusion, for like the paleontologist, the author must work with probabilities. Insofar as his characters follow a probable course of events, they are true to life and, in a sense, interact without the help of the author. That Thackeray meant his novels to be something more than believable illusionary worlds is clear when his conclusions are examined. In *The Newcomes*, for example, Thackeray retreats at the end from Pendennis's narrative to suggest that the sentimental world he has created has no basis in fact, although the reader may believe so if he wishes to delude himself, and in the well-known ending to *Vanity Fair*, Thackeray puts his "puppets"—his characters—back into their box.

Rather than following Samuel Taylor Coleridge's idea of "willing suspension of disbelief," Thackeray is philosophical, inviting the reader into a reconsideration of his own or of conventional beliefs and preconceptions. Certainly, Thackeray's satire is operative here, particularly in his *Punch* series, in *Catherine*, and in *The Luck of Barry Lyndon*, in which he deliberately spoofed popular historical, crime, and romantic novels, respectively. The reader is asked to look at more than literary conventions, however; he is asked to examine his own degree of hypocrisy and snobbery. In so doing, the reader is reminded again and again that if he laughs at his neighbors, he condemns himself. Thackeray's work is thus truly homiletic, both in a literary and in an extraliterary sense. Unlike many of his predecessors, he examined in detail the difficulties occasioned not only by marriage but also by other personal relationships; rather than assuming that a novel should end with marriage, he makes it his subject. Certainly, his personally tragic domestic situation and his affair with Jane Brookfield are reflected in Rachel Esmond's trials with her reckless husband in Henry Esmond's growing love for her. In the family chronicle *The Newcomes*, Thackeray looks at the misery occasioned by parental marriage choices; Mrs. Mackenzie (known as the "Campaigner"), a strongminded virago who runs her daughter's life, is modeled on Mrs. Shawe, Isabella's termagant mother. Finally, in *The Virginians*, he traces the development of family characteristics and family ties.

Another one of the many senses in which Thackeray's novels are educative is the way in which he redefines the word "gentleman" to apply not to a member of a particular social class, but rather to one who possesses a set of personal characteristics, such as clear-sightedness, delicacy, generosity, and humanitarianism. His upper-class upbringing in India as well as his Cambridge education coupled with his love of the high life would seem to mitigate against such a redefinition, but, in fact, it is the greengrocer's son, Dobbin, in *Vanity Fair* who is the gentleman, rather than the pompous, vain George Osborne, and it is Colonel Newcome who, despite his misguided attempts to settle his son Clive's happiness, emerges as the paradigmatical enemy to snobbery and to greed.

VANITY FAIR

Vanity Fair, whose title is taken from John Bunyan's *The Pilgrim's Progress*, (1678, 1684), proved to be Thackeray's most successful novel. Indeed, its attention to realistic detail and its panoramic sweep, to say nothing of the constant presence of the author-cum-narrator, caused many reviewers to label Thackeray "the Fielding of the nineteenth century." While neither the initial reviews nor the sales were immediately promising, interest in the serial grew steadily until the publication of the volume guaranteed the author a financial as well as a critical success. Rivaling Thackeray at the time was Charles Dickens, whose *Dombey and Son* (1846-1848) appealed to a wide audience; even Thackeray himself, upon reading the passage describing little Paul's death, despaired about writing "against such power." Thackeray, however, had his own power, that of the saritist who created "A Novel Without a Hero" and thus ran counter to his readership's expectations, and that of the moralist who included his reader and himself in his reflective view of society.

The hero that *Vanity Fair* must do without is the typically romantic hero. George Osborne (whose first name conjures up the dandified Regency court) is handsome, dashing, and well loved, but he is also vain, shallow, and pompous. After Joseph Sedley has gone bankrupt, George marries the pining Amelia Sedley only at the urging of his friend William Dobbin; during their honeymoon, he engages in a flirtation with Becky Sharp, herself newly married to Rawdon Crawley. Killed at the battle of Waterloo, George is cherished as a hero only by Amelia. Dobbin is at the other extreme: Gangly, awkward, and low in social standing, he is nevertheless possessed of compassion and understanding, yet he is so blinded by his selfless love for Amelia that he does not see until the end of the novel on how slight a character he has set his affection. Even Rawdon, who develops from a typical "heavy dragoon" who lives by his gambling into an affectionate father for his neglected son, lacks intellectual acumen, and, after his separation from Becky, accepts the post that her prostitution to Lord Steyne earned him.

As A. E. Dyson suggests, Thackeray is indeed writing "an irony against heroes"—and against heroines as well. Amelia and Becky are as different as George and Dobbin. Initally, Amelia seems to be a conventional heroine, but the reader who views her in that light will be shocked to discover that he is idealizing the passivity, self-sacrifice, and hero-worship that are the earmarks of neuroticism, the three characteristics well seen in her treatment of her son Georgy, who is absurdly spoiled despite Amelia's and her parents' penury. No wonder, then, that readers preferred "the famous little Becky puppet" for her wit and ambition. From the moment she rides away from Miss Pinkerton's finishing school, leaving Dr. Johnson's dictionary lying in the mud, her energy in making a place for herself in society is impressive. Failing to entangle Amelia's brother Jos, she eventually marries Rawdon, the favorite of his wealthy aunt, and only repines when Lord Crawley himself proposes—too late. She turns her very bohemianism into an asset as she gains entry into the best society, and while she claims that she too could be a "good woman on £5000 a year," her energy in luring dupes to Rawdon's card table, wheedling jewels from Lord Steyne, being presented to the king, and playing charades at a social affair, belies her claim. As John Loofbourow shows, as Becky comes into social ascendency, Amelia declines into obscurity. Amelia lacks Becky's energy, while Becky lacks Amelia's morality. In the end, when Dobbin has won his prize, Becky has devolved into a female picaresque rogue, traveling across the Continent from disreputable gaming table to questionable boarding house. Neither she nor Amelia qualifies as a heroine.

It is Thackeray's preface that reveals the moral purpose behind his satire. Posing as the "Manager of the Performance," Thackeray reminds his readers that they are embarked on a fictional journey through an emblematic Vanity Fair, an evocation related only partly to the original in Bunyan's work. Vanity Fair, for Thackeray, is a representation of the human condition; it is not for the reader, like Bunyan's Christian, to pass through and eschew its lures, but rather to experience it "in a sober, contemplative, not uncharitable frame of mind," for the reader and author alike are part of the fair. Thackeray's comments throughout serve the purpose of distancing the reader from the characters and forcing him to judge not only the created "puppets" but also his own preconceptions. If everyone is indeed part of the fair, to condemn the booth-owners' hypocrisy, or social climbing, or snobbery, or mendacity, is to condemn one's own failings. To be possessed of "charity"—to be able to pity others with the same care one has for oneself—this, Thackeray suggests, is the best that can be expected when the puppets are put back in the box.

THE HISTORY OF PENDENNIS

The subtitle of *The History of Pendennis—His Fortunes and Misfortunes, His Friends and His Greatest Enemy*—gives ample indication that the novel is a *Bildungsroman*. As Juliet McMaster points out, however, it is also a *Künstlerroman*; that is, a tale about the development of an artist. It is perforce autobiographical, detailing as it does the way in which a young man learns enough about the world and himself to become a writer of "good books." The novel is important in a study of Thackeray's technique, presenting, as it does, the background for the persona who was to narrate *The Newcomes* and showing Thackeray's struggles with Victorian prudery. Indeed, in his preface he complains that his readers, unlike those of Fielding, are unwilling to accept a truthful portrayal of human beings unless they are given "a conventional simper." Thackeray's reviewers, however, welcomed the novel, their only complaint being the cynicism with which he endowed Pen. Such cynicism refutes Henry James, Sr.'s remark that Thackeray "had no ideas," for Thackeray's wryness results from a consideration of political and religious turmoil, from the "skepticism" brought about by the 1848 French Revolution, and from the controversy occasioned by the Oxford movement and Cardinal John Henry Newman's conversion from Anglicanism to Catholicism. Clearly, one reason for Thackeray's contemporary appeal was that he reflected the very doubts of his own readers, for whom belief was an exercise in paradox.

The tension between the heart and the world that animates *The History of Pendennis* is well represented by the frontispiece to the first volume, in which a youthful figure is clasped on one side by a woman representing marital duty and on the other by a mermaid representing the siren lure of worldly temptations. Within the dictates of the plot, the same tension is demonstrated by the demands of Pen's sentimental mother, Helen Pendennis, who urges her son to marry the domestic Laura, her ward, and those of his uncle, Major Pendennis, who is willing to blackmail his acquaintance, Sir Francis Clavering, so that Pen can have a seat in Parliament and the hand of Clavering's wealthy but artificial daughter Blanche. Between the two, Pen must, as McMaster points out, find his own reality; he must acquire "his uncle's keen perception without the withering selfishness" and participate in his mother's world of emotions without engaging in "romantic illusion." Pen's education progresses primarily through his amours, but also through his choice of career, for to be a writer, he must determine the relationship between fact and fiction.

Pen's abiding interest in the nature of experience makes his involvement with an actress allegorical in nature. His first affair is with Emily Costigan (known as "the Fotheringay"), an Irish actress older than he and one who plays her parts serenely unconscious of their philosophical implications; her ignorance Pen passes off as "adorable simplicity." Extricated by his uncle, who "lends" Emily's father a small sum in return for Pen's love letters, Pen next enters Oxbridge, and then, influenced by his roommate, George Warrington, determines to study law and to become a writer. His affair with Fanny Bolton, the daughter of his landlady, is again one of an attraction to "adorable simplicity," and his consequent illness a kind of purgation. His attachment to Blanche Clavering is more serious and more dangerous, for Blanche is a social "actress" with whom Pen plays the role of world-weary lover. With her he believes he has matured because he is willing to compromise with disillusionment. His real moment of maturity comes, however, when he finds that he cannot put up with his uncle's worldliness, for in discovering that Clavering's second marriage is bigamous and that the Bar-

onet is paying blackmail money to his wife's first husband, the Major in turn blackmails Clavering to give up his seat in Parliament to Pen and to cede his estate to Blanche.

Pen's responsible decision to honor his proposal to Blanche despite the resultant scandal is, in fact, unnecessary, for she jilts him for a more suitable match, freeing him to marry Laura, whose steadfast, honest devotion represents the alternative to Blanche's sham affection. Laura, in fact, is Pen's muse, his living "laurel wreath"; she has insight and a critical faculty that force Pen to come face to face with himself. With her, Pen finally frees himself from both romantic illusion and worldly disillusionment.

HENRY ESMOND

Like Dickens, who turned from the largely unplotted "loose and baggy monsters" of his novelistic apprenticeship to produce the tightly controlled *Dombey and Son*, Thackeray moved from the looseness occasioned by serial publication to the careful construction of *The History of Henry Esmond, Esquire, a Colonel in the Service of Her Majesty Q. Anne*, more commonly known as *Henry Esmond*. While the novelist Anthony Trollope agreed with Thackeray that the book was his "*very* best," initial critical reaction was mixed, ranging from high praise for Thackeray's realism to a scandalized outcry against what Gordon Ray calls the "emotional pattern" of the work—Esmond's marriage to Lady Castlewood, his cousin and senior by eight years. All agreed, however, that the novel was profoundly moving. Much of its power is owing to its genesis: Written when Thackeray was recovering from his alienation from Jane Brookfield, the novel reflects his own emotional current, his nostalgia, his suffering, and his wish-fulfillment. In addition, *Henry Esmond* may be read on many levels—as historical fiction, as novel of manners, and as romance.

Superficially, Thackeray might seem an unlikely figure to write a historical novel, inasmuch as he composed a series of parodies of "costume dramas" (as he called them) for *Punch* and inasmuch as the historical novel was going out of fashion by 1852. Nevertheless, because Thackeray was steeped in seventeenth century history, the work has a verisimilitude that, in the view of some critics, allowed him to outstrip even Sir Walter Scott. The point of view he adopts, that of the first-person narrator, adds to the illusion. This tour de force is accomplished with a success that even Henry James, the master of psychological realism, might envy. The entire story is presented from the limited point of view of Esmond, the cheated heir of the Castlewood estate, who is adopted by his cousins, falls in love with the beautiful but irresponsible Beatrix Esmond, and for her sake joins the Jacobite cause; then, when Beatrix becomes the Pretender's mistress, he realigns himself on the side of the Stuarts, marries Beatrix's mother, and immigrates to America.

That Thackeray could, through a limited narrator, represent the complexity of Lady Castlewood's growing love for the innocent and unconscious Henry is remarkable in its own right. Thackeray's own memories of his boyhood helped him to re-create Henry's loneliness; his relationship with Jane Brookfield shaped his characterization of Lady Castlewood. As John Tilford points out, Thackeray prepares carefully for the marriage, doubtless aware that it challenged many readers' expectations and moral assumptions. Through nuances of dialogue, Rachel Castlewood's awareness of her feelings and of Henry's is revealed. A number of crucial scenes prepare for the denouement: Rachel's hysterical reaction to Henry's early affair with the blacksmith's daughter, an affair that brings smallpox to the family; her vituperation of Henry as he lies in prison for his involvement in a duel that killed Lord Castlewood, whose drinking, gambling, and hunting had contributed to a loveless marriage; and, finally, her overwhelming joy when she sees Henry after his long period of military service.

One early criticism of the novel was recorded by William Harrison Ainsworth, with whom Thomas Carlyle joined in objecting to the exultation of "sentiment above duty" in the novel; other critics found the comparison between the excitement of romantic love and marital unhappiness to be dangerous. The more sophisticated analysis of McMaster registers an "ironic tension" between "Rachel's moral rectitude and . . . the psychological damage" it can cause.

Like Henry James's Mme de Mauves, Rachel is possessed of a cool virtue based on a conviction of moral and intellectual superiority; as McMaster suggests, she may indeed welcome evidence of her husband's coarseness as a way of rationalizing her affection for Henry and may therefore be responsible for exacerbating her husband's untoward behavior. Thackeray does give both sides: While Castlewood, like Fielding's Squire Western, is rough and careless, pursuing a prodigal, adulterous life once his wife has lost her beauty to smallpox, he accuses her of pride and of a blighting coldness, and pleads for "the virtue that can forgive." Even Beatrix complains that her mother's saintliness provided so impossible a model that she was driven to ambitious selfishness. Such complaints themselves sound like rationalizations, however, for at the end of the novel, Rachel has undergone a long period of repentance. Having sent her temptation—Henry—away, she lives with the renunciation of happiness while he matures. Upon his return, then, she is no longer an angel, but, as he says, "more fondly cherished as woman perhaps than ever she had been adored as divinity."

THE NEWCOMES

Subtitled *Memoirs of a Most Respectable Family,* *The Newcomes* is a novel of manners that explores the way in which four generations of a nouveau riche family acquire social respectability. The novel, the first third of which is densely packed with background material and consequently slow-moving, is a deliberate return to the serial format that Thackeray had abandoned in *Henry Esmond*. While some modern critics object to the pace of this "monster," nineteenth century reviewers believed that, with this novel, Thackeray had outstripped even Dickens, whose antiutilitarian manifesto, *Hard Times* (1854), was running concurrently. To be sure, a number of reviewers noted some repetition in theme and characters, a charge against which Thackeray defended himself in the "Overture" but admitted to in private, acknowledging a failure of invention because of sheer exhaustion. One such "repetition," which is, in fact, a way of extending the scope of the novel, is that Pendennis is the "editor" of the Newcome memoirs. This device allows Thackeray not only to assume an objective stance from which his satire is more telling, but also to criticize the very social punctiliousness that Pendennis reveals, thereby achieving an advanced form of psychological analysis.

What provides the novel's "unifying structural principle," as McMaster notes, is "the repetition of the mercenary marriage and its outcome between various couples." This theme, however, is a manifestation of the larger examination of the nature of "respectability," as the subtitle implies. For Barnes Newcome, the banker, for the aristocratic Lady Kew, and even for her granddaughter, Ethel Newcome, affection and generosity are weighed against wealth and social position and found wanting. The touchstone figure is Colonel Thomas Newcome, Barnes's half brother; unworldly, honest, and loving, he is seen by Gordon Ray as a model of Christian humility. The underlying cynicism of the novel is underscored by the inability of the characters to gain happiness, whether they satisfy their acquisitiveness or rebel against such a value, for Thackeray reminds his readers that real fulfillment only exists in "Fableland."

To pursue the marriage theme is to understand that in Thackeray's world even the best intentions go awry. Certainly, the unhappiness that accrues in some relationships seems self-created: While the joining of money and class in Barnes's marriage to Lady Clara Pulleyn satisfies the dictates of the marriage market, Barnes's brutality drives his wife to elope with a former suitor. In contrast, Clive Newcome, the Colonel's son, is forbidden by Lady Kew to marry Ethel because his profession as an artist is unacceptable. Even Clive himself is infected by the view, for he neglects his modest muse to devote himself to society. For his part, the Colonel, seeing Clive's unhappiness, schemes to marry him to the sweet but shallow Rosey Mackenzie, the niece of his old friend James Binnie. The loveless though well-intentioned match is unhappy, for Clive longs for Ethel's companionship and the couple is tormented by the dictatorial Mrs. Mackenzie after the Colonel's bankruptcy.

Ethel, like Becky Sharp and Beatrix Esmond, is a complex heroine, one who, through much trial and error, weans herself from the respectable avarice she was reared to accept. In love with Clive despite her relations' objections, she nevertheless admits that she delights in admiration, fine clothes, and jewelry, and, although she despises herself for it, that she enjoys being a coquette. Her fine sense of irony about the marriage market, however, prompts her to wear a "sold" ticket pinned to her dress, much to the annoyance of her respectable relatives. At first affianced to Lord Frank Kew, she breaks the engagement; then, capitulating to social pressure, pursues the feebleminded Lord Farintosh, only to repent at the last moment when the devastation of Barnes's marriage, on which her own is to be patterned, is borne in upon her. In revulsion from her family's values, she devotes herself to Barnes's children and manages to divert some of the Newcome fortune to the impoverished Colonel and his son.

Ethel's "conversion" and Rosey's death do not, however, lead necessarily to a happy ending, for in the years of following Ethel hopelessly, of neglecting his painting, and, finally, of engaging in a loveless marriage, Clive has become less resilient, more demoralized. Indeed, a conventional ending to *The Newcomes* would be as unwieldy as the happy denouement that Dickens was persuaded to tack on to *Great Expectations* (1860-1861). All Thackeray does promise is that in "Fable-land . . . Ethel and Clive are living most comfortably together." As McMaster points out, "poetic justice does not operate in life, however it operates in romance and fairytale." In the end, Thackeray refuses to cater to weak sentimentality.

THE VIRGINIANS

Written while Thackeray was fighting a lingering illness, *The Virginians* is a long, formless novel, many of whose characters appear in earlier works. The weight of critical opinion, both contemporary and twentieth century, implies that Thackeray, as he well suspected, was at the end of his fictional powers. To Walter Bagehot, the novelist merely presented an "annotated picture," and, indeed, many complained about the plethora of details that substituted for imaginative creation. Thackeray's habit of digressing grew more pronounced, aided by his failure to preserve a distance between himself and his persona for the second half of the novel, the sardonic George

Warrington. Connected with such digressions was Thackeray's increasing propensity to justify himself in the eyes of his critics; such justification introduced in a work of fiction was as gratuitous, many felt, as the air of mordant rumination that colored the novel.

On the other hand, Thackeray's supporters cited his adept portraiture of character and his classical style. Geoffrey Tillotson's suggestion that all of Thackeray's works are like one long novel well represents this point of view. In reviving earlier characters and in introducing their descendants, Thackeray studies the development of character traits as well as repetitive familial situations. Beatrix Esmond, for example, having been mistress to the Pretender and the King and having buried two husbands, one a bishop, reappears as a fleshy old woman with a caustic tongue and piercing black eyes. The enigmatic George Washington in *The History of Pendennis* reappears in the person of his namesake; George and Henry Warrington are twin sons of Rachel, Henry Esmond's daughter.

Unfortunately, Thackeray was unable to pursue his original plan, which was to place the brothers on opposite sides in the Revolutionary War and to insert real-life sketches of such figures as Oliver Goldsmith and Dr. Samuel Johnson. The American section was foreshortened, although Thackeray's prodigious reading in American history lends it a remarkably realistic air—so realistic that some American readers were initially incensed that George Washington should be portrayed in so commonplace a light. The book falls into halves, the first reserved for the English adventures of the innocent, gullible Henry. As Gordon Ray points out, the theme, although difficult to discern, is "the contrast between American innocence and Old World corruption."

Henry becomes involved with his cousins at Castlewood, who welcome him as the heir of the Virginia estates, on the supposition that George has died in the battle of Fort Duquesne. Enticed into a proposal by the elderly Maria and encouraged to dissipate his fortune by his infamous cousins, Henry is rescued from debt by his twin, who had not died but was taken prisoner by the French. Deceived by his fortune-seeking relatives, Henry returns to Virginia to marry

the housekeeper's daughter. The second half, narrated by George, details his adventures in London. Kept on short funds by his mother, he marries Theo Lambert, the daughter of the gentlemanly General Lambert, a figure much like Colonel Newcome.

Even a brief plot outline of *The Virginians* reveals a number of Thackeray's recurring themes. The attraction of young men to older women is one: Just as Henry Esmond married Rachel, many years his senior, so his grandson becomes attached to Maria, and, conversely, so his mother, Mrs. Esmond Warrington, becomes attached to a much younger suitor. The dogmatic and clinging nature of the parent-child relationship is another, much-explored theme: Hetty Lambert gives up her love for Harry to nurture the General, who is loathe to let either of his daughters leave; Mrs. Esmond Warrington throws impediments in the way of George's marriage to Theo; even George himself meditates on his fear that his own daughters will eventually marry. In the final analysis, while *The Virginians* is justly faulted for its digressiveness, Thackeray's treatment of character and his mellow, pure style grant to this work what Gordon Ray calls "a modest vitality."

Overshadowed in modern assessments by his great contemporaries, Dickens and George Eliot, Thackeray is an essential figure in the history of the English novel, and his masterpiece, *Vanity Fair*, is among the great novels in the language. It is with this work that Thackeray is assured a place among the great authors in British literature.

Patricia Marks

OTHER MAJOR WORKS

SHORT FICTION: *The Yellowplush Papers*, 1837-1838; *Some Passages in the Life of Major Gahagan*, 1838-1839; *Stubb's Calendar: Or, The Fatal Boots*, 1839; *Barber Cox and the Cutting of His Comb*, 1840; *The Bedford-Row Conspiracy*, 1840; *Comic Tales and Sketches*, 1841 (2 volumes); *The Confessions of George Fitz-Boodle, and Some Passages in the Life of Major Gahagan*, 1841-1842; *Men's Wives*, 1843 (as George Savage Fitz-Boodle); *A Legend of the Rhine*, 1845 (as M. A. Titmarsh); *Jeames's Diary: Or, Sudden Wealth*, 1846; *The Snobs of England*, *by One of Themselves*, 1846-1847 (later as *The Book of Snobs*, 1848, 1852); *Mrs. Perkin's Ball*, 1847 (as Titmarsh); *"Our Street,'"*1848 (as Titmarsh); *A Little Dinner at Timmins's*, 1848; *Doctor Birch and His Young Friends*, 1849 (as Titmarsh); *The Kickleburys on the Rhine*, 1850 (as Titmarsh); *A Shabby Genteel Story and Other Tales*, 1852; *The Rose and the Ring: Or, The History of Prince Giglio and Prince Bulbo*, 1855 (as Titmarsh); *Memoirs of Mr. Charles J. Yellowplush [with] The Diary of C. Jeames De La Pluche, Esqr.*, 1856.

POETRY: *The Chronicle of the Drum*, 1841.

NONFICTION: *The Paris Sketch Book*, 1840 (2 volumes; as M. A. Titmarsh); *The Irish Sketch Book*, 1843 (2 volumes; as Titmarsh); *Notes of a Journey from Cornhill to Grand Cairo, by Way of Lisbon, Athens, Constantinople and Jerusalem, Performed in the Steamers of the Penninsular and Oriental Company*, 1846 (as Titmarsh); *The English Humourists of the Eighteenth Century*, 1853; *Sketches and Travels in London*, 1856; *The Four Georges: Sketches of Manners, Morals, Court and Town Life*, 1860.

BIBLIOGRAPHY

Bloom, Harold, ed. *William Makepeace Thackeray*. New York: Chelsea House, 1987. This critical anthology brings together major essays on Thackeray's main novels. Includes a chronology and a bibliography.

_____, ed. *William Makepeace Thackeray's "Vanity Fair."* New York: Chelsea House, 1987. In addition to Bloom's original introductory essay, the volume reprints, in the order in which they appeared, seven important previously published critical essays on the novel. Subjects range from Dorothy Van Ghent's evaluation of Becky Sharp to H. M. Daleski's consideration of the form of Thackeray's most important work.

Carey, John. *Thackeray: Prodigal Genius*. London: Faber & Faber, 1977. Takes a thematic approach, concentrating on his earlier writings and the shaping of Thackeray's imagination, especially its obsessive quality. The last two chapters relate this theme to the later fiction, *Vanity Fair* in particular. Indexed.

Clarke, Micael M. *Thackeray and Women*. DeKalb: Northern Illinois University Press, 1995. Examines Thackeray's treatment of female characters. Includes bibliographical references and an index.

Colby, Robert A. *Thackeray's Canvass of Humanity: An Author and His Public*. Columbus: Ohio State University Press, 1979. Colby seeks to capture Thackeray's "Protean" personality as expressed in his fiction. A very full text which contains a chronology.

Harden, Edgar F. *Thackeray the Writer: From Journalism to "Vanity Fair."* New York: St. Martin's Press, 1998. A thorough study of Thackeray's literary career.

_____. *"Vanity Fair": A Novel Without a Hero.* New York: Twayne, 1995. A clear, understandable review of the seminal novel. Excellent for any student of *Vanity Fair*.

Hardy, Barbara. *The Exposure of Luxury: Radical Themes in Thackeray*. London: Peter Owen, 1972. Takes a thematic approach to Thackeray's fiction, seeking to demonstrate the satiric and revolutionary feeling behind it. The themes covered include love, feasting, art and nature, and the exploitation of art.

Peters, Catherine. *Thackeray's Universe: Shifting Worlds of Imagination and Reality*. Boston: Faber & Faber, 1987. Relates Thackeray's fiction to his life, stressing particularly Thackeray's challenge to his society. A selected bibliography is provided.

PAUL THEROUX

Born: Medford, Massachusetts; April 10, 1941

PRINCIPAL LONG FICTION
Waldo, 1967
Fong and the Indians, 1968
Murder in Mount Holly, 1969
Girls at Play, 1969
Jungle Lovers, 1971
Saint Jack, 1973

The Black House, 1974
The Family Arsenal, 1976
Picture Palace, 1978
The Mosquito Coast, 1981
Half Moon Street: Two Short Novels, 1984
O-Zone, 1986
My Secret History, 1989
Chicago Loop, 1990
Millroy the Magician, 1994
My Other Life, 1996
Kowloon Tong, 1997

OTHER LITERARY FORMS

In addition to a steady stream of novels, Paul Theroux published collections of short stories, *Sinning with Annie and Other Stories* (1972), *The Consul's File* (1977), *World's End* (1980), and *The Collected Stories* (1997); a volume of criticism, *V. S. Naipaul: An Introduction to His Work* (1972); a memoir, *Sir Vidia's Shadow: A Friendship Across Five Continents* (1998); travel books, *The Great Railway Bazaar: By Train Through Asia* (1975) and *The Old Patagonian Express: By Train Through the Americas* (1979); and collections of children's stories, *A Christmas Card* (1978) and *London Snow: A Christmas Story* (1979). In addition to his books, Theroux wrote numerous reviews and articles, many of them based on his perceptions of events in the non-Western world; these are to be found in newspapers and periodicals such as *The New York Times Magazine*, the *Sunday Times* (of London), *Harper's*, and *Encounter*.

ACHIEVEMENTS

It is in the quirky nature of fame that Theroux, a prolific writer of novels, should be better known for his travel writing than for his fiction. *The Great Railway Bazaar* became a best-seller in 1975, gaining for Theroux both popular and commercial success. A second travel book, *The Old Patagonian Express*, published four years later, firmly established his popular reputation. Both offer the reader elegant and humane examples of a genre widely practiced between the world wars but not commonly seen today.

In the long run, however, Theroux's achievements will rest upon his fiction. He won a small share of

(1996 Newsday)

awards for his work, including four Playboy Editorial Awards for fiction (1972, 1976, 1977, and 1979), the Literature Award from the American Academy of Arts and Letters (1977), and the Whitbread Prize for Fiction (for *Picture Palace*, 1978). In 1982, he won the James Tait Black Memorial Prize and the *Yorkshire Post* Best Novel of the Year Award for *The Mosquito Coast*. In 1984, Theroux was inducted into the American Academy and Institute of Arts and Letters. *The Mosquito Coast* was released as a motion picture, starring Harrison Ford, in 1986; *Half Moon Street* was also turned into a film in 1986, starring Sigourney Weaver and Michael Caine.

Theroux writes in the best tradition of English literature, demonstrating a mastery of fictional conventions as well as a willingness to grapple with some of the thornier issues of modern life. Critics have compared him to, among others, Charles Dickens, Joseph Conrad, W. Somerset Maugham, Graham Greene, and Evelyn Waugh. Interested in neither the splashy innovations of a Donald Barthelme nor the lurid headline material of a Norman Mailer, Theroux is nevertheless a novelist to follow.

BIOGRAPHY

Paul Edward Theroux was born of French Canadian and Italian parentage in Medford, Massachusetts, in 1941, the third of the seven children of Albert and Anne Theroux. Literature and writing were important aspects of his early life. Albert Theroux, a leather salesman, read daily to the family from the classics and encouraged the publication of family newspapers. For his efforts, he was rewarded with two novelists: Paul, and his brother Alexander.

After conventional public schooling and a B.A. in English from the University of Massachusetts, Theroux volunteered for the Peace Corps in 1963 to escape the draft. He taught English in Malawi for two years until he was expelled for his unwitting involvement in the convolutions of African politics. From Malawi, Theroux went to Makerere University in Kampala, Uganda, where he lectured on seventeenth century English literature and maintained a careful political stance during the beginnings of Idi Amin's rise to power. At Makerere, Theroux met V. S. Naipaul, who became for a time his literary mentor. Theroux left Uganda in 1968 after being trapped in a street riot and went to Singapore, where he spent the next three years lecturing at the university.

Throughout this period, Theroux was writing prodigiously, both fiction and reportage, which he published in a variety of journals, both African and European. In 1967, he married Anne Castle, then also a teacher, and fathered two sons, Louis and Marcel. In 1972, judging himself able to earn his living by his pen alone, Theroux gave up teaching and moved his family to London. After he and his wife divorced, he returned to the United States, making his home in Massachusetts.

The Catholic background, the leftish political interests, the ten years in Africa and Asia, the friendship with V. S. Naipaul—these heterogeneous influences all left their mark on Theroux's fiction. At the same time, one notes how Theroux secularizes, liberalizes, and makes contemporary the Catholic ethic, turns the African experience into a metaphor for all social experience, and absorbs and makes his own the lessons of Naipaul.

ANALYSIS

Paul Theroux approaches his major theme—the ethical behavior of people in society—by way of postcolonial Africa and Southeast Asia, in stories that explore cultural interaction and the meaning of civilization. The three early African novels, *Fong and the Indians*, *Girls at Play*, and *Jungle Lovers*, set the scene, as it were, and suggest the terms for nearly all of his later fiction. These African novels offer not only a fictional portrait of the Third World struggling toward independence, but also a metaphor for all modern society and social ethics. In the apparently simpler world of East Africa, where white ex-patriot confronts black African, where Chinese meets Indian meets German meets American meets Australian, Theroux explores the ways individuals interact to form a social unit and the results, often absurd, of attempts to impose foreign values and ideas of civilization upon the primitive life of the jungle.

Although the later novels leave behind the specifically African setting, they continue to explore the theme of civilization versus jungle, expanding in particular upon the moral and ethical implications of certain kinds of social behavior. *The Family Arsenal* and *Saint Jack* provide instructive examples. In the former, Valentine Hood, an American ex-diplomat from Vietnam living in London, is struck by the domesticity displayed by the members of the terrorist band with which he lives: It is like a family. From this insight develop both the central theme of that novel and its plot structure. In *Saint Jack*, Jack Flowers creates a secular religion out of "giving people what they want." In *The Black House* and *The Mosquito Coast*, Theroux separates his protagonists from society to explore the meaning of exile, foreignness, and individualism. Yet underlying all of these fictions will be found the basic assumption that every human experience, from death to redemption, from fear to loneliness, from love to murder, must be understood in a social context.

FONG AND THE INDIANS

Fong and the Indians, the first of Theroux's African novels, is the witty tale of the business partnership between Sam Fong, a Chinese grocer, and Hassanali Fakhru, the Indian entrepreneur who rents him the store, supplies his goods, and, when business is poor, even becomes his customer. Fakhru dominates Fong's economic life, manipulating it for his own benefit by taking advantage of Fong's innocent incompetence as a businessman. Yet as the plot unfolds, it becomes clear the the relationship between Fong and Fakhru is far from one-sided. Moreover, it also becomes clear that this relationship is representative of all social and economic relationships. Each individual in a society suffers limitations of understanding that arise both from his own prejudices and from his cultural heritage. When two people meet to do business, they may well be speaking different languages, either literally or metaphorically. Misunderstandings are unavoidable, and the outcome of any action is unpredictable: Good intentions may or may not result in good consequences; the same is true of bad intentions. Chaos and absurdity reign when no one quite understands what anyone else is doing.

The plot of *Fong and the Indians* is an intricate comedy of errors involving Fong, the unwilling grocer; Fakhru, the capitalist swindler; and two CIA agents on a mission to convert suspected Communists. The fiction works as both a satirical portrait of African society today and an allegory in which the grocery business, the swindles, and the "good will" mission—artifices of civilization—are, in the context of African reality, revealed to be absurd. In *Fong and the Indians*, Theroux explores "civilization"; in later books, *Jungle Lovers*, *Girls at Play*, *The Black House*, and *The Mosquito Coast*, he explores the meaning of "Africa"—the reality of the jungle. At no time does Theroux become an apologist for the Third World, elevating primitive civilization over modern. Rather, he turns "jungle" into a metaphor for humanity's natural environment: The jungle is both dangerous and nurturing; it demands that its inhabitants concentrate upon basic human needs. Although the metaphor is most easily understood when Theroux sets his story in the literal jungle of Africa or Central America, there is "jungle" too in South London, in an English village, even in Florida.

In *Fong and the Indians*, Fakhru swindles Sam Fong by convincing him that canned milk represents

a victory of civilization. In Africa, however, canned milk makes no sense. Africans do not need it; Europeans prefer the fresh milk from Nairobi. Fong's only hope of becoming rich rests upon the wild improbability that the milk train will one day be wrecked. Aware of the absurdity, Fong accepts both the hope and the improbability of its fulfillment. Fong triumphs because he learns to love what he does not understand. He has the patience to submit, to accommodate his life to the requirements of survival. His change of diet, from the traditional Chinese cuisine he has maintained for all his thirty-seven years in Africa to a free, native one based on bananas and fried locusts, is at once a measure of his economic decline and an assurance of his ultimate triumph.

SAINT JACK

Theroux's ethic, then, appears to be based upon the virtue of inaction. Because human understanding is limited, all events appear ambiguous. Even innocently motivated attempts to improve the lot of humanity may prove unexpectedly destructive, such as Marais's attempt to bring revolutionary ideals to Malawi in *Jungle Lovers*, Valentine Hood's murder to rid the world of Ron Weech in *The Family Arsenal*, or even Maud Coffin Pratt's photographs of the pig feast and of her brother and sister in the mill in *Picture Palace*. Because all events are ambiguous, it is impossible to predict which actions will prove evil and which actions will prove good. Therefore, the only possible moral strategy is to take no action at all, to be patient and accommodate oneself to the unknowable mystery of the jungle.

Inaction, however, should not be confused with selfish laziness; rather it is an active, morally motivated inaction akin to the traditional Christian virtue of patience. Patience redeems the absurdity of the modern world, protecting humankind from despair and leading ultimately to a triumph of innocence and virtue that will in turn redeem society. This is the lesson of *Saint Jack*.

A middle-aged, balding, American ex-patriot, full of muddle, fear, and loneliness, Jack Flowers jumps ship in Singapore. A stranger and a misfit, Jack sees no hope of rescue; he does not believe in miracles. He is a modern man making a realistic appraisal of his chances in an unfriendly and dangerous world. Yet Jack wrests from this vision of despair an ad-lib ethic based upon fulfilling the desires of others. He becomes what others would have him be. Condemning no one, pardoning all, Jack participates in each person's unique fantasy. In the public world, he is called a pimp—he may even be a spy—but in his own private world, Jack is a saint: thoroughly reliable and incapable of cultural misunderstanding. He gives to each what everyone needs—pleasure, security, and forgiveness—and stands ready with whatever is needed to meet even an unexpected desire—be it pornographic pictures, the kind attentions of a good girl, or a game of squash. Jack shapes his own needs to match his companion's: He is the perfect friend and protector.

Jack's tattooed arms, emblazoned with Chinese obscenities and curses disguised as flowers, symbolize the way he eases the pain of human loneliness and fear by providing an illusion of hope and friendship and the reality of a temporary pleasure taken in safety. Pity, compassion, and a stubbornly innocent vision of human needs save Jack himself from doing evil and redeem the actions of all those he takes care of, even General Maddox himself.

The terms of this novel are coyly religious—Saint Jack, the manager of Paradise Gardens—but God is not really present in Singapore. What might in a Christian fiction be termed grace, is here good luck, and even Jack's redeeming power itself results, in the end, from his own fantasy. The effect is, on the one hand, tongue in cheek, and on the other, quite serious. Theroux appears to be walking the delicate line between a modern recognition that, in this absurd world, good and evil are meaningless categories and a commonsense realization that people need moral categories and at least an illusion of meaning in order to survive relatively sane.

THE FAMILY ARSENAL

The search for meaning and moral categories provides both the theme and the structure of *The Family Arsenal*. When the story opens, Valentine Hood has come to live with a group of unrelated people in South London. Their domesticity makes them a parody of the typical middle-class family: Mayo, the mother, a thief; Valentine, the father, a murderer; and Murf and Brodie, the teenage children, terrorist bombers. Early in the novel, many odd characters are introduced: Ralph Gawber, an accountant with a fondness for puzzles and a doomsday foreboding; Araba Nightwing, a radical actress who plays Peter Pan; Ron Weech, the hoodlum whom Hood chases and murders; Lorna Weech, his wife; Rutter, a gun-runner; and Lady Arrow. Initially, the relationships among these characters appear obscure if not irrelevant; yet as the plot develops, groupings take shape until the reader discovers, with Valentine Hood, that all are inextricably bound together by all sorts of dirty secrets, making them, in the words of one character, like one big family no one can quit.

The puzzlelike structure of this novel parodies the conventional thriller plot. Its purpose is, however, not action-packed adventure, but rather the slow revelation that, as Hood has suspected all along, inaction is best because all events (be they murder, theft, or bombing) are morally ambiguous. Thus, Hood changes from social avenger to listener. He develops an innocent vision of pity and love akin to Jack Flowers's that not only reveals the human bonds among all members and classes of society but also redeems his own guilt and saves at least some from the dangers and death that threaten them. By the end of the story, all is discovered and characters are regrouped into more pleasing families based on love rather than convenience.

Paralleling the revelation of relationships in the plot of *The Family Arsenal* is Hood's changing perception of the artistic organization of the stolen Van der Weyden that hangs in Mayo's closet. Mayo stole the painting believing that its theft would signal the beginning of social revolution. It does not: The world cares little about stolen artworks except as an interesting excuse for a headline. Yet, in an unexpected and very personal way, the painting does, in the end, play a revolutionary role in the story: It becomes the symbolic focus for the way art can organize seemingly disparate shapes and colors into a single beautiful whole. The Van der Weyden, like the tattoos on Jack's arms, suggests the resemblance between the personal vision of innocence that can redeem through pity and love and the vision of the artist that can change brutal reality into beauty.

PICTURE PALACE

The most extensive development of this theme occurs in *Picture Palace*, which becomes less a song of triumph for the artist's vision than a warning of the danger that arises when that vision becomes separated (as it necessarily must) from its real social context. Civilization versus the jungle, art versus reality—in Theroux's fiction these themes become almost versions of each other. The ethical effects of efforts by either art or civilization to improve human society are always unclear, dependent as much upon luck as fantasy. Instinctively, Maud Coffin Pratt seems to realize this tenet and locks away her photograph of Phoebe and Orlando in an incestuous embrace: To her, the picture represented love and innocent fulfillment, but when her brother and sister find it, they see only their own guilt and death. Unlike Jack Flowers (who can grab back his photographs of General Maddox) or Valentine Hood (whose revelations of family secrets save them in the end), Maud's personal vision of innocence redeems no one; indeed, it backfires completely, and she is left alone at the end of her life, famous but anonymous.

THE MOSQUITO COAST

In *The Mosquito Coast*, Theroux returns to the jungle milieu to explore further the consequences of extreme individualism, the separation of self from society and environment. With his perpetual motion ice machine, Allie Fox expends a mad energy trying to produce icebergs in order to impress the Indians with the superiority of his civilized genius. Needless to say, whether he floats the ice downstream to a native village or carries it by sledge across the mountains, the ice melts: The impressiveness of civilization disappears in the heat of the sun. Relying completely upon his own creativity, Fox, the Yankee inventor, may be seen as a type of the artist. His attempt to impose his personal vision of utopia upon the brutal reality of the jungle fails utterly; his story reads as a warning of the danger of art without social context.

Like Sam Fong's canned milk in *Fong and the Indians*, Fox's ice machine in *The Mosquito Coast* represents an absurd attempt to civilize the jungle; yet Fong is rewarded with riches (the milk train does wreck), while Fox dies mad and beaten on the beach of Central America. Both may be seen as emblems of the modern world, alone in a strange land, possessing nothing, trying to shape a life out of events that are mysterious, ambiguous, possibly dangerous, and probably absurd. Their differing responses to the jungle environment determine their different ends and provide the reader with the key to Theroux's view of social ethics.

Allie Fox rejects patience and accommodation; he rejects the mystery and the ambiguity of the jungle. He will build a bugless outpost of civilization; he would rather starve than eat a banana. In Theroux's world, it is poetic justice that Fox should misinterpret events and bring about the ruin of all that he has built. With true tragic irony, Fox learns from his failure not the value of accommodation, but only the need for an increased purity, an increased separation from the jungle, a separation doomed to failure. If Fong is the comic face of humanity, then Fox must be the tragic face.

O-ZONE

With *O-Zone*, Theroux fashions a future in which major American cities are sealed off from one another and aliens stalk the now-deserted outside. Despite Theroux's descriptive skills, however, critics disliked *O-Zone*—mainly because it had very little plot, which they believed had been sacrificed for Theroux's love of narrative (turned to better use in his travel writing).

MY SECRET HISTORY

About *My Secret History*, on the other hand, critics complained because the narrative takes the first third of the book to really begin. A long novel that is really six novellas grouped together, it follows a young man from Massachusetts who moves to Africa and, from there, to England. Andrew Parent (who changes his first name to "Andre" while in college) starts out as an altar boy in Boston, becoming first a Peace Corps volunteer in one African country, then a teacher in another African country, before finally deciding to become a writer, ultimately moving to London.

Ultimately, Andre becomes an international womanizer, as well as a successful writer, and the last chapter/novella concentrates on his facing the consequences of what he has done to his life. Theroux's cosmopolitan experiences are what fuel his characters, and that he draws from his own life is only natural for a writer. Some critics have believed that his work is too self-referential—that it is thinly disguised autobiography. Pointing to his mentor V. S. Naipaul's 1987 autobiographical novel *The Enigma of Arrival*, they have wondered whether *My Secret History* is a midlife crisis *roman à clef*.

Theroux's work, however, cannot be so easily categorized or dismissed. The progression of Theroux's novels demonstrates a marked coherence of interest and an increasing complexity of thematic and structural development. Although Theroux draws freely from the modern storehouse of pornography, violence, and antiheroism, he displays at the same time a real if not profound interest in some of the classic themes of Western literature—the source of good and evil, the use of pity and love in society, art, and reality. Technically, his work shows a similar melding of popular fiction (the gothic horror story, the thriller) with the structure and conventions of the classic novelists.

MY OTHER LIFE

Just as he resists any preconceived notions of a foreign culture he is about to enter, Theroux expects the same of readers who immerse themselves in his writings. "My secret is safe," he states in his introduction to *The Collected Stories*. The secret is his identity as a writer. To assign him to a category is to overlook the sense of separation that drives him in all directions in life. He is the consummate explorer who not only delights in discovery but also observes and records in imaginative detail. Yet as Theroux asks readers not to label him, he also reminds them that "My stories are the rest of me," and "I inhabit every sentence I write," statements that could be directed to his novel *My Other Life*. Written as a companion piece to *My Secret History*, the novel reflects what the author considers his "need to invent." In this case it is an "imaginary memoir" designed to portray his life as a series of short stories, a device that led one critic to refer to the work as another example of a Theroux novel being better for its parts than its whole.

THEROUX'S LATER NOVELS

The "other life" is a common theme throughout Theroux's works. He utilizes it to reveal the darker side of human nature, as exemplified in *Chicago Loop*, the story of Parker Jagoda, a respected Chicago businessman with a wife and children. Jagoda's sexual obsessions compel him to explore the baser instincts of like-minded people who inhabit other worlds within his city. Such obsessions often are at the core of his stories, as in *Millroy the Magician*, the satirical tale of a vagabond magician and his teenage sidekick who set out to rid a bloated America of its culture of consumption by advocating a biblical diet, in addition to other inventive schemes.

In *Kowloon Tong* Theroux resurrects the sense of separation and belonging that permeates earlier works such as *The Mosquito Coast*. He also returns to the Far East for his setting, specifically Hong Kong at the time Britain's rule over the colony was coming to a close. The central figure, Neville "Bunt" Mullard, symbolizes the internal conflicts and contradictions that invariably arise between colonists and the colonized. Among the latter is Mr. Hung, a mysterious Chinese figure whose efforts to take over Mullard's business expose the less appealing aspects of the two competing cultures.

Linda Howe, updated by William Hoffman

OTHER MAJOR WORKS

SHORT FICTION: *Sinning with Annie and Other Stories*, 1972; *The Consul's File*, 1977; *World's End*, 1980; *The London Embassy*, 1982; *The Collected Stories*, 1997

PLAY: *The Autumn Dog*, pr. 1981.

SCREENPLAY: *Saint Jack*, 1979 (with Peter Bogdanovich and Howard Sackler).

NONFICTION: *V. S. Naipaul: An Introduction to His Work*, 1972; *The Great Railway Bazaar: By Train Through Asia*, 1975; *The Old Patagonian Express: By Train Through the Americas*, 1979; *The Kingdom by the Sea: A Journey Around Great Britain*, 1983; *Sailing Through China*, 1983; *The Imperial Way*, 1985 (with Steve McCurry); *Sunrise with Seamonsters: Travels and Discoveries, 1964-1984*, 1985; *Patagonia Revisited*, 1985 (with Bruce Chatwin); *Riding the Iron Rooster: By Train Through China*, 1988; *To the Ends of the Earth: The Selected Travels of Paul Theroux*, 1990; *The Happy Isles of Oceania: Paddling the Pacific*, 1992; *The Pillars of Hercules: A Grand Tour of the Mediterranean*, 1995; *Sir Vidia's Shadow: A Friendship Across Five Continents*, 1998.

CHILDREN'S LITERATURE: *A Christmas Card*, 1978; *London Snow: A Christmas Story*, 1979.

BIBLIOGRAPHY

Barth, Ilene. "A Rake's Progress on Four Continents." *Newsday* June 1, 1989. This review of *My Secret History* gives a detailed plot summary of this lengthy novel. Barth compares it to Theroux's "prickly travelogues," noting the similarities between his fiction and his life.

Baumgold, Julie. "Fellow Traveler." *Esquire* 126 (September, 1996): 184. This informal conversation with Theroux provides some insight into the author's method of blending fact and fiction as part of his creative process.

Burns, Jim. "The Travels of Theroux: Seventeen Books Pay for a Lot of Train Tickets." *Herald Examiner* (Los Angeles), May, 1988. This interview with Theroux provides a good sketch of what motivates him to write, to travel, and to write about traveling. Some biographical information is also included.

Coale, Samuel. *Paul Theroux*. Boston: Twayne, 1987. Part of Twayne's United States Authors series, this book provides a comprehensive look at Theroux's work as well as providing a chronology of events in the author's life. Includes references for each chapter and a bibliography of both primary and secondary sources and an index.

Glaser, E. "The Self-Reflexive Traveler: Paul Theroux on the Art of Travel and Travel Writing." *Centennial Review* 33 (Summer, 1989): 193-206. This article provides more insight into what motivates Theroux's writing and traveling. This in-depth profile and interview of Theroux is invaluable in the light of the scarcity of book-length works about him; includes some references.

J. R. R. TOLKIEN

Born: Bloemfontein, South Africa; January 3, 1892
Died: Bournemouth, England; September 2, 1973

PRINCIPAL LONG FICTION

The Hobbit, 1937
The Lord of the Rings, 1955 (includes *The Fellowship of the Ring*, 1954; *The Two Towers*, 1954; *The Return of the King*, 1955)
The Silmarillion, 1977
The Book of Lost Tales I, 1983
The Book of Lost Tales II, 1984
The Lays of Beleriand, 1985
The Shaping of Middle-Earth, 1986
The Lost Road and Other Writings, 1987
The Return of the Shadow: The History of "The Lord of the Rings," Part One, 1988
The Treason of Isengard: The History of "The Lord of the Rings," Part Two, 1989
The War of the Ring: The History of "The Lord of the Rings," Part Three, 1990
Sauron Defeated, the End of the Third Age: The History of "The Lord of the Rings," Part Four, 1992
Morgoth's Ring, 1993
The War of the Jewels, 1994
The Peoples of Middle-Earth, 1996 (previous 12 novels collectively known as The History of Middle-Earth)

OTHER LITERARY FORMS

J. R. R. Tolkien's novels represent only a small part of the complicated matrix from which they evolved. During his lifetime, he published three volumes of novellas and short stories, *Farmer Giles of Ham* (1949), *Tree and Leaf* (1964), and *Smith of Wootton Major* (1967). Some of these tales had originally been bedtime stories for his own children, such as the posthumous *The Father Christmas Letters* (1976) or *Roverandom* (1998). *The Silmarillion* and *Unfinished Tales of Numenor and Middle-Earth* (1980) both contain stories Tolkien composed early in his life, material that sets the stage for the events in his novels. His poetry collections, *Songs for the Philologists* (1936), *The Adventures of Tom Bombadil* (1962), and *The Road Goes Ever On: A Song Cycle* (1967), link Tolkien's poetic formulations of Middle-earth's themes with the historical and linguistic themes of which both his professional work and much of his dreams were made, "the nameless North of Sigurd of the Völsungs, and the prince of all dragons." Tolkien's academic publications dealt with the history of the English language and Middle English literature: *A Middle English Vocabulary* (1922) and editions of *Sir Gawain and the Green Knight* (1925) with E. V. Gordon and the *Ancrene Wisse* (1962). His seminal essay "Beowulf: The Monsters and the Critics" (1936) and his only play, *The Homecoming of Beorhtnoth Beorhthelm's Son* (1953), offer fresh interpretations of ancient English epic poems.

Tolkien's novels have been adapted for cinema and television, and many, though not all, of his fragmentary stories, articles, and letters have been published since his death. His histories of Middle-earth, a remarkable invented mythology comprising chronicles, tales, maps, and poems, were edited as a series by his son, Christopher Tolkien. Volumes include *The Book of Lost Tales*, *The Lays of Beleriand*, *The Shaping of Middle-Earth*, and *The Lost Road and Other Writings*.

Achievements

Tolkien's fiction dismayed most of his fellow scholars at the University of Oxford as much as it delighted most of his general readers. Such reactions sprang from their recognition of his vast linguistic talent, which underlay both his professional achievements and his mythical universe. Tolkien led two lives at once, quietly working as an Oxford tutor, examiner, editor, and lecturer, while concurrently Middle-earth and its mythology were taking shape within his imagination.

For twenty years after he took First Class Honours in English Language and Literature at Oxford, Tolkien's

teaching and linguistic studies buttressed his scholarly reputation. Editing the fourteenth century text of *Sir Gawain and the Green Knight* with E. V. Gordon helped bring Tolkien the Rawlinson and Bosworth Professorship of Anglo-Saxon at Oxford in 1925. His lecture "Beowulf: The Monsters and the Critics" approached the Anglo-Saxon epic poem from an entirely new perspective and is considered a landmark in criticism of Western Germanic literature. As he was shaping his linguistic career, however, Tolkien was also formulating an imaginary language, which as early as 1917 had led him to explore its antecedents, its mythology, and its history, all of which he molded into the tales of *The Silmarillion*. Over the years, he shared them with friends, but he never finished putting them into a unified structure.

His preoccupation with Middle-earth and the practical demands of his teaching distracted Tolkien from scholarship, and between his celebrated essay *On Fairy Stories* in 1939 and his edition of the Middle English *Ancrene Wisse* in 1962, Tolkien published only fiction, a circumstance acknowledged with polite forbearance by most of Oxford's scholarly community, although his novels eventually met

(Houghton Mifflin Company)

with astonishing popular success. *The Hobbit*, originally a children's story, was published in 1937 after a six-year gestation, and by 1949, *The Lord of the Rings* was complete. Its sales, though steadily increasing after its publication in 1954-1955, did not soar until 1965, when an unauthorized American printing proved a disguised blessing, resulting in a campus cult responsible for the sale of three million copies by 1968.

Most critics of *The Lord of the Rings* have not achieved moderation. As W. H. Auden observed, "People find it a masterpiece of its genre, or they cannot abide it." Auden himself and C. S. Lewis, Tolkien's Oxford friend, headed the "masterpiece" faction, while Edwin Muir in England and Edmund Wilson in America deplored Tolkien's style and aims.

Honorary fellowships, an honorary Doctorate of Letters from Oxford and a C.B.E. from Queen Elizabeth all descended upon Tolkien with the unexpected wealth of his last years, which were nevertheless darkened by his reluctance to complete *The Silmarillion*. His reputation rests not on his academic talent or scholarly production, nor even on his brilliant linguistically oriented "mythology for England," but upon the novels that began as tales for his children and blossomed into a splendid imaginative tree of fiction whose roots feed upon the archetypes of northern European civilization and whose leaves shelter its finest aspirations.

BIOGRAPHY

John Ronald Reuel Tolkein was born in Bloemfontein, South Africa, on January 3, 1892. The piano-manufacturing firm of his father's family, originally descended from German aristocracy, had gone bankrupt, and the elder Tolkien had taken a South African bank position in hopes of improving his shaky finances. Tolkien's mother, Mabel Suffield, joined her husband at Bloemfontein, but when the climate strained Ronald's health, she took their two sons home to England in 1895. Less than a year later, Arthur Tolkien died in South Africa, leaving his widow and children nearly penniless.

In the summer of 1896, Mabel Tolkien rented a rural cottage at Sarehole Mill, close to Birming-

ham, and for the next four years she taught her boys French, Latin, drawing, and botany, to save school expenses. Much later, Tolkien called these "the longest-seeming and most formative part" of his life. Mabel Tolkien's attraction to Roman Catholicism led to her conversion in 1900, and she moved to a Birmingham suburb from which Ronald attended one of England's then leading grammar schools, King Edward's, on a scholarship. Already, he was demonstrating the fascination with ancient languages, which was to determine his career. He was involved in learning such northern European languages as Norse, Gothic, Finnish, and Welsh, as well as the Old and Middle English in which he achieved his academic reputation. He claimed this philological bent dated from the time he was five or six years old.

In 1904, his mother died at thirty-four, leaving her children in the care of Father Francis Morgan, her friend and pastor. Tolkien's devotion to his mother was inextricably intertwined with his own Catholic faith, and both played vital roles in the development of his fiction. Thus at sixteen, Ronald Tolkien looked back upon a series of grievous losses: his father, whom he considered as "belonging to an almost legendary past"; the Sarehole countryside he loved; his mother, whom he considered a martyr to her faith. Not surprisingly for a lonely boy, Tolkien fell in love early when he met Edith Bratt, another orphan, in his Birmingham boarding house. She was three years older than he, and she had just enough inheritance to support herself modestly while she dreamed of becoming a musician. Recognizing the boy's scholarly talent and fearing for his future, Father Morgan finally stopped all communication between Ronald and Edith until Ronald was twenty-one. Tolkien himself commented thirty years later, "Probably nothing else would have hardened the will enough to give such an affair (however genuine a case of true love) permanence." When he and Edith were reunited in 1913, they seemed to have little in common, but on the eve of his military departure to France in 1916, they were married.

By this time Tolkien had won a scholarship to Oxford University and graduated with first-class honors in 1913. He enlisted in the Lancashire Fusiliers in

1915, embarking for France in 1916. He survived the Battle of the Somme but was invalided back to England suffering from trench fever. While in a military hospital in 1917, Tolkien began *The Book of Lost Tales*, the genesis of *The Silmarillion*, although he dated the original ideas for the complete oeuvre from as early as 1910 and the original story of Beren and Tinuviel back to 1913. By 1918 he had read a version of "The Fall of Gondolin" to a college group.

After demobilization, Tolkien gained employment on the new *Oxford English Dictionary*, until in 1921 he was appointed to the University of Leeds in Yorkshire to lecture in Old English. While there he began to establish an academic reputation with his *Middle English Vocabulary* and an edition of *Sir Gawain and the Green Knight* done with Professor E. V. Gordon. On the strength of these and his connections back at Oxford, he was appointed the Rawlinson and Bosworth Professor of Anglo-Saxon Studies at Oxford in 1925, a post he held until 1945, when he was appointed Merton Professor of English Language and Literature at the same university. He held this post until his belated retirement in 1959. Various honorary degrees were bestowed upon him, and in 1938 he was Andrew Lang Lecturer at the University of St. Andrews, where he gave his famous lectures on fairy stories.

However, the central part of his life lay in his secret creation of the mythology of Middle-earth. It was initially the demands of his growing family (three boys and a girl) that brought any of this to light, particularly in *The Hobbit*, which was first drafted, according to his close friend and science-fiction novelist C. S. Lewis, by the beginning of 1930. Then it was through the influence of the Inklings, a club or group of like-minded university friends, that *The Hobbit* was reformulated and sent for eventual publication in 1937. The importance of the Inklings cannot be stressed enough, especially the friendship of C. S. Lewis, who encouraged Tolkien with *The Lord of the Rings* during World War II and immediately after, and who reviewed it in glowing terms. In a sense, Lewis was repaying the enormous debt he owed Tolkien for his conversion to Christianity. The Inklings continued till Lewis's death in 1963,

though the two men had drifted apart somewhat by then.

Even so, the vast bulk of Middle-earth mythology lay in a constant state of revision, expansion, and rearrangement, and despite the best efforts of friends and publishers, it was unpublished at his death. In fact, after the publication of *The Lord of the Rings* in 1956, he concentrated again on his academic work, and only after retirement did he make any serious inroads again into the mythology. In the end, it was left to his third son, Christopher, also an academic, to order the material and have it published, as he did with a number of incomplete academic studies. Tolkien's death in 1973 had been preceded by his wife's in 1971. They were both buried outside Oxford, their graves suitably inscribed with the names Beren and Lúthien. The year before his death he had been made Companion of the Order of the British Empire (C.B.E.) by Queen Elizabeth II.

ANALYSIS

Looking back around 1951 upon his Middle-earth, J. R. R. Tolkien commented, "I do not remember a time when I was not building it . . . always I had the sense of recording what was already 'there,' somewhere: not of inventing." He conceived of fantasy as a profound and powerful form of literature with intense philosophical and spiritual meaning, serious purposes, and eternal appeal. He believed the imagination, the mental power of making images, could be linked by art to "sub-creation," the successful result of imagemaking, and so he regarded the genuine artist as partaking in the Creator's divine nature.

Three major factors of Tolkien's personality and environment combined to shape the theory of fantasy underlying his novels, as first enunciated in the essay "On Fairy-Stories" (1938). His love of language for its singular rewards, his delight in the English countryside, and his shattering experience of trench warfare during World War I all provided the seeds for his three longest pieces of fiction. They also contributed to the points of view, astonishingly nonhuman and yet startlingly convincing, of *The Silmarillion*, *The Hobbit*, and *The Lord of the Rings*, where Elves and Hobbits illuminate the world of Men.

Even as a boy, Tolkien had been enchanted by Welsh names on railway coal cars, a sign of his unusual linguistic sensitivity, and as a mature scholar, he devoted himself to the mystery of the word in its northern manifestations. In "On Fairy-Stories," he wrote that "*spell* means both a story told, and a formula of power over living men." Tolkien cast his spells in the building blocks of words drawn from the imaginary languages he had been constructing as long as he could remember. The two languages he formulated for his Elves, the Elder Race, both derived from a common linguistic ancestor as human languages do, and this "nexus of languages" supplied the proper names for his fiction, so that despite their considerable length and complication they possess "cohesion, consistency of linguistic style, and the illusion of historicity." The last was possibly the greatest achievement of Tolkien's mastery of language in his novels, fostering vital credence in his imaginary world. He felt that the finest fairy stories "open a door on Other Time, and if we pass through . . . we stand outside our own time, outside Time itself, maybe." In his own childhood, a "troublous" one Tolkien said, he had "had no special 'wish to believe' "; he instead "wanted to know," as, perhaps, do his readers, aided by the resonance of his masterful use of words.

The memory of his years at Sarehole, the happiest of his boyhood, gave Tolkien an abiding love of nature, "above all trees," which formed the basis for one of his principal concepts, "the inter-relations between the 'noble' and the 'simple.'" He found "specially moving" the "ennoblement of the ignoble," a theme which recurs throughout his fiction. Tolkien's Elves practice love and respect toward nature, as do his Hobbits, "small people" connected closely to "the soil and other living things" who display both human pettiness and unexpected heroism "in a pinch." The Elves, Hobbits, and good Men are countered in Tolkien's Middle-earth by the threat of the machine, by which he meant "all use of external plans or devices," as opposed to "the development of inner powers or talents." The evil of the machine in Tolkien's eyes (he did not own a car after World War II) derived from the misguided human desire for power, itself a rebellion against the Creator's laws, a Fall from Paradise, another recurring theme in his fiction.

The horrors of World War I must have struck Tolkien as evil incarnate, with new military technology that devastated the countryside, struck down the innocent, and left no place for chivalry, heroism, or even common decency. Unlike Andrew Lang, an early Scottish collector of fairy tales, who felt children most often ask, "Is it true?," Tolkien declared that children far more often asked him of a character, "Was he good? Was he wicked?" Tolkien shared G. K. Chesterton's conviction that children "are innocent and love justice; while most of us are wicked and naturally prefer mercy." The child's stern perception of right and wrong, as opposed to the "mercy untempered by justice" which leads to "falsification of values," confirmed Tolkien's long-held inclination toward the steely world of the northern sagas, where human heroism faces inevitable defeat by the forces of evil, and the hero, according to Edith Hamilton, "can prove what he is only by dying." From his basic distrust of the machine and his firsthand memories of the Somme, Tolkien drew one of the major lessons of his fiction: "that on callow, lumpish and selfish youth peril, sorrow, and the shadow of death can bestow dignity, and even sometimes wisdom."

Reconciling this harsh northern *Weltbild* with his Roman Catholic faith did not seem to be difficult for Tolkien. An indispensable element of his theory of fantasy is the "sudden joyous 'turn'" of a "eucatastrophic" story, a moment in fiction accompanied by "a catch of the breath, a beat and lifting of the heart, near to (or indeed accompanied by) tears." By inserting the "turn" convincingly into his tale, the sub-creator "denies universal final defeat" and gives "a fleeting glimpse of Joy, Joy beyond the walls of the world, poignant as grief." Hence, Tolkien believed that such a joy was the "mark of the true fairy story," the revelation of truth in the fictional world the sub-creator built. It might even be greater, "a far-off gleam or echo of *evangelium* in the real world." Tolkien was able to see the Christian Gospels as "the greatest and most complete conceivable eucatastrophe," believing that in fantasy the human sub-creator might "actually assist in the effoliation and multiple enrichment of creation."

Tolkien's *The Silmarillion, The Hobbit,* and *The Lord of the Rings* form, as he always hoped, one coherent and archetypal whole. His "creative fantasy" effectively shows the three dissimilar faces his theory demanded: "the Mystical towards the Supernatural; the Magical towards Nature; and the Mirror of scorn and pity toward Man." Humanity's "oldest and deepest desire," the "Great Escape" from death, is satisfied in Tolkien's major fiction, not by denying Mortality but by accepting it gracefully as a gift from the Creator, a benefit to humankind that Tolkien's immortal Elves envied. The Elves' own magic is actually art, whose true object is "sub-creation" under God, not domination of lesser beings whose world they respectfully share. Scorn for fallen people (and fallen Elves and Hobbits as well) abounds in Middle-earth, but pity, too, for guiltless creatures trapped in the most frightful evil Tolkien could envision, evil that he believed arises "from an apparently good root, the desire to benefit the world and others—speedily— and according to the benefactor's own plans." Middle-earth lives forever in Tolkien's novels, and with it an affirmation of what is best, most true, and most beautiful in human nature.

For almost fifty years, mostly in the quiet academic atmosphere of Oxford, Tolkien built his resounding tales of "a body of more or less connected legend, ranging from the large and cosmogonic, to the level of romantic fairy-story." He consciously dedicated it simply "to England; to my country." The intellectual absorption with language he had always enjoyed gave him the starting place for his mythology, which he implemented in *The Silmarillion,* whose unifying theme is the Fall of Elves and Men. His happiness in the English countryside seems to have provided him the landscape from which *The Hobbit* grew, perhaps his most approachable "fairy-story" for both children and adults, illustrating the happiness to be gained from simplicity and the acceptance of the gift of mortality. The chivalric dreams of noble sacrifice shattered for Tolkien's generation by World War I were redeemed for him by his realization that the humble may effectively struggle against domination by the misguided technological values of modern civilization. The heroic legend of

The Lord of the Rings best illustrates Tolkien's resolution of the conflict between the northern values he had admired from youth and the Roman Catholic religion of hope and consolation to which he was devoted. Tolkien wanted to illuminate the simplest and the highest values of human existence, found in a human love that accepts and transcends mortality. Tolkien's "mythology for England," a unique gift of literature and language, has earned its immense popular success by appealing to humanity's eternal desire to understand its mortal lot. As Hilda Ellis Davidson commented of the great northern myths, so like Tolkien's own, "In reaching out to explore the distant hills where the gods dwell and the deeps where the monsters are lurking, we are perhaps discovering the way home."

The Silmarillion

Both in Tolkien's life and in the chronology of Middle-earth, the tales of *The Silmarillion* came first, but the book was not published until four years after his death. The volume called *The Silmarillion* contains four shorter narratives as well as the "Quenta Silmarillion," arranged as ordered chronicles of the Three Ages of Tolkien's Middle-earth by his son Christopher, following his father's explicit intention.

Tolkien began parts of *The Silmarillion* in 1917 after he had been invalided home from France. The work steadily evolved after more than forty years, and, according to Christopher Tolkien, "incompatibilities of tone" inevitably arose from his father's increasing preoccupation with theology and philosophy over the mythology and poetry he had originally favored. Tolkien himself never abandoned his work on *The Silmarillion,* even though he found himself unable to complete it. As Christopher Wiseman had suggested to Tolkien, "Why these creatures live to you is because you are still creating them," and so Tolkien painstakingly revised, recast, and polished these stories, unwilling to banish their characters from his imagination.

The Silmarillion opens with "Ainulindalë," a cosmogonical myth revealing the creation of Middle-earth by God ("Iluvatar") in the presence of the Valar, whom Tolkien described as angelic powers. He wanted "to provide beings of the same order . . . as the 'gods' of higher mythology" acceptable to "a mind that believes in the Blessed Trinity." The universe to which Middle-earth belonged was set in living motion by music, "beheld as a light in the darkness."

The short "Valaquenta" enumerates the individual Valar, whose personal responsibilities covered all created things of Middle-earth, stopping short of the act of creation itself. One of the Valar, Melkor, rebelled in the First Age; Tolkien believed that "there cannot be any 'story' without a fall." Melkor "began with the desire of Light, but when he could not possess it for himself alone, he descended . . . into a great burning." One of Melkor's servants was Sauron, who later embodied evil in the Third Age of Middle-earth.

The twenty-four chapters of the "Quenta Silmarillion" recount the legendary history of the immortal Elves, the First-Born of Iluvatar, whom Tolkien elsewhere called "rational incarnate creatures of more or less comparable stature with our own." After writing *The Lord of the Rings*, Tolkien clearly indicated that the Elves were "only a representation of an apprehension of a part of human nature" from which art and poetry spring, but, he said, "that is not the legendary mode of talking." The Elves originally share the Paradise of the Valar, Valinor, but the Elves suffer a fall from that grace in the "Quenta Silmarillion," the rebellion and exile to Middle-earth of one of the great families of Elves, led by their chief, the artificer Fëanor, who has captured the primal light of Iluvatar in the three Silmarils. Tolkien described these great jewels as aglow with the "light of art undivorced from reason, that sees things both scientifically (or philosophically) and imaginatively (or subcreatively) and 'says that they are good'—as beautiful." Fëanor's lust to possess the Silmarils for himself leads to their capture by Melkor, and in the struggle to redeem them, splendid deeds are performed by Beren, a Man of Middle-earth beloved of the Elvish princess Lúthien. Tolkien called this "the first example of the motive (to become dominant in Hobbits) that the great policies of world history . . . are often turned . . . by the seemingly unknown and weak." The union of Beren and Lúthien is the first between mortal Man and immortal Elf; they win Paradise to-

gether, and eventually Earendil the Elven Mariner closes the "Quenta Silmarillion" by bringing the gem Beren painfully rescued from Melkor to the land of the Valar. His Silmaril was set into the sky as its brightest star, while the others were lost in the depths of the earth and sea, and the First Age of Middle-earth came to its end.

Tolkien saw the Second Age of Middle-earth as dark, and he believed "not very much of its history is (or need be) told." The Valar continued to dwell at Valinor with the faithful Elves, but the exiled Elves with Fëanor were commanded to leave Middle-earth and live in the lonely Isle of Eressëa in the West. Some of them, however, ignored the order and remained in Middle-earth. Those Men of Middle-earth who had aided the Elves to redeem the Silmarils were given the Atlantis-like realm of Númenor as their reward, as well as lifespans three times the normal age of Men. Though Melkor was chained, his servant Sauron remained free to roam Middle-earth, and through his evil influence, both Men of Númenor and the Delaying Elves came to grief.

The decay of Númenor is told in the *Akallabeth*, a much briefer illustration of Tolkien's belief that the inevitable theme of human stories is "a Ban, or Prohibition." The long-lived Númenoreans were prohibited by the Valar from setting foot on "immortal" lands in the West. Their wrongful desire to escape death, their gift from Iluvatar, causes them to rebel and bring about their own watery destruction through the worship of Sauron, Melkor's servant. At the same time, the Elves who delayed in Middle-earth suffered the painful consequences of their flawed choice. Tolkien said they "wanted to have their cake without eating it," enjoying the perfection of the West while remaining on ordinary earth, revered as superior beings by the other, lesser races. Some of them cast their lot with Sauron, who enticed them to create three Rings of Power, in the misguided hopes of making Middle-earth another Valinor. Sauron secretly made another ring himself, one with the power to enslave all the others. The ensuing war between Sauron and the Elves devastated Middle-earth, but in the Last Alliance of Elves and Men against Sauron, the One Ring was lost. Tolkien calls this the "catastrophic end, not only of the Second Age, but of the Old World, the primeval age of Legend."

The posthumous collection called *The Silmarillion* ends with Tolkien's résumé "Of the Rings of Power and the Third Age," which introduces the motives, themes, and chief actors in the next inevitable war between Sauron and the Free Peoples of Middle-earth. Although *The Hobbit* and *The Lord of the Rings* have proved vastly more popular, and both can be enjoyed without the complicated and generally loftily pitched history of *The Silmarillion*, its information is essential to a thorough understanding of the forces Tolkien set at work in the later novels. Even more important, *The Silmarillion* was for Tolkien, as his son Christopher has said, "the vehicle and depository of his profoundest reflections," and as such, it holds the bejewelled key to the autobiography Tolkien felt was embedded in his fiction.

THE HOBBIT

Around 1930, Tolkien jotted a few enigmatic words about "a hobbit" on the back of an examination paper he was grading. "Names always generate a story in my mind," he observed, and eventually he found out "what hobbits were like." The Hobbits, whom he subsequently described as "a branch of the specifically *human* race (not Elves or Dwarves)," became the vital link between Tolkien's mythology as constructed in *The Silmarillion* and the heroic legend that dominates *The Lord of the Rings*. Humphrey Carpenter, Tolkien's official biographer, believes that Bilbo Baggins, hero of *The Hobbit*, "embodied everything he [Tolkien] loved about the West Midlands." Tolkien himself once wrote, "I am in fact a hobbit, in all but size," and beyond personal affinities, he saw the Hobbits as "rustic English people," small in size to reflect "the generally small reach of their imagination—not the small reach of their courage or latent power."

Tolkien's Hobbits appear in the Third Age of Middle-earth, in an ominously quiet lull before a fearful storm. Sauron had been overthrown by the Elflord Gil-galad and the Númenorean King Elendil, but since evil is never completely vanquished, Sauron's creatures lurk in the margins of Middle-earth, in the mountain-enclosed region of Mordor,

while a few Elves keep watch on its borders. Descendants of a few Númenoreans were saved from their land's disaster (Atlantean destruction was a recurrent nightmare for both Tolkien and his son Christopher), and they rule in the Kingdoms of Arnor in the North of Middle-earth and Gondor of the South. The former Númenoreans are allies of the Homeric Riders of Rohan, whose human forefathers had remained in Middle-earth when Númenor came to be. The three Elven Rings of Power secretly guard Rivendell and Lothlórien, which Tolkien called "enchanted enclaves of peace where Time seems to stand still and decay is restrained, a semblance of the bliss of the True West."

The Hobbits live in The Shire, in "an ordered, civilised, if simple rural life." One day, the Hobbit Bilbo Baggins receives an odd visitor, Gandalf the Wizard, who sends Bilbo off with traveling dwarves, as a professional burglar, in search of Dragon's Gold, the major theme of the novel. In the process, Tolkien uses the humble Hobbit to illustrate one of his chief preoccupations, the process by which "small imagination" combines with "great courage." As he recalled from his months in the trenches, "I've always been impressed that we are here, surviving, because of the indomitable courage of quite small people against impossible odds."

Starting from the idyllic rural world of The Shire, *The Hobbit*, ostensibly a children's book, traces the typical quest of the northern hero about whom Tolkien himself had loved to read in his youth. Gandalf shares certain characteristics with the Scandinavian god Odin, said to wander among people as an "old man of great height," with a long grey cloak, a white beard, and supernatural powers. Gandalf, like Odin, understands the speech of birds, being especially fond of eagles and ravens, and his strange savage friend Beorn, who rescues the Hobbits at one critical point, recalls the berserkers, bearskin-clad warriors consecrated to Odin who fought with superhuman strength in the intoxication of battle. The Dwarves of Middle-earth distinctly resemble their Old Norse forebears, skilled craftsmen who made treasures for the gods. Smaug the Dragon, eventually slain by the human hero Bard, is surely related to "the prince of all dragons" who had captured Tolkien's boyish imagination and who would reappear in *Farmer Giles of Ham*. The Germanic code of the *comitatus*, the warrior's fidelity unto death, celebrated in the tenth century Anglo-Saxon poem "The Battle of Maldon," inspired Tolkien's only play and applies to *The Hobbit*, too, since Bilbo's outward perils are overshadowed by the worst threat of all to the northern hero, the inward danger of proving a coward.

Bilbo's hard-won self-knowledge allows him to demonstrate the "indomitable courage of small people against great odds" when he saves Dwarves, Men, and Elves from suicidal war against one another, after the Dragon has been slain and its treasure freed. *The Hobbit* far exceeded its beginnings as a bedtime story for Tolkien's small sons, since it is also a fable about the child at the heart of every person, perceiving right and wrong as sternly as did the heroes of the North.

In late 1937, at the suggestion of his British publisher, Stanley Unwin, Tolkien began a sequel to *The Hobbit*. To the East, a malignant force was gathering strength in the Europe that even the mammoth sacrifices of World War I had not redeemed from oppression, and while Tolkien often cautions against interpreting his works allegorically, the apprehensive atmosphere of prewar England must have affected his own peace of mind. He described his intention in *The Lord of the Rings* as "an attempt to . . . wind up all the elements and motives of what has preceded." He wanted "to include the colloquialism and vulgarity of Hobbits, poetry and the highest style of prose." The moral of this novel, not a "trilogy" but, he stressed, "conceived and written as a whole," was "obvious": "that without the high and noble the simple and vulgar is utterly mean; and without the simple and ordinary the noble and heroic is meaningless."

THE LORD OF THE RINGS

The Lord of the Rings is a vast panoramic contest between good and evil, played out against the backdrop of Tolkien's mythology as presented in *The Silmarillion*. The One Ring of Sauron, long lost, was found by little Bilbo Baggins, and from him it passed to his kinsman Frodo, who becomes the central figure of the quest-in-reverse: Having found the Ring, the allied Men, Elves, Dwarves, and Hobbits must destroy it where it was forged, so that its power can never again dominate Middle-earth. Another quest takes place simultaneously in the novel, as the mysterious Strider who greets the Hobbits at Bree on the first stage of their perilous journey is gradually revealed as Aragorn, son of Arathorn and heir to Arnor in the North, descendant of Elendil who kept faith with the Valar; he is the human King of Middle-earth who must reclaim his realm. Sauron's minions rise to threaten the Ringbearer and his companions, and after many adventures, a great hopeless battle is fought before the Gates of Mordor. As Tolkien stated in "Of the Rings of Power and the Third Age," "There at the last they looked upon death and defeat, and all their valour was in vain; for Sauron was too strong." This is the paradoxical defeat-and-victory of the northern hero, whose glory is won in the manner of his death. As a practicing Christian, though, Tolkien had to see hope clearly in the ultimate struggle between right and wrong, "and help came from the hands of the weak when the Wise faltered." Frodo the Hobbit at last managed to carry the Ring to Mount Doom in spite of Sauron, and there it was destroyed, and "a new Spring opened up on Earth." Even then, Frodo's mission is not completed. With his three Hobbit companions, he has to return to the shire and undo the evil that has corrupted the hearts, minds, and landscape of that quiet region. Only after that may Frodo, with the Elves, depart for the far west.

In retrospect, Tolkien acknowledged that another central issue of *The Lord of the Rings* was "love in different modes," which had been "wholly absent from *The Hobbit*." Tolkien considered the "simple 'rustic' love" between Sam, Frodo's faithful batman, and his Rosie was *"absolutely essential"* both to the study of the main hero of the novel and "to the theme of the relation of ordinary life . . . to quests, to sacrifice, causes, and the 'longing for Elves,' and sheer beauty." The evidence of Tolkien's own life indicates the depth of his ability to love, like Beren, always faithful to his Lúthien. Such love that made all sacrifice possible forms the indestructible core of *The Lord of the Rings*, which moved C. S. Lewis to speak of "beauties which pierce like swords or burn like cold iron . . . a book that will break your heart."

Love exemplified in two important romances softens the necromancy and the battles of *The Lord of the Rings*: the poignant "mistaken love" of Eowyn for Aragorn, as Tolkien described it, and the novel's "highest love-story," the tale of Aragorn and Arwen, daughter of Elrond, leader of the Elves of Middle-earth. Eowyn is niece to Theoden, King of Rohan, the land of the horsemen Tolkien patterned after ancient Anglo-Saxon tribes he had first encountered through William Morris's *House of the Wolfings* (1889). In Theoden's decline, the shield-maiden Eowyn gives her first love to the royalty-in-exile she senses in Aragorn, and though he in no sense encourages her, Eowyn's tragedy is one only he can heal once he is restored as King. In contrast, Tolkien merely alludes to the love of Aragorn and Arwen in *The Lord of the Rings*, since it seems almost too deep for tears. Arwen must forsake her Elven immortality and join Aragorn in human death, paralleling the earlier story of Beren and Lúthien. Like Tolkien's own love for Edith, Aragorn's for Arwen is temporarily prevented from fruition until he can return to her in full possession of his birthright. The shadow of her possible loss lends stature to the characterization of Aragorn, the hero of *The Lord of the Rings*.

In 1955, Tolkien observed that "certain features . . . and especially certain places" of *The Lord of the Rings* "still move me very powerfully." The passages he cited sum up the major means by which the novel so strongly conveys love, redemption, and heroism achieved in the face of overwhelming odds. "The heart remains in the description of Cerin Amroth," he wrote, the spot where Aragorn and Arwen first pledged their love and where, many years later at the beginning of his fearful quest, "the grim years were removed from the face of Aragorn, and he seemed clothed in white, a young lord tall and fair." Tolkien magnifies this small epiphany of love through the eyes of the Hobbit Frodo. Another key episode, the wretched Gollum's failure to repent because Sam interrupts him, grieved Tolkien deeply, he said, for it resembled "the *real* world in which the instruments of just retribution are seldom themselves just or holy." In his favorite passage, however, Tolkien was "most stirred by the sound of the horns of the Rohir-rim at cockcrow," the great "turn" of *The Lord of the Rings*, a flash of salvation in the face of all odds that comes beyond hope, beyond prayer, like a stroke of unexpected bliss from the hand of the Creator.

The "turn" that makes *The Lord of the Rings* a "true fairy-story" in Tolkien's definition links fidelity to a vow, a Germanic value, to the Christian loyalty that animated many of the great Anglo-Saxon works Tolkien had spent his scholarly life studying. By weaving the immensely complex threads of Elves, Hobbits, Men, and Dwarves into his heroic legend of the last great age of Middle-earth, he achieved a valid subcreation, sharing in the nature of what for him was most divine.

THE HISTORY OF MIDDLE-EARTH
Tolkien's son Christopher undertook the massive task of editing and commenting on the many drafts and manuscripts Tolkien left unpublished. These volumes, grouped under the generic title of *The History of Middle-Earth*, became commentary of a painstaking, scholarly kind, such as Tolkien himself would have enjoyed, no doubt, though it leaves the average reader rather befuddled. Each volume reprints, compares, and comments on original draft material in chronological order. One interesting feature is the emergence of the *Annals*, running alongside the stories; another is the evolution of the Elvish languages and etymologies. Tolkien's original attempt to make this a mythology of England through the character of Aelfwine, an Anglo-Saxon who had somehow reached Middle-earth and then translated some of its material into Old English, can also be seen. *The Lost Road* (1937) emerges as a fragment produced as part of an agreement with C. S. Lewis for a science-fiction story on time travel that would complement a story by Lewis on space. The latter produced *Out of the Silent Planet* (1938), but Tolkien gave up on his, though the attempt to connect it to the *Akallabeth* can be seen clearly.

Christopher also edited the childhood stories and poetry; others have dealt with Tolkien's drawings, illustrations, and mapmaking predelictions. The production of such Tolkiana is perhaps in some danger of overshadowing the myth that gave it life. Tolkien saw all of his work as unfinished and imperfect. As

C. S. Lewis saw too in his *Chronicles of Narnia* (1950-1956), our myths can only ever be the first page of the Great Myth that goes on forever.

Mitzi M. Brunsdale,
updated by David Barratt

OTHER MAJOR WORKS

SHORT FICTION: *Tree and Leaf*, 1964, revised 1988; *Unfinished Tales of Numenor and Middle-Earth*, 1980 (Christopher Tolkien, editor); *The Book of Lost Tales*, 1983-1984.

PLAY: *The Homecoming of Beorhtnoth Beorhthelm's Son*, pb. 1953.

POETRY: *Songs for the Philologists*, 1936 (with E. V. Gordon et al.); *The Adventures of Tom Bombadil*, 1962; *The Road Goes Ever On: A Song Cycle*, 1967 (music by Donald Swann); *Poems and Stories*, 1980; *The Lays of Beleriand*, 1985.

NONFICTION: *A Middle English Vocabulary*, 1922; *The Letters from J. R. R. Tolkien: Selection*, 1981 (Humphrey Carpenter, editor); *The Monsters and the Critics, and Other Essays*, 1983.

CHILDREN'S LITERATURE: *Farmer Giles of Ham*, 1949; *Smith of Wootton Major*, 1967; *The Father Christmas Letters*, 1976; *Roverandom*, 1998.

TRANSLATIONS: *Sir Gawain and the Green Knight, Pearl, and Sir Orfeo*, 1975; *Finn and Hengest: The Fragment and the Episode*, 1982.

EDITED TEXTS: *Sir Gawain and the Green Knight*, 1925 (with E. V. Gordon); *Ancrene Wisse: The English Text of the Ancrene Riwle*, 1962; *The Old English Exodus: Text, Translation, and Commentary by J. R. R. Tolkien*, 1981.

MISCELLANEOUS: *The Tolkien Reader*, 1966.

BIBLIOGRAPHY

Carpenter, Humphrey. *Tolkien: A Biography.* London: Allen & Unwin, 1977. Written with access to Tolkien's unpublished letters and diaries, this mostly chronological narrative traces the development of the world of Middle-earth from Tolkien's philological work. Balances the details of his rather pedestrian life with the publishing history of Tolkien's writings. An extensive section of black-and-white photographs, a detailed bibliography, a family genealogy, and an index add to the value of this standard biography.

Crabbe, Katharyn W. *J. R. R. Tolkien.* Rev. ed. New York: Continuum, 1988. A study of Tolkien's writings (including a chapter on *The Silmarillion* and another on the posthumous History of Middle-earth series) unified by a vision of "the quest." After a brief biographical chapter, Crabbe considers Tolkien's use of languages to delineate character in his major works. Argues that his quest was for a suitable pre-Christian mythology which could ground the imaginative works of the future in a great mythic past for his beloved Britain.

Curry, Patrick. *Defending Middle-Earth: Tolkien—Myth and Modernity.* London: HarperCollins, 1997. Curry examines the relevance of Tolkien's mythological creation, especially in terms of its depiction of struggle of community, nature, and spirit against state. There are chapters on politics, ecology, and spirituality.

Foster, Robert. *The Complete Guide to Middle-earth: From "The Hobbit" to "The Silmarillion."* Rev. ed. New York: Ballantine, 1978. An alphabetical annotated compendium of each of the proper names in Tolkien's major works, including persons, places, and things, with page references to standard editions of each work. An invaluable reference, written from a perspective within the world created by Tolkien. The guide provides translations of Middle-earth tongues, chronologies as appropriate, and masterful summaries of complex events.

Hammond, Wayne, and Christina Scull. *J. R. R. Tolkien: Artist and Illustrator.* London: HarperCollins, 1995. A full commentary on Tolkien's illustrations for his major, minor, and unfinished stories. It brings out Tolkien's own skills as an artist and the quality of his visual imagination.

Isaacs, Neil D., and Rose A. Zimbardo, eds. *Tolkien and the Critics: Essays on J. R. R. Tolkien's "The Lord of the Rings."* Notre Dame, Ind.: University of Notre Dame Press, 1968. A collection of fifteen original and reprinted critical articles dealing with *The Lord of the Rings* as literature. Among the contributors, C. S. Lewis offers a paean to the author, critic Edmund Fuller allows that Tolkien's work lifts one's spirits, and translator Burton Raffel calls most of Tolkien's poetry "embarrassingly bad." An index of Middle-earth references completes a lively and accessible volume.

Reynolds, Patricia, and Glen GoodKnight, eds. *Proceedings of the J. R. R. Tolkien Centenary Conference, 1992*. Altadena, Calif.: Mythopoeic Press, 1995. As the title suggests, this is a collection of papers given at the Tolkien conference held at Keble College, Oxford, in 1992 and represents a significant collection of views on Tolkien.

LEO TOLSTOY

Born: Yasnaya Polyana, Russia; September 9, 1828
Died: Astapovo, Russia; November 20, 1910

PRINCIPAL LONG FICTION

Detstvo, 1852 (*Childhood*, 1862)
Otrochestvo, 1854 (*Boyhood*, 1886)
Yunost', 1857 (*Youth*, 1886)
Semeynoye schast'ye, 1859 (*Family Happiness*, 1888)
Kazaki, 1863 (*The Cossacks*, 1872)
Voyna i mir, 1865-1869 (*War and Peace*, 1886)
Anna Karenina, 1875-1877 (English translation, 1886)
Smert' Ivana Il'icha, 1886 (*The Death of Ivan Ilyich*, 1887)
Kreytserova sonata, 1889 (*The Kreutzer Sonata*, 1890)
Voskreseniye, 1899 (*Resurrection*, 1899)
Khadzi-Murat, 1911 (wr. 1904 *Hadji Murad*, 1911)

OTHER LITERARY FORMS

Leo Tolstoy's fiction, like that of many Russian writers, cannot be divided neatly into long fiction and short fiction. Tolstoy wrote only three full-length novels: *War and Peace, Anna Karenina*, and *Resurrection. Family Happiness, The Cossacks, The Kreutzer Sonata, Hadji Murad*, and the trilogy comprising *Childhood, Boyhood*, and *Youth* could be termed novellas or short novels; the distinction between the two is often ill-defined, but most readers would classify *The Cossacks*—the longest of this group—as a short novel. More problematic are the works which exceed the length of the traditional short story (as defined by English-language criticism) but not by a large margin. One such work is *The Death of Ivan Ilyich*, which may be regarded either as a novella (although it is about half the length of *Hadji Murad*, for example) or as a long short story. In turn, such well-known stories as "Khozyain i rabotnik" ("Master and Man"), "Dyavol" ("The Devil"), and "Otets Sergy" ("Father Sergius") are only slightly shorter than *The Death of Ivan Ilyich*.

The point of the foregoing is not to split terminological hairs but rather to emphasize the fact that the term "story," often loosely applied to Tolstoy's fiction, can be misleading. Tolstoy wrote relatively few "short stories" in the classic sense of the term; among those, some of the best known are "Nabeg" ("The Raid"), "Mnogo li cheloveku zemli nuzhno?" ("How Much Land Does a Man Require?"), and the stories collected in *Sevastopolskiye rasskazy* (1855-1856; *Sebastopol*, 1887). Finally, Tolstoy published a number of very short, moralistic tales, largely inspired by the religious reorientation which he experienced in the 1870's.

In addition to his fiction, Leo Tolstoy published a substantial body of nonfiction, particularly after his "conversion" to a new—and, in Orthodox terms, heretical—type of Christianity based on his idiosyncratic interpretation of the Gospels. In *Ispoved'* (1884; *A Confession*, 1885), he undertook a penetrating and negative self-evaluation, continued in *V chom moya vera* (1884; *What I Believe*, 1885), while detailing the tenets of this newfound faith. He began to dissect all around him, and specifically the world of art, which led to his two most famous literary essays: *Chto takoye iskusstvo?* (1898; *What Is Art?*, 1898) and *O Shekspire i o drame* (1906; *Shakespeare and the Drama*, 1906), in which Tolstoy attacked the world of Western art. Tolstoy is also the author of a voluminous correspondence stretching from his early adolescence to his death. His collected works appeared in Russia over a thirty-year period (1928-1958), in ninety volumes.

ACHIEVEMENTS

Tolstoy's literary career spanned sixty years of the most productive period in Russian literary history. Tolstoy was a "realist," in the sense that he focused chiefly on the outward physical aspects of human life. He was a master of the psycho-physical—that is, the depiction of the inner self of his characters through a carefully honed description of their physical being. From the first words of his diary to the very last, he perfected a style extraordinary for its logical precision and prosaic, unpoetic tone. His was a world of gray tones and pale colors rather than the black and white of his equally famous contemporary Fyodor Dostoevski. Tolstoy's fiction oscillates between the poles of memoir and invention, war and peace, moralism and neutrality. He is never light-hearted. His moralism, moreover, has frequently been misunderstood. He did not—as his great contemporary Ivan Turgenev thought—abandon fiction for moralism and moralistic essays. Rather, after 1880, he simply changed the emphasis in his fiction. He remained throughout his life a great artistic creator.

Tolstoy's influence has been enormous: By destroying Romantic conventions, he depoeticized the literary universe and gave it a sharpness, even a coarseness, that it theretofore had not known. One sees Tolstoy's influence in the stories of his contemporaries Nikolay Leskov and the great Anton Chekhov, and even in lesser figures such as Maxim Gorky. Tolstoy's impact, however, has been worldwide—in the Thomas Mann of *Buddenbrooks* (1901), in Marcel Proust, in James Joyce, in the ugliness of Stephen Crane's war, in the Saul Bellow of *The Adventures of Augie March* (1953), in the architectonic fiction of Mario Vargas Llosa. More than 150 years after his birth, Tolstoy remains a vital force in world literature.

BIOGRAPHY

Leo Nikolayevich Tolstoy's life was long and eventful, at times even overwhelming his work. Born the fourth child of a noble family, at its estate of Yasnaya Polyana in 1828, he was reared by a nanny, an aunt, a grandmother, and a succession of tutors. Tolstoy's mother—who, before her marriage, was Princess Marya Nikolayevna Volkonsky—died before his second birthday, leaving him only with idealized memories; his father, who died in 1837, left a much more distinct impression. Tolstoy's father, Nikolay Ilyich, a retired lieutenant-colonel, was very much the country gentleman, with a passion for hunting and little interest in literature. From his youth, Tolstoy himself had an extraordinary appetite for physical exercise, especially hunting. He was a naturally gifted linguist, and when he went to Kazan University, he entered as a student of Far Eastern languages but left without a degree. A voracious reader, he inclined toward moral dissatisfaction and self-analysis even as a young man; his diary, which he began on March 17, 1847 (he was then eighteen years old), reveals a constant battle between his reason and his soul.

Once he inherited the family estate, Tolstoy attempted in vain to help the peasants through social reform: He was always at war with the conventions of the world around him. Frustrated by his failure as a reformer, he went to Saint Petersburg, then to Moscow, leading the dissipated life of the young noble he was. Despite his considerable social exploits, he managed to earn a degree in literature and philosophy from the University of Saint Petersburg. His first work, written in 1851 but not published until many years after its completion, was "A History of Yesterday," an attempt to re-create in verbal detail a simple day in his life. It illustrates the central preoccupation of his literary existence: How can one transform the reality of events and the fantasy of dreams into words? This initial effort began an outpouring of fiction and nonfiction that dwarfs in volume the writing of any other Russian to this day.

In 1851, Tolstoy entered the army and traveled in the Caucasus—for him, as for many other Russian writers, a paradise on earth. Having become an officer, he became preoccupied with war and the behavior of the soldier during battle; he is said to have looked into the eyes of a soldier firing a gun to attempt a reading of his soul. After the siege of Sebastopol and the fall of the city late in 1855, Tolstoy's active military career was effectively at an end, although he did not officially resign his commission until September, 1856.

By the time of his marriage in 1862, Tolstoy had already achieved a substantial reputation in Russian literary circles. His wife was Sophia Andreyevna Behrs, the daughter of a court physician; at the time of their marriage, Tolstoy was thirty-four, Sophia only eighteen. Their first son was born in 1863; they were to have thirteen children in all. Happy and inspired, Tolstoy began thinking of a great cyclic novel, which was to become *War and Peace*. No sooner was it finished, however, than Tolstoy suffered a letdown: He plunged into a reading of the pessimistic German philosopher Arthur Schopenhauer, and he began to moralize on the great issues of life and death. This produced his second great novel, *Anna Karenina*, clearly a much more pessimistic work than *War and Peace*. Both books were immensely successful and made him world-famous.

As early as 1870, Tolstoy had begun to study Greek. In the years that followed, he read the Gospels as if for the first time. He began to believe that the Orthodox Church—and Christendom in general—had misinterpreted and distorted the teachings of Christ, and he advanced a revolutionary interpretation of Christianity based on his reading of Christ's own words. *A Confession* made him more than a literary figure; he became a prophet of sorts, preaching a religion the kernel of which is nonviolent resistance to evil. His passion for reform led him to visit slums, provide food for starving peasants, and appeal to the Czar for mercy for condemned terrorists. He openly associated with social outcasts; his family and relatives came to feel that he had betrayed them, and he was placed under police surveillance.

Concluding that the impulse to do good is killed by civilization and modern culture, Tolstoy asserted the sanctity of the Russian peasant. His outspoken views attracted a following of disciples, among the most prominent of whom was Vladimir Grigoryevich Chertkov, who was soon managing Tolstoy's literary affairs. This led to bitter and prolonged conflict between Chertkov and Tolstoy's wife over the copyrights to Tolstoy's books. Sophia Andreyevna wanted them for the children, while Tolstoy wished to give them up entirely. Meanwhile, Tolstoy sought to practice what he was preaching: He dressed as a peasant, worked in the fields, and gave up wine, meat, and tobacco, although not sex—despite his assault on sexual love in *The Kreutzer Sonata*.

Tolstoy's last full-length novel, *Resurrection*, was written to raise money to send a pacifist sect, the Dukhobors, to Canada. In the novel, Tolstoy continued his criticism of the Orthodox Church, which finally excommunicated him in 1901. His greatest artistic work of his final years, *Hadji Murad*, took Tolstoy back to the Caucasus he so loved. When the Revolution of 1905 shook Russia, he publicly condemned both sides. Angry at his wife, he willed control of his literary estate, without his wife's knowledge, to his daughter Alexandra. His last years were troubled: He had become a sort of world-conscience, and he was tortured by the fact that his life did not live up to his ideals; the almost constant hysteria of his wife added to his misery. Still, he retained a surprising vigor; he was planning a new novel shortly before his death. The manner of his death was indeed characteristic: Sick with pneumonia and confined to bed, he escaped, ostensibly to reach his beloved Caucasus, only to die in the Astapovo railroad station on November 20, 1910.

ANALYSIS

Leo Tolstoy's literary works may be viewed as repeated assaults on Romantic conventions. His view, expressed numerous times throughout his diary, was that such conventions blind both writer and reader to reality. Thus, his goal was to construct a new style, prosaic, matter-of-fact, but sharp and full of contrasts, like life itself. To depict all in motion, the inner world of people and the life surrounding them, is the basic creative method of Tolstoy. He sought to reveal the reality underneath by removing the veneer of custom. Precisely for that reason, Tolstoy was able to write *War and Peace*, a work depicting the ordinary life of an entire period of history in all of its movements, contradictions, and complexity.

Tolstoy, ever the moralist, sought to attain truth through art. In his conception, art is the great unmasker; as he wrote in his diary on May 17, 1896, "Art is a microscope which the artist aims at the mysteries of his soul and which reveals these mysteries common to all." The microscope focuses attention on the telling detail, the apparently meaningless gesture, the simplest expression. To Tolstoy, every inner thought, sense, and emotion was reflected in some physical detail; the resulting psychophysical method was to have a profound influence on later writers. Throughout Tolstoy's fiction, characters are reduced to one or two physical features; the palpable, the perceptible, the visible—this is the universe of Tolstoy.

Tolstoy believed that the literary patterns inherited from the Romantics did not get to the essence of meaning and were thus obsolete. His task: to destroy them. In his diary, he began a series of literary experiments: He made lists, he drew up columns, he numbered propositions in sequence. He was seeking a rational creative method—he wanted to construct narratives that were both factual, that is, true to experience, and aesthetically right.

Tolstoy's first artistic work, "A History of Yesterday," is telling in this respect. It is simply an account of uninteresting things that happen in the course of a day. Tolstoy's problem was to write down an accurate account of a full day: He verges on stream of consciousness as he follows his mental associations and perceives how one thing leads to another. To explain something, one must go back in time to explain its causes; this is Tolstoy the rational analyst. Moreover, there is the problem of what verbal expression does to what it describes. Thus, Tolstoy becomes a dual creator: He is not only the writer writing but also the analyst observing the writer writing. He continually makes remarks, interrupts them, questions himself. Tolstoy the analyst is also a creator, one who is attempting to impose rational order on a series that is nothing more than a random succession of human acts. He pushes analysis to extremes, and because he realizes that there is no limit in time to causation and that he could theoretically go back all the way to the beginning of history, he arbitrarily stops himself and leaves the fragment unfinished.

Thus, even at the beginning of his career, Tolstoy was experimenting with point of view and the literary re-creation of consciousness. This acute self-awareness runs through his oeuvre. As he said in his diary on February 29, 1897, a life that goes by without awareness is a life that has not been lived: "The basis of life is freedom and awareness—the freedom to be aware." To promote such awareness, Tolstoy sought to present things in a new way. To do so, he was obliged to distort, to make the familiar strange. It is no accident that when the Russian Formalist critic Viktor Shklovsky wanted to illustrate the technique he called *ostranenie* ("making strange," or "defamiliarization"), he turned first to the works of Tolstoy, perhaps the supreme practitioner of this device—as in the famous opera scene in *War and Peace* or the church service in *Resurrection*. In such passages, the reader sees familiar experiences as if for the first time. Art has become a path to truth: Tolstoy dissects reality and reconstructs it verbally in a new, more palpable form.

Tolstoy never abandoned this way of looking at reality: He portrayed cause and effect, in sequence. First he selected the facts to be described; then he arranged them. Before him, and even in a novelist such as Dostoevski, the artist's method was to show the result and then explain how it came to be—that is, to go back into the past after depicting the present. Tolstoy's method was the reverse: to show the cause and then the result. Show the wickedness of Napoleon and the strength of Mikhail Kutuzov, for example, and the reader can understand why Russia triumphed against the French.

Of Tolstoy's three full-length novels, only the last, *Resurrection*, is not representative of his distinctive method. This novel, which tells the tale of a repentant noble who seeks to resurrect the life of a young girl whom he once seduced, is full of moral strictures. Precisely because Tolstoy frequently forgot his psychophysical method, the novel fails as a work of art, in contrast to his two earlier and greater novels, which are examples of his method at its best.

WAR AND PEACE

If a conventional novel is a novel with a linear plot focused on one or two central characters, then *War and Peace* is a very unconventional novel. It has no single plot, and it includes more than 550 characters, some fifty of whom play important roles. *War and Peace* is like a gigantic epic, and while it may be called a historical novel, it is not a historical novel in

the vein of Sir Walter Scott: There is no great historical distance between the time of composition of the
book and the period depicted. It is a book of enormous contrasts, as suggested by the title: war and
peace, hate and love, death and life, hero and ordinary person, city and country. For Tolstoy, the world
of peace, love, life, and country was the ideal world,
but the world of war is the world of *War and Peace*.

The novel began as a story of the ill-fated Decembrist revolt, which took place after the death of
Czar Alexander I, in 1825, and before the accession
to power of his successor, Czar Nicholas I. Tolstoy
seeks to explain the events of 1825. Ever the rationalist, he realizes that to explain 1825, one must examine 1824; to explain 1824, one must examine 1823;
and so on. This reasoning (as in "A History of Yesterday") would have carried Tolstoy back to the beginning of time. Arbitrarily, he stopped in 1805 and began his novel there. He never reached 1825: The book
covers the period from 1805 to 1812, followed by a
twelve-year hiatus, after which the epilogue continues through 1824 to the eve of the 1825 Decembrist
revolt. Tolstoy's original plan was to write a family
rather than a historical novel, in which history was to
be the scenic decor in which families lived. There are
five complete versions of the novel: The first, entitled
"1805," does not resemble the fifth at all.

The book, rather than focusing on individual characters, concentrates on family blocks: Tolstoy used
the same contrast technique in portraying the families that he used in treating ideas and events. The
main backdrop of the action is the Napoleonic invasion of Russia. From the opening pages in the Moscow salon where Tolstoy first gives a glimpse of his
major noble figures, the echoes of the coming Napoleonic invasion can be heard. The reader will watch it
develop throughout the novel and will see it ultimately crumble as the great French army is conquered by the Russian climate and expanse.

The book poses two major questions, to both of
which it gives answers. First, under what circumstances do people kill one another and expose themselves to death? Tolstoy answers that they do so out
of self-preservation and duty. Second, in the battle
between life and death, who wins? Life wins, Tolstoy

answers, despite the ravages of time. Underlying the
whole narrative is a gigantic theory of history based
on the idea that the world spins not on the movements of single individuals (heroes) but rather on the
movements of masses of people. Thus, the Russian
mass will overwhelm the French army and its "hero,"
Napoleon. It will do this because its commanding officer, Kutuzov, understands that it is the movement of
the people that determines the course of history; he is
wisely passive. Tolstoy is uncompromisingly a fatal-
ist: Events occur as they do because they are fated to
do so; nothing that any single individual does can alter the course of fate. Thus, it is the fate of Russia to
undergo the great trials and tribulations of the Napoleonic horror, as it is the fate of Napoleon to lose the
crucial battle on Russian soil. Indeed, to underline
the importance of this theory, Tolstoy includes, at the
end of his novel, a famous epilogue in which he discusses the movements of masses. (Much has been
made of this epilogue, but it should be borne in mind
that Tolstoy himself omitted it from the 1873 edition
of the novel and that the evidence for it is in any case
given in the book itself.) *War and Peace* is thus a
book with a thesis.

The novel, completely static, in which scenes replace one another but do not flow in a continuous
stream, unfolds on two planes: the historical and the
familial. Tolstoy writes as if he were composing a
massive history of the period. There is an omniscient narrator with a severe national bent. Instead of
the description of personalities, one is given, as in
Homer's *Iliad* (c. 800 B.C.E.), the everyday facts of
human life: birth, marriage, family life, death, and so
on. There are no heroes; there is, rather, a sweeping
vision of human life, moving one critic to call the
book an "encyclopedia of human existence." The
novel is characterized by sheer bulk: It presents so
much material in such large blocks that the material
itself seems to go on after the story has ended. Because of the nontemporal scheme, the reader secures
less a feel of artistic framework imposed on all material than a sense of the vivid disconnectedness of real
life. Memorable and important as some of the characters may be, no single character dominates the book.
Only one is with us from beginning to end: Pierre

Bezukhov, the fat, awkward, and bespectacled illegitimate son of a very rich nobleman. His personal quest, to find the meaning of his life, unfolds with the book's events, but in no sense is the novel his story.

The reader looking for great "heroic" characters had best look elsewhere. Heroic characters are a dishonest Romantic convention. The novel contains no great sympathetic or unpleasant figures, none who is extraordinarily beautiful and extraordinarily appealing at the same time. Indeed, the two main contrasting families are combinations of good and bad. The Bolkonskys are a tense mixture of sensibility, intelligence, and narrow-mindedness. Andrey is a hero without a battle who claims to seek peace even though he is at home only at war. Maria—unattractive, mystical, totally devoted—exemplifies almost unjustifiable self-sacrifice. Both characters are dominated by an outwardly detestable father whose peace comes only through his own inner rage. The Rostovs, considerably steadier of mind and background, are a mixture of openness, altruism, and ignorant fear. Natasha is not beautiful, exceptionally intelligent, or extraordinarily adept, but she has unending charm and great possibilities of love. Her parents are wonderful, warm, loving, and foolish. Her brother Nicholas is handsome, intelligent, and dangerously narrow-minded. That Andrey and Natasha eventually come together and almost marry makes no sense, but then history does not have to make sense. That Pierre and Natasha do come together at the end of the novel does, however, make sense, for they share an openness common to virtually no one else in the book. Even the Kuragin family, so attractive and so given to extremes of behavior, is unheroic: The handsome Anatole, who almost marries Natasha, is last seen dying, his leg amputated; his sister Helen, the most beautiful woman in Russia, who marries Pierre and who seems so self-centeredly evil, is redeemed by her apparent willingness to realize that she is restless and can cause only misery to others.

Tolstoy does not write in black and white: All of his characters come in shades of gray, and all wind up fighting Tolstoy's own inner duel, the duel between reason and emotion. Tolstoy was convinced that a natural existence is the best; thus, Pierre and

Natasha survive because they are natural, while Andrey perishes because he is not. Kutuzov triumphs over Napoleon because he is more natural.

Tolstoy exploits to the utmost his famous psychophysical technique of showing people through various gestures and traits. Numerous characters come equipped with a single predominant feature that forever identifies them: the upper lip of Lise, the beautiful wife of Andrey, who dies in childbirth; the beautiful white shoulders of Helen; the looking-out-over-his-glasses of Pierre; the thick, little white hands of Napoleon; the dimpled chin of the French prisoner; the pimple on the nose of the man who leads the merchant delegation that meets Napoleon as he invades Moscow; the round face and composure of Platon Karatayev, the peasant whom Pierre meets in prison and whose roundness is a symbol of his moral completeness and of his ability to accept the world as it is.

Tolstoy rips away conventions: He redraws the world by changing the point of view of the observer. Just as he identifies characters by physical traits and cuts them down to size by knocking the hero out of them, so he destroys conventional perceptions of other elements of life. The battle of Austerlitz, in Tolstoy's description, consists only of a strange little sun, smoke, two soldiers in flight, one wounded officer, and finally Napoleon's little white hand. To Tolstoy, this was the real battle as seen by the soldier. In Tolstoy's view, battle as depicted by the likes of Scott had nothing to do with the real world: It was a result of conventions, and so Tolstoy deconventionalized it, as he did with opera. In placing Natasha, who has never before seen an opera, in an opera house, Tolstoy destroys the essence of opera by refusing to accept its conventions: Thus, a piece of cardboard on which a tree is painted is exactly that.

Tolstoy has rewritten the novel. It is not the form that existed before him, but a brand new one in which are combined philosophy, ordinary people, large masses and blocks of time. Curiously, *War and Peace* is frequently read to be an affirmation of life, but in fact it is all about death. It is death left at the end: The reader finds himself on the eve of the brutish Decembrist revolt where death awaits those, like Pierre, who will be involved. Moreover, the life that will be led as married couples by Pierre and Natasha, and Maria and Nicholas, is not a happy life: It is a life of conventions in which Natasha will bear children, Pierre will supply the finances, and so on.

As Tolstoy was completing *War and Peace*, he began to read more and more philosophy and more and more of the Bible. The cycle of pessimism which began in *War and Peace* and turned darker as the book wound toward its end culminated in the gloomy and tragic *Anna Karenina*.

ANNA KARENINA

Written between 1873 and 1877, *Anna Karenina* at first appears to be a completely different novel. The title immediately suggests that the book is centered on one dominant personality around which the book spins its plot. Anna's is the story of the fallen woman. Her fall is intertwined with moral and social questions of behavior, and like an expanding pool, the novel becomes all-encompassing of the Russian society of its day. What the book achieves is no less original than what *War and Peace* achieved: It is the classic story of the fallen woman, but it is combined as never before with the burning moral and social questions of the author's day.

The book begins with the pessimistic note with which *War and Peace* ended. It is a book about disorder. There are no happy couples and there are no happy events. Everything is discordant, as if fate had intended the world not to harmonize. Thus, Anna, who is married to a man whom she does not love, falls in love with a man, Vronsky, who cannot satisfy her. Because the story is contemporaneous with Tolstoy's time, he is able to introduce character types of his day that would not have appeared in *War and Peace*. Chief among them is Stiva Oblonsky, Anna's brother, a shameless opportunist and careerist; he exemplifies much of the evil in the Russian bureaucracy. It is he and his suffering family whom the reader sees first: The Oblonsky family introduces to the reader the themes of adultery (Stiva is a philanderer) and contemporary society.

From its opening lines, *Anna Karenina* is a serious and critical book. It develops many of the same contrasts that animate *War and Peace*—city and country, good and evil—but it also adds new con-

flicts: between sex and love, between guilt and truth. Sex, Tolstoy explains, as did Gustave Flaubert in *Madame Bovary* (1857), is a path to trouble. Anna follows her sexual instincts, and as those instincts are produced by modern society, they lead her to her doom. In *War and Peace*, everything seemed logical and sequential, as Tolstoy the rationalist led us from one event to another; in *Anna Karenina*, everything is irrational.

The world has become a system of irrational correspondences. Consider the scene in which Anna first meets Vronsky: Fate operates through signs. Vronsky and Anna look at each other and sense a curious bond. The reader is never told why, as would have been the case in *War and Peace*. The stationman is accidentally crushed to death: This is an omen which will culminate many pages later in the famous and gruesome suicide of Anna, when she throws herself beneath a train. Almost unconscious on her way to the station, she reviews her life and her affair with Vronsky in a long passage of stream of consciousness in which readers sense doom, in the form of the dead stationman, pulling her on. Tolstoy, always given over to interior monologues, now goes one step further and gives the free associations of a character bent on self-destruction. Unlike *War and Peace*, this book is unconscious mystery.

Anna Karenina is a long series of emotional collisions. Various pairs of people line up and contrast with one another: Anna-Vronsky, Stiva-Dolly (Stiva's suffering wife), Kitty-Levin. The latter pair is curious. Kitty, Dolly's younger sister, who is originally engaged to Vronsky, is a superficial version of Natasha, with all the playfulness and none of the true openness. Levin, long considered a mouthpiece for the author, is a continuation of a long line of such Tolstoyan moral spokesmen. At the end of the novel, however, one is left with a Levin who senses but a yawning gap in his existence. Nothing is resolved. Everything will go on as before—but in the absence of Anna, now dead.

Every one of the characters is seriously blemished. Anna has a capacity for genuine love, but she also uses people and ultimately cannot bear what fate has in store for her. Vronsky is honest and honorable but lacks real spirit and is not truly perceptive. Stiva is a foolish, fat bureaucrat, content to live in a class structure he does not understand. Anna's husband, Aleksei (note that both he and Vronsky have the same first name, another mysterious correspondence), is shallow and cold but at the death of Anna shows a magnanimity of spirit foreign to Vronsky. Kitty is romantic and playful but in the end conventional; she accepts what fate has done to her. Levin is well meaning and open, but he is a dead generalization, put in the book to make the case for living close to nature (which, in any case, bores him).

The book's tension is extreme. By contrasting the Anna-Vronsky story with that of Kitty-Levin, Tolstoy plays, as he did in the opera scene in *War and Peace*, with our sense of perception. In the famous scene in which Anna's husband discusses divorce with a lawyer who keeps trying (unsuccessfully) to catch a moth, the tension becomes almost unbearable. We are all alive in a world that simply does not care. Thus, the details which in *War and Peace* make up the tapestry of history appear here to form a set of incomprehensible correspondences. Since *Anna Karenina* is focused so clearly on one intrigue, however, it is considerably more conventional in form than *War and Peace*: Its aura of moral gloom is thus directly communicated. The world, Tolstoy is saying, is not worth preserving.

It is no wonder, then, that Tolstoy's next burst of creative energy was given over to nonfiction. In *Anna Karenina*, Tolstoy had blasted not only the Russian bureaucracy but also the school system, the Church, and even the peasantry; in his later work, he fully assumed the role of a social critic. Immediately following the completion of *Anna Karenina*, he burst forth in a fit of moral fervor with *A Confession*. As one critic put it, Tolstoy came under the power of his own method, and art retreated before the pressure of self-observation and analysis; his own soul became material for exposition and clarification. Tolstoy changed the proportions in his creative work and became more the moralist than ever before, but he never ceased being an artist, as any reader of *The Death of Ivan Ilyich* and even *Resurrection* well knows.

Philippe Radley

OTHER MAJOR WORKS

SHORT FICTION: *Sevastopolskiye rasskazy*, 1855-1856 (*Sebastopol*, 1887); *The Kreutzer Sonata, The Devil, and Other Tales*, 1940; *Notes of a Madman and Other Stories*, 1943; *Tolstoy Tales*, 1947.

PLAYS: *Vlast tmy*, pb. 1887 (*The Power of Darkness*, 1888); *Plody prosveshcheniya*, pr. 1889 (*The Fruits of Englightenment*, 1891); *Zhivoy trup*, pr., pb. 1911 (*The Live Corpse*, 1919); *I svet vo tme svetit*, pb. 1911 (*The Light Shines in Darkness*, 1923); *The Dramatic Works*, pb. 1923.

NONFICTION: *Ispoved'*, 1884 (*A Confession*, 1885); *V chom moya vera*, 1884 (*What I Believe*, 1885); *O zhizni*, 1888 (*Life*, 1888); *Kritika dogmaticheskogo bogosloviya*, 1891 (*A Critique of Dogmatic Theology*, 1904); *Soedinenie i perevod chetyrekh evangeliy*, 1892-1894 (*The Four Gospels Harmonized and Translated*, 1895-1896); *Tsarstvo Bozhie vnutri vas*, 1893 (*The Kingdom of God Is Within You*, 1894); *Chto takoye iskusstvo?*, 1898 (*What Is Art?*, 1898); *Tak chto zhe nam delat?*, 1902 (*What to Do?*, 1887); *O Shekspire i o drame*, 1906 (*Shakespeare and the Drama*, 1906); *The Diaries of Leo Tolstoy, 1847-1852*, 1917; *The Journal of Leo Tolstoy, 1895-1899*, 1917; *Tolstoi's Love Letters*, 1923; *The Private Diary of Leo Tolstoy, 1853-1857*, 1927; *"What Is Art?" and Essays on Art*, 1929; *L. N. Tolstoy o literature: Stati, pisma, dnevniki*, 1955; *Lev Tolstoy ob iskusstve i literature*, 1958; *Leo Tolstoy: Last Diaries*, 1960.

CHILDREN'S LITERATURE: *Azbuka*, 1872; *Novaya azbuka*, 1875; *Russkie knigi dlya chteniya*, 1875.

MISCELLANEOUS: *The Complete Works of Count Tolstoy*, 1904-1905 (24 volumes); *Tolstoy Centenary Edition*, 1928-1937 (21 volumes); *Polnoye sobraniye sochinenii*, 1928-1958 (90 volumes).

BIBLIOGRAPHY

Gustafson, Richard F. *Leo Tolstoy, Resident and Stranger: A Study in Fiction and Theology*. Princeton, N.J.: Princeton Univ. Press, 1986. Gustafson seeks to rescue Tolstoy from those who would classify him solely as a realist. By focusing on what he sees as the inherently and uniquely Russian attributes of Tolstoy's writing, Gustafson reunites the preconversion artist and the post-conversion religious thinker and prophet. The study's bibliography is divided between books devoted to Tolstoy and those focusing on Eastern Christian thought.

Orwin, Donna Tussig. *Tolstoy's Art and Thought, 1847-1880.* Princeton, N.J.: Princeton Univ. Press, 1993. Divided into three parts, which coincide with the first three decades of Tolstoy's literary career, Orwin's study attempts to trace the origins and growth of the Russian master's ideas. After focusing on Tolstoy's initial creative vision, Orwin goes on to analyze, in depth, *The Cossacks, War and Peace,* and *Anna Karenina.*

Smoluchowski, Louise. *Lev and Sonya: The Story of the Tolstoy Marriage.* New York: G. P. Putnam's Sons, 1987. With the publication of Sonya Tolstoy's diaries it became apparent that in order to understand Tolstoy, it is necessary to understand his marriage to the extraordinary Sonya. Smoluchowski does a good job of retelling the story, relying mainly on the words of the principals themselves.

Steiner, George. *Tolstoy or Dostoevsky: An Essay in the Old Criticism.* 2d ed. New Haven, Conn.: Yale University Press, 1996. This welcome reappearance of a classic study of the epic versus the dramatic, first published in 1959, carries only a new preface. In it, however, Steiner makes a compelling case for the reprinting, in the age of deconstructionism, of this wide-ranging study not just of individual texts, but of contrasting worldviews.

Tolstoy, Alexandra. *Tolstoy: A Life of My Father.* 1953. Reprint. New York: Octagon Books, 1973. Many of Tolstoy's offspring, relations, and peers wrote about him. This is a good place to begin for those who wish to understand why Tolstoy inspired such reverence in those around him.

Wilson, A. N. *Tolstoy.* New York: W. W. Norton, 1988. A. N. Wilson is a masterful biographer, and he produced a comprehensive, thought-provoking book of the great Russian master that is a joy to read. This 572-page work is generously illustrated and opens with a helpful and detailed chronology of Tolstoy's life and times.

WILLIAM TREVOR

Born: Mitchelstown, County Cork, Ireland; May 24, 1928

PRINCIPAL LONG FICTION

A Standard of Behaviour, 1958
The Old Boys, 1964
The Boarding-House, 1965
The Love Department, 1966
Mrs. Eckdorf in O'Neil's Hotel, 1969
Miss Gomez and the Brethren, 1971
Elizabeth Alone, 1973
The Children of Dynmouth, 1976
Other People's Worlds, 1980
Fools of Fortune, 1983
Nights at the Alexandra, 1987
The Silence in the Garden, 1988
Two Lives, 1991
Juliet's Story, 1991
Felicia's Journey, 1994
Death in Summer, 1998

OTHER LITERARY FORMS

In addition to novels, William Trevor wrote numerous short stories, a collection of which was published in 1992; some have appeared in *The New Yorker* and other magazines. Most critics recognize him as a master of both the short story and the novel. He also contributed to other genres. His nonfiction includes his memoirs, *Excursions in the Real World* (1993), and he wrote dozens of plays for the stage, radio, and television. Several of his television plays were based on his short stories.

ACHIEVEMENTS

Considered one of the most important storytellers in the English-speaking world, William Trevor became a member of the Irish Academy of Letters. His books won numerous awards: *The Children of Dynmouth, Fools of Fortune,* and *Felicia's Journey* won the Whitbread Award; *The Silence in the Garden* won the *Yorkshire Post* Book of the Year Award; *Reading Turgenev* (a novella included in *Two Lives*) was shortlisted for the Booker Prize; and *My House in Umbria* (the other novella included in *Two Lives*) was shortlisted for the *Sunday Express* Prize. Always aware of a moral vision, Trevor is known for his ability to combine this vision with sometimes chilling stories, usually about the psychology of eccentrics and outcasts of society.

BIOGRAPHY

Born William Trevor Cox, Trevor spent his childhood in provincial Ireland. After attending a number of Irish schools and later Trinity College in Dublin, he began his career as an instructor and sculptor, teaching history and art in Northern Ireland and England. He moved to London in 1960 to work as an advertising copywriter. Describing this period of his life (1960-1965) and this job, he noted the boredom he experienced as well as the reward of a job in which he was to write advertising copy: The company had given him a typewriter to work on, thus offering him the impetus to start writing stories.

He then moved to Devon, England, to write full-time in his home, an old mill surrounded by forty acres of land. Often described as an Anglo-Irish writer, he actually transcends that label, having once said that the advantage of living in England is that "it is sometimes easier to write about your own people from a foreign country," and having developed the pattern of spending half the year traveling in Italy or in Ticino, the nub of Switzerland that juts down into Italy. He would also visit Ireland often during the other half of the year.

ANALYSIS

William Trevor began to write fiction only in his thirties, and from then on he was one of the most revered and prolific writers in the English language. Influenced by the writings of Irishman James Joyce and Englishman Charles Dickens—writers from the two countries in which Trevor lived—he is known for his lyrical and psychologically rich fiction, in which a moral vision shines through with unusual clarity. With a wry and often macabre sense of humor, he develops characters, most of whom are social outsiders and eccentrics, and puts them into situations in which they must make decisions that irreversibly affect their lives and the lives of others. The story is always at the heart of Trevor's work, for he is a consummate narrator who weaves a tale which captures readers in his fictional web.

THE OLD BOYS

Trevor's second novel opens with a group of "old boys," a committee of an alumni association of an English public school that is five hundred years old. Since it is a tradition of the association that members do not serve on the committee until they are very senior, and that all members of the committee during a two-year term of office should have been at the school at the same time, this group is indeed appropriately described as "old boys." This small group of men, all between seventy and seventy-five, includes Mr. Turtle, Mr. Nox, Mr. Swabey-Boyns, Mr. Jaraby, General Sanctuary, Sir George Ponders, Mr. Sold, and Mr. Cridley. United by their memories, jealousies, anecdotes, and dislikes, they are holding an important meeting to decide the next chairman of the Old Boys' Association. The setting is contemporary London.

Mr. Jaraby wants the job. Mr. Nox does not want Jaraby to have it, and to prevent him from getting the position, he hires a detective to watch Jaraby, whom he suspects of frequenting prostitutes, and then gets a prostitute to approach Jaraby. Meanwhile the other old boys meet, talk, and reminisce. A number of events complicate the election process, including a visit that the committee makes to the school for Old Boys Day, and Turtle dies there. This death does not perturb the others, however, since they have become accustomed to the deaths of their old friends.

While the plotline is not completely unexpected—Jaraby is clearly an unpleasant character who gets what he deserves—the development of the characters is a rare accomplishment. Eccentric geriatrics, they offer Trevor the opportunity to explore old age with the skills that have become his trademarks: humor and compassion. The story is written largely in stylized dialogue, which some have criticized as artificial; however, it is consistent with the satiric tone of this novel, as well as its message about the persistence of smug, insular, superficial—and perhaps arti-ficial—groups of Old Boys at every level of society and within every country.

THE CHILDREN OF DYNMOUTH

At the heart of this novel is an aimless sadistic fifteen-year-old named Timothy Gedge, a virtual or-phan who wanders about the seaside town of Dyn-mouth trying to connect himself with other people. In his desperate quest for connections, he goes to funer-als, knocks on people's doors, and greets everyone he meets on the street. To fulfill his dream of participat-ing in a talent show, thus launching a career as a comic impersonator, he enlists the assistance of sev-eral people, all of whom he tries to blackmail: an ag-ing homosexual whose marriage he almost destroys, an adulterer who has been having an affair with Tim-othy's mother, and a twelve-year-old boy and his stepsister.

Timothy is unmasked at the end of the novel, and he surrenders his hope of becoming a famous come-dian. Yet he doesn't surrender everything. Instead, he takes on the fantasy of being the son of a couple more attractive than his own parents.

As in other Trevor novels, the characters of *The Children of Dynouth* are the focus. United in a town that is a veritable failure, they likewise share another unity: a dislike of Timothy, whose menacing omni-presence is unnerving and ominous. Although noth-ing is neatly resolved at the conclusion of this novel, there is the suggestion of redemption, insofar as the vicar's wife, unable to have a son, sees Timothy as that son. In his characteristic way, Trevor leaves a trail of memorable characters and unanswered ques-tions, both developed with humor and compassion.

TWO LIVES

The title of this book, which contains two novel-las, seems straightforward and simple. In fact, this book does trace the lives of two women, both cap-tives of their own lives and both attempting to find their escapes through literature. The first, *Reading Turgenev*, is a sorrowful love story about a woman trapped in Ireland; the second, *My House in Umbria*, is a kind of thriller about a woman trapped in Italy. Though different in style and setting, the two stories have thematic similarities, one of which is the com-plexity of being human and the ways in which hu-manity can encourage or discourage love and life.

Mary Louise Quarry is the heroine of *Reading Turgenev*, which opens with the following under-stated description: "A woman, not yet fifty-seven, slight and seeming frail, eats carefully at a table in a corner. Her slices of buttered bread have been halved for her, her fried egg mashed, her bacon cut. . . . She's privileged, the others say, being permitted to occupy on her own the bare-topped table in the cor-ner. She has her own salt and pepper."

This apparently "privileged" woman, who has been institutionalized for more than half her life, is preparing to leave the institution which has been both her confinement and her security. Irish authorities have decided that the patients will be better off in the community, and thus Mary Louise is facing a return to her husband, Elmer, and his two maiden sisters, Matilda and Rose. This trio has been getting along quite nicely without Mary Louise—just as they had before Elmer courted this unwanted intruder.

Moving back and forth in time, Trevor tells the story of Mary Louise Dallon, the twenty-one-year-old daughter of a poor Irish Protestant farmer, who tries to escape the boredom of country life by marry-ing tradesman Elmer Quarry, almost twice her age. He tells the story of Mary Louise Quarry, the an-guished wife whose husband is unable to consum-mate their marriage and whose sisters-in-law make daily life a living hell for her. Elmer retreats into al-coholism, and Mary Louise retreats into literature reading. She enters into a relationship, a chaste rela-tionship, with her invalid cousin Robert, who reads to her from Ivan Turgenev's novels. This dual relation-ship—with Robert and with Turgenev—allows her to escape the harsh reality of life with Elmer and his sis-ters. When Robert dies, Mary Louise plunges deep into herself and into literature, eventually to be insti-tutionalized and, as described in the opening lines, eventually to be released. Past and present, as well as reality and fantasy, converge in Mary Louise's life until they create a blurry universe within which she survives.

Her counterpart in Italy and in *My House in Um-bria* also deals with this blurry convergence and, like

Mary Louise Quarry, holds onto literature as a ballast amid the storms of memory and reality. Emily Delahunty, also in her mid-fifties, has lived a life that is even more fantastic than the formulaic romances she has begun to write in her middle age. Sold at birth by her natural parents, her adoptive father abused her sexually at an early age, and she eventually becomes a prostitute in Africa, where she saves enough money to buy a villa in Italy and begin writing her novels. On a trip to Milan, she travels in a railway carriage in which a terrorist bomb is planted. Unharmed by the explosion, she nonetheless is hurt in another way, for she develops writer's block, which prevents her from continuing her next novel, which she has planned to call *Ceaseless Tears*.

Deciding to offer shelter to the other victims of the bombing, she also chooses to write about these survivors, intending to write about reality instead of romance. Yet just as the distinction between these two views of life is a literary blur, so it becomes ambiguous for Emily Delahunty. As she narrates her story, and as she tries to write the stories of the others, Emily layers numerous scenes: from her past, her dreams, her romances, films, biblical stories, her fan mail from readers. The result is what she describes as the writer's challenge—and her own: "pieces of a jigsaw jumbled together on a table . . . that higgledy-piggledy mass of jagged shapes." Trying to assemble this mass, trying to write the story of her life and the lives around her, compels Emily to state what may be the moral of all William Trevor's fictions: "Survival's a complicated business."

The complications within these two novellas with their deceptively simple titles are testimony to Trevor's insistence that there are no neat resolutions to messy situations, no neat conclusions to fictions that resound with the complexities of human behavior. Even the obvious similarities between the novellas, including the focus upon two middle-aged women who escape into literature, is deceptively complicated, for Trevor said that he didn't plan to write a book comprising a pair of novellas about two women. In his words, "They just seemed to belong together. They seemed instinctively to contain echoes and reflections of each other. Most things in art of any kind happen by accident, and this is a case in point." That two lives should intersect by accident, and that two novellas should complement each other by accident is just one more mystery to add to the numerous other inexplicable dimensions of Trevor's fiction in general and *Two Lives* in particular.

DEATH IN SUMMER

Three deaths occur in the summer of this novel. Like many of Trevor's novels, including *Felicia's Journey*, which immediately precedes *Death in Summer*, this novel reads like a thriller, a mystery story that begins with one premature demise and ends with another. In between, Trevor explores the complex psychology of characters, some of whom live on the fringes of society, others of whom appear to be privileged but who are nonetheless also disconnected internally and externally.

At the heart of *Death in Summer* is Thaddeus Davenant, an emotional cripple who is scarred by a lonely childhood. His short-lived marriage was for money, and it leaves him with a daughter to care for, a mother-in-law who moves in to help with this care, and potential nannies who apply for a position within the household. One rejected applicant, Pettie, reveals herself as a person as troubled and lonely as Thaddeus, and their two social classes—his the privileged elite and hers the economically deprived—clash and collide. This collision course is complicated by still other factors: an older woman with whom Thaddeus had a brief affair and who re-enters his life, seeking financial help; the kidnapping of Thaddeus's daughter; and minor characters who are intriguing and critical to the ultimate outcome of the novel.

The outcome of the novel does not provide solutions to all the mysteries in this fiction. Indeed, William Trevor concludes this book characteristically—with unanswered questions as chilling as the events he chronicles. Like Emily Delahunty in *My House in Umbria*, Thaddeus Davenant and the other survivors in *Death in Summer* learn that survival is a complicated business, one that is dependent upon connections with others while at the same time threatened by those connections.

Marjorie Smelstor

OTHER MAJOR WORKS

SHORT FICTION: *The Day We Got Drunk on Cake and Other Stories*, 1967; *The Ballroom of Romance and Other Stories*, 1972; *The Last Lunch of the Season*, 1973; *Angels at the Ritz and Other Stories*, 1975; *Lovers of Their Time and Other Stories*, 1978; *Beyond the Pale and Other Stories*, 1981; *The Stories of William Trevor*, 1983; *The News from Ireland and Other Stories*, 1986; *Family Sins and Other Stories*, 1990; *Collected Stories*, 1992; *Ireland: Selected Stories*, 1995; *Outside Ireland: Selected Stories*, 1995; *Marrying Damian*, 1995 (limited edition); *After Rain*, 1996.

PLAYS: *The Elephant's Foot*, pr. 1965; *The Girl*, pr. 1967 (teleplay), pr., pb. 1968 (staged); *A Night Mrs. da Tanka*, pr. 1968 (teleplay), pr., pb. 1972 (staged); *Going Home*, pr. 1970 (radio play), pr., pb. 1972 (staged); *The Old Boys*, pr., pb. 1971; *A Perfect Relationship*, pr. 1973; *The 57th Saturday*, pr. 1973; *Marriages*, pr. 1973; *Scenes from an Album*, pr. 1975 (radio play), pr., pb. 1981 (staged).

NONFICTION: *A Writer's Ireland: Landscape in Literature*, 1984; *Excursions in the Real World*, 1993.

EDITED TEXT: *The Oxford Book of Irish Short Stories*, 1989.

BIBLIOGRAPHY

Firchow, Peter, ed. "William Trevor." In *The Writer's Place: Interviews on the Literary Situation in Contemporary Britain*. Minneapolis: University of Minnesota Press, 1974. An interview that includes discussion of the literary establishment in Britain, promising young writers, and literary agents.

Fitzgerald-Hoyt, Mary. "The Influence of Italy in the Writings of William Trevor and Julia O'Faolain." *Notes on Modern Irish Literature* 2 (1990): 61-67. Compares the two writers' use of Italian settings.

Morrison, Kristin. *William Trevor*. New York: Twayne, 1993. A useful study of Trevor's fiction, including a chronology of significant events in the author's life, a selected bibliography of his works, and a list of secondary works.

Schiff, Stephen. "The Shadows of William Trevor." *The New Yorker* 68, no. 45 (December 28, 1992/ January 4, 1993): 158-163. A profile of the writer and his works. Emphasizes Trevor's Irish heritage.

Schirmer, Gregory A. *William Trevor: A Study of His Fiction*. New York: Routledge, 1990. A general discussion, organized chronologically.

ANTHONY TROLLOPE

Born: London, England; April 24, 1815
Died: London, England; December 6, 1882

PRINCIPAL LONG FICTION

The Macdermots of Ballycloran, 1847
The Kellys and the O'Kellys, 1848
The Warden, 1855
Barchester Towers, 1857
The Three Clerks, 1858
Doctor Thorne, 1858
The Bertrams, 1859
Castle Richmond, 1860
Framley Parsonage, 1860-1861
Orley Farm, 1861-1862
The Small House at Allington, 1862-1864
Rachel Ray, 1863
Can You Forgive Her?, 1864-1865
Miss Mackenzie, 1865
The Belton Estate, 1865-1866
The Claverings, 1866-1867
The Last Chronicle of Barset, 1867
Phineas Finn, the Irish Member, 1867-1869
He Knew He Was Right, 1868-1869
The Vicar of Bulhampton, 1869-1870
The Eustace Diamonds, 1871-1873
Phineas Redux, 1873-1874
The Way We Live Now, 1874-1875
The Prime Minister, 1875-1876
The American Senator, 1876-1877
Is He Popenjoy?, 1877-1878
John Caldigate, 1878-1879
The Duke's Children, 1879-1880
Dr. Wortle's School, 1880
Ayala's Angel, 1881

The Fixed Period, 1881-1882
The Landleaguers, 1882-1883
Mr. Scarborough's Family, 1882-1883

OTHER LITERARY FORMS

Anthony Trollope's novels were frequently serialized in various periodicals such as *Cornhill Magazine* and *The Fortnightly Review*. They appeared subsequently in a two- or three-volume format. Trollope wrote several books of cultural reportage which were more than mere travelogues: *The West Indies* (1859), *North America* (1862), *Australia and New Zealand* (1873), and *South Africa* (1878), along with the more impressionistic *Travelling Sketches* (1865-1866). Three volumes of short stories appeared: *Lotta Schmidt and Other Stories* (1867), *An Editor's Tales* (1870), and *Why Frau Frohmann Raised Her Prices and Other Stories* (1882). He wrote sketches of clerical men in *Clergymen of the Church of England* (1865-1866) and detailed biographies of William Makepeace Thackeray, a longtime friend (1879), and Lord Palmerston, the prominent politician (1882). His own *Autobiography* appeared posthumously in 1883. He tried his hand at classical translation in an edition of *The Commentaries of Caesar* (1870). Trollope's letters were edited by Bradford A. Booth (1951), but 205 complete and three fragmentary letters remain unpublished at Princeton University.

ACHIEVEMENTS

Trollope was acknowledged during his lifetime as a prominent though not necessarily a weighty or enduring writer. He wished to entertain and he did so, at least until the late 1860's when *He Knew He Was Right* turned out to be a failure. His posthumous reputation was harmed by his *Autobiography*, which claimed that he wrote automatically, that his characters were imitations of commonly observed types, that he transcribed reality without much aesthetic control, and that he forced his production by his methodical habits of composition whatever the circumstances. These admissions brought upon him the wrath of the next generation of writers in the 1880's and 1890's who were imbued with more aesthetic doctrines of carefully contrived and consistent viewpoints, detailed representation of interior states, a conscious interplay of ideas, and a complex style to suit a more complex method of storytelling.

Later, Trollope suffered from those who deemed him a pedestrian realist padding his work with creaking plots, flat characters, prosaic situations, and dull prose. He was, and still is for much of the public, the novelist of a single work, *Barchester Towers*, but other writers and critics have not forgiven him for writing more than thirty novels and setting himself a goal to exceed in quantity if not in quality. Despite what seems to be a simple theory of fiction—the writer tries as closely as possible to make the reader's experience approximate his own, to make his characters and events appear to parallel actual life—Trollope was more sophisticated than he allows.

Walter Kendrick finds that before Trollope's *He Knew He Was Right*, his inner thought is not distinguished from outer events, consciousness is presented chronologically; and characters, at least by implication, appear without authorial intervention. Afterward, character becomes "a zone of space on a canvas" with changes of age, feeling, and appearance even while outside the narrative. Various linear plots

(Library of Congress)

create a spatial unity for the reader, and they become a mosaic on which the character exists. Fiction writing becomes a subject in the novel, and the characters are a warning against efforts to define their existence with the narrative. This view sees the characters as a complex interplay between narrative and reader. Nathaniel Hawthorne had a very different view of Trollope, equating him to a giant hewing a great lump out of the earth as the earth's inhabitants go about the business of putting it under a glass case. This comment leads, unfortunately, in the direction of Henry James's evaluation after Trollope's death that he had "a great deliberate apprehension of the real" but that his "great fecundity is gross and importunate."

Trollope is a mixture of several kinds of writer, sometimes realistic in the sociological way of Honoré de Balzac, analyzing class and caste, sometimes a comedian of manners and mores like Henry Fielding, at times a sentimental melodramatist like Charles Dickens, fairly often an ironist deliberately breaking fictional illusions like Thackeray, often introspective if not as equally learned as George Eliot, and periodically a brilliant chronicler of dementia like Joseph Conrad. This mixture is what creates havoc with critical response. Trollope is a master of convincing and accurate dialogue, good at retrospective interior analysis, and gifted with varieties of ironic voices. The building of his reputation, aided by Michael Sadleir's biography in the 1920's, was materially assisted by *The Trollopian* (now *Nineteenth Century Studies*), a journal devoted to studies of his novels, further work by scholars, such as Ruth apRoberts, Robert M. Polhemus and James R. Kincaid, and new critical techniques, which have given Trollope his present reputation as a leading English novelist.

BIOGRAPHY

Anthony Trollope, born on April 24, 1815, in London, seems to have owed his boisterous energy, booming voice, quarrelsome touchiness, and reticent sensitivity to a childhood of off-handed upbringing. C. P. Snow refers to him as "weighed down by 20 years of neglect and humiliation." His father was a

tactless and impractical barrister who had pretensions about being a landowner in Harrow. There, he established his family in an elegant though quickly declining farm, Julians, later the model for the experimental Orley Farm in the novel of that name. Trollope's mother, Frances, was the driving force of the family; she was closer to Trollope's oldest brother, Tom, than to Anthony: Anthony received neither much encouragement nor much regular affection from her. After starting his education at Sunbury School, with a brief stint at Harrow, Anthony was sent to Winchester, his father's old school, for three years. In 1827, the family was forced to move into a smaller house in Harrow for financial reasons.

Meanwhile, his mother made the acquaintance of a zealous utopian reformer, Fanny Wright, and went with her and three of her children—Henry, Cecilia, and Emily—to America. Their experiences there border on black comedy. Among other misfortunes, Frances, without past experience or common sense, started a fancy emporium or bazaar in Cincinnati; the building evolved into a grand structure modeled upon an Egyptian temple. The enterprise only succeeded in making the family penniless. Through the efforts of a painter friend, her husband, and son Tom, they managed to piecemeal their way home to England.

Anthony was removed from Winchester in 1830, which deprived him of the chance to enter Oxford University from which he might have entered into the clergy, the usual course at that time. He returned as a day student to Harrow School where the intense and entrenched snobbery made the shabby boy the butt of ridicule and persecution, and perhaps began his lifelong pattern of irritability. Also at that time, Trollope's father sank into petty miserliness and self-pitying moroseness, becoming more obsessively preoccupied with his scholarly work, an ecclesiastical encyclopedia.

The success of Frances's *The Domestic Manners of the Americans* (1832), a book adversely critical of American society, temporarily kept the family from bankruptcy, but her husband's financial mismanagement created more debts. To prevent his arrest for bankruptcy in 1834, the family, without Anthony, went to Bruges, Belgium. Any possible happiness they might have found was destroyed by tuberculosis, which killed Anthony's father, brother Henry, and sister Emily between 1834 and 1836. Frances Trollope was obviously too occupied with nursing to pay much attention to Anthony, but she did get him a tutoring position in Belgium for a short time. He returned to England where he survived in squalid lodgings in Marylebone, London, at a clerk's job in the main post office for seven years. At age twenty-six, he got the chance which changed his life, obtaining the post of deputy surveyor, the overseer of mail service, in western Ireland.

At Banaghar, he found a comfortable social milieu for the first time, though his manner with carriers and postmasters was brusque and his temper was at times violent. Trollope became a man jovial with companions, truculent with superiors, bullying with inferiors, and tender with close friends and family. In 1842, he married Rose Heseltine, an Anglo-Irish woman. Her bank-manager father, like one of Trollope's own shady characters, was an embezzler. A trusted partner, Rose handled Trollope's financial affairs, edited his manuscripts, and accompanied him on his journeys around the world. The portraits of solid, sensible, and compassionate wives and mothers found throughout his work, such as Lady Staveley in *Orley Farm*, suggest the type of woman Trollope had found in Rose.

Irish scenery and politics, and the models of his mother and his brother, Tom, led Trollope to his own fiction writing. Thus, not coincidentally, his first two novels have an Irish theme. In these years, Trollope also began rearing a family, two sons. Henceforth, Trollope's career ran on a dual path, pursuing his duties for the postal service and his writing.

Posted to southwest England in 1851 to correct faults in rural delivery, Trollope and his family led a roving existence for three years until he became his own boss as full surveyor in Belfast, at age thirty-nine. The experience of sleepy country towns and a current topic—the Anglican Church's misuse of endowed charity funds to create sizable incomes for administrators—resulted in the writing of *The Warden*, finished in Belfast and published in 1855; it was his first major success. When Trollope moved his family

to Dublin, he established a daily routine of writing. The successor to *The Warden, Barchester Towers*, his best-known novel, is a social comedy in the eighteenth century mock-heroic vein of Henry Fielding or Oliver Goldsmith.

During a visit to see his mother and brother in Italy, Trollope met a young American woman, Kate Field, and began a long and close friendship, mostly carried out by correspondence. C. P. Snow thinks that Trollope was impressed by the independent and self-assertive woman, who was rather unlike English women. Intrigued by Kate's advocacy of feminine freedom, in *Orley Farm* Trollope presents a woman who affronts social and moral conventions by an act of forgery to save the inheritance of her infant son. The motivation is a bit slick, but the fact that the resolute heroine succeeds against a determined male antagonist suggests that Kate's independence was sympathetically perceived.

Trollope went to North America during the early Civil War (1861-1862); a trip which resulted in a travel book. Like his mother's work, the book took a negative stance toward American institutions. He then published, among others, *Rachel Ray, The Last Chronicle of Barset*, and *The Claverings*, which gained Trollope his biggest sales price ever. His works were also being serialized in various periodicals, such as *The Fortnightly Review*. It became obvious, however, that Trollope's continued output led him to repeat themes and recycle characters.

Immersed as he was in writing and somewhat resentful of his position at the post office, Trollope resigned in October, 1867, after the offer of the editorship of a new journal, *St. Paul's Magazine*. He continued to do some work on behalf of the post office, however, since he went to Washington to negotiate a postal treaty in 1868. Trollope ran *St. Paul's Magazine* for three years before it went under financially. He was not temperamentally suited to deal with authors.

In his own writing, Trollope tended, as Walter Kendrick sees it, to turn toward more sensational materials, which other authors had discarded, but he was also experimenting in the psychological novel. In *He Knew He Was Right*, Trollope treats the subject of insanity and he presents a fascinating study of psychosis. Ruth apRoberts praises the novel for its economy and the supporting relationships of closely knit characters. Yet, Trollope's work began to command less popular attention, and he increasingly turned to the political world. He created Phineas Finn, an Anglo-Irish politician, who appears in the novel of that name in 1869 and reappears in *Phineas Redux*, part of the loose series sometimes referred to as the Palliser novels. Trollope, however, did not give up what is really his chief subject: conflict between the sexes.

In 1871, having sold Waltham House and given up his editorship, Trollope and his wife embarked on an eighteen-month visit to New Zealand and a stay with their son, Fred, a relatively unprosperous sheep-farmer in Australia. Trollope continued to write during their stay in the primitive sheep-station. A travel commentary and materials for *John Caldigate* were the result of the voyage, as well as further work on the novel *The Eustace Diamonds*. The Trollopes then settled in London where he wrote on the current topic of "the condition of England" in *The Way We Live Now* and *The Prime Minister*. Trollope presented his skeptical views about the ability of a democratic society to govern itself effectively.

The final stage of Trollope's life was a restless one in his sixties. He took another trip to Australia for eight months in 1875, returning through the United States and meeting with Kate Field. Then, he immediately went to South Africa to inspect the Boer territory with the encroaching British settlement based on gold and diamond exploitation. The Trollopes again returned to the land by moving into a refined farmhouse at Hartung, near Hastings, where Trollope worked on his autobiography. Along with other fiction, he wrote a mystery novel, *Mr. Scarborough's Family*, which was serialized before his death but published posthumously in 1883. Farm living aggravated Trollope's asthma which drained his energy, thus causing him to return to London. He was enjoying club life, dinners, and letters to his son, Henry, who was also a writer, when Trollope suffered a sudden stroke in the fall of 1882 that left him paralyzed, and a month later, on December 6, 1882, he died, at the age of sixty-seven.

ANALYSIS

Twentieth century criticism of Anthony Trollope acknowledged his affinity with comic satirists of the eighteenth century, and this affinity is reflected in his best-known work, *Barchester Towers*. There are two distinct worlds in the novel: that of London vanity, represented by Mr. Slope, the London preacher who comes to Barchester as the protégé of Mrs. Proudie; and that of the smaller, conservative rural world, represented by Archdeacon Grantly of Barchester Cathedral who opposes Mr. Slope with "high and dry" Anglicanism. At the end, Slope is rejected but so is the siren of the comic interlude, Signora Madeleine Vesey Neroni, daughter of the gentlemanly but parasitic, self-indulgent Dr. Vesey Stanhope, canon of the Cathedral.

BARCHESTER TOWERS

The novel is concerned with the pursuit of Eleanor Bold, a young prosperous widow and daughter of Mr. Harding, by Obadiah Slope, a brash and unctuous social climber. The newly vacant position of warden provokes a struggle between the Grantly forces and the Proudie forces (including Mr. Slope), with Mrs. Proudie at the head. In this strand of the plot, the mockheroic or mock-epic combat parodies the Miltonic epic tradition, with Grantly and his supporters as the rebel angels struggling against the tyrant Mrs. Proudie, with Slope as a kind of fallen angel. Slope is first supported by Mrs. Proudie in his efforts to prevent the return of the vacant post to Harding, but Slope, in his effort to attain favor with Eleanor Bold, eventually gets the position for Harding.

Slope is emasculated by Signora Neroni, who transfixes him with her bright eyes and silvery laughter during rural games and festivities at Ullathorne, the ancient seat of the Thornes and center of a static pastoral world. Seduced by her witchery, he is humiliated by this demoniac Eve and defeated by the godlike rebuff of Eleanor, who slaps his face as he presses his suit upon her. Further, he incurs the wrath of his patroness, Mrs. Proudie, with his attentiveness to Signora Neroni, who, although crippled, rules from a couch where she resides in state like Cleopatra. In this world of sham battles, Grantly celebrates his triumph, including a dean's position for Mr. Harding in a solemn conclave of the clergy.

The disputants in these mock-exercises practice their feints around innocent third parties: Bishop Proudie between Slope and Mrs. Proudie; Quiverful, the other candidate for the wardenship, a pathetically comic father of numerous children, between his determined wife and Slope; and Harding between Slope and Grantly. In this formally ordered structure, it is appropriate that Eleanor and Frances Arabin, the naïve Oxford academician, be matched by Miss Thorne, reaffirming the power of the old order, yet still contending with Proudies. The marriage of Eleanor and Arabin asserts the two worlds, old and new, country and city, innocent and corrupt.

The novel has a rich galaxy of minor characters. For example, there is Bertie Stanhope, the dilettante sculptor, who is pressed into proposing to Eleanor, but he undermines his own courtship by the candid admission of his motives; Mr. Harding, the unwilling tool of both Slope and Grantly, who takes such delight in the cathedral music that he mechanically saws an imaginary cello during moments of partisan plots and counterplots; and Mrs. Quiverful, who functions like a wailing chorus in a Greek tragedy, piteously reminding the world and Mrs. Proudie of the cruel difficulties of pinched means and a large family. Although Trollope did write important novels on more serious themes, *Barchester Towers* remains his best known, with its effective comic scenes, the balletlike entrances and exits, the lively irony, and the mock-heroic bathos. The orchestration of speaking styles ranging from the pomposity of the Archdeacon to the vacuity of Bertie Stanhope is another example of the buoyancy and playful wit that Trollope achieved only intermittently thereafter.

ORLEY FARM

Orley Farm was written during Trollope's middle period. Its central situation revolves around the plight of Lady Mason, the second wife of a rich man, who, twenty years earlier, forged a codicil to her dying husband's will so that it leaves Orley Farm, her sole economic support, to her and her young child, Lucius. The possession of the farm has become a matter of regret, as the suspicions of the legitimate heir, Joseph Mason, otherwise the inheritor of considerable wealth, eventuate in a trial to break the will.

The effort fails only because Lady Mason commits perjury. Using the omniscient viewpoint, Trollope shows both her guilt and her anguish in trying to provide security for her infant son. Lucius, as the novel opens, is a proud, priggish young man given to notions of scientifically reforming agricultural practice; he is well educated, theoretical, and self-righteous.

The novel's unusual perspective poses two main themes: first, how justice can be accomplished, and second, whether justice can actually be achieved. In setting human rights against legal rights, Trollope portrays Lady Mason's crime in the light of vested interests and the selfish motives of various people. Like C. P. Snow in a novel such as *The Masters* (1951), Trollope displays in *Orley Farm* an abstract ideal distorted and transformed by human emotions, calculations, and egotism. Joseph Mason is more concerned with defeating Lady Mason than enjoying the actual property; Sir Peregrine Orme, a highly respected landowner, proposes marriage to Lady Mason in order to extend the protection of his name, but even he is forced to realize the stain upon his honor if the truth should come out, and after Lady Mason refuses his offer, he, having been told the damning truth, keeps his promise to support her in her new trial. Another perspective is provided through Mr. Dockwrath, the country lawyer who discovers the evidence which necessitates the new trial, and hopes it will prove lucrative and will enhance his legal reputation. Lady Mason's solicitor, Mr. Furnival, carefully avoids definite knowledge of her guilt, though he suspects it, while also wishing she were proven guilty so that he might forgive her with pleasure. A less selfish attitude is seen in Edith Orme, Sir Peregrine's widowed daughter-in-law, who recognizes with compassion the necessity for Lady Mason's crime and the suffering it has entailed for her.

Trollope reveals some of his other typical thematic concerns in the subplots of *Orley Farm*. He explores various attitudes toward marriage and money in the romances of Peregrine, Jr., Lucius Mason, and Felix Graham, a poor barrister, with a variety of modern young women. The women's responses to the gentlemen's advances run from prudent calculation of worldly advantages to prudent reticence in acknowledging love until family wisdom approves it. Also, Trollope's impulses toward indulgence of children are exemplified in Lord and Lady Staveley, who, having made their way without worldly advantages, are willing to offer the same chance to their children by permitting the engagement of a daughter to Felix Graham, whose success has been impeded by his honesty. Trollope's conservatism is revealed through the reluctance of these young people to avow their love until they have consent from the Staveleys.

With regard to the central theme of moral and legal justice, purely through the oratorical skills of the trial lawyer, Lady Mason is found innocent of perjury, a finding wholly incorrect. The trial frees the guilty, turns the truthful into villains, makes the innocent bear the burden of deceit, challenges the loyalty of lawyers, and implicates the idealists posturings. The system has turned Lady Mason's desperate chicanery into heroism. It is somewhat anticlimactic that Trollope has the pure Edith Orme take Lady Mason to her heart and, from a sense of Christian charity, refuse to render judgment against her.

Meanwhile, Lady Mason's greatest trial has been alienation from Lucius who, unaware of her guilt, has attempted vigorous countermeasures to defend her honor rather than respecting her dignified silence. His discovery of the truth cuts deeply into his priggish pride, destroys his dreams of becoming a gentleman-farmer, and makes him restore the farm to Joseph Mason before departing abroad with his mother. Again, Trollope makes an ambivalent statement through this conclusion. Although forgiveness implies repentance and restitution, Lady Mason has not been, at least in public, repentant, and the restitution is as much a matter of pride as of justice. The effect is a tacit denial of Lady Mason's innocence and thus the aborting of the whole effort to save her reputation.

If the power of money, or the distortions of human choice and desire which money brings, is Trollope's major concern, the warfare of the sexes and the frustrations which that warfare brings are secondary themes in his novels. *Can You Forgive Her?*, the first of the Palliser series—which includes *Phineas Finn, Phineas Redux,* and *The Prime Minister,* each

grounded in politics—raises the issue of what sort of love a woman wishes in marriage or indeed whether marriage is a suitable institution. The novel presents the case of Alice Vavasour, a "new woman" who does not know what she wants in life but resents the demands of social propriety. She especially resents the expectation that she accept the marriage proposal of John Grey, whom she really does love, merely because everyone knows him to be a suitable partner. Her cousin, the heiress Lady Glencora McCluskie, has married Plantagenet Palliser, the dull younger son of a ducal family, to support his Liberal political career with her money; but she has fallen in love with the handsome Burgo Fitzgerald, an unconventional, ruinous, yet passionate charmer. Alice reinstitutes her former affection for her cousin George Vavasour, another charmingly irresponsible man who needs her money to campaign to keep his seat in Parliament. For Alice, the masculine excitement of politics makes George attractive, although she honestly admits his desire for her money.

The novel has low-comedy relief in Alice's aunt, Arabella Greenow, and her two suitors, a grocer with money and a retired military officer without it. Arabella means to have her own way, giving her lovers only as much liberty as she desires, choosing the officer because of "a sniff of the rocks and the valleys" about him. The comedy underscores the desire of Alice and Glencora, who, if they had a choice, would put themselves at the mercy of weak men.

In a melodramatic turn of the main plot, George knocks down his sister, Kate, for refusing to assist him in overturning their grandfather's will, which had left all the family property to her. This turn of the plot demonstrates, through George's furious masculine rage, the falsity of the normal economic subjugation of women, which has been reversed in Kate's case. Arabella Greenow, for her part, is also financially independent and can bargain her way into a satisfactorily romantic liaison balancing "rocks and valleys" against "bread and cheese."

Glencora, aware of being sold into matrimony, almost runs off with Burgo but is dissuaded at the last minute by the vigilance of Alice, who makes clear to Plantagenet the temptation he has given to his wife by his conduct. In an improbable reversal that displays Trollope's own romanticism, Plantagenet sacrifices his political hopes for a cabinet appointment in order to take her away from the scenes of her misery after she has confessed her infatuation. Indeed, he is even willing to provide Burgo, who becomes a frequenter of gambling tables, with an allowance at her behest when they encounter him abroad.

Plantagenet can make a sacrifice for Glencora because he has money and social position; George Vavasour, by contrast, is defeated in politics and exiled for lack of money. John Grey, meanwhile, has interposed himself in Alice's arrangement with George so that her fortune is not at stake. This conduct, chivalrous in one sense, paternalistic in another, results in George's challenging him to a duel. The Victorian world is not that of Regency rakes, however, and George's blustering challenge is physically rebuffed, and he is sent away degraded. Alice finally accepts John Grey in a contrite mood. Although Grey has kindly intentions, Alice's undefined longings for autonomy anticipate those Henrik Ibsen made memorable through Nora Helmer in *A Doll's House* (1879), where Nora sacrifices love in the effort to mould her own destiny.

If the future of his heroines seems to lie within conventional marital arrangements or respectable spinsterhood secured by inherited money, Trollope's questioning title for the novel seems to turn the issue of feminine aspiration somewhat ambivalently to the reader. He has shown women challenging the decorum of prudent emotions and affections based on money, but only the ungenteel Mrs. Greenow succeeds in mastering her destiny through financial manipulation.

THE EUSTACE DIAMONDS

In *The Eustace Diamonds*, Trollope shows the psychologically damaging effects of survival in an upper-class and aristocratic hierarchy, a society that channels affections and loyalties in terms of property and money, where people struggle for ascendancy, domination, and power, while subscribing to Romantic illusions of unfettered expression and creative self-development. The narrator ironically undercuts the Romantic pretensions as the novel delineates the un-

realistic strategies of men and women coping with the moral corruption of social ambition. They seek security, status, prestige, and elegance while evincing pretentiousness, snobbery, envy, and parasitism. Trollope takes an anarchic pleasure in those egotistical characters who subvert institutions by undermining the rules of conduct, stretching them to the point of fatuity.

In the novel, Lizzie Eustace appropriates the diamonds without specific authority from her late husband, Sir Florian, and uses them as weapons against the respectable family lawyer, Mr. Camperdown, and the man she intends as her second husband, the morally honorable Lord Fawn. The diamonds become a symbol of Lizzie's inner rage against the world, a rage arising from self-doubt prompted by the excessive demands of her own idealized views of herself. While denying that ownership of the necklace gives her any pleasure, Lizzie simultaneously insists that she will throw the diamonds away while guarding them zealously. When the box in which she ostentatiously houses them is stolen, Lizzie claims that the necklace has been stolen as well. The lie is psychologically predictable. The diamonds exemplify her attitudes toward herself, toward Lord Fawn whom she despises for his complete disdain of the diamonds, and toward Frank Greystock, her champion before the world, whom she has lured away from his serious attentions to Lucy Morris. The supposed theft is Lizzie's symbolic punishment for a guilt which will be lessened if the diamonds are believed stolen, but it is also an aggrandisement of her own self-esteem since secretly she knows they are still in her possession. The diamonds, however, are stolen in a second robbery, which ends Lizzie's control of the situation.

Lizzie's desire for social domination gains dimension through the narrator's ironic moral judgment and through the close-ups of the omniscient viewpoint that reveal her own rationalizations and fears. Seeking support, Lizzie confesses to Lord George, hoping that he will be cynically brutal, but instead she receives his weak acknowledgment of her supposed cunning. When the police discover the truth, Lizzie prefers the illusion of submitting to the police administrator to the reality of confronting her own self-destructive behavior. Lizzie then tries desperately to reestablish control by triumphing over someone: She reproaches Mrs. Carbuncle, her friend; breaks her engagement with Lord Fawn, ignoring his earlier efforts to end the relationship and pretending to be heartlessly jilted; offers herself to Lord George, who also refuses her; and finally bids for the attentions of Frank Greystock through his need for money, yet Frank is simply provoked into promising he will abandon her utterly if she persists.

Yielding to a fantasy logic, Lizzie entertains a marriage proposal from Mr. Emilius, an impudent and sanctimonious popular preacher whom she had once refused. She deliberately accepts him knowing that he is a fraud and admitting that his bogus qualities attract her. Lizzie's limited knowledge of how the world operates is supported by Emilius's brazen effrontery, which will offer her a new chance for social domination.

The secondary characters are drawn with an equal sense of psychological aberration. For example, there is the cynical honesty of Lord George, which conceals a fearful vacillation that abhors responsibility yet is resolute in pushing his companion, Sir Griffin Tewett, into marriage with Lucinda Roanoke. Alternately submissive and aggressive, he turns vindictive in denouncing Lizzie for the damage she has caused his reputation by creating suspicions of his complicity in her concealment of the necklace. He is also forgiving, on the other hand, of Mrs. Barnacle, his former mistress, for her good intentions in encouraging her niece, Lucinda, to marry for money. Lord George appears cognizant of obligations assumed by others though irresolute in taking them upon himself. Further, he shows the unreality of Lizzie's dreams; but his own conduct is the model of a romantic neurosis. Other examples of psychologically crippled characters are Lucinda, who suffers from strong sexual repression and emotional sterility, and Sir Griffin, cool, vindictive, and arrogant, who is repelled by anyone who would love him.

These characters are set up in contrast to the more conventional ones, such as Mrs. Hittaway, who reflect the pathological tendencies that a materialis-

tic society encourages. The baffled efforts of Lizzie, Lord George, Sir Griffin, and Lucinda to deal with destructive self-deception reflect the results of social forces inhibiting real creative growth in understanding. V. S. Pritchett has criticized Trollope for being "a detailed, rather cynical observor of a satisfied world," and that "we recognize that he [Trollope] has drawn life as people say it is when they are not speaking about themselves." C. P. Snow commented that an exploratory psychological writer such as Trollope "has to live on close terms with the blacker— including the worse—side of his own nature." *The Eustace Diamonds* is the record of Trollope's endurance of a mental nature that was divided. Pritchett has accused Trollope of not capturing or presenting the depth of moral experience. This may reflect a demand for a more complex style, a more intensive depiction of the intricacies of moral struggle, and a more insistent emphasis on values. Snow, however, perceived the simple, direct style as cutting out everything except the truth. Trollope was not temperamental or self-advertising, but as a novelist he covers a wide range of social, institutional, and religious issues and controversies constituting the fabric of Victorian society. He dramatizes the moral and intellectual dilemmas often arising from them and has considerable insight as well as the ability to present the sheer flux of mental life, which anticipates later developments in the work of James Joyce, Virginia Woolf, and Dorothy Richardson.

Roger E. Wiehe

OTHER MAJOR WORKS

SHORT FICTION: *Tales of All Countries*, 1861, 1863; *Lotta Schmidt and Other Stories*, 1867; *An Editor's Tales*, 1870; *Why Frau Frohmann Raised Her Prices and Other Stories*, 1882.

NONFICTION: *The West Indies*, 1859; *North America*, 1862; *Clergymen of the Church of England*, 1865-1866; *Travelling Sketches*, 1865-1866; *The Commentaries of Caesar*, 1870 (translation); *Australia and New Zealand*, 1873; *South Africa*, 1878; *Thackeray*, 1879; *Lord Palmerston*, 1882; *Autobiography*, 1883; *The Letters of Anthony Trollope*, 1951 (Bradford A. Booth, editor).

BIBLIOGRAPHY

Felber, Lynette. *Gender and Genre in Novels Without End: The British Roman-fleuve*. Gainesville: University Press of Florida, 1995. Discusses Trollope's Palliser novels, Dorothy Richardson's *Pilgrimage*, and Anthony Powell's *Dance to the Music of Time*. An excellent study.

Hall, N. John. *Trollope: A Biography*. Oxford, England: Clarendon Press, 1991. One of several biographies of Trollope that have appeared since the mid-1980's, Hall's book draws heavily on the great Victorian's own words—not surprising, as Hall also edited the two-volume edition of Trollope's *Letters* (1983)—and pays particular attention to Trollope's travel writing and his final decade.

_____, ed. *The Trollope Critics*. Basingstoke, England: Macmillan, 1981. Of a number of critical anthologies, this is probably the best for introductory purposes. Includes twenty leading Trollope critics and covers a wide range of topics. An excellent bibliography is provided.

Halperin, John. *Trollope and Politics*. New York: Macmillan, 1977. This study focuses on each of the six Palliser novels and includes several more general chapters. Contains a select bibliography and indexes.

Mullen, Richard, and James Munson. *The Penguin Companion to Trollope*. New York: Penguin, 1996. A thorough guide to Trollope's life and works. With an index and Trollope bibliography.

Pollard, Arthur. *Anthony Trollope*. Boston: Routledge & Kegan Paul, 1978. Pollard seeks to put all of Trollope's novels and a variety of miscellaneous works within the context of his life and time. Stresses Trollope's evocation of his age and his guiding moral purpose. Includes an index.

Terry, R. C., ed. *Trollope: Interviews and Recollections*. New York: St. Martin's Press, 1987. This invaluable collection is a useful adjunct to the numerous biographies of Trollope. Terry collects forty-six memories of Trollope by a host of individuals who knew him at various points in his life. These selections are arranged in roughly chronological order, starting with his granddaughter Muriel's reminiscences about Anthony's mother and ending—again with Muriel—with images of Anthony as an old man. Terry also includes critical evaluations of Trollope's work.

Wright, Andrew. *Anthony Trollope: Dream and Art*. Basingstoke, England: Macmillan, 1983. This brief study of fifteen of Trollope's novels sees them as contemporary fictions, transfiguring life in a certain way. Contains a bibliography and an index.

IVAN TURGENEV

Born: Orel, Russia; November 9, 1818
Died: Bougival, France; September 3, 1883

PRINCIPAL LONG FICTION

Rudin, 1856 (*Dimitri Roudine*, 1873; better known as *Rudin*, 1947)

Asya, 1858 (English translation, 1877)

Dvoryanskoye gnezdo, 1859 (*Liza*, 1869; also as *A Nobleman's Nest*, 1903; better known as *A House of Gentlefolk*, 1894)

Nakanune, 1860 (*On the Eve*, 1871)

Pervaya lyubov, 1860 (*First Love*, 1884)

Ottsy i deti, 1862 (*Fathers and Sons*, 1867)

Dym, 1867 (*Smoke*, 1868)

Veshniye vody, 1872 (*Spring Floods*, 1874; better known as *The Torrents of Spring*, 1897)

Nov, 1877 (*Virgin Soil*, 1877)

The Novels of Ivan Turgenev, 1894-1899 (15 volumes)

OTHER LITERARY FORMS

Ivan Turgenev's fame as a writer rests primarily on his narrative prose works, which, aside from his novels, include novelettes, novellas, and short stories, the latter a genre in which he excelled and became prolific. In 1847, he began putting together a collection of stories, published in 1852 and bearing the title *Zapiski okhotnika* (*Russian Life in the Interior*, 1855; better known as *A Sportsman's Sketches*,

(Library of Congress)

libretti, essays, articles, autobiographical pieces and memoirs, and even a semiscientific study on nightingales.

ACHIEVEMENTS

In the world of letters, Ivan Turgenev stands out as a naturalist, although not in the hammering manner of Émile Zola, the depressing manner of Thomas Hardy, or the milder, veristic manner of Giovanni Verga. Even if the words "idealization" and "sentimentality" are often used in connection with Turgenev, his "Nature school" tonality has neither the idealizing tendency of Sergey Aksakov nor the sentimental tendency of Dmitri Grigorovich, both of whom were his compatriots and contemporaries. On the surface, these qualities are there; when one digs further, they are not. If, on the one hand, the reader luxuriates in his intensely felt descriptions of nature, he is, on the other hand, struck by Turgenev's devastating irony (especially as applied to the upper classes) and by the uncompromising realism of his portrayals (of all classes, including the peasantry). Turgenev's worldview—more exactly, the view of his Russia, whose social history his novels chronicle for two decades—is not optimistic. His most famous hero, the controversial Bazarov in *Fathers and Sons*, is a nihilist; otherwise, his "heroes" are nonheroes, that is, "superfluous men." His heroines appear affirmative only in the perhaps important but not exhilarating sense of loyalty and self-sacrifice. Turgenev's sentimental hue coats a tragic substance, and his instinctive idealism is pared by a naturalistic objectivity.

One reason for the initial, positive flavor is the constant appearance of the love motif and the delicate treatment of that special aspect of it, its awakening. Another is the luringly sensual way in which nature fits Turgenev's creative scheme, particularly landscapes which may or may not shape a background to events but which reflect, along with his compassion for the serfs, what may well be the author's most genuine inspiration of all. Finally, there is the softening effect produced by a manicured style; a sense of language and its need for immediate communication at the proper level; the use of several ad-

1932), highly admired by Leo Tolstoy, which includes many of Turgenev's well-known pieces. Turgenev's naturalism was well adapted to the portrayal of the life of poor countryfolk—enough to evoke compassion while inciting indignation at their lot.

Turgenev tried his hand at drama, too, achieving reasonable success with *Gde tonko, tam i rvyotsya* (1912; *Where It Is Thin, There It Breaks*, 1924), *Kholostyak* (1849; *The Bachelor*, 1924), *Provintsialka* (1851; *A Provincial Lady*, 1934), and especially *Mesyats v derevne* (1855; *A Month in the Country*, 1924), a play whose innovations in many ways adumbrate those of Anton Chekhov.

Turgenev began writing poetry as a student and had some verses published in 1838. Toward the end of his life, he assembled a collection of his poetic works entitled *Senilia* (1882, 1930; better known as *Stikhotvoreniya v proze; Poems in Prose*, 1883, 1945).

The total profile of Turgenev's literary activities encompasses other forms as well, including opera

jectives to enhance descriptiveness, individualizing it through incorrectness or strange words or French phrases; and the author's care not to allow an idea to become so involved that it mars the basic tenet: clarity (Turgenev liked the short sentence as much as he disliked the metaphor). He was a craftsman.

Turgenev profited from his many and admired Western friends and writers, Alphonse Daudet, George Sand, Gustave Flaubert, Prosper Mérimée, and Henry James among them. Despite his preoccupation with things Russian, he is the most "Western" of Russian authors and among the most tempered, the least given to extremes, even when he presents the peasants as far more human than their masters. To speak of his friends' influence, however, would be to stretch the point, for, in his homeland, there were also Alexander Pushkin, Mikhail Lermontov, Tolstoy, Aleksandr Ivanovich Herzen, and Fyodor Dostoevski (who hated Turgenev, as shown by the character Karmazinof in Dostoevski's *The Possessed*, 1871-1872)—to mention but a few Russian writers. Turgenev unquestionably felt an aesthetic and cultural affinity with the West, and he surely believed in the Europeanization of Russia, but he was his own artist, and he wrote his own way as a creator who could see and say more through his personal optic than through varied imitation.

Turgenev's irony notwithstanding, moderation shaped this optic, a moderation that could come down hard on both sides of an issue (why else were both conservatives and radicals outraged at the portrayal of Bazarov?). Yet it was a moderation that implied that, whatever the desirability of Romantic idealism and the rationality of what is reasonable, there are no answers to life's problems. The important thing is to maintain a balanced, liberal altruism. In his speech entitled "Gamlet i Don Kikhot" (1860; "Hamlet and Don Quixote," 1930), Turgenev showed that Don Quixote's accomplishments are secondary to the way he feels about people, to his sense of ideal and of sacrifice, his ability to act on indignation, although his fantasy makes him appear a madman. Hamlet, on the other hand, is the total egocentric, doubting, hesitating, and calculating, more concerned with his situation than with his duty. Only the Fates "can show us

whether we struggled against visions, or against real enemies." The Knight of the Woeful Countenance made more of an impact on society than did the Prince of Denmark. Turgenev tended to emphasize the social over the human side of things, though one must be cautious in accepting this observation without qualification.

BIOGRAPHY

Ivan Sergeyevich Turgenev was born in Orel and spent his early childhood on his mother's estate in Spasskoye. His father, Sergey Turgenev, a former cavalry officer, belonged to the nobility—the fallen nobility—and had acquired solvency with his marriage to a rich heiress, Varvara Petrovna Lutovinova. Unfortunately, this lady was unhappy, matching energy with despotism, loveless toward her husband and harsh toward her servants and three sons. Ivan's passion for reading sometimes managed to keep him out of the reach of her capricious cruelty. German and French tutors taught him their languages, and he listened eagerly when an old servant read to him from Gavriil Derzhavin, Lermontov, Pushkin, and others.

He began the study of philosophy at the University of Moscow, but after his father's death, when the family moved to Saint Petersburg and he transferred to the university there, his literary inclinations began to take hold. He met P. A. Pletnev, the new editor (after Pushkin's death) of the journal *Sovremennik*, and published some poetry. Even after he made poetry secondary to prose, he never discarded its sense, either in his lyric view of life (not merely in his descriptions of nature) or in his refinement of style.

In 1838, Turgenev headed westward, first to Berlin, where his attendance at the university (in the faculty of philosophy) was incidental to the various friendships he made with "Westernizers" such as Nikolay Stankevich, Herzen, Timofey Granovsky, Mikhail Bakunin, and other "progressives," who believed, as opposed to the more orthodox "Slavophiles," that Russia's cultural future lay in emulating the best of Western civilization. Turgenev became one of them ideologically, especially after wider travels in Europe that took him as far south as Rome and

Naples. Indeed, after returning to his homeland in 1841, trying his hand at civil service and deciding on a career in writing, he returned to the West in 1847. Despite the encouragement of Vissarion Belinsky, he had known more failures than successes in composing verse (much in the Romantic tradition) and came to see realistic narrative prose as his likely avenue as a creative writer. His mother expressed her dissatisfaction with his expressed vocation, as she did in response to his infatuation with the widowed French singer Pauline Viardot (with whom, and with whose family, he formed a strange but close lifetime relationship), by withdrawing financial support, but in 1847 Turgenev proved his point with his first literary success, the short story "Khor and Kalinych." As his short stories continued to appear, with consistent success, he became confirmed in his decision and in his Western thrust. In 1850, he inherited a large fortune. By his mother's seamstress, he had an illegitimate daughter, who was reared by Pauline and named Paulinette and about whom he was very sensitive (he challenged Tolstoy to a duel—unfought—over an uncomplimentary remark about her). With Pauline providing the music, he also wrote some libretti for light opera. He never married the French diva, but clearly she meant much to him: "Oh, thou, my only friend, oh thou whom I love so deeply and so tenderly," he wrote of her in a poem.

A Sportsman's Sketches was published in 1852. Turgenev, while following in the footsteps of Nikolai Gogol, Lermontov, and the early Dostoevski, aimed at accurate portrayal of the serfs, without idealizing them and without highlighting the negative side; this was well in the tradition of Honoré de Balzac, Sand, and especially Berthold Auerbach, whose *Schwarzwälder Dorfgeschichten* (1843-1860; *Black Forest Village Stories*, 1869), complete with local language, explored the lives and traditions of the German peasants. It is believed that Czar Alexander II was influenced by Turgenev's stories on the occasion of the Emancipation of the Serfs in 1861. The stories, however, had also displeased the censors under Alexander II's predecessor, Nicholas I, and as a result of an article on Gogol's death, Turgenev was arrested, detained in Saint Petersburg, and then forced to reside

for eighteen months on his Spasskoye property. He left it in 1853, and a few years later also left Russia—almost for good.

It was then that Turgenev the novelist emerged; his first novel, *Rudin*, appeared in 1856. He was already well known in Russia, France, and Germany, as well as England and Italy. The novels that followed, like the first, all written abroad but all concerned with the social and political problems of Russia, were awaited and discussed—and polemically debated, because, rather than engage in philosophical flights and metaphysical views of the human condition, Turgenev engaged immediate, recognizable issues realistically. In addition, the usual controversy between Westernizers (including Nikolay Dobrolyubov and N. G. Chernyshevsky) and Slavophiles (including Aleksey Khomyakov, Ivan Kireyevsky, Yury Samarin, the Aksakovs, and even, though with greater circumspection, Dostoevski) continued to rage, to the point that *Fathers and Sons* was deemed by some a criticism of the new generation. The fact was that at that time, because of the rapid interactions of shifting events and cultural conditions, opinions could change monthly. Hence, the intellectual points of reference in Turgenev's earlier novels are different from those in later novels.

When critics, as some have tended to do, overstress the social importance of Turgenev's novels, they siphon off a good part of his vitality as an artist, for it is not only the social commentary that makes Balzac, Alessandro Manzoni, or Jane Austen great writers. Turgenev's handling of nature and character development alone—without elevating his works' psychological attributes to the level of Dostoevski or James—together with his sense of style and structure, are enough to welcome him to the writers' pantheon. His ability in character portrayal is evident in his comedies, so well interpreted by the young actress Maria G. Savina, with whom he fell madly in love in his twilight years. In his novels, short stories, and plays, however, he remained ultimately the poet rather than the social critic, as his deep and private interest in collecting his prose poems near the end of his life, with no intention of publishing them, suggests—indeed, symbolizes. It is fitting that he returned briefly to Russia in 1880 to deliver a telling lecture in honor of the poet Pushkin, whose monument was being unveiled. Turgenev died of cancer at the home of Pauline Viardot, to whom he had dictated his last story, "An End," in 1883.

ANALYSIS

The idealistic generation of the 1830's and 1840's, the so-called superfluous men and victims of the Russia of Nicholas I, comes to the fore in Ivan Turgenev's first novel, *Rudin*.

RUDIN

It is a philosophically articulate generation, little given to action. Dmitri Rudin fascinates and charms the household of Daria Mikhailovna Lasunskaia with his poetic linguistic abilities and his brilliant capacity for discussion drawing on keen aphorisms and on German Transcendentalists (including Georg Wilhelm Friedrich Hegel), so that instead of staying overnight, he remains for several months. In time, he declares his love for the young Natasha, yet, as the vainglorious human figure he is (something her "lioness" mother and patroness of the arts comes to discern), he withdraws spinelessly, though aware that his love is returned, when he learns of Lasunskaia's opposition. He departs, leaving Natasha hurt.

The story is told by his friend Leznev, not always sympathetically, and it is probable that Turgenev originally wanted to satirize the budding anarchist Bakunin (the novel's original, satiric title was "The Genius"). As such, Rudin would have emerged not as a superfluous man but simply as an unsavory boaster. Events in Russia changed quickly, however: Bakunin's arrest, the death of the admired historian Granovsky, who liked the rebel, and other circumstances invited an "Epilogue" (1855-1856) and finally a last paragraph (1860). Here Rudin dies in the Paris barricades of 1848 in a kind of hero's apologia, in which, from a vain failure, he becomes a tragic failure, a true superfluous man, full of remorse over his treatment of Natasha and conscious that he is "sacrificing [himself] for some nonsense in which [he does not] believe." Now the Russian radicals protested (again the events were changing) against what they believed was an ideological acquiescence to older values. This was a typical Turgenevian situation: the incarnation of a problem in a hero by the writer and the argumentative reaction to it by society.

One answer to the plight of the superfluous man is the return to the soil, to the Russian homeland, "tilling it the best way one can," a task which can be accomplished with a deep sense of religion. *A House of Gentlefolk*, published in 1859—a Slavophile novel which was enormously well received and stirred no polemics—provides this answer. The European-educated nobleman Fedor Ivanovich Lavretsky has remained spiritually Russian and returns to his homeland from Paris when his frivolous wife, Varvara Pavlovna Korobine, beguiled by the delights of the French capital, is unfaithful to him. His goal is to organize his lands with humility, seeing to the well-being of the serfs. He comes across a distant cousin, the serious, religious, and dutiful Liza Kalitina, one of Turgenev's most idealized portrayals—recalling Pushkin's Tatyana in *Eugene Onegin* (1825-1832, 1833)—of Russian womanhood. Although the shadow of Varvara cannot be dispelled, they fall in love. The impossible union appears briefly possible when a newspaper account reports Lavretsky's wife's death; the story is incorrect, however, and Varvara appears at his home in Russia, only to leave the country estate and move on to the social pleasures of Saint Petersburg, where she acquires a new lover. Lavretsky becomes a model landlord, and Liza retires to a convent.

While the plot is typically sparse, the characterization is typically rich: Vladimir Nikolaevich Panshin, the deceptively charming and egotistical young careerist (a pro-Western foil to Lavretsky), who courts Liza before Lavretsky's appearance; her wealthy and widowed provincial mother, Maria Dmitrievna Kalitina; her old German music teacher, Christopher Lemm, a man of unrecognized talent reluctantly living in Russia; Lavretsky's despotic and narrow-minded father; his harsh and fierce Aunt Glafira; his idealistic and poor university friend, Mikhyalevich, who speaks nobly about the duties of landed gentry toward the country and the peasants—these figures and others are to be added to the characters of Lavretsky, Varvara, and above all Liza herself, an array of portraits that pleased the artistic reader and an espousing of ideas that pleased the social forces of the time (the model landlord for the radicals, the Russian consciousness for the Slavophiles, the profound faith and devotion, rectitude, and determination of Liza for those seeking a sociomoral message, like Turgenev's good, religious friend Countess Elizabeth Lambert).

On the Eve

On the Eve is also relatively plotless yet sensitive in its character-drawing; it turns one's eyes back to the West, though the heart of the story throbs in Bulgaria through the most ideal pair of lovers Turgenev ever conceived. There is a contrast between the trifling pedantry of young Russians and the vital commitment of youth elsewhere: The elegant and superficial Pavel Yakovlich Schubin, a fine-arts student, represents the French leaning, while the awkward but good and learned Andrei Petrovich Bersenyev represents the German. Both pursue the superior and beautiful Elena Nikolaevna Strahof, an ardent and noble-minded daughter of a dissipated aristocrat and a faded society belle. Her willpower is no match for her wooers, and it is not surprising that when the Bulgarian patriot Dmitri Insarov passes through (his cause is the liberation of Bulgaria from the Turks), she falls in love with him. Both of his parents having been victims of the Turks, Insarov, though not of sound health, is regarded as the leader of the coming revolt. (The "eve" of the revolt could be the approaching Crimean War and the forthcoming reforms of Alexander II which followed that war.)

Because he returns her love, Insarov fears on the eve of the conflict that Elena is distracting him from his mission and leaves her, but she seeks him out and tells her that her idealism will make her forsake everything for him and his cause. They marry and leave for Bulgaria but get only as far as Venice before he dies. Elena follows the coffin to Bulgaria, where, having no country now, she joins the Sisters of Mercy, who act as army nurses. Turgenev said that he derived the plot outline from a manuscript handed to him by one V. V. Karataev, who left for Crimea at the outbreak of the war in 1853. It would be reading something into the novel that is not there to see in the Bulgarian Insarov a forerunner of the Russian revolutionary hero, as it would be incorrect to see in the

self-sacrificing and idealistic Elena, who is reminiscent of Anita, the wife of the famous Italian patriot Giuseppe Garibaldi, whom Turgenev much admired, a prototype of the revolutionary heroine. In their own way, one religious and one secular, Liza and Elena are the same. At first, the novel disappointed the public, which expected to see the willful Russian man dedicated to a noble cause; the protagonists pointed westward, as it were, the way Ivan Goncharov's active Stolz, a German, pointed away from the dreamy Russian Oblomov. Yet here again, the value of the work is better sought less in the ideological orientation than in the series of types it presented—in other words, in the characterization (see, for example, Uvar Ivanovich).

Fathers and Sons

Time and again, discussion of Turgenev's novels focused on his social concerns, relegating the artistic side of his endeavors, characterization (which, to be sure, is central to the communication of these concerns), to a secondary plane. Hence, his most famous novel, *Fathers and Sons*, completed in 1861, around the time of the Emancipation of the Serfs, and published with some modifications supposedly prompted by publisher M. N. Katkov in 1862, aroused widespread polemics about the ideological facets of the characters, particularly Bazarov, rather than about the balanced objectivity of the characterizations themselves. There is no doubt that Turgenev liked what his "nihilist" (a term which, while not coined by the author, gained currency through this novel) protagonist stood for, but there is equally no doubt that he did not like the way that he stood for it.

Evgeni Bazarov, a medical student, and his friend, Arkadi Kirsanov, stop at the latter's provincial home after a three-year absence. The widowed father, who has taken up with a peasant girl and is a mismanaging member of the landed gentry, especially after the Emancipation, lives with Arkadi's uncle, a frustrated and intolerant ex-officer of the guard. In this sedentary, conservative atmosphere, whose ineffectualness represented everything that the younger generation—the materialistic and utilitarian "new men and women" that Chernyshevsky (in his novel *Chto delat'?*, 1863; *What Is to Be Done?*, 1866) and Dobrolyubov (in his essay "Chto takoye Oblomovshchine," 1859-1860; "What Is Oblomovism?," 1903) praised with such ingenuous dullness—could not stand, the insolently cynical and aggressive libertarian views of Bazarov, let alone his uninhibited manner, are hardly received with smiles. In the words of his less militant friend Arkadi, Bazarov "bows before no authority and accepts no principle without examination." His intellectually cold and antiromantic attitude toward women shocks the old Kirsanov brothers. Yet, when the students leave the estate, Bazarov meets a widow at a ball, Ana Odintsova, and falls in love with her, despite much self-struggle, in the sentimental, unmaterialistic way he most despised. She eludes him; Arkadi's admiration for his friend cools as he, too, leaves him, preferring to shape his life according to more traditional values. Now Bazarov goes to his own provincial parents (an ex-army doctor and an uneducated daughter of the lower nobility), lovable if rather naïve, who both love him and fear him. Through an infection sustained in a finger while performing an autopsy on a tubercular body, left unattended because of a lack of cauterizing medication as well as his own apathy, young Bazarov dies.

In the contrast between two generations, the novel divided Russia between "fathers" and "sons." Neither group liked what it read, and both forgot about the fine lines of character, the accurate descriptions of milieus, and the impressive landscapes. The two generations looked at rebellion or not, authority or not, tradition or not, the need to live (to Live) or not, the necessity for change (progress) or not, and in so doing betrayed their desire to have things stated black and white terms: The revolutionaries were scum or could do no wrong; the conservatives were dangerous regressives or the sole pillars of moral strength. Turgenev made Bazarov not sufficiently satanic for the "sons" and not sufficiently godly for the "fathers." His liberalism appreciated the social-minded impetus of Bazarov's ideas, and at times he gave his protagonist moving, human touches, but Turgenev also gave him offensive, elitist attitudes toward the "oafs" he would use to do the dirty work. Bazarov's quixotic integrity and relentless single-mindedness under the banner of a social cause are not enough to offset his brash intemperance and lack of rational circumspection. Turgenev, like all true creators of types, drew from life synthetically, making his characters composites of what they represented. Bazarov's brutal cynicism and his anticlimactic end, almost making him a pointless victim of his "new realism" founded on science, encouraged the interpretation that Turgenev had parodied Chernyshevsky and Dobrolyubov by caricaturing the revolutionary—an act of faithlessness in the "new men and women." Yet such had not been his intent. Rather, his purpose had been to demonstrate the gap between generations, but more than that, on a more universal level that his immediate reading public by and large missed, to suggest the transience of all ideology—social, political, economic, even moral—in the light of the eternal and fundamental realities of love and death.

SMOKE

This same stress on milieu and characterization examined at arm's length (except for the author's mouthpiece Potúgin), but now with an even more intensified appreciation of the natural setting, obtains in *Smoke*, and the same displeasure on the parts of both radicals and conservatives ensued. Turgenev's idea of putting together a simple love story outside the homeland, in Baden-Baden, the meeting spot of the European international set, merged with a desire to follow up his observations on postreform Russia, on the biases interfering with the reform itself, the lack of depth of both revolutionaries and aristocracy, and the continuing controversy between Slavophiles and Westernizers. Too many things to say, perhaps, between the covers of one book, but Turgenev, whose career had already peaked, tried it anyway.

The love story involves the protagonist Grigóry Mikhailovich Litvinov and his former fiancée, Irína Pavlovna. Shortly before their wedding was to take place, Irína, embarrassed by her impoverished situation, and after a successful appearance at a high-society ball, jilted Litvinov and married for rank a fatuous and unattractive young general, Ratmírov. Now in Baden-Baden, Litvinov awaits the arrival of his new betrothed, his cousin Tátiana Petrovna Shestova, whose mother will accompany her. Irína is there, too, and the old love is rekindled; she and Litvinov plan to run away together—a plan which Litvinov divulges to the saddened Tátiana—but at the last moment, the general's wife changes her mind, thus disrupting Litvinov's life for a second time. Disconsolate, the latter returns to Russia, where his dedication to work succeeds in bringing about a reconciliation with Tátiana—unconvincing as this happy ending (unusual for Turgenev) sounds.

Innocent and naïve enough as a story, and whatever its autobiographical innuendos (the author had almost married his cousin Olga Turgeneva after a parting from Pauline Viardot in 1850), the novel hits hard at two groups of people: the hypocritical, mercenary, rabble-rousing intellectuals who call themselves radicals, and the vapid, narrow-minded bosses—the "planters"—who do not mend their ways after the Emancipation as far as the serfs are concerned. In addition, a good part of the book deals with arguments quite extraneous to the story line: the long discourses by Potúgin, who upholds intransigently the Westernizing ideology as opposed to the cultural distinctiveness of Russia in which the Slavophiles believed. Aleksandr Herzen, with whom Turgenev had crossed swords and who could not embrace the Potúgin-Turgenev philosophy, ultimately seemed sympathetic to the novel (unlike publisher Katkov, who found this occasion to break away from the outspoken author), but the spiritualistically and nationalistically irritable Dostoevski found reason to be thoroughly vexed by it. The point, however, had been made: Matters Russian were enveloped in a symbolic smoke, whether in the cultural ineffectiveness inside the homeland or in its citizens' flavorless lives in Germany. Superfluous men abounded. Turgenev had lived too long away from this homeland to understand what was going on there—this became the facile charge, obviously a weak one, since what he had to say aroused such furor and such partisan passions.

VIRGIN SOIL

Without relinquishing his interest in portraying types, Turgenev then turned to depicting the new (post-Alexander II) Russia in his longest and most complex novel, *Virgin Soil*, about the "going to the people" period of the mid-1870's. At the University

of Saint Petersburg, there is a student, the revolutionary Nezhdánov, the illegitimate son of a nobleman. Nezhdánov, earns his living as preceptor at the home of a high dignitary and self-fancying though cautious liberal, Sipyágin. There Nezhdánov meets Sipyágin's crafty and attractive wife and a pair that shares his political persuasion: Sipyágin's poor niece Marianna and his fanatical brother-in-law Markélov, who loves the niece, though his love is unrequited. In fact, Marianna, who dislikes the Sipyágin couple, is drawn in her quest for freedom to Nezhdánov and his revolutionary goals. He, however, is too introspective for action and unsure of those goals, even of loving Marianna. A manager of a paper factory, Solómin, an active, progressive, but practical man, shields Nezhdánov and Marianna (they have fled the Sipyágin household) from the authorities. While Markélov tries to incite insurgency, Nezhdánov distributes pamphlets and attempts ineffectually to stir up revolution, and Marianna does her share by teaching the peasants' children. Attempts are aborted, the intellectuals are suspected by the peasants themselves, Markélov is arrested, and Nezhdánov, dramatically facing his besetting weakness—his inability to decide and to act, whether in a political or a personal context (as Leonard Schapiro has aptly said, "the tragedy of a Hamlet who longs to be a Don Quixote"—escapes arrest through suicide. Solómin and Marianna go into hiding and marry.

Turgenev's message was not revolution, as some of his contemporaries sought to demonstrate, but rather the Solómin brand of compassionate and sober evolution, constantly, efficiently, and practically working toward a diminishing of inequality. Only the educated class, not the well-intentioned and liberal gentry, will bring about reform, unless the gentry develop a true capacity for action and self-sacrifice. Around Solómin, the novel's hero, and the other frontline characters drift a host of secondaries—as usual, as important in the Turgenevian scheme as the primaries, for the message would lack both formation and relief without them: the homely and poor student revolutionary Mashurina, the lively but spineless Páklin (who speaks the author's mind), the wealthy and illiberal landlord Kollomietsev, the old aristocrats Fimushka and Fomushka, Sipyágin's beautiful man-eating wife, and many more. Again, Turgenev drew from reality, and his fundamental greatness continues today to lie in his naturalistic characterizations (alongside his stylistic and descriptive powers), without which he could not feel any confidence in his own ideas. He himself once wrote:

> When I do not have concrete figures before my eyes I am immediately disoriented and don't know where to go. I always feel that an idea opposite to my own could be affirmed with equal reason. But if I speak of a red nose or of a white hair, then the hair is white and the nose is red. No dialectics will be able to alter this state of things.

Jean-Pierre Barricelli

OTHER MAJOR WORKS

SHORT FICTION: *Zapiski okhotnika*, 1852 (*Russian Life in the Interior*, 1855; better known as *A Sportsman's Sketches*, 1932); *Povesti i rasskazy*, 1856.

PLAYS: *Neostorozhnost*, pb. 1843 (*Carelessness*, 1924); *Bezdenezhe*, pb. 1846 (*A Poor Gentleman*, 1924); *Kholostyak*, pr. 1849 (*The Bachelor*, 1924); *Zavtrak u predvoditelya*, pr. 1849; *Nakhlebnik*, wr. 1849, pb. 1857; *Razgovor na bolshoy doroge*, pr. 1850 (*A Conversation on the Highway*, 1924); *Mesyats v derevne*, wr. 1850, pb. 1855 (*A Month in the Country*, 1924); *Provintsialka*, pr. 1851 (*A Provincial Lady*, 1934); *Gde tonko, tam i rvyotsya*, wr. 1851, pr. 1912 (*Where It Is Thin, There It Breaks*, 1924); *Vecher v* Sorrente, wr. 1852, pr. 1884 (*An Evening in Sorrento*, 1924); *The Plays of Ivan Turgenev*, pb. 1924; *Three Plays*, pb. 1934.

POETRY: *Parasha*, 1843; *Senilia*, 1882, 1930 (better known as *Stikhotvoreniya v proze; Poems in Prose*, 1883, 1945).

NONFICTION: "Gamlet i Don Kikhot," 1860 ("Hamlet and Don Quixote," 1930); *Literaturnya i zhiteyskiya vospominaniya*, 1880 (*Literary Reminiscences and Autobiographical Fragments*, 1958); *Letters*, 1983 (David Lowe, editor); *Turgenev's Letters*, 1983 (A. V. Knowles, editor).

MISCELLANEOUS: *The Works of Iván Turgenieff*, 1903-1904 (6 volumes).

BIBLIOGRAPHY

Costlow, Jane T. *Worlds Within Worlds: The Novels of Ivan Turgenev*. Princeton, N.J.: Princeton University Press, 1990. A useful discussion of Turgenev's long fiction. Includes bibliographical references and an index.

Freeborn, Richard. *Turgenev: The Novelist's Novelist*. Oxford, England: Oxford University Press, 1963. One of the best studies of Turgenev's development as a novelist.

Knowles, A. V. *Ivan Turgenev*. Boston: Twayne, 1988. An excellent introductory study, with a biographical sketch, chapters on the start of Turgenev's literary career, the establishment of his reputation, his first three novels, and a separate chapter on *Fathers and Sons*. Subsequent chapters on his later novels, letters, final years, and his place in literature. Includes chronology, notes, and an annotated bibliography.

Muchnic, Helen. *Russian Writers Notes and Essays*. New York: Random House, 1971. Contains two brief but useful introductory essays on Turgenev's life and fiction.

Pritchett, V. S. *The Gentle Barbarian: The Life and Work of Turgenev*. New York: Random House, 1977. A graceful biography by a great man of letters. Pritchett provides considerable insight into Turgenev's literary sensibility.

Troyat, Henri. *Turgenev*. New York: Dutton, 1988. A sound narrative biography by a seasoned biographer. Troyat examines closely the contradictions of Turgenev's character and how they relate to his work. A perfect introductory book, written in an accessible but nevertheless learned style. Provides notes, bibliography, illustrations, and detailed index.

Waddington, Patrick, ed. *Ivan Turgenev and Britain*. Providence, R.I.: Berg, 1995. Essays on Turgenev's reputation in England and in America, including reviews by distinguished critics such as Frank Harris, Virginia Woolf, and Edmund Gosse. Waddington provides a comprehensive introduction, explaining the historical context in which these reviews appeared. With extensive notes and bibliography.

Walder Dennis, ed. *The Realist Novel*. New York: Routledge, 1995. Examines English realistic fiction, such as Jane Austen's *Pride and Prejudice*, Mary Wollstonecraft Shelley's *Frankenstein*, Charles Dickens's *Great Expectations*, and Turgenev's *Fathers and Sons*.

Woodward, James B. *Turgenev's "Fathers and Sons."* London: Bristol Classical Press, 1996. Part of the Critical Studies in Russian Literature series, this is an excellent study of the novel. Provides bibliographical references and an index.

SCOTT F. TUROW

Born: Chicago, Illinois; April 12, 1949

PRINCIPAL LONG FICTION

Presumed Innocent, 1987
The Burden of Proof, 1990
Pleading Guilty, 1993
The Laws of Our Fathers, 1996
Personal Injuries, 1999

OTHER LITERARY FORMS

Although known primarily as an author of best-selling mystery novels, early in his career Scott F. Turow published short stories written while he was an undergraduate at Amherst College. In 1977 Turow published a compelling nonfiction account of his first year as a law student, *One L. One L* became required reading for prospective law students and eventually sold more than three million copies. Turow would continue to write and publish book reviews, articles for legal journals, and newspaper articles on topics ranging from politics to sports.

ACHIEVEMENTS

Turow won the Crime Writers' Association Silver Dagger Award in 1988 for *Presumed Innocent*. Paperback rights to *Presumed Innocent* sold for a record three million dollars, and Turow was paid one million dollars for the motion picture rights, which was unprecedented for a first novel. Turow's remarkable success with *Presumed Innocent*, coupled with his determination to remain a practicing lawyer, started an interest in legal fiction written by lawyers, especially Turow and novelist John Grisham. Turow's success helped create a new market for courtroom drama, and, in Turow's wake, scores of lawyers and law students began tinkering with writing fiction. Turow was often hailed as an author who had transcended his genre, whose work was consistently literary yet nonetheless had mass audience appeal.

BIOGRAPHY

The eldest of two children, Scott F. Turow was born into an upper-middle-class Jewish family in Chicago, the son of a physician and a former public school teacher. When he was in his teens his family moved from a largely Jewish neighborhood in the city to the suburbs. Turow's father, a former Army doctor, treated depression and devoted most of his time to his work, and Turow's relationship with him was somewhat strained. Largely inspired by his mother, who had written unpublished short stories and novels and published a self-help book, Turow decided he would pursue a career as a writer. He enrolled in Amherst College in Massachusetts in 1966, where he majored in English and studied with Tillie Olsen, a noted writer of Jewish and feminist short stories. Turow graduated summa cum laude and in 1970 entered the master's program in creative writing at Stanford University, where he continued to study with Olsen.

In 1971, Turow married Annette Weisberg, a painter and teacher who also had grown up in the suburbs of Chicago; the couple would eventually have three children. Turow was awarded the appointment of E. H. Jones Lecturer in Creative Writing at Stanford, but after three years as a teacher he began to feel that life in academia kept him too far removed from the real world. Turow had become interested in the law, intrigued by research into legal matters he had done for his first novel, *The Way Things Are* (which was eventually rejected by twenty-five publishers). Turow decided to apply to law school and was accepted into Harvard Law School in 1975. Turow felt that the legal system was to some degree

(CORBIS/Bettmann)

taking on the role once played by organized religion in American culture; practitioners of the law were vital modern-day arbiters of truth and defenders of right against wrong. Receiving his law degree in 1978, he accepted a job as an assistant United States attorney in the U.S. Court of Appeals in Chicago. There, Turow became involved with "Operation Greylord," an investigation into corruption in the court system, and helped to prosecute several police officers, lawyers, and judges.

Often noted for his remarkable discipline, Turow successfully juggled his legal career, growing family, and literary pursuits, writing *Presumed Innocent* during the hours he traveled on a commuter train between his office and his suburban home. Realizing that he could not both maintain his grueling work schedule and complete the book, on his wife's advice Turow resigned his job with the U.S. attorney's office and accepted a position with Sonnenschein Nath & Rosenthal, a private Chicago law firm. Before starting work there, he took three months off to finish *Presumed Innocent.*

Presumed Innocent's record-breaking success made Turow a wealthy man. Although he continued

to work as a lawyer and was determined to maintain his two careers, soon after the publication of *Presumed Innocent* he asked Sonnenschein Nath & Rosenthal to allow him to work part-time. He remained employed with the firm while writing his next three best-selling novels.

ANALYSIS

Presumed Innocent is in some respects a typical murder mystery, beginning with the gruesome murder of a beautiful woman and tracing the investigation of her death and the criminal trial of the accused, with a surprise twist at the end. Turow drew upon his own investigations of police and political corruption to create realistic characters and gripping courtroom scenes. However, *Presumed Innocent* is much more than a potboiler; the story encompasses several compelling themes: the intricacies of the legal practice, the elusive quality of truth and how well the truth is revealed by the legal process, and the common notions that anyone can be corrupted and everyone has at least one dark secret. These ideas are central to all of Turow's fiction, although each of his subsequent works would take a different approach to exploring these themes. Turow's later novels introduce a greater range of characters, examine these characters' failures in greater depth, and address more convoluted aspects of courtroom tactics, crime, and criminal behavior. Each book features a corpse, but the mystery of "whodunit" increasingly became secondary to Turow's delight in legal maneuvering and his concerns with larger questions of character.

PRESUMED INNOCENT

When *Presumed Innocent* begins, the beautiful, ambitious Carolyn Polhemus, a Kindle County deputy prosecuting attorney, has been brutally raped and murdered in her apartment. Chief Prosecuting Attorney Raymond Horgan asks deputy P.A. Rusty Sabich to investigate and prosecute Polhemus's murder. Horgan's campaign for reelection is faltering, and he believes the Polhemus murder must be resolved quickly or his opponent Nico Della Guardia will point to it as evidence of weakness in Horgan's administration.

Sabich reveals that he had a brief affair with Polhemus and pursued her obsessively for some months afterwards; he has admitted as much to his wife Barbara. Police detective Dan Lipranzer, Sabich's best friend, begins an investigation into Polhemus's death but is taken off the case as it becomes clear that Della Guardia is running his own investigation and that Sabich is a suspect. Sabich is charged with Polhemus's murder and brought to trial with attorney Alejandro "Sandy" Stern defending him and Horgan's old friend Judge Larren Lyttle presiding.

Raymond Horgan testifies against Sabich, angry because he believes Sabich murdered Polhemus and thus jeopardized Horgan's chances at reelection. A key piece of evidence, a glass with Sabich's fingerprints on it found at the crime scene, is lost and cannot be produced at the trial. On his own, Sabich investigates Polhemus's background and her murder, uncovering a long-past bribery scam and discovering that Polhemus had also had affairs with Horgan and with Lyttle. Stern is able to discredit prosecution witnesses and show that Sabich might have been framed for Polhemus's murder, and the case is dismissed.

Although Turow's prose can turn purple as the introspective Sabich watches his life fall apart, for the most part *Presumed Innocent* is a gripping and fast-moving novel that indeed transcends the murder-mystery formula. Rather than introducing a set of individuals with motives to kill the victim and moving through a process of elimination to find the killer, *Presumed Innocent* creates a many-layered world where the "coppers'," judges', and lawyers' motives and perceptions seem to shift depending on Sabich's current knowledge of them; nearly every noble act is countered by something reprehensible in the character's past.

The courtroom scenes and Sabich's consultations with his lawyer offer fascinating insight into legal tactics and explore a theme that Turow would revisit in his later works: the ambiguity and simple human recalcitrance that plague the person who searches for the truth. Even after the murderer's identity is revealed, the difficulty of knowing what really happened is reemphasized as Sabich and his friend Lipranzer disagree about the murderer's intentions. Did the killer intend to frame Sabich and watch him go to jail, or was there another, more subtle motive behind the murder? Sabich, in fact, guessed the identity of Polhemus's killer midway through the novel, without revealing his knowledge to his lawyer, his best friend, or readers. When readers discover that Sabich has known for some time who killed Polhemus, his character is thrown into a different light, and readers are invited to do what Sabich has done throughout the novel, to reexamine someone else's thoughts and actions based on a new revelation, a new piece of the whole truth.

The novel concludes as Sabich considers why he was drawn to the ultimately coldhearted, calculating Polhemus. Sabich concludes that he desired her because of her denial of truth about herself: She "had suffered vastly—and had claimed in every visible aspect of her being to have triumphed over it all." He "reached for Carolyn" out of a helpless attraction to her own doomed hope that she was not the person she ultimately proved to be.

THE LAWS OF OUR FATHERS

In Turow's second and third novels, *The Burden of Proof* and *Pleading Guilty*, Turow departed ever further from the traditional murder mystery or courtroom drama. Turow's fourth novel, *The Laws of Our Fathers*, continued to move away from the page-turning fiction that launched his career and was instead an attempt to revisit a work he had once set aside in order to finish *Presumed Innocent*.

Ghetto gang leader and drug dealer Ordell Trent, also known as Hardcore, confronts a white woman who has driven to his neighborhood in an unexplained attempt to meet with him; evidently Hardcore was expecting someone else, but before he can convince her to flee she is gunned down by another gang member, and a third gang member—a teenage girl—is injured at the scene. The murdered woman is identified as June Eddgar, ex-wife of state senator Loyall Eddgar. Hardcore turns state's evidence to reduce the sentence for his own involvement with the murder, claiming that June Eddgar's son Nile set up the meeting in the ghetto and conspired to have his mother killed.

In *The Laws of Our Fathers*, Turow builds a story around a secondary character from an earlier work, just as he did with *Presumed Innocent*'s defense attorney Sandy Stern in his second novel, *The Burden of Proof*, where Sonia "Sonny" Klonsky appeared as a prosecuting attorney and love interest for Stern. *The Laws of Our Fathers* catches up with Sonny several years later, divorced from her poet husband, struggling with single motherhood and sitting as a state court judge in Kindle County, where she feels out of place even among her clerical staff.

The murder of June Eddgar and the trial of Eddgar's son reunites Sonny with several people she knew in the late 1960's, when Sonny and the Eddgars lived in the same apartment building. June Eddgar and her ex-husband Loyall were then leftist radicals, focusing every moment of their lives on launching a political revolution. Seth Weissman was Sonny's uneasy live-in boyfriend, caught up in the Eddgars' radical politics and awaiting the revolution while trying to wring some kind of commitment out of the determinedly distant Sonny. Seth's best friend Hobie Tuttle was an increasingly isolated young African American man, angrily renouncing his friendship with Seth as he became more involved with drugs and with the Black Panther Party.

Sonny had lost touch with Seth and Hobie; now she learns that Seth writes a syndicated column about the faded idealism of the 1960's, continually mourning his generation's shattered expectations, and remains friends with Hobie, now a finely dressed defense attorney who appears in Sonny's court to represent Nile Eddgar. Because of her past associations with the Eddgars, Sonny repeatedly offers to recuse herself from hearing the case against Nile Eddgar; however, the prosecution and defense attorneys not only urge her to remain, but also, during a legal wrangle in the courtroom, request a bench trial, meaning that no jury will be called and Judge Klonsky will decide the verdict herself.

The trial features much showboating by Hobie and much indignant screaming by prosecuting attorney Tommy Molto (a minor character from *Presumed*

Innocent). Sonny leans first toward convicting Nile and then toward acquitting him. She feels increasingly compromised as she becomes romantically involved with Seth, wondering if he is using her to glean information for Hobie, and is pressured by another judge to protect Loyall Eddgar. When Hobie declares in court that he might move for a mistrial, Sonny takes advantage of his theatrics and grants him the mistrial on the spot.

Three-quarters through the novel, the trial is suddenly over; however, the trial and its outcome are not the central focus of the story. The crime and the trial are simply vehicles for reuniting the Eddgars, Seth, Sonny, and Hobie and examining the people they have become. Most of the story is told from either Seth's or Sonny's point of view, shifting backward and forward in time from the 1960's to 1995. Neither the judge nor the journalist has known the truth about the Eddgars or learned the truth about Hardcore; the legal process has not uncovered the events that led to June Eddgar's death. In the book's last few chapters the narrative is transferred in quick succession to Hardcore, Nile, Loyall Eddgar, and June Eddgar, and the reader learns how June happened to meet with Hardcore and how she was killed.

Much of the novel is devoted to the character's struggles to leave behind the legacies of their parents and find happiness by improving upon or rejecting the past. Sonny worries daily that her career is making her an absentee mother like her own mother Zora, a McCarthy-era activist and radical organizer who adored Sonny but could literally forget about her while making a political point. The Eddgars' political fanaticism left Nile Eddgar an aimless shell of a man, willing to become involved with Hardcore because the gang leader's charisma reminded him of his father's. Seth's parents survived the Auschwitz Nazi concentration camp, and their distrust of authority is reflected in Seth's willingness to accept the Eddgars' belief that they are constantly under surveillance and to become involved in political revolution. Seth's own children determine to become practicing Jews, resolving Seth's alienation from his parents even as their legacy is confirmed.

Maureen J. Puffer-Rothenberg

OTHER MAJOR WORKS

NONFICTION: *One L*, 1977; "The Prosecutor's Function in Sentencing," 1983 (with Dan Webb); "RICO Forfeiture in Practice: A Prosecutorial Perspective," 1983 (with Webb); "Why Competence Isn't Enough: Law Schools Teach Skills. Now They Must Teach What It Really Means to Be a Lawyer," 1988.

BIBLIOGRAPHY

Bennett, Julie K. "The Trials of a Novelist." *North Shore* 10, no. 9 (September, 1987): 46-49. Examines Turow's life and work.

Gray, Paul. "Burden of Success: As a High-Powered Lawyer and Novelist, Scott Turow Has Become the Bard of the Litigious Age." *Time*, June 11, 1990, 68- 73. Discusses the aspects of Turow's legal fiction.

Lundy, Derek. *Scott Turow: Meeting the Enemy.* Toronto: ECW Press, 1995. An admiring examination of Turow's background and his work. Discusses Turow's personal views on life, authorship, fame, and the law, and provides analyses of Turow's early short stories and first three novels.

AMOS TUTUOLA

Born: Abeokuta, Nigeria; 1920
Died: Ibadan, Nigeria; June 8, 1997

PRINCIPAL LONG FICTION

The Palm-Wine Drinkard, 1952
My Life in the Bush of Ghosts, 1954
Simbi and the Satyr of the Dark Jungle, 1955
The Brave African Huntress, 1958
Feather Woman of the Jungle, 1962
Ajaiyi and His Inherited Poverty, 1967
The Witch-Herbalist of the Remote Town, 1981
The Wild Hunter in the Bush of Ghosts, 1983 (wr. c. 1948)
Pauper, Brawler, and Slanderer, 1987

OTHER LITERARY FORMS

While excerpts from Amos Tutuola's novels have appeared in numerous anthologies of African literature, he published only a handful of "short stories," most of which until the 1980's were either earlier or later versions of tales included in the novels. They include "The Elephant Woman," which appeared in *The Chicago Review* in 1956; "Ajayi and the Witchdoctor," which appeared in *The Atlantic Monthly* in 1959; "The Duckling Brothers and Their Disobedient Sister," which appeared in *Présence africaine* in 1961; "Akanke and the Jealous Pawnbroker," which appeared in *Afriscope* in 1974; and "The Pupils of the Eyes," which appeared in *Confrontation: A Journal of Third World Literature* in 1974. In 1984, two new stories about a character called Tort, the Shell Man, were published in a popular fantasy anthology in the United States, indicating the possibility of an entirely new audience in the 1980's. Those stories, "The Strange Fellows Palm-Wine Tapster" and "Tort and the Dancing Market Woman," published in *Elsewhere*, reprise themes found in Tutuola's earliest writings.

ACHIEVEMENTS

Tutuola, who was unknown to both African and Western readers at the time of the publication of *The Palm-Wine Drinkard*, occupies a unique place in the literary world. While his novels have been praised by serious writers and literary critics, he is, quite literally, one of a kind. Despite a limited command of standard English (which, coupled with his depictions of a "backward" and "superstitious" Africa, has drawn the wrath of many educated Africans), he produced a body of work that stands at the very beginning of the increasingly impressive body of anglophone African literature. Combining the rich folkloric traditions of his Yoruba people with a powerful imagination, his stories supply the Nigerian Bushman with heroes and heroines who face television-handed ghosts, half-bodied babies, bloodthirsty satyrs, and witch-mothers.

Few writers have achieved such serious attention while remaining as unsophisticated in their literary style as did Tutuola. There is no question that Tutuola is, in the truest sense of the word, a "natural," yet he is more than a literary curiosity. In a number of ways, he is a crossroads figure. He succeeded as a writer not by imitating the West but by depending upon local sources (mixed with a number of influences from the West but never overwhelmed by them). This helped create a climate in which other Africans could write about the African experience and be accepted both in their own nations and abroad. His dependence upon Yoruba folk stories, and such Yoruba-language writers as Chief D. O. Fagunwa, continues to draw attention to the richness and variety of African folk traditions. The depth of Tutuola's debt to those folk stories and the writings of Fagunwa has yet to be fully explored. Extensive passages in several of Tutuola's books appear to be in large part translated or paraphrased from Fagunwa's *The Forest of a Thousand Daemons: A Hunter's Saga* (1950), a title which in itself suggests both Tutuola's second published novel, *My Life in the Bush of Ghosts*, and his first-written novel, *The Wild Hunter in the Bush of Ghosts*. It cannot be said, however, that Tutuola was merely plagiarizing. In a sense, he continued—on paper—the time-honored storytellers' practice of drawing upon existing and remembered material to make the old tales new again. Moreover, Tutuola's stories are possessed of a human warmth that makes them more than simply entertaining embellishments of the folk heritage. Despite hardships—which sometimes make the sufferings of Job appear insignificant—his men and women persevere and eventually triumph against all odds. Like all great cultural heroes, they stand up to a potentially destructive universe and struggle to preserve themselves and their people. Their mythic successes are rather like Tutuola's own achievement—wildly unexpected and strangely gratifying.

BIOGRAPHY

There was little in Amos Tutuola's early life to indicate that he would be a world-famous author. Born in 1920, in Abeokuta, Nigeria, in the township of Iporo-Ake, he was an eager listener to the folktales related to him in the evenings by his mother and his aunt. At the age of ten, he was enrolled in the nearby Salvation Army School, where he first began to study English. English is the official language of Nigeria (whose forty million people speak many different African languages), but Tutuola's first language was Yoruba. Furthermore, the everyday "English" spoken by uneducated Nigerians is either pidgin or affected by West African idiom. Like many other Nigerians, Tutuola combined the deep grammar of his native language with English surface grammar. "I had no other work more than to drink," for example, the statement made by the Palm-Wine Drinkard at the start of his story, is typical Yoruba syntax.

When his family could no longer afford to send him to school, Tutuola began to work as a houseboy for a government clerk. In return for his services, the clerk enrolled Tutuola in Ake Central School and, later, in Lagos High School. There, Tutuola became familiar with the Yoruba writings of Fagunwa and simplified versions of such classics as John Bunyan's *The Pilgrim's Progress* (1678, 1684). Apparently, he was not an outstanding student, for he decided to leave school and learn the trade of blacksmith, finding a job as a metalworker for the Royal Air Force at Oshodi. When this job ended, the only work Tutuola could find was as a junior messenger for the Labour Department in Lagos in 1946. Much of his time was spent sitting in the offices, waiting for messages to carry. To combat his boredom, he began scribbling down stories on scraps of paper. Around 1948, he sent his first completed manuscript, *The Wild Hunter in the Bush of Ghosts*, to a photography publisher in London, The Focal Press. The book, he explained to them in a letter, was written to accompany a collection of photographs of ghosts. Those photographs, he said, would follow shortly. The photographs turned out to be of drawings of ghosts, and The Focal Press dumped both text and "ghost photos" into their files. There they remained for more than thirty years.

Although Tutuola may have been discouraged by that early failure (which he did not mention to anyone for decades), he continued to write. Upon seeing an advertisement for books from The United Society for Christian Literature in a newspaper, he decided to send to that organization a manuscript, the first draft of which had been written in lead pencil over the course of several days. After three months of enlarging the story, he made a copy of it in ink and sent it off. The organization did not publish books but, making one of those small decisions which have unexpectedly large effects, they sent the manuscript on to the publishing house Faber and Faber. Slightly more than a year later, in 1952, it was published as *The Palm-Wine Drinkard*. Three months after its publication, Faber and Faber received a second Tutuola manuscript. After a small amount of editing by Geoffrey Parrinder, it was published as *My Life in the Bush of Ghosts*. It is clear now that it drew freely on Tutuola's memories of his first, "lost" manuscript.

Enchanted by his fresh West African idiom, critics praised the book and went so far as to urge other African writers to follow Tutuola's example—a difficult task; indeed, Tutuola himself found it hard to do. He continued for a time to work as a messenger (who was visited now and then by distinguished white scholars, to the disapproving surprise of his employers) but was now concerned about his own shortcomings. He acknowledged that his English was imperfect and attended night school to improve it. His renown brought him a great deal of attention, but he remained a shy, retiring person. A job working as a storekeeper for the Nigerian Broadcasting Corporation was given to him in 1956, and in 1957, he arranged to be transferred to the Ibadan offices of the corporation so that he could work with Professor Collis at the University of Ibadan in producing a play version of *The Palm-Wine Drinkard*. This version was translated into Yoruba and successfully staged throughout West Africa in the early 1960's.

Married in 1947 and the father of several children, Tutuola was never comfortable playing the part of a celebrity. He had little to say to interviewers and did not like to go on lecture tours or even have much to do with other writers (though he was a self-effacing charter member of the Mbari Club, a seminal writers' and publishers' group in Nigeria). A six-month scholarship was offered to him in 1963 by West Germany, but he did not accept it.

By the time his third novel was published, there was some improvement in his standard of English, but there was also a growing disenchantment with Tutuola's work. Africans continued to criticize both his bad habits and his borrowings, and Europeans intimated that his "improvement" had a negative effect upon his work, which they also criticized for being repetitive. To some, he was now deliberately childish, whereas before he had been pleasingly childlike.

By the 1970's, however, Tutuola was again receiving praise from both African and European critics, who were beginning to see his writings for what they were: not true novels, but linked stories in the monomythic tradition. Some see him as the equivalent for world literature of the *akpala kpatita* (professional storyteller) of Nigeria. (Jorge Amado, the popular Brazilian writer, shows the influence of Tutuola in his own writing.) This renewed and more balanced attention directed toward Tutuola is surely one of the factors which led to his publishing a book in 1981, the first in more than a decade, and an extended tour of the United States in the 1980's, during which he spoke and took part in symposia. When, thanks to some fine scholarly detective work on the part of Bernth Lindfors, the handwritten original manuscript of Tutuola's first novel, *The Wild Hunter in the Bush of Ghosts*, was tracked down and then published in 1983, both scholars and biographers of the Yoruba writer had to do considerable backtracking. Published by Three Continents Press with a typeset script facing photocopies of the original handwritten pages, it is significant as a minor work at an early stage of Tutuola's development. Furthermore, as its discoverer Bernth Lindfors puts it in his introduction to the book, it is "the first long piece of prose fiction written for publication in English by a Nigerian author." Tutuola died on June 8, 1997.

ANALYSIS

Although it is certainly possible to enjoy Amos Tutuola's novels on their own merits—merits which include economy of language, a strong storytelling voice, a marvelous self-assurance on the part of his narrators (almost always in the first person), fantastic imagination, and virtually nonstop action—it is useful to look at him within the context of Yoruba culture. The Yorubas are a people of western Nigeria who both have embraced Western culture and have remained intensely connected to traditional ways. The sixteen million Yoruba people make up about 20 percent of the population of Nigeria, Africa's most populous nation and one of its best educated. Although Christianity is the religion of virtually all Yoruba people, there is a deep undercurrent of animism and, like Tutuola's narrators, contemporary Yoruba people see nothing unusual in a world where churches coexist with magical charms (*juju*) and the deepest and most impassable jungles (the bush) are filled with spirits, both those of the dead and those of nonhuman beings. Yoruba folklore is characterized by a belief in a distant though benevolent Supreme Deity and the presence on the earth of numerous smaller "gods," and powers, often anthropomorphic. It is still common practice for both adults and children to sit around in the evening and listen to folk stories much like those in Tutuola's books. In some cases, they do so while drinking palm-wine, the mildly alcoholic sap of the palm-wine palm, which can be drunk straight from the tree.

Inexpensive or "free" primary education in British-style schools, often run by churches, was common when Tutuola was a child, and this exposure, from his tenth year until his late teens, provided Tutuola with the necessary tools—literacy and a knowledge of literary forms (from simplified classics in the schools to books published in Yoruba)—to begin his career as a writer. One thing which those schools did not give him, though, was the confidence of one who knows a good story and is not afraid to tell it. It was that self-assurance (so clearly echoed in the gentle strength of all of his various protagonists) which led a junior clerk, a man in a lowly position in an extremely class-conscious colonial society, to dare to send his first writings to a publisher.

THE PALM-WINE DRINKARD

The Palm-Wine Drinkard begins with the narrator telling us a bit about himself. "I was a palm-wine drinkard since I was a body of ten years of age. I had no other work more than to drink palm-wine in my life." These first words hardly prepare us for the

mythic dimensions of the character which we see later in the book, but the prodigious amounts of palm-wine he consumes (225 kegs every twenty-four hours) give us the hint that he is no ordinary human. When his palm-wine tapster falls from a tree and dies, the Drinkard sees that the only thing he can do is seek out his tapster in the land of the Dead. This sets the mythic tone of the book and all the rest of Tutuola's work. The Drinkard enters the bush, a netherworld inhabited by spirits and strange creatures. His first encounter, with an old man who sets him the Herculean task of capturing Death, reveals to us the Drinkard's superhuman powers. His other name, he tells us, is "Father of gods who could do everything in this world," and his success in capturing Death (who then escapes, which is why "we are hearing his name about in the world") proves that his title is no idle boast. His next exploit is to rescue his wife-to-be from a skull who has borrowed body parts to masquerade as a "Complete Gentleman." Thereafter, he and his wife continue on his quest, but not before she becomes pregnant (in her thumb) and gives birth to a miraculous and dangerous half-bodied child who must be destroyed before they can continue on their way. They do eventually reach the town of the Dead, despite the menace of such beasts as a "Spirit of Prey" with eyes like searchlights and with the help of the Drinkard's powerful jujus and such beings as the Faithful Mother, whose servants buy the Drinkard's death and rent his fear.

Novelistic plot development in the conventional sense does not exist in this or Tutuola's other romances; the various episodes are almost interchangeable. The Drinkard, however, does learn a lesson at the end of the novel. His tapster has now (like a student in a European school or an apprentice blacksmith) "qualified" as a full dead man. He cannot return to the living. Instead, he gives the Drinkard and his resourceful wife, who has developed into something of a Sibyl, a miraculous egg. The Drinkard and his wife return to the land of the living. There he finds a famine and, sending a sacrifice to Heaven, brings rain to the people—an ending which seems to recapitulate the conclusion of a traditional creation story.

In one of the best analyses of Tutuola's style, Bernth Lindfors concludes that his books are not novels at all; instead, they are, in content, structure, and style, concatenated folktales. Both African and English critics have noted the structure of the quest and the rite of passage which also characterize Tutuola's extended narratives. They always begin with the introduction of a main character; the sending out of that character into the world, where many hardships are encountered; the overcoming of all obstacles; and the return of the hero or heroine in triumph. This structure is both that of *The Pilgrim's Progress* and that of the epic stories of Yoruba (and other African) cultural heroes as they overcome death, use their personal magic to change themselves into animals or objects, and travel through a world fully as hostile as real life. To describe either Tutuola's stories or African folklore as escapism, in fact, is quite inaccurate. The worlds of Simbi, of the Brave Huntress, and of the Drinkard are graphically horrifying. They are no more an escape than would be a series of vivid nightmares.

The flavor of the stories is that of the naïve tall tale. Almost anything is possible in such accounts, even turning oneself into a stone and then throwing oneself to escape. The reader (or the listener, for the voice in Tutuola is that of an oral storyteller) is carried along by the headlong rush of events, the total acceptance of this illogical world by the narrators (who always live well within this world, playing and winning by its rules), the humor and humanity which are among the author's greatest virtues. Furthermore and here both Tutuola's Christian faith (which is very real) and the folktale tradition come into play—these are moral tales. There are always lessons to be learned. No one commits a foolish action without having to pay the consequences. Good is always eventually rewarded; evil is always strong but eventually defeated. There is a clear structure to each of Tutuola's books, a beginning and an end which are carefully linked. The Drinkard's search for his tapster ends with his finding him and learning a lesson as a result of all of his efforts—a lesson which was unexpected on the protagonist's part but which the reader responds to and understands. *My Life in*

the Bush of Ghosts begins with the central character not knowing what "good" or "bad" or hatred is. It ends, after twenty-four years of trials and wandering in the bush, with these words: "This is what hatred did."

A cornucopia of horrifically memorable menaces confronts Tutuola's protagonists in each of the books. Indeed, this may be one of the more serious of Tutuola's failings, the very abundance of monsters and fabulous encounters in each of his stories (although those monsters are invariably memorable and individually characterized with surprising economy). After a certain point, especially when one reads a series of Tutuola's novels in a short space of time, events and characters begin to blur and one feels overwhelmed. It was probably with this overabundance in mind that the dramatic version of *The Palm-Wine Drinkard* was created out of only eight of the twenty episodes found in the book. In his essay "Amos Tutuola: A Nigerian Visionary," Gerald Moore characterizes the first two novels as quest romances and ties them to the monomyth of Joseph Campbell's *The Hero with a Thousand Faces* (1949). Considering that Tutuola's stories follow the pattern of Yoruba storytelling sessions, only a bit more extended, and those stories often relate creation myths, it is not surprising that Moore should find that pattern.

MY LIFE IN THE BUSH OF GHOSTS

It is difficult to use conventional critical apparatus in dealing with Tutuola. It is equally difficult to summarize easily any of his books, for they consist, like his first book, of a loosely organized, helter-skelter collection of fantastic events that have their own logic. *My Life in the Bush of Ghosts* presents its readers with another character like the Drinkard, but possessed of less magic. He is, however—like the Drinkard—resourceful, plucky, and often very shrewd. He is not fortunate enough to have a wife like the Drinkard's, but Tutuola makes up for that in the characters of both Simbi and the Brave African Huntress in his later books. They are women of purpose, wonderfully self-reliant, and as capable as his male heroes. Simbi engages in heroic combat with a "Satyr" (Tutuola's names for his mythic creatures are often drawn from Western mythology but have nothing at all to do with the original beings in Western myth) who is ten feet tall, covered with blood and feathers, "an impatient and ill-tempered, impenitent and noxious creature." The Brave African Huntress vows death to all the "pygmies" (small creatures which resemble the various dwarflike forest creatures of African myth rather than human beings) who have either killed or "detained" her four brothers. She proceeds to do so with bloodthirsty efficiency, burning the pygmy town, blowing it up with gunpowder, and then picking off the pygmies one by one with her gun as they run from the ruins. After rescuing her brothers, she proceeds to sell the minerals found in the Jungle of the Pygmies and becomes wealthy.

The world which is inhabited by the characters in all of Tutuola's writing is an interesting one in another way. It contains no Caucasians. Aside from one brief reference to a set of footprints made in the rocks near Ife by "the first white men who had traveled from heaven through that rock to the earth," one finds no Europeans in his books. Instead, the books are set in an African Africa, albeit an Africa affected by Western inventions and institutions such as newspapers, gunpowder, the Methodist Church, and airplanes. Though it may be unintentional, certain sections of Tutuola's novels—such as the description of the Dead Cousin who has become a Methodist bishop in the "10th Town of Ghosts"—seem to be parodies of real events in Nigerian history. More often than not, Western objects appear in Tutuola's similes—as when he compares the sound of the skulls chasing the Drinkard to "a thousand petrol drums pushing along a hard road." His is thus not an ideal Africa, but one rather like the West Africa of the early nineteenth century, when the influence of the slave trade had deepened rivalries between such African states as Oyo and Dahomey and created a climate of continual warfare and uncertainty.

In the midst of this world, Tutuola's heroes and heroines are much like many Yoruba people of today, men and women who deal with an increasingly complicated world with pragmatism, shrewdness, and even humor.

Joseph Bruchac

OTHER MAJOR WORKS

SHORT FICTION: "The Elephant Woman," 1956; "Ajayi and the Witchdoctor," 1959; "The Duckling Brothers and Their Disobedient Sister," 1961; "Akanke and the Jealous Pawnbroker," 1974; "The Pupils of the Eyes," 1974; "The Strange Fellows Palm-Wine Tapster," 1984; "Tort and the Dancing Market Woman," 1984; *Yoruba Folktales*, 1986; *The Witch Doctor and Other Stories*, 1990.

BIBLIOGRAPHY

Achebe, Chinua. "Work and Play in Tutuola: *The Palm-Wine Drinkard.*" *Okike* 14 (1978): 25-33. A perceptive article by one of Africa's greatest novelists.

Armstrong, Robert G. "Amos Tutuola and Kola Ogunmola: A Comparison of Two Versions of *The Palm-Wine Drinkard.*" *Callaloo* 3 (1980): 165-174. A useful source study and comparison.

Collins, Harold R. *Amos Tutuola*. Boston: Twayne, 1969. A standard introductory study, with chronology, notes, and bibliography.

Heywood, Christopher, ed. *Perspectives on African Literature*. New York: African Publishing Corporation, 1971. See the essay by A. Afolayan, "Language and Sources of Amos Tutuola," which assesses the writer's contribution to Yoruba literature from a Yoruba perspective.

Irele, Abiola. *The African Experience in Literature and Ideology*. London: Heineman, 1981. Irele's chapter "Tradition and the Yoruba Writer: Daniel O. Fagunwa, Amos Tutuola, and Wole Soyinka," should be compared to Afolayan's essay in Heywood.

Langford, Michele, ed. *Contours of the Fantastic in Two West African Novels*. New York: Greenwood Press, 1990. Contains Joyce Watford's essay, "Techniques of the Fantastic in Two West African Novels."

Lindfors, Bernth, ed. *Critical Perspectives on Amos Tutuola*. Washington: Three Continents Press, 1975. An excellent source for discussions of individual novels.

Onyeberechi, Sydney E. "Myth, Magic and Appetite in Amos Tutuola's *The Palm-Wine Drinkard.*"

MAWA Review 4 (1989): 22-26. Often cited as one of the best studies of Tutuola's masterpiece.

Owomoyela, Oyekan. *Amos Tutuola Revisited.* New York: Twayne, 1999. An excellent introduction to Tutuola's life and works. Good for the beginning student.

Palmer, Eustace. "Twenty-Five Years of Amos Tutuola." *International Fiction Review* 5 (1978): 15-24. A good overview of the novelist's career and his reputation.

Quayson, Ato. *Strategic Transformation in Nigerian Writing.* Bloomington: Indiana University Press, 1997. Contains "Treasures of an Opulent Fancy: Amos Tutuola and the Folktale Narrative." A sound treatment of an important element in the writer's fiction.

MARK TWAIN
Samuel Langhorne Clemens

Born: Florida, Missouri; November 30, 1835
Died: Redding, Connecticut; April 21, 1910

PRINCIPAL LONG FICTION

The Gilded Age, 1873 (with Charles Dudley Warner)
The Adventures of Tom Sawyer, 1876
The Prince and the Pauper, 1881
Adventures of Huckleberry Finn, 1884
A Connecticut Yankee in King Arthur's Court, 1889
The American Claimant, 1892
Tom Sawyer Abroad, 1894
The Tragedy of Pudd'nhead Wilson, 1894
Personal Recollections of Joan of Arc, 1896
Tom Sawyer, Detective, 1896
Simon Wheeler, Detective, 1963
Mark Twain's Mysterious Stranger Manuscripts, 1969 (William M. Gibson, editor)

OTHER LITERARY FORMS

In addition to his novels, Mark Twain wrote a great deal of short fiction, which can be divided, al-though often only very arbitrarily, into short stories, tales, and humorous sketches. One of the best examples of his short stories is "The Man That Corrupted Hadleyburg," and one of the best examples of his humorous sketches is the jumping frog story. Somewhere between the story and the sketch are tales such as "Captain Stormfield's Visit to Heaven." Twain also wrote speeches and essays, both humorous and critical. Representative of his best satiric essays, which range from the very funny to the very sober, are "Fenimore Cooper's Literary Offenses" and "To the Person Sitting in Darkness." The first of these is a hilarious broadside against Cooper's style and invention in which Twain is obviously enjoying himself while at the same time continuing his ongoing war against the romanticizing of the past. "To the Person Sitting in Darkness," considered by some to be his finest piece of invective, is his attack upon what he saw as the exploitation of the Philippines following the Spanish-American War by, in his words, "The Blessings-of-Civilization Trust." Early in his career, he wrote the travel sketches and impressions, *The Innocents Abroad* (1869), *Roughing It* (1872), and *A Tramp Abroad* (1880), and later, *Following the Equator* (1897). Two of his most important books are autobiographical, *Life on the Mississippi* (1883) and *Mark Twain's Autobiography,* published after his death in various editions in 1924.

ACHIEVEMENTS

The coincidental appearance of Halley's comet in the years of Twain's birth and death, 1835 and 1910, has been much remarked. A historical event, however, in contrast to the cosmic one, occurring very near the midpoint of his life, provides a better symbol for his career and his achievement than does the mysterious, fiery comet. In 1869, at Promontory Point, Utah, a golden spike was driven to complete the first North American transcontinental railroad. The subsequent settling of the great midwestern center of the continent and the resulting transformation of a frontier society into a civilized one, a process people thought would take hundreds of years, was to be effected in several decades. Twain's life spanned the two Americas, the frontier America that produced so much of the national mythology and the emerging urban, industrial giant of the twentieth century. At the heart of Twain's achievement is his creation of Tom Sawyer and Huck Finn, who embody that mythic America, midway between the wilderness and the modern super-state.

Tom and Huck, two of the nation's most enduring characters, give particular focus to Twain's turbulent, sprawling, complex career as journalist, humorist, entrepreneur, and novelist. The focus is dramatic because the two characters have made their way into the popular imagination with the abiding vitality of legend or folklore. They have been kept before generations of Americans in motion pictures, television, cartoons, and other popular art forms as well as in their original form in the novels. The focus is also symbolic because of the fundamental dualism which the two characters can be seen to represent on the personal, the literary, and the cultural planes.

On the personal plane, Tom and Huck represent aspirations so fundamental to Twain's life as to make them seem rather the two halves of his psyche. Like good and bad angels, they have been taken to represent the contending desires in his life: a strong desire for the security and status of material success on the one hand, set against the deeply ingrained desire for freedom from conventional social and moral restraints on the other. It has been conjectured that steamboat piloting was perhaps the most satisfying of Twain's occupations because it offered him high degrees of both respectability and freedom. Although the character of Tom, the symbol of perennial boyhood, can be easily overburdened by this perspective, there is in him the clear outline of the successful, settled, influential man-of-affairs-to-be. If Tom had grown up, he—like Twain himself—might well have made and lost a fortune in the publishing business and through investments in the Paige typesetter. He almost certainly would have been a successful professional or businessman. He would most likely have traveled abroad and would have been eager to associate with nobility at every opportunity. It is relatively easy to imagine Tom growing up. It is in-

(Library of Congress)

structive to realize that it is almost impossible to imagine Huck's doing so.

On the literary plane, the two may also be seen as representing contending forces, those of the two principal literary schools of the period, the Romantic and the realistic. Surely, Twain's pervasive attacks upon Romantic literature are somewhat compulsive, reminiscent of Nathaniel Hawthorne's preoccupation with the Puritans. Both protest too much. Twain is one of America's foremost Romantics, even if he did see himself as a realist, and even if he did engage much of his time in puncturing the sentimental balloons of the disciples of Sir Walter Scott, Cooper, and the graveyard poets. He was both Romantic and realist, and Tom and Huck emerge almost allegorically as symbols of the two major literary schools of the late nineteenth century.

Tom as the embodiment of socially conforming respectability and as a disciple of Romantic literature contrasts illustratively with Huck as the embodiment of the naturally free spirit, who is "realistic" in part because of his adolescent honesty about such things as art, royalty, and the efficacy of prayer. It is the symbolic dualism on the historical plane, however, that brings into sharpest focus the nature of Twain's central and most enduring achievement. On the historical plane, his two central characters reflect most clearly Twain's principal legacy to posterity: the embodiment in fiction of that moment in time, a moment both real and imaginary, given some historical particularity by the driving of the golden spike at Promontory Point in 1869, when America was poised between the wilderness and the modern, technological state. In this context, Tom represents the settlements that were to become the towns and cities of the new century, and Huck represents the human spirit, freer, at least in the imagination, in the wilderness out of which the settlements were springing. At the end of *Adventures of Huckleberry Finn*, Twain sends Huck on that impossible mission that has been central to the American experience for centuries, when he has him decide to "light out for the territory" before Aunt Sally can "adopt" and "civilize" him.

Twain the humorist and satirist, Twain the silver-mining, typesetting entrepreneur, Twain the journalist, the family man, the anguished, skeptical seeker after religious faith—all must be taken into consideration in accounts of the nature of his achievements. Without Tom Sawyer and Huck Finn, he would have made his mark as a man of his time, a man of various and rich talents. Most likely, his reputation would rest today largely upon his talents as a humorist and satirist, and that reputation still figures largely in assessment of his overall achievement. With Tom and Huck, however, his achievement is given the depth and dramatic focus of a central contribution to the national mythology. Huck's "voice" is frequently compared to the voice of Walt Whitman's "Song of Myself" (1855). Such comparisons rest in part upon rhetorical similarities between the two voices, similarities in what has been called the "vernacular mode." More significantly, they derive from the similarities of the achievements of the poet and the novelist in the establishing of historically and culturally distinctive American "voices" in poetry and fiction. Tom Sawyer and Huck Finn loom large on the nine-

teenth century literary horizon. They stand, along with Cooper's Natty Bumppo and Chingachgook, Hawthorne's Hester Prynne and Arthur Dimmesdale, and Whitman's persona in "Song of Myself," as the principal characters of the emerging national literature. Twain's contribution to that body of literature is at the deepest center of his achievement as a major American writer.

Biography

Mark Twain was born Samuel Langhorne Clemens in Florida, Missouri, in 1835. He first used the pen name "Mark Twain," taken from the leadsman's cry for two fathoms of water, in 1862.

Twain's father was a Virginia lawyer, and the family was of poor but respectable southern stock. In 1839, the family moved to Hannibal, Missouri, the Mississippi River town that provided the source material and background of some of Twain's best-known fiction. After his father died in 1847, Twain left school to become an apprentice in the printing shop of his brother Orion. From 1853 to 1856, Twain worked as a journeyman printer in St. Louis, New York, Philadelphia, Keokuk, and Cincinnati. Between 1857 and 1860, he acquired much of his knowledge of the Mississippi River as a pilot, beginning that short though richly productive career under the tutelage of a senior pilot, Horace Bixby. He was a Confederate volunteer for several weeks after the Civil War began. In 1861, he left for the Nevada Territory with his brother Orion, where he drifted into prospecting and journalism, beginning his career as a reporter with the *Virginia City Territorial Enterprise*, and continuing it with the San Francisco *Morning Call*.

Twain's literary career and the beginning of his fame might be said to have begun in 1865 with the publication in the New York *Saturday Press* of "Jim Smiley and His Jumping Frog" (later known as "The Celebrated Jumping Frog of Calaveras County"). As a journalist, he went to the Sandwich Islands in 1866 and to Europe and the Holy Land in 1867. The latter of the two provided him with the experiences which he shaped into his first book, *The Innocents Abroad*. *Roughing It*, his narrative of pioneers striving to establish civilization on the frontier, appeared in 1872, and his first novel-length fiction, written with Charles Dudley Warner, *The Gilded Age*, came in 1873.

In 1870, Twain married Olivia Langdon. After beginning their married life in Buffalo, New York, they resettled in Hartford, Connecticut, in 1871. Their infant son Langdon died in 1872, the year Susy, their first daughter, was born. Her sisters, Clara and Jean, were born in 1874 and 1880. Twain's most productive years as a novelist came in this middle period when his daughters were young and he was prospering. *The Adventures of Tom Sawyer*, *The Prince and the Pauper*, *Adventures of Huckleberry Finn*, and *A Connecticut Yankee in King Arthur's Court*, were all written during this highly productive period.

By 1890, Twain's financial fortunes were crumbling, mostly owing to bad investment in his own publishing firm and in the Paige typesetter. In 1891, Twain closed the Hartford mansion, sold the furniture, and went to Europe to economize. In 1896, after he completed a round-the-world lecture tour, his daughter Susy died, and his wife, Livy, shortly afterward suffered a nervous collapse from which she never recovered. Twain blamed himself for bringing on his beloved family the circumstances that led to both tragedies. His abiding skepticism about human nature deepened to cynicism and found expression in those dark stories of his last years, such as "The Man That Corrupted Hadleyburg," "The Mysterious Stranger," and the essay "What Is Man?" He died in 1910 at the age of seventy-four in Redding, Connecticut.

ANALYSIS

It is instructive to note that the most pervasive structural characteristic of Mark Twain's work, of his nonfiction as well as his fiction, is dualistic. That observation is not worth much without detailed application to specific aspects of particular works, but even before turning to particulars, it is useful to consider how many "pairs" of contending, conflicting, complementary, or contrasting characters, situations, states of being, ideas, and values run through Twain's work. One thinks immediately of Tom and Huck, of

Huck and Jim, of Huck and Pap, of Aunt Sally and Miss Watson, of the prince and the pauper, of the two sets of twins in *The Tragedy of Pudd'nhead Wilson*. One thinks of boys testing themselves against adults, of youth and adulthood, of the free life on the river contrasted with the settled life of the river towns, of the wilderness and civilization, of the promises of industrial progress against the backdrop of the humbler, traditional rural setting, of Eden and everything east of Eden, and, finally, of good and evil.

The tonal quality of Twain's works is also dualistic. The jumping frog story is almost pure fun. "The Mysterious Stranger," first published in bowdlerized form after Twain's death, is almost pure gloom. Most of Twain's fiction comes between the two, both chronologically and thematically. Except for *The Gilded Age*, which he wrote with Charles Dudley Warner, the novels, from *The Adventures of Tom Sawyer* to the final two, *The Tragedy of Pudd'nhead Wilson* and *Personal Recollections of Joan of Arc*, fall within the thematic and tonal extremes established by the short fiction. That is, Tom's adventures take place in the hallowed light of innocence and virtue beyond the reach of any truly effective evil forces, while Roxy's adventures in *The Tragedy of Pudd'nhead Wilson*, are of almost unrelieved gloom. *Adventures of Huckleberry Finn* is midway between the extremes, with its blending of the light and affirmation that shine so brightly in Twain's childhood idyll with the darkened vision of the later years.

THE ADVENTURES OF TOM SAWYER

Nearly everyone agrees that *The Adventures of Tom Sawyer*, Twain's second novel, is an American classic, and nearly everyone agrees that there is no accounting for its success. It is at the same time a novel of the utmost simplicity and of deep complexity. The novel is a marvelous boy's adventure story, a fact given perspective by Twain's observation that "it will be read only by adults." That is, the essence of childhood can be savored only after the fact, only after one has passed through it and can look back upon it. Popularizations of Tom's adventures are produced for children, but the continuing vitality of the novel depends upon the adult sensibility and its capacity and need for nostalgic recollection. Twain plays on all the strings of that sensibility as he guides the reader through Tom's encounters with the adult world, represented by Aunt Polly and Judge Thatcher, through Tom's romance with Becky, and finally to the adventurous triumph over evil in the person of Injun Joe.

Aunt Polly is the perfect adult foil for a perfect boyhood. Not only does she provide the emotional security that comes from being loved in one's place, but she also serves as an adult Tom can challenge through his wits, thereby deepening his self-confidence about his place in the adult world. The fence whitewashing episode is surely one of the best known in American literature. In it, Tom not only outwits his friends, whom he persuades to whitewash the fence for him, but also successfully challenges the adult world which, through Aunt Polly, assigned the "boy's chore" to him in the first place. The episode also provides Twain an opportunity to exercise his irony, which, in contrast to much that was to come in the later fiction, is serenely gentle here. Judge Thatcher represents the secure, if somewhat pompous, authority of the adult world beyond the domestic circle. The much desired recognition of that authority is achieved with decisive pomp when the Judge makes the treasure found in the cave legally Tom's and Huck's.

The romance with Becky is almost pure idyll, although the young lovers' descent into the cave inevitably raises speculations about deeper implications. While Injun Joe as evil incarnate is believable enough to raise the hair along the back of the necks of adults as well as children, especially when the last candle burns out in the cave, there is never any doubt that Tom and Becky will be saved, that good will triumph—never any doubt, that is, for the adult sensibility, secure beyond the trials and tribulations of adolescent infatuation and terror.

The book as childhood idyll is really a simple matter, but that does not diminish the significance of that dimension of the work. Rather, it affirms an understanding of the book's success on that level. There is more to be considered, however, especially in terms of the companion piece to come, *Adventures of Huckleberry Finn*. The poignance of *The Adven-tures of Tom Sawyer* is attributable in part to the fact that it is an imaginative reconstruction of youthful experience from the perspective of early middle age. The actual historical frame of the re-creation adds its own deeply poignant dimension to the book. The American national experience was clearly in the transitional state between frontier and modern society when the novel was published in 1876. Twain's idyll of boyhood is set in a time and place in history calculated to deepen the significance of the adult's backward recollection of a time of innocence and joy. The American wilderness was never Eden, but that image has haunted the American imagination from at least the time of James Fenimore Cooper's creation of his frontiersman, Natty Bumppo, down to at least the time of Robert Frost's creation of his travelers through the dark, lonely woods.

Finally, in part because it is one of those many pairings of characters so pervasive in Twain's work, Tom's relationship with his half-brother, Sid, should be noted. The relationship is instructive in that it foreshadows that of the later Tom-Huck relationship. Sid is the "model" boy who serves as Twain's foil for Tom's adventuresome independence. While Tom is never good in the subservient, lap-dog sense that Sid is, there is a kind of lateral movement of his character from the early to the later novel; in *The Adventures of Tom Sawyer*, Tom plays off the foil of Sid's pious "respectability," while in *Adventures of Huckleberry Finn*, Tom, himself, has moved over to provide a similar foil for Huck's freedom.

THE PRINCE AND THE PAUPER

Unlike its predecessor, *The Prince and the Pauper* is a "children's book" which has remained simply that, a book for children. Twain professed to have taken great joy in the writing of it, probably in part because of the relief he felt upon completing the troublesome *A Tramp Abroad*. His wife and children admired the book, as did William Dean Howells and the reviewers for the New York *Herald*, the Boston *Transcript, The Atlantic Monthly*, and the *Century*. Nevertheless, the novel holds little interest for the mature reader except in terms of its relationship to the two superior novels which preceded and followed it.

Its plot hinges upon one of Twain's most explicit pairings, that of Prince Edward with the pauper Tom Cantry. The switching of these look-alike adolescents in the England of Henry VIII allows the Prince to learn what poverty and hardship are like in the alleyways of his kingdom and the pauper to satirize, through his innocence, the foibles of royalty and court life. Neither the satire nor the compassion, however, ring true. It is almost as if Twain were finding his way from his first classic to his second through this experiment, set in a time and place far removed from his native Mississippi River valley.

With that contrast in mind, it is perhaps reasonable to see the prince and the pauper as another Sid and Tom, another Tom and Huck, all of the sets representing at various removes those two basic drives of Twain's nature for respectability and freedom. Huck and Tom Cantry, the pauper, are "freer" than are Tom and Prince Edward, although the relationships are not that simple, since the members of each pair are attracted like magnetic opposites to their mates. This attraction is made most explicit in *The Prince and the Pauper*, where the two actually exchange places. Later in his career, in *The Tragedy of Pudd'nhead Wilson*, Twain made a comparably explicit exchange with wholly tragic consequences. In *The Prince and the Pauper*, it is all play with little consequence at all except for the exigencies of a contrived, melodramatic plot. Twain's truest pairing, that of Huck and Jim, was yet ahead of him.

ADVENTURES OF HUCKLEBERRY FINN

Adventures of Huckleberry Finn is almost universally hailed as Twain's best book, as well as one of the half dozen or so American classics of the nineteenth century. This is not to say that the novel is without defects. The ending, in particular, presents some very real problems, structurally, thematically, and rhetorically. The very high place of the novel, however, is generally conceded. This success depends upon several considerations. In the first place, the novel continues the mythic idyll of American boyhood begun with *The Adventures of Tom Sawyer*. That connection and that continuation by itself would have insured the book a place in the national archives if not the national heart. Most agree, however, that its

success derives from even deeper currents. *Adventures of Huckleberry Finn* is Twain's best book because, for whatever reasons, he brought together in it, with the highest degree of artistic balance, those most fundamental dualities running through his work and life from start to finish. The potentially destructive dualities of youth and age, of the need for both security and freedom, of the wilderness and civilization, of innocence and corruption, all are reconciled by means of an aesthetic transformation. Historical, realistic dualities as well as psychological and moral dualities are brought into an artistic synthesis, into a novel, the most distinctive feature of which, finally, is its own modal duality, played out in the terms of a delicate balance between lyricism and satire.

Huck's relationship with Jim, the runaway slave, is central to the novel's narrative, to its structure, and to its theme. Escaping "down" the river, a cruel irony in itself, provides the episodic structure, which is the narrative thread that holds together the developing relationship between the two runaways on the raft. The escape, the quest for freedom, is literal for both Huck and Jim as they flee from Pap and Jim's owner, Miss Watson. It may also be seen as symbolic on several planes: historical, philosophical, and moral. The historical setting of the novel is that pivotal era in American history when the new nation was being carved out of the wilderness. The flight down the river is a flight from the complexities of the ever-expanding, westward-moving settlements of the new civilization. The continuing vitality of the novel depends in part upon the survival in the twentieth century of the need for that imaginative escape. Like Henry David Thoreau's Walden Pond, Huck's Mississippi River, originally an escape from what may now seem some of the simpler strictures of society, continues to serve the American psyche as an imaginative alternative to modern civilization.

The philosophical dimensions of the rapidly disappearing frontier are those of nineteenth century Romanticism. Celebrating their freedom on the raft from the legal and social strictures of the town along the river, Huck and Jim are at the same time affirming the central Romantic thesis concerning people's need to return to nature and to the natural self.

There are two kinds of Romanticism in the novel: that which Tom espouses in his adolescent preoccupation with adventure, and that which Huck practices on the river under the stars and, most significantly, in the final resolution of the problem of Jim as a runaway slave. Twain holds up Tom's bookish Romanticism as childish at best and, for the most part, as silly. This attack on Romanticism—a secondary theme in *Adventures of Huckleberry Finn*, where Twain sends the derelict steamer, the *Walter Scott*, to its destruction on a rock—was one of Twain's lifelong preoccupations. It was continued with a vehemence later in *A Connecticut Yankee in King Arthur's Court*, but its deep-running, destructive potential for Twain is harnessed in *Adventures of Huckleberry Finn*. The satire is there, but it is in the largely playful terms of the antics of the King and the Duke, their mangling of Shakespeare, and the graveyard art and poetry of Emmeline Grangerford. This playful treatment of one of his serious themes results in part from the fact that Twain is here working a deeper vein of Romanticism in the person of his supreme fictional creation, Huck.

The moral climax of the novel comes in chapter 31, when Huck decides that he will "go to hell" rather than turn in Jim. The difficulties with the ending of the book derive largely from that relatively early resolution of its central theme. Shortly thereafter, Huck is reunited with Tom, who is responsible for all the preposterous plans to save Jim, who, ironically, no longer needs to be saved. There are real problems here with the plot, with motivation, and with the prose itself, which is no longer sustained by the lyricism of Huck's accounts of life on the raft. The artistic achievement of the climax, however, makes such problems pale into relative insignificance. Twain embodies in Huck and dramatizes in his decision a principal line of American political and moral thought which has its roots in Thomas Jefferson and Thomas Paine, its "philosophical" development in Ralph Waldo Emerson and Thoreau, and its aesthetic transformation at the hands of Twain and Whitman. Huck is the embodiment of both the political and the Romantic ideals of common humanity, with no past or roots, whose principal guide is expe-

rience rather than tradition. He is one of the principal literary symbols of that fundamental American mythical dream of moral rejuvenation in the Edenic wilderness of the "new" continent. He stands at the center of nineteenth century American literature and at the center of Twain's achievements.

In *Adventures of Huckleberry Finn*, Twain's attack upon the Romantic glorification of the past is a peripheral theme. In *A Connecticut Yankee in King Arthur's Court*, it is central and devastating, both in the novel itself and in its signaling of the direction in which Twain's thought and creative energies were heading. Although this too is a boy's book of a kind, there is about it none of the idyllic radiance of *Adventures of Tom Sawyer* nor the harmonious balancing of opposites of *Adventures of Huckleberry Finn*. Rather, there is finally outright war between the forces of the feudal past and those of the progressive present, with considerable ambiguity about which is to be considered the good and which the evil.

There is no doubt that the reader's sympathies at the outset are with the Yankee mechanic, Hank Morgan, who, after a blow on the head, wakes up in King Arthur's England of 528 C.E. After saving himself from execution as a witch by "commanding" a total eclipse of the sun, he vies successfully with Merlin for power and prestige at court. He is like Huck in his commonsense responses to life in general, and in particular to the romantic claims of the feudal society in which he finds himself. He is unlike Huck in his vigorous progressivism, in his determination to bring the fruits of nineteenth century democracy and technology to feudal England. He introduces explosives, sets up schools to train workmen in the mechanical arts, gives instruction in journalism to his page with an eye to a national press, and stretches telephone lines haphazardly across the countryside. His talents, taken for magic for the most part, earn for him the title "the Boss," and the abiding enmity of Merlin, whom he replaces at court. He plans to declare a republic after Arthur's death, and the sixth century kingdom enjoys all the fruits of progress: schools, trains, factories, newspapers, the telephone and telegraph. The end of the story, however, just before Hank returns to his own century, pictures anything but the envisioned utopia. Arthur dies in a battle with Lancelot, Camelot is reduced to shambles, and Hank fortifies himself in a cave against the surviving chivalry of England. One of his final concerns is with the pollution caused by the dead bodies piled in the trenches around his fortress. The repressive, superstitious nightmare of feudal society has been compounded by the fearful efficiency of nineteenth century technology.

The ambiguity of the ending of the novel is symptomatic. The artistic balance of *Adventures of Huckleberry Finn* is no longer in evidence. Twain, always something of an allegorist, was by 1889 becoming more and more a polemicist, increasingly more interested in conflicts between abstract ideas and values than in the development and portrayal of human characters in all their complexities. Hank can be identified with Huck in terms of their common sense and their human values, but the big difference between them is that Huck's chief concern is with another human being while Hank's is with an abstraction called feudalism.

THE TRAGEDY OF PUDD'NHEAD WILSON

Twain was to do some of his most important writing in the last two decades of his life, including short fiction and social and moral criticism. His best novels, however, were completed in 1875 and in the 1880's. Of those coming after 1889, *The Tragedy of Pudd'nhead Wilson* is the most readable and the most consistent with the principal direction of his deepening cynicism about the "damned human race." The novel's only really interesting character is Roxy, a slave woman who switches her son with that of her owner Percy Driscoll to save her child from eventually being sold "down river." The whole of the dark tale that follows indicates, in Maxwell Geismar's words, how much "irony and tragedy have taken over the center stage in [Twain's] comic proscenium of life."

Lloyd N. Dendinger

OTHER MAJOR WORKS

SHORT FICTION: *The Celebrated Jumping Frog of Calaveras County, and Other Sketches*, 1867; *Mark Twain's Sketches: New and Old*, 1875; *The Stolen White Elephant and Other Stories*, 1882; *The £1,000,000 Bank-Note and Other New Stories*, 1893; *The Man That Corrupted Hadleyburg and Other Stories and Essays*, 1900; *A Double-Barrelled Detective Story*, 1902; *Extracts from Adam's Diary*, 1904; *King Leopold's Soliloquy: A Defense of His Congo Rule*, 1905; *Eve's Diary*, 1906; *The $30,000 Bequest and Other Stories*, 1906; *A Horse's Tale*, 1906; *Extract from Captain Stormfield's Visit to Heaven*, 1909; *The Curious Republic of Gondour and Other Whimsical Sketches*, 1919; *Letters from the Earth*, 1962; *Mark Twain's Fables of Man*, 1972 (John S. Tuckey, editor); *Life as I Find It*, 1977 (Charles Neider, editor).

PLAYS: *Colonel Sellers*, pr. 1874; *Ah Sin*, pr. 1877 (with Bret Harte).

NONFICTION: *The Innocents Abroad*, 1869; *Roughing It*, 1872; *A Tramp Abroad*, 1880; *Life on the Mississippi*, 1883; *Following the Equator*, 1897; *How to Tell a Story and Other Essays*, 1897; *My Début as a Literary Person*, 1903; *What Is Man?*, 1906; *Christian Science*, 1907; *Is Shakespeare Dead?*, 1909; *Mark Twain's Speeches*, 1910 (Albert Bigelow Paine, editor); *Mark Twain's Letters*, 1917 (2 volumes; Paine, editor); *Europe and Elsewhere*, 1923 (Paine, editor); *Mark Twain's Autobiography*, 1924 (2 volumes; Paine, editor); *Sketches of the Sixties*, 1926 (with Bret Harte); *The Adventures of Thomas Jefferson Snodgrass*, 1926; *Mark Twain's Notebook*, 1935 (Paine, editor); *Letters from the Sandwich Islands, Written for the Sacramento Union*, 1937; *Letters from Honolulu, Written for the Sacramento Union*, 1939; *Mark Twain in Eruption*, 1940 (Bernard De Voto, editor); *Washington in 1868*, 1943; *The Love Letters of Mark Twain*, 1949 (Dixon Wecter, editor); *Mark Twain to Mrs. Fairbanks*, 1949 (Dixon Wecter, editor); *Mark Twain of the Enterprise: Newspaper Articles and Other Documents, 1862-1864*, 1957 (Henry Nash Smith and Frederick Anderson, editors); *Traveling with the Innocents Abroad: Mark Twain's Original Reports from Europe and the Holy Land*, 1958 (Daniel Morley McKeithan, editor); *Mark Twain-Howells Letters: The Correspondence of Samuel L. Clemens and William D. Howells, 1872-1910*, 1960 (Henry Nash Smith and

William M. Gibson, editors); *Mark Twain's Letters to His Publishers, 1867-1894*, 1967 (Hamlin Hill, editor); *Clemens of the Call: Mark Twain in San Francisco*, 1969 (Edgar M. Branch, editor); *Mark Twain's Correspondence with Henry Huttleston Rogers, 1893-1909*, 1969 (Lewis Leary, editor); *Mark Twain Speaking*, 1976 (Paul Fatout, editor).

MISCELLANEOUS: *The Portable Mark Twain*, 1961 (Bernard De Voto, editor); *The Writings of Mark Twain*, 1968 (25 volumes); *Collected Tales, Sketches, Speeches, and Essays, 1891-1910*, 1992 (Louis J. Budd, editor).

BIBLIOGRAPHY

Giddings, Robert, ed. *Mark Twain: A Sumptuous Variety.* Totowa, N.J.: Barnes & Noble Books, 1985. A useful collection of critical essays about Twain and his works.

Lauber, John. *The Inventions of Mark Twain.* New York: Hill & Wang, 1990. Very well written and often humorous, this biography reveals Twain as an extremely complex, self-contradictory individual. Includes an annotated bibliography.

Long, E. Hudson, and J. R. LeMaster. *The New Mark Twain Handbook.* New York: Garland, 1985. A very useful work which discusses Twain's career, his development as a mythic figure, and the literature on his life and writings. Each section contains an extensive bibliography.

Miller, Robert Keith. *Mark Twain.* New York: Frederick Ungar, 1983. Links events in Twain's life to critical analyses of his major works and summarizes viewpoints of Twain scholars. Miller also offers his own conclusions about Twain's attitudes. Includes a helpful chronological table.

Paine, Albert Bigelow. *Mark Twain: A Biography.* 3 vols. New York: Harper and Brothers, 1912. Though long out of print, this remains the standard, and best, biography of Twain.

Rasmussen, R. Kent. *Mark Twain A-Z.* New York: Facts on File, 1995. An impressive reference tool. Virtually every character, theme, place, and biographical fact can be researched in this compendious volume. Contains a complete chronology.

ANNE TYLER

Born: Minneapolis, Minnesota; October 25, 1941

PRINCIPAL LONG FICTION

If Morning Ever Comes, 1964
The Tin Can Tree, 1965
A Slipping-Down Life, 1970
The Clock Winder, 1972
Celestial Navigation, 1974
Searching for Caleb, 1976
Earthly Possessions, 1977
Morgan's Passing, 1980
Dinner at the Homesick Restaurant, 1982
The Accidental Tourist, 1985
Breathing Lessons, 1988
Saint Maybe, 1991
Ladder of Years, 1995
A Patchwork Planet, 1998

OTHER LITERARY FORMS

In addition to her novels, Anne Tyler published more than forty short stories, including several in *Harper's*, *Mademoiselle*, *The New Yorker*, *Seventeen*, and the *Southern Review*. There is no collection to date, although two stories appeared in the O. Henry Prize volumes for 1969 and 1972 and others in the first edition of the Pushcart Prize anthology (1976), *Best American Short Stories* (1977), *Stories of the Modern South* (1978, 1981), *The Editor's Choice: New American Stories* (1985), *New Women and New Fiction* (1986), *Louder than Words* (1989), and several anthologies of American literature published by major publishing houses for use in college and university courses. Tyler also wrote several autobiographical and personal essays, one for *The Washington Post* in 1976 and another for *The Writer on Her Work* (1980), edited by Janet Sternburg. In 1975, her reviews of current fiction, criticism, and biography began appearing in major newspapers and magazines, including the *Boston Globe*, the *Chicago Sun-Times* and the *Chicago Tribune*, the *Detroit News*, *The New Republic*, *The New York Times Book Review*, *USA Today*, and *The Washington Post*.

ACHIEVEMENTS

Despite praise for the truth of her characterizations and her eye for details, Tyler did not receive much national recognition for her fiction until the publication of her sixth novel, *Searching for Caleb*. Prior to 1976, the largest segment of her audience was in the South, although her short stories appeared in prestigious national magazines throughout the 1960's and 1970's. All of her novels except *A Slipping-Down Life* have been published abroad. Besides English editions, translations into Danish, French, German, Italian, and Swedish have appeared. Still, the American academic and critical communities were slow to appreciate Tyler's work. Her strong supporters include John Updike, who favorably reviewed her novels for *The New Yorker*, beginning with *Searching for Caleb*, and Reynolds Price, Tyler's professor at Duke University, who also reviewed her work.

In 1976, Tyler began to receive increasing recognition. In 1977, the American Academy and Institute of Arts and Letters cited her as a novelist of excellence and promise. *Earthly Possessions* and *Morgan's Passing* also received largely favorable national reviews. While a few critics, including Updike, expressed some disappointment in *Morgan's Passing*, the Writers Workshop of the University of Rochester awarded it the sixth annual Janet Heidinger Kafka prize for fiction by an American woman.

With the publication of *Dinner at the Homesick Restaurant*, her first novel to make the best-sellers list, Tyler at last acquired full national stature. Benjamin DeMott's front-page notice in *The New York Times Book Review* pointed to the novel's wit and the depth of Tyler's psychological insight and characterizations. DeMott saw the book as clear evidence of Tyler's having joined the ranks of major novelists. Updike reiterated this praise, citing *Dinner at the Homesick Restaurant* as a work of considerable power. As a result of this increasing recognition and

praise, scholarly studies of Tyler's work, including her early novels, began to appear. Tyler's reputation as a major contemporary American novelist was fixed with the publication of *The Accidental Tourist*, which won the 1985/1986 National Book Critics Circle Award for fiction. The successful film version of the novel increased Tyler's popularity with the reading public. *Breathing Lessons* was nominated for the National Book Award and won the 1989 Pulitzer Prize for fiction.

BIOGRAPHY

Anne Tyler was born in Minneapolis, Minnesota, on October 25, 1941, to Phyllis Mahon, a social worker, and Lloyd Parry Tyler, an industrial chemist. She was the oldest of four children, the only girl. Both parents were Quakers dedicated to finding an ideal community, a quest that produced the theme of frustrated idealism in Tyler's fiction. As a consequence of her parents' idealism, Tyler spent most of her early years, from infancy until age eleven, in various rural Quaker communes scattered throughout the midwestern and southern United States. When

(Diana Walker)

she was six, the family was settled in Celo, North Carolina—a large, isolated valley commune virtually independent of the outside world and unquestionably the setting for Tyler's short story "Outside," which appeared in the *Southern Review* in 1971.

Tyler later wrote of the impact of her early years on her fiction. Unable to sleep at night and needing to amuse herself, she began telling herself stories at age three. Her isolation in the rural communes in which she lived as a child contributed to the themes of isolation and community dominant in her novels. Additionally, growing up in North Carolina, where she spent summers tying tobacco, she listened carefully to the stories of the tobacco handlers and tenant farmers. Later, she was able to capture the cadences of everyday speech in her fiction, realizing that the stories these workers told could form the basis for literature. She was also to rely heavily on the North Carolina tobacco country as the setting for her early novels, especially *The Tin Can Tree* and *A Slipping-Down Life*.

When Tyler was eleven, she and her family moved to Raleigh, where they finally settled into an "ordinary" middle-class existence. There, Tyler attended Broughton High School and received encouragement in her writing. She also discovered the work of Eudora Welty, which was to have great influence on Tyler's own fiction.

In September, 1958, Tyler entered Duke University as an Angier Duke Scholar majoring in Russian. She was encouraged by Reynolds Price, who taught her freshman composition and later introduced her to his agent. At Duke, Tyler helped edit the *Archive* (the student literary magazine), published three early stories there, acted in several productions of the Wesley Players, and learned a great deal about the craft of fiction from reading Leo Tolstoy and the other major Russian novelists. She twice received the Anne Flexner award for creative writing at Duke and was graduated Phi Beta Kappa, just three years after entering, in 1961.

In September, 1961, Tyler began work on a master's degree in Russian at Columbia University, an experience that provides some of the background for *If Morning Ever Comes*. She completed the course-work for the degree but quit before writing her thesis. The following summer she spent in Maine, supporting herself by working on a schooner and proofreading for a local newspaper.

In 1962, Tyler returned to Duke University as the library's Russian bibliographer. That fall, she met her future husband, Taghi Modarressi, an Iranian child psychiatry student at the Duke Medical Center. The couple married in May, 1963, three months after the publication of Tyler's first short story in a national magazine. They moved to Montreal, Canada, that spring; during their four years there, Tyler wrote her first novel, taught herself Persian in anticipation of living in Iran, and worked as a librarian at the McGill University law library. In September, 1965, she gave birth to her first child, Tezh, a girl. The publication of *The Tin Can Tree* followed the next month.

In June, 1967, the Modarressis moved to Baltimore, Maryland. While Tyler's short stories continued to appear frequently in national publications between 1965 and 1970, her third novel was not published until January, 1970, first in condensed form in *Redbook* and later that same year in its entirety by Alfred A. Knopf. Between *The Tin Can Tree* and *A Slipping-Down Life* came one other book—*Winter Birds, Winter Apples*—which was not published. A second daughter, Mitra, was born in November, 1967, in Baltimore. A dedicated mother and a productive, organized writer, Tyler managed her dual careers for years by writing in the mornings while her children were at school. Although Tezh moved to New York and Mitra to San Francisco, Tyler and her husband continued to live in Baltimore. Taghi Modarressi died there of lymphoma in April, 1997, at age sixty-five. Tyler continued to reside in, and set her fiction in, Baltimore.

Analysis

In *The Writer on Her Work*, Anne Tyler discusses the importance of her having lived as a child in "an experimental Quaker community in the wilderness." For her, this early experience of isolation and her later effort "to fit into the outside world" provided the "kind of setting-apart situation" the writer requires for aesthetic distancing. Tyler's early isolation and struggle to belong also provided both the style and material for her fiction: the ironic distance characteristic of her prose as well as the subject of the individual's relationship to the community, particularly to other members of one's own household and family. Most of Tyler's short fiction and all of her novels published to date, from *If Morning Ever Comes* to *A Patchwork Planet*, concern the intricacies of family relationships and the isolation of the individual within the family. For Tyler, families clearly provided not only her major source for learning about the world as a child, but also fertile ground for studying how people endure the pain of loss and disappointment of life, adjust to living with others, and yet continue to love. All of the major conflicts and central themes of her novels evolve from this concern with the family and the individual's relationship to the community.

In this regard, Tyler falls clearly within the southern literary tradition with its emphasis on family life and history. As Paul Binding points out in *Separate Country: A Literary Journey Through the American South* (1979), Tyler, like her mentor Reynolds Price, relies on interaction and "badinage between members of a family or between people who know one another well in order to illuminate personality." Tyler does not, however, evoke or write of a regional past. She focuses on the present, narrating the past to provide a personal or familial, not a regional, history. Nor are her characters and families symbolic figures. They are, instead, idiosyncratic personalities, truthfully depicted, memorable yet atypical. In all but her first three novels and, to an extent, *Ladder of Years*, Tyler's setting is not the small towns and rural landscapes so often considered synonymous with southern life. Rather, her terrain is the border city of Baltimore and the decay and transience of modern urban life. Price, in fact, has said that she is the closest thing the South has to an urban novelist, indicating Tyler's somewhat unusual position among late twentieth century American writers: a southerner with a traditional interest in family, community, and the past; a modern woman fascinated with change and drawn to urban life; a writer with faith in humankind's ability to love and endure yet keenly aware of

the difficulties of contemporary life, particularly the failure of communication within the family.

In her concern for familial relationships, Tyler's novels raise the existential issues of freedom and commitment. Significantly, hers is a compassionate art without explicit moral judgment—an absence of judgment for which some critics have faulted her. The effect of this gentle portrayal of serious themes is ironic: The disturbing failure of Tyler's characters to understand fully and to be understood by those they love is counterbalanced by a witty, carefully detailed style. Violence is usually absent from her work as well, and so are the grotesques found in the fiction of Flannery O'Connor and Carson McCullers. The most disfigured character in Tyler's work—Evie Decker, the fat teenager in *A Slipping-Down Life* who carves a local rock singer's name in her forehead—is compassionately portrayed. Like Eudora Welty, Tyler populates her novels with ordinary people, all of whom, she comments in *The Writer on Her Work*, are mildly eccentric in some way and "have something unusual" at their centers, something "funny and strange" and "touching in unexpected ways." From Ben Joe Hawkes in *If Morning Ever Comes*, who reads upside down to relieve boredom, to the elusive and difficult black sheep of her fictional families—Caleb and Duncan Peck, Morgan Gower, Cody Tull, and Barnaby Gaitlin—Tyler warmly and humorously portrays a wide spectrum of fascinating yet ordinary human beings.

Tyler's view of human nature, her talent for realistically capturing generations of squabbling families, her keen ear for dialogue, and her interest in character and the isolation of the individual within the family derive from various sources. Her own "setting apart" experience in the North Carolina wilderness, her early childhood habit of telling herself bedtime stories for rest and amusement, and her long periods listening to tenant farmers' stories contributed substantially to her art. Shy, quiet, and keenly observant, she listened carefully to the stories the workers told. Later, she could call up the words of her own characters. "Having those voices in my ears all day," she has written, "helped me to summon up my own characters' voices." Additionally, with Reynolds Price as her teacher and Eudora Welty as a model, Tyler saw early in her career the rich source of literary materials offered by commonplace experience. Paul Binding also cites the influence of Tyler's study of the Russian masters, particularly Ivan Turgenev and Anton Chekhov, as a basis for her tolerant and warm portrayal of multiple generations of entangled and eccentric families. Finally, perhaps most prominent is Tyler's own witness to her parents' idealism, their quest for a perfect community throughout her youth, and later their apparently easy adjustment to an ordinary existence in a middle-sized southern city. Like her own father, whom she describes in *The Writer on Her Work*, the heroes of Tyler's novels are those who are "infinitely adapting" and always "looking around . . . with a smile to say, `Oh! So this is where I am!'" They are complex people, enriched and deepened by experience—Elizabeth Abbott in *The Clock Winder*, Justine Peck in *Searching for Caleb*, Charlotte Emory in *Earthly Possessions*, Jenny Tull in *Dinner at the Homesick Restaurant*, Maggie Moran in *Breathing Lessons*, and Delia Grinstead in *Ladder of Years* best represent the type—able to enjoy life because they view themselves and others with tolerance and wit.

In an interview with Clifford Ridley for the *National Observer*, Tyler commented that she did not particularly "like either" of her "first two books" because "they seem so bland." Ben Joe Hawkes, the hero of *If Morning Ever Comes*, is "a likable guy; that's all you can say about him." While it is true that Ben Joe lacks the zaniness and interest which some of Tyler's later characters exhibit, his struggle to deal with his family, to recognize both his own independence and theirs, and to come to terms with the past and the psychological distance that isolates people even within an intimate group, provides a basis for understanding Tyler's later work and her place within the southern literary tradition. *If Morning Ever Comes* had its origins in two short stories: "I Never Saw Morning," which appeared in the April, 1961, *Archive* and was later collected in *Under Twenty-five: Duke Narrative and Verse, 1945-1962* (1963), edited by William Blackburn; and "Nobody Answers the Door," which appeared in the fall, 1964, issue of the

Antioch Review. Both involve incidents suggested by the novel but occurring prior to the time of its opening. With the novel, they indicate Tyler's strong sense of the continuity of her characters' lives.

IF MORNING EVER COMES

As in later novels, the plot and subject of *If Morning Ever Comes*, Ben Joe's five-day journey home to Sandhill, North Carolina, from Columbia University, where he is a law student, evolve from family conflict. The family of women Ben Joe has left behind— six strikingly independent sisters, a proud mother, and a spry, seventy-eight-year-old grandmother, the first of Tyler's zanies—fail to tell him what is happening at home. Jenny, the family letter-writer, is all business. No one mentions the illegitimate son whom Ben Joe's father left behind with a mistress when he died, nor the support payments Ben Joe personally delivered for years before he left for New York. The family treats lightly even the fact that Ben Joe's oldest sister, Joanne, has taken her child, left her husband, and returned home after seven years. Their behavior and their failure to understand Ben Joe's concern and worry point clearly to the theme of the individual's isolation within the family, here a male in an entire family of women.

On the surface, *If Morning Ever Comes* is a simply structured novel covering less than a week in the life of its hero. As one critic has observed, however, going home is "only partly a spatial relocation." Ben Joe, like other southern literary heroes, "from Quentin Compson to Jack Burden," must return home "to embrace the spiritual crisis" created by an unsettled past and attempt to forge a future shaped by that very past. In this regard, *If Morning Ever Comes* is clearly a southern novel. That it draws on a sharp contrast between the peaceful North Carolina setting and the briskness of New York, as well as the hero's discomfort and sense of dislocation in the North, is also suggestive of Tyler's southern literary roots.

THE TIN CAN TREE

Although not widely reviewed nor acclaimed, *The Tin Can Tree* is a moving novel which expands and deepens Tyler's treatment of family relationships and the individual's struggle to remain committed in the face of significant loss and change. Just as Ben Joe

Hawkes in *If Morning Ever Comes* remained committed to his family despite their pride and reticence, and to his father's memory despite the elder Hawkes's unfaithfulness, so also the characters in *The Tin Can Tree*, the members of three separate families sharing one house—the Pikes, the Greens, and the Potters—must deal with the commonly experienced grief at the death of the Pikes's six-year-old daughter, Janie Rose, adjust, and resume the task of living. Tyler's achievement here is that she captures eight different characters' varying responses to grief while avoiding the sentimental and maudlin. She opens the novel with the close of the funeral service, thus deliberately focusing on life, rather than death, and the resumption of the tasks of everyday living.

In addition to this theme of grief, *The Tin Can Tree* explores the background and interactions of James and Ansel Green and Joan Pike, Janie Rose's cousin. The study of James's commitment to his ailing brother Ansel, the two brothers' alienation from their family, and Joan's distance from her own elderly parents as well as her unresolved romantic involvement with James, give the novel a depth lacking in *If Morning Ever Comes*, with its heavy focus on one central character. As one reviewer noted, *The Tin Can Tree* illustrates Tyler's talent for bringing "into focus a remarkable range of human traits and emotions." Lou Pike's depressive withdrawal and immobility after her daughter's death, her husband's worried yet practical concern, their son Simon's sense of rejection and neglect, Joan's uncertainty and anger at James and his brother Ansel—all acquire full portraiture. A love of detail permeates the book, from the Potter sisters' eccentric way of wearing hats and gloves even when visiting only at the other end of the porch to the details of Janie Rose's behavior, her "tin can tree" made in honor of God during a religious period and her wearing layer upon layer of underwear on "her bad days." Such details make the characters real and Janie Rose's death more immediate and painful.

The Tin Can Tree is also the first Tyler novel to draw explicitly on the author's tobacco-field experience. Joan Pike, a school secretary, spends part of her summers handling tobacco in the warehouses, as Tyler herself did as a teenager. Besides providing elements of plot and characterization, the Tobacco Road landscape mirrors the sterility of the characters' lives following Janie Rose's death and provides a spokesman for the novel's theme. "Bravest thing about people, Miss Joan," one of the tobacco tiers says, "is how they go on loving mortal beings after finding out there's such a thing as dying." Unlike Erskine Caldwell, whose stereotypical white trash characters are often farcical grotesques, Tyler deepens the Tobacco Road landscape by a compassionate, detailed account of the grief of several families at the death of a child. Hers is a fiction of psychological insight, not a document for social change. *The Tin Can Tree*, as one critic observed, is "a novel rich in incident that details the closing of a family wound and the resumption of life among people stunned by the proof of mortality."

A SLIPPING-DOWN LIFE

In her third novel, *A Slipping-Down Life*, Tyler returned to the existential themes of the individual's isolation, his struggle for identity, and the lack of understanding and meaningful communication among people living closely together. Set in the fictional towns of Pulqua and Farinia, North Carolina—suspiciously similar to the actual town of Fuquay-Varina near Raleigh—it was the last of the Tyler's books set entirely in North Carolina but also the first to portray the barrenness of familial relationships in a clearly modern setting. While most of *If Morning Ever Comes* and all of *The Tin Can Tree* are set in peaceful, remote areas where family life, though troubled, seems unaffected by distinctly modern problems, *A Slipping-Down Life* draws heavily on the impact of modern American culture and media on family life. Also, where Tyler's first two novels covered only a few days in the lives of the principal characters, *A Slipping-Down Life* chronicles one full year in the life of its heroine—a fat, dowdy, teenage girl named Evie Decker—indicating a development in Tyler's ability to handle character over an extended period of time.

Originating in a "newspaper story about a fifteen-year-old girl in Texas who'd slashed 'Elvis' in her forehead," the novel traces Evie's barren interaction with her father, her only living relative, as well as the development and dissolution of a relationship with a local rock singer named Bertram "Drumstrings" Casey, the first of Tyler's unadmirable yet likable antiheroes—exploitative and selfish yet touchingly shy and dependent on his parents and Evie. Evie's entanglement with Drum, leading eventually to their marriage, is initiated by her carving the name "Casey" in her forehead with a pair of nail scissors, and ends with the couple's separation, the death of Evie's family, and her discovery of Casey in bed with another woman. Throughout, Evie thinks of herself as though she were acting on a stage set, taking her cues from the soap operas she watches daily with Clotelia, the Deckers' sullen maid and Evie's sometime chiding surrogate mother. Like Joan Pike in *The Tin Can Tree* and later Tyler heroines—Justine Peck in *Searching for Caleb* and Charlotte Emory in *Earthly Possessions*—Evie is an only child faced with growing up alone in a dark, stifling household and creating an identity without the companionship and aid of siblings or understanding parents.

Besides its characterizations, *A Slipping-Down Life* is also noteworthy for capturing at least part of the American experience in the 1960's: the lonely world of teenagers, the generation gap, the high school student's unending quest for popularity and romance, as well as a small town's tawdry local rock scene, featuring the chilled air in a roadside house, painfully loud music, necking couples, and the smell of stale beer. As one reviewer observed, *A Slipping-Down Life* captures "a *way* of life, a way that is tacked upon teenage bulletin boards, sewn to dresses 'decorated with poodles on loops of real chain,' enclosed in high-school notebooks containing *Silver Screen* magazine."

THE CLOCK WINDER

Tyler's first three novels all involve some type of journey home during which a central character confronts both the distance between himself and his family and the difficulties of unresolved past conflicts. Ben Joe's journey from New York to Sandhill in *If Morning Ever Comes* fits this pattern, as do James Green's trip to Caraway, North Carolina, in *The Tin Can Tree* and, in *A Slipping-Down Life*, Evie

Decker's return to her father's house following his death. A similar trip occurs in *The Clock Winder*. A novel characterized by Sarah Blackburn as having all the "virtues" of southern writing—"an easy, almost confidential directness, fine skill at quick characterization, a sure eye for atmosphere, and a special nostalgic humor"—*The Clock Winder* was at the time of its publication Tyler's most ambitious work, tracing the intricate relationships of a large cast of characters over an entire decade. It was also her first novel set in Baltimore.

The diverse, eccentric, eight-member Emerson family of Baltimore and their one adopted member, Elizabeth Abbott, clearly form one of those "huge," "loving-bickering" southern families Tyler told Clifford Ridley she hoped to create in writing *If Morning Ever Comes*. Mrs. Emerson—a skinny, fragile widow—is unrelenting in nagging her children about their neglected duties to her. She is, consequently, estranged from all but one: Timothy, a pressured medical student who, with his twin Andrew, is one of the most neurotic and disturbed characters in Tyler's novels. Into this entangled, crisis-prone family, Elizabeth Abbott brings the very skills she is unable to practice with her own family in Ellington, North Carolina. Tolerant, practical, dextrous, and witty—the first of Tyler's "infinitely adapting" heroines based on her own father—Elizabeth is a handyman and a godsend for the nervous Mrs. Emerson. In Ellington, she is a bumbler, a rebellious college dropout, and a painful reminder of failure to her minister father. Her life at home is bleak, ordinary, and restricted. Commitment to the Emersons, despite their family feuds, offers interest and freedom from the Abbott family's dicta, an opportunity to form a new identity and life free of reminders of past mistakes.

Besides expanding character, setting, and time frame, *The Clock Winder* is unusual among Tyler's first four works for its use of violence and its experimentation with point of view. Timothy Emerson commits suicide by shooting himself in Elizabeth's presence, sending her home to her family for several years. Later, after her return to Baltimore, his twin shoots her, though he causes only a flesh wound. Also, where earlier Tyler novels used omniscient point of view focusing largely on one major character—the exception is *The Tin Can Tree*, in which Joan Pike and James Green serve alternately as centers of consciousness—*The Clock Winder* shifts perspective among many characters, some of them minor. In one chapter, the reader witnesses the succession of disconnected thoughts, the confusion of physical sensations, and the temporal disorientation accompanying Mrs. Emerson's stroke. Another presents the views of the youngest Emerson, Peter, who appears only in the final chapter of the novel. These shifts in point of view result in an intimate portrait not only of the novel's central character, Elizabeth, but also of the Emersons—a varied, contrasting family of idiosyncratic individuals.

CELESTIAL NAVIGATION

With *Celestial Navigation*, Tyler moved her novels to a totally urban landscape. Eight months after the novel's publication, she told a Duke University audience that she "could no longer write a southern novel" since she had lived away from the South too long to capture realistically the "voices" and behavior of the people who live there. Set almost exclusively in a seedy Baltimore boardinghouse "smack in the middle" of a deteriorating inner-city neighborhood, *Celestial Navigation* is Tyler's portrait of the artist. It covers thirteen years in the central character's life, expanding the study of character development found in earlier novels and illustrating her increasing skill in handling point of view. The various boarders narrate firsthand their experiences and relationships to other residents. Additionally, since it focuses largely on boarders rather than kin, somewhat like *The Tin Can Tree* with its three families unrelated by blood, and since it includes the common-law marriage of its hero, *Celestial Navigation* redefines the meaning of family ties as characterized in Tyler's novels. It also intensifies the isolation of the protagonist. Jeremy Pauling, the artist-hero of the novel and the owner of the rooming house, is so reclusive that for years he has not left the city block where he lives. His principal ties are not with his two sisters in Richmond, neither very understanding of his peculiar artistic temperament, but with the boarders with whom he lives.

The caring family of boarders the novel studies, however, are essentially isolated strangers living in private rooms. They are mostly older people with severed family connections or no remaining kin. Ironically, they exhibit more tolerance and unquestioning respect for the peculiarities and privacy of one another than do many blood-related members. Mrs. Vinton, an aged spinster who works in a bookstore, stays on to care for Jeremy years after the others move or die, yet she never interrupts his trance-like states or work. With the other boarders—the elegant widow Mrs. Jarrett, the nubile Mary Tell, the young Olivia, and the fractious old Mrs. Somerset shuffling about in slippers—Mrs. Vinton is a testament to Tyler's talent for realistically capturing a gallery of idiosyncratic yet identifiably ordinary people.

The real achievement of *Celestial Navigation*, though, is Jeremy Pauling. He is one of Tyler's minor grotesques. A pale, pudgy sculptor, he rarely speaks and withdraws for days at a time to his secluded bedroom-studio. The novel works as Jeremy's story, however, partly because Tyler gives him a full range of emotions—including sexual attraction to several female boarders and a love for the children he has by his common-law marriage. She also views him with both compassion and humor and lets the reader see him from several points of view. Tyler shifts to third-person point of view to narrate Jeremy's chapters, since Jeremy himself is incapable of communicating his impressions in the coherent manner of the other characters. Tyler has said that the character of Jeremy is based in part on a shy, easily flustered little man she helped one day in the library where she worked, but she added several of her own traits to the character: a dread of telephones and doorbells (something retained from her isolated childhood) and, most important, her own artistic vision, an eye for the "smallest and most unnoticed scenes on earth," very much like those details Tyler captures in *Celestial Navigation*.

SEARCHING FOR CALEB

Searching for Caleb marked a turning point in Tyler's career. It was her first novel to receive national recognition, at a time when Tyler's own reviews began to appear in national publications. As Walter

Sullivan commented in 1977 when reviewing *Searching for Caleb* for the *Sewanee Review*, Tyler "retained" in her work "a kind of innocence . . . a sense of wonder at all the crazy things in the world and an abiding affection for her own flaky characters." *Searching for Caleb* was also evidence that Tyler had retained her southern literary roots and her delight in huge families and the range of human characters those families produce. Something of a combined family history and detective story, the novel is one of Tyler's most ambitious works, tracing five generations of one large, dichotomous, and extremely long-lived clan, the Pecks of Baltimore, from the 1880's through 1973. As in *The Clock Winder* and *Celestial Navigation*, Tyler shows her strong fascination with urban life, a result perhaps of her own early life in remote areas. She also returns to Roland Park, one of Baltimore's oldest residential neighborhoods and the main setting of *The Clock Winder*.

As the title suggests, *Searching for Caleb* involves a quest for the vanished Caleb, the great uncle of the novel's protagonists, Duncan and Justine Peck, and the half-brother of their grandfather, Daniel Peck. Representing one side of the family, Caleb, Justine, and Duncan are outcasts of a sort: spirited, talented, imaginative, and free individuals unable or unwilling to live as family rules dictate. Caleb becomes a musician, Justine a fortune-teller. Duncan, her husband and first cousin, leads an unsettled life as a mechanic and jack-of-all-trades, foreshadowing Morgan Gower, the hero of *Morgan's Passing*. Like Morgan and, later, Barnaby Gaidlu of *A Patchwork Planet*, Duncan dismays his family.

The other side of the family, the Pecks of Roland Park, headed by Daniel, are uniformly humorless and restricted. The women, though educated, are unthreatening; the men, all attorneys educated at Johns Hopkins, drive black Fords and dress in Brooks Brothers suits. They are, above all, clannish, living side by side in similar Roland Park houses. For them, family tradition and training—in effect, the past—are inescapable. Even Daniel's late-life quest for his half-brother evolves from his ties to family and an unsettled conflict. It represents a delayed response to the question frequently asked in his childhood: "Daniel, have you seen Caleb?"

Searching for Caleb, like Tyler's earlier novels, also illustrates the author's belief in the need for human adaptability, tolerance, and love. Justine epitomizes the philosophy. She weathers a dark and uncertain childhood with a depressive mother, frequent moves with her restless husband, the death of both parents and her grandfather, and the loss of her one daughter in marriage to a Milquetoast minister. Yet, she remains spirited and continues to love her family. She insists on visiting Roland Park, a longing Duncan cannot understand, and she is committed to finding Caleb, not only out of a love of travel and adventure but also to share the experiences with her grandfather and to find her own roots. With its focus on community and family and its delineation of the unsettled conflicts of the past impacting on the present, *Searching for Caleb* indicates Tyler's own roots in the family of southern literature.

EARTHLY POSSESSIONS

When it appeared in 1977, *Earthly Possessions* was Tyler's most unfavorably received novel. Among disapproving reviewers, Roger Sale in *The New York Times Review of Books* saw the book as "a cartoon" of sorts, with the life of Charlotte Emory, the protagonist, "reduced . . . by her own hand" until all "possible anguish is . . . lost." The reason for this response is no doubt the sardonic nature of Charlotte herself, an entrapped housewife who sets out to leave her husband but gets kidnapped instead in a bungled bank robbery. Such reversals characterize Charlotte's life and have led her to "loosen" her hold so that she sees everything from an ironic distance. Charlotte, moreover, is the novel's only narrator, and she tells her life-story in chapters alternating perfectly with those narrating her experiences with Jake Simms, her kidnapper, on their trip south from Clarion, Maryland, Charlotte's hometown. Along the way, Tyler captures the fragmentation and transience of modern life, reflected in a string of drive-in restaurants, banks, and films. The triumph of the novel is not, as in earlier Tyler works, characterization, but the panorama of contemporary American life that the book captures during this journey of hostage and kidnapper.

With its contrapuntal chapters, *Earthly Possessions* is Tyler's most highly structured novel, the first to be told entirely in the first person by one narrator. The result is an artificial temporal arrangement and a restricted focus, one lifetime as compared with those of eight or nine Emersons, five generations of Pecks. Also, the reader is always in the presence of two somewhat unsavory characters: a nail-biting, minor league criminal and a stoical, cynical woman. All might have come from the pen of Flannery O'Connor but for the touchingly human flaws Tyler draws. Neither Jake nor Charlotte, despite their failings, is morally culpable. What they share is a common, impractical desire for freedom from the entanglements of life: for Charlotte, marriage complete with a house full of relatives and in-laws, rooms of furniture (earthly possessions), even sinners from the mourner's bench at her husband's church; for Jake, jail for a petty crime and a pregnant girl friend. Heading south to rescue Mindy Callendar, Jake's Kewpie-doll girl friend, from a home for unwed mothers, Jake, Charlotte realizes, is like herself "criss-crossed by strings of love and need and worry." Even Charlotte and Jake's relationship grows into a type of commitment. Eventually the two share the driving as well as their troubles. Any "relationship," Tyler told Marguerite Michaels in an interview for *The New York Times Book Review*, even one "as bizarre as" that of "a bank robber and hostage could become . . . bickering [and] familiar. . . . Anything done gradually enough becomes ordinary."

Earthly Possessions, despite its problems, shares with *The Tin Can Tree* and *Celestial Navigation* a redefinition of family ties. With Tyler's other novels, it also illuminates the problems and conflicts of the individual within a close relationship, whether familial or not, and focuses on the eccentric nature of ordinary lives, the ordinariness of the bizarre.

In her eighth novel, Tyler returned to the heart of Baltimore for her setting and to a central character, Morgan Gower, who is strikingly eccentric. Reviewers compared him with Saul Bellow's Henderson and Joseph Heller's Major Major. He also resembles Duncan Peck as well as other Tyler protagonists. Like those heroes, Morgan is in conflict with his family: seven daughters who find him embarrassing, a slovenly though good-natured wife, a senile mother, and a depressed, inert sister. Like Ben Joe Hawkes, Morgan feels trapped and misunderstood in a house cluttered with "the particles of related people's unrelated worlds" and full of women with whom he is unable to communicate satisfactorily. While his family insists on going about life unconsciously, Morgan, spirited and highly inventive, faces a mid-life crisis that calls for a change. He must also come to terms with his past, the consequences of marrying Bonny for her money as well as his father's inexplicable suicide when Morgan was a teenager. Like Duncan Peck, Morgan is a kind of mechanical genius who takes up various projects, then drops them—"a tinkering, puttering, hardware sort of man." Like the renegade Pecks, he eventually abandons his Baltimore family to take up a new life and identity with a traveling amusement company.

Despite these resemblances to other Tyler heroes, Morgan is a unique creation, the product of Tyler's maturing vision of life. Her understanding of his sexual attraction to a young puppeteer and her portrayal of his frustration with his wife suggest a depth of insight into the problems of marriage, a depth lacking in the early *If Morning Ever Comes*. Morgan is also a complex character, a genuine impostor who tries on identities complete with appropriately matching costumes. At times he is "Father Morgan, the street priest of Baltimore"; at other times, he is an immigrant with family still abroad, a doctor who delivers a baby in the backseat of a car—any role in which people will accept him. Though most of this role-playing is harmless, Morgan is an antihero lacking a firm identity, a modern eccentric who revels in the anonymity and emptiness of decaying city neighborhoods and a man who assumes a false identity to take up life with another man's wife without benefit of divorce. Not surprisingly, reviewers found it difficult to like Morgan, but few found him unbelievable.

Tyler's increasing skill in capturing and making believable such a character testifies to her maturation as a writer. As John Leonard commented in *The New York Times* when reviewing the novel, readers "are obliged to care" about Tyler's "odd people" "because their oddities are what we see at an angle in the mirror in the middle of a bad night." Drawing from selected everyday scenes covering twelve years in Morgan's life, Tyler roots her novel firmly in the here and now. Morgan becomes believable because he is not always posing. He reads the morning paper over coffee, affectionately slaps his wife on her rear end, smokes too much, attends a daughter's wedding, despairs over a quarrel-filled family vacation, works in a hardware store, and comes down with a terrible cold. Tyler's is a realistic art illuminating family conflict and solidly based in the ordinary details of life.

Dinner at the Homesick Restaurant

Of all Tyler's novels, *Dinner at the Homesick Restaurant* most inspires comparison with the work of Flannery O'Connor. The title is reminiscent of O'Connor's wit and irony, and the mood of the novel, as one reviewer noted, is that of "O'Connor's Gothic South" with its "sullen, psychic menace." At her best, as in *Celestial Navigation*, Tyler captures the pain, anxiety, and isolation beneath the surface of ordinary lives. At times, however, particularly in *Earthly Possessions* but also *Morgan's Passing*, she treats this pain lightly, thus denying a sense of genuine struggle. In *Earthly Possessions*, Charlotte is flippant and ironic; in *Morgan's Passing*, Morgan is a zany, the mood quick and light. *Dinner at the Homesick Restaurant*, representing what John Updike called a "darkening" of Tyler's art, presents the other side of the coin from *Morgan's Passing*, not only in mood but also in story line. Its focus is not the husband who abandons his family to find a new life, but the family he left behind. It is a stunning psychological portrait of the Tulls, Pearl and her three children, and the anger, guilt, hurt, and anxiety they feel growing up in an uncertain world without a father. All carry their pain through life, illustrating more profoundly than any of Tyler's earlier books the past's haunting influence on the present.

Covering thirty-five years, three generations of Tulls, the novel opens with Pearl on her deathbed. This first chapter, reminiscent of Katherine Anne Porter's short story, "The Jilting of Granny Weatherall," depicts Pearl as a stoical, frightened woman who has weathered a youth filled with dread of being an old maid, a quick marriage, and a lonely struggle to rear three "flawed" children: Cody, the oldest boy, a troublemaker from childhood, "prone to unreasonable rages"; Jenny, the only girl, "flippant" and "opaque"; Ezra, his mother's favorite, a gentle man who has not "lived up to his potential," but instead has become the ambitionless owner of the Homesick Restaurant. Not one of Pearl's children has turned out as she wished. Consequently, she, like other Tyler characters, feels "closed off" from her family, the very children to whom she has devoted her life. Later chapters reveal why, focusing on each of the children in turn and tracing the evolution of their lives as well as their fear of their mother's rages. All, like their mother, end up in some way "destroyed by love."

Tyler's compassionate portrayal of her characters and her characteristic humor do mitigate the darkness of this novel. Although Pearl, her forehead permanently creased from worry, verbally and physically abuses her children, Tyler lets the reader understand the reasons for Pearl's behavior, even though he may not forgive her, and shows a far mellower Pearl in old age. Jenny, after struggling through medical school, two marriages, and a nervous breakdown, is nursed back to health by her mother. Cody spares no expense in caring for his family, even though he is unable to forgive Pearl for mistreating him as a child. The teenager Cody plays cruel but funny tricks on his brother Ezra—partly out of resentment of Ezra's being the favorite, but also from Cody's own pain and sense of rejection. Taking slats from Ezra's bed, Cody strews the floor with pornographic magazines so Pearl will think Ezra the kind of disappointment she finds Cody to be. Later, after stealing Ezra's sweetheart, he recognizes not only his guilt but also his love for his brother. These tales fill out the dark psychological portrait Tyler draws, making *Dinner at the Homesick Restaurant*, like many of Tyler's earlier books, a confirmation of life's difficulty as well as of the value of love.

The Accidental Tourist

A mood of dark comedy pervades *The Accidental Tourist*. It is the only Tyler work in which a murder occurs, and a sense of the inexplicable, tragic nature of reality moves the plot and forms a backdrop for the novel. The book opens with Macon and Sarah Leary returning from a truncated beach vacation and the sudden announcement by Sarah that she wants a divorce. Macon, the central character, is a forty-four-year-old writer of guidebooks for businessmen who find themselves in foreign places but prefer the familiarity of home. The logo for the series, entitled Accidental Tourist, is a winged armchair, a motif suggesting Macon's attitude toward the disruptions of travel. In the opening pages of *The Accidental Tourist*, the reader learns of the death of Macon and Sarah's twelve-year-old son, Ethan, who was killed in a robbery at a burger stand. Besides their grief at the death of their son, Macon and Sarah must confront the permanent jarring of their world by the random nature of the crime: The robber shot Ethan as an afterthought; Ethan and his friend had impulsively stolen away from a summer camp. With Sarah's leaving, Macon's life tailspins, yet he strives desperately to maintain control, to reduce life to its simplest terms. He sleeps in one sheet sewn together like a body bag and showers in his shirt to save on laundry. In a spirit of fun, Tyler gives Macon an alter ego, a Welsh corgi, Edward, who becomes increasingly surly as Macon's life disintegrates. Through Edward, Tyler introduces the unpredictable Muriel Pritchett, a dog trainer set on finding a father for her sickly son, Alexander.

Told from a limited third-person point of view, *The Accidental Tourist* displays Tyler's art at its best: her eye for idiosyncratic behavior and the accidental quality of reality, her focus on family as the center of life's triumphs and tragedies. The family here is not only Macon and Sarah but also Macon's siblings: his sister Rose, whose romance with Julian Edge, Macon's publisher, forms a dual plot to Macon's romance with Muriel, and his two brothers, Charles and Porter. For part of the novel, Tyler centers on the Leary siblings, all marred by their mother's carefree abandonment of them. Both Charles and Porter are divorced, and Rose now maintains her grandparents' home for her brothers. What is striking about the house is its orderliness—every item in the kitchen is shelved in alphabetical order—and its changelessness. When Macon breaks a leg in a freak accident,

he returns to his siblings and resumes life just as if he had never been married, had a child, and lived away for years. The characteristics of families, Tyler suggests, are permanently etched. It is the occurrences of life that constantly shift.

BREATHING LESSONS

In *The Accidental Tourist*, Anne Tyler depicted the dissolution of a twenty-year marriage following the violent death of the Learys' son. In *Breathing Lessons*, she presents the opposite: the duration of Ira and Maggie Moran's marriage for twenty-eight years. Told primarily through flashbacks as the couple journeys to the funeral of a friend, the novel covers nearly thirty years in one September day and contrasts the Morans' courtship and marriage with the relationship of their son, Jesse, and his former wife, Fiona. From its beginning, *Breathing Lessons* concerns not only Ira and Maggie's bickering, love, and tolerance for each other but also Maggie's struggle to reconcile Jesse and Fiona.

Set in Pennsylvania and Baltimore, the novel has three principal divisions, each told from a restricted third-person point of view. The first and third sections focus on Maggie's consciousness, while the middle section, which constitutes something of an interlude, centers on Ira's thoughts. The first section wittily depicts the music and mores of the 1950's. The second part depicts a side trip in which Ira and Maggie temporarily become involved with an elderly black man who has separated from his wife of more than fifty years. This section also provides Ira's family history and his response to his wife and children. Tyler reveals here a masterful handling of exposition through internal thought sequences and flashbacks. The novel's third section, which introduces the characters of Fiona and Leroy, her daughter, returns to Maggie's thoughts and her memories of Jesse and Fiona's relationship. A return to Baltimore with Fiona and Leroy completes the section, suggesting the cyclical nature of experience, a central theme in the novel.

In *Breathing Lessons*, Tyler continues to balance a lighthearted view of human nature with a depth of insight into the darker side of marriage. Maggie and Ira's marriage, while offering a sound balance of two contrasting personality types who can bicker and then reconcile, has its dark side also: a "helpless, angry, confined feeling" which Maggie experiences "from time to time." Ira, too, realizes that marriage involves "the same old arguments, . . . the same old resentments dragged up year after year." The joyful side of Tyler's fiction is her fondness for zany characters, her keen eye for the bizarre in human behavior, which she observes with amused detachment, and her finely tuned ear for human speech. *Breathing Lessons* offers many examples, beginning with the zesty, lowerclass names of her characters: Serena, Fiona, Duluth. Maggie herself belongs to a long line of lively, unpredictable Tyler heroines—most expert caretakers—beginning with Granny Hawkes in *If Morning Ever Comes*, Tyler's first novel. In fact, in both her acute observations of others and her repeated attempts "to alter people's lives," Maggie resembles her creator, the fiction writer who manipulates the lives of her characters to fill her plot.

Saint Maybe

The "darkening" of Tyler's work continues in *Saint Maybe* despite its lovably offbeat characters and unambiguously happy ending. Possible marital infidelity, chi¹d neglect, and suicide set the novel moving. The Bedloes are an "ideal, apple-pie" family, determined to be happy and "normal." Trouble invades their Eden in the form of Lucy, a sexy single mother who marries the elder son Danny, bringing along two young children and, most likely, another she is carrying when she meets her new groom. She also brings an insatiable restlessness. The Bedloes welcome the addition to the fold, proclaiming their son fortunate to have found "a ready-made family." It is the seventeen-year-old protagonist Ian, Danny's younger brother, who questions Lucy's virtue, a query with lethal consequences: Danny's suicide when he sees himself a cuckold and Lucy's when she forfeits a bleak future with an overdose of pills.

Guilt over the tragedy he believes he has caused drives Ian to join the Church of the Second Chance, a congregation of born-again Christians who pursue active atonement for their failings. Obsessively seeking forgiveness, Ian drops out of college at nineteen to raise his brother's orphaned stepchildren. Christ-

like, he forswears sexual activity and pursues carpentry. He leads a martyred though by no means solitary existence over the next twenty-three years. As with many Tyler heroes, Ian lacks self-awareness: He cannot recognize his own goodness, does not understand that he has paid any debt in full. Yet when at forty-two he marries Rita diCarlo, a character reminiscent of Muriel Pritchett, Macon Leary's freewheeling lifeline in *The Accidental Tourist*, Ian is delightfully surprised to realize that he has not spent his years paying a penance but leading a rich—if unorthodox—life.

Ladder of Years

Ladder of Years tells the story of forty-year-old Cordelia Grinstead's circular flight from her upper-middle-class life in Baltimore. Until she simply walks away from her husband and teenage children during their vacation, Delia has never left home. Having passively married her father's assistant, who chose her as a helpmate in assuming the family medical practice, Delia lives her married life in her girlhood home, where she suffocates under the weight of domesticity. Her presence is defined by the demands of the family she nurtures, yet her children's increasing self-sufficiency threatens her with obsolescence. Fleeing home, Delia embarks on a journey toward self-discovery, a quest reminiscent of Charlotte Emory's in *Earthly Possessions*. She initially revels in her spare new existence in a small Maryland town, but as with other of Tyler's would-be renegades from the hearth, the caregiver's habits of heart and mind reassert themselves. Realizing that she has recreated the very role she believed she had shed, Delia embraces her identity as a nurturer and returns home, aware finally of her family's genuine yet unvoiced appreciation.

A Patchwork Planet

A Patchwork Planet revisits *Saint Maybe*'s theme of debt and repayment. Black sheep Barnaby Gaitlin is a former juvenile delinquent who, to the shame of his affluent parents, was arrested in his youth for breaking into the homes of their wealthy Guilford neighbors. To keep her son out of jail, Margot Gaitlin (born Margo Kazmerow, "just a Polish girl from Canton") swallowed her pride to beg and buy her neighbors' silence. Barnaby's freedom cost $8,700, a sum his embittered mother continually holds over him. Though Barnaby eventually repays this debt, he learns that self-respect cannot be purchased.

A handyman who performs odd jobs for an assortment of crotchety yet colorful senior citizens, Barnaby stumbles across a client's "Twinform" while tidying her attic. The mannequin—shaped and painted to resemble the owner—was invented by his great-grandfather as an aid to foolproof dressing: By first modeling an outfit on a "double," one could gauge and adjust the effect of the intended apparel. Barnaby is intrigued by this premise of the trial run, and he imputes his many mistakes to his failure to hold metaphoric dress rehearsals for his life. He is convinced that he lacks necessary information for successful living, a need which prompted the boyhood burglaries during which he would examine his victims' photographs and diaries for clues to how they managed their lives. He remains rudderless at thirty, wavering between intentionally disappointing his parents through exaggerated irresponsibility and straining to please them, nearly marrying the unsuitably staid Sophia Maynard because she lends him the respectability he lacks.

Barnaby sinks to an emotional low when he is wrongly accused of theft, a crime Sophia believes him guilty of and a charge that he feels he vicariously deserves. However, in the homemade blanket alluded to in the novel's title, Barnaby finds the expansive perspective from which to accept the love and faith that his clients rightly place in him. On an elderly woman's quilt he sees that Earth is "makeshift and haphazard, clumsily cobbled together, overlapping and crowded and likely to fall into pieces at any moment." He is moved to accept and forgive his own failings as a universal condition of his humanity. The novel ends with his resolute goodbye to the girlfriend who doubted his goodness: "Sophia, you never did realize. I am a man you can trust."

Stella A. Nesanovich,
updated by Theresa M. Kanoza

BIBLIOGRAPHY

Gullette, Margaret M. *Safe at Last in the Middle Years—The Invention of the Midlife Progress Novel: Saul Bellow, Margaret Drabble, Anne Tyler, and John Updike*. Berkeley: University of California Press, 1988. Devotes a chapter, originally published as a separate essay in the *New England Review*, to Tyler's presentation of the conflicts of adulthood in her novels.

Petry, Alice Hall. "Bright Books of Life: The Black Norm in Anne Tyler's Novels." *The Southern Quarterly* 31, no. 1 (Fall, 1992): 7-13. A study of Tyler's favorable portrayals of African Americans as wise and knowing characters.

Robertson, Mary F. "Anne Tyler: Medusa Points and Contact Points." In *Contemporary American Women Writers: Narrative Strategies*, edited by Catherine Rainwater and William J. Scheick. Lexington: University Press of Kentucky, 1985. A discussion of the narrative form of Tyler's novels, focusing on her disruption of the conventional expectations of family novels.

Salwak, Dale, ed. *Anne Tyler as Novelist*. Iowa City: University of Iowa Press, 1994. A collection of essays addressing Tyler's development, attainments, and literary reputation. Contributors include John Updike and Linda Wagner-Martin. Novels discussed range from *If Morning Ever Comes*, Tyler's first published novel, to her twelfth, *Saint Maybe*.

Stephens, C. Ralph, ed. *The Fiction of Anne Tyler*. Jackson: University Press of Mississippi, 1990. A collection of essays selected from papers given in 1989 at the Anne Tyler Symposium in Baltimore and representing a range of interests and approaches.

Voelker, Joseph C. *Art and the Accidental in Anne Tyler*. Columbia: University of Missouri Press, 1989. The first book-length study of Anne Tyler's fiction, this volume focuses on the development of Tyler's aesthetics and her treatment of character, particularly her view of selfhood as mystery and of experience as accidental.

U

SIGRID UNDSET

Born: Kalundborg, Denmark; May 20, 1882
Died: Lillehammer, Norway; June 10, 1949

PRINCIPAL LONG FICTION

Fru Marta Oulie, 1907

Fortaellingen om Viga-Ljot og Vigdis, 1909 (*Gunnar's Daughter*, 1936)

Jenny, 1911 (English translation, 1921)

Varen, 1914

Kransen, 1920 (*The Bridal Wreath*, 1923)

Husfrue, 1921 (*The Mistress of Husaby*, 1925)

Korset, 1922 (*The Cross*, 1927; previous 3 novels collectively known as *Kristin Lavransdatter*)

Olav Audunssøn i Hestviken and *Olav Audunssøn og hans børn*, 1925-1927 (*The Master of Hestviken*, 1928-1930, 1934; includes *The Axe*, 1928, *The Snake Pit*, 1929, *In the Wilderness*, 1929, and *The Son Avenger*, 1930)

Gymnadenia, 1929 (*The Wild Orchid*, 1931)

Den brændende busk, 1930 (*The Burning Bush*, 1932)

Die Saga von Vilmund Vidutan und seiner Gefährten, 1931

Ida Elisabeth, 1932 (*Ida Elizabeth*, 1933)

Den trofaste husfru, 1933 (*The Faithful Wife*, 1937)

Madame Dorthea, 1939 (English translation, 1940)

OTHER LITERARY FORMS

Sigrid Undset's literary works include short stories, poetry, drama, essays, and autobiographies. In her youth, she favored shorter forms, following her first novel with a one-act play, *I graalysningen* (1908; in the grey light of dawn); a volume of lyrics, *Ungdom* (1910; youth); and four collections of short fiction, *Den lykkelige alder* (1909; the happy age), *Fattige skjæbner* (1912; humble existences), *Splinten av trold speilet* (1917; the splinter from the magic mir-

ror), and *De kloge jomfruer* (1918; the wise virgins). She wrote in German and English as well as in her native Norse, and her numerous articles, essays, and speeches reflected the major social and spiritual concerns from which her fiction grew, such as her *Samtiden* article "Nogen kvindesaks-betragtninger" ("Reflections on the Suffragette Movement") in 1912 and the collection *Et kvindesynspunkt* (1919; a woman's point of view).

The passionate interest in medieval Scandinavian history that had inspired Undset's sagalike *Gunnar's Daughter* not only led to her mammoth mature novels *Kristin Lavransdatter* and *The Master of Hestviken* but also merged with her conversion to Roman Catholicism, to which she testified fervently in the essays collected in *Kimer i klokker* (1924; the bells are ringing), *Katolsk propaganda* (1927; Catholic propaganda), *Begegnungen und Trennungen: Essays über Christentum und Germanentum* (1931; meetings and partings: essays on Christianity and Germanism), and *Etapper I and II* (1929, 1933; *Stages on the Road*, 1934). In *De søkte de gamle stier* (1936; they sought the ancient paths) and *Norske helgener* (1937; *Saga of Saints*, 1934), she explored the lives of great European defenders of the faith. As one of Nazi Germany's first and strongest opponents, Undset assailed totalitarian aims in "Fortschritt, Rasse, Religion" ("Progress, Race, Religion"), an essay that appeared in *Die Geföhrdung des Christentums durch Rassenwahn und Judenverfolgung* (1935), an anti-Nazi anthology published in Switzerland. Later, from the United States, she continued to attack Nazism and all other forms of modern paganism in the collections *Selvportretter og landskapsbilleder* (1938; *Men, Women, and Places*, 1939), *Tillbake til fremtiden* (1942; *Return to the Future*, 1942), and *Artikler og taler fra krigstiden* (1953; wartime articles and speeches). Her warm friendship with America and the American people is also reflected in her essays "Skjønne Amerika" ("Beautiful America"), "Amerikansk litteratur" ("American Literature"), and "Common Ground," all of which were written during World War II.

Toward the end of her life, Undset published several autobiographical fragments, of which the most detailed are *Elleve år* (1934; *The Longest Years*,

1935) and *Happy Times in Norway* (1942). Her last works, like her first, dwell upon her Christian Scandinavian heritage, and her last theoretical and historical essays, "Scandinavia and the New World" (in *The People's Century*, 1942), "Brotherhood," and "Scandinavian Literature," written in the early 1940's, all stress the peculiarly Scandinavian response to life she celebrated in her novels: "[The] preference for the realities of life . . . [the] interest in the innate disparities which condition our development."

ACHIEVEMENTS

The reality of Undset's early life was the necessity of leaving school and earning her living in an Oslo law office; the innate disparities between Undset and her office-mates were her ambition to write about the Middle Ages and her ability to comprehend all that she observed around her. When the draft of *The Master of Hestviken* that she completed in 1905 was rejected, Undset turned to the contemporary situations of working women with *Fru Marta Oulie*. *Jenny*, a novel depicting a woman defeated both in love and in artistic vocation, aroused indignant tirades from suffragettes. Undset attended one such meeting and noted "the essence of comedy. . . . [I] waited for them to start beating one another about the head with their handbags, but unfortunately it never got so far." Undset's bold realism offended some readers, but according to Andreas H. Winsnes, even more upsetting was her characterization of her heroine Jenny as more closely dependent on her sexual nature than are the men in the novel, a view which seemingly reduced woman's claim to equality. Despite this objection, Einar Skavlen and other Norwegian critics praised the novel's painstaking revelation of the "slow process of change" in Jenny's thoughts and feelings.

Ten years later, Undset's *Kristin Lavransdatter* and *The Master of Hestviken*, two multivolume novels treating the Norway of the thirteenth and fourteenth centuries with no less vital realism, received the highest critical acclaim and were translated into every major European language. Undset received the Nobel Prize in Literature in 1928 for these novels, and on them her reputation beyond Norway largely rests. In *Kristin Lavransdatter*, European critics recognized a new dimension of historical fiction, with insights into love and marriage realistically portrayed in the context of an essentially moral universe. With *The Master of Hestviken*, Undset achieved a still greater triumph, a profound insight into the psychological ramifications of guilt which Sigurd Hoel has compared favorably with Fyodor Dostoevski's portrait of Raskolnikov in *Crime and Punishment* (1866).

By 1945, Undset was exhausted from her own battles against Nazi Germany. She returned to Norway to find her home at Lillehammer sadly devastated by the wartime occupation, but on her sixty-fifth birthday, King Haakon awarded her Norway's highest honor, the Grand Cross of the Order of Saint Olav, "for eminent services to literature and to the nation."

(The Nobel Foundation)

BIOGRAPHY

Sigrid Undset was born at Kalundborg, Denmark, on May 20, 1882. Her father, Ingvald Undset, a famous Scandinavian archaeologist, had reacted against the provincial surroundings of his rural boyhood at Østerdal in Norway and the confining atmosphere of Norwegian Lutheranism. Undset's beautiful and intellectual mother, Anna Charlotte Gyth, had been reared by an indulgent Danish aunt and retained both a *grande dame* air and a rationalistic outlook after her marriage to Ingvald Undset, already not a well man. Not surprisingly, Sigrid Undset experienced only perfunctory religious training as a child.

In 1884, the Undsets moved to Christiania (now Oslo), where Undset's liberal parents allowed her to follow her own precocious interests. Her father's illness often shadowed the childhood memories she recorded in *The Longest Years*, which ends at his death when she was eleven, but her home was filled constantly with the atmosphere of the Middle Ages. She often read aloud to her father from medieval texts, perhaps only half understanding but wholly spellbound by the stern power and the splendor of Old Norse poetry, as in the Hávarðar Saga, which she read to him the day before he died:

> Drag Þú mér af hendi
> hring enn rauða,
> faer Þú enni engu
> Ingibjorgu.
> Sá mun henni
> hugfastr tregi,
> ǫr ǫk ǫigi kǫm
> til Uppsala.
> (Draw from my arm
> the ring so red,
> carry it back
> to Ingibjorg.
> It will be to her
> a deep-set grief,
> when I return not
> to Uppsala.)

At sixteen, Undset began to support herself and her family. Her ten years in an Oslo office made her familiar at first hand with the day-to-day struggles of ordinary women. She educated herself by reading voraciously, not only of Norway's past, but also of the history of all Western Europe; in addition, she read widely in English literature. Her first literary attempt, a long medieval novel that later evolved into *The Master of Hestviken*, was rejected, and she turned to the problems of modern women, opening *Fru Marta Oulie* with the theme of marital conflict which she never abandoned in her fiction: "I have been unfaithful to my husband."

The first phase of Undset's literary activity extended through World War I as she unflinchingly portrayed women torn between their desire for independence and their yearning to be fulfilled in love and marriage. In 1912, she had married the divorced artist Anders C. Svarstad in Belgium. Despite his impetuosity, he was highly sensitive to color and artistic technique, a quality he shared with Undset. While rearing their three children and Svarstad's three from his former marriage, Undset wrote continuously, describing herself occasionally as "a bad housewife" and criticizing the egotistic materialism of the times that led to the evasion of responsibility. She saw the unwed, self-sufficient woman as abnormal: "A woman can become nothing better than a good mother, and nothing much worse than a bad one." The moral position she was developing by 1918 depended on woman's traditional role: "The normal human being . . . has always had a central shrine, the fireside of his home, and from there he has kindled all his altar-fires."

As she worked on her great medieval novels, Undset was increasingly drawn to the altar of the Roman Catholic Church, which she already considered in 1918 "the bearer of those ideals which cannot die." Her marriage was disintegrating under insurmountable stresses, and in 1925, shortly before her formal conversion, it was annulled: "I had nothing else to do but . . . ask to be instructed in all that the Catholic Church taught as true."

Between the two world wars, Undset firmly fixed her criticism of contemporary culture upon her religious ideals. Many commentators feel the fiction she wrote during this time was impaired by her attempts to solve all human problems through the Catholic faith alone, but her essays reveal a concurrent preoccupation with the incommensurability of God and humans, the basic theme of all of her writing. By 1938, she was also able to acknowledge and praise D. H. Lawrence's recognition of "the consequences of the mechanisation of our existence—a slow death from the loss of our vital warmth."

Nazism for Undset was only one manifestation of that menace, and in her last novel, *Madame Dorthea*, she concentrated on the eighteenth century in the rationalistic spirit she had inherited from her mother. On her way to America during World War II, Undset traveled across the Soviet Union, which she later assessed as "a nationalist and imperialist state . . . under the thumb of Josef Stalin." One of Undset's last works was the deceptively childlike memoir *Happy Times in Norway*, a celebration of traditional, home-centered Norwegian culture. Upon Undset's death in 1949, she was hailed as a Christian universalist, a relentless enemy of pseudoliberalism and irresponsible individualism.

ANALYSIS

From her first work to her last, the central issue of Sigrid Undset's fiction is loyalty. At first, she depicted the loss of a wife's loyalty in *Fru Marta Oulie*, then Jenny's loss of faith in herself which led to suicide. In her epic medieval novels, Undset analyzed the development of the sense of loyalty to others, to self, and finally to God, which motivates all lesser relationships in Christian morality. Once she had accepted her religion, Undset could write, "The history of the Church is like a paradigm which illustrates the fate of the divine when it comes into human hands." Her later novels reflect contemporary concerns in her basic religious context, for as Winsnes has observed, she invariably judges the human torments of conscience that stem from disloyalty by the standard of her Catholic faith.

At the beginning of her career, Undset felt that William Shakespeare's Brutus was "the noblest figure in all literature," because when he saw he had lost everything on the field at Philippi, he "found no man but he was true to me." Undset commented in 1914, "Brutus feels such triumphant joy . . . because

he can now say for certain that disloyalty, which is for him the ugliest sin, has never come near him." Such perfect idealism, she knew, could not be found in the life she saw around her, but she developed the typical situation of her fiction from oaths, pacts, vows, and covenants upheld or abused. From the outset, she linked the abstract concept of fidelity to one of humankind's most powerful and bedeviling drives, the urge for sexual fulfillment. In "Fru Hjelde" ("Mrs. Hjelde"), one of her earliest short stories, Undset framed her message lyrically: "in the brief moment when love's caresses are new and make the blood flutter, you must understand and take control of all your life." A companion story, "Fru Waage," more realistically stresses the human need to make reparation: "better to pay for a precious hour of happiness with a whole lifetime of penance and prayer than to go on fretting oneself into grey hairs and bitterness."

The pagan Scandinavia to which her father's work drew Undset worshiped gods who knew they themselves would die in flaming *Götterdämmerung*. Because the eventual defeat of good by evil was inevitable, only the manner in which the northern hero died could matter, and the old Nordic tales resound with the song of two-handed battle swords carving bitter destiny into the personal immortality of the saga. As she immersed herself in Scandinavian folklore and history in preparation for *Kristin Lavransdatter*, her reading of the thirteenth century *Njáls saga* became a turning point in Undset's life, she said, because she recognized there the intense psychological pressure exerted on the individual by the old pagan familial society. She came to believe, as she wrote in *Saga of Saints*, that the thirst for loyalty engendered by the ancient Germanic code, however noble its individual exemplifications, was fatally limited by the lack of "a door which leads to freedom for the soul of every human being, even though his deeds . . . have their inevitable consequences and defeat here on earth."

Undset's ideal gradually changed from the pagan moralist Brutus to the Christian humanist Thomas More, who served his God before his king even unto death. In *De søkte de gamle stier*, a collection of sketches of "almost forgotten soldiers of Christ," Undset declared that the eventual victory of the good depends on "whether the wills of individual men and women are directed into an effort to do God's will— even if in life they have not been able to . . . without wavering, deviation and interruption."

KRISTIN LAVRANSDATTER

Undset's *Kristin Lavransdatter* traces the life of a well-born woman of medieval Norway through youth in *The Bridal Wreath*, maturity in *The Mistress of Husaby*, and old age with *The Cross*. As in all of her fiction, Undset's characters are developed in an immensely detailed social and cultural milieu. By the time she wrote *Kristin Lavrandsdatter*, Norwegian scholars such as Magnus Olsen and Sigurður Nordal had applied modern research methods to Scandinavian history, and Undset praised their respect for medieval documents as "examples of literary art," the basis for her re-creation of medieval Nordic life.

THE BRIDAL WREATH

In *The Bridal Wreath*, Undset simultaneously depicted youthful love and mature marriage, both impeded by the tragic consequences of broken vows. Kristin's father, Lavrans Björgulfsson, all of his life had been devoted to doing the will of God, but the wife he took at his family's wish came to him secretly flawed by a previous affair. That hidden sin had to be faced and overcome before Lavrans and Ragnfrid could die at peace with God and each other. Kristin herself is betrothed to the good though dull Simon Darre, but she forces her father to break the vow and weds instead the dashing Erlend Nikulausson, a breach of faith which haunts them the remainder of their lives.

THE MISTRESS OF HUSABY

As *The Mistress of Husaby*, Erlend's manor, Kristin bears son after son in mounting frustration at Erlend's apparent lack of concern for their future. As she labors to rear their children and improve their estate, Erlend is drawn into a gallant yet abortive attempt to free Norway from the Swedish throne. Because Erlend fails and loses his inheritance, he must live on Kristin's land; his innate nobility, however, allows him to forget old injuries to an extent that Kristin, fatally, cannot.

THE CROSS

In *The Cross*, Kristin's unwillingness to forgive causes Erlend's needless death. They are separated, and he is living at his last holding, a little hut on the mountain at Haugen, when she visits him there briefly and conceives their last child. At its birth, the country-folk accuse her of adultery, and in returning to defend her honor, Erlend is killed. Kristin's sons grow away from her, and she at last accepts the pilgrim's road to faith, dying of bubonic plague after she has nursed the poor and outcast as a lay sister in a convent not far from the road where she last saw the houses at Haugen, "high on the topmost mountain ridge."

In the story of Kristin Lavransdatter and Erlend Nikulausson, Undset championed the new, emerging Norway against the old. Kristin slowly and painfully wins her Christian faith, but Erlend perishes, unshriven, through the violence of his Scandinavian warrior's values. The old code of the sagas required the individual himself to execute the justice which he was due, but Undset's traditionally Christian orientation insisted upon the will of God before the will of people. Upon secretly plighting their troth, Erlend swears to Kristin, "May God forsake me if woman or maid ever rests in my arms, before I can possess you with law and honour." Kristin, however, replies, "May God forsake me if ever I take another man in my arms as long as I live." To Erlend, people's law and honor are tragically uppermost; to Kristin, even though she does not fully understand until she bears her own cross, God's law is finally all.

THE MASTER OF HESTVIKEN

Despite the great success of *Kristin Lavransdatter*, Undset considered the tetralogy *The Master of Hestviken* her masterpiece. Set in a slightly earlier historical period, *The Master of Hestviken* hinges on the conflict between ancient family honor and the new code in which Church and State, rather than the individual, must defend the law. While Kristin's redemption is earned by overcoming the pride that injures others, the long saga of Olav Audunssøn of Hestviken strikes inward to the tender spot of conscience, where a person stands loneliest before his God. Olav's revolt demonstrates the special Norse meaning of contrition as a power for rejuvenation.

Henrik Ibsen hinted at such pagan redemption in *Rosmersholm* (1886), when Rebecca West recognizes that "What I have sinned—it is fit I must expiate," as she goes "gladly" to her death with Rosmer. Undset carried Olav's redemption to its Christian extreme beyond physical death: "here on earth it would never be his to see the radiance of a standard under which he might fight."

THE AXE

The Axe, the first volume of the tetralogy, exposes the bloody family feuds that underlie Olav's exile from Norway and Ingunn, to whom he was betrothed as a child. Olav is nominally Christian, but when Ingunn's relatives deny their marriage, he kills one of them and must flee to Denmark. While waiting for Olav, Ingunn is trapped by a clever young rogue by whom she becomes pregnant; she confesses to Olav on his return. To preserve his own reputation, Olav secretly kills the youth who seduced Ingunn.

THE SNAKE PIT

In *The Snake Pit*, Olav returns with Ingunn to Hestviken on the Oslo-fjord, where his life comes to resemble the old carving on the hall doorpost of Gunnar of the *Volsunga saga*, stricken by the one snake he could not charm. Olav's human loyalty to Ingunn and to Duke Haakon, whom he follows on an expedition to Norway, helps him restore his estate, but this is a pale shadow of his loyalty to God as Lord, which to Olaf only confirms the old morality. He still takes no account of the man he secretly killed: "He had had to kill so many a better man in battle, and never taken it to heart." At Ingunn's death, Olav thinks of confession, but he draws back, not knowing whether something prevents him or whether "after all he dared not come forward."

IN THE WILDERNESS

Olav's middle years are spent *In the Wilderness*, as he now knows that he has chosen the path of Cain. Leaving Hestviken, he at last visits London and wins some respite from the snake gnawing at his breast: "It was not that he now thought less of his sin, but that he himself bulked far less in his own eyes." After he returns to defend Hestviken against marauding Swedes, the snake ceases to tear at his heart: "He saw now it was not his suffering that destroyed the happi-

ness of his life . . . sufferings that are of some *avail*, they are like the spearpoints that raise the shield on which the young king's son sits when his subjects do him homage."

THE SON AVENGER

The final act of Olav Audunssøn's divine comedy is *The Son Avenger*, in which Olav reaches the end of his human resources and places himself, helpless, at the mercy of God. In solemn irony, Ingunn's illegitimate son Eirik helps Olav to contrition. Olav "must stand forth and could not declare one deed that he had performed from full and unbroken loyalty," but in a final ecstatic vision, "the very rays from the source of light" high on the hill above the fjord "broke out and poured down over him." Olav's loyal spirit had bowed at last before its true Lord.

Darker in spirit than *Kristin Lavransdatter* but no less evocative, *The Master of Hestviken* displays the essentially conservative theological position Undset adopted toward the psychological complex of guilt. Other views of Olav's tragic life are possible; as Sigurd Hoel noted in 1928, both the psychological theory of dangerously suppressing one's emotions and the biological explanation that certain minds are "disposed to melancholia, remorse, and all that is tragic," but Hoel concludes that Undset regarded Olav's "fixed ideas of sin and guilt" strictly from the religious viewpoint: "Olav's fate is the fate of one who disobeys the voice of God."

The twin purposes of Christianity and realism animated all of Undset's work. Inspired by the intense attention to detail, the concentration upon personal loyalty, and the breadth of background of the Scandinavian family saga, she joined to these the considerable insight she achieved through her acceptance of Catholic tradition. She felt herself more at home in the Middle Ages than in modern civilization, and through her vividly realized characterizations of Kristin Lavransdatter and Olav Audunssøn and the wealth of their environments no less than by her contemporary novels, she achieved a moral refuge for all who seek the personal relationship of faith, the only fellowship she thought worthwhile: the fellowship of individual souls in God.

Mitzi M. Brunsdale

OTHER MAJOR WORKS

SHORT FICTION: *Den lykkelige alder*, 1909; *Fattige skjæbner*, 1912; *Splinten av trold speilet*, 1917; *De kloge jomfruer*, 1918; *Four Stories*, 1969.

PLAY: *I graalysningen*, wr. 1908 (one act).

POETRY: *Ungdom*, 1910.

NONFICTION: *Et kvindesynspunkt*, 1919; *Kimer i klokker*, 1924; *Katolsk propaganda*, 1927; *Etapper I and II*, 1929, 1933 (*Stages on the Road*, 1934); *Begegnungen und Trennungen: Essays über Christentum und Germanentum*, 1931; *Elleve år*, 1934 (*The Longest Years*, 1935); *De søkte de gamle stier*, 1936; *Norske helgener*, 1937 (*Saga of Saints*, 1934); *Selvportretter og landskapsbilleder*, 1938 (*Men, Women, and Places*, 1939); *Happy Times in Norway*, 1942; *Tillbake til fremitiden*, 1942 (*Return to the Future*, 1942); *Artikler og taler fra krigstiden*, 1953.

BIBLIOGRAPHY

Bayerschmidt, Carl F. *Sigrid Undset*. New York: Twayne, 1970. An introductory study, with chapters on the life, early works, social novels, middle age, and later novels. Includes notes and bibliography.

Beyer, Harald. *A History of Norwegian Literature*. Edited and translated by Einar Haugen. New York: New York University Press, 1956. See Harald Beyer's succinct essay on Undset's place in the history of Norwegian realism.

Brunsdale, Mitzi. *Sigrid Undset: Chronicler of Norway*. New York: Berg, 1988. Provides a useful introduction to Norway and Norwegian literature, a short biography of Undset, analysis of her early novels and later masterpieces, and a final chapter assessing her achievement. With chronology, notes, and a bibliographical essay.

Gustafson, Alrik. *Six Scandinavian Novelists*. Minneapolis: University of Minnesota Press, 1968. Gustafson criticizes many of Undset's beliefs—particularly concerning religious matters—but he is a subtle interpreter of her fiction.

Hudson, Deal W., ed. *Sigrid Undset on Saints and Sinners—New Translations and Studies: Papers Presented at a Conference Sponsored by the Wethersfield Institute, New York City, April 24,* 1993. San Francisco: Ignatius Press, 1993. Contains essays entitled "A Life of Sigrid Undset," "Sigrid Undset: Holiness and Culture," and "In the Blood: The Transmission of Sin in *The Master of Hestviken*."

Lytle, Andrew. *Kristin: A Reading*. Columbia: University of Missouri Press, 1992. Lytle's reading aims to recover an appreciation for what he deems a neglected twentieth century classic. Lytle, a novelist and critic, provides an especially sensitive, indeed a model, reading of a complex literary work.

Solbakken, Elisabeth. *Redefining Integrity: The Portrayal of Women in the Contemporary Novels of Sigrid Undset*. New York: Peter Lang, 1992. Examines Undset's feminism and treatment of female characters in the long fiction.

Winsnes, A. H. *Sigrid Undset: A Study in Christian Realism*. Reprint. Westport, Conn.: Greenwood Press, 1970. A reprinting of this 1953 critical study, which is an accessible biography that illuminates the backgrounds of many of Undset's important novels. Written in consultation with Undset.

JOHN UPDIKE

Born: Shillington, Pennsylvania; March 18, 1932

PRINCIPAL LONG FICTION

The Poorhouse Fair, 1959
Rabbit, Run, 1960
The Centaur, 1963
Of the Farm, 1965
Couples, 1968
Bech: A Book, 1970
Rabbit Redux, 1971
A Month of Sundays, 1975
Marry Me: A Romance, 1976
The Coup, 1978
Rabbit Is Rich, 1981
Bech Is Back, 1982

The Witches of Eastwick, 1984
Roger's Version, 1986
S., 1988
Rabbit at Rest, 1990
Memories of the Ford Administration,
   1992
Brazil, 1994
In the Beauty of the Lilies, 1996
Toward the End of Time, 1997
Bech at Bay: A Quasi-Novel, 1998
Gertrude and Claudius, 2000

(Davis Freeman)

OTHER LITERARY FORMS

Since publishing his first story in *The New Yorker* in 1954, Updike has truly become a man of letters, publishing in virtually every literary genre—poetry, short fiction, novel, essay, drama, art criticism, and autobiography. His first short-story collection, *The Same Door*, appeared in 1959; many more followed, including *The Afterlife and Other Stories* in 1994. Updike's play *Buchanan Dying* was published in 1974. His poetry has appeared in many volumes of his own, beginning with *The Carpentered Hen, and Other Tame Creatures* (1958), as well as in anthologies. Updike published his first nonfiction prose collection in 1965; most of his nonfiction works are collections of essays and criticism, but the autobiographical *Self-Consciousness: Memoirs* appeared in 1989 and the single-themed *Golf Dreams: Writings on Golf* was published in 1996.

ACHIEVEMENTS

One of the major figures to emerge in American fiction after World War II, John Updike is widely acclaimed as one of the most accomplished stylists and prolific writers of his generation. Showing remarkable versatility and range, his fiction represents a penetrating chronicle in the realist mode of the changing morals and manners of American society. Updike's work has met with both critical and popular success. His first novel, *The Poorhouse Fair*, was awarded the Rosenthal Award of the National Institute of Arts and Letters in 1960. In 1964, he received the National

Book Award for *The Centaur*. He was elected the same year to the National Institute of Arts and Letters. A number of his short stories have won the O. Henry Prize for best short story of the year and have been included in the yearly volumes of *Best American Short Stories*. In 1977, he was elected to the prestigious American Academy of Arts and Letters. In 1981, his novel *Rabbit Is Rich* won the Pulitzer Prize for Fiction and the American Book Award. That same year, he was awarded the Edward MacDowell Medal for literature. While Updike's novels continue the long national debate on the American civilization and its discontents, perhaps more significant is their depiction of restless and aspiring spirits struggling within the constraints of flesh, of time and gravity—lovers and battlers all. For Updike (writing about the novel in an essay), "Not to be in love, the capital N novel whispers to capital W western man, is to be dying."

BIOGRAPHY

The only child of Wesley and Linda Grace (née Hoyer) Updike, John Updike spent the first thirteen years of his life living with his parents and grandparents in his maternal grandparents' home in Shillington, Pennsylvania, in rather strained economic conditions. In 1945, the Updikes had to move to the family farm in Plainville, ten miles away from Shillington. Updike's father supported the family on his meager salary as a mathematics teacher at the high school. His mother had literary aspirations of her own and later became a freelance writer. A number of short stories, such as "Flight," and the novels *The Centaur* and *Of the Farm* drew upon this experience. As a youth, Updike dreamed of drawing cartoons and writing for *The New Yorker*, an ambition he fulfilled in 1955. Updike went to Harvard University in 1950 on a full scholarship, majoring in English. He was editor of the Harvard *Lampoon* and was graduated in 1954 with highest honors. In 1953, he married Radcliffe student Mary Pennington, the daughter of a Unitarian minister; they were to have four children.

After a year in Oxford, England, where Updike studied at the Ruskin School of Drawing and Fine Art, he returned to the United States to a job offered him by E. B. White as a staff writer with *The New Yorker*, for which he wrote the "Talk of the Town" column. In April of 1957, fearing the city scene would disturb his development as a writer, Updike and his family left New York for Ipswich, Massachusetts, where he would live for the next seventeen years and which would serve as the model for the settings of a number of stories and novels. During this time, Updike was active in Ipswich community life and regularly attended the Congregational Church. In 1974, the Updikes were divorced. In 1977, Updike remarried, and he and his new wife, Martha Bernhard, settled in Georgetown, Massachusetts.

During the late 1950's and early 1960's, Updike faced a crisis of faith prompted by his acute consciousness of death's inevitability. The works of such writers as Søren Kierkegaard and, especially, Karl Barth, the Swiss orthodox theologian, helped Updike come to grips with this fear and to find a basis for faith. Religious and theological concerns pervade Updike's fiction. In a real sense, like Nathaniel Hawthorne's writing more than one hundred years earlier, Updike's fiction explores for his time the great issues of sin, guilt, and grace—of spiritual yearnings amid the entanglements of the flesh.

Updike's success as a writer enabled him to travel under government auspices. In 1964-1965, Updike traveled to Russia, Romania, Bulgaria, and Czechoslovakia as part of the U.S.S.R.-U.S. Cultural Exchange Program. In 1973, he traveled and lectured as a Fulbright lecturer in Ghana, Nigeria, Tanzania, Kenya, and Ethiopia. Updike's Bech novels and *The Coup* reflect those journeys.

ANALYSIS

A writer with John Updike's versatility and range, whose fiction reveals a virtual symphonic richness and complexity, offers readers a variety of keys or themes with which to explore his work. The growing and already substantial body of criticism Updike's work has engendered, therefore, reflects a variety of approaches. Alice and Kenneth Hamilton were among the first critics to give extensive treatment to the religious and theological elements in Updike's fiction. Rachel Burchard explores Updike's fiction in terms of its presentations of authentic quests for meaning in our time, for answers to age-old questions about humanity and God, and of its affirmation of human worth and hope despite the social and natural forces threatening defeat of the human enterprise. Considering technique as well as theme, Larry Taylor treats the function of the pastoral and antipastoral in Updike's fiction and places that treatment within a long tradition in American literature. British critic Tony Tanner discusses Updike's fiction as depicting the "compromised environment" of New England suburbia—the fear and dread of decay, of death and nothingness, and the dream of escaping from the complications of such a world. Edward Vargo focuses upon the recurrence of ritualistic patterns in Updike's fiction, the struggle to wrest something social from an increasingly secularized culture. Joyce Markle's thematic study of Updike's fiction sees a conflict between "Lovers," or Life-givers, and the embodied forces of convention, dehumanizing belief, and death.

In a 1962 memoir entitled "The Dogwood Tree: A Boyhood," Updike discusses his boyhood fascination with what he called the "Three Great Secret Things: Sex, Religion, and Art." Critic George W. Hunt contends that "these three secret things also characterize the predominant subject matter, thematic concerns, and central questions found throughout his adult fiction." Detailing Updike's reliance upon the ideas of Søren Kierkegaard and Karl Barth, Hunt's study is interested in the religious implications of Updike's work. A more sociological interest informs Philip Vaughan's study of Updike's fiction, which, to Vaughan, provides readers with valid depictions of the social conditions—loneliness, isolation, aging, and morality—of our time. David Galloway sees Updike's fiction in existential terms, seeing Updike's protagonists as "absurd heroes" seeking meaning in an inhospitable universe. More impressionistic but quite suggestive is Elizabeth Tallant's short study of the fate of Eros in several of Updike's novels. Believing that a thesis or thematic approach does not do full justice to Updike's work, Donald J. Greiner examines Updike's novels more formalistically in order to "discuss the qualities that make Updike a great writer."

Using a comparative approach, George Searles discusses Philip Roth and Updike as important social realists whose work gives a true sense of life in the last half of the twentieth century. To Searles, Updike's overriding theme is cultural disintegration—questing but alienated protagonists confronting crises caused by a breakdown of the established order. Jeff Campbell uses Updike's long poem *Midpoint* (1969) as a key to an analysis of Updike's fiction. Seeing Updike as an "ironist of the spiritual life," Ralph C. Wood discusses Updike's fiction—along with the fiction of Flannery O'Connor, Walker Percy, and Peter De Vries—as depicting the "comedy of redemption," a study deeply indebted to the theology of Karl Barth.

In a compendious study of American fiction since 1940, Frederick R. Karl offers a useful overview of Updike: "Updike's fiction is founded on a vision of a compromised, tentative, teetering American, living in suburban New England or in rural Pennsylvania; an American who has broken with his more disciplined forebears and drifted free, seeking self-fulfillment

but uncertain what it is and how to obtain it." While this rather global description fairly represents the recurring condition in most of Updike's novels, it does not do justice to the complex particularities of each work. Nevertheless, it does point to the basic predicament of nearly all of Updike's protagonists—that sense of doubleness, of the ironic discrepancy of the fallen creature who yet senses, or yearns for, something transcendent. Updike's people are spiritual amphibians—creatures in concert with two realms, yet not fully at home in either. Updike employs an analogous image in his novel *The Centaur*—here is a creature that embodies the godly with the bestial, a fitting image of the human predicament in Updike's fiction. His fiction depicts the ambiguity of the "yes-but" stance toward the world, similar to the paradox of the "already and the not-yet." In his fine story "The Bulgarian Poetess" (1966), Updike writes: "Actuality is a running impoverishment of possibility." Again there is a sense of duplicity, of incompleteness. In such a world, problems are not always solved; they are more often endured if not fully understood. Yet even the curtains of actuality occasionally part, unexpectedly, to offer gifts, as Updike avers in his preface to *Olinger Stories: A Selection* (1964)—such gifts as keep alive a vision of wholeness in an often lost and fragmented world.

THE POORHOUSE FAIR

Updike's first novel, *The Poorhouse Fair*, may seem anomalous in comparison with the rest of his work. In fact, the novel depicts a collision of values that runs throughout Updike's work. As in so much of Updike's fiction, the novel is concerned with decay, disintegration, a loss or abandonment of vital traditions, of values, of connection to a nurturing past. This opposition is embodied in the two principal characters: ninety-four-year-old John Hook, former teacher and resident of the poorhouse, and Stephen Conner, the poorhouse's prefect. The novel is set in the future, sometime in the late 1970's, when want and misery have virtually been eliminated by a kind of humanistic socialism. Such progress has been made at a price: sterility, dehumanization, spiritual emptiness, and regimentation. In a world totally run by the head, the heart dies. Hook tells Conner, in response to the prefect's avowed atheism: "There is no goodness, without belief." Conner's earthly paradise is a false one, destroying what it would save. The former prefect, Mendelssohn, sought, as his name would suggest, to fulfill the old people's spiritual needs in rituals and hymn singing.

Out of frustration with Conner's soulless administration, the old people break into a spontaneous "stoning" of Conner in the novel's climax. In effect, Conner is a corrupt or perverted martyr to the new "religion" of godless rationalism. The incident symbolizes the inherent desire and need for self-assertion and individualism. Conner's rationalized system is ultimately entropic. The annual fair is symbolic of an antientropic spirit in its celebration of the fruits of individual self-expression—patchwork quilts and peach-pit sculptures. In its depiction of an older America—its values of individuality, personal dignity, and pride—being swallowed up by material progress and bureaucratic efficiency, the novel is an "old" and somber book for a young author to write. In effect, Updike depicts an America become a spiritual "poorhouse," though materially rich. It is Hook, one of the last links to that lost America, who struggles at the end for some word to leave with Conner as a kind of testament, but he cannot find it.

THE CENTAUR

In a number of stories and the novels *The Centaur* and *Of the Farm*, Updike draws heavily upon his experiences growing up in Shillington, Pennsylvania. Both novels—though very different from each other—concern the reckoning of a son with a parent, in the case of *The Centaur* with his father and in *Of the Farm* with his mother, before he can proceed with his life. This is emotional and spiritual "homework" necessary for the son's passage to maturity, to freedom from the past, yet also to a new sense of responsibility. As in all Updike's fiction, this passage is difficult, complex, and ambiguous in its resolution.

The Centaur is arguably Updike's most complex novel, involving as it does the complicated interweaving of the myth of Chiron the centaur with the story of an adolescent boy and his father one winter in 1947. Although the novel won the National Book

Award, its reception was quite mixed. A number of reviewers thought the use of myth to be pretentious and not fully realized, while others praised the author's achievement. The novel is part *Bildungsroman*, a novel of moral education, and part *Künstlerroman*, a novel of an artist seeking his identity in conflict with society and/or his past. Operating on different levels, temporally and spatially, the nine chapters of the novel are a virtual collage, quite appropriate for the painter-narrator, nearly thirty, self-described as a "second-rate abstract expressionist," who is trying to recover from his past some understanding that might clarify and motivate his artistic vocation. Peter Caldwell, the narrator, reminisces to his black mistress in a Manhattan loft about a three-day period in the winter of 1947, fourteen years earlier. On the realistic level, Peter tells the story of his self-conscious adolescence growing up an only child, living on a farm with his parents and Pop Kramer, his grandfather. His father is the high school biology teacher and swim coach, whose acts of compassion and charity embarrass the boy. On the mythic level, the father is depicted as Chiron the centaur, part man and part stallion, who serves as mentor to the youthful Greek heroes. As such, he suffers for his charges. By moving back and forth between the mythic and the realistic levels, Peter is able to move to an understanding of his father's life and death and to a clarification of his own vocation.

Just as Chiron sacrifices his immortality—he accepts death—so that Prometheus may be free to live, so too does George give his life for his son. While George is obsessed with death, it is doubtful that his sacrifice takes the form of death. Rather, his sacrifice is his willingness to go on fulfilling his obligations to his family. In reflecting upon this sacrifice by his father, Peter, feeling a failure in his art, asks: *"Was it for this that my father gave up his life?"* In the harsh reappraisal his memory provides, Peter is learning what he could not know as an adolescent. Love, guilt, and sacrifice are somehow inherent in the very structure of life. It is this that his mythicized father reveals to him in the very act of his narrating the story. For many critics, George Caldwell's sacrificial act frees the son to resume his artistic vocation with courage.

For others, the novel is a mock epic showing in Peter the artist, the son of a scientist father and the grandson of a preacher, a loss of the metaphoric realm that makes great art possible and that leaves Peter diminished by his confinement to the earth alone. However the end is taken, the mythic element of the narrative richly captures the doubleness of human existence so pervasive in Updike's fictions.

OF THE FARM

A short novel, *Of the Farm* is another tale of the intricacy of love, guilt, sacrifice, and betrayal. In *The Centaur*, Peter Caldwell, stalled and failing in his artistic vocation, goes home through a creative act of the memory and imagination to recover his lost vision, a basis to continue his work. Peter can fulfill his Promethean charge because his father was Chiron. In contrast, *Of the Farm*'s Joey Robinson goes home to get his mother's blessing on his recent remarriage. Joey seeks forgiveness of the guilt he bears for the acts of betrayal that have constituted his life. He betrays his poetic aspirations by becoming an advertising executive and betrays his marriage to Joan and his three children through adultery and divorce. Bringing home for his domineering mother's approval his sensuous new wife, Peggy, sets the stage for more betrayals and recriminations. As the weekend progresses, Peggy and Joey's mother vie for Joey's soul. Joey cannot please both women or heal the wounds of his past betrayals. For Joey, Peggy is the "farm" he wishes to husband. At the end, failing to win his mother's blessing, Joey and Peggy return to their lives in the city, leaving Joey's mother to die amid the memorials of her own unrealized dreams. If the novel is an exploration of human freedom, as the epigraph from Jean-Paul Sartre would suggest, the reader sees that freedom escapes all the characters, bound as they are by conflicting desires, guilt, and obligation.

RABBIT, RUN

When Updike published *Rabbit, Run* in 1960, a story of an ex-basketball player and his floundering marriage set in the late 1950's, he had no intention of writing a sequel. Yet, Updike returned to Harry "Rabbit" Angstrom once every ten years for four novels—*Rabbit Redux* (1971), *Rabbit Is Rich* (1981),

and *Rabbit at Rest* (1990)—as a kind of gauge of the changes occuring in American culture. This series of novels is among the most popular of his work.

For *Rabbit, Run*, Updike uses a quote from Pascal for an epigraph: "The motions of Grace, the hardness of heart; external circumstances." Updike has commented that those three things describe our lives. In a real sense, those things also describe the basic movements and conflicts in the Rabbit novels. From *Rabbit, Run* to *Rabbit at Rest*, as the titles themselves suggest, Rabbit's life has been characterized by a series of zigzag movements and resistances and yearnings, colliding, often ineffectually, with the external circumstances of a fast-paced and changing world. *Rabbit, Run* takes place in the late 1950's, when Harry Angstrom, a former high school basketball great nicknamed Rabbit, at twenty-six finds himself in a dead-end life: with a job selling items in a dime store and a marriage to a careless and boozy woman. Wounded by the stifling boredom of everyday life and the cloying pressures of conforming and adapting to his environment, so characteristic of the 1950's, Harry wonders, confusingly, what has happened to his life. The disgust he feels about his present life is aggravated by his memories of when he was "first-rate at something" as a high school basketball great. Out of frustration, Rabbit bolts from his life-stifling existence, feeling that something out there wants him to find it. The novel is the study of this nonhero's quest for a nonexistent grail. Rabbit's zigzagging or boomeranging movements from wife Janice to mistress Ruth, the part-time prostitute, wreaks havoc: Janice accidentally drowns the baby; Ruth is impregnated and seeks an abortion. Pursued by the weak-faithed, do-gooder minister Eccles and failed by his old coach Tothero, Rabbit has no one to whom he can turn for help. Rabbit, like so many of Updike's protagonists, is enmeshed in the highly compromised environment of America, locked in the horizontal dimension yet yearning for something transcendent, the recovery of the vertical dimension. For Rabbit, the closest he can come to that missing feeling is sex, the deep mysteries of the woman's body replacing the old revelations of religion. Rabbit, though irresponsible, registers his refusal to succumb to such a world through movement, his running replacing the lost territories of innocent escape.

RABBIT REDUX

Ten years later, in *Rabbit Redux*, Rabbit has stopped running. He is back home with Janice and works as a typesetter. It is the end of the 1960's, and Rabbit watches the Moon landing on television as well as the upheavals of civil rights, campus demonstrations, and the Vietnam War. Rabbit feels that the whole country is doing what he did ten years earlier. As Janice moves out to live with her lover Stavros, Rabbit and his son Nelson end up as hosts to Jill, a runaway flower-child, and a bail-jumping Vietnam veteran and black radical named Skeeter. This unlikely combination allows Updike to explore the major cultural and political clashes of the 1960's. This time Rabbit is more a passive listener-observer than an activist searcher. Skeeter's charismatic critiques of the American way of life challenge Rabbit's unquestioning patriotism and mesmerize him. As a result, Rabbit is helpless when disaster comes—his house is set on fire and Jill dies inside. Rabbit helps Skeeter escape. Fearing for her lover's heart, Janice returns to Rabbit. Unlike the restless figure of the first novel, Rabbit now seems to have capitulated or resigned himself to those powerful "external circumstances" from which he once sought escape. Rabbit bears witness, numbingly, to a disintegrating America, even as it puts a man on the Moon. America's spiritual landscape is as barren as that on the Moon. The novel ends with Rabbit and Janice asleep together. Perhaps they can awake to a new maturity and sense of responsibility for what they do in the world.

RABBIT IS RICH and RABBIT AT REST

In the first two Rabbit novels, Rabbit was out of step with the times—running in the placid 1950's, sitting in the frenetic 1960's. In *Rabbit Is Rich*, he is running again, but this time in tune with the rhythms of the 1970's. Rabbit now jogs, which is in keeping with the fitness craze that began in the 1970's. He and Janice are prospering during the decade of inflation and energy crises. They own a Toyota agency and are members of a country club. Rabbit plays golf and goes to Rotary Club lunches. Instead of newspapers, as in *Rabbit Redux*, he reads *Consumer Reports*,

the bible of his new status. The ghosts of his past haunt him, however: the drowned baby, the child he did or did not have with Ruth, memories of Jill and Skeeter. The chief reminder of the sins of his past is his son Nelson, returning home, like something repressed, to wreak havoc on the family's new affluent complacency. Like his father of old but lacking Rabbit's conscience and vision, Nelson has a quest for attention that practically wrecks everything that he touches: his father's cars, his relationships. Rabbit can see himself in Nelson's behavior and tries to help him avoid recapitulating Rabbit's mistakes, but communication is difficult between them. With Skylab falling and America held hostage by Iranians, the present is uneasy and anxious, the future uncertain. Characteristically, Rabbit turns to sex to fill the spiritual void. He and Janice make love on top of their gold Krugerrands. Rabbit lusts for the lovely Cindy, but in the wife-swapping escapade during their Caribbean holiday, Rabbit gets Thelma Harrison instead and is introduced to anal sex—a fitting image of the sense of nothingness pervading American culture at the end of the "Me Decade." Updike does not end there. He leaves Rabbit holding his granddaughter, "another nail in his coffin," but also another chance for renewal, perhaps even a motion of grace, a richness unearned.

The sense of exhaustion—of a world "running out of gas" in so many ways—that pervades *Rabbit Is Rich* becomes more serious, even terminal, in *Rabbit at Rest*. The fuzzy emptiness and mindlessness of the 1980's pervade the novel, even as so much is described in such vivid detail. Rabbit and Janice now winter in Florida, and Nelson runs the car dealership. Rabbit sustains himself on junk food and endless television viewing, images of the emptiness of American life under Ronald Reagan. He suffers a heart attack and undergoes an angioplasty procedure. His son's cocaine addiction and embezzlement of $200,000 from the business shock the family. Yet this often coarse and unsympathetic man continues to compel the reader's interest. He wonders about the Dalai Lama then in the news. As the Cold War dissipates, Rabbit asks: "If there's no Cold War, what's the point of being an American?" The man called

"Mr. Death" in *Rabbit, Run* now must face death in his own overblown body and contemplate it in relation to a world he has always known but that now is no more. Can such a man find peace, an acceptance and understanding of a life lived in such struggle and perplexity? In *Rabbit Is Rich*, Harry confesses to Janice the paradox of their lives: "Too much of it and not enough. The fear that it will end some day, and the fear that tomorrow will be the same as yesterday." In intensive care in Florida, at the end of *Rabbit at Rest*, Rabbit says, "Enough." Is this the realization and acceptance of life's sufficiency or its surplus? A confession of his own excesses and indulgences, or a command of sorts that he has had enough? These are only a few of the questions raised by the Rabbit novels.

MARRY ME

Many critics praise Updike for being the premier American novelist of marriage. Nearly all of his fiction displays the mysterious as well as commonplace but ineluctable complexities and conflicts of marriage. It is one of Updike's major concerns to explore the conditions of love in our time. His fiction is his updating and reworking of the Tristan and Isolde myth, about which Updike had commented in his review of Denis de Rougement's book *Love in the Western World* (1956)—lovers whose passion is enhanced by the obstacles needed to be overcome to fulfill it; the quest for an ideal lover who will assuage the fear of death and the longing for the infinite; the confusions of *eros* and the death wish. Many of Updike's male protagonists are aspects of both Tristan and Don Juan in their quest for a life-enhancing or death-denying passion. Such are the ingredients in the novels *Couples, Marry Me: A Romance*, and *The Witches of Eastwick*. All the novels are set in the 1960's—the spring of 1962 to the spring of 1963 in *Marry Me*, the spring of 1963 to the spring of 1964 in *Couples*, and probably 1969 for *The Witches of Eastwick*. In their various ways, each novel tries to answer the question, "After Christianity, what?" Human sexuality is liturgy and sacrament of the new religion emerging in America in the 1960's—a new end of innocence in a "post-pill paradise." The three novels make an interesting grouping because all deal

with marriages in various states of deterioration, and all explore the implications of "sex as the emergent religion, as the only thing left," Updike says. While not published until 1976, *Marry Me* was actually written before *Couples*. In fact, one story seems to lead right into the other. *The Witches of Eastwick* explores the theme from a woman's perspective.

Both Jerry Conant of *Marry Me* and Piet Hanema of *Couples* are educated professionals, married with children, and live in upper-middle-class suburbs of great cities. They are both suffering spiritually, longing for an affirmation from outside their selves, for some sort of blessing and certainty. As Jerry says, "Maybe our trouble is that we live in the twilight of the old morality, and there's just enough to torment us, and not enough to hold us in." The mortal fear that such an insight inspires leads both men to desperate quests for a love that will mend or heal their spiritual brokenness or emptiness. *Marry Me* takes place during the second year of the Kennedy administration, when the charm of the Camelot myth still captivated the country. Significantly, Updike calls *Marry Me* a "romance" rather than a novel, in order to suggest an attempt to use the freer form to explore the ambiguities of love, marriage, and adultery. The novel ends in ambiguity, with no clear resolution. In fact, there are three possible endings: Jerry with his lover Sally in Wyoming, Jerry with his wife Ruth in France, and Jerry in the Virgin Islands alone, on the island of St. Croix, symbolizing perhaps Jerry's self-immolation.

COUPLES

Couples takes place during the last year of the Kennedy presidency, including his assassination, and is thus a much more cynical book, harsher and darker than *Marry Me*. A certain light has gone out in the land; death and decay haunt the imagination. In contrast to *Marry Me*, choices are made and lives reconstitute themselves in a kind of cyclical way at the end of *Couples*. These two rather weak men fail at their quest to find in the flesh what they have lost in the spirit. Both men are believers and churchgoers, and both face a crisis in their faith. The church, committed to secularity and worldliness, fails them. Their respective wives are naturalistic and feel at home on earth and offer them little surcease to their anxiety. In *Marry Me*, Jerry must contend with Sally's husband Richard, an atheist with one blind eye, who insists on clear-cut decisions. For Jerry, however, every choice involves a loss that he cannot tolerate. In *Couples*, Piet is pitted against Freddy Thorne, the self-proclaimed priest of the new religion of sensuality. To Freddy, it is their fate to be "suspended in . . . one of those dark ages that visits mankind between millennia, between the death and rebirth of gods, when there is nothing to steer by but sex and stoicism and the stars." The many adulteries among the ten couples of *Couples* lead finally to divorce and disintegration of the secular paradise of Tarbox, the fictional suburb of the novel. Piet leaves his unattainable but earthbound wife, fittingly named Angela, for the sensuous Foxy Whitman, whose abortion of Piet's child Freddy arranges. When his church is destroyed by fire, Piet is freed from his old morality and guilt and the tension inherent in his sense of fallenness. Yet the satisfaction obtained with Foxy is a foreclosure of the vertical hope and is a kind of death. Both novels depict the failure of sex as a religion as well as the profound disappointments with love in its romantic or secular forms. Such may be Updike's answer to the question he posed: "After Christianity, what?"

THE WITCHES OF EASTWICK

The setting of *The Witches of Eastwick* is a small town in Rhode Island during the first year or so of Richard Nixon's presidency, an era of protest and discontent. Three divorcees, Alexandra Spofford, Jane Smart, and Sukie Rougemont, discover the power of sisterhood and femininity and become witchlike in their powers. The delicate balance of their friendship is upset by the entrance of the apparently demoniac Darryl Van Horne, who takes them all as his lovers. The novel's three parts, "The Coven," "Malefica," and "Guilt," suggest a progression from their new-found power and independence through an encounter with the demoniac to a rediscovery of responsibility through an awareness of guilt. Like Updike's many male protagonists, the three women must come to grips with death before they can reconstitute a meaningful life. Van Horne is a satanic figure whose machinations lead to a dissipation of the women's

powers. When he chooses the young Jennifer Gabriel for his wife, the women employ their powers to create a curse to bring about Jennifer's death. When she does die, the women feel guilt, even though it is not clear that their curse caused the girl's cancer. Van Horne preaches a sermon on the evilness of a creation saturated with disease and leaves town with Jennifer's brother, Christopher. The three women disband and find their way into suitable marriages. Such use of witchcraft allows Updike to explore the nature of evil and its connections with nature, history, and technology. The ambiguities of feminism are examined in the context of the moral and social confusions of the late 1960's in an effort to break down the destructive and outmoded polarities of the patriarchical tradition.

BECH and THE COUP

The first two Bech books—*Bech: A Book* and *Bech Is Back*—and *The Coup* are novels and stories resulting from Updike's travels to Eastern Europe and to Africa. Each work offers the author an opportunity to develop a very different persona from those of his domestic novels, as well as the chance to explore another aspect of "otherness" and "difference." *Bech: A Book* is a collection of seven stories about a middle-aged and very successful Jewish novelist, Henry Bech, and his various experiences both abroad and in America. The collection is framed by the fiction of Updike writing about an actual person contemporary with him. The book has a foreword by the putative author as well as two appendices. Such devices afford Updike an opportunity for humorous satire of the literary life in America. Bech emerges as a strong and believable character struggling with the failure of his success as a writer in a success-plagued culture. In *Bech Is Back*, Updike creates seven more stories about Bech's travels and his wrestling with the ambiguities of fame, fortune, and human worth, the protagonist's success with women an index of his success and worth as a writer. He must struggle with the question of whether he has sold out his talent for the marketplace, defiling both. Felix Ellellou, the protagonist of *The Coup*, is a bold creation for Updike, a black Islamic Marxist whose memoirs constitute the novel. Now in exile, the former president of the fictional sub-Saharan nation of Kush recounts the story of his rise and fall and of his perpetual struggle to avoid the ambiguous gifts of American aid. He fears not only the junk food but also the forces of secularity and materialism that will ultimately make of his beloved Kush a spiritual wasteland. He virtually stands alone in his resistance to the so-called benefits of American civilization, toward which he admits ambivalence. In Ellellou, one can see an African version of Updike's body-spirit conflict so prevalent in his fiction. For Ellellou, freedom must be freedom from material possessions, yet he anguishes over his people's poverty-stricken plight. He believes that it is better to die in poverty than from spiritual loss. In privation, he believes, the spirit will soar. Despite Ellellou's stoicism, his faith is plagued by doubts. He suspects that the new world religion will be godless and entropic. Updike's African novel is a replay of the author's critical interrogation of the moral and spiritual failures of the West.

A MONTH OF SUNDAYS, ROGER'S VERSION, and S.

Updike's concern with love, marriage, and adultery in so much of his fiction links him to Nathaniel Hawthorne's great novel *The Scarlet Letter* (1850), America's first great treatment of the complex social and religious consequences of adulterous love. Three novels in particular treat different dimensions of that adulterous triangle of Hawthorne's novel—*A Month of Sundays*, *Roger's Version*, and *S.* Hawthorne's Dimmesdale is updated in the figure of the Reverend Tom Marshfield, the exiled protagonist of *A Month of Sundays*. Roger Lambert of *Roger's Version*, the professor of theology specializing in heresies, is Updike's treatment of Hawthorne's Roger Chillingworth. Sarah Worth of *S.* is a contemporary depiction of Hawthorne's Hester, the truly noble and strong character of *The Scarlet Letter*. Hawthorne's Dimmesdale is crushed by his inability to integrate the body-and-soul division. So, too, does Updike's Marshfield suffer from this split in a novel with many allusions to *The Scarlet Letter*. Marshfield marries the former Jane Chillingworth, whose father was Marshfield's ethics instructor. The retreat center is managed by Ms. Prynne, who reads the diary entries of Marshfield and his fellow clerical exiles. The novel

traces Marshfield's integration of body and spirit, a mending of Marshfield's fragmented self, enabling him to return to his ministry as a true helper to the faithful. Roger Chillingworth in *The Scarlet Letter* was the cuckolded husband seeking revenge for his wife's adultery. In *Roger's Version*, Roger Lambert imagines that his wife Esther is having an affair with Dale, the computer science graduate student trying to prove God's existence by computer. Dale is a kind of innocent, a fundamentalist seeking technological support for his faith. By the end, Dale's project has failed, as Roger believed it would, and Dale returns to Ohio, his faith demolished. Yet, Dale's project provoked Roger to revivify his own faith and to engage his world more responsibly than he has. Updike's Sarah Worth of *S.* is certainly one possible version of a late twentieth century Hester Prynne. Sarah is a woman who has taken her life fully into her own hands without shame or illusion. After bolting from her faithless but wealthy physician husband, Sarah goes to an ashram in Arizona for spiritual renewal. That proves to be a false endeavor, but Sarah survives intact (and with much of the cult's money). Loving and compassionate yet willful and worldly, Sarah Worth dares to follow her own path.

TOWARD THE END OF TIME

Ever the chronicler of societal obsessions, Updike in 1997 provided his readers with a millennial book, *Toward the End of Time*. In this, his twentieth novel, the year is 2020, and the Sino-American nuclear war has recently destroyed the North American infrastructure and the U.S. government. In a universe of two moons and new life-forms, the "metallobioforms" that rose up out of the nuclear slime, the normal order of things seems to have come undone. Updike's protagonist, Ben Turnbull, seems at times to assume the identities of such disparate entities as an ancient Egyptian tomb robber and a medieval monk, and he is having an affair with a dark-eyed young woman whom he suspects is also a doe. Updike spends considerable time mulling over the mysteries of quantum mechanics and string theory, implying that such abstractions may contain the key to the enigma of time. In the end, though, the drama of Ben's post-millennial existence seems an elaboration of the sublunary obsessions of other Updike protagonists. The story of this sixty-six-year-old retired financial adviser could almost serve as a coda to the *Rabbit* books.

BECH AT BAY

With *Bech at Bay: A Quasi-Novel*, Updike ended the saga of another of his favorite alter egos, the now septuagenarian Henry Bech. Like its predecessors, this "quasi-novel" consists of a series of linked stories concerning the crabbed but accomplished—and now superannuated—Jewish novelist. *Bech at Bay* finds Bech at the heart of late twentieth century American literary life; however, that life, like Bech himself, seems to have lost nearly all its vitality. The mood is set in the book's opening section, "Bech in Czech," in which Bech finds himself on a book tour in the gloom of Prague, haunted by the uneasy feeling that he is no more than a character in someone else's book. In another episode, Bech is tapped to head an elite artistic organization called "The Forty"—a group not unlike the American Academy of Art and Letters, which Updike served as chancellor—but finds himself presiding over its demise when the elderly existing members refuse to admit any new blood.

Nonetheless, Bech has not lost all his imaginative powers. In "Bech Noir," he fantasizes the murders of critics who have abused him. Then, in the volume's finale, Bech is awarded the Nobel Prize. Delivering his acceptance speech before the Swedish Academy, Bech asserts his vitality by holding aloft his newborn daughter for the audience's edification. The gesture is, if nothing else, life affirming. Exactly how Bech—a "semi-obscure" writer with a slim body of work—arrived at this pinnacle of literary recognition is no clearer than the import of Bech's entire literary saga. Updike may be saying that for his fictional counterpart, this jaded urban Jew with writer's block, life and sex trump art. As the title of the book tells the reader, this last installment of the Bech series is a quasi-novel, and Henry Bech seems often to be merely a mask for his creator. The epigraph, "Something of the unreal is necessary to fecundate the real," which Updike borrows from Wallace Stevens, points to the correspondence between creator and creation.

With the astonishing variety and richness of his narratives, John Updike's fiction constitutes a serious exploration and probing of the spiritual conditions of American culture in the late twentieth century. The fate of American civilization is seen in the condition of love—its risks and dangers as well as its possibility for gracious transformation.

John G. Parks, updated by Lisa Paddock

OTHER MAJOR WORKS

SHORT FICTION: *The Same Door*, 1959; *Pigeon Feathers and Other Stories*, 1962; *Olinger Stories: A Selection*, 1964; *The Music School*, 1966; *Museums and Women and Other Stories*, 1972; *Problems and Other Stories*, 1979; *Too Far to Go: The Maples Stories*, 1979; *Trust Me*, 1987; *Brother Grasshopper*, 1990 (limited edition); *The Afterlife and Other Stories*, 1994.

PLAYS: *Three Texts from Early Ipswich: A Pageant*, pb. 1968; *Buchanan Dying*, pb. 1974.

POETRY: *The Carpentered Hen, and Other Tame Creatures*, 1958; *Telephone Poles and Other Poems*, 1963; *Midpoint and Other Poems*, 1969; *Tossing and Turning*, 1977; *Facing Nature*, 1985; *Mites and Other Poems in Miniature*, 1990; *A Helpful Alphabet of Friendly Objects*, 1995.

NONFICTION: *Assorted Prose*, 1965; *Picked-Up Pieces*, 1975; *Hugging the Shore: Essays and Criticism*, 1983; *Just Looking: Essays on Art*, 1989; *Self-Consciousness: Memoirs*, 1989; *Odd Jobs: Essays and Criticism*, 1991; *Golf Dreams: Writings on Golf*, 1996; *More Matter: Essays and Criticism*, 1999.

BIBLIOGRAPHY

Detweiler, Robert. *John Updike*. Boston: Twayne, 1984. This is an expanded and revised edition of Detweiler's 1972 study of Updike's fiction. It is an excellent introductory survey of Updike's work through 1983. It contains a chronology, biographical sketch, analysis of the fiction and its sources, a select bibliography, and an index. It provides a good discussion of religious and theological themes in the fiction.

O'Connell, Mary. *Updike and the Patriarchal Dilemma: Masculinity in the Rabbit Novels*. Carbondale: Southern Illinois University Press, 1996. Examines the themes of men, masculinity, and patriarchy in Updike's Rabbit series. Includes an index and bibliography.

Rogers, Michael. "The Gospel of the Book: *LJ* Talks to John Updike." *Library Journal* 124, no. 3 (February 15, 1999): 114-116. Updike expounds on books, contemporary writers, and the state of publishing at the end of the twentieth century.

Schiff, James A. *Updike's Version: Rewriting "The Scarlet Letter."* Columbia: University of Missouri Press, 1992. Schiff explores the influence of Hawthorne's novel on Updike's oeuvre. Contains an index and bibliography.

Trachtenberg, Stanley, ed. *New Essays on "Rabbit, Run."* Cambridge, England: Cambridge University Press, 1993. Essays in this collection address Updike's notable novel and such themes as middle-class men in literature. With bibliographical references.

Uphaus, Suzanne Henning. *John Updike*. New York: Frederick Ungar, 1980. An introductory analysis of Updike's fiction through 1979. Biographical information, a chronology, notes, bibliography, and an index.

Wood, Ralph C. *The Comedy of Redemption: Christian Faith and Comic Vision in Four American Novelists*. Notre Dame, Ind.: University of Notre Dame Press, 1988. A sophisticated theological analysis of Updike's Rabbit novels as well as *The Centaur* and *Couples*, along with a treatment of the fiction of Flannery O'Connor, Walker Percy, and Peter De Vries. The book contains notes and an index.

V

Mario Vargas Llosa

Born: Arequipa, Peru; March 28, 1936

Principal long fiction

La ciudad y los perros, 1962 (*The Time of the Hero*, 1966)

La casa verde, 1965 (*The Green House*, 1968)

Los cachorros, 1967 (novella; *The Cubs*, 1979)

Conversación en la catedral, 1969 (*Conversation in the Cathedral*, 1975)

Pantaleón y las visitadoras, 1973 (*Captain Pantoja and the Special Service*, 1978)

La tía Julia y el escribidor, 1977 (*Aunt Julia and the Scriptwriter*, 1982)

La guerra del fin del mundo, 1981 (*The War of the End of the World*, 1984)

La historia de Alejandro Mayta, 1984 (*The Real Life of Alejandro Mayta*, 1986)

¿Quién mató a Palomino Molero?, 1987 (*Who Killed Palomino Molero?*, 1987)

El hablador, 1987 (*The Storyteller*, 1989)

Elogio de la madrastra, 1988 (*In Praise of the Stepmother*, 1990)

Lituma en los Andes, 1993 (*Death in the Andes*, 1996)

Los cuadernos de don Rigoberto, 1997 (*The Notebooks of Don Rigoberto*, 1998)

Other literary forms

In addition to his novels, Mario Vargas Llosa has written works of literary criticism. Two of his best-known critiques are *Gabriel García Márquez: Historia de un deicidio* (1971) and *La orgía perpetua: Flaubert y "Madame Bovary"* (1975). He has also written several works of short fiction, most of which are included in the collected work *Los jefes* (1959; *The Cubs and Other Stories*, 1979). In 1981, he published his first play, *La señorita de Tacna*. In *Cartas a un Novelista* (1997), Llosa outlines novelistic structure using examples of James Joyce's *Ulysses* (1922) and Marcel Proust. He published *Claudio Bravo: Paintings and Drawings* (1997), about the Chilean-born painter, and *Making Waves* (1996), a collection of essays on a wide variety of topics.

Achievements

In the course of an energetic life, Vargas Llosa has created the image of the writer as activist, and both his works and his life conform to his perception of that role. A prolific writer, he is also a constant traveler as a member of literary juries, newspaper commentator, peripatetic professor of Latin American fiction at English and North American universities, soccer enthusiast, and investigator of Amazonian texts. During the years spanned by his career, Vargas Llosa's fiction has outlived the theory that the sudden explosion of vitality in Latin American fiction in the 1960's was a mere "boom." He has explored new areas of reality in each successive novel. The enthusiasm which characterizes his appreciation for Gustave Flaubert, William Faulkner, the novels of chivalry, and the fiction of his peer, Gabriel García Márquez, has developed new affinities within the cultural milieu of Latin America, a continent not always open to such influences in the past. Vargas Llosa eloquently decries the pejorative influence of politics upon literature, and he simultaneously articulates political opinions which are not always the most popular; he has both supported and excoriated the Cuban Revolution. The Sartrean formulation of praxis could find no clearer illustration than the adventurous life of Vargas Llosa.

Vargas Llosa was a Fellow at the Woodrow Wilson Center and the recipient of numerous awards, including the Premio de la Crítica Española (1963 and 1967), the Ritz Paris Hemingway Award (1985), the Cervantes Prize for literature (1994), and the Jerusalem Prize (1995). He hosted the Peruvian television program *The Tower of Babel*.

Biography

Jorge Mario Pedro Vargas Llosa was born in Arequipa, Peru, in March of 1936. As a child, he endured an unstable family life, his mother compensating for his having been abandoned by his father. The family moved to Bolivia and later to Piura, a city in northern Peru which would later figure importantly in *The Green House* and in *Captain Pantoja and the Special Service*. Eventually, they moved to Lima, where Vargas Llosa was enrolled in the Leoncio Prado Military Academy. The trauma related to his schooling at this military institution found its later expression in Vargas Llosa's first novel, *The Time of the Hero*.

In 1951, Vargas Llosa began to work for the newspaper *La crónica*; he would later employ his insight into the journalistic life in *Conversation in the Cathedral*, *Aunt Julia and the Scriptwriter*, and *The War of the End of the World*. He studied at the San Miguel School in Piura, and the student strike that he organized there is reflected with unusual immediacy in "Los jefes" ("The Leaders"). He participated more seriously in the literary milieu, collaborating on newspapers and literary magazines, and he, Luis Loayza, and Abelardo Oquendo edited the journals *Cuadernos de composición* and *Literatura*. He married Julia Urquidi and saved the delicious parody of his own romance for *Aunt Julia and the Scriptwriter*.

The short story "El desafío" ("The Challenge") earned for Vargas Llosa a trip to France in 1958. A scholarship to the University of Madrid gave him the opportunity to study the novel of chivalry, prototype of the modern novel, a form that has continued to interest him. After a collection of his stories, *The Cubs and Other Stories*, was published in Barcelona in 1959, Vargas Llosa returned to Paris. He completed the first draft of *The Time of the Hero* while he was working at Berlitz, at Agence France-Presse, and at the French Radio-Television Network (ORTF). His work for the ORTF provided the necessary entrée to the many Latin American writers in Paris, where Vargas Llosa met Julio Cortázar, Jorge Luis Borges, and Carlos Fuentes; it also took him to Cuba, where he met Carlos Barral, whose publishing house in Barcelona would subsequently issue all of Vargas Llosa's novels.

In 1962, Vargas Llosa entered *The Time of the Hero* in the competition for the Biblioteca Breve Prize. The following year, he won that prize as well as the Premio de la Crítica Española. He began work on *The Green House* and on the novella *The Cubs*. The extraordinary critical reception which *The Time of the Hero* received was amplified in 1965, when he published *The Green House*. He moved to London to take a professorship at Queen Mary College. In 1967, *The Cubs* appeared, but its reception was overshadowed by the three prizes won by *The Green House*, the most important of which was the Rómulo Gallegos Novel Prize. He traveled to Caracas for the awarding of the Gallegos, and in a ceremony that was an international event, he delivered the speech in which he clearly assumed the role of artist as public conscience. He met García Márquez at the ceremony, thereby initiating a friendship which would have both literary and personal significance. Vargas Llosa's confrontation with the fiction of García Márquez produced the *Historia de un deicidio* (history of a deicide), an explication of his as well as of García Márquez's aesthetics, and it would later encourage the gift for satire which he suppressed until *Captain Pantoja and the Special Service*.

(AP/Wide World Photos, EFE)

Vargas Llosa traveled extensively in 1968, including a stint as writer in residence at Washington State University. At that time, he was revising *Conversation in the Cathedral*, which he would publish in 1969. He moved to Barcelona in 1970 and continued his exploration of García Márquez's fiction. Two screenplays and *Captain Pantoja and the Special Service* were finished in 1973. In 1974, Vargas Llosa returned to Lima, where he worked on the correspondence and fiction of Flaubert, a preoccupation which resulted in the publication of *La orgía perpetua: Flaubert y "Madame Bovary"* in 1975. In this second volume of literary criticism, Vargas Llosa both celebrated the achievement of Flaubert and developed his own concept of the art of fiction. As president of the International Association of Poets, Playwrights, Editors, Essayists, and Novelists (PEN Club), Vargas Llosa spent much of 1976 and 1977 traveling. In 1977, he lectured at the University of Oklahoma during an international symposium, was Visiting Fellow at Cambridge University, and published *Aunt Julia and the Scriptwriter. Texas Studies in Literature and Language* devoted a special issue to Vargas Llosa's fiction, and the winter, 1978, issue of *World Literature Today* presented the papers of the Oklahoma symposium.

In the fall of 1980, Vargas Llosa, Fuentes, and Juan Goytisolo were the subjects of a symposium organized by José Miguel Oviedo at the University of Indiana. The essays from the symposium later were published in numbers 116 and 117 of *Revista iberoamericana*. During this period, Vargas Llosa was at work on a vast novel set in Brazil, which he published in 1981 as *The War of the End of the World*. Vargas Llosa declined an offer of the premiership in Peru in 1984. In 1990, he mounted an ultimately unsuccessful campaign for the presidency of Peru, running for the Liberty Movement Party. He lost to Alberto Fujimori, an agricultural engineer and son of Japanese immigrants. Vargas Llosa is also a football commentator.

ANALYSIS

The fictional world of Mario Vargas Llosa is one of complex novels, of murals of characters, of actions whose significance the reader must determine, of vast edifices that aspire to become total realities. Vargas Llosa's vision of reality is consistently binary, as can be seen from the titles of some of his works. The tension created by the opposition between the two realities is felt both by the characters within the novels and by the reader, and it is the prime factor in the dramatic nature of Vargas Llosa's style. In his early short stories and in his first novel, he focused the narrative on existential gestures, those acts or words which irrevocably set into action the course of a character's fate. As his novels grew more complex, Vargas Llosa concentrated on long dialogues that gave the intricate structures their cohesion. When he turned to humor and satire, Vargas Llosa reverted to the emphasis on gestures, tag words, and brief but revealing verbal interchanges between characters. *The War of the End of the World* resembles those massive descriptions of entire epochs which characterized fiction in the nineteenth century (which is precisely the period that gives life to the novel's plot). Vargas Llosa, then, has never contented himself with one style; rather, he has continued to adjust his narrative procedure to the subject at hand.

The influences to which Vargas Llosa has submitted himself for apprenticeship are, with the exception of the Peruvian José María Arguedas, either European or North American. This aspect of his development, in combination with an original use of cinematic techniques, gives his fiction its distinctive flavor. Beneath the glittering surface of technique, there are constants within Vargas Llosa's novels. The murals of characters always present doubles, characters whose fates are connected and whose ends always provide moral points of reference for the society configured in the novels. Insofar as the real or psychic death of one of the doubles is significant for society as a whole, these characters function as scapegoats, those generally unfortunate beings who must atone for the sins of their society. The marginality of these figures sometimes obscures the tragic nature of their fates and of Vargas Llosa's concept of fiction itself. In his exploration of *Madame Bovary* (1857), Vargas Llosa provides the most succinct explication of his aesthetics: "The greatest satisfaction that a novel can provide is to provoke my admiration for an act of nonconformity." As one considers his canon, it becomes clear that, no matter how complex the fictional structure becomes, the vital spark for the novel's action is the act of nonconformity.

THE TIME OF THE HERO

In his first novel, *The Time of the Hero*, Vargas Llosa was already the narrative perfectionist that his readers have come to expect. He had outgrown the personal trauma produced by his experiences in the Leoncio Prado, gaining the maturity to make of that terrifying institution a microcosm for the corruption of society as a whole. The military hierarchy and those secret hierarchies which the cadets (the "dogs") form give him the structure that houses the plot, which, set in motion by a dice game, works itself out with the irrevocability of a classical tragedy. In this most Sartrean of his novels, Vargas Llosa uses multiple narrators. Each of the significant characters has his moment on the stage, a moment which Vargas Llosa explores dramatically as the character converses with himself and as he comes into conflict with other characters.

The crisis of adolescence is the natural subject for a *Bildungsroman*, and it is a theme to which Vargas Llosa returned in *The Green House, Conversation in the Cathedral*, and *Aunt Julia and the Scriptwriter*. *The Time of the Hero* concentrates upon the moment in adolescence when one's roles suddenly become limited, when the mask freezes to the face, when the violence of the games becomes mortal—the moment Jean-Paul Sartre termed the time of election, when one becomes the self one has chosen to be. Vargas Llosa explores the moment when desire becomes reality, not only for the adolescents but also for their officers and for the power structure of Peru. By stressing the limited options available to the cadets and by revealing the hideous strength of the social hierarchies into which they must blend, he creates a narrative web of tragic intensity. Character is fate, and the adolescents' furious attempts to enter adult reality only bring about disaster.

The cadets at the Leoncio Prado are from varying social strata, thereby providing Vargas Llosa with the perfect mechanism for including the structure of the entire country within his range of vision. The cadets form a small cell (the "Circle") to ensure their survival. The cell selects an emissary to carry out its desires, and, through a series of mistakes, the cell is implicated in the complete subversion of the rules of the school and even in the death of a cadet. The guilt associated with the responsibility for the cadet's death spreads through the school like a cancerous growth. The moral implications of the cadet's murder can be realized most clearly in the reactions of three characters: Gamboa, the perfect officer; Alberto, the author of pornographic novels and the typical bourgeois; and the Jaguar, the invincible strong man who created the Circle. Each of them comes to terms with the harsh reality of the Leoncio Prado and with the even harsher reality of death itself. The defeat suffered as a result of the confrontation with the Leoncio Prado indelibly marks each of them: Gamboa's career is ruined because he disputes his superior officers' decisions; Alberto returns to the artificial paradise of the bourgeois suburb instead of becoming the writer he should have been; and the Jaguar escapes through his love for Terry, but his life is constantly threatened by the corruption surrounding it. The fragmented conversations, the disjointed interior monologues, the sudden connections between disparate events, the constant tension between adolescent and adult realities—all of these aspects create a dramatic field upon which the battles for honor are lost.

THE GREEN HOUSE

The Green House is a more complex novel, but it is built on the binary concept found in *The Time of the Hero*. The Peruvian jungle and the desert city of Piura are the contrasting environments that reiterate the hellish milieu of the Leoncio Prado. The social hierarchies are as solidly in place in the jungle as they are in Lima, and the "heroic" characters who succeed in forming their private paradise eventually re-create the same infernal structures. Five plots are interwoven in *The Green House*: the tale of the Indian child Bonifacia; the life of the Indian chief, Jum; the career of Anselmo and his romance with the blind deaf-mute Antonia; the fortunes of the multinational bandit Fushía; and the tragedy of Sergeant Lituma. *The Green House* initiated the period of Vargas Llosa's exploration of Faulknerian themes and techniques; it has the alternating plots, the sudden character metamorphoses, the insistence on fate in the manipulation of the plot, and the exploration of the perverse precincts of the human soul which are Faulkner's hallmarks. *The Green House* was also the first novel in which Vargas Llosa revealed his fondness for the chivalric romance, as the careers of Fushía and Anselmo illustrate. Flaubert's influence is also evident here, particularly in the character of Bonifacia, who might be termed the Madame Bovary of the Peruvian jungle.

The theme of exploitation connects the five plots and is the basis for the interaction of all the characters; Vargas Llosa builds a multilayered society based upon exploitation on physical, material, and moral levels. Only two of the novel's many characters escape appropriation by others for ends which they cannot control. Anselmo, who calculatedly installs a bordello (the Green House of the title) in the desert near Piura, is capable of the most courtly romance, and he spends his life after the destruction of the Green House wondering if Antonia did, indeed, reciprocate his love. After his infamous career as robber baron and absolute ruler of an island of pleasure, Fushía is reduced to utter dependence on his friend Aquilino, who ferries him by boat to the leper colony where he will end his ignoble life. The conversation between Aquilino and Fushía during the course of their river journey is pure metaphysics, and it provides the poetic thread that prevents the fragmentation which the novel's multiple plots would otherwise create.

Anselmo's Green House is destroyed by fire, only to rise again like the phoenix. Each of the plots ends in the utter defeat of the characters, but the characters themselves never give up. Although each is severely embattled by the structures in which he is trapped, the character nevertheless persists in being himself, in exploiting the possibilities of his role to the limit of its potential ramifications. Although Vargas Llosa rarely allows his creatures to become heroic, in their stubborn election of a self in conflict with all other selves and with society itself, his characters do forge an active role in a narrative realm which would de-

mand their complete domination. Considered as a whole, the novel's entire cast is making the same trip as Fushía, down the slow river of death. Some of them—including Fushía himself, Anselmo, and Aquilino—are fortunate enough to enjoy the supreme gift in Vargas Llosa's fiction: the pleasures of friendship.

CONVERSATION IN THE CATHEDRAL

Conversation in the Cathedral presents Vargas Llosa's bleakest enactment of the strategies of nonconformity. Lima at all levels is the stage for an endless struggle which Vargas Llosa symbolizes in the conflict between fathers and sons. The nefarious career of the political strongman Cayo Bermúdez infects and eventually destroys the life of every character in the novel. The most vital of the many interwoven plots is that which concerns a young newspaperman, Santiago Zavala, and his discovery that his ostensibly bourgeois father is the infamous Bola de Oro. Vargas Llosa constructs this enormous novel's edifice upon the running dialogue between Santiago and his father's former chauffeur, a dialogue which takes place in a seedy dive called the Cathedral. The atmosphere of the prose resembles that of Faulkner's *Sanctuary* (1931); there is even a character named Popeye. The vast nature of the reality configured in the narrative once again reminds the reader of Flaubert and his eye for re-creating the minutiae of mundane existence; at the same time, the novel is a kind of allegory of an oppressive political situation all too common in Latin America. Coming to realize just how pervasive is Bermúdez's influence throughout Lima, Santiago must acknowledge that his father's capitalistic gambling provides significant sustenance for Bermúdez's power, that his father's moral decay is the real field upon which the family's honor is lost. His *anagnorisis* does not lead to the triumph typical of Greek drama but instead to the deliberate election of mediocrity; Santiago will forever hide himself in the gray streets and mean bars of Lima's underside.

Whereas Vargas Llosa captured the definitive gestures of adolescence in *The Time of the Hero* and those of maturity in *The Green House*, he captures in *Conversation in the Cathedral* the desperate grimace of a society in need of a complete revolution. Like Faulkner's *Absalom, Absalom!* (1936), the novel suggests that humanity's design, no matter how grand or intricate, only attracts destruction from the gods. Santiago comes to know his father, and thereby to know himself, only to understand that his life was destroyed even before it began.

CAPTAIN PANTOJA AND THE SPECIAL SERVICE

In *Captain Pantoja and the Special Service*, military hierarchies supply the structure upon which Vargas Llosa weaves the tragicomic career of Pantaleón Pantoja, the archetypal military man whose perfectionism is his downfall. Although the thematic preoccupation is much like that of *The Time of the Hero*, the tone is radically different. Vargas Llosa treats injustice, corruption, and defeat, but he presents them with humor and satire rather than as the components of tragedy. Captain Pantoja is given the curious task of devising a system to provide "ladies of the night" to the Peruvian military forces stationed at hardship posts in the jungle. He attacks his task with gusto and rigor, and he succeeds beyond the greatest expectations of his officers. The fact that his family is destroyed and his life completely changed restrains Pantoja not at all.

Although Vargas Llosa abandons his usual practice of avoiding a protagonist in this novel, he does provide Pantoja with the customary double that has characterized his plots. The jungle also harbors a religious fanatic, Brother Francisco, whose career holds up a dark mirror to Pantoja's and whose death at the hands of his followers reflects the danger inherent in Pantoja's success. In this novel, Vargas Llosa extends the use of dream sequences as vehicles for the expression of the subconscious, and Pantoja's surreal nocturnal voyages eloquently reveal the distress caused by his new life.

Pantoja's downfall is engineered by the radio announcer Sinchi, an egomaniac who cannot tolerate competition from Pantoja's kingdom of pleasure. Vargas Llosa deftly uses the cliché-ridden texts of Sinchi's radio broadcasts to exaggerate the boredom of daily life in the towns lost in the jungle. Sinchi's delirious diatribes are, however, no match for the monomaniacal military reports in which Pantoja mar-

shals ever-increasing statistics to convince his officers in Lima of the success of his system. These parodies were anticipated in the pornographic novels of Alberto in *The Time of the Hero*, and they are carried to a hyperbolic extreme in *Aunt Julia and the Scriptwriter.*

Pantoja is eventually defeated by the very numbers which he has assembled to validate his reports. His moral decay becomes evident to the whole region as he enjoys a brief but intense affair with an irresistible Brazilian, one of his fleet of "visiting ladies." Rather than make of Pantoja the tragic figure that Gamboa is in *The Time of the Hero*, Vargas Llosa makes him the pawn of even more comic generals, thereby implying that the most powerful institution in Peru can be reduced to a hierarchy of absurd buffoons.

AUNT JULIA AND THE SCRIPTWRITER

In counterpoint closely resembling the structure of Faulkner's *The Wild Palms* (1939), *Aunt Julia and the Scriptwriter* alternates the story of a young writer, Mario Varguitas (whose name clearly echoes that of the author), with the fortunes of Pedro Camacho, a writer of radio serials. As he serves his apprenticeship as a writer, Varguitas gradually explores the mysteries of love with his "Aunt" Julia, the recently divorced sister-in-law of his Uncle Lucho. His success in both endeavors parallels the decline of Camacho. An obvious difference of tone characterizes the two modes of narration. Varguitas recounts his experiences with humor, and as his romance progresses, that humor is extended to hyperbole. Both the texts of Camacho's serials and the episodes concerning Camacho in Varguitas's narration are marked by ferocious satire. Varguitas narrates the episodes of his romance in a linear fashion, but the history of Pedro Camacho is presented obliquely, through the texts of increasingly alienated soap operas. The characters in Camacho's texts exhibit all the repressed elements of his seething unconscious. Inasmuch as his texts are connected thematically rather than by the characters, they provide the opportunity for Vargas Llosa to bring back former characters and favorite subjects—Sergeant Lituma reappears and undergoes an apotheosis, and a savage is once again confronted with the modern city, recapitulating one of the major themes of *The Green House*.

The desperate isolation of Pedro Camacho and the subsequent sublimation of that loneliness into the texts of his soap operas carry the same import as does the radical isolation of Quentin Compson in Faulkner's *The Sound and the Fury* (1929). Unlike Quentin, however, Camacho does not kill himself; instead, he becomes even more mediocre than before, becoming as invisible as Santiago Zavala in *Conversation in the Cathedral*. In his last appearance in the novel, he is a completely changed man, and his magnificent voice is all that remains of his former personality. Varguitas does not become invisible; rather, he perfects himself by perfecting his craft, constantly rewriting his short stories, and his escape from the grimy world of second-class journalism is assured. After all, he becomes the author of the novel the reader is reading.

THE WAR OF THE END OF THE WORLD

After the writing of *The Green House*, Brazil hovered on the horizon of Vargas Llosa's fiction as a potential paradise for adventurers. After the relatively lighter novels, *Captain Pantoja and the Special Service* and *Aunt Julia and the Scriptwriter*, Vargas Llosa returned to the novel of massive complexity in *The War of the End of the World*, a work based on the same historical events that formed the background for Euclydes da Cunha's influential novel *Os sertoes* (1902; *Rebellion in the Backlands*, 1944)—indeed, Vargas Llosa dedicated his novel to Cunha. In a manner reminiscent of Leo Tolstoy, Vargas Llosa recounts the military campaign of the Brazilian government to obliterate the utopian community established at Canudos. The unrest in the north of Brazil at the end of the nineteenth century provides the stage for the war of wills and of concepts of reality, and the struggle between gigantic forces threatens the very fabric of society itself. Canudos is established by a religious zealot, Antonio the Counselor, as a refuge for those citizens whose reality is consistently denied by the modern state.

Vargas Llosa's analysis of the problems of the state demands an excursion into the eighteenth century, and the character of the Barón de Cañabrava

conveys the unresolved problems which that century bequeathed to the nineteenth. The pilgrims following Antonio take over land owned by the Barón de Cañabrava as a site for their city, so that the struggle extends even beyond that between the modern government and the military to encompass that fundamental disagreement between owners of vast tracts of land and the humble masses who own nothing. Only gradually does the government come to understand the desperate nature of the military campaign to expel the religious community from Canudos; the two principal antagonists in the struggle, Antonio the Counselor and the military commander Moreira Cesar, suffer from no such illusions. Each of them understands that this is a battle to the death, a war of the end of the world. Although the struggle is protracted and both leaders are killed, there is never any doubt as to which side will emerge triumphant. The victory of the status quo gives an additional poignancy to the sacrifices of the individual characters, created with Vargas Llosa's customary vividness.

Just as Faulkner in *Absalom, Absalom!* used several distinct literary styles to capture the distinct worldviews of various narrators, so Vargas Llosa employs a variety of styles to create the complex community of Canudos. The rational, eighteenth century life of the Barón de Cañabrava, the picaresque world of the reformed thieves and murderers who form the army of the Counselor, the chivalric romances of the enigmatic beauty Jurema on the way to Canudos—all are narrated in a style appropriate to the interior world of the characters. Galileo Gall, the ludicrous phrenologist seduced by the idea of revolution, is one of the most bizarre characters. As Gall ineffectively attempts to transplant the European mystique of revolution à la Pierre Joseph Proudhon and Mikhail Bakunin to an environment already leavened by the Counselor's revolution of the interior world, Vargas Llosa produces the necessary vehicle for a thorough examination of the apocalypse, a subject latent in his fiction since *The Green House*.

The character of a myopic journalist whose constant sneezing interrupts even the most serious moments of the campaign against Canudos serves Vargas Llosa as a roving camera, one whose lens analyzes and freezes the vast scope of the action. The journalist functions as the conscience of the society embattled by the alternative reality of Canudos. He constantly meditates on the secret motivations of the deadly campaign to exterminate the community. His glasses are shattered during a skirmish, and he is reduced to helpless dependence upon his friends. Without the use of his eyes, the journalist must intuit the actions around him with his other senses, and he moves like an amoeba through the frightful violence of the last days of Canudos. Because the journalist sees events no one else can see, he serves as a bridge between characters and events. His role gives continuity and a sense of completion to a novel that might otherwise become too diffuse.

In *The War of the End of the World*, Vargas Llosa has returned to the epic style which he forged in *The Green House* and *Conversation in the Cathedral*. He lightens the somber atmosphere with the antics of Galileo Gall and the nearsighted journalist, but the novel's tone is ultimately dark and despairing. The concept of individual honor is swallowed up by the larger struggles of the military hegemony and religious fanaticism. Even the war of the end of the world, the apocalypse itself, does not change the fundamental structure of society or the future of the hapless individuals trapped within it.

Seen as a whole, Vargas Llosa's fictions revolve around a set thematic structure organized around bipolar opposites. Clearly established in his first novel, his style has nevertheless evolved to include humor, satire, and the exploration of the subconscious. Vargas Llosa's world is one of male domination. The feminine characters serve primarily as bridges to other characters or as sporadic amusements for the more vital males. Although certain females—Bonifacia in *The Green House*, the Brazilian in *Captain Pantoja and the Special Service*, and the vivacious Aunt Julia—escape their roles and reveal aspects of themselves beyond their stereotypes, they are temporary phenomena.

The incorporation of symbolic space has increased in Vargas Llosa's fiction; from the foggy precinct of the Leoncio Prado, he has proceeded to incorporate the jungle, the desert, and Lima itself, with

all of its infernal layers. *The War of the End of the World* makes concrete the Brazil which heretofore in his fiction existed only as a region of dreams. No matter how complex the stage becomes, however, Vargas Llosa's characters are condemned to being themselves and to carrying out individual acts of nonconformity against the rigid hierarchies that would otherwise annihilate them. Even as they are defeated, Vargas Llosa's characters find a way to affirm themselves.

THE REAL LIFE OF ALEJANDRO MAYTA

The Real Life of Alejandro Mayta is based on the Trotskyite revolutionary Alejandro Mayta, who led an uprising against the Peruvian government in 1958. The novel is a reconstruction and fictionalization of Mayta's life. Vargas Llosa uses his story in the context of modern Peru and its social unraveling. He opens and closes the novel on the garbage dumps outside of Lima, a clear reference to the detritus that threatens the culture's ability to sustain its humanity.

IN PRAISE OF THE STEPMOTHER

In Praise of the Stepmother offers a detached, cold view of sexuality and its perversities through the story of the aging insurance executive Don Rigoberto, his second wife, sexy Dona Lucretia, and his young son, Alfonso. Aware of the possibility that he may resent her replacement of his mother, Lucretia attempts to gain Alfonso's favor; however, the two become sexually involved. "Fonsito" later writes an essay detailing his seduction of Lucretia and lets his father read it. Llosa describes Don Rigoberto's fastidious toilet habits, and his seeming compliance with the liaison between his new wife and son, until the maid discovers that Alfonso has set out from the beginning to seduce his stepmother as a way of ridding himself and the household of her presence. He claims that his goal was to restore the household's original order: his father and the maid all to himself.

THE NOTEBOOKS OF DON RIGOBERTO

The Notebooks of Don Rigoberto, a sequel to *In Praise of the Stepmother*, is set in Lima, where Don Rigoberto fills ledgers with his fantasies and sexual obsessions. Vargas Llosa purposely plays with the division between fiction and reality as Rigoberto's entries are soon confused with details of Lucretia's attempts to resist her stepson's advances. He describes high-flown scenes with his wife, such as having her portray the subjects of famous, sexually titillating paintings. The portrayal of Alfonso is one of a sexually astute wolf in sheep's clothing. Barely on the cusp of adolescence, he visits his outcast stepmother to show her his drawings and discuss artist Egon Schiele, whose own art reflected a certain perversity and lustiness. She feigns outrage at his impudence after he "tricks" her into a sexual liaison. The scene ends with the boy leaving, Lucretia masturbating on the bidet, and then unexpectedly, Don Rigoberto giving scrupulous instructions to the architect of his new house on how to accommodate his art and book collection. Such juxtapositions of Lucretia's carnal weaknesses and her husband's near-obsessive attention to his art and literature are clearly Vargas Llosa's favorite topics, as he skillfully weaves together Lucretia's erotic experiences, Schiele's life and art, and Rigoberto's sensual musings.

Mary E. Davis, updated by Nika Hoffman

OTHER MAJOR WORKS

SHORT FICTION: *Los jefes*, 1959 (*The Cubs and Other Stories*, 1979).

PLAYS: *La señorita de Tacna*, pb. 1981; *Kathie y el hipopótamo*, pb. 1983; *La Chunga*, pb. 1987; *Three Plays*, pb. 1990.

NONFICTION: *La novela en América Latina: Dialogo*, 1968; *Literatura en la revolución y revolución en literatura*, 1970 (with Julio Cortázar and Oscar Collazos); *La historia secreta de una novela*, 1971; *Gabriel García Márquez: Historia de un deicidio*, 1971; *El combate imaginario*, 1972; *García Márquez y la problemática de la novela*, 1973; *La novela y el problema de la expresión literaria en Peru*, 1974; *La orgía perpetua: Flaubert y "Madame Bovary,"* 1975; *José María Arguedas: Entre sapos y halcones*, 1978; *La utopia arcaica*, 1978; *Entre Sartre y Camus*, 1981; *A Writer's Reality*, 1991 (Myron I. Lichtblau, editor); *Fiction: The Power of Lies*, 1993; *Pez en el agua*, 1993 (*A Fish in the Water: A Memoir*, 1994); *Making Waves*, 1996; *Cartas a un Novelista*, 1997; *Claudio Bravo: Paintings and Drawings*, 1997 (with Paul Bowles).

BIBLIOGRAPHY

Booker, M. Keith. *Vargas Llosa Among the Postmodernists*. Gainesville: University Presses of Florida, 1994. One of the most comprehensive treatments of Vargas Llosa's work. Includes chapters such as "The Reader as Voyeur" and "Literature and Modification."

Cevallos, Francisco Javier. "García Márquez, Vargas Llosa, and Literary Criticism: Looking Back Prematurely." *Latin American Research Review* 26, no. 1 (1991): 266-275. An interesting article about Vargas Llosa and his peer Gabriel García Márquez.

Farnsworth, Elizabeth. "Peru: A Nation in Crisis." *World Policy Journal* 5, no. 4 (Fall, 1988): 726-746. A helpful overview of the many challenges Peru faced as of mid-1988, including details of the opposition's 1990 electoral strategies. Farnsworth examines Vargas Llosa's United Left.

_____. "The Temptation of Mario." *Mother Jones* 14, no. 1 (January, 1989): 22-28. A smartly written popular biography of Vargas Llosa, set in the middle of his 1990 presidential campaign.

Kristal, Efra'n. *Temptation of the Word: The Novels of Mario Vargas Llosa*. Nashville: Vanderbilt University Press, 1999. Kristal examines the overarching reasons for Vargas Llosa's political passions and divides Vargas Llosa's writing career into sections corresponding to results of his ideas on capitalism and the decline of the Cuban Revolution.

Texas Studies in Literature and Language 19, no. 4 (Winter, 1977). Special issue devoted to the author. Specific studies on such works as *The Time of the Hero* and others on more general topics concerning his work.

Williams, Raymond Leslie, William Gass, and Michel Rybalka. "The Boom Twenty Years Later: An Interview with Mario Vargas Llosa." *Latin American Literary Review* 15, no. 29 (January/June, 1987): 201-206. Among many interviews with the author, this one is particularly noteworthy because of Vargas Llosa's candid comments concerning his own work.

World Literature Today 52, no. 1. (Winter, 1978). This special issue on Vargas Llosa has three main sections: an introduction, with texts by editor Ivar Ivask and Vargas Llosa, with a chronology; a collection of essays by various critics; and a bibliography of works about and by the author.

GIOVANNI VERGA

Born: Catania, Sicily; September 2, 1840
Died: Catania, Sicily; January 27, 1922

PRINCIPAL LONG FICTION

Amore e patria, 1857
I carbonari della montagna, 1861-1862 (also as *I carbonari della montagna: Sulle lagune*, 1975; includes *Sulle lagune*)
Una peccatrice, 1866
Storia di una capinera, 1871
Eva, 1873
Eros, 1874
Tigre reale, 1875
I Malavoglia, 1881 (*The House by the Medlar Tree*, partial translation, 1890, 1953; complete translation, 1964)
Il marito di Elena, 1882
Mastro-don Gesualdo, 1889 (English translation, 1893, 1923)
Dal tuo al mio, 1906

OTHER LITERARY FORMS

Giovanni Verga was a writer of short stories and a playwright as well as a novelist. "Nedda" is the story of a Sicilian peasant girl who harvests olives and suffers the buffets of bad fortune until at length she thanks the Virgin Mary that her baby has been taken and will no longer suffer on earth. This story, written in 1874, prompted Luigi Capuana to predict that Verga had opened "a new seam in the mine of Italian literature." In *Primavera ed altri racconti* (1876; springtime and other stories), Verga attempts a certain realism by occasionally reproducing the Milanese dialect of his characters. *Vita dei campi* (1880; *Under the Shadow of Etna*, 1896) contains some of his finest stories, such as "La lupa" ("The She-Wolf"), in which a woman drives her son-in-law to kill her as the result of her continual sexual proddings; in 1896, Verga transformed this story into a play. Also included in this collection is "Cavalleria rusticana" (literally meaning "rustic chivalry" but known in English only by its Italian name), the tragedy of Turiddu at the hands of the cuckolded Alfio, each one cooperating with fate to work out the other's destruction. Also notable in this collection is "Fantasticheria" ("Reverie"), in which a man and a woman compare the merits of the world of high society with the unsullied world of the peasant, and the man in the story argues eloquently for the superiority of the latter. *Novelle rusticane* (1883; translated by D. H. Lawrence in 1925 as *Little Novels of Sicily*) explores in its twelve stories the peasant's struggle to survive and his victimization by nature and society. In "La libertà" ("Liberty"), for example, in which the peasants rebel and slaughter their oppressors, they are immediately cowed by the enormity of their vengeance and are soon made into willing victims by those who execute the law. "Pane nero" ("Black Bread"), more a short novel than a story, is striking for the contrast its peasants provide to the idealism of the Malavoglia family; the fear of poverty in these peasants drives them to ignore all scruples in their search for material necessities. In *Per le vie* (1883; through the streets), Verga writes of the struggles of the urban Milanese poor; these stories seem to lack the brilliance of his stories set in Sicily. In "Camerati" ("Buddies"), Verga takes a dim view of the Socialist ideas which were coming into vogue in Northern Italy on the grounds that they merely complicate the problems that they are out to solve.

All of his life, Verga dreamed of being a successful playwright; although he did not write many plays, some of them were successful. In 1883, he rewrote "Cavalleria rusticana" as a one-act tragedy, which was performed the next year in Turin with the finest actors in Italy at the time, Eleanora Duse, Cesare Rossi, and Tebaldo Checchi. It was the greatest success of Verga's career as a writer and, in 1889, was transformed into an opera by composer Pietroc Mascagni. "The She-Wolf," rewritten into a two-act trag-

(Library of Congress)

ACHIEVEMENTS

Verga is generally viewed as the second greatest novelist Italy has produced, after Alessandro Manzoni. His objectivity, his efforts to infuse new life into the petrified, tradition-shackled Italian language, his compassion for humanity, and his conception of society as controlled by immutable economic laws have made an indelible impression on the Italian writers who followed him, especially on the neorealists. One of the landmark works of the neorealist cinema is Luchino Visconti's *La terra trema* (1948), based on Verga's novel *The House by the Medlar Tree*. The tragic vision elaborated in his best novels, however, has less appeal than his short stories. Abroad he is best known as the source of the libretto *Cavalleria rusticana* (1884), and his stories, such as "The She-Wolf," "Conforti" ("Consolation"), "Black Bread," "Liberty," and "Cos'è il re" ("So Much for the King"), are frequently anthologized; he is among the few modern Italian writers included with any regularity in textbooks of literature published in the United States.

Although his dramatic works were not many, Verga was the only fully successful writer of tragedy in Italian theater between Count Vittorio Alfieri and Luigi Pirandello. *Cavalleria rusticana* is a work of monumental importance in the history of Italian theater, for it ushered in a new age of realistic drama dealing with contemporary problems after centuries of plots based on medieval themes.

In his best novels, Verga achieved a perfect synchronization of style and story and created a language capable of conveying the feelings of his Sicilian peasant characters that his Italian readers could understand. Verga steeped himself in the customs and the psychology of Sicily and then proceeded to convert the Sicilian dialect of his characters into a crystalline and unartificial Italian. Generally remaining within the bounds of standard Italian, Verga preserved successfully syntactic features of his native dialect, such as the tendency to repeat the verb at the end of a sentence, as in "Per voi tirerei tutta la casa, tirerei" ("For you I would lift the whole house up, I really would") from "Cavalleria rusticana." Gabriele D'Annunzio would later imitate this feature of Verga's language in his own short stories.

edy, premiered as *La lupa* in Turin in 1896 with some success, and for a time Mascagni considered using it also as the basis of an opera. *In portineria* (the porter's lodgings) is a stage adaptation in two acts taken from a story in *Per le vie*; when it premiered in Milan in 1885, it was a failure. *La caccia al lupo* (1901; *The Wolf Hunt*, 1921) and *La caccia alla volpe* (1901; the fox hunt) are companion pieces that explore instances of marital infidelity among the poor and among the rich; predictably, Verga is more successful portraying the story set in the world of the Sicilian peasant than the one set in the empty world of high society. *Dal tuo al mio* (1903; what's yours is mine), which deals with a confrontation between sulfur miners and the barons who own the mines, and which puts forth the self-interest motive as the source of all actions, was later reconstructed by Verga as a less effective short novel in 1906. There is no complete edition of the plays of Verga, although the one-volume *Teatro*, published by Mondadori in 1912, is a valuable collection of the better ones.

BIOGRAPHY

Giovanni Verga was the eldest of five children born to Giovanni Battista Verga Catalano and Caterina di Mauro. The Vergas were upper middle class, descended from a Spaniard, Lajn Gonzalo de Vergas, who came to Sicily in the thirteenth century. The elder Giovanni Verga was cultured and well read, and he dabbled in the occult; Verga's mother was regarded as an intellectual and was a cousin of Domenico Castorina, a local writer. Both of Verga's parents were cautiously liberal in that they opposed the Bourbon monarchy that held a tyrannical sway over southern Italy at that time. Although born and reared in Catania, Verga spent much of his life in Vizzini, where his father owned considerable property. There the family sought refuge in summers to avoid outbreaks of cholera and political violence. In 1850, Verga went to a secular school directed by Antonino Abate, where he read Dante, Petrarch, Torquato Tasso, Ludovico Ariosto, Ugo Foscolo, and Manzoni, as well as the bombastic writings of Catania's own Castorina.

Although Abate favored the union with Italy, unlike some Sicilians, who desired an independent Sicily, he wished to see an Italian republic rather than a monarchy. His student, Verga, on the other hand, was so grateful when the troops of Giuseppe Garibaldi made a unified Italy possible that he accepted the idea of a monarchy easily. A unified Italy, however, did not bring all it had seemed to promise. When the new leaders began to break up the ancient feudal estates, as the land-hungry peasants had hoped, the fragmented estates were purchased by members of the middle class, who by this means were able to elevate themselves, to the total exclusion of the peasants, who no longer had even the rights of use that they had enjoyed under the previous system. There occurred savage attacks upon the gentry by an embittered and defrauded peasantry, and although Verga himself had to flee their unleashed wrath, somehow there took root deep within him a remarkable compassion for the plight of this unfortunate class of people, and it was precisely this empathy that led him to greatness as a writer.

To please his father, Verga entered the University of Catania to study law, but he soon was bored and began to apply himself to writing fiction. Because these first literary efforts were mildly successful, he decided to move to the Italian mainland in order to perfect his Italian and his literary style. Following the tradition of writers such as Alfieri, Foscolo, and Manzoni, who purified their Italian by taking up residence in the country's linguistic capital, Verga chose to move to Florence, which in 1865 was also the country's interim political capital. He mastered Italian, as was his goal, but skillfully preserved the rhythms and syntax of the dialects and, although he used outright idioms that had to be italicized within his texts less and less frequently as he matured as a writer, he succeeded in substituting Italian words for dialect in such a way as to preserve even the lexical flavor of the original speech.

In Florence, Verga renewed his acquaintance with Luigi Capuana, from Mineo, and Mario Rapisardi, from Catania; he also became acquainted with Francesco Dall'Ongaro, a respected critic and writer. At the Dall'Ongaro residence, Verga met Giselda Fojanesi, soon to be Rapisardi's wife and subsequently Verga's mistress. Verga saw her during his frequent visits to Catania, where she and her husband returned to live, until December, 1883, when Rapisardi discovered the infidelity and sent Giselda back to Florence, whereupon Verga ended the liaison. *Storia di una capinera* (story of a blackcap), written in 1869, was published in Milan in 1871, and in November, 1872, Verga moved to Milan, where he associated with members of the *Scapigliatura* literary group, making friends with Giuseppe Giacosa, Giacomo Puccini's foremost librettist, and with Arrigo Boito, who wrote libretti for Verdi. The school of the *Scapigliati* (the "disheveled," or those against the establishment) reacted against bourgeois traditions and sought greater originality, subjectivity, and immediacy in their writing. Although Verga probably did not ever consider himself a member of this group, it is in the impulse that they gave to him that much of their own historical importance lies. Verga enjoyed his years in Milan, where he wrote several trivial novels featuring erotic escapades among the rich, usually set in Florence or Milan; only the publication of "Nedda" in 1874 gave an inkling of his potential greatness. The decade 1880 to 1890 was a glorious one for Verga; during this period, he published two great novels, *The House by the Medlar Tree* and *Mastro-don Gesualdo*, in addition to a number of masterpieces of short fiction. Still, the critical reception of his works was not enthusiastic, and this depressed him.

In 1889, Giovanni Targioni-Tozzetti and Giovanni Menasci took Verga's "Cavalleria rusticana" and turned it into a libretto for the then-unknown Pietro Mascagni. Verga was consulted beforehand and gave his consent without specifying what share of the royalties he wished. When the opera proved successful, Verga initiated a lawsuit that ended in 1893 with the court awarding him the one-time sum of 143,000 lire. A few years later, Verga brought suit again, claiming that his agreement to the 1893 terms had been fraudulently induced. The litigation, at great cost to Verga, dragged on until 1915. It was said invidiously that Verga lost interest in his writing because he enjoyed litigating more; if the assertion is untrue, certainly the fact of the litigation served to take his personal focus away from his writing to worldly matters.

Disillusioned by what he viewed as the failure of his literary career and moved by nostalgia for the Sicilian countryside, Verga left Italy for Catania in 1893. From Sicily he continued to travel, especially to Milan, but he no longer maintained an apartment there and stayed instead in hotels. The return home failed to revitalize Verga's interest in the cycle of five novels that he was planning; although the plot of the third novel, "La duchessa di Leyra" (the duchess of Leyra), was already worked out, he never finished it. In his last decades of life, he had the consolation of his friendship with the younger Federico De Roberto, author of the historical novel *The Viceroys* (1894), who came to play Boswell to Verga's Johnson. De Roberto published a series of newspaper articles on Verga after his death that left no doubt that Verga had been considered the most important person in De Roberto's life.

In Rome in 1881, Verga had met Dina Castellazzi, wife of the count of Sordevolo, and the relationship that developed between them was to last the rest of Verga's life. The more than seven hundred letters he wrote to her from Catania are the primary source of information on the last two decades of his life. Although she became a widow in 1891 and wanted Verga to marry her, he was unwilling and remained a bachelor.

As he became more withdrawn in old age, Verga became more politically conservative. His stance against demonstrations that could disrupt the political order of Italy hardened. When Luigi Capuana and De Roberto publicly faulted the Italian government for its inefficiency in handling the earthquake that destroyed Messina and Reggio di Calabria in 1908, Verga, fearing to trigger a secession movement in Sicily, remained silent. His inability to understand the march of time began to interfere with his art. In his play *Dal tuo al mio*, about the suppression of a strike at a sulfur mine and the turncoat loyalties of the mine's foreman, his message that greed is the incontrovertible source of evil in a world devoid of idealism has by now become doctrinaire and boring. Although politics as such interested Verga only sporadically, in 1920, Prime Minister Giovanni Giolitti made Verga a Senator of the Kingdom, following a tradition begun in 1860 when Alessandro Manzoni was similarly invested.

Verga died on the morning of January 27, 1922, having suffered a cerebral hemorrhage three days earlier. De Roberto scarcely left Verga's bedside those three days; afterward he made a thorough search for the manuscript of "La duchessa di Leyra," which everyone expected to appear as a finished product, but he found only the first chapter and a few pages of the second. In a letter in 1899, Verga had complained of difficulties ("May God help me with this Duchess!") he was having with the Duchess's language, the international, stilted, and pretentious language of the upper classes. For the novelist who had mastered the medium used by the peasants, the medium of his own class was an insurmountable obstacle; whereas in his pre-maturity novels, he had openly permitted himself to react against the false world of this privileged group, his self-imposed adherence to Verism kept him, at this point, from expressing his unutterable disdain and thus from completing a possible masterpiece.

ANALYSIS

Giovanni Verga's first novels were romantic, predictable, and superficial. His masterpieces of Verism were written between 1880 and 1890, and for the last thirty years of his life, though full of good intentions, he produced relatively little. In one of his earliest novels, *Una peccatrice* (a sinner), which could be called an autobiography of wish fulfillment (in the story, a young Sicilian, footloose in the big city, achieves both literary fame and the beautiful woman he loves), the author strives for a veneer of realism by claiming that his story comes from authentic documents that have come into his possession. Although Verga in his maturity would disown this novel, the writer's task to re-create reality is already taken seriously in it. *Storia di una capinera* tells the story of a young girl forced to become a nun against her will, in the manner of Denis Diderot's *The Nun* (1796). For years Verga's most widely read novel, it consists of letters allegedly written by the girl herself. The blackcap of the title is a fragile bird Verga claims to have seen once and been reminded of later when he learned the girl's story.

In the preface to *Eva*, Verga again asserts the veracity of what he writes, although this time not insisting that it is true, but rather that it could have happened. Although the character of Eva is lost in the bombast of the novel's conventionalities, Eva's speech is precise and reflects her personality. Further, Eva's decision to leave Enrico for a rich lover stems from Verga's firm belief that love, without the social coercion afforded by marriage or without the nostalgia caused by separation, cannot survive routine when lovers live together. Also emphasized is the incontestable power of financial security to nurture art and love.

Hardly an advance over *Eva*, *Tigre reale* (royal tigress) concerns a consumptive Russian lady who lives in Florence and falls in love with a young Sicilian. Despite its title, another early novel, *Eros*, is the most complex of this group and the one least trammeled by the unreality of the dreamlike eroticism that fascinated the early Verga. The aristocratic Alberto, a type Verga never again explored in his novels, grows up without a family, searches for love,

makes many mistakes, and ends his life with a gunshot. Although the often realistic and colloquial language coincides with character, Verga as author obtrudes upon the reader his strong dislike for the aristocratic world he is portraying.

The appearance in 1874 of the short story "Nedda" marked the point at which Verga abandoned his autobiographical theme of aristocrats searching for love and began to seek a commoner world apparently closer to his heart, the world of the Sicilian "primitive." It was at this point that Verga joined the literary movement known as Verism, the Italian equivalent of the realistic and naturalistic schools in France. Verga had long followed French literary trends closely and admired Émile Zola, Gustave Flaubert, and Guy de Maupassant. The views of Maupassant, whose success did much to stimulate interest in the short story in Italy, were especially compatible with Verga's concept of good writing. In fact, there developed between the two a mutual respect, and Maupassant even offered at one time to write a preface for *Little Novels of Sicily* when it appeared in French translation.

Verga's cardinal rules of good writing were in the process of emerging: The story must tell itself without evidence of or interference from the author, and language must coincide in every way with the characters who are speaking. The spare narrative style that Verga achieved in his best work, however, did much to alienate the critics, who were also put off by his pessimism and the harshness of his vision. The characteristics of the Italian novel had been set by Manzoni thirty years earlier, and it was unacceptable for a novelist to deviate from this norm. Certainly Manzoni had written of the harshness of real-life situations, but the harshness of Manzoni is balanced by his deep religious belief, a feeling absent in Verga's writing.

Verga's intent, expressed as early as 1878 and clearly based on the inspiration of Honoré de Balzac's *The Human Comedy* (1829-1848) and Zola's *The Rougon-Macquart Family* (1871-1893), was to compose a cycle of five novels to be called "La marea" (the tide)—later changed to *I vinti* (the doomed)—which would scrutinize successive stages in people's struggle for material security. The first novel of the cycle, *The House by the Medlar Tree*, would involve the struggle of a Sicilian family for minimal needs alone. The search would evolve to outright greed for riches typified by a middle-class character, Mastrodon Gesualdo, in the second book of the series. "La duchessa di Leyra" (begun in 1907), still with a Sicilian setting, would explore aristocratic vanity in Palermo, and "L'onorevole Scipioni" (the honorable Scipioni) would study political ambition in Rome. Finally, "L'uomo di lusso" (the man of wealth) would portray a character who possesses all these desires and is consumed by them. These last two titles were only projected works; Verga never completed his planned five-volume series.

THE HOUSE BY THE MEDLAR TREE

The first book of the cycle was to be named after its main character, "Padron 'Ntoni" (master 'Ntoni), but Verga decided at the last minute to name the novel after the family, *I Malavoglia* (an emphasis lost in the title of the English translation). The tragic error of the Malavoglias, a family of fishermen, is their speculation in a shipload of lupine (a forage crop), to be paid for from profits yet to be made. A storm at sea sinks their boat, the *Provvidenza*, and causes the loss of the lupine cargo and the death of Master 'Ntoni's son Bastianazzo. Because the debt must be paid, their cherished house by the medlar tree is lost and the family risks disintegration. The tragedy pervades the book, but the poetic psychology of their moral code, especially their family ties, raises the book far beyond the commonplace and gives it a rare dignity. True to Verga's belief that an author must not interfere in his story, the major characters do all the narrating, and the minor characters act as a chorus for the reader, commenting on events in a colloquial style that sounds more like spoken than written speech. The story is told from the inside by all the characters rather than by a single voice. There is little description per se, and what there is seems as if it were spoken by some unidentified villager using the same language as the other speakers. Verga does not furnish the reader with character descriptions; instead, he gives only names and gestures. Those events which are not witnessed, such as the sinking

of the *Provvidenza*, are left to the reader's imagination through the subsequent conversation of the villagers.

Consistent with Verga's aim of precision and factuality, the reader knows exactly when each event in the novel takes place. Master 'Ntoni was born in 1801 and the youngest of his grandchildren in 1864. The setting is Aci-Trezza, ten miles north of Catania in eastern Sicily, where nearly the entire plot unfolds and whose pervasive atmosphere serves a function not unlike that of Egdon Heath in Thomas Hardy's *The Return of the Native* (1878). When Master 'Ntoni's grandson, also named 'Ntoni, is inducted into the Italian navy, he is sent to Naples, the former capital of the Kingdom of the Two Sicilies, which the new Kingdom of Italy has recently incorporated and superseded; there he is struck by the many sensations and temptations of the metropolis. Although these years of unification were exciting ones in the history of the Italian nation, the villagers here are ignorant of current events. The military service that is required by the new Italian government imposes a terrible drain of human power on a hardworking family such as the Malavoglias. When Master 'Ntoni, in his attempts to gain an exemption for his grandson, speaks with Don Franco, the town pharmacist and one of the few villagers who knows anything about politics, the pharmacist blames conscription on the monarchy and speaks in favor of the republic, whereupon Master 'Ntoni begs him to start his republic soon, "as though Don Franco kept a republic up his sleeve."

Master 'Ntoni's character is revealed in his frequent use of proverbs (which in Italian are used more freely than in modern colloquial English), such as "To pull an oar, the five fingers must work together" and "Before you can be a Pope, you must learn to be a sacristan." Master 'Ntoni is the "thumb" (the only indispensable finger) and "Pope" of these metaphors, and his son Bastianazzo, though big and burly, takes orders from his father the patriarch. Bastianazzo's wife Maruzza, called "La Longa," is good at bearing and rearing their five children: 'Ntoni, a big oaf of twenty; Luca, who has more sense but who is killed in military service at the naval Battle of Lissa in 1866; Alessi, who resembles grandfather 'Ntoni and who will carry on the family name and honor; Mena, an industrious young woman; and Lia, who is not yet "fish, flesh nor fowl."

After the loss of the lupine, the moneylender, Uncle Crucifix, demands his money. Uncle Crucifix is a tyrant who reappears with amplifications as Mazzaro in the story "La Roba" ("Property") in *Little Novels of Sicily* and as Mastro-don Gesualdo, the most complex and the most tragic of the three. Tyrant that he is, however, Uncle Crucifix is respected in the village, because he is rich and because he "sticks to his trade." Master 'Ntoni, after exhausting all honest methods open to him to repay the debt, agrees to surrender his beloved house by the medlar tree. The sunken *Provvidenza* has been recovered and will be repaired so that eventually the Malavoglia family will be able to buy back the house. At this point, the story becomes less that of a debt that must be paid, and more a story of personal heroism, a story in which Master 'Ntoni looms like a giant, strong in his faith that he will be able to recover the house and unswerving in his courage.

The grandson 'Ntoni, who is not a bad person and who does genuinely love his family, cannot see the sense in fighting a losing battle when there are opportunities elsewhere and soon gets involved in smuggling coffee, sugar, and silk kerchiefs. When the local customs official, Don Michele, catches up with him, 'Ntoni knifes him in the chest and is brought to trial. When he sees his namesake brought to trial as a criminal, Master 'Ntoni has a stroke and, just as his grandson Alessi brings him word that the house by the medlar tree is about to be theirs again, he dies. Alessi is destined to carry on the family name and is Verga's reaffirming symbol of faith in tradition and hard work.

The defense lawyer at the trial argues that there had been no smuggling and that young 'Ntoni wished only to restore the family honor, because Don Michele had seduced his sister, Lia. This does irreparable damage to Lia's reputation; in order to avoid dishonor, she is forced to leave home and is actually forced into prostitution by the very villagers who claim to abominate sexual promiscuity. Because no self-respecting man in the village would marry a prostitute's sister, this also condemns Mena to spinsterhood. Mena will take a room in the attic and wait to help rear Alessi's children when they come. Young 'Ntoni must go away as well, but Alessi and Mena carry on in the same house almost as if nothing had happened. Although many of their number have been lost, the disasters that have befallen the Malavoglia family have not destroyed their faith in life.

Despite its fatalism, the book is filled with irony and humor. The very name Malavoglia, which suggests both "ill-will" and "sloth," has little application to the family members themselves; the boat, *Provvidenza*, is hardly providential for the family; and there is little redemption in the undisguised greed of Uncle Crucifix. There is humor in some of the marriages that occur in the course of the novel: Uncle Crucifix meets his nemesis when he marries La Vespa, who blithely squanders the money that he has amassed in his long career, and Brasi Cipolla, who feels he can no longer marry Mena because of the family's reputation, is stuck with the worthless Mangiacarrube.

MASTRO-DON GESUALDO

Mastro-don Gesualdo, Verga's other masterpiece, the second of his projected cycle of novels and the last one completed, is the epic of a self-made man impelled toward the acquisition of greater and greater wealth. The title is applied to him sarcastically by the villagers in order to remind him of his humble origins, since "Mastro" (mastercraftsman; in this case, stonemason) and "don" (landowning gentleman) are sociologically incompatible ideas. Everyone in the novel is obsessed by greed, but Gesualdo also sees his wealth as a means to power. As in Verga's earlier masterpiece, the use of proverbs underscores the philosophies of the characters: "The world belongs to those who have money," and "Everyone works in his own interest." Gesualdo's goal is to be admitted into the bourgeoisie, a class that would not tolerate him if it were not for his riches. He marries the aristocratic but penniless Bianca Trao—even though she has already been seduced by her cousin, Baron Ninì Rubiera—simply for the prestige the marriage will give him in business deals. "La roba" (property) is an obsessive symbol for Gesualdo, and it is significant that on his wedding night he applies this very word, in its second sense of "stuff," to Bianca ("Fine stuff you are!").

After his marriage to Bianca, Gesualdo must give up his mistress, the faithful Diodata, by whom he has fathered two children and for whom he provides a dowry to ensure her subsequent marriage. Count Ninì Rubiera, who, unbeknown to Gesualdo, is the father of his "daughter" Isabella, falls in love with an actress and applies to Gesualdo for a loan. Gesualdo obliges happily, seeing in this still another way to acquire property. Later he forces his daughter Isabella to marry the duke of Leyra from Palermo, who has an illustrious name but who is badly in need of Isabella's dowry.

The specter of death haunts the last quarter of the book. The tubercular Bianca is dying. The peasants rebel against the rich, who in order to save their own property try to divert the attention of the furious crowds to the upstart Gesualdo. Once his own cancerlike disease is diagnosed, Gesualdo fights furiously against the thought of death. He is finally taken to Palermo by the duke of Leyra, where, under surveillance, he will not be able to rewrite his will in favor of his illegitimate children. Because the character Gesualdo never loses awareness of the great price his riches have cost him, because his own interest has often included interest in many other people, and because of the detachment from his riches that he achieves while in Palermo, he is a character with whom the reader can ultimately sympathize. "I want to clear my accounts with God" are his last words.

For many years after the appearance of *Mastro-don Gesualdo*, critics argued over which of the two Verga masterpieces was the greater. It is now generally agreed that *The House by the Medlar Tree* is the more powerful narrative, yet in content rather than style and for the stature of its hero, *Mastro-don Gesualdo* deserves to be appreciated in its own right.

Jack Shreve

OTHER MAJOR WORKS

SHORT FICTION: *Primavera ed altri racconti*, 1876; *Vita dei campi*, 1880 (*Under the Shadow of Etna*, 1896); *Novelle rusticane*, 1883 (*Little Novels of Sicily*, 1925); *Per le vie*, 1883; *Vagabondaggio*, 1887; *I ricordi del capitano D'Arce*, 1891; *Don Candeloro e Cia.*, 1894; *Del tuo al mio*, 1905 (adaptation of his play); *Cavalleria Rusticana and Other Stories*, 1926; *The She-Wolf and Other Stories*, 1958.

PLAYS: *Cavalleria rusticana*, pr., pb. 1884 (based on his short story; *Cavalleria Rusticana: Nine Scenes from the Life of the People*, 1893); *In portineria*, pb. 1884 (based on his short story "Il canario del N. 15"); *La Lupa*, pr., pb. 1896 (based on his short story); *La caccia al lupo*, pr. 1901 (based on his short story; *The Wolf Hunt*, 1921); *La caccia alla volpe*, pr. 1901; *Dal tuo al mio*, pr. 1903; *Teatro*, pb. 1912; *Rose caduche*, pb. 1928 (wr. 1873-1875).

NONFICTION: *Lettere al suo traduttore*, 1954; *Lettere a Dina*, 1962, 1971; *Lettere a Luigi Capuana*, 1975.

BIBLIOGRAPHY

Alexander, Alfred. *Giovanni Verga*. London: Grant & Cutler, 1972. This biography should be used with some caution. Although Alexander provides important factual material, his interpretations seem highly speculative and sometimes unpersuasive.

Alexander, Foscarina. *The Aspiration Toward a Lost Natural Harmony in the Work of Three Italian Writers: Leopardi, Verga, and Moravia*. Lewiston: The Edwin Mellen Press, 1990. Provides biographical notes and bibliography.

Bergin, Thomas G. *Giovanni Verga*. New Haven, Conn.: Yale University Press, 1931. Reprint. Westport, Conn.: Greenwood Press, 1969. Still considered one of the best treatments of Verga in English.

Cecchetti, Giovanni. *Giovanni Verga*. Boston: Twayne, 1978. A solid introductory study with chapters on Verga's formative years and his maturity, with separate chapters on *The House by the Medlar Tree* and *Mastro-don Gesualdo*. Includes chronology, notes, and an annotated bibliography.

Hemmings, F. W. J., ed. *The Age of Realism*. Baltimore: Penguin Books, 1974. Contains an essay, "Giovanni Verga: From 'Verismo' to Realism." A short but perceptive discussion of Verga's career, situating him in the context of European realism.

Kennard, Joseph Spencer. *Italian Romance Writers.* New York: Brentano's, 1906. Rather elementary but still useful for the beginning student.

Ragusa, Olga, ed. *Verga's Milanese Tales.* New York: S. F. Vanni, 1964. Valuable for its translations of Verga's prefaces to his work and for the translation of Luigi Pirandello's essay on Verga.

Williams, D. A., ed. *The Monster in the Mirror: Studies in Nineteenth-Century Realism.* Oxford, England: Oxford University Press, 1978. Contains an insightful essay on Verga's *Mastro-don Gesualdo.*

JULES VERNE

Born: Nantes, France; February 8, 1828
Died: Amiens, France; March 24, 1905

PRINCIPAL LONG FICTION

Cinq Semaines en ballon, 1863 (*Five Weeks in a Balloon*, 1876)

Voyage au centre de la terre, 1864 (*A Journey to the Centre of the Earth*, 1872)

De la terre à la lune, 1865 (*From the Earth to the Moon*, 1873)

Voyages et aventures du capitaine Hatteras, 1864-1866 (2 volumes; includes *Les Anglais au pôle nord*, 1864 [*English at the North Pole*, 1874], and *Le Désert de glace*, 1866 [*Field of Ice*, 1876]; also as *Adventures of Captain Hatteras*, 1875)

Les Enfants du capitaine Grant, 1867-1868 (3 volumes; *Voyage Round the World*, 1876-1877; also as *Captain Grant's Children*, includes *The Mysterious Document*, *Among the Cannibals*, and *On the Track*)

Vingt mille lieues sous les mers, 1869-1870 (*Twenty Thousand Leagues Under the Sea*, 1873)

Autour de la lune, 1870 (*From the Earth to the Moon . . . and a Trip Around It*, 1873)

Une Ville flottante, 1871 (*A Floating City*, 1876)

Aventures de trois russes et de trois anglais, 1872 (*Meridiana: The Adventures of Three Englishmen and Three Russians in South Africa*, 1873)

Le Tour du monde en quatre-vingts jours, 1873 (*Around the World in Eighty Days*, 1873)

Docteur Ox, 1874, 1876 (in *Dr. Ox's Experiment and Master Zacharius*, 1876)

L'Île mystérieuse, 1874-1875 (3 volumes; includes *Les Naufrages de l'air*, *L'Abandonné*, and *Le Secret de l'île*; *The Mysterious Island*, 1875)

Le "Chancellor," 1875 (*Survivors of the "Chancellor,"* 1875)

Michel Strogoff, 1876 (*Michael Strogoff*, 1876-1877)

Hector Servadac, 1877 (English translation, 1878)

Les Cinq Cents Millions de la Bégum, 1878 (*The Begum's Fortune*, 1880)

La Maison à vapeur, 1880 (*The Steam House*, 1881; includes *The Demon of Cawnpore* and *Tigers and Traitors*)

La Jangada, 1881 (2 volumes; *The Giant Raft*, 1881; includes *Down the Amazon* and *The Cryptogram*)

Mathias Sandorf, 1885 (English translation, 1886)

Robur le conquerant, 1886 (*The Clipper of the Clouds*, 1887)

Sans dessus dessous, 1889 (*The Purchase of the North Pole*, 1891)

Le Château des Carpathes, 1892 (*The Castle of the Carpathians*, 1893)

L'Île à hélices, 1895 (*Floating Island*, 1896; also as *Propeller Island*, 1965)

Face au drapeau, 1896 (*For the Flag*, 1897)

Le Sphinx des glaces, 1897 (*An Antarctic Mystery*, 1898; also as *The Mystery of Arthur Gordon Pym*)

Le Village aérien, 1901 (*The Village in the Treetops*, 1964)

Maître du monde, 1904 (*Master of the World*, 1914)

La Chasse au météore, 1908 (*The Chase of the Golden Meteor*, 1909)

Les naufrages du "Jonathan," 1909 (*The Survivors of the "Jonathan,"* 1962)

Le Secret de Wilhelm Storitz, 1910 (*The Secret of Wilhelm Storitz*, 1965)

(Library of Congress)

L'Étonnante Aventure de la mission Barsac, 1920
(2 volumes; *Into the Niger Bend*, 1919; *The City
in the Sahara*, 1965)

OTHER LITERARY FORMS

Jules Verne's initial ambition was to be a playwright, and several of his plays and operettas were
produced in Paris during the 1850's. The first was *Les
Pailles rompues*, produced by Alexandre Dumas, *père*,
in 1850, which also appeared in print. Others were the
librettos *Colin Maillard* (1853) and *Les Compagnons
de la Marjolaine* (1855). Various short stories appeared in periodicals during the same period; some
were collected along with the novelette "Une Fantasie
du docteur Ox" in 1874. A collection of later stories
was assembled for publication by Verne's son, Michel
Verne, appearing under the title *Hier et demain* (1910;
Yesterday and Tomorrow, 1965). Verne also wrote various nonfictional works on the history of exploration
and took over from Théophile Lavellée a multivolume
project called *Géographie illustrée de la France et de*

ses colonies, which was issued from 1867 to 1868.
Many of his novels were adapted to dramatic form and
were usually represented as collaborations when produced or subsequently published as plays. Of his early
articles, the most important is an essay on Edgar Allan
Poe which he published in 1864 in the journal *Musée
des familles*.

ACHIEVEMENTS

Verne is remembered today chiefly as one of the
two most notable writers of science fiction *avant la
lettre*. I. O. Evans describes him as the "founder" of
science fiction, and Peter Costello calls him the "inventor" of science fiction. The claim is justified, but
it should be remembered that Verne did not see himself in this way—he was quite sincere in seeing no
real literary relationship between his own work and
that of H. G. Wells, with whom he was frequently
compared during the last decade of his life. What
Verne actually set out to do, consciously and method-
ically, was to use geography as an ideative resource
in the same way that Alexandre Dumas, *père*, had
used history. Only a fraction of his work can be described as science fiction, yet all of it fits into a single
pattern that is suggested by his use of the term *les
voyages extraordinaires* as a kind of series title for his
oeuvre. The medium that he invented and developed
might more appropriately be called "the novel of
imaginary tourism"; the science fiction element in
his work arose out of his occasional ambitions to
send his tourists to places never before visited by humans (the North Pole, the moon, and cave systems
beneath the earth's surface). In some instances, he had
to devise new modes of travel—Barbicane's space-
gun and Robur's flying machine—but, for the most
part, he was content to employ conventional means
of transport or slightly more luxurious versions of already existing machines (balloons and submarines).

There is a sense in which Verne's reputation has
been distorted by the emphasis on his achievements
as a precursor of modern science fiction. He has been
described by Franz Born as "the man who invented
the future" and by Peter Haining as "the master
of prophecy," but these descriptions are plainly absurd. Apart from two whimsical essays and his last,

most somber, short story, "L'Eternel Adam" (written c. 1900 and included in *Yesterday and Tomorrow*; "The Eternal Adam"), Verne wrote nothing set in the future. Many of his novels deal with achievements not yet accomplished in the real world, but they were all achievements which Verne believed to be perfectly possible in the context of his own times. Even in his own day, Verne was hailed as the inventor, in his imagination, of technological devices later realized, but Verne always disclaimed any such achievement. In relation to the most commonly quoted example—the submarine described in *Twenty Thousand Leagues Under the Sea*—Verne pointed out, when questioned, that there had been submarines around for at least sixty years (he had probably seen *Le Plongeur*, built in 1864, on display at the Paris Exhibition of 1867) and that all the innovations he had attributed to the *Nautilus* actually remained unrealized.

Verne's real achievement was simply to notice the impact that the revolution in transportation was having upon the world. When he saw the *Great Eastern* under construction in London in 1859, he had the wit to realize what a difference steamships would make to the business of travel and to the accessibility of distant parts of the world. He realized that a revolution in exploration was under way quite as important as the great navigations of the fifteenth and sixteenth centuries, and that new technologies would shrink the world very dramatically. If his novel *Around the World in Eighty Days* seemed sensational, it was only because of the ignorance of the audience; Thomas Cook had already advertised the first tour around the world for anyone who cared to go, and a Bostonian named George Francis Train had already gone around the world in eighty traveling days, though his total journey time was extended by a few sojourns in foreign jails.

Verne's enthusiasm for the Industrial Revolution was undoubtedly based upon a one-sided view of its consequences; the same might be said, however, of the many writers who saw and bemoaned the social consequences of the revolution—the growth of the industrial poor—without realizing the historical significance of technological advancement. Verne had little to say about the future of technology, but he was aware of the fact that the process of innovation would continue and would be important in its impact on human affairs. This makes him a wiser man than most of the political economists of the day—including Karl Marx—who grossly underestimated, or even mistook, the significance of technological change.

Verne has never been taken very seriously as a novelist. Partly this is because he was considered popular, and thus vulgar—all the more so because Pierre-Jules Hetzel, his publisher, dealt mainly in juvenile fiction. In Britain, Verne's books were published in butchered translations as "boys' books," and it is only in recent years that unmutilated translations of a few of his more famous works have become available. In France, interest in Verne has revived. Michel Butor wrote an excellent essay entitled "The Golden Age in Jules Verne" (1960), and even Roland Barthes paid wry homage to Verne in one of the brief essays in *Mythologies* (1957). The contribution made by Verne to nineteenth century consciousness is now openly acknowledged, if not universally admired. The literary skills displayed in Verne's novels are limited, and the very processes of change which he was celebrating have robbed his stories of their excitement and conviction, leaving to them only historical interest and a certain naïve charm. For these reasons, modern readers have great difficulty in reading Verne for pleasure; his appeal is anchored in a lost past from which today's reader is far removed. Nevertheless, his achievements, seen in their appropriate historical context, should not be underestimated.

BIOGRAPHY

Jules Verne was born in 1828, the son of Pierre Verne, a lawyer, and Sophie, née Allotte de la Fuye. He was born in Nantes, on the Île Feydeau, an island in the Loire River that has since been connected to the bank. His family appears to have been a bastion of middle-class respectability, desperately concerned with keeping up appearances. This fact appears to have had a profound effect upon Verne's life, a subtle but important influence on his work, and to be the cause of some misrepresentation in the biographies written by members of his family—even the one published in 1973 by Jean Jules-Verne (his grandson).

Verne's life story seems to have been one of constant and unsuccessful rebellion against the standards and lifestyle that his family tried to impose upon him. He never escaped the clutches of middle-class respectability and seems to have spent the last forty years of his life maintaining a facade for the sake of the expectations of his family. Under such circumstances, it is perhaps not surprising that he took full advantage of the opportunity to become a voyager in the imagination—a champion escapist.

Verne studied law in his father's office for a while before going to Paris, ostensibly to continue his studies there. Actually, he wanted to be a playwright, and he threw himself into the bohemian life of the student quarter of the Left Bank, where he met Victor Hugo and Alexandre Dumas, *père*. Dumas encouraged his literary endeavors and produced Verne's first one-act comedy at the Théâtre Historique. Verne's attempts to establish himself in the literary world were, however, less than wholly successful. While he wrote plays, short stories, and operettas in the early 1850's, he was for three years secretary of the Théâtre Lyrique, but by the end of 1855, he had had enough. In 1856, he planned to marry a young widow, Honorine Morel, and in order to be able to support her, he asked his father to buy him a share in a stock-broking business.

This business provided Verne with an income, but he still had other ambitions and began collecting articles which he hoped might help him to carve out a niche for himself as a novelist exploiting geography in the same way that Dumas had exploited history. He traveled extensively, visiting Britain in 1859 and Scandinavia in 1861, and produced more light plays with music. His son Michel was born in August, 1861.

Around this time, Verne appears to have become partly estranged from his wife. They had no more children and occupied separate beds, but they continued to maintain the appearance of a happy marriage. Verne retreated more and more frequently to his club—the Cercle de la Presse Scientifique—where he met and became friendly with Félix Tournachon, a photographer and aeronaut who used the pseudonym "Nadar." Out of the interest in aeronautics inspired by this association came a documentary novel about ballooning, which Verne took to the publisher Hetzel (who himself wrote, under the pseudonym P. J. Stahl) in 1862. Hetzel suggested sweeping revisions, which Verne carried out in only two weeks. Verne put to Hetzel, soon after the publication of *Five Weeks in a Balloon*, his idea for an extended series of *les voyages extraordinaire*, and Hetzel encouraged him to go ahead. By September, 1863, when the Verne family moved to Auteuil, Verne was well established as a novelist. He was, however, apparently under great personal strain. He suffered a good deal from stress-related facial paralysis, which eventually had to be relieved by electric shock treatment.

Verne seems to have been grateful to Hetzel, and his first biographer, Marguerite Allotte de la Fuye (his niece), alleges that Hetzel treated him with the utmost generosity. In fact, Hetzel's financial records reveal that Hetzel made about five times as much from Verne's books as Verne did and, though Verne eventually became quite well off, his family certainly struggled for a while in the 1860's and may have suffered mild financial embarrassments later in his career, when his sales fell off dramatically.

In 1870, Ferdinand de Lesseps solicited the Légion d'Honneur for Verne; it was awarded in 1870 immediately before the fall of the Third Republic. He was honored by the Académie Française in August, 1872, but was never elected to it. During the Franco-Prussian War, Verne set up a coast-guard unit at Crotoy, where he had been living for some years, and afterward had to return to the Bourse for a while because of the effect of the war on the book trade. This did not last long, however, and in 1872, he settled permanently in Amiens, devoting himself from then on to full-time writing.

Verne's son Michel proved a great disappointment to him. As a boy, Michel was delinquent, and he was estranged from his parents for a long time, living a turbulent personal life. When he finally settled down, however, he and his father were reconciled. Michel's third son, Jean Jules-Verne, eventually became one of Verne's biographers.

Verne's main relaxation during his years at Amiens was his involvement with a series of small boats, all of which he called *St. Michel*, the third and last of which he bought in 1877. He spent a great deal of time on these boats, and the third one was actually large enough to allow him to undertake some voyages of his own. He visited Britain and Scandinavia in 1877, went cruising in the Baltic in 1880, and toured parts of the Mediterranean in 1884. On the last trip, in particular, he was exposed to a great deal of publicity and was hailed as a celebrity wherever he went. He tried to avoid this, but his wife reveled in it and frustrated his attempts to remain unnoticed. He sold the third *St. Michel* in 1886, possibly because of financial problems—throughout the 1880's, sales of his new books plummeted. Whereas, at the peak of his career, *Around the World in Eighty Days* had sold more than a hundred thousand copies in the trade edition, by 1880, his new works frequently sold less than twenty thousand copies, and the books he wrote in the last decade of his life sold less than ten thousand copies.

In March, 1886, Verne was shot in the foot by a would-be assassin—his nephew Gaston. Gaston was confined to an asylum; the incident was so shocking to the family that Peter Costello, in his 1978 biography, reports that no one will discuss the matter even today. Verne remained lame for the rest of his life, but that did not prevent him from going into local politics the following year. This represented a modest emergence from his shell, in that he stood as a radical, undoubtedly offending his staunchly conservative family. It is interesting that Verne's political radicalism is occasionally evident in his wry asides but is never given free expression in his works. The same is true of his religious beliefs. Though his family was staunchly Catholic (and the family biographers maintain that Verne was also), Verne appears to have become an agnostic, if not an atheist, as early as the 1850's. Religiosity was part of the facade which he maintained throughout his life, and his novels do very little to suggest his true opinions, except in certain sly remarks. This self-conscious hypocrisy is, at times, willfully subverted by the author, as in *The Village in the Treetops*, in which a token denial of belief in Darwinism is then made to look absurd by a story about apes with quasi-human intelligence—living "missing links." The difficulty of penetrating this

facade was increased when Verne, in 1898, burned a number of his personal papers, including manuscripts and account books.

Even after Verne's death, the business of keeping up appearances continued. Michel became his father's literary executor and seems to have taken a hand in revising one or two of his manuscripts for posthumous publication. The authorship of the novel translated into English in two volumes as *Into the Niger Bend* and *The City in the Sahara*, in particular, is rather dubious. A ghostwriter named Georges Montignac may well have been involved, as well as Michel. Certain other works published under Jules Verne's name are most likely the work of Michel, although this may apply only to shorter pieces.

What is remarkable about Verne's life, insofar as it affected his literary career, was the extent to which everything that really mattered to him remained private. He was a man whose "real" life was lived inside his head, quite disconnected from the daily routine of going through the motions of respectable middle-class life. Even in his books, his innermost thoughts remain covert, peeping out only occasionally, and then in disguise. The best of his fantasies concern ordinary people snatched by circumstance into isolation and imprisonment, which they accept with relief and guilty joy. He was the archetypal armchair traveler, a man who found solace in his dreams and worked to add a special verisimilitude to those dreams, researching indefatigably to fill in their background. He pretended to be satisfied with his lot in life, but his stories are the work of a deeply disappointed and frustrated man.

ANALYSIS

Most of Jules Verne's novels, including the ones for which he is best known, are imaginary travelogues whose initial appeal to the reader is that they will show him the remote regions of the world and allow him to participate in adventures which could only take place there. In the first ten years of his career, Verne's imaginary travels took him to all the most inaccessible corners of the globe: Captain Hatteras went to the North Pole; the children of Captain Grant circumnavigated the Southern Hemisphere; and the protagonists of *Five Weeks in a Balloon* and *Meridiana* crossed darkest Africa at a time when "darkest" still meant obscure and unknown. Other characters undertook still bolder voyages: Axel and Professor Lidenbrock never did reach the center of the earth, but they did get under its skin, and though Barbicane and his companions failed to land on the moon (mercifully, as they had no means of return), they did get a trip around it.

We know today that all these stories are unrealistic, but Verne's audience could not know that, and they were compelled to be impressed by the elaborate methods Verne used to create an atmosphere of verisimilitude. His attention to detail, particularly the detail of scientific instrumentation and measurement, gives his travelers a vital sense of purpose. They are researchers, collecting information with the same intellectual curiosity and dedication that guided Verne's collecting of research materials. It may well be that the scientifically minded heroes have less serious companions who are along for the ride (and who usually provide comic relief), but there is no doubt as to where the real value of the works is located.

A JOURNEY TO THE CENTRE OF THE EARTH

The best of the early works is *A Journey to the Centre of the Earth*, because it is at once the most painstaking, the most imaginative, and the most elegantly plotted. The notion of an enclosed world inhabited by primeval monsters is one that has been copied many times since, and though it is the kind of wild invention of which Verne rather disapproved (he never did anything similar again), it seems perfectly appropriate to this particular literary exercise. Significantly, however, *A Journey to the Centre of the Earth* was not the most popular of the early works, and it does not enjoy the highest reputation—that distinction goes to *Twenty Thousand Leagues Under the Sea*.

TWENTY THOUSAND LEAGUES UNDER THE SEA

There are many reasons for the popularity of *Twenty Thousand Leagues Under the Sea*. The undersea world which it displays is bound to seem meager, and sometimes laughable, to modern readers who have seen and become familiar with films made by Jacques Cousteau. The contemporary reader knows

what a strange and wonderful world it is, and how many bizarre inhabitants it has. In 1870, however, there was no underwater photography, the first skin-diving equipment had not yet been designed, and the undersea world was as alien as the planet Mars. The mysterious menace of the sea was legendary and had been spectacularly recalled to the public attention in 1861, when the French naval vessel *Alecton* encountered a so-called giant octopus (actually a giant squid), which the crew nearly succeeded in harpooning and hauling aboard.

In fact, *Twenty Thousand Leagues Under the Sea* is the least reliable of all Verne's novels as far as its informational content is concerned. Almost every invention in it, no matter how modest, missed the mark. Although the illustrations imply that the diving suits in the novel are rather like the pressurized suits which later became widespread, in reality the ones Verne describes would be lethal. Despite the credit given to Verne for "inventing" the modern submarine, the *Nautilus* is rather an absurd vessel, in terms of its scientific plausibility. All of this, of course, would not have affected the contemporary reader, who could quite easily swallow the whole story, hook, line, and sinker.

Quite apart from these considerations, however, the book offers powerful attractions. Captain Nemo and the *Nautilus* may not be particularly realistic, but they are most certainly charismatic. They are only disguised as rational creations; in fact, they are myth-figures whose significance reveals a good deal about the spirit of Verne's work.

Barthes, in *Mythologies*, claims that what Verne's characters are always seeking is seclusion, and that the many vessels which are employed in his stories are to be seen not so much as the means of reaching faraway destinations, but rather as microcosmic private worlds where "claustrophilic" heroes can live in comfort, safe from the chaotic and confusing world which flows by outside the windows. In this respect, the *Nautilus* is by far the best of the Verne ships. It has every possible comfort—Nemo not only has the best of everything, but his best also reaches a standard unknown to the aesthetes of Paris. It is also sealed tight; Aronnax is so completely enclosed that he is a helpless prisoner—even the power of self-determination has been taken away from him, so that he can relax utterly and completely into a security greater than anything he has undergone since the womb.

This desire for seclusion and the retreat into a private microcosm is by no means all there is to Verne—it is often the case that his characters cannot seclude themselves and are forced to fight a dogged battle for survival—but it is something that shows up strongly in his romantic and most personal stories. The fantasy of being held prisoner by a benevolent captor, maintained in luxury, and removed from the hurly-burly of the actual world is a common one, and in *Twenty Thousand Leagues Under the Sea*, it finds almost perfect expression. The wonders and dangers of the undersea world are most important here as a kind of emphatic counterpoint, standing in for the uncertainties of life. Nemo's obsessive crusade against the world's shipping is basically a strategy of rejection and retreat which, though it can be admired, envied, and temporarily shared, must ultimately be refused as a viable mode of conduct. The real world, after all, does have to be faced; one cannot help but deal with it even if one's dealings constitute a facade and one's heart is elsewhere.

THE MYSTERIOUS ISLAND

It is significant that Captain Nemo makes his reappearance in Verne's own favorite among his novels—the long and languid *The Mysterious Island*. This was the first and best of Verne's several Robinsonades, in which the island on which the protagonists are cast away becomes an ideal microcosm where (with a little help from an unknown friend) they carefully reconstruct a world of middle-class comfort. Significantly, it is an all-male world strongly reminiscent of a gentlemen's club. The discovery, late in the novel, that the *Nautilus* is hidden deep in the bowels of the island is a magnificently naïve emphasis of the fact that, in terms of Verne's private mythology, the island and the submarine are really the same in terms of their function.

The Mysterious Island belongs to the second decade of Verne's career, a decade in some ways very different from the first. It commenced with the most

popular of his nonfantastic works, *Around the World in Eighty Days*, which constitutes a travelogue rather different from his earlier ones in that the emphasis is on speed rather than leisurely seclusion. Significantly, it is from the closed world of a Victorian club that Phileas Fogg emerges, and to which he intends to return in the minimum possible time, once he has demonstrated that the world can be encircled (and therefore, in a sense, brought under control) on an unexpectedly tight schedule.

The travelogues that Verne wrote after *Around the World in Eighty Days* are markedly different in character from those which he wrote before. The emphasis on scientific research is largely abandoned, though the characters are always subject to occasional lapses into careful observation of odd phenomena and debates about their significance. There are no more expeditions of the kind undertaken by Professor Lidenbrock—Verne takes care to provide his characters with more urgent and more personal motives for travel and thus begins to rely more and more on shipwreck and catastrophe as motive forces.

It may be significant that the highly self-indulgent *The Mysterious Island* was followed by the grim horror story *Survivors of the "Chancellor,"* the story of a ship beset by a chain of catastrophes leaving the survivors to face further appalling ordeals. The contrast reflects the tension in Verne's work to which Barthes does not do full justice—the author was quite well aware of the cozy romanticism which occasionally dominated his stories, and he shared with Barthes the suspicion that there was something unhealthy about it and that it might even be something to be despised. It is almost as if, after 1874, Verne made a conscious effort to distance his work from his own daydreams, to free himself from dependence on their emotional charge in order to become a genuine literary craftsman. He went on after *Survivors of the "Chancellor"* to write the adventure story *Michael Strogoff*, whose plot is built around a journey but which can under no circumstances be accounted a novel of imaginary tourism. When, in *Hector Servadac*, he made a conscious return to imaginative territory similar to that covered in *From the Earth to the Moon . . . and a Trip Around It*, he was noticeably halfhearted about it and allowed the novel to decay into confusion. Not until 1881, when he published *The Giant Raft*, did he really recapture something of the spirit of his early travel-adventure novels.

The Begum's Fortune

One of the most interesting experiments of this second decade was *The Begum's Fortune*, an exercise in social speculation in which an enormous inheritance split between two legatees is used to build two very different cities—the utopian Frankville and the militaristic Stahlstadt. In imagining this sharp contrast between the ideals of a French social scientist and a German militarist, Verne was reflecting upon the intellectual legacy of the Franco-Prussian War, but his vision of Stahlstadt proved to be rather more prophetic than he would have wished. Verne was, in reality, interested in politics and in town planning—there was a streak of authentic utopianism in him—but that was one of the few occasions when he allowed his interest to affect his literary work, and it does so only in a rather stylized manner; both Frankville and Stahlstadt are deliberately oversimplified almost to the point of caricature, as if to emphasize the fact that Verne had no wish to deal in serious speculations about the possible future developments in French or German society. He seems to have believed that there would be a kind of impropriety in so doing, and this belief may be connected with his curiously hostile reaction to the idea that he belonged in the same literary category as Wells.

For the whole of his career as a novelist, Verne maintained a steady productivity. His books were released at the rate of one or two a year, and he left behind enough of a stockpile for the publishers to maintain this schedule for five years after his death. The decline in his popularity in the 1880's, however, reflected a genuine decline in the appeal of his work. He might with justification have wondered at that, believing himself to be demonstrating much greater versatility in his work, but it is ironically true that he echoed his earlier vitality only when he was virtually plagiarizing himself. Many of his later works are interesting, for one reason or another, but few of them are really memorable. *The Clipper of the Clouds* and its sequel, *Master of the World*, are effective pastiches of *Twenty Thousand Leagues Under the Sea*, reduced dramatically in effect by virtue of the fact that the skies patrolled by the flying machine are no substitute for the submarine world of the *Nautilus*. A rather more interesting "microcosmic fantasy" is provided in *Propeller Island*, but Verne deliberately does not treat the notion too seriously.

Interesting for a different reason is *The Castle of the Carpathians*, in which Verne set out to write a gothic romance, albeit of a rationalized nature. Because of his association with science fiction and his use of scientific apparatus in assuring the verisimilitude of his early travelogues, Verne's interest in Romantic fiction of a more exotic character is often overlooked entirely, though he was a great admirer of Poe and E. T. A. Hoffmann. In *An Antarctic Mystery*, Verne provided a continuation of Poe's classic *The Narrative of Arthur Gordon Pym* (1838), and the best of his own early works of short fiction, *Maître Zacharius: Ou, L'Horloger qui a perdu son âme* (1854, 1976; *Dr. Ox's Experiment and Master Zacharius*, 1876) is plainly a pastiche of Hoffmann. Both *The Castle of the Carpathians* and *An Antarctic Mystery*, however, show how difficult Verne found it to create any real sense of supernatural threat. Both stories are rationalized, but they are pedestrian and mundane even before the climactic "explanations." The fact that Verne could be interested in this kind of fantasy, and yet be incapable of writing it, is symptomatic of the fact that his work became steadily more detached from any real core of personal feeling; it became gradually more self-conscious and artificial, a product of intellectual craftsmanship with no real roots in his own beliefs and feelings. By the 1880's, if not earlier, Verne seems to have made a decision that his writing was to be a commercial activity, a way of making a living, rather than a mode of self-expression. Only work published before 1875— and not all of that—really shows any measure of imaginative vigor. For all of its carefulness and frequent cleverness, all the later work is rather lifeless.

Verne's Later Works

In the work of Verne's last years, a certain bleakness becomes gradually more evident. The misanthropy glimpsed in some of his earlier novels (in the character of Captain Nemo, for example) also gained rather freer expression. Members of the ape race in *The Village in the Treetops*, with their primitive caricature-religion, offer a challenge to human vanity, and a much more explicit condemnation of human traits is to be found in the criticisms of materialism which occur in several of the posthumous novels as satirizations of gold-lust. This censure is most evident in *The Chase of the Golden Meteor*, which has a very moral ending in which the scientist-hero sinks the golden meteor rather than allow any of his greedy rivals in the pursuit to get their hands on it. It is perhaps more telling, however, in *The Survivors of the "Jonathan,"* in which the anarchist hero's attempts to found a utopian community are confounded by the discovery of a vicinity of gold. This novel is one of the few in which Verne's radical political sympathies are made unmistakably explicit. A rather different kind of bitterness is seen in *The Secret of Wilhelm Storitz*, in which a jilted lover uses unusual means in order to get back at the woman who rejected him. This downbeat streak in Verne's last period culminated in the short story "The Eternal Adam," a tale of historical cycles of decline and fall which gives voice to an almost Spenglerian pessimism. This is pure science fiction, but it is the work of a very different man from the young Verne who wrote *A Journey to the Centre of the Earth*.

It seems odd to write of a man whose work has been read by millions—a man who is possibly the most translated French writer of all time—that he kept very much to himself. Despite his involvement in a closely knit web of family relationships (which he seems to have regarded as a burdensome oppression), he was essentially a loner. His heroes are mostly independent and detached men who escape into situations in which they enjoy the undemanding companionship of tolerable acquaintances, but in which they have abundant opportunity to be by themselves, observing and meditating upon the world around them. Verne's main appeal is to the reader's longing to "get away from it all," and the key to his great popularity as a writer is that it is precisely that impulse toward escape which drives many people to the activity of reading.

It is by no means surprising that a man with such a personality should have been so interested in science and technology, because it is very often men of such temperament who find contemplation of the abstract world of knowledge congenial. Painstaking research and attention to detail are the prerogatives of individuals willing and able to withdraw habitually from the routines of human intercourse. One may regret that Verne did not "put himself into" his works to any great extent, with the exception of *Twenty Thousand Leagues Under the Sea* and *The Mysterious Island*. One may also regret, especially if one values Verne primarily for his contribution to the emergent genre of scientific romance, that he kept such a disciplined rein on his imagination after the early extravagances of *A Journey to the Centre of the Earth* and *From the Earth to the Moon . . . and a Trip Around It*. These, however, are facets of the man's character, which undeniably has its puzzling aspects.

Verne was not a great writer, but he was a unique and interesting one. He is a literary phenomenon who remains even today something of an enigma despite the fact that his books are straightforward tales of adventure, mostly lacking in depth. Though his work was wide enough in its appeal to generate many imitations, there remains something inimitable about his best books—and not merely the naïveté that the passage of time has rendered impossible. There is a Vernean esprit which remains his alone.

Brian Stableford

OTHER MAJOR WORKS

SHORT FICTION: *Maître Zacharius: Ou L'Horloger qui a perdu son âme*, 1854; *Docteur Ox*, 1874, 1976; *Dr. Ox's Experiment and Master Zacharius*, 1876; *Hier et demain*, 1910 (*Yesterday and Tomorrow*, 1965).

PLAYS: *Les Pailles rompues*, pr. 1850; *Colin Maillard*, pb. 1853 (libretto); *Les Compagnons de la Marjolaine*, pr. 1855 (libretto).

NONFICTION: *Géographie illustrée de la France et de ses colonies*, 1867-1868 (with Théophile Lavellée); *Histoire des grandes voyages et grand voyageurs*, 1870-1873 (3 volumes; with Gabriel Marcel; *Celebrated Travels and Travellers*, 1879-1881).

BIBLIOGRAPHY

Butcher, William. *Verne's Journey to the Centre of the Self: Space and Time in the Voyages Extraordinaires*. London: Macmillan, 1990. A comprehensive study of Verne's science fiction, with detailed notes and a comprehensive bibliography.

Costello, Peter. *Jules Verne: Inventor of Science Fiction*. New York: Scribner's, 1978. A readable biography that puts the fiction in historical context. Includes a bibliography.

Jules-Verne, Jean. *Jules Verne*. New York: Taplinger, 1976. Written by Verne's grandson, this readable and entertaining biography draws on material in the family archives and explores Verne's methods and the experiences that led to his stories and novels. Also a good portrait of the times in which Verne lived and wrote. Includes detailed bibliography and index.

Lottmann, Herbert. *Jules Verne: An Exploratory Biography*. New York: St. Martin's Press, 1996. A graceful study by a veteran biographer of many French subjects. The detailed notes reflect extensive new research.

Lynch, Lawrence. *Jules Verne*. New York: Twayne, 1992. A reliable introductory study with chapters on Verne's early life, his early fiction, his period of masterpieces, and his final fictions. Includes an appendix listing film adaptations of Verne, detailed notes, a chronology, and an annotated bibliography.

Martin, Andrew. *The Mask of the Prophet: The Extraordinary Fictions of Jules Verne*. Oxford, England: Clarendon Press, 1990. Attempts to recapture Verne for modern readers, focusing on his fictions of subversion and law and disorder, and on the prophetic nature of fiction itself.

GORE VIDAL
Edgar Box

Born: West Point, New York; October 3, 1925

PRINCIPAL LONG FICTION

Williwaw, 1946
In a Yellow Wood, 1947
The City and the Pillar, 1948, revised 1965
The Season of Comfort, 1949
A Search for the King: A Twelfth Century Legend, 1950
Dark Green, Bright Red, 1950
The Judgment of Paris, 1952, revised 1965
Death in the Fifth Position, 1952 (as Edgar Box)
Death Before Bedtime, 1953 (as Box)
Death Likes It Hot, 1954 (as Box)
Messiah, 1954, revised 1965
Julian, 1964
Washington, D.C., 1967
Myra Breckinridge, 1968
Two Sisters: A Memoir in the Form of a Novel, 1970
Burr, 1973
Myron, 1974
1876, 1976
Kalki, 1978
Creation, 1981
Duluth, 1983
Lincoln, 1984
Empire, 1987
Hollywood: A Novel of America in the 1920's, 1990
Live from Golgotha, 1992
The Smithsonian Institution, 1998

OTHER LITERARY FORMS

Gore Vidal wrote short stories as well as novels, and he is known as a master essayist, having regularly published collections of essays. Vidal also wrote or adapted plays during the so-called golden age of television, and he wrote screenplays during the last days of the Hollywood studio system.

ACHIEVEMENTS

Gore Vidal is considered a leading American literary figure. While primarily a novelist, he has mastered almost every genre, except poetry. He won success in films, in television, and on Broadway. Many readers consider him a better essayist than novelist, though Vidal emphatically rejects that judgment.

While many of his contemporaries focused their

writings on mundane details of everyday life, Vidal continued to write the novel of ideas. He maintained his focus on the largest questions: What is the nature of Western civilization? What flaws have prevented the United States from achieving its democratic promise? How does a free individual live an intellectually fulfilling and ethically proper life in a corrupt society? These concerns are reflected not only in his writing but also in his political activities, including a bid for the U.S. Senate in 1982. Vidal won a National Book Award in 1993 for his collection of essays *United States: Essays, 1952-1992*, and his books are routinely included in "best" lists and course syllabi.

BIOGRAPHY

Eugene Luther Vidal was born on October 3, 1925 (he took the name Gore when he was fourteen). He was born at West Point, where his father, Eugene, taught aeronautics at the military academy. Eugene Vidal helped establish civil aviation in the United States and later became the director of air commerce in the administration of Franklin D. Roosevelt. Gore's mother, Nina, was a beautiful socialite, the daughter of powerful Oklahoma senator Thomas P. Gore. Soon after Gore's birth, the family moved to Senator Gore's mansion in Washington, D.C. Gore Vidal, one of the most learned of contemporary writers, never went to college. His education began at the home of Senator Gore: The senator, who was blind, used his grandson as a reader and in return gave him free run of his huge library. In 1935, the Vidals were divorced, and Nina married Hugh D. Auchincloss, a member of a prominent family of bankers and lawyers. Gore Vidal then moved to the Auchincloss estate on the Potomac River in Virginia. Here his education included rubbing shoulders with the nation's political, economic, and journalistic elite.

Vidal was brought up removed from real life, he says, protected from such unpleasant realities as the effects of the Great Depression. He joined other patrician sons at St. Albans School, after which he toured Europe in 1939, then spent one year at Los Alamos School in New Mexico, before finishing his formal education with three years at Phillips Exeter Academy in New Hampshire.

(Jane Bown)

In 1943, Vidal joined the army and served on a transport ship in the Aleutian Islands. His military service gave him subject matter and time to write his first novel, *Williwaw*. He finished his second book, *In a Yellow Wood*, before he left the army. In 1946, he went to work as an editor for E. P. Dutton and soon published *The City and the Pillar*. Good critical and popular response brought him recognition as one of the nation's best young authors. He used Guatemala as his home base from 1947 to 1949 and then bought an old estate, Edgewater, on the Hudson River in New York. He wrote five more novels before he was thirty years old.

Meanwhile, a controversy engulfed him and shifted his life and career. *The City and the Pillar* had dealt with homosexuality; because of this, the literary establishment removed him from its list of "approved" writers, and critics largely ignored his next few novels. To earn money in the 1950's, he wrote mysteries under the name Edgar Box and wrote scripts for the major live television dramatic series. He also became a successful screenwriter, with such films as *The Catered Affair* (1956) and *Suddenly Last Summer* (1959, with Tennessee Williams). In addition, he wrote plays. He achieved major Broadway successes with *Visit to a Small Planet: A Comedy Akin to a Vaudeville* (1957) and *The Best Man: A Play About Politics* (1960).

These were his years of "piracy," Vidal says, aimed at gaining enough financial security to allow him to return to his first love, novels. His years in Hollywood and on Broadway established Vidal's public reputation for sophisticated wit and intelligence. He ran for Congress in 1960, supported by such famous friends as Eleanor Roosevelt, Joanne Woodward, and Paul Newman. Although he was defeated, he ran better in his district than did the Democratic presidential candidate, John F. Kennedy. Vidal shared a stepfather with Jacqueline Kennedy and had become friends with the Kennedy family; this connection pulled him further into public affairs.

In 1964, Vidal published *Julian*, his first novel in ten years. It was a major critical and public success. Many best-sellers followed, including *Myra Breckinridge*, *Burr*, *Creation*, and *Lincoln*.

Conflict over civil rights, the Vietnam War, and the Watergate scandal made the 1960's and 1970's one of the most tumultuous periods in American political history. Vidal's essays, published in major journals, established his reputation as an astute and hard-hitting social critic. His acid-tongued social commentary brought him to many television guest shows, where he made many friends and enemies. He had spectacular public feuds with members of the Kennedy family and with such fellow celebrities and authors as William F. Buckley, Jr., Norman Mailer, and Truman Capote. In 1968 he was a cofounder of the New Party, and in 1970-1972 he was cochair of the People's Party. In 1982, he ran for the U.S. Senate in California, and, out of a field of eleven in the Democratic primary, came in second, behind Governor Jerry Brown.

The range and breadth of Vidal's interests showed in *United States*, a thousand-page collection of his essays which won the National Book Award for 1993. Here one finds literary discussions ranging from readings of Henry James and William Dean Howells to attacks on those of his contemporaries (John Barth, Thomas Pynchon) whom he calls "the academic hacks," novelists writing only for an audience of literature professors. He also attacks what he calls the "heterosexual dictatorship" and the United States' increasingly grandiose and imperial self-image.

Palimpsest: A Memoir (1995) was a book that Vidal said he had sworn never to write, a personal memoir. He revealed his family background and told of his struggles with establishments literary and political, concluding with his view of his quarrel with the Kennedy family. In a lyrical passage, he spoke of the great love of his teenage years, a classmate named Jimmie Trimble who died in World War II. In the 1990's Vidal added a new aspect to his public persona by appearing as a character actor in several films, including *Bob Roberts* (1992), *With Honors* (1994), *The Shadow Conspiracy* (1996), and *Gattaca* (1997).

In 1998 Vidal was embroiled in further public debate as a member of the committee that selected the Modern Library's one hundred best twentieth century English-language novels. One of many controversial aspects of the list was the absence of those writers he called academic hacks. Vidal insisted that his role was only to make recommendations and that he bore no responsibility for the final selections.

ANALYSIS

In an age and country that have little room for the traditional man of letters, Gore Vidal has established that role for himself by the force of his writing and intelligence and by his public prominence. He is a classicist in writing style, emphasizing plot, clarity, and order. Iconoclastic wit and cool, detached intelligence characterize his elegant style.

Because Vidal knows most contemporary public figures—including jet-setters, Wall Street insiders, and Washington wheeler-dealers—many readers comb his writing to glean intriguing bits of gossip. *Two Sisters: A Memoir in the Form of a Novel*, for example, is often read as an account of the lives and loves of Jacqueline Kennedy Onassis and her sister, Lee Bouvier. Some people search Vidal's writing for clues to his own life and sexuality.

Vidal draws from his own rich experience as he creates his fictional world, yet he is a very private person, and he resists people's urge to reduce everyone to a known quantity. Vidal refracts real people and events through his delightfully perverse imagination. The unwary gossipmonger can easily fall into Vidal's many traps.

If one can with certainty learn little from Vidal's fiction about such famous people as the Kennedys, readers can learn much about his major concern, the nature of Western civilization and the individual's role within it. He is interested in politics—how people make society work—and religion, the proper perspective on life as one faces death. In his early novels, one can see Vidal's interest in ideas. Vidal's young male protagonists find themselves entering a relativistic world in which all gods are dead. A "heterosexual dictatorship" and a life-numbing Christian establishment try to impose false moral absolutes. Society tempts the unwary by offering comfort and security and then removes the life-sustaining freedom of those who succumb to the temptation.

THE CITY AND THE PILLAR

In writing his third novel, Vidal probed the boundaries of society's sexual tolerance. The result, *The City and the Pillar*, affected the rest of his career. To Vidal, the book is a study of obsession; to many guardians of moral purity, it seems to glorify homosexuality. In American fiction, either homosexuality had been barely implied or the homosexual characters had been presented as bizarre or doomed figures. In contrast, Vidal's protagonist is an average young American man, confused by his homosexual proclivities and obsessed with the memory of a weekend encounter with another young man, Bob Ford. While Bob regards the weekend as a diversion to be enjoyed and forgotten, Jim enters the homosexual world. If he is doomed, it is not because he prefers men to women, but because he is obsessed with the past. When he finally meets Bob again and tries to revive the affair, Bob rejects him. Enraged and humiliated, Jim kills Bob. Vidal later issued a revised edition in which Jim forces Bob to submit sexually; in the emotional backwash from the confrontation, Jim realizes the sterility of his obsession.

Vidal later said that he could have been president had it not been for the homosexual label applied to him. Readers assumed that Vidal must be the character he invented. Vidal is a sexual libertarian who believes that sex in any form between consenting adults is a gift to be enjoyed. He believes, furthermore, that a "heterosexual dictatorship" has distorted human sexuality. "There is no such thing as a homosexual or a heterosexual person," Vidal says. "There are only homo- or heterosexual acts. Most people are a mixture of impulses if not practices, and what anyone does with a willing partner is of no social or cosmic significance." In 1948, people were not ready for that message. Although the book was a best-seller, such powerful establishment journals as *The New York Times* eliminated him from the list of "approved" writers. His next few books were failures, critically and financially.

THE JUDGMENT OF PARIS

Two of the books ignored after *The City and the Pillar*, *The Judgment of Paris* and *Messiah*, later found admirers. In these novels Vidal began to develop the style that is so recognizably his own. Moreover, it is in these two books that Vidal fully expresses his philosophy of life: "I have put nearly everything that I feel into *The Judgment of Paris*, a comedic version, and *Messiah*, a tragic version of my sense of man's curious estate."

In *The Judgment of Paris*, Vidal retells the ancient myth of Paris, who was asked by Zeus to choose the most beautiful of three goddesses: Hera (power), Athena (knowledge), and Aphrodite (love). In the novel, Philip Warren, an American innocent, meets Regina Durham (Hera) in Rome, Sophia Oliver (Athena) in Egypt, and Anna Morris (Aphrodite) in Paris. Regina and Sophia offer him, respectively, political power and life of the intellect. To Philip, political power rests on manipulation of people, and intellectual life requires the seclusion of the scholar from humanity. He chooses love, but he also leaves Anna Morris. His choice implies that one must accept no absolutes; nothing is permanent, not even love. One must open oneself to love and friendship and prepare to accept change as one moves through life.

MESSIAH

Many readers consider *Messiah* an undiscovered masterpiece. Religion, the human response to death and nothingness, has been a major concern in Vidal's fiction, especially in *Messiah*, *Kalki*, and *Creation*. *Messiah* is narrated by Eugene Luther, an old man secluded in Egypt. He is a founding member of a new religion that has displaced Christianity and is spreading over the world. Luther, who has broken with the church he helped build, scribbles his memoirs as he awaits death. The movement was built around John Cave, but Cave was killed by his disciples and Cave's word was spread by an organization using modern advertising techniques. One can readily find in *Messiah* characters representing Jesus Christ, Saint Paul, Mother Mary, and Martin Luther. The process by which religious movements are formed interests Vidal. *Messiah* shows, by analogy, how the early church fathers manipulated the Gospels and the Christ figure for their own selfish needs.

JULIAN

With *Julian*, Vidal again examines the formation of a religious movement, this time looking directly at Christianity. Julian the Apostate, Roman emperor from 361 to 363 C.E., had long been the object of hatred in the West, because he had tried to reverse the Christianization of the empire. In the nineteenth and twentieth centuries, Julian began to attract admirers who saw him as a symbol of wisdom and of religious toleration.

Julian, reared as a Christian, lived in an age when the modern Christian church was taking shape. Warring prelates conducted abstract debates that robbed religion of its mystery and engaged in persecutions that ignored Jesus' message of love and peace. Julian was trained as a philosopher. His study of ancient wisdom awakened in him love and respect for the gods of the ancient world and for the Eastern mystery religions then being suppressed by Christianity. When he became emperor, Julian proclaimed religious toleration and tried to revive "paganism."

Like Paris before him and Philip Warren after, Julian was offered the worlds of intellect, love, and power. Julian chose power, but he tempered the absolute authority of emperor with love and wisdom. He was also a military genius who, like Alexander the Great, was tempted by the dream of world conquest. He was killed during an invasion of Persia.

Vidal constructs his novel as a fictive memoir written by Julian and presenting Julian's own view of himself and his world. The novel opens in 380 C.E., seventeen years after Julian's death. Two friends of Julian, the philosophers Libanius of Antioch and Priscus of Athens, correspond as they prepare Julian's memoirs for publication. Their letters and comments on the manuscript provide two other views of the events described by Julian. Because they are writing as the Emperor Theodosius is moving to destroy the ancient religions, Julian's life takes on a special poignancy. Vidal's major point, says biographer Ray Lewis White, is that modern people of the West are the descendants of the barbarians who destroyed the classical world, and that the modern world has yet to be civilized. If Julian had lived, Vidal believes, Christianity might well have remained only one of several Western religions, and Western civilization might now be healthier and more tolerant than it is.

CREATION

In 1981 Vidal took readers even further back into history in *Creation*. In 445 B.C.E., Cyrus Spitama, an elderly Persian diplomat to Athens and grandson of the Persian prophet Zoroaster, begins to dictate his memoirs to his nephew, the philosopher Democritus. Cyrus is angry after hearing the historian Herodotus give his account of the Persian-Greek war, and he decides to set down the truth.

Here Vidal traces the earliest foundations of Western civilization and the formation of major world religions. Cyrus, a diplomatic troubleshooter for the Persian court, takes the reader on a tour of the ancient world. He knows Persian emperors Darius and Xerxes; as a traveler to China and India, he meets the Buddha and Confucius, and he remembers his own grandfather, Zoroaster. In Athens he talks with such famous figures as Anaxagoras and Pericles and hires Socrates to repair his wall. In *Creation*, Vidal shows the global interaction of cultures that goes back to the ancient world. He rejects the provincialism that has allowed historians to wall Western civilization off from its Asian and African sources.

BURR

This master of historical fiction also turned his attention to the United States. Starting with *Washing-*

ton, D.C., Vidal began a sequence of novels covering United States history from its beginning to the post-World War II era. In chronological sequence, the novels are *Burr, Lincoln, 1876, Empire, Hollywood*, and *Washington, D.C.* Vidal's iconoclastic view of the past may have shocked some readers, but in the turmoil of the Vietnam and Watergate era, many people were ready to reexamine United States history. At a time when many Americans held that the old truths had failed, Vidal said that those truths had been hollow from the start.

Burr is one of the most widely admired of Vidal's novels. Aaron Burr, the preeminent American maverick, appealed to Vidal personally. *Burr* is narrated by Charlie Schuyler, who in 1833 is a twenty-five-year-old clerk in Burr's law office. He is an aspiring author who writes for William Leggett and William Cullen Bryant, editors of the *New York Evening Post*. Disliking Martin Van Buren, President Andrew Jackson's heir apparent, Leggett and Bryant set Charlie to work running down the rumor that Van Buren is the illegitimate son of Burr; if the rumor is true, they can use the information to destroy Van Buren. The seventy-seven-year-old Burr responds warmly to Charlie's overtures to write about his life. In the next few years, Burr gives the young writer copies of his journal and dictates to him his memories of the past.

Although Vidal's portrait of the Founding Fathers shocks some readers, his interpretation is in line with that of many of the nation's best historians. Vidal reminds the reader that Burr was one of the most able and intelligent of the Founding Fathers. Vidal allows Burr, from an insider's viewpoint, to demystify the founders of the republic. George Washington, Alexander Hamilton, Thomas Jefferson, and the other Founding Fathers created the republic, Burr says, because it satisfied their personal economic and political interests to do so.

Burr admires some of his contemporaries, especially James Madison and Andrew Jackson, but he detests Thomas Jefferson. Jefferson is a ruthless man who wants to create a nation "dominated by independent farmers each living on his own rich land, supported by slaves." What Burr cannot excuse is Jefferson's cant and hypocrisy:

Had Jefferson not been a hypocrite I might have admired him. After all, he was the most successful empire-builder of our century, succeeding where Bonaparte failed. But then Bonaparte was always candid when it came to motive and Jefferson was always dishonest.

What are the motives of the Founding Fathers? Burr tells Alexander Hamilton: "I sense nothing more than the ordinary busy-ness of men wanting to make a place for themselves. . . . But it is no different here from what it is in London or what it was in Caesar's Rome." The Founding Fathers write the Constitution because it suits their purposes, and they subvert it when it suits their purposes.

Burr makes no secret of his opportunism, although he does regret his mistakes. He should have realized that the world is big enough for both Hamilton and himself, he says. Instead, Vice President Burr kills Hamilton in a duel and is then accused by Jefferson of heading a plot to break up the United States and establish himself as the king in a new Western empire.

Charlie does find evidence that Van Buren is Burr's son, but Charlie, having come to love the old man, refuses to use it. Van Buren rewards him with a government position overseas.

LINCOLN and 1876

With *Lincoln*, Vidal surprised those who expected him to subject the Great Emancipator to the same ridicule he had directed at Washington and Jefferson. Vidal's Lincoln is a cold, remote, intelligent man who creates a unified, centralized republic that is far different from the one envisioned by the Founding Fathers. In *1876*, Charlie Schuyler returns to the United States from Europe, where he has lived since 1837. He left in the age of Jackson and returns in the age of Ulysses S. Grant to a booming industrializing, urbanizing nation. He watches, in the American centennial year, as the politicians steal the presidential election from Democrat Samuel J. Tilden. He sees members of the ruling class using the rhetoric of democracy but practicing it as little as they had in the days of Washington and Jefferson.

EMPIRE

In *Empire*, Vidal paints wonderful world-portraits

of Henry Adams, Henry James, William Randolph Hearst, John Hay, and Theodore Roosevelt, along with the fictional characters of newspaper publishers Caroline and Blaise Sanford and Congressman James Burden Day. The creation of the internal empire, begun by Jefferson's Louisiana Purchase, had already made a shambles of the American democratic promise. Now Roosevelt and other American leaders begin to look overseas for new areas to dominate. Their creation of the overseas empire lays the groundwork for the increasingly militarized republic that emerges in the twentieth century.

HOLLYWOOD

Many of these same figures appear in *Hollywood*, set a few years later, in the administrations of Woodrow Wilson and Warren Harding. While the forging of the American empire continues, Vidal turns his gaze on a new force that is corrupting the democratic promise, the mass media. Newspaper publisher Hearst and the Sanfords have long understood the power of the press, but Hearst and Caroline Sanford see that the new medium of film has potential power beyond the printed page. Instead of reporting events, film could create a new reality, within which newspapers and politicians would have to work.

WASHINGTON, D.C.

In *Washington, D.C.*, Blaise Sanford, his son Peter, Senator James Burden Day, and his assistant, Clay Overbury, are locked in a political and moral drama. Senator Day, a southern conservative, much like Senator Gore, opposes the new republic being created by Franklin Delano Roosevelt, Harry Truman, and Dwight D. Eisenhower. He has a chance to be president but lacks money. Burden Day gives in to temptation and takes a bribe; his presidential bid fails, and later Clay Overbury, using his knowledge of the bribe, forces Day out of the Senate and takes his seat. Overbury is a young man who cares nothing for friends or ideas or issues. Winning personal power is the only thing that interests this politician, who is modeled on John F. Kennedy.

As Day is dying, he says to the spirit of his unreconstructed southern father: "You were right. . . . It has all gone wrong." Aaron Burr would have understood what he meant.

MYRA BRECKINRIDGE

If most scholars approved of Vidal's well-researched historical fiction, many readers were shocked at *Myra Breckinridge*. Myra opens her book with the proud proclamation: "I am Myra Breckinridge whom no man will ever possess." She maintains her verve as she takes readers on a romp through popular culture. Because the novel is dead, she says, there is no point in writing made-up stories; the film of the 1940's is the high point of Western artistic creation, although it is being superseded by a higher art form, the television commercial. Myra has arrived in Hollywood to fulfill her destiny of reconstructing the sexes. She has a lesson to teach young would-be stars such as Rusty Godowsky and old cowboy stars such as Buck Loner:

> To be a man in a society of machines is to be an expendable, soft auxiliary to what is useful and hard. Today there is nothing left for the old-fashioned male to do, . . . no physical struggle to survive or mate. . . . [O]nly in travesty can he act out the classic hero who was a law unto himself, moving at ease through a landscape filled with admiring women. Mercifully, that age is finished. . . . [W]e now live at the dawn of the age of Women Triumphant, of Myra Breckinridge!

Beneath the gaiety of Myra's campy narrative, a serious purpose emerges. Her dead homosexual husband, Myron, had been abused and humiliated by many males. Myra carries out her plan to avenge Myron, and to revive the Female Principle, by forcing Buck Loner to submit to her demands to take over his acting studio, and by raping with a dildo the macho, all-American stud Rusty.

Myra is brought down by an automobile accident, which upsets her hormonal balance. Her breasts vanish, and she sprouts a beard; she is, in fact, Myron, after a sex-change operation. As the book ends, Rusty is a homosexual, and Myron/Myra is married and living happily with Rusty's former girlfriend. In a sequel, *Myron*, Myron and Myra struggle for domination of the single body and again have much to say about popular culture, the mass media, and human sexuality.

Perhaps as respites from the scrupulous historicity

of the American history novels, Vidal interspersed them with fantasies in which reality was plastic and ever-changing. In *Myron*, characters were likely to find themselves in the midst of the old films they were watching. *Duluth* represented a deliberately postmodernist interpenetration of an actual Duluth with a serial television show also called *Duluth*.

LIVE FROM GOLGOTHA

Live from Golgotha continued the motif of a reality subject to random change. It is set in 96 C.E., but the first century is being manipulated by forces from the twentieth, operating through psychic channelers and the Hacker, whose computer manipulations apparently can destroy not only records of the past but even memories of those records. Indeed, there is a plan afoot to return to the Crucifixion, televise it live, and perhaps even change the events.

Timothy, the narrator, is the biblical Timothy to whom St. Paul wrote epistles. He has been chosen to preserve the Gospel story in the face of these computerized depredations, though his knowledge of the event is at best secondhand, coming from Paul, who knows it only through a vision. The story departs radically from the standard biblical story. Timothy and Paul are actively bisexual, as are most of the first-century people depicted. Jesus is thought to have been morbidly obese. Anachronistic terms such as "Mossad" and "intifada" abound. Future figures such as Mary Baker Eddy and Shirley MacLaine make appearances.

Timothy eventually learns that the actual Jesus was a Zealot, a political revolutionary. With electronic assistance, Jesus framed Judas, the fat man Paul saw in the vision, and fled to the twentieth century. There he became the Hacker in order to clear out images of "gentle Jesus meek and mild." He plans to start Armageddon through a nuclear attack on Arab capitals. Timothy uses more advanced technology to prevent Jesus's escape from arrest. The Crucifixion takes place, with the real Jesus, but Japanese technicians add to the image a rising sun and the mother goddess Amaterasu. *Live from Golgotha* was condemned for its irreverence and blasphemy, as well as for the outlandishness of its central conceit, but many readers nevertheless enjoyed its wit

and its lusty portrayal of the first-century Roman world.

THE SMITHSONIAN INSTITUTION

Vidal's next novel, *The Smithsonian Institution*, also dealt with retroactive time change, but of a political rather than a theological sort. T., a thirteen-year-old mathematics prodigy in 1939, is summoned to the Smithsonian Institution to take part in a secret scientific experiment. He soon learns that the apparent wax dummies that are part of the project are actually living people. Indeed, T. is seduced by Mrs. Grover Cleveland. T. has an Einstein-like ability to visualize equations dealing with time. Anxious to ward off the coming of World War II because it would lead to the development of terrifying new weapons, the scientists secretly in charge of the Smithsonian (with the assistance of the supposed wax dummies of political leaders) plan to use T.'s ideas to construct a time machine and change the past so that the war will not occur. After one trip that only makes things worse, T. returns to a war in which he saves an alternate version of himself and enables the war to be concluded more quickly, without the weapons development.

Some commentators have said that the audience Vidal created for himself with his highly regarded historical novels was destroyed by *Myra Breckinridge* and *Myron* and by his later campy fantasies *Kalki* and *Duluth*. Yet Vidal continued to write one best-seller after another, and his books have steadily gained critical admirers. Vidal's books, essays, and television appearances stimulated, intrigued, and angered a large part of his audience, yet his appeal as a writer and public figure remained compelling. As long ago as 1948, with *The City and the Pillar*, Vidal made a decision to live his life and conduct his artistic career in his own way. To many admirers, he is a symbol of freedom. The turmoil of the modern age makes his civilized voice of reason seem more necessary than ever before. Often accused of cynicism, Vidal responded that he is a pessimist and a realist who also believes that people can, or must act as if they can, take action to make the world better.

William E. Pemberton,
updated by Arthur D. Hlavaty

OTHER MAJOR WORKS

SHORT FICTION: *A Thirsty Evil: Seven Short Stories*, 1956.

PLAYS: *Visit to a Small Planet: A Comedy Akin to a Vaudeville*, pr. 1957; *The Best Man: A Play About Politics*, pr. 1960; *Romulus: A New Comedy*, pr., pb. 1962; *An Evening with Richard Nixon*, pr. 1972.

SCREENPLAYS: *The Catered Affair*, 1956; *Suddenly Last Summer*, 1959 (with Tennessee Williams); *The Best Man*, 1964.

NONFICTION: *Rocking the Boat*, 1962; *Reflections upon a Sinking Ship*, 1969; *Homage to Daniel Shays: Collected Essays, 1952-1972*, 1972; *Matters of Fact and of Fiction: Essays, 1973-1976*, 1977; *The Second American Revolution and Other Essays, 1976-1982*, 1982; *At Home: Essays, 1982-1988*, 1988; *The Decline and Fall of the American Empire*, 1992; *Screening History*, 1992; *United States: Essays, 1952-1992*, 1993; *Palimpsest: A Memoir*, 1995; *Gore Vidal, Sexually Speaking: Collected Sex Writings*, 1999.

MISCELLANEOUS: *The Essential Vidal*, 1999 (Fred Kaplan, editor).

BIBLIOGRAPHY
Baker, Susan, and Curtis S. Gibson. *Gore Vidal: A Critical Companion*. Westport, Conn.: Greenwood Press, 1997. A helpful book of criticism and interpretation of Vidal's work. Includes bibliographical references and index.

Dick, Bernard F. *The Apostate Angel: A Critical Study of Gore Vidal*. New York: Random House, 1974. An entertaining and perceptive study, based on interviews with Vidal and on use of his papers at the University of Wisconsin at Madison. Dick focuses on Vidal's work rather than on his biography. The book contains footnotes and a bibliography.

Kiernan, Robert F. *Gore Vidal*. New York: Frederick Ungar, 1982. This study of Vidal's major writings tries to assess his place in American literature and gives astute descriptions of the Vidalian style and manner. The book, which uses Vidal's manuscript collection, contains a brief note and bibliography section.

Parini, Jay, ed. *Gore Vidal: Writer Against the Grain*. New York: Columbia University Press, 1992. Vidal's distaste for much of the academic study of contemporary fiction has been mirrored in a lack of academic study of his work. Jay Parini sought to redress the balance by compiling this work, which deals with both Vidal's fiction and nonfiction. The book reprints chapters from the Dick and Kiernan studies referenced here, as well as encomia and reviews by such writers and critics as Louis Auchincloss, Italo Calvino, and Harold Bloom. In addition, there are eight newly commissioned essays, including essays by James Tatum and Donald E. Pease.

Stanton, Robert J., and Gore Vidal, eds. *Views from a Window: Conversations with Gore Vidal*. Secaucus, N.J.: Lyle Stuart, 1980. A compilation of interviews excerpted and arranged along themes. Vidal comments on his and other authors' works, on sexuality, and on politics. Vidal edited the manuscript and made corrections, with changes noted in the text.

VOLTAIRE
François-Marie Arouet

Born: Paris, France; November 21, 1694
Died: Paris, France; May 30, 1778

PRINCIPAL LONG FICTION

Zadig: Ou, La Destinée, Histoire orientale, 1748 (originally as *Memnon: Histoire orientale*, 1747; *Zadig: Or, The Book of Fate*, 1749)
Le Micromégas, 1752 (*Micromegas*, 1753)
Histoire des voyages de Scarmentado, 1756 (*The History of the Voyages of Scarmentado*, 1757; also as *History of Scarmentado's Travels*, 1961)
Candide: Ou, L'Optimisme, 1759 (*Candide: Or, All for the Best*, 1759; also as *Candide: Or, The Optimist*, 1762; also as *Candide: Or, Optimism*, 1947)

L'Ingénu, 1767 (*The Pupil of Nature*, 1771; also as
　Ingenuous, 1961)
L'Homme aux quarante écus, 1768 (*The Man of
　Forty Crowns*, 1768)
La Princesse de Babylone, 1768 (*The Princess of
　Babylon*, 1769)

OTHER LITERARY FORMS

Voltaire is probably the most prolific and versatile
writer of any age. He wrote in all the literary forms,
and he wrote in them concurrently. His numerous
plays fill 6 volumes, and his correspondence 102 volumes. He was especially active toward the end of his
life, when, living at Ferney, and in his eighties, he
wrote pamphlets; one of his best philosophical poems, *Épître à Horace* (1772); and many plays. He
went to Paris at the age of eighty-three, shortly before he died, to see a production of his latest classical
tragedy, *Irène* (1778). At the time of his death, he
was at work on a new play and rewriting others.

In many ways, Voltaire wished to be considered as
a defender of the classical tradition. His plays are
mainly classical, embodying the unities and dealing
with highborn heroes. *Œdipe* (1718; *Oedipus*, 1761)
was widely acclaimed in Voltaire's day, as were *Zaïre*
(1732; English translation, 1736) and *Mérope* (1743;
English translation, 1744, 1749). Yet Voltaire also introduced devices and techniques that ultimately led
to the demise of classical theater, including local
color, such as red togas for members of the Senate
in *Brutus* (1730; English translation, 1761) and real
cannon fire in *Adélaïde du Guesclin* (1734). Voltaire's later plays include a certain amount of tearful
sensibility that was a characteristic of Denis Diderot's bourgeois dramas.

Voltaire composed many kinds of poetry. As a
young man, he achieved much acclaim with his epic
poem *La Ligue* (1723) and *La Henriade* (1728, a
rewriting of *La Ligue*; *Henriade*, 1732). *Henriade*,
which narrates Henry IV's successful struggle against
the Catholic League, was reprinted through the beginning of the nineteenth century. Today, these poems
have no appeal. Voltaire also wrote satiric and philosophical poetry, including *Le Mondain* (1736; *The
Man of the World*, 1764). This poem caused a scandal

(Library of Congress)

with its suggestion that a pleasurable life on earth is
the only positive happiness one can grasp and that one
should enjoy it rather than wait for a life after death.
This element of audacious irreverence is a quality
that spices all of Voltaire's work and was what his admirers appreciated. Voltaire's *Épître à Horace* is one
of the best of Voltaire's philosophical epistles.

Voltaire has some renown as a historian. His *Le
Siècle de Louis XIV* (1751; *The Age of Louis XIV*,
1752) reveals meticulous research and a journalistic
bent. Voltaire praises the reign of Louis XIV in order to criticize the reign of Louis XV. *Essai sur les
mœurs* (1756, 1763; *The General History and State
of Europe*, 1754, 1759) presents a philosophical review of historic events. Other nonfiction works popu-
larize the accomplishments of Sir Isaac Newton in
science and of John Locke in philosophy (*Éléments
de la philosophie de Newton*, 1738; *The Elements
of Sir Isaac Newton's Philosophy*, 1738). In *Lettres
philosophiques* (1734; originally published in English as *Letters Concerning the English Nation*,
1733; also as *Philosophical Letters*, 1961), Voltaire,

with his powerful satire, praises English customs and institutions as a method of criticizing French society of his day. Censorship, which outlawed much of Voltaire's work, not only added to the satirist's celebrity but also increased the sales price of his books. The articles that Voltaire wrote for *Dictionnaire philosophique portatif* (1764, enlarged 1769; *A Philosophical Dictionary for the Pocket*, 1765; also as *Philosophical Dictionary*, 1945, enlarged 1962) were also offensive to the establishment, full of his propaganda on the subject of fanaticism, judicial corruption, and social oppression.

Achievements

Voltaire's career spanned sixty years, and during that time he achieved great fame and even greater notoriety. Voltaire's literary ambitions were revealed when he chose *Œdipe* as the subject of his first tragedy. His ambition was to rival Pierre Corneille, and at the age of twenty-four he was already hailed as a worthy successor to both Jean Racine and Corneille. In the theater, Voltaire considerably delayed the demise of classical tragedy, and he remained an extremely popular dramatist of the age. Between 1745 and 1803, his plays were staged many more times than those of Corneille and Racine. Today, however, Voltaire's plays are no longer of interest to audiences.

Voltaire also enjoyed success in the field of poetry. *La Ligue* was so highly acclaimed that it put epic poetry back in fashion. Voltaire's love of the classical tradition stemmed, no doubt, from his Jesuit education at Louis-le-Grand. His poetry also brought him prestige at court and financial rewards. After the successful production of *La Princesse de Navarre* in 1745, performed at the wedding of Louis XV, Voltaire was given the post of royal historiographer and a pension of two thousand francs a year, and later was made a gentleman of the King's Chamber. The following year, 1746, Voltaire achieved another ambition when he was finally elected to the Académie Française. He had been denied this privilege several times before because of the various scandals he had caused. Madame du Châtelet tried to protect him from his own indiscretion; she once locked up his outrageous *La Pucelle d'Orléans* (1755, 1762; *The*

Maid of Orleans, 1758; also as *La Pucelle: Or, The Maid of Orleans*, 1785-1786), a scurrilous writing on the subject of Joan of Arc.

Voltaire's philosophical and satiric writings, such as his tales and pamphlets, not only brought him literary fame but also endangered his liberty. For this reason, Voltaire lived much of his life in exile or on the French-Swiss border.

One of the most astonishing aspects of Voltaire is his schizophrenic outlook. He dearly wished to have access to the noble classes (which accounts for his name change), while at the same time he despised the inequality inherent in the privilege of noble birth. A champion of the classical tradition, Voltaire inadvertently eroded its hold on his century by his innovations in drama and the novel. It is surprising that a champion of French classical tragedy and epic poetry should be the prime mover in introducing the latest developments in English literature, philosophy, and science into France. Voltaire's efforts to create a climate for liberty of thought and belief did eventually ameliorate conditions in France. The Encyclopedists, with Voltaire at their head, were ultimately responsible for producing a climate of critical thinking and a desire for reform that culminated in the French Revolution. Voltaire's *Philosophical Letters* were burned in public because they did not display the respect due "authority." Voltaire nevertheless would have been horrified to see the revolutionary tide sweep away this authority, even though it was corrupt. He enjoyed the cultivated nobility and the gracious support this class gave to the arts; he would have had no faith in the judgment of unrefined and poorly educated republicans. Still, the new ideas he had promulgated traveled through France and even to North America. Like John Locke, many of whose ideas are to be found in the American Bill of Rights and the Constitution, Voltaire contributed to political philosophy as it was developing in Europe and even in the United States.

It is through his satiric and philosophical writings that Voltaire exercised that influence. Whereas his effect on literature disappeared at the beginning of the nineteenth century, his emphasis on reason and critical thinking still dominates the French mind. The ideals of liberty of thought and justice are his legacy.

BIOGRAPHY

Voltaire was born in Paris in 1694 as François-Marie Arouet. His father was a highly placed official and belonged to the upper-middle class. Voltaire received an excellent classical education at the Jesuit school of Louis-le-Grand in Paris, where he displayed a talent for writing poetry. He also probably acquired his taste for theater there.

The Abbé de Châteauneuf, Voltaire's godfather, introduced the twelve-year-old boy to the Society of the Temple, which was the domain of worldly libertines. Voltaire's taste for witty irreverence and for luxurious living was definitely encouraged by this company. In 1711, Voltaire became a law student. As early as 1716, his satiric writing, aimed at the Regent and the poet Antoine Houdar de la Motte, caused Voltaire to be exiled twice to the provinces. In 1717, after writing a second time satirizing the Regent, Voltaire was imprisoned (fairly comfortably) in the Bastille for eleven months. During this stay, he completed *Oedipus* and began to write *La Ligue*. Upon leaving prison, he changed his name to de Voltaire. He became famous with the success of *Oedipus* in 1718 and *La Ligue* in 1723, and as a result he was invited to the literary and social circles of the wealthy. He even became a habitué of the court and had three of his plays, *Oedipus, Mariamne* (1724; English translation, 1761), and *L'Indiscret* (1725) performed as part of the celebrations for Louis XV's marriage in 1725.

Late in 1725, Voltaire had a dispute with the chevalier de Rohan, who ridiculed Voltaire's use of a false aristocratic name. Angered by a beating at the hands of Rohan's men, Voltaire challenged the noble to a duel. None of Voltaire's aristocratic friends supported him in the matter, which increased Voltaire's hatred of the unfairness of privilege. A *lettre de cachet* (a letter of arbitrary arrest issued by the King) sent him to the Bastille. Soon—in May, 1726—Voltaire was allowed to go into exile in England, where he spent three years frequenting the literary circles of the day. There he wrote his *Philosophical Letters*, prepared four tragedies, and published *Henriade*. Voltaire returned to France in 1729 and once again gained access to literary circles. In 1730, his play

Brutus was produced. The influence of William Shakespeare, acquired in England, is obvious in Voltaire's drama. *Zaïre* was presented in 1732 and *Adélaïade du Guesclin* in 1734. In the same year, Voltaire also took a great risk when he published his highly critical *Philosophical Letters* for the first time in France.

From 1734 to 1744, Voltaire lived in the du Châtelet castle at Cirey, where Madame du Châtelet, Voltaire's mistress, restrained Voltaire's volatile literary indiscretions somewhat. This period proved to be a most productive one. Voltaire wrote several plays during this time, including *Alzire* (1736; English translation, 1763) and *Mérope*. He also wrote his provocative *The Man of the World* while at Cirey. Both Madame du Châtelet and Voltaire took an interest in physics, chemistry, and astronomy; it is at Cirey that Voltaire wrote *The Elements of Sir Isaac Newton's Philosophy*.

For the three years following 1744, Voltaire was involved in life at court. His protectress, Madame de Pompadour, was, like him, of a humble background. The king and queen always distrusted Voltaire. After a thoughtless remark, Voltaire was obliged to flee the court and go to the summer home of the duchesse du Maine, the Château d'Anet at Sceaux. In *Zadig*, Voltaire satirizes life at court.

In 1747, Madame de Châtelet died in childbirth. Voltaire was extremely pained by this loss. There was no longer a reason to remain in France, and Voltaire spent the years from 1750 to 1753 at the court of Frederick the Great of Prussia. He published *The Age of Louis XIV* in Berlin in 1751. There he also wrote his satiric philosophical tale *Micromegas*. Although he had hoped to discover in Frederick his ideal of the "enlightened" monarch, Voltaire was as independent as Frederick was authoritarian, and the visit soon ended. These two men still respected each other greatly, however, and continued to correspond.

In 1755, Voltaire moved to Les Délices, an estate near the Swiss border. He lived there from 1755 to 1760, and it was there that, still in a depressed frame of mind, he wrote *Candide*.

From 1760 until his death, Voltaire resided in Ferney, on French soil, although situated very close to the Swiss border. Voltaire was extremely active during this period. He wrote some six thousand letters, as well as pamphlets, plays, and tales. In closing his letters, he usually wrote "Écrasez l'infâme" (crush the vile), by which he meant that superstition and intolerance must be eliminated. He wrote philosophical tales here, waging his battle against the usual targets; *Ingenuous* appeared at this time, as did many other philosophical tales. Voltaire championed the causes of the Calas and Sirven families and also of La Barre; all three were cases of a miscarriage of justice and of religious persecution.

Voltaire, taking his own advice at the end of *Candide*, did much to improve the region of Ferney. He built a church, installed a tannery, and established a watchmaking industry. He even had his area exempted from the salt tax.

In 1778, at the age of eighty-three, Voltaire went to Paris in triumph to watch a production of *Irène*. The popularity of Voltaire was at its highest, and the accolades and honors he received during his sojourn proved too much for him. He died shortly thereafter.

ANALYSIS

Voltaire was the most influential writer in eighteenth century France. He epitomizes the philosopher of the *siècle des lumières*, the Age of Enlightenment; his curiosity embraces all the developments of his day, whether French or otherwise European, scientific or literary. His faith in human reason does not waver, although his optimism about human progress often does. His writings reflect the changing literary tastes of the century as he defends a waning classical tradition while himself introducing the most outrageous innovations. His theater particularly embodies both of these tendencies, whereas his tales tend to exploit traditional literary forms in order to introduce a unique type of satiric philosophical story.

Voltaire's long fiction includes many rather short stories, which have been called indiscriminately *romans philosophiques* (philosophical novels) or *contes philosophiques* (philosophical tales). Henri Coulet indicates that Voltaire himself used the term *histoire* (story). Because satire such as Voltaire's depends on economy of style and the tales have no real development of plot or character, they are limited in length by the genre itself.

CANDIDE

Candide is considered to be the most perfect example of the philosophical novel, revealing Voltaire's brilliant irony and vivacious wit. All the tales are humorous tragicomedies and include incidents that are by turns absurd, grotesque, poetic, romantic, and shocking. The unifying element is always the philosophical theme that Voltaire is stressing. Voltaire began writing his tales at the age of forty-five, when his ideas were firmly established; hence, the concerns and reforms he seeks to address remain fairly constant throughout the tales. Despite the fact that these stories are meant to appeal primarily to the intellect, they are eminently entertaining. Voltaire's writings are rooted firmly in the humanistic rationalism of the first half of his century rather than in the literature of pre-Romantic sensibility, which made its appearance in the late 1700's.

Henri Bénac's suggestion that the tales fall into four chronological groups related to the development of Voltaire's thought is widely accepted. Bénac proposes that the first two groups—of 1747 to 1752 and 1756 to 1759—reveal Voltaire's growing realization that war must be waged against evils such as intolerance, injustice, corruption, and ignorance. The first group includes such stories as *Le Monde comme il va* (1748; revised as *Babouc: Ou, Le Monde comme il va*, 1749; *Babouc: Or, The World as It Goes*, 1754; also as *The World as It Is: Or, Babouc's Vision*, 1929), *Memnon: Or, Human Wisdom*, and *La Lettre d'un Turc* (1750); *Zadig* and *Micromegas* are the best known of the group. The second group includes *History of Scarmentado's Travels*, which is the outline of *Candide*. In the third group figure *Jeannot et Colin* (1764; *Jeannot and Colin*, 1929), *Le Blanc et le noir* (1764; *The Two Genies*, 1895), and, best known, *Ingenuous, The Man of Forty Crowns*, and *The Princess of Babylon*. According to Bénac, the tales in this third group are, like Voltaire's pamphlets, weapons in his war against oppression of all kinds. In the last group, Bénac sees Voltaire searching for a morality on which to base a humane and free society. Tales in this period include *L'Histoire de Jenni* (1775) and

Les Oreilles du Comte de Chesterfield (1775; *The Ears of Lord Chesterfield and Parson Goodman*, 1826).

ZADIG

The concerns of the early tales recur throughout all the stories, but Voltaire presents the different tales with a rich range of tones. *Zadig*, like other tales of this early group, is imbued with sunny humor and gaiety despite the sardonic irony that underscores the misfortunes of the hero. Voltaire sketches his hero Zadig with an unusually delicate touch, and some passages dazzle momentarily with rare poetry: "He marveled at these vast globes of light which to our eyes appear to be only feeble sparks. . . . His soul flew up into the infinite and, detached from his senses, contemplated the immutable order of the universe."

Memnon: Histoire orientale contained fifteen chapters that reappeared in *Zadig* in 1748. The story of Zadig is in the picaresque tradition, which is to say that the hero, on his travels, meets with many adventures. The plot of such a tale is of necessity episodic and highly imaginative. Zadig, a wealthy, virtuous, and handsome young Babylonian, is about to marry the beautiful young Semire, who loves him "passionately." When a jealous youth, Orcan, attempts to abduct Semire, Zadig bravely rescues his betrothed, receiving a wound that might mean the loss of an eye. Instead of expressing her gratitude, Semire protests that she hates one-eyed men, and she promptly marries Orcan. Zadig recovers quickly and marries another woman, Azora, whose faithfulness he puts to the test by pretending to have died. Unfortunately, Azora fails the test. Zadig encounters difficulties with the law when he makes scientific deductions from observing the tracks of the queen's dog and the king's horse, leading a huntsman to deduce that Zadig stole the animals. Zadig eventually becomes the king's prime minister.

His next misfortune arises through no fault of his own: Queen Astarté falls in love with him. The king, in jealousy, plots to kill them both, and Zadig has to flee. As he arrives in Egypt, he sees an Egyptian beating a woman, who asks Zadig to save her. In the ensuing fight, Zadig kills his adversary. Zadig is arrested and imprisoned for this act, then sold as a slave and taken to Arabia by his master, Sétoc, with whom he becomes close friends. Zadig dissuades a young widow from burning herself on her husband's funeral pyre, as is the religious custom. He also persuades an Egyptian, an Indian, a Chinese, a Greek, and a Celt to worship the same Supreme Being. Zadig is accused of impiety by Arabian priests and condemned to be burned. The young widow whom he saved now helps him escape.

Zadig next goes to the island of Serendib (Ceylon) on behalf of Sétoc. He makes a good impression on the king of the island and helps him to find an honest minister. On his travels, Zadig meets the brigand chief Arbogad and learns that King Moabdar has gone mad and been killed, and Astarté has disappeared. Zadig eventually discovers Astarté, who is a captive of Ogul, who is sick with an imaginary illness. Zadig cures Ogul, and the two return to Babylon, where peace is restored. Zadig wins a tournament that is held to decide who shall be the new king of Babylon and marry Astarté. Zadig wins the tournament but is cheated, and his rival claims the victory. In the middle of his despair, Zadig meets a hermit who reveals to him the secret of happiness, and Zadig learns to accept the ways of Providence. Zadig guesses the correct answers to the riddles and finally marries Astarté.

Zadig the hero—whose name in Arabic means "just"—attempts to be happy in a world where goodness is frustrated by absurd and illogical interventions of fate. At one point, Zadig says: "I was sent to execution because I had written verses in praise of the King; I was on the point of being strangled because the Queen had yellow ribbons; and here I am a slave with you because a brute beat his mistress. Come, let's not lose heart; perhaps all this will end."

The absurdity of Zadig's world, which is out of control and beyond the powers of logical explanation, is not the horror evoked in Franz Kafka's fiction; unlike Kafka, Voltaire does not attempt to create a sense of dreamlike but undeniable reality in either setting or characterization. Voltaire's exotic Eastern novel is in the tradition of the fifteenth century

A Thousand and One Nights, translated from the Arabic by Antoine Gallard and much in vogue after the success of *Persian Letters* (1721), by Charles de Montesquieu. The events are as unreal as those of the fairy tale, and the sensibility of the reader is not touched by Zadig's dilemmas. Instead, Voltaire disturbs the comfort of the reader's reason, logic, and innate sense of order and justice; the irony of Voltaire is at work. The frustration of Zadig becomes that of his audience. The knight Itobad steals Zadig's white suit of armor during the night, leaving his green suit in its place so that Zadig cannot claim the hand of Astarté, and Zadig cannot prove that he is the victor of the tournament, because the combatants must conceal their identities until a victor is proclaimed. Zadig has often been punished unjustly for being good, and here he is once again cheated of a happiness that is almost within his grasp. The audience is robbed of an anticipated happy ending and is frustrated by this anticlimax.

Voltaire was a master of the art of satire, and he often made use of anticlimax as an effective satiric technique. Zadig, after bewailing a list of horrifying punishments he has narrowly escaped, says, "Come, let's not lose heart; perhaps all this will end. . . ." This anticlimactic statement satirizes both Zadig's naïve optimism and the ridiculous optimism of the philosophers Gottfried Wilhelm Leibniz and Friedrich August Wolf—that "this is the best of all possible worlds"—which was much in vogue in the eighteenth century.

This leitmotif, the attack on optimism, is one of the many minor satiric barbs that Voltaire uses to spice his tale. Other satiric attacks abound in *Zadig* and reappear throughout the tales. Eighteenth century readers, usually belonging to the nobility and upper-middle class, took delight in synthesizing the apparent subject of Voltaire's narrative with the real and often audacious object of its satire. Voltaire makes a dangerous allusion to the court when the fisherman tells Zadig how archers "armed with a royal warrant were pillaging his house lawfully and in good order." The ironic effect is achieved by the surprising juxtaposition of "pillaging" and "lawfully." Voltaire's irony had its basis in reality: He had been forced to flee the court at Versailles after making disparaging remarks about the courtiers being cheats. In *Zadig*, Voltaire also frequently satirizes the judicial system and judges who are "abysses of knowledge," who "prove" Zadig looked out of a window even though Zadig has answered none of their questions.

Voltaire's anticlericalism and antireligious bent often figure in the satire of *Zadig*. Almona the Arab widow intends to burn herself on her husband's funeral pyre, as the Brahman religion demands. Zadig the philosopher reasons her out of this plan, convincing her that she is about to take a ridiculous course in order to satisfy her vanity and not her religious principles. Zadig also persuades Sétoc that it is ridiculous to worship shining lights (the stars), and he demonstrates his reasons by kneeling and appearing to worship lighted candles. The "bonzes," who represent the monks, "chanted beautiful prayers to music, and left the state a prey to the barbarians." Zadig's rationalism (and Voltaire's) is primarily concerned with people's practical problems in society.

Voltaire's primary philosophical theme, however, is people's concern with destiny. Zadig vacillates between hope and despair as fate deals him many adverse blows. Despite his ingenuity and virtue, which he displays when he acts as the prime minister of King Moabdar, Zadig is presented as the plaything of destiny. The fisherman's story and the hermit incident reinforce the supremacy of this philosophical question as the main theme. How do philosophers explain the sufferings of a good person in the hands of a malevolent destiny? Voltaire resolves this problem happily with a *deus ex machina* ending. The angel Jesrad, representing divine intervention, tells Zadig to stop his questioning and simply worship Providence. Most men, Jesrad explains, form opinions with limited knowledge. Zadig's virtue triumphs, and he wins his queen and rules with "justice and love. Men blessed Zadig and Zadig blessed heaven." The skies of Zadig remain free of the blackness of *Candide*.

MICROMEGAS

Micromegas, which appeared in 1752, is a philosophical tale in a more literal sense, being primarily a vehicle for ideas on relativity. It is a very short tale, with almost no action (in stark contrast to the episodic *Zadig*) and only two main protagonists. Micromegas (which is Greek for "little big one") is a very tall inhabitant of the planet Sirius who has been banned from court for writing a book about insects which the "Mufti" of his planet has found to be heretical. He goes on an interplanetary voyage, finally arriving on the planet Saturn, where he meets a dwarf. (Voltaire intended his readers to recognize in the dwarf a caricature of his own enemy, Bernard le Bovier de Fontenelle.) The two travelers arrive on Earth and finally discover minute humans in a boat. The travelers attend a banquet at which various forms of philosophical credos are represented, allowing Voltaire to launch a satiric attack on the theories of Aristotle, René Descartes, Nicolas Malebranche, and Leibniz. Voltaire approves of the philosophy of the follower of John Locke. A storm develops, and the philosophers fall into the pocket of Micromegas. Although the giant is angry that such small creatures have so much pride, he gives a book to the philosophers; its pages, however, are blank. Voltaire gives the closing line to the dwarf (his enemy, Fontenelle), who, upon receiving the blank book—supposedly a philosophical treatise revealing the final truth about things—says, "Ah . . . that's just what I suspected." This last line was extremely offensive to Fontenelle, because it implied that he agreed that all of his metaphysical speculations over the past years had been wasted effort—that such truths were impossible to discover and prove. This attack on metaphysics is the main thrust of Voltaire's satire in *Micromegas*. Voltaire ridicules the philosophers in the boat, implying that "our little pile of mud" is relatively unimportant when seen in relation to the rest of the cosmos and that the opinions of its inhabitants are hence practically worthless. The philosophers in the boat all talk at once and all have different opinions. Voltaire shows that this kind of truth is "relative" to the person uttering it, and unreliable.

Voltaire's *Micromegas* is in direct imitation of Jonathan Swift's *Gulliver's Travels* (1726), and Montesquieu had previously used this type of travel story in *Persian Letters*. Voltaire, then, used an established subgenre, the fictional travelogue, as a vehicle for social commentary: The traveler in a strange land, seeing things for the first time, has no prejudice and puts into a new perspective situations that have been seen in only a certain way for centuries. This fresh perspective opens the way for critical appraisal and reform.

In *Micromegas*, Voltaire makes little effort to convince the reader of the reality of his story; the tale must be accepted as fantasy. The satire is less complicated, less adroit, and less sparkling than it is in *Zadig*. The main purpose of the satire is to address subjects of great interest to Voltaire's contemporaries; little of the subject matter of *Micromegas* is of interest to the modern reader. These two early works, *Zadig* and *Micromegas*, do, however, share a lighthearted spirit of enjoyment as Voltaire ridicules general stupidity and personal enemies. In these works, too, Voltaire formulated what would become the constant subjects of his satiric attacks throughout his tales.

CANDIDE

Candide belongs to the second group of tales described by Bénac and is distinguished by its radical pessimism and bitter irony, in contrast to the sunny atmosphere of the previous two tales. *Candide* is considered the epitome of the philosophical tale, and it remains highly relevant today. Unlike Voltaire's other writings, *Candide* is still read everywhere. The tale's atmosphere is dark and often despairing. Voltaire was shocked by the horrors and atrocities of the Seven Years' War, which began in August, 1756, when Frederick the Great invaded Saxony. The Lisbon earthquake in 1755 also horrified Voltaire, causing him to reflect on what kind of Providence could inflict death on the innocent and guilty alike. The optimistic philosophy of Leibniz and Wolf seemed totally absurd in the midst of so much human suffering.

The satire in *Candide* is directed above all against this optimistic philosophy, epitomized in the character Pangloss. The characters in this tale are caricatures, deformed so that each represents only one characteristic or outlook. Candide, the hero, represents naïve, good, and reasonable humanity. The philosopher Martin symbolizes a cynical Manichaeanism which acknowledges the power of evil as well as of good in the world. James, who represents real human goodness and charity, is allowed to drown in stormy seas after rescuing a sailor who had attempted to murder him. Such is the bitter mood of the tale.

The form of this novel is basically picaresque, as in *Zadig*, but Voltaire also parodies the novel of adventure and the novel of sentiment. The characters continually die horrible deaths after suffering gruesome tortures in various lands, but they somehow miraculously (and ridiculously) reappear, having been saved or cured. Their tearful reunions are a parody of the sentimental literature which Samuel Richardson's *Pamela* (1740-1741) introduced to France from England and which infiltrated the bourgeois dramas of Diderot, and indeed of Voltaire's own theater. These reappearances also reinforce the central unity of the novel. There is a finely orchestrated rhythm which unifies the entire tale; it is not simply that the main aim of the satire holds the tale together, as in the other stories. The fates (and philosophies) of secondary characters affect the hero in a rhythmic ebb and flow of alternating hope and despair, which echo across the desolate landscape of a sad humanity in the throes of war, persecution, and suffering.

A gloss of the incidents in the tale reveals that there is no development of character or plot as such, and it underlines the rapid and vertiginous pace of the tale's episodes. This brisk pace lightens the seriousness of the atrocities being described, preventing the reader from dwelling on them or taking them to heart. Hence, Voltaire employs a technique of diminution, undercutting the value and dignity of human life.

Candide lives happily in a château in Westphalia with the baron of Thunderten-tronckh. Pangloss, the disciple of the optimistic philosophy of Leibniz, also lives there as tutor, as does Cunegonde, the baron's beautiful daughter, whom Candide loves. Candide agrees with Pangloss that all works out for the best in this wonderful world at the château. The baron, however, discovering the two lovers embracing, chases Candide out of the château. He is carried off forcibly to join an army and fight. After deserting, he goes to Holland, where he meets Pangloss, who has become a beggar and is barely recognizable with the sores of

a terrible disease. Candide learns that all the people of the château have been killed.

Candide takes Pangloss to his benefactor, James the Anabaptist, who restores the sick man. The three then set sail for Lisbon, where James has a business engagement. On the way to Lisbon, their ship is wrecked in a storm, and James is drowned, while a sailor who had tried to murder him is saved. In Lisbon, Pangloss and Candide live through an earthquake that kills thirty thousand people. As Candide and Pangloss wander through the destroyed city, Pangloss attempts to comfort the citizens with his philosophy that "all is for the best"—a philosophy which, as Voltaire makes clear in his juxtaposition of Pangloss's theories to the suffering about him, is ludicrous if not cruel. Overhearing Pangloss's remarks, an officer of the Inquisition questions Pangloss about his belief in Original Sin and Free Will. Pangloss, sputtering his rationalizations, is arrested along with Candide—"one for having spoken, the other for having listened with an air of approval." Pangloss is hanged, but Candide is saved by the timely arrival of Cunegonde, who has escaped from the massacre of her family.

As things are beginning to seem more hopeful, Candide is obliged to kill two people, and he has to flee to America. He takes refuge with some Jesuits in Paraguay, where he miraculously meets Cunegonde's brother, who has also escaped the massacre at the château and has become a priest. Although he embraces Candide as a brother, his mood suddenly shifts when Candide announces that he intends to marry Cunegonde, and in the ensuing fight, Candide kills the brother of his beloved. After similiar incidents in Eldorado, Surinam, Venice, and Constantinople, Candide finally finds Cunegonde. After all of her suffering, she has become very ugly, but, true to his word, Candide marries her. He then takes the advice of a wise old Turk and installs himself and his companions in an estate. He refuses to ask any more philosophical questions about evil and suffering in favor of hard work and practical reality; thus the novel's famous closing line: ". . . we must cultivate our garden."

In 1759, the year that *Candide* was published, Voltaire bought Ferney, an estate on the French-

Swiss border, which has led critics to surmise that Candide's conclusions about work and the happiness to be found in practical progress are those of Voltaire.

Once Voltaire was installed at Ferney, he gained confidence and energy and bombarded his public and his enemies with pamphlets, essays, plays, and stories, waging numerous legal battles on behalf of those persecuted for religious reasons. *Ingenuous* was written during this last, very active period of Voltaire's life. Although Voltaire was seventy-three years old when he wrote this work, his incredible intellectual and creative vigor had not diminished.

INGENUOUS

Ingenuous is one of the weapons Voltaire used in his unremitting battle against intolerance and injustice and belongs to the third group of novels delineated by Bénac. Voltaire's confidence had returned, and he wrote with a sure hand; none of the tales which follow *Candide* can rival the grandeur of *Ingenuous*.

Ingenuous is the most romantic of Voltaire's stories, and its plot is narrative rather than episodic. The tone of the story is more naturalistic, as are the characters. The device of a voyage is used again; the religious and social systems of France in the time of Louis XIV are seen through the eyes of the Huron stranger, who, without prejudice and with candid reasoning, questions institutions and beliefs that have been taken for granted and must now be considered from a new perspective.

The character of the Huron is in the tradition of the "noble savage" popularized by a missionary, baron de Lahontan, who praised the uncorrupted American Indian. The unity of the tale lies in the unfolding of the story of two lovers: Hercules Kerkabon (as the Huron is later named) and Mademoiselle de St. Yves. The satire used here also unites with the central love theme, targeting the corrupt Catholic Church and its priests, monks, and practices, which are instrumental in separating the lovers and ruining their chance for happiness. Voltaire also satirizes the court officials and Jansenism.

Voltaire's wit has a somewhat subdued tone throughout *Ingenuous*; the satire resides in the calmly reasoned arguments of the Huron, who questions all the basic doctrines of Jesuit and Jansenist alike. Voltaire, using the Huron as his mouthpiece, explains very simply all of his objections to the two religions. At the time of writing this tale, Voltaire was involved in the trials of the Calas family, the Sirven family, and La Barre, and his hatred of religious persecution and his anger at the injustices meted out by a corrupt judicial system were therefore as intense as they had ever been.

The story reflects the century's taste for cosmopolitanism. The Huron has been reared by a Huron tribe in Canada and arrives on the Lower Brittany coast in 1689. It is "discovered" that he is the lost child of the Abbé Yerkabon and his sister. Their brother went to Canada as a soldier and was killed by the Iroquois. The Abbé claims Hercules as his nephew and baptizes him as a Catholic. The beautiful Mademoiselle de St. Yves acts as his godmother. Hercules later falls in love with Mademoiselle de St. Yves but cannot marry his godmother, because the Church forbids it. Mademoiselle de St. Yves is sent to a convent, and Hercules, who is by now a hero for helping to defend the French against an English attack, goes to Versailles to engage the king's help in his marriage scheme. At Versailles, he is arrested and imprisoned in the Bastille, where he meets Gordon, a Jansenist. After much study and discussion, he converts Gordon to Deism. Now Mademoiselle de St. Yves goes to Versailles to save Hercules, but she must submit to a government minister in order to obtain her lover's release. She never recovers from the shame and dies of her chagrin. Hercules is tempted to take his own life but recovers himself and becomes an excellent officer and philosopher. The tale does not end with the expected happy ending for the lovers, but Voltaire suggests that even if ambitions and ideals cannot be attained, there are compromises that can be made and one can be tolerably happy—a message similar to that of *Candide*.

THE MAN OF FORTY CROWNS

The Man of Forty Crowns, published the year after *Ingenuous*, displays a strong contrast in style. The two tales have in common the underlying interest of Voltaire in practical things. In *Ingenuous*, Voltaire has Hercules recover from his loss and become a good soldier; in *The Man of Forty Crowns*, Voltaire has his protagonist discuss tax reform with a mathematician. There is a great difference, however, between these polemics and those of *Ingenuous*. In the later tale, Voltaire writes for a clever and agile mind able to follow the mathematical bent of his arguments. There is scarcely a plot or an appealing character to enliven the discussion. Voltaire, as usual, satirizes monks (who do not pay taxes), despotic monarchs, unfair judicial systems, and ignorant people who think they know more than they do. This highly polemical tale, amusing for Voltaire's eighteenth century circle, is of little interest today; not even the odd humorous remark, such as the suggestion that smiles and songs be taxed, can redeem the lack of relevance or interest of this story for a modern reader.

Voltaire's tales do suffer a slight impoverishment in translation. The musicality of the French language offsets the dryness of the succinct, economic prose and the laconic, pointed understatement. Polemical tales such as *The Man of Forty Crowns* particularly suffer in English translation.

Of Voltaire's many tales (some two dozen in all), *Candide* remains the most popular. Perhaps it has universal appeal because the evils it portrays persist in today's world. Wars are still waged in the name of religious causes, and political prisoners continue to be tortured and cast into jail without trial. Unfortunately, Voltaire is no longer here to provoke people's consciences and fire their minds with his energetic fury. Without him, the genre of the philosophical tale lies in disuse.

Avril S. Lewis

OTHER MAJOR WORKS

SHORT FICTION: *Le Monde comme il va*, 1748 (revised as *Babouc: Ou, Le Monde comme il va*, 1749; *Babouc: Or, The World as It Goes*, 1754; also as *The World as It Is: Or, Babouc's Vision*, 1929); *Memnon: Ou, La Sagesse humaine*, 1749 (*Memnon: Or, Human Wisdom*, 1961); *La Lettre d'un Turc*, 1750; *Le Blanc et le noir*, 1764 (*The Two Genies*, 1895); *Jeannot et Colin*, 1764 (*Jeannot and Colin*, 1929); *L'Histoire de Jenni*, 1775; *Les Oreilles du Comte de Chesterfield*, 1775 (*The Ears of Lord Chesterfield and Parson Goodman*, 1826).

PLAYS: *Œdipe*, pr. 1718 (*Oedipus*, 1761); *Artémire*, pr. 1720; *Mariamne*, pr. 1724 (English translation, 1761); *L'Indiscret*, pr., pb. 1725 (verse); *Brutus*, pr. 1730 (English translation, 1761); *Ériphyle*, pr. 1732; *Zaïre*, pr. 1732 (English translation, 1736); *La Mort de César*, pr. 1733; *Adélaïade du Guesclin*, pr. 1734; *L'Échange*, pr. 1734; *Alzire*, pr., pb. 1736 (English translation, 1763); *L'Enfant prodigue*, pr. 1736 (verse; prose translation *The Prodigal*, 1750?); *La Prude: Ou, La Grandeuse de Cassette*, wr. 1740, pr., pb. 1747 (verse; based on William Wycherley's play *The Plain Dealer*); *Zulime*, pr. 1740; *Mahomet*, pr., pb. 1742 (*Mahomet the Prophet*, 1744); *Mérope*, pr. 1743 (English translation, 1744, 1749); *La Princesse de Navarre*, pr., pb. 1745 (verse; music by Jean-Philippe Rameau); *Sémiramis*, pr. 1748 (*Semiramis*, 1760); *Nanine*, pr., pb. 1749 (English translation, 1927); *Oreste*, pr., pb. 1750; *Rome sauvée*, pr., pb. 1752; *L'Orphelin de la Chine*, pr., pb. 1755 (*The Orphan of China*, 1756); *Socrate*, pb. 1759 (*Socrates*, 1760); *L'Écossaise*, pr., pb. 1760 (*The Highland Girl*, 1760); *Tancrède*, pr. 1760; *Don Pèdre*, wr. 1761, pb. 1775; *Olympie*, pb. 1763; *Le Triumvirat*, pr. 1764; *Les Scythes*, pr., pb. 1767; *Les Guèbres: Ou, La Tolérance*, pb. 1769; *Sophonisbe*, pb. 1770 (revision of Jean Mairet's play); *Les Pélopides: Ou, Atrée et Thyeste*, pb. 1772; *Les Lois de Minos*, pb. 1773; *Irène*, pr. 1778; *Agathocle*, pr. 1779.

POETRY: *La Ligue*, 1723; *La Henriade*, 1728 (a revision of *La Ligue*; *Henriade*, 1732); *Le Temple du goût*, 1733 (*The Temple of Taste*, 1734); *Le Mondain*, 1736 (*The Man of the World*, 1764); *Discours en vers sur l'homme*, 1738 (*Discourses in Verse on Man*, 1764); *Poème de la loi naturelle*, 1752 (*On Natural Law*, 1764); *La Pucelle d'Orléans*, 1755, 1762 (*The Maid of Orleans*, 1758; also as *La Pucelle: Or, The Maid of Orleans*, 1785-1786); *Le Désastre de Lisbonne*, 1756 (*Poem on the Lisbon Earthquake*, 1764); *Le Pauvre Diable*, 1758; *Épître à Horace*, 1772.

NONFICTION: *An Essay upon the Civil Wars of France . . . and Also upon the Epick Poetry of the European Nations from Homer Down to Milton*, 1727;

Histoire de Charles XII, 1731 (*The History of Charles XII*, 1732); *Le Temple du goût*, 1733 (*The Temple of Taste*, 1734); *Letters Concerning the English Nation*, 1733; *Lettres philosophiques*, 1734 (originally published in English as *Letters Concerning the English Nation*, 1733; also as *Philosophical Letters*, 1961); *Discours de métaphysique*, 1736; *Éléments de la philosophie de Newton*, 1738 (*The Elements of Sir Isaac Newton's Philosophy*, 1738); *Vie de Molière*, 1739; *Le Siècle de Louis XIV*, 1751 (*The Age of Louis XIV*, 1752); *Essai sur les mœurs*, 1756, 1763 (*The General History and State of Europe*, 1754, 1759); *Traité sur la tolérance*, 1763 (*A Treatise on Religious Toleration*, 1764); *Dictionnaire philosophique portatif*, 1764, enlarged 1769 (as *La Raison par alphabet*, also known as *Dictionnaire philosophique*; *A Philosophical Dictionary for the Pocket*, 1765; also as *Philosophical Dictionary*, 1945, enlarged 1962); *Commentaires sur le théâtre de Pierre Corneille*, 1764; *Avis au public sur les parracides imputés aux calas et aux Sirven*, 1775; *Correspondence*, 1953-1965 (102 volumes).

MISCELLANEOUS: *The Works of M. de Voltaire*, 1761-1765 (35 volumes), 1761-1781 (38 volumes); *Candide and Other Writings*, 1945; *The Portable Voltaire*, 1949; *Candide, Zadig, and Selected Stories*, 1961; *The Complete Works of Voltaire*, 1968-1977 (135 volumes; in French).

BIBLIOGRAPHY

Ayer, A. J. *Voltaire*. New York: Random House, 1986. See the first chapter on Voltaire's life and character, and chapter 5 on *Candide*.

Hearsey, John E. N. *Voltaire*. New York: Barnes & Noble, 1976. See chapter 17, "*Candide*."

Howells, Robin. *Disabled Powers: A Reading of Voltaire's Contes*. Amsterdam: Editions Rodopi, 1993. See chapter 4, "*Candide* as Carnival." Includes a bibliography.

Mason, Haydn. *Candide: Optimism Demolished*. New York: Twayne, 1992. Divided into two parts: the literary and historical context (including critical reception); and a reading (the book's view of history, philosophy, personality, structure, and form). With notes and an annotated bibliography.

_____. *Voltaire*. New York: St. Martin's Press, 1975. See chapter 3 for a discussion of Voltaire's long fiction. Other chapters discuss his career as dramatic critic and dramatist, historian, poet, polemicist, reformer, philosopher, and correspondent. Contains chronology, detailed notes, bibliography, and index. An excellent introductory study.

Richter, Peyton, and Ilona Ricardo. *Voltaire*. Boston: Twayne, 1980. A sound introductory study, including a chapter on Voltaire's life, his place as an eighteenth century philosopher, his poetry, and his relevance for the twentieth century. See chapter 5 for a discussion of Voltaire's fiction. The chronology and annotated bibliography make this a particularly useful book.

Ridgway, R. S. *Voltaire and Sensibility*. Montreal: McGill-Queens University Press, 1973. See chapter 8 for a discussion of the relationship between Voltaire's personality and Candide's.

Torrey, Norman L. *The Spirit of Voltaire*. New York: Columbia University Press, 1938. See especially chapter 3 for Torrey's discussion of Voltaire's personality and his writing of *Candide*. Includes notes and index. Voltaire's tales tend to exploit traditional literary forms in order to introduce a unique type of satiric philosophical story.

Williams, David. *Voltaire: Candide*. London: Grant & Cutler, 1997. A thorough study guide to the seminal text. With bibliographical references.

KURT VONNEGUT, JR.

Born: Indianapolis, Indiana; November 11, 1922

PRINCIPAL LONG FICTION

Player Piano, 1952
The Sirens of Titan, 1959
Mother Night, 1961
Cat's Cradle, 1963
God Bless You, Mr. Rosewater: Or, Pearls Before Swine, 1965

(Jill Krementz)

*Slaughterhouse-Five: Or, The Children's Crusade,
    a Duty-Dance with Death*, 1969
*Breakfast of Champions: Or, Goodbye Blue Mon-
    day*, 1973
Slapstick: Or, Lonesome No More!, 1976
Jailbird, 1979
Deadeye Dick, 1982
Galápagos, 1985
Bluebeard, 1987
Hocus Pocus, 1990
Timequake, 1997
God Bless You, Dr. Kevorkian, 1999 (novella)

Other literary forms

Although known primarily for his novels, Kurt Vonnegut, Jr., also wrote for Broadway and television and published a children's book and several books of essays.

Achievements

Critical acclaim eluded Vonnegut until *Slaughterhouse-Five* was published in 1969. An immediate best-seller, it earned for Vonnegut respect from crit-ics who had previously dismissed him as a mediocre science-fiction writer. Vonnegut has been honored as the Briggs-Copeland Lecturer at Harvard University, as a member of the National Institute of Arts and Letters, and as the Distinguished Professor of English Prose at the City University of New York. Through his insightful and sympathetic treatment of the psychologically and morally crippled victims of the modern world, Vonnegut earned a reputation as one of the greatest humanist writers of his time.

Biography

Kurt Vonnegut, Jr., was born in Indianapolis, Indiana, in 1922. Both the location and the era of his birth helped shape his distinctive worldview. Growing up in the American heartland in the calm interval between the world wars, Vonnegut had a brief vision of a middle-class world that embraced the values of honesty, decency, and human dignity. For Vonnegut, this was the world as it should be, a world unravaged by violence and war, a world untouched by technology. This period of childhood happiness was, however, merely the calm before the storm in this life that would be rocked by a series of personal and national disasters: the suicide of his mother on Mother's Day; his prisoner-of-war experience in World War II; the deaths of his sister and brother-in-law; the dissolution of his first marriage; the bombings of Dresden and Hiroshima; the assassinations of President John F. Kennedy and the Rev. Martin Luther King, Jr.; the Vietnam War; the death of his first wife, with whom he had maintained a close friendship; and the death of his brother Bernard. All the heartaches of his family and his nation reverberate through Vonnegut's work, while the artist, through his fiction, stands as advocate for a saner, calmer world.

During the Depression years, Vonnegut's family suffered emotional and financial setbacks. When Vonnegut entered Cornell University in 1940, his father forbade him to study the arts and chose instead for his son a career in science, a career with guaranteed job security. In 1943 Vonnegut left Cornell to enlist in the army, despite his own public opposition to the war. Less than one year later, he was captured by the Germans and, in 1945, survived one of the greatest massacres of the war, the Allied fire-bombing of Dresden. This horror pursued Vonnegut for twenty-three years, until he worked through the pain by writing *Slaughterhouse-Five*.

After the war, Vonnegut married and began studies in anthropology at the University of Chicago. After three years, he left college and took a job as a publicist with General Electric (GE), where his brother worked as a physicist. Vonnegut's background in science and his disillusionment at GE influenced his first two novels, *Player Piano* and *The Sirens of Titan*, both parables of dehumanization in a technological society.

Between 1952 and 1998, Vonnegut wrote more than a dozen novels, numerous essays, a Broadway play, and a musical work, *Requiem*, which was performed by the Buffalo Symphony. He and Joe Petro III had a showing of twenty-six of their silk-screen prints in Denver in 1996. Despite his varied artistic talents, however, Vonnegut has always been known for his fiction. Vonnegut remarried in 1978; he and his wife, Jill Krementz, settled in New York.

ANALYSIS

In his novels, Kurt Vonnegut, Jr., coaxes the reader toward greater sympathy for humanity and deeper understanding of the human condition. His genre is satire—sometimes biting, sometimes tender, always funny. His arena is as expansive as the whole universe and as tiny as a single human soul. Part philosopher, part poet, Vonnegut, in his fictive world, tackles the core problem of modern life: How can the individual maintain dignity and exercise free will in a world overrun by death and destruction, a world in which both science and religion are powerless to provide a solution? The reader will find no ready answers in Vonnegut, only a friendly guide along the questioning path.

Vonnegut has, himself, behaved with a commendable sense of responsibility, dignity, and decency: He has labored long to show humankind its ailments and to wake it to the work it has to do. He admits to his and his family's having lived comfortably while so many of the world's population suffered, but in quoting the words of American socialist Eugene Debs in

his dedication to *Hocus Pocus*, he seems to define the position that he himself has taken as human being and as author and public figure for half of the twentieth century: "While there is a lower class I am in it. While there is a criminal element I am of it. While there is a soul in prison I am not free." He has spoken out in many forums for many causes and for all of humankind, and his has been a wide audience.

PLAYER PIANO

Ilium, New York, sometime in the near future, provides the setting for Vonnegut's first dystopian novel, *Player Piano*. Ilium is a divided city. On one side of the river live the important people, the engineers and managers who program and run the computers and machines that run people's lives. On the other side of the river, Homestead, live the downtrodden inhabitants of the city, those locked into menial, dehumanizing jobs assigned to them by the central computer.

Paul Proteus, the protagonist, is the brilliant young manager of the Ilium Works, a man being groomed for even greater success. Yet just as Ilium is a divided city, so is Paul divided about his life and his future. Paul suffers a growing discontent with his job at the Ilium Works, where people have been replaced by machines and machines are supervised by computers. Outwardly, Paul has no reason for worry or doubt. He has the best job and the most beautiful wife in Ilium, he is being considered for the highest post in his company, and he is climbing the ladder of success. Nevertheless, Paul's uneasiness increases. At first he seeks escape, settling on a farm in an attempt to get back to nature and free himself from his automatic life. He finds, however, that he has become an automaton, completely out of touch with the natural world, and his attempt at escape fails.

Finally, Paul is drawn to the other side of the river. His sympathy for the dehumanized masses and his acknowledgment of complicity in their plight drive Paul to join the masses in armed revolution. The fighters take to the streets, frantically and indiscriminately destroying all machines. The revolution fails, leaving Paul disillusioned and defeated, realizing that he has been manipulated by leaders on both sides of the conflict. Now he must surrender and face execution.

Paul's manipulation, first by those who would replace person with machine and then by those who would destroy the machines, is symbolized by the "player piano" of the title. The simplest of machines, the player piano creates its music without the aid of human beings, neatly rendering the skilled musician obsolete. Paul is entranced by the music of the player piano, in his fascination manipulated by the machine just as it manipulates its ivory keys.

The most striking symbol of the story, however, is the small black cat befriended by Paul as it wanders aimlessly through the Ilium Works. The cat, symbol of all that is natural and pure, despises the monstrous factory machines. The doomed animal is helplessly sucked into an automated sweeper, which spits it down a chute and ejects it outside the factory. Miraculously, it survives, but as Paul races to its rescue, the cat is roasted on the factory's electric fence, symbolizing humanity's destruction by the forces of technology. With characteristic Vonnegut irony, however, *Player Piano* ends on an affirmative note. Although the price of escape is its life, the cat does escape the Ilium Works. Near the end of the novel, Paul sees beautiful flowers growing outside the factory—flowers rooted in cat excrement, signifying ultimate rebirth and a glimmer of hope for Paul and his world.

MOTHER NIGHT

In his third novel, *Mother Night*, Vonnegut peers even more deeply into the human soul, exploring the roots of human alienation, probing an individual's search for his "real" identity, and uncovering the thin veil that separates reality from illusion. The story is told as the memoirs of Howard W. Campbell, Jr., a self-proclaimed "citizen of nowhere." A successful writer and producer of medieval romance plays, Campbell sees himself as a sensitive *artiste*. Nevertheless, he allows himself to be recruited by Major Frank Wirtanen to be an American double agent posing as a Nazi radio propagandist in Germany. Secretly, Campbell sends coded American messages in his propaganda broadcasts, but he does not understand the code and never comprehends the messages he transmits. Still unaware, he even transmits the news of his beloved wife's death.

Publicly, Campbell is reviled as a traitorous Nazi hatemonger, but he does not mind, because he enjoys being on the radio. Eventually, though, he begins to lose touch with his "real" self. Is he the sensitive artist, the cruel Nazi, or the American patriot? Like Paul Proteus, Campbell allows himself to be manipulated by those around him. With no will or identity of his own, Campbell is easy prey for those who would use him for their own ends.

Two of Campbell's manipulators are his postwar friend George Kraft and his sister-in-law Resi, who poses as Campbell's long-lost wife, Helga. George and Resi are actually Russian spies plotting to capture Campbell and transport him to Russia. They abandon this plan, however, when they realize their love for Campbell, and they finally attempt to escape to freedom with him. Before the three can flee together, however, the Russians are arrested by American agents. Campbell is arrested as well but is soon freed by his friend Frank Wirtanen.

Gripped by existential fear at finding himself a free man, Campbell appeals to a Jewish couple in his apartment building, a doctor and his mother, both survivors of Auschwitz. Campbell begs to be tried for his crimes against the Jews and soon finds himself awaiting trial in a Jerusalem prison. Before Campbell goes to trial, Frank Wirtanen sends a letter on his behalf, explaining how he had recruited Campbell and honoring him as an American patriot. Yet Campbell can never be a truly free man until he purges his conscience. Upon his release from prison, he is nauseated by the prospect of his freedom, knowing that he is one of the many people "who served evil too openly and good too secretly." In his failure to resist evil and his openness to manipulation by others, Campbell had given up his free will and lost his ability to choose. Coming to this realization, he finally asserts his will to choose and ironically chooses to die, vowing to hang himself "for crimes against himself."

CAT'S CRADLE

Equally dark is Vonnegut's fourth novel, *Cat's Cradle*. In addition to its broad parody of science and religion, *Cat's Cradle* expands on Vonnegut's earlier themes of the dangerous misuse of science and technology, humans' moral responsibility in an immoral world, and the importance of distinguishing reality from illusion. The parodic tone is set in the very first line, "Call me Jonah," bringing to mind the Old Testament Book of Jonah. Like that Jonah, this protagonist (really named John) faithfully pursues God's directives but never truly comprehends the order behind God's plan. Continuing the parody, John encounters the Bokononist religion, whose bible, The Books of Bokonon, proclaims in its first line, "All of the true things I am about to tell you are shameless lies," an obvious inversion of the Johannine maxim "You will know the truth, and the truth will make you free" (John 8:32). In the world John inhabits, the only real freedom is the ultimate freedom—death.

John is writing a book, "The Day the World Ended," an account of the bombing of Hiroshima. His obsession with the destruction of Hiroshima foreshadows his involvement in the eventual destruction of the world by "ice-nine," a substance that converts liquid into frozen crystals. In *Cat's Cradle*, the atomic bomb and ice-nine are both the doomsday toys of an amoral scientist, Dr. Felix Hoenikker. Hoenikker pursues his work so intensely that he has little time for his three children, who grow up to be emotionally warped and twisted Products of Science. Hoenikker's only legacy to his children is the ice-nine he was brewing in the kitchen before his sudden death on Christmas Eve. After their father's death, the three children—Angela, Frank, and Newt— divide the ice-nine among themselves, knowing that it is their ticket to a better future. Newt, a midget, barters his ice-nine for an affair with a Russian ballerina. The homely Angela uses her portion to buy herself a husband. Frank gives his to Miguel "Papa" Monzano, dictator of the Caribbean Republic of San Lorenzo, in exchange for the title of general and the hand of Monzano's beautiful adopted daughter, Mona.

Pursuing information on the Hoenikker family, John finds himself in San Lorenzo, where he is introduced to Bokononism. The people of San Lorenzo are desperately poor, for the soil of the island is as unproductive as the Sahara. The island's teeming, malnourished masses find their only comfort in Bokononism, which urges them to love and console one another. John finds that, ironically, the religion started as a game by the island's founders. Knowing no way to lift the country from its destitution, they decided to give the people hope by inventing a religion based on *foma*, or comforting lies. The religion encouraged people to find strength in their *karass*, groups of people with whom they are joined to do God's mysterious will. To strengthen the faith of the people, Bokononism was outlawed, its founder banished on pain of death. As the people's faith grew, so did their happiness and their dependence on *foma*, until all the inhabitants of the island were "employed full time as actors in a play." For the inhabitants of San Lorenzo, illusion had become reality.

Soon after his arrival on the island, John finds that Papa Monzano is critically ill; it is expected that "General" Frank Hoenikker will succeed Papa and take the beautiful Mona as his bride. Secretly, though, Frank has no desire to rule the island or marry Mona. He is a simpering mass of insecurities, hiding behind his fake title. Frank's life, like everything around him, has been a lie: He has bought a false sense of dignity, which he wears like a military uniform, but inside he is gripped with fear, the same fear that pulses through the veins of the dying dictator. Papa and Frank become symbols for all people, running scared and grasping at false comforts as they confront brutal reality. Faced with the horror of an agonizing death, Papa clutches his vial of ice-nine, his last illusion of security and power. Uttering the desperate cry, "Now I will destroy the whole world," he swallows the poison and turns himself into an ice-blue popsicle. Papa's power proves illusory, however, as John and the Hoenikker children clean up the mess and seal off Papa's bedroom.

John, Frank, Angela, and Newt inform the staff that Papa is "feeling much better" and go downstairs to watch a military celebration. Despite their success at covering up Papa's death and hiding their secret, John and the Hoenikker children sense impending doom. As all the islanders watch the military air show, a bomber careens out of control and bursts into flame, setting off a massive explosion and landslide. As his castle disintegrates, Papa Monzano's body is propelled from the bedroom closet, plunging into the waiting sea, infecting all with ice-nine.

As the story ends, only John, Newt, and Bokonon remain, awaiting their imminent death. John recalls Angela's heroic end, remembering how she had clutched her clarinet bravely and played in the face of death, music mocking terror. John dreams of climbing the highest mountain and planting some magnificent symbol. As his heart swells with the vision of being the last man on the highest mountain, Newt mocks him and brings him back to earth. The story concludes with the last verse of The Books of Bokonon, in which Bokonon mourns human stupidity, thumbs his nose at God, and kills himself with ice-nine.

Like many of Vonnegut's satirical writings, *Cat's Cradle* functions as humanity's wake-up call. For Vonnegut, heroism is not a dream; dignity is not an illusion. Still, he understands all too well the fear that grips a man on the brink of action, the torpor that invades the soul. In his frustration, all the artist can do is plod on, calling out his warnings as he goes.

SLAUGHTERHOUSE-FIVE

Vonnegut's efforts to touch the soul of humanity are most fully realized in his sixth novel, *Slaughterhouse-Five*, his most touching and brilliant work. Incorporating all Vonnegut's common themes—the nature of reality and illusion, the question of free will and determinism, the horror of humankind's cruelty to itself, the vision of life as an ironic construct—*Slaughterhouse-Five* produces "an image of life that is beautiful and surprising and deep." This often-misunderstood novel leads the reader on a time-warped journey, as popular films say, "to hell and back." Emotionally suffocated by his experience in World War II, Vonnegut waited twenty-three years to tell the story of his capture by the Germans and his survival of the Allied firebombing of Dresden, the calculated annihilation of a quarter of a million refugees and civilians in an unguarded city.

As befits a tale of such distorted experience, *Slaughterhouse-Five* breaks all novelistic conventions. The story is divided into ten sections, spanning the years from 1944 to 1968. Opening with a simple, first-person narrative, Vonnegut describes his return to Dresden in 1967. He recounts his life after the war,

discusses his wife and children, and relives a conversation with his old war buddy Bernard V. O'Hare, in which he reveals why *Slaughterhouse-Five* is subtitled *The Children's Crusade*. In the original Children's Crusade of 1213, Catholic monks raised a volunteer army of thirty thousand children who were intent on traveling to Palestine but instead were sent to North Africa to be sold as slaves. In the end, half the children drowned en route and the others were sold. For Vonnegut, this incident provides the perfect metaphor for all wars: hopeless ventures fought by deluded children. Thus Vonnegut prepares the reader for this personal statement about the tragedy of war. Nevertheless, the reader finds himself unprepared for the narrative shape of the tale.

Breaking from his reverie, Vonnegut reads from a Gideon Bible the story of Lot's wife, turned to a pillar of salt for looking back on Sodom and Gomorrah. To Vonnegut, her reaction was tender, instinctively human, looking back on all those lives that had touched hers, and he adopts Lot's wife as a metaphor for his narrative stance. *Slaughterhouse-Five* will be a tale told by a "pillar of salt." Vonnegut assumes the role of a masked narrator, a disinterested party, allowing himself the aesthetic distance he needs to continue his painful journey. Yet, when the reader turns to chapter 2, he finds another surprise, as chapter 2 begins, "Listen: Billy Pilgrim has come unstuck in time."

To increase his emotional distance from the story, Vonnegut, the masked narrator, tells not his own story but the story of pathetic Billy Pilgrim, Vonnegut's mythical fellow soldier. Through time travel over which he has no control, Billy is forced to relive the chapters of his life, in seemingly random order. For Billy, as for Vonnegut, his war chronology is too unsettling to confront head on. Instead of assimilating his life experiences, Billy unconsciously tries to escape the memory of them by bouncing back and forth in time from one experience to another. Not until the end of the tale can he face the crucial moment, the horror of Dresden.

The reader first sees Billy as a forty-six-year-old retired optometrist living in Ilium, New York. Billy's daughter, Barbara, thinks that he has lost his mind.

Billy has given up interest in business and devotes all of his energies to telling the world about his travels to the planet Tralfamadore. Two years earlier, Billy had been captured by aliens from Tralfamadore and had spent six months on their planet. Billy's belief in Tralfamadorian philosophy is the great comfort of his life, and he is eager to share this philosophy with the world. The aliens taught Billy, the optometrist, a better way to "see." On Tralfamadore, time is not linear; all moments are structured and permanent, and death is merely one moment out of many moments in a person's life. The Tralfamadorians do not mourn the dead, for even though one may be dead in one moment, he or she is alive and happy in many others. The Tralfamadorians respond to life's temporary bad moments with a verbal shrug, "So it goes." Their world is a world without free will, without human responsibility, without human sorrow. On an intellectual level, Billy hungrily embraces their philosophy, yet deep inside him (as inside Vonnegut) stirs the need to reconstruct his life, to reconcile his past. So, armed with Tralfamadorian detachment, Billy steps back in time to where it all began.

It is 1944, and Billy, a night student at the Ilium School of Optometry, is drafted into action in World War II. No soldier is more unsuited to war than is Billy. Timid and friendless, he is a chaplain's assistant, a hapless soul with a "meek faith in a loving Jesus which most soldiers found putrid." Billy's marching companion is Roland Weary, a savage young man, even by military standards. Weary's father collects ancient instruments of torture, and Weary regales Billy with gruesome tales of cruelty, giving the gentle boy an unwanted view of a monstrous world. Weary, a callous, stupid killing machine, is the natural result of humanity's barbarity. Although physically robust, he is morally depleted, a symbol of the spiritually bankrupt world into which poor Billy has been thrust. Billy—kind, sensitive, tenderhearted—has no natural defenses against the barbarity which surrounds him, so he becomes unstuck in time.

After a brief respite of time travel, Billy returns to the war. He and Weary have been captured behind German lines, taken prisoner by two toothless old men and two young boys. The Germans are accom-

panied by a guard dog, a female German shepherd named Princess who had been stolen from a farmer. Princess and Billy are confused and shivering from the cold. Of the whole motley group, only the barbarous Weary belongs at war. Billy, Princess, the old men, and the young boys symbolize helpless humanity in the grip of military madness.

Billy and his fellow prisoners, including Vonnegut and Bernard V. O'Hare, are taken to a prisoner-of-war camp before their transport to Dresden. As Billy recalls these moments of his life, he is moved to time travel many times. He flashes forward to 1948, when, emotionally shattered by his war experience, he checks himself into a veterans' hospital for mental patients. Here the reader is introduced to Valencia Merble, Billy's unlovely fiancée, and Eliot Rosewater, his fellow mental patient. In the hospital, Eliot and Billy devour the science-fiction novels of Kilgore Trout. They are drawn to Trout's work for the same reason Billy is drawn to the philosophy of Tralfamadore: Human experience on earth has been too disturbing; life seems meaningless. Escaping to the world of science fiction relieves the pressure, enabling Eliot and Billy to "reinvent" themselves in a kinder universe.

Before Billy returns to his war story, he again relives his adventures on the planet Tralfamadore, where he spends six months in the Tralfamadore Zoo, displayed in a glass cage. Here Billy learns of his own death in 1976. He will be murdered by Paul Lazarro, a former inmate in Billy's prisoner-of-war camp. The maniacal Lazarro, incorrectly blaming Billy for the death of Roland Weary, has plotted revenge since 1944. Naturally, Billy's innocence makes his meaningless death doubly absurd. At this time, Billy also learns of the eventual destruction of the world by the Tralfamadorians. While testing a new rocket fuel for their spacecraft, they accidentally blow up the universe. "So it goes."

When Billy returns to his war story, he and his fellow American soldiers are in Dresden, working in a factory producing vitamin syrup for pregnant women. Yet soon there will be no pregnant women in Dresden. The American soldiers are quartered underground in a former pig butchery—slaughterhouse number five. On the night of February 13, 1945, Billy (and Vonnegut) nestles safely in the shelter while the city is flattened by British and American firebombs. The next morning, the prisoners go aboveground, finding the city as lifeless as the surface of the moon. Only the one hundred American prisoners and their guards had survived.

In chapter 10, Vonnegut himself returns as narrator. It is 1968. In the intervening years, Billy has survived an airplane crash in which all of his fellow passengers have died. Valencia, frantically hurrying to see Billy in the hospital, has died of accidental carbon-monoxide poisoning. Robert Kennedy and Martin Luther King, Jr., have been assassinated. The Vietnam War is raging.

Finally, Vonnegut takes the reader back to Dresden. He and Billy are there, where the prisoners of war are digging for bodies, mining for corpses. Billy's digging companion dies of the dry heaves, unable to face the slaughter. Billy's friend Edgar Derby is executed for stealing a teapot. When the corpse mines are closed down, Billy, Vonnegut, and their companions are locked up in the suburbs to await the end of the war. When the war is over, the freed soldiers wander out into the street. The trees are blooming, and the birds are singing; springtime has finally arrived for Kurt Vonnegut.

Looking back on the novel, the reader realizes that Billy's time travels have been more than simply a coping device; they provide a learning tool as well. The jumble of events to which Vonnegut subjects Billy are not random and meaningless. Even if Billy remains blankly ignorant of the connections between events in his life, both the reader and the author learn about emotional survival in the modern world. For Vonnegut, who has called himself "the canary in the coal mine," Billy's story is a parable and a warning to all humankind: a warning that men and women must resist the temptation to abandon their free will, as Billy had, and an exhortation to keep one's dignity in the face of modern dehumanization.

That *Slaughterhouse-Five* is a story of survival may seem contradictory or ironic, but that is always Vonnegut's approach. It would be hard for the reader to imagine more death than he witnesses here—the slaughter in Dresden and the deaths of Billy, his wife, his father, and assorted soldiers, all culminating in the foretelling of the destruction of the universe by the Tralfamadorians. Yet the reader comes to understand that everything about Vonnegut's tale is ironic. Edgar Derby is executed, amid the Dresden corpse mines, for stealing a teapot; Billy, sitting in a slaughterhouse, is saved from destruction. No wonder Billy sees himself as the plaything of uncontrollable forces. Yet Vonnegut knows better. Billy, comfortably numbed by Tralfamadorian philosophy, never reinvents himself—but Vonnegut does. Writing this book enabled the author to face his past, his present, and his future. In fact, after writing *Slaughterhouse-Five*, Vonnegut proclaimed that he would never *need* to write another book. *Slaughterhouse-Five* embodied for Vonnegut the spirit of the phoenix: his soul, through his art, rising from the ashes.

After the spiritual and psychological rejuvenation wrought by *Slaughterhouse-Five*, Vonnegut became a totally unfettered artist in his next two books, *Breakfast of Champions* and *Slapstick*. In *Breakfast of Champions*, he sets all of his characters free, disdaining his role as puppeteer. Admitting that, in English poet John Keats's words, he had been "half in love with easeful Death," he asserts that he has rid himself of this dangerous fascination. In *Slapstick*, he becomes frankly autobiographical, abandoning his aesthetic distance, eschewing all masks, facing his uncertain future and painful past with calm equanimity.

GALÁPAGOS

In *Galápagos*, called by Vonnegut himself his best novel, the ghost of Leon Trotsky Trout, son of Kilgore Trout, calmly tells the story of humankind from 1986 to a point one million years in the future. He tells of the end of humankind as known by its "bigbrained" twentieth century readers and of the new Adam and Eves and their new Eden. Satirist and atheist that he is, Vonnegut idealizes no part of or party to his story. Knowledge is still the poisoned apple, but naturalist Charles Darwin, not God, is the featured figure of this final record of human life as known to its recorder.

Leon Trout died in the construction of the luxury liner the *Bahia de Darwin*, the launching of which is advertised as "the nature cruise of the century." Worldwide crises, however, cause all but a paltry few to withdraw their names from the list of passengers and crew. The cruise itself is begun by accident, and Mary Hepburn, not the figurehead captain, Adolf von Kleist, guides it to its destination. This unaware Adam and sterile-but-godlike Eve, with six Kankabono girls "from the Stone Age," begin the new race according to Darwin's (and God's?) dictum: Having eaten of the rotten apple, humankind, with its big, self-destructive brain, is no longer fit to survive; it is a matter of shrink and swim or die. Humankind thus becomes small-brained fisherkind as witnessed by the curious ghost of Leon Trout—who can now, having so witnessed, travel through the blue tunnel into the Afterlife.

Satirist, moralist, and spokesperson for humankind that he is, Vonnegut, as Jonathan Swift before him, has offered in *Galápagos* his modest proposal to a humankind bent on its own destruction. He has also offered as epigraph to his tome the words of Anne Frank: "In spite of everything, I still believe people are really good at heart."

TIMEQUAKE

In *Timequake* Vonnegut has humankind, because of a glitch in time, replay years 1991 to 2001 "on automatic pilot." He speaks as failed author of a ten-year project, *Timequake One*. Kilgore Trout, whom he personally identifies as his alter ego and as lookalike to his father, plays a crucial role in this novel. Vonnegut reprises his authorial roles as science-fiction writer, fiction writer, autobiographer, and spokesman for humankind.

Vonnegut's fictional story shows characters living and dying, living and dying again, and then waking and reeling from the reintroduction of free will. When humanity is roused from its ten years on automatic pilot, Trout becomes its hero. Because people have had no free will for ten years, they have forgotten how to use it, and Trout shows them the path to readjustment. Trout's words, for which he is celebrated, are: "You were sick, but now you're well again, and there's work to do."

Vonnegut's epilogue honoring his "big brother Bernie," who died toward the end of *Timequake*'s

composition, calls to mind his prior references to saints he has known who, in an indecent society, behave decently. His references throughout *Timequake* and this final tribute to Bernard Vonnegut seem a recommendation of that gentle man to the status of saint.

Karen Priest, updated by Judith K. Taylor

OTHER MAJOR WORKS

SHORT FICTION: *Canary in a Cat House*, 1961; *Welcome to the Monkey House*, 1968; *Bagombo Snuff Box: Uncollected Short Fiction*, 1999.

PLAY: *Happy Birthday, Wanda June*, pb. 1970.

TELEPLAY: *Between Time and Timbuktu: Or, Prometheus-5, a Space Fantasy*, 1972.

NONFICTION: *Wampeters, Foma, and Granfalloons (Opinions)*, 1974; *Palm Sunday: An Autobiographical Collage*, 1981; *Fates Worse than Death: An Autobiographical Collage of the 1980's*, 1991.

CHILDREN'S LITERATURE: *Sun Moon Star*, 1980 (with Ivan Chermayeff).

BIBLIOGRAPHY

Allen, William Rodney. *Understanding Kurt Vonnegut*. Columbia: University of South Carolina Press, 1991. Allen's study, part of the Understanding Contemporary American Literature series, places Vonnegut, and especially *Slaughterhouse-Five*, in the literary canon. Contains an annotated bibliography and an index.

Broer, Lawrence R. *Sanity Plea: Schizophrenia in the Novels of Kurt Vonnegut*. Ann Arbor: University of Michigan Press, 1989. The comprehensive work covers all Vonnegut's major fiction from the perspective of psychology, viewing Vonnegut's characters as psychologically damaged by the traumas of the modern . The book lacks a chronology but has an excellent introduction, an index, and a thorough bibliograpworldhy.

Giannone, Richard. *Vonnegut: A Preface to His Novels*. Port Washington, N.Y.: Kennikat Press, 1977. This comprehensive work covers all Vonnegut's major fiction up to 1977. Giving special treatment to the unity of Vonnegut's themes, this book has an outstanding introduction, a brief chronology, a brief bibliography, and a brief index.

Klinkowitz, Jerome. *"Slaughterhouse-Five": Reforming the Novel and the World*. Boston: Twayne, 1990. This book contains the most thorough and most modern treatment available of *Slaughterhouse-Five*. With care and insight, Klinkowitz debunks earlier, fatalistic interpretations of the novel. Features a comprehensive chronology, a thorough bibliography, and an index.

_____. *Vonnegut in Fact: The Public Spokesmanship of Personal Fiction*. Columbia: University of South Carolina Press, 1998. Klinkowitz makes a case for Vonnegut as a sort of redeemer of the novelistic form, after writers such as Philip Roth declared the novel dead. He traces Vonnegut's successful integration of autobiography and fiction in his body of work. Provides an extensive bibliography and an index.

Merrill, Robert, ed. *Critical Essays on Kurt Vonnegut*. Boston: G. K. Hall, 1990. Merrill claims to have compiled "the most comprehensive collection of criticism on this author yet assembled." An index is provided.

Mustazza, Leonard, ed. *The Critical Response to Kurt Vonnegut*. Westport, Conn.: Greenwood Press, 1994. Presents a brief history of the critical response to Vonnegut and critical reviews. A selected bibliography and an index are provided.

Schatt, Stanley. *Kurt Vonnegut, Jr.* Boston: Twayne, 1976. This volume is notable for its discussion of Vonnegut's plays and short stories, as well as its retrospective of Vonnegut's life, entitled "The Public Man." It also offers a comprehensive treatment of the fiction, a brief chronology, a bibliography, and an index.

W

JOHN WAIN

Born: Stoke-on-Trent, Staffordshire, England;
    March 14, 1925
Died: Oxford, England; May 24, 1994

PRINCIPAL LONG FICTION

Hurry on Down, 1953 (pb. in U.S. as *Born in
    Captivity*)
Living in the Present, 1955
The Contenders, 1958
A Travelling Woman, 1959
Strike the Father Dead, 1962
The Young Visitors, 1965
The Smaller Sky, 1967
A Winter in the Hills, 1970
The Pardoner's Tale, 1978
Young Shoulders, 1982 (pb. in U.S. as *The Free
    Zone Starts Here*)
Where the Rivers Meet, 1988
Comedies, 1990
Hungry Generations, 1994

OTHER LITERARY FORMS

A complete man of letters, John Wain published short stories, poetry, drama, many scholarly essays, and a highly respected biography in addition to his novels. Wain's writing reflects his determination to speak to a wider range of readers than that addressed by many of his modernist predecessors; it reflects his faith in the common reader to recognize and respond to abiding philosophical concerns. These concerns include his sense of the dignity of human beings in the midst of an oftentimes cruel, indifferent, and cynical world. His concern is with a world caught up in time, desire, and disappointment.

Significant among Wain's writings other than novels are several collections of short stories—including *Nuncle and Other Stories* (1960), *Death of the Hind Legs and Other Stories* (1966), *The Life Guard* (1971), and *King Caliban and Other Stories* (1978)—and volumes of poetry, such as *Mixed Feelings* (1951), *A Word Carved on a Sill* (1956), *Weep Before God: Poems* (1961), *Wildtrack: A Poem* (1965), *Letters to Five Artists* (1969), *The Shape of Feng* (1972), *Feng: A Poem* (1975), and *Open Country* (1987). Wain also published criticism that communicates a sensitive and scholarly appreciation of good books. Readers should pay particular attention to *Preliminary Essays* (1957), *Essays on Literature and Ideas* (1963), *A House for the Truth: Critical Essays* (1972), *Professing Poetry* (1977), and his autobiography, *Sprightly Running: Part of an Autobiography* (1962). Most readers believe that *Samuel Johnson* (1974) is the best and most lasting of all Wain's nonfiction. In this monumental biography, many of the commitments reflected in Wain's other writings come through clearly and forcefully.

ACHIEVEMENTS

John Wain is noted for his observance of and compassion for human sorrow. *Young Shoulders*, an examination of the ramifications of a fatal accident on the people left behind, won the 1982 Whitbread Best Novel Award.

BIOGRAPHY

Although his world was that of the twentieth century, John Wain was very much an eighteenth century man. He delighted in pointing out that he and eighteenth century writer Samuel Johnson were born in the same district ("The Potteries") and in much the same social milieu; that he attended the same university as Johnson (Oxford, where he served from 1973 to 1978 as Professor of Poetry); and that he knew, like Johnson, the Grub Street experiences and "the unremitting struggle to write enduring books against the background of an unstable existence." What chiefly interests the critic in surveying Wain's formative years are the reasons for his increasingly sober outlook. Wain's autobiography, *Sprightly Running*, remains the best account of his formative years as well as offering engaging statements of many of his opinions. In it, the reader finds some of the profound and lasting effects on Wain's writing of his childhood, his adolescence, and his years at Oxford.

John Barrington Wain was born on March 14, 1925, in Stoke-on-Trent, Staffordshire, an industrial city given over to pottery and coal mining. Here, as in other English cities, a move upward in social status is signaled by a move up in geographical terms. Therefore, the Wain family's move three years later to Penkhull—a manufacturing complex of kilns and factories and, incidentally, the setting for Wain's third novel, *The Contenders*—marked a step up into the middle-class district.

From infancy, Wain had a genuine fondness for the countryside. He immersed himself in the sights and sounds and colors of rural nature, all of which made an impression on him that was distinctive as well as deep. This impression developed into an "unargued reverence for all created life, almost a pantheism." On holidays, he and his family traveled to the coast and hills of North Wales—an association which carried over into his adult years, when, at thirty-four, he married a Welsh woman. His feeling for Wales—for the independent life of the people, the landscape and mountains, the sea, the special light of the sun—is recorded in *A Winter in the Hills*. Here and elsewhere is the idea that nature is the embodiment of order, permanence, and life. Indeed, the tension between the nightmare of repression in society and the dream of liberation in the natural world is an important unifying theme throughout Wain's work.

The experience of living in an industrial town also left an indelible imprint upon Wain's mind and art. His exposure to the lives of the working class and to the advance of industrialism gave him a profound knowledge of working people and their problems, which he depicts with sympathy and humanity in his fiction. Moreover, Wain's experiences at Froebel's Preparatory School and at Newcastle-under-Lyme High School impressed on him the idea that life was competitive and "a perpetual effort to survive." He found himself surrounded and outnumbered by people who resented him for being different from themselves. His contact with older children, schoolboy bullies, and authoritative schoolmasters taught Wain that the world is a dangerous place. These "lessons of life" were carried into his work. The reader finds in Wain's fiction a sense of the difficulty of survival in an intrusive and demanding world. The worst of characters is always the bully, and the worst of societies is always totalitarian. Beginning with *Hurry on Down*, each of Wain's published novels and stories is concerned in some way with the power and control that some people seek to exercise over others.

To cope with these injustices as well as with his own fears and inadequacies during his early years, Wain turned to humor, debate, and music. For Wain, the humorist is above all a moralist, in whose hands the ultimate weapon of laughter might conceivably become the means of liberating humankind from its enslavement to false ideals. Thus, his mimicry of both authorities and students was used as the quickest way to illustrate that something was horrible or boring or absurd. In both *Hurry on Down* and *The Contenders*, the heroes use mockery and ridicule to cope with their unjust world.

Wain's interest in jazz also influenced his personal and literary development. He spoke and wrote often of his lifelong enthusiasm for the trumpet playing of Bill Coleman, and he admitted that Percy Brett, the black jazz musician in *Strike the Father Dead*, was created with Coleman in mind. Accompanying this interest was a growing interest in serious writing and reading. Unlike many youths, Wain did not have to endure the agonizing doubt and indecision of trying to decide what he wanted to do in life. By the age of nine, he knew: he wanted to be an author. He began as a critically conscious writer who delighted in "pastiche and parody for their own sake," though he had problems maintaining a steady plotline. Wain matched his writing with voracious reading. His early interest in the novels of Charles Dickens, Tobias Smollett, Daniel Defoe, and others in the tradition of the English novel influenced his later literary style. Like these predecessors, Wain approached his characters through the conventional narration of the realist, and his concerns were social and moral.

The second major period in Wain's life occurred between 1943, when he entered St. John's College, Oxford, and 1955, when he resigned his post as lecturer in English at Reading University to become a full-time writer. Two friends made in his Oxford period especially influenced his writing. One was Philip Larkin, whose "rock-like determination" provided an inspiring example for Wain. The other friend was Kingsley Amis, whose work on a first novel inspired Wain to attempt writing a novel in his spare time. Wain wrote his first novel, not particularly because he wished to be a novelist, but to see if he could write one that would get into print. In 1953, Frederick Warburg accepted *Hurry on Down*, and its unexpected success quickly established Wain as one of Britain's promising new writers.

Wain's exhilarating experience with his first book was, however, poor preparation for the sobering slump that followed. Ill health, divorce proceedings, and the drudgery of a scholar's life pushed him into a crisis of depression and discouragement. He tried to climb out of this crisis by leaving the university for a year and retreating to the Swiss Alps. There, he let his imagination loose on his own problems. The result was *Living in the Present*, a depressing book of manifest despair and disgust. Out of this period in his life, Wain developed a profound awareness of love and loneliness, union and estrangement. The essential loneliness of human beings, and their more or less successful attempts to overcome their loneliness by love, became major themes in his later fiction.

Although Wain was never sanguine about the human condition or the times in which he lived, his life was to be more fulfilling than he anticipated at this time. As a result of his year of self-assessment, in 1955 Wain did not return to the junior position he had held at the University of Reading but instead began working fulltime at his writing. Little more than a decade later, his reputation had become so well established that he could reenter the academic world as a visiting professor. Eventually Wain was appointed Professor of Poetry at Oxford University, a post he held from 1973 to 1978.

Sprightly Running, published in 1962, was evidence that Wain was much more contented than he had been seven years before. He was now happily married to Eirian James, an intelligent, insightful woman who provided him with companionship and sometimes help with his work (she coedited *The New Wessex Selection of Thomas Hardy's Poetry* in 1978).

They had three sons. Their life together ended only with Eirian's death in 1987. The following year, Wain married Patricia Dunn.

Despite ill health and diminished vision, Wain labored on courageously at what proved to be his final project, three novels that together constitute the Oxford Trilogy. On May 24, 1994, Wain died of a stroke at the John Radcliffe Hospital in Oxford.

ANALYSIS

As a novelist, John Wain has been described as a "painfully honest" writer who always, to an unusual degree, wrote autobiography. His own fortunes and his emotional reactions to these fortunes are, of course, transformed in various ways. His purpose is artistic, not confessional, and he shaped his material accordingly. As Wain himself stated, this intention is both pure and simple: to express his own feelings honestly and to tell the truth about the world he knew. At his best—in *Hurry on Down*, *Strike the Father Dead*, *A Winter in the Hills*, and *The Pardoner's Tale*—Wain finds a great many ways to convey the message that life is ultimately tragic. Human beings suffer, life is difficult, and the comic mask conceals anguish. Only occasionally is this grim picture relieved by some sort of idealism, some unexpected attitude of unselfishness or tenderness. What is more, in all his writings Wain is a thoughtful, literate man coming to terms with these truths in a sincere and forthright manner.

To understand something of Wain's uniqueness as a novelist, the reader must look back at least to the end of World War II. For about ten years after the war, established writers continued to produce successfully. English novelists such as Aldous Huxley, Graham Greene, Evelyn Waugh, C. P. Snow, and Anthony Powell had made their reputations before the war and continued to be the major literary voices that time. Most of them had been educated in "public" schools, then at Oxford or Cambridge, and were from upper- or upper-middle-class origins. Their novels were likely to center around fashionable London or some country estate. Often they confined their satire to the intellectual life and the cultural as well as social predicaments of the upper-middle class.

A combination of events in postwar England led to the appearance of another group of writers, soon referred to by literary journalists as the "Angry Young Men." Among these writers was John Wain, who, along with Kingsley Amis, John Braine, John Osborne, Angus Wilson, Alan Sillitoe, and others, turned away from technical innovations, complexity, and the sensitive, introspective protagonist to concentrate on concrete problems of current society. Thus, in the tradition of the eighteenth century novel, Wain fulfills most effectively the novelist's basic task of telling a good story. His novels move along at an even pace; he relies upon a simple, tightly constructed, and straightforward plot; clarity; good and bad characters; and a controlled point of view. The reader need only think of James Joyce and Franz Kafka, and the contrast is clear. What most of Wain's novels ask from the reader is not some feat of analysis, but a considered fullness of response, a readiness to acknowledge, even in disagreement, his vision of defeat.

Wain's typical protagonist is essentially an "antihero," a man at the mercy of life. Although sometimes capable of aspiration and thought, he is not strong enough to carve out his destiny in the way he wishes. Frequently, he is something of a dreamer, tossed about by life, and also pushed about, or at least overshadowed, by the threats in his life. Wain's Charles Lumley (*Hurry on Down*) and Edgar Banks (*Living in the Present*) bear the marks of this type. Often there is discernible in his characters a modern malaise, a vague discontent, and a yearning for some person or set of circumstances beyond their reach. Sometimes, this sense of disenchantment with life as it is becomes so great that the individual expresses a desire not to live at all, as Edgar Banks asserts in *Living in the Present* and as Gus Howkins declares in *The Pardoner's Tale*.

Wain is also accomplished in his creation of place and atmosphere. In *Strike the Father Dead*, he fully captures the grayness of a London day, the grayness of lives spent under its pall, the grayness of the people who wander its streets. When Wain describes an afternoon in which Giles Hermitage (*The Pardoner's Tale*) forces himself to work in the subdued light at

home, when Arthur Geary (*The Smaller Sky*) walks the platforms at Paddington Station, when Charles Lumley walks in on a literary gathering, or when Roger Furnivall (*A Winter in the Hills*) makes his way home through the Welsh countryside—at such moments the reader encounters Wain's mastery of setting and atmosphere.

The themes communicated through Wain's novels are, like his method, consistent. It is clear that he sees the eighteenth century as a time of dignity, pride, and self-sufficiency—qualities lacking in the twentieth century. Like Samuel Johnson, Wain defends the value of reason, moderation, common sense, moral courage, and intellectual self-respect. Moreover, his fictional themes of the dignity of the human being, the difficulty of survival in the modern world, and the perils of success have established him principally as a moralist concerned with ethical issues. In later works, the value of tradition, the notion of human understanding, and the ability to love and suffer become the chief moral values. In all his novels, he is primarily concerned with the problem of defining the moral worth of the individual. For all these reasons, Wain is recognized as a penetrating observer of the human scene.

One final point should be noted about Wain's capacities as a novelist. Clearly, the spiritual dimension is missing in the world he describes, yet there is frequently the hint or at least the possibility of renewal, which is the closest Wain comes to any sort of recognized affirmation. Charles Lumley, Joe Shaw, Jeremy Coleman, and Roger Furnivall are all characters who seem to be, by the end of their respective stories, on the verge of rebirth of a sort, on the threshold of reintegration and consequent regeneration. In each case, this renewal depends on the ability of the individual to come to terms with himself and his situation; to confront and accept at a stroke past, present, and future; and to accept and tolerate the contradictions inherent in all three. Wain's sensitive response to the tragic aspects of life is hardly novel, but his deep compassion for human suffering and his tenderness for the unfortunate are more needed than ever in an age when violence, brutality, and cynicism are all too prevalent.

HURRY ON DOWN

In his first novel, *Hurry on Down*, Wain comically perceives the difficulties of surviving in a demanding, sometimes fearful world. Detached from political causes and progress of his own life, the hero is a drifter, seeking to compromise with or to escape from such "evils" as class lines, boredom, hypocrisy, and the conventional perils of success. Although the novel carries a serious moral interest, Wain's wit, sharp observations, and inventiveness keep the plot moving. His comedy exaggerates, reforms, and criticizes to advocate the reasonable in social behavior and to promote the value and dignity of the individual.

Hurry on Down has the characteristic features of the picaresque novel: a series of short and often comic adventures loosely strung together; an opportunistic and pragmatic hero who seeks to make a living through his wits; and satirical characterization of stock figures rather than individualized portraits. Unlike the eighteenth century picaro, however, who is often hardhearted, cruel, and selfish, Wain's central character is a well-intentioned drifter who compromises enough to live comfortably. His standby and salvation is a strong sense of humor that enables him to make light of much distress and disaster. Lumley's character is revealed against the shifting setting of the picaresque world and in his characteristic response to repeated assaults on his fundamental decency and sympathy for others. He remains substantially the same throughout the novel; his many roles—as window cleaner, delivery driver, chauffeur, and the like—place him firmly in the picaresque tradition. Lumley's versatility and adaptability permit Wain to show his character under a variety of circumstances and in a multiplicity of situations.

Lumley's character is established almost immediately with the description of his conflict with the landlady in the first chapter. The reader sees him as the adaptable antihero who tries to control his own fate, as a jack of all trades, a skilled manipulator, an adept deceiver, an artist of disguises. Wain stresses Lumley's ingenuity rather than his mere struggle for survival; at the same time, he develops Lumley's individual personality, emphasizing the man and his adventures. The role that Lumley plays in the very first scene is one in which he will be cast throughout the story—that of a put-upon young man engaged in an attempt to cope with and outwit the workaday world.

The satire is developed through the characterization. Those who commit themselves to class—who judge others and define themselves by the class structure—are satirized throughout the novel. Surrounding the hero is a host of lightly sketched, "flat," stock figures, all of whom play their predictable roles. These characters include the proletarian girl, the American, the landlady, the entrepreneur, the middle-class couple, and the artist. In this first novel, Wain's resources in characterization are limited primarily to caricature. The comedy functions to instruct and entertain. Beneath the horseplay and high spirits, Wain rhetorically manipulates the reader's moral judgment so that he sympathizes with the hero. In the tradition of Tobias Smollett and Charles Dickens, Wain gives life to the grotesque by emphasizing details of his eccentric characters and by indicating his attitude toward them through the selection of specific bodily and facial characteristics.

Wain has also adopted another convention of eighteenth century fiction: the intrusive author. The active role of this authorial impresario accounts for the distance between the reader and the events of the novel; his exaggerations, his jokes, and his philosophizing prevent the reader from taking Lumley's fate too seriously. In later novels, Wain's authorial stance changes as his vision deepens.

Any discussion of comic technique in *Hurry on Down* leads inevitably to the novel's resolution. Ordinarily, readers do not like to encounter "perfect" endings to novels; nevertheless, they are not put off by the unrealistic ending to this novel because they know from the beginning that they are reading a comic novel which depends upon unrealistic exaggeration of various kinds. Elgin W. Mellown was correct when he called the novel "a pastiche: Walter Mitty's desire expressed through the actions of the Three Stooges—wish fulfillment carried out through outrageous actions and uncharacteristic behavior." The reader feels secure in the rightness of the ending as a conclusion to all the comic wrongness that has gone on before.

STRIKE THE FATHER DEAD

In *Strike the Father Dead*, Wain further extended himself with a work more penetrating than anything he had written before. Not only is it, as Walter Allen said, a "deeply pondered novel," but it is also a culmination of the promises inherent in Wain's earlier works. Plot, theme, character, and setting are integrated to tell the story of a son who breaks parental ties, thereby freeing himself to make his own way in life as a jazz pianist. Pointing to the foibles of his fellowman and probing the motives of an indignant parent, Wain's wit and sarcastic humor lighten this uncompromising study of the nonconformist's right to assert his nonconformity.

Two later Wain novels—*A Winter in the Hills* and *The Pardoner's Tale*—continue and elaborate upon many of the central themes of his fiction, but they surpass the earlier novels in richness and complexity. Both novels exhibit, far more than do his earlier writings, an interest in the tragic implications of romantic love; a greater complexity in character development allows Wain to portray convincingly men whose loneliness borders on self-destruction. Each novel is not simply another story of isolation or spiritual desolation, although it is that. Each hero is cast into a wasteland, and the novel in a sense is the story of his attempts to find the river of life again, or possibly for the first time. One of the themes that develops from this period in Wain's career is that personal relationships are the most important and yet most elusive forces in society.

The plot of *Strike the Father Dead* is arranged in an elaborate, seven-part time-scheme. Parts 1 and 6 occur sometime late in 1957 or early in 1958; part 2 takes place in the immediate prewar years; and the other divisions follow chronologically up to the last, which is set in 1958. The scene shifts back and forth between a provincial university town and the darker, black-market-and-jazz side of London, with a side trip to Paris.

Wain narrates the story from the points of view of four characters. The central figure, Jeremy Coleman, revolts against his father and the academic establishment in search of self-expression as a jazz pianist. Alfred Coleman, Jeremy's father and a professor of classics, is an atheist devoted to duty and hard work. Eleanor, Alfred's sister and foster mother to Jeremy, is devoted to Jeremy and finds comfort in innocent religiosity. Percy Brett, a black American jazz musician, offers Jeremy his first real parental leadership. Like Ernest Pontifex, in Samuel Butler's *The Way of All Flesh* (1903), Jeremy escapes from an oppressive existence; he has a passion for music, and once he has the opportunity to develop, his shrinking personality changes.

Strike the Father Dead marks a considerable advance over *Hurry on Down* in the thorough rendering of each character and each scene. By employing a succession of first-person narrators, Wain focuses attention more evenly on each of the figures. The result is that the reader comes away knowing Jeremy even better, because what is learned about him comes not only from his own narration but from other sources as well. Inasmuch as there are three central characters, *Strike the Father Dead* represents a larger range for Wain. Each interior monologue is a revelation; the language is personal, distinctive, and descriptive of character.

In the manner of a *Bildungsroman*, *Strike the Father Dead* is also a novel which recounts the youth and young manhood of a sensitive protagonist who is attempting to learn the nature of the world, discover its meaning and pattern, and acquire a philosophy of life. Setting plays a vital role in this odyssey. The provincial and London backgrounds and the accurate rendering of the language make the novel come alive. *Strike the Father Dead* moves between two contemporary worlds—a world of rigidity and repression, represented by Alfred, and a world of creativity, international and free, represented by London and Paris. The first world oppresses Jeremy; the second attracts and draws him. He dreams about it and invents fictions about it. Central to this new world is Jeremy's love of jazz. For him, the experience of jazz means beauty, love, life, growth, freedom, ecstasy—the very qualities he finds missing in the routine, disciplined life of Alfred.

Although *Strike the Father Dead* tells the story of a British young man who becomes successful, the success is to a certain extent bittersweet. In his triumphs over his home circumstances, Jeremy loses something as well. There are various names given to it: innocence; boyhood; nature; the secure, predictable life at home. The world beyond the academic life waits for Jeremy, and he, unknowingly, does his best to bring it onstage. With such a life comes a developing sense of injustice, deprivation, and suffering. These concerns become focal points in Wain's subsequent novels, as he turns toward the impulse to define character and dilemma much more objectively and with greater moral responsibility.

A WINTER IN THE HILLS

With its setting in Wales, *A Winter in the Hills* marked a departure from Wain's first seven novels, all of which were centered in England. The story expresses, perhaps more comprehensively than any other, Wain's feelings for the provincial world, its cohesion and deep loyalties, and its resistance to innovation from outside. Here the reader finds Wain's sympathy for the underdog, his respect for decency and the dignity of humanity, and his affirmation of life; here, too, is expressed Wain's deep interest in the causes and effects of loneliness and alienation.

The reader's first inclination is to approach the novel as primarily a novel of character, the major interest and emphasis of which is the constantly developing character of Roger Furnivall himself. Using third-person narration, Wain keeps the focus on his main character as he progresses straight through several months that constitute a time of crisis in his life. Through most of the novel, Roger struggles doggedly against a combination of adverse circumstances, always in search of a purpose. Outwardly, he forces himself on Gareth, for example, as a way of improving his idiomatic Welsh. Inwardly, he "needed involvement, needed a human reason for being in the district." The guilt he carries because of his brother's suffering and death helps to propel him into a more active engagement with contemporary life. His conflict with Dic Sharp draws him out of his own private grief because he is helping not only Gareth, but also an entire community of people.

The reader learns about Roger in another way, too: Wain uses setting to reveal and reflect the protagonist's emotions and mental states. Roger's walk in the rain down the country roads, as he attempts to resolve his bitterness and disappointment at Beverley's rejection of him, is vividly depicted. It carries conviction because Roger's anxiety has been built up gradually and artistically. The pastoral world is a perpetually shifting landscape, and Wain depicts its shifts and contrasts with an acute eye for telling detail. Especially striking are the sketches of evening coming on in the Welsh hills, with their rocks and timber and vast expanses of green. Such descriptions help to convey Roger's yearning for happiness in a world which seems bent on denying it to him.

One major theme of the book is the invasion of the peaceful, conservative world of Wales by outsiders who have no roots in the region, and therefore no real concern for its inhabitants. These invaders are characterized by a sophisticated corruption that contrasts sharply with the unspoiled simplicity and honesty of the best of the natives. A related theme is the decline of the town: its economic insecurity, its struggle to resist the progressive and materialistic "cruelty, greed, tyranny, the power of the rich to drive the poor to the wall." Through Roger's point of view, Wain expresses his opposition to the pressures—economic, political, cultural—that seek to destroy the Welsh and, by implication, all minority enclaves. Thus, *A Winter in the Hills* is more than a novel about the growth of one human being from loneliness and alienation to mature and selfless love; it is also a powerful study of the quality of life in the contemporary world, threatened by the encroachments of bureaucracy, greed, and materialism.

THE PARDONER'S TALE

The somewhat optimistic resolution of *A Winter in the Hills* stands in stark contrast to that of *The Pardoner's Tale*, Wain's most somber novel. In no other work by Wain are the characters so lonely, so frustrated, or so obsessed with thoughts of mutability, lost opportunities, and death. The novel is really two stories: a first-person tale about Gus Howkins, an aging Londoner contemplating divorce, and a third-person narrative (the framing narrative) about Giles Hermitage, an established novelist and bachelor living in an unnamed cathedral town, who gets involved with the Chichester-Redferns, a woman and daughter, while he is working out the story of Howkins. It is the interplay between these two stories which constitutes the plot of *The Pardoner's Tale*.

Giles Hermitage is obviously the figure with whom Wain is the most intimately involved. He is a highly idiosyncratic figure with very recognizable weaknesses; he is easily discouraged (there is an early thought of suicide), and he resorts to excessive drinking. The root cause of his death wish and of his drinking is loneliness. Like Wain's earlier heroes, he is very much a modern man: vague in his religious and humanitarian aspirations, rootless and alienated from the social life of the community in which he lives, and initially weak and confused in his relationships with women. Plagued by anxiety, depression, vague discontent, and a sense of inner emptiness, he seeks peace of mind under conditions that increasingly militate against it. Add to his problems the ever-growing urge toward self-destruction, and the reader begins to recognize in this novel a truly contemporary pulsebeat. Hermitage is a stranger in a world that does not make sense.

Unlike Wain's earlier heroes, however, Hermitage tries to make sense of the world through the medium of his writing by stepping back into what he calls "the protecting circle of art." His approach to writing is autobiographical, personal, even subjective. The hero of his novel is a mask for himself. The author is creating a character who is in his own predicament, and the agonies he endures enable him to express his deepest feelings about life. In Hermitage, Wain presents a character who tries to create, as artists do, a new existence out of the chaos of his life.

The remaining major characters in *The Pardoner's Tale* bear family resemblances to those in other of Wain's novels. If the part of the lonely, alienated hero so effectively carried in *A Winter in the Hills* by Roger Furnivall is here assigned to Giles Hermitage, then the role of the manipulator is assigned in this novel to Mrs. Chichester-Redfern. Although a good deal less ruthless than Dic Sharp, she nevertheless seeks to exploit the hero.

The process by which Mrs. Chichester-Redfern is gradually revealed through the eyes of Hermitage is subtle and delicate. At first merely a stranger, she

comes to seem in time a calculating and educated woman, the innocent victim of a man who deserted her, a seventy-year-old woman grasping for answers to some vital questions about her own life. She summons Hermitage under the pretense of wanting to gain insight into her life. From these conversations, the reader learns that she, like Hermitage, is confronted and dislocated by external reality in the form of a personal loss. Also like the hero, she desires to come to some understanding of her unhappy life through the medium of art. Her true motive is revenge, however, and she wants Hermitage to write a novel with her husband in it as a character who suffers pain. Then, she says, "there will be that much justice done in the world."

In addition to the alienated, lonely hero and the manipulator, most of Wain's fiction portrays a comforter. In his latest novel, the comforter is embodied in Diana Chichester-Redfern, but the happiness Diana offers is only temporary. In this novel, love is reduced to a meaningless mechanical act: Diana, also, is living in a wasteland.

The basic tension of this novel is a simple and classic one—the life-force confronting the death-force. As surely as Mrs. Chichester-Redfern is the death-force in the novel, Diana is the active and life-giving presence. She is depicted as an abrasive, liberated, sensual, innately selfish modern young woman who stands in positive contrast to the deathlike grayness of her mother. She is earthy and fulfilled, accepting and content with her music (playing the guitar satisfies her need for proficiency), her faith (which takes care of "all the moral issues") and her sexuality (which she enjoys because she has no choice). Diana goes from one affair to another, not in search of love (she claims she "can't love anybody") but out of a need for repetition. Diana defines love and meaning as the fulfillment of a man or woman's emotional requirements. To her, love does not mean self-sacrifice; rather, love is synonymous with need.

The world of *The Pardoner's Tale* is thus the archetypal world of all Wain's fiction: random, fragmented, lonely, contradictory. It is a world in which wasted lives, debased sexual encounters, and destroyed moral intelligences yield a tragic vision of futility and sterility, isolation from the community, estrangement from those who used to be closest to one, and loneliness in the midst of the universe itself.

YOUNG SHOULDERS

Amid all this, Wain's unflinching honesty and his capacity for compassion make his definition of the human condition bearable. Both characteristics are evident in *Young Shoulders*. Again, Wain focuses on senseless waste. A plane of English schoolchildren crashes in Lisbon, Portugal, killing everyone aboard. Seventeen-year-old Paul Waterford, whose twelve-year-old sister Clare was one of the victims, describes his journey to Lisbon with his parents, their encounters with other grief-stricken relatives, the memorial service they attend, and their return to England. Because he is still untainted by convention, Paul feels free to see the other characters as they are, often even to find them funny; however, he has to admit that he can be wrong about people. The seemingly calm Mrs. Richardson, a teacher's widow, collapses during the memorial service; the restrained Janet Finlayson howls in the hotel lobby that God is punishing them all; Mr. Smithson, whom Paul assessed as a man on his way up, goes crazy on the tarmac; and everyone depends upon Paul's parents: the mother Paul saw only as a drunk and the father Paul dismissed as hopelessly withdrawn.

Because Wain has the eighteenth century writer's hunger for universals, we may assume that the real subject of *Young Shoulders* is not how individuals behave in the face of tragedy but what the young protagonist and, by extension, the reader has learned by the end of the novel. Paul comes to see that human beings avoid acknowledging their emotions in so many ways that an outsider's judgment is likely to be inaccurate. He also recognizes the extent to which he deludes himself, whether by imagining a utopian society he will govern or by addressing "reports" to Clare, thus denying that she is dead. By losing his innocence, Paul gains in compassion.

THE OXFORD TRILOGY

With its single plotline, its compressed time scheme, and its limited cast, *Young Shoulders* is much like a neoclassical play. By contrast, the three novels composing the Oxford Trilogy have an epic quality, as indeed they must if they are to "describe and dramatize the Oxford that has been sinking out of sight, and fading from memory, for over thirty years," as Wain states in his preface to the final volume. The series does indeed cover three decades. *Where the Rivers Meet* introduces the protagonist Peter Leonard and takes him through his undergraduate years at Oxford; *Comedies* begins in 1933, with Leonard's appointment as a fellow, and ends after World War II; and *Hungry Generations* covers Leonard's life from 1947 to 1956. There is a multitude of characters, ranging from Oxford intellectuals to the patrons of the pub that Leonard's parents run, each with definite ideas about local politics, world news, and the progress of society. Wain's honesty is reflected in the way he permits all the characters to speak their minds; his compassion is revealed in his attempt to understand even the least appealing of them. These qualities, along with his creative genius and his consummate artistry, should ensure for John Wain a permanent place in twentieth century literary history.

Dale Salwak,
updated by Rosemary M. Canfield Reisman

OTHER MAJOR WORKS

SHORT FICTION: *Nuncle and Other Stories*, 1960; *Death of the Hind Legs and Other Stories*, 1966; *The Life Guard*, 1971; *King Caliban and Other Stories*, 1978.

PLAYS: *Harry in the Night: An Optimistic Comedy*, pr. 1975; *Johnson Is Leaving: A Monodrama*, pb. 1994.

TELEPLAY: *Young Shoulders*, 1984 (with Robert Smith).

RADIO PLAYS: *You Wouldn't Remember*, 1978; *A Winter in the Hills*, 1981; *Frank*, 1982.

POETRY: *Mixed Feelings*, 1951; *A Word Carved on a Sill*, 1956; *A Song About Major Eatherly*, 1961; *Weep Before God: Poems*, 1961; *Wildtrack: A Poem*, 1965; *Letters to Five Artists*, 1969; *The Shape of Feng*, 1972; *Feng: A Poem*, 1975; *Poems for the Zodiac*, 1980; *Thinking About Mr. Person*, 1980; *Poems, 1949-1979*, 1981; *Twofold*, 1981; *Open Country*, 1987.

NONFICTION: *Preliminary Essays*, 1957; *Gerard Manley Hopkins: An Idiom of Desperation*, 1959; *Sprightly Running: Part of an Autobiography*, 1962; *Essays on Literature and Ideas*, 1963; *The Living World of Shakespeare: A Playgoer's Guide*, 1964; *Arnold Bennett*, 1967; *A House for the Truth: Critical Essays*, 1972; *Samuel Johnson*, 1974; *Professing Poetry*, 1977; *Samuel Johnson 1709-1784*, 1984 (with Kai Kin Yung); *Dear Shadows: Portraits from Memory*, 1986.

CHILDREN'S LITERATURE: *Lizzie's Floating Shop*, 1981.

EDITED TEXTS: *Contemporary Reviews of Romantic Poetry*, 1953; *Interpretations: Essays on Twelve English Poems*, 1955; *International Literary Annual*, 1959, 1960; *Fanny Burney's Diary*, 1960; *Anthology of Modern Poetry*, 1963; *Selected Shorter Poems of Thomas Hardy*, 1966; *Selected Shorter Stories of Thomas Hardy*, 1966; *Thomas Hardy's "The Dynasts,"* 1966; *Shakespeare: Macbeth, a Casebook*, 1968; *Shakespeare: Othello, a Casebook*, 1971; *Johnson as Critic*, 1973; *The New Wessex Selection of Thomas Hardy's Poetry*, 1978 (with Eirian James).

BIBLIOGRAPHY

Gerard, David. *John Wain: A Bibliography*. London: Mansell, 1987. Contains a critical introduction to Wain's writings and a comprehensive list of his books and contributions to books and periodicals. Also includes other critical and biographical references and reviews of works by Wain.

Gindin, James. "The Moral Center of John Wain's Fiction." In *Postwar British Fiction: New Accents and Attitudes*. Berkeley: University of California Press, 1962. Gindin contends that Wain creates characters who always exhibit dignity and moral commitment. Considers Wain's first four novels and his stories in the volume *Nuncle and Other Stories*. In an introductory essay, Gindin evaluates Wain in the context of other authors from the 1950's.

Hague, Angela. "Picaresque Structure and the Angry Young Novel." *Twentieth Century Literature* 32 (Summer, 1986): 209-220. Hague views Wain's *Hurry On Down* as erroneously grouped with the "Angry Young Men" novels of the 1950's. She compares Wain's heroes with those in the novels of Kingsley Amis and Iris Murdoch; all are essentially loners who, like the picaresques of the eighteenth century, respond to tensions between traditional values and societal change.

Heptonstall, Geoffrey. "Remembering John Wain." *Contemporary Review* 266 (March, 1995): 144-147. An appreciation of the author and a thoughtful assessment of his place in the literary tradition. Though Wain has fallen out of favor with critics, it is argued that his works will continue to appeal to the public and that his worth will be recognized by future generations. An excellent overview.

Rabinovitz, Rubin. "The Novelists of the 1950's: A General Survey." In *The Reaction Against Experiment in the English Novel, 1950-1960*. New York: Columbia University Press, 1967. Rabinovitz places Wain in the context of novelists who embraced traditional values rather than those who experimented with unconventional ideas or forms, aligning Wain's novels with those of Arnold Bennett and eighteenth century picaresque novelists.

Salwak, Dale. *Interviews with Britain's Angry Young Men*. San Bernardino, Calif.: Borgo Press, 1984. This useful resource characterizes Wain as an "eighteenth century man." Engages Wain in a discussion of the role of criticism in the author's life, his goals as a writer, his response to the phenomenon of the Angry Young Men, and the sources and themes in several of his novels.

_____. *John Wain*. Boston: Twayne, 1981. After a chapter introducing Wain's life and art, the text contains four chapters on his novels, focusing on his early works, *Hurry on Down* and *Strike the Father Dead*, and two of his late works, *A Winter in the Hills* and *The Pardoner's Tale*. "Other Fiction, Other Prose" covers Wain's stories, poems, and biographical works. A selected bibliography completes the text.

Taylor, D. J. *After the War: The Novel and English Society Since 1945*. London: Chatto & Windus, 1993. An attempt to define the nature of postwar writing. Wain is grouped with William Cooper and Kingsley Amis as being antimodernist, or opposed to the psychological emphasis and stylistic complexity of James Joyce and Virginia Woolf, and antiromantic.

ALICE WALKER

Born: Eatonton, Georgia; February 9, 1944

PRINCIPAL LONG FICTION

The Third Life of Grange Copeland, 1970
Meridian, 1976
The Color Purple, 1982
The Temple of My Familiar, 1989
Possessing the Secret of Joy, 1992
By the Light of My Father's Smile, 1998

OTHER LITERARY FORMS

Alice Walker published several volumes of short fiction, poetry, and essays in addition to her novels. Walker was an early editor at *Ms.* magazine, in which many of her essays first appeared. Her interest in the then little-known writer Zora Neale Hurston led to her pilgrimage to Florida to place a tombstone on Hurston's unmarked grave, to Walker's editing of *I Love Myself When I Am Laughing . . . And Then Again When I Am Looking Mean and Impressive: A Zora Neale Hurston Reader* (1979), and to her introduction to Robert Hemenway's *Zora Neale Hurston: A Literary Biography* (1977).

ACHIEVEMENTS

Walker's literary reputation is based primarily on her fiction, although her second book of poetry, *Revolutionary Petunias and Other Poems* (1973), received the Lillian Smith Award and a nomination for a National Book Award. Her first short-story collection, *In Love and Trouble:*

Stories of Black Women (1973), won the Rosenthal Award of the National Institute of Arts and Letters. In addition, she received a Charles Merrill writing fellowship, an award for fiction from the National Endowment for the Arts, and a Guggenheim Fellowship. She was also a Bread Loaf Scholar and a fellow at the Radcliffe Institute. *The Third Life of Grange Copeland* was widely and enthusiastically reviewed in publications as varied as *The New Yorker*, *The New Republic*, and *The New York Times Book Review*, although journals aimed primarily at a black readership were often silent or critical of the violence and graphic depiction of rural black life. With the publication of *Meridian*, Walker's second novel, her work as a poet, novelist, essayist, editor, teacher, scholar, and political activist came together. *Meridian* was universally praised in scholarly journals, literary magazines, popular magazines, and black-oriented journals. Some critics, mainly black male reviewers, objected again to the honest, straightforward portrayals of black life in the South and to Walker's growing

(Jeff Reinking/Picture Group)

feminism, which they saw in conflict with her commitment to her race. Walker's third novel, *The Color Purple*, was widely acclaimed; feminist and *Ms.* editor Gloria Steinem wrote that this novel "could be the kind of popular and literary event that transforms an intense reputation into a national one," and Peter Prescott's review in *Newsweek* began by saying "I want to say at once that *The Color Purple* is an American novel of permanent importance." These accolades were substantiated when Walker received both the American Book Award and the 1983 Pulitzer Prize for fiction.

BIOGRAPHY

Alice Walker was born in Eatonton, Georgia, on February 9, 1944, the last of eight children of Willie Lee and Minnie Lou Grant Walker, sharecroppers in rural Georgia. Her relationship with her father, at first strong and valuable, became strained as she became involved in the civil rights and feminist movements. A moving depiction of her estrangement from her father occurs in her essay "My Father's Country Is the Poor," which appeared in *The New York Times* in 1977. For Walker, a loving and healthy mother-daughter relationship has endured over the years. An account of that relationship is central to her essays "In Search of Our Mothers' Gardens" and "Lulls—A Native Daughter Returns to the Black South" and in Mary Helen Washington's article "Her Mother's Gifts," in which Walker acknowledges that she often writes with her mother's voice—"Just as you have certain physical characteristics of your mother . . . when you're compelled to write her stories, it's because you recognize and prize those qualities of her in yourself."

One of the central events in Walker's childhood was a BB gun accident which left her, at age eight, blind in one eye. Scar tissue from that wound, both physical and psychological, seems to have left her with a compensating acuteness of vision, despite the conviction that she was permanently disfigured. Walker was affected enough by the accident to say in a 1974 interview with John O'Brien, "I have always been a solitary person, and since I was eight years old (and the recipient of a disfiguring scar, since cor-

rected, somewhat), I have daydreamed—not of fairy-tales—but of falling on swords, of putting guns to my heart or head, and of slashing my wrists with a razor." Walker's partial blindness allowed her to attend Spelman College in Atlanta on a scholarship for the handicapped, following her graduation from Butler-Baker High School in 1961. She left Spelman after two years—which included summer trips to the Soviet Union and to Africa as part of a group called Experiment in International Living—for Sarah Lawrence College, from which she graduated in 1965.

Walker's political activity governed her movements during the years immediately following her college graduation: She spent the summer of 1965 in the Soviet Union and also worked for civil rights in Liberty County, Georgia. The next year she was a case worker for New York City's Department of Social Services, and then a voter-registration worker in Mississippi. In 1967, she married Melvyn Leventhal, a civil rights lawyer, and moved to Jackson, Mississippi, where she continued her civil rights work, lived in the heart of the South as part of an interracial couple, and taught at Jackson State University, while continuing to write stories, poems, and essays. She taught at Tougaloo College in Mississippi for a year before returning to the East, where she was a lecturer in writing and literature at Wellesley College, an editor at *Ms.* magazine, and an instructor at the University of Massachusetts at Boston. By 1977, she had divorced her husband, accepted a position as associate professor of English at Yale University, and written six books.

After *The Color Purple* won critical acclaim in 1986, Walker and her family shared the success with Eatonton. Walker's sister established The Color Purple Educational Scholarship Fund, and Walker adopted three elementary schools to help provide needed supplies for students who maintained above-average grades. Walker continued her activities in political forums as well, working for civil rights and protesting against nuclear weapons. She became an avid objector to female genital mutilation ("female circumcision") in Africa through public speaking and through her novel *Possessing the Secret of Joy* and her nonfiction book *Warrior Marks: Female Genital*

Mutilation and the Sexual Blinding of Women (1993), which focus on the horrors and scars of this practice.

Walker also used her success to help other female writers. She advocated women's literature classes and helped promote neglected female and black writers. In 1984, Walker began her own publishing company, Wild Trees Press. Throughout the 1980's and 1990's she lived in Northern California, where she continued to write stories, essays, poems, and novels.

ANALYSIS

The story of Alice Walker's childhood scar provides the most basic metaphor of her novels: the idea that radical change is possible even under the worst conditions. Although she was never able to regain the sight in one eye, Walker's disfigurement was considerably lessened:

> I used to pray every night that I would wake up and somehow it would be gone. I couldn't look at people directly because I thought I was ugly. . . . Then when I was fourteen, I visited my brother Bill [who] took me to a hospital where they removed most of the scar tissue—and I was a *changed person*. I promptly went home, scooped up the best-looking guy, and by the time I graduated from high school, I was valedictorian, voted "Most Popular," and crowned queen!

The idea that change and personal triumph are possible despite the odds is central to all of Walker's writing. Her work focuses directly or indirectly on the ways of survival adopted by black women, usually in the South, and is presented in a prose style characterized by a distinctive combination of lyricism and unflinching realism. Walker's women attempt not merely to survive, but to survive completely with some sense of stability, despite the constant thread of family violence, physical and mental abuse, and a lack of responsibility on the part of the men in their lives. Walker is simultaneously a feminist and a supporter of civil rights, not only for black Americans, but also for minorities everywhere.

Walker's vision was shaped in part by a work from the first flowering of black writing in America: Jean Toomer's *Cane* (1923). She said in 1974 about Toomer's book that "it has been reverberating in me

to an astonishing degree. *I love it passionately*; could not possibly exist without it." Like *Cane*, the first part of which centers mainly on women in the South, Walker's novels are made up of nearly equal parts of poetry, portraiture, and drama, broken up into a series of sections and subsections. Other important literary influences on Walker include Zora Neale Hurston, from whom she inherited a love of black folklore; Flannery O'Connor, who wrote of southern violence and grotesqueries from her home in Milledgeville, Georgia, less than ten miles from Walker's childhood home; and Albert Camus, whose existentialism speaks to the struggle for survival and dignity in which Walker's characters are engaged. Walker herself defined her "preoccupations" as a novelist: "The survival, the survival *whole* of my people. But beyond that I am committed to exploring the oppressions, the insanities, the loyalties, and the triumphs of black women." *The Third Life of Grange Copeland*, on the surface a novel about the cycle of rage and violence torturing the lives of a father and his son, is as much about the recipients of that rage—the women and children whose lives are directly affected. Although the novel is unremitting in its picture of desperate poverty's legacy of hatred, hopelessness, and cruelty, it concludes optimistically with Ruth Copeland's hope for a release from sorrow through the redemption promised by the early days of the Civil Rights movement and by the knowledge and love inherited at the sacrifical death of her grandfather.

THE THIRD LIFE OF GRANGE COPELAND

Writing in 1973, Walker observed that her first novel, *The Third Life of Grange Copeland*, "though sometimes humorous and celebrative of life, is a grave book in which the characters see the world as almost entirely menacing." This dark view of life is common to Grange Copeland, the patriarch of a family farming on shares in rural Georgia, his son Brownfield, and the wives and daughters of both men. For all these characters, the world is menacing because of the socioeconomic position they occupy at the bottom of the scale of the sharecropping system. Father and son menace each other in this novel because they are in turn menaced by rage born out of the frustration of the system. Although the white people of the book are nearly always vague, nameless, and impersonal, they and the system they represent have the ability to render both Grange and Brownfield powerless.

It is not accidental that these characters' names have agricultural connotations. "Grange" suggests a late nineteenth century association of farmers, a feudal farm and grain storage building, and a combination of graze and range, while "Brownfield" and "Copeland" are self-explanatory—for the inability to cope with the land is what leads both male characters along virtually parallel paths. For the father, the mere appearance of the white farm boss's truck is enough to turn his face "into a unnaturally bland mask, curious and unsettling to see." The appearance of the truck causes the son to be "filled with terror of this man who could, by his presence alone, turn his father into something that might as well have been a pebble or a post or a piece of dirt." Although Grange is, in this same image, literally a piece of land, he eventually returns to the South and learns to live self-sufficiently, farming a section of soil he tricked his second wife into giving to him. Brownfield, in contrast, is never able to escape from the sharecropping system, although he sees that, like his father, he is "destined to be no more than overseer, on the white man's plantation, of his own children." Brownfield is able to live obliviously on a farm in Georgia, content to blame all of his problems on others. The poor rural black workers of this novel are themselves little more than a crop, rotated from farm to farm, producing a harvest of shame and hunger, cruelty and violence.

Unlike the men of the novel, the women are menaced by both blacks and whites, by both the agricultural system and the "strange fruit" it produces. Margaret, Grange's first wife, is both physically and mentally degraded by her husband and then sexually exploited by a white truck driver, resulting in her second pregnancy. Unable to cope with this situation, Grange deserts his family, after which his wife poisons both her child and herself. Following his father's pattern, Brownfield marries and begins to work the land, but after "a year when endless sunup to sundown work on fifty rich bottom acres of cotton land

and a good crop brought them two diseased shoats for winter meat." he too begins to abuse his wife. Although Brownfield's wife, Mem, is a schoolteacher intelligent enough to try to break the cycle of raising others people's crops, her brief rebellion against her husband's malevolent beatings and mental tortures is a failure: He is able to subjugate her through repeated pregnancies that sap her rebellion as they turn her once rich and strong body into a virtual wasteland of emaciation. Because her body, which represents the land of the South, is still able to produce children despite its depleted condition, Brownfield is enraged enough to murder her in retaliation for her physical shape: "he had murdered his wife because she had become skinny and had not, with much irritation to him, reverted, even when well-fed, to her former plumpness. . . . Plumpness and freedom from the land, from cows and skinniness, went all together in his mind." Despite his irrational abuse of her, Mem is not ashamed "of being black though, no matter what he said. . . . Color was something the ground did to the flowers, and that was an end to it."

What the ground did to these generations of southern black people is the subject of Walker's novel—the whole lurid history of violence, hatred, and guilt that she chronicles in this story of one family's griefs. By the book's end, Brownfield Copeland has murdered his wife and an unnamed albino baby, while Grange Copeland has murdered his son Brownfield—first spiritually, then physically—and indirectly has killed his first wife and her infant.

Walker's characters are allegorical representations of the classic modes of survival historically adopted by black Americans in dealing with their oppression. Brownfield identifies with whites by daydreaming of himself on a southern plantation, sipping mint juleps, and then by bargaining for his freedom with the sexual favors of black women. Both of Grange's wives attempt to be true to the white stereotype of black women as promiscuous sexual beings, free of any moral restraints. Brownfield's wife, Mem, attempts the passive resistance advocated by Martin Luther King, Jr., but she is destroyed by what her husband calls "her weakness . . . forgiveness, a stupid belief that kindness can convert the enemy." Brownfield's daughter, Daphne, who calls herself the Copeland Family Secret Keeper, tries the strategy of inventing a falsely romantic history of the past, of the good old days when her father was kind, echoing those historical revisionists who try to argue that slavery was not that bad. Brownfield's other daughters try to stay away from their father altogether, regarding him "as a human devil" of whom they were afraid "in a more distant, impersonal way. He was like bad weather, a toothache, daily bad news."

Each of the title character's three lives (at home in the South as a sharecropper married to Margaret; in the North as a hustler of alcohol, drugs, and women; and finally back in the South as a farmer married to Josie and rearing his granddaughter Ruth) parallels a traditional survival strategy, which Grange summarizes as follows, "The white folks hated me and I hated myself until I started hating them in return and loving myself. Then I tried just loving me, and then you, and *ignoring* them much as I could." To put it another way, Grange tries at first to adapt to the system by believing what whites say about blacks; then he turns to the classic escape of the runaway slave— heading North to freedom; finally, he tries the technique of praising black life while ignoring whites altogether. A large part of the novel's devastation is caused by the repeated use of these techniques, not against whites, but against other members of the Copeland family. Only Ruth, the granddaughter through whom Grange seeks redemption, is able to deal with whites in an intelligent, balanced, nondestructive yet independent way. She has learned from her grandfather, and from her family history, that pure hatred becomes self-hatred, and violence begets self-violence; she therefore becomes the novel's symbol of the new black woman, ready to assume her place in black history as a courageous worker in the Civil Rights movement which the rest of her family has been groping to discover.

MERIDIAN

Walker's second novel, *Meridian*, picks up chronologically and thematically at the point where her first novel ended. *Meridian* describes the struggles of a young black woman, Meridian Hill, about the same age as Ruth Copeland, who comes to an awareness of power and feminism during the Civil Rights movement, and whose whole life's meaning is centered in the cycles of guilt, violence, hope, and change characteristic of that dramatic time. Thematically, *Meridian* picks up the first novel's theme of self-sacrificial murder as a way out of desperate political oppression in the form of the constant question that drives Meridian Hill—"Will you kill for the Revolution?" Meridian's lifelong attempt to answer that question affirmatively (as her college friends so easily do), while remaining true to her sense of responsibility to the past, her sense of ethics, and her sense of guilt of having given to her mother the child of her teenage pregnancy, constitutes the section of the novel entitled "Meridian." The second third of the novel, "Truman Held," is named for the major male character in the narrative. The third major section of the novel, "Ending," looks back at the turmoil of the Civil Rights movement from the perspective of the 1970's. Long after others have given up intellectual arguments about the morality of killing for revolution, Meridian is still debating the question, still actively involved in voter registration, political activism, and civil rights organization, as though the movement had never lost momentum. Worrying that her actions, now seen as eccentric rather than revolutionary, will cause her "to be left, listening to the old music, beside the highway," Meridian achieves release and atonement through the realization that her role will be to "come forward and sing from memory songs they will need once more to hear. For it is the song of the people, transformed by the experiences of each generation, that holds them together."

In 1978, Walker described *Meridian* as "a book 'about' the Civil Rights movement, feminism, socialism, the shakiness of revolutionaries and the radicalization of saints." Her word "about" is exact, for all of these topics revolve not chronologically but thematically around a central point—the protagonist, Meridian Hill. In some ways, Meridian *is* a saint; by the book's end she has sustained her belief in the Civil Rights movement without losing faith in feminism and socialism, despite family pressures, guilt, literally paralyzing self-doubts, the history of the movement, and the sexism of many of its leaders.

In contrast, Truman Held represents those males who were reported to have said that "the only position for a woman in the movement is prone." Although Truman Held is Meridian's initial teacher in the movement, she eventually leaves him behind because of his inability to sustain his initial revolutionary fervor, and because of his misogyny. Unlike Brownfield Copeland, Truman argues that women are of less value than they should be, not because of skinniness, but because "Black women let themselves go . . . they are so fat." Later in the novel, Truman marries a white civil rights worker whose rape by another black man produces disgust in him, as much at his wife as at his friend. When Truman seeks Meridian out in a series of small southern hamlets where she continues to persuade black people to register to vote and to struggle for civil rights, he tells her that the movement is ended and that he grieves in a different way than she. Meridian answers, "I know how you grieve by running away. By pretending you were never there." Like Grange Copeland, Truman Held refuses to take responsibility for his own problems, preferring to run away to the North.

Meridian's sacrificial dedication to the movement becomes a model for atonement and release, words that once formed the working title of the book. *Meridian* could also have been called "The Third Life of Meridian Hill" because of similarities between Meridian's life and Grange Copeland's. Meridian leads three lives: as an uneducated child in rural Georgia who follows the traditional pattern of early pregnancy and aimless marriage, as a college student actively participating in political demonstrations, and as an eccentric agitator—a performer, she calls herself—unaware that the movement is ended. Like Grange Copeland in another sense, Meridian Hill is solid proof of the ability of any human to change dramatically by sheer will and desire.

Meridian is always different from her friends, who, filled with angry rhetoric, ask her repeatedly if she is willing to kill for the revolution, the same question that Grange asked himself when he lived in the North. This question haunts Meridian, because she does not know if she can or if she should kill, and because it reminds her of a similar request, posed in a similar way by her mother: "Say it now, Meridian, and be saved. All He asks is that we acknowledge Him as our Master. Say you believe in Him . . . don't go against your heart." In neither case is Meridian able to answer yes without going against her heart. Unlike her college friends and Truman Held, who see the movement only in terms of future gains for themselves, Meridian is involved with militancy because of her past: "But what none of them seemed to understand was that she felt herself to be, not holding on to something from the past, but *held* by something in the past."

Part of the past's hold on her is the sense of guilt she feels about her relationships with her parents. Although her father taught her the nature of the oppression of minorities through his knowledge of American Indians, her strongest source of guilt comes from her mother, who argues, like Brownfield Copeland, that the responsibility for *all* problems stems from outside oneself: "The answer to everything," said Meridian's mother, "is we live in America and we're not rich." Meridian's strongest sense of past guilt comes from the knowledge she gains when she becomes pregnant: "it was for stealing her mother's serenity, for shattering her mother's emerging self, that Meridian felt guilty from the very first, though she was unable to understand how this could possibly be her fault."

Meridian takes the form of a series of nonchronological sections, some consisting of only a paragraph, some four or five pages long, that circle around the events of Meridian's life. The writing is clear, powerful, violent, lyrical, and often symbolic. Spelman College, for example, is here called Saxon College. The large magnolia tree in the center of the campus, described with specific folkloric detail, is destroyed by angry students during a demonstration: "Though Meridian begged them to dismantle the president's house instead, in a fury of confusion and frustration they worked all night, and chopped and sawed down, level to the ground, that mighty, ancient, sheltering music tree." This tree (named The Sojourner, perhaps for Sojourner Truth) expands symbolically to suggest both the senseless destruction of black ghettos by blacks during the turmoil of the 1960's, and also Meridian Hill herself, who receives a photograph years later of The Sojourner, now "a gigantic tree stump" with "a tiny branch, no larger than a finger, growing out of one side." That picture, suggesting as it does the rebirth of hope despite despair, also evokes the last vision of Meridian expressed by the now-shamed Truman Held: "He would never see 'his' Meridian again. The new part had grown out of the old, though, and that was reassuring. This part of her, new, sure and ready, even eager, for the world, he knew he must meet again and recognize for its true value at some future time."

THE COLOR PURPLE

Like her first two novels, *The Color Purple* has an unusual form. *The Color Purple* presents the author's familiar and yet fresh themes—survival and redemption—in epistolary form. Most of the novel's letters are written by Celie, an uneducated, unloved, black woman living in rural Georgia in the 1920's; Celie's letters are written in what Walker calls "black folk English," a language of wit, strength, and natural humor. Ashamed of having been raped by her stepfather, a man whom Celie thinks at the time is her father, she begins to send letters to God, in the way that children send letters to Santa Claus, because her rapist told her to tell nobody but God. Although her early letters tell of rape, degradation, and pain, of her stepfather's getting rid of the two children born of his cruelty, the tone is nevertheless captivating, ironic, and even humorous. Soon the despair turns into acceptance, then into understanding, anger, rebellion, and finally triumph and loving forgiveness as the fourteen-year-old Celie continues to write until she reaches an audience, some thirty years later. Like the author, who began writing at the age of eight, and who has turned her childhood experience in rural Georgia into three novels of violence, hatred, understanding, love, and profound hope for the future, Celie is a writer, a listener, a thinker, and a promoter of Walker's constant theme: "Love redeems, meanness kills."

Like Meridian Hill, Celie compares herself to a tree. After her stepfather's repeated rapes, Celie is sold into a virtual state of slavery to a man who beats her, a man she neither knows, loves, nor talks to, a man she can never call anything but Mr. ——, an ironic throwback to the eighteenth century English epistolary novel. Celie tries to endure by withholding all emotion: "I make myself wood. I say to myself, Celie, you a tree. That's how come I know trees fear man." Like The Sojourner, or like the kudzu vine of the deep South that thrives despite repeated attempts to beat it back, Celie continues to express her fears and hopes in a series of letters written in a form of black English that is anything but wooden. The contrast between the richly eccentric prose of Celie's letters and the educated yet often lifeless sentences of her sister Nettie's return letters supports Walker's statement that "writing *The Color Purple* was writing in my first language." The language of the letters is at first awkward, but never difficult to follow. As Celie grows in experience, in contact with the outside world, and in confidence, her writing gradually becomes more sophisticated and more like standard written English, but it never loses its originality of rhythm and phrase.

Based on Walker's great-grandmother, a slave who was raped at twelve by her owner, Celie works her way from ignorance about her body and her living situation all the way through to an awakening of her self-worth, as well as to an understanding of the existence of God, the relations between men and women, and the power of forgiveness in uniting family and friends. Much of this transformation is brought about through the magic of a blues singer named Shug Avery, who guides Celie in understanding sexuality, men, and religion without causing her to lose her own fresh insights, naïve though they are.

The letters that make up the novel are something like the missives that the protagonist of Saul Bellow's novel *Herzog* (1964) writes but never sends, in that they are often addressed to God and written in an ironic but not self-conscious manner. Because of the combination of dark humor and despair, the letters also evoke memories of the desperate letters from the physically and spiritually maimed addressed to the hero of Nathanael West's *Miss Lonelyhearts* (1933). Although Celie is unlettered in a traditional sense, her ability to carry the complicated plot forward and to continue to write—first without an earthly audience, and then to her sister, whom she has not seen for more than twenty years—testifies to the human potential for self-transformation.

Discussing Celie's attempts to confirm her existence by writing to someone she is not certain exists, Gloria Steinem says, "Clearly, the author is telling us something about the origin of Gods: about when we need to invent them and when we don't." In a sense, Shug Avery becomes a god for Celie because of her ability to control the evil in the world and her power to change the sordid conditions of Celie's life. Early in the book, when Celie is worrying about survival, about rape, incest, beatings, and the murder of her children, her only source of hope is the name "Shug Avery," a name with a magical power to control her husband. Not even aware that Shug is a person, Celie writes "I ast our new mammy bout Shug Avery. What it is?" Finding a picture of Shug, Celie transfers her prayers to what is at that point only an image: "I see her there in furs. Her face rouge. Her hair like somethin tail. She grinning with her foot up on somebody motocar. Her eyes serious tho. Sad some. . . . An all night long I stare at it. An now when I dream, I dream of Shug Avery. She be dress to kill, whirling an laughing." Shug Avery becomes a god to Celie not only because she is pictured in the first photograph Celie has ever seen, but also because she is dressed in a style that shows a sense of pride and freedom.

Once Celie's sister's letters begin to appear, mailed from Africa, where Nettie is a missionary, the ironic connection between the primitive animism of the Africans and Celie's equally primitive reaction to Shug's picture becomes clear. Although Nettie has crossed the ocean to minister to a tribe of primitive people, her own sister is living in inhuman conditions in Georgia: ignorance, disease, sexism, lack of control of the environment, and the ever-increasing march of white people. When Shug explains her own animistic religious beliefs—which include the notion that God is not a he or a she, but an it (just as Celie once thought Shug Avery was an it)—Celie is converted to a pantheistic worship that makes her early identification with trees seem less naïve.

When the narrator of Herman Melville's "Bartleby the Scrivener" tries to explain Bartleby's with-

drawal from life, he thinks of the dead letter office in which the scrivener was rumored to have worked, and says, "On errands of life, these letters speed to death." In contrast, Celie's and Nettie's letters, ostensibly written to people long thought to be dead, speed across the ocean on errands of life, where they grow to sustain not merely the sisters in the book, but all those lucky enough to read them. As the author says of *The Color Purple*, "It's my happiest book . . . I had to do all the other writing to get to this point." For the reader who has gotten to this point in Walker's career by reading all of her other books, there is no question that Alice Walker's name could be substituted for Celie's in the author's statement about her most recent novel: "Let's hope people can hear Celie's voice. There are so many people like Celie who make it, who come out of nothing. People who triumph."

POSSESSING THE SECRET OF JOY

The novels *By the Light of My Father's Smile* and *Possessing the Secret of Joy* share strong characters whose sexual identities suffer in order to conform to the society in which they live. Only through death can Tashi and Mad Dog become complete and escape the male-dominated world and its restrictions.

Walker combines fact and fiction in *Possessing the Secret of Joy* to illustrate the effects that female genital mutilation has on the women who are subjected to the procedure. The main character, Tashi, an African tribal woman, willingly undergoes the tribal ritual of genital mutilation in a desire to conform to her culture and feel complete. This procedure leaves her physically and mentally scarred. Tashi realizes that the procedure destroyed her emotionally and made her feel as if she were something other than her true self. After her mutilation, she marries Adam Johnson and moves to America. She is renamed Evelyn Johnson, and her chapter headings shift from "Tashi" to "Evelyn" in order to demonstrate the conflict within her as she struggles to find her true identity. The conflict leads her to madness.

Tashi strives to understand her insanity and to interpret her recurring nightmares of a tower. With the help of her therapists, Mzee and Raye, and the members of her family, Tashi realizes the reasons for her insanity and gradually becomes stronger and able to face her nightmares and what they represent. The chapters are told through the eyes of all the main characters, a technique that provides insight into the effect that Tashi has on those around her. Through its main characters, Tashi, Olivia, and Adam, *Possessing the Secret of Joy* is connected to, but is not a sequel to, Walker's previous novels *The Color Purple* and *The Temple of My Familiar.*

BY THE LIGHT OF MY FATHER'S SMILE

Walker's sixth novel, *By the Light of My Father's Smile,* follows the Johnson family on a journey through life, and to rebirth through death. Magdalena, referred to as Mad Dog, discovers her sensuality and its connection with her spirituality while living with her parents in Mexico. Her parents are pretending to be missionaries in order to do an anthropological study of the Mundo people. Magdalena is acutely aware of her emotions and sensuality, but she is severely beaten by her father when he discovers her sexual activity.

Magdalena's sister Susannah, shadowed by Magdalena's anger and frustration, is awakened to her true desires by her friend Irene, who is able to survive and accept life on her own terms despite the restrictions placed on her by her society. Susannah realizes that her unhappiness is the result of having been "sucked into the black cloth" and hypocrisy of the world. Each member of the Johnson family suffers through life searching for true love and happiness, which they find only in death. The story moves between the spiritual world and physical world as the father watches his two daughters come to terms with their anger and their true spirits. As characters pass into the spiritual world, they are enlightened to their failings in the physical world and make amends with those they have injured. Only when acceptance of each soul is obtained can the four family members cross the river and live in eternity.

Timothy Dow Adams,
updated by Mary A. Blackmon

OTHER MAJOR WORKS

SHORT FICTION: *In Love and Trouble: Stories of Black Women,* 1973; *You Can't Keep a Good Woman Down,* 1981; *The Complete Stories,* 1994.

POETRY: *Once: Poems,* 1968; *Five Poems,* 1972; *Revolutionary Petunias and Other Poems,* 1973; *Goodnight, Willie Lee, I'll See You in the Morning: Poems,* 1979; *Horses Make a Landscape Look More Beautiful,* 1984; *Her Blue Body Everything We Know: Earthling Poems, 1965-1990,* 1991.

NONFICTION: *In Search of Our Mothers' Gardens: Womanist Prose,* 1983; *Living by the Word: Selected Writings, 1973-1987,* 1988; *Warrior Marks: Female Genital Mutilation and the Sexual Blinding of Women,* 1993; *The Same River Twice: Honoring the Difficult,* 1996; *Anything We Love Can Be Saved: A Writer's Activism,* 1997.

CHILDREN'S LITERATURE: *Langston Hughes: American Poet,* 1974; *To Hell with Dying,* 1988; *Finding the Green Stone,* 1991.

EDITED TEXT: *I Love Myself When I Am Laughing . . . And Then Again When I Am Looking Mean and Impressive: A Zora Neale Hurston Reader,* 1979.

BIBLIOGRAPHY

Bloom, Harold, ed. *Alice Walker: Modern Critical Views.* New York: Chelsea House, 1989. A book-length compilation of the best of criticism on Walker. Authors Diane F. Dadoff and Deborah E. McDowell explore the resonant Zora Neale Hurston/Alice Walker relationship. Naturally radical feminism is addressed in this study, and Bloom discusses the mother/daughter motif in Walker's works.

Christian, Barbara. *Black Feminist Criticism.* New York: Pergamon Press, 1985. Throughout the book there are references to the characters in Alice Walker's novels. Chapters 2 and 6 focus entirely on Walker's female characters and the motifs in her work, in particular growth through pain. Chapter 17 discusses her novel *Meridian,* and chapter 15 her novel *The Color Purple.* The book is a valuable resource for black literature as well as for insights into Walker's characterization.

Gates, Henry Louis, Jr., and K. A. Appiah, eds. *Alice Walker: Critical Perspectives Past and Present.* New York: Amistad, 1993. Contains reviews of Walker's first five novels and critical analyses of several of her works of short and long fiction. Also includes two interviews with Walker, a chronology of her works, and an extensive bibliography of essays and texts.

Gentry, Tony. *Alice Walker.* New York: Chelsea House, 1993. This biography is geared toward the high school student. The text is simple to read but thorough in providing biographical information about Walker and discussing her writing. A chronology and brief bibliography are also included.

Montelaro, Janet J. *Producing a Womanist Text: The Maternal as Signifier in Alice Walker's "The Color Purple."* Victoria, B.C.: English Literary Studies, University of Victoria, 1996. Examines themes of feminism, motherhood, and African American women in literature.

Winchell, Donna Haisty. *Alice Walker.* New York: Twayne, 1992. Provides a comprehensive analysis of Walker's short and long fiction. A brief biography and chronology precede the main text of the book. Each chapter refers to specific ideas and themes within Walker's works and focuses on how Walker's own experiences define her characters and themes. Following the narrative is a useful annotated bibliography.

DAVID FOSTER WALLACE

Born: Ithaca, New York; February 21, 1962

PRINCIPAL LONG FICTION

The Broom of the System, 1987
Westward the Course of Empire Takes Its Way, 1989 (novella)
Infinite Jest, 1996

OTHER LITERARY FORMS

Wallace's writing showcases a remarkable talent, as adept at the novel as at the short story and as skillful in fiction as nonfiction. In *Girl with Curious Hair* (1989), his first collection of short stories, Wallace demonstrates his keen eye for representing the complexities of life in the late twentieth century. As an essayist, he published detailed philosophical explorations of the death of the author and on the love-hate relationship between fiction and television in America, as well as humorous travel reports, such as "In Quest of Managed Fun," a chronicle of his misadventures aboard a mass-market luxury Caribbean cruise liner. During his visit to the Illinois State Fair in "Getting Away from Already Being Pretty Much Away from It All," Wallace weaves his way among pungent livestock and nauseating rides and indulges in too many prize-winning desserts when he is mistaken for a contest judge. Other essays, including personal profiles of film director David Lynch and tennis player Michael Joyce, provide insights into artistry and excellence.

ACHIEVEMENTS

Wallace achieved a remarkable degree of recognition early in his career. In addition to numerous prizes awarded for individual short stories, he was honored with several prestigious awards, including the Whiting Foundation's Writers' Award in 1987, a National Endowment for the Arts Writer's Fellowship in 1989, the Lannan Foundation Award for Literature in 1996, and the MacArthur Foundation Fellowship in 1997. His cultural analysis of rap music, *Signifying Rappers: Rap and Race in the Urban Present* (written with Mark Costello), was nominated for the 1991 Pulitzer Prize in Nonfiction.

BIOGRAPHY

Born in Ithaca, New York, in 1962, David Foster Wallace was raised in central Illinois, where his father was a philosophy professor at the University of Illinois in Urbana, and his mother was an English teacher. Growing up among the geometric grids of rural Illinois farmland, Wallace developed an acute sense of angles, which, he argues in the essay "Derivative Sport in Tornado Alley," enabled him to become a successful player on the competitive junior tennis tournament circuit between the ages of twelve and fifteen. At Amherst College, his father's alma mater, Wallace majored in philosophy, specializing in math and logic and writing a part of *The Broom of the Sys-*

tem for his senior thesis project before graduating summa cum laude in 1985. After graduation, he completed the novel and received an M.F.A. degree in 1987 from the University of Arizona. Wallace's early success contributed toward some self-destructive experimentation in his personal life, which a few reviewers speculate might have provided some of the material on addiction that appears in *Infinite Jest*. Wallace emerged from this downward spiral around 1990. An editor at *The Review of Contemporary Fiction* and a contributing editor for *Harper's*, Wallace became an English professor at Illinois State University in Normal, Illinois.

ANALYSIS

Wallace's name is often linked with innovative postmodernist authors, such as John Barth, Robert Coover, and Thomas Pynchon; however, his writing incorporates the intricate intellectual hilarity of these authors at the same time as it includes a postironic sincerity and a puzzlement with the predicament of living in postmodern America. Throughout his writing, Wallace examines themes of loneliness and desire, detachment and self-awareness, and mass culture and spectacle. Claiming that books are saturated with the uniform sameness of the messages in commercial media, Wallace maintained that fiction's role for the contemporary reader is "[to make] the familiar *strange* again." Knowledge is learned through language. To this end, Wallace's work foregrounds narrative as an act that mediates our experience of the world through language. His short stories are often fragmented and defy simple summary, while his long fiction involves twisting multidirectional sentences and interconnecting plots that rely heavily on contingency and uncertainty. His work is uncompromising in its use of multiple points of view and disparate plot lines that are often left unresolved, but rather than merely frustrating readers' expectations, this openness demands that readers collaborate with the author in the experience of taking meaning from the text.

THE BROOM OF THE SYSTEM

Wallace's first novel, published in 1987, employs diverse viewpoints and narrative styles that fore-shadow the same techniques in his later work, from the short story "Order and Flux in Northampton" to the masterfully encyclopedic *Infinite Jest*. Set in the near-future (around 1990), *The Broom of the System* is a bizarre quest narrative, populated by characters with strange names—Biff Diggerence, Candy Mandible, Clint Roxbee-Cox, Rex Metalman, Judith Preitht—and even stranger events, which have encouraged critical comparisons with Thomas Pynchon's *The Crying of Lot 49* (1966). The central character, Lenore Stonecipher Beadsman, is emotionally adrift on the edge of the Great Ohio Desert (abbreviated G.O.D.). As Lenore struggles to understand the mysterious disappearance of her grandmother, also named Lenore Beadsman, who has vanished from a Cleveland nursing home with twenty-five other elderly residents, she must also deal with her enigmatic and manipulative family. The elder Lenore and the other patients feel lost in a meaningless, static existence, until Lenore, Sr., manages to persuade the Stonecipheco baby-food company, run by Lenore, Jr.'s father, to develop Infant Accelerant, a drug that is reputed to increase the rate of language acquisition in children. The elder Lenore has learned about the drug from a nurse whose husband researched the product, and she steals the test data from the Stonecipheco corporation, feeding the samples to her granddaughter's pet cockatiel, Vlad the Impaler. The bird develops enhanced speaking abilities and at the end of the novel seems destined for stardom on the Reverend Hart Lee Sykes's *Partners with God* television program.

Lenore's grandmother was once a student of the philosopher Ludwig Wittgenstein, whose *Tractatus Logico-Philosophicus* (1921) concerns the possibilities and limits of language as a medium for representing things in the world. Significantly, the novel's linguistic system revolves around the relevance of words themselves: Definitions, misunderstandings—including one character who calls his telephone a "lymph node" so that he can tell his family he does not own a "phone"—and stories proliferate throughout Wallace's text. The younger Lenore is a switchboard operator for a publishing company, engaged in a halfhearted affair with her boss, Rick Vigorous.

While Lenore feels comforted when Rick reads her the stories he has received for the literary magazine he publishes, she also feels disoriented, imagining that she has no identity except as a character in the stories other people tell about her. A minor character sums up this difficulty of finding a stable identity amid the confusion of an ever-changing world: "How to begin to come to some understanding of one's place in a system, when one is a part of an area that exists in such a troubling relation to the rest of the world, a world that is itself stripped of any static, understandable character by the fact that it changes, radically, all the time?" While critics of *Infinite Jest* complained that that novel lacks narrative resolution, readers of *The Broom of the System* often feel the novel's rapid conclusion is too contrived. Whereas Wallace chooses to end *Infinite Jest* without neatly summing up the story, in this novel, he does not allow readers to forget that their experience of the text is mediated, as the plot that Lenore (and readers) have been attempting to understand through the fragmented pieces of Wallace's narrative is miraculously explained.

WESTWARD THE COURSE OF EMPIRE TAKES ITS WAY

Published as part of *Girl with Curious Hair*, Wallace's novella *Westward the Course of Empire Takes Its Way* parodies John Barth's "Lost in the Funhouse" (1967), a classic metafictional story that debunks the illusion that realistic fiction presents an unmediated view of life. A fictional patricide of its metafictional forefather, *Westward the Course of Empire Takes Its Way* presents a cogent account of the absorption of Barth's once-transgressive metafictional aesthetic by contemporary commerical culture. The story recounts the journey of D. L. Eberhardt and Mark Nechtr to Collision, Illinois, for the televised reunion of every person who has ever appeared in a McDonald's restaurant commericial. D. L., a self-proclaimed postmodernist who constructs poems made entirely of punctuation, and Mark, a talented but blocked writer, are students of Professor Ambrose (a stand-in for Barth) in the East Chesapeake Tradeschool Creative Writing Program. Accompanying D. L. and Mark is Tom Stern-

berg, a claustrophobic actor who has one eye turned around in his head, although the narrator informs us, "He doesn't talk about what the backward eye sees."

The other plot line of *Westward the Course of Empire Takes Its Way* describes a successful advertising executive's courting of Professor Ambrose and his scheme to license a nationwide chain of funhouse franchises. While Wallace praises the groundbreaking work of Barth and Coover, he sharply criticizes the imitators of these metafictional masters, who borrow experimental techniques for no substantive thematic purpose. According to Wallace's diagnosis, television usurped metafiction's business of irony and self-reference and thus robbed the metafictional novel of its power to critique televisual culture. What worries Wallace in *Westward the Course of Empire Takes Its Way* is not Professor Ambrose's "selling out," but that "they want to build a Funhouse for lovers out of a story that does not love."

INFINITE JEST

The media frenzy surrounding the publication of *Infinite Jest* hailed Wallace's massive novel as the literary spectacle of the 1990's. Set in a dystopian postmillennial near-future—when the calendar is subsidized (years are sponsored: "Year of the Tucks Medicated Pad," "Year of the Whisper-Quiet Maytag Dishmaster," "Year of the Depend Adult Undergarment") and huge catapults launch garbage projectiles into a Canadian wasteland nicknamed the Great Concavity—*Infinite Jest* presents a huge cast of characters and their stories. As an encyclopedic novel, it is a compendium of filmmaking, pharmacology, postmillennial politics, and literary history, supplemented with hundreds of footnotes that Wallace uses to fracture the surface of the primary text.

One of the novel's main stories concerns Don Gately, an ex-burglar and oral narcotics addict, who is trying to break his addiction at the Ennet House Drug and Alcohol Recovery House (the redundancy is telling). The other major story chronicles the elite Incandenza family: Hal, a tennis prodigy who memorizes dictionaries; his two brothers, Orin, a professional football punter, and Mario, a dwarf; and their father, James, an "après-garde" filmmaker who committed suicide by sticking his head in a microwave oven.

To deal with his loneliness after his father's suicide, Hal loses himself in tennis and drugs, a pattern that is replicated throughout the novel, as every character struggles with some form of addiction. The novel's title, which alludes to Hamlet's graveyard tribute to Yorick from William Shakespeare's 1600-1601 play, refers to the title of one of James's films, which showcases an entertainment so spectacular that anyone who watches it becomes instantly addicted. Enraged by U.S. president Johnny Gentle's plan to catapult American garbage into their country, a group of wheelchair-bound Canadian assassins smuggle the tape into the United States.

The mysterious film features Joelle van Dyne, who was Orin's girlfriend before he lost her to his father; in the novel's present, she is a radio host who appears at Ennet House after a suicide attempt, where Don falls in love with her. Despite numerous connections between different narrative threads, the novel eludes a clear-cut ending, circling instead back to its beginning. Near the end of the novel, Wallace posits an inclusive vision of a "radical realism" that contains "every single performer's voice" in the foreground. To Wallace's credit, the novel, which contains at least fifteen different points of view, does not degenerate into meaningless chaos. Like James Incandenza's "anticonfluential" film, Wallace's *Infinite Jest* has been called "a stubborn and possibly intentionally irritating refusal of different narrative lines to merge into any kind of meaningful confluence," reflecting Wallace's refusal to artificially reduce the complexities of his characters' lives into a neat resolution.

Trey Strecker

OTHER MAJOR WORKS

SHORT FICTION: *Girl with Curious Hair*, 1989; *Brief Interviews with Hideous Men: Stories*, 1999.

NONFICTION: *Signifying Rappers: Rap and Race in the Urban Present*, 1990 (with Mark Costello); *A Supposedly Fun Thing I'll Never Do Again: Essays and Arguments*, 1997.

BIBLIOGRAPHY

Blythe, Will, ed. *Why I Write: Thoughts on the Practice of Fiction*. Boston: Little, Brown, 1998. This collection of twenty-five essays on fiction writing includes Wallace's "The Nature of the Fun."

Bruni, Frank. "The Grunge American Novel." *The New York Times Magazine*, March 24, 1996, 38-41. Offers an author profile of Wallace in the midst of the excitement generated by the publication of *Infinite Jest*. Nominates him as the literary spokesman for the 1990's generation.

LeClair, Tom. "The Prodigious Fiction of Richard Powers, William T. Vollmann, and David Foster Wallace." *Critique* 38, no. 1 (Fall, 1996): 12-37. Compares Wallace's *Infinite Jest* with the ambitious novels of his contemporaries, Richard Powers's *The Gold Bug Variations* (1991) and William T. Vollmann's *You Bright and Risen Angels* (1987). LeClair explores the root of the word "prodigious," demonstrating how these authors display a vast range of encyclopedic information in their fiction in order to reorient readers with the natural world.

Olsen, Lance. "Termite Art: Or, Wallace's Wittgenstein." *The Review of Contemporary Fiction* 13, no. 2 (Summer, 1993): 199-215. Explores how Wallace employs the philosophy of Ludwig Wittgenstein in *The Broom of the System* in the process of questioning language and its relationship to the world.

Wallace, David Foster. "*E Unibus Pluram: Television and U.S. Fiction*." In *A Supposedly Fun Thing I'll Never Do Again: Essays and Arguments*. Boston: Little, Brown, 1997. Argues that the self-conscious irony of metafictionist writing has been absorbed by the mass media. Asserts that innovative art must posit new values rather than merely expose false ones. An indispensable text for students of twentieth century American literature.

_____. "An Interview with David Foster Wallace." Interview by Larry McCaffery. *The Review of Contemporary Fiction* 13, no. 2 (Summer, 1993): 127-150. Discusses the ways authors can engage television and other contemporary media, the role of fiction in postliterary culture, and Wallace's complex relation to the literary postmodernism of the 1960's and 1970's.

EDWARD LEWIS WALLANT

Born: New Haven, Connecticut; October 19, 1926
Died: Norwalk, Connecticut; December 5, 1962

PRINCIPAL LONG FICTION

The Human Season, 1960
The Pawnbroker, 1961
The Tenants of Moonbloom, 1963
The Children at the Gate, 1964

OTHER LITERARY FORMS

The brevity of Edward Lewis Wallant's literary career did not allow for a long list of publications. He did contribute three short stories to the *New Voices* series: "I Held Back My Hand" appeared in *New Voices 2* (1955), "The Man Who Made a Nice Appearance" in *New Voices 3* (1958), and the posthumously published "When Ben Awakened" in *American Scene: New Voices* (1963). Wallant also wrote an essay on the art of fiction which was published posthumously in the *Teacher's Notebook in English* (1963). In addition, there is a sizable collection which includes unpublished manuscripts, the final drafts of his first two unpublished novels, some half-dozen short stories, various drafts of his published novels, the first act of a play, his journal and his notebooks, and miscellaneous loose notes and fragments. All these papers are on deposit at the Beinecke Library at Yale University.

ACHIEVEMENTS

Wallant's literary output was so small and his career so short that it is difficult to assess his place in postwar American fiction. Wallant's work is best seen in its relationship to kindred works in the late 1950's and early 1960's. Although he is still little known to the public, Wallant's four novels rank with J. D. Salinger's *Franny and Zooey* (1961), Saul Bellow's *Henderson the Rain King* (1959), Bernard Malamud's *A New Life* (1961), and Ken Kesey's *One Flew over the Cuckoo's Nest* (1962) as examples of what has been described as the "New Romanticism." Wallant's novels reflect an outlook on life that led him to write about the unfortunate, the outcast, and the common person, whom he portrayed with compassion and dignity. His unwaveringly realistic perception of life and its often painful demands leaven his general optimism. In each of his fictions, Wallant's central character is shocked out of a moral lethargy and into action on behalf of his fellow human beings. This shock is preceded by a submersion into the contemporary human condition, which provides Wallant the opportunity to explore the interconnections and disconnections of modern urban life. He was a committed writer whose commitment acknowledged the darker side of the lives of his characters. It is not surprising, then, that while some critics should emphasize the positive nature of Wallant's work, his "happy endings" and his optimism, there should also be those who find in his work a note of despair and a presentiment of his own early death. It was Wallant's achievement to fuse the qualities of an old-fashioned novelist with the perceptions of a modern urban realist. The combination resulted in novels that offer a particularly clear view of the 1960's.

BIOGRAPHY

Edward Lewis Wallant was born in New Haven, Connecticut, on October 19, 1926. His father, who was invalided by mustard gas during World War I, was almost continuously hospitalized during Wallant's early years, and he died when his son was six. Wallant, an only child, was reared in a shabby although respectable middle-class neighborhood by his mother, Anna, and two aunts. Except for his Russian-born grandfather, who told him stories of the old country, it was a household without adult males. During his years at New Haven High School, Wallant held a number of jobs including plumber's assistant, delivery boy for a drugstore across the street from a Catholic hospital, and hot-dog hawker at Yale football games. Although his academic career in high school was not remarkable, he did attend briefly the University of Connecticut. He soon left, however, to join the navy.

The final months of World War II found Wallant serving as a gunner's mate in the European theater of operations; after his discharge from the navy in 1946, he enrolled in Pratt Institute to prepare for a career as an artist. In 1947, he married Joyce Fromkin, a girl he had known since childhood; in 1948, they moved to Brooklyn. After his graduation from Pratt in 1950, he was hired by the L. W. Frohlich advertising agency, where he became art director for the Westinghouse account. In the same year, he also enrolled in creative writing courses at the New School for Social Research, where he studied with Harold Glicksberg and Don Wolfe. Under their guidance, Wallant wrote a group of short stories and a novel, "Tarzan's Cottage," which was never published.

In 1953, Wallant moved to the advertising agency of Doyle, Kitchen, and McCormick. He also moved his family from New Rochelle, New York, where a son, Scott, had been born in 1952, to Norwalk, Connecticut, where, in 1954, his daughter Leslie was born. In 1955, his short story "I Held Back My Hand" appeared in *New Voices 2: American Writing Today*, edited by his writing instructor, Don Wolfe. It was his first publication. During the late 1950's, Wallant submitted to various publishers his early novels "Tarzan's Cottage" and "The Odyssey of a Middleman," but neither met with any success. Wallant changed jobs a third time in 1957, moving to McCann Erikson as an art director, a position he was to hold until shortly before his death. His second daughter, Kim, was also born the same year. Another story, "The Man Who Made a Nice Appearance," was published in 1958 in *New Voices 3*, edited by Charles Glicksberg.

Wallant's third novel was accepted within twenty-four hours of its submission to Harcourt, Brace. Originally entitled *A Scattering in the Dark*, it appeared in 1960 retitled as *The Human Season*. Although it received few reviews, some were enthusiastic and helped to create a small, underground reputation for his work. In spite of its limited commercial success, the novel received the Harry and Ethel Daroff Memorial Fiction Award from the Jewish Book Council for the best novel on a Jewish theme. The publication of *The Pawnbroker* in 1961, also by Harcourt, Brace, established Wallant's reputation as a novelist. The book was nominated for a National Book Award, and the screen rights were sold to Sidney Lumet, who in 1965 made a critically acclaimed film starring Rod Steiger.

The modest success of *The Pawnbroker* came at a crucial period in Wallant's life. For years, he had balanced his work as an advertising art director with his after-hours vocation of writing, and he was having increasing difficulty in reconciling his two lives. A resolution of sorts seemed imminent when he received a Guggenheim Fellowship in 1962, which allowed him to travel in Europe and to write full time. For three months, he traveled abroad. Joyce joined him briefly in Italy, and then Wallant went on to Spain. He returned home with the idea for a comic novel, to be called *Tannenbaum's Journey*, based on his travels. He also resolved to devote his life to full-time writing and resigned his position with McCann Erikson. He took a small room in New York to use as a retreat for his work. In spite of feeling tired, Wallant was excited by his prospects; the European trip had given him inspiration. Then, quite suddenly, he was stricken by a viral infection and lapsed into a coma. He died of an aneurysm of the brain a week later on December 5, 1962.

At the time of his death, Wallant had two novels, *The Tenants of Moonbloom* and *The Children at the Gate*, under consideration by Harcourt, Brace, and it fell to his editor, Dan Wickenden, to see these projects through the press. *The Tenants of Moonbloom* was published in 1963, as were two other pieces: a story, "When Ben Awakened," in *American Scene: New Voices*, again edited by Don Wolfe, and an essay, "The Artist's Eye," for the *Teacher's Notebook in English*. *The Children at the Gate*, although written before *The Tenants of Moonbloom*, was not published until 1964.

ANALYSIS

Just before his death, Edward Lewis Wallant wrote: "I suggest that most people are nearsighted, myopic in their inability to perceive the details of human experience." It was a condition he found perfectly normal; there is simply too much energy used up in everyday life, having families, supporting oneself, and living in a community, for much insight into the lives of fellow human beings, except as they relate to one's own immediate needs. Yet there are times, Wallant noted, when people experience an unrecognized yearning to "know what lies in the hearts of others." "It is then," he wrote, "that we turn to the artist, because only he can reveal even the little corners of the things beyond bread alone." It is revealing that Wallant, first trained as a graphic artist, should title the one essay in which he set forth his artistic credo "The Artist's Eye." In this essay, Wallant explores the relationship between the observable, everyday world and the interpretation of that world through the writer's heightened sense of awareness.

In all four of Wallant's published novels, this theme of heightened perception is central. The protagonist, who has become emotionally insulated from life, experiences a reawakening of feelings and rejoins the world around him. This spiritual and emotional rebirth comes as the result of the death of someone who has become close to the protagonist. The impact of this death, which often happens in a shocking way and with suddenness, penetrates the emotional barriers Wallant's characters erect against the onslaught of modern, urban life: Joe Berman escapes the past, Sol Nazerman is rescued from both the past and the dim recesses of his pawnshop, Angelo DeMarco gets beyond his streetwise sassiness, and Norman Moonbloom overcomes his inertia and learns to act. In each case and with each novel, Wallant takes his readers into the lives of his characters and reveals the little corners of the human heart.

THE HUMAN SEASON

Wallant's first novel, *The Human Season*, is the story of a middle-aged, middle-class man who must come to grips with himself following the death of his wife. Joe Berman is recognizably a twentieth century Everyman who lives a life barely distinguishable from that of his neighbors. He is a Russian Jew

who immigrated to America when he was a little boy, and he seemingly has attained the American Dream, founding his own plumbing business, owning his own modest home, marrying, and fathering three children. His wife, Mary, of "obligatory blonde, American prettiness," as one critic has described her, dies prior to the beginning of the novel, leaving him alone to face life and his largely unrecognized emotions. The structure of the novel intensifies the tension between past and present by alternating scenes from the present, in which Wallant skillfully renders Berman's daily life through a series of highly detailed episodes, with incidents from the past, each of them exposing some traumatic memory. In their reverse progression into the earlier years of Berman's life, these dreams deepen one's understanding not only of Berman's character but also of the formation of his emotional paralysis. Beginning on April 30, 1956, the day of Mary's fatal stroke, they recede back to September, 1907, when Berman was a little boy of nine living in Russia. The dreams contrast sharply in their emotional vividness with the increasingly comatose quality of Berman's present life. He has become an automaton, living without connection in an environment increasingly alien to him. He lashes out at the objects that remind him of his wife's delicacy and sensitivity as he succumbs to his "numbing, disorienting grief." Finally, Berman tries to kill himself.

As he becomes more and more blind to the real world, the world of his dreams, his past, becomes more vivid until it begins to intrude into his present, waking life. Increasingly, Wallant returns to images of the natural sources of Berman's earlier feelings in his memories of his father and of his life in Russia. Although there is a pastoral quality to these memories. Wallant does not suggest a return to some agrarian ideal. Berman's dreams remind him of his human capacities and inaugurate his search for something that will approximate the bond with the nature of his youth. Among the dreams are recollections of his father and Judaism. Berman realizes how neglectful he was of his own son, who was killed in the war, and how estranged from the healing qualities of his Jewishness he had become. The death of his wife, after all, merely provides a catalyst for his sickness, causing his self-doubt and sense of alienation to surface. The initial moment of his illumination quite literally comes as a shock: In an attempt to fix a faulty television set, Berman is thrown across the room, and in his fear and astonishment, he begins to pray in a jumble of English, Yiddish, and Russian. In that moment, he discovers the meaning of all the months of his suffering. He is alone.

It is from this revelation that he begins to reconstruct his life, one which will be authentic and will result in a new self. He discovers a craving for people; his dreams no longer haunt him but provide him with soothing images which strengthen his zest for self-renewal. In a scene that elevates the fiction to a mythical dimension, Berman is born again as he walks home in the rain after having "witnessed" the life around him. As the novel ends, Berman is waiting in his empty house for his son-in-law to take him home for a family dinner. In this final chapter, Wallant convincingly depicts a poignant example of people's infinite capacity for self-renewal.

THE PAWNBROKER

Wallant abandoned work on a comic fiction, *Gimple the Beast*, to write his second novel, *The Pawnbroker*. As in his first novel, the central character is a middle-aged, Jewish immigrant. Sol Nazerman, however, did not arrive in America as a youth; instead, the forty-five-year-old ex-professor from the University of Krakow fled Europe and the death camps in which he had been a prisoner during World War II. Now he is the operator of a pawnshop in a black ghetto in New York City. The shop is owned by a minor underworld figure who uses it as a drop point for the transferral of illegal money. Nazerman is aware of the criminality of the operation but does not protest. He uses his income to support his sister and her family, who live in the suburbs. He also contributes to the support of his mistress, Tessie Rubin, who lives with her dying father. The novel brings together the nightmare world of the concentration camp as Nazerman remembers it with the corrupt urban world of the pawnshop.

As in *The Human Season*, the central character has walled himself off from the pain and suffering of the world around him. Amid the grotesques who visit

his shop, Nazerman remains a private, isolated man. The novel is the story of his spiritual reawakening, which is largely brought about through the intervention of Jesus Ortiz, the black, Catholic assistant who works in the business, and whose energy and ambition awaken sympathy from Nazerman. The death of Ortiz during an attempted robbery of the shop, which occurs on the fifteenth anniversary of the destruction of Nazerman's family in the death camps, provides the shock that penetrates the insulation with which Nazerman has wrapped his feelings in order to maintain his delicate sense of survival. He recognizes the part he willingly plays in the chain of human exploitation of which his pawnshop is a microcosm, and he is forced to acknowledge the community of grief to which he belongs and from which he has so long isolated himself. The novel concludes with three acts of atonement for Nazerman as he rejoins the world. He telephones his nephew, Morton, and asks him to become his new assistant, thereby opening a father-son relationship with the young man who has been wanting it for so long. After the phone call, Nazerman sleeps and dreams, not a nightmare as he usually does, but a dream in which he is able to lay the dead past to rest. Finally, he, like Berman, learns to mourn and goes to Tessie to help her grieve over the death of her father. As in the previous novel, this act is an important sign of his rebirth.

The connections between Wallant's first two novels are more than superficial. The two protagonists, who have much in common, experience similar awakenings. Both novels interweave dreams with the narrative thread. Both men must expiate their guilt over the death of their sons. Berman never did respond to his son, who died in the war unaware of his father's love; Nazerman must seek forgiveness for the guilt he feels for the death of his son, who slipped out of his grasp and suffocated on the floor of a cattle car on their way to the death camp. Both men are finally free from their past when they can fully and properly mourn the dead; then they can rebuild their lives again in the present. *The Pawnbroker* is the darkest of Wallant's books and seems to have provided a release for the marvelously comic voice of the last two novels.

THE CHILDREN AT THE GATE

During the summer of 1961, while he was awaiting the outcome of his Guggenheim application, Wallant underwent a radical shift in attitude concerning his vocation as a writer. In the little more than six months he took to complete the manuscript of *The Pawnbroker*, he drafted the first version of *The Children at the Gate*, a completed version of which was left with his editor before he began his European travels with the fellowship money.

The novel concerns the relationship between the literal-minded, nineteen-year-old Angelo DeMarco, who makes the rounds of a Catholic hospital to take orders among the patients for the pharmacy where he works, and Sammy Cahan, a clownish Jew who is an orderly in the hospital. DeMarco, who clings to a rationalism as a defense against the horrors of his life—his disabled sister, his fatherless home, his obsessively religious mother, and the dying patients among whom he must spend his days—is redeemed by the antics of Cahan, whose essentially emotional view of life provides DeMarco with his spiritual change. Unlike Berman and Nazerman, Cahan seems to have inherited his life-giving vision, which he is able to spread throughout the hospital. As with the pawnshop and later the apartment houses of *The Tenants of Moonbloom*, the hospital setting provides a microcosm for the world's suffering humanity against which the drama of the central character's spiritual growth can take place. Once again, it is a death, Cahan's, which shocks DeMarco awake to the final recognition of his stifling life and the possibility of rebirth, a recognition which is made concrete in DeMarco's ministrations to his retarded, childlike sister, who has been raped by their father. Like Berman and Nazerman before him, DeMarco reveals his growing humanity through his acts of kindness and tenderness.

The centrality of the dream-world which played so important a part in the previous novels is replaced here by a living world of dreams which DeMarco must shatter before abandoning his barricade of toughness. It is no coincidence that he first discovers Cahan in the children's ward at the hospital, for it is the childlike simplicity of the orderly, his trust and innocence, which DeMarco must rediscover in order to be reborn. *The Children at the Gate* reveals the intermingling of Christian and Jewish myths which Wallant used to such great effect in all of his novels. It is not only the accumulation of religious artifacts or references in the novel but also Cahan's portrayal as the religious fool and his martyrdom in the Christlike crucifixion on the hospital gates which sets the tone. Just as the death of the assistant, Ortiz, in *The Pawnbroker* precipitated Nazerman's rebirth, so here Cahan's death reveals to DeMarco the path he must follow. The roles of teacher and priest, the relationship between suffering and redemption, and the confluence of death and rebirth form a religious nexus which gives this book its especially powerful message of commitment, community, and love.

Although there were comic elements in *The Children at the Gate*, it was only in *The Tenants of Moonbloom* that Wallant's comic genius flowered. His last novel exhibits a certainty of handling and a smoothness of execution which were the results of his growing confidence as a writer. Wallant had thrown over his job as an advertising man and had made a commitment to literature.

THE TENANTS OF MOONBLOOM

The Tenants of Moonbloom traces the emergence of Norman Moonbloom, an introverted rent collector who manages four decrepit apartment buildings for his brother, and who emerges from his passivity as the result of his contact with the urban flotsam and jetsam who inhabit his apartments. Moonbloom, who is thirty-three at the time of the story, has finally settled down after years of college and a number of majors. He is a rather average young man who has spent his life retreating from people, and although he would prefer to hide in the womblike security of his apartment, his tenants persistently intrude on his consciousness. Finally unable any longer to retreat from the world, Moonbloom plunges into his past, like Berman and Nazerman, to search for a base upon which he can build a relationship with life. Through a series of seemingly disconnected visions, Moonbloom awakens to an understanding of the humanity which he shares with even the most bizarre of his tenants. He launches a "holy war" of rehabilitation in order to try to respond to the needs of those human beings placed into his trust.

Through a series of jolts, not unlike the ones received by Wallant's other antiheroes, delivered by the various inhabitants of Moonbloom's apartments, he is transformed. This is accomplished during three visits he makes to his tenants. Each successive visit further shocks him into responding. His reaction culminates in the frenzy of activity in which he engages to bring the buildings and by extension the lives of his tenants up to some sort of standard. Although Moonbloom, a former rabbinical student, is Wallant's final Christ-figure, this novel relies far less than its predecessors, most notably *The Children at the Gate*, on biblical imagery and allusions, despite Moonbloom's messianic zeal to convert his tenants into full-blown human beings. In his last novel, Wallant was to integrate the comic and the tragic. As one critic has written, Wallant moved from being a cautious optimist to become "the comic celebrant of man's capacity to live an energetic, courageous, and spiritually dedicated existence."

Wallant's reputation rests firmly on a small body of fiction which he wrote with much passion and energy. Necessarily, this reputation has been enhanced by the tragedy of his untimely death and the unfulfilled promise of his career. His prose reflects a joyful celebration of life, life in all of its manifest complexities. Although he has often been compared to two other Jewish writers, Bruce Jay Friedman and Nathanael West, Wallant did not succumb to the absurd fantasies of the first nor to the despair of the second. Perhaps his importance as a modern novelist is best summarized by a critic who wrote that it was his cautious refusal to accept "the existential despair and the universal isolation of modern man" which distinguished him from his contemporaries and led him to affirm quietly the worth and joy of life. Wallant's novels are a testament to the continuing resilience of the human spirit.

Charles L. P. Silet

BIBLIOGRAPHY

Ayo, Nicholas. "The Secular Heart: The Achievement of Edward Lewis Wallant." *Critique: Studies in Modern Fiction* 12 (1970): 86-94. Compares Wallant to Fyodor Dostoevski to convey his grim realism and emphasis of changes of heart, looking expressly at the religious element in Wallant's characters.

Baumbach, Jonathan. *The Landscape of Nightmare: Studies in the Contemporary Novel*. New York: New York University Press, 1965. Baumbach compares *The Pawnbroker* and *The Tenants of Moonbloom* as examples of fictional structures in which characters must make a "truce with the nightmare of survival," a truce they achieve despite the brutality of the world.

Galloway, David. *Edward Lewis Wallant*. Boston: Twayne, 1979. The only book-length treatment of Wallant. Like other volumes in the Twayne series, Galloway's includes a chronology, notes, and an annotated bibliography.

Gurko, Leo. "Edward Lewis Wallant as Urban Novelist." *Twentieth Century Literature* 20 (October, 1974): 252-261. Examines Wallant's metaphoric use of the city, which is ugly, perverted, dangerous, and cruel. Gurko claims, however, that in its sprawling vitality, the city also contains "seeds of its own reconstruction."

Lewis, Robert W. "The Hung-Up Heroes of Edward Lewis Wallant." *Renascence* 24 (1972): 70-84. This substantial discussion examines all four of Wallant's novels, especially *The Pawnbroker*, paying particular attention to an analysis of Wallant's sensitive, intellectual characters and to his themes of suffering and rebirth. Lewis also looks at Wallant's use of myth.

Schulz, M. F. "Wallant and Friedman: The Glory and Agony of Love." *Critique: Studies in Modern Fiction* 10 (1968): 31-47. Offers a comparison of Wallant and Bruce Jay Friedman, particularly in their use of humor and the theme of love. Schulz finds Wallant's characters to be examples of growth in sensibility and his novels to be affirmations of order and rebirth.

Stanford, Raney. "The Novels of Edward Wallant." *Colorado Quarterly* 17 (1969): 393-405. Examines some of Wallant's characters and themes, concentrating especially on *The Tenants of Moon-*

bloom and *The Pawnbroker*. Wallant's characters tend to undergo rebellion that leads to their rebirth. Stanford includes a discussion of Wallant's realistic detail.

JOSEPH WAMBAUGH

Born: East Pittsburgh, Pennsylvania; January 22, 1937

PRINCIPAL LONG FICTION

The New Centurions, 1970
The Blue Knight, 1972
The Choirboys, 1975
The Black Marble, 1978
The Glitter Dome, 1981
The Delta Star, 1983
The Secrets of Harry Bright, 1985
The Golden Orange, 1990
Fugitive Nights, 1992
Finnegan's Week, 1993
Floaters, 1996

OTHER LITERARY FORMS

In addition to several "nonfiction novels" (*The Onion Field*, 1973; *Lines and Shadows*, 1984; *Echoes in the Darkness*, 1987; *The Blooding*, 1989), Joseph Wambaugh wrote screenplays for the filming of *The Onion Field* (1979) and *The Black Marble* (1980). He also served as creative consultant for television productions of *The Blue Knight* and the series *Police Story*.

ACHIEVEMENTS

Wambaugh is widely regarded as an outstanding storyteller and the greatest novelist in the field of "police procedure" novels. All of his fiction and nonfiction works have been best-sellers, and he was awarded the Mystery Writers of America Special Award in 1973. Critics have praised Wambaugh's ability to combine objectivity and empathy in realistic depictions of life in a police force. No other novelist has so effectively conveyed the feelings of horror, isolation, despair, frustration, and helplessness experienced daily by police officers, as well as their reactions to these intense psychological pressures. The heroism and cowardice, anger and compassion, dedication and laziness, insight and ignorance of the average police officer on the beat have been brought vividly to life by Wambaugh. His believable portraits of policemen and policewomen are matched by cogent explorations of the sociopathic personalities of the criminals they battle, all of which draw the reader into a complete and compelling world of drugs, crime, alcoholism, and social and moral decay.

BIOGRAPHY

Joseph Aloysius Wambaugh, Jr., was born in 1937 in East Pittsburgh, Pennsylvania, the son of a small-town police chief. Following in his father's footsteps was not young Wambaugh's original intention. He entered the U.S. Marine Corps in 1954 and soon thereafter married his high school sweetheart, Dee Allsup. Discharged in 1957, Wambaugh settled in Ontario, California, where he became a steelworker and went to college part-time at night. He planned to be a teacher and eventually completed both a B.A. and an M.A. in English. In 1960, however, while in his senior year at California State College in Los Angeles, Wambaugh suddenly decided to become a policeman. For the next fourteen years, he worked as a detective in the Los Angeles Police Department (LAPD) and was eventually promoted to sergeant, despite several well-publicized run-ins with his superiors. These conflicts were occasioned by the publication of Wambaugh's first novel, *The New Centurions*, in which the hierarchy of the LAPD was irreverently satirized.

Wambaugh continued to be both detective and novelist until 1974. By this time, he had become so famous that his celebrity status had begun to limit his job effectiveness. He regretfully gave up police work for full-time writing. In 1983 Wambaugh moved from Los Angeles, dividing his time between the suburban areas of Orange County and Palm Springs. In 1993 he moved further south to the Point Loma district of San Diego.

ANALYSIS

All Joseph Wambaugh's novels deal with police officers, primarily in Southern California. Their environment is completely outside both the experience of most middle-class Americans, for it is populated with drug dealers, drifters, pimps, prostitutes, addicts, panhandlers, murderers, and thieves. Supplementing the "bad guys" are the outcasts, outsiders, and victims: welfare mothers and their families, abused children, old and crippled pensioners, illegal immigrants, the mentally incompetent, and the chronically disaffected. Middle-class values have disappeared, and what are usually considered normal attitudes and behaviors seem nonexistent. In the cultures of the barrio, in the ghetto, and even among the wacky rich, police officers are charged with representing and upholding a legal system overwhelmed by the morass of modern society. Because Wambaugh himself was a veteran of the streets, the reader experiences his world through the mind of a policeman: It is full of darkness, desolation, and, above all, a sense of helplessness, for the fate of an individual, as well as the solution to a case, often turns upon trivial, capricious accidents.

This depressing background of urban decay sets the stage on which Wambaugh presents several themes. The most persistent is that real police work is very different from typical public perceptions influenced by television, motion pictures, and traditional police stories, which depict cops as superheroes who always get the bad guys and put them away. Again and again, Wambaugh's police officers express their frustration with juries who demand to know why it takes three officers with nightsticks to subdue a single, unarmed suspect, or why a police officer did not "wing" a fleeing felon rather than shoot him to death. Everyday people who have never had a real fistfight or attempted to aim a weapon at a moving target simply do not understand the realities of these situations. Police officers are not superhuman;

they are normal people thrown into extremely abnormal situations.

Often, it seems as if the police are at war with a judicial system that elevates form over substance and technicalities over the determination of guilt or innocence. To the average patrol officer, vice-squad officer, or homicide detective, the courts are arenas where shifty, politically motivated defense lawyers and prosecutors conspire to overturn common sense, where judges and juries view police procedures and conduct with twenty-twenty hindsight, and where the rights of the defendant have triumphed over the suffering of victims. It is the average officer who most often encounters the anguish and suffering of those victims. These experiences alienate and isolate police officers from the rest of "normal" society.

Within the police force itself, the officers on the street are responsible to a hierarchy of "brass" who, for the most part, have never themselves worked a

(Library of Congress)

beat. In Wambaugh's view, the brass are primarily concerned with ensuring their own advancement and have little concern for the welfare of their officers. He paints high-level officers, often with brutal humor, as buffoons who spend much of their time trying to seduce female officers, avoiding real responsibility, and protecting their reputations.

Given that he is a street veteran himself, Wambaugh's sympathies clearly lie with his former comrades, yet what makes his novels extraordinary is his realistic appraisal of these officers, warts and all. Many of them are crude racists, and most resent the forced acceptance of women on the force, which began in the 1960's. Attempting to shield themselves from the sheer terror and pain intrinsic to their jobs, they exude cynicism and disgust with nearly everything and everybody, even themselves. They respond to the daily brutality they encounter, and which they must occasionally employ, with gallows humor, sexual promiscuity, alcoholism, and, far too often, "eating their pieces"—suicide.

THE NEW CENTURIONS

Wambaugh's first novel, *The New Centurions*, follows the progress of three rookies from their training at the Los Angeles Police Academy in the summer of 1960 to their accidental reunion in the Watts riots of August, 1965. Serge Duran is a former athlete and former marine who has attempted to escape his Chicano heritage, Gus Plebesly is an undersized overachiever who is exceedingly afraid of failure, and Roy Fehler thinks of himself as a liberal intellectual making merely a temporary detour from an academic career in criminology. In their development as police officers, all three face situations that force them to examine their beliefs about themselves. Initially assigned as a patrolman in a barrio precinct, Duran meets a Hispanic woman who teaches him not to be ashamed of his ethnic identity. Under the tutelage of a veteran patrolman, Kilvinsky, Plebesly gains the professional and personal assurance to become a competent officer. Fehler, however, fails to reconcile his intellectual views with the emotional realities of race relations on the street: He blinds himself to his own prejudices, tying himself into a psychological knot. His failure is dramatically sym-

bolized at the end of the novel, when he is shot and dies.

The plot of *The New Centurions* develops chronologically and in episodes focusing on each of the rookies in turn. As Duran, Plebesly, and Fehler receive new assignments, Wambaugh takes the opportunity to display the operational peculiarities of the various divisions within the police force—street patrols, vice, homicide, juvenile, and narcotics—as well as to introduce a host of minor characters, both police and civilians, who reveal all the quirks and propensities of their world. Whenever a new character appears, Wambaugh adds believability and depth by interrupting the narrative to discuss some incident that has shaped this person's life and attitudes. These brief digressions are often darkly humorous and also allow Wambaugh to illustrate further the vicissitudes of life in the LAPD.

It is apparent that Wambaugh regards the Watts riots as a kind of watershed for civilized society and the rule of law. Until the summer of 1965, the police force generally dealt with specific crimes committed by and against individuals. The Watts riots, however, represented a fundamental rejection of the structures of lawful authority by almost the entire black community, and the department was astonished and overwhelmed by the senseless violence of mobs of ordinarily law-abiding citizens. At the end of the book, it is clear that, though a few officers seem to have guessed that some sort of qualitative change in social attitudes had occurred, most assumed that the situation would soon return to normal.

THE BLUE KNIGHT

One of the main themes of *The Blue Knight*, Wambaugh's second novel, is that the situation did not, in fact, return to normal. Hostile media coverage of the riots focused upon the LAPD's lack of community-relations efforts, incompetence, and alleged brutality, while government investigations reported widespread racism and corruption throughout the department. Stung by criticism, department executives became increasingly image-conscious and ordered significant changes in training and operational procedures. One result was that the time-honored tradition of the individual policeman walking his beat was replaced by the two-person patrol-car unit. In the past, officers generally had been granted a large amount of latitude in dealing with situations on their beats and were usually trusted to keep order as they saw fit. The wise policeman developed a commonsense attitude, allowing certain kinds of violations to slide while others were dealt with immediately and often severely. The new breed of patrol officer, however, was supposed to stay close to his unit, maintain constant radio communication with his precinct, and limit his activities to those precisely within the law. The new policy was intended to ensure both the safety and the good behavior of officers, whose individual initiative was drastically curtailed.

The Blue Knight takes place in the midst of the transition from the old to the new; its main character is a traditional beat officer, William H. "Bumper" Morgan, a twenty-year veteran on the brink of retirement. Wambaugh examines Bumper's last three days on the police force, using the first-person viewpoint to help the reader perceive events directly through Bumper's eyes and ears. Though Bumper has been forced to trade walking his beat for driving a police unit, he insists on working alone and spends most of his shift out of his car and out of radio contact with his precinct.

Bumper's long experience has made him something of a sociologist and philosopher, and his observations represent Wambaugh's slightly irreverent tribute to the old police view of the world. As he makes his rounds, Bumper recalls for the reader many of the events of his twenty years on the force, as well as what he learned from them. Through these recollections, he reveals the essence of his approach to successful police work: Never give or accept love, and always remain impersonal and uninvolved on the job. Unfortunately, Bumper's philosophy is a self-delusion. The excitement and danger of police work isolate him from everything and everyone outside of his beat, the only environment in which he is truly in control. In fact he is so completely involved that his life is nothing but his job. Thus, at the end of the story, despite postretirement plans for marriage and a cushy position as a corporate head of security, Bumper decides that he cannot give up his badge.

Though Bumper is clearly meant to be a sympathetic character, Wambaugh also endows him with flaws. He is overweight and indulges himself in vast feasts provided free by the restaurateurs on his beat. He is crude and flatulent, angry and vengeful, egotistic and very expansive in interpreting his powers as a representative of the law. Like many police officers, he imbibes copious amounts of liquor and is certainly no paragon of sexual morality. Sometimes, despite his experience, he even makes stupid mistakes, such as allowing himself to be drawn alone into a dangerous confrontation with student demonstrators. Bumper is softhearted but also tough, violent, and often frustrated. Ultimately, he appears as a tragic figure, unable to break with a career that casts him as a permanent outsider.

THE CHOIRBOYS

After leaving the LAPD in 1974, Wambaugh apparently felt the need to give free rein to some of the anguish and bitterness he felt about his career as a police officer. These emotions are expressed in his third novel, *The Choirboys*, which differs significantly from his previous works in both style and substance. In its structure, grim humor, and overall feeling of hopelessness, *The Choirboys* resembles Joseph Heller's *Catch-22* (1961), with the LAPD substituted for Heller's Army Air Corps. Like the military officers in *Catch-22*, the ten officers who make up the "choirboys" are losers and misfits: several alcoholics, a sadist, a masochist, a violent racist, and the like. Each chapter introduces a new character and relates a series of especially harrowing incidents that lead to the calling of a "choir practice," in which the group meets in a park to get drunk and vie for the sexual favors of two overweight waitresses. Choir practice allows the officers to let off steam and serves as a coping device against the horrifying realities they have faced. The sessions frequently get out of hand, however, and eventually lead to the unintended death of a civilian and the suspension of several of the group.

With its uninhibited street language, unrestrained cynicism, emotional violence, and unrelieved sense of futility, *The Choirboys* is saved only by the brutal hilarity of its bumbling protagonists and the ironies they suffer. The situations into which Wambaugh's policemen stumble are so outrageous that the reader cannot take them very seriously. Thus, even though Wambaugh's characters are incisive and believable, the world in which they operate is so impossibly awful that the reader maintains the objectivity necessary for laughter.

THE BLACK MARBLE

After *The Choirboys*, Wambaugh's novels became both more conventional in structure and more sentimental in tone. His main characters are still losers, and the sense of blind fate and the prominence of coincidence continue to dominate his plots, but, in the end, his protagonists seem to be at least somewhat redeemed; the climaxes always result in some kind of catharsis. Each of his succeeding books revolves around a single case, a kind of puzzle that is resolved not through brilliant police work, but through dogged determination and serendipitous accidents. An excellent example is his next novel, *The Black Marble*, whose hero is Sergeant Andrei Mikhailovich Valnikov, an absentminded, broken-down alcoholic who is also a consummate and very touching gentleman. Valnikov was once a top homicide detective, but after he investigated a string of cases of sexually abused and brutally murdered children, he developed constant nightmares and started drinking to forget. Eventually, he suffered a breakdown and was reassigned to the robbery division.

Valnikov is paired with Natalie Zimmerman, an ambitious female detective who is bitter generally about the discriminatory attitude of the LAPD toward women and specifically about being stuck with Valnikov. She believes that her Russian-born partner is not only a drunk but crazy as well, especially when he begins to devote all of his still-considerable abilities to the solution of a case she regards as ridiculous: the theft of a prize schnauzer. Wambaugh follows their misadventures in discovering that the dog has been stolen by a trainer seeking to extort money from the owner, a formerly wealthy divorcée now unable to pay the ransom. As always in a Wambaugh novel, along the path to the solution of the case the reader becomes acquainted with a cast of wacky police officers and civilians, until Valnikov finally catches the criminal and wins the love and respect of his partner.

All Wambaugh's subsequent novels have followed the pattern established by *The Black Marble*: the often-coincidental solution of a crime by not-very-heroic police officers or former officers. Though he himself regarded *The Choirboys* as his best work, it is not representative of his style. In later novels Wambaugh solidified his reputation as a master of the crime novel with stories featuring the flawed characters, dark humor, intricate plots, and dangerous constructions exhibited in his earlier works. With each succeeding narrative, the tone becomes even more in keeping with its backdrop, from the illusory appeal of Hollywood in *The Glitter Dome* to the stark realities of inner-city life in *The Delta Star* to the haunting environs of the Palm Springs desert in *The Secrets of Harry Bright*.

THE GOLDEN ORANGE and FUGITIVE NIGHTS

With *The Golden Orange* and *Fugitive Nights*, the author enters into the "ex-cop" phase of his work in the persons of Winnie Farlowe and Lynn Cutter, both former officers and heavy drinkers who become drawn into complicated crimes requiring a considerable application of their skills. All the while they must strive to surmount the accumulation of personal demons engendered and nurtured by years of police work. In both novels the upscale settings, of Newport Harbor in *The Golden Orange* and Palm Springs in *Fugitive Nights*, serve as an effective foil for the trademark cop chatter and streetwise daring of the author's heroes. In the ex-cop's world, saloons serve as substitute offices where former officers and off-duty policemen congregate to conduct business and male bonding on the side. Wambaugh's ex-cops are tough yet vulnerable, especially when they place their trust in others who, on the surface, seem worthy of it. In *The Golden Orange*, the moment arrives for one of the author's gritty veterans to address what he terms the Cop's Syllogism, a condition that could be applied to nearly all of Wambaugh's fictional constructions. It simply states, "People are garbage. I am a person. Therefore———." Once the syllogism is avowed, only something bad can happen. It "has led thousands of burned-out, overwhelmingly cynical members of the law enforcement business into alcoholism or drug addiction, police corruption, or suicide." It affirms why, in an interview, the author took issue with the notion that his works are police procedurals. "I was the first person, I think, to write a book about cops that was not a police procedural," he said. "A police procedural is a novel that attempts to show how a cop acts on the job. I wasn't interested so much in that. So, I turned it around. I thought I'd like to show how the job acts on the cop."

FINNEGAN'S WEEK

In *Finnegan's Week* another of Wambaugh's hero-detectives, Finbar Finnegan, teams up with Nell Salter, a district attorney's office investigator, and Bobbie Ann Doggett, a navy law enforcement official, to solve a crime involving a stolen truck loaded with lethal pesticide. As usual, the drinks, jokes, sexual repartee, salty dialogue, and verbal and physical clashes flow freely. At times they almost careen out of control, whipsawing the reader to a conclusion that is judicious and sensible.

FLOATERS

Floaters features an aquatic theme, as Wambaugh pairs a couple of harbor cops and vice officers in an investigation of a scheme by a business tycoon to sabotage a competitor's entry in the America's Cup yachting race. As in previous works, the author demonstrates a knack for juxtaposing characters who are very different. In addition to the unlikely cops, there is a yachting enthusiast, an expensive call girl and masseuse, a vicious pimp, and a band of rowdy Australian crewmen. Though the plot is slow paced at the beginning, the events leading up to the climax are vintage Wambaugh. In all his fiction, Wambaugh has explored essentially the same themes: the basic humanity of police officers and the pressures they face, the decline of traditional values in modern society, and the haphazard and accidental nature of fate.

Thomas C. Schunk,
updated by William Hoffman

OTHER MAJOR WORKS

SCREENPLAYS: *The Onion Field*, 1979; *The Black Marble*, 1980.

NONFICTION: *The Onion Field*, 1973; *Lines and Shadows*, 1984; *Echoes in the Darkness*, 1987; *The Blooding*, 1989.

BIBLIOGRAPHY

Donahue, Deirdre. "Wambaugh, Veteran of the Cop Beat." *USA Today*, May 8, 1996, p. 1D. This article discusses the popularity, due to their accuracy, of Wambaugh's books among police officers. Wambaugh also is described as being more mellow in his later works and injecting more humor into them.

Jeffrey, David K. "Joseph Wambaugh." In *American Novelists Since World War II*. Vol. 6 in *Dictionary of Literary Biography*, edited by James E. Kibler, Jr. 2d ser. Detroit: Gale Research, 1980. Jeffrey is the only scholar who has devoted much attention to Wambaugh. Here he has culled a brief biography from newspaper articles and offers some analysis and criticism of Wambaugh's works to 1978. Like many critics, Jeffrey admires Wambaugh's ability but does not like police officers. Thus, he is somewhat hostile to Wambaugh's more romantic novels such as *The Black Marble*, in which the hero is ultimately vindicated.

"Joseph Aloysius Wambaugh, Jr." In *Current Biography Yearbook: 1980*, edited by Charles Moritz. New York: H. H. Wilson, 1981. In addition to a brief biography, this article contains excerpts of press interviews with Wambaugh and critical evaluations of his works.

Meisler, Andy. "Paranoid Among the Palms." *The New York Times*, June 13, 1996, p. C1. In this interview Wambaugh offers his observations on what he considers the erosion of the American judicial system in the late twentieth century. He also provides an overview of his own career as a Los Angeles detective and novelist.

Van Dover, J. K. *Centurians, Knights, and Other Cops: The Police Novels of Joseph Wambaugh*. Brownstone Mystery Guides 19. San Bernardino, Calif.: Brownstone Books, 1995. Van Dover examines Wambaugh's novels in chronological order, from *The New Centurions* through *Finnegan's Week*. He also includes a primary bibliography, general index, and character index.

"Wambaugh." In *Authors in the News*. Vol. 1, edited by Barbara Nykoruk. Detroit: Gale Research, 1979. A compilation of newspaper stories about

Wambaugh. Includes two fairly substantial interviews with the writer while he was still a police officer.

ROBERT PENN WARREN

Born: Guthrie, Kentucky; April 24, 1905
Died: West Wardsboro, near Stratton, Vermont; September 15, 1989

PRINCIPAL LONG FICTION
Night Rider, 1939
At Heaven's Gate, 1943
All the King's Men, 1946
World Enough and Time: A Romantic Novel, 1950
Band of Angels, 1955
The Cave, 1959
Wilderness: A Tale of the Civil War, 1961
Flood: A Romance of Our Time, 1964
Meet Me in the Green Glen, 1971
A Place to Come To, 1977

OTHER LITERARY FORMS

Robert Penn Warren wrote successfully in so many genres that Charles Bohner called him "the pentathlon champion of American literature." In addition to his novels, he published short stories, numerous volumes of poetry, and a considerable amount of nonfiction. Warren's fiction and his poetry often consider the same philosophical themes: the meaning of history, the loss of innocence and the recognition of evil in the fallen world, and the difficulty of finding a moral balance in a world in which traditional Christian values seem to be faltering. For example, in his book-length poem *Brother to Dragons: A Tale in Verse and Voices* (1953), Warren begins with a historical event—a brutal murder of a slave by Thomas Jefferson's nephew, Lilburne Lewis—and creates a philosophical examination of people's fallen nature. Warren does something very similar in his novel *World Enough and Time.* The story is based on a

murder which occurred in 1825, but the novel, like the poem, becomes an examination of people's fall from innocence and the difficulty of establishing moral ideals in a fallen world.

Warren's concerns over history and morality are also evident in his earliest, nonfiction works. In his first book, a biography, *John Brown: The Making of a Martyr* (1929), Warren contends that Brown did not tread the path of morality quite so righteously as Ralph Waldo Emerson had thought he had; in his fallen condition, Brown mistook his own egotism for pure idealism. Warren's neo-orthodox insistence on people's fallen nature and his skepticism about the possibilities of pure idealism, both of which are reflected in his novels, led him to accept the traditionalist attitudes of the Southern intellectuals who made up the "Fugitive Group," and he contributed to the agrarian manifesto *I'll Take My Stand* (1930). Warren did, however, espouse a more liberal attitude toward racial matters in his later nonfiction works *Segregation: The Inner Conflict in the South* (1956) and *Who Speaks for the Negro?* (1965).

Warren's social criticism ultimately proved less influential than his literary criticism. His *Selected Essays* (1958) contains perceptive studies of Samuel Taylor Coleridge's *The Rime of the Ancient Mariner* (1798), Joseph Conrad's *Nostromo* (1904), William Faulkner, Ernest Hemingway, and Katherine Anne Porter. These essays are important not only for what they say about these authors but also for what they reveal about Warren's own work. Even more important than these essays, however, was Warren's collaboration with Cleanth Brooks. Their textbooks, *Understanding Fiction* (1943) and *Understanding Poetry* (1938), helped to change substantially the way literature was taught in the United States.

Warren continued to publish literary criticism at intervals throughout his life; indeed, *New and Selected Essays* appeared in the year of his death, 1989. Yet with a poetry-writing career that spanned fifty years, he was at least equally well known as a craftsman in that genre. His poems have been widely anthologized, and he is recognized as one of the United States' foremost twentieth century poets.

ACHIEVEMENTS

For most readers Warren's name is probably most associated with his novel *All the King's Men*, for which he won both the Pulitzer Prize for Fiction and the National Book Award. He also won the Robert Meltzer Award from the Screen Writers Guild for the play based on that novel. Warren's short story "Blackberry Winter" has also been highly acclaimed and widely anthologized. Other readers think of Warren primarily as a poet, and with good reason; he won the Pulitzer Prize for Poetry twice, first for *Promises: Poems 1954-1956* (1957), which also won the Edna St. Vincent Millay Prize and the National Book Award for Poetry, and a second time for *Now and Then: Poems 1976-1978* (1978). *Selected Poems: New and Old, 1923-1966* (1966) won the Bollingen Prize from Yale University, and *Audubon: A Vision* (1969) won the Van Wyck Brooks Award and the National Medal for Literature. Warren was elected to the American Philosophical Society in 1952 and to the American Academy of Arts and Sciences in 1959. He was named first poet laureate of the United States in 1986.

BIOGRAPHY

Robert Penn Warren's background and experience had a tremendous impact upon the thematic concerns of his fiction. He demonstrated the need, common to so many Southern writers, to cope with the burden of the past. He also wrote out of a scholar's familiarity with and devotion to certain prominent literary artists, past and present, particularly the Elizabethan and Jacobean dramatists, Joseph Conrad, William Faulkner, and T. S. Eliot. His academic studies, pursued in a long career as an English professor, may have had a great deal to do with the structure of his works and their typically tragic mode. His recurring subject, however, was the peculiar experience of the South; a love-hate relationship with a dying heritage runs throughout his work.

Born to Robert Franklin and Anna Ruth Penn Warren on April 24, 1905, in the tiny Kentucky town of Guthrie, Warren grew up in an almost classic Southern situation. His father, a banker and businessman struggling to support a large family, did not ini-

(Washington Post/D.C. Public Library)

tially fire the young Warren's imagination as his grandfather did. The emotional bond between Warren and his maternal grandfather, Gabriel Thomas Penn, ripened during long summers spent on his grandfather's tobacco farm. Here, Warren experienced the pastoral charms of agrarian life, soaked up the nostalgic glow of the American Civil War from his grandfather, and absorbed the rhetoric and humor that permeates the Southern storytelling.

Gabriel Thomas Penn had been a cavalryman during the Civil War, and many an afternoon with his grandson was spent reliving the legendary time. It is not surprising that the boy looked upon the Civil War as America's great epic, as imbued with nobility and tragedy as Homer's *Iliad* (c. 800 B.C.E.) He was not blind, however, to the irony and ambiguity of his grandfather, as representative of the values of the aristocratic horse soldier. Warren has commemorated his realization that the romantic image of the Confederate cavalryman had its darker side in the poem "Court Martial" in *Promises: Poems 1954-1956*, which is about his grandfather's hanging of bushwhackers without benefit of legal trial. Because this poem was written much later, however, it is possible that the ambiguous view of the grandfather was partially constructed from a more mature understanding. The event, however, was a true one that evidently made a deep impression on the young Warren. In any case, Warren was absorbing background for a number of later novels, such as *Wilderness: A Tale of the Civil War* and *Band of Angels*. In neither of these does he write as an apologist for the Old South, but he does expose the moral shortcomings of Northerners, much as he does in his early biography of John Brown.

Warren was also absorbing the local tales of tobacco war, when the growers of dark-fired tobacco banded together to boycott the tobacco company that regulated prices. Warren's first novel, *Night Rider*, was written from childhood memories of such local stories. Warren's brother Thomas, who became a grain dealer, knew all the farmers of the region and was adept at repeating such tales.

The young Warren loved nature; collected butterflies, snakes, rocks, and leaves; and aspired to paint animals (an interest reflected in his poem about John Audubon). Later, he hunted with his brother and learned taxidermy. These experiences were more important, perhaps, to the content of his poetry than to his fiction. In spite of his persistent affinity for nature, he usually recognized in his fiction its essential amorality: "The blank cup of nature," he calls it in *World Enough and Time*.

In spite of the contribution to his early imaginative development by his grandfather and his agrarian milieu, the influence of Warren's father was subtle and pervasive, perhaps more significant in the long run to the human relationships explored in his novels. Ambiguous father-son relationships appear over and over in such novels as *All the King's Men, The Cave, At Heaven's Gate*, and *A Place to Come To*. None is modeled after Warren's actual relationship to his own father, but they reflect a combination of admiration, guilt, and mystery that suggests some deep personal involvement in the issues they raise.

Warren often admitted to an odd sense of guilt about "stealing his father's life." Robert Franklin Warren had wanted to be a lawyer and a poet but had become a businessman instead, because of financial responsibilities not only to his own family but also to a family of half brothers and sisters left without a provider when his father died. One of Warren's favorite reminiscences was about finding a book with some poems written by his father in it and carrying it with delight to him. His father summarily confiscated the book, and his son never saw it again. Warren thought perhaps his father had been embarrassed or pained at this reminder of a goal long since set aside. According to Warren, his father never regretted the obligations that dictated the terms of his life. Indeed, he took joy in them. Warren speaks with an admiration bordering on awe of the seemingly effortless rectitude of his father and of the ideal relationship between his father and mother.

As the result of an accident when he was fifteen years old, Warren lost the sight of one eye and was thus prevented from pursuing a career as a naval officer, as he had planned. Warren went, instead, to Vanderbilt University and came under the influence of John Crowe Ransom and the Fugitives, a group of academics and townspeople who met regularly to discuss philosophy and poetry. Ransom soon recognized Warren's unusual ability and encouraged him to write poetry.

Warren was graduated summa cum laude from Vanderbilt in 1926 and pursued an M.A. at the University of California at Berkeley. While there, he became an ardent student of Elizabethan and Jacobean drama, which perhaps struck a responsive chord in an imagination already steeped in the violence and melodrama of Southern history. He started to work on a doctorate at Yale University but left as a Rhodes scholar for Oxford, England, where he received a Bachelor of Letters degree in 1930.

During this period, Warren wrote his first book, *John Brown: The Making of a Martyr*. To some extent, this book grew out of an impulse shared with a number of his Vanderbilt friends and other writers of the so-called Southern Renaissance. They were concerned about the exclusively Northern bias of most historians dealing with events leading up to and during the Civil War and its aftermath. Certainly, Warren presents a jaundiced view of the radical abolitionist. Brown seems to have provided a nucleus for Warren's meditations about the effects of power and the misuses of altruism which were to be explored in a number of later novels, especially *Night Rider* and *All the King's Men*. He also wrote his first fiction while at Oxford, a short story called "Prime Leaf," about the impact of the Kentucky tobacco war on an old man, his son, and his grandson. The old man has a role similar to that of the elder Todd in *Night Rider*, the wise man who bows out of the organization when it resorts to vigilante tactics.

Warren taught at a number of universities, including Louisiana State, where he lived in the legendary ambience of the Southern demagogue Huey Long, whose presence lies behind the fictional Willie Stark of *All the King's Men*. Warren later said that he knew nothing about the real Huey Long, but the mythical Huey was on everyone's lips. Even casual conversations often dwelt upon questions of power and ethics, of means and ends, of "historical costs." In an essay entitled "All the King's Men: The Matrix of Experience," in John Lewis Longley's *Robert Penn Warren: A Collection of Critical Essays* (1965), Warren writes:

> Melodrama was the breath of life. There had been melodrama in the life I had known in Tennessee, but with a difference; in Tennessee the melodrama seemed to be different from the stuff of life, something superimposed upon life, but in Louisiana people lived melodrama, seemed to live, in fact, for it, for this strange combination of philosophy, humor and violence. Life was a tale that you happened to be living—and that "Huey" happened to be living before your eyes.

These remarks demonstrate that Warren was not primarily a historical novelist, but rather a classicist, fascinated with the universal patterns in particular experience. Thus, he discouraged close comparisons between Willie Stark and Huey Long, pointing out that he wrote the first version of the story as a verse drama in Italy, as he watched Benito Mussolini, another man of the people, consolidate his power.

In Warren's writing career, the years from 1943 to 1950, though a dry period for poetry, were productive ones for fiction and literary criticism. Besides *All the King's Men*, he produced *At Heaven's Gate*, about the unscrupulous liaison between government and industry, and *World Enough and Time*, about a nineteenth century murder case. When Warren was poetry consultant for the Library of Congress in 1944-1945, Katherine Anne Porter, who was fiction consultant that year, threw on his desk the confession of Jeroboam Beauchamp, hanged for murder in Kentucky in 1826. Porter announced cryptically that she was giving him a novel. This was, indeed, the germ for his most complex novel, *World Enough and Time*.

Warren's dry period in poetry eventually ended after he divorced his first wife, Emma Brescia, married the writer Eleanor Clark, and fathered two children. He began writing excellent poetry and produced several more novels. A long association with Yale University began in 1950.

In 1986 Warren was named the United States' first poet laureate, a post he held for two years. He died of cancer in 1989, at his summer home near Stratton, Vermont.

ANALYSIS

Often, what Robert Penn Warren said about other writers provides an important insight into his own works. This is especially true of Warren's perceptive essay "The Great Mirage: Conrad and *Nostromo*" in *Selected Essays*, in which he discusses the enigmatic speech of Stein in Joseph Conrad's *Lord Jim* (1900):

> A man that is born falls into a dream like a man who falls into the sea. If he tries to climb out into the air as inexperienced people endeavor to do, he drowns— *nicht wahr?* . . . No! I tell you! The way is to the de-

structive element submit yourself, and with the exertions of your hands and feet in the water make the deep, deep sea keep you up.

Warren interprets the dream here as "man's necessity to justify himself and his actions into moral significance of some order, to find sanctions." The destructiveness of the dream arises from humans' nature as egotistical animals with savage impulses, not completely adapted to the dream-sea of ideas. The one who learns to swim instead of drowning in the unnatural sea of ideas is he who realizes that the values he creates are illusion, but that "the illusion is necessary, is infinitely precious, is the mark of his human achievement, and is, in the end, his only truth." Warren calls *Nostromo* "a study in the definition and necessity of illusion." This phrase could also describe most of Warren's works of fiction.

Warren's classification of thematic elements in Conrad's stories could also be applied to his own. Warren writes that Conrad is concerned with the person who lacks imagination but clings to fidelity and duty (like the old captain in *Youth*, 1902), the sinner against human solidarity and the human mission (like Kurtz in *Heart of Darkness*, 1902, and Decoud in *Nostromo*), and the redeemed individual (Jim in *Lord Jim* and Dr. Monygham in *Nostromo*). Warren says that Conrad is most interested in the latter—"the crisis of this story comes when the hero recognizes the terms on which he may be saved, the moment, to take Morton Zabel's phrase, of the 'terror of the awakening.'"

One might note that in Warren's novel *At Heaven's Gate*, Jerry's dirt-farmer father fits the pattern of natural rectitude, while Slim Sarrett, the nihilistic, cynical artist, is certainly the sinner against human solidarity. No one seems to be redeemed in *At Heaven's Gate*, though Jerry might have a chance in a hypothetical future, since he has acquired considerable self-knowledge. Mr. Munn in *Night Rider* has also stripped away his own illusions, but he dies, like William Shakespeare's Macbeth, without redemption. In other novels of this period, however, Burden in *All the King's Men*, and perhaps even the murderer in *World Enough and Time*, achieve some kind of abso-

lution. Warren and Conrad share this deep obsession with the need for redemption, and though the sentiment is religious and may be expressed in Christian imagery, it is consistently humanistic in emphasis. The world they both recognize is a naturalistic one, but people must live in two worlds, the world of facts and the world of ideas, which they create themselves. Warren's notion of submission to the realm of ideas is analogous, perhaps, to Ernest Hemingway's code of the hunter, the fisherman, the bullfighter, or the soldier, which provides existential meaning in a meaningless world.

Warren's early novels, particularly *Night Rider, All the King's Men*, and *World Enough and Time*, which critics generally agree are his best, trace a pattern of increasing complexity in the theme of people's vacillation between the fantasy of dreams and the reality of facts. After *World Enough and Time*, which is almost too densely packed and convoluted in theme, Warren relaxed his insistence that everything must be said on the subject of illusion and reality in one novel. Later works, such as *Meet Me in the Green Glen* and *Wilderness: A Tale of the Civil War*, though not conspicuously different in theme, concentrate on a particular manifestation of the problem—on the nature of love in *Meet Me in the Green Glen*, and on the nature of altruism in *Wilderness*.

Actually, Warren's examination of the apposition between the world of ideas and the world of facts begins in his first book, *John Brown: The Making of a Martyr*. Warren portrays the militant abolitionist as not so much obsessed with freeing slaves as with starring in his own myth. Brown is encouraged in this role by the unqualified praise of Ralph Waldo Emerson, whom Warren believed to be a writer of empty words, with little perception of the real world; Warren quotes Emerson as saying of Brown, "He is a man to make friends wherever on earth courage and integrity are esteemed—the rarest of heroes, a pure idealist, with no by-ends of his own." Warren did not for a moment believe that Brown was a "pure idealist"; moreover, Warren had a continuing distrust of "pure idealists," whoever they might be. In his fiction, Warren was inclined to show abstract idealists as lacking in self-knowledge, capable of self-righteous violence because they refuse to acknowledge their own irrational impulses. The best example of this personality-type in Warren's fiction is Adam Stanton, in *All the King's Men*, who assassinates Willie Stark because Willie, the man of fact, seduced Adam's sister.

John Brown, however, as a man who uses exalted ideas to inflate his own self-image, is more akin to Warren's Professor Ball, Dr. MacDonald, and Mr. Munn of *Night Rider*; Bogan Murdock, the industrialist, and Slim Sarett, of *At Heaven's Gate*; and Wilkie Barron, the manipulative false friend of Jeremiah Beaumont, in *World Enough and Time*. Willie Stark, though categorized by Jack Burden as the "man of fact," in contrast to Adam Stanton, the "man of idea," has his own idealistic dream of the people's hospital, free to anyone who needs it. Whether that dream was truly altruistic, however, or tinged by the secret need for a personal monument to his existence, is ambiguous.

NIGHT RIDER

Thus, Warren suggests that the self is itself part of the dream-sea of ideas. Warren's protagonists are often initially passive persons whose emptiness is filled by other more dynamic personalities. Having acquired a somewhat fictitious self under such influence, they proceed to act in the real world as though that dream were true—often with tragic results. Thus, Mr. Munn seems an innocuous, ordinary young lawyer when he first appears in *Night Rider*, but he is drawn irresistibly to his more dynamic friend, Mr. Christian, who has a legitimate concern for the plight of the tobacco growers at the mercy of the price-controlling tobacco company. Munn learns to savor his new role as labor leader. He is ripe, then, for indoctrination by more conniving, professional agitators, Professor Ball and Dr. MacDonald, who preach a secret society that will scrape the fields of uncooperative growers and punish backsliders who dare to violate the embargo. What begins as a lawful strike by the downtrodden majority becomes lawless action by a vigilante group that destroys crops, burns warehouses, and commits murder. In the case of Munn, the crisis of this psychic change in direction comes

when he realizes that his assigned task to assassinate the tobacco farmer Bunk Trevelyon, whom he once defended in court on a murder charge, is not only his "duty" to the group; it also satisfies something very personal in himself that he has not yet recognized. Trevelyon had committed the murder of which he was once accused, and the African American who was hanged for that murder was innocent. Trevelyon thus becomes the symbol for Munn's half-conscious cooperation in framing the African American, or, to use another favorite term of Warren, Munn's original sin. In this ritual of retribution, the shared myth of community justice fuses with Munn's private myth of killing the shadow-self, an act of both self-condemnation and deliberate concealment of a secret crime.

After this private confrontation and ritual killing of his shadow-self, Munn makes no more moral objections to anything Ball and MacDonald want to do. The three lead a concerted assault on the company warehouses, which results in a number of casualties. One person who dies is young Benton Todd, who had been an ardent admirer of Munn. Moreover, Todd hoped to marry Mr. Christian's daughter, Lucille, who has been having a secret affair with Munn. If Trevelyon symbolizes the murderous shadow-self that Munn has hated to acknowledge, Benton Todd suggests the lost idealism, the better dream that Munn has betrayed.

Munn's subsequent flight to the West to escape prosecution for a murder he did not commit might have resulted in redemption, but it does not. The pattern of redemption is presented to him obliquely by the story of Proudfit, the impoverished farmer who is sheltering Munn. Proudfit tells of his own checkered career in the West, as a buffalo hunter and hide-tanner, with companions as rough and wild as himself. Eventually, however, he lives in peace among American Indians. When he becomes ill, the Native Americans care for him, using all their resources of natural healing and religious ritual. In his fever, he eventually has a vision of Kentucky, where he was reared, and a young woman waiting beside a stream. His strength then begins to return, so he leaves the Native American friends and goes back to find the very woman he saw in his vision, now his wife, and the very hill he saw, which is now his farm.

Proudfit's story is both an engrossing dialect narrative and a unique version of the underlying myth of death and resurrection. Proudfit's humble redemption contrasts with the myth of sin and damnation implied in Munn's career. Both Proudfit and Munn have a period of withdrawal (Proudfit, among the American Indians; Munn, on Proudfit's remote farm), time to rethink their past lives and future goals. This experience is analogous, perhaps, to the withdrawal and contemplation that the mythic hero undergoes before he returns to his homeland as a new man. Munn, however, is not transformed. He does become mildly obsessed with the innocent African American who died in Trevelyon's stead, but he cannot even remember the man's name. Perhaps his inability to name the scapegoat is intended to suggest Munn's distance from the redemption offered by Christ's sacrifice. This does not mean that Warren was advocating Christianity; he was admitting, at least, a moral vacuum where traditional values have been eliminated in a society concerned primarily with power and wealth.

ALL THE KING'S MEN

The polarity of idea and fact receives more explicit development in *All the King's Men*. Again, an essentially passive person, Jack Burden, feeds emotionally on a more dynamic personality, Willie Stark. Burden calls himself—somewhat cynically—an idealist, but his idealism consists mostly of a fastidious preference for not getting his hands dirty with some of Stark's more questionable political maneuvers. Stark is good naturedly tolerant of Burden's moral preferences, since he has Tiny Duffy to do his dirty work.

Burden considers himself a good judge of character and motives, but when a cherished image about the purity and goodness of his old girlfriend, Anne Stanton, is proven to be false, he is devastated and lost in self-doubt. Anne, who is quite a passive, unfulfilled person herself, has become Stark's mistress. Burden's first impulse is to flee, to escape, to drown, to fall into what he calls the Great Sleep. From this symbolic death, Burden is born again into a bleak but emotionally insulating belief in the Great Twitch—an

understanding of the world as completely amoral and mechanistic, wherein no one has any responsibility for what happens. Here, indeed, Burden has stepped out of the fantasy of dreams into the reality of facts.

Burden can now consent to let Stark use the information he has uncovered concerning Judge Irwin's long-forgotten political crime. Burden soon discovers how brutal the world of fact can be, when Judge Irwin's suicide reveals that the judge was actually Burden's own father. Hardly recovered from this blow, Burden recognizes a measure of responsibility for the deaths of Willie Stark and his best friend, Adam Stanton, who is shot by Willie's bodyguard after the assassination. Through his passivity and noninvolvement, Jack Burden had virtually handed over Anne Stanton to his more dynamic boss, and thus set the stage for assassination.

The novel is a fascinating study of symbiotic relationships, of which the most striking is that between Willie Stark, the practical politician, and Adam Stanton, the puritanical idealist and perfectionist. Warren also suggests a politically symbiotic relationship between the demagogue and the people he represents. In social terms, the world of *All the King's Men* is more complex than that of *Night Rider*. Munn's career is essentially that of the tragic hero, the good but not exclusively good man who is corrupted by power. Willie Stark, however, is sustained not only by his own drive for power but also by the concerted will of his constituency, who feel themselves to be socially and politically helpless. He is probably more significant as an antidote to their depression than as an answer to their physical needs. Even though Willie wants to change the world of facts for their benefit— build roads, bridges, a free hospital—it is for his psychological impact, exemplifying the triumph of the common person over the privileged elite, that he is beloved. Thus, even the man of facts floats in the symbolic sea of ideas.

WORLD ENOUGH AND TIME

If the relationship between dream and reality is complicated in *All the King's Men*, in *World Enough and Time* it becomes intricately complex. Seldom have human aspirations been so relentlessly exposed, one after another, as frail illusions. Though it might be termed a historical novel, because it is based loosely on an actual event, or a philosophical novel, because it comments repeatedly on the abstract meaning of human behavior and aspiration, *World Enough and Time* is better termed a psychological novel, or more precisely, perhaps, an examination of the psychological motivations for philosophizing. It is certainly not, like Andrew Marvell's poem "To His Coy Mistress," to which the title ironically alludes, a neat argument for seizing pleasures while one may. It is not a neat argument for any philosophical position, but it illuminates the sequential confusion of a reasonably thoughtful, well-meaning person trying to identify himself and justify his actions.

Jeremiah Beaumont, the orphaned son of an unsuccessful Kentucky farmer in the early nineteenth century, becomes the loved protégé of Colonel Cassius Fort, a well-known lawyer and statesman of the region. Jerry's exalted view of Colonel Fort receives a cruel blow from his dashing friend Wilkie Barron, a popular man-about-town and dabbler in politics. Wilkie tells Jerry of a beautiful woman he once loved in vain, who was seduced by an older man who had come to console her when her father died. When the young woman, Rachel Jordan, had a stillborn child, the older man abandoned her. The knave who wronged her was the unimpeachable Colonel Fort.

The persuasive Wilkie succeeds in promoting in a somewhat passive Jerry a romantic vision of wronged womanhood. From this point on, Jerry creates his own drama of love and revenge, though Wilkie continues to manipulate him in ways he never understands until near the end of his life. Jerry repudiates Colonel Fort, his surrogate father, and woos and eventually wins the lovely Rachel, who is in a neurotic state of depression, not because of the supposed perfidy of Colonel Fort but because of her baby's death. Jerry, blind to the real source of her despondency, hounds her into commanding him to defend her honor. Fort refuses a duel with Jerry, however, and the honorable vengeance seems destined to fizzle. Rachel is again pregnant, and Jerry is fitting into the comfortable role of country squire. An unknown messenger brings to Rachel a slanderous handbill in which Colonel Fort, presumably denying to his polit-

ical opponents his affair with Rachel, claims that Rachel had slept with a slave. Fort had gallantly claimed paternity of the child as a chivalric gesture. This shocking document, which is actually a forgery written by Wilkie Barron, precipitates Rachel's labor, and Jerry's child is also born dead. Jerry, in remorse, kills Fort—not openly in a duel, as he had planned, but secretly, letting it appear to be a political assassination.

Jerry's trial is a bewildering process where deceit and truth become inextricably mixed. Wilkie Barron appears, however, and reveals Jerry's vow to kill Fort, the reaction Wilkie had himself orchestrated even before Jerry had met the wronged lady. All is lost, and Jerry is sentenced to hang. Rachel comes and stays with him in his basement jail cell, where they indulge in a passionate interlude—a veritable frenzy of love in the face of imminent death.

The unpredictable Wilkie appears at the last minute, after the lovers have unsuccessfully tried to commit suicide by drinking laudanum. Wilkie rescues them and sends them west to live in the desolate island refuge of a notorious bandit. This is a return to nature, but a nature devoid of its original innocence, incapable of healing the scars of "civilization." Jerry sinks into a bestial pattern and Rachel into insanity, eventually killing herself. Jerry, who finds out that the slanderous handbill came from Wilkie Barron, is himself murdered as he seeks to find his way back to the hangman, resigned now to the most austere prize of all—neither love nor honor, but simply knowledge.

The flight to the West seems an almost gratuitous extension of suffering, especially since the real Jereboam Beauchamp, who murdered Colonel Solomon Sharp in 1825, did hang for his crime. The real trial and death of Beauchamp and his wife, Ann Cook, were only slightly less miserable, however, than Warren's fictional account.

Warren's extension to allow further demoralization of the lovers does help to explore all possible approaches to the problem of reconciling the ideal and the real. At first, Jerry believes that the idea must redeem the world: The mental context defines the object. Unfortunately, this route leads to an idealism divorced from action and allows a further evil to develop in the world—the death of his child. Then he believes that the world will redeem the idea—that is, the act of killing Fort will vindicate the idea of honor. In his flight to the West, he commits a third error, the opposite to his first: to deny the idea completely and embrace the physical world—"to seek communion only in the blank cup of nature."

Perhaps this tortured journey through innocence and experience should arrive at some reconciliation of opposites, but, if so, that too seems more dream than reality. "There must be a way whereby the word becomes flesh," muses Jerry in his last days. Even so, "I no longer seek to justify. I seek only to suffer." If this is not a particularly lucid analysis of philosophical possibilities, it may nevertheless be true psychologically to the mental and moral confusion in which people live. Perhaps it is intended to represent that "terror of the awakening" which Warren finds in Conrad's *Lord Jim* when the "hero recognizes the terms on which he may be saved. . . ."

In his later novels, Warren continued to deal with the tension between the ideal and the real. The central mystery is usually the self, which the protagonist does not know except through a painful dialectic between exalted idea and gross fact. The protagonist also suffers from an inability to identify his real father or the real home where he belongs. Jack Burden and Jeremiah Beaumont both have several surrogate fathers, but they are responsible for the deaths of those to whom they owe the greatest filial loyalty. In *At Heaven's Gate*, Jerry Calhoun rejects his real father, the man of natural rectitude and love, and gives his devotion to Bogan Murdock, who, in Conrad's phrase, is hollow at the core.

A PLACE TO COME TO

Even in Warren's last novel, *A Place to Come To*, the protagonist's first act is to despise his father and flee from his homeland; his last is to return to his hometown and make peace with the gentle stepfather he had never wanted to meet and the deaf father who had humiliated him as a child. As Warren wrote in "The Ballad of Billie Potts," the son must always return to the father, who often represents the flawed and fallen world which is our heritage.

WILDERNESS

The struggle between the ideal and the real in Warren's later novels is most explicit in *Wilderness: A Tale of the Civil War*, about an idealistic young Jew from Bavaria who comes to the United States to fight for the freedom of the slaves. When his father, a political prisoner in Berlin, dies, Adam Rosenzweig realizes that he has "lived only in the dream of his father's life, the father's manhood, the father's heroism." The trip to America is a way to star in his own heroic story. Adam's career in America is a progress in disillusionment; the telltale symbol of the compromising world of physical fact is his clubfoot, which he has desperately sought to hide in a specially constructed boot. If *World Enough and Time* is Warren's most complex treatment of idealism, *Wilderness* is his most direct treatment of this recurring subject, uncluttered by secondary themes or plots. Some critics prefer it for that reason, though it lacks the depth and humanity of Warren's earlier epic treatment of romantic idealism.

MEET ME IN THE GREEN GLEN

Meet Me in the Green Glen is a pastoral novel about the nature of love. The love of a homeless young Italian immigrant for a dowdy country wife begins with carnal passion devoid of any attempt to idealize sexual attraction. The ironically named Angelo has distinct similarities to Conrad's "natural man," Nostromo, who lives in the physical world with little thought of any other. In fact, Angelo protects himself from any really serious bond with Cassie, the frustrated wife of a paralyzed man, casting her in the more tawdry dream of "scarlet woman" with gifts of a tight red dress and cosmetics. Only at the last, when she pleads for his life in court by confessing to the murder of her husband, of which Angelo is accused, does he recognize a love that transcends the merely physical. Just as Adam in *Wilderness* becomes more human when he admits the strength of flawed reality, so Angelo becomes more human when he recognizes the strength of dreams. In spite of Cassie's confession, Angelo is condemned to die, because, in his ignorance of the racial situation, he violates the mores of the community. Cassie, unable to save her lover, drifts off in the dream-sea of ideas, forgetting the sordid elements of their affair and only retaining the dream that transcends the body's need.

In these and other episodes in his fiction, Warren showed his fascination with what he called, in his Conrad essay, "the Great Mirage." It is a dark vision which sees all human values as illusions, yet insists—with the passion that fueled six decades of creative work—that such illusions are necessary, and that humanity must continue to invent itself.

Katherine Snipes

OTHER MAJOR WORKS

SHORT FICTION: *Blackberry Winter*, 1946; *The Circus in the Attic and Other Stories*, 1947.

PLAYS: *Proud Flesh*, pr. 1947; *All the King's Men*, pr. 1958.

POETRY: *Thirty-Six Poems*, 1935; *Eleven Poems on the Same Theme*, 1942; *Selected Poems 1923-1943*, 1944; *Brother to Dragons: A Tale in Verse and Voices*, 1953; *Promises: Poems 1954-1956*, 1957; *You, Emperors, and Others: Poems 1957-1960*, 1960; *Selected Poems: New and Old, 1923-1966*, 1966; *Incarnations: Poems 1966-1968*, 1968; *Audubon: A Vision*, 1969; *Or Else—Poem/Poems 1968-1974*, 1974; *Selected Poems 1923-1975*, 1976; *Now and Then: Poems 1976-1978*, 1978; *Being Here: Poetry 1977-1980*, 1980; *Rumor Verified: Poems 1979-1980*, 1981; *Chief Joseph of the Nez Percé*, 1983; *New and Selected Poems 1923-1985*, 1985.

NONFICTION: *John Brown: The Making of a Martyr*, 1929; *Modern Rhetoric*, 1949 (with Cleanth Brooks); *Segregation: The Inner Conflict in the South*, 1956; *Selected Essays*, 1958; *The Legacy of the Civil War: Meditations on the Centennial*, 1961; *Who Speaks for the Negro?*, 1965; *Democracy and Poetry*, 1975; *Portrait of a Father*, 1988; *New and Selected Essays*, 1989.

EDITED TEXTS: *An Approach to Literature*, 1936 (with Cleanth Brooks and John Thibault Purser); *Understanding Poetry: An Anthology for College Students*, 1938 (with Brooks); *Understanding Fiction*, 1943 (with Brooks); *Faulkner: A Collection of Critical Essays*, 1966; *Randall Jarrell, 1914-1965*, 1967 (with Robert Lowell and Peter Taylor); *American Literature: The Makers and the Making*, 1973 (compiled by Warren, Brooks, and R. W. B. Lewis).

BIBLIOGRAPHY

Blotner, Joseph. *Robert Penn Warren: A Biography*. New York: Random House, 1997. Blotner's is the first of what will almost certainly be many biographies following Warren's death in 1989. Blotner began his work while Warren was still alive and had the good fortune to have the cooperation not only of his subject but also of the larger Warren family. Blotner's book is straightforward and chronological; it makes a good beginning.

Bohner, Charles. *Robert Penn Warren*. 1964. Rev. ed. Boston: Twayne, 1981. An excellent all-purpose introduction, divided into thematic sections with subdivisions. Provides a chronology, notes, and an index. Also includes a bibliography in which secondary sources receive brief summaries regarding their merit and suitability.

Burt, John. *Robert Penn Warren and American Idealism*. New Haven, Conn.: Yale University Press, 1988. Burt describes his work as traversing "regions" of Warren's work: the elegies, the narrative poems, and three major novels—*Night Rider, All the King's Men*, and *World Enough and Time*. What unifies these works, Burt maintains, is Warren's ambivalence about experience, an ambivalence endemic to American idealism.

Clark, William Bedford. *Critical Essays on Robert Penn Warren*. Boston: G. K. Hall, 1981. This study provides reviews, from *John Brown* (1929) to Harold Bloom on *Brother to Dragons: A New Version* (1979). Separate essays include James Justus showing how Warren has created a myth out of the figure of Samuel Taylor Coleridge's Ancient Mariner and Victor Strandberg demonstrating that Warren reconciles an awareness of evil with a Whitmanesque unity of being.

Gray, Richard, ed. *Robert Penn Warren: A Collection of Critical Essays*. Englewood Cliffs, N.J.: Prentice-Hall, 1980. Many of the essays in this collection date from the 1960's, and about two-thirds of them deal with Warren's novels. Represented in the volume are a number of recognized

Warren specialists, among them James Justus, Leonard Casper, and Victor Strandberg. A competent and comprehensive essay prefaces the volume, which contains a short bibliography helpful to the general student.

Ruppersburg, Hugh. *Robert Penn Warren and the American Imagination*. Athens: University of Georgia Press, 1990. Ruppersburg considers the Warren opus an attempt to define a national identity. He focuses, in particular, on *Brother to Dragons*, *Audubon: A Vision*, and *Chief Joseph of the Nez Percé*. Subscribing to Warren's notion that he was not a historical writer, Ruppersburg also attempts to place Warren in a contemporary context, emphasizing such modern American concerns as civil rights and nuclear warfare.

Walker, Marshall. *Robert Penn Warren: A Vision Earned*. New York: Barnes & Noble Books, 1979. Offers a comprehensive treatment of Warren's canon well into the seventh decade of his life. Discussion and analysis are provided for major and minor works as Walker traces the development of Warren's thought over a period of roughly fifty years, taking into consideration the contributions of a number of earlier critics. A chronology and a bibliography are attached.

FRANK WATERS

Born: Colorado Springs, Colorado; July 25, 1902
Died: Taos, New Mexico; June 3, 1995

PRINCIPAL LONG FICTION

Fever Pitch, 1930 (also known as *The Lizard Woman*)
The Wild Earth's Nobility, 1935
Below Grass Roots, 1937
The Dust Within the Rock, 1940
People of the Valley, 1941
River Lady, 1942 (with Houston Branch)
The Man Who Killed the Deer, 1942
The Yogi of Cockroach Court, 1947

Diamond Head, 1948 (with Branch)
The Woman at Otowi Crossing, 1966
Pike's Peak: A Family Saga, 1971 (completely rewritten, one-volume novel based on *The Wild Earth's Nobility*, *Below Grass Roots*, and *The Dust Within the Rock*)
Flight from Fiesta, 1986

OTHER LITERARY FORMS

In addition to his long fiction, Frank Waters wrote a number of books which combine history, ethnography, mythology, and speculative essay. All of these are centered in the American Southwest, and all deal, in whole or in part, with American Indian subjects. Of these, *Book of the Hopi* (1963) comes closest to ethnography in the strict sense, being the actual Hopi versions of their mythology, ritual, and belief, which Waters recorded from the words of tribal spokesmen. *Masked Gods: Navaho and Pueblo Ceremonialism* (1950) covers analogous material in relation to the Navaho and Pueblo tribes, and contains substantial sections in which these traditional beliefs are compared to the teachings of the Far East (particularly Tibetan Buddhism) and with the findings of nuclear scientists. *Pumpkin Seed Point: Being Within the Hopi* (1969) is a personal account of Waters's three-year residence among the Hopi, while he was compiling material for *Book of the Hopi*. *Mexico Mystique: The Coming Sixth World of Consciousness* (1975) treats the history, myth, and science (particularly calendrical) of Mexico. *Mountain Dialogues* (1981) is more eclectic in style, a series of essays ranging in subject matter from the relation of mind and matter to the bipolar symbolism reflected in the land around Waters's New Mexico home.

Waters's three biographies all deal with Western subjects: *Midas of the Rockies: The Story of Stratton and Cripple Creek* (1937) is the biography of Winfield Scott Stratton; *To Possess the Land* (1973) is the biography of Arthur Rockford Manby. *The Earp Brothers of Tombstone* (1960) is based on the recollections of Mrs. Virgil Earp and material from Waters's own research.

In 1946, Waters published *The Colorado* as part of the Rivers of America series (Farrar and Rinehart), and in 1964, an art monograph, *Leon Gaspard*. From 1950 to 1956, he was a regular contributor to the *Saturday Review* with reviews of books about the West. Numerous periodicals contain his essays on ethnography, history, and literary criticism, as well as a few short stories.

ACHIEVEMENTS

Waters gave the American Southwest its finest and most complete literary rendering. In both his fiction and his nonfiction, he sought to give literary vitality to the "spirit of place" imbuing that section of the American continent and to show how this spirit variously affects the different races who live there, finding its expression in mythology, lifestyle, architecture, and ritual, all reflecting, in their different ways, the "vibratory quality of the land itself." Whether he portrays life by presenting the facts of history (as in his nonfiction), or in the symbols of his novels, or whether he writes about the mythological realm which occupies the zone between the two, his work captures the deep resonance of his locale, and thus the significance of place, per se, to people's development.

Waters is probably best known for his work on and about American Indians, and he was one of the few writers whose work has earned the respect of both the literary establishment and the American Indian communities. He was also one of the few writers who could work successfully both in ethnography and in prose fiction. His firsthand knowledge of the Indian tribes of the Southwest and his deep respect for their traditions and their instinctual attunement to their locale made it possible for Waters to write about these matters without romanticism, and thus to reveal not only the rugged dignity of their lives but also the value of their wisdom.

Thus, *The Man Who Killed the Deer*, Waters's most popular novel, has long been recognized as a classic in the literature on the Native American, just as *Book of the Hopi* is a landmark in ethnography. In the late twentieth century, the relevance and quality of his other work resulted in a greater degree of recognition, made tangible by the republication of much of his fiction.

BIOGRAPHY

Frank Waters was born on July 25, 1902, and spent most of his childhood and youth in Colorado Springs. These years provided much of the material for his early novels *The Wild Earth's Nobility, Below Grass Roots*, and *The Dust Within the Rock* and consequently for their revised version, *Pike's Peak*. Waters's grandfather became the model for Joseph Rogier, the main character of these books, and Waters's boyhood experience in the Cripple Creek mining camps provided much of the background. His experiences as an engineering student at Colorado College (from 1922 to 1925) and as a day laborer in the Salt Creek oil fields are also incorporated into these early novels.

After his work at Salt Creek, Waters traveled to California, where he was employed by the telephone company in the border town of Calexico-Mexicali. It was there, among imported Chinese laborers, opium dens, and general degradation, that he came across Tai Ling, who became the protagonist of *The Yogi of Cockroach Court*. This novel was actually drafted before the above-mentioned Colorado novels, but technical problems prevented its completion until some years later.

The move to California marks a dividing line in Waters's treatment of his material. The personal experiences from before the move went into novels of a semiautobiographical nature. Those which drew their material from after the move were not autobiographical, though they continued to draw their characters from people Waters knew, their settings from places where he had lived, and even their incidents from actual events. (The ending of *The Yogi of Cockroach Court*, for example, was taken directly from newspaper accounts.)

Waters moved to the town of Mora in the Sangre de Cristo Mountains of New Mexico. There he wrote *The Dust Within the Rock* and planned *People of the Valley*, drawing again on his youth in Colorado. The latter novel takes its material from the Mora locale, an isolated valley that is inaccessible for most of the year and which was settled by Spanish-speaking people from Mexico. It was in Mora, too, that Waters witnessed the rituals of the Penitente cult, which he incorporated into the novel.

After leaving Mora, Waters moved to Taos. From there, in the late 1930's, he drew the material (again, based on actual events) for *The Man Who Killed the Deer* and later for two nonfiction works, *Masked Gods* and *Mountain Dialogues*. He continued to make Taos his home, returning there after the war and working as editor for *El Crepusculo*, a local Spanish-English newspaper; he also worked from 1953 to 1956 as an information consultant at the Los Alamos Scientific Laboratory. These latter two positions are reflected in *The Woman at Otowi Crossing*, though it is evident from *Masked Gods*, published sixteen years earlier, that Waters had long been concerned with the curious juxtaposition of atomic research facilities and Indian kivas in the Four Corners area.

In 1977 Waters was married to Barbara Hayes; thereafter the couple divided their time between homes in Taos and Tucson, Arizona. In his later years Waters devoted his attention principally to the writing of nonfiction; he died on June 3, 1995.

ANALYSIS

The writing of Frank Waters is always concerned with the bipolar tensions which underlie human existence: male and female, reason and instinct, conscious and unconscious, progress and tradition, linear and nonlinear, matter and energy (or spirit). His fictional characters are involved in efforts to reconcile these polarities, either within themselves or in the world of events. The search for reconciliation is inseparable from what Waters called "the spirit of place," for once one is able to embody the unconscious rhythms of one's locale, one may move more completely toward the reconciliation of bipolar tensions.

In another sense, his work is a continuing attempt to give literary expression to this spirit of place. Viewed sociologically, his novels show how this spirit imbues the various racial types of the Southwest. The spirit of place is found in the blood, is experienced as a "blood-power" from which one can never quite break free. Because of these instinctual or biological ramifications, the novels about "racial types" are not mere sociological studies, but expressions of a spiritual search.

Waters said that the three novels *People of the Valley, The Man Who Killed the Deer*, and *The Yogi of Cockroach Court* express his interest in the racial types of the West: the Spanish or Mexican, the Native American, and the mestizos, or those of mixed blood. *The Woman at Otowi Crossing*, which deals primarily with Caucasians, completes this study of racial types. *Pike's Peak: A Family Saga* portrays the mingling of various racial types, but here Pike's Peak itself is portrayed as an active agent.

Thus, this late novel makes graphic what in the previous novels was a subtle but powerful undercurrent: In all of Waters's work, the earth itself plays a dominant role. It is the matrix which reconciles polarity. Fruitful and destructive by turns, benevolent or menacing, it resists people's efforts at domination or comprehension, yet demands of them that continuing process of individuation which is inseparable from the reconciliation of polarity. The earth, the source of life, embodies a mystery which cannot be overcome but must be understood through faith. As the beginning and end of people's essential polarities (such as life and death, summer and winter), it is both a material fact and a rhythmic energy with which one must be in harmony.

Harmony, however, does not indicate a static equilibrium. Waters's novels end with reconciliation, yet the reconciliation leads to ongoing movement. As Waters points out in an explication of the Nahuatl hieroglyph "Ollin" ("Movement"), the tension between dualities results in movement. This movement is found not only in the processes of the natural world but also inside the heart of people. This ancient Nahuatl concept is reflected in all of Waters's novels. The central reconciliation is in the human heart, as the characters attempt to find that harmony in movement that enables them to be part of the great pattern of Creation.

PEOPLE OF THE VALLEY

People of the Valley was Waters's first nonautobiographical novel to be published. The most obvious social polarity—progress and tradition—is the main impetus of the plot. The government is going to build a dam which will uproot all the people of the Beautiful Blue Valley. The name is significant: The color blue symbolizes the abiding faith of the people in their traditional ways and in the faithful fruitfulness of the valley itself. (This symbolic use of the color blue returns in other novels, most notably *The Man Who Killed the Deer*, where Dawn Lake, the center of the Pueblo religious life, is referred to as the "Blue Eye of Faith.") In this period, when their faith is threatened, the people of the valley look to Maria, a local bruja, for her reaction and her strength, her wisdom and her faith.

Maria has been in the Beautiful Blue Valley for as long as anyone can remember and has become, in the minds of its inhabitants, synonymous with the valley itself. She knows its secrets and its cures and has lived through its periods of fruitfulness and flood. She is, then, an embodiment of the spirit of place; by turns, she is a goad and a comfort, a shrewd business-woman and a prophet. As the story progresses (a chapter is devoted to each period of her life), it becomes clear why she is the repository of the implicit faith of the people: She is trusted because of her own implicit trust in the earth, in the essential trustworthiness of its rhythms, even of its floods. Because she accepts the earth in all of its many moods, she is the spokesperson for its wisdom. Like the earth, she can be sharp and repelling, or healing and comforting. Like the earth, she accepts all who come to her, whether as lovers, questioners, or even husbands. Within change, however, she abides in a faith that grows, year by year.

In addition, Maria makes the welfare of the earth—of the valley—synonymous with her own welfare. She has reconciled the duality of self and other by making her own wealth inseparable from that of the valley, and hence of its people. The clearest example of this comes from her early life, when, destitute, she survived by gathering discarded wheat-seed from the local fields. This seed she divided into superior and inferior. The latter she used for food; the former she kept until spring, when she would trade it for a double measure to be collected at the next harvest. This process she repeated yearly. Because she kept the best seed for replanting, the wealth of the valley's wheat increased; because she received a double measure at harvest, her own wealth increased as well. Her

wealth, however, was never monetary; rather, it was in the natural yield of the earth, and in the faith that such a yield is sufficient for all purposes.

In the end, it is this faith that makes Maria significant. Faith, too, is the essence of the people of the valley, and of their traditions. Without such faith, life there is not possible. This faith, as she points out, is not a concept, but a baptism into life itself, into the rhythmic experience of harmony, which comes from giving oneself wholly to the spirit and energy of one's locale, the spirit of place. The significance of the dam is that it stops the flow of faith, which is likened to water. Faith refreshes life and gives it meaning; the dam causes stagnation, a break in natural rhythms. The example of Maria shows, however, that if one's faith is deep enough, it will not be disrupted by surface events. In the end, this faith is in the heart, and what one sees in the external world corresponds to one's inner nature.

THE MAN WHO KILLED THE DEER

The idea of faith carries over into Waters's next novel, *The Man Who Killed the Deer*. Whereas Maria had grown slowly into her faith, and had never been torn from it, Martiniano must find a faith within the exacerbated polarities of his nature. The disruptions of progress had not come to Maria until she was an old woman; they come to Martiniano during his formative years. Because of this, his search is one of finding what he has lost, not simply deepening what he already knows.

Half Apache and half Pueblo, Martiniano's mixed blood indicates the duality of his nature, the spirit of independence and rebellion opposed to the spirit of acceptance and harmony. Sent away to a government school at an early age and thus deprived of his initiation into the kiva at the proper age, Martiniano must be taught to find harmony, not only with his world but also within himself, where the pole of masculine independence has not recognized the pole of the female imperative.

The story of the novel is, on the surface, a simple one. Martiniano has killed a deer out of season, against regulations of the United States government as it is against those of the pueblo. The matter seems simple, but as the story unfolds, it becomes clear that the apparently simple event has many layers. It is not so much that Martiniano has broken the white person's law, but that his insistence on his own independence of action indicates an inner disharmony and a lack of wisdom. It indicates, finally, a lack of connection with the mystery of life itself. In place of this connection is a belief that a person can be free when alone, when cut off from society or the earth, from the source of faith, symbolized by the lake in the mountains above the pueblo, "The Blue Eye of Faith," the center of the pueblo's religious-ceremonial life.

The deer that Martiniano has killed becomes for him a totem, appearing to him in various places and guises to demonstrate that there is something in his situation that he cannot defeat by confrontation, something that he first must understand, to which he must submit. Eventually, the deer appears in his wife, Flowers Playing; as she grows with child, with the mystery of life, Martiniano begins to lose connection with her.

Martiniano learns, slowly, that even his own sense of manhood is held in bondage to the feminine part of his being and that until he reconciles this polarity, he will never feel fully alive. This is best symbolized by the description of the Deer Dance (in a passage found in both *The Man Who Killed the Deer* and *Masked Gods: Navaho and Pueblo Ceremonialism*). Flowers Playing is one of the Deer Mothers in the ceremony, the embodiment of the mystery of organic life. The Deer Dance symbolizes how the male force of independence and escape is held bondage, unwillingly but necessarily, by "the female imperative," the rhythms of Earth that are deeper than the ego. The dance offers another vantage on the spirit of place, here appearing as the "blood power" from which people can never break free and upon which they are dependent for the development of wisdom.

There is another sense in which Martiniano's action was not done in isolation: His killing of the deer has repercussions that are felt in the wider sphere of politics. It has made more difficult the pueblo's case for restoration of Dawn Lake. As the pueblo elders point out again and again, one person's action is like a pebble dropped into a pool; the ripples extend far beyond the action itself. The effort of the elders en-

ables Martiniano to see that much wider whole, of which he is an integral part and without which he is an incomplete human being.

The pueblo elders embody a different way of knowing from that of the white race which has control of the lake. The polarity is rational-linear opposing nonrational, nonlinear. The method of the elders is intuitive, and, while it does not deny the validity of rational methods (any more than the female imperative denies the validity of the male drive for independence), it does indicate a deeper level of wisdom. The elders know the eventual result of their legal disputes over Dawn Lake far before these results come over the telegraph, even when all indications (relayed, of course, over the telegraph) point to the futility of their case.

To the elders—as, it seems, to Waters himself—linear or rational knowledge is not as encompassing or effective as the more intuitive method which comes so naturally to the Indians. The difference between these two methods of knowing is a duality to which Waters returns in later books, particularly *The Woman at Otowi Crossing*. It is interesting to note, in this context, that just as the pueblo elders correctly predicted that they would regain their Dawn Lake, so Waters himself, in his novel, predicted the actual political event; for just as in the novel the Native Americans regain rights to their lake, so, thirty years later, did they do so in fact, through a congressional decision in December of 1970.

THE YOGI OF COCKROACH COURT

Waters's next novel, *The Yogi of Cockroach Court*, takes the working of polarities one step further to juxtapose Eastern mysticism (particularly Buddhist) to life in a Mexican border town. Sociologically, Waters is here concerned with the mestizo culture. Barby is an example of this type. Orphaned as a child, he is brought up by Tai Ling, who runs a small shop, The Lamp Awake, beside the prostitute district, Cockroach Court. The name of the shop itself introduces the duality of light and dark, associated respectively with the clarity of the mind and the darkness of the senses. Tai Ling is repeatedly pictured meditating by his lamp, amid the swirl of a violent, dark world.

Barby and Guadalupe (Barby's lover, and another person of mixed blood) cannot detach themselves from that dark world, which to Tai Ling is the result of blindness, the working out of karma. Their relationship is a tempestuous one, fueled by Barby's impotent desire for control. This impotence results from Barby's rootless feeling of inferiority, from his inner division. Where Barby is at the mercy of his internal division, Guadalupe is at the mercy of external ones. In the daytime, she is alive in the absorption in her own physical vitality; at night, she comes under the domination of Barby.

These complexities are interwoven with the life of Tai Ling, whose lamp illumines the darkness of the physical world in which he sits, even as his search for a way to transcend the play of polarities illumines the darkness of his mind. Inherent in Tai Ling's search for transcendence, however, is yet another polarity: The life of transcendence is itself polarized with life in a physical body. In this way, Tai Ling is still involved in duality, or karma, and in the end, just as Barby cannot dominate Guadalupe except in darkness, so Tai Ling cannot subdue the ongoing karma of the physical world until the darkness of death surrounds him.

Both Barby and Tai Ling bring about their own deaths by attempts to conquer the physical world. The difference between them is nevertheless a significant one: Barby dies while blinded by passion, aggression, and ignorance; Tai Ling, whose mind is clearer, finally sees and accepts his inner polarity, accepts his karma and his situation, and sees the folly of trying to transcend the world by separating oneself from it. Tai Ling, therefore, achieves a reconciliation, and though it comes at the moment of death, there is great hope in it, as Tai Ling finally comes to a unity with his world, comes to true knowledge.

Tai Ling's realization is not a rational one. He uses rationality to dissect his ego, but his realization is intuitive. He speaks of the difference between those who see that life's journey is a spiral and those whose vision is so limited that the curve of the spiral seems a straight line. To people of unconsidered action, whose vision is limited to the rational, horizontal plane, all seems linear, not cyclic. The person of contemplation, however, sees the nonlinear nature of things which underlies the linear but does not negate it. Thus, the treatment of two ways of knowing is here given an additional perspective.

The Yogi of Cockroach Court was published in 1947. *The Woman at Otowi Crossing*, Waters's next novel, was published in 1966. The intervening years saw the publication of *Masked Gods, The Earp Brothers of Tombstone: The Story of Mrs. Virgil Earp, Leon Gaspard*, and *Book of the Hopi*. In addition, Waters had worked as the editor of a local newspaper and at the Los Alamos Scientific Laboratory as a consultant. His deepening knowledge of and feeling for Pueblo traditions, as well as his firsthand knowledge of the activities at Los Alamos, are both brought to expression in the later novel.

THE WOMAN AT OTOWI CROSSING

The Woman at Otowi Crossing deals primarily with Anglos and thus completes the cycle of novels dealing with racial types. It also brings many of Waters's concerns into a contemporary focus. As in previous books, the action develops out of the tension between polarities. The developing, intuitive awareness of Helen Chalmers is juxtaposed to the development of the atomic bomb on the mesa above her. Both developments signal people's evolutionary potential, and both involve the unification of matter and energy.

Helen Chalmers has come from a broken marriage to operate a small teahouse at the edge of Pueblo Indian land. Coincident with the beginning of the Los Alamos Research Laboratory—called "The Project"—she discovers a growth on her breast. Her assumption that it is cancerous, and the resultant immediacy of death, triggers in her a chain reaction of explosively expanding awareness, an explosion which radically alters her view of the world around her and her relationship with it.

The scene of Helen's discovery ends with Facundo, a member of the pueblo kiva, tossing pebbles against her window. The moment is significant, for in the kiva, the American Indians continue their attempt to understand and ensure the unity of matter with energy, or spirit. Facundo's response to Helen's condition is one of immediate comprehension, but his response is undramatic. He simply points to the sun, the source of life, empowered by the same unity of energy and matter that the people of the project seek to harness. Facundo's emphasis, however, is on the presence of that process, that reality, in each moment.

Thus, Helen's task becomes what will eventually become the task of everyone: to integrate her newfound knowledge with the tangible events of her life. The discovery of the bomb requires the same integration; the two discoveries together create a new world order in which one must learn to live. Again, the methods of the Native Americans point the way to reconciliation, for they have shown how the development of insight and the knowledge of the unity of matter and spirit can be integrated into, and are in fact a necessary part of, a stable, viable society.

Waters draws a number of additional parallels between the activities of the Pueblo kiva and those of the project. Both are shrouded in secrecy, and both have their selected initiates who take on new identities vis-à-vis the rest of their society. (Members of the kiva take on the identity of cosmic forces; men of the project take on new, common names: Niels Bohr becomes Nicholas Baker.) Both kiva and project exclude women, and in both there is an attempt to empower the mystery of life, to make use of the unity within the duality represented by matter and energy, matter and spirit. (These parallels echo Waters's speculations in *Masked Gods*, where he writes of the common search of all people, whether in a Tibetan monastery, an Indian kiva, or an atomic research laboratory.)

Along with these parallels, however, the book demonstrates obvious differences as well. Primary among these is that the rituals of the Pueblo are to ensure the ongoing life of all creatures, whereas the activity of the project is directed toward death. The method of the kiva, being intuitive and nonrational, includes and embraces polarity, whereas the method of the project, being rational, divides one entity from another. Even this polarity, however, can result in a reconciliation, not in the external world, necessarily, but within the individual heart. The scientists involved in creating the bomb are presented in warm,

human terms. Gaylord, a young scientist and the lover of Helen Chalmers's daughter, comes to a more intuitive, even mystical awareness as a result of his exposure to radiation.

PIKE'S PEAK

Pike's Peak is a kind of summing up of Waters's work. This may be understood literally, because the novel is a rewritten and shortened version of three early novels, the titles of which are retained as major divisions of the new novel. It may also be understood symbolically, because in its panoramic scope, *Pike's Peak* encompasses many of Waters's lifelong concerns.

Joseph Rogier, the protagonist, is largely a fictionalized version of Waters's grandfather; Waters himself, like the character March (grandson of Rogier and part Native American), spent much of his youth in the mining camps of Cripple Creek, went to college as an engineering student, and worked in the Salt Creek oil fields. The novel transcends the category of autobiographical fiction, however, because of Waters's use of symbolism, in particular that of Pike's Peak itself, which stands as both tangible fact and intangible symbol. A mystery to be understood, an ungraspable meaning which one feels impelled to grasp, it stands at the borderline between the conscious and the unconscious, at once numinous and tangible.

The peak both draws and repels Rogier, who seeks within it for its golden heart. The pull is irresistible, and in his effort to plumb the peak, Rogier slowly lets go of all his social responsibilities. His building firm deteriorates, his family becomes neardestitute; he loses the respect of the community and becomes an object of mockery. His search is an obsession, not for mere gold, and not for riches (though he is not above their temptation), but for the symbolic golden heart, within himself as it is within Pike's Peak, shining in the center of the dense granite, or in the center of the flesh.

The method of his search combines the rational and the irrational. The obsession is irrational, and at its service he places his considerable rational gifts and material wealth. Yet, despite his knowledge of engineering and geology, he cannot strike a significant vein, while men of lesser knowledge, and without his material resources, make seemingly lucky strikes, literally at the drop of a hat. Rogier's situation has parallels to that of Martiniano, for he, like Rogier, finds something in his search that he cannot conquer by rational means or external manipulation. Rogier's attempts to find gold—symbolic or literal—lead him increasingly deeper into darkness and isolation. Like the deer for Martiniano, the peak for Rogier becomes a sort of totem, appearing as a lure, as a guide, or as an obstacle—a truth he cannot grasp, but which is constantly within his sight.

The tragedy of Rogier is that his view of the world is linear. As a miner, he has literal and symbolic tunnel vision. By going straight ahead, mining a vertical shaft, he hopes to find the essence of the mystery symbolized by the mountain itself. Its apparent tangibility as real gold draws him irresistibly, but Rogier's linear viewpoint blinds him to the world around him, isolating him from the sympathies and understanding of his family. His search for truth takes place at the expense of human warmth and community, and he finds, as does Martiniano, that such obsessive pride—even if it seems to be a search for truth—is doomed to futility. Where Martiniano is finally able to understand his folly and arrange for his son to enter the kiva and so live in the harmony it had taken him so long to achieve, Rogier dies in psychological isolation, unable to release his passion into genuine human community.

For all that, however, the tragedy contains a triumph. March, Rogier's grandson, carries on a search encompassing many of Rogier's ideals. Of mixed blood, March shows promise of reconciling the intuitive ways of his American Indian blood with the rational methods of his grandfather. Despite himself, Rogier has passed on to March a profound respect for depth and knowledge; one feels for him a deep sympathy, because for all his gruffness, even his selfishness, he has somehow managed to give March a profound respect for enduring value and the determination to search for it, for the enduring gold within the dense rock of material being.

The search for eternal value in the midst of flux is a final polarity. Tai Ling sought it in his meditation,

Maria found it in her inseparability from natural cycles; even Martiniano found it by acquiescing to the Pueblo's ways. For Helen Chalmers, the search was for a way to integrate eternal value into the apparently mundane particulars of everyday living. Thus, even the discovery of eternal verities is not a final resting point. The eternal is continually juxtaposed to and interwoven with the mundane, and just as the action of the novels is given impetus by this polarity, so the movement of the world both rises from it and expresses it. As each new layer is peeled off, new polarities emerge.

Waters's writing reveals an attempt to penetrate and illuminate these symbolic and literal layers, and to find within movement the enduring values of human life. His characters seek these values within the temporal, within enduring change, the first cause and final truth. Thus, in Waters's novels, the Nahuatl hieroglyph "Ollin" comes to literary expression: that eternal movement comes from the tension between polarities. The reconciliation between polarities is found in the movement of tangible existence—in concrete substance, not abstract form; in the harmony within activity that expresses harmony with greater cycles, such as those of society, of one's locale, or of the earth. In this sense, the expression of the spirit of place is an expression of the unity of humankind, for all are subject to the same enduring, cyclic existence. In a wider sense, Waters's writing is rightly considered mystical, concerned with the oneness of people with others, with the earth, with all that exists.

Tim Lyons

OTHER MAJOR WORKS

NONFICTION: *Midas of the Rockies: The Story of Stratton and Cripple Creek*, 1937; *The Colorado*, 1946; *Masked Gods: Navaho and Pueblo Ceremonialism*, 1950; *The Earp Brothers of Tombstone: The Story of Mrs. Virgil Earp*, 1960; *Book of the Hopi*, 1963; *Leon Gaspard*, 1964; *Pumpkin Seed Point: Being Within the Hopi*, 1969; *To Possess the Land: A Biography of Arthur Rockford Manby*, 1973; *Mexico Mystique: The Coming Sixth World of Consciousness*, 1975; *Mountain Dialogues*, 1981; *Brave Are My People: Indian Heroes Not Forgotten*, 1993.

BIBLIOGRAPHY

Blackburn, Alexander. *A Sunrise Brighter Still: The Visionary Novels of Frank Waters*. Athens: Ohio University Press, 1991. Chapters on each of Waters's novels, with an introduction that surveys the writer's purposes and his career and a conclusion arguing that Waters is a major American writer. Includes detailed notes and extensive bibliography.

Davis, Jack L. "The Whorf Hypothesis and Native American Literature." *South Dakota Review* 14 (Summer, 1976): 59-72. Benjamin Lee Whorf's notion of linguistic relativity, that perception is determined by the structure of language, is tested by analyzing Waters's *The Man Who Killed the Deer* in comparison to N. Scott Momaday's *House Made of Dawn*. Waters's plot represents the great gap between white and Native American cultures and parallels Whorf's conclusion drawn from a study of Hopi language. The difference between Whorf and Waters is Waters's emphasis on the nonverbal dimensions of pueblo consciousness which become mystical and communal. Like Momaday, Waters believes that great change is required for Western civilization to discover a fellowship through the nonverbal experience in pueblo culture.

Deloria, Vine, Jr., ed. *Frank Waters: Man and Mystic*. Athens: Ohio University Press, 1993. Memoirs of Waters and commentaries on his novels, emphasizing his prophetic style and sense of the sacred.

Hoy, Christopher. "The Archetypal Transformation of Martiniano in *The Man Who Killed the Deer.*" *South Dakota Review* 13 (Winter, 1975-1976): 43-56. The character Martiniano must undergo a fundamental psychological change to reconcile the conflict between his newly acquired white values and his native ones, which occurs when he tries to return to his pueblo culture. This change can be explained in reference to the archetype of the Great Mother, as developed by Carl Jung and Erich Neumann.

Lyon, Thomas J. *Frank Waters*. New York: Twayne, 1973. Fills a critical vacuum by analyzing Waters's themes and artistic style. After sketching Waters's life, Lyon examines his nonfiction, showing him to be a writer of ideas with a sacred theory of the earth and Hopi mythic values. Focuses on seven novels as narrations of these ideas, from *Fever Pitch* to *Pike's Peak*, and also discusses his minor works, including the biography of *The Earp Brothers of Tombstone*, the children's biography of Robert Gilruth, his book reviews, and his essays on writing. The last chapter summarizes the book's thesis and calls for more study of Waters's work. Contains a chronology, notes and references, a selected annotated bibliography, and an index.

Malpezzi, Frances. "A Study of the Female Protagonist in Frank Waters' *People of the Valley* and Rudolfo Anaya's *Bless Me, Ultima*." *South Dakota Review* 14 (Summer, 1976): 102-110. These two novels portray stereotypical *machismo* cultures and also present positive images of women, such as Maria in *People of the Valley*. Maria is respected for her authority and power, grows stronger with age, and displays dignity in her acceptance of death. She arranges the migration of her people and prepares her own spiritual migration. A heroic and inspiring person, Maria is an example of an androgynous character liberated from stereotype.

South Dakota Review 15 (Autumn, 1977). A special Frank Waters issue, containing the essays: "The Sound of Space," by John Milton; "Frank Waters' *Mexico Mystique*: The Ontology of the Occult," by Jack L. Davis; "Frank Waters and the Visual Sense," by Robert Kostka; "Frank Waters and the Concept of 'Nothing Special,'" by Thomas J. Lyon; "Teaching *Yoga* in Las Vegas," by Charles L. Adams; "Frank Waters and the Mountain Spirit," by Quay Grigg; "The Conflict in *The Man Who Killed the Deer*," by Christopher Hoy; "Mysticism and Witchcraft," by Waters; and "Frank Waters," by John Manchester.

EVELYN WAUGH

Born: London, England; October 28, 1903
Died: Combe Florey, England; April 10, 1966

PRINCIPAL LONG FICTION

Decline and Fall, 1928

Vile Bodies, 1930

Black Mischief, 1932

A Handful of Dust, 1934

Scoop, 1938

Put Out More Flags, 1942

Brideshead Revisited, 1945, 1959

Scott-King's Modern Europe, 1947

The Loved One, 1948

Helena, 1950

Men at Arms, 1952

Love Among the Ruins: A Romance of the Near Future, 1953

Officers and Gentlemen, 1955

The Ordeal of Gilbert Pinfold, 1957

The End of the Battle, 1961 (also known as *Unconditional Surrender*)

Basil Seal Rides Again: Or, The Rake's Regress, 1963

Sword of Honour, 1965 (includes *Men at Arms*, *Officers and Gentlemen*, and *The End of the Battle*)

(Library of Congress)

OTHER LITERARY FORMS

Evelyn Waugh wrote seven travel books, three biographies, an autobiography, and numerous articles and reviews. The only completed section of Waugh's planned three-volume autobiography, *A Little Learning* (1964), discusses his life at Oxford and his employment as a schoolmaster in Wales—subjects fictionalized in *Brideshead Revisited* and *Decline and Fall*. The autobiographical background for virtually all of Waugh's novels is evident in his travel books, his diaries, and his letters. His articles and reviews for English and American periodicals include a wide range of topics—politics, religion, and art—and contribute to his reputation as a literary snob, an attitude Waugh himself affected, especially in the 1940's and 1950's.

ACHIEVEMENTS

Waugh was esteemed primarily as a satirist, especially for his satires on the absurdly chaotic world of the 1920's and 1930's. His ability to make darkly

humorous the activities of the British upper class, his comic distance, and his vivid, at times brutal, satire made his early novels very popular among British and American literary circles. His shift to a more sentimental theme in *Brideshead Revisited* gave Waugh his first real taste of broad popular approval—especially in America—to which he reacted with sometime real, sometime exaggerated, snobbishness. Waugh's conservative bias after the war, his preoccupation with religious themes, and his expressed distaste for the "age of the common man" suggested to a number of critics that he had lost his satiric touch. Although his postwar novels lack the anarchic spirit of his earliest works, he is still regarded, even by those who reject his political attitudes, as a first-rate craftsman of the comic novel.

BIOGRAPHY

Evelyn Arthur St. John Waugh was born in Hampstead, a suburb of London, in 1903 to Arthur and Catherine Waugh. He attended Lancing College from 1917 to 1924 and Hertford College, Oxford, from

1921 to 1924, from which he left without taking a degree. Although Waugh turned to writing novels only after aborted careers as a draftsman, a schoolmaster, and a journalist, his family background was literary; his father directed Chapman and Hall publishers until 1929, and his older brother Alec published his first novel, *The Loom of Youth*, in 1917.

Waugh's years at Oxford and his restless search for employment during the 1920's brought him experiences which were later fictionalized in several of his novels. After leaving Oxford in 1924, he enrolled in the Heatherley School of Fine Art, where he aspired to be a draftsman; later in that year, he was apprenticed to a printer for a brief period. His employment as a schoolmaster in Wales in 1925 and in Buckinghamshire in 1926 formed the background for his first novel, *Decline and Fall*. His struggle to establish himself as a writer and his participation in the endless parties of London's aristocratic youth during the last years of the 1920's are fictionalized in his second novel, *Vile Bodies*.

In 1927, Waugh was engaged to Evelyn Gardner and, despite the objections of her family, married her in 1928 when his financial prospects seemed more secure after the publication of his life of Dante Gabriel Rossetti and his first novel. In 1929, while Waugh was working in seclusion on *Vile Bodies*, his wife announced that she was having an affair; the couple, temperamentally unsuited to each other, were divorced that year.

The next seven years of Waugh's life were a period of activity and travel. Two trips to Africa in 1930 and 1931 resulted in a travel book and provided Waugh with the background of *Black Mischief*. A journey through Brazil and British Guiana in 1932 resulted in another travel book and his fourth novel, *A Handful of Dust*. In addition, Waugh traveled to the Arctic and once more to Africa; he was a correspondent for the London *Times*, reviewed books for *The Spectator*, and wrote a biography of Edmund Campion, a British-Catholic martyr. During this unsettled period, Waugh converted to Roman Catholicism in 1930, an event which provided much of the stability of his later life. In 1933, he met Laura Herbert, a Catholic, whom he married in 1937, after securing an annulment of his previous marriage from the Catholic Church.

Waugh's experiences during World War II are fictionalized in *Put Out More Flags* and the *Sword of Honour* trilogy. After several months unsuccessfully seeking military employment, Waugh joined the Royal Marines in 1939 and was part of an ineffectual assault on Dakar in 1940. Later in 1940, Waugh joined a commando unit with which he served in the Middle East, taking part in the battle of Crete in 1942. In 1943, after an injury in parachute training, Waugh was forced to resign from the commandos, and, in 1944, he was granted military leave to write *Brideshead Revisited*. In the last year of the war, he served as a liaison officer with the British Military Mission in Yugoslavia, where he struggled against the persecution of Roman Catholics by the partisan government.

Waugh's life from 1945 to 1954 was relatively stable. The success of *Brideshead Revisited*, a Book of the Month Club selection in America, brought him moderate financial security and several offers from filmmakers. Although none of these film offers materialized, they resulted in the trip to Hollywood in 1947 that inspired *The Loved One*, and in several commissioned articles for *Life*. During this nine-year period, Waugh published four short novels and the first volume of the World War II trilogy. In the first three months of 1954, on a voyage to Ceylon, Waugh suffered the mental breakdown that he later fictionalized in *The Ordeal of Gilbert Pinfold*.

Waugh led a relatively reclusive life during the last ten years, avoiding the public contact that had made him notorious earlier. In this period, he finished the war trilogy and published a biography of Ronald Knox, another travel book on Africa, the first volume of his autobiography, a revision of *Brideshead Revisited*, and the recension of the war trilogy into a single volume; he also began several other projects which were never completed. Waugh died on Easter Day in 1966.

ANALYSIS

Evelyn Waugh's novels are distinguished by the narrative detachment with which they survey the madness and chaos of the modern age. His characters participate in a hopeless, often brutal, struggle for stability which hardens them to the absurdities of civilization and leads them, ultimately, to an unheroic retreat from the battle of life. Ironic detachment, thus, is Waugh's principal comic technique and his principal theme as well.

Because each of Waugh's novels reflects actual experiences, the nature of this detachment changes through the course of his career. In his early works, which satirize the havoc and instability of the 1920's and 1930's, he achieves comic detachment by splicing together the savage and the settled, the careless and the care-ridden, the comic and the tragic. Victims and victimizers alike are caught in the whirlwind of madness. Waugh's satiric method changes in his postwar novels: Comically ineffectual characters still wage battle against the absurdities of life, but one is more aware of their struggle to maintain or recapture spiritual and moral values amid the absurdity. Waugh maintains comic distance in these novels by recommending a quiet sort of spiritual heroism as the only source of people's happiness in the uncertain postwar world.

DECLINE AND FALL

Waugh's first novel, *Decline and Fall*, traces the misadventures of Paul Pennyfeather, a temperate, unassuming student of theology at Scone College, Oxford. He is "sent down" for indecent behavior when drunken members of the university's most riotous (and, ironically, most aristocratic) club assault him, forcing him to run the length of the quadrangle without his trousers. Like Voltaire's Candide, Pennyfeather is an innocent victim temperamentally ill suited for the world into which he is thrust. Indeed, *Decline and Fall* owes much to *Candide* (1759): its Menippean satire, its cyclical "resurrection" of secondary characters, and the hero's ultimate resignation from life.

The action itself provides a thin framework for Waugh's satire on modern life. Pennyfeather finds employment, as Waugh himself did, as a schoolmaster in Wales—the only occupation, Pennyfeather is told, for a young man dismissed from the university for indecent behavior. At Llanabba Castle, he meets three characters with whose stories his own is interlaced: Grimes, a pederast and bigamist who pulls himself out of the continual "soup" he gets into by feigning suicide; Prendergast, a doubting cleric who becomes a "modern churchman" and is eventually murdered by a religious fanatic; and Philbrick, the school butler, a professed imposter, jewel thief, and arsonist who manages to secure a continual life of luxury by his preposterous stories about his criminal life. At Llanabba, Pennyfeather also meets Margot Beste-Chetwynde, a rich socialite to whom he becomes engaged; he is arrested the afternoon of their wedding for unknowingly transporting girls to France for her international prostitution ring. His innocent association with Margot thus leads to his conviction for another act of "indecent behavior," this time leading to a prison sentence in Blackstone Gaol—a "modern" penal institution.

What strikes one about the novel is not the injustices served Pennyfeather, but the very madness of the world with which his innocence contrasts. Characters with criminal designs—Margot, Philbrick, and Grimes—are unaffected by changes in fortune; those in charge of social institutions—Dr. Fagan of Llanabba Castle and Sir Lucas-Dockery of the experimental prison—are eccentrically out of touch with reality. Their absurdity, when contrasted with Pennyfeather's naïve struggle, defines Waugh's theme: The only sanity is to become cautiously indifferent to the chaos of modernism. At the end of the novel, when Pennyfeather returns to Oxford under a new identity and continues his study of the Early Church, he assumes the role of a spectator, not a participant, in the madness of life.

Although *Decline and Fall*'s narrative structure is more derivative and its characters less fully rounded than those of Waugh's later novels, it displays techniques typical of his fiction at its best. The callous descriptions of the tragic—little Lord Tangent's death from Grimes's racing pistol or Prendergast's decapitation at Blackstone Gaol—and their fragmented interlacement into the plot are hallmarks of Waugh's comic detachment. Tangent's slow death from gangrene is presented through a series of casual offstage reports; the report of Prendergast's murder is incongruously worked into verses of a hymn sung in the prison chapel, "O God, our Help in Ages Past." The tragic and the savage are always sifted through an ironic filter in Waugh's novels, creating a brutal sort of pathos.

A HANDFUL OF DUST

Waugh's fourth novel, *A Handful of Dust*, was his first to present a dynamically sympathetic protagonist. Pennyfeather, from *Decline and Fall*, and Adam Symes, from *Vile Bodies*, attract one's interest largely because they provide a detached perspective from which one can observe the chaos of modern civilization. Basil Seal in *Black Mischief*, although a participating rogue, is amiable largely because of his comic disregard for the mischief he makes. Tony Last of *A Handful of Dust*, however, is a fully sympathetic character as well as a pathetic victim of the modern wasteland to which the title alludes. Unlike Paul Pennyfeather, Tony is not simply an observer of social chaos: His internal turmoil is set against the absurdity of external events, and in that respect, his quest for lost values anticipates that of Charles Ryder in *Brideshead Revisited* and of Guy Crouchback in *Sword of Honour*.

Waugh's theme is the decadence of tradition, emblematized, as it is in many of Waugh's novels, by the crumbling estates of the aristocracy. Tony's futile effort to maintain his Victorian Gothic estate, Hetton Abbey, thus symbolizes his struggle throughout the plot. He is wedded to the outmoded tradition of Victorian country gentlemen, while his wife, Brenda, embraces the social life of London. She eventually cuckolds Tony by having an affair with the parasitic John Beaver, whose mother, an interior decorator, sees in her son's affair an opportunity to "modernize" Hetton with chromium plating and sheepskin carpeting.

The pathos one feels for Tony is ultimately controlled by the absurd contexts into which Waugh sets the pathetic scenes. When his son, John Andrew, dies in a riding accident, Tony is left emotionally desolate, yet the cause of the accident is ironic; John Andrew's horse is startled by a backfiring motorcycle, a modern "horse." Later, one is made brutally aware of the irony of Tony's grief when one learns of Brenda's

initial reaction to the news of her son's death: She assumes it was John Beaver, her lover, not John Andrew, her son, who died. In the same way, Tony's later divorce from Brenda empties him of values he traditionally respected. He consents to the legal convention that he should give evidence of his infidelity, even if his wife has been the unfaithful partner. His evidence incongruously turns into an uncomfortable weekend with a prostitute and her daughter at Brighton, and the absurdity of this forced and inconsummate infidelity further defines Tony's loneliness. Ironically, it provides him with a means to deny an exorbitant divorce settlement that would force him to sell Hetton Abbey.

In the end, Tony searches for his Victorian Gothic city in the jungles of South America and suffers a delirium in which his civilized life at Hetton Abbey is distorted; these scenes are made comically pathetic by interlaced scenes of Brenda in London trying to regain the civilized life she lost in her estrangement from Tony. Ultimately, she does not find in London the city she sought, nor does Tony in South America. Tony does find, instead, an aberration of his vision; he is held captive by an illiterate who forces him to read aloud from Charles Dickens's novels in perpetuity.

Perhaps Waugh's emotional reaction to his own divorce from Evelyn Gardner prior to the publication of the novel accounts for the increase of pathos in *A Handful of Dust*. Perhaps Waugh realized that thinness of characterization in his earlier novels could lead only to stylistic repetition without stylistic development. Whatever the reason, this novel depicts characters struggling for moral equilibrium in a way that no previous Waugh novel had done.

BRIDESHEAD REVISITED

Brideshead Revisited is different from Waugh's earlier novels in two important ways. First, it is the only novel Waugh finished which employs the first-person point of view. (He had attempted the first person in *Work Suspended* in 1942, but either the story itself faltered, or Waugh could not achieve a sufficient narrative detachment to complete it.) Second, *Brideshead Revisited* was the first novel in which Waugh explicitly addressed a Roman Catholic theme: the mysterious workings of divine grace in a small aristocratic Catholic family. As a result, it is Waugh's most sentimental and least funny novel. Although it departed radically from his earlier satires, it was Waugh's most popular and financially successful work.

The narrative frame creates much of what is sentimental in the novel but also provides a built-in detachment. Charles Ryder's love for Sebastian Flyte during his years at Oxford in the 1920's and for Julia Mottram, Sebastian's sister, a decade later, live vividly in Ryder's memories when he revisits the Brideshead estate during a wartime bivouac. His memories tell the story of Sebastian's and Julia's search for happiness, but because they are remembered by an emotionally desolate Ryder, the novel is a study of his spiritual change as well.

Before he meets Sebastian, Ryder is a serious-minded Oxford undergraduate, not unlike Paul Penny-feather at the end of *Decline and Fall*. Like Penny-feather, he is drawn into a world for which he is unprepared, yet unlike Waugh's earlier protagonist, Ryder is enthralled by a make-believe world of beauty and art. The Arcadian summer Ryder spends with Sebastian at Brideshead and in Venice are the most sumptuously written passages in any of Waugh's novels, reflecting—as Waugh admitted in his 1959 revision of the novel—the dearth of sensual pleasures available at the time of its composition. The change in style also reflects a change in theme. Sebastian's eccentricities about his stuffed bear, his coterie of homosexual "aesthetes," and his refusal to take anything seriously would have been the object of satire in Waugh's earlier novels. In *Brideshead Revisited*, however, the absurdities are sifted through the perspective of a narrator aware of his own desperate search for love. When Sebastian's make-believe turns to alcoholism, the narrator himself becomes cynically indifferent.

Ryder's love for Julia ten years after he has left Brideshead is an attempt to rediscover the happiness he lost with Sebastian. One is more aware, in this second half of the narration, of Ryder's cynicism and of the discontentment which that cynicism hides. When he and Julia fall in love on a transatlantic voyage back to England, they are both escaping mar-

riages to spouses whose worldly ambitions offer no nourishment for the spiritual emptiness each feels. Julia's return to the Church after the deathbed repentance of her father causes Ryder to realize that he has fathomed as little about Julia's faith as he had about Sebastian's. The narration itself thus ends on a note of unhappiness which recalls the separation of Ryder and Sebastian. In the epilogue following Ryder's memories, however, Waugh makes it clear that the narrator himself has converted to Catholicism in the intervening years. Ryder sees in the sanctuary light of the chapel at Brideshead the permanence he sought with Sebastian and Julia and finds contentment, if not hope for the future.

It is easy to overstress the religious implications of the novel. Indeed, many critics find Julia's hysteria about sin, Lord Marchmain's return to the Church, and Ryder's conversion strained. Some, such as Edmund Wilson, see the novel as an adulation of the British upper classes. *Brideshead Revisited*, however, is less a Roman Catholic novel than it is a lament for the past and a study in spiritual and artistic awakening. It was a turning point in Waugh's fiction: His novels after *Brideshead Revisited* dealt less with the absurdity of life and more with the spiritual values that have disappeared as a result of the war.

THE LOVED ONE

Perhaps the grimmest of Waugh's satires, *The Loved One* presents a sardonic vision of American culture. Its principal satiric target is Forest Lawn Memorial Park—a place that in many ways served for Waugh as the epitome of American pretensions to civilization. In "Half in Love with Easeful Death," an essay Waugh wrote for *Life* in 1947 after his visit to Hollywood, Waugh describes Forest Lawn as it would appear to archaeologists in the next millennium: a burlesque necropolis, like the tombs of the pharaohs in its aspirations, but, in fact, the product of a borrowed, devalued culture. His version of Forest Lawn, Whispering Glades, is a distorted wonderland in which the cosmetic and the artificial substitute for beauty and in which banality is glorified and substitutes for the poetic vision.

It is fitting that the protagonist, Dennis Barlow, be a poet—even though an unproductive one who has been seduced to Hollywood by a consultantship with Megalo Studios. Like many of Waugh's other protagonists, he is the filter through which one sees absurdities satirized. Like Basil Seal in *Black Mischief* and *Put Out More Flags*, he is an opportunist, flexible enough to engineer a profit for himself out of the chaotic world into which he is thrust. His vision is grimly sardonic, however, in a way that even Seal's is not.

When he first enters Whispering Glades, he is intrigued, as Seal would be, by its absurd glamour and by the potential of using that glamour to improve his own position at The Happier Hunting Grounds, a pet mortuary where he is employed. Whispering Glades, however, has a far deeper attraction; it would be the kind of place, if it were real, that would appeal to any poet, but Barlow is enchanted by its very fraudulence. At the human-made Lake Isle of Innisfree (complete with mechanized humming bees), Barlow falls in love with a mortuary cosmetician and enchants her by the very fact that he is a poet. The enchantment is false, just as everything is at Whispering Glades; he sends her plagiarized verses from *The Oxford Book of English Verse* and pledges his troth to her by reciting a stanza from Robert Burns's "A Red, Red Rose" at The Lover's Nook near the Wee Kirk o' Auld Lang Syne.

If plagiarism lies at the heart of Barlow's involvement at Whispering Glades, it also lies at the heart of Whispering Glades itself and the characters who work there—even though the place and the people are possessed by the utmost seriousness. The girl with whom Barlow falls in love is named Aimee Thanatogenos. Although she professes to be named after Aimee McPherson—the American huckster of religion whom Waugh satirized in *Vile Bodies*—her given name and her surname both translate into the euphemism that embodies all of Whispering Glades's false coating: "The loved one." Her enchantment with Barlow eventually takes the form of a burlesque tragedy. She is torn between Barlow and the head mortician, Mr. Joyboy—a poet of a different sort, whose special art is preparing infant corpses.

Aimee's tragedy results from a bizarre sequence of events, comic in its effects. When she discovers Joyboy's mother fixation and Barlow's fraudulence, she seeks advice from her oracle, the Guru Brahmin, an advice columnist. When the Guru, Mr. Slump— fired from his job and in an alcoholic funk—advises Aimee to jump off a roof, she kills herself in the more poetic environment of Whispering Glades. Her suicide by drinking embalming fluid gives a doubly ironic force to her name and to the title of the novel. The tragedy ends with a darkly humorous catharsis. Joyboy, fearful that Aimee's death on his table might mar his lofty position at Whispering Glades, consents to Barlow's extortion and to Barlow's plan to cremate their beloved Aimee at The Happier Hunting Grounds. The novel's conclusion, thus, strikes the grimmest note of all: Barlow sits idly by, reading a cheap novel, while the heroine—a burlesque Dido— burns in the furnace.

In some ways, *The Loved One* is atypical of Waugh's postwar novels. In *Scott-King's Modern Europe* and the *Sword of Honour* trilogy, Waugh turns his satiric eye to political issues. *The Loved One*, however much it satirizes American values, transcends topical satire. Barlow lacks the spiritual potential of Charles Ryder in *Brideshead Revisited*, even though he displays Ryder's callousness. Barlow is an artist in search of beauty, but he leaves California, ironically, with an artist's load far different from what he expected. It is the view of an ironist, like Waugh himself, who could hardly make a better travesty of Whispering Glades than it makes of itself.

SWORD OF HONOUR

The *Sword of Honour* trilogy, like *Brideshead Revisited*, is infused with a predominantly religious theme; it traces Guy Crouchback's awakening to spiritual honor—a more active form of spiritual growth than Charles Ryder experienced. Like *Brideshead Revisited*, *Sword of Honour* is more somber and more deliberately paced than Waugh's satires in the 1920's and 1930's, but it shares with his early works a detached satiric framework. Each volume is composed at a distance of ten or more years from its historical occurrence and, as a result, reflects a greater consciousness of the long-range implications of the absurdities presented.

MEN AT ARMS

Men at Arms concerns the chaos of Britain's first entry into the war, much like Waugh's wartime satire *Put Out More Flags*. One is immediately aware, however, of the difference in Waugh's detachment. *Put Out More Flags* was the product of a writer in his mid-thirties looking wryly at the days of peace from the middle of the war. Its protagonist, Basil Seal, is a mischief-making opportunist for whom greater chaos means greater fun and profit; the novel satirizes the madness of a world which leaves the characters trapped in the ever-changing insanity of war. *Men at Arms*, however, and, indeed, the entire trilogy, looks back from the perspective of the author's later middle age, with a sense of disappointment at the final results of the war. Appropriately enough, Guy is an innocent at the outset of the war, not a mischief maker like Basil Seal. He is a middle-aged victim who is literally and figuratively cast into a battle for which he is ill prepared.

Guy's heroic illusions are shattered in three successive stages through the separate volumes of the trilogy. *Men at Arms* concerns Guy's search for the self-esteem he lost eight years earlier after his divorce from his wife. As an officer-trainee in the Royal Corps of Halberdiers, Guy temporarily finds self-respect, but the elaborate traditions of the Halberdiers and his traineeship at commandeered preparatory schools cause Guy to revert to adolescence. His physical awkwardness, his jealousy of fellow trainees, his vanity about growing a mustache, his ineffectual attempt to seduce his former wife on Saint Valentine's Day, and the blot he receives on his military record at the end of the novel all seem more appropriate for a schoolboy than for an officer preparing to lead men into battle.

As in Waugh's earlier novels, the comedy of *Men at Arms* depends not on the protagonist, but on the events and characters that he encounters. Apthorpe, a middle-aged *miles gloriosus*, and Ben Ritchie-Hook, Guy's brigadier, represent two forms of the military insanity for which Guy trains. Apthorpe's preoccupation with boots, salutes, and his portable field latrine, the "Box," makes him an unlikely candidate for leading men into battle; Ritchie-Hook, whose only no-

tion of military strategy is to attack, makes an elaborate game out of officer training by booby trapping Apthorpe's "Box"—a prank which causes Apthorpe to sink deeper into his madness. The confrontation between Apthorpe and Ritchie-Hook defines an absurd pattern which recurs later in the trilogy. Seeming madmen control the positions of power, and the protagonist is unwittingly drawn into their absurd worlds.

OFFICERS AND GENTLEMEN

Officers and Gentlemen further trains Guy in the illogic of military life, this time focusing on the efforts of gentlemen soldiers to re-create the comforts of their London clubs during the war. The novel ends on a more somber note, however, than did *Men at Arms*. Guy finds temporary solace in the commando unit to which he is transferred after his disgrace as a Halberdier and believes again that he will find some honorable role to play in the war, but the British defeat at Crete at the end of this volume negates whatever notions of honor he entertained.

Even more than *Men at Arms, Officers and Gentlemen* relentlessly travesties *esprit de corps* and pretentions to heroism. Ian Kilbannock's gentlemanly service as a military journalist, for example, is to transform the ineffectual Trimmer into a propaganda hero for the common person. Julia Stitch's yacht, the *Cleopatra*, brings the comforts of the English social world to the Mediterranean war. The burrowing Grace-Groundling-Marchpole absurdly continues the secret file he began in *Men at Arms* about Guy's supposed counterintelligence activities. All of these events occur while England is suffering the first effects of German bombing and while the British disgrace at Crete looms ahead.

For a time, Guy imagines that the commandos are the "flower of England"; he even sees Ivor Claire as the ideal soldier, the kind of Englishman whom Hitler had not taken into account. The flower withers, however, in the chaotic retreat of British forces from Crete. Although Guy himself manages to maintain an even keel through most of the ordeal, the officers with whom he serves prove unheroic. His commander, "Fido" Hound, suffers a complete mental collapse in the face of the retreating troops; Ivor

Claire, unable to face the prospect of surrendering, deserts his men and flees to India, where he is protected by his genteel birth. Eventually, Guy unheroically joins a boat escaping from the island and, exhausted, suffers a mental collapse. Guy initially resists Julia Stitch's efforts to cover up Claire's disgrace, but eventually destroys his own diary recording the orders to surrender when he learns that nothing will be done about Claire's desertion and when he learns of England's alliance with Russia. Unlike the first volume, the second volume ends with Guy's realization that he is an ineffectual player in a war that has lost a sense of honor.

It is curious to note that Waugh announced in the dust-jacket blurb for *Officers and Gentlemen* that, although he had planned the series for three volumes, he wanted his readers to regard it as finished with this second volume. The grimness of Guy's disillusionment thus sheds a somber light on Waugh's personal dilemma during the mid-1950's. After completing about a third of the draft of this second volume, Waugh suffered the mental collapse fictionalized in *The Ordeal of Gilbert Pinfold*. Guy's hallucination at the end of *Officers and Gentlemen* probably owes some of its vividness to the madness Waugh himself endured in 1954, and perhaps the numbness that affects Guy at the end of the novel reflects Waugh's own consciousness of his failing physical and mental powers.

THE END OF THE BATTLE

Men at Arms and *Officers and Gentlemen* each deflate Guy's illusions about honor. *The End of the Battle* follows the same pattern in terms of wartime politics and in terms of Guy's military life, but in personal terms, Guy achieves a kind of unheroic, unselfish honor by the end of the novel. As a soldier, Guy accomplishes nothing heroic; even his efforts to liberate the Jewish refugees from partisan Yugoslavia is unsatisfying. Although most of the refugees are liberated, the leaders of the group—the Kanyis—are imprisoned and presumably executed. Guy's struggle with the Yugoslavian partisans and his disgust at Britain's alliance with the Communist-bloc countries further define the dishonorable end that Guy and Waugh see in the war.

Unlike the two previous volumes, however, *The End of the Battle* ends on a note of tentative personal hopefulness, effected by Guy's renewed Roman Catholic faith. In the first two novels of the trilogy, Guy's religion lay dormant—a part of his life made purposeless since his divorce from Virginia. In *The End of the Battle*, the death of Guy's piously religious father causes Guy to realize that honor lies not in the "quantitative judgments" of military strategy, but in the spiritual salvation of individual souls. Guy's efforts to rescue the Yugoslavian Jews is selflessly honorable, even if ultimately futile. His remarriage to Virginia, who is pregnant with Trimmer's baby, is directed by the same sense of honor. Guy has little to gain emotionally from his remarriage; he does it for the preservation of the child's life and, implicitly, for the salvation of its soul. It is a different sort of heroism than he sought at the beginning of the war, possible only because Virginia has died.

Sword of Honour is, in many ways, a fitting climax to Waugh's literary career. It poignantly expresses his reverence for religious values yet recognizes the anomalous existence of those values in the modern world. It burlesques the eccentric and the absurd, yet moves beyond superficial satire to a more deeply rooted criticism of postwar politics. It displays Waugh's masterful ability to capture minor characters in brisk, economical strokes while working them thematically into the emotional composition of the protagonist. Waugh's importance as a novelist lay in his ability to achieve this kind of economy in a traditional form. He kept alive, in short, a tradition of the comic novel that reaches back to the eighteenth century.

James J. Lynch

OTHER MAJOR WORKS

SHORT FICTION: *Mr. Loveday's Little Outing*, 1936; *Tactical Exercise*, 1954; *Charles Ryder's Schooldays and Other Stories*, 1982.

NONFICTION: *Rossetti: His Life and Works*, 1928; *Labels*, 1930; *Remote People*, 1931; *Ninety-two Days*, 1934; *Edmund Campion: Jesuit and Martyr*, 1935; *Waugh in Abyssinia*, 1936; *Robbery Under the Law*, 1939; *The Holy Places*, 1952; *The Life of the*

Right Reverend Ronald Knox, 1959; *Tourist in Africa*, 1960; *A Little Learning*, 1964; *The Diaries of Evelyn Waugh*, 1976 (Christopher Sykes, editor); *The Letters of Evelyn Waugh*, 1980 (Mark Amory, editor).

BIBLIOGRAPHY

Carens, James F., ed. *Critical Essays on Evelyn Waugh*. Boston: G. K. Hall, 1987. Contains twenty-six essays divided into three sections: general essays, essays on specific novels, and essays on Waugh's life and works. In his lengthy introduction, Carens provides a chronological overview of Waugh's literary work and a discussion of Waugh criticism. This well-indexed book also contains a bibliography of Waugh's writings and a selective list of secondary sources.

Cook, William J., Jr. *Masks, Modes, and Morals: The Art of Evelyn Waugh*. Rutherford, N.J.: Fairleigh Dickinson University Press, 1971. Considers Waugh's novels squarely in the ironic mode, tracing Waugh's development from satiric denunciation to comic realism to romantic optimism to ironic realism. Cook provides lengthy analyses of the novels, which he suggests move from fantasy to reality and from satire to resignation. Well indexed and contains an excellent bibliography, which also lists articles.

Crabbe, Katharyn. *Evelyn Waugh*. New York: Continuum, 1988. Crabbe's book is most helpful: She provides a chronology of Waugh's life, a short biography, and five chapters of detailed criticism on Waugh's major novels. Crabbe reads *The Ordeal of Gilbert Pinfold* as an autobiographical novel. A concluding chapter on style is followed by a bibliography and a thorough index.

Davis, Robert Murray. *Evelyn Waugh: Writer*. Norman, Okla.: Pilgrim Books, 1981. Drawing from previously unavailable manuscript materials, Davis examines Waugh's fiction in terms of his artistic technique, his extensive revisions, and his reworking of his novels. After an opening chapter on Waugh's biography of Dante Gabriel Rossetti, Davis focuses exclusively on the novels, *Brideshead Revisited* and *Sword of Honour* in particular. Well documented and well indexed.

Hastings, Selina. *Evelyn Waugh: A Biography*. Boston: Houghton Mifflin, 1994. An excellent one-volume biography. Hastings notes that hers is not an academic biography such as Stannard has written, but a lively attempt to recapture Waugh's personality as it seemed to him and to his friends.

Lane, Calvin W. *Evelyn Waugh*. Boston: Twayne, 1981. Indispensable for Waugh scholars, Lane's relatively short volume contains a detailed chronology, a biography stressing the factors influencing his literary career, and lengthy treatments of Waugh's novels. Stresses Waugh's irony, satire, and conversion to Catholicism, which greatly influenced his fiction after 1930. Lane's selected bibliography contains articles, annotated book-length studies, and four interviews with Waugh.

Stannard, Martin. *Evelyn Waugh*. New York: W. W. Norton, 1987. A scholarly, well-documented account of Waugh's early literary career, Stannard's biography provides valuable publication details about the novels and utilizes Waugh's diaries and letters. Also contains many photographs and illustrations, a genealogical chart of Waugh's ancestry, a selected bibliography, and an excellent index.

_____. *Evelyn Waugh: No Abiding City, 1939-1966*. London: Dent, 1992. The second volume of a meticulous, scholarly biography. Includes notes, bibliography, illustrations, and two indexes: a general index and one of Waugh's work.

FAY WELDON

Born: Alvechurch, England; September 22, 1931

PRINCIPAL LONG FICTION
The Fat Woman's Joke, 1967 (pb. in U.S. as . . . *And the Wife Ran Away*, 1968)
Down Among the Women, 1971
Female Friends, 1974
Remember Me, 1976
Words of Advice, 1977 (pb. in England as *Little Sisters*, 1978)

(AP/Wide World Photos)

Praxis, 1978
Puffball, 1980
The President's Child, 1982
The Life and Loves of a She-Devil, 1983
The Shrapnel Academy, 1986
The Rules of Life, 1987
The Hearts and Lives of Men, 1987
The Heart of the Country, 1987
Leader of the Band, 1988
The Cloning of Joanna May, 1989
Darcy's Utopia, 1990
Growing Rich, 1992
Life Force, 1992
Affliction, 1993 (pb. in U.S. as *Trouble*, 1993)
Splitting, 1995
Worst Fears, 1996
Big Women, 1997 (pb. in U.S. as *Big Girls Don't Cry*, 1997)

OTHER LITERARY FORMS

Fay Weldon began her writing career with plays for radio, television, and theater, but she soon transferred her efforts to novels, for which she is best known. She has also published short stories, a biography of Rebecca West, and an introduction to the work of Jane Austen in fictional form, *Letters to Alice on First Reading Jane Austen* (1984).

ACHIEVEMENTS

In addition to a successful career as an advertising copywriter, Fay Weldon has enjoyed a long career as a television scriptwriter, a playwright (for television, radio, and theater), and a novelist. Her radio play *Spider* (1972) won the Writers' Guild Award for Best Radio Play in 1973, and *Polaris* (1978) won the Giles Cooper Award for Best Radio Play in 1978. Weldon has earned growing acclaim for her humorous fictional explorations of women's lives and her biting satires that expose social injustice, and her novel *Praxis* was nominated for the Booker Prize, a prestigious literary award in England. In 1983, Weldon became the first woman chair of judges for the Booker Prize. She was again recognized for her many achievements in 1997, when she received the Women in Publishing Pandora Award. Although her works often focus primarily on the lives of women, Weldon comments on a wide-ranging number of issues with relevance to all. Her work reveals a deep yet unsentimental compassion for all human beings, an understanding of their weaknesses and foibles, and a celebration of their continued survival and ability to love one another in the face of adversity.

BIOGRAPHY

Fay Weldon was born into a literary family in the village of Alvechurch, England, in 1931. Her mother, her maternal grandfather, and her uncle were all published novelists. While still a child, Weldon emigrated with her family to New Zealand, where she grew up. When she was six years old, her parents

(Frank Thornton Birkinshaw, a doctor, and Margaret Jepson Birkinshaw) were divorced; Weldon continued to live with her mother and sister. This experience of being reared by a single mother in an era that did not easily accommodate single-parent families gave Weldon early insight into the lot of women who flouted social norms. When she was fourteen, Weldon, her mother, and her sister joined her grandmother in London. These were years of hardship in postwar England, but the strong and independent women of the family set a good example. Weldon was able to observe, at first hand, both the trials women faced and the importance of family and of humor in overcoming these difficulties.

In 1949, Weldon earned a scholarship to St. Andrews University in Scotland, and in 1952 she was graduated with an M.A. in economics and psychology. In 1955, she had her first son, Nicholas, whom she supported as a single mother. Weldon's literary ambitions had not yet crystallized—though she had begun writing—so she drifted into a series of writing jobs: propaganda for the Foreign Office; answering problem letters for a newspaper; and, finally, composing advertising copy. In this last career she was quite successful, producing many jingles and slogans that would become household sayings and honing her talent for concision, wit, and catchy, memorable phrasing.

In 1960, she married Ronald Weldon, a London antiques dealer, and together they settled in a North London suburb, where they had three children: Daniel (born 1963), Thomas (born 1970), and Samuel (born 1977). Beginning in the mid-1960's, Weldon combined professional and family responsibilities with a burgeoning career as a writer. Her efforts were at first directed toward writing plays. Her one-act play "Permanence" was produced in London in 1969 and was followed by many successes. For British television networks, Weldon has written more than fifty plays, as well as other scripts, including an award-winning episode of *Upstairs, Downstairs*.

Writing for television led to fiction: Weldon's first novel, *The Fat Woman's Joke*, in 1967, had begun as a television play. Her third novel, *Female Friends*, solidified her reputation. In the 1970's, Weldon left her job in advertising. She was able to devote more of her time to writing, earning further acclaim for *Praxis* in 1978. *The President's Child*, in 1982, was an even bigger best-seller, thanks to its "thriller" quality, while *The Life and Loves of a She-Devil*, in 1983, introduced Weldon's work to a mass audience when it was made into a motion picture, *She-Devil* (1990), starring Meryl Streep and Roseanne Barr.

In addition to her novels, in the 1980's and 1990's Weldon also published collections of her short fiction, including *Moon over Minneapolis: Or, Why She Couldn't Stay* (1991) and *Wicked Women: A Collection of Short Stories* (1995). She also put her comic gifts to work in three books for children, *Wolf the Mechanical Dog* (1988), *Party Puddle* (1989), and *Nobody Likes Me* (1997). Meanwhile, after the author and her husband of thirty-four years were divorced in 1994, she married Nicholas Fox and settled down in London. There she continued to write and to crusade for writers' rights and to attack the two great enemies of her profession, censorship and exploitation by unscrupulous publishers.

ANALYSIS

In her fiction, Fay Weldon explores women's lives with wit and humor. She is caustic in her implicit condemnation of injustice but avoids preaching by satirizing both sides of every issue and by revealing the gulf between what characters say and what they do. Despite their realistic settings, her novels blend fable, myth, and the fantastic with satire, farce, and outlandish coincidence to produce tragicomedies of manners.

Weldon's admiration for writers such as Jane Austen (whose work she has adapted for television) is expressed openly in *Letters to Alice on First Reading Jane Austen*, but it is also evident from the parallels in Weldon's own work. In a typical Weldon novel, a limited cast of characters interacts in a well-defined setting. A series of misunderstandings or trivial coincidences initiates the action, which then takes on a momentum of its own, carrying all along with it until an equally trivial series of explanations or coincidences brings closure and a resolution that restores all to their proper place. The theme is often a minor domestic drama, such as a marital crisis, rather than an epic upheaval, but such personal interactions are seen to represent in microcosm society as a whole and therefore have a universal appeal.

. . . AND THE WIFE RAN AWAY

This structure is present even in Weldon's early work, no doubt because it is a formula that works well for television. In her first novel, originally entitled *The Fat Woman's Joke*, but renamed . . . *And the Wife Ran Away* for its American publication in 1968, Weldon takes as her subject the crisis in the marriage of a middle-aged, middle-class couple, Esther and Alan Wells, when Alan decides to have an affair with his young and attractive secretary, Susan. The beginning of Alan's affair coincides with Esther and Alan's decision to go on a diet, a symbolic attempt, Weldon suggests, to recapture not only their lost youthful figures, but also their youthful love, ambition, and optimism. Infidelity, the novel therefore subtly suggests, is related to aging and to a more deep-seated identity crisis. Weldon frequently uses hunger or the satisfaction of food as a metaphor for other, more metaphysical and intangible, needs, and this theme recurs in a number of her works (for example, in the short story "Polaris," 1985).

The influence of Weldon's background as a scriptwriter (and the novel's origin as a play) is also evident in its form. Esther, who has left her husband at the opening of the novel, recounts her version of events to her friend Phyllis, as she gorges herself on food to compensate for the self-denial she has suffered during the diet. Esther's narrative is intercut with scenes of Susan telling her version to her friend Brenda. The novel is thus almost entirely conveyed through dialogue describing flashbacks seen from the perspective of the female characters. This technique is evident elsewhere in Weldon's early work—for example, in *Female Friends*, where parts of the novel are presented in the form of a script.

THE LIFE AND LOVES OF A SHE-DEVIL

The Life and Loves of a She-Devil stands as one of Weldon's most accomplished works. It represents the themes that are the hallmark of Weldon's fiction (a concern with women's lives and the significance of human relationships such as marriage) while encompassing her use of fantasy in one of her most carefully constructed and formally satisfying novels. The plot tells the story of a middle-class, suburban housewife, Ruth, whose accountant husband leaves her for a rich and attractive writer of romance novels. Unlike the typical wife, however, Ruth does not simply bow to the inevitable. When her husband calls her a "she-devil" in a moment of anger, this becomes her new identity, and she musters a formidable array of resources to live up to it. Through a series of picaresque adventures, she makes the life of her husband Bobbo and his new love Mary Fisher impossible, has Bobbo framed and then imprisoned for embezzlement, destroys Mary's ability and will to write, and finally undergoes massive plastic surgery so that she looks just like the now-dead rival Mary and can assume her place in Bobbo's broken life. The configuration at the end of the novel thus mirrors the beginning, but with the variation that the power dynamics of the relationship have been inverted: Ruth is now in command, while Bobbo has been humiliated and accepts his fate like a downtrodden wife.

The tale not only presents a certain kind of symmetry reminiscent of fairy stories but also evokes a poetic magic in the telling of it. Many of the chapters begin with a variation on the opening line of the novel: "Mary Fisher lives in a High Tower, on the edge of the sea." These incantations, repeated with variations, have the hypnotic quality of a witch's spell, reinforcing both Ruth's supernatural power and her obsession with Mary Fisher (whose residence in a tower evokes a fairy-tale princess). This poetic refrain also unifies the narrative and gives a cyclical structure to the plot.

THE SHRAPNEL ACADEMY

At first glance, *The Shrapnel Academy* appears to be a variation on the theme of the "country house weekend" plot, a staple of British literature. A group of characters, most of them unknown to one another, are seen arriving at the Shrapnel Academy, a military institute, for a weekend. Bad weather will ensure that they remain confined to the academy, cut off from the outside world and forced to confront one another and the problems that arise.

While many novelists fail to acknowledge the presence of the host of servants who make such country weekends possible, Weldon's novel takes the reader below stairs and into the lives of the hundreds of illegal immigrant servants and their extended families and camp followers. *The Shrapnel Academy* could thus be subtitled "Upstairs, Downstairs," like the television series about an upper-class Edwardian family and its servants (to which Weldon contributed an award-winning episode). *The Shrapnel Academy* strays far beyond the realist conventions of the television series, however, and by presenting the clash between shortsighted, class-based militarism and the struggle for survival and dignity in the microcosm of the academy, Weldon succeeds in painting an apocalyptic allegory.

The Shrapnel Academy illustrates how Weldon avoids assigning blame by showing how character flaws and opportunity combine to create problems. Despite the black humor of this novel, Weldon's moral universe is not one of black and white. The reader is made to sympathize with the choices of the militarists and is shown the complicity of the victims so that simplistic judgments become impossible. As in most of Weldon's novels, no one villain is responsible for the misfortunes that befall the characters; instead, everyone bears some degree of responsibility for the accumulation of trivial choices and decisions that combine to make up the "frightful tidal wave of destiny." The theme of destiny increasingly preoccupies Weldon; it is one of the major themes in *The Cloning of Joanna May*, for example, in which the role of coincidence is the subject of mystical and metaphysical speculation.

Many thematic and stylistic elements of Weldon's work also recur in *The Shrapnel Academy*, such as the revenge fantasy theme, food symbolism, and the revision of mythology and fable. Since war affects everyone—increasingly, Weldon argues, women and children—the militaristic theme of *The Shrapnel Academy* should not be construed as belying a male-oriented narrative. Weldon uses the female characters in this novel to offer characteristic insight into the position of the various women above stairs—Joan Lumb, the officious administrator, the General's mistress Bella, Shir-

ley the unquestioning and dutiful wife, Muffin the fluff-brained assistant—as well as the often anonymous women who are raped, die in childbirth, or become prostitutes in the "third world" below stairs.

Formally, too, the novel displays typical characteristics of Weldon's work (short narrative passages with aphoristic asides, the use of dialogue), as well as innovative and experimental qualities. Weldon interrupts the narrative at frequent intervals, sometimes to offer a satirical summary of military history, highlighting advances in warfare or giving accounts of famous battles. Weldon brings out the absurdity of celebrating such "progress" and uses her fine wit to draw the reader's attention to the Orwellian doublespeak and the underlying assumptions of military thinking. At other times, Weldon interpellates the reader directly, apologizing for the delay in getting on with the story or inviting readers to put themselves in the place of one of the characters—invitations that pointedly drive home the lesson that the reader is no better than the characters he or she is inclined to judge. Weldon even interrupts the story to offer a recipe for cooking pumpkin, only one of the ways Weldon breaks with the conventional codes of narrative (elsewhere she offers lists, timetables, and even a seating plan and a menu).

LIFE FORCE

Weldon also breaks with her readers' expectations, as in *Life Force*, which, instead of being an indictment of male callousness and infidelity, is a lusty tribute to male sexuality. The central figure in the book is Leslie Beck, a man with no virtues except his power to please women through the skillful use of his huge genitalia and his equally outsized imagination. Structurally, *Life Force* follows the pattern established in Weldon's earlier novels: It begins with a seemingly unimportant incident that stimulates the narrator to relive and reassess complex relationships. That incident eventually becomes a crucial element in a dramatic resolution, in which a woman avenges herself upon a man who has wronged her.

When Leslie Beck turns up at the Marion Loos Gallery, carrying a large painting by his late wife Anita, it does not seem possible that this unappealing, sixty-year-old man could for so long have been the Lothario of upper-middle-class London. However, the owner of the gallery, who at this point is the first-person narrator, explains to the reader why she is so shocked when she sees the unimpressive painting that her former lover expects her to sell on his behalf. Its subject is the bedroom and the bed in which Leslie once gave Marion so much pleasure. Naturally, the painting prompts Marion to recall her involvement with Leslie and to wonder how much Anita knew about the affair.

However, nothing in this novel is as straightforward as it seems. In the second chapter, not only does Weldon change narrators, now telling the story through the eyes of Nora, another of Beck's former lovers, but also she has Nora admit that it was she, not Marion, who actually wrote the first chapter, simply imagining herself as Marion. Although the two narrators continue to alternate as the book progresses, from time to time the author reminds us that Marion's narrative is Nora's fiction, based as much on gossip and guesses as on fact. Thus, Weldon suggests that since the only approach to truth is through what human beings see and say, what we call reality will always include as much fiction as fact.

TROUBLE

After *Life Force*, in which she showed both genders as being controlled by their own animal instincts, Weldon again turned her attention to a society that permits men to victimize women. The protagonist of *Trouble*, which was published in England under the title *Affliction*, is Annette Horrocks, a woman who, after ten years of trying, has finally become pregnant, only to find that her once-devoted husband Spicer has become monstrous. Not only does he now seem to loathe Annette, but also none of his tastes, opinions, and prejudices are what they were just a few months before.

Eventually, Annette discovers the source of the problem: Spicer has been seduced by a pair of unscrupulous, sadistic New Age psychiatrists. Before she is finally cured of what she comes to recognize as her addiction to Spicer, Annette loses her home, her baby, and very nearly her mind. If in *Life Force* Weldon shows the battle of the sexes as essentially comic, in *Trouble* Weldon tells a story with tragic overtones. Again she points out how vulnerable women are in a society that believes men have a monopoly on the truth, but in this case she shows what can happen when the male version of reality is reinforced by the self-seeking therapy industry, the primary target of satire in this novel.

Weldon's fiction has developed from dialogue-based, scriptlike narratives to a style that resembles more conventional forms of the novel, although still with a characteristic lack of reverence for the conventions of storytelling. Her themes have expanded from domestic dramas and personal relationships to topical questions of national and international import, but without abandoning the belief that the personal remains the minimal unit of significance at the base of even the largest human networks. Humor has remained a constant feature of her work, her delicious wit and sharp irony the armor that protects her from charges of overseriousness, preaching, or doctrinaire political stances.

Melanie Hawthorne,
updated by Rosemary M. Canfield Reisman

OTHER MAJOR WORKS

SHORT FICTION: *Watching Me, Watching You*, 1981; *Polaris and Other Stories*, 1985; *Moon over Minneapolis: Or, Why She Couldn't Stay*, 1991; *Wicked Women: A Collection of Short Stories*, 1995; *A Hard Time to Be a Father*, 1999.

PLAYS: *Permanence*, pr. 1969; *Time Hurries On*, pb. 1972; *Words of Advice*, pr., pb. 1974; *Friends*, pr. 1975; *Moving House*, pr. 1976; *Mr. Director*, pr. 1978; *Action Replay*, pr. 1979 (also known as *Love Among the Women*); *I Love My Love*, pr. 1981; *After the Prize*, pr. 1981 (also known as *Wordworm*).

TELEPLAYS: *Wife in a Blonde Wig*, 1966; *The Fat Woman's Tale*, 1966; *What About Me*, 1967; *Dr. De Waldon's Therapy*, 1967; *Goodnight Mrs. Dill*, 1967; *The Forty-fifth Unmarried Mother*, 1967; *Fall of the Goat*, 1967; *Ruined Houses*, 1968; *Venus Rising*, 1968; *The Three Wives of Felix Hull*, 1968; *Hippy Hippy Who Cares*, 1968; *£13083*, 1968; *The Loophole*, 1969; *Smokescreen*, 1969; *Poor Mother*, 1970; *Office Party*, 1970; *On Trial*, 1971 (in *Upstairs, Downstairs* series); *Old Man's Hat*, 1972; *A Splinter* *of Ice*, 1972; *Hands*, 1972; *The Lament of an Un-married Father*, 1972; *A Nice Rest*, 1972; *Comfortable Words*, 1973; *Desirous of Change*, 1973; *In Memoriam*, 1974; *Poor Baby*, 1975; *The Terrible Tale of Timothy Bagshott*, 1975; *Aunt Tatty*, 1975 (adaptation of Elizabeth Bowen's story); *Act of Rape*, 1977; *Married Love*, 1977 (in *Six Women* series); *Pride and Prejudice*, 1980 (adaptation of Jane Austen's novel); *Honey Ann*, 1980; *Watching Me, Watching You*, 1980 (in *Leap in the Dark* series); *Life for Christine*, 1980; *Little Miss Perkins*, 1982; *Loving Women*, 1983; *Redundant! Or, The Wife's Revenge*, 1983.

RADIO PLAYS: *Spider*, 1972; *Housebreaker*, 1973; *Mr. Fox and Mr. First*, 1974; *The Doctor's Wife*, 1975; *Polaris*, 1978; *Weekend*, 1979 (in *Just Before Midnight* series); *All the Bells of Paradise*, 1979; *I Love My Love*, 1981.

NONFICTION: *Letters to Alice on First Reading Jane Austen*, 1984; *Rebecca West*, 1985.

CHILDREN'S LITERATURE: *Wolf the Mechanical Dog*, 1988; *Party Puddle*, 1989; *Nobody Likes Me*, 1997.

EDITED TEXT: *New Stories Four: An Arts Council Anthology*, 1979 (with Elaine Feinstein).

BIBLIOGRAPHY

Barreca, Regina, ed. *Fay Weldon's Wicked Fictions.* Hanover, N.H.: University Press of New England, 1994. This important volume contains thirteen essays by various writers, in addition to five by Weldon. The editor's introduction provides a useful overview of Weldon criticism. Indexed.

Cane, Aleta F. "Demythifying Motherhood in Three Novels by Fay Weldon." In *Family Matters in the British and American Novel*, edited by Andrea O'Reilly Herrera, Elizabeth Mahn Nollen, and Sheila Reitzel Foor. Bowling Green, Ohio: Bowling Green State University Popular Press, 1997. Cane points out that in *Puffball*, *The Life and Loves of a She-Devil*, and *Life Force*, dysfunctional mothers produce daughters who are also dysfunctional mothers. Obviously, it is argued, Weldon agrees with the feminist position about mothering, that it cannot be improved until women cease to be marginalized.

Mitchell, Margaret E. "Fay Weldon." In *British Writers*. Supplement 4 in *Contemporary British Writers*, edited by George Stade and Carol Howard. New York: Scribner's, 1997. A very comprehensive study of Weldon's life and work. A lengthy but readable analysis is divided into sections on "Weldon's Feminism," "The Personal as Political," "Nature, Fate, and Magic," "Self and Solidarity," and "Fictions." Contains a biographical essay and a bibliography.

Weldon, Fay. "Towards a Humorous View of the Universe." In *Last Laughs: Perspectives on Women and Comedy*, edited by Regina Barreca. New York: Gordon and Breach, 1988. A short (three-page) article about humor as a protection against pain, with perceptive comments about class-related and gendered aspects of humor. Although Weldon herself does not draw the connections specifically, the reader can infer much from her comments about the role of humor in her own work.

Wilde, Alan. "'Bold, But Not Too Bold': Fay Weldon and the Limits of Poststructuralist Criticism." *Contemporary Literature* 29, no. 3 (1988): 403-419. The author focuses primarily not on Weldon's work but on literary theory, using *The Life and Loves of a She-Devil* as an arena to pit poststructuralism against New Criticism. The argument is at times obscure, but Wilde offers some useful comments regarding moderation versus extremism in this novel.

H. G. WELLS

Born: Bromley, Kent, England; September 21, 1866
Died: London, England; August 13, 1946

PRINCIPAL LONG FICTION
The Time Machine: An Invention, 1895
The Wonderful Visit, 1895
The Island of Dr. Moreau, 1896

The Wheels of Chance: A Holiday Adventure, 1896

The Invisible Man: A Grotesque Romance, 1897

The War of the Worlds, 1898

When the Sleeper Wakes: A Story of the Years to Come, 1899

Love and Mr. Lewisham, 1900

The First Men in the Moon, 1901

The Sea Lady, 1902

The Food of the Gods, and How It Came to Earth, 1904

Kipps: The Story of a Simple Soul, 1905

In the Days of the Comet, 1906

The War in the Air, and Particularly How Mr. Bert Smallways Fared While It Lasted, 1908

Tono-Bungay, 1908

Ann Veronica: A Modern Love Story, 1909

The History of Mr. Polly, 1910

The New Machiavelli, 1910

Marriage, 1912

The Passionate Friends, 1913

The Wife of Sir Isaac Harman, 1914

The World Set Free: A Story of Mankind, 1914

Bealby: A Holiday, 1915

The Research Magnificent, 1915

Mr. Britling Sees It Through, 1916

The Soul of a Bishop: A Novel—with Just a Little Love in It—About Conscience and Religion and the Real Troubles of Life, 1917

Joan and Peter: The Story of an Education, 1918

The Undying Fire: A Contemporary Novel, 1919

The Secret Places of the Heart, 1922

Men like Gods, 1923

The Dream, 1924

Christina Alberta's Father, 1925

The World of William Clissold: A Novel at a New Age, 1926 (3 volumes)

Meanwhile: The Picture of a Lady, 1927

Mr. Blettsworthy on Rampole Island, 1928

The King Who Was a King: The Book of a Film, 1929

(Library of Congress)

The Autocracy of Mr. Parham: His Remarkable Adventure in This Changing World, 1930

The Buplington of Blup, 1933

The Shape of Things to Come: The Ultimate Resolution, 1933

The Croquet Player, 1936

Byrnhild, 1937

The Camford Visitation, 1937

Star Begotten: A Biological Fantasia, 1937

Apropos of Dolores, 1938

The Brothers, 1938

The Holy Terror, 1939

Babes in the Darkling Wood, 1940

All Aboard for Ararat, 1940

You Can't Be Too Careful: A Sample of Life, 1901-1951, 1941

OTHER LITERARY FORMS

H. G. Wells's short stories appear in such collections as *The Stolen Bacillus and Other Incidents* (1895), *Tales of Space and Time* (1899), *The Country* of the Blind and Other Stories* (1911), and *A Door in the Wall and Other Stories* (1911). *The Outline of History: Being a Plain History of Life and Mankind* (1920) and *Experiment in Autobiography: Discoveries and Conclusions of a Very Ordinary Brain Since 1866* (1934) extended his literary range. His sociological essays include *A Modern Utopia* (1905) and *Mind at the End of Its Tether* (1945).

Achievements

Wells is best known for his science-fiction novels, some having been adapted as popular films. A socialist and Fabian, he was a spokesman for women's rights and international peace movements, for which he wrote books of advocacy in essay and fictional form. He was also an effective novelist of social satire and comedy.

Biography

Herbert George Wells was born in 1866 at Bromley in Kent, England, to Joseph and Sarah Neal Wells. He attended a commercial academy from 1874 to 1880. Having run away from his apprenticeship in a drapery shop, he taught in a preparatory school. Then he attended the London Normal School of Science from 1884 to 1887, studying biology under T. H. Huxley. In 1891 he was married to Isabel Mary Wells, and he published "The Rediscovery of the Unique." *The Time Machine* brought him fame in 1895, the same year that he divorced Isabel to marry Amy Catherine Robbins.

In 1901, Wells's son George Philip was born; Frank Richard followed in 1903. In 1914, having visited Russia, Wells published a prophecy, *The War That Will End War*; that year his son Anthony West was born to Rebecca West. After visiting soldiers on the front lines of World War I, Wells supported a "League of Free Nations," and he entered the propaganda effort against Germany. In 1920 he made another trip to Russia, to meet Vladimir Ilich Lenin, and published *Russia in the Shadows*.

Wells was defeated as a Labour candidate for Parliament in 1922, and Amy Catherine died in 1927. He coauthored a book on biology before visiting Russia and the United States in 1934 to meet Joseph Stalin and President Franklin Delano Roosevelt. In 1935 he wrote film scenarios for *Things to Come* and *The Man Who Could Work Miracles*. In 1938 Orson Welles's radio broadcast of *The War of the Worlds* frightened people in the United States, paving the way for Wells's successful lecture tour there in 1940. Wells died in London on August 13, 1946.

Analysis

H. G. Wells's early scientific romances begin with *The Time Machine* (1895) and conclude with *The First Men in the Moon* (1901). His social satire and comic romance commence with *Kipps* (1905) and end with *The History of Mr. Polly* (1910). Didactic fiction dominated his last decades, from *Ann Veronica* (1909) to *You Can't Be Too Careful* (1941). Throughout is a struggle between science and socialism. Visions of doom alternate with calls for reform and renewal; individuals acquire knowledge of science but lose control of their destinies.

The Time Machine

Wells's early novels are journeys of ironic discovery. The enduring point of *The Time Machine* is in the Time-Traveller's frightening discovery in the year 802701. He encounters the Eloi, who have been terrorized by the Morlocks, molelike creatures who prey upon the flesh of the Upper-worlders. They are the fruits of an evolutionary process of separating capitalists from workers. Before he returns to his own time, the Time-Traveller accidentally moves even further into the future, to an Earth about to fall into a dying Sun.

The Island of Dr. Moreau

Edward Prendick, narrator of *The Island of Dr. Moreau*, is a castaway, grateful to reach Moreau's island—until he realizes its horrors. He thinks that Moreau is turning people into animals, but when he finds the Beast-people, he realizes his mistake. Moreau explains that pain is animality, and he excises pain to humanize animals, but they kill him as they revert to their animal natures. Prendick barely escapes becoming an animal before he returns to civilization, where he has anxiety attacks about people's animality.

Pessimism is never far from the surface of Wells's writing. Losing faith in reason, he turned to prophetic satire, as in *The Invisible Man*. In this story, Griffin, having failed to anticipate the awful effects of losing visibility, has lapsed in ethical responsibility because he had no training or economic opportunity to make better use of his knowledge. Lacking love, he lacks constructive purpose for his power. His invisibility represents knowledge itself, as either destructive or constructive. Knowledge and power combine without sympathy in *The War of the Worlds* to result in catastrophe. The narrator is a frightened man struggling to compete for survival of the fittest. He believes that the Martians are little more than brains, dispassionate reason threatening annihilation. All brain with no sympathy threatens civilization, but so does instinct with no brain. The Martians near success, when suddenly they die, ironically having succumbed to the tiniest life form, bacteria.

THE FIRST MEN IN THE MOON

Wells reverses the cosmic journey in *The First Men in the Moon*, as Bedford accompanies eccentric scientist Cavor to mine the Moon, adding private enterprise to science. The heroes find an intoxicating mushroom, which prompts Bedford to speculate that his private motive for profit will produce public benefits—even for the Moon itself. This madly grandiose notion is subverted when Bedford and Cavor are captured by the antlike Selenites, who live under the surface of the Moon. When Bedford escapes alone to Earth, Cavor sends messages that he is to be executed to prevent Earth inhabitants from returning with their violent ways, to do to the Moon what Wells had envisioned in *The War of the Worlds*, where Earth was invaded by Martians.

THE FOOD OF THE GODS, AND HOW IT CAME TO EARTH

The Food of the Gods, and How It Came to Earth edges beyond science and humor into socialism and satire. Experiments with Boomfood on a chicken farm cause mass destruction through the creation of giant chickens, rats, and wasps; human babies become giants, and ordinary mortals grow terrified. Wells is on the giants' side, because they can make a new world by destroying the faults of the old. People accommo-

date to preserve old ways, but they shut their eyes to truth, eventually causing a crisis of choice between old and new. The story ends as the giants prepare for a war with the little people.

IN THE DAYS OF THE COMET

With *In the Days of the Comet* Wells presents a more optimistic view of changes that can be made in the world. Willie Leadford describes life before the great "change," when a comet turned Earth into paradise. The power of the novel, however, is in the rhythm of rage and hate that accelerates as Willie pursues the woman he loved, to kill her and her new lover. This momentum is accented by other accelerating events, including economic crisis and war with Germany. The comet changes all, including Willie and his beloved, Nettie, who offers to live with both lovers. In a new world, people learn to accept polygamy as natural and right.

KIPPS

Kipps: The Story of a Simple Soul is a story like Charles Dickens's *Great Expectations* (1860-1861). The aunt and uncle who reared Kipps expected him to become a store clerk; Kipps has not been very skilled at anything he has undertaken, and he proves no better at handling an unexpected inheritance. Kipps has a dreary existence: He gains no real pleasure from life, not even from reading. Life in lower-middle-class commercial and shopkeeping society is without substance, imagination, or purpose. Kipps's first thought is to buy a banjo, though he cannot play it. Thinking more seriously of his prospects, he asks his art teacher to marry him, and she proceeds to teach him to speak and dress properly. Kipps tries and hopes, until he encounters an old love, Ann Pornick, working as a maid. He snubs her and in his guilt asks her forgiveness; she not only forgives him, but also marries him. Thus, Kipps has stumbled through mistake after mistake, from education to apprenticeship to courtship and marriage. Finally, when he loses most of his fortune, he and his wife resign themselves to a restricted life and open a bookshop.

Wells's satire is directed at Kipps for trying to be more than he can be, for misplacing values in a system of manners; indeed, Wells intensely scorns the social superficialities. The protagonist of *Tono-*

Bungay, George Ponderevo, has much in common with Kipps, but George is less simple and more reflective. His early life is like Kipps's (and Wells's) in that he resists training for trade, shows a talent for science, marries above his class, divorces, and rediscovers a childhood romance, through scenes of satirical analysis of the social snobs, religious bigots, and capitalist cutthroats of England. More sympathetic is ambitious Uncle Teddy, who makes a fortune with Tono-Bungay, a bogus medicine, and launches a disastrous career in the "romance of modern commerce." George Ponderevo is more a master of his destiny than is Kipps. After the collapse of his uncle's financial empire, George turns to engineering as a means of commitment to scientific objectivity. He is beyond society and governments, as he is alone in the world of love.

Science triumphs over socialism and capitalism in *Tono-Bungay*, while individual vitality triumphs over all ideas in *The History of Mr. Polly*, another of Wells's best comic novels from his middle period. This story begins with a discontented middle-aged shopkeeper, Mr. Polly, contemplating his boredom, indigestion, and proud misuse of English. He decides to burn his shop and cut his throat. Having succeded in his arson but having forgotten to cut his throat, he deserts his wife for happy obscurity as a fat woman's handyman, forgetting the life he detested. Although Mr. Polly is an absurd creature, surrounded by stupid, unambitious people, he is sympathetic because he rebels against that absurdity and stupidity. Wells rewards Mr. Polly well for his rebellion.

Ann Veronica

Wells also rewards the heroine of his infamous novel *Ann Veronica*, which takes up more fully themes of free love and women's rights. Ann Veronica Stanley rebels against her father's authority and flees to London, where she attends university lectures in biology. Having thrown herself into the cause of women's suffrage, she is arrested and imprisoned. Then she elopes with her biology instructor, a married man, to Switzerland. This unconventional woman, however, receives a very conventional reward: She marries her lover, has children, and becomes reconciled with her father.

Having put new ideas into old literary forms with *Ann Veronica*, Wells set the direction of his writing for the rest of his life. In his later novels, ideas, argument, debate, and intellectual analysis become prominent, often at the expense of literary form. Feminist causes give way to issues of world peace in books dealing with the world wars, the one that was and the one to come. *Mr. Britling Sees It Through* is one of the best, though it is a troubling confusion of political despair and comic resignation. Touches of good humor keep the book going with scenes of absurdity, as when Mr. Britling tries to drive his car or Mr. Direck tries to understand British manners. This good humor erodes, however, under the pressure of the events of World War I. Mr. Britling's son is killed, his children's German tutor also is killed, and his private secretary is terribly wounded. The war nearly destroys Mr. Britling, but he sees it through, clinging to a religious hope of divine struggle through human suffering. He commits himself to the cause of world peace, but in the course of writing a letter to the German parents of his children's tutor, he gradually gives way to outrage against Germany and finally collapses in grief. The novel ends when Mr. Britling gets up from his writing to look out his window at the sunrise.

Such an ending hints of an uncertainty in Wells's own commitment to hope. His novels analyze the dead end of civilization and call for redirection through peaceful applications of scientific discoveries. Wells's bitterness at the barbarism of World War I emerges again in *Mr. Blettsworthy on Rampole Island*, whose hero, driven by an unhappy love affair and a failing business, travels to forget. This is one of Wells's most interesting later works, combining anthropology and psychology with experimentation in form. Mr. Blettsworthy's experience with cannibals on Rampole Island may be a fantasy of his madness or an insight into reality, but his experience on the battlefield of World War I is a plunge into an all-too-real madness. Blettsworthy's romantic life of optimism finally yields to a cynical discontent with reality. His perspective is not, however, Wells's final word, since Blettsworthy's business partner, Lyulph Graves, speaks at the end for a philosophy of "creative stoicism," like the attitude which is assumed by

Mr. Britling and, perhaps, by Wells himself. Certainly there were differing points of view in Wells's imagination. These differences may express intellectual confusion, but they gave substance to his fiction and saved it from succumbing utterly to his tendency to preach.

THE AUTOCRACY OF MR. PARHAM

The opposition of Blettsworthy and Graves is repeated in the relationship of Mr. Parham with Sir Bussy Woodcock in *The Autocracy of Mr. Parham*, which envisions a time when humankind might destroy itself through another barbarous world war. Mr. Parham voices the Fascist call (by Benito Mussolini) to traditional discipline and order as a way to prevent self-destruction; Sir Bussy expresses suspicion of dictatorship, social discipline, and intellectual utopias. Wells employs an entertaining device for exposing the differences between his protagonists: He brings them into a fantasy of the future as the result of a séance.

Possessed by a Nietzschean force calling itself the "Master Spirit," Mr. Parham's ego is loosed upon the world as the British dictator Lord Paramount. He goes to war with the United States and Germany, aiming for Russia, but he cannot command the obedience of Sir Bussy, who refuses to use a powerful new gas to destroy the opposition. After the séance, Mr. Parham discovers that Sir Bussy has had a dream very much like his own fantasy. Wells's use of comic irony is very strong in the conclusion, as Mr. Parham is deflated by Sir Bussy's plans to preach peace through the very means by which Mr. Parham had hoped to reach the world himself: journalism. Mr. Parham is a smug intellectual who knows where the world ought to go, if it would only follow his instructions; Sir Bussy is a muddled businessman, limited by the contingencies of immediate events and satisfied with the disorganized vitality that distresses Mr. Parham. This difference between creative capitalism and intellectual autocracy is imaged as a difference in personalities caught in a play of life's ironies.

Wells's scientific romances display an optimistic hope for a future made better by scientific discoveries, countered by the pessimistic doubt that humankind could make the necessary choices for social and political progress. Wells shows sympathy and scorn for the stunted characters of his middle novels, for Kipps, George Ponderevo, and Mr. Polly; he exposes their inadequacies, largely as products of a narrow, stultifying environment, but he also rescues them in life-affirming conclusions. Finally, between the great wars, H. G. Wells, like his Mr. Britling, "saw it through," exercised the "creative stoicism" of Lyulph Graves, and occasionally managed to rise above his pamphleteering style to produce entertaining novels of lives muddled by uncertainty, conflict, and contradiction.

Richard D. McGhee

OTHER MAJOR WORKS

SHORT FICTION: *The Stolen Bacillus and Other Incidents*, 1895; *The Plattner Story and Others*, 1897; *Thirty Strange Stories*, 1897; *Tales of Space and Time*, 1899; *The Vacant Country*, 1899; *Twelve Stories and a Dream*, 1903; *The Country of the Blind and Other Stories*, 1911; *A Door in the Wall and Other Stories*, 1911; *The Short Stories of H. G. Wells*, 1927; *The Favorite Short Stories of H. G. Wells*, 1937.

NONFICTION: *Text-Book of Biology*, 1893 (2 volumes); *Honours Physiography*, 1893 (with Sir Richard A. Gregory); *Certain Personal Matters*, 1897; *A Text-Book of Zoology*, 1898 (with A. M. Davis); *Anticipations of the Reaction of Mechanical and Scientific Progress upon Human Life and Thought*, 1902 (also known as *Anticipations*); *The Discovery of the Future*, 1902; *Mankind in the Making*, 1903; *A Modern Utopia*, 1905; *Socialism and the Family*, 1906; *The Future in America: A Search After Realities*, 1906; *This Misery of Boots*, 1907; *New Worlds for Old*, 1908; *First and Last Things: A Confession of Faith and Rule of Life*, 1908; *The Great State: Essays in Construction*, 1912 (also known as *Socialism and the Great State*); *The War That Will End War*, 1914; *An Englishman Looks at the World: Being a Series of Unrestrained Remarks upon Contemporary Matters*, 1914 (also known as *Social Forces in England and America*); *God, the Invisible King*, 1917; *The Outline of History: Being a Plain History of Life and Mankind*, 1920; *Russia in the Shadows*, 1920; *The Salvaging of Civilization*, 1921; *A Short History of the*

World, 1922; *Socialism and the Scientific Motive*, 1923; *The Open Conspiracy: Blue Prints for a World Revolution*, 1928; *Imperialism and the Open Conspiracy*, 1929; *The Science of Life: A Summary of Contemporary Knowledge About Life and Its Possibilities*, 1929-1930 (with Julian S. Huxley and G. P. Wells); *The Way to World Peace*, 1930; *What Are We to Do with Our Lives?*, 1931 (revised edition of *The Open Conspiracy*); *The Work, Wealth, and Happiness of Mankind*, 1931 (2 volumes); *After Democracy: Addresses and Papers on the Present World Situation*, 1932; *Evolution, Fact and Theory*, 1932 (with Huxley and G. P. Wells); *Experiment in Autobiography: Discoveries and Conclusions of a Very Ordinary Brain Since 1866*, 1934 (2 volumes); *The New America: The New World*, 1935; *The Anatomy of Frustration: A Modern Synthesis*, 1936; *World Brain*, 1938; *The Fate of Homo Sapiens: An Unemotional Statement of the Things That Are Happening to Him Now and of the Immediate Possibilities Confronting Him*, 1939; *The New World Order: Whether It Is Obtainable, How It Can Be Attained, and What Sort of World a World at Peace Will Have to Be*, 1940; *The Common Sense of War and Peace: World Revolution or War Unending?*, 1940; *The Conquest of Time*, 1942; *Phoenix: A Summary of the Inescapable Conditions of World Reorganization*, 1942; *Science and the World Mind*, 1942; *Crux Ansata: An Indictment of the Roman Catholic Church*, 1943; *'42 to '44: A Contemporary Memoir upon Human Behaviour During the Crisis of the World Revolution*, 1944; *Mind at the End of Its Tether*, 1945.

CHILDREN'S LITERATURE: *The Adventures of Tommy*, 1929.

Bibliography

Bergonzi, Bernard. *The Early H. G. Wells: A Study of the Scientific Romances.* Manchester, England: University Press, 1961. Bergonzi examines Wells's *fin de siècle* milieu and analyzes the scientific romances to *The First Men in the Moon*; he concludes that the early writings deserve recognition. Includes a bibliography, an appendix providing texts of "A Tale of the Twentieth Century" and "The Chronic Argonauts," notes, and an index.

Costa, Richard Hauer. *H. G. Wells.* Rev. ed. Boston: Twayne, 1985. A sympathetic survey of Wells's career and influence, with an emphasis on the major novels in the context of literary traditions before and after Wells. A chronology, a review of contemporary trends in Wells criticism, notes, an annotated bibliography, and an index strengthen this helpful book.

Hammond, J. R. *An H. G. Wells Chronology.* New York: St. Martin's Press, 1999. A guide to Well's life and work. Includes bibliographical references and an index.

_____. *An H. G. Wells Companion.* New York: Barnes & Noble, 1979. Part 1 describes Wells's background and his literary reputation. Part 2 is an alphabetical listing and annotation of every title Wells published. Part 3 provides succinct discussions of his short stories; part 4 contains a brief discussion of book-length romances, and part 5 addresses individual novels. Part 6 is a key to characters and locations. There is also an appendix on film versions of Wells's fiction and a bibliography. An indispensable tool for the Wells scholar.

Haynes, Roslynn D. *H. G. Wells: Discoverer of the Future.* London: Macmillan, 1980. This is a thorough study of the influence of science on Wells's fiction and sociological tracts. It shows how science helped Wells to achieve an analytical perspective on the problems of his time, from art to philosophy. A bibliography and an index follow notes for the text.

Huntington, John, ed. *Critical Essays on H. G. Wells.* Boston: G. K. Hall, 1991. Essays on his major writings, including *Tono-Bungay* and *The History of Mr. Polly*, as well as discussions of his science fiction and his treatment of social change, utopia, and women. Includes an introduction but no bibliography.

Smith, David C. *H. G. Wells: Desperately Mortal: A Biography.* New Haven: Yale University Press, 1986. The most scholarly biography of Wells, covering, with authority, every aspect of his life and art. Includes very detailed notes and bibliography.

EUDORA WELTY

Born: Jackson, Mississippi; April 13, 1909

PRINCIPAL LONG FICTION

The Robber Bridegroom, 1942
Delta Wedding, 1946
The Ponder Heart, 1954
Losing Battles, 1970
The Optimist's Daughter, 1972

OTHER LITERARY FORMS

In spite of her success and acclaim as a novelist, Eudora Welty always regarded herself as essentially a writer of short stories. In an interview that appeared in the fall, 1972, issue of the *Paris Review*, she said, "I'm a short-story writer who writes novels the hard way, and by accident." In 1980, all of her previously collected short fiction and two uncollected stories were published in one volume, *The Collected Stories of Eudora Welty*. Another new collection, *Moon Lake and Other Stories*, was published in the same year, and *Retreat* was released in 1981. Prior to that, some had appeared in *Short Stories* (1950) and in *Selected Stories of Eudora Welty* (1954). Other early short-story collections are *A Curtain of Green and Other Stories* (1941); *The Wide Net and Other Stories* (1943); *The Golden Apples* (1949), regarded by some as a loosely structured novel, but considered by Welty to be a group of interconnected stories; and *The Bride of the Innisfallen, and Other Stories* (1955). Welty also published numerous essays and reviews, some of which were collected in *The Eye of the Story: Selected Essays and Reviews* (1978). In addition, she published a book for children, *The Shoe Bird* (1964), and books of her own photographs, *One Time, One Place* (1971) and *Eudora Welty: Photographs* (1989). A memoir, *One Writer's Beginnings*, appeared in 1984.

ACHIEVEMENTS

Although it was not until she wrote *Losing Battles* and *The Optimist's Daughter* that Welty's name began to appear on the best-seller lists, her work had long been recognized and appreciated by discerning readers. In five decades of writing and publishing, she received nearly every major award for fiction offered in the United States. Among them are the prestigious William Dean Howells Medal of the Academy of Arts and Letters for "the most distinguished work of American fiction" for the years 1950 through 1955, the National Institute of Arts and Letters Gold Medal for the Novel in 1972, the Pulitzer Prize for Fiction in 1973, and the National Medal for Literature at the American Book Awards ceremony in 1980. In addition, she was awarded several honorary doctorates, Guggenheim Fellowships, special professorships, and membership in the National Institute of Arts and Letters.

Uninterested in either fame or fortune, Welty simply wanted the opportunity to write and the assurance that there are readers who enjoy her work. She repeatedly expressed gratitude to such writers and editors as Robert Penn Warren, Cleanth Brooks, Albert Erskine, Ford Madox Ford, and Katherine Anne Porter, who were among the first persons of influence to recognize her ability and to promote interest in her early stories. Warren, Brooks, and Erskine accepted some of her first stories for *The Southern Review* and thus opened the door for subsequent publication in such magazines as *The Atlantic Monthly*, *Harper's Bazaar*, and *The New Yorker*. This exposure to a national audience also facilitated the publication of her first volume of stories.

BIOGRAPHY

Eudora Alice Welty was born in Jackson, Mississippi, on April 13, 1909. She would spend most of her life in Jackson. She was the only daughter of Christian Webb Welty and Mary Chestina Andrews Welty; she had two younger brothers. Soon after their marriage in 1904, Welty's parents moved to Jackson. Her father, who came from Ohio, where his father owned a farm, was president of the well-established Lamar Life Insurance Company. Her mother, a West Virginian, was descended from pre-Revolutionary War Virginia stock, engendered by country preachers, teachers, and lawyers. Welty, who claimed that she would feel "shy, and discouraged at the very thought" of a biography about her, felt that a "private life should be kept private." Still, though she insisted that it is the writer's work, not his or her life, that is important, she did finally write a memoir of her family history and her early years, *One Writer's Beginnings*, which was published in 1984 and received positive critical comment.

Perhaps one reason she suggested that her own biography would not "particularly interest anybody" is that she lived for the most part in the mainstream of American society. As Katherine Anne Porter aptly observes in her introduction to *A Curtain of Green*, Welty is not the "spiritual and intellectual exile" that typifies the modern artist. She attended Central High School in Jackson, then went for two years to Mississippi State College for Women, in Columbus, before transferring to the University of Wisconsin in 1927. After graduating with a bachelor of arts degree in English in 1929, she enrolled in the School of Business at Columbia University, where she studied advertising for a year. By then, the country was in the throes of the Depression, and she returned to Jackson to seek work. During the next several years, she held a variety of jobs in advertising, radio scriptwriting, and part-time newspaper work. She also began writing stories. Possibly the most important of those early jobs was the position of "Junior Publicity Agent" with the Works Progress Administration from 1933 to 1936. In this position, Welty was required to travel extensively through Mississippi doing newspaper stories on various WPA projects. Her work involved taking photographs, talking with a great variety of people, and, perhaps most important, listening to them. As Welty herself confessed, she had a "good ear" and a visual imagination, qualities that enabled her to hear and observe things and people during those three years that she would use in her fiction throughout her life.

A number of the photographs she took while on her WPA assignment were displayed for a month in the Lugene Gallery in New York, a small camera shop. Later, some of them appeared in her published collection of photographs *One Time, One Place*. Only after several years of discouraging rejection slips did Welty finally publish a story, "Death of a Traveling Salesman," in a small magazine called *Manuscript* in 1936. Soon after that, her talent was discovered by Robert Penn Warren, Albert Erskine, and Cleanth Brooks. Then, John Woodburn of Doubleday, Doran, and Company became interested in her work, and with his support, her first collection of short stories, *A Curtain of Green and Other Stories*, was published in 1941. The next year, her first novel, *The Robber Bridegroom*, appeared. Two of her books have been successfully adapted for the stage, *The Ponder Heart* as a New York stage play in 1956 and *The Robber Bridegroom* as a Broadway musical in 1974.

Humane, thoughtful, and generous, Welty modestly accepted the many honors that came to her. Scarcely a year would pass after 1940 in which she would not received a major award of some kind. She also gave abundantly of her time to schoolchildren, scholars, interviewers, and aspiring writers. She was active in community causes in Jackson, gave scores

(Richard O. Moore)

of lectures and readings, assisted numerous charities, and even provided recipes for cookbooks.

Welty asserted in a famous article, "Place in Fiction," in *The South Atlantic Quarterly* (1956), that a deep sense of place is vital to a writer's development. She herself spent her entire adult life in the neo-Tudor house her father built in 1926 across the street from the campus of Belhaven College in Jackson. In fact, as a young woman she would listen, through the open window of her bedroom, to the melodious sounds emanating from the music building on the Belhaven campus. Music, as well as the visual arts, became an important motif in her fiction. Welty said that aspects of two women characters in her fiction most greatly illustrate qualities of her own life—the high regard for art held by Miss Eckhart, the piano teacher in "June Recital" (in *Golden Apples*), and the great concern of Laurel McKelva Hand (*The Optimist's Daughter*) with her family's past. However, Laurel, unlike Miss Eckhart, is able to deal with her conflicts and achieves "a separate peace."

During the years of severe unrest over civil rights issues, Welty's critics attacked her for not actively taking up that cause in her fiction. She answered those critics eloquently in a 1965 *Atlantic Monthly* essay entitled "Must the Novelist Crusade?" However, in *The New Yorker* the next year, Welty published a short story, "Where Is the Voice Coming From?," attacking the ugly racism of the South that resulted in the murder of a black civil rights leader.

In her introduction to *The Collected Stories of Eudora Welty*, Welty expresses characteristic gratitude for the help and encouragement she received during her career. In her memoir she speaks of her good fortune in being reared in a family that encouraged the reading of books. She had a particular love for myths, fairy tales, and legends, and she believed it her good fortune to have grown up in a region where, as she said, people love talking and delight in a good yarn. Even though she was teased as a child for having a "Yankee" father, her work is deeply rooted, like its creator, in the South as a place. Still, neither she nor her fiction could be called "regional" in any narrow sense of the term. In fact, she balked at the regionalist title. Her work, for all its down-home south-

ern flavor, attests the universality of her vision and the capacity of her art to elude easy labels. Her subject is not the South, but humanity.

ANALYSIS

Paramount in Eudora Welty's work is the sense of what "community," or group membership, means in the South and how it is expressed through manners, attitudes, and dialogue. Clearly, it provides a special way of seeing and responding. In Welty's published essays and interviews, certain concerns keep surfacing—the relationship between time and place and the artistic endeavor; the importance of human relationships in a work of fiction; the necessity for the artist to be grounded in real life and yet be aware of life's "mystery"; the value of the imagination; and the function of memory. These concerns find expression in her work principally in the tension between what is actual, what is seen and heard in a specific time and place, and what is felt or known intuitively. Welty uses the sometimes conflicting demands of the community and the self, the surface life and the interior life, to describe this tension in her novels. On the one hand is the need for community and order; on the other is the need for the separate individual life which often works against community and order.

Typically, a Welty novel swings between overt action, including dialogue, and individual contemplation. This is especially evident in *Delta Wedding*, where Welty almost rhythmically alternates dialogue and action with the inner musings of her principal female characters. In *The Optimist's Daughter*, only Laurel Hand's thoughts are set against the exterior action, but it becomes apparent that her father, as he lies unmoving in his hospital bed, is silently contemplating the mystery of life and human relationships for perhaps the first time in his life. Her mother, too, near the end of her life, had begun speaking out the painful things she must have harbored for many years in her dark soul. Even Edna Earle Ponder in *The Ponder Heart* seems to talk incessantly to keep the inner life from raising itself into consciousness. In *Losing Battles*, where Welty says she consciously tried to tell everything through speech and action—she had been accused of obscurantism in previous works—

the pattern still emerges. Instead of swinging between action and cerebration, however, this novel swings between action and description. Still, the effect is surprisingly similar, though the pages of action and dialogue far outnumber the pages of description and the transitions between the two modes of narration are very abrupt. Even so, the young schoolteacher who chooses love and marriage against her mentor's advice slips occasionally into Welty's meditative mode. The alternation of thought and action is also the basic structural pattern of the stories in *The Golden Apples*.

Thus, in Welty's novels, external order is established through speech and action that sustain community, either the social or family group. In fact, the novels are often structured around community rituals that reinforce the group entity against outside intrusions and shore up its defenses against its most insidious foe, the impulse to separateness in its individual members. *Delta Wedding* is set entirely in the framework of one of these community-perpetuating rituals. For the moment, the wedding is everything, and members of the group pay it homage by gathering, giving gifts, feasting, and burying their individual lives in its demands. *Losing Battles* is also framed by a community ritual, the family reunion. The threat from individual outsiders is felt constantly, and the family takes sometimes extreme measures to ward off influences that might undermine its solidarity. There are at least two rituals that provide structure for *The Ponder Heart*, the funeral and the courtroom trial. The first of these is conducted in enemy territory, outside the acceptable group domain; the second is conducted in home territory, and acquittal for the accused member of the group is a foregone conclusion. A funeral is also the major external event of *The Optimist's Daughter* and becomes the battleground in a contest for supremacy between two opposing groups or communities. Several of the stories or chapters in *The Golden Apples* are also structured around community rituals, including the June piano recital, the girls' summer camp, and the funeral.

In addition to these large, highly structured observances, there are the multitude of unwritten laws that govern the group. Welty's community members attach great importance to certain objects and practices: a treasured lamp given to the bride, a handcrafted breadboard made for a mother-in-law, the establishment of family pedigrees, the selection of one male member of the community for special reverence and heroic expectation, the protection of the past from intrusion or reassessment, and, perhaps most important of all, the telling of stories as an attestation of the vitality and endurance of the group.

Underlying all of this attention to ritual and group expectation, however, is the unspoken acknowledgment that much of it is a game the participants have agreed to play, for their own sake and for the sake of the community. Some of the participants may be fooled, but many are not. Aware but fearful, they go through the motions of fulfilling community requirements in an effort to hold back the dark, to avoid facing the mystery, to keep their individual selves from emerging and crying for existence. They sense themselves to be at what Welty calls "the jumping off place" and are afraid to make the leap in the dark. They agree to pretend to be fooled. They tell stories instead of rehearsing their fears and uncertainties. The bolder ones defy the group and either leave it or live on its periphery. In every book, there are moments when a character confronts or consciously evades the dark underside of human personality and experience, and memory becomes a device for dealing with the effects of that confrontation or for evading it.

Paradoxically, storytelling, an important ritual for securing the past and bolstering community against passion, disorder, the intimations of mystery, and the erosive effects of individual impulses and yearnings, assists in the breakdown of the very group it was intended to support. The risk of indulging in rituals is that they sometimes set people to thinking and reevaluating their own individual lives and the lives of others close to them. The ritual is performed by the group, but it may stir the solitary inner being to life and to the kind of probing contemplation that jeopardizes the group's authority. Such a countereffect may be triggered by the storytelling ritual even though that ritual is meant to seal up the past for ready reference whenever the group needs reinforcement. Because storytelling relies on memory, it can become an exercise of the individual imagination. It tends to lapse, as one commentator observes, "into the memory of a memory" and thus shifts sides from the group's activities into the realm of mystery. The community's habit of setting up straw men for heroes can similarly erode community solidarity because it too relies upon imagination and memory. It glorifies the individual rather than the group spirit.

As Welty presents this conflict, then, between the self and the group, and between the intuitive and the actual, she writes into her work a sense of foreboding. The community, especially the traditional southern community, is doomed. It cannot forever maintain itself on the old terms, for it is dependent upon the acquiescence of separate individuals who seem increasingly impervious to the efforts of the group to contain them. Welty's work also suggests that some of the things the community prizes and perpetuates are merely gestures and artifacts with little intrinsic value or meaning. When the meanings behind what a community treasures have been lost or forgotten, that community cannot long endure. In actively laboring to exclude others, the group works against its own best nature, its capacity for loving and caring. Threats to order and community may indeed come from the outside, but Welty insists that the more serious threats come from the inside, from that part of the human heart and mind that seeks to go its own way.

THE ROBBER BRIDEGROOM

Welty's first novel, *The Robber Bridegroom*, is quite unlike her others. Its most noticeable differences are its setting in a much older South, on the old Natchez Trace in the days of bandits and Native Americans, and its fairy-tale style and manner. Even with these differences, Welty establishes what becomes her basic fictional stance. She achieves tension between the actual and the imaginary by freighting this very real setting with fabulous characters and events. The legendary characters are transformed by Welty's imagination and deftly made to share the territory with figures from the Brothers Grimm. Welty indicated the double nature of her novel, or novella, when in an address to the Mississippi Historical

Society she called it a "Fairy Tale of the Natchez Trace." A favorite of William Faulkner, the book is a masterpiece, a delightful blend of legend, myth, folklore, and fairy tale that swings from rollicking surface comedy and lyrical style to painful, soul-searching explorations of the ambiguities of human experience. Although it deals with love and separateness—Robert Penn Warren's terms for the conflicting needs of communities and individuals in Welty's work—it does not deal with them in the same way that the later novels do. Clement Musgrove, a planter whose innocence leads him into marriage with the greedy Salome and an excursion into humanity's heart of darkness, learns what it is like to face the cold, dark nights of despair comfortless and alone. His daughter, Rosamond, is beautiful and loving, but she is also an inveterate liar who betrays her husband's trust in order to learn his "real" identity. Jamie Lockhart, who leads a double life as both bandit and gentleman, keeps his true identity hidden even from her whom he loves. Thus, like so many Welty characters, the principal actors in *The Robber Bridegroom* have interior lives that threaten the equilibrium of their exterior worlds.

In another sense, too, *The Robber Bridegroom* is closely linked with Welty's other novels. In writing the book, Welty testifies to the value of stories and the storytelling ritual that buttresses community, a theme that reappears in all of her novels. She finds common ground with her readers in this novel by spinning a yarn full of their favorite childhood fairytales. Then, too, fairy-tale worlds, imaginative though they are, sustain surface order, for they are worlds of sure answers, of clear good and evil, of one-dimensional characters, and of predictable rewards and punishments. As such, they confirm what the community collectively believes and perpetuates. Just as imagination, intuition, and the ponderings of the individual human soul jeopardize the codes a community lives by in other Welty novels, so do they undercut the basic assumptions of the fairy tale in this novel. Here, answers are sometimes permanently withheld, people are complex and unpredictable, the richest prize is found in human relationships rather than in kingdoms and gold, appearances are deceiving, and evil may lie in unexpected places. It is worthy of note that Welty began her novel-writing career with a book that delights in the fairy tale at the same time that it questions community assumptions about fairy-tale morality.

DELTA WEDDING

The tension between community expectations and individual yearnings and apprehensions is central to *Delta Wedding*. The narrative takes place in the Mississippi delta country, during the week of Dabney Fairchild's wedding. The Fairchild family, after whom the nearby town is named, is of the social elite and has moderate wealth, mostly in property. The wedding provides an occasion for the family to gather and exercise the rituals and traditions that bind them together and strengthen their sense of community. The wedding itself is the principal ritual, of course, with its attendant food preparation, dress making, rehearsal, and home and yard decorating. Welty's eye for manners and ear for speech are flawless as the Fairchilds deliberate over the consequences of George Fairchild's having married beneath him and Dabney's seemingly unfortunate repetition of her father's mistake. The Fairchilds still claim George, however, even though they have little use for his wife, Robbie Reid, and they will continue to embrace Dabney in spite of her choosing to marry an outsider, Troy Flavin. It is the habit of community to maintain order by defining and placing people and things in relation to itself. A person either does or does not have legitimate ties to the group.

The Fairchilds also repeat family stories in order to keep the past secure and give stability to the present. Their current favorite story is also one that makes a hero out of the male heir-apparent. George's dead brother was apparently more remarkable than he, but George is the one survivor, and the family's hopes rest with him. At least a dozen times in the book, some version is told of George's staying on the railroad track with his mentally retarded niece whose foot was caught in the rails. Instead of leaping to safety with the others, he stayed to face the oncoming train. Luckily, the engineer of the Yellow Dog was able to stop the train in time. By choosing to stay with Maureen instead of answering his wife's plea to save himself, George made a reflexive choice for honor and blood over marital obligation. Later, he again chooses family over wife when he comes for the prewedding activities instead of looking for his absent, heartbroken wife.

Running counter to the speech and actions that affirm order and community, however, is an undercurrent of threat to that order. Welty intersperses the overt actions and attitudes of the family, especially of the aunts, whose sole desire is to perpetuate the clan structure, with individual ruminations of other female characters who are part of that structure and yet somewhat peripheral to it. Ellen, who married into the Fairchilds and has never dared resist them, has moments of personal doubt that would be regarded as treasonous were they known by her aunts. Dabney also wonders, in a brief honest moment, about the homage paid to the wedding ritual for its own sake. Further, she accidentally breaks a treasured lamp, a family heirloom given her by the aunts as a wedding present. Little Laura, having lost her mother, has also lost her basic tie to the family. From her position on the edge of the Fairchild clan, she questions the community tenets that exclude her. Even George seems ready to violate community expectations by his apparent willingness to deprive two of the aunts of their home.

The novel's essential statement, then, is that the community is losing its hold. In an interview published in 1972 by *The Southern Review*, Welty is asked the question: "Is Shellmound [the home of the Fairchilds] with its way of life and its values doomed?" She replies, "Oh, yes. I think that was implicit in the novel: that this was all such a fragile, temporary thing. At least I hope it was." She adds, "Well, you're living in a very precarious world without knowing it, always." The community's position is inexorably altered in the face of individual yearning and independent action.

THE PONDER HEART

There are two large community rituals in *The Ponder Heart*: the funeral of Bonnie Dee Peacock and the trial of Uncle Daniel Ponder for her murder. Such narrative matter sounds ominous enough to one unfamiliar with Welty's capacity for comedy, but to the initiated, it promises a hilarious display of southern talk and manners. Still, *The Ponder Heart* is troubled, as Welty's other novels are, by an ominous current running beneath its surface action. Like the Fairchilds of *Delta Wedding*, the Ponders have social position and wealth—perhaps greater than that of the Fairchilds. They are on the decline, however, in spite of the efforts of Edna Earle Ponder, Welty's first-person narrator, to maintain the family and its image. Symbolic of the failing family or community image that Edna Earle seeks to perpetuate and protect are two buildings which the family owns, the Beulah Hotel, run by Edna Earle, and the Ponder home a few miles out of town. In the end, both buildings are virtually empty. The family has shrunk to two members, and the future holds no promise.

The storyline tells of middle-aged Uncle Daniel's taking to wife young Bonnie Dee Peacock, losing her, regaining her, losing her again, reclaiming her, and then finally losing her by tickling her to death in the aftermath of an electric storm. Uncle Daniel's mental age is considerably lower than his chronological age, but he is blessed with a generous nature. He gives away everything he can get his hands on, and has to be watched continually. Not that Edna Earle cares to restrain him very much, for he is the revered scion, like George in *Delta Wedding*, without whose approbation and presence the community would totter. Her duty is to protect and sustain Daniel, and she will not even permit herself private doubts over what that duty requires. The entire novel is the report of her conversation about Uncle Daniel with a visitor who is stranded at the Beulah. Clearly, Edna Earle's talk and actions are designed to maintain order and community as she has known them all her life. She believes that if she relaxes her vigil, the structure will collapse.

The ritual of the Peacock funeral is important because it is grossly inferior to the Ponder notion of what constitutes a funeral. The Peacocks are what the Ponders (except Daniel, who in his innocence would not know the difference) would call "country"; in other words, they are regarded as comically inferior beings who have no business marrying into the Ponder family. The trial is more to Edna Earle's liking,

though it is threatened by the presence of the low-bred Peacocks and a prosecuting shyster lawyer who is an outsider. Edna Earle gets caught in a lie designed to protect Daniel, but the day is saved when Daniel begins passing out greenbacks in the courtroom. The jury votes for acquittal in record time, and Daniel cheerily dispenses the whole family fortune. He discovers to his sorrow afterward, however, that people who have taken his money can no longer face him. Thus, in the end, Daniel, who wanted nothing more than company and an audience for his stories, is left lonely and friendless. Though Edna Earle tries to inject new hope through the promise of a new audience—her captive guest at the Beulah—doom is on the horizon for the Ponders even more surely than it was for the Fairchilds. The collapse of community structure in this novel, as in *Delta Wedding*, can be laid partly to the failure of the community's rather artificial system of supports—rituals, traditions, family stories, pedigrees, and a family "hero." It must also be laid, however, to the fact that Uncle Daniel, in his innocence, breaks away and acts as an individual. He is not capable of the contemplation that undermines community in *Delta Wedding*, but neither can he be restrained to act as a member of the group instead of as himself.

LOSING BATTLES

In *Losing Battles*, Welty partially turns the tables on what she had done with the conflict between community and self in her previous two novels and in *The Golden Apples*. Here, she shows that community, though mildly ruffled by individual needs and doubts, can prevail when it is sustained by strong individuals who are also loyal group members. Welty indicates in a *Southern Review* interview that she deliberately chose as her setting the poorest section of Mississippi during the time of the Depression, so that her characters would be shown on a bare stage with themselves as their only resource, without "props to their lives." Thus, the artificial structures built of money and status that support community in *Delta Wedding* and *The Ponder Heart* are not available to the Vaughn-Beecham-Renfro clan in *Losing Battles*. Perhaps that is one reason for their greater durability.

The story is told almost entirely through dialogue and action, interlaced with occasional lyrical descriptions of setting and even less frequent ruminations of the story's principal outsider, Gloria Renfro, the hero's wife. The action takes place entirely in one day and the following morning, with details of the past filled in through family storytelling. Jack Renfro, the young grandson who has been exalted by family hope and expectations, bears some resemblance to George Fairchild and Daniel Ponder. On him lies the chief burden of sustaining the family, of guaranteeing its survival as a unit. He returns home from the state penitentiary to the waiting family reunion that is celebrating old Granny Vaughn's birthday. He finds there not only his bride, but a baby daughter he has never seen. The family has believed, has had to believe, that things will be better once Jack has returned home. Jack himself believes it, and, as Welty indicates, the others take their faith from his. Through a series of wild, funny episodes—and more than a few tender moments—the family prevails. Welty says that in this comic novel she intended to portray the indomitability, the unquenchable spirit of human beings. Folks such as these may be losing the battles, but they are still fighting them, and that is what counts.

Welty describes "the solidity of the family" as "the strongest thing in the book." She also recognizes that, in a clan such as this, a character sometimes has to be himself or herself before he or she can reinforce the unity of the group. Welty says that such a "sticking together" as is seen in *Losing Battles* "involves both a submerging and a triumph of the individual, because you can't really conceive of the whole unless you *are* an identity." The extended family of *Losing Battles* engages in rituals to maintain itself just as the Fairchild family does in *Delta Wedding*. It acknowledges milestones reached by its members, milestones such as weddings and ninetieth birthdays; it tells stories; it creates a hero; and it works painstakingly to establish and affirm blood relationships with any who might seek entrance into the group. All is done with the honor of the clan—or the individual as member of the clan—in mind, whether it is going to jail or rescuing a car from a cliff on Banner Top.

In spite of the prevailing unity and the optimistic conclusion to the novel's events, there are small rumblings of individual assertion against community. Gloria loves Jack, but she does not want to be a member of his family. She envisions a smaller community, made up of just her, Jack, and their baby, Lady May. The group, however, will not allow her to build a community of her own. Against her will, it tries to reconstruct a parentage for her that would make her a blood relation. The relatives perform a rather cruel ritual of pouncing on her and forcing her to eat watermelon, but she remains adamant. She also remains steadfast in her admiration for Miss Julia Mortimer, the schoolteacher who picked Gloria as her successor and who fought a losing battle all her life against the joyful ignorance of the likes of Jack's family.

Thus, there are several influences in the book that threaten, though not seriously, the sense of community. Gloria and her child, and Miss Julia, are the most obvious ones. It becomes apparent, though, in the very style of the narration, which repeatedly turns from family action and talk to brief imaginative description, that the ordering of the actual and the real according to community necessity does not entirely carry the day. There is another side to experience, the imaginative, the intuitive—a part of the individual soul that resists allegiance.

The Optimist's Daughter

In *The Optimist's Daughter*, Welty returns to a more balanced combination of action and contemplation. The book's perceiving eye is Laurel Hand, daughter of Becky and Judge McKelva. The abiding question for Laurel is why, after the death of the intelligent, sensitive Becky, the Judge took for a wife a crass, tasteless woman half his age. Laurel helplessly watches her father's still form as he silently reviews his life in a hospital room, ironically set against the backdrop of the Mardi Gras festival. She repeats her helpless watch as he lies in his coffin at Mount Salus while his wife, Wanda Fay Chisom, performs her gnashing, wailing ritual of bereavement and his old friends perform their ritual of eulogy. The Chisom family, who nod appreciatively as Fay grossly mourns, are the same breed as the Peacocks in *The Ponder Heart*, entirely out of context in the McKelva home. Laurel, however, is equally uncomfortable with her own group's rites of community preservation—telling stories about the Judge that make a hero of him, despising the intrusive outsider, urging Laurel to stay and bolster the old relationship. Laurel's husband Phil was killed in military service many years ago, and Laurel herself is working in Chicago, but the women who were bridesmaids at her wedding have kept that group intact and still refer to themselves as "the bridesmaids."

Laurel's last night at home is spent in anguish. Trapped by an invading chimney swift in rooms full of memories, she is caught hopelessly in the past. In the course of the night, she is forced to examine the protective structure she had built around her parents' marriage and her own. In doing so, she must allow memory and imagination to reinterpret the past which she had wanted to keep sealed away in the perfection of her own making, and she must relinquish her old idea of what constitutes group unity and loyalty. The Wanda Fays of the world will always claim their space, will always intrude. The secret for surviving their intrusion, Laurel discovers, is to withdraw one's protective walls so that the Fays have nothing to knock down. Laurel at last allows truth to dismantle the edifice of community as she had conceived it, and she finds, through the imagination and the heart, a new source of strength in watching the artificial construct tumble. Thus, the foreboding and pessimism arising from the impending doom of community in *Delta Wedding* and *The Ponder Heart*, diverted for a time in the paradoxical optimism of *Losing Battles*, are to some extent reversed in Laurel's final acceptance in *The Optimist's Daughter*. *The Golden Apples* had foretold such an outcome, for a number of its characters must also deal with the relationship between their individual lives and the group life.

The miracle of Welty's work is the skill with which her imagination bears on the actual and makes a reconciliation out of the conflicting demands of the community and the private life, out of that which can be perceived by the senses and that which can be known only intuitively. For Welty, the actual is mainly the realities of Mississippi life. In her work, however, the reality of Mississippi becomes a springboard rich with possibilities for an imagination that knows how to use time and place as doorways to the human heart.

Marilyn Arnold, updated by Philip A. Tapley

OTHER MAJOR WORKS

SHORT FICTION: *A Curtain of Green and Other Stories*, 1941; *The Wide Net and Other Stories*, 1943; *The Golden Apples*, 1949; *Short Stories*, 1950; *Selected Stories of Eudora Welty*, 1954; *The Bride of the Innisfallen, and Other Stories*, 1955; *The Collected Stories of Eudora Welty*, 1980; *Moon Lake and Other Stories*, 1980; *Retreat*, 1981.

NONFICTION: *Music from Spain*, 1948; *The Reading and Writing of Short Stories*, 1949; *Place in Fiction*, 1957; *Three Papers on Fiction*, 1962; *One Time, One Place: Mississippi in the Depression, a Snapshot Album*, 1971; *A Pageant of Birds*, 1974; *The Eye of the Story: Selected Essays and Reviews*, 1978; *Ida M'Toy*, 1979; *Miracles of Perception: The Art of Willa Cather*, 1980 (with Alfred Knopf and Yehudi Menuhin); *One Writer's Beginnings*, 1984; *Eudora Welty: Photographs*, 1989; *A Writer's Eye: Collected Book Reviews*, 1994 (Pearl Amelia McHaney, editor).

CHILDREN'S LITERATURE: *The Shoe Bird*, 1964.

BIBLIOGRAPHY

Devlin, Albert J. *Eudora Welty's Chronicle: A Story of Mississippi Life*. Jackson: University Press of Mississippi, 1983. Devlin analyzes certain works, such as *Delta Wedding*, in great detail. He offers insightful criticism and suggests that Welty's writing contains a historical structure, spanning from the territorial era to modern times.

Evans, Elizabeth. *Eudora Welty*. New York: Frederick Ungar, 1981. Presents a reliable but not comprehensive overview of Welty's life and work.

Manning, Carol S. *With Ears Opening Like Morning Glories: Eudora Welty and the Love of Storytelling*. Westport, Conn.: Greenwood Press, 1985. An advanced book offering a critical interpretation of Welty's writing. Manning believes that the root of Welty's creativity is the southern love of storytelling. Offers a select bibliography.

Mortimer, Gail L. *Daughter of the Swan: Love and Knowledge in Eudora Welty's Fiction.* Athens: University of Georgia Press, 1994. Concentrates primarily on the short stories and discusses one novel, *The Optimist's Daughter,* in detail.

Vande Kieft, Ruth M. *Eudora Welty.* Rev. ed. Boston: Twayne, 1987. Vande Kieft offers an excellent critical analysis of Welty's major works, an overview of Welty's career, and an annotated secondary bibliography. A well-written, useful study for all students.

Waldron, Ann. *Eudora: A Writer's Life.* New York: Doubleday, 1998. The first complete but unauthorized biography of Welty. Offers a balanced study of her life as well as sensitive and sensible analyses of her short stories and novels.

Westling, Louise Hutchings. *Sacred Groves and Ravaged Gardens: The Fiction of Eudora Welty, Carson McCullers, and Flannery O'Connor.* Athens: University of Georgia Press, 1985. Westling examines the lives and works of Welty and the other authors in terms of their common concerns as women, such as their relationships with men and with their mothers. Offers a provocative and original viewpoint.

Weston, Ruth D. *Gothic Traditions and Narrative Techniques in the Fiction of Eudora Welty.* Baton Rouge: Louisiana State University Press, 1994. Examines Welty's fiction, especially the novels *Losing Battles* and *Delta Wedding,* in terms of its relation to "myth, . . . 'mystery and magic,'" inspired by Welty's acquaintance with the literary gothic tradition.

FRANZ WERFEL

Born: Prague, Czechoslovakia; September 10, 1890
Died: Beverly Hills, California; August 26, 1945

PRINCIPAL LONG FICTION

Nicht der Mörder, der Ermordete ist schuldig: Eine Novelle, 1920 (*Not the Murderer,* 1937)

Verdi: Roman der Oper, 1924 (*Verdi: A Novel of the Opera,* 1925)

Der Tod des Kleinbürgers, 1927 (novella; *The Man Who Conquered Death,* 1927; also as *The Death of a Poor Man,* 1927)

Der Abituriententag: Die Geschichte einer Jugendschuld, 1928 (*Class Reunion,* 1929)

Barbara: Oder, Die Frömmigkeit, 1929 (*The Pure in Heart,* 1931; also as *The Hidden Child,* 1931)

Die Geschwister von Neapel, 1931 (*The Pascarella Family,* 1932)

Kleine Verhältnisse, 1831 (novella; *Poor People,* 1937)

Die vierzig Tage des Musa Dagh, 1933 (*The Forty Days of Musa Dagh,* 1934)

Höret die Stimme, 1937 (*Hearken unto the Voice,* 1938)

Twilight of a World, 1937 (novellas)

Der veruntreute Himmel: Die Geschichte einer Magd, 1939 (*Embezzled Heaven,* 1940)

Das Lied von Bernadette, 1941 (*The Song of Bernadette,* 1942)

Stern der Ungeborenen: Ein Reiseroman, 1946 (*Star of the Unborn,* 1946)

Cella: Oder, Die Überwinder, 1954 (wr. 1937-1938)

OTHER LITERARY FORMS

In addition to the novels listed above, Franz Werfel authored the novellas included in the collection *Geheimnis eines Menschen* (1927; *Saverio's Secret,* 1937). Werfel's voluminous lyric work was published in a number of collections, among them the influential expressionist ones, *Der Weltfreund* (1911; friend to the world), *Wir sind* (1913; we are), *Einander* (1915; to one another), and *Der Gerichtstag* (1919; Judgment Day). In addition, Werfel wrote a number of internationally successful dramas: an adaptation of Euripides' *The Trojan Women* (415 B.C.E.) entitled *Die Troerinnen des Euripides* (1915); *Spiegelmensch* (1920; mirror man), dealing with the theme of the alter ego; *Bocksgesang* (1921; *Goat Song,* 1926), a mythic drama; *Juárez und Maximilian* (1924; *Juárez and Maximilian,* 1926), a drama about the Habsburg emperor of Mexico, which became Werfel's first interna-

(CORBIS/Bettman)

tional success; and *Paulus unter den Juden* (1926; *Paul Among the Jews*, 1928), which treats the historical moment when Christianity broke away from Judaism. Werfel's greatest American success was *Jacobwsky und der Oberst* (1944; *Jacobwsky and the Colonel*, 1944), the story of a Polish officer and a Jew who manage to escape from advancing German troups in France. Most works have appeared in *Gesammelte Werke* (1948-1975; collected works), edited by Adolf D. Klarmann.

ACHIEVEMENTS

During his early career, Werfel was one of the most outstanding representatives of German expressionism, giving voice to the world-embracing attitude of this literary movement. This feeling of oneness with all humankind is best exemplified by his famous verse line: "My only wish is to be related to you, O Man!" His drama *Spiegelmensch* incorporated one of the most popular expressionist themes, that of the alter ego, which was to find its way into many con-

temporary films, such as *The Cabinet of Dr. Caligari* (1919). Today, however, Werfel is remembered primarily for his novels, which made him one of the most widely read German-speaking writers of his time.

Werfel's main achievement in his novels lies not in his language or his style, which is traditional and similar to that of other writers of the 1930's and 1940's, but rather in his insistence on the importance of people (no doubt a heritage of expressionism) and his belief in the importance of people's spiritual well-being. He is concerned about people finding their places in relation to other people and to God rather than about their material welfare. Werfel fought against all materialistic, areligious, agnostic, and nihilistic elements of his time, including science and technology, against an "age that with mockery, anger and indifference is turning away from these ultimate values of our life," as Werfel himself put it. This insistence on the validity of metaphysics was at the same time the reason for his declining popularity during the late 1950's and the 1960's, when a settling of accounts with the German Nazi past and a present of newly gained affluence became the hallmark of social-critical German literature.

BIOGRAPHY

Franz Werfel was born in 1890 in the city of Prague, the son of a wealthy Jewish glove manufacturer and merchant. During his high school years in Prague, he became a personal friend of Willy Haas and Max Brod, who were also to become writers. After his graduation, Werfel attended lectures on law and philosophy at the German University of Prague. His mandatory one-year military service was spent in an artillery regiment in Prague. His father's attempt to make him a merchant by sending him as an apprentice to a freight company in Hamburg failed: Werfel showed no inclination or talent for becoming a merchant. In 1911, his first book of poetry, *Der Weltfreund*, appeared, evidently influenced by Walt Whitman's *Leaves of Grass* (1855, 1856, 1860, 1867, 1871, 1876, 1881-1882, 1889, 1891-1892).

Because of the success of this collection, Werfel was able to obtain a position as an editor with the Kurt Wolff publishing company in Leipzig in the fall of 1912, where he stayed until 1914—an extremely productive time. In July of 1914, he had to follow the call to arms; during the first months of World War I, he wrote a number of antiwar poems. In 1917, he was ordered to the war press headquarters in Vienna, where a number of other authors, among them Rainer Maria Rilke, Hugo von Hofmannsthal, Robert Musil, Peter Altenberg, and Franz Blei, were able to survive. During this time, he met Alma Mahler—the widow of composer Gustav Mahler, then the wife of the architect Walter Gropius. During the revolutionary turmoil at the end of the war, Werfel participated in mcctings and rallies of the leftist Red Guards, which had been founded by young authors, an activity which he later regretted.

The years from 1918 to 1938 Werfel spent in and around Vienna, interrupted only by a number of extended trips. In 1925, for example, he and Alma took a long trip to the Middle East which inspired Werfel to write the drama *Paul Among the Jews*. Conversations with the dramatist Hermann Sudermann at the Italian Riviera, who told him about the hardships of his youth, induced him to write the novel *Class Reunion*. During a visit to Paris in the spring of 1928, Werfel conceived the idea of writing the novel *The Pure in Heart*. In July, 1929, Werfel and Alma were married. On a second trip to the Middle East in 1929, he was so overcome by the plight of the half-starved Armenian refugee children in Damascus that he decided to write a novel on the persecution of the Armenian people by the Turks, *The Forty Days of Musa Dagh*. The story of *The Pascarella Family* had its origin in a long conversation which Alma had had with an Italian woman in a hotel in Santa Margherita, Italy. The idea for *Hearken unto the Voice* evolved when in 1936 Werfel was rcstlcssly pacing the streets of Locarno: Looking for new material, he bought himself a Bible and by chance began reading the Book of Jeremiah.

During March, 1938, when Adolf Hitler annexed Austria in the Anschluss, Werfel was in Italy. He did not return to Austria but instead met Alma in Milan, from where they traveled to Zurich. Shortly thereafter, their exile led them to Paris. Apart from essays for newspapers and magazines, Werfel was then working on the novel *Embezzled Heaven*, which appeared in 1939, issued by the émigré publishing company Bermann-Fischer in Stockholm. After suffering a heart attack, Werfel moved to Sanary-sur-Mer, a French fishing village where a number of other prominent German exile writers were living, including Lion Feuchtwanger, Robert Neumann, Friedrich Wolff, and Arnold Zweig. After Belgium capitulated on May 28, 1940, Alma and Werfel went to Marseilles and from there to Lourdes, where Werfel vowed to write a book on Saint Bernadette if he should succeed in reaching America. Finally, the Werfels managed to get to Portugal and from there to the United States, where they arrived on October 13, 1940; a home which friends had rented was waiting for them in Los Angeles. Werfel immediately started working on *The Song of Bernadette*—which, against his expectations, became his greatest success as a novelist. His drama *Jacobwsky and the Colonel*, which first appeared in English translation, was equally successful in the United States. Werfel was able to complete the utopian novel *Star of the Unborn* ten days before his death on August 26, 1945, in his home in Beverly Hills.

ANALYSIS

Although it is impossible to label the entire work of Franz Werfel with the name of one conventional literary movement, his early work (before 1924) clearly shows all the characteristics of expressionism. The style of the work of his middle period (1925-1938) is similar to that of other neorealistic writers of the time. His novels written during his exile show an increased interest in strictly Christian-Catholic themes, similar to the work of Catholic authors such as Stefan Andres, Gertrud von Le Fort, and Elisabeth Langgässer. In his late work *Star of the Unborn*, the mythic element becomes stronger, paralleling other works of the time, such as Thomas Mann's trilogy *Joseph and His Brothers* (1933-1943) or Hermann Hesse's utopian *Magister Ludi* (1943; also known as *The Glass Bead Game*).

There are a number of themes which characterize

Werfel's work in particular and which, in combination, set it apart from the works of his contemporaries. The father-son conflict, typical of the expressionist period, is not only the hallmark of the work of the early Werfel, but it permeates even some of the works of his middle period, such as *The Pure in Heart* and *The Forty Days of Musa Dagh*. The same applies to the theme of Judgment Day, which is not only the main theme of the expressionist Werfel but also part of many of his works in the form of forensic self-justifications and the scrutinizing of one's conscience. Not only *Not the Murderer* but also *Class Reunion* and *Mirror Man* are prime examples. Finally, in *Star of the Unborn*, Judgment Day takes place without the use of fictional mediating characters. Many of Werfel's works contain a strong musical element which encompasses their language and structure. The novel *Verdi*, with its musical theme and structure, is the best example. Another structuring device found in many of Werfel's works is a clearly defined polarity between protagonist and antagonist.

Although Werfel, like Franz Kafka, was not convinced of the value of psychoanalysis, his works lend themselves very well to psychoanalytical interpretation, because people's motivations and their consciences are at the center of Werfel's concerns. Indeed, Werfel was a profoundly religious writer. Under the childhood influence of his Czech nursemaid, he was exposed to Catholicism early in his life. He did accept Christianity, but he was never baptized. Christian religion pervades his writings, from an early essay, *Die christliche Sendung: Ein offener Brief an Kurt Hiller* (1917; the Christian mission: an open letter to Kurt Hiller), to *Star of the Unborn*. Using Christianity and a concern about people as a point of departure, Werfel is against all modern ideologies, against all "-isms" (Communism, Marxism, national socialism, militarism, materialism), against technology and all attempts to make people subservient to institutions. In all of his works, humankind is at the center—people's consciences, their relationships to other people and to God.

NOT THE MURDERER

The most typically expressionist of Werfel's early prose works is *Not the Murderer*, which, in the Ger-

man subtitle, Werfel calls a novella. The work nevertheless has all the earmarks of a short novel. Consequently, critics have either simply called it Werfel's first novel (Annemarie von Puttkamer) or his first major book of prose (Lore B. Foltin, Werner Braselmann). The book is a first-person narrative. The fictional, supposedly autobiographical narrator is Karl Duschek, the son of an Austrian officer, who first tells about his difficult childhood. His father has sent him to a military academy with only one goal in mind: to make him an officer. Whereas the father manages to advance to the rank of general, the son becomes a lieutenant who excels in his unmilitary attitude and behavior. He finally joins a group of anarchists who plan to assassinate the Russian czar. After having been arrested during a raid, Karl is brought before his father, who humiliates him in front of other officers by hitting him in the face with his riding whip. In the evening, Karl returns and threatens his father with a dumbbell, chasing the old man around the table. When the father surrenders, Karl does not kill him. After his imprisonment for resisting arrest, Karl immigrates to America. Before he leaves, he returns to an amusement park which he had once visited with his father and learns that the son of an amusement-stand owner had been arrested for killing his father. He remembers that it was here that he himself had thrown a ball into his own father's face, and he realizes that he had meant to hurt him. He sends a letter to the public prosecutor pointing out the general, classical nature of the case before him.

The title of the book goes back to an old Albanian proverb. Werfel got the idea for the plot from an actual killing that took place in the Viennese Prater amusement park, which had in fact prompted him to write a letter to the public prosecutor. The letter contained in the book is an only slightly adapted version of the original. The main theme is one of the most popular themes of German expressionism, the father-son conflict, which was treated in plays such as Walter Hasenclever's *Der Sohn* (1914; the son). In Foltin's interpretation, Werfel sees the father problem as the basic problem of state, society, and military—the basic problem of any kind of authority. He has the speaker of the anarchists explain it to Karl as underlying religion (God as the father of people); the state (the king or president as the father of the citizens); the court (judges and police supervisors as the fathers of those whom human society calls criminals); the army (the officer is the father of the soldiers); the industry (the entrepreneur is the workers' father). *Patria potestas*, authority, is unnatural, is the negative principle as such. Werfel takes these thoughts up again in a letter to the public prosecutor in which he states that every father is Laius, the sire of Oedipus, thus suggesting an interpretation in Freudian terms. Independent of the social level, the guilt of the sons necessarily presupposes the guilt of the fathers. In his letter, Duschek/Werfel not only examines his own conscience but also indicts the generation of the fathers for defending its authority and its inability to abdicate control. He sees the guilt of the generation of the sons who fight their fathers because they are the fathers. Werfel does not support the anarchists' fight—he was against the kind of political activism which many expressionists advocated—but he analyzes what he conceives as being a patriarchal world order.

The father-son conflict is a theme that occupied other writers from Prague, too. There are, for example, numerous parallels between *Not the Murderer* and Franz Kafka's works, particularly *The Sentence* (1913, 1916; also as *The Judgment*) and *Letter to His Father* (1952, written 1919). Later, in *The Pure in Heart*, Werfel took up the father-son problem again; it is also one of the main themes of the novel *The Forty Days of Musa Dagh*, which deals with the gruesome persecution of the Armenian people by the Turkish government in 1915-1916.

THE FORTY DAYS OF MUSA DAGH

Based on a detailed study of historical source material, *The Forty Days of Musa Dagh* remains one of Werfel's best-known works. When the order for relocation reaches five Armenian villages on the Syrian coast, the majority of the inhabitants decide to resist. Five thousand of them collect food and barricade themselves on the Musa Dagh (the Mountain of Moses), which lends itself well to defense purposes. Under their leader Gabriel Bagradian,

they succeed in fighting back several assaults by Turkish troops, and in the end, the survivors are saved by warships of the Allied powers and brought to Egypt.

Only Gabriel Bagradian himself stays behind (and is killed by the Turks), because for him the events have completed his life—or rather, the process of self-finding which is central to the story. Thus, the novel is not only the heroic epic of the Armenian people but also the story of an individual, Gabriel Bagradian, who has lived as a scholar in Paris for many years and has become an "abstract" man, who is theoretical and culturally refined, and who has lost his emotional contact with his people, the Armenians. In the course of the novel, he returns to his origins, finds his identity as an Armenian, and learns to fulfill his duty as the leader of his people. He forgets about his cultured exterior refinement and becomes a practical politician, administrator, and officer who, with the help of his fellow citizens, simple farmers and artisans, manages temporarily to hold at bay the military forces of a large country. His counterpart is his French wife Juliette, who can live only in luxury and ultimately falls prey to the advances of a Greek adventurer. In spite of his love for his son Stephan, Gabriel fails to understand him; Stephan tries to prove himself in various deeds of daring until he is captured and murdered by the Turks.

Werfel did not intend to write a historical epic, restricting himself to historical, social, or political forces and their interaction, but primarily a novel about people and their search for self-understanding. Therefore, to criticize Werfel for making the process of Gabriel Bagradian's "way to himself" too important in relation to the historical events, the heroic fight of a small group of Armenians, is asking something of him which is counter to his nature and intention. *The Forty Days of Musa Dagh* is both a historical epic about the last stand of a group of Armenians against the Turks and the story of a fictional Armenian leader who returns to his true self.

Because the book contains numerous instances in which Werfel parallels the persecution of the Armenians with the persecution of the Jews, the work was received throughout the world and even in Germany as a prophetic book dealing with the fate of the Jews. Its greatest appeal, of course, was to the Armenian people, and even today the novel is a best-seller in Armenian translation.

The lifelong religious struggle of the Jew Werfel, who believed in Christ, had earlier found expression in the play *Paul Among the Jews*. It had manifested itself in the naïvely pious maid Barbara and her intellectual counterpart, the Jew Alfred Engländer, who believed in Christ, in *The Pure in Heart*, and also in *Hearken unto the Voice*, when Jeremiah, who resists his calling, becomes a prophet and admonisher in his time. In this manner, Werfel met the challenge of national socialism by drawing from Jewish antiquity, just as Lion Feuchtwanger did with *Josephus* (1932) and as Thomas Mann did in the trilogy *Joseph and His Brothers*. During his exile, Werfel continued writing novels with religious themes, but with a decidedly Catholic content. The first of these novels is *Embezzled Heaven*, which consists of two parts. First are the memories of the exiled writer, who now lives in Paris and remembers the family of the Argans and their generous hospitality in Grafenegg, Austria. He remembers the seemingly happy summer of 1936, which comes to an abrupt end with the accidental death of the Argans's son. The author interprets the ensuing collapse of the family as the "revenge of the spirit of the times," which encompasses the inevitable catastrophe, the dissolution of Europe's intellectual world. The old bohemian maid of the Argans is Teta Linek, who slowly moves to the center of attention. She is certain to gain eternal life because she believes she is to have the priestly mediation of her nephew Mojmir, who has been studying theology at her expense. At the age of seventy, however, she finds out that Mojmir has swindled her out of her money so that her life plan is ruined. She embarks on a pilgrimage to Rome during which she meets the young chaplain Johannes Seydel. In confession to him, she realizes that she lacked love, that she merely wanted to buy God's grace. Although she suffers a stroke in an audience with the pope, her life is not lived in vain, because she has discovered meaning in love in her relationship with Seydel.

Interesting, too, is the intertwining of her fate with the political happenings of the time, the annexation of Austria and the narrator's exile, to which he alludes time and again. Viewed from that perspective, Teta's case becomes a model for our time, which has "embezzled heaven"; which has revolted against metaphysics by making time, work, and money more important than religion; and which has replaced metaphysics by such substitute religions as Communism and national socialism. Werfel himself advances this interpretation in a conversation between the exiled author and the chaplain on one of the last pages of the book.

THE SONG OF BERNADETTE

The focus of Werfel's next novel, *The Song of Bernadette*, seems, at first glance, to be totally different. Faithful to his vow, Werfel tells the story of the fourteen-year-old girl Bernadette Soubirous, who, on February 11, 1858, saw a "lady" in the cave of Massabielle near Lourdes, France, and did not change her story when questioned by secular and church authorities. The lady calls herself "the immaculate conception." The miracle of a spring which originated in the cave after it had been announced by the lady leads to healings. Bernadette is ultimately (posthumously) canonized in 1933.

In this novel, there is no inner struggle in Bernadette, who always remains the same: a girl who believes and does not question. Thus, Werfel places emphasis on the mystery of the appearance and on the innocence of his heroine. He defends simple, unquestioning belief in a world of intellectual doubt.

The Song of Bernadette is structured according to the rosary, in five divisions of ten chapters each. Accordingly, the fiftieth chapter bears the heading "The Fiftieth Ave." Against Werfel's expectations, the novel became his greatest international success.

STAR OF THE UNBORN

Star of the Unborn, Werfel's last work, is a utopian novel. The subtitle, *Ein Reiseroman*, means "a travelogue"; thereby, Werfel placed his novel in the tradition of Daniel Defoe, Jonathan Swift, and Dante. F. W., the narrator, is summoned by means of spiritualism from the realm of the dead into the astromental world of California in the year 101945.

He is the guest of honor at a wedding between members of two respected astromental families. He is greeted and guided by his former friend B. H. (Willy Haas), who has learned the art of reincarnation in the monasteries of Tibet. The astromentals have overcome all natural threats to human existence, such as sickness, poverty, and even death. They live in underground quarters and take in liquid food only. There is only one language left in the world. All work is performed in the Workers' Park, which has hills, valleys, springs, and herds of diminutive sheep and goats, whereas the landscape of the astromentals is flat. The astromental university, the Djebel, is an artificial mountain which the boys enter and do not leave before the end of their lives at the age of two hundred. Death itself has been eliminated in favor of retrogenesis in the winter-garden inside the earth, where two-hundred-year-old people are developed back into children, embryos, and finally into marguerites if everything goes well. When the astromentals are defeated in a war with "the jungle" at the outskirts of the astromental world, where primitive, barbaric people live, they go to the winter-garden in order to avoid natural death. Only one boy refuses and accepts death, thus redeeming the astromental world by believing in something that cannot be proven. F. W. and B. H. manage to leave the winter-garden, and F. W. finally finds himself in his home in Beverly Hills.

Star of the Unborn is a highly religious novel which contains the total of Werfel's thinking and beliefs, as Hermann Hesse's *The Glass Bead Game* embodies that writer's thought. Like many other utopian novels, it includes the author's criticism of his own time by painting a picture of another world. In contrast to other utopias, however, the astromental world is by no means perfect. Rather, it constitutes the final result of the development of our world, should the contemporary tendencies be allowed free rein and development. As the Grand Bishop points out to F. W., the nineteenth and twentieth centuries were much better than the astromental era because the latter is much more removed from God. The old civilizations accepted suffering and death, whereas the astromental one tries to avoid work, suffering, and death, thus

defying the curse of the archangel. The astromentals cannot experience deep emotions, neither suffering nor true happiness. What presented itself as progress turns out to be the opposite in religious terms, an argument that is much more powerful than the regret about lack of diversity and fullness of life. F. W. realizes quickly that philosophy and metaphysics have not made any progress whatsoever. The final representatives of the astromental era characteristically are the Grand Bishop and the Jew of the Era, who are witnesses to an eternal community between Jews and Christians which, according to Werfel, was to outlast all changes of history.

Although one might criticize some parts of the book for being silly, tedious, or pointless, in many other parts Werfel shows more imagination and fantasy than in any other work. The ironic tone and the humor pervading it takes away from the seriousness of the reflections and discussions, adding a touch of lightness to the whole. Star of the Unborn is, without a doubt, Werfel's most mature book and his legacy as a thinker.

Hans Wagener

OTHER MAJOR WORKS

SHORT FICTION: *Geheimnis eines Menschen*, 1927 (*Saverio's Secret*, 1937); *Erzählungen aus zwei Welten*, 1948-1952 (part of *Gesammelte Werke*).

PLAYS: *Der Besuch aus dem Elysium*, pb. 1912; *Die Versuchung*, pb. 1913; *Die Troerinnen des Euripides*, pb. 1915 (a free adaptation of Euripides' *The Trojan Women*); *Die Mittagsgöttin*, pb. 1919; *Spiegelmensch*, pb. 1920; *Bocksgesang*, pb. 1921 (*Goat Song*, 1926); *Schweiger*, pb. 1922 (English translation, 1926); *Juárez und Maximilian*, pb. 1924 (*Juárez and Maximilian*, 1926); *Paulus unter den Juden*, pr., pb. 1926 (*Paul Among the Jews*, 1928); *Das Reich Gottes in Böhmen*, pr., pb. 1930 (*The Kingdom of God in Bohemia*, 1931); *Der Weg der Verheissung*, pb. 1935 (*The Eternal Road*, 1936); *In einer Nacht*, pr., pb. 1937; *Jacobwsky und der Oberst*, pr. 1944 (*Jacobwsky and the Colonel*, 1944).

POETRY: *Der Weltfreund*, 1911; *Wir sind*, 1913; *Einander*, 1915; *Der Gerichtstag*, 1919; *Poems*, 1945 (Edith Abercrombie Snow, translator).

NONFICTION: *Die christliche Sendung: Ein offener Brief an Kurt Hiller*, 1917.

MISCELLANEOUS: *Gesammelte Werke*, 1948-1975 (16 volumes).

BIBLIOGRAPHY

Foltin, Lore B., ed. *Franz Werfel*. Stuttgart, Germany: Metzler, 1972. A detailed bibliographical compilation of Werfel's work and the commentary on it.

_____, ed. *Franz Werfel: 1890-1945*. Pittsburgh: University of Pittsburgh Press, 1961. Essays by scholars analyzing the major aspects of Werfel's work.

Huber, Lothar. *Franz Werfel: An Austrian Writer Reassessed*. New York: Berg, 1989. See especially the essays "Franz Werfel and Kafka" and Peter Stephan Jungk's and J. M. Ritchie's essays on Werfel's fiction. Includes detailed notes and a bibliography.

Jungk, Peter Stephan. *Franz Werfel: A Life in Prague, Vienna, and Hollywood*. New York: Grove Weidenfeld, 1987. A very fine study of Werfel's life and work, illuminating the contexts in which he wrote his popular fiction. Jungk has a good command of Werfel's world and how it differs from that of later generations of readers. With a chronology, detailed notes, and bibliography.

_____. *A Life Torn by History: Franz Werfel 1890-1945*. London: Weidenfeld and Nicolson, 1990. An excellent look at Werfel's life and times.

Michaels, Jennifer E. *Franz Werfel and the Critics*. Columbia, S.C.: Camden House, 1994. Part of the Studies in German Literature, Linguistics, and Culture series, this is a good look at criticism of Werfel.

Steiman, Lionel B. *Franz Werfel: The Faith of an Exile from Prague to Beverly Hills*. Waterloo, Ontario: Wilfrid Laurier University Press, 1985. Chapters on Werfel and World War I, his marriage to Alma Mahler, *The Forty Days of Musa Dagh*, and his vision of history. Includes detailed notes and comprehensive bibliography.

Wagener, Hans. *Understanding Franz Werfel*. Columbia: University of South Carolina Press, 1993.

See chapter 4, which contains a detailed study of Werfel's prose works, with each major title receiving a separate discussion. Provides notes and an annotated bibliography.

GLENWAY WESCOTT

Born: Kewaskum, Wisconsin; April 11, 1901
Died: Rosemont, New Jersey; February 22, 1987

PRINCIPAL LONG FICTION

The Apple of the Eye, 1924
The Grandmothers: A Family Portrait, 1927
The Pilgrim Hawk: A Love Story, 1940
Apartment in Athens, 1945

OTHER LITERARY FORMS

Glenway Wescott's first published work was *The Bitterns: A Book of Twelve Poems* (1920); another volume of poetry, *Natives of Rock: XX Poems, 1921-1922* appeared in 1925. Two of his short stories were privately published in France by friends as separate books: *. . . Like a Lover* (1926) and *The Babe's Bed* (1930). A collection of stories with a long title essay, *Good-bye, Wisconsin*, was published in 1928. Other books include a variety of forms: *Fear and Trembling*, a collection of essays (1932); *Twelve Fables of Aesop* (1954); and *Images of Truth: Remembrances and Criticism* (1962). Several uncollected poems and stories appeared in literary journals over the years, along with a number of personal and critical essays. Perhaps Wescott's most imaginative work is "The Dream of Audubon: Libretto of a Ballet in Three Scenes," in *The Best One-Act Plays of 1940* (1941), which holds the key to Wescott's extensive use of bird imagery and symbolism.

ACHIEVEMENTS

After his beginnings as a published poet, Wescott often reviewed books of poetry and fiction. His critical pieces reveal that from the time of his earliest experiments in prose fiction, he was forming his idea of the novel and the aims of the art that it best embodied: to present images of reality and the truth of experience.

Even after his first two novels were published, critics disagreed as to whether Wescott *was* a novelist. The skepticism had several causes, mostly related to form. The first section of his first novel, *The Apple of the Eye*, was published separately as the story "Bad Han" in two parts in *The Dial*. Wescott then expanded it with two more parts to make a novel. *The Grandmothers*, accepted as a novel by the Harper's Prize judges, was a series of portraits of individual characters. Today, these books are recognized as formally innovative: They focus on the process of self-discovery, and they are unified by the relation of the parts to the experience of the protagonist.

The short stories in *Good-bye, Wisconsin* seemed to support the critics' judgment that Wescott was essentially a short-story writer and their further pigeonholing of him as a regional realist attacking the narrowness of culture in the Midwest and as a typical expatriate writer. Doubts about Wescott's capacities as a novelist were permanently laid to rest, however, with the triumph of *The Pilgrim Hawk*, which was hailed as a masterpiece of its genre and later reprinted in two anthologies of great short novels. *The Pilgrim Hawk*, set in France, and the next novel, *Apartment in Athens*, showed that Wescott could go beyond regional materials. The latter, however, although chosen by the Book of the Month Club, was not a critical success, probably because its propagandistic aims were too obvious.

Wescott spent many years in service to literature. He was president of the National Institute of Arts and Letters, 1958-1961. He wrote and delivered a number of introductory and presentation speeches, later published in the Proceedings of the American Academy of Arts and Letters. He also became a member of the National Commission for the United Nations Educational, Scientific, and Cultural Organization (UNESCO). As a public man of letters, he gave many talks and readings, appeared on radio and television, participated in symposia and writers' conferences, and served on various committees for the Institute and the Authors' Guild. He edited *The Maugham*

Reader (1950) and *Short Novels of Colette* (1951), writing the introduction for the latter.

At times considered an unfashionable writer, Wescott should be read in any survey of the great decades of the American novel from 1920 to 1940. A revival of critical interest in his work is long overdue.

BIOGRAPHY

Glenway Wescott was born in Kewaskum, Wisconsin, on April 11, 1901, the first of six children. According to the autobiographical portrait of Alwyn Tower in *The Grandmothers*, he was a sensitive, imaginative, and solitary child. His nature was antipathetic to the physical and cultural poverty of the farm life in which he spent his boyhood. At age thirteen, because of difficulties with his father, he left home and lived with an uncle and others while going to high school.

(Library of Congress)

In 1917, Wescott entered the University of Chicago, began writing poetry, and soon joined the Poetry Club. The following year, he became engaged, but he did not marry then or later; the engagement was broken in 1921. During this period, Wescott tried fiction, beginning the story "Bad Han," which became part of his first novel.

Because of ill health, Wescott withdrew from the University of Chicago after a year and a half, thus ending his formal education. Shortly thereafter, he went to New Mexico for an extended visit with Yvor Winters, a period which he referred to as one of the happiest of his life.

In 1920, after a visit to his family, Wescott went to Chicago to stay with Monroe Wheeler, with whom he was to share his travels abroad and much of his life in the United States and to whom he dedicated his 1962 volume of essays. He traveled with Wheeler to New York City, then to England and Germany, before returning to the United States and embarking on a career of serious writing.

In 1925, Wescott moved to France, beginning eight years as an expatriate but returning yearly for a visit to his family. He used the experience of an expatriate looking back at his pioneer family in Wisconsin as the framework for *The Grandmothers*, which was written during the first year of his stay abroad. Winning the prestigious Harper's Prize, the book was a critical and popular success. With the publication of a volume of short stories the following year, Wescott's position in the forefront of talented young writers seemed assured.

During his stay abroad, Wescott spent extended periods in Germany, leading him to write the essays in *Fear and Trembling* and later, during wartime, to try to explain the German character in the novel *Apartment in Athens*. In 1933, Wescott moved back to the United States, dividing his time between New York City and the farm in New Jersey where his family had moved. He went to Europe with his brother and the latter's bride, Barbara Harrison, in 1935 and again traveled abroad in 1938, before finally settling in America.

The year 1940 marked a period of renewed creativity for Wescott with the appearance of his ac-

claimed short novel *The Pilgrim Hawk*, a ballet libretto, several lyrical essays, and, in 1945, *Apartment in Athens*, a war novel set in Greece (which Wescott had never visited). Thereafter, he produced less, leading the life of a public man of letters. Besides the distractions of that role, he suggested another reason for his diminished literary output in later life, saying, "I am an incorrigibly copious letter-writer, and doubtless have wasted time in that way."

His father, with whom he eventually became reconciled, died in 1953, and his mother, to whom he was extremely devoted, died in 1960. Wescott lived on the family farm in rural New Jersey until he died on February 22, 1987.

ANALYSIS

When Glenway Wescott left his native Wisconsin, returned, and left again, each time it was to move farther east, first to Chicago, then New York, then Europe. It was also to plunge into the major literary currents of the day: imagism in poetry, regionalism in fiction, criticism of American culture and society by the expatriates, focus on the self as a major theme, revolt against traditional forms and experiments with new ones. If he was typical of the young writers of the 1920's, then he was also—like F. Scott Fitzgerald, Ernest Hemingway, and William Faulkner—a distinctive voice whose contributions to this innovative period of American fiction should be studied along with those of his greater contemporaries.

THE APPLE OF THE EYE

Published when Wescott was twenty-three, *The Apple of the Eye* was considered an impressive, although not faultless, first novel by such reviewers as Kenneth Burke and Ruth Suckow. In content, it is a typical initiation story, following the self-discovery of the hero, Dan Strane, as he rebels against midwestern puritanism, finds an affirmative meaning in life, and departs to live it his own way. In form, the novel is more original, with its tripartite structure. Its style reveals, even this early, the author's mastery of what Ira Johnson calls the "lyric, disciplined, imagistic prose of sensibility."

Book 1 elaborates on a sort of legend that Wescott's mother once told him about an old servant.

Hannah Madoc, called "Bad Han," is a "secular saint" who accepts love and lives life as it comes, without the common tortures of guilt. Han's lover, Jules Bier, influenced by his father, leaves her to marry Selma Duncan, who represents puritanism, the "evasion of experience." Book 2 introduces Rosalia and tells of her love affair with Dan's new friend, Mike Byron. Mike begins Dan's initiation by explaining that while puritanism appeals to the imagination, it is unhealthy in its division of the flesh from the spirit. Dan turns away from his beloved mother and her religion, while Mike initiates in him an awareness of the pleasures of sensuality. Meanwhile, Mike's and Rosalia's affair gains momentum, then dies, and Rosalia is deserted by Mike. Maddened by sorrow and guilt, she dies in the marsh.

In book 3, Dan's uncle, Jules Bier, retells the story of Bad Han as an object lesson in what is wrong with the local religious views, which have brought Rosalia and others tragedy. Bad Han becomes a powerful symbol, leading Dan to feel he is her spiritual son. Completing his separation from the sterile, frustrating environment, he departs for college, at the same time realizing that he has been blessed by experiencing several kinds of love and has felt a "sense of awakening."

Dan Strane is the first of Wescott's several autobiographical portraits. The natural setting, the rural poverty, the roughness of farm life, the puritanism, all were elements of the author's boyhood against which he rebelled. Even some of the most intimate aspects of Dan are tied to Wescott's life: the devotion to the mother, the conflict with the father, the despair and thoughts of suicide (Wescott had attempted suicide when he was eighteen), the implied homosexual attachment.

Most striking for a first novel is Wescott's lyrical style, with its piling of images into central symbols with many facets. The meaning of a symbol such as the marsh changes with the season of the year and the perception of it by a character or the omniscient narrator. It appears variously fecund, barren, ominous, even sexual. Bad Han, herself a creature of the marsh, also assumes symbolic import. A natural symbolist from the beginning, Wescott grew ever more powerful in his control of this tool of meaning, reaching finally its near-perfect use in *The Pilgrim Hawk*.

Even in this first novel, bird imagery and symbolism are pervasive, with passages about bitterns, turkeys, pigeons, wild geese, and crows. Later, in his ballet libretto, "The Dream of Audubon," Wescott sums up the key to his bird symbolism: "We are all hunters; and our heart's desire, whatever it may be, is always somehow a thing of air and wilderness, flying away from us, subject to extinction in one way or another."

THE GRANDMOTHERS

In addition to the search for self-knowledge, Wescott was preoccupied with the search for an organic form to fit his materials; in his second novel, *The Grandmothers*, he found one of great originality. An expatriate poet, Alwyn Tower, puts together a series of individual histories to create a family portrait. As a third-person participant-narrator, looking back from the "tower" of Europe at his origins, Alwyn treats time as fluid, moving from the self-present to the self-past when as a child he heard fragments of stories from his paternal grandmother. His curiosity roused, he watched his grandparents' life, caught glimpses of their past life, and now as an adult is able imaginatively to re-create it, as he does the lives of his parents and of other relatives. The task the adult Alwyn sets himself, at his desk in a Riviera hotel, is a purposeful search for usable knowledge needed by the self, the "all" that he will "win": "For the personages in rocking-chairs, the questionable spirits leaning over his cradle, had embodied not only the past, but the future—his own wishes and fears; and he was not to be content until an everyday light had unveiled all their faces."

Devoting himself to the acceptance of life and the creation of art, once he has exorcised their spirits, Alwyn can find meaning where they failed. His close examination of the family, and all the misguided ambition, anxiety, pride, and stubbornness of its members, remembered and imagined with compassion, will result finally in the detachment needed for the full creation of the self.

The first chapter shows Alwyn as a small boy in Wisconsin, remembered by the adult Alwyn in Europe, sensing the rich, mysterious layers of family history in his grandmother's rooms, hearing hints and half-explanations, and being tantalized by curiosity about the whole of the stories. In the second chapter he sees the Towers as making up a "composite character, the soul of a race; something so valuable that one recognized it only as an atmosphere, a special brightness, or a peculiar quality of the temperaments and customs and fortunes of Americans; as if it were the god of place." Despite his affinity for Europe, Alwyn loves his country and his family; in fact, he feels they are one and the same.

In the next twelve chapters, the narrator reconstructs and reflects on the lives of family members in the two preceding generations. The reader learns snatches of their stories as the boy learns them. Such suspense as there is in the essentially plotless book comes from waiting with him to get the answers: Why did his grandmother Rose marry Henry Tower instead of his brother Leander, who was her sweetheart before he went off to war? What happened to their brother Hilary, who went with Leander and never came home? Why did his Aunt Flora look like "a girl of thirty" and die early? These questions and more are answered in relation to love, family, religion, and historical context, although whether the answers are actually remembered or are imagined is always a guess.

Through this one family, Wescott explores the many ways of love and how it makes the Towers its victims. Henry and Rose, the grandparents, each lose their first romantic love: Henry, when his first wife, Serena, dies; Rose, when Leander will not marry her and she has to settle for his brother. Rose marries her second choice, Henry, because she wants to escape from her own family of rough boys, and she wants "nothing in the world . . . but to be acceptable" to the Towers. Throughout the novel, events and their interpretation hinge on the family—its honor (the boys go to fight in the Civil War); its pride (the one who deserts cannot come home); its narrowness (James cannot choose a career in music); its prejudices (the spinster cannot marry a Catholic). For its members, love of family and of place are all-important and almost identical. Even though it means facing Rose,

whom he jilted, Leander decides to return to Hope's Corner from California. The deserter, Evan, returns for visits, even though he knows his father will spurn him. Hope's Corner, poor as it is, symbolizes what has been the dream of the American pioneers, now changed: "The West, that point of the compass which had glittered with hope like a star, came to resemble the East—the light went out of it. . . . Every hope had a rendezvous with disappointment."

"Mother" and "home" are important themes in the novel. In its beginning, the author protagonist hears a drunken sailor on the quay below crying, "I want my mother!" While exploring memory, Alwyn discovers that, beginning with Rose and certainly including his own mother, the strong women who have married the Tower men have been their salvation, and he proclaims America a matriarchy. He finds in himself some of the characteristics of the Tower men and realizes that he will have to accommodate them somehow in his artist self.

Many kinds of love abound in these portraits, but in the conclusion, Wescott develops the theme of incest, making of it a complex metaphor for what Alwyn is doing. He looks back from the "tower" of Europe at his nineteenth year, when he spent many nights watching by the bed of his dying grandmother, Rose Tower. His other grandmother, Ursula Duff, in the confusion of age has called him by the name of her eldest son and also called him her sweetheart. He thinks of this as oracular, "a menace or a promise" that must be interpreted. In the effort, he mediates on the incest taboo, and he also recalls the tradition that the breaking of that law may sometimes create a legendary hero—or god. This idea, in turn, symbolizes his way of becoming self-created: "Memory was incest. . . . The desire to understand was, after all, desire." If the word *mother* "meant that which had produced one," then it included the wilderness, Wisconsin, the family, its "squalor, ideals, manias, regrets, sensuality, what consolations there had been." He had broken the law by going back to what had produced him, going back in imagination and going forward again: "Alwyn thought with rather unreasonable pride that he had become a man in as nearly as possible the way that men had become heroes or gods."

THE PILGRIM HAWK

In his third autobiographical novel, *The Pilgrim Hawk*, Wescott again treats the themes of the self and love, again evokes their essences through symbolism, and for the second time places the development of the story inside the consciousness of a narrator, this one with a first-person viewpoint. Here the self is not, as in *The Grandmothers*, primarily a member of a family or an evolving artist, but a practicing artist exploring the difficulties of his vocation and probing the extent of his talent as well as his own problems of love.

Geographically, there is a reversal: The narrator, Alwyn Tower, the protagonist of *The Grandmothers*, has been an expatriate in France but is now in America about ten years later, looking back at that other place and time. The historical context is the world on the verge of war; he visualizes gun emplacement in the idyllic countryside he once visited. Again, the structural framework makes possible a double layering of time. Tower remembers what happened on one May afternoon and how he speculated on the meaning of the events; in present time, he meditates and elaborates still further on those meanings.

On that day, Alwyn Tower is at the home of his friend Alexandra Henry (who later meets and marries his brother), when the Irish Cullens arrive. From the beginning, all attention is centered on Lucy, the pilgrim hawk Madeleine Cullen carries on her leather-encased wrist. The bird, along with the lore of falconry, is fascinating to Tower. Even more so is the conundrum of the triangular relationship of the two Cullens and the hawk. Tower sees the hawk, its needs and activities, as vastly symbolic, even of certain aspects of himself.

The events of that day, presented chronologically, can be summarized briefly as following the patterns established by the hawk. The account is interspersed with the reflective analogies drawn by the narrator. He first notes Lucy's "hunger," which can be a "painful greed, sick singlemindedness"; it reminds Tower of "human hungers, mental and sentimental," for example, his own hunger to be a literary artist, which, because no one warned him that he did not have enough talent, "turned bitter, hot and nerveracking."

Then, because his work has not been going well, he thinks of her as "an image of amorous desire," which would be a "natural consolation" to the weary artist.

The hawk bates—that is, throws herself headlong off her perch on the wrist and hangs helpless, upside down. While Mrs. Cullen brings her under control and soothes her, the narrator meditates on the woman's apparent need to dominate, and the group debates the value of independence. Larry Cullen, who is tethered to his wife as firmly as Lucy is, says that such yearning for freedom is the only human characteristic of hawks.

Later in the novel, Tower hears Cullen express embarrassingly frank sexual feelings toward his wife, as well as resentment at the way Lucy, constantly on his wife's arm, interferes with his embraces while traveling. These comments about sexual desire continue the hunger imagery. Tower, also, has been thinking of his own need for love: "Old bachelor hungry bird, aging-hungry-man-bird, and how I hate desire, how I need pleasure, how I adore love, how difficult middle age must be!"

With his jealousy fully roused, Cullen goes to free Lucy, who has been left weathering in the garden. Thus he, in his own way, bates. Having observed the act, Tower quietly informs Mrs. Cullen, and she is able to recapture the bird.

Jealousy also erupts in a subtriangle: Jean, the cook, is enraged by the flirtation of his wife, Eva, with Ricketts, the Cullens's chauffeur. Disturbed by both episodes, the Cullens leave early, only to return immediately. Mrs. Cullen enters the house with the news that her husband has tried to shoot someone; whether the chauffeur—of whom he is also jealous—or himself is not clear. In other words, he has bated again. She goes to toss the gun into the pond in the garden and returns to make a final farewell. Tower and Alexandra linger on the scene, discussing what it all has meant, at the same time concluding from sounds in the garden that Jean and Eva have been reconciled.

The ridiculousness of Mrs. Cullen's appearance while she enacts this drama with Lucy still clutching her wrist makes the bird, too, seem funny to Tower; he begins to unload all the symbols he has piled on her and to see more realistically. The narrator is amused at "how often the great issues which I had taken this bird to augur come down in fact to undignified appearance, petty neurasthenic anecdote." The bird's—and Cullen's—"poor domestication" reminds him of "the absurd position of the artist in the midst of the disorders of those who honor and support him, but who can scarcely be expected to keep quiet around him for art's sake." So it goes, while brick after brick of the carefully built, towering symbol is pulled down.

In his final meditations, the narrator becomes ashamed of the intricate theories he has spun during the afternoon and dubious about their validity. They may be only projections of the artist's self. He calls them "guessing," "cartooning," "inexact and vengeful lyricisms" and says, "Sometimes I entirely doubt my judgment in moral matters; and so long as I propose to be a story-teller, that is the whisper of the devil for me." While Alex absents herself to attend to household duties, he tries to "compress the excessive details of the afternoon into an abstraction or two," even though he knows that "abstraction is a bad thing, innumerable and infinitesimal and tiresome."

Abstraction—that is, the expression of truth in statement rather than in images—is what Wescott could not or would not give up. In William H. Rueckert's opinion, "Without absurdity, it can be said that Wescott slays himself as an artist in this work." The work itself remains a jewel of art.

APARTMENT IN ATHENS

Wescott, through the persona of Alwyn Tower in *The Pilgrim Hawk*, appeared to reject further attempts at the art of fiction. Meanwhile, however, he had thought about what the ideal novel should be like: objective, written "with precise equivalents instead of idioms, a style of rapid grace for the eye rather than sonority for the ear," one out of which the self, its prejudices, and its parochial origins "will seem to have disappeared." His next book, *Apartment in Athens*, is a traditional novel, and it suffers by comparison with his more original works.

The chief problem with the novel is its didacticism, arising from its design as propaganda. Since he was ineligible for the draft, Wescott said, he wanted

to contribute to the war effort by embodying in a novel his understanding of the German mentality gained on several visits to Germany. He got the idea of setting the story in Athens in meetings with a hero of the Greek underground who was visiting in the United States.

When a Nazi officer, Captain Kalter, is billeted in the apartment of the Helianoses, a Greek family of four, they become his "slaves," constantly harassed and abused. Somehow, though, the parents, an aging couple, find their love renewed by the experience. After leave in Germany, Kalter comes back a changed man, and the Helianoses are baffled by his kindness. When he reveals that he has lost his whole family in the war, Mr. Helianos offers sympathy and blames Hitler, whereupon the Nazi flies into a rage, beats him, and has him arrested. With her husband in jail, Mrs. Helianos and her children, Alex and Leda, expect more abuse, but Kalter, although obviously declining in health, continues to be kind. When he commits suicide, he leaves a note to a friend in the military suggesting that his death may be charged against this Greek family and used to get information from them about the underground. His friend declines to pursue the suggestion. Helianos is executed anyway. His wife, who has refused to become involved in the Resistance, now joins it and resolves to dedicate her children also to the eventual freedom of Greece.

Told in plain style, from the omniscient point of view, thus without the voice and play of intellect of a participating narrator, *Apartment in Athens* is not an artistic success. Although Edmund Wilson praised this novel and it was a Book-of-the-Month Club selection, it lacks the rich imagery and symbolism of Wescott's previous novels, and it is also marred by long stretches of exposition and argument. One chapter amounts to a lecture by Kalter on the Nazi view of German superiority in all things; another is mostly given over to a letter from prison expressing the views of Helianos on the threat of Germany and the prospects of Greece.

Wescott found his materials in his own life, primarily among the people of the farms and small towns of Wisconsin, with their hard work, cultural poverty, and puritanical outlook, but he wrote of them with nostalgia and compassion rather than with the satiric venom of many midwestern writers of the period. He dwelt on the themes of self, love, family, and home, showing how they interacted with one another and the environment to determine the fate of his characters. His major theme was the self-discovery of the artist, a participant-narrator, in his two best novels, who is also an expatriate. Because of the established distance in time and place, the narrator is able to reflect not only on the events he is recounting but also on himself as an artist. The memories are laden with rich imagery, often linked in a matrix of symbols in the narrator's mind. When Wescott abandoned his distinctively subjective, symbolic style, he seemed to have lost his impulse as a storyteller, although he continued to be active as a man of letters.

Eileen Tarcay

OTHER MAJOR WORKS

SHORT FICTION: . . . *Like a Lover*, 1926; *Good-bye, Wisconsin*, 1928; *The Babe's Bed*, 1930; *Twelve Fables of Aesop*, 1954.

POETRY: *The Bitterns: A Book of Twelve Poems*, 1920; *Natives of Rock: XX Poems, 1921-1922*, 1925.

NONFICTION: *Elizabeth Madox Roberts: A Personal Note*, 1930; *Fear and Trembling*, 1932; *A Calendar of Saints for Unbelievers*, 1932; *Images of Truth: Remembrances and Criticism*, 1962.

EDITED TEXTS: *The Maugham Reader*, 1950; *Short Novels of Colette*, 1951.

BIBLIOGRAPHY

Beach, Joseph Warren. *The Twentieth Century Novel: Studies in Technique*. New York: Appleton-Century-Crofts, 1932. The entry on Wescott discusses his technique in *The Grandmothers* and likens this work to that of Joseph Conrad. Beach faults Wescott for his lack of visual information that characterizes "the born writer of fiction," although concedes other strengths in the book.

Cowley, Malcolm. *Exile's Return*. New York: Viking Press, 1951. A notable book on the expatriate movement of the 1930's, which explores writers

who were once called the "lost generation." Helpful in placing Wescott in this movement and defining his relation to the times.

Johnson, Ira. *Glenway Wescott: The Paradox of Voice*. Port Washington, N.Y.: Kennikat Press, 1971. A full-length, valuable study of Wescott, with extensive critical commentary on his major works, complete with bibliography and plot summaries of his novels. The commentary on Wescott's fiction assesses his technique and evaluates the artistic merit of his works. Includes a discussion of his essays in *Images of Truth*. An indispensable guide for the Wescott scholar.

Kahn, Sy Myron. "Glenway Wescott: A Bibliography." *Bulletin of Bibliography* 22 (1956-1959): 156-160. Part 1 presents an exhaustive bibliography of Wescott's writings up to 1954; part 2 is selective bibliography of critical commentary on Wescott, including major articles and noteworthy reviews. A valuable resource for the Wescott scholar.

Rosco, Jerry. "An American Treasure: Glenway Wescott's *The Pilgrim Hawk*." *The Literary Review* 31 (1988): 133-142. An excellent discussion of a neglected masterpiece.

Rueckert, William H. *Glenway Wescott*. New York: Twayne, 1965. A useful introduction to the works of Wescott—both poetry and fiction—chronicling his development as a writer. Includes commentary on the "dry years" between 1933 and 1939, during which time Wescott, having returned to America from Europe, wrote very little that was published. Largely a sympathetic study of Wescott but points out that his ideas on the novel are limiting and this has affected his work. Contains a selected bibliography.

NATHANAEL WEST
Nathan Weinstein

Born: New York, New York; October 17, 1903
Died: El Centro, California; December 22, 1940

PRINCIPAL LONG FICTION

The Dream Life of Balso Snell,
    1931
Miss Lonelyhearts, 1933
A Cool Million: The Dismantling
    of Lemuel Pitkin, 1934
The Day of the Locust, 1939

OTHER LITERARY FORMS

Nathanael West often used the short-story form for preliminary sketches of characters and themes that later appeared in his novels. Between 1930 and 1933 especially, he wrote stories with a broader focus and in a more sophisticated style than his first work, *The Dream Life of Balso Snell.* The stories include "The Adventurer," "Mr. Potts of Pottstown," "Tibetan Night," and "The Sun, the Lady, and the Gas Station," all unpublished. After the publication of *Miss Lonelyhearts* in 1933, West also worked as a scriptwriter in Hollywood for several years, producing such works as *Born to Be Wild* (1938) and *Men Against the Sky* (1940).

(New Directions)

ACHIEVEMENTS

Since West's death in an automobile accident in 1940, his work has steadily gained critical attention. His characters' hysterical pitch of loneliness, their frustration, and their inability to find a source of relief have gradually interested a wide audience, especially since World War II. Stripped of their professional masks, the people in West's novels reveal a talent for cruelty. They tease, exploit, or murder to ensure their own survival in a world reminiscent of T. S. Eliot's *The Waste Land* (1922), but their world is without Eliot's hint of redemption or spirituality. In *Miss Lonelyhearts,* the world is dead; in *The Day of the Locust,* it is corrupt and jaded, a modern Sodom which West symbolically destroys. This last novel was made into a film in the 1970's; although it never became a box-office hit, West would have approved of its powerful treatment of dreamers and misfits.

BIOGRAPHY

Nathanael West was born Nathan Weinstein in New York City on October 17, 1903. His father's and mother's families had known one another before they immigrated to the United States from Russia. His father's side used construction skills learned in the old world to become successful contractors in the new country, taking advantage of the building boom of the turn of the century. His mother's side was well educated, and Anna Wallenstein Weinstein wanted her son Nathan and her two daughters to have all the perquisites of an upwardly mobile, middle-class life. Soon after settling in New York City, the Weinsteins learned to enjoy their comforts and to value them highly. They also assumed that their son would receive the finest possible education, pursue a professional career, or at least join the family business. West was an avid reader but a much less ambitious student. He attended a variety of grammar schools before his parents placed him in DeWitt Clinton High

School. West, however, preferred exploring Central Park during the day and the theater district in the evenings. He was particularly attracted to the vaudeville shows, his first exposure to techniques such as slapstick and stereotypes which he later used in his fiction.

West was not very disciplined, but his clever and adventurous nature helped to get him into Tufts University without a high school diploma. After one unsuccessful year there, he attended Brown University. West's biographer attributes Brown's acceptance of West to a complicated mismatching of transcripts with another student whose name was also Weinstein, though whether this was planned or accidental is not absolutely certain. Whatever the case, West was graduated from Brown in 1924 with a degree in philosophy, which he earned in only two and a half years.

Neither West nor his parents had much nostalgia for their Jewish Lithuanian roots; instead, they concentrated on rapid assimilation. In 1926, he legally changed his name to Nathanael West. Even so, the subject of roots still appears in most of his work. The degree of corruption in Lemuel Pitkin's hometown in *A Cool Million* is nothing compared to what he finds elsewhere in the country. The protagonist in *Miss Lonelyhearts* suffers from acute isolation despite his efforts to communicate, and this seems to stem from his earliest memories of childhood; he is estranged from his Baptist upbringing and has only a single comforting memory of his youth. Tod Hackett in *The Day of the Locust* leaves the East Coast, where he was an undergraduate at the Yale School of Fine Arts, for Hollywood. He observes other new arrivals and decides that they have come to California to die in one way or another. Although he does not include himself in this category, it is clear that he too succumbs to the superficial glitter and wastefulness.

West's parents encouraged him to pursue a dependable career, but their son was not interested, and he convinced them to send him to Paris in 1926. He enjoyed the artistic and literary circles there, but signs of the coming Depression were being felt in the construction industry and West had to return to New York after three months. Relatives managed to find him a job as a night manager of a midtown hotel, providing West with an income, a place to write, and a steady flow of guests to watch. West found these people fascinating, and so it is not surprising that seedy hotels and their transient occupants find their way into *The Day of the Locust*. Working as a night manager also gave West time to revise *The Dream Life of Balso Snell*, which he had begun while in college. William Carlos Williams liked the manuscript and recommended that Moss and Kamin publish it; five hundred copies were printed in 1931.

S. J. Perelman, also a student at Brown, married West's sister Laura. Through Perelman, who worked at *The New Yorker*, West met other writers and artists. It was also through his brother-in-law that West conceived of the controlling idea for *Miss Lonelyhearts*. Perelman knew a writer named Susan Chester who gave advice to readers of *The Brooklyn Eagle*. The three of them met one evening in 1939, and she read samples of the letters. West was moved by them and eventually used an advice-to-the-lovelorn column and a tormented newspaper columnist for what is probably his most famous novel. *Miss Lonelyhearts* was published by Liveright in 1933.

West soon went to Southern California to work on film scripts. His experience with the less glamorous aspects of Hollywood and the film industry, with the masses of aspiring actors and actresses, with people who had little talent to begin with, but compensated for that with their dreams, helped provide the themes, landscapes, and characters of West's final novel, *The Day of the Locust*. In 1940, West married Eileen McKenney, the sister of Ruth McKenney, who worked with Perelman at *The New Yorker*. West's careless driving was known to all his friends, and a few months after his marriage, he and his wife were killed in an automobile crash.

ANALYSIS

Although all of Nathanael West's fiction is concerned with certain recurring themes, it gradually matures in tone, style, and subject. *The Dream Life of Balso Snell*, his first novel, has a clever but sarcastic and ugly adolescent tone. *The Day of the Locust*, his last novel, is also satirical and sarcastic, but its greater maturity and empathetic tone make it both disturbing and profoundly moving.

West's Miss Lonelyhearts dreams that he is a magician who does tricks with doorknobs: He is able to make them speak, bleed, and flower. In a sense, this conceit explains all of West's work. His protagonists travel across dead landscapes which they try to revivify. In *The Dream Life of Balso Snell*, the landscape is mechanical, wooden, purely farcical; in *A Cool Million*, West shows one American town after another, all equally corrupt. *Miss Lonelyhearts* is set in the dirt and concrete of New York City, and *The Day of the Locust* is set in the sordid but irresistible Southern California landscape. West's typical protagonist is a quester, intent on bringing life wherever he travels; Miss Lonelyhearts especially is obsessed with the challenges of a savior. The task of making a dead world bloom, however, seems hopeless. Life may surface in a moment of communication or lovemaking, but something is likely to go awry, as the moment reverses itself into an unnatural distortion. For example, as Miss Lonelyhearts tries to comfort an old man he meets in Central Park, he suddenly has the urge to crush and destroy him. Shrike, his employer at the newspaper office, compares making love to his wife with sleeping with a knife in his groin. This dichotomy is at the heart of West's vision. Characters driven by benevolent ambitions are thwarted—by themselves, by those in need of their help, by cosmic and divine indifference—until they become grotesque parodies of their original selves. Innocence and success can be recalled only through dreams. At best, the world is passively dead; at worst, it is aggressively violent.

THE DREAM LIFE OF BALSO SNELL

The quester of *The Dream Life of Balso Snell* does not take himself seriously, and the novel itself seems to be an extended literary joke. Balso Snell describes a dream in which he encounters the famous wooden horse of the Greeks in ancient Troy. A brash and distinctly modern tour guide leads him through the interiors of the horse, which quickly become the subject of numerous adolescent witticisms. The inside of the horse expands to a landscape that Balso explores for the rest of his dream. West's purpose is humor and parody, which he accomplishes mercilessly although unpleasantly, beginning even with the title of this first book. Following his "path," Balso meets a Catholic mystic, and West has the opportunity to mock the literary lives of saints. Then Balso meets a schoolboy who has just hidden his journal in the trunk of a nearby tree. Balso reads its entries, which serve as a parody of the nineteenth century Russian novel. Balso then meets the boy's teacher, Miss McGeeny, who has been busily writing a biography of a biographer's biographer; West parodies another literary genre.

The Dream Life of Balso Snell is not a significant work of fiction, but it is useful for readers to appreciate how quickly West's style and perspective deepened. His later novels have the same piercing quality, and West never lost his tendency to satirize, but the later novels are finely and precisely directed. West's later fiction also has the same motifs—quester, mechanical or obsessive journeys, dreams, and suffering humanity—but West examines them much more seriously in the later novels.

MISS LONELYHEARTS

West is in superb control of his material in *Miss Lonelyhearts*, published only two years after *The Dream Life of Balso Snell*. The vituperative tone of the earlier work is balanced by greater development of plot and diversity of character. Following his preference for fast action and exaggeration, West uses comic-strip stereotypes: the meek husband and the bullying wife, Mr. and Mrs. Doyle; the bullish employer, Shrike, and his castrating wife Mary; and Miss Lonelyhearts's innocent but dumb girl friend Betty. Miss Lonelyhearts himself is only somewhat more developed, primarily because he is in almost every episode and because the third-person voice sardonically presents his private thoughts.

As in *The Dream Life of Balso Snell*, a central quester travels a barren landscape. Between the newspaper office and the local speakeasy is Central Park. As Miss Lonelyhearts walks across it, he realizes that there should be signs of spring but, in fact, there are none to be seen. Then he recalls that last year, new life seemed wrenched from the soil only in July. Miss Lonelyhearts's job as a newspaper columnist thrusts him into the position of a quester, and he makes a highly unlikely candidate. Simultaneously attracted to and repelled by his mission to assuage the grief of his readers, he makes attempts to get close to some of them, such as Mr. and Mrs. Doyle, but he then suddenly feels a compulsion to keep separate from them. This dichotomy keeps him in motion, reeling him like a puppet from one person's apartment to another, building a pressure that is released only when Miss Lonelyhearts has a final breakdown.

In each new location, the newspaperman tries to make a meaningful connection with another human being. Strict chronology becomes vague as the protagonist's state of mind becomes increasingly disturbed. He reaches toward Betty when they are sitting on the couch in her apartment but suddenly has no interest in her. He does remain sexually interested in Mary Shrike, but she refuses his advances as long as they stay in her apartment, and in the restaurant she teases him sadistically. He telephones Mrs. Doyle, a letterwriter, saying he will advise her in person. He exploits her unhappiness to satisfy his own need but, not surprisingly, is disappointed in the results. Rather than help others, the quester of this novel uses them as targets for venting his own anger. As he is increasingly frustrated in his task of bringing beauty and gentleness into the world, Miss Lonelyhearts takes to the isolation of his own room.

Another kind of quest occurs here, one that parodies the earlier quest. Rather than embark on further quests from one location to another in New York City, Miss Lonelyhearts hallucinates a journey; his bed serves as his mode of transportation. It appears to him a perfect world and a perfect journey, sanctioned by God, who finally communicates to him that he has chosen the right conclusion to his quest. Miss Lonelyhearts feels that he has become a rock, perfect in its design not because God has helped to create it, but because it is impenetrable to all but its own existence. It is ironic that the driven quester actually drives himself into a blissful delusion of isolation.

Reality intrudes. Mr. Doyle, incensed at being cuckolded, rushes up the stairs to the apartment. Miss Lonelyhearts rushes down the stairs, hoping to meet him and welcome what he assumes is Doyle's con-

version. Instead, there is a scuffle and Doyle's gun fires. Only in dreams do doorknobs blossom and human beings turn into gentle and compassionate creatures—at least in West's novels. Miss Lonelyhearts dies, a victim of his own miscalculation.

A COOL MILLION

The protagonist of *A Cool Million: Or, The Dismantling of Lemuel Pitkin*, is another miscalculating quester. Pitkin is an idealistic young man who leaves his hometown to seek his fortune. The fact that the immediate cause of his departure from Ottsville, Vermont, is the dishonest foreclosing of his mother's mortgage does not dampen his enthusiastic belief that his nation is the land of limitless possibilities. He has faith in himself and in those who insist they are using him for his own good.

Mr. Shagpole Whipple, ex-president of the United States and now director of the Rat River National Bank in Ottsville, becomes Lemuel's earliest supporter. He advises his young friend that America "is the land of opportunity," a land that "takes care of the honest and the industrious." Lemuel is inspired and sets out in what becomes a parody of the Horatio Alger myth. On the train to New York City, he enjoys a conversation with a Mr. Mape, who was left "a cool million" by his father. Lemuel is impressed, especially since, he explains, he must make his fortune starting with only the thirty dollars in his pocket. By the end of the trip, he has been divested of that thirty dollars. Lemuel is the fall guy for another scheme, so that he, and not the thief, is apprehended by the police, brought to trial, and declared guilty. Being sent to prison is only the first of a long series of misfortunes. Lemuel is always someone's dupe or prey, but he bounces back to try again, although he repeatedly gets nothing out of his adventures. In fact, the more he travels, the less he has. Lemuel loses his teeth, his scalp, his eye, part of a hand, one leg; each time there is someone close by who can benefit from his new loss. Lemuel is used by entrepreneurs and thieves of all varieties.

A Cool Million is fast-paced and episodic. Its characters are pure stereotypes—the ingenuous dupe, the patriot, the innocent young girl, the deceitful villain. Everyone and everything is satirized: midwesterners, Jews, southerners, capitalists, and socialists. *A Cool Million* shows how West was beginning to use his material for clearly defined purposes and to control his sharpedged humor and black comedy in order to make a point. This novel, however, remains a minor work in comparison to *Miss Lonelyhearts* and *The Day of the Locust*. In these works, pathos emerges from West's stereotypes and seems all the more powerful because of its sources. *A Cool Million* is clever and biting but not poignant or profound.

THE DAY OF THE LOCUST

West is at his best in *The Day of the Locust*. Tod Hackett, the central quester, comes to Hollywood from the East to learn set and costume designing. The people he gets to know are desperately in need of beauty, romance, and renewal, but, as in *Miss Lonelyhearts*, the harder they struggle to achieve these goals, the farther away they are.

The story is about dreamers who have traveled to what they believe is the dream capital of America, which West portrays as the wasteland of America. In addition to Tod, there is Faye Greener, beautiful but exploitative, making up in vanity what she lacks in intelligence. Homer Simpson is a thickheaded but sincere middle-aged bachelor from the Midwest. He has run from his one attempt to break through his dull-witted loneliness because the memory of failure is too painful. Characters such as Faye and Homer are particularly successful; although they are stereotypes, they still have something unpredictable about them. This quality usually manifests itself involuntarily by a spasm or quirk. For example, Faye is obviously a second rate actress, but Tod sees through her tawdry facade to a deep archetypal beauty. Faye is unaware of any such quality; even if she knew, she would not appreciate it, because it has almost nothing in common with the self she has created. Homer Simpson has difficulty controlling parts of his body. He does not fall asleep easily because waking up is so arduous. His hands seem disassociated from his psyche; he has to put them under cold running water to rouse them, after which his fingers seem to follow their own rhythms. Like Faye, he has a structural purity without means to express it. Like Miss Lonelyhearts, his emotions swell in intensity, causing pres-

sure that eventually must find release.

Faye becomes Tod's obsession. If he is a quester, she is his grail, and a most difficult challenge. Tod can neither support her nor further her acting career. Instead, he becomes a voyeur, watching her tease Earle Shoop, the cowboy from Arizona, and Miguel, the Mexican. He settles for simply painting Faye in a mural he calls "The Burning of Los Angeles." Tod observes that people come to California to die, despite their ambitions, and the mural reflects their disappointments. In the mural, a mob chases Faye, who seems oblivious to imminent danger and maintains a calm, detached expression. Those who realize they have failed need to express their anger, and those who think they have succeeded exist in a state of happy but dangerous ignorance. As in all of West's fiction, the challenge is as impossible as turning doorknobs into flowers. As the dreamers recognize the gap between their desires and accomplishments, thwarted ambition leads to frustration, and frustration to violence. The power of *The Day of the Locust* derives from the last few chapters, which describe the mindless and destructive product of such frustrated dreams.

It is the evening of a motion-picture premiere; violet lights run across the sky, and crowds of fans are kept under control by police barricades. The premiere provides the opportunity for fans to see face-to-face the "stars," the ones who have made it. The tension is too great, however, and the control too tenuous. The crowd begins to charge toward the theater, and Tod is caught in the pressure. *The Day of the Locust* is a tight, "pressured" novel, but all gives way at the end. As the crowd surges, it builds up strength from the people whose lives are filled with boredom and mistakes. There is mass pandemonium. Homer, moving like a robot, mechanically and swiftly murders a child who has been teasing him. Tod, submerged in the crowd, is hurt, but steadies himself at the base of a rail. In agony, he begins to think about his mural, "The Burning of Los Angeles," until reality and his thoughts merge. He thinks of the burning city, of mobs of people running into the foreground with baseball bats, and he and his friends fleeing from the mob. He actually believes he is painting the flames when policemen grab him from the rail and lift him into a police car. When the siren begins, Tod is not sure whether he or the siren has been making the noise. In effect, he succumbs to the chaos around him.

The Day of the Locust is a bleak novel, reflecting West's belief that recognizing limitations is difficult for humanity, which prefers to think that all things are possible. West shows limitations to be everywhere: within the masses; within the questers trying to save them; within the arid landscape itself. As the limitations prove insurmountable, natural ambitions and desires for harmony are inverted. Love becomes pantomime and compassion a veil for selfish and sadistic purposes. West's characters and settings desperately need to be renewed, but the job of salvation is difficult, one that West's protagonists fail to achieve.

Miriam Fuchs

OTHER MAJOR WORKS

SCREENPLAYS: *Follow Your Heart*, 1936 (with Lester Cole and Samuel Ornitz); *The President's Mystery*, 1936 (with Cole); *Ticket to Paradise*, 1936 (with Jack Natteford); *It Could Happen to You*, 1937 (with Ornitz); *Born to Be Wild*, 1938; *I Stole a Million*, 1939; *Five Came Back*, 1939 (with Jerry Cady and Dalton Trumbo); *Men Against the Sky*, 1940.

BIBLIOGRAPHY

Bloom, Harold, ed. *Nathanael West.* New York: Chelsea House, 1986. This useful collection includes essays on all of West's work in what Bloom hopes is a representative selection. S. E. Hyman's essay is a valuable introduction to West. Contains a bibliography.

_____, ed. *Nathanael West's "Miss Lonelyhearts."* New York: Chelsea House, 1987. This valuable collection offers nine essays from a variety of viewpoints on *Miss Lonelyhearts.* Includes a chronology and a bibliography.

Martin, Jay, ed. *Nathanael West: A Collection of Critical Essays.* Englewood Cliffs, N.J.: Prentice-Hall, 1971. This collection contains some brief critical commentaries by West himself as well as analyses by others. Martin's introductory essay is a useful summary; some of the others presuppose a fairly sophisticated reader. Selected bibliography.

Siegel, Ben, ed. *Critical Essays on Nathanael West.* New York: G. K. Hall, 1994. Divided into two sections—reviews and essays. In addition to the comprehensive introduction surveying West's life and career, the essay section provides studies of individual novels and of West's work as a whole. Notes and index but no bibliography.

Veitch, Jonathan. *American Superrealism: Nathanael West and the Politics of Representation in the 1930's.* Madison: University of Wisconsin Press, 1997. Contains separate chapters on each novel as well as an introduction discussing the "crisis of representation in the 1930's." Includes very detailed notes but no bibliography.

Widmer, Kingsley. *Nathanael West.* Boston: Twayne, 1982. Widmer's general introduction concentrates on "West as the prophet of modern masquerading, role-playing, and its significance" while offering useful analyses of West's work. Lengthy notes and an annotated bibliography are provided.

Wisker, Alistair. *The Writing of Nathanael West.* New York: St. Martin's Press, 1990. Chapters on each novel and a series of appendices on various aspects of West's work, including his handling of violence, his unpublished fiction, and revisions of his work. Includes notes and bibliography.

PAUL WEST

Born: Eckington, England; February 23, 1930

PRINCIPAL LONG FICTION
A Quality of Mercy, 1961
Tenement of Clay, 1965
Alley Jaggers, 1966
I'm Expecting to Live Quite Soon, 1970
Caliban's Filibuster, 1971
Bela Lugosi's White Christmas, 1972

Colonel Mint, 1972

Gala, 1976

The Very Rich Hours of Count von Stauffenberg, 1980

Rat Man of Paris, 1986

The Place in Flowers Where Pollen Rests, 1988

Lord Byron's Doctor, 1989

The Women of Whitechapel and Jack the Ripper, 1991

Love's Mansion, 1992

The Tent of Orange Mist, 1995

Sporting with Amaryllis, 1996

Terrestrials, 1997

Life with Swan, 1999

The Dry Danube: A Hitler Forgery, 2000

O.K.: The Corral, the Earps, and Doc Holliday, 2000

OTHER LITERARY FORMS

Paul West is a remarkably prolific novelist whose literary interests also include poetry, criticism, and other nonfiction. In addition to his books of verse, *Poems* (1952), *The Spellbound Horses* (1960), and *The Snow Leopard* (1964), West has published memoirs: *I, Said the Sparrow* (1963) recounts his childhood in Derbyshire; *Words for a Deaf Daughter* (1969), one of West's most popular works, poignantly relates the experiences of his deaf daughter, Mandy; and *Out of My Depths: A Swimmer in the Universe* (1983) describes the author's determination to learn to swim at middle age. His short stories were collected in *The Universe and Other Fictions* in 1988. Besides his numerous essays and book reviews in dozens of periodicals, journals, and newspapers, West has published *The Growth of the Novel* (1959), *Byron and the Spoiler's Art* (1960), *The Modern Novel* (1963), *Robert Penn Warren* (1964), *The Wine of Absurdity: Essays in Literature and Consolation* (1966), and a series of books entitled *Sheer Fiction* (vol. 1, 1987; vol. 2, 1991; vol. 3, 1994). *A Stroke of Genius: Illness and Self-Discovery* was published in 1995.

ACHIEVEMENTS

When West arrived on the literary scene as a novelist, he was regarded as an author who possessed a compelling voice but also as one who wrote grotesque and verbally complex fictions. The unevenness of critical reaction cannot overshadow, however, the regard with which serious readers have approached his work, and a list of his fellowships and awards clearly indicates a writer of significant stature: He is the recipient of a Guggenheim Fellowship (1962), a *Paris Review* Aga Kahn Prize for Fiction (1974), the National Endowment for the Humanities Summer Stipend for science studies (1975), the National Endowment for the Arts Fellowship in Creative Writing (1980), the Hazlett Memorial Award for Excellence in the Arts (1981), the American Academy and Institute of Arts and Letters Award in Literature (1985), and a National Endowment for the Arts Fellowship in Fiction (1985). In 1998 the French government decorated him Chevalier of the Order of Arts and Letters. Besides teaching at Pennsylvania State University from 1962 to 1995, West was a visiting professor and writer-in-residence at numerous American universities. As his fiction has developed, West has shown himself to be a highly imaginative, experimental, and linguistically sophisticated writer. Critics usually commend him for his original style and note the striking diversity of his oeuvre.

BIOGRAPHY

Paul Noden West was born in Eckington, Derbyshire, on February 23, 1930, one of two children, into a working-class family. After attending local elementary and grammar schools, West went to Birmingham University, then to Lincoln College, Oxford, and in 1952 to Columbia University on a fellowship. Although profoundly attracted to New York life, West was forced to return to England to fulfill his military service in the Royal Air Force and there began his writing career. Once he concluded his service, West taught English literature at the Memorial University of Newfoundland, wrote a volume of poems, and did considerable work for the Canadian Broadcasting Corporation. In 1962 he was awarded a Guggenheim Fellowship and returned to the United States, where he took up permanent residence. He was a member of the English and comparative literature faculties at Pennsylvania State University from 1962 to 1995, dividing his time each year between teaching and writing in New York. Upon his retirement, he devoted himself to writing and guest lectureships at Goucher College, University of Miami, Cornell University, and the United States Air Force Academy. He prefers the United States to England, and he has become an American citizen.

ANALYSIS

Paul West has long insisted that what is most important to him as a writer is the free play of the imagination. What the imagination invents, he contends, becomes something independent and actual. West himself states the case most clearly when noting that "elasticity, diversity, openness, these are the things that matter to me most." Thus his fictions often revolve, both thematically and structurally, around the interplay between the individual and his or her imagination and an absurd, threatening universe. Often these fictions rely heavily upon dreams of one sort or another, with characters living in their dreams or living out their dreams or becoming confused about where dreams leave off and the world begins.

Consequently, West's fictions often abound with a sense of precariousness as characters who are constrained in one form or another struggle to free themselves and find their places in the world. Sanity frequently becomes the central issue in these lives, with protagonists taking on the forces of conventionality in their private wars with the drab and mundane. Typical West heroes are outsiders, often marginal or largely inconsequential figures, who will not or cannot conform to the forces about them and who, in striking out on their own, pay steep prices for their individuality.

A QUALITY OF MERCY

A Quality of Mercy, West's first novel and a work which he largely disowns, deals with a collection of embittered and failed lives overseen by Camden Smeaton, the novel's central consciousness. The novel is otherwise unmemorable except insofar as it anticipates concerns West more successfully developed in later novels: alienation, immersion in dream and illusion, the idea of an irrational universe, and the use of stylistic fragmentation.

TENEMENT OF CLAY

On the other hand, *Tenement of Clay*, West's second novel, stands as a far more accomplished work, controlled, stylistically inventive, morally probing. Here West introduces the reader to the voices of two narrators, each of whom is compelling and unique. The work is divided into three chapters, the two shortest forming a frame offered by Pee Wee Lazarus, a dwarf wrestler whose direct idiom immediately assaults the reader and demands his attention. His desire is to "involve" the reader in his tale, a story that revolves around Papa Nick, narrator of the middle section, who along with Lazarus meets a taciturn giant he names Lacland. Lacland appears to have no home or clear destination, so Nick takes him back to his rooms, where Nick presides over a private flophouse for local bums. Kept in the darkened basement, Lacland soon develops, under Lazarus's perverse tutelage, a sexual appetite and his own abusive language. After a series of horrible misadventures, Lacland reverts to his despondency and silence and eventually becomes Nick's legal ward.

All these events, extreme and dramatic as they may appear, actually operate as a backdrop to Nick's personal turmoil. For years he has carried on a fitful relationship with Venetia, a former film actress, who exhorts him to abandon his altruism toward the derelicts and to run off with her to a life of leisure. When Nick physically collapses from the burden of Lacland and Lazarus's escapades, Venetia nurses him back to health, leaves him when he returns to his bums, and dies in a car crash in Florida.

The novel's soul comes in the form of Nick's constant ruminations, which offer a way of coping with and sometimes solving the dilemmas of his existence. Gradually the line between straight narration and Nick's hallucinations begins to dissolve; the two become one, and the reader learns something fundamental about this world: Dream and reality invade each other; there is no escaping one for the other.

The novel is furthermore important for the moral questions it raises. Perhaps the most telling of these involves one's responsibilities to other human beings; in particular terms, is Nick responsible for the lives he admits into his home? As Lacland and Lazarus demonstrate, Nick has assumed the role of a Dr. Frankenstein and created his own monsters, whom he has unwittingly unleashed upon the world. Is the answer to this dilemma incarceration? Lacland's temporary internment in the basement suggests that it is not.

For Nick, these are the questions that finally come with life itself, and his failure to arrive at any fixed solution suggests a form of authorial honesty about the complexity of modern existence. In this context, the epigraph from Samuel Beckett makes sense: "If there were only darkness, all would be clear. It is because there is not only darkness but also light that our situation becomes inexplicable."

The novel's title comes from a passage in John Dryden's *Absalom and Achitophel* (1681-1682), and certainly the images of tenements abound in the work: All the buildings in this metropolis Lazarus calls New Babylon, especially Nick's flophouse, the grave into which Venetia is lowered, and the human body itself, which contains and in many cases entraps the spirit. In their concerns with their corporeal selves, most of these characters miss the important questions Nick poses throughout. Life, then, amounts to inhabiting one vast tenement, and the point is never escape, but how one chooses to live that life.

ALLEY JAGGERS

With his next novel, *Alley Jaggers*, West moved even further into depicting a consciousness at odds with the rest of the world. Alley is as compelling a narrator as Lazarus or Nick, and like them he speaks in a language that is distinct and unique, an idiom that oddly combines Irish brogue, Midlands accent, and personal argot.

Alley is a profoundly frustrated little man who realizes that his job and marriage are unfulfilling but who has no idea how to remedy his situation. He spends his most satisfying moments dreaming of horses and the elaborate names owners concoct for them and creating airplanes in his attic retreat. Alley wants desperately to make an impression of some kind, and one of his creations, an androgynous, semihuman form emitting a silent scream, both intrigues his fellow workers and stands as an effigy of his own condition.

Eventually his boredom and frustration explode into violence when he accidentally kills a young woman during an unsuccessful sexual tryst. In fear and confusion, he wraps her body in plaster and makes a companion for his own statue. When the police inevitably discover the body, Alley has finally and inadvertently stumbled into prominence: In the police he finds his first willing audience in years.

West's purpose here is far more sophisticated than the old cliché of the criminal as artist or as misunderstood noble creature. Instead, Alley represents the alienated individual, the small person cut off from any meaningful existence who struggles in hopeless confusion to make his life somehow mean something. Unfortunately, Alley is locked in the prison of himself, both convict and jailer at once, and remains in fundamental confusion about what to do. Nevertheless, his most vital moments are spent in his imagination, which is infinitely more extravagant and vital than his quotidian existence.

I'M EXPECTING TO LIVE QUITE SOON

The second novel in the Jaggers trilogy, *I'm Expecting to Live Quite Soon*, represents an entirely different turn in West's career. Here he not only shifts his attention from Alley to his much maligned wife, Dot, but also creates a more controlled, straightforward type of narrative. The real daring in this work comes in West's attempt to enter the consciousness of a woman, to take the same world of the first novel and shift the perspective to see through the eyes of another member of the family.

Where Alley was frustrated and irresponsible to anyone outside himself, Dot lives a life of devotion and caring: attending to Alley's irascible mother, ministering to her dying father in a nursing home, and visiting Alley in the mental hospital. Like Alley, she needs a release from boredom and conventionality, which eventually she achieves through immersion in her sensual self. The measure of her change can be seen in her eventual decision to throw over her old life and run away to Birmingham with Jimsmith Williams, a black bus-driver.

BELA LUGOSI'S WHITE CHRISTMAS

Bela Lugosi's White Christmas, the final volume in the trilogy, finds Alley (now referred to as AJ) in analysis with Dr. Withington (With) in a state institution. Who is counseling whom becomes vague as With is drawn increasingly into AJ's fractured mind, and the two eventually reverse roles, thus effecting AJ's temporary freedom and With's incarceration.

More than any of the previous novels, this one dramatically stakes its claim to stylistic and linguistic experimentation. Attempting to enter AJ's mind as fully as possible, West fashions one of his densest, most verbally complex fictions. While the reader is often at a loss to understand the exact meaning of many passages, what one does comprehend is AJ's indefatigable desire to experience as much as he can as quickly as he can. The result is criminal melee with AJ commandeering a bulldozer and digging up graves in search of his dead father, threatening customers in a bar, sodomizing and murdering a cow, covering himself with the animal's blood and sawdust, and starting a fire in a factory near his mother's home.

AJ's immersion in his own mind becomes so complete that, like a Beckett character, he reaches a state of almost total silence by the end of the novel. Once again, West examines the line between madness and sanity, originality and convention, but like all of his fictions, the work is no polemic; AJ is neither saint nor hopelessly depraved misanthrope but a tortured human being who desperately wants "a bit of individuality." The work is also significant for the fact that West actually intrudes on the fiction in spots, first in a long footnote in which he explains the eccentricities of his characters' names and ends by noting that "in this text, optical illusion is empirically sound," and later in another footnote announcing his own presence throughout the narrative. The point in both cases is to assert artifice as a fictional construct: Fictions are both stories about people and about fiction itself.

CALIBAN'S FILIBUSTER

West deals with some of these same concerns in *Caliban's Filibuster*, the novel that was published immediately before *Bela Lugosi's White Christmas*. This work represents West at his most experimentally extreme as he takes his deepest plunge into an individual's consciousness. Cal, the narrator, is yet an-

other of West's profoundly frustrated protagonists, in this case a failed novelist-cum-screenwriter who chafes at bastardizing his talent for decidedly mercenary ends. As he travels over the Pacific Ocean with his companions Murray McAndrew, a ham actor, and Sammy Zeuss, a crass film producer and Cal's employer, voices representing various of Cal's divided selves carry on endless debates about his artistic aspirations. Thus the reader is not only taken fully into the character's mind but also given access to the dimensions of his troubled psyche.

To appease these voices and satisfy himself, Cal concocts three separate yet interdependent scenarios in which he and his companions play significant roles. In creating these tales, Cal attempts to convince himself of his abused talent and also to distance himself from his experience, like a viewer before a screen in a theater watching versions of his own life. Like Caliban, his Shakespearean namesake in *The Tempest* (1611), Cal seethes with revenge, cursing those who control him. On his behalf, however, readers must regard his filibuster as an attempt to retain his individuality, which he sees as being eroded by the sterile conventions of his profession.

One way to view the novel is as West's paean to language itself, for it abounds in extravagant verbal complexities: anagrams, puns, malapropisms, acronyms, rhymes, and alphabet games. Language operates not only as Cal's professional tool but also as his saving grace; it literally keeps him sane, affording him the diversity of experience that the world denies. Like so many of West's heroes, Cal feels himself trapped, contained by forces which inexorably press against and threaten to destroy him. Language becomes his one potent defense.

COLONEL MINT

In *Colonel Mint*, West operated from a seemingly straightforward, but by no means uncomplicated, premise: An astronaut in space claims that he has seen an angel. Whether he has or not is beside the point; instead, the fact that he *thinks* he has and that others want to disabuse him of this belief becomes the subject of this alternately humorous and morally serious work. For his comment Mint is shunted off to the hinterlands of Washington State and is forced to undergo endless hours of interrogation. If he recants he can go free; otherwise, he must indefinitely remain a prisoner of the space program.

The more Mint refuses to cooperate, the more clever and depraved the methods used against him become. After threats, physical beatings, and sexual sadism fail to make Mint waver, his tormentor, General Lew R., begins—like Dr. With in *Bela Lugosi's White Christmas*—gradually to assume Mint's point of view. He wonders what it would be like to see an angel, what exactly an angel is, and finally he accepts, though he cannot empirically confirm, that Mint has seen an angel.

When the two men escape from the interrogation compound for the wilds of the surrounding woods, it appears they have defeated the forces of conformity and conventional thinking. As is the case in so many of West's fictions, however, those forces track the characters down and exact payment: Lew R. is shot and Mint is frozen. Thus, in this novel, to assert one's individuality becomes tantamount to political treason, and the response of the state is swift, final, and utterly unforgiving.

Stylistically the novel is far more straightforward than *Caliban's Filibuster*, but in at least one important respect it recalls a feature of *Bela Lugosi's White Christmas*. The tone of the novel, for all of its physical and psychological horror, is remarkably level, often nonchalant and conversational. Here the narrator, not necessarily the author, addresses the audience directly a number of times. For example, early in the work, when the reader begins to doubt the plausibility of Mint's abduction, the narrator anticipates one's objections by remarking, "You might ask, now, where is the humanity in all this; where sweet reason went. . . ." The effect here and later in the work, when the intrusions continue, is one of complicity; the audience cannot remain at the safe distance of voyeur but must participate, psychologically and emotionally, in the events that transpire. The forces of conformity involve everyone, and the audience becomes uncomfortably aware of this throughout the narrative.

Gala

In *Gala*, West extends the range of his experimentation but also returns to some familiar territory as he develops fictionally the situation described in *Words for a Deaf Daughter*. Here, novelist and amateur astronomer Wight Deulius and his deaf child Michaela construct a model of the Milky Way in their basement. The reader takes a stellar journey through the universe, moving increasingly toward what appear to be the limits of the imagination.

What is especially intriguing about this work is the form West's experimentation takes. Recalling the practice of earlier novels, but especially *Caliban's Filibuster*, West fashions a unique structure for the fiction. Where in the latter work he relies upon the International Date Line and the color spectrum (different sections of the novel are devoted primarily to different colors), in *Gala* elements of physics and the genetic code symbols offer the pattern for the story. West explains this practice when remarking, "I am a compulsive exotic and structural opportunist. I have no idea what structures I will choose next—although I do feel that they will probably be from nature rather than from society."

The Very Rich Hours of Count von Stauffenberg

In his ninth novel, *The Very Rich Hours of Count von Stauffenberg*, West once again shifted focus and style to re-create the details of one of Adolf Hitler's would-be assassins. The novel represents the best in historical fiction, a seemingly effortless blending of fact, elaboration, and pure fantasy, with the result that history becomes for the reader felt experience rather than a catalog of dry, distant details. As West points out in a preface, Stauffenberg is important not only for his public persona but also as someone whose military experience recapitulates, to greater or lesser degrees, that of West's father and all those who lived through World War II. Thus the reader comes to understand an important feature of this writer's fiction, which he expresses as follows: "Whatever I'm writing evinces the interplay between it and my life at the moment of writing, and the result is prose which, as well as being narrative and argumentative and somewhat pyrotechnical, is also symptomatic."

While the narrative, on the surface, seems markedly different from the novels which immediately precede it, one can also see characteristic West concerns emerging. For example, most of the novel places the audience squarely in Stauffenberg's mind as he copes with his war wounds, struggles to express the abiding love he feels for his wife and family, ponders the responsibilities that come with his social and military class, and rages increasingly at the psychopathic perversity of Hitler, the displaced paperhanger. West manages to avoid the obvious trap of the revisionist historian who might be tempted to make Stauffenberg into a martyr or saint. Instead, he emerges as a deeply committed, idealistic man but also one whose psyche is profoundly bruised and disturbed by the events of which he finds himself a part.

The structure of this novel is also just as experimental as that of earlier novels. West had been reading a number of medieval books of hours, lay breviaries that offer devotional prayers alongside richly illuminated paintings. Stauffenberg's rich hours are the last thirty-six of his life; the novel, however, does not stop with his execution. West imaginatively allows the count to speak to the audience from the grave, becoming, then, the most authoritative and omniscient of narrators describing those turbulent last months of the Third Reich.

RAT MAN OF PARIS

Rat Man of Paris, his most popular novel, found West exploring yet again the effects of the Third Reich on the life of yet another alienated, marginal figure, in this case a boulevardier of modern Paris who spends his time accosting passersby with a rat he conceals in his overcoat. Étienne Poulsifer, the rat man, has survived the Nazi occupation and destruction of his childhood village, and he carries about with him the emotional and psychological baggage of his horrifying past, as well as the rats which serve as metaphor for that growing legacy.

When he learns of Klaus Barbie's extradition to France, Poulsifer confuses him with the Nazi commander responsible for his parents' death and goes on a personal campaign to become the conscience of an entire nation. Watching all this is Sharli Bandol, Rat Man's lover, who desperately tries to bring some order and love into the chaos of his condition. The birth of a son appears to temper Poulsifer's extremism, but

to the end he retains his eccentricity and thus his individuality.

Like *The Very Rich Hours of Count von Stauffenberg*, *Rat Man of Paris* carefully examines the interplay between personal and public trauma, and as West puts it, "Everybody who's born gets the ontological shock, and some people get the historical shock as well, and he has both. Because he has the historical shock, he has the ontological shock even worse, and this has blighted his life." Thus the rat man stands as a contemporary Everyman, radically imperfect, overwhelmed by the world in which he finds himself, but tenaciously determined to make something of his existence.

Also like other of West's protagonists, Poulsifer demonstrates the vitality of the creative imagination. Were it not for his wild musings, the delight he takes in yoking utterly disparate things together in his mind, he would be consumed by history and dreary conventionality. In many ways he is the last free man, an essential primitive who refuses the definitions and restrictions of others for a life created on his own terms.

TERRESTRIALS

West's sixteenth novel, *Terrestrials*, was actually a story over which he had labored for twenty years or more. It involves a pair of American pilots flying a secret reconnaissance jet over Africa. During one routine flight, they are forced to eject over the Danakili Desert. One of the men is put to work by members of a local tribe in the grueling duties of a salt-mining crew, while the other is stranded in his ejection capsule on the ledge of a nearby mountain. Miraculously they are both rescued, ferried off to Turkey, and "debriefed" by junior officers they despise who question their loyalty. They are then returned to the United States and are kept on a base for more questioning. Eventually they escape, open an air touring business, and evade an assassination attempt.

On the surface the plot may seem confusing and unspectacular; however, plotting is neither the novel's primary concern nor the source of its achievement. The novel is a bold attempt to evince some of what two minds undergo as a result of life-altering trauma. Each is oppressed with guilt, feeling that he has betrayed the other, and although the two are not actually friends, they are devoted to and dependent upon each other. They grow closer as a result of their shared experience. In many ways the novel can be seen as a paean to friendship and near-filial devotion, and it asserts the intimate interconnectedness of all life.

LIFE WITH SWAN

Another intimate portrait can be found in *Life with Swan*, a *roman à clef* about West's early courtship and years with his spouse of more than twenty years, poet and naturalist Diane Ackerman (an anagram of her name—Ariada Mencken—is used for the female character's). Set in the 1970's, the novel follows a middle-aged professor as he falls in love with a younger woman, against the advice of many of his friends and colleagues. The two begin a life that saves him from his excesses. Their mutual fascination with astronomy develops into a full-blown passion and culminates with their being witnesses, at the behest of Raoul Bunsen (a character who is an echo of cosmologist Carl Sagan), to the launches of the Viking spacecraft to Mars and the Voyager to Jupiter. If *Terrestrials* is a paean to friendship, *Life with Swan* is a companion piece that examines and glorifies the saving grace of unselfish love. The prose is lush and extravagant, every page lovingly adorned with West's incomparable lyricism.

Throughout his career, West has drawn criticism for his own stylistic eccentricities and rich verbal texturings. The usual complaint holds that he is self-indulgent and willfully obscure. While indeed his fiction makes considerable demands of his audience, he is anything but deliberately perverse or obscure. In fact, West consistently attempts to reach and communicate with his audience, to involve them, in each of his rich fictional stories. His note at the beginning of *Tenement of Clay*, the interview appended to *Caliban's Filibuster*, the footnotes in *Bela Lugosi's White Christmas*, the moments of direct address in *Colonel Mint*, the announcement in the middle of *Gala* of the novel's particular structure, and the preface to *The Very Rich Hours of Count von Stauffenberg*—all demonstrate that West is fully aware of his audience and always desirous of its sympathetic participation

in the fictional experience. West is committed to the proposition that writing matters and that good writing must present its own unique experience. As he says in his essay "In Defense of Purple Prose," "The ideal is to create a complex verbal world that has as much presence, as much apparent physical bulk, as the world around it. . . . This is an illusion, to be sure, but art *is* illusion, and what's needed is an art that temporarily blots out the real."

David W. Madden

OTHER MAJOR WORKS

SHORT FICTION: *The Universe and Other Fictions*, 1988.

POETRY: *Poems*, 1952; *The Spellbound Horses*, 1960; *The Snow Leopard*, 1964.

NONFICTION: *The Growth of the Novel*, 1959; *Byron and the Spoiler's Art*, 1960, 2d ed. 1992; *I, Said the Sparrow*, 1963; *The Modern Novel*, 1963; *Robert Penn Warren*, 1964; *The Wine of Absurdity: Essays in Literature and Consolation*, 1966; *Words for a Deaf Daughter*, 1969; *Out of My Depths: A Swimmer in the Universe*, 1983; *Sheer Fiction*, 1987; *Portable People*, 1990 (drawings by Joe Servello); *Sheer Fiction*, vol. 2, 1991; *Sheer Fiction*, vol. 3, 1994; *A Stroke of Genius: Illness and Self-Discovery*, 1995; *My Mother's Music*, 1995; *The Secret Lives of Words*, 2000.

EDITED TEXT: *Byron: Twentieth Century Views*, 1963.

BIBLIOGRAPHY

Bryfonski, Dedria, and Laurie Lanza Harris, eds. *Contemporary Literary Criticism*. Vol. 14. Detroit: Gale Research, 1980. Contains extracts from reviews of West's works, including *Gala* and *Words for a Deaf Daughter*, from such sources as *The Washington Post*, *The New York Times Book Review*, and *The Nation*. Most of the reviews are favorable, addressing West's intelligent writing as both an advantage and a disadvantage. One reviewer praises *Words for a Deaf Daughter*, calling it a "sympathetic book for anyone who feels responsible for someone else." Another review describes *Gala* in terms of its "startling, dazzling meditations."

Lucas, John. "Paul West." In *Contemporary Novelists*, edited by James Vinson. London: St. James Press, 1976. Lucas discusses the Alley Jaggers sequence of novels, which "deservedly won his reputation as an original novelist," although he faults them for their lack of psychological study. Mentions West's highly acclaimed study of Lord Byron's poetry and *Bela Lugosi's White Christmas*. Lists West's works up to 1975 and includes a statement by West.

McGuire, Thomas G. "The Face(s) of War in Paul West's Fiction." *War, Literature, and the Arts: An International Journal of the Humanities* 10, no. 1 (Spring/Summer 1998): 169-186. Traces the persistence of West's rumination on warfare and conflict. Three principal novels—*The Very Rich Hours of Count von Stauffenberg*, *The Place in Flowers Where Pollen Rests*, and *Rat Man of Paris*—form the basis of the argument. The journal also contains an interview with West and three of the author's short fictions.

Madden, David W. "Indoctrination to Pariahdom: Liminality in the Fiction of Paul West." *Critique* 40, no. 1 (Fall, 1998): 49-70. Examines five of West's novels to explain the confusions and violence found so frequently there. The essay argues that each novel presents characters suspended in a liminal state from which they have difficulties extracting themselves.

_____, ed. *The Review of Contemporary Fiction* 11, no. 1 (Spring, 1991). A special half-issue devoted to West. Contains thirteen essays, an interview, and a primary bibliography of West's work up to *The Women of Whitechapel*, examining his novels from a variety of perspectives. The collection also features three short fictions from West.

_____. *Understanding Paul West*. Columbia: University of South Carolina Press, 1993. A book-length study on West that provides an overview of his work through *The Women of Whitechapel*. Intended as an introductory study to West's life and fiction, it traces the development of the themes of identity, artistic creation, and imagination's freedom.

Pope, Dan. "A Different Kind of Post-Modernism." *The Gettysburg Review* 3, no. 4 (Autumn, 1990): 658-669. Looks at West's 1988 short story collection, *The Universe and Other Fictions*, in the company of Rick DeMarinis's *The Coming Triumph of the Free World* and T. Coraghessan Boyle's *If the River Was Whiskey*. A fine sustained consideration of West's short fiction.

Saltzman, Arthur M. "Beholding Paul West and *The Women of Whitechapel*." *Twentieth Century Literature: A Scholarly and Critical Journal* 40, no. 2 (Summer, 1994): 256-271. Examines West's fourteenth novel in terms of the author's wit and inventive verbal energy and the uneasy balance between ontology and linguistic inventiveness.

West, Paul. "Paul West." In *Contemporary Authors: Autobiography Series*, edited by Mark Zadrozny. Vol. 7. Detroit: Gale Research, 1988. A beautifully written autobiography, filled with rich images and information about West's early life, his ideas about writing, and other writers who became his friends. Includes a bibliography of his works.

REBECCA WEST
Cicily Isabel Fairfield

Born: London, England; December 21, 1892
Died: London, England; March 15, 1983

PRINCIPAL LONG FICTION
The Return of the Soldier, 1918
The Judge, 1922
Harriet Hume: A London Fantasy, 1929
War Nurse: The True Story of a Woman Who Lived, Loved, and Suffered on the Western Front, 1930
The Harsh Voice, 1935
The Thinking Reed, 1936
The Fountain Overflows, 1956
The Birds Fall Down, 1966
This Real Night, 1984
Cousin Rosamund, 1985
Sunflower, 1986

(Library of Congress)

OTHER LITERARY FORMS

Although Rebecca West excelled in a variety of literary genres, she first came to prominence as a book reviewer, a role that she continued throughout her life. From her first critique, which appeared in *The Freewoman* in 1911, to her last, which appeared in the *London Sunday Telegraph* on October 10, 1982, West wrote almost one thousand reviews. Several of these appear in the collection *The Young Rebecca* (1982). Her first book, *Henry James* (1916), which is an evaluation of James's contributions to literature, was considered an audacious project for a young woman. This fearless honesty and willingness to write bluntly about sacrosanct persons and ideas marked her entire career. Since that bold debut, West published several other notable works of literary criticism. *The Strange Necessity: Esays and Reviews* (1928), a collection of essays from the *New York Herald Tribune* and the *New Statesman*, introduced one of West's recurring themes: the necessity of art in human life. *The Court and the Castle* (1957), based on her lectures at Yale, describes the role of the arts in government and society from the time of William Shakespeare to Franz Kafka.

West was also a prominent journalist and social commentator. Her coverage of the Nuremberg Trials (the trials of Nazi war criminals following World War II) appeared in *A Train of Powder* (1955). One of her most famous books, *Black Lamb and Grey Falcon* (1941), a combination travelogue, history, and sociopolitical commentary on the Balkans, is still considered essential reading for those who wish to understand the complexities of that area.

ACHIEVEMENTS

Rebecca West was a writer of great perception, encyclopedic knowledge, extensive interests, and great curiosity. It is hard to categorize her work because of its variety and complexity. As a result, West's individual works, both fiction and nonfiction, have not received the critical analysis and acclaim that they deserve. However, she often received recognition for the body of her work. Certain universal themes permeate her writing: the nature of art, the frauds and weaknesses of the social system, the causes and results of treason and betrayal. West received numerous honors because of her ability to accurately portray the social milieu of the twentieth century. In 1937, West was made a member of the Order of St. Sava by Yugoslavia. The French government named her a Chevalier of the Legion of Honor in 1959. She became Dame Commander, Order of the British Empire, in 1959 and was made a Companion of Literature for the Royal Society of Literature in 1968. The American Academy of Arts and Letters inducted her as an honorary member in 1972. She also received the Women's National Press Club Award for journalism.

BIOGRAPHY

Rebecca West was born Cicily (Cissie) Isabel Fairfield, the youngest of three daughters of Charles

Fairfield and Isabella Mackenzie. Charle[?] pursued several careers, including journa[?] failed to succeed at any of them. In 1901, [?] doned his family in order to pursue yet anothe[?] in Sierra Leone. Although he returned to Englar[?] ter a few months, he never again lived with his family. Still, West admired her father's Anglo-Irish gentility and charm, finding him a strong and romantic figure. Throughout her life she wrote fondly of him and frequently justified his poor treatment of his family. After his departure, the family was forced to move to Isabella Mackenzie's family home in Edinburgh. West described this as a period of deprivation. Although the family had enough income to survive, they were caught between social classes, not fitting into any established social level. All three of the Fairfield daughters embraced feminism. West's first job, in 1911, was writing for *The Freewoman*, a weekly publication focusing on women's issues. In the spring of 1912, she adopted a pseudonym, Rebecca West, a character she had once played in Henrik Ibsen's play *Rosmersholm* (1886). The character, a strong woman, mistress of a married man, convinces her lover to join her in suicide. Later, West said that this had been a hasty decision and that she liked neither the play nor the character. However, the name took hold, and to all but her family, Cissie had become Rebecca West.

West's reviews gained for her the attention of the London literary establishment. After reading her review of his novel *Marriage* (1912), H. G. Wells wished to meet its author. Although he was married, the two embarked on an intense ten-year affair. On August 4, 1914, West gave birth to a son, Anthony Panther West. Both West and Wells kept his true parentage from their son for many years, primarily since Wells did not wish to make the affair public. West even acquired adoption papers for Anthony in order to formalize her status as his parent. Anthony West was particularly bitter about his mother's role in his life, often criticizing her in the press. The relationship between West and Wells was a tempestuous one. They frequently disagreed on social, political, and literary issues, as well as the details of their relationship and on child rearing. In addition, West often felt trapped by motherhood and was resentful of the freedom Wells had. Her literary career, however, met with growing success in both England and the United States. Her first novels received favorable comment. By 1923, her affair with Wells was ending, and she began a brief, unsuccessful liaison with newspaper magnate Max Beaverbrook.

In 1930, West married Henry Andrews, a banker she had met the previous year. Andrews worked for Schroder, a German banking firm. Both he and West became increasingly disturbed by the growing Nazi influence. Andrews, sympathetic to the plight of the Jews, helped many escape from Germany, a role which eventually caused the bank to fire him. During the 1930's, West became fascinated with the politics, history, and social mores of Yugoslavia. This increased her determination to encourage Britain to adopt an active role in combating the Nazi threat. In 1941, *Black Lamb and Grey Falcon*, West's monumental portrait of Yugoslavia, appeared to popular acclaim.

After World War II, West published several works examining treason and justice. Her stance during the late 1940's and 1950's isolated her from many of her literary acquaintances, because she felt Communism was a greater threat than Senator Joseph McCarthy and the United States' House Committee on Un-American Activities. On November 3, 1968, Henry Andrews died. In spite of illnesses that crippled her during the 1970's, West continued working until her death in 1983.

ANALYSIS

Rebecca West never received the same acclaim for her novels as for her critical and journalistic work. While her novels were praised for their complexity, West was often criticized for over-intellectualizing her stories. Critics frequently state that her novels lack action. In fact, all her novels are characterized by extended internal monologues. In addition, West uses long, complex sentences; she has frequently been compared to Henry James in both subject matter and style. A West novel demands the reader's close attention. Most of her novels take place during the Edwardian era or explore the values and social behavior of that period. Within this background, her fiction examines the relationships between men and women, most of which seem doomed to failure. Her stories are presented through a feminine perspective; West's usual narrator is a young woman who is intelligent, sensitive, and clever.

THE RETURN OF THE SOLDIER

The title character of her first short novel, *The Return of the Soldier*, is Chris Baldry, a shell-shocked soldier who is suffering from amnesia. However, this is a story about love rather than war. The novel opens as Chris's wife, Kitty, and his cousin Jenny, the narrator, wait to receive a letter from the war front. Instead they are visited by Margaret Grey, a shabbily dressed woman, who tells them that she has received a message from Chris. As a result of his injuries, Chris has forgotten the last fifteen years of his life, including his marriage, the death of his child, and his comfortable life in Baldry Hall. He remembers only Margaret, whom he had loved passionately fifteen years earlier, despite the difference in their social class.

When Chris returns, he fails to recognize his wife, and he is desperately unhappy; the present has become a prison, keeping him from the person he loves—Margaret. Eventually he arranges to see her, finding that in spite of the ravages that years of poverty have caused, he is truly at ease only with her. Margaret, however, recognizes that because of their obvious class differences the two of them cannot hope for a life together and helps him regain his memory. Ironically, this allows him to resume his former life, and he realizes that he was never content. In addition, since he is now cured, he can return to his life as a soldier. The recovery of memory proves to be more tragic than its loss. *The Return of the Soldier* has the strengths common to West's novels: insight into the nature of romantic relationships, vivid descriptions of the influence of social background, and an insightful examination of human nature.

THE JUDGE

West's second novel, *The Judge*, a longer, more complex work, is divided into two sections: The first explores a young woman's coming of age, while the second centers around the tortured relationships in her fiancee's family. Several critics complain that these sections differ so much in style and content that they do not form a satisfactory whole. The first part of the novel, set in Edinburgh, contains many autobiographical elements. The main character, Ellen Melville, a secretary for a law firm, is clever, independent, and involved in the woman suffrage movement. She emerges from youth into womanhood, dealing with problem employers and becoming involved with Richard Yaverland, whom she sees as a romantic hero. Ellen is both charming and intriguing as she learns somewhat bitter lessons about a woman's role in society. The engagement between Ellen and Richard leads to the second section of the novel, where the subject and mood shift dramatically.

The focus moves from Ellen to Richard's mother, Marion. West concentrates on Richard's illegitimate birth and its consequences. During her pregnancy, Marion is attacked by a group of villagers. In desperation, she allows herself to be married to Peacey, the butler of the man she loves. He eventually rapes her, and she bears a second child, Roger, a pale and pathetic figure beside his more vigorous brother. Marion, whose relationship with Richard contains strong sexual overtones, commits suicide in order to allow Richard and Ellen to become free of his ties to her and to his past. Roger blames his brother for the death. When the two fight, Richard kills his brother. In spite of the dramatic content, the novel has been criticized for its length and lack of action.

HARRIET HUME

West's previous novels utilized the Freudian psychological realism of many twentieth century novels. In her third novel, *Harriet Hume*, she changes her style, creating a fantasy. The two main characters, Harriet, a pianist, and Arnold Condorex, a politician, both have weaknesses that jeopardize their careers: Harriet's hands are too small to span the keys of the piano as she would like; Condorex was not born to a family with power and social class. However, they succeed in spite of their difficulties. Their relationship is complicated by Arnold's need to be involved with a woman who will aid his political career and by the fact that Harriet possesses psychic powers, which enable her to read the mind of her lover. The novel traces their meetings throughout the years, describing both the fascination they have for each other and the differences in the values that each has embraced. The novel is a fable illustrating some of the main themes of West's work: the necessity of art in love and life, as well as the complex reasons men give to justify betrayal.

THE FOUNTAIN OVERFLOWS

The Fountain Overflows is the first of a four-novel series West planned to write centering around the Aubrey family, patterned on her own family. Only the first appeared before her death; *This Real Night* and *Cousin Rosamund* were published posthumously. She never completed the fourth novel. *The Fountain Overflows* is a childhood memory. It describes the Aubrey children's survival after their father deserts them: Cordelia, the oldest; the twins Mary and Rose; and Richard Quin, the youngest member of the family. Filled with vivid detail, it contains not only a rich portrait of family life but also a murder and several supernatural occurrences, all presented from a child's perspective. West's subject and style in this novel has been compared to the richly textured writing of Charles Dickens and Arnold Bennett.

THE BIRDS FALL DOWN

The Birds Fall Down, one of the most popular of West's novels, marks another departure in subject matter. The story, set in 1905, is narrated by Laura Rowen, an eighteen-year-old whose grandfather, a Russian grandduke, has been unfairly exiled by the czar. The main plot deals with treachery and betrayal, set against the backdrop of the political turmoil in Russia during this period. Clearly, however, West is developing themes she explored in her history book *The Meaning of Treason* (1947). As Laura journeys through France with her grandfather, he learns that his trusted aide is a double agent responsible for his disgrace. Her grandfather has a stroke and dies, while Laura has to struggle to escape from the traitor. The secondary plotline describes her father's affair, a betrayal of his wife and family which runs a parallel course to the treachery on the international level.

Mary E. Mahony

OTHER MAJOR WORKS

NONFICTION: *Henry James*, 1916; *The Strange Necessity: Essays and Reviews*, 1928; *Lions and Lambs*, 1928; *D. H. Lawrence*, 1930; *Arnold Bennett Himself*, 1931; *Ending in Earnest: A Literary Log*, 1931; *St. Augustine*, 1933; *A Letter to a Grandfather*, 1933; *The Modern Rake's Progress*, 1934; *Black Lamb and Grey Falcon*, 1941 (travel); *The Meaning of Treason*, 1947 (history; rev. as *The New Meaning of Treason*, 1964); *A Train of Powder*, 1955 (history); *The Court and the Castle*, 1957 (literary criticism); *The Vassall Affair*, 1963; *McLuhan and the Future of Literature*, 1969; *The Young Rebecca: Writings of Rebecca West*, 1982 (journalism); *1900*, 1982; *Family Memories*, 1987

MISCELLANEOUS: *Rebecca West: A Celebration*, 1977.

BIBLIOGRAPHY

Deakin, Motley F. *Rebecca West*. Boston: Twayne, 1980. Clear examination of major genres and themes in West's writing. Provides detailed commentary on theme, character, style, and setting in West's novels.

Glendinning, Victoria. *Rebecca West: A Life*. New York: Alfred A. Knopf, 1986. Detailed account of West's life, focusing particularly on the early years. Provides insight into West's development as a writer.

Orel, Harold. *The Literary Achievement of Rebecca West*. London: Macmillan, 1986. Analyses West's life and her critical stance. Compares and contrasts characters, style, idiom, and recurring themes in her novels.

Rollyson, Carl E. *The Literary Legacy of Rebecca West*. San Francisco: International Scholars Publications, 1998. A thorough book of criticism and interpretation of West. Includes bibliographical references and an index.

_____. *Rebecca West: A Life*. New York: Scribner, 1996. Detailed biography discussing West's importance to twentieth century literature, tracing the development of her long career and illustrating the connections between her fiction and nonfiction.

Scott, Bonnie Kime. *Refiguring Modernism.* 2 vols. Bloomington: Indiana University Press, 1995. The first volume of this set discusses women of 1928, and the second volume offers postmodern feminist readings of Virginia Woolf, Djuna Barnes, and West.

Wolfe, Peter. *Rebecca West: Artist and Thinker.* Carbondale: Southern Illinois University Press, 1971. Evaluates problems and achievements in West's novels, arguing the early novels lack satisfactory plot development while the later novels are stylistically and thematically superior.

EDITH WHARTON

Born: New York, New York; January 24, 1862
Died: St.-Brice-sous-Forêt, France; August 11, 1937

PRINCIPAL LONG FICTION

The Touchstone, 1900
The Valley of Decision, 1902
Sanctuary, 1903
The House of Mirth, 1905
Madame de Treymes, 1907
The Fruit of the Tree, 1907
Ethan Frome, 1911
The Reef, 1912
The Custom of the Country, 1913
Summer, 1917
The Marne, 1918
The Age of Innocence, 1920
The Glimpses of the Moon, 1922
A Son at the Front, 1923
Old New York, 1924
The Mother's Recompense, 1925
Twilight Sleep, 1927
The Children, 1928
Hudson River Bracketed, 1929
The Gods Arrive, 1932
The Buccaneers, 1938

OTHER LITERARY FORMS

In addition to her novels, of which several had appeared serially in *Scribners, The Delineator,* and *The Pictorial Review,* Edith Wharton published eleven collections of short stories and three volumes of poetry as well as a variety of nonfiction works. She wrote an early and influential book on interior decorating, *The Decoration of Houses* (1897, in collaboration with architect Ogden Codman, Jr.), a short book on the art of narrative, *The Writing of Fiction* (1925) published originally in *Scribner's Magazine,* and a delightful if highly selective autobiography, *A Backward Glance* (1934), which includes among other things an amusing account of Henry James's circumlocutory manner of speech. Wharton, an indefatigable traveler, recorded accounts of her travels in *Italian Villas and Their Gardens* (1904), *Italian Backgrounds* (1905), *A Motor-Flight Through France* (1908), and *In Morocco* (1920). During World War I, she wrote numerous pamphlets and letters to inform Americans about French and Belgian suffering and to enlist sympathy and support. Articles she wrote to explain the French people to American soldiers were later collected in the volume *French Ways and Their Meaning* (1919), and accounts of her five tours of the front lines were published under the title *Fighting France from Dunkerque to Belfort* (1915). Wharton also published a great many short stories, articles, and reviews that have never been collected. A number of her stories and novels have been adapted for the stage, motion pictures, and television, and have also been translated into French, Italian, Spanish, German, Danish, Finnish, and Japanese.

ACHIEVEMENTS

Unlike Henry James, whose readership was small and intensely discriminating, Wharton managed to attract a large audience of general readers and at the same time command the interest of critics and fellow writers as well. Among her admirers were Sinclair Lewis and F. Scott Fitzgerald; Bernard Berenson, the art critic; and Percy Lubbock. Wharton's popularity remained high almost to the end of her career in the 1930's, but critical enthusiasm began to diminish after 1920, when the quality of her fiction declined.

Even in the early years, 1905 to 1920, when Wharton's best fiction was being published, there were reservations expressed or implied by those who thought her a follower of and to some extent a lesser James, a charge easier to disprove than to eradicate. The truth is, that, though Warton learned from James—and a few of her novels, particularly *Madame de Treymes*, reflect Jamesian themes as well as techniques—Wharton had her own manner as well as her own subject, and as she grew older, she continued to discover differences between her fiction and James's. It should also be pointed out (whether in praise or blame will depend on the critic) that James was a more dedicated artist than Wharton; his fiction had a finish and a coherence to be found in only a half-dozen of her novels; moreover, Wharton sometimes

(Library of Congress)

skated on the thin ice of superficiality, and in one novel, *The Glimpses of the Moon*, plunged through. Toward the end of her career, she also grew increasingly out of touch with life in the postwar world, much of which offended her. Her long residence in France, moreover, not only cut her off from the life of her fellow countrymen, but also—since she spoke French or Italian almost exclusively—loosened her grasp of English, so much so that a critic such as the young Edmund Wilson could complain that there were awkward phrases even in her masterpiece *The Age of Innocence*.

Wharton's major talent was for social observation. Unlike James, whose interest was ultimately metaphysical and whose novels were often invented from the slightest hints and employed few details, she filled her novels with precise accounts of the decoration of houses, of dress and of dinner parties, describing them often down to the cut of a waistcoat

and the contents of the soup tureen. This is not to say that such details were signs of superficiality, but rather that Wharton's fiction depended heavily on the notation of manners and were the result of direct observation. Wharton tended to write—again, unlike James—out of her own direct experience. Even novels such as *Ethan Frome* and *Summer*—both set in provincial New England, and so different from the world she inhabited in New York and Paris—were created with remarkable attention to surface details, of which the famous cut glass, red pickle dish of Zeena's in *Ethan Frome* is a familiar example.

Wharton's fiction, it now appears, was (again, unlike James's) significantly autobiographical. Even the novels of provincial life, so different on the surface, treated issues that came out of the tensions of her own restricted upbringing and her unhappy marriage. Marriage was one of Wharton's principal subjects and provided her with a way of exploring and dramatizing her two main themes: the entrapment of an individual, as R. W. B. Lewis puts it in his *Edith Wharton: A Biography* (1975), and the attempt by an outsider, often a vulgar lower-class individual, to break into an old, aristocratic society. There is a sense in which these two themes are contradictory; the first one implies a point of view that identifies with the individual rather than with society; the second one judges from the point of view of society. The apparent contradiction, however, merely points up the range and boundaries of the author's sensibility. In some novels, *Ethan Frome* and *The House of Mirth*, for example, Wharton writes with sympathy of the trapped individual; in others, *The Custom of the Country*, and *The Children*, she writes from the standpoint of a traditional society. In her best novels, there is both sympathy for the trapped individual and the invocation of an outside claim—marriage vows, moral code, traditional manners—with the balance of sympathy tipped to the individual.

Wharton's major work was written between 1905, the year *The House of Mirth* was published, and 1920, when *The Age of Innocence* appeared. Interesting novels were still to come: *The Mother's Recompense, The Children*, and *The Buccaneers*, which has the best qualities of her earlier fiction; but the major works of the late 1920's and early 1930's, *Hudson River Bracketed* and *The Gods Arrive*, betray a serious falling off of energy and of talent. In these novels, Wharton was attempting to judge the contemporary world by the values of the past, but was so out of sympathy with the life around her and so out of touch with its manners that her representation of it in these later books can hardly be taken seriously.

Despite this later decline, however, and despite the undeniable influence of James on some of her early work, Wharton produced a considerable body of original fiction, high in quality and superior to most of what was being published at the time. Her fiction also influenced other, younger American writers, notably Sinclair Lewis and F. Scott Fitzgerald. After a long decline in readership and a period of critical indifference, there now appears to be a renewal of interest in her writing, both by critics and scholars of the American novel and by feminist scholars interested in extraliterary issues.

BIOGRAPHY

Edith Wharton was born Edith Newbold Jones on January 24, 1862, in New York City. Her parents, George Frederic and Lucretia Rhinelander Jones, were descendants of early English and Dutch settlers and belonged to the pre-Civil War New York aristocracy, families whose wealth consisted largely of Manhattan real estate and who constituted in their common ancestry, landed wealth, and traditional manners a tightly knit, closed society. With the industrial expansion that occurred during and immediately after the Civil War, the old society was "invaded" by a new class of self-made rich men such as John Jacob Astor and Cornelius Vanderbilt. Whereas the old society had lived unostentatiously, observing, outwardly at least, a strict code of manners—the women presiding over a well-regulated social life and the men making perfunctory gestures at pursuing a profession—the new rich spent lavishly, built expensive, vulgar houses, and behaved in ways the old order found shockingly reprehensible. With its energy, its money, and its easier morality, the new order inevitably triumphed over the old, and this displacement of New York society constituted one of the chief subjects of Wharton's fiction, particularly in *The House of Mirth* and *The Custom of the Country*.

Wharton was educated at home by governesses, and later, tutors, and it was expected that she would assume the role young women of her class were educated to play, that of wife, mother, a gracious hostess. From an early age, however, Wharton showed intellectual and literary talents which, along with an acute shyness, kept her at the edge of conventional social life and later threatened to consign her at the age of twenty-three to a life of spinsterhood—the worst fate, so it was thought, that could befall a young woman of her class. After one engagement had been called off (because the young man's mother opposed it), and a promising relationship with a young lawyer, Walter Berry (who later became a close friend), had failed to develop romantically, Wharton married a man twelve years her senior, Edward ("Teddy")

Robbins Wharton, a friend of her favorite brother.

Teddy Wharton was a socially prominent Bostonian without a profession or money of his own; Henry James and other friends in England were later incredulous that Wharton could marry a man so obviously her intellectual inferior and so incompatible in his interests; nevertheless, the marriage in the beginning must have been a liberation, both from the social pressure to marry and from her mother's domination. Wharton was close to her father, but there was a coolness between her and her mother that is frequently reflected in her fiction in the portrayal of mother-daughter relationships. By marrying Teddy, she was at last free to come and go as she pleased, to establish her own residence, which she did on a grand scale at Lenox, Massachusetts, and to travel abroad as often as she liked, In time, however, the marriage to Teddy became irksome, partly from lack of deep affection for him, but also because of his increasing bouts of depression and, later, his financial and sexual irresponsibilities. After revelations of his mismanagement of her estate and his adulterous affairs, she divorced Teddy in 1913. In his research for the biography of Wharton, Lewis uncovered the fact that she herself had had a brief but intense affair in 1908 with an American journalist named Morton Fullerton, and that that relationship had a profound influence on her fiction.

Wharton had lived and traveled in Europe as a child with her parents and after her marriage had visited abroad as often as possible, alternating the seasons between her house at Lenox and an apartment in Paris, with shorter visits to England and rural France. In 1903, when she met James in England, there began an important friendship, with frequent visits and exchanges of letters and motor trips in Wharton's powerful automobile. The Whartons always traveled in luxury, and their style and Edith's energy quite overwhelmed James at the same time he delighted in them. Like James, and for somewhat the same reasons, Wharton became in time an expatriate, giving up the newer, rawer life of America for the rich, deeply rooted culture of Europe. She felt at home in the salons and drawing rooms of Paris and London, where art and literature and ideas were discussed freely, where women were treated by men as equals, and where life itself was more pleasing to the senses and to the contemplative mind. Wharton also felt that in Europe, respect for the family, for manners, for learning, and for culture, even among the poorer classes, was very much alive.

Even before the final break with Teddy, Wharton had lengthened her frequent stays abroad and, finally, in 1911, allowed the house at Lenox to be sold. When World War I broke out, she remained in Paris and devoted her time, energy, and money to the relief of French and Belgian refugees; in 1916, she was officially recognized for her services to her adopted country by being made a Chevalier of the Legion of Honor. After the war, she bought a house just north of Paris and, later, another in the south of France. She made only one more trip home, in 1923, to receive an honorary degree at Yale. The remainder of her life was spent abroad.

According to those who knew her well, Wharton was a highly intelligent, well-read, brilliant conversationalist, somewhat remote at first, though the grand manner that many complained of was apparently a way of covering up her deep shyness. She read and spoke Italian and French fluently, and her salons in both Paris and Saint Claire were gathering places for literary, artistic, and social luminaries of the time, including such well-known figures as F. Scott Fitzgerald, Bernard Berenson, Jean Cocteau, Aldous Huxley, and Kenneth Clark. Despite the hectic pace of her social life and her frequent travels, Wharton continued to write regularly, turning out novels and short stories and articles, most of which sold well and brought her a great deal of money. She suffered a slight stroke in 1935, which for a time curtailed her activities; two years later, she was fatally stricken. After a short illness, she died at her home in St.-Brice-sous-Forêt, August 11, 1937. Her body was buried in a cemetery at Versailles, beside the grave where the ashes of her old friend Walter Berry had been buried earlier.

ANALYSIS

On a surface level, there is a surprising variety in the kinds of characters and the aspects of life with which Edith Wharton was familiar. In *The House of*

Mirth, for example, one of her best novels, she was able to create characters such as the Trenors and the Van Osburghs, who belong to opposite ends of the upper level of old New York society, as well as Nettie Struther, the poor working-class girl who befriends Lily Bart when she has sunk from the glittering world of Fifth Avenue social life to a seedy, boardinghouse existence. In *The Fruit of the Tree*, she created not only the world of the fashionable Westmores, but also the factory milieu in which the foreman John Amherst attempts to bring industrial reform. In *The Reef*, she could treat life in a French chateau, as well as in a sordid hotel in Paris, and in her two brilliant short novels, *Ethan Frome* and *Summer*, she managed to depict a life in rural Massachusetts that she could only have known by observation, rather than by direct experience.

It must be admitted, however, that Wharton is at times less than convincing. Some critics consider her attempt to deal with factory life in *The Fruit of the Tree* inept, even ludicrous, though others believe it entirely adequate; and certainly the life of impoverished Nettie Struther is delineated with nothing like the thoroughness of Lily Bart's, whose upper-class milieu Wharton knew at firsthand. Still, the extent of Wharton's social range and her ability to create realistic characters from a background quite different from her own is impressive, unrivaled in American fiction of the time.

As for variety of character types, one might cite in particular those to be found in *The House of Mirth*, in the range of male characters—from the fastidious Selden to the rapacious Gus Trenor and the socially ambiguous and vulgar Simon Rosedale, all of them suitors for Lily's attention. Both *Ethan Frome* and *Summer* present a more limited range, but both contain sharply realized and distinctly differentiated characters, including the powerful Ethan, the pretty young Mattie, and Zeena, the neurasthenic wife of Ethan. In *Summer*, Charity Royall, the mountain girl, is vividly created, as is her feckless young lover and her elderly guardian and attempted seducer, Lawyer Royall.

Despite this surface breadth, this impressive range of social observation, Wharton's novels have a rather narrow thematic focus. It has been said that Edith Wharton's chief theme is entrapment. Blake Nevious, in *Edith Wharton: A Study of Her Fiction* (1953), points out how this theme is implicit in the principal relationships among characters in many of the novels, in which a superior nature is caught in a wasteful and baffling submission to an inferior nature. It was a situation that Wharton herself must have experienced, not only with a mother who was obsessed with fashion and propriety, but also in a society narrowly given up to the pursuit of pleasure. It was a situation in which she later found herself in her marriage to Teddy, who disliked and resented her interest in social and intellectual life. In novel after novel, one sees this same situation treated—superior individuals trapped in relationships with their inferiors and prevented from extricating themselves by a finer sensibility.

THE HOUSE OF MIRTH

In *The House of Mirth*, Lily Bart is impoverished by the bankruptcy and later the death of her father and is obliged to recoup her fortune in the only way open to her, by attempting to marry a rich man. Lily's situation was not Wharton's, but the social pressures on her must have been similar: to make a suitable marriage, with social position certainly, and, if possible, money as well. In the novel, Lily is given a choice that Wharton apparently did not have: an offer of marriage from an emancipated young lawyer of her own class (though Walter Berry, a lawyer, was thought at one time to have been Wharton's suitor). Wharton chose a passionless marriage with Teddy; Lily was not allowed that solution. Selden deserts her at the crucial moment, and she dies of an overdose of sleeping medicine.

In her autobiography *A Backward Glance*, Wharton stated that her subject in *The House of Mirth* was to be the tragic power of New York society in "debasing people and ideas," and Lily Bart was created in order to give that power dramatic scope. Lily's entrapment by society and her eventual destruction are not the final story. Lily overcomes the limitations of her upbringing and aspirations and acts on principle. She has in her possession a packet of letters which could be used to regain her social position, but the letters would involve the reputation of Selden. She also has a ten-thousand-dollar inheritance which could be used to establish herself in a profitable business, but she burns the letters and uses the money to repay a debt of honor. Lily dies, but in choosing death rather than dishonor, she has escaped entrapment.

THE AGE OF INNOCENCE

In *The Age of Innocence*, published fifteen years after *The House of Mirth*, the underlying conflict is the same, though the tone of the novel and the nature of the entrapment are somewhat different. Here, the trapped individual is a man, Newland Archer, a young lawyer who is engaged to marry May Welland, a pretty and shallow young woman of respectable old New York society of the 1870's and 1890's. This is the world of Wharton's young womanhood, a society that is narrow and rigid and socially proper. Into this limited and self-contained world, she brings Ellen Olenska, a cousin of May, who belongs to this world by birth but left it years before and has since married a Polish count. Ellen has now separated from her husband, who has been notoriously unfaithful, and has returned to the bosom of her family for support and comfort. Archer is engaged by the family to help her in her quest for a divorce settlement. The inevitable happens. Archer and Ellen fall in love. Archer is attracted by Ellen's European sophistication, her freedom of thought and manners, and her refusal to take seriously the small taboos of New York society. Archer considers breaking with May and marrying Ellen. The family, sensing his defection, contrive with other members of the society to separate the lovers and reunite Archer with May, his conventional fiancée. Social pressure forces Ellen to return to Europe, and Archer is again thinking of pursuing Ellen; then May announces that she is expecting a baby. Archer is finally and permanently trapped.

As though to drive home the extent to which Archer has been defeated, Wharton takes him to Paris years later. His son is grown, his wife dead, and Ellen Olenska is now a widow living alone. Archer makes an appointment to see Ellen but gets only as far as a park bench near her apartment. At the last minute, he decides to send his son to see her, while he remains seated on the bench, telling himself that it would be more real for him to remain there than to go himself to see Ellen. The trap has done its work.

While one can see resemblances between Ellen and Wharton—the expatriation, the charm, the liberated views, perhaps even the slight French accent with which Ellen speaks—Archer is also Wharton, or that side of her that could never entirely escape the past. *The Age of Innocence* was thought by some reviewers to be a glorification of the past, which it clearly is not. Wharton does evoke with some nostalgia the old New York of her youth, but she also sets forth with delicate but cutting irony that society's limitations and its destructive narrowness. Archer has led an exemplary life, one is led to believe, but the happiness he might have had was gently but firmly denied him. Whereas a more popular novelist might have allowed Archer to be reunited with Ellen at the end of the novel, Wharton insists that that would be unreal; for her, personal happiness in the real world is the exception rather than the rule.

ETHAN FROME

Two of Wharton's best novels—also two of her shortest—both deal with protagonists trapped by passionless marriages. The earliest of these, *Ethan Frome*, is about a Massachusetts farmer married to an older, neurasthenic wife, whose pretty young cousin has come to work for her. The inevitable again happens. Ethan falls in love with Mattie and dreams about running away with her. Ethan's jealous wife, however, arranges for Mattie to be sent away, and Ethan is obliged to escort her to the train station. It is winter, and the lovers stop for a brief time together. They embrace, realize the inevitability of separation, and decide to kill themselves by coasting down a steep hill into a great elm tree. During the ride down the steep hill, Ethan accidentally swerves the sled; a crash occurs, in which the lovers are seriously injured but survive. Mattie becomes a whining invalid, while Zeena, the neurotic wife, takes over the running of the household, and Ethan, who is severely disfigured, feels himself like a handcuffed convict, a prisoner for life.

As Lewis has pointed out, the situation in *Ethan Frome* is very much like the situation in Wharton's own life at the time. If one shifts the sexes, Frome is Wharton trapped in a loveless marriage with the neurasthenic Teddy and passionately in love with a younger man who shared her interests and feelings, Morton Fullerton. The violent ending, of course, may be seen as Wharton's passionate statement about her own desperate situation. The success of *Ethan Frome*, however, does not depend on making such biographical connections; the book is a brilliantly re-alized work of realistic fiction that owes its power not to some abstractly conceived pessimistic philoso-phy of life, but to Wharton's successful transposi-tion of her own emotional life into the language of fiction.

SUMMER

Summer was published six years after *Ethan Frome* and was called by Wharton and her friends the "hot Ethan." As in *Ethan Frome*, there is a triangle: Lawyer Royall, elderly guardian of Charity, a pretty young mountain girl, and a visiting architecture stu-dent, Lucius Harney. During the idyllic summer months, an intense and passionate affair takes place between Charity and Harney. Harney returns to Bos-ton, and Charity is left to face her guardian, who is also in love with her, and the prospect of an illegal abortion. The novel concludes with a reconciliation between Charity and her guardian and a secure if pas-sionless marriage with him. While it would be a mis-take to overemphasize biographical parallels, they are unmistakable. The affair of Charity and Har-ney suggests Wharton's earlier affair with Fullerton, while the intrusive presence of the fatherly Lawyer Royall suggests Teddy's irksome claims on Whar-ton's loyalties. An interesting alteration of chronol-ogy is in making the marriage with the older man fol-low the affair rather than precede it, as it had in Wharton's own life. *Summer* was written four years after the Whartons were divorced, and by then, she may have had time to view her marriage to Teddy more dispassionately, as the practical solution it must originally have been. Like Lily's death, the surrender to marriage is a defeat as well as a moral triumph.

Summer is one of Wharton's finest novels, written according to her own testimony, in a state of "cre-ative joy" and reflecting in its characters, scenes, and symbolic structures, the deep well of the unconscious that seems to nourish the most powerful works of American fiction.

THE REEF

The Reef, published the year before the Whartons' divorce, and commonly acknowledged to be Whar-ton's most Jamesian novel, again deals with conflicts between the individual and society and the problems of marriage. In this novel, however, the society is re-mote; the inheritor of the society's standards, Anna Leath, an American widow of a French nobleman, is reunited with an old friend, George Darrow, also an American, a lawyer, living in Europe. Anna and Darrow become engaged and are about to be married when Anna discovers that Darrow has had an affair with Sophy Viner, her daughter's governess, a girl of a lower class, and that Sophy, who is also her step-son's fiancée, is still in love with Darrow. For Dar-row, the situation is a matter of diplomatic maneuver-ing, of steering his way between the two women and the stepson, but for Anna, it presents a moral di-lemma involving, on the one hand, an inherited code of conduct, which tells her that Darrow must be abandoned, and a personal one, which tells her not to give him up. The moral complexities of the novel are a good deal more complicated than summary can in-dicate—indeed, are so ambiguous that one is hard pressed to decide where the author stands. It is possi-ble, however, to see in this novel situations parallel to Wharton's earlier involvement with Fullerton, and a possible moral dilemma over her own infidelity. In a sense, Wharton is Sophy Viner, but Sophy (and Wharton's affair with Fullerton) seen in the light of a later moral judgment, Wharton is also Anna, attempt-ing to accept the break with conventional morality that led to Darrow's affair with Sophy. The trap in which Anna finds herself is doubly baited, and no matter which way she turns, she must fall, either morally or emotionally. The fact that Anna chooses Darrow after all suggests the same kind of compro-mise other Wharton protagonists have made, Justine of *The Fruit of the Tree* and Charity Royall of *Sum-mer* especially, both of whom were betrayed by the weakness of the men they loved but settled for what was finally available.

THE CUSTOM OF THE COUNTRY

The Custom of the Country is a different sort of work, influenced by the French realist Honoré de Balzac rather than by Henry James; it attempts to deal, as did Balzac, with the destruction of an aristocracy by the invasion of uncivilized materialists. The protagonist of the novel, Undine Spragg, is a handsome young woman from Apex, a city in the American Middle West. Undine's father made a great deal of money in Apex and now has come East to try his hand in New York City. The Spraggs move into an expensive, vulgar hotel, and the parents would be content to exist on the fringes of New York society, but Undine, who is as ambitious as she is vulgar, manages to meet and then marry Ralph Marvel, an ineffectual member of old New York society. When life with Marvel grows boring, Undine becomes the mistress of a richer and more aggressive New York aristocrat, Peter Van Degen; when Van Degen drops her, she manages to snare the son of an old aristocratic French family, the Marquis de Chelles. Undine marries de Chelles, but she has learned nothing, being without taste, manners, or ideas; her sole interest is in amusing and gratifying herself. As soon as she gets what she thinks she wants, she becomes dissatisfied with it and wants something she decides is better. She grows tired of having to fit herself into the demands of the feudal aristocracy into which she has married; when she attempts to sell family heirlooms, whose value she does not understand, her husband divorces her. Her third husband is a perfect match, a hard-driving vulgar materialist from Apex, Elmer Moffat, whose chief interest is in buying up European art. Moffat also aspires to an ambassadorial post, but is barred because he is married to Undine, a divorced woman.

The Custom of the Country is regarded by some critics as among Wharton's best fiction, but, as Blake Nevius has observed, during the course of the novel, Undine ceases to be a credible character and becomes an "inhuman abstraction." Clearly, she came to represent everything that Wharton detested in the America of 1912, and, at a deeper and vaguer level, perhaps also expressed Wharton's fear and resentment at the displacement of her own class by more energetic and less cultivated outsiders. The fact that such fears were real enough and the implicit social criticisms valid, does nothing to alter the fact that, measured against books such as *The House of Mirth, Ethan Frome, Summer*, and *The Reef, The Custom of the Country* is crude and unconvincing. James had been right years earlier in advising Wharton to write about that part of the world she knew best, for in attempting to deal with the Middle West in *The Custom of the Country*, and later, in *Hudson River Bracketed* and *The Gods Arrive*, with bohemian circles about which she knew very little, she condemned herself to superficiality and caricature. It is difficult to take seriously Undine Spragg of *The Custom of the Country* or Advance Weston, the protagonist of *Hudson River Bracketed* and *The Gods Arrive*, who is said to be from Pruneville, Nebraska, and later Hallelujah, Missouri, and Euphoria, Illinois. Caricature is an expression of outrage, not understanding.

THE BUCCANEERS

Fortunately, the last of Wharton's novels, *The Buccaneers*, published the year after her death, was a return to the territory of her earlier fiction, old New York of the 1870's. The novel was unfinished at her death and lacks the coherence of her best early work, but she could still write with the sharpness and scenic fullness that had characterized *The House of Mirth* and *The Age of Innocence*.

Wharton was a novelist of manners, then, not a chronicler of large social movements, and her real subject was the entrapment of superior individuals who keenly feel the pull of moral responsibility. Her talents for social observation, for noting subtleties of dress and decoration, for nuance of voice and phrase, and for language—precise and yet expressive—were essential instruments in the creation of her novels. Wharton has been unduly charged with pessimism; her characteristic tone is ironic, the product of a sensibility able to see and feel the claims on both sides of a human dilemma. If her voice faltered in her later years and she conceded too much to the popular taste for which she increasingly wrote, she nevertheless produced some of the finest American fiction published in the first two decades of the century, and her name deserves to stand with those of James and F. Scott Fitzgerald, who outrank her only at their best.

W. J. Stuckey

OTHER MAJOR WORKS

SHORT FICTION: *The Greater Inclination*, 1899; *Crucial Instances*, 1901; *The Descent of Man*, 1904; *The Hermit and the Wild Woman*, 1908; *Tales of Men and Ghosts*, 1910; *Xingu and Other Stories*, 1916; *Here and Beyond*, 1926; *Certain People*, 1930; *Human Nature*, 1933; *The World Over*, 1936; *Ghosts*, 1937; *The Collected Short Stories of Edith Wharton*, 1968.

POETRY: *Verses*, 1878; *Artemis to Actæon*, 1909; *Twelve Poems*, 1926.

NONFICTION: *The Decoration of Houses*, 1897 (with Ogden Codman, Jr.); *Italian Villas and Their Gardens*, 1904; *Italian Backgrounds*, 1905; *A Motor-Flight Through France*, 1908; *Fighting France from Dunkerque to Belfort*, 1915; *French Ways and Their Meaning*, 1919; *In Morocco*, 1920; *The Writing of Fiction*, 1925; *A Backward Glance*, 1934; *The Letters of Edith Wharton*, 1988; *The Uncollected Critical Writings*, 1997 (Frederick Wegener, editor).

BIBLIOGRAPHY

Ammons, Elizabeth. *Edith Wharton's Argument with America*. Athens: University of Georgia Press, 1980. Ammons proposes that Wharton's "argument with America" concerns the freedom of women, an argument in which she had a key role during three decades of significant upheaval and change. This engaging book examines the evolution of Wharton's point of view in her novels and discusses the effect of World War I on Wharton. Contains a notes section.

Bell, Millicent, ed. *The Cambridge Companion to Edith Wharton*. Cambridge, England: Cambridge University Press, 1995. Essays on *The Age of Innocence*, *Summer*, *The House of Mirth*, *The Fruit of the Tree*, and *The Valley of Decision*, as well as on Wharton's handling of manners and race. Bell gives a critical history of Wharton's fiction in her introduction. Includes a chronology of Wharton's life and publications and a bibliography.

Bendixen, Alfred, and Annette Zilversmit, eds. *Edith Wharton: New Critical Essays*. New York: Garland, 1992. Studies of *The House of Mirth*, *The Fruit of the Tree*, *Summer*, *The Age of Innocence*, *Hudson River Bracketed*, and *The Gods Arrive*, as well as on Wharton's treatment of female sexuality, modernism, language, and gothic borrowings. There is an introduction and concluding essay on future directions for criticism. No bibliography.

Benstock, Shari. *No Gifts from Chance: A Biography of Edith Wharton*. New York: Scribner's, 1994. A valuable work by a noted Wharton scholar, this supplements but does not supplant Lewis's biography. Divided into sections on "The Old Order," "Choices," and "Rewards." Includes a chronology of works by Wharton, a bibliography, notes, and index.

Dwight, Eleanor. *Edith Wharton: An Extraordinary Life*. New York: Abrams, 1994. A lively succinct biography, copiously illustrated. Includes detailed notes, chronology, and bibliography.

Gimbel, Wendy. *Edith Wharton: Orphancy and Survival*. New York: Praeger, 1984. Drawing upon psychoanalytic theories and feminist perspectives, Gimbel analyzes the four works that she sees as key to understanding Wharton: *The House of Mirth*, *Ethan Frome*, *Summer*, and *The Age of Innocence*. The analyses of these works, with their deeply psychological overtones, are well worth reading.

Lewis, R. W. B. *Edith Wharton: A Biography*. 2 vols. New York: Harper & Row, 1975. An extensive study on Wharton, who Lewis calls "the most renowned writer of fiction in America." Notes that Wharton thoughtfully left extensive records, made available through the Beinecke Library at Yale, on which this biography is based. Essential reading for serious scholars of Wharton or for those interested in her life and how it shaped her writing.

Lindberg, Gary H. *Edith Wharton and the Novel of Manners*. Charlottesville: University Press of Virginia, 1975. Presents Wharton's style with a keen understanding of the ritualism of the social scenes in her work. Strong analytical criticism with a good grasp of Wharton's use of irony.

PATRICK WHITE

Born: London, England; May 28, 1912
Died: Sydney, Australia; September 30, 1990

PRINCIPAL LONG FICTION

Happy Valley, 1939
The Living and the Dead, 1941
The Aunt's Story, 1948
The Tree of Man, 1955
Voss, 1957
Riders in the Chariot, 1961
The Solid Mandala, 1966
The Vivisector, 1970
The Eye of the Storm, 1973
A Fringe of Leaves, 1976
The Twyborn Affair, 1979
Memoirs of Many in One, 1986

OTHER LITERARY FORMS

Patrick White first attempted to achieve literary success as a playwright in London in the 1930's. His work was largely rejected, partly, he implied in his autobiographical memoir, *Flaws in the Glass: A Self-Portrait* (1981), because of lack of connections in the theatrical world (although he did not deny that his talent was immature at that time). In particular, he noted that an effort to dramatize *The Aspern Papers* (1888), Henry James's famous novella based on an incident in the life of Lord Byron's mistress, might have succeeded had it found a sponsor, thanks to James's dialogue. Later, however, White successfully published a number of plays, mostly in the 1960's and 1980's; one play, *The Ham Funeral* (1961), received much attention.

White's short-story collections, *The Burnt Ones* (1964) and *The Cockatoos: Shorter Novels and Stories* (1974), bring together the best of his shorter fiction published originally in Australian literary journals (for the most part); White also published in *The London Magazine*, where, among others, the fine stories "Clay" and "A Cheery Soul" appeared. White experimented with writing film scripts; one was filmed and received some mildly favorable reviews. His autobiographical memoir, already mentioned, mixes poetic impressionism with trenchant satire.

ACHIEVEMENTS

White's stature as a novelist was already considerable, among discerning critics and discriminating readers in the English-speaking world, before it was confirmed by his reception of the Nobel Prize in Literature in 1973. The books that established White's reputation after World War II were *The Aunt's Story*, which has been widely recognized as a masterpiece, *The Tree of Man*, and the virtually unforgettable *Voss*. At the same time, White's fiction, though accessible to the general reader, unlike the work of such modernist masters as James Joyce and William Faulkner (or contemporary "experimental" fiction), never achieved a wide readership. It is uncompromisingly addressed to the same discerning public that re-

(The Nobel Foundation)

spects Joyce, D. H. Lawrence, Thomas Mann, and Marcel Proust.

If rather philistine criticism from intellectual readers as well as from the general public in Australia and elsewhere began in the 1960's, after *Riders in the Chariot, The Aunt's Story* is almost universally admired, and *The Tree of Man, Voss, Riders in the Chariot, The Vivisector, The Eye of the Storm*, and *A Fringe of Leaves* all have admirers who regard them as virtual classics. White's transformation of Australian history into epic and tragic vision in *The Tree of Man, Voss*, and *A Fringe of Leaves* is brilliant, and his vision of the fragmented world of the twentieth century is equally impressive, especially in *The Vivisector* and *The Eye of the Storm*. White's major successes ultimately assure their author a place beside the masters of prose fiction in English, including Joyce, Lawrence, and Graham Greene.

BIOGRAPHY

Patrick Martindale White was born in Wellington Court, London, on May 28, 1912, of parents whose affluence allowed them the opportunity to travel and enjoy the social pretensions available to prosperous Australians able to play the role of landed gentry. White's father, Victor (Dick) White, was one of several brothers who enjoyed prosperity in the family grazier business. Although the Whites could trace their lineage to respectable yeoman stock in Somerset, it was only in Australia that they achieved such success. Ironically, their social aspirations so far as the mother country was concerned were forever tainted by their status as "colonials" and Australians, the former penal colony being one of the least prestigious of the British dominions. White's mother was a Withycombe, and it is to the maternal connection that White attributed most of his imaginative and poetic gifts. At the same time, White disliked his strong-willed and socially ambitious mother, Ruth. Toward his father, White was more ambivalent; he pitied Victor White for his weakness but found him impossible because he hid his emotions behind his social role as a landed gentleman.

Resenting and distrusting his parents as he did, and contemptuous of their social ambitions and their

inclination to conceal their humanity behind public personae, White felt as much an outsider and rebel against the class to which he was born as is his painter hero, Hurtle Duffield, in *The Vivisector*, a working-class child adopted by a prosperous Sydney family.

White tended as a child to identify with his nanny and her working-class husband, a circumstance that helps to account for the persistent scorn and irony in his fiction directed toward the assumptions and manners of the Australian upper class. Not only was White an "outsider" in relationship to the Australian affluent class, but also he found that his status in English boarding schools, and later at Cambridge, was that of an outsider, by virtue of his Australian citizenship and accent. Hence, throughout his career, White as artist played the role of an outsider in a double sense, a condition intensified by his frequent alternation of residences between Australia and England in childhood and youth. White's major concentration at Cambridge was modern languages, primarily German, an interest augmented by time spent on the Continent, in the Germany of the Weimar Republic in its waning days, and in the early years of Adolf Hitler's rule, during summer vacations from 1932 to 1935. One German city, Hanover, is depicted in White's fiction as the archetypal German cathedral town from which White's characters Voss and Himmelfarb both originate.

After coming down from Cambridge, White spent a bohemian period in London in the middle and late 1930's, lodging mainly in Ebury Street, where he wrote three unsatisfactory novels and attempted without success to begin a career in the theater as a playwright. During this time, White fell under the influence of various intellectual friends and apprentice artists, the most important being the Australian expatriate Roy de Maistre, who was, like White, homosexual. (White seems to have accepted his homosexuality in his boarding school adolescence, and to have had little difficulty over it at the Cambridge and London of the 1930's.) In 1939, White's unsatisfactory first novel, *Happy Valley*, was published, and soon White voyaged to America to try his hand in New York literary circles and to begin a period of dissipation that lasted for several months. During this New York period, he completed his strong second novel, *The Living and the Dead*, a book that shows him mastering and exorcising some of the literary and cultural influences of his youth. The decision of White's working-class hero, Joe, to go to Spain to fight on the Loyalist side, is a symbol of commitment; it reflects White's own decision, reached after much guilt and self-analysis, to return to England (unlike some other English expatriates, such as W. H. Auden) and to offer himself to the campaign against Hitler.

Receiving a commission in the Royal Air Force's intelligence division, White spent the majority of his war years in North Africa, Alexandria, the Middle East, and Greece. It is clear that his years in the war were a significant rite of passage for him. He gained decisiveness and self-reliance as well as maturity; equally important, he met Manoly Lascaris, a Greek whose mother had been British; Lascaris was to become White's lover and homosexual spouse. Eventually, White and Lascaris decided on permanent residence in Australia, and White arrived there in 1947 with the manuscript of *The Aunt's Story* as a kind of "talisman." Hence, White was an Australian by a conscious choice, however reluctant the choice may have been. At the same time, his country was not always overwhelmed by White's decision, for although White used the Australian heroic past extensively in his fiction, he continued to be an outsider whose work did not always display clear relationships with Australian literary traditions.

White's long career in Australia flourished primarily at two residences: the small "farm" called "Dogwoods," really only a house, some outbuildings, and a few acres at Castle Hill, just outside Sydney and later incorporated into it. In 1963, however, White moved to Martin's Road in Sydney. In the Castle Hill period, White and Lascaris kept some cattle and tried to support themselves, at least partially, by some gardening. In later years, White's writing provided some support.

After five novels and a book of short stories, White was awarded the Nobel Prize in Literature in 1973. He used the money to establish a fund for

struggling Australian writers of some talent and literary ambition. His later life was marked by increasing fame and some travel and by considerable attention from the media and from academic critics and scholars. He died in Sydney on September 30, 1990.

ANALYSIS

Patrick White's fiction is concerned with the psychological depth and the emotional density of experience, and with the perceptions of the solitary self. This obsession with the isolated self in its search for fulfillment, its quest for an experience of unity and the divine, and its attempts to resolve the contradictions of its social heritage and its sexual nature, provides the central drama in White's fiction. On the one hand, White's fiction is rich in its command of the nuances of dialogue and social intercourse; it is possible to discuss his work in terms primarily of the novel of manners and social comedy. On the other hand, White's fiction is the work of an author obsessed with tragic vision and a religious quest. After *The Aunt's Story*, White's novels contain characters who struggle and overcome obstacles to understanding and vision, and whose lives culminate in a visionary or mystical affirmation. Stan Parker in *The Tree of Man* testifies to the unity of holiness of being; Elizabeth Hunter finds the eye of God in the center of her storm; Rod Gravenor in his final letter to Eddie Twyborn asserts the reality of love and faith in God. Such affirmations, though they represent White's own beliefs, if his autobiographical statements are to be accepted, are nevertheless to be seen as dramatic statements, paradoxical assertions aimed at overcoming doubts and confusion, and ultimately as aesthetically correct as the statements of faith in the poetry of the seventeenth century metaphysical poets. Despite all the parallels with Victorian novelists who write family novels with complicated plots, White was essentially a religious visionary akin to poets such as T. S. Eliot and W. H. Auden, and one very much at odds with the dominant spirit of his age.

HAPPY VALLEY

White's first published novel, *Happy Valley*, is regarded by most critics as a failure, and the judgment is accurate. The novel deals with the passions and defeats of a group of characters in an Australian rural setting, but White is not entirely in control of his characters and plot, nor of his own style. The characters are mostly flawed romantics, somewhat obsessed by sex and erotic entanglements, and their emotions are often operatic and even Wagnerian in scope. The novel lacks the saving grace of White's magisterial and sophisticated irony, which tends to control the style in the later books and prevent both author and characters from lapsing into the excesses of emotion. White, however, does use the Australian landscape effectively as a dramatic backdrop for human drama played out under the eye of an inscrutable cosmos.

THE LIVING AND THE DEAD

The Living and the Dead, the second published novel of White's prewar apprenticeship, shows considerable improvement. The novel, set in England, primarily London, casts a critical and retrospective look at the 1930's, but like many novels of the period by English and American writers, it displays a movement from empty intellectualism and social snobbery to political and ideological commitment on the part of some characters. The central figures in the book are Elyot and Eden Standish and their feckless and snobbish mother. Elyot and Eden provide an ironic contrast: Eloyt is a skeptical rationalist who wants to withdraw from experience, while Eden is a romantic who accepts life with its attendant suffering. Each finds a suitably ironic reward: Eden gains love with a working-class hero, only to lose him when he departs to join the Loyalist cause in the Spanish Civil War; Elyot, fearing involvement with others, is doomed to a life of loneliness until he finds himself exposed to the suffering he has tried to avoid by the death of his mother and the departure of his sister for Spain. Ironically, the experience of tragedy helps to heal Elyot's loneliness and alienation; at the end of the novel, he finds a satisfying release from the prison of himself.

Brian Kiernan in *Patrick White* (1980) has pointed out that there are many influences of T. S. Eliot's early poetry evident in the novel; London is Eliot's "Unreal City" of *The Waste Land* (1922), for example. It might be added that Elyot Standish is White's most Prufrockian character; he represents the same kind of paralyzed and life-evading intellectual that Eliot satirized in his early poetry, and White's portrayal indicates his own aversion to such a figure.

If Elyot is skillfully drawn, his mother, with all her vulgarities and superficialities, is equally effective, and her final spasmodic affair with an English jazz musician is poignant, as is the description of her final illness. Less effectively depicted, but still successful, are Eden, Elyot's romantic sister, and Wally Collins, the itinerant jazz musician just back from America, who is presented as representative of the rootless and uncommitted modern urban person. The weakest figure of all is Joe Barnett, the working-class hero, who is too obviously inspired by the abstraction of the virtuous proletarian which afflicted much of the fiction of the 1930's.

The emphasis on commitment and release from alienation with which the novel concludes is handled with much aesthetic tact and restraint. The adoption of the Loyalist cause in Spain is portrayed as more of a humanist commitment than an acceptance of an ideological or religious imperative, although no doubt White's sympathies were leftist. While White's characters find an exit from the modern wasteland through tragic self-sacrifice, the novel does not provide any assurance that the solution found is an enduring one, either for the characters who accept it or for the author.

THE AUNT'S STORY

With his next novel, *The Aunt's Story*, White established himself as a novelist of stature with a mature tragic vision. One of the most difficult things for a novelist to do, White believed, is to make a "virtuous woman" an interesting character. White accomplished this feat with Theodora Goodman, the aunt, who to all outward appearances lives an uneventful life, save for its tragic denouement. The real "story" of the spinster aunt is rendered through White's depiction of her inner life; despite Theodora's apparently barren existence, her experience is rich indeed.

Theodora's tale is told in three economically narrated sections: an Australian sequence called "Meroe"; a European interlude, "Jardin Exotique"; and a climactic American adventure, "Holstius." In these sections, Theodora's childhood, youth, and maturity are portrayed. She has a strong, rather masculine sensibility, and an imaginative nature with deep psychological insight, in an unprepossessing feminine body.

In part 1, Theodora's journey from innocence to the experience of young adulthood is chronicled. The contrast between the heroine's strong desire for individuality and the conventional femininity and conformity of her sister is strongly marked. At boarding school in adolescence, Theodora develops one of her strongest relationships, a friendship with the sensitive Violet Adams, who, like Theodora, is fascinated by art and poetry. Theodora here reveals her intense and rather hard inner nature: She would like to be a poet, but her chosen subject would be landscapes and studies of rocks.

In her childhood and youth, too, Theodora shows more love for her father's country estate than for the city: Meroe is the "Abyssinia," or happy valley of innocence, which provides a romantic metaphor for her years of growth and maturation. Later, following World War I, when Australia, after a brief emergence from its provincial slumber, relapses into a comfortable vacuous middle-class existence, Theodora lives in Sydney and cares for her mean-spirited and snobbish mother in the latter's failing years. In this period, the mysterious murderer Jack Frost provides some excitement and titillation for a bored middle-class population, and serves as a symbol of the mysterious Jungian shadow she longs to encounter. Her major chance for the conventional felicity of marriage and children occurs when she is courted by the apparently strong and manly Huntly Clarkson. Yet in a role reversal typical of many later White novels, Huntly soon is revealed as weak and somewhat feminine in his relationship with the resolute Theodora. Her skillfulness and strength strike a deathblow to their courtship.

Released from an unrewarding life by the death of her mother, Theodora finds herself free to seek her destiny abroad, and her journey of initiation to Europe constitutes the central action in part 2, "Jardin Exotique," where she encounters a group of European eccentrics in a "grand hotel" setting on the French Riviera. Here Theodora exercises her talent for living, which had been suppressed and frustrated in Australia. She enters imaginatively into the lives of her companions, identifying with them and living their exotic histories vicariously. Her friends, a seedy group of expatriates, have all built up myths of romantic pasts. Theodora not only is a responsive and sympathetic consciousness for them but also is able to enrich their illusions by her own imagination. Ironically, however, each fantasy life proves to have been an artful lie near the end of part 2, leaving Theodora with the sense of having been cheated when the pathetic reality of a character's past is revealed. The final irony occurs when the Hotel du Midi is destroyed by fire, probably a symbol of the coming war.

This section, rich in fine characterizations and virtuoso stylistic divertissements, is White's portrait of the Europe of the 1930's and his moral evaluation of it. Theodora, at first seduced by Europe and its illusions of a glamorous past and then disillusioned by the emptiness of its reality, emerges from the experience morally tested and unscathed, but still an unfulfilled and psychologically incomplete personality. It is not until part 3, "Holstius," that Theodora confronts her own tragic destiny.

Part 3 takes place in America, where Theodora is overwhelmed by a sense of the vastness of the American continent and her own sense of isolation. A chance encounter with a traveling salesman on a train near Chicago results in a conversation that is symbolic: The salesman boasts of America's size and population in the best Babbitt or booster style, while Theodora is impressed with the abstractness of the individual self in a country where enormous numbers—of square miles, people, and sums of money—seem to dominate.

Leaving the train in the mountains of Colorado, Theodora wanders into a lonely canyon, driven by an urge to confront the unknown side of her inner self at last. Alone, at night, she hallucinates an experience of mythic force: a meeting with a stunted little man, almost like a folklore dwarf, who informs her that his name is "Holstius" (a name that perhaps both combines and caricatures the Jungian "animus" or male self in a woman, and the idea of "wholeness"). In Theodora's encounter with the imaginary Holstius, the masculine side of her nature emerges and speaks to her at last, and her inner conflicts appear to be resolved. The confrontation is traumatic, however, and the cost of it is the loss of Theodora's sanity, for the next day a nearby farmer and his family are forced to take charge of her, regarding her as mad.

The Aunt's Story is an expression of mature tragic vision, a novel which explores the possibilities and anguish of the solitary self in search of wholeness and fulfillment, in a more assured manner than White's first two published novels. Unlike *The Living and the Dead*, it envisions self-discovery and self-fulfillment as a private quest, to which the changing political and social winds are incidental, almost irrelevant. In this respect, and in its hints of a symbolism drawn partly from Jungian psychology, as well as in its masterful weaving of a subtle texture of imagery, *The Aunt's Story* marks the beginning of White's maturity as an artist.

THE TREE OF MAN

White's next three novels were much larger in scope and intention, epic in length at least. They also project a vision of the Australian past and of the middle twentieth century present influenced by that past. The first, *The Tree of Man*, tells the saga of Australia's pioneer past, as seen through three generations, but mainly through the experience of Stan and Amy Parker, homesteaders who wrest a farm from the wilderness. Stan and Amy are attractive characters, although rather conventional, and their lives are given a depth not found in most novels of pioneer life. Moreover, White provides splendid comic relief through their foils, the irresponsible O'Dowds, so that despite its length, the novel has considerable popular appeal, unlike much of White's fiction. Yet while Stan and Amy's life as lonely settlers in the outback often possesses a beauty and quiet dignity, their later lives are frustrating, and their sense of progress and achievement is dissipated in the disappointing lives of their children, and in Amy's later estrangement from her husband.

A brilliant reversal of perspective occurs in the closing pages. Here, the aged Stan Parker, apparently a neglected and forgotten failure living in a suburb of Sydney, rises to heights of tragic dignity. Accosted

by an annoying fundamentalist evangelist, Parker rejects the easy formula for salvation the latter offers and asserts his own faith: He identifies God with a gob of spittle. To the evangelist, this is a blasphemous comment, and some have tended to treat it as a defiant and rebellious one, but, as William Walsh and some other critics have claimed, Parker's statement is a confession of faith in the ultimate goodness of life and of the holiness of being. This event marks the beginning of the paradoxical but assured religious affirmation that surfaces at crucial moments in most of White's subsequent novels.

Voss

The sense of an impressive tragic vision is heightened and intensified in White's next novel, *Voss*, which is, like *The Aunt's Story*, one of his better-known works. It describes its hero's Faustian ambition to be the first to conquer the Australian continent by leading an exploratory expedition across it. Voss's noble failure (based on an actual expedition led by the explorer Ludwig Leichardt) is counterbalanced by his mystical love for Laura Trevelyan, which transforms him from an exponent of the heroic and resolute will (like that celebrated by Friedrich Nietzsche in the late nineteenth century) to a more chastened and forgiving spirit. At the end, Voss is ready to accept his failure and death with a sense of Christian (or at any rate, religious) resignation.

Although a humorless and often exasperating character, Voss is a dynamic force who entices stolid Australian businessmen into financing his enterprise. Yet his nature is more complex than most of the unimaginative bourgeois Australians realize; only Laura, a complicated young woman who privately rebels against conventional Christianity and the age's worship of material progress, perceives the hidden sensitivities and beauty of Voss's character.

In the early stages of the novel, Laura and Voss seem to be in conflict, as their opposed but complementary natures seem to strike sparks from each other. Once Voss and his companions embark on their heroic journey in the Australian desert, however, Laura and Voss appear to communicate by a mystical or telepathic bond. Jungian psychology would consider each a person who has partially suppressed his hidden self: Voss has repressed his latent feminine qualities by devotion to the ideals of the masculine will; Laura has suppressed her masculine alter ego in the service of femininity. Their mystic communication enlarges and fulfills both their natures.

Defeated by the Australian climate and landscape, the treachery of his companions, and his own miscalculations, Voss's expedition culminates in his tragic death. Yet the heroic grandeur of Voss's failure is impressive; White's hero has a strength and ambition beyond that of the protagonists of many modern novels, and in his defeat he gains some of the humanity that he had so obviously lacked.

RIDERS IN THE CHARIOT

Voss's acceptance of the Southern Cross as a symbol of his transformation from Nietzschean ideals to a more humane and forgiving outlook prompted some to assume that White himself was espousing doctrinal and institutional Christianity in *Voss*. This is not so, but White does affirm his personal religious vision—a synthesis of Jungian thought, Christian and Jewish mysticism, and poetic vision. His next novel, *Riders in the Chariot*, is perhaps White's most ambitious attempt to present the religious vision that undergirds all the fiction after *The Tree of Man*. *Riders in the Chariot* draws its title from Ezekiel's biblical vision of the chariot, but its prophetic and at times apocalyptic tone comes partially from William Blake, whose visionary conversation with Isaiah and Ezekiel in *The Marriage of Heaven and Hell* (1790) provides an epigraph. The four main protagonists, two men and two women (one black or "abo" painter, one Jewish mystic, one evangelical Christian, and one nature mystic) are all outcast visionaries, who combine to make a gigantic and impressive human mandala.

Himmelfarb is a scholar who turns from enlightened rationalism to the dense but powerful mystical images of the Cabala, including the "blue fire" of some Cabalist treatises. White's other seekers in the novel are religious questers who follow different and perhaps equally valid paths to their epiphanies and revelations. Miss Hare's nature mysticism is a naïve affirmation of being that resembles the kind of mysti-

cism preached and celebrated by Ralph Waldo Emerson and Walt Whitman. By contrast, Mrs. Godbold's way is that of orthodox Christian piety, and Alf Dubbo's path is that of the romantic transcendentalist vision, as proclaimed by Blake and others.

Riders in the Chariot asserts the primacy of mystical search over conventional life, and it is also Blakean in its harsh indictment of evil in the modern world and in modern history. Evil is seen in various forms in this novel: It is the anti-Semitism and later the Nazism that Himmelfarb encounters; it is the smug self-righteousness of decaying puritanism in Miss Hare's tormentor, Mrs. Jolley; it is the narcissistic upper-class arrogance and contempt for the less fortunate shown by Mrs. Chalmers-Robinson; it is the feeble and thwarted religiosity of the Reverend Pask and his sister. Above all, it is the working-class bigotry and mule-headed chauvinism with its suspicion of outsiders shown by the Australian workmen, who reenact the crucifixion as a blasphemous joke on Himmelfarb on Good Friday. Primarily, White is inclined in this novel to see evil as a kind of spiritual blindness or lack of vision "of the infinite" as Blake's epigraph says, although the malice demonstrated by Mrs. Jolley and White's laborers is hard to explain in such simple terms. Nevertheless, White's sense of the overwhelming presence of evil in the modern world, especially "moral evil," or evil for which humans are responsible, is one of the most convincing features of the book. Equally strong is the sense of moral goodness or innocence in his four central characters, however much they may occasionally surrender to their flaws. Whether one is interested in White's attempt to portray the different paths of mysticism, it is hard to forget the strength of his portraits of four characters who remain admirable while enduring great suffering.

THE SOLID MANDALA

White devoted the early and middle years of the 1960's to works that were smaller in scale. In *The Solid Mandala*, which White considered one of his three best novels, his idiosyncrasies emerge more noticeably than in earlier works. This novel affirms White's Jungian religious vision more strongly than ever, and to underscore the theme for the obtuse reader, the noble example of Fyodor Dostoevski is invoked by Arthur Brown, the inarticulate visionary who is in part a spokesman for White. Arthur is set in contrast with his tragic brother, Waldo, a minor fiction-writer and critic hampered by excessive rationalism and rendered creatively impotent by fear of his emotions and imagination. Ironically, after failing as a writer and ruining his life by aloofness from humanity, Waldo is ambushed by his repressed sexuality near the end: He becomes a pathetic transvestite wearing his late mother's discarded dresses, and thus expressing the thwarted feminine side of his nature.

Arthur Brown's life also ends pathetically in a lonely old age, yet Arthur, one of White's holy simpletons or divine fools, lives a spiritually fulfilled, if obscure and misunderstood, existence. Arthur has a mystical sympathy with animals and nature and with some of the other less articulate characters, especially Dulcie Feinstein, a rich young woman to whom both brothers are attracted. A close communion also exists between Arthur and Mrs. Poulter, a working-class woman who is a kind of surrogate mother and wife to him. Arthur finds meaning in existence through his apprehension of mandalas, the Jungian symbol for the unity and holiness of all being, and of all innocent and life-enhancing forms of existence. Two major mandala symbols dominate Arthur's experience: a large green marble, or "solid mandala," which appears to him to be symbolic of the holiness toward which humanity should strive; and a mystic dance in the shape of a mandala he performs with Mrs. Poulter.

Arthur and Waldo both lead tragic lives, if judged by conventional human standards, and each is an incomplete person: Arthur, the mystic and visionary, lacks a well-developed rational mind; while Waldo, the rationalist, is dead to all spiritual and transcendental existence. The story is thus a fable about the tragic split in humanity between the rational and the mystical faculties of the mind, between—if some psychologists, such as Robert Ornstein, are to be believed—the left and the right sides of the human brain. Yet despite the tragic nature of his novel, White makes Arthur much the more attractive of the two brothers, and reaffirms once more one of the themes of *Riders in the Chariot* and other novels: If a choice must be made between reason and mysticism, the path of the mystic, however despised in a rationalistic and technological age, is the more rewarding and redemptive road.

Although beneath the rough and grainy surface of *The Solid Mandala* there are surprising riches and pleasures, its sometimes crabbed and eccentric nature might have suggested to some that White had fallen into a creative decline in the 1960's. The three remarkable novels that followed, however, proved that the converse was true: *The Vivisector, The Eye of the Storm*, and *A Fringe of Leaves* not only testify to an impressive sustained surge of creative power but also show White in more masterful control of his material and of his artistic form than ever before.

THE VIVISECTOR

The Vivisector describes the life of a rebellious and obsessed painter, Hurtle Duffield, who triumphs over enormous obstacles—an obscure background, a stultifying upper-class education, the cultural sterility of the Australian environment, numerous unhappy love affairs—to achieve triumph as a modern artist, a master of the techniques of Impressionism, Surrealism, and Abstract Impressionism, who successfully shapes Australian material into a solid series of enduring works.

In terms of form, *The Vivisector* is one of White's more daring gambles, for it ostensibly follows the shapeless biographical narrative mode of some of the most primitive works of fiction, tracing Duffield's development from his childhood to his death through a series of selected incidents and periods. Yet close inspection of *The Vivisector* shows that White has made a sophisticated use of a naïve narrative form in his treatment of Duffield's struggle. For example, Duffield's experience is rendered in terms of his relationship to a series of Jungian anima figures who serve as lovers, supports, and muses. These range from his crippled foster sister, Rhoda Courtney, a childhood rival but a supporter of his old age; through Ponce Nan, a vital but tragic prostitute; and Hero Pavloussi, the wife of a Greek businessman with whom he enjoys a brief, passionate, but unsatisfying romance.

As a painter, Duffield is a tireless worker and committed visionary whose paintings recapitulate many motifs familiar to White's readers. At one point, Duffield perfects his craft by painting rocks; the action suggests the need to come to terms with the intractable and substantial nature of the visible and phenomenal world. In his early stages, Duffield is a rebellious and defiantly blasphemous painter who charges God with being the great "vivisector," an unfeeling and cruel being who experiments with human suffering as a scientist dismembers animals—or as Duffield and other artists approach human life, seeing it as raw material for art. Guilt over the suicide of Nan, however, for which he feels partially responsible, and compassion for the frustrated homosexual grocer Cutbush, whom he paints as a Surrealist figure machine-gunning lovers, work in Duffield a more tolerant and forgiving nature, and his work at last becomes more a kind of worship than blasphemy. In his last period, weakened by strokes, he becomes obsessed with painting in indigo and is characterized by a wry humility and kindness. Duffield thinks of his final, fatal stroke as a moment when he is "indiggodd," or departing "into God."

THE EYE OF THE STORM

If *The Vivisector* is rich in vital characterizations and frequently possesses the exuberance of Duffield's raw energy, *The Eye of the Storm* is a splendidly controlled performance which demonstrates once more that when he chose, White could display a sure mastery of the techniques of the English novel of manners as practiced by such writers as E. M. Forster. *The Eye of the Storm* is constructed around the social comedy of the last days of Elizabeth Hunter, a regal but selfish matriarch of Sydney society who at eighty-six is slowly dying in her home on Moreton Drive while her son and daughter scheme to have her removed from the care of her nurses and placed in a nursing home. As is usual with White, however, the social comedy of the novel's surface masks tragedy and religious vision: in this case, the Learesque tragedy of Mrs. Hunter and her two children, and the crisis of faith suffered by her remarkable nurse, Sister Mary de Santis. Although the present time of the novel amounts to only a few days,

White's narration re-creates, through the memories of the characters, the spiritual and psychological histories of their entire lives. Elizabeth Hunter, like White himself the talented offspring of a grazier, has during her life grown from a grazier's wife with social aspirations into a lady of poise and charm. At the same time, this majestic woman is portrayed as a dominating and selfish mother whose poise and beauty have given her untalented and unattractive daughter, Dorothy, an inferiority complex and driven her talented but narcissistic son to become both a successful London actor and a pathetic womanizing failure in private life.

Mrs. Hunter in later life, however, has been transformed during a hurricane on Brumby Island, when, abandoned and alone, she experienced a numinous epiphany in the still of the eye of the storm. As a result, she has become a compassionate, understanding, and deeply religious woman, although her piety is of the unchurched kind. This transformation lends a Learlike poignancy to her last days, when the poorly concealed malice of Basil and Dorothy is embodied in their effort to move her to a nursing home. The irony in this situation is heightened by the fact that Basil Hunter longs to play Lear himself, as the capstone of his career. Another tragic irony is Dorothy's idolizing of the Duchess of Sanseverina in Stendhal's *The Charterhouse of Parma* (1839): Longing to be a masterful woman like the Sanseverina, Dorothy resents her mother, whose social poise and personality recall that Stendhal heroine. The tragic irony in the actions of the children comes to a climax in their sentimental journey to their home ranch, where they finally surrender to their loneliness and huddle together in an act of incest during the night.

In contrast to the bleak and loveless lives of Basil and Dorothy, Mrs. Hunter finds solace in the loving care of Mary de Santis, her nurse and a reluctant believer in Greek Orthodox Christianity. Sister de Santis's care aids Mrs. Hunter in her final days, and in turn, Sister de Santis finds her own provisional faith reaffirmed by an epiphany of numinous divine immanence at the end of the novel in a mystic moment of water, birds' wings, and morning light, recalling biblical images of revelation.

An interesting and partially comic minor plot in *The Eye of the Storm* involves another of Elizabeth Hunter's nurses, the youthful Flora Manhood, who finds herself caught between resentment of her male lover and a temptation to join her cousin in a lesbian affair. Yet, despite White's obvious sympathy for Flora and her lesbian inclinations, the matter is resolved by her decision to remain heterosexual, while lesbianism is treated with a touch of comic irony. It is curious that White, himself a practicing homosexual, was able to treat homosexuality with enormous sympathy, yet finally imply the desirability of a traditional heterosexual identity.

Without a doubt, *The Eye of the Storm* is one of White's most carefully crafted and formally satisfying novels, and the one that most closely approximates the Jamesian ideal of complete mastery of novelistic form. This novel, which might have been considered the crowning work of a lesser career, was followed by other equally challenging works.

A Fringe of Leaves

There are many impressive strengths of *A Fringe of Leaves*. Like *Voss*, this epic tale is inspired by the Australian past, specifically the experience of Eliza Fraser, a heroic woman who survived shipwreck, the loss of husband and companions, and captivity by aborigines, to return to civilization and become a legendary heroine. White's heroine, Ellen Gluyas Roxborough, is a woman of enormous appetite for living, who undergoes numerous metamorphoses on her road to destiny. At first an imaginative Cornish farm girl who longs to journey to some mystical or fabled sacred place such as Tintagel, Ellen marries a dry country squire, Austin Roxborough, and is made over, on the surface at least, into a polished eighteenth century lady and a dutiful adornment to her husband's estate near Winchester. On a sentimental journey to Australia (or "Van Diemen's Land") to visit her husband's rakish brother, Garnet, Ellen's inner self emerges, first in a brief affair with Garnet, then in the ordeal of survival of shipwreck and capture by "savages."

The shipwreck and the captivity sections form the heart of the narrative. In the shipwreck, Ellen gradually has her civilized self stripped from her, along with her clothing, which is removed layer by layer. Later, after losing her husband and becoming a captive of the Australian natives, Ellen is obliged to confront her own authentic humanity. Her will to survive is indomitable; to cling to her sense of being human, she weaves a "fringe of leaves" as a kind of primitive clothing and an assertion of her belonging to a human realm above the world of nature. Yet a central question for her is the question of her relationship to her captors. Is she of the same order as the dark-skinned aborigines? The question is answered when she participates in a ritual feast at the center of the novel; it is a rite of cannibalism which not only provides physical nourishment but also, ironically, a sense of religious fulfillment. At the center of her "heart of darkness," Ellen finds her essential humanity.

The captivity section—which one critic has compared to the captivity narratives of prisoners of the American Indians—is followed by an idyllic interlude which represents a return to innocence for Ellen. In this episode, Ellen meets an escaped convict, murderer Jack Chance, who in London had brutally murdered his wife, but atones for that by falling in love with Ellen. With Jack, Ellen enjoys her most satisfying sexual relationship, but this Edenic experience, like all others, must end when Ellen crosses the Brisband River (likened to a snake) that separates the Australian wilderness from the settled country.

In the resolution of the novel, Ellen is both a heroine to other pioneers, especially the women, and a penitent. In her own eyes, her guilt over her participation in the cannibal rite and the betrayal of Jack is great, but her will to live triumphs over her sense of unworthiness and self-immmolation. At the close of the novel, it is clear she will return to routine and ordered life by marrying a pleasant, but somewhat inarticulate, Australian settler.

In its depiction of the indestructible will to survive, *A Fringe of Leaves* is a masterpiece, perhaps White's finest novel. Its central character, Ellen Roxborough, may well become one of the unforgettable heroines of literature.

The Twyborn Affair

Although *A Fringe of Leaves* has received much favorable comment, White's subsequent novel, *The*

Twyborn Affair, was the object of a different reception, especially in America. This work is one of White's most controversial, for it attempts to deal with homosexual experience more candidly than ever before in White's fiction. Moreover, the novel is an interesting experiment in technique, because it is constructed of three sections which are essentially self-contained units, yet which also attempt to form a greater unity of a lengthy novel covering several decades.

Eddie Twyborn, the hero (and sometimes heroine) of the novel, is presented as a feminine personality in the body of a handsome male: an unusual "prisoner of sex" whose incarceration is indeed tragic. In part 1, Eddie Twyborn appears as the transvestite lover of a likable older man, a somewhat decadent Greek living in France in the pre-World War I period. The couple are spied upon by Joanic Golson, a friend of Eddie's upper-class, overbearing Australian mother, and there is a certain amount of rather strained social comedy here until the affair ends with the death of Twyborn's Greek lover. In part 2, Twyborn returns to Australia after the war as a decorated hero and tries living as a working man in the outback on a sheep ranch. There, he becomes emotionally entangled with the brutal foreman, Don Prowse, who finally rapes him, and with the owner's wife, who falls in love with him, misunderstanding his sexual nature while beguiled by his charm and sensitivity.

The failure to live peacefully as a man in part 2 is followed by Twyborn's life in London in part 3, where he surfaces in the late 1930's in female dress. This time, he is the madam of a brothel patronized by the rich and fashionable, and he becomes something of a celebrity. During this period, he suffers from a thwarted love for his patron, Lord Gravenor, who is finally revealed as homosexual also. A touching reconciliation with his selfish mother, now humbled by age and living in London alone, provides a kind of tragic recognition scene at the novel's end. This is followed by Twyborn's death in the London blitz.

Undoubtedly, Eddie Twyborn—the name is an obvious pun on "twice-born"—is one of the most interesting homosexual heroes in literature, and perhaps White's theme, the irony of a feminine nature in a male body, has never been treated with such insight.

The novel's eccentricities, however, are pronounced, and the social comedy in Parts 1 and 3 often becomes tiresome. Like White's other major novels, the work achieves a kind of tragic dignity, despite its flaws, yet it appears vastly inferior to his other novels published in the 1970's.

White's strengths as a writer are many. He is a masterful stylist, and his characterizations are psychologically complex and memorable. His skill at social comedy is complemented by contempt for the arrogance of wealth and power. Beyond these gifts, however, White sought to create tragic fictional works on the Greek or Shakespearean scale in an age of irony and a diminished or disappearing tragic vision. White's fiction also, in the works following *The Aunt's Story*, articulates the author's own prodigious mythology and majestic religious vision. It is a vision drawing on numerous disparate sources—Blake and the Cabala, Carl Jung, Dostoevski, and the Bible—but it forms a synthesis which affirms the importance of a search for transcendence and the significance of mystical experience. Both his vision and his novels are likely to stand the test of time.

Edgar L. Chapman

OTHER MAJOR WORKS

SHORT FICTION: *The Burnt Ones*, 1964; *The Cockatoos: Shorter Novels and Stories*, 1974; *Three Uneasy Pieces*, 1987.

PLAYS: *Return to Abyssinia*, pr. 1947; *The Ham Funeral*, wr. 1947, pr. 1961; *The Season at Sarsaparilla*, pr. 1962; *A Cheery Soul*, pr. 1963; *Night on Bald Mountain*, pr. 1963; *Four Plays*, pb. 1965 (includes the preceding four plays); *Big Toys*, pr. 1977; *Signal Driver*, pr. 1982; *Netherwood*, pr., pb. 1983; *Shepherd on the Rocks*, pr. 1987.

SCREENPLAY: *The Night of the Prowler*, 1976.

POETRY: *The Ploughman and Other Poems*, 1935.

NONFICTION: *Flaws in the Glass: A Self-Portrait*, 1981; *Patrick White Speaks*, 1989; *Patrick White: Letters*, 1996 (David Marr, editor).

BIBLIOGRAPHY

Beatson, Peter. *The Eye in the Mandala, Patrick White: A Vision of Man and God*. London: P.

Elek, 1976. One of the early books on White that, unlike other early studies, does more than survey his life and fiction. Bases the analysis of the novels on a cosmology derived from eclectic psychological theories and the teachings of world religions. The discussion is divided into the three worlds White's fiction represents: the world of being, the human world, and the natural world.

Bliss, Carolyn. *Patrick White's Fiction: The Paradox of Fortunate Failure.* New York: St. Martin's Press, 1986. This original study treats the fiction as a paradox, arguing that the individual failure so often expressed in the characters' lives does at times lead to their redemption. The theme of redemption through failure is then linked to the writing itself, on which White, according to Bliss's examination of the stylistic elements, imposes failure and at the same time creates a distinctive style. An extensive secondary bibliography is included.

Edgecombe, Rodney Stenning. *Vision and Style in Patrick White: A Study of Five Novels.* Tuscaloosa: University of Alabama Press, 1989. The five novels addressed in this study are *Voss, Riders in the Chariot, The Solid Mandala, The Vivisector,* and *The Eye of the Storm,* considered by Edgecombe to be White's greatest. Links these books by exploring the metaphysical thoughts they share and examines White's distinctive style. This style affirms his novels' thematic emphasis on alienation, isolation, and the subsequent search for a vision to free the individual from spiritual imprisonment.

Marr, David. *Patrick White: A Life.* New York: Knopf, 1992. Written with White's cooperation. The biographer had complete freedom. Even though a dying White found the biography painful reading, he did not ask the author to change a word. A monumental accomplishment, with detailed notes, bibliography, and helpful appendices.

Morley, Patricia. *The Mystery of Unity: Theme and Technique in the Novels of Patrick White.* Montreal: McGill-Queen's University Press, 1972. This early study is the only one that places White's work in the mainstream of European writing. Also shows how his fiction makes use of the international tradition along with the archetypes of Western literature. Morley argues that, through his intertextuality, White gives a unified view of a world beset by pain and suffering, but one that will offer salvation for those who seek it.

Weigel, John A. *Patrick White.* Boston: Twayne, 1983. Introduces White and his work by tracing his life and discussing each of his novels, as well as his plays. Although introductory and general, the book serves well the beginning reader of White's fiction. Includes a secondary bibliography and a chronology.

Williams, Mark. *Patrick White.* New York: St. Martin's Press, 1993. An excellent introduction to the life and works of White. Includes bibliographical references and an index.

Wolfe, Peter. *Laden Choirs: The Fiction of Patrick White.* Lexington: University Press of Kentucky, 1983. While not taking any particular thematic stand, this book offers a substantial analysis of each of White's novels. Focuses in part on White's style, demonstrating how it affects narrative tension, philosophical structure, and the development of character.

_____, ed. *Critical Essays on Patrick White.* Boston: G. K. Hall, 1990. A wide-ranging collection edited by one of White's most astute critics. Includes a section of autobiographical essays by White and a helpful bibliography.

T. H. WHITE

Born: Bombay, India; May 29, 1906
Died: Piraeus, Greece; January 17, 1964

PRINCIPAL LONG FICTION

Dear Mr. Nixon, 1931 (with R. McNair Scott)
First Lesson, 1932 (as James Aston)
They Winter Abroad, 1932 (as Aston)
Darkness at Pemberley, 1932

Farewell Victoria, 1933

Earth Stopped: Or, Mr. Marx's Sporting Tour, 1934

Gone to Ground, 1935

The Sword in the Stone, 1938

The Witch in the Wood, 1939

The Ill-Made Knight, 1940

Mistress Masham's Repose, 1946

The Elephant and the Kangaroo, 1947

The Master: An Adventure Story, 1957

The Candle in the Wind, 1958

The Once and Future King, 1958
(tetralogy; includes *The Sword in the Stone, The Witch in the Wood, The Ill-Made Knight*, and *The Candle in the Wind*)

The Book of Merlyn: The Unpublished Conclusion to "The Once and Future King," 1977

(William Foster)

OTHER LITERARY FORMS

T. H. White's first literary productions were two poetry collections. Several short stories enclosed within the satirical frame narrative of *Gone to Ground* were reprinted along with later items in the posthumously issued *The Maharajah and Other Stories* (1981). The majority of White's nonfiction books celebrate his strong interest in field sports; *The Goshawk* (1951), which describes his experiments in falconry, is the most notable. The title of *The Godstone and the Blackymor* (1959) refers to a legendary monument on the island of Inniskea. White also wrote two book on famous scandals, *The Age of Scandal: An Excursion Through a Minor Period* (1950) and *The Scandalmonger* (1952).

ACHIEVEMENTS

White labored long and hard in relative obscurity before achieving literary success. His most successful work, *The Sword in the Stone*, was considered by many a children's book. White intended from the very beginning, however, that the story should be the introduction to a comprehensive modern rendering of the Arthurian legend, and the second and third

volumes became increasingly adult in their concerns and much darker in their implications. The fourth part languished unpublished for nearly twenty years, but after it was finally revised to form the conclusion of *The Once and Future King* the collection was eventually recognized as a masterpiece of modern fantasy. Even that version lacked the original fifth part, however, which remained unpublished for another nineteen years—thirteen years after the author's death. Although the animated film of *The Sword in the Stone* (1963) and the film version of the *Once and Future King*-based stage musical *Camelot* (1967) have reached a far wider audience than the original novels, the Arthurian sequence can now be seen as a work comparable in ambition and quality to the similar endeavors of fantasy novelist J. R. R. Tolkien.

BIOGRAPHY

Terence Hanbury White was born in Bombay, the son of a district supervisor of police and the grandson of a judge. He spent his first five years on the Indian subcontinent before returning to England with his mother Constance. His childhood was difficult because Constance—who eventually obtained a judicial separation from her husband but not the divorce that would have allowed her to marry her live-in lover—was mentally disturbed, and White was frightened of her. Removal to Cheltenham College in 1920 provided no relief; mistreatment from classmates maintained his misery, but he still won admission to Queen's College in Cambridge. He might have been happier there were it not for anxieties about his own condition, in which homosexual feelings and alcoholism were further confused by the total loss of his early religious faith and irrepressible sadomasochistic fantasies. As if this were not enough, he contracted tuberculosis while in his second year at Cambridge, and his teachers had to donate money to send him to Italy to convalesce; it was there that he wrote his first novel.

White returned from Italy in much better condition. His determination to stay fit and healthy cemented his interest in field sports, but his triumph over physical frailty was shadowed by an exaggerated awareness of his mortality, which added furious fuel to all his activities. After obtaining a first-class degree with distinction in 1929 he became a schoolmaster for a while—concluding with a four-year stint at one of England's best public schools, Stowe, in 1932-1936, before the autobiographical potboiler *England Have My Bones* (1936) sold well enough to win him a commission to deliver a book every year to his publisher, Collins. He rented a gamekeeper's cottage on the Stowe estate in order to pursue his new career.

Fearful of conscription into a war he desperately did not want to be involved in, White moved to Ireland (which remained neutral throughout World War II) in 1939, lodging in Doolistown in County Meath and at Sheskin Lodge in County Mayo. In these two locations, living as an exile, he wrote the fourth and fifth parts of the Arthurian series, but Collins ended

the book-per-year arrangement after issuing *The Ill-Made Knight*; the subsequent hiatus in his career lasted until 1946. In that year he relocated to the Channel Islands, living briefly in Jersey before settling in Aldernay in 1947; he died in his cabin, apparently of heart failure, while on a Mediterranean cruise in 1964.

ANALYSIS

White's first five novels, one of which was written in collaboration with R. McNair Scott and two of which were concealed under the pseudonym James Aston, were all naturalistic. The only one which is now remembered is his nostalgic panorama of the Victorian era, *Farewell Victoria*, which was also the only one not solidly rooted in his own experiences. The first he wrote, *They Winter Abroad*—the third published, under the Aston pseudonym—is of some interest for the insight it offers into his youthful state of mind.

EARTH STOPPED and GONE TO GROUND

Earth Stopped is a satiric comedy paying respectful homage to the works of English novelist Robert Smith Surtees, whose addiction to hunting, shooting, and fishing White shared. White's similarly addicted friend Siegfried Sassoon had introduced him to a reprint of Surtees' 1845 novel *Hillingdon Hall* in 1931. Sassoon's autobiographical novel *Memoirs of a Fox-Hunting Man* (1928) reflects sarcastically on the fact that he had been sent to a sanatorium to save him from a court-martial when he refused to return to the front after being wounded in action in 1917, and his influence on White's attitudes was profound. *Earth Stopped* introduces the inept revolutionary Mr. Marx into a Surtees-like party gathered for a weekend's sport at an English country house. The party remains blithely good humored until the final chapters, when a world war abruptly precipitated by the forces of communism and fascism breaks out, at which point "the universe split open like a pea-pod, informed by lightning but far transcending thunder."

The story continues in *Gone to Ground*, in which the survivors of the house party swap tall tales while they hide from the catastrophe, taking psychological refuge in fantasy while taking physical refuge underground. Although its prophetic pretensions were supposedly impersonal, this provided an ironic metaphorical account of the subsequent shape of White's life and career. The book ends with the conclusion of the final tale—reprinted in *The Maharajah and Other Stories* as "The Black Rabbit"—in which Keeper Pan, who was the inventor of panic as well as the god of nature, asserts his ultimate dominion over the objects of human sport.

THE ONCE AND FUTURE KING

Anticipation of a new world war, which many imaginative people expected to put an end to civilization, overwhelmed English fantastic fiction in the late 1930's. Other English writers were writing apocalyptic fantasies far more terrifying than *Earth Stopped*, but White decided to go in the opposite direction, becoming a connoisseur of playful escapism. The account of the boyhood and education of Arthur set out in *The Sword in the Stone* is as firmly rooted in personal experience as White's earliest novels are, but it is a calculated magical transformation of the oppressions that afflicted the author and his ultimate redemption from them.

The Sword in the Stone begins with an exotic schoolroom syllabus devised for the future Sir Kay by his governess, who cannot punish her noble student but can and does take out her frustrations on his whipping boy, "the Wart," who is not recognized as the future embodiment of England and the chivalric ideal until he acquires a far more inspiring tutor in Merlyn. The debt that White owed to his tutor at Cambridge and longtime correspondent L. J. Potts is acknowledged in the fact that Merlyn, whose prophetic gifts result from living his life in reverse, actually served as a Cambridge tutor in the twentieth century, which lay in his distant past.

The account of the childhood of Gareth and his brothers contained in *The Witch in the Wood* is far darker—in spite of comic relief provided by the alcoholic lapsed saint Toirdealbhach and King Pellinore's obsessive pursuit of the Questing Beast—because their lustful, neglectful, and unbalanced mother is a transfiguration of White's own. The characterization of Lancelot in *The Ill-Made Knight* probably owes something to Siegfried Sassoon as well as to White's

perception of himself, and it is significant that the text explicitly compares the greatest of all the Arthurian knights to one of the great sportsmen of the late 1930's, the Australian cricketer Donald Bradman. Lancelot's obsessive anxiety that his forbidden love for Guenever will sap the strength that makes him England's champion and deny him the chance to find the Holy Grail is a transfiguration of White's anxieties about his homosexuality and terror of military service (both of which were implicated in his decision to live as a recluse as soon as it became economically viable).

Given the deep personal significance of the first three volumes, it is hardly surprising that the dourly harrowing *The Candle in the Wind*, which White wrote in the latter months of 1940, is saturated with his anxiety for the blitzkrieg-devastated England that he had left and the civilization that it represented. He wrote to Potts on December 6, 1940, that he had discovered that "the central theme of the *Morte d'Arthur* is to find an antidote to war." In the fifth volume, Arthur goes underground with his old tutor, and they analyze the dismal failure of the Grail quest and look for a new way forward. While they do so, in *The Book of Merlyn*, they are surrounded by the animals Arthur loved so much as a boy, and Keeper Pan is certainly present in spirit, if not in person. Two key sequences from *The Book of Merlyn* were transposed into the version of *The Sword in the Stone* contained in *The Once and Future King*, and other elements were grafted onto the new version of *The Candle in the Wind* to supply the sense of an ending, but these devices distorted the balance and meaning of the whole, which was not published in its intended form.

J. R. R. Tolkien set out to expand his children's fantasy *The Hobbit* (1937) into an epic at almost exactly the same time White began to elaborate *The Once and Future King*. Tolkien was a Catholic and an Old English scholar who carefully excluded everything that had arrived in Britain with the Norman conquest (1066) from the mythos of his fantastic secondary world, Middle-Earth; however, it was precisely that imported tradition of chivalric romance that White chose for the heart of his own exercise. There is, therefore, a curious sense that the two resultant masterpieces of fantasy are as complementary and opposed as the universities of Oxford, which was Tolkien's home, and Cambridge, White's spiritual home, to which he remained anchored by his correspondence with L. J. Potts. One might also compare and contrast *The Once and Future King* with the fantasies of an older Cambridge man who was also troubled by inescapable sadomasochistic fantasies, John Cowper Powys, who eventually followed up the Grail epic *A Glastonbury Romance* (1932) with a more explicit transfiguration of Arthurian myth, *Porius* (1951), which was never issued in its entirety. Powys tackled the problem of designing a mythology for the much-conquered island of Britain by producing his own syncretism of Anglo-Saxon and Anglo-Norman elements with earlier Celtic and Greek myths.

All three of these writers were trying to construct or reconstruct a neomythological epic for an island that had somehow never contrived to produce a real one, which would also embody and allegorize the crisis at which the contemporary British nation had arrived in the pause between World War I and World War II. Of the three, White's is by far the most lighthearted but also—by virtue of its precipitous plunge into tragedy in *The Candle in the Wind*—the most emotional. It is perhaps ironic that Tolkien, who was not nearly as committed to the politics of escapism as White, should have become the parent of a whole genre of escapist fantasy, while White became best known as the inspirer of a Walt Disney film and a musical comedy. Thanks to the University of Texas edition of *The Book of Merlyn*, however, modern readers and critics have the opportunity to reconstruct White's masterpiece as he intended it to be read, and to judge its true worth as an epic for the isle of Britain.

LATER NOVELS

The three fantasies that White wrote after he recovered from the disappointment of Collins's initial refusal to publish *The Candle in the Wind* are best regarded as footnotes to the main sequence of his novels, displaying a gradual acceptance of the fact that he was seen as a children's writer. *The Elephant and the Kangaroo* is an allegorical comedy in which an English atheist in Ireland witnesses a visitation by

the archangel Michael and sets out to build an ark in response to the threat of an impending second deluge. In *Mistress Masham's Repose*, a young girl discovers descendants of the Lilliputians of Jonathan Swift's *Gulliver's Travels* (1726) living on an island and sets out to defend them from commercial exploitation by Hollywood filmmakers. *The Master* is a science-fiction story for children, whose juvenile heroes thwart the eponymous island-based villain's plans for world domination.

Brian Stableford

OTHER MAJOR WORKS

SHORT FICTION: *The Maharajah and Other Stories*, 1981.

POETRY: *Loved Helen and Other Poems*, 1929; *The Green Bay Tree: Or, The Wicked Man Touches Wood*, 1929.

NONFICTION: England Have My Bones, 1936 (autobiography); *The Age of Scandal: An Excursion Through a Minor Period*, 1950 (anecdotes); *The Goshawk*, 1951; *The Scandalmonger*, 1952 (anecdotes); *The Godstone and the Blackymor*, 1959 (autobiography); *America at Last*, 1965 (autobiography).

TRANSLATION: *The Book of Beasts*, 1954 (of medieval bestiary).

BIBLIOGRAPHY

Brewer, Elisabeth. *T. H. White's "The Once and Future King."* Cambridge, England: D. S. Brewer, 1993. Examines White's work and other Arthurian romances, historical fiction, and fantastic fiction. Includes bibliography and an index.

Crane, John K. *T. H. White.* New York: Twayne, 1974. A competent overview of White's work. For the beginning student.

Irwin, Robert. "T. H. White." *The St. James Guide to Fantasy Writers.* Detroit: St. James Press, 1996. A good summary account of White's fantasies.

Kellman, Martin. *T. H. White and the Matter of Britain.* Lewiston, N.Y.: E. Mellen Press, 1988. The second volume of a series on the historical novel, Kellman studies the Arthurian legend in detail.

Manlove, C. N. *The Impulse of Fantasy Literature.* Kent, Ohio: Kent State University Press, 1983.

The chapter on White carefully relates his work to the book's other subjects and the tradition of British fantasy.

Warner, Sylvia Townsend. *T. H. White: A Biography.* London: Cape/Chatto & Windus, 1967. A sensitive biography, whose central conclusions are summarized in Warner's introduction to *The Book of Merlyn.*

JOHN EDGAR WIDEMAN

Born: Washington, D.C.; June 14, 1941

PRINCIPAL LONG FICTION

A Glance Away, 1967
Hurry Home, 1970
The Lynchers, 1973
Hiding Place, 1981
Sent for You Yesterday, 1983
The Homewood Trilogy, 1985 (includes
    Damballah, *Hiding Place*, and *Sent for You
    Yesterday*)
Reuben, 1987
Philadelphia Fire, 1990
The Cattle Killing, 1996
Two Cities, 1998

OTHER LITERARY FORMS

An intensely lyrical novelist, John Edgar Wideman has also published numerous short stories based upon family members, friends, and neighbors from his childhood community of Homewood, a long-standing all-black subdivision of Pittsburgh, Pennsylvania. Twelve of these pieces are presented as letters in his critically acclaimed collection *Damballah* (1981), which has also been published with two of his novels as *The Homewood Trilogy*. Wideman's autobiographical *Brothers and Keepers* (1984) blends facts with fictionalized characters and incidents as the author scrutinizes his own relationship to his brother, Robert Wideman, imprisoned for life in Pennsylvania's Western State Penitentiary. *Fever* (1989), a collection of twelve stories, combines themes of family and community with those of displacement, estrangement, and cultural loss. Uncollected poetry, reviews, and essays on black American literature by Wideman abound in the foremost scholarly journals and literary digests.

ACHIEVEMENTS

When he emerged upon the literary scene in the late 1960's, Wideman stood out from his peers as a black American writer who did not address exclusively themes of racial conflict and militant nationalism. He concentrated instead on individual psychological struggles that transcend color lines. His earliest novels having been enthusiastically received; he was lauded as a successor to William Faulkner.

After being asked to teach African American literature and essentially having to "teach himself" the field, Wideman began to overtly centralize racial themes in his writing, most radically with the publication of *The Lynchers*, which begins with a chronology of 116 historically documented lynchings. His primary critical acclaim, however, came with the publications of the Homewood series, engendered by the death of his grandmother, Freeda French, in 1973. *Sent for You Yesterday*, the final work of the Homewood trilogy, received the 1984 Faulkner Award for Fiction from PEN, the International Association of Poets, Playwrights, Editors, Essayists, and Novelists. Through the 1990's, Wideman remained the only author to have received two PEN/Faulkner awards, receiving the second for *Philadelphia Fire*. In addition, he was awarded the Lannan Literary Fellowship for Fiction in 1991 and a MacArthur Foundation Award (a "genius grant") in 1993.

In spite of favorable reviews of his fiction, some critics have accused Wideman of indulging in an unconventional style at the expense of theme. More often than not, though, his experimentation extends meaning by illustrating the impact of the past in addition to the inextricable bonds among generations. His autobiographical *Brothers and Keepers*, which displays some of his innovative techniques, earned a National Book Critics Circle Award nomination. In 1998, Wideman won the prestigious Rea Award, sponsored by the Dungannon Foundation and estab-

(University of Wyoming)

he received his B.Ph. degree from Oxford University in 1966, specializing as a Thouron Fellow in the eighteenth century novel. He then spent one year as a Kent Fellow at the University of Iowa Writers' Workshop, subsequently returning to lecture at his alma mater, Pennsylvania. While writing and teaching literature at the University of Wyoming, he endured the conviction of his oldest son Jacob, on charges of fatally stabbing another youth during a camping trip in Arizona. This tragedy recalls the imprisonment of his brother Robert for involvement in a robbery and killing. His daughter Jamila, having inherited her father's basketball prowess, garnered a position playing in the Women's National Basketball Association (WNBA) professional league. In 1986 Wideman became professor of English at the University of Massachusetts, Amherst. In the 1980's and 1990's he frequently contributed articles and review essays to *The New York Times Book Review* and to popular magazines such as *TV Guide*, *Life*, and *Esquire*.

lished to honor a short story author "for literary power, originality, and influence on the genre." Wideman's critical accolades have been profuse, but it is his range of style, continual formalistic innovation, and his powerful prose that warrant his consideration as one of the best American writers of his generation.

BIOGRAPHY

Born in Washington, D.C., on June 14, 1941, John Edgar Wideman initially aspired to be a professional basketball player. Consequently, he served as both a Benjamin Franklin Scholar at the University of Pennsylvania and captain of the school's championship basketball team. A member of Phi Beta Kappa, he was graduated from the University of Pennsylvania in 1963 with a B.A. in English. Promptly selected as only the second black Rhodes Scholar in history,

ANALYSIS

The recurring thematic emphasis in John Edgar Wideman's novels is on the way history, both collective and personal, and the stories that arise from that history, shape notions of reality. From homosexual college professors to ghetto junkies, Wideman's characters are often uncomfortable with their places in history and unsure that they even understand those few traditions that they do observe. Therefore, they shuttle between the imaginary and the real in order to rediscover the past, revive it, or at least preserve whatever parts they do recall. Despite Wideman's literary beginnings in the racially turbulent 1960's, when blacks in America articulated their estrangement from Africa, his white as well as black characters crave the rootedness that distinguishes those who have come to terms with their backgrounds. Shifting from the anonymous northern cities of his first three novels to the clearly delineated Homewood of *Hiding Place* and *Sent for You Yesterday*, Wideman nevertheless consistently indicates that ignorance of heritage results in isolation and psychological turmoil. The same observation is later applied to Philadelphia, specifically Osage Avenue.

Wideman forgoes strictly chronological plot development, adopting instead an intricate experimental style consisting of stream-of-consciousness narrative, long interior monologues, dream sequences, surrealistic descriptions, and abrupt shifts in time, diction, and points of view. Beginning each novel almost exclusively *in medias res*, he employs a technique influenced by the works of T. S. Eliot, James Joyce, and Jean Toomer, yet indisputably original. In *The Lynchers*, for example, he illustrates the traditionally victimized status of black Americans with a preface that cites more than one hundred documented lynchings. Reeling between their own ravaged communities and impenetrable white ones, the black protagonists of his first two novels, *A Glance Away* and *Hurry Home*, occupy a jumbled landscape where blues clubs coexist with biblical icons. Similarly, in *Hiding Place* and *Sent for You Yesterday*, Wideman retells the stories of his ancestors until a shack or a cape acquires the same expressive quality as a cross. As the author himself explains, "You can call it experimentation, or you can call it ringing the changes. . . . I value spontaneity, flexibility, a unique response to a given situation. . . . Getting too close to the edge but then recovering like the heroes of the Saturday matinee serials. That's excitement."

A GLANCE AWAY

Dedicated to "Homes," Wideman's first novel, *A Glance Away*, creates thematic excitement with its treatment of two drifting men coming to terms with their pasts. After a year spent at a rehabilitation center for drug addicts, Eddie Lawson, a disillusioned young black man, returns to his listless, decaying urban neighborhood. Rather than celebrating, however, he spends his gloomy homecoming confronting the goblins that drove him to the brink in the first place: his mother Martha Lawson's idealization of his dead older brother, his girlfriend Alice Smalls's rejection of him for sleeping with a white woman, and his own

self-disgust over abandoning a secure postal job for menial, marginal employment. Dejected and defeated by nightfall, he drags himself to grimy Harry's Place in order to cloak his memories in a narcotic haze. There, he is reconciled by his albino friend Brother Smalls with another outcast named Robert Thurley, a white college professor struggling with his own record of divorce, alcoholism, and homosexuality. Though discrepancies between wealth and power divide the two homeless men, each manages to urge the other to maintain his faith in people despite his guiltridden history.

A Glance Away generated much favorable critical response in particular for Wideman's depiction of the alienated Thurley. In trying to disavow his personal past, this connoisseur of food and art embraces a surfeit of creeds and cultures. "In religion an aesthetic Catholic, in politics a passive Communist, in sex a resigned anarchist," he surrounds himself with treasures from both East and West and indulges in a smorgasbord of the globe's delicacies. Yet as a real measure of the displacement that these extravagances so futilely conceal, he quotes lines from T. S. Eliot's "The Love Song of J. Alfred Prufrock" (1917), in which a similarly solitary speaker searches for intimacy in a world bereft of its cultural moorings.

Emphasizing his protagonists' self-absorption and the estrangement of their family members and friends, Wideman abandons strictly chronological plot development in favor of lengthy interior monologues. Conversations tend to be short; more likely than not they are interrupted by unspoken flashbacks and asides. Using speech to measure isolation, the author portrays both Eddie and Thurley as incapable of communicating adequately. Eddie, for example, becomes tongue-tied around a group of southern travelers, shuddering in his bus seat instead of warning them as he wishes for the reality of the Northern mecca that they seek. Similarly, despite the empowering qualities of a gulp of Southern Comfort, Thurley delivers a lecture on Sophocles' *Oedipus Tyrannus* (c. 429 B.C.E.) fraught with "futility and detachment, . . . introspection and blindness." In one brilliant play on this speechlessness, both men suddenly converse as if they were actors on a stage. This abrupt emphasis on what is spoken—to the exclusion of private thoughts—stresses each person's imprisonment within him- or herself. Flowing from a weaker artist's pen, *A Glance Away* would have become a mere exercise in allusive technique and stream-of-consciousness style. On the contrary, it reads with the effortless ease of a masterfully crafted lyrical poem. Key to its success is Wideman's careful alliance of form and content, not to mention his insightful treatment of a rootlessness that transcends the barriers of race.

HURRY HOME

The same compact length as the novel which precedes it, *Hurry Home* similarly focuses upon the theme of rootlessness. Its ambitious protagonist, the honors graduate Cecil Otis Braithwaite, is in many ways an upscale Eddie Lawson with a wife and an advanced degree. After slaving through law school, supporting himself with a meager scholarship and his earnings as a janitor, Cecil has lost his aspirations and his love for his girlfriend, Esther Brown. In search of something more, he escapes from his wedding bed to Europe, where he roams indiscriminately for three years among its brothels as well as its art galleries. In the tradition of Robert Thurley of *A Glance Away*, two white men as displaced as Cecil attempt to guide him: Charles Webb, belatedly in search of an illegitimate son, and Albert, a mercenary in Webb's employ who has also abandoned a wife. Too lost to save themselves, however, this pair can offer no enduring words of solace to Cecil.

Hurry Home is more sophisticated than *A Glance Away* in its treatment of the isolation theme. It suggests, for example, that the upwardly mobile Cecil is not merely disturbed by his personal past; he is estranged as well from his African and European cultures of origin. On the other hand, nowhere does *Hurry Home* convey the hope that pervades its predecessor. Cecil travels more extensively than does Eddie to reclaim his past, yet he gains no key to it to speak of. Confronting his European heritage merely confirms his status as "a stranger in all . . . tongues." He flees to the African continent by boat, "satisfied to be forever possessed," only to be forever rebuffed from a past that "melts like a wax casing as I am

nearer . . . the flame." When he returns at last to his Washington, D.C., tenement, the fruitlessness of his journey is underscored. There, he finds all the same as when he first entered following his miserable nuptials. Symbolically limning his rootlessness, he switches vocations, abandoning the tradition-steeped protocol of the bar for the faddish repertoire of a hairdresser. Thus, "hurry home," the catchphrase for his odyssey, is an ironic one. Cecil really can claim no place where a heritage nurtures and sustains him, no history that he can truly call his own.

Hurry Home displays a masterful style commensurate with that of the later Homewood novels. In addition to a more controlled stream-of-consciousness technique, recurring Christian symbols, icons of Renaissance art, and fragments from Moorish legend powerfully indicate Cecil's fractured lineage. This second novel being a more refined paradigm than the first, Wideman seemed next inclined to break new ground, to address intently the racial polarization that had unsettled American society by the early 1970's, producing that period's most influential published works.

THE LYNCHERS

Distinguished from the previous two novels by its bawdy humor and portrayal of a professional black woman, *The Lynchers* is set in the generic northeastern slum, pockmarked by the self-inflicted wounds of the 1960's, that has become a Wideman trademark. Central to the action are four frustrated black men: Willie "Littleman" Hall, an unemployed dwarf; Leonard Saunders, a ruthless hustler turned repressed postal clerk; Thomas Wilkerson, a plodding fifth-grade schoolteacher; and Graham Rice, an introspective janitor with a persecution complex. Disenchanted with the superficial changes that the Civil Rights movement has wrought—the "job here or a public office there, . . . one or two black faces floating to the top"—these four conclude that violence is the only means to effect a lasting alteration of the white power structure. With Littleman as the ringleader and mastermind, they plan to flex the latent power of the black community and turn the tables on their oppressors by kidnapping and lynching a white policeman.

The plot falls apart, however, once Littleman is badly beaten by the authorities for delivering a militant speech at Woodrow Wilson Junior High School. Suspicion, distrust, and doubt override the remaining conspirators so that they foil themselves instead of their "white butcher pig" enemy. Thus, in a perverse way the weapons of the executioner do revert to black hands. Lynching becomes a symbol of frustration turned inward, of despairing hearts made so taut in their efforts to beat more freely that they burst.

Unlike *A Glance Away* and *Hurry Home, The Lynchers* is a total immersion into blackness. Perhaps the critics wanted another black-white character dichotomy, for their assessments of this novel were at best mixed. Nevertheless, Wideman again displays strong gifts of characterization without diminishing the theme's universal appeal. A continuation of his preoccupation with rootlessness, *The Lynchers* showcases men who feel acutely that they belong nowhere. Wilkerson, for example, is the Cecil type, the black professional who is alienated from his working-class roots, condescended to by whites possessing similar educational backgrounds, and unwelcome in the clubs and restaurants that they patronize. Saunders, like Eddie, is a marginally good citizen, at once attracted to and repelled by "the life" of conning and thieving. In an intricate new twist to this scenario, Wideman depicts the older generation as a group as anchorless as the young. For example, Wilkerson's father, a drunk and a philanderer, stabs a longtime friend to death.

In its familiar inner-city setting and cast of alienated men (a passing reference is even made to Cecil Braithwaite as Littleman's lawyer), *The Lynchers* recalls Wideman's preceding works. In its use of a symbol generated exclusively from the black experience, it acts as a transition between these two novels and Wideman's fourth and fifth endeavors. No longer primarily gleaning symbols from Christianity and the European classics, here Wideman unifies his montage of dialogues with "the hawk," a symbol indigenous to the men's own harsh environment. This frigid, anthropomorphic wind that lashes the streets indicates the blacks' powerlessness and the hollow bravado of their ill-fated intrigue. They cannot even abduct the police officer without using one of their own people, his black girlfriend, Sissie, as a pawn.

HIDING PLACE

After an eight-year interval during which he researched black American literature and culture, Wideman applied folk sources more fully than ever before in *Hiding Place*, one of the three works of fiction which make up *The Homewood Trilogy*. Challenged to enlarge his black readership without limiting the universal relevance of his themes, he chose to emphasize one black family based largely on his own Homewood clan. In this novel's swift, uncomplicated plot, Tommy Lawson, a tough, wisecracking youth from the black neighborhood of Homewood, is running from the police for his involvement in a robbery and killing. He seeks refuge among the weedy plots and garbage piles of desolate Bruston Hill, a once-fertile area to which his ancestor Sybela Owens fled from the South and slavery with Charlie Bell, her white owner's recalcitrant son. In the lone residence at the crest of the Hill, a rotting wooden shack sardonically known as "that doghouse," the reclusive "Mother" Bess Owens reluctantly offers her sister's great-grandson a temporary haven. After Tommy regains the courage to elude the authorities eager to convict him for a murder that he did not commit, Bess reaffirms her ties to her kin and ends her self-imposed isolation. Not knowing whether Tommy is dead, has escaped, or has been captured, she burns her shack and prepares to reenter Homewood to retell Tommy's tragic story so that another like it might never happen again.

Though Bess does not leave her longtime home until the novel's final chapter, *Hiding Place* is as much the story of her isolation from family as it is one of Tommy's. Just as Tommy has shirked his responsibilities as a husband, father, and son, Bess has turned her back upon the younger generations of kin whose ways are alien to her. Widowed and childless, she has retreated into an archaic lifestyle, shunning the twentieth century amenities of electricity and phones, in order to avoid intimacy with others. Physically rooting herself among Bruston Hill's ruins, she has been running from the present in her mind by focusing her thoughts on the past, especially the deaths of loved ones that have occurred. Only when she becomes involved in Tommy's affairs does she rekindle her active commitment to the family.

In *Hiding Place*, Wideman's style dramatically differs from those of the canonized white writers who were his early models. With a method many reviewers have compared to jazz, his characters unfold the histories of five generations of Lawsons and Frenches. Bess herself repeats certain key events in the family history several times; one of her favorites is the one in which Mary Hollinger revives her cousin Freeda French's stillborn baby by plunging it into the snow. Yet like a jazz improvisation, where instruments alternately play solo and play together, she retells the tale each time in a different way, varying her approach to it with different bits of superstition, mysticism, and folklore. Even Wideman's Clement, an inarticulate orphan similar to Benjy Compson in William Faulkner's *The Sound and the Fury* (1929), bears the unique stamp of the black American experience. As the author himself avows, Clement's assimilation into Homewood reflects the nature of the black community as a tolerant extended family.

Its legacy of songs, tales, and superstitions notwithstanding, the Homewood that finally draws Bess back is a model of urban blight, a "bombed out" no-man's-land of "pieces of buildings standing here and there and fire scars and places ripped and kicked down and cars stripped and dead at the curb." This dying landscape, and in a similar way Bess's ramshackle Bruston Hill homestead, proclaims the present descendants' dissociation from their ancestors and one another. In *Sent for You Yesterday*, the final installment of *The Homewood Trilogy* and the 1984 PEN Faulkner Award winner for outstanding fiction, this undercurrent becomes the novel's predominant theme. Carl French and his lover Lucy Tate relate the stories of a Homewood gone by to the latest generation of listeners, as if the recovery of the past is integral for the entire community's survival and solidarity.

SENT FOR YOU YESTERDAY

Sent for You Yesterday cannot be divided easily into main story and subplots. All the episodes in it are major in scope and significance. The most memorable ones include the saga of the piano player Albert Wilkes, who slept with a white woman and murdered a white policeman; the tragedy of Samantha, whose college education could not shield her from grief and madness; and the bittersweet adventures of the resilient Brother Tate, an albino and best friend of Carl who communicates only with gestures and scat sounds. Retold by Carl's nephew Doot, a former Homewood resident modeled largely after Wideman himself, each tale conveys a lesson to a younger generation. More than mere exempla, however, the stories emphasize the cyclic nature of the human condition: Each generation rises to further, alter, and often reenact the accomplishments of its predecessors. Thus, Uncle Carl's street in Homewood becomes to Doot "a narrow, cobbled alley *teeming* with life. Like a wooden-walled ship in the middle of the city, like the ark on which Noah packed two of everything and prayed for land." This determination to survive that the ark imagery calls to mind impels Carl and Lucy to share Homewood's history. By remembering past lives, by preserving traditions, they ensure their own enduring places in the memories of their heirs.

REUBEN

Traditions preserved and memories presented from black America's African past form the backbeat of *Reuben*, Wideman's next novel of community and interracial struggle. From a rusting trailer that his clients describe as part office, part altar to the gods, the dwarf Reuben serves the poor of Homewood in need of a lawyer, a psychologist, a warrior, or a priest. Like West African *griots* or oral scribes, who commit to unerring memory genealogies, triumphs, faults, and names, Reuben relies upon a mix of law and bureaucratic legerdemain that he has heard from his own employers and remembered. Like an obliging ancestral spirit shuttling prayers from this world to the next, Reuben negotiates pacts between the ghetto's bombed-out streets and the oak, plush, and marble interiors of City Hall. As he prescribes legal strategies and bestows grandfatherly advice, he also steers his clients to confront and abandon the views that have overturned their lives. When words and contracts alone will not do, Reuben rustles deep within collective memory and knots a charm: "A rag, a bone, a hank of hair. Ancient grains of rice. . . ." Reuben transforms garbage into power, excrement into nourishment, gristle into life. He preaches reincarnation and the nature of things dead to rise again, and he catalyzes his clients to seek similar transformations in themselves.

Infused with magic and spiritualism, *Reuben* also is illustrated by the ravaged images of the inner city. Wideman likens ghetto buildings to the rat-infested holds of slave ships and the people in those buildings to roles of both predator and prey. Much of the Homewood population resembles a coffle of freshly branded slaves, slaves who are bound by laws instead of chains, by the welfare system or underworld crime instead of a plantation economy. Others are human versions of rats—snitching, beating, starving, stealing, and otherwise pestering their neighbors with an eat-or-be-eaten mentality. "There were historical precedents, parallels," Reuben understands. "Indian scouts leading long-hairs to the hiding places of their red brethren. FBI informers, double agents, infiltrators of the sixties. An unsubtle variation of divide and conquer." In this bleak landscape, the game of divide and conquer has changed little since enslavement.

PHILADELPHIA FIRE

Philadelphia Fire, *The Cattle Killing*, and *Two Cities* are framed within a geographic shift from Pittsburgh to Philadelphia. In keeping with Wideman's fluid notion of history and myth as mutually interlocking categories of representation, *Philadelphia Fire* recasts the 1985 police bombing of the building occupied by the radical MOVE organization. John Africa, MOVE's leader, is represented as Reverend King, who is described as "a nouveau Rousseau." King leads a rebellion against the infringement on African American individual and communal rights couched in the guises of "urbanization" and "integration" by espousing an ideology that embraces a return to nature and a rejection of modern material values. Elsewhere, Wideman asserts that "the craziness of MOVE is their sanity; they were saying no to the system . . . it makes perfect sense. So the myth of integration is analogous to the prophecy of the cattle killing."

THE CATTLE KILLING

This prophecy serves as the guiding metaphor for the novel *The Cattle Killing*, and it refers to the lies told to the African Xhosa people in order to make them believe that to combat European oppression they must kill their cattle. The cattle are their life force, and their destruction leads to the near annihilation of Xhosa culture. The people die as their cattle die, struck down because they believed the lie of the prophecy: "The cattle are the people. The people are the cattle." Wideman subtly extends this metaphor to consider the problem of intraracial crime ravaging American inner cities and connects contemporary circumstances with the diseased and disintegrating conditions surrounding the yellow fever outbreak of eighteenth century Philadelphia.

In all three instances—in Africa, in Philadelphia, in black urbania—there is a potential for annihilation because of an epidemic fueled by hysteria, exacerbated by racist ideology and carried out by those who believe the "lie" and perpetrate their self-destruction. The narrator of *Cattle Killing*, Isaiah, called "Eye," is an obvious recasting of the biblical figure who prophesies the downfall of the nation of Israel. He is a prophet who warns of false prophecies—in this case, the lie of integration, which is, intricately entwined with modernization and its attenuating conspicuous consumption, the theme foregrounded in *Philadelphia Fire*. This text's distinction from *Philadelphia Fire*, however, lies in the vision of hope with which readers are left; *The Cattle Killing* is also a love story.

TWO CITIES

The Cattle Killing and the following novel, *Two Cities*, mark a thematic shift for Wideman. Though harkening back to the theme of love (a kind of communal love) inherent in the Homewood trilogy, the novels transcend that representation, exploring the healing potential of intimate, spiritual love. *Two Cities*, which links Philadelphia and Pittsburgh, Cassina Way and Osage Avenue, explores the difficulty of loving in troubled times. It overwhelmingly endorses the embracing of love, not merely physical love but also self-love, love of community, and love of life, as the only viable means of refusing and subverting the lies which have threatened to destroy the African American community.

From the beginning of his extensive literary career, critics have often compared Wideman's prose to the experimental fictions of the eighteenth century English writer Laurence Sterne. The sociable Sterne had befriended Ignatius Sancho, a gregarious former slave, a prodigious correspondent, and host of one of London's most popular salons. Sancho admired Sterne's mock humility and imitated his wit and playful style. In turn, Sterne admired the double entendre, self-scrutiny, and flair for detail in the letters of his African friend.

In Wideman's novels, the voices of the African Sancho and the Englishman Sterne converge. These works present black America from the perspectives of the enslaved and the descendants of the enslaved, as well as from the vantage of those whites who served as either tormentors and oppressors or benefactors and friends. These works warn of the potholes where our elders slipped before, and they expose the reader to the vistas that one often fails to notice and enjoy. They achieve Wideman's goal of "expanding our notions of reality, creating hard, crisp edges you can't swallow without a gulp."

Barbara A. McCaskill,
updated by Heather Russell Andrade

OTHER MAJOR WORKS

SHORT FICTION: *Damballah*, 1981; *Fever*, 1989; *The Stories of John Edgar Wideman*, 1992; *All Stories Are True*, 1992.

NONFICTION: *Brothers and Keepers*, 1984; *Father-along: A Meditation on Fathers and Sons, Race and Society*, 1994.

BIBLIOGRAPHY

Bennion, John. "The Shape of Memory in John Edgar Wideman's Sent for You Yesterday." *Black American Literature Forum* 20, nos. 1 and 2 (Spring/Summer, 1986): 143-150. Bennion argues that the reader's struggle to grasp the "foreign and familiar" aspects of Wideman's *Sent for You Yesterday* mirrors the struggle the characters undergo to apprehend their experiences. One's ordering of reality is made possible only through a complex negotiation between order and chaos.

Coleman, James W. *Blackness and Modernism: The Literary Career of John Edgar Wideman.* Jackson: University Press of Mississippi, 1989. The book contends that Wideman's fiction has evolved from a modernist emphasis on alienation and despair to a postmodernist portrayal of black communities that are strong and sustaining. Coleman evaluates the fiction for its fantasy, surrealism, magic, ritual, folklore, and mainstream influences. He appends an interview with Wideman on changes in the fiction.

_____. "Going Back Home: The Literary Development of John Edgar Wideman." *CLA Journal* 27 (March, 1985): 326-343. Coleman considers how Wideman transforms his childhood neighborhood into myth that unifies and directs *The Homewood Trilogy*. Once they can connect to their ancestors' lives, alienated and isolated characters in the books can revitalize themselves and rejoin their communities. Important is Wideman's use of gospel music, scat songs, dreams, oral stories, blues, the numbers game, street vernacular, and other aspects of black American folk culture.

Dubey, Madhu. "Literature and Urban Crisis: John Edgar Wideman's *Philadelphia Fire.*" *African American Review* 32 (Winter, 1998): 579-595. Dubey examines *Philadelphia Fire* in relation to its implicit critique of urban renewal and its attenuating glorification of consumption and excess, legitimation of law and order, and the resulting dispossession, displacement, and segregation of the city's inhabitants. Dubey suggests that while Wideman's invocation of the MOVE organization and its resistance to urbanization provides an important critique, the text resists positing a nationalist or utopian vision to counterbalance the vision undergirding urban renewal.

Mbalia, Doreatha D. *John Edgar Wideman: Reclaiming the African Personality.* London: Associated University Presses, 1995. Examines the African influences on Wideman's work. Includes bibliographical references and an index.

Rushdy, Ashraf. "Fraternal Blues: John Edgar Wideman's Homewood Trilogy." *Contemporary Literature* 32, no. 3 (Fall, 1991): 312-345. Rushdy begins by suggesting that the narrator of the trilogy utilizes three modes of narrating which are depicted in the three texts, *Damballah*, *Hiding Place*, and *Sent for You Yesterday*, respectively: letters, stories, and "the blues." He argues that the narrative voice gains an understanding of self when it finds a "blues voice." Rushdy discusses "achieving a blues mind," which, he asserts, is based upon impulses borrowed from blues, jazz, and gospel music.

Samuels, Wilfred D. "Going Home: A Conversation with John Edgar Wideman." *Callaloo* 6 (February, 1983): 40-59. This interview investigates how Wideman has found creative inspiration in his family history, African heritage, and black American folk culture. He discusses his concern for reaching black American readers and his transition from mainstream academic pursuits to the study of black American literature.

TuSmith, Bonnie. *Conversations with John Edgar Wideman*. Jackson: University Press of Mississippi, 1998. Compiles interviews with Wideman that span thirty-five years. The interviews are framed around the publication of his various novels, short stories and autobiographical works. In her introduction, TuSmith represents Wideman as a man committed to his craft, compassionate about his subjects, and engaged in refining and revising his acts of representation.

Wideman, John Edgar. "The Black Writer and the Magic of the Word." *The New York Times Book Review*, January 24, 1988, 1, 27-28. Wideman explains his commitment to preserving black American patterns of speech. He shows that the double entendre and sound variation in the English of black American speakers are conscious attempts to establish self-esteem and respond to the manipulations of whites. He contends that black writers have been frustrated by publishers and critics who measure their worth according to fluctuating standards of literate speech.

Wilson, Matthew. "The Circles of History in John Edgar Wideman's *The Homewood Trilogy*." *CLA Journal* 33 (March, 1990): 239-259. Wilson argues the Homewood sequence as a nontraditional family chronicle. The essay examines interconnections among individual family histories, events from American enslavement, and the histories of the Fon and Kongo cultures. A central theme of the trilogy is that black Americans resist annihilation and vanquish the oppressive acts of whites by telling their own stories and exposing their authentic histories.

ELIE WIESEL

Born: Sighet, Transylvania (now Romania); September 30, 1928

PRINCIPAL LONG FICTION

L'Aube, 1960 (novella; *Dawn*, 1961)
Le Jour, 1961 (novella; *The Accident*, 1962)
La Ville de la chance, 1962 (*The Town Beyond the Wall*, 1964)
Les Portes de la forêt, 1964 (*The Gates of the Forest*, 1966)
Le Mendiant de Jérusalem, 1968 (*A Beggar in Jerusalem*, 1970)
Le Serment de Kolvillàg, 1973 (*The Oath*, 1973)
Le Testament d'un poète juif assassiné, 1980 (*The Testament*, 1981)
Le Cinquième Fils, 1983 (*The Fifth Son*, 1985)
Le Crépuscule, au loin, 1987 (*Twilight*, 1988)
L'Oublié, 1989 (*The Forgotten*, 1992)

OTHER LITERARY FORMS

After the appearance in 1956 of *Un di Velt hot geshvign* (in French as *La Nuit*; *Night*, 1960), Elie Wiesel published more than twenty works. Other works include *Les Juifs de silence* (1966; *The Jews of Silence*, 1966), a personal testimony of his trip to Russia; *Le Chant des morts* (1966; *Legends of Our Time*, 1968), *Entre deux soleils* (1970; *One Generation After*, 1970), and *Un Juif aujourd'hui* (1977; *A Jew Today*, 1978), collections of essays and short stories; several volumes of biblical portraits and Hasidic tales; plays, such as *Zalmen: Ou, La Folie de Dieu* (1968; *Zalmen: Or, The Madness of God*, 1974) and *Le Procès de Shamgorod tel qu'il se déroula le 25 février 1649* (1979; *The Trial of God: As It Was Held on February 25, 1649, in Shamgorod*, 1979); and a cantata, *Ani Maamin: Un Chant perdu et retrouvé* (1973; *Ani Maamin: A Song Lost and Found Again*, 1973). Some of his later works, the biblical portraits and Hasidic tales, although written in French, were originally published in the English translation by his wife, Marion Wiesel.

ACHIEVEMENTS

Elie Wiesel is one of the most important figures in the genre known as "the literature of the Holocaust." He brings to literature a new literary vocabulary, rooted in the Bible, that is at once mystical, legalistic, theological, and historical. As a survivor of the Holocaust, he considers himself to be a messenger from the dead to the living, and, as a witness, he bears testimony both to the unfathomable events of the death camps and to the current, unfolding history of his people. Wiesel's work, parochial in context, is universal in perception. It speaks to all humankind, for all participated, either actively or silently, in the supreme trial of their humanity. He views the Holocaust as touching upon every facet of one's life and interests, and he perceives humanity's major problem to be survival in the post-Holocaust world.

As a writer, Wiesel is preoccupied with the inadequacy of language, but not in the abstract manner of many contemporary writers. Language affirms a belief in humankind and attests its grandeur. The Holocaust negates humanity. It represents a misuse of language; the failure of imagination; the rule of the depraved; the suspension of the senses, of beliefs, of time; the inversion of order. To capture the Holocaust in language is to impose upon it a decorum which in itself is a betrayal of those victimized by this satanic maelstrom. Wiesel believed, when he began to write, that the tale nevertheless must be told, because the murderer murders not only his victim but also him-

(The Nobel Foundation)

self. He says, "At Auschwitz, not only man died, but also the idea of man." Awareness of the Holocaust may save the world from self-obliteration.

Wiesel raises questions that are unanswerable, questions intended to arouse the consciousness of a people, the progeny of the indifferent observers of the decade of the 1940's. He also vies with God, not as a defiant disbeliever, but as a believer in the biblical tradition of the prophets who have challenged God, remonstrated with Him, and protested heavenly decrees. There is no gaiety in Wiesel's works. There is laughter, but it is not a joyous laughter. It is the laughter of a madman defying his creator. Writers, theologians, and humanists of all faiths are attempting to come to terms with the problems he presents.

Writing, for Wiesel, is not simply intended as a moral lesson for the post-Holocaust generations. It is also, and perhaps primarily—as he explains in the essay "Mes Maîtres" ("My Teachers"), in *Legends of Our Time*—a monument to the unburied dead, to the millions whose celestial cemeteries are bereft of tombstones.

Wiesel's first publication, *Night*, is in the form of a memoir of his Holocaust experiences. Wiesel did not have an easy time publishing his initial work. It originally appeared in 1955 as an eight-hundred-page manuscript in Yiddish entitled *Un di Velt hot geshvign* (and the world was silent) and was published in Argentina by a Yiddish press. It was then condensed to a little more than one hundred pages, translated into French, given the title *La Nuit*, and, with the help of Wiesel's close friend François Mauriac, published in France in 1958. It was an instant success. Stella Rodway translated the French version into English, but major publishing houses in the United States rejected the manuscript because the subject matter was "too sad" to appeal to the general public. Finally, in 1960, Hill and Wang accepted the manuscript for publication. Wiesel would continue to write in French; his later books were translated into English by his wife, Marion. The exception is his eyewitness account of his trip to Russia, *The Jews of Silence*, which was originally written in Hebrew as a series of journalistic articles for an Israeli newspaper. It was thereafter put together in its present form. Some of Wiesel's essays first appeared in various magazines prior to their appearance in *Legends of Our Time* and *A Jew Today*.

Wiesel is a celebrated lecturer sought after by various organizations, conferences, and campuses; he served on the boards of numerous national and international organizations; he holds honorary doctoral degrees from more than forty colleges and universities and has received awards for literary, academic, and humanitarian contributions from thirty-five organizations. In 1983 he won the Belgian International Peace prize, and in 1986 he received the Nobel Peace Prize.

BIOGRAPHY

Eliezer Wiesel, the third child and only son of Shlomo and Sarah Wiesel, was born in the village of Sighet, in Transylvania, on September 30, 1928. He had two older sisters, Bea and Hilda, and one younger one, Tzipporah. His parents were Orthodox Jews. As a child, Eliezer was a profound believer in God and spent his days in religous studies. His father, though religious, was a man of culture and a rational humanist. He taught his son to believe in humanity and saw to it that he learned secular subjects, such as Latin, mathematics, and physics, as well as religious ones. His mother was more spiritual. She taught her son a love of God. The constant argument in the Wiesel home was whether their son should be a professor or a rabbi. Wiesel's maternal grandfather, Dodye Feig, was a Hasid. The young boy would visit with his grandfather to listen to the tales of the Hasidim and the miracles wrought by the rabbis. Eliezer's talent as a storyteller had its beginnings in the stories told to him by his grandfather. He also evinced an appreciation for music and took violin lessons at an early age. After the war, he earned his keep as a choirmaster. His cantata, *Ani Maamin*, with a musical score by Darius Milhaud, is one of the most moving works to be produced about the Holocaust. At the age of twelve, he studied the Cabala under the tutelage of his master, Moshe. Wiesel's first work, *Night*, commences with the serenity of his youth. The portrait of his grandfather and the conflicting attitudes of his parents are subjects of essays to be found in *Legends of Our Time* and *A Jew Today*.

The tranquillity of Wiesel's life was disturbed in the spring of 1944. Although the war in Europe had been going on since 1939, Hungary was one of the last countries to be invaded by the Germans. The inhabitants of the town of Sighet, protected as they were by the Carpathian mountains and isolated from the events taking place, did not recognize or believe that disaster was imminent. Immigration, when it was still possible, had never been seriously considered. Suddenly, in a matter of weeks, ten thousand Jews were first placed in ghettos and then deported to Auschwitz. For Wiesel, one of the most bizarre aspects of the deportation was the apathy and indifference of the general public. Friends and neighbors turned their backs on the people who had lived with them for generations. Wiesel deals with this in his novel *The Town Beyond the Wall* and also in various essays and lectures.

The four-day ride in the sealed boxcar, the arrival at Auschwitz, the separation of families, his last glimpse of his mother and younger sister, the concentration-camp experience (including the loss of faith), the stripping away of his humanity, the march to Buchenwald, the death of his father, and finally liberation by the Americans in April, 1945, are tersely rendered in *Night*. Various aspects of this experience are reflected upon by some of the characters of his other novels and by Wiesel directly in some of his essays. The Holocaust itself, while it remains the impetus and muted background of all his writings, does not appear again as the bulk of any particular work. Instead, Wiesel turns from the memoir to the novel form, from fact to fiction, as his protagonists search, as he has done, for a way to live in the post-Holocaust world with the burden of the unimaginable behind them and with the guilt of living confronting them.

When Wiesel was liberated, at the age of sixteen and a half, he refused to be repatriated to the town that had evicted its Jews one year earlier. Instead, he joined a transport of children that was going to France at the invitation of Charles de Gaulle. Upon his arrival in France, he made the decision that he must testify to what he had experienced, but not until he understood it fully himself. He knew it would take time to prepare himself for that testimony, perhaps ten years. He realized that he needed better communication skills and a keener understanding of what had happened. Meanwhile, he vowed not to speak of his experience of the Holocaust. (This vow of silence later became the subject matter for his novel *The Oath*.) In France, Wiesel learned that his two older sisters were alive. At Versailles, he became acquainted with François Wahl, a young philosopher at the Sorbonne, who taught him French by having Wiesel read French classical literature and classics translated into French. Wiesel moved to Paris in 1946. There, he earned his livelihood as a choir director and as a teacher of the Bible. In 1948, he enrolled at the Sorbonne to study philosophy, the humanities, and literature, hoping to find the answers to the theological, philosophical, and humanistic questions that were plaguing him. His studies broadened his horizons but did not present him with solutions,

and he was becoming restless. Fortunately, he landed a job as Paris correspondent for the Israeli newspaper *Yediot Aharonot*, and the next few years were spent traveling in North America, South America, Europe, North Africa, Asia, and the Middle East. As a journalist, Wiesel covered the Israeli War of Independence, which forms the background of his novella *Dawn*. In 1952, Wiesel traveled to India on an assignment. While in India, he wrote a dissertation comparing the Hindu, Christian, and Jewish religions. He also decided to teach himself English at that time.

One of Wiesel's assignments brought him back to Paris, where he met François Mauriac, who convinced him that he must break his vow and start telling his story. The result of this meeting was *Night*, a memoir in the form of a novella. The years after his liberation and the meeting with Mauriac are reflected in his essay "An Interview Unlike Any Other," in *A Jew Today*.

In 1956, Wiesel was sent to New York to cover the United Nations. He also began writing articles in Yiddish for the *Jewish Daily Forward*. During his first summer in New York, he was almost killed by a taxicab while crossing Times Square. He required weeks of hospitalization and months of recuperation. He could move about only with the help of a wheelchair. This experience became the subject of the novella *The Accident*, which he wrote while he was housebound. During that time, his French visa expired, and he applied for American citizenship.

Wiesel returned to Sighet in 1965. He arrived in the middle of the night. It was an unbearable experience for him, poignantly and searingly related in an essay entitled "Le Dernier Retour" ("The Last Return"). The retailing of this incident also appears in the collection *Legends of Our Time* and in "The Watch," in *One Generation After*, and it is recorded with great accuracy in his novel *The Town Beyond the Wall*. Wiesel could not bring himself to spend more than twenty-four hours in the city he had left so abruptly some twenty years before.

Wiesel's first visit to Russia, in 1965, resulted in three works, each in a different form: *The Jews of Silence*, a compilation of newspaper articles concerning this trip; *Zalmen*, a play dealing with the anguish of the rabbi of the Moscow synagogue; and *The Testament*, a novel begun during his trip but set against the background of the Stalinist purge of Jewish writers and poets in 1952. Wiesel returned to Russia again in 1979, as chairman of the President's Commission on the Holocaust.

From 1948 on, Wiesel made several trips to Israel in his capacity as correspondent for *Yediot Aharonot*. His participation in the June, 1967, war provided the impetus for the novel *A Beggar in Jerusalem*. He returned to Israel in 1968, this time to be married in Jerusalem, to Marion Erster Rose, a Viennese, a concentration-camp survivor also, and a linguist.

Wiesel joined the faculty at City College of New York in 1972, first as a visiting professor teaching courses on Jewish literature, the Holocaust, and Hasidism, and then, in 1973, as Distinguished Professor. Thereafter, he would teach at Boston University, as an Andrew Mellon professor of the humanities.

ANALYSIS

Elie Wiesel said that all his works are "commentary" on *Night*, his one work that deals directly with the Holocaust. His novels are odysseys of a soul fragmented by the Holocaust, in quest of tranquillity, an attempt to move away from the night reaching the shores of day. The key to understanding Wiesel, then, is his memoir in the form of a novella, *Night*. It is a slim volume which records his childhood memories of his hometown and his experiences in the concentration camp. It also contains the themes, images, and devices which recur throughout his work.

NIGHT

The opening chapter of *Night* begins with the social setting of Wiesel's native village of Sighet in Transylvania—its inhabitants, their customs, their beliefs—and his first meeting with Moché, the beadle, a character who forms a link to all his other works. Events occur rapidly. The disruption of normalcy with the invasion of the Germans, the forcing of the Jews into ghettos, their deportation, and the obliteration of the Jewish community are recorded tersely but accurately.

From the moment the Jews of Sighet leave the tranquil setting of their native village until they are liberated, time is suspended. The concentration camp is a universe like no other. There, every day is a waking nightmare. Each day is a repetition of deprivation, starvation, cremation; death, either by torture, gunshot, or fire, is the only certainty. The boys look like old men; the men cry like children. Existence depends upon endurance, regardless of age.

Not only is the town obliterated and time obliterated, but also the individual is transformed into an unrecognizable substance. The bestial inhumanity of the victimizers, the divorce from social, moral, and humanistic constraints, marks their apotheosis in the kingdom of Hell. The inmates of the concentration camp's universe are metamorphosed also. The tattooing of numbers on their arms indelibly brands them as objects of inventory, to be used as long as they work well and to be disposed of when they malfunction. *Night* describes this transformation. Early in the work, Wiesel says of himself that he "had become a completely different person." The work ends after the war. He has survived and has been liberated; he looks into the mirror and sees a corpse staring back at him. The corpse becomes part of his life, and the tension of his works rests upon separating himself from the corpse, which means finding a place for himself among the living and giving the corpse a proper burial in the form of a literary monument. Separating himself from the corpse is not an easy task. It involves personal, social, and theological issues: assuaging his own guilt for having survived and coming to terms with an indifferent society and an indifferent God, Who allowed the Holocaust to take place. His future works chart his attempt at reconciliation with life, reintegration into society, rediscovery of his religious heritage, and reaffirmation of his belief in God, in spite of everything. This is accomplished by the use of a dual character or alter ego. In each novel, the personality of the protagonist, a survivor of the Holocaust, is complemented by that of the antagonist, usually someone who was not directly involved in the war. They lead separate lives until their paths cross and their souls fuse. The antagonist then disappears; his existence is no longer necessary.

Within the biographical-historical-psychological framework of Wiesel's works are recurring metaphors, characters, and themes. The Holocaust, the overriding presence in Wiesel's oeuvre, is metaphorically night. The sealed, unlit boxcar bearing Wiesel and his townspeople arrived at Auschwitz at midnight. For the victims, night describes the abyss to which they were consigned; for the oppressors, it indicates the depravity of the soul; for the world, it represents the failure of enlightenment, the blackness in which the world was engulfed during the Holocaust period. For Wiesel, night is a physical and psychological condition. As a victim, he moved like a shadow through the kingdom of Death, communicating with corpses. As a survivor, the corpses still haunt him. In Auschwitz, time lost its significance, and night became the only frame of reference. Night continues to circumscribe the parameters of confinement for the protagonists in *The Town Beyond the Wall*, *The Gates of the Forest*, *A Beggar in Jerusalem*, *The Oath*, and *The Testament*.

The lasting effects of the devastation on the psyche are summed up by Wiesel in an incantatory paragraph which appears early in *Night*:

> Never shall I forget that night, the first night in camp which has turned my life into one long night, seven times cursed and seven times sealed. Never shall I forget that smoke. Never shall I forget the little faces of the children, whose bodies I saw turned into wreaths of smoke beneath a silent blue sky.

Having pledged never to forget, Wiesel makes memory an important aspect of all his writings. His characters, especially his protagonists, are haunted by their memories. Memory controls their lives and motivates their actions. It is also a bridge to their future.

Moché, the beadle of *Night*, survives the massacre of the first roundup of Jews and returns to Sighet to tell the tale and warn the others concerning their impending doom. The townspeople, however, refuse to believe him and think he has gone mad. Moché appears in every book; his role is usually that of messenger in the tale he tells. Madness is an essential element in all Wiesel's works. On the one hand, it is indicative of the malady that struck the world during the Holocaust years. Wiesel, however, treats his madmen sympathetically. Their madness is not clinical but mystical. They are visionaries, saints, or messengers, endowed with the task of saving the world. As such, they become one with humankind, God, and creation. Wiesel's point is that madness can be a force of evil or good. Hitler and his Nazis were mad. Their madness was employed to destroy the world. Most of Wiesel's madmen want to bring about the Messiah; they want to redeem the world.

Another theme that is paramount in Wiesel's works is that of silence. Wiesel's ten years of silence after his liberation afforded him the opportunity for reflection and meditation on past events and future actions. He followed a carefully conceived plan not to speak. It was not that he had nothing to say or that he was indifferent; his decision was prompted by the knowledge that no words could describe what had taken place. His silence was intended as an "eloquent silence, a screaming silence, a shouting silence." Wiesel broke his silence when he decided to write, and in each of his novels, excepting *The Town Beyond the Wall*, the protagonist is confronted with a similar problem and makes a similar decision. Related to the theme of silence is the theme of responsibility, which is expressed in breaking the silence.

To evoke accurately the ravaged soul of the survivor in the post-Holocaust world, Wiesel creates a society of characters different from those one is used to meeting in novels. The characters are beggars, witnesses, messengers, storytellers, and chroniclers.

THE TOWN BEYOND THE WALL

The Town Beyond the Wall, Wiesel's first novel after his three novellas, depicts his attempt to go home again. After his liberation from Buchenwald, Wiesel refused to return to his native town. He became, like the beggars or messengers in his stories, a *navenadnik*, a wanderer, a lost soul traveling throughout the world to find an inner peace and a place that he could call home. He traveled for ten years and finally, albeit accidentally, settled in the United States. It became home for him, however, only when he could totally and irrevocably sever his ties with his hometown. No matter where he went, he was drawn to the memories of his childhood, the familiarity and tranquillity of those days. He had to return at least once in order to realize that the Sighet of his youth no longer existed.

It was a journey, as Wiesel says, to "nothingness."

The Town Beyond the Wall is divided into four parts and is presented in a series of reveries which help the protagonist cope with the torture imposed upon him by his captors during his confinement in prison. Michael, a survivor of the Holocaust, has returned to his hometown of Szerencseváros with the aid of his friend, Pedro. The town is now under Communist rule, and he has entered it illegally. He is betrayed, imprisoned, and—because he remains silent and will not inform on his friend—is given the standard treatment, a torture called "The Prayer," which consists of keeping a prisoner on his feet facing a wall until he speaks or loses consciousness. In order to surmount the pain, Michael devises a method of transcending time by moving back and forth in his consciousness so that the present recedes to his subconscious level and the past moves forward into his consciousness. The reflections relating to his hometown are twice filtered, first as they are told to Pedro and then as he recalls them during his "prayers."

The pendular movement between different levels of consciousness, so that time is obliterated, is suggestive of Wiesel's imprisonment in the concentration camp. It is as if Wiesel is saying that time exists only in society. Once removed from society, people are also removed from time. In fact, they have no need for it. Time stops for them, but because time continues to move on for the world beyond their confinement, they will never be able to retrieve it.

Night hovers over *The Town Beyond the Wall*, as it hovered over Wiesel's first work. The protagonist is enveloped in a physical and psychological darkness. With his eyes closed, shutting out all light and consciousness, he evokes the nightmare world of his past, the fears of his childhood, his reflections on the Holocaust, the death of those who influenced him— Moché, the madman; Varady, his neighbor; Kalman, his teacher; his father; Yankel, his friend from the concentration camp—and the bleakness of life in France. An aspect of this nightmare world is his divided consciousness. This is suggested by the time and place in which he meets Pedro: in Tangiers, an hour before midnight in a dimly lit café, which is under a sign of a black cat. Pedro is his antagonist. He

is what Saul Bellow would call "the Spirit of Alternatives." They walk the city together late at night. Pedro listens to Michael, providing him with alternatives to his dilemmas, answers to his questions, and a *modus vivendi*. He is a good friend. Their identities, at the conclusion, fuse, and when Michael is imprisoned, Pedro disappears, living only in Michael's memory in the form of an attitude toward life.

Through his relationship with Pedro, Michael comes to realize that silence in the form of indifference is destructive. People affirm their humanity when they involve themselves with or share in the anguish of humankind. To be a spectator of life is to deny life. That was the reason for Michael's return to Szerencseváros. He wanted to confront the spectator, the man who watched his Jewish neighbors being humiliated, looked on as the children cried of thirst, and then turned his back without any expression of emotion. That is why, at the end of the novel, he decides that he must reach out to his cellmate, who has rejected the world and now exists as a mute on the periphery of life. Michael knows that by restoring an interest in existence to his silent companion, he is also asserting his own essence, giving meaning to his own life. Wiesel later expands on this theme in *The Oath*.

In *The Town Beyond the Wall*, silence is viewed as detrimental. In the opening section, when Michael reflects upon his childhood friendship with the renegade Varady, he notes that the community expresses its hatred for him through silence. In the next chapter, Michael's failure to respond to his friend's need results in Yankel's committing suicide. In the third section, Michael tells the tale of a mother and child who attempt to flee the Germans by hiding in the wagon of hay owned by a friendly neighbor who offers to take them to safety. He tells them that their lives depend on their being silent. Silence, however, did not help them; they were killed when the Hungarian officers repeatedly stuck their bayonets through the hay. In the conclusion, Michael's silence, while it may have saved the life of Pedro, may also have cost him his own life.

Wiesel expresses his own equivocation regarding silence in this novel. Words may betray, words may deceive, but speech remains the only expression of civilized people. Language, when properly used and properly understood, is instructive and a means of creating a bond between people. It may not save the world, but it may save one human being. This is the lesson Wiesel learned from Mauriac, which caused him to break his vow.

Madness is presented as the opposite of silence. One takes refuge in being mute, the other in being vocal. The silent one sees without responding; the madman sees and reacts, usually through the use of words which other characters cannot comprehend or which they refuse to comprehend. Wiesel elaborates on this theme in the scene at the insane asylum in *A Beggar in Jerusalem*. In *The Town Beyond the Wall*, Pedro prevents Michael from joining the cadre of madmen. He tells him, "To see liberty only in madness is wrong." Madness is seen as a force of evil in this work. Michael's cellmate is mad; he sees things that are not there and says things that do not make sense, and he finally attempts to kill a third cellmate, Menachem.

It is significant that *The Town Beyond the Wall* ends in the cell. Michael is still a prisoner of his past. He is reaching out toward others, attempting to find his own identity, but he has not yet been able to do so. Wiesel's next novel deals with this problem; each of his novels, excluding *The Testament*, charts his journey away from *Night*.

THE GATES OF THE FOREST

While *The Town Beyond the Wall* examines the possibility of going home and acknowledges the impossibility of doing so, *The Gates of the Forest* concentrates on retrieving a lost name and the identity that goes with it. This novel also begins with night and imprisonment. The opening setting is not a cell but a cave in the forest. It is springtime, with its intimations of rebirth and regeneration, but the war once again casts its shadowy reflection over the entire work. Gavriel, a seventeen-year-old Jewish youth, has escaped deportation and is hiding from the German and Hungarian police. He has assumed the name of Gregor to increase his chances of remaining alive. His father was with him in hiding but had gone in search of food three days earlier, and he has not re-

turned. Prior to his leaving, he had admonished his son not to break his silence and betray his whereabouts. A stranger, another Jew, makes his way to Gregor's hideout. The man has no name, and Gregor gives him his. The entire work is devoted to searching out the efficacy of silence and its relationship to an individual's identity.

The Gates of the Forest is also divided into four sections, alternating between the forest and the city. The first two sections establish the protagonist as a man of various masks. In the first section, he gives his name to a stranger who first jeopardizes and then saves his life. In section 2, he assumes two guises: that of a deaf-mute bastard child and that of the betrayer of Christ. After escaping from the forest, Gregor seeks refuge with Martha, the peasant woman who used to work for them. It is her idea that he disguise his identity and become the child of her wayward sister, Ileana. He assumes yet another identity in this village, when the school principal decides to stage a Passion play and bestows upon him the part of Judas. Section 2 concludes with Gregor proclaiming his true self—Gavriel. Now that he has pronounced his name, he has to labor at reclaiming his identity. The second half of the work is devoted to transforming the personality of Gregor into that of Gavriel: the estranged individual into a man of God. He does this by intimately relating to his own people and by refusing to be other than what he is. He joins a Jewish partisan group in the forest. When the war is ended, he meets Clara, who was also a partisan, and marries her. In New York, Gregor joins in a Hasidic celebration and gains an audience with a Hasidic Rebbe. He confronts him with all the problems that have afflicted him since the war, especially his inability to believe in God after what has happened. The Rebbe's answers provide him with a "gate" to the future. It is in the synagogue after his meeting with the Rebbe that Gavriel reclaims his name and his identity as a man of God.

The Rebbe and the stranger are Gregor's antagonists. The stranger at the beginning of the novel has the name Gavriel—"Man of God"; the Rebbe, at the end of the work, *is* the man of God. The stranger disappears early in the work, and Gregor's search for him proves futile. He thinks he sees Gavriel at the Rebbe's house of study, but it is an illusion, a dream. He sees, or dreams that he sees, only another stranger. He insists that the stranger listen to his story. The act of telling the story restores Gavriel's identity. He awakens from his dream knowing what he has to do: help Clara lay her ghosts to rest and restore his relationship with God. The work ends with his recitation of Kaddish, which, while it is a prayer for the dead, affirms the greatness of God. Once again, Wiesel concludes that silence is not a solution. Through the use of words, people not only speak to God but also become "messengers to heaven."

There is in this novel, as in all Wiesel's novels, much autobiographical detail. Wiesel, as Gavriel-Gregor, the storyteller, presents his attitude toward the Germans, the Christians, and Europe itself, as well as the humanism of his father, the mysticism of his childhood, the isolation and ignorance of the Jews of Transylvania regarding their fate, his inability to cry, his guilt as a survivor, his going to France immediately after the war, his becoming a journalist and traveling to North Africa, the Far East, and the United States, his refusal to say Kaddish upon the death of his father, and his inability to believe in a God who remained silent during the Holocaust. Above all, this work charts the author's slow but certain return to religion and the Hasidism of his childhood. The visits to the Hasidic Rebbe are autobiographical, as is the search for a master or teacher. Wiesel continues to study with a Talmudic master and maintains a close relationship with a Hasidic rebbe in Brooklyn, New York.

Night, in this work, is significant as a general obfuscation of identity. The novel begins at night, in the cave with the protagonist who bears an assumed name, and it concludes in the morning, as Gavriel finds himself. Madness is a force of evil. It connotes the failure of rationality and describes the malady of the times, the frenzy of the mob. It is a condition from which one must be saved. Clara is on the verge of madness, and Gregor attempts to rescue her. The masters (or teachers), the stranger Gavriel, and the Rebbe are storytellers, and storytellers always bear messages. Gregor is both witness and messenger. In

his role as Judas, he is witness to the madness of the peasants. Upon entering the partisan camp, he is a messenger bearing news from the outside, telling the group about the massacre of the townspeople. Later, he brings word of the death of Leib, leader of the partisans.

The work concludes in the season of winter with the ushering in of a new day. In its reconciliation with the past, the "gates of the forest" open onto a new life for Wiesel and his protagonists while not fully closing upon the darkened phase of his youth.

A BEGGAR IN JERUSALEM

A Beggar in Jerusalem is a difficult novel. It is lyric, mystical, sensitive, yet powerful. Written in a mood of ecstasy, the seven-hundred-page first draft was condensed to its present length of slightly more than two hundred pages.

A Beggar in Jerusalem was galvanized by two crucial events in Wiesel's post-Holocaust life: a trip to Israel in 1967 and his marriage in 1968. At the outbreak of the Six-Day War in 1967, between the Arabs and Israelis, with its threat of extermination of the Jews once again, Wiesel went to Israel as a journalist. This work captures and records a victorious moment in Jewish history, the reunification of Jerusalem and, with it, the securing of the Wailing Wall. It also transmits the texture of this experience, the significance that Jerusalem embodies for Wiesel and the Jewish people. It is an emotional presentation, communicating the yearning of a people, the fulfillment of dreams, the "returning" home to Jerusalem. Wiesel was married in 1968 in a synagogue near the Wall. The novel is also a dedication to his wife, Marion. As such, it looks backward into his past and forward into the future. Like *The Town Beyond the Wall* and *The Gates of the Forest*, it, too, is a quest. In this novel, the search is for a new being. Wiesel does not want to rid himself of his past; it becomes an integral part of his life. The new being has to integrate his past experiences with his present identity and his future with his wife.

Silence is not a major issue in this work. It is the telling of tales and memory that are paramount. *A Beggar in Jerusalem* shifts between time periods, suggesting that contemporary events are meaningful only in the perspective of history. The joy of conquest is tempered with the sadness of two millennia of Jewish suffering. As in all Wiesel's works, the Holocaust forms the background and molds and shapes the events of this hauntingly beautiful novel. It is a paean to Jerusalem, but it does not extol the victors. There is no gaiety, no victory celebration. It is a somber novel which concentrates on the anticipation and fear which precede war, acknowledges the human torment which follows war, and focuses on the collective responsibility of humankind.

The aftermath of war is not glorious; instead of heroes, the novel offers a strange array of beggars, vagabonds, madmen, and storytellers. All are Holocaust survivors who left the camps with nothing, had no home to which to go, were unwanted by everyone, and were treated like beggars everywhere—displaced persons whose lives take on meaning in the sharing of experiences. The beggars—Moché, the madman, among them—meet at night. They exchange tales of anguish as they debate God's justice and their own human condition.

David, the narrator of the work, is also a survivor of the Holocaust. As a representative of the past, he is the witness and the teller of tales. He interrupts the present tale of the Six-Day War with memories, the collective experiences of his people, and stories he has heard from others. He is a beggar and seeks out the company of other beggars, survivors like himself. This narrator-beggar ironically bears the name of the King of Israel, David. David's antagonist, Katriel, is an Israeli officer. He represents the present, a new generation which believes that it can alter its destiny. The work begins as a search for Katriel, who disappears after the war. David's and Katriel's stories move along separate lines, yet they are related. They meet during the war in the army camp and enter into a pact whereby they will remain together, each helping the other to conquer his fear. The survivor will bear witness for the other. They remain together for the war and the victory. They are together at the Wailing Wall, and both observe the custom of writing a wish on a piece of paper which is slipped into a crack in the wall. The destiny of the antagonists of *The Town Beyond the Wall* and *The Gates of the For-*

est befalls Katriel: He vanishes. No one knows what has happened to him. Actually, the personalities of Katriel and David have fused at the Wall in Jerusalem. The present has joined the past to create a new being. That David and Katriel are now one is suggested when David repeats to Malka, Katriel's wife, a story about a beggar told to him by Katriel. He then asks her, "But do you know who the beggar was? Sometimes I tell myself he was Katriel, he was I."

In this novel, Wiesel ends his quest. He no longer searches for a home. He has come to realize the validity of the words of a wandering preacher whom he met as a young boy—that all roads lead to Jerusalem. He also recalls the words of Katriel: "One doesn't go to Jerusalem, one returns to it." He no longer searches for identity or a new being; it has been reshaped by Jerusalem, "the city which miraculously transforms man into pilgrim; no one can enter it and go away unchanged." At the conclusion of *A Beggar in Jerusalem*, both the protagonist and his creator find that Jerusalem, the city of peace, is a concept one carries within oneself.

In *The Town Beyond the Wall* and *The Gates of the Forest*, the protagonists learn of the necessity to involve themselves in the life of other human beings. In *A Beggar in Jerusalem*, Wiesel moves from the single individual to the community: The beggars are comforted by the others in their group, Jewish people everywhere offer their support to the threatened Jewish state, and Israel wins the war, as the narrator states, with the aid of the six million who died.

THE OATH

Responsibility, both individual and collective, is the major theme of *The Oath*. In the works that preceded *The Oath*, especially *The Town Beyond the Wall* and *The Gates of the Forest*, the dramatic tension created by the desire for silence gave way to the practical need to speak, yet Wiesel continued to question his decision to speak. In *One Generation After*, he suggests that the horrors of the Holocaust might have been transmitted more eloquently and consequently more effectively by the abjuration of speech. Had the survivors "remained mute, their accumulated silences would have been unbearable: the impact would have deafened the world." *The Oath* addresses itself to this issue. It, too, is a personal statement in which Wiesel works out his own problems regarding his decision to break his vow of silence. *The Oath* seems to resolve the tensions created in the desire for silence, recognizing the futility of explanation and the need for speech. It does not, however, conclude Wiesel's concern with the issue, which he takes up once again in *The Testament*.

THE TESTAMENT

The Holocaust marked the destruction of East European Jewish life and culture. Not long after World War II, another area of Jewish culture was liquidated. On August 19, 1952, Stalin climaxed his infamous purge of Yiddish artists in the Soviet Union. On that day, thirty Yiddish writers were executed simply because they were Jewish. Hundreds more had been murdered earlier or were killed shortly afterward. These artists were consigned to oblivion, but Wiesel commemorates their achievements and bemoans their loss in *The Testament*. In so doing, he helps "the dead vanquish death."

Like Wiesel's earlier novels, *The Testament* is animated by the dramatic and dialectical tension between silence, or the "futility of all explanation," and the need to recount or bear witness. In this work, father and son are in opposition to each other. The father, Paltiel Kossover, an obscure poet, has substituted the god of Communism for the God of his forefathers, only to realize, too late, that his zeal is misdirected, that the new god has rejected him, and that his destiny is linked to his own people. This is the legacy he transmits to his son, in the form of a testament written in jail prior to his execution. The son, Grisha, a mute—he bit off his tongue so that he would not be able to testify against his father—reads the father's testament in an apartment in Jerusalem, to which he has come in 1972. The document was saved by a witness to the execution, Zupanev, a jailer who is determined not to allow Paltiel Kossover's memory to be obliterated.

The testament binds the present to the past, links the current tragedy to its historical predecessors. Zupanev says that Grisha, as a mute, is an "ideal messenger"—ideal because no one suspects him—who will be able to assimilate the events of the document

into his consciousness and then recount them to future generations. Grisha's role as an effective witness is diminished, nevertheless, by his inability to speak.

Among Wiesel's novels, *The Testament* is the harshest in outlook and the darkest in vision. All his other works end on a note of optimism. This one does not. Only the setting of Jerusalem illuminates the night of the novel. The work begins in hope, at the Lod airport, with the ingathering of the Russian exiles. It ends in death and in memory and indicates that Wiesel has little faith in the writer's ability to change humanity and human nature. It is his testament that "mankind didn't change." Nevertheless, Wiesel continues to write. One explanation for his persistence is suggested by the prologue to *The Testament*, which recounts an anecdote concerning a Just Man and his desire to correct injustice. He says: "In the beginning, I thought I could change man. Today, I know I cannot. If I still shout today, if I still scream, it is to prevent man from ultimately changing me."

THE FORGOTTEN

The Holocaust and its aftermath would remain powerful themes in Wiesel's writings, as he shows again in *The Forgotten*. The forgotten of the title refers to that which is forgotten as well as to he who is forgotten, for memory, remembrance, and mental and psychological forgetting are all important leitmotifs.

Professor Elhanan Rosenbaum, Malkiel's increasingly sick and senile father, is rapidly losing his memory. To hold on to his dissolving past, he sends Malkiel to his native Carpathian village to retrace the family origins, a mission for which the son is highly qualified. As a *New York Times* reporter, Malkiel specializes in the dead, whether the victims of the Cambodian killing fields or the mighty of the obituary page. In President Nicolae Ceausescu's Romania the reporter meets a philosophical Jewish gravedigger, who, through his tales told in the style of Hebraic storytellers, is both a witness of Nazi horrors and Jewish heroism and a repository of Jewish folklore and memory. Malkiel learns of his grandfather's self-sacrifice and of his father's courage and also of the fact that, as in so many German-occupied countries, most people actively participated in tracking and killing Jews or did nothing to save them. He also learns that the young Elhanan did not speak out while a comrade took revenge on their worst enemy by raping his widow, a silence that would haunt his father forever.

During lucid moments the father tells the son of his illegal entry into Palestine with Talia, his future wife, and of the intoxicating first days of Israel's independence, which symbolically and dramatically coincide with Malkiel's birth and Talia's death. Woven with the moving and passionate plea not to forget the dead are Malkiel's torturing liaisons with Inge the German and Leila the Arab, each of whom revives a special memory of hatred and pain. On the other hand, Tamar, his Jewish colleague and lover, presents him with a more difficult dilemma when she questions conduct and ethics of modern-day Israel.

Only through legends, stories, eyewitness accounts—in short, words—can one hope to triumph over forgetfulness and ultimately death itself. From the power of words the spinner of tales survives, and so does his message, however incomplete and lost in the fog of memory. To seize and reassemble those shattered fragments of Elhanan's failing memory, Wiesel uses various narrative devices—letters, flashbacks, journal entries, tape recordings, prayers, unspoken dialogues—complemented by parables taken from Hasidic and Talmudic scholars.

Beginning with the publication of *Night* in 1956, Wiesel established himself as the bard of the Holocaust. *The Forgotten*, though, shines with a luminosity that was often absent from his earlier works, as if Wiesel had come out of his own Night Kingdom, scathed of course, but also full of hope and optimism. All is remembered; nothing is forgotten: "Thanks to him [Elhanan's grandson yet to be born], I shall live on; thanks to you, Abraham lives."

L. H. Goldman, updated by Pierre L. Horn

OTHER MAJOR WORKS

SHORT FICTION: *Le Chant des Morts*, 1966 (essays and short stories; *Legends of Our Time*, 1968); *Entre deux soleils*, 1970 (essays and short stories; *One Generation After*, 1970); *Un Juif aujourd'hui*, 1977 (essays and short stories; *A Jew Today*, 1978).

PLAYS: *Zalmen: Ou, La Folie de Dieu*, pb. 1968 (*Zalmen: Or, The Madness of God*, 1974); *Le Procès de Shamgorod tel qu'il se déroula le 25 février 1649*, pb. 1979 (*The Trial of God: As It Was Held on February 25, 1649, in Shamgorod*, 1979).

NONFICTION: *Un di Velt hot geshvign*, 1956 (in Yiddish), 1958 (in French as *La Nuit*; *Night*, 1960); *Les Juifs du silence*, 1966 (travel sketch; *The Jews of Silence*, 1966); *Discours d'Oslo*, 1987; *Evil and Exile*, 1990; *From the Kingdom of Memory: Reminiscences*, 1990; *A Journey of Faith*, 1990 (with John Cardinal O'Connor); *Tous les fleuves vont à la mer*, 1994 (memoir; *All Rivers Run to the Sea*, 1995); *Mémoire à deux voix*, 1995 (*Memoir in Two Voices*, 1996); . . . *et la mer n'est pas remplie*, 1996 (memoir; *And the Sea Is Never Full*, 1999).

MISCELLANEOUS: *Célébration hassidique*, 1972 (biographical sketches and stories; *Souls on Fire*, 1972); *Ani Maamin: Un Chant perdu et retrouvé*, 1973 (cantata; *Ani Maamin: A Song Lost and Found Again*, 1973); *Célébration biblique*, 1975 (biographical sketches and stories; *Messengers of God: Biblical Portraits and Legends*, 1976); *Four Hasidic Masters and Their Struggle Against Melancholy*, 1978 (biographical sketches and stories); *Images from the Bible*, 1980 (biographical sketches and stories); *Five Biblical Portraits*, 1981 (biographical sketches and stories); *Paroles d'étranger*, 1982 (biographical sketches and stories); *Somewhere a Master*, 1982 (biographical sketches and stories); *Signes d'Exode*, 1985; *The Six Days of Destruction: Meditations Towards Hope*, 1988 (with Albert H. Friedlander); *Silences et mémoire d'hommes: Essais, histoires, dialogues*, 1989; *Sages and Dreamers: Biblical, Talmudic, and Hasidic Portraits and Legends*, 1991.

BIBLIOGRAPHY

Abramowitz, Molly, comp. *Elie Wiesel: A Bibliography*. Metuchen, N.J.: Scarecrow Press, 1974. Dated but still valuable annotated bibliography of works by and about Wiesel.

Berenbaum, Michael. *The Vision of the Void: Theological Reflections on the Works of Elie Wiesel*. Middletown, Conn.: Wesleyan University Press, 1979. Although discussing works published before 1979, this is an excellent study of the Jewish tradition as evident in Wiesel's religious writings.

Cargas, Harry James, ed. *Responses to Elie Wiesel.* New York: Persea Books, 1978. A perceptive collection of articles and book chapters that present specific aspects of Wiesel's thought and influence, including those on the non-Jewish world.

Estess, Ted L. *Elie Wiesel.* New York: Frederick Ungar, 1980. Despite its brevity, this general introduction is well argued and often insightful.

Patterson, David. *In Dialogue and Dilemma with Elie Wiesel.* Wakefield, N.H.: Longwood Academic, 1991. In a series of fascinating interviews, Wiesel speaks not only about the Holocaust but also about his audience, his craft, and his mission as a writer and witness.

Rittner, Carol, ed. *Elie Wiesel: Between Memory and Hope.* New York: New York University Press, 1990. A balanced collection of provocative essays, written by scholars from different disciplines.

Sibelman, Simon P. *Silence in the Novels of Elie Wiesel.* New York: St. Martin's Press, 1995. This study of a dominant theme in Wiesel is thorough, intelligent, and stimulating.

Stern, Ellen Norman. *Elie Wiesel: Witness for Life.* New York: Ktav Publishing House, 1982. A fine and useful biography that deals more with the man than with his writings.

OSCAR WILDE

Born: Dublin, Ireland; October 16, 1854
Died: Paris, France; November 30, 1900

PRINCIPAL LONG FICTION

The Picture of Dorian Gray, 1890 (serial), 1891 (expanded)

OTHER LITERARY FORMS

Oscar Wilde wrote in a number of literary forms. His earliest works were poems published in various journals and collected in a volume entitled *Poems* in 1881. His later and longer poems, including *The Sphinx* (1894), were occasionally overwrought or contrived, but his final published poem, *The Ballad of Reading Gaol* (1898), is regarded by many as a masterpiece. Wilde wrote two collections of fairy tales, *The Happy Prince and Other Tales* (1888) and *A House of Pomegranates* (1891). He wrote several plays, most notably the comedies *Lady Windermere's Fan* (1892), *A Woman of No Importance* (1893), the successful farce *The Importance of Being Earnest* (1895), and the controversial and temporarily banned *Salomé* (1893). Finally, Wilde wrote a few short stories, including "The Canterville Ghost" (1887) and "Lord Arthur Savile's Crime" (1887).

ACHIEVEMENTS

Oscar Wilde's works remain popular a century after his death. This is due in part to the enduring beauty of his poetry and his prose, as well as the timeless insight he offers about art and morality. Wilde's conclusions are presented with such easy elegance and wit that readers enjoy the seduction of the narrative. No doubt Wilde's provocative statements and iconoclastic poses, as well as the notoriety of his trial, helped to immortalize his life and thus to sustain interest in his writings for generations. Wilde received Trinity College's Berkeley Gold Medal for Greek in 1874, and he won the Newdigate Prize for Poetry in 1878.

BIOGRAPHY

Oscar Wilde was born to ambitious, successful Irish parents in Dublin in 1854. As a young man he attended Trinity College, and in 1874 (at age twenty) he entered Magdalen College, Oxford, on a scholarship. Wilde was drawn to art criticism and literature in his studies, and he was strongly influenced by several mentors, most notably writers John Ruskin and Walter Pater. At college Wilde discovered, developed, and began to refine his extraordinary gifts of creativity, analysis, and expression. These he pressed into the service of aestheticism, an iconoclastic artistic movement promoted by Pater, which advocated "the love of art for art's sake." Wilde would come to personify aestheticism, with all its intellectual refine-

(Library of Congress)

social functions he so frequently attended, that gained for him sustained public attention. Wilde was a gifted speaker with a keen sense of timing and an ability to lampoon societal standards with his humorous remarks.

The Victorian public's amusement with Wilde's contrarianism turned to contempt in 1895. In this year the Marquis of Queensberry, furious over the writer's continuing relationship with his son, accused Wilde of being a "sodomite." Wilde ill-advisedly sued for libel, maintaining that he was not, in fact, homosexual. The Marquis, to support his claim about Wilde's homosexuality, entered into court various letters and other pieces of evidence. When Queensberry's lawyer was about to produce as witnesses young male prostitutes who had had sexual relations with Wilde, Wilde's lawyer withdrew from the suit. Queensberry was acquitted by the jury. Almost immediately after the trial, Wilde was arrested for violation of England's sodomy laws. By now the public had all but deserted Wilde, and after his conviction even most of his friends disavowed him. Wilde spent two years in prison for his offenses.

Upon his release from prison in 1897 Wilde left England to live in exile, finally locating in Paris. He lived under the alias Sebastian Melmoth, attempting to expunge his notoriety as the humiliated Oscar Wilde. Yet his spirits and his health had been broken by his prison sentence, and Wilde died within three years, at age forty-six.

ment, provocative posing, and hedonistic excess.

Wilde married Constance Lloyd in 1884 and with her had two sons. Although throughout his short life Wilde evinced great love and devotion to his wife and sons, he grew increasingly involved in sexual liaisons with men. Most notably and tragically, Wilde became engrossed in an obsessive and rocky homosexual friendship with Lord Alfred Douglas, the son of the Marquis of Queensberry. Douglas helped to lead Wilde deeper into London's homosexual underworld. While Douglas at times seemed to genuinely love Wilde, he periodically became impatient, selfish, and abusive toward his older friend. Still, Wilde remained, with increasing recklessness, committed to Douglas.

During the second half of the 1880's Wilde wrote poems, plays, and stories with increasing success. To a large extent, however, it was his provocative and radical remarks, made at public lectures and at the

Analysis

Wilde began his literary efforts with poetry, which was a common approach in his day. He published *Ravenna*, in 1878. He would write little poetry after the release of *Poems* in 1881. For the next several years he gave lectures in Europe and America, establishing his name on both sides of the Atlantic. He also assumed the editorship of a monthly magazine, *The Lady's World*, which was rechristened *The Woman's World*.

In the late 1880's Wilde wrote two collections of fairy tales, as well as a number of short stories, essays, and book reviews. He steadily gained attention as a writer, social critic, and, most of all, aesthete. Literary critics frequently were unenthusiastic, or even hostile, toward his works, finding them to be overly contrived or recklessly immoral. It is true that Wilde's writing can at times assume a baroque ornamentation and artificiality. There is no doubt that Wilde's characteristic indolence (which he exaggerated for show) constrained his ability to see his works through to the final stages of editing and polishing. It is true also that Wilde's writing frequently ridiculed social conventions, mores, and morals. Yet Wilde was indisputably an ingenious analyst of art and culture, possessing a mastery of prose and verse, and equipped with a keen sense of paradox.

THE PICTURE OF DORIAN GRAY

Oscar Wilde's only novel was published in its complete form in 1891. It is not a long book, and some of its features reflect the writer's haste or carelessness. However, the story is a fascinating and engaging one, at once depicting basic elements of human nature and conjuring fantastic, almost gothic images. Its plot is rather simple, but the ideas and issues that the narrative presents are complex and even profound. Perhaps for this reason the book has stood the test of time.

The story centers on three figures: an artist (Basil Hallward), his clever but impudent friend (Lord Henry Wotton), and a young, attractive, and impressionable man (Dorian Gray). Basil paints a full-length portrait of young Dorian and presents it to him as a gift. Lord Henry, who meets Dorian for the first time at Basil's studio, talks at length about the supreme value, but transience, of youth. Immediately drawn to Lord Henry's theories, Dorian observes the just-completed portrait of himself and remarks on "how sad it is" that he "shall grow old, and horrible, and dreadful. But this picture will remain always young. . . . If it were only the other way!" In the first section of the book, therefore, Wilde sets up a framework to examine some fundamental ideas about art and beauty: the transience of beauty, the inevitability of aging and death, the goal of the artist to "capture" beauty in art, and the corruptive influence of ideas, among others.

Wilde uses Lord Henry whom Wilde later declared to be a depiction of how the public perceived

Wilde—to provide the corruptive theories and ideas. Throughout the book Lord Henry utters clever aphorisms and paradoxes in Wilde's celebrated wordplay. Dorian is infatuated by Lord Henry and appears receptive to his theories and values. Readers soon see evidence of the corruptive influence of those theories and values in Dorian's behavior. Dorian becomes smitten by a young actress in a seedy theater. He returns with Basil and Lord Henry to watch her perform, but this time he is disappointed by her acting. After the performance the actress declares to Dorian that he has helped her see how false is her world of acting—the false world of the stage—and she declares her love for him. Dorian, however, spitefully dismisses her, claiming that she had thrown away her artistic genius and poetic intellect. Now, she "simply produce(s) no effect."

Upon returning home, Dorian observes a slight change in the portrait Basil had painted of him. Dorian notes a "touch of cruelty in the mouth." It becomes evident that the painting shows the outward signs of sin and of aging, while Dorian himself does not change appearance. Although first horrified by this, Dorian eventually learns to take advantage of the situation. The narrative traces an ever-worsening degradation of Dorian Gray's soul. He lives for sensations and self-gratification, without regard for the consequences of his actions upon others. He is seemingly unbound by any sense of morality—indeed, the very notion of violating moral strictures seems to be an attractive prospect for him. Near the climax of the story Dorian goes so far as to murder Basil.

The story thus raises provocative questions about morality and self-imposed restraint. If a person could be assured that any indulgences, including gluttony, sexual abandon, and avarice, would have no effect upon one's earthly body, would self-control survive? What opportunities and temptations are imposed upon one who possesses unusual and eternal beauty? What is the relationship between virtue and constraint? What are the consequences of unexposed moral degradation? Indeed, what are the causes of immorality?

The Picture of Dorian Gray aroused enormous indignation in Wilde's contemporaries, and it was treated especially harshly by most critics. There seemed to be a consensus that the book itself was immoral, that it could corrupt readers, and that it somehow promoted decadent behavior. Yet one can easily arrive at the opposite conclusion. The story clearly emphasizes the costs of self-indulgent, immoral behavior. It literally shows this in the changes that appear in the painting, which is understood to portray the condition of Dorian's soul. The story also makes a point of noting the harm done to others by Dorian's misbehavior: reputations ruined, hearts broken, suicides induced, murders committed. In no way does the book portray the corruption of Dorian Gray in a glamorous or seductive way. Instead, the effect is to repulse the reader.

The book might be somewhat corruptive in its suggestion that immorality may be less a choice than simply a product of circumstances. We have no reason to believe that Dorian Gray is intrinsically evil; rather, if the book's basic premise that one's soul is normally reflected in one's appearance, then the introduction of Dorian as possessing "youth's passionate purity" conveys the idea that he is especially innocent. Ironically, Wilde himself was accused of corrupting a young man (Lord Alfred Douglas), and his writings (including *The Picture of Dorian Gray*) were held up as evidence of his dangerous ideas. That Wilde responded that he believed there was no such thing as an immoral book, only a badly written one, compounds the irony.

The fatalistic view of sin (which might be consistent with Wilde's religious upbringing, such as it was) is further evidenced when Dorian is unable to change his course toward the end of the book. He feels his past starting to catch up with him as people he has wronged, or their defenders, begin to identify him and his actions. Resolving to abandon his ways, Dorian decides to do a good deed; he cancels an arranged plan to go off with (and undoubtedly take advantage of) a young female acquaintance. Yet when he subsequently examines the portrait for evidence of his good deed, he detects only a smirk of hypocrisy.

In a conclusion laden with symbolism, Dorian considers his situation hopeless. He reflects that "there [is] a God who called upon men to tell their sins to earth as well as to heaven." Yet he cannot fathom how he could ever confess his sins, and he recognizes that even his attempt to do good sprung from a hypocritical desire to experience new sensations. In desperation, he decides to drive a knife into the loathsome painting, which reflects all his sins. The servants downstairs hear a scream, and when they enter the room they see the portrait, restored to its original beauty, hanging on the wall. Dorian Gray lies on the floor with a knife in his heart, looking just as the figure in the loathsome portrait had moments earlier.

The conclusion creates a striking and stark symmetry, although how it answers the questions raised earlier is unclear. Still, the ending is satisfying in that it allows reality to finally come out of hiding. The parallels to Wilde's life are exceptional. While Wilde noted that the character of the languid iconoclast Lord Henry reflected how people viewed Wilde, he also asserted that it was the artist, Basil, whom Wilde actually resembled, and that it was Dorian himself whom Wilde wanted to be.

Steve D. Boilard

OTHER MAJOR WORKS

SHORT FICTION: "The Canterville Ghost," 1887; *The Happy Prince and Other Tales*, 1888; *The House of Pomegranates*, 1891; *Lord Arthur Savile's Crime and Other Stories*, 1891.

PLAYS: *Vera: Or, The Nihilists*, pb. 1880; *The Duchess of Padua*, pb. 1883, *Lady Windermere's Fan*, pr. 1892; *Salomé*, pb. 1893 (in French, pb. 1894 (in English); *A Woman of No Importance*, pr. 1893; *An Ideal Husband*, pr. 1895; *The Importance of Being Earnest: A Trivial Comedy for Serious People*, pr. 1895; *A Florentine Tragedy*, pr. 1906 (one act; completed by T. Sturge More); *La Sainte Courtisane*, pb. 1908.

POETRY: *Ravenna*, 1878; *Poems*, 1881; *Poems in Prose*, 1894; *The Sphinx*, 1894; *The Ballad of Reading Gaol*, 1898.

NONFICTION: *Intentions*, 1891; *De Profundis*, 1905; *Letters*, 1962 (Rupert Hart-Davies, editor).

MISCELLANEOUS: *Works*, 1908; *Complete Works of Oscar Wilde*, 1948 (Vyvyan Holland, editor); *Plays, Prose Writings, and Poems*, 1960.

BIBLIOGRAPHY

Calloway, Stephen, and David Colvin. *Oscar Wilde: An Exquisite Life*. New York: Welcome Rain, 1997. A brief, heavily illustrated presentation of Wilde's life.

Ellmann, Richard. *Oscar Wilde*. New York: Alfred A. Knopf, 1988. A biography of Wilde, drawing much insight from Wilde's published works. The book is extensively documented and footnoted and makes use of many of Wilde's writings and recorded conversations. Includes bibliography and appendices.

Hardwick, Michael. *The Drake Guide to Oscar Wilde*. New York: Drake, 1973. A description, with excerpts, of a number of Wilde's writings. Also includes a brief biography and an alphabetical index of descriptions of the major characters in the stories and plays.

Harris, Frank. *Oscar Wilde*. New York: Carrol and Graf, 1997. A biography written by one of Wilde's dedicated friends. Although hardly an objective work, Harris's book, written in the first person, provides details and insights about Wilde's life that many books do not.

Hyde, H. Montgomery. *Oscar Wilde: A Biography*. New York: Farrar, Straus & Giroux, 1975. Detailed discussion of Wilde's life, with emphasis on his trials and his exile. Many passages in this book draw upon published essays, poems, letters, and even testimony at Wilde's trial. Includes bibliography.

(Library of Congress)

THORNTON WILDER

Born: Madison, Wisconsin; April 17, 1897
Died: Hamden, Connecticut; December 7, 1975

PRINCIPAL LONG FICTION

The Cabala, 1926
The Bridge of San Luis Rey, 1927
The Woman of Andros, 1930
Heaven's My Destination, 1934
The Ides of March, 1948
The Eighth Day, 1967
Theophilus North, 1973

OTHER LITERARY FORMS

Thornton Wilder is as well known for his plays as for his fiction. *Our Town* (1938), *The Merchant of Yonkers* (1938, revised as *The Matchmaker*, 1954), and *The Skin of Our Teeth* (1942) are some of his best known. Collections of his short plays were published in *The Angel That Troubled the Waters and Other Plays* (1928) and *The Long Christmas Dinner and Other Plays in One Act* (1931). *A Life in the Sun,* commonly known as *The Alcestiad*, was published in 1955, and a collection of his essays, *American Characteristics and Other Essays*, was published in 1979. A set of cullings from his diaries, *The Journals of Thornton Wilder, 1939-1961*, was released in 1985.

ACHIEVEMENTS

Wilder began his career as a teacher and in a sense never gave up the practice of that profession. He attempted to persuade generations of readers of the power of love, the need for individual integrity, the importance of maintaining faith in people's essential goodness. His clear style and straightforward narrative earned for him a broad readership, transcending categories of age, class, or education. Though detractors have labeled him middle class and middlebrow, he received enthusiastic praise throughout his career from such critics as Edmund Wilson, Malcolm Cowley, Edmund Fuller, Henry Seidel Canby, and John Updike. Wilder has been less a subject of scholarly research than some of his contemporaries—F. Scott Fitzgerald and Ernest Hemingway, for example—yet he has remained widely read since his first novel was published in 1926, and his versatility as a writer—of two Pulitzer-Prize-winning full-length plays and dozens of short plays—has brought him worldwide recognition.

Wilder won a Pulitzer Prize for fiction in 1928, the first National Medal for Literature in 1964, and a National Book Award in 1967, besides being the recipient of several honorary doctorates.

BIOGRAPHY

Thornton Niven Wilder was born in Madison, Wisconsin, on April 17, 1897, the son of Amos Parker Wilder and Isabella Thornton Niven Wilder. His father, a newspaper editor, moved the family to Hong Kong in 1906 when he was assigned a diplomatic post there. The young Wilder attended the Kaiser Wilhelm School, then the China Inland Mission Boys' School, where he harbored a brief desire to become a missionary himself. When his family returned to the United States, settling in California, he continued his education at the Thacher School in Ojai, then Berkeley High School, where he first be-

gan to write plays and act in class productions. In 1915, he entered Oberlin, a school his father chose because it was less socially elite than his own alma mater, Yale. At Oberlin, Wilder continued his involvement in theatrical productions and contributed prolifically to the college's literary magazine. After two years there, Wilder was allowed by his father to enroll at Yale, where, after a period of homesickness for Oberlin, he again proved himself, in the words of professor and literary critic William Lyon Phelps, to be "a star of the first magnitude . . . unusually versatile, original, and clever." Wilder was graduated with no specific career goals in mind. His father, believing a European experience would be broadening, sent him to study at the American Academy in Rome for a summer. Meanwhile, he searched for a suitable job for his son and found one at Lawrenceville, a preparatory school in New Jersey. There, when his French classes were over, Wilder began a novel with the working title *Memoirs of a Roman Student*, to be published as *The Cabala* in 1926. In the same year, Wilder took advantage of Lawrenceville's proximity to Princeton to earn his master of arts degree. He took a year's leave of absence from teaching and began work on a new novel, *The Bridge of San Luis Rey*, published to enormous acclaim in 1927, and earning Wilder his first Pulitzer Prize.

In 1929, Wilder was invited to teach at the University of Chicago by an Oberlin classmate, Robert Hutchins, who had just been named president of the prestigious Illinois university. Wilder was writing intensely: *The Woman of Andros* was published in 1930, a collection of short plays in 1931, and *Heaven's My Destination* in 1934. He remained at the University of Chicago until the mid-1930's, teaching one semester and writing during the next. More and more, he was drawn to the theater. He completed *The Merchant of Yonkers*, later revised as *The Matchmaker* (and still later transformed into the Broadway musical *Hello, Dolly!*) in 1937 and then turned to a more serious play, *Our Village*, soon retitled *Our Town*. This play was met with great enthusiasm when it opened in New York in 1938 and earned Wilder his second Pulitzer Prize.

The political upheaval in Europe, soon to involve

America, found its way into Wilder's next play, *The Skin of Our Teeth*, which evoked a deep response in audiences both in the United States and abroad; the play was awarded a Pulitzer Prize in 1942. Wilder served in the army during World War II, and emerged with his optimism intact and his faith in humanity unshaken.

In the late 1940's, Wilder again turned to fiction, dealing with the problem of authority and dictatorship in *The Ides of March*. This novel reflected his talks with Gertrude Stein, whom Wilder had met in 1934 when Stein was lecturing at the University of Chicago. They shared ideas on the problem of identity and the creation of a believable reality for readers. Stein attempted to deal with these problems in her own book, *Ida, a Novel* (1941); Wilder took as his subject Julius Caesar.

In 1950, Wilder delivered the Charles Eliot Norton lectures at Harvard, then traveled—always a stimulation and joy for him—and worked on *The Alcestiad*, his retelling of the Greek legend of Alcestis. In the early 1960's, he retreated to Arizona to write *The Eighth Day*. By the end of the decade, his pace had slowed. He worked on short plays and completed his quasi-autobiographical *Theophilus North*. He died in his sleep on December 7, 1975.

ANALYSIS

Thornton Wilder's seven novels, written over nearly fifty years, show a remarkable consistency in theme and tone. His early books, contemporaneous with Theodore Dreiser's *An American Tragedy* (1925) and Sinclair Lewis's *Arrowsmith* (1925), are far from the realism and naturalism which dominated American literature in the 1920's and 1930's. Though he joined groups active in civil rights and social justice, these themes did not find their way into his works in the manner of John Dos Passos or John Steinbeck. His later works, similarly, show none of the interest in psychoanalysis which may be found in the works of Sherwood Anderson, for example, none of the angry intensity of a Norman Mailer.

Wilder chose not to comment on contemporary politics, social problems, psychological angst, or cultural changes, preferring instead to mine those

themes he considered of utmost importance: love, brotherhood, tolerance, and faith. His faith was expressed not in strictly Judeo-Christian terms, but in humanistic convictions which incorporated diverse religious beliefs. Without being didactic, Wilder wished to educate, to inspire, to allow his readers to move beyond an obsession with the individual case to a consideration of humankind and its history. His second novel, *The Bridge of San Luis Rey*, is representative of the themes which recur throughout his works, and his final statement in that book well expresses his one abiding conviction: "There is a land of the living and a land of the dead and the bridge is love, the only survival, the only meaning."

THE CABALA

Though Wilder drew on his memories of Rome for his first novel, *The Cabala*, the book is a fantasy, only incidentally autobiographical. The "Cabala" is an aristocratic social circle in which two Americans find themselves involved. These two, Samuele and James Blair, represent Wilder's interest in duality of personality which recurs in later works and results in part from his having been born a twin (his sibling was stillborn). Samuele is a typical Wilder character: innocent, sensitive, stable, with a deep strain of common sense. Blair is the dry intellectual so obsessed by books that he fears real life.

Samuele is the vehicle by which a number of episodes are linked, since he is asked by various members of the Cabala to intervene in the lives of others. First, he is called in to restrain the impetuous and licentious Marcantonio, but fails: The young man engages in incest and then kills himself. Then, Samuele must console the lovely young Alix, unfortunate enough to fall in love with James Blair. Finally, he must deal with the royalist Astrée-Luce in her plot to "prop up" and empower cynical Cardinal Vaini. Samuele is baffled by these obsessed and decadent characters, and is hardly satisfied by an explanation offered to him that the group is possessed by ancient gods who have passed on their power to unsuspecting mortals. Finally, on advice from Vergil's ghost, Samuele returns to America. For Wilder, Europe, for all its richness of culture, was too deeply mired in the past to allow the spirit to grow. Samuele could thrive only in America, a country of youth and intellectual freedom.

THE BRIDGE OF SAN LUIS REY

In his second novel, *The Bridge of San Luis Rey*, Wilder again uses a structure of separate episodes linked by one thread, this time the collapse of an ancient bridge over a chasm in Peru. Again, he offers a religious figure, but instead of the jaded Cardinal, there is the sympathetic brother Juniper, who searches for meaning in the deaths of those who perished: the Marquesa de Montemayor; Pepita, her maid; Esteban, a young Indian; Uncle Pio, an aging actor, and his ward Jaime. Brother Juniper finds that the five were victims of love, and those who survive are forced to a change of consciousness by the deaths of those they spurned or misjudged.

As in *The Cabala*, Wilder explores twinness in the tale of Esteban and his twin brother Manuel. The two are extraordinarily close, and when Manuel falls in love with a woman, Esteban becomes despondent. Yet he nurses his brother faithfully after Manuel is injured, suffering his delirious ravings until Manuel dies. Nearly mad with grief, Esteban first assumes his dead brother's identity, then attempts suicide, only to die when the bridge collapses. A sea captain, Alvarado, had offered to sign him on his crew, and tried to console him by reminding him, "We do what we can. We push on, Esteban, as best we can. It isn't for long, you know. Time keeps going by. You'll be surprised at the way time passes." Wilder was always conscious of the brevity of life and the need, therefore, to cling to love where one finds it. In *The Bridge of San Luis Rey*, he urges the celebration and fulfillment of love as the only meaning in the world.

THE WOMAN OF ANDROS

From eighteenth century Peru, Wilder moved to pre-Christian Greece in his third novel, *The Woman of Andros*, again dealing with love; its theme, as in *The Bridge of San Luis Rey*, is "How does one live? . . . What does one do first?" Society on the island of Brynos was not essentially different, according to Wilder, from that of his own America. When Chrysis, the central character, says "Lift every roof, and you will find seven puzzled hearts," she speaks of people's bewilderment in the face of the unknown, their search for communion, their need for love—basic human struggles which are not rooted in any particular time or place.

In 1930, however, a number of critics were disappointed with this message. In a time of economic and social crisis, Wilder seemed to retreat into yet another esoteric setting, far removed from the urgencies of the day. One critic writing in *The New Republic* dubbed Wilder a "Prophet of the Genteel Christ" who wrote for a wealthy elite not interested in social problems. The article touched off a month of debate, with letters supporting or attacking Wilder appearing in each issue of the journal. At the end of December, Wilder finally received his greatest support when Sinclair Lewis, accepting the Nobel Prize for Literature, praised his fellow writer "who in an age of realism dreams the old and lovely dreams of the eternal romantic."

HEAVEN'S MY DESTINATION

Throughout the controversy, Wilder remained silent. He was sensitive to the criticism, however, and in his next novel attempted to find a setting and characters which would appear relevant to his own time. *Heaven's My Destination* concerns the misadventures of George Marvin Brush, a salesman of religious textbooks, who travels across Depression-ridden America preaching, moralizing, and interfering in the lives of ordinary citizens. Converted to Bible Belt Christianity by a woman evangelist at Shiloh Baptist College, he has proceeded to spread his own fundamentalist version of the Gospel wherever he goes. Wilder returned to the episodic structure of his first two novels in presenting George's adventures in picaresque form. Unlike Don Quixote, however, with whom George has been compared, Wilder's protagonist is rarely endearing, more often exasperating.

George is different from the "normal" Americans with whom he interacts, yet Wilder is satirizing not only his earnest hero, but also those who spurn him. George, after a while, becomes depressed by his society and exclaims, "It's the world that's crazy. Everybody's crazy except me; that's what's the matter. The whole world's nuts." Why, asks this ardent believer, is God "so slow" in changing things?

For all his misconceptions, George does act upon truly humanistic beliefs. He takes a vow of poverty and occasionally of silence, refuses his interest from the bank and dislikes raises in pay. "I think everybody ought to be hit by the depression equally," he says, as he gives away his money. Like Samuele, George maintains his integrity in an environment which threatens to corrupt him and is selfless in his efforts to aid those who need him—even if they protest against his interference.

George Brush was Wilder's answer to the critics who dismissed his previous works, and in a sense, he gave them what he thought they deserved—a priggish, monomaniacal American overreacting to mundane occurrences. Even with such a cartoon-strip character, however, Wilder could not help but imbue him with gentleness and humility, and for Edmund Wilson, George Brush emerged as a "type of saint . . . and therefore a universal character."

In part, it was George's earnestness, his reluctance to see evil and his determination to do good, that caused Wilder to exclaim, "I'm George Brush." Certainly his persistent faith in humanity unites him with his character, but there is further correspondence in Brush's essential isolation, the loneliness which causes him to reach out for companionship. For Wilder, such isolation was characteristically American; solitude was to be treasured, but loneliness was threatening. He once noted an adage which he thought well expressed the American spirit: "If you can see the smoke from your neighbor's chimney, you're too near." In his next novel, thirteen years later, he created yet another lonely, questing character, but this time Wilder eschewed satire and humor to deal seriously with people powerful before the world, yet powerless before death.

THE IDES OF MARCH

The Ides of March, written just after World War II, deals with an archetypal dictator, Julius Caesar. Here, Wilder aimed to revive the spirit of the man from a palimpsest of historical and fictional treatments. The novel, therefore, becomes a study in identity and a technical challenge in creating for readers a believable reality. In structure, *The Ides of March* differs sharply from Wilder's previous work. He assembles fictionalized letters, diary entries, messages, and documents in an effort to offer a vibrant picture of Roman life. Caesar himself is a man obsessed not only with power but also with death, and he must learn how to celebrate life faced with a dark world and an uncaring universe.

Wilder contrasts Caesar with his friend and counselor Lucius Turrinus, who offers a philosophy which was by then familiar to Wilder's readers: "The universe is not aware that we are here," Lucius tells Caesar. "Hope has never changed tomorrow's weather." Yet love could change the world, and Caesar comes to exclaim, "I wish to cry out to all the living and all the dead that there is not part of the universe that is untouched by bliss."

Caesar's urge to seize life and live it to the fullest causes his companions to label him rash and irreverent; but he feels himself to be above them because he has clearly envisioned his own death, and in so doing believes himself "capable of praising the sunlight." Wilder transfers to the Roman dictator much of the sentiment expressed in his play *Our Town*, where Emily Webb dies and is allowed to return to Earth for one day. Only then does she realize how wonderful life is, how desperately she wants to live, and how foolish most people are in squandering their brief existence. Caesar refuses to be foolish; perhaps he will be ruthless, impetuous, temperamental, passionate—but he will live each moment.

The Ides of March had two major inspirations: the war itself, with its focus on the use and misuse of power, the character of a dictator, and the death of innocents; and a personal confrontation with death—first that of Wilder's friend and mentor Edward Sheldon, a playwright whose character informs Lucius Turrinus, and upon whose wisdom Wilder often relied; then, and most important, the death of his mother, his most ardent supporter and admirer.

THE EIGHTH DAY

After *The Ides of March* was published, Wilder devoted nearly two decades to his plays; not until 1967 would he write another novel. In *The Eighth Day*, Wilder returned to an American setting, the turn-of-the-century Midwest, and to traditional narrative. He carefully unfolds the tale of John Barrington Ashley, tried for the murder of his neighbor, Breckenridge Lansing, and found guilty. Five days after being sentenced to death, he escapes with the help of an unknown accomplice. Five years later, Ashley is found innocent on the basis of new evidence. Ashley's flight, which takes him to Chile, is contrasted with the life of his wife and children in a small town which barely tolerates the outlaw's family.

Wilder's concern, however, is not with one family's history, but with the archetypal family, and Ashley represents not one wronged citizen, but the man of the Eighth Day, a new man with faith in humanity and a strong commitment to working toward a better future. Wilder tells his readers that faith and action can bring about a better life. Throughout the novel, he assigns several characters to speak for him, most notably Dr. Gillies, a country physician, who observes:

> Nature never sleeps. The process of life never stands still. The creation has not come to an end. The Bible says that God created people on the sixth day and rested, but each of those days was many millions of years long. That day of rest must have been a short one. Man is not an end but a beginning. We are at the beginning of the second week. We are children of the eighth day.

On the eighth day, people must begin to forge their own futures, and though Dr. Gillies knows that there will be "no Golden Ages and no Dark Ages," still he believes in the power of each individual to work toward the collective fate of humankind.

Because the novel is concerned essentially with imparting a message, the characters—as in *The Cabala* and *Heaven's My Destination*—are not fully realized individuals, but instead are one-dimensional representations of predictable types. The Ashley family, ignored and rebuffed by their neighbors, never lose their aristocratic elegance. They persist in their nightly reading of William Shakespeare even when economic problems would seem severe enough to lower their morale. Here, Wilder pleads for art as the true salvation of humankind, its highest achievement, "the only satisfactory products of civilization."

Through Dr. Gillies, who echoes the sentiments of Chrysis in *The Woman of Andros* and Lucius in *The Ides of March*, Wilder reminds his readers that they occupy only a brief span of time when contrasted with eternity and so must exhibit proper humility. They are small specks in a vast universe, and their duty is not to enhance their own egos, but to work together toward a higher good. "We keep saying that 'we live our lives,'" Dr. Gillies exclaims. "Shucks! Life lives us." Wilder had sent this message for forty years; he insisted again, in the turbulent, self-conscious, self-indulgent late 1960's, on attempting to awaken his readers to his own values.

THEOPHILUS NORTH

Wilder was seventy when *The Eighth Day* was published, the time of a writer's life when he might consider writing his autobiography or memoirs. Wilder, however, chose not to reveal his memories or bare his soul; instead, he wrote a last novel, *Theophilus North*, with a protagonist, he once told an interviewer, who was what his twin brother might have been if he had lived.

Theophilus may be Wilder's imaginary brother, but his life bears striking similarities to that of Wilder himself. He has lived in China, attended Yale, and spent a summer in Rome; after teaching at a boys' preparatory school in New Jersey, he leaves his job to explore life and goes to Newport, Rhode Island—a town where Wilder often vacationed—to set his new course. Like Samuele, Theophilus is gentle, well mannered, polite, helpful. These traits endear him to the Newport natives, and he is asked to intervene in several lives. The structure here, as in many previous Wilder novels, is one of loosely linked episodes.

Theophilus succeeds in such tasks as separating mismatched lovers, liberating an aging man from the manipulation of his daughter, allowing a shrewish wife to mend her ways, extricating one man from his unwitting involvement with criminals, bringing home a wayward husband, finding a lover for a maimed young man, and impregnating a woman whose husband is sterile. Throughout, Theophilus is a typical Wilder hero—a man of good will, of faith, of sincerity. *Theophilus North* is Wilder's only novel in which sexuality is of central importance. The sexual episodes are conducted offstage and seem unbelievable and strained. Theophilus, in his seductions and in his everyday relationships with his neighbors, is curiously unaffected and uninvolved. Though he displays emotion, he seems to lack passion.

Wilder's characters, from Samuele to John Ashley, from the circle of Roman aristocrats to Newport society, remain thin and superficial, emblems rather than specific, rounded human beings. Such characterization was in keeping with Wilder's conviction that each individual was, in the long history of the human race, of but little importance. His trials, anguish, suffering, and joy were not significant when placed in the context of all human suffering and all human joy. Rather than writing about individual human beings, Wilder chose to write about humanity; rather than dealing with the intricacies of individual lives, he chose to compress those lives into brief episodes to demonstrate the multiplicity of life.

Wilder, deeply philosophical and reflective, was always the teacher, the educator, with an abiding concern for the future of humanity. "Hope," he wrote in *Theophilus North*, "is a projection of the imagination; so is despair. Despair all too readily embraces the ills it foresees; hope is an energy and arouses the mind to explore every possibility to combat them." In all his works, he exuded hope and, even in dark times, urged his readers to work together in faith and in love.

Linda Simon

OTHER MAJOR WORKS

PLAYS: *The Trumpet Shall Sound*, pb. 1920; *The Angel That Troubled the Waters and Other Plays*, pb. 1928 (includes 16 plays); *The Happy Journey to Trenton and Camden*, pr., pb. 1931 (one act); *The Long Christmas Dinner*, pr., pb. 1931 (one act; as libretto in German, 1961; translation and music by Paul Hindemith); *The Long Christmas Dinner and Other Plays in One Act*, pb. 1931 (includes *Queens of France*, *Pullman Car Hiawatha*, *Love and How to Cure It*, *Such Things Only Happen in Books*, and *The Happy Journey to Trenton and Camden*); *Lucrece*, pr. 1932 (adaptation of André Obey's *Le Viol de Lucrèce*); *A Doll's House*, pr. 1937 (adaptation of

Henrik Ibsen's play); *The Merchant of Yonkers*, pr. 1938 (adaptation of Johann Nestroy's *Einen Jux will er sich machen*); *Our Town*, pr., pb. 1938; *The Skin of Our Teeth*, pr., pb. 1942; *The Matchmaker*, pr. 1954 (revision of *The Merchant of Yonkers*); *A Life in the Sun*, pr. 1955 (commonly known as *The Alcestiad*; act four pb. as *The Drunken Sisters*); *Plays for Bleecker Street*, pr. 1962 (3 one-acts: *Someone from Assisi*; *Infancy*, pb. 1961; and *Childhood*, pb. 1960).

SCREENPLAYS: *Our Town*, 1940 (with Frank Craven and Harry Chantlee); *Shadow of a Doubt*, 1943 (with Sally Benson and Alma Revelle).

NONFICTION: *The Intent of the Artist*, 1941; *American Characteristics and Other Essays*, 1979; *The Journals of Thornton Wilder, 1939-1961*, 1985.

TRANSLATION: *The Victors*, 1948 (of Jean-Paul Sartre's play *Morts sans sépulture*).

BIBLIOGRAPHY

Blank, Martin, ed. *Critical Essays on Thornton Wilder*. New York: G. K. Hall, 1996. A solid collection of criticism on Wilder. Includes bibliographical references and an index.

Blank, Martin, Dalma Hunyadi Brunauer, and David Garrett Izzo, eds. *Thornton Wilder: New Essays*. West Cornwall, Conn.: Locust Hill Press, 1999. A contemporary look at Wilder and his oeuvre.

Castronovo, David. *Thornton Wilder*. New York: Ungar, 1986. Two chapters on Wilder's early and later novels. A useful introductory study, including chronology, notes, and bibliography.

Goldstein, Malcolm. *The Art of Thornton Wilder*. Lincoln: University of Nebraska Press, 1965. An early and still useful introduction to Wilder's novels and plays. A short biographical sketch is followed by an in-depth look at his work through the one-act play *Childhood* (1962). Includes bibliographical notes and an index.

Goldstone, Richard H. *Thornton Wilder: An Intimate Portrait*. New York: Saturday Review Press, 1975. An intimate portrait of Wilder by a close friend who had written previous studies on the subject, had access to personal documents, and interviewed family and friends. Includes notes, a selected bibliography, and an index.

Harrison, Gilbert A. *The Enthusiast: A Life of Thornton Wilder*. New York: Ticknor & Fields, 1983. A chatty biographical study of Wilder by a biographer who was provided access to Wilder's notes, letters, and photographs. Harrison successfully recreates Wilder's life and the influences, both good and bad, that shaped him.

Simon, Linda. *Thornton Wilder: His World*. Garden City, N.Y.: Doubleday, 1979. A solid biographical study of Wilder that includes examinations of his published works and photographs, notes, a bibliography, and an index.

Walsh, Claudette. *Thornton Wilder: A Reference Guide, 1926-1990*. New York: G. K. Hall, 1993. A complete guide to Wilder and his works. Includes bibliographical references and an index.

Wilder, Amos Niven. *Thornton Wilder and His Public*. Philadelphia: Fortress Press, 1980. A short critical study of Wilder by his older brother, who offers an inside family look at the writer. A supplement includes Wilder's "Culture in a Democracy" address and a selected German bibliography.

John A. Williams

Born: Jackson, Mississippi; December 5, 1925

PRINCIPAL LONG FICTION

The Angry Ones, 1960 (also known as *One for New York*)
Night Song, 1961
Sissie, 1963
The Man Who Cried I Am, 1967
Sons of Darkness, Sons of Light: A Novel of Some Probability, 1969
Captain Blackman, 1972
Mothersill and the Foxes, 1975
The Junior Bachelor Society, 1976
!Click Song, 1982
The Berhama Account, 1985
Jacob's Ladder, 1987
Clifford's Blues, 1999

OTHER LITERARY FORMS

Known primarily as a novelist but also a short-story writer, John A. Williams has produced an extraordinary number of nonfiction pieces, many of them journalistic. He was among the first African Americans of his generation to write a fact book about Africa, *Africa: Her History, Lands, and People* (1962). His treatment of 1960's social issues can be found in *The Protectors* (1964), containing stories about narcotics agents, and *This Is My Country Too* (1965) documents Williams's travels throughout the United States in 1963-1964, from articles serialized in *Holiday* magazine. A controversial work, *The King God Didn't Save* (1970) is a critical look at civil rights leader Martin Luther King, Jr.'s public and private life, and *The Most Native of Sons* (1970) treats the life of the famed black novelist Richard Wright. A comprehensive compilation of articles, some autobiographical, was published in *Flashbacks: A Twenty-Year Diary of Article Writing* (1973). Williams also produced an award-winning book of poetry, *Safari West* (1998), the play *Last Flight from Ambo Ber* (1981), dealing with the Falashas in Ethiopia, and the libretto for the opera *Vanqui* (1999).

ACHIEVEMENTS

One of the most prolific and influential writers of his era, Williams infused his works with self-exploration, reflecting the collective social experience of African Americans. He lectured widely, contributed extensively to anthologies, and edited numerous collections, such as *The Angry Black* (1962), *Beyond the Angry Black* (1967), *Amistad 1* (1970), *Amistad 2* (1971), *Yardbird No. 2* (1978), *Introduction to Literature* (1985), *Street Guide to African Americans in Paris* (1992), and *Bridges: Literature Across Cultures* (1994). In the 1970's, he was a contributing editor for such publications as *American Journal* and *Politicks*, and in the 1980's he served in a similar capacity for the distinguished, groundbreaking publication *Journal of African Civilizations*.

Williams was the recipient of numerous awards, beginning with his recognition in 1962 by the National Institute of Arts and Letters. His other honors and achievements include the Richard Wright-Jacques

Roumain Award (1973), the National Endowment for the Arts Award (1977), the Lindback
Award for Distinguished Teaching, Rutgers University (1982), the American Book Award for
!Click Song (1983), the New Jersey Literary Hall
of Fame Michael Award (1987), the American
Book Award for *Safari West* (1998), and induc-
tion into the National Literary Hall of Fame
(1998).

BIOGRAPHY

John Alfred Williams was born near Jackson,
Mississippi, in Hinds County, to Ola and John
Henry Williams. Williams's mother, whose African name means "Keeper of the Beautiful House"
or "He Who Wants to Be Chief," had been born
in Mississippi; his father's roots were in Syracuse, New York, where the couple met. When
Williams was six months old, he returned with
his mother to Syracuse. The family resided in
the multiethnic Fifteenth Ward, and Williams attended Washington Irving Elementary, Madison
Junior High, and Central High School. Joining
the navy in 1943, Williams served in the Pacific,
and after discharge in 1946 and his return to Syracuse he completed his secondary education, followed by a brief term at Morris Brown College
in Atlanta and then enrollment at Syracuse University, where he studied creative writing. In 1947, he
married Carolyn Clopton, with whom he had two
sons, Gregory and Dennis. In 1950, Williams earned
his B.A. and continued at Syracuse to pursue graduate study. During this period, he worked at a variety
of jobs—foundry work, social work, public relations,
insurance, radio and television—while developing as
a journalist. Following the failure of his marriage in
1952 and a brief stay in California in 1954, he was
determined to become a professional writer. In 1946,
he contributed pieces to the Syracuse newspaper, the
Progressive Herald, continuing through 1955 as a reporter for the *Chicago Defender*, the *Pittsburgh Cou-
rier*, the *Los Angeles Tribune*, and the *Village Voice*.

After moving to New York in 1954, he worked for
a vanity publisher, Comet Press, in 1955-1956 and at
Abelard-Schuman in 1957-1958. In 1958, Williams

(Library of Congress)

was Director of Information for the American Com-
mittee on Africa, a reporter for *Jet* magazine, and a
stringer for the Associated Negro Press. Based in
Barcelona for a period, he was employed in 1959 by
WOV Radio in New York; his first published novel,
The Angry Ones, appeared in 1960.

Though Williams was nominated in 1962 for the
Prix de Rome by the American Academy of Arts and
Letters, his name was withdrawn for reasons that
Williams attributed to his upcoming interracial marriage. In 1963 Williams contributed an article to *Eb-
ony* magazine and began writing for *Holiday*. An Africa correspondent for *Newsweek* in 1964, in 1965 he
married Lorrain Isaac, with whom he had a son,
Adam. Williams began his career in higher education
in 1968, teaching at the College of the Virgin Islands
and the City College of New York. He held positions
at the University of California at Santa Barbara, Uni-

versity of Hawaii, Boston University, New York University, University of Houston, and Bard College. From 1979 to 1994 he taught at Rutgers University while continuing his literary activities. Following the publication of *Safari West* in 1998, his long-awaited novel, his first in twelve years, *Clifford's Blues*, was published.

ANALYSIS

Williams's novels draw on personal experience, though they are not strictly autobiographical; they reflect the racial issues facing American society, especially during the civil rights period. Williams writes in the clear, readable prose of the journalist; his plot structures mix linear time with flashback passages to achieve a seamless continuity. His characters have been writers, jazz musicians, black mothers, and military veterans, and his themes have addressed the hardships of the black writer, the expatriate in Europe, black family life, interracial relationships, and political conspiracy. The presentation of jazz is a frequent element, and New York City is a repeated setting, though Williams has also depicted the Caribbean and Africa.

THE ANGRY ONES

Williams's initial novel is a first-person narrative drawing on autobiographical elements. Like Williams, Stephen Hill, the African American main character, is a World War II veteran, who works for a vanity press in New York. Early in the novel, Williams refers to African and Native American origins and jazz contexts. The novel is principally about Steve's relationships with his employer, coworkers, and friends. One of Steve's closest associates is Linton Mason, a white former collegemate and editor at McGraw-Hill. The novel uses Lint's success in publishing to indicate the racial divide, sexual jealousy, and the benefits of being white in racist America. Another theme is the search for a meaningful relationship, the choice between interracial and intraracial love. The causes of black "anger" are linked to Steve's frustrating attempts to rise within the company run by Rollie Culver and, generally, the treatment of black men in New York's publishing world, symbolized by the suicide of Steve's black friend

Obie Roberts. The novel presents racism through the day-to-day experiences of the main character.

NIGHT SONG

Set in Greenwich Village, New York, in the 1950's, *Night Song* is a "jazz novel" that mirrors the life of famed alto saxophonist Charlie Parker through the portrayal of Eagle (Richie Stokes), a drug-addicted musician who retains the capabilities of jazz performance despite his debilitation. Eagle befriends the alcoholic David Hillary, an out-of-work white college professor employed in the jazz café run by Keel Robinson, a former black preacher and Harvard graduate involved in an interracial relationship with Della. Each of the characters is fractured, most notably Eagle, whose alcoholism and addiction are implicitly the result of the racist treatment of the black artist. Williams portrays David as a savior and betrayer of Eagle; David's "healing" is the ironic result of his association with Eagle, Keel, and Della.

SISSIE

Titled after the mother of two principal characters, Iris and Ralph, *Sissie* is divided into four parts. Through memories, the novel presents the stories of Iris, Ralph, and Sissie Joplin, with Sissie's history revealed in parts 3 and 4, resulting in a Joplin family saga. Iris's story, her failed marriage, her career in Europe, and her relationship with the jazz musician called Time, is the first extended flashback. Ralph's recollections, his experiences in the service, his struggle as a writer in New York, are presented through psychoanalysis, a device that reveals racial issues from the viewpoint of a white psychologist, a symbol of societal norms. Sissie Joplin, a matriarchal figure, has an affair that threatens the stability of her marriage, which undergoes numerous challenges, such as the difficulty of surviving economic hard times and the struggle to find personal fulfillment through love. Sissie is ultimately the catalyst for Ralph and Iris's recognition of their family's conflicted yet sustaining experiences.

THE MAN WHO CRIED I AM

Williams's best-received and perhaps most influential work, *The Man Who Cried I Am* revolves around Max Reddick, an African American writer reunited in Amsterdam with his Dutch ex-wife, Margrit. Williams presents, within a twenty-four-hour time period, the downward spiral of Reddick, a Chester Himes figure, who is suffering from colon cancer. Through flashbacks, Reddick's recollections of a thirty-year past present the social experience of black Americans through the civil rights era. The novel portrays Reddick's association with Harry Ames, a character based on black novelist Richard Wright, who has uncovered the King Alfred Plan, a plot to place America's black population in concentration camps. Other characters in the novel also resemble actual black writers or political figures, such as Marion Dawes, a James Baldwin type; Paul Durrell, a Martin Luther King, Jr., replica; and Minister Q, a Malcolm X parallel. Furthermore, Williams develops African characters, such as Jaja Enzkwu, who reveals the King Alfred Plan to Harry Ames. The involvement of the Central Intelligence Agency (CIA) in Reddick's death points to an international conspiracy against black people, demonstrating Williams's tragic vision of global race relations.

CAPTAIN BLACKMAN

An exploration of black contributions in American wars, this novel employs a narrative strategy in which time is fluid. At the outset, Captain Blackman, a Vietnam soldier who teaches his troops the history of black Americans in the military, is wounded and trapped by the Viet Cong. His hallucinations are used to develop scenes in various periods of American wars, from the American Revolution through Vietnam. In these settings, Blackman experiences battle and the racial circumstances affecting black troops. The novel mixes fictional characterizations with historical fact, as in the reference to the Battle of Bunker Hill in the American Revolution. Williams portrays a possible nuclear armageddon, in which black people become the forces of control, though the reversal of power from black to white is itself part of the dream visions of Blackman.

!CLICK SONG

Considered by Williams at the time to be the novel in which he achieved the most effective coalescence of his literary intentions, *!Click Song*, titled after a vocal sound found in the Xhosa language of South Africa, parallels two writers, one black, the other white and Jewish. Using flashbacks, manipulating linear time, the narrative develops the literary careers of Cato Douglass and Paul Cummings. Divided into three sections, "Beginnings," "Middle," and "Endings," *!Click Song* uses the first-person narrator, Cato, as a representation of the journey of the black American writer. Beginning with the funeral of Paul, who committed suicide, the novel returns to the undergraduate experiences of the two veterans pursuing creative writing, circumstances that suggest the author's biography. Parallels to Williams's life are inescapable, especially in the treatment of Cato's career. However, Williams goes beyond mere autobiography by using Cato to symbolize the black artist who resists cultural falsehood, as in the closing section in which Cato in the 1960's offers a countertext to the withholding of information about black culture by major museums.

JACOB'S LADDER

Jacob's Ladder explores the predicament of an African American military attaché, Jacob Henry (Jake), caught in the turmoil of American destabilizing efforts in Pandemi, a fictitious West African country, where he had spent part of his youth as the son of a black American missionary. Resembling Liberia, Pandemi is ruled by Chuma Fasseke, Jake's childhood friend. The government of Chuma Fasseke has replaced that of the Franklins, a family descended from nineteenth century repatriated African Americans. The novel also offers a parallel to Nigeria in the portrayal of Taiwo Shaguri, the head of state of Temian. Containing elements of an espionage thriller, *Jacob's Ladder* proposes that an African country can attain nuclear capabilities. Williams humanizes Jake and Fasseke, creating a work deeper than clandestine intrigue. The final sections describe the fall of Fasseke and the takeover of the nuclear power plant by his opposition, assisted by the CIA. The epilogue uses the ironic device of the press release to show the perspective of the international press.

Joseph McLaren

OTHER MAJOR WORKS

PLAYS: *Last Flight from Ambo Ber*, pr. 1981; *Vanqui*, pr. 1999 (libretto).

POETRY: *Safari West*, 1998.

NONFICTION: *Africa: Her History, Lands, and People*, 1962; *The Protectors: The Heroic Story of the Narcotics Agents, Citizens, and Officials in Their Unending, Unsuing Battles Against Organized Crime in America and Abroad*, 1964 (as J. Dennis Gregory with Harry J. Anslinger); *This Is My Country Too*, 1965; *The Most Native of Sons: A Biography of Richard Wright*, 1970; *The King God Didn't Save: Reflections on the Life and Death of Martin Luther King, Jr.*, 1970; *Flashbacks: A Twenty-Year Diary of Article Writing*, 1973; *Minorities in the City*, 1975; *If I Stop I'll Die: The Comedy and Tragedy of Richard Pryor*, 1991; *Way B(l)ack Then and Now: A Street Guide to African Americans in Paris*, 1992 (with Michel Fabre).

EDITED TEXTS: *The Angry Black*, 1962; *Beyond the Angry Black*, 1966; *Amistad 1*, 1970 (with Charles F. Harris); *Amistad 2*, 1971 (with Harris); *The McGraw-Hill Introduction to Literature*, 1985 (with Gilbert H. Muller); *Bridges: Literature Across Cultures*, 1994 (Gilbert H. Muller, author).

BIBLIOGRAPHY

Cash, Earl A. *John A. Williams: The Evolution of a Black Writer*. New York: Third Press, 1975. This text is the first book-length study of Williams's works, covering the nonfiction and the novels through *Captain Blackman*.

Gayle, Addison, Jr. *The Way of the New World: The Black Novel in America*. Garden City, N.Y.: Doubleday, 1975. Gayle addresses the shift from protest to history in *The Man Who Cried I Am* and *Captain Blackman*.

Muller, Gilbert H. *John A. Williams*. Boston: Twayne, 1984. Containing a chronology and thematic approach, this study is a comprehensive treatment of Williams's life and work through *!Click Song*.

Nadel, Alan. "My Country Too: Time, Place, and Afro-American Identity in the Work of John Williams." *Obsidian II* 2, no. 3 (1987): 25-41. This article examines selected nonfiction and fiction, showing political orientation and modernist patterns.

Ramsey, Priscilla R. "John A. Williams: The Black American Narrative and the City." In *The City in African-American Literature*, edited by Yoshinobu Hakutani and Robert Butler. Madison, N.J.: Fairleigh Dickinson University Press, 1995. Focusing on urban realities, this study offers an overview of selected Williams novels.

Reilly, John M. "Thinking History in *The Man Who Cried I Am*." *Black American Literature Forum* 21, no. 1/2 (1987): 25-42. Reilly considers Williams's novel in relation to naturalism and history.

Ro, Sigmund. "Toward the Post-Protest Novel: The Fiction of John A. Williams." In *Rage and Celebration: Essays on Contemporary Afro-American Writing*. Atlantic Highlands, N.J.: Humanities Press, 1984. This essay argues that Williams's novels develop from protest fiction to novelistic treatments of 1960's racial issues.

A. N. WILSON

Born: Stone, England; October 27, 1950

PRINCIPAL LONG FICTION

The Sweets of Pimlico, 1977
Unguarded Hours, 1978
Kindly Light, 1979
The Healing Art, 1980
Who Was Oswald Fish?, 1981
Wise Virgin, 1982
Scandal, 1983
Gentlemen in England, 1985
Love Unknown, 1986
Incline Our Hearts, 1988
A Bottle in the Smoke, 1990
Daughters of Albion, 1991
The Vicar of Sorrows, 1993
Hearing Voices, 1995
A Watch in the Night: Being the Conclusion of the Lampitt Chronicles, 1996
Dream Children, 1998

OTHER LITERARY FORMS

Despite the regularity with which A. N. Wilson produces novels, he has never been limited to that form alone. He is one of the best-known journalists in Great Britain, having served as literary editor to *The Spectator*, the prestigious weekly journal of conservative social and political opinion, and as the literary editor of the *Evening Standard*. His own writing has not been confined to reviewing books, and he is often a commentator on social and political subjects. Wilson has a special interest in religion, and aside from his occasional essays on that subject, he published a study of the layman's dilemma in matters of Christian belief, *How Can We Know?* (1985), and historical biographies of Jesus and of the apostle Paul. He taught at the University of Oxford and wrote biographies of writers Sir Walter Scott, John Milton, Hilaire Belloc, Leo Tolstoy, and C. S. Lewis. He has also published volumes of essays and reviews, *Pen Friends from Porlock* (1988) and *Eminent Victorians* (1989), as well as children's books, mostly about cats, such as *Stray* (1987) and *The Tabitha Stories* (1997).

ACHIEVEMENTS

The Sweets of Pimlico gained for Wilson the John Llewelyn Rhys Memorial Prize in 1978, and *The Healing Art* won three prizes, including the Somerset Maugham Award for 1980 and the Arts Council National Book Award for 1981. *Wise Virgin* brought him the W. H. Smith Annual Literary Award in 1983, and his study of Scott, *The Laird of Abbotsford: A View of Sir Walter Scott* (1980), won the Rhys prize for him once again. Another of his biographies, *Tolstoy* (1988), won the Whitbread Award in 1988.

There are several formidable writers in Wilson's generation, but it is possible to distinguish Wilson as one of the best of the satirists and, as such, one of the most perceptive commentators on Great Britain in the last quarter of the twentieth century. Given his talent, and his capacity to comment attractively (if sometimes improperly) on the excesses of his society, it is not surprising that he has become something of a public personality, the literary figure most often identified with the "Young Fogeys," that amorphous group of literary, social, and political figures who espouse the principles of landowning Toryism and look with nostalgia back to the old Empire and to the days when High Anglicanism was a spiritual power in the land. Part of their conservatism is sheer mischief-making, part of it a matter of temperament and class, but in Wilson's case, it is a love for the aesthetic detail of what he sees as a richer and more caring society (which does not stop him from making wicked fun of it).

BIOGRAPHY

Andrew Norman Wilson, born in Stone, Staffordshire, England, in 1950, was educated at Rugby, one of the great English public schools, and at New College, Oxford. He won the Chancellor's Essay Prize in 1971 and the Ellerton Theological Prize in 1975. He was a lecturer in English at New College and at St. Hugh's College, Oxford, from 1976 to 1981. He was then appointed literary editor of *The Spectator* for two years and later became the literary editor of the *Evening Standard*. In addition to his fiction, his nonfiction, and his children's books, he has published in *The Times Literary Supplement*, *New Statesman*, *Daily Mail*, *Observer*, and the *Sunday Telegraph*. In 1992, he narrated *Jesus Before Christ*, a presentation by Thames Television Production which presents a demythologized approach to Jesus' life. His declaration of loss of faith and departure from the Church of England in the early 1990's ran parallel with events in the lives of a number of major characters throughout the corpus of his fiction. His new understanding and interpretation of Jesus and Saint Paul are presented in his biographies, published in 1992 and in 1997 respectively, of those early Christian figures. During his second year of studies at Oxford, Wilson married Katherine Duncan-Jones, one of his tutors in English at Oxford's Somerville College and a specialist in Renaissance literature. Early in the marriage they became the parents of two daughters. After the marriage ended in divorce, he married Ruth Guilding, an art historian whom he met in 1989 when filming a television episode of *Eminent Victorians*, which he was narrating. Wilson was made a Fellow of the Royal Society of Literature in 1981 and is also a member of the American Academy of Arts and Letters.

ANALYSIS

A. N. Wilson's novels are part of the tradition of sophisticated wittiness—sometimes comic, sometimes satiric—which explores the English caste system (with particular emphasis upon the middle and upper-middle classes), long a subject for English letters, particularly in the 1930's. The promise that World War II would not only stop international tyranny but also destroy the British social hierarchy did not, in fact, come true. Great Britain may have fallen on hard times economically, and may have become less important politically, but the class structure, though shaken, would prevail.

THE SWEETS OF PIMLICO

Evelyn Waugh was the foremost social satirist prior to the war and until his death in 1966, commenting on the dottier aspects of life among the well-born, the titled, the talented, and the downright vulgar climbers and thrusters, determined to ascend the greasy pole of social, political, and economic success. Wilson's first novel, *The Sweets of Pimlico*, might well have been written by a young Waugh. Thinly plotted, but written with astringent grace and wide-ranging peripheral insights into the fastidious improprieties of the privileged, it tells of the queer love life of Evelyn Tradescant (whose surname alone is appropriately bizarre, but whose credentials are established by the fact that her father is a retired diplomat, Sir Derek Tradescant, of some minor political reputation).

By chance, Evelyn tumbles (literally) into an association with a much older man, Theo Gormann—wealthy, pleased by the attentions of a young woman, and mysteriously ambiguous about his past, which seems to have involved close association with the Nazis before the war. While Theo urges his peculiar attentions on Evelyn, so does his closest friend, John "Pimlico" Price, and Evelyn learns that everybody seems to know one another in varyingly confusing ways. Her father and mother remember the Gormann of Fascist persuasion, and her brother, Jeremy, is also known to Theo through his connection with Pimlico,

who proves to be an occasional male lover of Jeremy, who in his last year at Oxford is doing little work but considerable loving, including a sudden excursion into incest with Evelyn. Wilson is teasingly and sometimes feelingly successful in exploring the sexual brink upon which Evelyn and Theo hover in their relationship and which convinces Theo to give part of his estate to Evelyn. Pimlico, the present heir, knows that someone is being considered as a joint recipient of the estate, but he never suspects Evelyn, and Theo dies before the will is changed. All is well, however, since Evelyn and Pimlico decide to marry. It is farce of high order in which coincidence, arbitrary behavior, and sophisticated silliness are mixed with moments of genuine tenderness (but not so tender as to overcome the sly mockery of money and influence in the smart set of south London).

UNGUARDED HOURS and KINDLY LIGHT

In his next two novels, *Unguarded Hours* and *Kindly Light*, Wilson eschews the underplayed wit of *The Sweets of Pimlico* for comic excess, reminiscent of P. G. Wodehouse in its extravagant playfulness. These theological comedies are strongly cinematic in their incident and character and they display, if ridiculously, Wilson's strong interest in, and deep knowledge of, English Anglicanism and its constant flirtation with Roman Catholicism as well as his affectionate enthusiasm for the detail, the knick-knackery of religious ceremony and trapping. The two novels ought to be read in the proper chronological order, since the hero escapes in a balloon at the end of *Unguarded Hours* and begins in the next one, having floated some distance away, once again trying to make his way into the clerical life.

THE HEALING ART

The Healing Art, one of Wilson's most admired works, reveals how wide his range can be, not only tonally but also thematically. The novel is a "black comedy" in the sense that acts which normally offend are portrayed in such a way that readers enjoy the improprieties without worrying about the moral consequences. Two women, one a university don, one a working-class housewife, meet while having surgery for breast cancer and comfort each other, despite the fact that they otherwise have nothing in common.

Their doctor, overworked but peremptory, unfeeling, and vain, may have misread the women's X rays and deems one of them cured and the other in need of chemotherapy. The gifted, handsome, successful younger woman, informed of her possibly fatal condition, refuses treatment, energetically determined to live out her life quickly and to explore her personal relations with some fervor. In the process, she learns much about herself and her male friends and becomes involved in a love affair with the cast-off, occasional mistress of the man whom she presumed was, in fact, her lover (even if such love had not, to the moment, been consummated).

Wilson juxtaposes the range of experience open to a woman of the upper middle class, searching for some meaning for the last days of her life, surrounded by the many pleasures and alternatives of her world, to the life of a working-class woman, supposedly healthy, but obviously wasting away and ignored by family and by the medical profession as something of a nuisance. The cruelty of it all is subtly explored by Wilson, and the final ironies for both women are unnervingly sad and comic. Wilson proves with this novel that he is serious, and sensitive, particularly in dealing with the emotional lives of the two women.

WHO WAS OSWALD FISH?

In *Who Was Oswald Fish?*, which might be called a contemporary black fairy tale, coincidence simply struts through the novel. The mysterious Oswald Fish, a turn-of-the-century architect and designer whose one church—a Gothic ruin in the working-class district of Birmingham—is to be the center of life and death for the parties drawn together to decide its fate, proves to be related to everyone who matters (and some who do not). In the retrieval of Fish's reputation from the neglect and indifference of twentieth century tastelessness and vulgarity, one suicide, one manslaughter, and two accidental deaths occur, the latter two in the rubble of his lovely old church. No one means any harm (although there are two children in this novel who could put the St. Trinian's gang to flight). Fanny Williams, former pop star and model and survivor of the English rock revolution of the early 1960's, is, in the late 1970's, famous again as the owner of a chain of trash-and-trend novelty shops

dealing in Victorian nostalgia, and she is determined to protect the ruined church from demolition at the hands of soulless civic planners. Sexy, generous, and often charmingly silly, her life is an extravagant mess, a whirlpool of sensual, slapstick nonsense in which some survive and some, quite as arbitrarily, drown. Behind the farcical escapades lies Wilson's deep affection for the rich clutter of Victoriana juxtaposed to the new efficiency.

WISE VIRGIN

After the comic excesses of *Who Was Oswald Fish?*, Wilson pulled back into the narrower range of his early work in *Wise Virgin*. There has always been a sense that not only Waugh but also Iris Murdoch influenced him (*The Sweets of Pimlico* had been dedicated to her and to her husband, the literary critic John Bayley), particularly in the way in which she uses love as an unguided flying object, which can strike any character in the heart at any moment. Love tends to strike arbitrarily in Wilson's fiction, for he, like Murdoch, enjoys tracing the madness of fools in love. Also reminiscent of Murdoch, Wilson works interesting technical detail into his novels, often, as has been stated, of the religious world, but in *Who Was Oswald Fish?* his interest in Victorian architecture and objets d'art predominates and adds amusingly to the texture of the novel. In *Wise Virgin*, Wilson utilizes his own special knowledge as a literary scholar, since his protagonist, Giles Fox, is a medievalist, working on a definitive edition of an obscure text, *A Treatise of Heavenly Love*, on the relation of virginity and the holy life. Fox, irascible, snobbish, and sometimes vicious, has two virgins on his hands, his daughter, whom he has sought to educate without benefit of twentieth century influence, and his assistant, Miss Agar, who is determined to marry him.

Wilson has been accused of gratuitous cruelty in the way in which he allows his characters to comment upon the gracelessness of contemporary British society, and it is true that Fox is a master of the unfair comment and is insensitive to the possibility that some kinds of stupidities, particularly in the less privileged classes, are only innocent gaucheries. Certainly Fox is an unattractive protagonist, but he is also a man who has suffered much, having lost one wife in childbirth and another in a motor accident, and having himself gone blind in midcareer. He is something of a twentieth century Job (although more deserving of punishment), and the tone and plot of the novel suggest black comedy bordering on tragedy. On the lighter side, Wilson satirizes Fox's sister and brother-in-law, who, suffering from that peculiar kind of arrested development which strikes some people as cute, indulge interminably in the baby talk of the schoolboys whom the husband teaches in a public school, clearly based upon Wilson's own school, Rugby.

GENTLEMEN IN ENGLAND

Gentlemen in England takes place in the late Victorian period of which Wilson is so fond. With this work, Wilson has written a trick novel, partly in the tradition of Thomas Keneally and E. L. Doctorow, in which actual historical events and characters intrude on, and affect, the action. Wilson, however, refuses to use obvious historical allusions carefully chosen to satisfy the vanities of intelligent, well-informed readers. Much of the historical structure requires a deep knowledge of Victorian England. For example, although the novel definitely takes place in 1880, the exact date is never stated but must be gathered from certain facts mentioned by the characters. Allusions to George Eliot and Henry James might be easy to pick up, but those to public figures of the time, such as Charles Bradlaugh, E. B. Pusey, and Sir Charles Wentworth Dilke, require a formidable cultural memory.

The story centers on a father who has lost his Christian faith in the face of Darwinism; a son who is flirting with the late stages of the Oxford movement in religion, with the more theatrical experiments of High Anglicanism, and with the revival of the Roman Catholic Benedictine movement; and a daughter pursued by a disciple of Alma-Tadema, the popular painter of the time. Wilson recounts their family drama in a Victorian style, most reminiscent of the works of Anthony Trollope—slightly arch, witty, but restrainedly so, and inclined to overripe ironies. Like Victorian furniture and design, it is rich and heavy to the point of ponderousness.

Inside this lovingly detailed, historically accurate structure, Wilson plays out pure farce: A mother, still beautiful in early middle age, falls in love with a young painter, who falls in love with the daughter, who is half in love with her mother's old lover, who is half in love with both of them, and who is Wilson's way into the real world of London life. Called, with obvious intent, Chatterway, the former lover is intimately associated with the major figures of London life in that particularly lively year, 1880. *Gentlemen in England* is, in many ways, a work which illustrates Wilson's manipulative curiosity about the ways in which novels can be pushed and pulled about. Kingsley Amis has similar ideas, and his *Riverside Villas Murder* (1973) anticipated Wilson in its careful recreation of a 1930's-style English murder mystery in which content, structure, and language were scrupulous imitations of the real thing.

This awareness of the novel as a form which could be used in many ways allows Wilson many humorous moments. In *Who Was Oswald Fish?*, he introduces, in a minor role, Jeremy Tradescant, who was the sexually confused brother of Evelyn, the heroine of *The Sweets of Pimlico*. He goes even further in making a comment on the fate of Evelyn's marriage to Pimlico Price, incomprehensible to all but those who have read the earlier novel. Wilson introduces into *Gentlemen in England* a genuinely thoughtful discussion of the problem of Christian faith, which is tonally at odds with the clutter of Victorian sexual high jinks. He has, in short, no sense of decorum, not because he does not know, but because he knows so well. Sometimes, as in *Scandal* and *Love Unknown*, he seems to have returned to social satire; the latter novel is puzzling until one recognizes that it is based upon the most pathetic kind of popular romance. Wilson is off again, manipulating the genre, enriching junk literature by imposing first-class literary technique on banality and turning it into something it hardly deserves.

THE LAMPITT CHRONICLES

In a vein similar to his other novels, Wilson's five novels that comprise the Lampitt Chronicles focus on a group of middle- and upper-class English whose lives become intertwined through a variety of typically Wilsonian "coincidences." With its ironic overview of twentieth century English society, this *roman-fleuve* quintet chronicles the life of the first-person narrator, Julian Ramsey, and the lives of several members of the upper-class Lampitt family.

The first two novels recount the early events in Julian's life. In *Incline Our Hearts*, a twelve-year-old orphaned Julian is living with his Uncle Roy, the vicar at Timplingham. Roy, obsessed with the Lampitt family, continuously recounts "Lampitt-lore" to Julian, who develops an interest in James Petworth ("Jimbo") Lampitt, a minor Edwardian writer whose death begins the novel. This hilarious commentary on English snobbery and English institutions follows Julian at school (the "English Gulag") and through his adolescence. *A Bottle in the Smoke*, a darker satire, records Julian's marriage to Anne, a Lampitt niece. Some of the exasperation, confusion, and emptiness over modern relationships between the sexes expressed in poet T. S. Eliot's *The Waste Land* (1922) is echoed here (and in the next three novels).

The satire continues in *Daughters of Albion*, as Julian becomes "Jason Grainger" on the nationally popular radio series *The Mulberrys*. Raphael Hunter (Jimbo's biographer, who outraged the family by presenting Jimbo as a homosexual) successfully sues a would-be Blakean poet, Albion Pugh, for accusing him of murdering Jimbo. Interspersed with his satire on the world of publishing, radio, and television, Wilson, through both the narrator and Pugh, presents ideas about myth, Christianity, Jesus, and Saint Paul, which later find their nonfiction counterparts in Wilson's religious biographies.

Hearing Voices is a mystery as well as a comedy of manners. Ramsey, asked to write an authorized biography of the Lampitts, goes to America to do research, and he marries for the second time (unsuccessfully). The murder of the American tycoon who had bought Jimbo's literary papers remains unsolved, as Wilson's emphasis continues to be on human interactions.

In *A Watch in the Night: Being the Conclusion of the Lampitt Chronicles*, Ramsey, in his late sixties and at peace with himself, addresses dramatist William Shakespeare—as Saint Augustine does God in his *Confessiones* (397-400; *Confessions*, 1620)—as he reflects on his life and its intersection with the lives of countless characters. This Proustian sum-

mary clarifies major and minor ambiguities in the earlier novels (and resolves the murders).

Although Wilson's satiric tone varies in his novels from caustic to gentle, his works are generally amusing, perceptive about the human condition, and memorable for their characters (despite their chaotic lives). His insight into English society and its institutions, past and present, reflects the deep confusions not only of contemporary England but also of twentieth century Western civilization. Whether he should be grouped primarily with Angus Wilson and Evelyn Waugh for serious farce, with Iris Murdoch and Joyce Cary for analytical comedy, or with Kingsley Amis for caustic irony, it is clear that Wilson is one of the twentieth century's major English authors.

Charles H. Pullen,
updated by Marsha Daigle-Williamson

OTHER MAJOR WORKS

NONFICTION: *The Laird of Abbotsford: A View of Sir Walter Scott*, 1980; *The Life of John Milton*, 1983; *Hilaire Belloc*, 1984; *How Can We Know?*, 1985; *Pen Friends from Porlock*, 1988; *Tolstoy*, 1988; *Eminent Victorians*, 1989; *C. S. Lewis*, 1990; *Jesus*, 1992; *The Rise and Fall of the House of Windsor*, 1993; *Paul: The Mind of the Apostle*, 1997; *God's Funeral: The Decline of Faith in Western Civilization*, 1999.

CHILDREN'S LITERATURE: *Stray*, 1987; *The Tabitha Stories*, 1988; *Hazel the Guinea Pig*, 1989.

EDITED TEXTS: *The Faber Book of Church and Clergy*, 1992; *The Faber Book of London*, 1993.

BIBLIOGRAPHY

CSL: The Bulletin of the New York C. S. Lewis Society 10, no. 8/9 (June/July, 1990): 1-16. Introduction is by Jerry L. Daniel, and articles are by John Fitzpatrick, George Sayer, and Eugene McGovern. The entire issue is devoted to reviews of Wilson's 1990 biography of C. S. Lewis, which are mostly unfavorable because of disagreement with his biographical approach and speculative interpretation.

Landrum, David W. "Is There Life After Jesus? Spiritual Perception in A. N. Wilson's *The Vicar of Sorrows*." *Christianity and Literature* 44 (Spring/Summer, 1995): 359-368. A discussion of Wilson's first novel after he declared his unbelief in Christianity. Wilson deals much more seriously here with the problem of evil and other difficult religious questions than in his other fiction.

Weales, Gerald. "Jesus Who?" *The Gettysburg Review* 6, no. 4 (Autumn, 1993): 688-696. A comparison of Gore Vidal's treatment of Christ in his novel *Live from Golgotha* (1992) to Wilson's treatment of Christ in *Jesus*.

Weinberg, Jacob. "A. N. Wilson: Prolific to a Fault." *Newsweek* 112 (September 13, 1988): 75. A short but well-written essay, interspersed with comments by Wilson, on his novels and biographies. Also concerns Wilson as a "Young Fogey," a term used to describe young members of the Conservative party in England.

Wilson, A. N. "PW Interviews A. N. Wilson." Interview by Michele Field. *Publishers Weekly* 231 (May 15, 1987): 262-263. In the course of this interview, Wilson discusses his Anglo-Catholicism, the inevitable comparison of his works with those of Evelyn Waugh, the "cruel" nature of his novels, and his views on the writing of biography. Also contains much valuable biographical information.

Wolfe, Gregory. "Off Center, on Target." *Chronicles* 10, no. 10 (1986): 35-36. Wolfe's essay concerns Wilson's affinities with Evelyn Waugh, particularly in terms of their style and in their perspectives on Western Christianity. Sees Wilson as in the tradition of P. G. Wodehouse, who epitomized the light comic novel, but in Wilson's hands that novel becomes a vehicle for satire and social criticism.

ANGUS WILSON

Born: Bexhill, East Sussex, England; August 11, 1913
Died: Bury St. Edmunds, Suffolk, England; June 1, 1991

PRINCIPAL LONG FICTION
Hemlock and After, 1952
Anglo-Saxon Attitudes, 1956
The Middle Age of Mrs. Eliot, 1958
The Old Men at the Zoo, 1961
Late Call, 1964
No Laughing Matter, 1967
As If by Magic, 1973
Setting the World on Fire, 1980

OTHER LITERARY FORMS

Angus Wilson started his literary career in 1946, at the age of thirty-three, by writing short stories. The earliest stories were published in *Horizon*. *The Wrong Set and Other Stories* (1949), *Such Darling Dodos and Other Stories* (1950), and *A Bit off the Map and Other Stories* (1957) deal with the same problems and use the same imagery as his novels. Wilson also wrote drama, and in the 1970's, he became a leading reviewer of fiction. His literary journalism and criticism for *The Spectator*, *The Observer*, and *London Magazine* center mainly on the problem of the English novel. The range of writers he discussed in articles, introductions, or lectures is extremely wide and includes, among others, the Victorians, the Bloomsbury Group, Aldous Huxley, D. H. Lawrence, John Cowper Powys, Leo Tolstoy, Fyodor Dostoevski, Irving Shaw, Robert Penn Warren, and William Golding. He also published three full-length literary monographs: *Émile Zola: An Introductory Study of His Novels* (1952), *The World of Charles Dickens* (1970), and *The Strange Ride of Rudyard Kipling* (1977). Wilson's many lectures and articles display his concern with a wide range of problems relevant to the second half of the twentieth century. Most important for the study and understanding of his art is the volume *The Wild Garden: Or, Speaking of Writing* (1963), which contains lectures given in California in 1960. Some of his criticism was collected in *Diversity and Depth in Fiction: Selected Critical Writings of Angus Wilson* (1983). Travel pieces written over several decades are collected in *Reflections in a Writer's Eye* (1986).

ACHIEVEMENTS

Most critics agree that by the 1980's, Wilson had secured a place among the most distinguished contemporary British novelists. He even became recognized outside the English-speaking world, particularly in France. In the 1960's and 1970's, the number of interviews with the artist increased, signifying his growing recognition among critics. Whether the critics use Stephen Spender's terminology of "modern" and "contemporary," or speak of experimental, psychological, aesthetic, or modern versus the traditional, sociological English novel, they all try to assess Wilson in relation to these categories. Some contend that Wilson's main concern rests with the sociological aspects of human life, but almost all critics concede that his interest goes beyond social issues. Without abandoning his commitment to depicting reality, Wilson was always committed to probing deeper into the dark depths of the human self. This concern with the inner self separates him sharply from the "angry" writers who also wrote in the 1950's: Kingsley Amis, John Wain, and Alan Sillitoe. Wilson, however, was dedicated to experimenting both in content and method. In his novels and critical writings, he emerged as a champion for a new type of novel, standing between the traditional and the experimental.

BIOGRAPHY

Angus Frank Johnstone Wilson was born in Bexhill, Sussex, on August 11, 1913, the sixth son of a middle-class family. His father was of Scottish extraction; his mother came from South Africa, and he spent some time there as a child. In constant financial troubles, his parents tried to maintain pretense and appearance, which left a deep impression on Wilson: At a very early age, he became aware of the chasm separating the real world and the world of fantasy into which many people escape to avoid the unpleasant facts of their lives. Frequently lonely (he was thirteen years younger than his next older brother), he realized that his clowning ability made him popular with the schoolchildren. He attended prep school in Seaford; from there he went to Westminster School and then to Merton College, Oxford. At the University of Oxford, his history training was on the Marxist line; that fact and his left-wing political activities in the 1930's account for his Labour sympathies.

In 1937, he started work at the British Museum, and, with an interruption during World War II, he

(Camera Press Ltd./Archive Photos)

stayed there until 1955. During the war, he was associated with an interservice organization attached to the Foreign Office, and for a while he lived in the country in a home with a Methodist widow and her daughter. During this time, he had a serious nervous breakdown; his psychotherapist suggested creative writing as therapy. In 1946, Wilson rejoined the staff at the British Museum and, at the same time, started writing seriously. His first published writing, the short story "Raspberry Jam" (1946), reflects his personal crisis and foreshadows the dark atmosphere of most of his work to come. The whole experience at the British Museum, situated in London's sophisticated Bloomsbury district and especially his job as Deputy Superintendent at the Reading Room, provided him with an understanding and knowledge of the cultural establishment and of the management of cultural institutions, which he used later in *The Old*

Men at the Zoo. Also, observing scholars, book addicts, and eccentric visitors to the Reading Room gave him material for creating some of his fictional characters, such as Gerald Middleton in *Anglo-Saxon Attitudes.*

In 1952, he published his first novel, *Hemlock and After,* and a critical monograph, *Émile Zola.* He gave talks on the novel for the British Broadcasting Corporation that were later published in *The Listener.* In 1955, a contract with Secker and Warburg as well as his ongoing reviewing activity for *The Spectator* and *Encounter* made it possible for him to resign his post at the British Museum. He then retired to the Sussex countryside, thus reviving his childhood garden-dream. As a result of his freedom from job-related responsibilities, he published four novels in a rapid sequence: *Anglo-Saxon Attitudes, The Middle Age of Mrs. Eliot, The Old Men at the Zoo,* and *Late Call.* Furthermore, his participation in the cultural and literary life of England as a journalist, critic, and lecturer became more extensive. In 1963, he started his association with the University of East Anglia as a part-time lecturer, becoming professor in 1966. Also in 1966, he became Chairman of the Literary Panel of the Arts Council of Great Britain. In 1967, he lectured at Berkeley, California, as a Beckerman Professor, and in the same year *No Laughing Matter* appeared.

In 1968, he was made Commander of the British Empire and Honorary Fellow of Cowell College of the University of California at Santa Cruz. He honored the Dickens Centennial in 1970 with *The World of Charles Dickens.* Between 1971 and 1974, he served as Chairman of the National Book League while receiving two more distinctions in 1972, becoming a Companion of Literature and a Chevalier de l'Ordre des Arts et des Lettres, the latter a sign of his growing reputation in France. A sixth novel, *As If by Magic,* appeared in 1973; in it he made use of his teaching experience and involvement with young intellectuals. He continued to live in the country, his many activities including travel. His Asian journey resulted in his book *The Strange Ride of Rudyard Kipling.* He was John Hinkley Visiting Professor at The Johns Hopkins University in 1974, and, in 1977,

Distinguished Visiting Professor at the University of Delaware; he also lectured at many other American universities. In 1980, he published another novel, *Setting the World on Fire.* His manuscripts, deposited at the Library of the University of Iowa, provide ample material for future researchers.

After suffering a stroke, Wilson died on June 1, 1991, in a nursing home in the southeast of England. He was seventy-seven years old.

ANALYSIS

"Self-realization was to become the theme of all my novels," declared Angus Wilson in *The Wild Garden.* Self-realization does not take place in a vacuum; the process is closely linked with a person's efforts to face and to cope with the world. Wilson's childhood experience, among déclassé middle-class people living in a fantasy world, initiated the novelist's interest in the conflict between two worlds and in the possibility or impossibility of resolving the conflict. The rapidly changing scene in England as the Edwardian Age gave way to the postwar 1920's, with the cultural dominance of Bloomsbury, and then to the radical leftist 1930's, impressed on him the urgency of such a search. His encounter with Marxism at Oxford intensified Wilson's tendency to see the world as one of opposing forces. The dichotomy of town and country, of the classes, and of old and new forms the background of Wilson's fiction as the remnants of Edwardian England disappeared and the dissolution of the British Empire left the island nation searching for its place in the modern world.

In *The Wild Garden,* Wilson describes his creative writing process in terms of a dialectic; he reveals that he "never felt called upon to declare allegiance to either fantasy or realism," but then he adds that "without their fusion I could not produce a novel." Wilson is desperately looking for syntheses to all kinds of conflicts and insists that self-realization is an absolute necessity to achieve them. His own breakdown as well as Sigmund Freud's impact on his generation pushed Wilson in the direction of psychoanalysis and the search for identity. In an age of tension, violence, and suffering, he insists on the necessity of self-realization in order to overcome despair.

Wilson's heroes all have crippled, wasted lives and broken families, and the novelist explores their "cherished evasions." Bernard Sand in *Hemlock and After* has to be shocked into self-knowledge by facing sadism in his own nature; Gerald Middleton, in *Anglo-Saxon Attitudes*, gets a new chance for a satisfactory, if not happy, life in old age when he is ready to resume responsibility as a scholar and to reveal a shameful hoax. Both of these heroes are presented in their private and public lives because, in Wilson's view, both of these aspects of life are equally important to modern people. This view of human life in the dialectic of the private and the public is even more important for Meg Eliot, the heroine of *The Middle Age of Mrs. Eliot*; after many frustrations she emerges at the end of the novel as a career woman. Similarly, Sylvia Calvert in *Late Call* discovers a meaningful [retirement] life of her own, independent of her family.

Wilson was a very "British" writer with a subtle sense for the typical English understatement, while his Hegelian drive for reconciliation of conflicts agrees with the spirit of the traditional English compromise. He was constantly searching for ways to save the remnants of the liberal, humanistic values that have remained dear to him in a world that did not seem to have any use for them. His heroes and heroines, saved from final disintegration, are restored to some kind of meaningful life through self-knowledge and are brought closer to other people in defiance of loneliness and despair.

HEMLOCK AND AFTER

In his first novel, *Hemlock and After*, Wilson extends the exploration of the theme of self-knowledge to both the private and public life of his hero. The novel is about Bernard Sand's troubled conscience, a most private matter; but Bernard is an important public figure, described as "the country's own ambassador to the world outside," and a successful, self-confident novelist who organizes a subsidized writers' colony, Valden Hall, in order to support young talent. Overtly successful, his family life is in shambles. His wife, Ella, lives in "neurotic misery"; his son is a staunch conservative in strong disagreement with Bernard's liberal views; his unmarried daughter,

a journalist, feels lonely and unhappy. As an indication of the overhanging disaster, Bernard's first novel is entitled *Nightmare's Image*.

In the title, "Hemlock" suggests poisonous wrong, evil, and even violence. Poisoning and violence occur in a "massacre of innocence," as related to Eric, Bernard's young homosexual partner, and to the little girl Elzie, whom the disreputable Mrs. Curry wants to make available to Hugh Rose. Wilson deliberately links the fate of the two young people by calling them both "rabbits." Rose and Mrs. Curry strike their deal at the "Lamb" Inn.

The word "After" in the title refers to the aftermath of knowledge: self-knowledge. A crucial scene occurs at the end of book 1 when a still complacent and self-confident Bernard watches the arrest of young homosexuals at Leicester Square and is shocked suddenly by the discovery that he experienced sadistic enjoyment in watching the terror in the eyes of those youths. This discovery has a devastating effect on Bernard's life and destroys not only him but also Valden Hall. The long-awaited opening of the young artists' colony becomes a total disaster, as its erupting violence grows into a symbol of the modern predicament. Wilson describes the scene as one of chaos, disorder, disappointment, strain, and hostility.

After this startling event, Bernard's life goes downhill very rapidly; self-knowledge paralyzes his will, and he is entirely unable to act. The discovery of sadistic tendencies makes him suspect of his own motives. He realizes with frightening clarity the abyss of the human soul and is driven to utter despair about the motivation behind any action. He has a horrifying vision of the subtle difference between intention and action, and as a consequence, Bernard loses his determination to deal with Mrs. Curry. At the same time, Ella almost miraculously recovers from her nervous breakdown and, after Bernard dies, acts on his behalf in arranging efficient management at Valden Hall and a prison sentence for Rose and Mrs. Curry. Rose commits suicide in prison, while Mrs. Curry earns an early release with her good behavior. It is briefly indicated that she might continue her former activity; thus the Epilogue ends the novel on an ambiguous note of qualified optimism.

ANGLO-SAXON ATTITUDES

The title *Anglo-Saxon Attitudes*, derived from Lewis Carroll's *Alice's Adventures in Wonderland* (1865), suggests a typically English atmosphere; it is Wilson's most Victorian novel, a broad social comedy. At the same time, it displays experimental technique in the use of the flashback, which provides all the background to Gerald Middleton's crisis in his private and public life. The hero, a sixty-year-old failure, is a historian. In the beginning of the novel, sitting by himself at a Christmas party given by his estranged wife, Inge, Gerald overhears broken sentences of conversation that remind him of the most significant episodes of his life. Wilson makes it very clear that self-knowledge is important for Gerald; it is both a psychological need to him and a matter of "intellectual honesty," a duty to the professional community of historians.

Gerald's crisis of conscience concerns a cruel hoax that occurred back in 1912 when he participated with a team in an excavation. Young Gilbert Stokeway, a disciple of T. H. Hulme and Wyndham Lewis and the son of the leader of the team, put a fake idol in the tomb under research at Melpham. His hoax was successful, and the fake came to be hailed as a pagan idol. At that time, Gerald was a Prufrock-like antihero: disabled physically by a sprained ankle, and disabled emotionally by his love for Gilbert's wife, Dollie. His affair with her played an important role in his silence about the fake idol. Gerald's feelings of guilt center on "the two forbidden subjects of his thoughts," his marriage and the hoax. His life, "rooted in evasion," appears to him empty, meaningless, and futile. His professional career fell victim to his decision not to reveal the hoax. Because of his affair with Dollie, he evaded dealing with Inge's inadequacies as a mother.

In fact, none of the minor characters has a happy, self-fulfilling life. While Gerald still believes in the liberal tradition, neither of his sons adheres to his beliefs. His elder son, Robert, a businessman, stands rather to the right and the younger son, John, is a radical, and they have violent clashes whenever they meet. Both sons are unhappy in their personal relationships as well. Robert is married to the conventional Marie-Hélène but loves the more modern Elvira Portway. John has a short-lived homosexual relationship with an unruly young Irishman, Larry, who is killed in a wild drive in which John loses a leg. Gerald's daughter, Kay, has a serious crisis in her marriage to the smart right-wing young sociologist, Donald. Wilson employs specific imagery to drive home to the reader the overwhelming atmosphere of frustration of all these people. Expressions such as "flat and dead" and "deadly heaviness" abound, referring to the behavior of people at parties when communication is impossible. Gerald's house is "noiseless as a tomb," and during the Christmas party at the home of the "Norse Goddess" Inge, all those present "shivered" in spite of the central heating.

Realizing the failure of his family, Gerald has to admit that he is to take the blame; when he selected Inge to be his wife, he decided for second-best. Yet, at the end, Gerald manages to pull himself out of his dead life. By revealing the hoax, he succeeds in restoring his professional status, and after a long silence, he becomes active again in research. The novel, however, like *Hemlock and After*, ends on a note of qualified optimism as Gerald remains estranged from his family. The picture of Gerald's life, combined with the divergent subplots, reveals a world in which relationships do not last, where options are limited.

THE MIDDLE AGE OF MRS. ELIOT

Critics believe that they can recognize Wilson in most of his central characters; the novelist, however, admits the connection only in the case of Meg Eliot, the heroine of his third novel, *The Middle Age of Mrs. Eliot*. "Meg," he says, "is in large part modelled on myself," while David Parker's nursery recalled to Wilson childhood memories of a garden of a friendly family.

Meg Eliot, a well-to-do barrister's childless, worldly, spoiled wife, experiences sudden tragedy when her husband dies from a gunshot wound as he tries to protect a local minister. The novel depicts Meg's nervous breakdown and painful recovery: her journey to self-knowledge. She is first revealed to be holding desperately to her old friends; yet, their lives are no more secure than hers. Lady Pirie in her "decaying genteel jail" is preoccupied with her son only; bohemian Polly Robinson lives a kind of "animated death"; and Jill Stokes is obsessed with the memory of her dead husband. These "lame ducks" cannot help Meg, nor can drugs. Meg's brother, David Parker, who runs the nursery with his homosexual partner, is sheltered in the pleasant quiet atmosphere, which suggests a return to lost innocence. Yet, Wilson is ambiguous about the validity of the garden image, since David's nursery is commercial, an irony in itself. Meg cannot share her brother's lifestyle, his abnegation of action and the human world. Wilson does not censure David for his contemplative lifestyle, but it is evident that he prefers Meg's choice "to be with people!"

Meg is determined to find meaning in life, in a life with people. She is strikingly reminiscent of George Eliot's heroines; similar to them, she used to live in self-delusion and is shocked into consciousness by the "remorse of not having made life count enough" for her husband. Moreover, again like the Victorian woman, she returns to a fuller life. Two factors are important in her recovery. First, she refuses any kind of opium, a George Eliot ideal; second, she is determined to build herself a meaningful, useful life. While she admits that she "used to be Maggie Tulliver," she also resembles Gwendolen Harleth from Eliot's *Daniel Deronda* (1876). She shares with her an unhappy childhood and the horrors of remorse, but she shares also in Gwendolen's way of redemption. Like the Victorian heroine, Meg too had to learn in a painful way that the outside world could intrude into her life at any time and destroy it if she is taken unaware. As she takes a paying secretarial job, Meg is full of confidence in her farewell letter to David: "At any rate in a few years at least, the modern world won't be able to take me by surprise so easily again."

THE OLD MEN AT THE ZOO

From the omniscient narrator of his early works, Wilson shifts to a more modern device in *The Old Men at the Zoo* by creating a first-person narrator in Simon Carter. In the beginning of the novel, Simon is a gifted, dedicated yet disabled naturalist, very much like Gerald Middleton at the time of the excavation.

He is prevented from continuing research in Africa because of amoebal dysentery. He joins the London Zoo as an administrator at a crucial time when the zoo itself becomes a battleground of conflicting ideas, reflecting a conflict of values in British politics. Wilson creates an armed conflict between England and Allied Europe, followed by a Fascist invasion of England when all standards of civilized behavior collapse and give way to brutality. When the war breaks out, the Fascists want to put on a spectacle with prisoners of war fighting the zoo animals. Simon is horrified, but as he later tries to drive the animals to safety, he finds himself killing his favorite badgers to feed a boy and his mother.

Almost an antihero, trying to avoid any kind of involvement with people, an administrator following orders, Simon emerges at the end of the novel ready to face the world, to be involved with people, even running for director. Because of his loyalty to the zoo under three different administrations, representing three different political ideologies, some are inclined to view him as a Vicar of Bray. In the twentieth century, however, many people had to face Simon's fundamental dilemma: whether to follow orders or to take up independent responsibility. Simon's American-born wife, Martha, disapproves of his behavior; she would like him to give up his job. Simon refuses, saying, "What do you think I am, a weathercock?" There is cruel irony in this remark; however, Wilson's irony is not pointed at Simon but rather at the general human predicament of a rapidly changing world in which choices are limited and people are continuously bombarded with dilemmas.

Simon's only independent action is his attempt to save the animals, which ends in disaster. In him, Wilson presents modern society struggling with despair in a desperate race to catch up with challenges. Simon's painful adjustment commands respect; he almost achieves heroic status when, after all the horrors and violence, he describes this modern world as "a demie-paradise." In this sense, *The Old Men at the Zoo* is Wilson's least pessimistic novel.

NO LAUGHING MATTER

No Laughing Matter is one of Wilson's most complex novels and requires close reading. The narrative is interwoven with dramas, enacted by the characters and reflecting various dramatic styles, including the absurd. Pastiches and parody of writers are important features of the novel, and literary references abound. John Galsworthy's 1922 *A Forsyte Saga*-like family chronicle of the Matthews family, the novel is also a historical document covering the twentieth century to 1967. The father, Billy Pop, a Micawber of the twentieth century, is a failure in his writing profession and ineffectual in his family life, letting his selfish wife dominate the children. All six of them have a crippled childhood and are deprived of privacy. By the end of the novel, they all achieve some kind of success in their professional lives; some even attain fame, such as Rupert, the actor, and Quentin, the political journalist, later a celebrated television commentator. Success does not make him lovable, and his cynicism, enjoyed by a million common viewers, questions the role of the media.

The final scene, in 1967, brings the whole clan together. While Margaret and her brother Marcus, a homosexual art dealer, are discussing and quarreling about Margaret's art, Hassan, who will inherit Marcus's cooperatively run scent factory, makes a final statement: the last words of the novel. He considers Marcus's ideas of a cooperative absurd. Hassan admires "ambition, high profit and determined management." His coldly calculating thoughts cast a dark shadow on the future; they underline once again Wilson's skepticism about the survival of liberal humanistic ideals in the modern world.

A strong moral sense links Wilson to George Eliot, and his sense of the caricature and the grotesque shows affinities with his favorite author, Charles Dickens. At the same time, his fiction is full of experiments into new literary methods. With almost each novel, Wilson made an important step forward in his search for new techniques. Tragedy and laughter coexist in his novels; there is tragedy in the private lives of the characters, but Wilson has a grotesque view of people's behavior, and his ability to create atmosphere through concentrating on speech habits promotes laughter.

In his commitment to duty, in his moral seriousness, Wilson is definitely akin to George Eliot, but he differs from the Victorian in that he cannot believe in "meliorism." George Eliot firmly maintained that self-awareness would lead to self-improvement and in consequence, to the individual's improved performance in the human community. Wilson is much more skeptical. Like E. M. Forster, he, too, is painfully aware of the decline of liberal hopes. In *The Middle Age of Mrs. Eliot*, he came to the sad conclusion that "self-knowledge had no magic power to alter," and in his sixth novel, he killed magic with finality.

AS IF BY MAGIC

In *As If by Magic*, magic, the ultimate evasion, is destroyed forever for the two central characters. Moreover, this time they are not middle-aged or elderly intellectuals paralyzed by frustration; they are young people. Wilson's teaching experience in Britain and America caused him to concentrate on the young, the future generation. Hamo Langmuir is a dedicated young scientist on a worldwide fact-finding tour to study the benevolent affects of his "magic" rice, destined to solve the problem of starvation in underdeveloped countries. His goddaughter, Alexandra Grant, in the company of her fellow hippies, is also on a world tour in search of an occult answer to all human problems. A bewildered Hamo must find out that his magic rice solution has introduced a farming method for which natives are not yet prepared and, consequently, it is causing more damage than good. Hamo falls victim to the anger of a crowd at a moment when he is ready to get involved in the human aspects of research. He, like Alexandra, who gets to Goa at the same time, had to learn through experience that the intrusion of Western ways into radically different cultures can cause disruption and many unnecessary tragedies. At the end of the novel, a sober Alexandra, cured of her hippie ways, resumes the responsibility of building a normal life for her son, a legacy of the hippie venture. A millionaire through an inheritance, she is ready to support and subsidize food research, but she knows by now that the possibilities are limited and that no easy answers are available; magic of any kind is only for the neurotics who are unable to face reality or for the power-hungry who use it to dominate others.

SETTING THE WORLD ON FIRE

Wilson's concern with human nature and with what it means for the future of the world dominates *Setting the World on Fire*. This novel is a family chronicle like *No Laughing Matter* but more condensed, more limited in time (1948-1969) and in the number of characters. Indeed, the writer concentrates on two brothers, Piers and Tom, the last generation of an old aristocratic family. Literary references are replaced by other arts: theater, music, architecture, and painting. Piers hopes to dedicate his life to the theater, and as a promising student, he earns the admiration of family, friends, and teachers with his stage-managing and directing abilities. The final part of the novel is about the preparations for the first performance of a new play, with the younger brother Tom supporting Piers as best he can in the hectic work. Everything is set for success when, unexpectedly, Scotland Yard intervenes and orders the premises emptied because of a bomb threat. The author of the play, an old employee of the family, masterminded the plot, simultaneously aimed at the family and at the government.

Tom saves Piers's life by knocking him down, but he himself gets killed. On his way home from the hospital where Tom died, Piers is on the verge of a breakdown and about to give up hope as well as artistic ambitions, because what good are the wonders of art in "a chaotic universe"? He calms down, however, and decides to stage the play anyway; he must not "lose the power to ascend the towers of imagination," he says. The tragedy brought Piers to a fuller realization of his duty as an artist, which means doing the only thing left to him: to create in, and for, a world threatened by chaos, violence, and destruction.

Wilson, a mixture of a twentieth century Charles Dickens, George Eliot, and E. M. Forster, with an increasingly dark vision of the modern predicament, rededicated himself, the artist, to his moral obligation. He continued writing in a desperate attempt to impose some kind of order on chaos and, by making people aware, to try to save humankind from itself.

Anna B. Katona

OTHER MAJOR WORKS

SHORT FICTION: *The Wrong Set and Other Stories*, 1949; *Such Darling Dodos and Other Stories*, 1950; *A Bit off the Map and Other Stories*, 1957; *Death Dance: Twenty-five Stories*, 1969.

PLAY: *The Mulberry Bush*, pr., pb. 1956.

NONFICTION: *Émile Zola: An Introductory Study of His Novels*, 1952; *For Whom the Cloche Tolls: A Scrapbook of the Twenties*, 1953 (with Philippe Jullian); *The Wild Garden: Or, Speaking of Writing*, 1963; *Tempo: The Impact of Television on the Arts*, 1964; *The World of Charles Dickens*, 1970; *The Strange Ride of Rudyard Kipling*, 1977; *Diversity and Depth in Fiction: Selected Critical Writings of Angus Wilson*, 1983; *Reflections in a Writer's Eye*, 1986.

BIBLIOGRAPHY

Conradi, Peter. *Angus Wilson*. Plymouth, England: Northcote House, 1997. A very fine introduction to Wilson's work, including a biographical outline, a section on his stories, chapters on his major novels, notes, and a very useful annotated bibliography.

Drabble, Margaret. *Angus Wilson: A Biography*. New York: St. Martin's Press, 1995. Written by a fine novelist and biographer, this book is a sympathetic, well-researched, and astute guide to Wilson's life and work. Includes notes and bibliography.

Faulkner, Peter. *Angus Wilson: Mimic and Moralist*. New York: Viking Press, 1980. Follows a chronological approach to Wilson's writings, including pertinent biographical background and evaluations of one or two main works each chapter in order to illustrate the evolution of Wilson's art. Also contains a bibliography of Wilson's major publications and selected secondary sources.

Gardner, Averil. *Angus Wilson*. Boston: Twayne, 1985. The first full-length study of Wilson published in the United States, representing a well-rounded introduction to Wilson's fiction. Includes a biographical sketch and analyses of Wilson's stories and novels through 1980. Contains a useful annotated bibliography of secondary sources.

Halio, Jay L. *Angus Wilson*. Edinburgh: Oliver & Boyd, 1964. The first full-length study of Wilson, this slender volume covers Wilson's writing through *The Wild Garden*. After a biographical sketch, Halio examines Wilson's fiction in chronological order. Concludes with a chapter on Wilson's literary criticism.

_____. ed. *Critical Essays on Angus Wilson*. Boston: G. K. Hall, 1985. Includes an overview of Wilson's writings, several reviews of his work, three interviews with the author, and fourteen essays that offer a diverse study of Wilson's individual works as well as his career as a whole. The selected bibliography draws readers' attention to further resources.

Stape, J. H., and Anne N. Thomas. *Angus Wilson: A Bibliography, 1947-1987*. London: Mansell, 1988. This thorough and indispensable resource includes a foreword by Wilson and a useful chronology of his life. Part 1 is a bibliography of works by Wilson, including books, articles, translations of his works, and interviews. Part 2 is a bibliography of works about Wilson.

ETHEL WILSON

Born: Port Elizabeth, South Africa; January 20, 1888
Died: Vancouver, British Columbia, Canada; December 22, 1980

PRINCIPAL LONG FICTION

Hetty Dorval, 1947
The Innocent Traveller, 1949
The Equations of Love, 1952
Lilly's Story, 1953
Swamp Angel, 1954
Love and Salt Water, 1956

OTHER LITERARY FORMS

Eleven short stories and eight essays by Ethel Wilson were published in magazines between 1937 and 1964. Two of the stories, "Hurry, Hurry!" and "Mrs. Golightly and the First Convention," were later anthologized, and two others, "I Just Love Dogs" and "The Window," were selected for *Best British Short Stories of 1938* and *Best American Short Stories: 1959*, respectively. These four stories, three of the others, and one of the essays, along with nine stories and an essay not previously published, were collected in *Mrs. Golightly and Other Stories* (1961). Besides the stories and essays, seven excerpts from novels also appeared separately as short stories in magazines. One of these, "Miss Tritt," from *The Equations of Love*, was anthologized as a short story.

ACHIEVEMENTS

Wilson was among the Canadian authors of the 1930's who broke away from the frontier tradition of provincial and didactic romances. She adapted to Canadian backgrounds the universal themes and methods of the realistic and psychological novel. She was one of the first Canadians to achieve a critical reputation abroad, not indeed as a major novelist, but certainly as an important minor one. Her novels are in the main current of the British and French realistic tradition, especially that of the early twentieth century, showing affinities with the works of E. M. Forster, Virginia Woolf, Arnold Bennett, Ivy Compton-Burnett, and Marcel Proust. Nevertheless, she maintained strong individuality in both theme and form. She wrote that authors can be "endangered by the mould or formula becoming apparent, and then the story has no life." Without being innovative, therefore, her novels have a great deal of variety of theme and approach, so that they are difficult to classify.

Perhaps because Wilson did not attempt to follow literary trends, and perhaps also because she began publishing relatively late in her life, when she was nearly fifty, her works did not have a dramatic impact on Canadian letters. She was publishing out of her generation, and her realism and understatement seemed somewhat old-fashioned to those authors of the 1930's who were following naturalistic trends. Still, she was influential in raising the quality of the art in Canada and in quietly introducing the theme of women "finding themselves" in some sense, well before the theme became popular among feminists. Her heroines are not necessarily strong or aggressive but they mature, meet the vicissitudes of their lives with determination and ingenuity, and for the most part succeed in small but important ways. Wilson's treatment of this theme and her impeccable craftsmanship contributed significantly to the maturing of the novel in Canada.

BIOGRAPHY

Ethel Davis Wilson was born in Port Elizabeth, South Africa, on January 20, 1888, to Robert William Bryant and Lila (Malkin) Bryant. Her mother died when she was only two, and her father took her to Staffordshire, England, to be reared by her maternal grandmother and successive aunts and uncles. Her family members were involved in a number of literary activities, including reading, journalism, and translation, and were acquainted with Matthew Arnold and Arnold Bennett. This literary atmosphere no doubt stimulated her interest in letters, and the literary allusions and quotations in her works demonstrate a comprehensive familiarity with the English tradition. Her father died when she was ten, and she went to Vancouver, British Columbia, to join her grandmother, who had moved there. Many of these family and early personal experiences are recounted in *The Innocent Traveller*, the semibiographical novel based on the life of her aunt.

In Vancouver, Wilson attended Miss Gordon's School, but she was sent to Trinity Hall School in Southport, England, for her secondary education. In 1907, she was graduated from Vancouver Normal School with a Second Class Teacher's Certificate. Between 1907 and 1920, she taught in Vancouver elementary schools.

On January 4, 1921, Wilson married Dr. Wallace Wilson. Their marriage was a happy one, marked by a good deal of traveling in Canada, Europe, and around the Mediterranean, and the successful development of both their careers. Dr. Wilson became a respected physician; he studied internal medicine in Vienna in 1930, represented Canada at the British Medical Association's convention in 1938 and at the World Health Organization in Paris in 1947, and was

president of the Canadian Medical Association in 1946 and 1947. The relationship between the Wilsons may have provided details for the happy marriages and the deepening love relationships in *Hetty Dorval, Lilly's Story*, and *Love and Salt Water*. The love of travel is also obvious in her work; travel is healing, broadening, and sensitizing to her characters, and Wilson's ability to describe the essential atmosphere of various locales is one of her strongest attributes.

Wilson published her first short story in 1937, and another in 1939 before her career was interrupted by World War II. Although Dr. Wilson was in the Canadian Army and Wilson herself served by editing a Red Cross magazine between 1940 and 1945, she made little use of wartime experiences in her novels, except tangentially in *The Innocent Traveller* and *Love and Salt Water*. Only the short story "We Have to Sit Opposite" deals specifically with wartime problems.

It is likely that Wilson's career in writing was encouraged by ill health. She was a victim of arthritis, which by 1956 had become so severe that she could not walk around in London, as she described in her essay "To Keep the Memory of So Worthy a Friend." She wrote, "One of the advantages of being lame is that one can sit and think. . . . And so I often think and think." In her last three novels, several major characters suffer handicaps, either physical or psychological, which affect their relationships with others in various ways and which must be transcended. No doubt her own disability enabled her to interpret this theme sympathetically.

The late 1940's and the 1950's were Wilson's most productive years, all of her novels and most of her short stories and essays being written or published during that period. At the peak of her success, after the publication of *Swamp Angel*, she received three awards: an honorary doctorate from the University of British Columbia in 1955, a special medal from the Canada Council in 1961 for contributions to Canadian Literature, and the Lorne Pierce Gold Medal from the Royal Society of Canada in 1964.

Dr. Wilson died in 1966, and Ethel Wilson lived in retirement in Vancouver until her death in 1980.

ANALYSIS

Although Ethel Wilson's canon is small, it is of high quality. The writing style is direct, simple, and expressive. Only occasionally, in the early books, does the diction or syntax call attention to itself as excellent. In general, only if one should try to paraphrase a passage or change a word would he become aware of that rightness of style that is typical of an artist. Passages describing the beauty of nature are most immediately impressive. Wilson's account of the train journey of the Edgeworths across Canada to Vancouver, in *The Innocent Traveller*, offers a vivid impression of the countryside and evokes the haunting vastness of the plains and forests stretching northward from the train track to the arctic circle. Magnificent descriptions of the Northern Lights occur in more than one book, and the mist-shrouded or sun-brightened mountains of the Vancouver area are sketched with a sensitive pen. Less frequent but equally impressive are descriptions of unsightly scenes, such as the interior of the slovenly Johnson apartment in *Tuesday and Wednesday* (published in *The Equations of Love*). It is not only in description, however, that Wilson excels; her humor is deft, ironic, and humane in passages such as the chapter "Nuts and Figs," from *The Innocent Traveller*, in which Great-Grandfather Edgeworth, in his declining days, proposes to two worthy lady friends in one afternoon and is refused, to the gratification of all three. Thoughtful and philosophical passages are also subtly presented, so that except for a few intrusive statements in the early, less integrated books, the concepts are suggested through economical language and apt symbols.

For Wilson, nature is not only a major inspiration for description, but also a method of characterization. Most of her protagonists are close to nature. Their ability to love and the essential civilization of their emotions are measured by their appreciation of the beauties and dangers of the Canadian mountains, forests, and waters. One notable exception is the garrulous Topaz Edgeworth, who exists in her human relationships rather than in nature, and the other is Hetty Dorval, an antagonist, whose appreciation of nature is one of the deceptive charms of her evil. Wilson's characters are firmly rooted in their environments and grow out of them. Her attitude toward them is dispassionately empathetic; they are clearly and humorously drawn, with subtle complexities. All are believable, and the best of them are memorable. She develops understanding of even her most unsympathetic characters, to the extent that plot is often weakened because she is drawn into digressions about the characters, about whom she cares more than she cares about careful plot structure. Topaz Edgeworth, Nell Severance, Lilly Hughes, and Maggie Lloyd are her most convincing creations, and it is the success of their characterization which causes *The Innocent Traveller*, *Lilly's Story*, and *Swamp Angel* to be her best novels.

If style and characterization are what make Wilson's novels outstanding, the plots are what keep them from being great. Plotting appears always to have been difficult for Wilson. Her admirers defend the inconsequentiality of her plots as true to life, expressing a philosophy about the fortuitous connections, or lack of connections, between the events in a person's history. Wilson minimizes suspense as a plot device; in fact, she often uses a technique of revealing future events, since causality interests her more than suspense. Still, the novels that are most effectively plotted, *Lilly's Story* and *Swamp Angel*, are recognized to be her best.

THE EQUATIONS OF LOVE

The title of Wilson's third book, *The Equations of Love*, suggests her recurring themes as a novelist. The typical protagonist of a Wilson novel is orphaned or otherwise separated from her family, as Wilson herself was as a child. Deprived of parental love, she becomes independent but lonely. This typical protagonist usually takes a journey, which is both a literal "trip"—aboard ship or into the Canadian wilderness—and an interior voyage of self-discovery. She is both soothed and awed by her insignificance in the natural world, which is beautiful but indifferent. Out of her new self-awareness, she learns to give of herself and to build a relationship, usually but not necessarily marriage, that brings new meaning to her life, either happiness or philosophical maturity. Love is the solution to this symbolic orphanhood, yet love, too, is imperfect. Orphanhood leaves its mark, and people make do with various "equations of love." This sense of irrevocable loss, of necessary compromise, saves Wilson's love-stories from sentimentality without veering toward cynicism. There is nobility in the aspiration toward love and self-subordination, triumph in even the flawed achievement of those graces. Wilson is impressed by the human ability to transcend egotism through whatever equation of love is possible to each individual.

HETTY DORVAL

For a first novel, *Hetty Dorval* is exceptionally good, although a melodramatic climax undercuts the subtleties of its characterization. It introduces Wilson's recurring themes: orphanhood, egotism, and love; the tempering of the ego by nature or travel; the lasting impact of momentary impressions or casual coincidences; the emotional maturation of a young woman. It is the story of Frances Burnaby, and the influence of Hetty Dorval on her maturation. Hetty crosses Frankie's path only a half-dozen times, but the temptation that she represents is very strong. The two are parallel in certain important respects: Both are only children, and both are reared with considerable protection and privilege. Both are attracted by elements of wildness, such as the turbulent Thompson River and the flight of wild geese. Frankie, however, has been reared by her parents with friends and loving discipline. By contrast, illegitimate Hetty's mother, Mrs. Broom, has hidden her maternal role, and with it her model of a loving relationship, to give Hetty a superior social standing: She has pretended to be Hetty's nurse and later her lady's maid, so that Hetty has learned tyranny and self-indulgence. Hetty is seraphically beautiful, with selfish charm, concerned only with her own pleasures. Frankie's mother calls her "The Menace" even before she knows Hetty's full story. Hetty's beauty and charm and her elemental wildness attract Frankie as a child. Even though the younger girl gives up the older woman's friendship, in obedience to her parents' orders, she does not understand the evil in Hetty's character. As she grows up and gains experience, however, in each subsequent contact with Hetty she learns more and comprehends more fully the destruc-

tiveness of Hetty's egotism. Frankie's full comprehension of what is morally wrong with Hetty's way of life comes when Richard Tretheway, the man she loves, falls in love with Hetty, and she has to decide what action she should take.

Three of the major characters in the story are orphaned: Frankie loses her father during the course of the story; Richard has lost his mother before Frankie meets him; and Hetty is a psychological orphan, having no publicly acknowledged father or mother. Each has dealt with the problems of isolation in a different way. Frankie grows to love the Tretheway family and builds new familial relationships with them; Richard has tried to substitute as a mother to his younger sister Molly; and Hetty has turned to self indulgence and the collection and abandonment of men. Each of these compensatory behaviors is one possible equation of love, but Hetty's is not honest or giving. The traits in Frankie's character that are similar to Hetty's are finally subordinated in Frankie as she learns to love. Although Hetty comments near the end of the book about their kinship, Frankie has moved beyond Hetty in self-control and compassion, and has thus ended her egocentric solitude.

THE INNOCENT TRAVELLER

Wilson's second novel, *The Innocent Traveller*, is a radical departure from her archetypal plot line. Topaz Edgeworth is not a solitary orphan, but a beloved child in a large and close family. Family is an all-pervasive concept throughout the book; characters are designated according to their role in the family, which changes as they age. Father becomes Grandfather and finally Great-Grandfather Edgeworth. Topaz herself is defined successively in terms of child, daughter, sister, aunt, and great-aunt. Topaz does lose her mother when she is young, but Father marries Mother's sister, and the family continues with virtually imperceptible interruption. Topaz continues to live with her father until she is middle-aged, and after his death, she lives with her older sister in much the same role of dependent daughter. Even with the death of the sister, she lives with her niece in virtually the same role, as if she were daughter to her niece. Although she moves to Canada, the wilderness does not impress her, nor does the new environment broaden her sympathies. *The Innocent Traveller* is a happy book, Topaz a happy woman, with a sense of warmth and security very different from the solitary mood of the other novels. Complementing this happy mood are glowing descriptions of the English and Canadian landscapes and sensitive expressions of a generous, witty, and perceptive philosophy.

What this book contributes to analysis of Wilson's thematic development is the contrast it provides with her recurring story of orphanhood and reconciliation. Topaz is never orphaned; she also never matures. Topaz is characterized as a delightfully irrepressible child, a lovable nonconformist, but gradually (and only between the lines), an irresponsible eccentric, and finally an irritating, futile burden on her family. She is loved, but she does not love deeply in return; she is an affectionate family member, but she does not feel the needs and tragedies of others. She remains childishly egocentric to the last of her life. After her death, "there is no mark of her that I know, no more than the dimpling of the water caused by the wind . . . and when we met together . . . perhaps no one remembers, until afterwards, to mention her name." The contrast between Topaz and Wilson's typical orphaned protagonists is striking. Topaz is never independent and never feels solitary; therefore, she never comes to value loving relationships. She never goes off alone to come to terms with herself and her universe; therefore, she never comes to terms with society. She never feels insignificant in nature; therefore, she never feels the need to establish significance through commitment and love. Having realized these themes from the converse and happy side, Wilson was prepared to use them more powerfully in *The Equations of Love* and *Swamp Angel*.

TUESDAY AND WEDNESDAY

Tuesday and Wednesday, a novella, the first part of *The Equations of Love*, deals with grotesque and pitiable "equations" in a mood of dark humor or satire. It is the story of the marital reelationship of Myrt and Mort Johnson, no longer a marriage of love, but an equation of shared resentment and frustration, lightened by moments of sensuality and a habitual tender impulse. Mort is shiftless, envious, self-deceived, but good-natured and capable of friendship. Myrt is self-pitying, domineering, lazy, sporadically sensual, often spiteful, but kind when it is no trouble to be kind. They live apart from most human contacts; Mort is too feckless and Myrt too lazy to entertain. They have no family except one aunt and one orphaned cousin, Victoria May Tritt, to whom they are indifferently kind because she is even more lonely and repressed than they are. This kindness passes in her mind as beneficence, and her gratitude constitutes a kind of love for them. Mort has a friend, Eddie, whom Myrt dislikes because of his drinking and brawling, but the two men share a bond of camaraderie and wishful thinking. These are the relationships which pass for love in the seedy near-slums of the city.

One evening, Mort meets Eddie, drunk; during a search in the dark for Eddie's lost suitcase, the inebriated Eddie falls off a pier and drowns. Mort, in his efforts to save his friend, falls into the water and is dragged under by Eddie to his death. Witnesses testify to Eddie's drunkenness, and the police conclude that both men were drunk, reporting the accident to Myrt in those terms. In her typical spite and self-pity, Myrt is not grieved, but affronted by Mort's drinking, abandoning her, and damaging her reputation by his association with the brawling Eddie. To salvage her self-esteem, she bitterly adopts the role of martyr. Victoria May has seen the meeting of Eddie and Mort, however, and knows that Mort was not drunk. In her love for both Myrt and Mort, she tells not only that part of the story but also the fiction that Mort dived after Eddie in a heroic attempt to save his friend. Thus, in her love for this unlikely pair, she both redeems Mort and comforts his wife by recalling Myrt's love for Mort, restoring her self-esteem, and establishing her right to grieve.

Even though *Tuesday and Wednesday* is darkly satirical, the story is in some ways the clearest of Wilson's statements about the success, however flawed, of the human drive for love as a solution to loneliness. Antagonistic though they may be, Myrt and Mort nevertheless love each other in their own way and cling together against their isolation. Mort's love for Myrt, with so little to thrive on, is sad and admirable. Myrt's need for Mort to pierce the shell of her egotism is believable and moving. Victoria May is almost heroic in her lie for Mort. Such unsatisfactory substitutes for love are pitiable, but they transcend the dingy and uninspiring atmosphere in which these characters live.

LILLY'S STORY

Lilly's Story, the second half of *The Equations of Love*, approaches the equations in a more positive way, although the heroine begins even more unpromisingly than Myrt and Mort. Lilly is an abandoned child, growing up like an alley cat. Never having experienced love, she expects none, and her first equation of love is the lust she excites to acquire food and stockings from men. Running away from the police, she gets a job as a waitress in a small town some distance from Vancouver and finds another equation of love, a man who provides her some temporary security, like "a kennel into which a bitch crawls." When this man leaves, and she finds she is pregnant, she goes to another small town farther into the wilderness and gets a job as a maid.

In this new environment, Lilly knows love for the first time, her love for her baby; and for her baby's sake, she invents a dead husband and behaves with such circumspection that she earns the respect of the couple whom she serves. Respect is a new equation of love. In this wilderness location, she also learns a new identification with nature which she could not have known in the slums of Vancouver. She lets Eleanor grow up in touch with this natural environment. Lilly also admires the pretty home and gentle manners of her employers, and she allows Eleanor, her child, to receive training from Mrs. Butler, determined that Eleanor will have a better life than her own. Eventually, Lilly leaves the Butlers and finds employment as housekeeper in a hospital. She and the Matron become close friends, and Lilly begins to build relationships that are overcoming her circle of self-protection. Eleanor grows into a lady and goes to nursing school, where she meets and marries a young lawyer. It is from this marriage that Lilly learns what love can be and what she has missed, when she sees Eleanor "come up to her husband with her face raised, and on her face a revealed look that Lilly had never seen on Eleanor's face nor on any face. . . . She

had lived for nearly fifty years, and she had never seen this thing before. So this was love, each for each, and she had never known it." Soon after this, a threat from Lilly's past drives her to Toronto, where she meets a widower and marries him, not with the passion that she has observed in Eleanor, but at least with "the perfect satisfaction which is one equation of love."

Lilly could be another Mrs. Broom (*Hetty Dorval*), but instead of hiding her motherhood and spoiling her child, Lilly drags herself out of that egocentric circle in order to prevent egocentrism in Eleanor, and in so doing, she finds loving relationships which almost transform her. Lilly starts off too badly and is too warped by her orphanhood ever to be totally transformed by love, but at least her story is a triumph of the power of love over egocentrism.

SWAMP ANGEL

Maggie Lloyd, is triply solitary: The protagonist of *Swamp Angel*, her mother died when she was a baby, her young husband in the war, and her baby and her father shortly thereafter. Maggie, unlike Wilson's other orphaned heroines, is never trapped in egocentrism by her loneliness. She has too much giving in her nature, and makes a second marriage out of compassion. Her story opens when she leaves that mistaken equation of marriage and goes into the wilderness, not to find but to reestablish herself. She finds a job as cook and assistant manager to a fishing lodge owner who has been lamed and can no longer manage alone. His wife, Vera, is the orphan in this story who has been warped and damaged by her loneliness. Vera finds no comfort in the beauty of the wilderness that restores Maggie after her separation. Vera, to the contrary, longs to return to the city from which she came, and instead of building new relationships that might redeem her, she nags at her husband and grows jealous of his admiration for Maggie. She eventually tries to commit suicide but cannot, and the story ends with Maggie trying to think how to break through Vera's egocentrism to help her. Another pair of "orphans" in this story are Maggie's friends Nell Severance and her daughter Hilda. Although their story constitutes a subplot, in some ways they are more important to the theme than is Vera.

Nell is a widow who has had more than her share of excitement and romance. She used to be a juggler on the stage, and she met and married a man she loved deeply. Because of her career and eventful marriage, however, she neglected Hilda to the extent that Hilda has always felt a degree of isolation and alienation from her mother. Nell's loved memento from her past life is a small revolver, the Swamp Angel, which was part of her juggling act. Hilda has always resented the revolver, as it reminds her of her neglect as a child, but she has never told her mother of her feelings: This is her gift of love to her mother. Nell is aware of Hilda's aversion to the gun, although she does not know the reason; one day she boxes it and sends it to Maggie: This is her gift of love to her daughter. Hilda goes away on a vacation, and comes back with new self-knowledge and recognition of her love for Albert Cousins, whom she marries not long before Nell dies. Thus, she builds new relationships to end her sense of solitude. These are very loving relationships, successful resolutions to the problems of isolation.

Swamp Angel makes use of two important symbols which specify more clearly than any of Wilson's earlier books the meanings of wilderness/egotism and orphanhood/love. While in the wilderness, Maggie goes swimming. She feels happy, strong, elemental, and in control of her movements. She can swim wherever she wishes; she is alone and completely independent. She also realizes, however, that this feeling is an illusion: She is not a god. The water is sensual and comforting, but it could drown her as impartially as it now buoys her. She swims back to her boat and returns to the lodge, to the things of civilization and the friends she serves in her job. The other key symbol is the Swamp Angel itself. It is a symbol of Nell's past, and she clings to it until she realizes that it makes Hilda uncomfortable. She gives it to Maggie to discard, reflecting that the symbol is less important than the reality, which cannot be taken away, but which grows less important as she grows nearer to death. Like the water in which Maggie swims, the gun symbolizes independence and control, but it also symbolizes egotism. In giving it away, Nell severs herself from the past in order to build a better rela-

tionship with her daughter. Unlike Maggie and Nell, Vera clings to her past, cannot find herself in nature, and so cannot build loving relationships with her husband and son. She tries to drown herself in the same lake where Maggie swims and where she throws Nell's gun.

Ethel Wilson's books can be summed up as minor masterpieces of style, insightful, witty, believable, and intelligent. They are prevented from being major works by faults in plotting, and they have not had a great influence upon literary trends. Nevertheless, they are all readable and entertaining, and the best are compelling. They deserve renewed attention in this age of increased receptivity to literature by and about women.

Carol I. Croxton

OTHER MAJOR WORKS

SHORT FICTION: *Mrs. Golightly and Other Stories*, 1961.

MISCELLANEOUS: *Ethel Wilson: Stories, Essays, and Letters*, 1987 (David Stouck, editor).

BIBLIOGRAPHY

Bhelande, Anjali. *Self Beyond Self: Ethel Wilson and Indian Philosophical Thought*. Mumbaim, India: S.N.D.T. Women's University, Bharatiya Vidya Bhavan, 1996. Examines the Indic influences on Wilson and her philosophy.

McAlpine, Mary. *The Other Side of Silence: A Life of Ethel Wilson*. Madeira Park: Harbour Publishing, 1989. The first biography.

McPherson, Hugo. "Fiction: 1940-1960." In *Literary History of Canada: Canadian Literature in English*, edited by Carl Frederick Klinck. 2d ed. Vol. 2. Toronto: University of Toronto Press, 1976. Wilson's fiction is discussed in the context of a supposed "search for identity" thought to infuse Canadian literature's development in the mid-twentieth century. McPherson notes a contrary individuality in Wilson's writing that transcends her failure at times to reconcile her creative impulses as both "artist and sibyl."

Mitchell, Beverley. "Ethel Wilson." In *Canadian Writers and Their Works: Fiction Series*, edited by Robert Lecker, Jack David, and Ellen Quigley. Vol. 6. Toronto: ECW PRESS, 1985. Wilson's life and complete works are thoroughly examined. An exhaustive bibliography follows Mitchell's straightforward, readable analysis, making this study a must for Wilson readers.

Pacey, Desmond. *Ethel Wilson*. New York: Twayne, 1967. This thorough, readable overview of Wilson's long and short fiction is not deeply analytical, but it does consider Wilson's lightly ironic vision and her valuable contribution to Canadian literature despite her relatively short publishing history. Despite its age, the book still contains some useful insights. A selected bibliography and an index are included.

Woodcock, George. "Innocence and Solitude: The Fictions of Ethel Wilson." In *Modern Times*. Vol. 3. in *The Canadian Novel*, edited by John Moss. Toronto: NC Press, 1982. Woodcock discusses Wilson's originality and vision as they are expressed in her novels and novellas.

_____. "On Ethel Wilson." In *The World of Canadian Writing: Critiques and Recollections*. Vancouver, British Columbia: Douglas and McIntyre, 1980. Slightly revised since its 1974 publication, this reflective personal essay enumerates the strengths of Wilson's personality and her unique works. This volume contains an index of the names of authors mentioned or treated in the book.

P. G. WODEHOUSE

Born: Guildford, Surrey, England; October 15, 1881
Died: Southampton, Long Island, New York; February 14, 1975

PRINCIPAL LONG FICTION
The Pothunters, 1902
A Prefect's Uncle, 1903
The Gold Bat, 1904
The Head of Kay's, 1905
Love Among the Chickens, 1906

Not George Washington, 1907 (with Herbert Westbrook)
The White Feather, 1907
Mike: A Public School Story, 1909 (also known as *Enter Psmith*, *Mike at Wrykyn*, and *Mike and Psmith*)
The Swoop: How Clarence Saved England, 1909
Psmith in the City: A Sequel to "Mike," 1910
A Gentleman of Leisure, 1910 (also known as *The Intrusion of Jimmy*)
The Prince and Betty, 1912
The Little Nugget, 1913
Something Fresh, 1915 (also known as *Something New*)
Psmith Journalist, 1915 (revision of *The Prince and Betty*)
Uneasy Money, 1916
Piccadilly Jim, 1917
Their Mutual Child, 1919 (also known as *The Coming of Bill*)
A Damsel in Distress, 1919
The Little Warrior, 1920 (also known as *Jill the Reckless*)
Indiscretions of Archie, 1921
The Girl on the Boat, 1922 (also known as *Three Men and a Maid*)
The Adventures of Sally, 1922 (also known as *Mostly Sally*)
The Inimitable Jeeves, 1923 (also known as *Jeeves*)
Leave It to Psmith, 1923
Bill the Conqueror: His Invasion of England in the Springtime, 1924
Sam the Sudden, 1925 (also known as *Sam in the Suburbs*)
The Small Bachelor, 1927
Money for Nothing, 1928
Summer Lightning, 1929 (also known as *Fish Preferred* and *Fish Deferred*)
Very Good, Jeeves, 1930
Big Money, 1931
If I Were You, 1931
Doctor Sally, 1932
Hot Water, 1932
Heavy Weather, 1933
Thank You, Jeeves, 1934

Right Ho, Jeeves, 1934 (also known as
    Brinkley Manor: A Novel About Jeeves)
Trouble Down at Tudsleigh, 1935
The Luck of the Bodkins, 1935
Laughing Gas, 1936
Summer Moonshine, 1937
The Code of the Woosters, 1938
Uncle Fred in the Springtime, 1939
Quick Service, 1940
Money in the Bank, 1942
Joy in the Morning, 1946
Full Moon, 1947
Spring Fever, 1948
Uncle Dynamite, 1948
The Mating Season, 1949
The Old Reliable, 1951
Barmy in Wonderland, 1952 (pb. in U.S. as
    Angel Cake)
Pigs Have Wings, 1952
Ring for Jeeves, 1953 (also known as *The Re-
    turn of Jeeves*)
Jeeves and the Feudal Spirit, 1954 (also
    known as *Bertie Wooster Sees It Through*)
French Leave, 1956
Something Fishy, 1957 (also known as *The
    Butler Did It*)
Cocktail Time, 1958
Jeeves in the Offing, 1960 (also known as *How
    Right You Are, Jeeves*)
Ice in the Bedroom, 1961
Service with a Smile, 1961
Stiff Upper Lip, Jeeves, 1963
Biffen's Millions, 1964 (also known as *Frozen
    Assets*)
Galahad at Blandings, 1965 (also known as *The
    Brinkmanship of Galahad Threepwood: A
    Blandings Castle Novel*)
Company for Henry, 1967 (also known as *The
    Purloined Paperweight*)
Do Butlers Burgle Banks? 1968
A Pelican at Blandings, 1969 (also known as *No
    Nudes Is Good Nudes*)
The Girl in Blue, 1970
Jeeves and the Tie That Binds, 1971 (also known
    as *Much Obliged, Jeeves*)

(Courtesy D.C. Public Library)

Pearls, Girls and Monty Bodkin, 1972 (also known
    as *The Plot That Thickened*)
Bachelors Anonymous, 1973
The Cat-Nappers: A Jeeves and Bertie Story, 1974
    (also known as *Aunts Aren't Gentlemen*)
Sunset at Blandings, 1977

OTHER LITERARY FORMS

In addition to writing more than ninety novels,
P. G. Wodehouse wrote hundreds of short stories,
some eighteen plays (of which ten were published),
the lyrics for thirty-three musicals, and a vast, uncollected body of essays, reviews, poems, and sketches.
So much of Wodehouse's early work has been lost
that it is impossible to measure his total literary output, and collections of his stories published under the
title "Uncollected Wodehouse" are likely to appear
with some frequency for the next twenty years. He
also wrote two comic autobiographies, *Performing*

Flea: A Self-Portrait in Letters (1953; revised as *Author! Author!*, 1962) and *America, I Like You* (1956; revised as *Over Seventy: An Autobiography with Digressions*, 1957).

ACHIEVEMENTS

Wodehouse has always been regarded as a "popular" writer. The designation is just. "Every schoolboy," wrote Ogden Nash, "knows that no one can hold a candle to P. G. Wodehouse." His novels and short stories were among the best-selling works of their generation, but it should be remembered that Wodehouse's appeal transcended his popular audience. Many of the major writers of the twentieth century have professed a deep admiration for the art of "Plum," as Wodehouse was known to his friends and family. T. S. Eliot, W. H. Auden, Bertrand Russell— all were fanatic enthusiasts of Wodehouse. Hilaire Belloc said that he was the greatest writer of the twentieth century, and Evelyn Waugh offered the following tribute to his genius: "Mr. Wodehouse's idyllic world can never stale. He will continue to release future generations from captivity that may be more irksome than our own." It is unfortunately true that critics and readers who expect high seriousness from their literary pleasures will never quite approve of one who makes a light-hearted mockery of most of England's and America's most sacred cows. F. R. Leavis, the celebrated English scholar, pointed to the awarding of an honorary doctorate to Wodehouse as proof of declining literary standards. Other critics have been even more emphatic in their deprecation of Wodehouse's lack of seriousness. For sheer enjoyment, however, or what Dr. Johnson called "innocent recreation," no one can touch P. G. Wodehouse.

BIOGRAPHY

Pelham Grenville Wodehouse was born in Guildford, Surrey, on October 15, 1881, the third of four sons born to Henry Ernest and Eleanor Deane Wodehouse. Wodehouse's father was a member of the English Civil Service and spent most of his working years in Hong Kong; indeed, it was a mere chance that Wodehouse was not born in Hong Kong.

Whether it was miscalculation or the event was premature, his birth occurred during one of his mother's rare and rather brief visits to England.

Wodehouse was reared away from his parents; they were, he often remarked, like distant aunts and uncles rather than parents. Wodehouse entered Dulwich College at the age of twelve and remained there for the next six years. The school was not prominent in the sense that Harrow and Eton were prominent; it was simply a good middle-class school. The headmaster was the most impressive figure, and may have served as the model for Wooster's nemesis, the Reverend Aubrey Upjohn; the headmaster was not impressed with his student. He once wrote to Wodehouse's parents: "He has the most distorted ideas about wit and humour. . . . One is obliged to like him in spite of his vagaries." The vagaries, apart from the student's drawing match figures in his classical texts, are unrecorded. In those final years at Dulwich, Wodehouse had found his vocation. He was appointed editor of the school paper and sold his first story to a boy's weekly, *The Public School Magazine*. The story won first prize for fiction in that year.

Following graduation in 1900, Wodehouse went to work for the London branch of the Hong Kong and Shanghai Bank. His work there was not a complete disaster for the banking industry, but very nearly so. Wodehouse was no good at checks and balances and served only as an unpleasant distraction for those who were. At night, he continued to write fiction and reviews or plays and was given a position on the *Globe* in 1902, the year the first of his many novels was published. *Punch* accepted an article from him the next year, and a second novel was also published in 1903. From that time, Wodehouse averaged more than a novel, several short stories, and either a play or musical a year. In 1914, Wodehouse married Ethel Rowley, a widow with one child. The marriage was a happy one, and the author frequently expressed his gratitude to his wife for the support she had given to his work. For the Wodehouse reader, however, the following year had a much greater significance: *Something New*, the first of the Blandings novels, was published. A few years later, *My Man Jeeves* (1919) appeared, the first of the Jeeves and Wooster saga.

Novels and stories appeared with an unfailing regularity, and in the next two decades, Wodehouse became an acknowledged master. In 1939, Oxford paid tribute to his greatness by conferring on him the honorary Doctorate of Letters (D.Litt.). The doctorate meant that Jeeves, Wooster, Emsworth, and the rest were accepted as part of the heritage of English literature. The London *Times* supported the Oxford gesture, noting that the praise given to Wodehouse the stylist was especially apt: "Style goes a long way in Oxford; indeed the purity of Mr. Wodehouse's style was singled out for particular praise in the Public Orator's happy Horatian summing up of Mr. Wodehouse's qualities and achievements."

Wodehouse and his wife had lived in France throughout much of the 1930's, and though war with Germany was believed imminent, he returned to France after he received the doctorate at Oxford. In 1940, he was taken prisoner by the Germans. In various prison camps, he made a series of broadcasts over German radio which were interpreted as a form of collaboration with the enemy. Wodehouse was innocent of all the charges, but it was perhaps his innocence, the vital ingredient in most of his heroes, that almost undid him. The closest Wodehouse came to collaboration was his remark to the effect that he was not unhappy in prison, for he was able to continue his work. One scholar has called that broadcast "clearly indiscreet," but those who have read the Wodehouse letters know that he scarcely thought about anything else beside his work.

After his release, Wodehouse eventually returned to America, where he took permanent residence; he was naturalized in 1955. In 1973 he was knighted, and he died in 1975 at the age of ninety-four.

ANALYSIS

Few of P. G. Wodehouse's novels are ever far from the school environment, for the plots of the later Jeeves and Blandings series of novels frequently derive from the desire of one schoolmate, usually Bertie Wooster, to help another. Yet the early school novels represent a distinct type within the body of Wodehouse's fiction.

THE SCHOOL NOVELS

Perhaps, as one scholar has observed, these eight school novels are no more than "bibliographical curiosities," in that only the most ardent fan of Wodehouse would be led to read them after the later work had been written. Still, the works are different in tone and theme. The novels are set at Wrykyn College, which seems to closely resemble Dulwich, the author's alma mater. The emphasis is on sports, and this emphasis gives a serious tone to the work. Boys are measured largely by their athletic skills. One might suggest that the ever-present sports motif was a symbol of the particular virtues of youth: comaradeship, loyalty, and perseverance. Enlarging upon these virtues, Wodehouse was following what was almost a cliché in the boy's fiction of the time. The cliché, however, was one particularly congenial to the author, who once noted that he would never be able to write his autobiography, for he had not had one of the essentials in the background of an autobiographer— "a hell of a time at his public school."

Wodehouse loved Dulwich College, and the eight school novels are a record of his affection. The schoolmasters are a decent group, the boys, with few exceptions, are generous and loyal, and the setting of the college is one of great beauty. The distinctive element in the novels is the happiness which pervades them, and the reader need only remember George Orwell's, Graham Greene's, and Evelyn Waugh's accounts of their own school days to notice the sharp difference between Wodehouse and many of his contemporaries. The only curiosity about the novels is not the absence of horror and malice, but that no one in the school novels seems to have learned anything at Wrykyn. It should also be remembered that many of Wodehouse's most celebrated idiots are graduates of Oxford and Cambridge.

Wodehouse once said of his work: "I believe there are two ways of writing novels. One is mine, making a sort of musical comedy without music and ignoring life altogether." The Blandings series of novels is perhaps the best example of the author's determined resistance to "real life." These twenty-odd novels are centered on the beautiful estate of Lord Emsworth, who serves as unwilling host to almost everyone who goes in and out of his ancestral home. Lord Emsworth is old and absentminded, and his affections are limited to his younger brother Galahad, his roses, and his pig, the Empress of Blandings. This pig, as Emsworth remarks several times in each of the novels, has won the silver prize for being the fattest in Shropshire County. Only Galahad can really appreciate the high distinction that has been conferred on the Empress, and one feels that even he is not very serious about the pig. Yet the Empress is very nearly the catalyst for all of the actions that take place in the novels. She is stolen, which makes it imperative to effect a rescue; she is painted an outrageous color and introduced into strange bedrooms to make the recipients of such favors "more spiritual" in their outlook; and on one occasion, her portrait is done at the behest of Lord Emsworth.

THE BLANDINGS NOVELS

This last episode in the life of the Empress occurs in one of the best of the Blandings novels and is a fair measure of the formula used by Wodehouse in the series. *Full Moon*, in which the portrait is commissioned, has all of the characteristics of the Blandings novels. Emsworth has the insane idea that the pig's portrait should be done by an eminent painter, but they have all turned down his request. While this action is debated, Lady Constance, Emsworth's sister, has come to the castle with a young lady in tow. Her intent is to keep the young woman away from the man to whom she has become foolishly engaged, foolishly because the fellow does not have any money, which is the essential requisite for a good marriage in the mind of Lady Constance. Galahad arranges to have the young man invited to the castle on the pretext that he is Edwin Landseer, celebrated painter of animal pictures, including "Pig at Bey." Galahad's ruse works for a while, but the young man's painting is rejected by Emsworth, who complains that the painting makes the Empress look as if she had a hangover. The young man is ejected from Blandings but soon returns, wearing a beard resembling an Assyrian monarch. He makes a tragic mistake when he gives a love note to one of Emsworth's other sisters, thinking that she is a cook. He is again thrown out. By the novel's end, however, he has suc-

cessfully won the hand of his beloved, and the sisters are all leaving the estate. Galahad has once more succeeded in spreading "sweetness and light" in all directions, except that of his usually irate sisters.

There are few variations in the Blandings series. At least one and sometimes as many as three courtships are repaired; the pig is safe from whatever threatens it; the sisters have been thwarted in usually about five ways by Galahad; and Lord Emsworth has the prospect of peace and quiet in front of him at the novel's end. Yet Emsworth, Galahad, the sisters, and a host of only slightly less important or interesting characters are among the most brilliant comic figures in the whole of English literature. In writing the Blandings novels, Wodehouse followed his own precept: "The absolute cast-iron rule, I'm sure, in writing a story is to introduce *all* your characters as early as possible—especially if they are going to play important parts later." Yet his other favorite maxim that a novel should contain no more than one "big" character—is seldom observed in the Blandings series. Each of the characters has his own element of fascination, and each is slightly crazy in one way or another. As absurd and funny as is Lord Emsworth's vanity about his pig, it is only a little more so than his sisters' vanity about their social position and wealth. If the formula for this series does not vary, neither does the uniform excellence of each novel in the series.

THE JEEVES AND WOOSTER NOVELS

More than a dozen novels use Jeeves and Bertie Wooster as the main characters. These novels have commonly been regarded as Wodehouse's "crowning achievement," but the author once noted that the idea of the latent greatness of Jeeves came to him very slowly. In his first appearance in a short story, he barely says more than "Very good, Sir." Jeeves is the manservant to Bertie Wooster, who is preyed upon by aunts, friends, and women who wish to help him improve his mind as a prerequisite to marriage with him. Wooster has been dismissed as silly and very stupid. Compared to Jeeves, perhaps he is both, but he is also extremely generous with both his money and time, and it is his unfailing willingness to help others that invariably places him in the precarious situation that is the main plot. Wooster is an Oxford graduate, but detective novels are most demanding reading. He never uses a word of more than two syllables without wondering whether he is using the word properly. Wooster is the "big" character in the Jeeves series, and such a character, according to Wodehouse, is worth "two of any other kind."

The marriage motif is very much a part of the Wooster and Jeeves saga, but frequently the central issue of this series is helping Bertie keep away from the wrong woman. It is not quite accurate to describe him as one of "nature's bachelors," for he has been engaged to nearly a score of females and is threatened with marriage in nearly every one of the novels in the series. Some of these women are insipid and poetic, others are coarse and athletic; the worst are intellectual women who want to improve his mind. He is assigned books to read that he finds boring and incomprehensible, told never to laugh aloud, and threatened, after marriage, with having his membership in the Drones Club revoked. Bertie is quite content with the state of his mind and soul. At the threat of marriage and all the other threats that the novels present, Jeeves comes to the rescue. In spite of Bertie's chronic need of Jeeves's aid, he is ostensibly the main character in the novels and one of Wodehouse's most brilliant creations. It is through the eyes of Bertie that the reader observes and passes judgment on what is taking place in the novel. Such a process was an enormous technical difficulty for his creator: Wooster must be stupid and generous in order for the plot to develop, but not so stupid that the reader casts him off.

The character of Jeeves, perfect as it is, is one of the most traditional aspects of Wodehouse's craft, for the wise servant of a stupid master is a hoary cliché. Jeeves has never been to Oxford, and he has no aristocratic blood flowing in his veins to spur him into action. His central motive for rescuing Bertie and the legions of others who come to him for counsel is a manifestation of what is called in this series of novels "the feudal spirit." Though not a university man, Jeeves knows French, Latin, and the whole of English literature. He quotes freely from the Shakespearean tragedies, and even has at his disposal a host of obscure lines from obscure poets in Latin and English. He is not a gloomy person, but Benedictus de Spinoza is his favorite author. He is well acquainted with psychology, and his rescue of Bertie or others in trouble frequently derives from his knowledge of the "psychology" of the individuals in question. He is moved by the feudal spirit, but he is tipped in a handsome way by his employer for services rendered, and he accepts the just praises of all whom he serves.

The series is also distinguished by a host of lesser figures who threaten to jostle Bertie out of his role as the main character. Gussie Fink-Nottle is an old schoolmate of Bertie, and he is engaged to a particularly insipid woman, Madelaine Basset, a romantic intellectual. She has a poetic phrase for everything, and drives Bertie and all who know her crazy merely by opening her mouth. Madelaine is one of Bertie's former girl friends, and she imagines that Bertie is still in love with her. The hero's duty is to see that the pending nuptials between Gussie and Madelaine take place, but Gussie, who is even less intelligent than Bertie, keeps fouling things up. Bertie goes at once to his aid, but nothing works until Jeeves puts his brain to the trial.

EULALIE SOEURS

Jeeves never fails in his destined role as guardian angel to Wooster, but the plots frequently have an additional twist. Jeeves, though not omniscient as a character, has recourse to a body of information that none of the others shares. As a butler and member of a London club for butlers, he has access to a private collection of anecdotes supplied by other butlers about their masters. It is a point of honor for a manservant to supply all vital information about his employer—tastes, eccentricities, and even weaknesses—so that others will be well advised before taking employment with the same person. The collection has something about almost every rich male in England, and when affairs take on a desperate note, Jeeves is dispatched to London to find out something about the adversary that might serve as blackmail. Thus, one of the silliest of Wodehouse's creations, a proto-Fascist named Spode who is inclined to bully everyone and especially Wooster, is disarmed when it is discovered that he designs ladies' underwear. As Wooster is being threatened with decapitation by Spode, he mentions the name of Spode's company, *Eulalie Soeurs*, and the man is silent and servile, though it is only at the very end and with the bribe of a trip around the world that Jeeves tells Wooster the meaning of that magic phrase.

The Jeeves novels, then, have at least three plots running through them, and it is in his scrupulous concern for the development of the plot that the author exhibits one of his greatest talents. The key to Wodehouse's concerns for the logic and probability of his plots derives, perhaps, from his lifelong interest in detective novels; Wodehouse frequently avowed that they were his favorite kind of reading. The plots of the great Wodehouse comedies develop like that of a superb mystery: There is not an extraneous word or action in them.

THE PSMITH NOVELS

For most Wodehouse readers, the Blandings and Jeeves series of novels represent the highest level of Wodehouse's art, but there are many other novels that do not fit into either category. In 1906, Wodehouse published *Love Among the Chickens*, which has in it the first of Wodehouse's several "nonheroes," Ukridge. Ukridge has almost no attractive qualities. He does not work; rather, he lives by his wits and is able to sponge off his friends and from many who scarcely know him. Another character who figures prominently in several novels is Psmith. The name is pronounced "Smith," and its owner freely admits that he added the *P* to distinguish himself from the vast number of Smiths. The name is one mark of the young man's condescending arrogance, but he is helpful toward all who seek his assistance. A Psmith novel usually ends with the marriage of a friend or simply a bit of adventure for the central figure. Psmith does not hold a regular job, and like many of the other young male protagonists in Wodehouse novels, he seems to be a textbook study in the antiwork ethic. The heroes in the Psmith series, like the central figure himself, are not ignorant or stupid men, but the novelist's emphasis is on their old school ties and on physical excellence. They are, as one critic noted, "strong, healthy animals." They are good at sports and they triumph over poets and other intellectual types. On occasion, they may drink heavily, but they make up for an infrequent binge by an excess of exercise.

Evelyn Waugh once suggested that the clue to Wodehouse's great success was the fact that he was unaware of the doctrine of original sin. In the Wodehouse novel, virtue is inevitably triumphant, and even vice is seldom punished with anything that might be called severity. In Wodehouse's catalog of bad sorts, one group alone stands out: intellectual snobs. In his frequent descriptions of such types, Wodehouse may have consciously been responding to the disdain with which intellectuals have usually treated his work; in turn, the author had almost no sympathy for the group that he often described as "eggheads." Whatever may have been his motivation, the athletes and the innocents invariably triumph over those who carry on about their own minds or some esoteric art form. It is therefore hard to agree with critics such as George Orwell who find elements of snobbery in the Wodehouse novels. It is true that the creator of Blandings Castle loved big houses and grand vistas, but the aristocrats are too obviously flawed in intellect or temper for any to assume Wodehouse was on their side. It may be, however, that Wodehouse was an inverse snob in his treatment of intellectuals, both male and female. None of them succeeds in his fiction.

There is nothing like a consensus over the source or qualities of Wodehouse's greatness as a writer. Scholars have traced Wooster and Jeeves back through English literature to authors such as Ben Jonson, but source studies do not account for Wodehouse's genius. He has been called the laureate of the Edwardian age, but there is little resemblance between the Edwardian world and that of P. G. Wodehouse. For most readers, the triumph of a Wodehouse novel is in its artistry of presentation. All the aspects of fiction—good story, effective characters, and dialogue which is often brilliant—are present. Wodehouse once summed up his career as well as anyone ever has: "When in due course Charon ferries me across the Styx and everyone is telling everyone else what a rotten writer I was, I hope at least one voice will be heard piping up: 'But he did take trouble.'" Wodehouse did indeed take trouble with his work, but given the rich abundance of that work and the incredible smoothness of each volume, the reader would never know.

John R. Griffin

OTHER MAJOR WORKS

SHORT FICTION: *Tales of St. Austin's*, 1903; *The Man Upstairs, and Other Stories*, 1914; *The Man with Two Left Feet, and Other Stories*, 1917; *My Man Jeeves*, 1919; *The Clicking of Cuthbert*, 1922 (also known as *Golf Without Tears*); *Ukridge*, 1924 (also known as *He Rather Enjoyed It*); *Carry on, Jeeves!* 1925; *The Heart of a Goof*, 1926 (also known as *Divots*); *Meet Mr. Mulliner*, 1927; *Mr. Mulliner Speaking*, 1929; *Jeeves Omnibus*, 1931 (revised as *The World of Jeeves*, 1967); *Mulliner Nights*, 1933; *Blandings Castle and Elsewhere*, 1935 (also known as *Blandings Castle*); *Mulliner Omnibus*, 1935 (revised as *The World of Mr. Mulliner*, 1972); *Young Men in Spats*, 1936; *Lord Emsworth and Others*, 1937 (also known as *The Crime Wave at Blandings*); *Dudley Is Back to Normal*, 1940; *Eggs, Beans, and Crumpets*, 1940; *Nothing Serious*, 1950; *Selected Stories*, 1958; *A Few Quick Ones*, 1959; *Plum Pie*, 1966; *The Golf Omnibus: Thirty-one Golfing Short Stories*, 1973; *The World of Psmith*, 1974.

PLAYS: *A Gentleman of Leisure*, pr. 1911 (with John Stapleton); *Oh, Lady! Lady!*, pr. 1918; *The Play's the Thing*, pr. 1926 (adaptation of Ferenc Molnár); *Good Morning, Bill*, pr. 1927 (adaptation of László Fodor); *A Damsel in Distress*, pr. 1928 (with Ian Hay); *Baa, Baa, Black Sheep*, pr. 1929 (with Hay); *Candlelight*, pr. 1929 (adaptation of Siegfried Geyer); *Leave It to Psmith*, pr. 1930 (adaptation with Hay); *Anything Goes*, pr. 1934 (with Guy Bolton and others); *Carry On, Jeeves*, pb. 1956 (adaptation with Bolton).

NONFICTION: *William Tell Told Again*, 1904 (with additional fictional material); *Louder and Funnier*, 1932; *Bring on the Girls: The Improbable Story of Our Life in Musical Comedy, with Pictures to Prove It*, 1953 (with Guy Bolton); *Performing Flea: A Self-Portrait in Letters*, 1953 (revised as *Author! Author!* 1962; W. Townend, editor); *America, I Like You*,

1956 (revised as *Over Seventy: An Autobiography with Digressions*, 1957).

EDITED TEXTS: *A Century of Humour*, 1934; *The Best of Modern Humor*, 1952 (with Scott Meredith); *The Week-End Book of Humor*, 1952 (with Meredith); *A Carnival of Modern Humor*, 1967 (with Meredith).

BIBLIOGRAPHY

Green, Benny. *P. G. Wodehouse: A Literary Biography*. New York: Rutledge Press, 1981. This very useful study, arranged chronologically, traces the connections between Wodehouse's personal experiences and his fictional creations. Illustrations, a chronology, notes, a bibliography, and an index are included.

Hall, Robert A., Jr. *The Comic Style of P. G. Wodehouse*. Hamden, Conn.: Archon Books, 1974. Provides a discussion of three types of Wodehouse's stories, including school tales and juvenilia, romances and farces, and the various sagas. The fascinating, detailed analysis of Wodehouse's narrative techniques and linguistic characteristics is indispensable for anyone interested in understanding his style. Contains an index and a bibliography.

Phelps, Barry. *P. G. Wodehouse: Man and Myth*. London: Constable, 1992. Phelps has uncovered much new information in this sympathetic biography. He also provides an unusual number of useful appendices including a Wodehouse chronology, family tree, and bibliography.

Sproat, Iain. *Wodehouse at War*. New Haven, Conn.: Ticknor & Fields, 1981. This volume is necessary to those studying the sad war events that clouded Wodehouse's life and to those interested in exploring the individual psychology that produced such comic delight. Sproat, a politician as well as a fan, vindicates Wodehouse's innocence in the infamous Nazi broadcasts, which are reprinted here. Includes appendices of documents in the case.

Usborne, Richard. *After Hours with P. G. Wodehouse*. London: Hutchinson, 1991. A collection of entertaining pieces on Wodehouse's life and death written somewhat in the spirit of Wodehouse himself.

_____. *Wodehouse at Work to the End*. 1961. Rev. ed. London: Barrie & Jenkins, 1976. Includes individual chapters on Wodehouse's major series characters, very helpful appendices of lists of his books, plays, and films, and an index. For the diehard fan, each chapter is followed by a brief section called "Images," with humorous quotations from the works. The introduction refers to other secondary sources.

Voorhees, Richard J. *P. G. Wodehouse*. New York: Twayne, 1966. An excellent introductory volume on Wodehouse, with chapters on his life, his public school stories, his early novels, the development of his romantic and comic novels, a description of the Wodehouse world, and a discussion of the place of that world in British literature. A chronology, notes and references, and a bibliography of primary and secondary sources are provided.

(Nancy Crampton)

LARRY WOIWODE

Born: Carrington, North Dakota; October 30, 1941

PRINCIPAL LONG FICTION

What I'm Going to Do, I Think, 1969
Beyond the Bedroom Wall: A Family Album, 1975
Poppa John, 1981
Born Brothers, 1988
Indian Affairs, 1992

OTHER LITERARY FORMS

Larry Woiwode is known primarily for his longer fiction, but he also frequently published short stories in such prominent literary periodicals as *The Atlantic Monthly* and *The New Yorker*; several of his stories were chosen for anthologies of the year's best. He has written book reviews and essays for many newspapers, including *The New York Times*. *The Neumiller Stories* (1989), a collection of thirteen previously un-

collected stories, including three penned in the 1980's, expands the "family album" of narratives about the Neumiller clan that Woiwode began in his novels *Beyond the Bedroom Wall* and *Born Brothers*. He also published a well-received book of poetry, *Even Tide* (1977).

ACHIEVEMENTS

Woiwode's first novel, *What I'm Going to Do, I Think*, won for him the prestigious William Faulkner Foundation Award for the "most notable first novel" of 1969 and the American Library Association Notable Book award in 1970 and brought him immediate critical attention. It was a best-seller and was translated into several foreign languages. His second novel, *Beyond the Bedroom Wall*, actually begun before *What I'm Going to Do, I Think*, was nominated for both the National Book Award and the National Book Critics Circle Award, and it won the American Library Association Notable Book award in 1976. It became an even bigger commercial and critical success than his first novel. Woiwode's third novel, *Poppa John*, however, was much less successful commercially and critically. The novel's premise and protagonist indeed represented a departure from the regional narrative Woiwode had successfully employed in his previous fiction, but it did earn the Cornerstone Best Book of the Year Award in 1982.

Poppa John notwithstanding, critics are quick to credit Woiwode's idiosyncratic, family-centered narratives with helping indirectly to rehabilitate the family chronicle, a genre long considered out of fashion. After a decade of relative publishing silence, Woiwode returned to this narrative genre in *Born Brothers* and *The Neumiller Stories*. Woiwode's evolving canon of Neumiller narratives depicts prodigal sons and daughters who, no matter where they tread, fulfill their destiny in rediscovering their roots and the family relationships which nurtured them early in their lives. Woiwode unabashedly admires the traditional nuclear family, and his fiction underscores the value of finding one's way by retracing one's steps. His narrative strength is thus seen in the fact that, even among readers accustomed to despondent, "lost" protagonists preoccupied with discovering the mysteries of life in the squalor of the city or some illicit relationship, Woiwode can make such old-fashioned premises seem startlingly fresh and appealing.

In the ebb and flow of many a writer's career, an acclaimed "first novel" often permanently overshadows subsequent efforts, and the disappointment with—and apparent dearth of fresh ideas that followed after—the publication of *Poppa John* provoked many critics and readers to wonder if Woiwode had lost his narrative vision. Such concerns were answered with the publication of *Born Brothers* and *The Neumiller Stories*.

BIOGRAPHY

Larry Alfred Woiwode (pronounced "why-woodee") was born in Carrington, North Dakota, October 30, 1941, and spent his early years in nearby Sykeston, a predominantly German settlement amid the rugged, often forbidding north-midwestern terrain. No doubt the beauty as well as the stark loneliness of this landscape heightened the author's appreciation

for the effect of nature upon individual character. At the age of ten, he moved with his family to Manito, Illinois, another evocatively Midwestern environment capable of nurturing the descriptive powers of a budding fiction writer.

He attended the University of Illinois for five years but failed to complete a bachelor's degree, leaving the university in 1964 with an associate of arts in rhetoric. He met his future wife, Carol Ann Patterson, during this period and married her on May 21, 1965. After leaving Illinois, Woiwode moved to New York City and supported his family with freelance writing, publishing in *The New Yorker* and other prestigious periodicals while working on two novels.

He was a writer-in-residence at the University of Wisconsin, Madison, and had extended teaching posts at Wheaton College (Illinois) and at the State University of New York at Binghamton, where he served as a faculty member (intermittently) beginning in 1983. In 1977, he was awarded the Doctor of Letters degree from North Dakota State University. He and his family returned to North Dakota in 1978 to maintain an organic farm.

ANALYSIS

To understand Larry Woiwode's craft and achievement, one must finally recognize the essentially religious character of his narratives and their thematic structure. He is an advocate for restoring a moral, even religious voice to modern letters. While believing that the most important human questions are, in fact, religious ones, Woiwode rejects the notion that there can be legitimate, compelling "novels of ideas", for him, such fiction connotes mere propagandizing. Woiwode handles such questions not by placing philosophical soliloquies in the mouths of sophisticated, worldly protagonists, but by creating authentically ordinary characters, and settling them comfortably into the concrete and utterly mundane world of daily life.

In achieving this effective depiction of what might be called heightened normality, Woiwode's prose is consistently active, alive, and unassuming, approaching at times the crisp clarity of Ernest Hemingway but touched with a finely tuned lyricism. While

Woiwode has sometimes been criticized for lapsing too easily into didacticism or marring an otherwise evocative scene with excessive detail, his keen eye for the extraordinary ordinariness of life makes his narrative vision compelling and believable.

As a novelist, Woiwode stands apart from most of his contemporaries in refusing to drown his characters in the angst-ridden excesses that have become so conventional in the modern American novel. His characters are not helpless victims of their times but participants in them; they are accountable not so much for what has happened to them but for what they do in response to their circumstances. Their conflicts, from Chris Van Eenanam's enigmatic search for manhood in *What I'm Going to Do, I Think* to Poppa John's drive to recover his self-identity, are not merely contrived psychological dramas played out inside their own consciousness, but compelling confrontations with the very concrete world of everyday life. This is a world which registers as authentic to the reader precisely because of Woiwode's gift for realism.

Woiwode's characters eventually recognize that the answers to their dilemmas are only partly in themselves. In the reestablishment of personal trust in friendships and the nostalgia of forgotten familial relationships, they recover a sense of balance and worth in themselves. However obliquely, each major Woiwode character finds himself in a quest for a transcendent moral order, a renewed trust in God and humanity that would give him a reference point for his life. This quest animates their rejection of narcissism and a search for a love and security that only marital and familial relationships can foster.

Woiwode's willingness to affirm that these relationships are central to self-fulfillment and to the stability of American culture makes him unique among a generation of writers whose thematic concerns tend to focus on their characters' dehumanization in society and alienation from family life and marital fidelity. Woiwode thus belongs in the company of self-consciously moralistic writers such as Walker Percy and Saul Bellow, who are more interested in the ways human beings survive and thrive in a fallen world than in the ways they capitulate to it.

When compared with other writers of his caliber, Woiwode cannot be considered a particularly prolific author. Yet two of his novels were critically acclaimed, national best-sellers, and they are among the best American novels written after 1960. The publication in consecutive years of *Born Brothers* and *The Neumiller Stories* seems to have redeemed Woiwode from the ambivalent response to *Poppa John*, and Woiwode's reputation as an important American writer in the second half of the twentieth century seems secure.

WHAT I'M GOING TO DO, I THINK

Woiwode's first novel, *What I'm Going to Do, I Think*, is an absorbing character study of two newlyweds, each of whom is originally drawn to the other as opposites proverbially attract. Chris Van Eenanam, the protagonist, is a listless mathematics graduate student, an unhappy agnostic unsure of his calling in life. The novel's title accentuates his self-doubt and indecision, echoing something Chris's father once said in observing his accident-prone son, "What I'm going to do, I think, is get a new kid." Ellen Strohe, his pregnant bride, is a tortured young woman, dominated by the overbearing grandparents who reared her after her parents' accidental death. Neither she nor Chris can abide their interference and meddling.

Despite the fact that little action takes place "live" before the reader, the psychological realism in Woiwode's use of compacted action and flashbacks and the patterned repetition of certain incidents carry the reader along as effortlessly as might a conventionally chronological narrative. The reader learns "what happens" primarily as events filter through the conversations and consciousness of Chris and Ellen Van Eenanam during their extended honeymoon at her grandparents' cabin near the northwestern shore of Lake Michigan.

In this retreat from the decisions Chris elects not to face, the couple, now intimate, now isolated, confront a grim modern world, which has lost its faith in a supreme being fully in control of his created universe. This loss is exemplified most dramatically in the lives of Chris and Ellen as they try to sort out the meaning of affection and fidelity in their new relationship as husband and wife and as potential parents. Ellen's pregnancy is at first a sign of a beneficent nature's approval of their union, but later, as each has a premonition of their unborn child's death, it becomes a symbol of an ambivalent world's indifference to their marriage and its apparent fruitlessness.

In the absence of a compensatory faith even in humankind itself, a secondary faith arguably derived from faith in God, Chris and Ellen come to realize that they have lost their ability to navigate a hostile world with lasting, meaningful relationships. Neither mathematics nor nature can fill the vacuum left by an impotent faith whose incessant call is to fidelity and perseverance without passion or understanding. In a suspenseful epilogue which closes the novel with an explanation of what has happened to them in the seven years following their marriage, Chris and Ellen return to their honeymoon cabin. Chris retrieves the rifle he has not touched in many years, and, as the action builds toward what will apparently be his suicide, he repeats to himself the beginning of a letter (suicide note?) that he could not complete: *"Dear El, my wife. You're the only person I've ever been able to talk to and this is something I can't say. . . ."*

As he makes his way to the lake, he fires a round of ammunition into a plastic bleach container half-buried in the sand. In the novel's enigmatic final lines, Chris fires "the last round from his waist, sending the bullet out over the open lake." This curious ending seems intended by Woiwode to announce Chris's end of indecision—a recognition that his life can have transcendent meaning only in embracing fully his marriage commitment to Ellen.

BEYOND THE BEDROOM WALL

The expansiveness and comic vitality of Woiwode's second novel, *Beyond the Bedroom Wall*, offer a marked contrast to *What I'm Going to Do, I Think*. In *Beyond the Bedroom Wall*, Woiwode parades sixty-three characters before the reader by the beginning of chapter 3. True to its subtitle, *A Family Album*, *Beyond the Bedroom Wall* is a sprawling, gangly work of loosely connected snapshots of the Neumiller family. An engaging homage to the seemingly evaporating family unit at the end of the twentieth century, the novel's "plot" is nearly impossible to

paraphrase, consisting as it does of some narrative, some diary entries, and even its protagonist Martin Neumiller's job application for a teaching position. Since Woiwode published nearly a third of the forty-four chapters of *Beyond the Bedroom Wall* as self-contained short stories in *The New Yorker*, it is no surprise that the book reads as a discontinuous montage of events, images, and personalities.

The novel opens in part 1 with the funeral of Charles Neumiller, a German immigrant farmer who had brought his family to America before the war, and it continues, to part 5, closing with stories of the third generation of Neumillers in 1970, bringing the Neumiller family full circle from birth to life to death. Yet it is Martin Neumiller, Charles's son, a god-fearing, devoutly Catholic man and proud son of North Dakota, whose adventures and misadventures give the novel any unity it possesses. "My life is like a book," he says at one point. "There is one chapter, there is one story after another." The eccentric folks he encounters in and out of his extended family form a burlesque troupe of characters who boisterously sample both the joys and the sorrows of life on Earth. In the Neumiller "family album," Woiwode lends concreteness to his notion that reality is a fragile construction, one that sometimes cannot bear scrutiny "beyond the bedroom wall," that is, beyond the dreamy world of sleep, of its visions of what might be. Woiwode intimates that whatever hope there may be for fulfilling one's dreams, it is anchored in "walking by faith, and not by sight," by trusting in and actively nurturing family intimacy.

The rather sentimental, "old-fashioned" quality Woiwode achieves in this family chronicle, his evocation of once-embraced, now-lamented values, prompted critic and novelist John Gardner to place Woiwode in the company of literature's greatest epic novelists: "When self-doubt, alienation, and fashionable pessimism become a bore and, what's worse, a patent delusion, how does one get back to the big emotions, the large and fairly confident life affirmations of an Arnold Bennett, a Dickens, a Dostoevski? *Beyond the Bedroom Wall* is a brilliant solution."

Woiwode's eye for the rich details of daily life enables him to move through vast stretches of time and space in executing the episodic structure in this novel. His appreciation for the cadences of midwestern speech and his understanding of the distinctiveness of prairie life and landscape and its impact on the worldviews of its inhabitants recall other regional writers such as Rudy Wiebe and Garrison Keillor at their best.

POPPA JOHN

Poppa John is shockingly short when compared with the massive *Beyond the Bedroom Wall*, and is more a novella than a novel. The book takes its title from the character Ned Daley played for many years on a popular television soap opera. His immense popularity beginning to overshadow the show itself, he is abruptly written out of the show in a dramatic "death." Ned thus finds himself suddenly unable to recover a sense of purpose, so long has he lived within the disguise of Poppa John, the fiery father figure, who often quoted Scripture to his television family. Now close to seventy, outspoken and Falstaffian in appearance and behavior, he seeks his deeply lost identity. Ned to his wife, but Poppa John to everyone else, he is lost in the malevolent nostalgia of growing old without self, or self-respect.

The novel opens two days before Christmas, a few months after Poppa John's television "death." Facing the Christmas season with wife, Celia, broke, broken, and without prospects for the future, the couple wander New York City, squandering their savings on gifts they had always wanted to buy for each other. Forced to "be himself," he finds he has leaned too heavily on the preacherlike Poppa John character, and his life begins to unravel. He is finally forced to face his own inconsistencies, his doubts, and even his sins, as Ned, an "elderly boy," is incapable of trusting in a life beyond the present. Speeding to a climax in its closing pages, the novel depicts Poppa John "coming to himself" on Christmas Day, realizing that he, after all these years, does believe in God, and therefore can come to believe in himself.

Poppa John perhaps deserved a better critical reception than it received; as a more than interesting attempt to portray an elderly actor's disintegrating life, it contains some of Woiwode's most lyrical scenes. In the end, however, it remains an unsatisfy-

ing chronicle—in part because the complexity apparent in Poppa John's character is never fully realized, presented as it is in a very compressed time frame. While Poppa John emerges as a potentially authentic character in the early parts of the novella, Woiwode gives the reader little insight into the motivations which would prompt his sudden conversion experience at the climax of the story.

BORN BROTHERS

In *Born Brothers*, Woiwode returns to the characters, setting, and moral center that brought him his greatest and most uniformly favorable critical attention. Woiwode begins what he calls not a sequel but a "companion volume" to *Beyond the Bedroom Wall* in the middle of the twentieth century, the narration filtered through the consciousness of Charles Neumiller, a lost soul searching his memories for a meaning to life and a purpose for living it. He finds both in exploring his relationship with his brother Jerome. Charles's fragmentary childhood memories in fact become the narrative building blocks for the often elliptical and multiperspective chronicle that unravels before the reader in an even more challenging sequence than that of *Beyond the Bedroom Wall*. *Born Brothers* contains less a plot than a chain of remembrances; as family members and their ahistorical interactions with Charles are paraded before the reader in a kind of visual patchwork, one is compelled to enter Charles's consciousness and see the world through his convoluted epistemology.

Despite his outward sophistication and sense of being, Charles is obsessed with suicide; he seems incapable of conceiving of a meaningful order outside the family structure that had shaped his life and has now dissipated with the death of his mother and the collapse of his marriage. In part, it is Woiwode's intent to explain American society's apparent moral disintegration—rampant promiscuity, unwanted pregnancy, and divorce—by reference to the absence of strong family ties. Charles longs for the bond of brotherhood he once shared—or thinks he shared—with elder brother Jerome. That idyllic childhood in North Dakota, free from the cares and stresses modern, industrial life, allows to impinge without provocation upon Charles's consciousness. Charles's strange career as a "radio personality" who is both the interviewer and the interviewee is somehow emblematic of his need for conversion, for freedom from self. He needs an "outside," a reference point, which, Woiwode hints, will come only from faith in the transcendent God whose eternal family Charles is invited to join.

Woiwode makes few compromises for the reader unwilling to attend to—or, perhaps eavesdrop upon—Charles Neumiller's open-ended musings. To refer to his ramblings as stream-of-consciousness narration is to give too precise a labeling, for not merely a consciousness is under consideration here but the history of a mind and a life as well. The journey to and through that history is not one that the casual reader will be inclined to take, which underscores the main criticism of Woiwode's prose shared even by critics sympathetic to his family chronicle: his apparent inattention to the toll his often exhaustive detail takes on both his characters and his readers. Jonathan Yardley's judgment seems most apt: "It's a pity to see a writer of Woiwode's talent and humanity stuck, at mid-career, in the endless exploration and re-exploration of material that has yielded its last fresh insight if not its last lovely sentence."

INDIAN AFFAIRS

With its broken sequence of scenes and lack of exposition or resolution of conflicts, *Indian Affairs* has elements of a postmodern novel. Woiwode uses this style to reflect the inner turmoil of Chris Van Eenanam, the main character of *What I'm Going to Do, I Think*. Chris and his wife Ellen return to an isolated cabin in the Michigan woods so that he can write his Ph.D. dissertation on American poet Theodore Roethke's natural philosophy and poetry. Mundane interruptions such as cutting firewood, installing a water pump, shopping, and tavern hopping distract him. A gang of drunken Native American teenagers threatens him when he does not supply them with beer, and a mysterious stalker forces him to keep a loaded gun. On a deeper level, Chris undergoes an identity crisis—a need to affirm his masculinity, to cope with religious and moral dilemmas, and to resolve the conflict of whether his roots are Caucasian or American Indian.

Chris and Ellen's childless seven-year marriage has brought them no sense of permanence or hope for the future. Although they are thirty years old, Chris is still a graduate student, and they are dependent upon Ellen's wealthy grandparents for use of the cabin. Ellen's previous miscarriage and her ensuing barrenness symbolize the status of their marriage. Ellen resolves her unhappiness by recording her thoughts in a journal. Meanwhile, she joins a feminist discussion group, goes to a bar without an escort, and tries the hallucinogen peyote to ease her feelings of emptiness. Her conflicts disappear when she becomes pregnant again.

Chris spends much time with his bachelor friend Beau Nagoosa, a Chippewa Indian who has dropped out of white culture to build his own cabin. He supports himself as a woodcutter and justifies stealing wood on absentee landowners' property by telling himself it was once Native American land. Beau resents the invasion of white real-estate promoters, who claim to represent Volunteers in Service to America (VISTA), yet he accommodates them and compromises his ideals.

Chris and Beau discuss humanity's role within the spiritual harmony of the natural world. For Chris, Roethke's claim that objects in nature are sentient is synonymous with Native American beliefs. Beau introduces Chris to peyote, which stimulates vivid sensory perceptions and fantasies but renders both Chris and Beau unable to cope with their real problems. Frustrated by chaotic events in his life and dissatisfied with the prospect of returning to academe in New York, Chris is overcome with depression. Feeling that nothing can guide him now except his own instincts, Chris decides to adhere to a line from one of Roethke's poems, "I'll be an Indian." Chris's future role as a teacher or leader is ambiguous.

As Chris begins to identify more strongly with his own Blackfoot Indian heritage and feel reverence for the natural world, conflicts escalate between the segregated white and Native American communities. The natural environment shrinks as urban development expands. Tribal leadership does not extend beyond exhibition dancing at powwows. American Indian families disintegrate, alcoholism and drug use destroy lives, and teenage youths engage in threat-making and violence. Woiwode's realistic and tragic portrayal of Native American life offers no solution to the problems.

To fully appreciate Woiwode's book, readers should have read *What I'm Going to Do, I Think* and have more than a passing acquaintance with the philosophies and writings of Theodore Roethke and Vine Deloria, an American Indian cultural nationalist. Woiwode's underlying theme is that modern Native Americans lack effective leaders to guide them.

Bruce L. Edwards, Jr.,
updated by Martha E. Rhynes

OTHER MAJOR WORKS

SHORT FICTION: *The Neumiller Stories*, 1989; *Silent Passengers: Stories*, 1993.

POETRY: *Even Tide*, 1977.

NONFICTION: *Acts*, 1993; *What I Think I Did: A Season of Survival in Two Acts*, 2000.

BIBLIOGRAPHY

Connaughton, Michael E. "Larry Woiwode." In *American Novelists Since World War II*, edited by James E. Kibler, Jr. 2d series. Detroit: Gale Research, 1980. An assessment of Woiwode's gift for regional fiction that explores the themes and narrative style of his first two novels.

Gardner, John. Review of *Beyond the Bedroom Wall*, by Larry Woiwode. *The New York Times Book Review* 125 (September 28, 1975): 1-2. An enthusiastic review of what most critics believe is Woiwode's best novel; Gardner's plaudits won a wide audience for Woiwode beyond the small circle of intellectuals who had hailed his first novel.

Jones, Timothy. "The Reforming of a Novelist." *Christianity Today*, October 26, 1992, 86-89. In this interview, Woiwode discusses his view of the nonreligious, humanistic approach of the East Coast literary establishment and the fact that his most recent writing includes greater emphasis on a religious view of such issues as belief and doubt.

Nelson, Shirley. "Stewards of the Imagination: Ron Hanson, Larry Woiwode, and Sue Miller." *Christian Century*, January 25, 1995, 82-86. An inter-view with three novelists in which they discuss their works and careers as well as the role of religion in their lives and writing. Includes an excerpt from Woiwode's *Poppa John*.

Pesetsky, Bette. Review of *Born Brothers* by Larry Woiwode. *The New York Times Book Review* 93 (August 4, 1988): 13-14. An affirmative evaluation of Woiwode's narrative mode and a defense of the novel's difficult thematic structure.

Woiwode, Larry. "An Interview with Larry Woiwode." *Christianity and Literature* 29 (1979): 11-18. An early, revealing interview in which Woiwode discusses those influences which shaped his narrative vision. Notable is his discussion of the centrality of family to his characterizations.

CHRISTA WOLF

Born: Landsberg an der Warthe, Germany; March 18, 1929

PRINCIPAL LONG FICTION

Der geteilte Himmel: Erzählung, 1963 (*Divided Heaven: A Novel of Germany Today*, 1965)
Nachdenken über Christa T., 1968 (*The Quest for Christa T.*, 1970)
Kindheitsmuster, 1976 (*A Model Childhood*, 1980; also as *Patterns of Childhood*, 1984)
Kein Ort: Nirgends, 1979 (*No Place on Earth*, 1982)
Kassandra: Erzählung, 1983 (*Cassandra: A Novel and Four Essays*, 1984)
Störfall: Nachrichten eines Tages, 1987 (*Accident: A Day's News*, 1989)
Sommerstück, 1989
Medea: Stimmen, 1996 (*Medea: A Modern Retelling*, 1998)

OTHER LITERARY FORMS

Christa Wolf's reputation rests primarily upon her novels. Her short stories were collected into one volume in 1980, *Gesammelte Erzählungen*, updated and translated in 1993 as *What Remains and Other Stories*. Her most important essays, reviews, speeches, and interviews are found in *Lesen und Schreiben: Aufsätze und Betrachtungen* (1971; *The Reader and the Writer: Essays, Sketches, Memories*, 1977), *Lesen und Schreiben: Neue Sammlung* (1980), *Die Dimension des Autors* (1987; *The Author's Dimension*, 1993), and *Auf dem Weg nach Tabou* (1994; *Parting from Phantoms*, 1997). She has also collaborated on the screenplays of several East German films, and with her husband, Gerhard Wolf, wrote the script for *Till Eulenspiegel* (1972). Wolf has also published her correspondence with author Brigitte Reimann, *Sei gegrüßt und lebe: Eine Freundschaft in Briefen, 1964-1973* (1993) and her correspondence with author Franz Fühmann, *Monsieur, wir finden uns wieder: Briefe, 1968-1984* (1995).

ACHIEVEMENTS

Before publishing her first short story, "Moskauer Novelle," Wolf had prepared for her own literary career by working for several years as a reader and reviewer for a variety of East German publications. She rose to the position of editor of *Neue deutsche Literatur*, the periodical of the German Writers' Union (1958-1959). Her fame began with her first novel, *Divided Heaven*, a work which evoked lively discussion in both East and West Germany and which quickly became known beyond the borders of the two German states. She received the National Prize III Class of the Academy of the Arts in 1964 for this novel. In 1972, she shared with Walter Kempowski the Wilhelm Raabe Prize of the city of Brunswick and in 1980 received the prestigious Georg Büchner Prize from the German Academy of Language and Poetry in Darmstadt. In the spring of 1974, she was Max Kade Writer-in-Residence at Oberlin College, Ohio. In 1983, Wolf was a guest professor at Ohio State University, where she received an honorary doctorate. In 1985 she was made an Honorary Fellow of the Modern Language Association of America (MLA). In 1987, the City of Munich, Germany, awarded her its Geschwister-Scholl Prize, which comes with twenty thousand German marks. Wolf's fortunes then suffered a temporary reversal, and in

1993 the City of Munich attempted to revoke the prize. In 1992-1993, Wolf was a research fellow at the Getty Center for the History of Art and the Humanities in Santa Monica, California. Wolf is an internationally recognized author, the recipient of many invitations, honors, and awards. In 1997, Wolf was the first German to receive the Salon du Livre prize at the Bordeaux Book Fair. She is widely recognized as one of the most significant contemporary German writers by many of her literary peers as well as by critics, Germanists, and the reading public.

The political controversy surrounding several of her works has tended at times to obscure or distort their actual import while at the same time revealing one of their most important thematic concerns: the role and significance of literature in the contemporary technological world. She is a politically engaged writer in the broadest sense of the term. The honesty and the sensitivity with which she has examined the influence of the modern state and of modern society on the individual have struck responsive chords in her readers at home and abroad and have caused those with political axes to grind to regard her as friend or foe, depending on the direction of political currents. Her own self-confidence and clarity of artistic purpose, however, have enabled her to prevail over those who seek to use her works for their own short-range goals.

BIOGRAPHY

Christa Wolf was born Christa Margarete Ihlenfeld, the daughter of a grocer, March 18, 1929, in Landsberg an der Warthe, Germany, now Gorzów, Poland. Her middle-class background and her uneventful youth are remarkable only insofar as they might be seen as typical for many Germans of her generation: those old enough to have been influenced by the twelve years of Nazi rule, but too young at the end of the war to have participated actively in it. Wolf's autobiographical novel *Patterns of Childhood* deals largely with these twelve years and explores the connections that exist between the committed Socialist of the 1970's and the sixteen-year-old girl who confided to her diary that she would die if the Führer should. The flight of Wolf's family westward from her birthplace is documented in *Patterns of Child-hood* as well as in several of her other prose pieces. Allusions to her own years of studying German liter-ature in Jena and Leipzig (1949-1953) may be recog-nized in *The Quest for Christa T.*

She joined the Socialist Unity Party (SED) in 1949, the year that East Germany was founded as a separate state with that party at its head. In 1951, she married Gerhard Wolf, a fellow Germanist and histo-rian, and in the next years had two daughters, Annette (born in 1952) and Katrin (born in 1956). Her work as a reviewer and editor continued throughout these years. In 1959, she followed the suggestion of the SED leadership that writers go to work in the facto-ries in order to gain working-class experience ("the Bitterfeld way to literature"). She worked for a time in a train-car manufacturing plant in Halle. This, along with the overnight construction of the Berlin Wall on August 13, 1961, became the background for *Divided Heaven*.

Wolf's public activities and her literary concerns became increasingly connected during the 1960's and 1970's. Her conviction that the writer must be personally and actively involved in the workings of his or her society was expressed not only themati-cally and theoretically in her writings of these years but also in her life. In early 1963, her name was put on the candidate list for the Central Committee of the SED. At the December, 1965, plenary meeting of this body, she defended writers who acknowledged in their works that certain aspects of socialism were as yet unrealized in East German life. This topic had be-gun to concern her as well, as *The Quest for Christa T.* was soon to show. The defense of such literary works helped to bring her into disfavor with Party functionaries, so that in April of 1967, her name was no longer on the SED Central Committee candidate list. Not until 1971 did the political climate in East Germany change enough to allow Wolf's attitudes to be accepted. However, she was removed from the leadership of the Berlin branch of the Writers' Union for having cosigned an open letter protesting the ex-patriation of the poet Wolf Biermann in 1976. Unlike some other prominent writers and intellectuals who signed the letter, Wolf remained in East Germany

and enjoyed the freedom to write, lecture, and travel abroad. She chose to refrain from further criticism of the regime.

East German Communism collapsed, and Germany was peacefully reunified on October 3, 1990. Wolf was then free to publish her account of the costly and absurd surveillance that had intruded into her life for years. The slim volume *Was Bleibt: Erzählung* (1990; what remains) gave rise to a journalistic attack out of all proportion to the content of the book. The press, not the academics, in West Germany criticized Wolf for not having taken a stronger stand against the Communist regime. Fuel was added to the flames when it became known that Wolf had cooperated with the East German police as a social informant be-tween 1959 and 1962. The facts that she passed on only inconsequential information and came under surveillance herself were ignored. Instead, journalists tried to discredit all of Wolf's work. In an effort to counteract this politically motivated unfairness, her publisher, Luchterhand, put out a thick volume of documentation in 1993, *Akteneinsicht Christa Wolf Zerrspiegel und Dialog* (examining the files on Christa Wolf, distorting mirrors and dialogues). Edited by Hermann Vinke, it contains the state secu-rity files on Wolf from 1955 to 1964 and many arti-cles and letters written by others in her defense.

Wolf's collection of essays and speeches, *Parting from Phantoms*, ends with an essay on Germany. Wolf states that the German people did not want the country to be divided into two separate states, East and West, from 1949 to 1990. Now that Germany is reunified, the time has come to work together.

ANALYSIS

In her interview with East German critic Hans Kaufmann (in 1974; reprinted in *Lesen und Schreiben: Neue Sammlung*), Christa Wolf used the term "sub-jective authenticity" to describe what she believes should be the methodology and the goal of contem-porary prose writers: the intense involvement of the author's self in the work, along with an absolutely straightforward presentation of reality, as much as this is possible—given the unavoidable subjectivity of the author. Such an approach to writing prohibits the establishment of distance between the author and the work, the reading public, and society as a whole. It implies that the process of writing is more important than the finished product and therefore prevents the commercialization of literature toward which modern marketing tends. For Wolf, the relationship of the author to the work becomes paradigmatic for the relationship between literary language, on the one hand, and modern secular language, on the other, and between the individual's need for self-realization and the pressures for conformity in the technological age. By bridging the gap between author and work through subjective authenticity, Wolf asserts that an intensely reciprocal relationship between author and reader, reader and work is created. At the same time, the dangerous erosion of language in a technological and scientific age is diminished, and the alienation of the individual from society may be abated.

In her acceptance speech for the Georg Büchner Prize in 1980, Wolf warned against alienation of inner, personal life from outer, materialistic life in a contemporary, technological world. She claimed that the dichotomy between the languages of these worlds is not merely a symptom of the separation of the places of work and of living, of the material from the spiritual, but that it has now become a perpetuator of this alienation. Ultimately, it is a threat to the continuation of the human race. The one-sided positive evaluation of modern technology and material advances has been accompanied by a parallel devaluation of the spiritual side of life and its expression in literary language. A deep skepticism toward modern science and technology is an important theme in Wolf's fiction, particularly in the short stories "Neue Lebensansichten eines Katers" ("The New Life and Opinions of a Tomcat") and "Selbstversuch" ("Self-Experiment"). The writer, says Wolf, must combat these modern tendencies by reaffirming the validity of a committed individual viewpoint and its subjective expression in language. The subjectivity of the individual author, because it is founded in the real world and has its purpose outside itself, can thus be a model for individual self-realization. It is not surprising that Wolf's novels all deal with the general problem of individual self-realization within various so-

cial contexts. Thematically as well as stylistically, Wolf intends her works to effect "the production of new structures of human relationships in our time," as she told Kaufmann.

In order to examine the problem of modern alienation and as part of the process of developing subjective authenticity, Wolf has drawn heavily on her own life as a literary source. She has looked at East German society in order to understand alienation in herself and others (*Divided Heaven* and *The Quest for Christa T.*). She wrote *Patterns of Childhood* in order to understand herself better as part of a whole generation of Germans who have been alienated from an important era of their lives and history. She has turned to the lives and times of others at the beginning of the technological age, around 1800, when she believes the alienation of the spiritual from the material in art and life and within the modern world in general began. In *No Place on Earth*, she uses the figures of two writers, Heinrich von Kleist and Karoline von Günderode, both early victims of the alienation between art and life, both eventual suicides.

The writer (often represented by the narrator/author) is the quintessential figure in Wolf's works, and the process of narration is often presented as the fundamental act which can reconcile the material with the spiritual, the real with the ideal. The striving toward a whole world which underlies her ideas about writing gives Wolf's work the utopian impulse which she has said is necessary for full human life here and now. The parallels with the philosophical thought of Ernst Bloch (author of *Das Prinzip Hoffnung*, 1954-1959; *The Principle of Hope*, 1986), a professor in Leipzig during Wolf's study there, may be seen in Wolf's concept of utopianism as an attitude of active commitment to contemporary issues. In the foreword to her 1980 edition of Günderode's works, Wolf says, "Writers are, and this is not a lament, predestined to be sacrificial victims and self-sacrificers." They, through language, can bridge the chasm between materialism and spirituality, although they pay a heavy price in the process.

The selection of the long-neglected poet Günderode as the subject not only of the novel but also of this significant essay fits another pattern in Wolf's work: her preoccupation with female figures. Women are the main characters in all her novels and short stories. Where men play prominent roles, it is either as problematic, inwardly torn figures (*Divided Heaven* and *No Place on Earth*) or as destructive forces. Wolf has said that she has focused on female figures because she naturally can identify more readily with women. More than this, however, she has claimed historical reasons for her depiction of women and men in seemingly stereotypical fashion. She asserts that women, because they have been excluded from power in the last two centuries, have also largely escaped the inner alienation from which modern men suffer. They are therefore a potential force for changing and even for saving contemporary human society. The problematic condition of the writer in the modern world is intensified when the writer is a woman.

Wolf, in examining the experiences of earlier women writers (Günderode and Bettina von Arnim) and of incipient, if failed, contemporary women writers (Christa T.), is also examining herself and her own situation. She understands this aspect of her writing as a natural result of an examination of history (women's position in bourgeois society). Her own experiences of the consequences of this historical development then go into her works as part of a general dialogue about women in the Socialist state and as part of her striving for subjective authenticity.

Wolf's life and work are closely intertwined. She maintained her optimism and hope in Socialist society while recognizing its inadequacies. Other East German colleagues were not able to stay on this narrow path without incurring official disfavor. Wolf's own frictions with Party functionaries can be seen as proof of the actuality, pertinence, and commitment of her writing. Certainly most of her work would not have taken form without her intense inner and outer involvement with her surroundings. Yet it is not limited to this involvement. Like all good literature, it goes beyond the configurations of time and place in which it is based to address issues of timeless human interest: the conflict between the individual and society, the problem of self-knowledge, and the endeavor to "heal the world" through writing, as Wolf once put it.

DIVIDED HEAVEN

The immediate acclaim which was accorded Wolf's first novel, *Divided Heaven*, in both East and West Germany was largely the result of the Cold War climate of the day. The presentation of an unhappy love affair against the background of divided Berlin was interpreted in the West as a veiled protest against this political act. The defection of the negatively portrayed male protagonist and the affirmation of the positive heroine-narrator's life in the East was regarded in East Germany as properly supportive Socialist Realism, in spite of the ideological blurring of the heroine's motivation and the ambivalent Socialist zeal displayed by some of the secondary figures. That the novel is not about divided Germany but about "the reasons people leave one another," as Wolf said, has become clearer in recent years.

The thematic relationship to her later works is also apparent now. Manfred and Rita drift apart because they represent, as Alexander Stephan stated in his study *Christa Wolf* (1976), the two basic attitudes toward life possible for members of contemporary industrial society. Wolf oversimplifies the dichotomy to some extent by making Manfred the heir of bourgeois materialism and Nazi opportunism through his family, while the two years of Rita's life chronicled in the book almost become a condensation of the Marxist view of historical process: from a close connection to nature through the spiritual and psychological disruptions of bourgeois intellectualism and late capitalism to the healing world of contemporary everyday socialism.

The problems addressed in the book, however, are not so black and white. In *Divided Heaven*, Wolf begins her examination of the elements within Socialist society which prevent individuals from realizing themselves fully. Rita may make the "right" decision in the official view when she parts from Manfred in West Berlin, the day before the Wall is constructed, but her reasons remain unclear to her for some time. Indeed, only several months later, while recuperating from a suicide attempt made soon after the lovers' parting, does she become convinced of the correctness of her decision to participate actively and confidently in the construction of true socialism in her state. Manfred, on the other hand, represents those modern individuals who have become cynical, apathetic, and indifferent to life, alienated by the frustration of their efforts to effect social change, perhaps, or lured by the appeal of fitting into the comfortable routine of a materialistic consumer society. In many ways, Manfred is the central character of the novel. Certainly his self-awareness, his original enthusiasm about contributing to his society, and his ultimate failure to do so make him a more interesting figure than Rita, and also link him closely with the heroine of *The Quest for Christa T.*

In *Divided Heaven*, Wolf had not yet mastered the subjective narrative technique which she used to such advantage in her next novel, although the rather conventional flashback and montage techniques featured in *Divided Heaven* were fairly shocking to East German sensibilities at a time when the insistence on strict Socialist Realist literary principles was only beginning to weaken. More interesting is Wolf's attempt, here supported mainly by repeated imagery and leitmotifs, to show a development toward self-awareness on the part of Rita through her narration of and reflection on the past. This interest in the mutual influence between the narrator and the text prefigures the complex narrative stance of *The Quest for Christa T.* In many ways, *Divided Heaven* is most interesting now for its relationship to later works by Wolf. It established her reputation, for some of the wrong reasons, as an internationally important East German writer, a reputation which needed her next major work, however, to be fully justified.

THE QUEST FOR CHRISTA T.

When Wolf's second novel, *The Quest for Christa T.*, appeared in 1968, it sold out immediately in East Germany. The Luchterhand edition the next year was eagerly awaited and greeted with positive reviews in the West. Within East Germany, however, only two reviews, largely critical, were published, and almost six years passed before a second edition was printed. *The Quest for Christa T.*, like its protagonist, came on the scene before its time. Only several years after its appearance did internal East German cultural politics acknowledge the need for constructive criticism within Socialist society. The potential for social criticism can be seen in one of the main themes of the novel: the question of how an individual can gain self-realization yet also be a productive member of a planned and carefully organized society. The background of East German Socialist society is essential to the novel, unclearly delineated as it seems at times, and unpolitical as the heroine seems to be. Christa T., the incurable individual, believes in the rightness of the new world that socialism is to build yet finds it impossible to develop a role for herself that will make her a useful member of the new society without necessitating her conforming to and stultifying within some given role. Left to assert her individualism outside a social context, she dies.

The extent to which Christa T.'s dilemma reflects Wolf's own experience is unclear; certainly, a close relationship exists among Wolf, Christa T., and the unnamed narrator, the latter's friend and a writer like Wolf. In "Selbst-interview" ("Self-Interview," in *The Reader and the Writer*), Wolf acknowledged the near-identity of the three. The biographical background of the novel is sufficiently complex to encourage what becomes an intermingling of personae: Both the narrator and Christa T. share elements of Wolf's biography, and Wolf has claimed that there was a real "Christa T." from whose life and posthumous papers she drew some of the facts and citations included in the work.

Aside from such factual cross-influences, the process of narration encourages identification of the narrator and the author with Christa T. This identification becomes one of the main themes of the novel. The narrator tries to be just to the person Christa T. was—indeed, to "rethink" her and thus let her go on living, for, she says, "we need her now." The English title does not transmit the wordplay which indicates this double function of the reflective, narrative process: both *nachdenken* (to reflect on) and *nach-denken* (to seek and re-create in thought). Christa T., ordinary and insignificant though she may seem, is the proper material for such a reciprocal, productive process. Unwilling and unable to compromise or commit herself and insistent on the necessity of conscience and fantasy for the continuation of the human race, she is an admonition to the narrator/author to maintain her own integrity and not to fall into complacency and self-satisfaction. Christa T.'s life is also a warning to her society. Her failure to find a useful place within it stems from the inconsistencies which result when a society calls for "new human beings" without making their development possible. The narrative process discloses the importance of Christa T. not only to the narrator/author but also to the reader and the society to which she so longed to contribute.

Closely connected to the theme of narration as a creative and healing process is that of writing, for Christa T. is an aspiring writer, a role she shares with Wolf and the narrator. It is through writing that she seeks to close the "gaps" in life through which the cold, dark, destructive forces pour. For Christa T., as for the narrator and for Wolf herself, writing is a way of constructively processing the past, present, and future. Unlike Wolf herself, Christa T. lacks the strength to prevail against her time, which is still marked by many of the characteristics of the bourgeois and Nazi past. Yet the basic tone of the work is one of optimism, just as Christa T. also maintained her optimism and hope for a better future. Critic Andreas Huyssen is correct to point to the utopian philosophy of Ernst Bloch in connection with *The Quest for Christa T.* A better future is posited by the example of Christa T. and by the changes within herself which the narrator/author acknowledges as a consequence of her reflections on her dead friend. The effect on the reader is to be similar: Christa T. is needed to point the way to a better society in which individual integrity is allowed to take its place as an important contributing factor to the whole.

The tentative quality of Wolf's narrative style in *The Quest for Christa T.* is marked by "the difficulty of saying I," in the heroine's words. The difficulty stems in part from Christa T.'s own reluctance to commit herself to any role. This transmits itself to the narrator, who attempts to be absolutely accurate and at the same time nonautocratic in her statements in order to allow Christa T. to live again on her own terms. This effort causes her to draw closer to and understand her protagonist better and in turn invites a similar effort on the part of the reader to become an active participant in the text. In this novel, Wolf's

subjective authenticity is at its best: the provocative evocation of an individual within an identifiable milieu; the weaving of a relationship among author, narrator, protagonist, and reader; and the general utopian impulse pointing the way to a reconciliation of individual fulfillment with common social goals.

PATTERNS OF CHILDHOOD

The question of "how we became who we are"— which Christa T. poses—underlies all Wolf's novels. In *Patterns of Childhood*, her autobiographical third novel, Wolf attempts to examine the most problematic period for Germans of her generation: the twelve years of National Socialism. Once again, as in *The Quest for Christa T.*, she is interested in understanding not only the past as such but also its implications for the present and the future. The narrative structure plays an important role here as well. Although the narrator, the protagonist, and the author are the same person, Wolf seems to want to establish some distance between them. She does so by giving her younger self a different name, Nelly Jordan, and, more important, by speaking of this younger self in the second person. In addition, she uses a complex time structure in which there are three levels: the past of Nelly Jordan, from the age of four to sixteen (1933-1945); a trip to her former home of Landsberg, Poland, in July of 1971 along with her husband, brother, and daughter Lenka; and the present, in which she is writing the novel, from November, 1972, until May, 1975.

The evocation of the Nazi years is very convincing, with the scrupulous concern for honesty and completeness which has become characteristic of Wolf's narrative style. The integration of the past with the present is less successful. Wolf attempts to make such connections, for example, through the criticism of contemporary East German institutions and practices voiced by her brother and Lenka, which gives rise to suspicions of continued Fascist tendencies in the Socialist state. She also alludes to historical events in Vietnam and Chile which occur during the writing of the work. The parallelism of such events to others which occurred in the Nazi state is not convincing, mainly because it does not seem to promote the increased self-knowledge which is the goal of the narration. The critical stance toward such events taken by the adult Nelly Jordan as narrator/author does not seem to have its origins in the child she evokes in her reflections. What is missing is the postwar transformation of the Bund Deutscher Mädel girl of the Hitler era to the Freie Deutsche Jugend member of East Germany, as Alexander Stephan points out in *Christa Wolf: Forschungsbericht* (1979).

Wolf's attempts to make a personal examination of her own past into a process which would enlighten the present and instruct the future are only partly successful here. This does not mean that her methodology of subjective authenticity, which she pursues here, too, is faulty. Rather, the reason for this partial success probably lies in the enormously problematic nature of the past she is attempting to illuminate. Wolf's novel is a significant attempt to deal with this extremely difficult part of German history as personal history, and it certainly succeeds as personal testimony of that sort. Her efforts to deal with her youth in Nazi Germany as honestly as possible, acknowledging the incomprehensibility of her participation, limited though it was, certainly can provoke an examination of conscience on the part of those Germans who may believe they have "mastered the past." Wolf offers no answer to the question of why so many Germans offered no resistance to the Nazi regime. It is a mark of her uncompromising honesty that one is left with the rather helpless feeling which Wolf herself seems to have experienced after the war when a freed Communist prisoner asked: "Just where were you the whole time?"

NO PLACE ON EARTH

The utopian import of *No Place on Earth* is indicated by its German title, *Kein Ort* (no place) and *Nirgends* (nowhere), being literal translations of the Greek term *utopia*. Here, Wolf uses in even more radical form than in her previous works the narrative technique associated with her subjective authenticity. She goes beyond her own past and social environment to examine the lives and times of two writers in the German Romantic era: Heinrich von Kleist and Karoline von Günderode. In her opening lines, she establishes the pertinence of these figures for herself. They are predecessors, for she has their "blood in her

shoes." Wolf presents these writers as early victims of the alienation of the artist from society. The deep alienation from the self which ensued led to their youthful suicides. Their fate has broad implications, for it is a prophetic foreshadowing of that awaiting all those who cherish spiritual values in an increasingly materialistic world.

Wolf creates a fictional meeting between Kleist and Günderode in Winkel along the Rhine in 1804. The couple's conversation and inner thoughts are interspersed with commentary by the narrator/author; at times it is difficult to be sure who is speaking. Again Wolf attempts to establish through narrative structure and style a close relationship between subject and object. She succeeds in this by projecting feelings and thoughts into these figures which are consistent with the excerpts from their diaries and letters that she also weaves into the text. Wolf locates here the historical source of problems we are familiar with from her other works. As in *The Quest for Christa T.*, the artist is the one to sense the alienation between the spiritual and the material and is the most likely to be destroyed by it.

One is reminded of Christa T. when Günderode speaks of the necessity of hope, for, as she says, "when we stop hoping, that which we fear will certainly come." The belief that love can heal the self-alienation which modern materialistic life causes is also posited by Günderode, and this is an important theme in Wolf's fiction, especially in "Unter den Linden" and "Self-Experiment." Again in *No Place on Earth*, a utopian power and vision are ascribed to literature, a power to remind human beings of the need to work continually toward their self-realization and a dynamic vision of humankind which, as Günderode says, is "contradictory to the spirit of every era." Kleist and Günderode may, like Christa T., have "died of their time," but our recognition of this, evoked by Wolf's re-creation of them, can become a first step in ending the historical process which began in their generation.

SOMMERSTÜCK

Wolf's apolitical novel *Sommerstück* (summer play) portrays private life in the North German province of Mecklenburg. After dissident writer Wolf

Biermann was expelled from Communist East Germany in 1976, Wolf refrained from further criticism of the regime. She and her family moved to an island where collective farmers coexisted peacefully with intellectuals in self-imposed exile from the cities. The quiet of the land brought unexpected healing. Wolf's disclaimer at the end of *Sommerstück* is qualified by the coincidence that another writer from the group, Sarah Kirsch, described it more directly in her chronicle *Allerlei-Rauh* (1988).

Wolf uses Kirsch's poem "Raubvogel" (bird of prey) as an epigraph for *Sommerstück* and works the themes into the novel. At the peak of summer, Luisa admires a hawk diving through the sunlight and ascending again with its prey in its talons. "Raubvogel süß ist die Luft/ So stürz ich nicht noch einmal durch die Sonne" (The air is sweet as a bird of prey/ I will not plunge through the sunlight like this again).

The novel is written retrospectively, capturing the poignant essence of a summer so perfect that the characters want to hold and preserve it forever. Wolf's narrative technique of writing from different characters' perspectives creates a broad composite picture, while there are hints of events and interactions not expanded upon. The reader wants to know more and so shares the sense of loss and nostalgia. The people are gone, and their houses burned to the ground.

MEDEA

Medea was Wolf's first major work after the reunification of Germany in 1990, after which Wolf became the focal point of a general attack on East German literature. Those who are critical of her see the novel as an allegory of her situation and an attempt at self-vindication. Text-immanent analyses show that the novel is concerned with a perennial problem of human nature, the dichotomy between the female emphasis on healing and the male lust for power.

The Medea of Greek mythology killed her brother, her two sons, and her former husband's new wife. Wolf's retelling has the brother dismembered by superstitious hags, the sons stoned by a mob, and the new wife drowning in a well. Central to all these incidents are issues of succession, to the throne of either Medea's native Colchis or her adopted home, Cor-

inth. Only after the fact are the deaths falsely attributed to Medea, as calumny conveniently discredits the woman who knows too much.

Wolf's significant addition to the plot is Medea's unearthing of yet another political murder. Her incautious pursuit of this knowledge brings about her downfall. In retrospect, Medea sees she was wrong to leave Colchis, because Corinth is no better. One king has his son killed, the other king his daughter. Wolf creates multifaceted intrigue by writing from the viewpoints of six different people, none of whom has all the facts. No one, not even a reclusive sculptor, escapes unscathed from the machinations of those determined to remain in power at any cost.

Linda Schelbitzki Pickle, updated by Jean M. Snook

OTHER MAJOR WORKS

SHORT FICTION: *Moskauer Novelle*, 1961; *Unter den Linden: Drei unwahrscheinliche Geschichten*, 1974; *Gesammelte Erzählungen*, 1980 (*What Remains and Other Stories*, 1993); *Was Bleibt: Erzählung*, 1990.

SCREENPLAYS: *Der geteilte Himmel*, 1964 (with Gerhard Wolf); *Fräulein Schmetterling*, 1966 (with Wolf); *Till Eulenspiegel*, 1972 (with Gerhard Wolf).

NONFICTION: *Lesen und Schreiben: Aufsätze und Betrachtungen*, 1971 (*The Reader and the Writer: Essays, Sketches, Memories*, 1977); *Fortgesetzter Versuch: Aufsätze, Gespräche, Essays*, 1979; *Lesen und Schreiben: Neue Sammlung*, 1980; *Die Dimension des Autors: Essays und Aufsätze, Reden, und Gespräche 1959-1985*, 1987 (partial trans. *The Fourth Dimension: Interviews with Christa Wolf*, 1988); *Ansprachen*, 1988; *The Author's Dimension: Selected Essays*, 1993; *Sei gegrüßt und lebe: Eine Freundschaft in Briefen 1964-1973*, 1993; *Auf dem Weg nach Tabou: Texte 1990-1994*, 1994 (*Parting from Phantoms: Selected Writings, 1990-1994*, 1997); *Monsieur, wir finden uns wieder: Briefe, 1968-1984*, 1995.

BIBLIOGRAPHY

Finney, Gail. *Christa Wolf*. New York: Twayne, 1999.
    A thorough introduction and overview of Wolf's life and works.

Fries, Marilyn Sibley, ed. *Responses to Christa Wolf: Critical Essays*. Detroit: Wayne State University Press, 1989. Twenty-one excellent essays in English. Conference proceedings of the special session on Christa Wolf at the 1982 Modern Language Association of America convention. Contains a list of secondary articles and books and review articles on each of Wolf's books.

Love, Myra N. *Christa Wolf: Literature and the Conscience of History*. New York: Peter Lang, 1991. Deals with the main works up to *Cassandra* from different theoretical points of view. Presupposes familiarity with all the works.

Resch, Margit. *Understanding Christa Wolf: Returning Home to a Foreign Land*. Columbia: University of South Carolina Press, 1997. Separate sections clearly identified in the table of contents provide good analyses of all the major works up to 1990. Contains a useful chronology, a list of selected articles in English, and an annotated bibliography of critical works.

Smith, Colin E. *Tradition, Art, and Society: Christa Wolf's Prose*. Essen, Germany: Die blaue Eule Verlag, 1987. Provides lists that cannot be found elsewhere: the seven books edited by Wolf between 1959 and 1985, her many reviews, essays, and articles from 1952 to 1985, and conversations and interviews from 1959 to 1984. Secondary literature is conveniently subdivided into the literature on specific works. Each chapter deals with a single work.

Wallace, Ian, ed. *Christa Wolf in Perspective*. Atlanta: Rodopi, 1994. Eleven of the thirteen essays are in English. They deal with individual works, with Wolf's politics, and with themes and imagery. Written after Wolf came under attack from Western journalists.

THOMAS WOLFE

Born: Asheville, North Carolina; October 3, 1900
Died: Baltimore, Maryland; September 15, 1938

PRINCIPAL LONG FICTION

Look Homeward, Angel, 1929
Of Time and the River, 1935
The Web and the Rock, 1939
You Can't Go Home Again, 1940
The Short Novels of Thomas Wolfe, 1961 (C. Hugh Holman, editor)

OTHER LITERARY FORMS

During his lifetime Thomas Wolfe published four major works: two novels, *Look Homeward, Angel* and *Of Time and the River*; a collection of short stories, *From Death to Morning* (1935); and his description of his life as a creative artist, *The Story of a Novel* (1936). In addition to his major works, he also sold a few lengthy stories to magazines; *Scribner's Magazine* published "A Portrait of Bascom Hawke" (April, 1932) and "The Web of Earth" (July, 1939). Both of these have since been republished as short novels in *The Short Novels of Thomas Wolfe* (1961), a collection edited by C. Hugh Holman. Because Wolfe viewed each piece of his writing as only a part of some larger design, he frequently adapted past material to meet a present need. For example, he modified "A Portrait of Bascom Hawke" for later inclusion in *Of Time and the River*, and "The Child by Tiger" (1937), a short story he published in *The Saturday Evening Post*, appeared two years later with changes in point of view in *The Web and the Rock*. After his death, Wolfe's editor at Harper's, Edward Aswell, put together three posthumous books from two large packing cases of unfinished manuscript that Wolfe left behind. Two of these books—*The Web and the Rock* and *You Can't Go Home Again*—are novels; the third is a volume of stories, entitled *The Hills Beyond* (1941). Wolfe began his career (unsuccessfully) as a playwright with *The Mountains*, which he wrote in 1920 but which was not published until 1940 by the University of North Carolina at Chapel Hill, Wolfe's alma mater. Wolfe's letters and notebooks have also been published, allowing for firsthand insight into his personal and creative life.

ACHIEVEMENTS

Wolfe captured the essence of what it meant to be

young in his time with the publication of *Look Homeward, Angel*. He further influenced readers of the Depression-plagued 1930's with stories he published in magazines such as *The New Yorker, Harper's Bazaar, Redbook, Scribner's Magazine*, and *The Saturday Evening Post*. Widely read in America and abroad, Wolfe was a well-respected author during his lifetime, a man who in a very real sense lived the part of the driven artist. Wolfe is still read, even if not to the extent of his more significant contemporaries, Ernest Hemingway, William Faulkner, and F. Scott Fitzgerald. In retrospect, Wolfe's achievement is especially remarkable when one considers that his literary life spanned little more than a decade. In 1957, Faulkner ranked Wolfe above all of his contemporaries: "My admiration for Wolfe is that he tried the best to get it all said; he was willing to throw away style, coherence, all the rules of preciseness to try to put all the experience of the human heart on the head of a pin." Wolfe's weaknesses are now recognized, but he is still praised for his strengths. A balanced view of his work has emerged, and his reputation as an important figure in twentieth century American literature is secure.

(Library of Congress)

BIOGRAPHY

Born on October 3, 1900, in Asheville, North Carolina, Thomas Wolfe was the youngest of the seven surviving children of Julia Elizabeth Westall and William Oliver Wolfe. Of Pennsylvania Dutch-German stock, Wolfe's father was a man of intense vitality, a stonecutter who instilled in Wolfe a love of language, whether it be the high rhetoric of Elizabethan poetry or the low vernacular of the mountain people surrounding Asheville. Wolfe's mother was more attuned to the values of commerce than her husband (she was forever speculating in real estate). In fact, one biographer has termed the match an "epic misalliance." Domestic relations in the Wolfe household were often strained; young Wolfe grew up a witness to his father's drunken rampages and his mother's ensuing resentment. From this family cauldron came much of the autobiographical material Wolfe poured forth in *Look Homeward, Angel*.

In September of 1912, Wolfe entered the North State Fitting School, where he came under the influence of his teacher, Margaret Roberts (Margaret Leonard in *Look Homeward, Angel*). Roberts encouraged Wolfe's voracious appetite for reading by introducing him to the best of English literature. In 1916, at the precocious age of fifteen, Wolfe entered the University of North Carolina at Chapel Hill. Six feet tall and still growing (he would eventually reach six feet six inches), Wolfe was a skinny, long-legged youth, sensitive to the criticism of his older classmates. Wolfe's first year at Chapel Hill was unremarkable, but he eventually made a name for himself as an excellent student and a campus literary figure. In March of 1919, *The Return of Buck Garvin*, a play Wolfe had written in a dramatic writing course, was performed by the Carolina Playmakers, with Wolfe performing in the title role.

After graduating in 1920, Wolfe entered Harvard University to pursue his interests as a playwright. He was especially attracted by the famous workshop given by playwright George Pierce Baker (whom he would later depict as Professor Hatcher in *Of Time and the River*). Wolfe hoped to make a literary name for himself, but after a series of setbacks, he accepted an appointment as an instructor in English at the Washington Square College of New York University and began teaching in February of 1924, continuing to do so intermittently until 1930.

In October of 1924, Wolfe made his first trip to Europe. Many of his experiences there he later incorporated into *Of Time and the River*. Returning to New York in August of 1925, Wolfe met Aline Bernstein, a wealthy married woman who was involved in the theater world of New York. For the next seven years, Wolfe participated in a stormy on-and-off again affair with Bernstein, who was seventeen years his elder. She was the mother-mistress Wolfe seemed to need; certainly, she inspired *Look Homeward, Angel*, which he commenced while abroad with Bernstein in July of 1926.

The popular image of Wolfe as a literary lion is in part caused by the critical success he achieved with *Look Homeward, Angel* but is based mostly on his personal appearance and habits. Often dressed in shabby clothes, he was known to prowl the streets of Brooklyn, where he had settled after another trip abroad in 1931. One night while wandering the streets he was overheard to say, "I wrote ten thousand words today! I wrote ten thousand words today!" Although Wolfe resented efforts to publicize his eccentricities, it was inevitable that his behavior and fame would make him a legendary figure.

In December of 1933, Wolfe began work on what was to become *Of Time and the River*. It was also during this period that Maxwell Perkins, Wolfe's editor at Scribner's, worked closely with the author on the formation of the novel. Wolfe incorporated his experiences at Harvard, in Europe, and with Bernstein into *Of Time and the River*, which picks up the Eugene Gant story where *Look Homeward, Angel* concludes. In 1937, after critics had raised questions concerning Perkins's influence on his work, Wolfe left Scribner's for Harper and Brothers. His editor at Harper's was Edward C. Aswell, and Wolfe left two large crates containing nearly a million words of manuscript with him before leaving on a tour of

the West in May of 1938. In July, Wolfe fell ill with pneumonia and was hospitalized near Seattle. In September, having been transferred to The Johns Hopkins Hospital in Baltimore, he underwent brain surgery for complications he suffered from tuberculosis. He died on September 15, 1938.

ANALYSIS

Throughout Thomas Wolfe's fiction there is evidence of a powerful but sometimes uncontrolled mind at work. Few would argue Wolfe's genius, but many have questioned how well he directed it. Part of the difficulty may have come from his self-professed intention to create an American mythology. The result would be the record of an individual, lonely and lost in the flux of time, forever exploring the diversity of American life. Partly because of his early death and partly because of his own difficulties in giving form to ideas, Wolfe never managed to unify the vast body of his work. Add to this the considerable amount of influence his editors exerted upon his manuscripts, and some intriguing questions still remain about the interrelationships of segments in the writings and the final form of his novels.

Wolfe wrote with passionate intensity, producing vast quantities of manuscript. His central themes focus on a lonely individual, the isolated artist, in search of self-discovery and the true meaning of the American experience. In *Look Homeward, Angel*, the first of these themes is most pronounced, for this is autobiography very thinly veiled. The story of Eugene Gant is in many ways the story of Thomas Wolfe. After the publication of *Look Homeward, Angel*, which was generally well received, some critics began to raise questions concerning the novel's weaknesses, especially the obvious attempt by Wolfe to capture experience at the expense of artistic control. It was not until 1936, however, that the landmark case against Wolfe would be launched with the publication in the *Saturday Review* of "Genius Is Not Enough," Bernard De Voto's indictment of Wolfe and his fiction.

De Voto was responding to *The Story of a Novel*, Wolfe's extremely frank account of his own life as a writer and the work that went into *Of Time and the*

River. For Wolfe, writing was a chaotic experience, something done with great pain and toil. De Voto acknowledged that Wolfe was a genius "of the good old-fashioned, romantic kind, possessed by a demon, driven by the gales of his own fury, helpless before the lava-flood of his own passion"; he further argued, however, that such genius was in and of itself not enough. Today the legacy of De Voto's remarks remains manifest in a series of stereotypes: By some readers (especially academics), Wolfe is still thought of as one who never controlled his rhetoric, as one who was unable to organize his work, and as one who sometimes pushed autobiography to the limits of reporting.

To illustrate Wolfe's lack of rhetorical restraint, De Voto pointed to *Of Time and the River*, commenting that Wolfe invested each experience he described with so much raw emotion that a midnight snack took on the same importance as the death of Oliver Gant. As De Voto stated, "If the death of one's father comes out emotionally even with ham-on-rye, then the art of fiction is cockeyed." As for the charge that Wolfe was a writer who never exerted sufficient control over his material, De Voto and others have cited the sprawling sections of his mammoth novels where there is supportive evidence that episodes stand by themselves rather than in relation to others. The extent of Wolfe's involvement with his editors (Maxwell Perkins at Scribners from 1928 to 1937; Edward Aswell at Harper's from 1937 to 1938) also raises questions about his own ability to revise and organize his novels.

Perhaps the most revealing example of editorial influence on Wolfe's fiction concerns *Of Time and the River*. While Wolfe was working on the novel, Perkins met with him day and night for more than a year in an attempt to help him gain control over the voluminous amount of material he had written. Often Perkins would ask Wolfe to go home and cut a section, only to find that he would return with an episode thousands of words longer. In one of the most dramatic decisions any editor has made with a figure as significant as Wolfe, Perkins, without Wolfe's final approval, sent the manuscript of *Of Time and the River* to the printer in September of 1934. Perkins

made the decision because he felt the novel was as complete as Wolfe could make it and that Wolfe needed to get on with other work. Whatever the reasons, the ultimate responsibility for the publication of any book rests squarely upon the writer. Because Wolfe was so deferential to his editor and because he was unable or unwilling to see his novel through to the end, he opened himself to questions concerning his craftsmanship, questions which are still being asked today.

Finally, there remains the issue of autobiography in Wolfe's novels. Wolfe himself claimed that autobiography was a part of any serious creative work, but there are in his novels, especially *Look Homeward, Angel*, sections that read like a mere diary. There is also a great deal of artistic invention in his novels, and certainly almost all writers use material based on their own experiences; nevertheless, many of Wolfe's depictions were so thinly fictionalized that individuals were easily recognized, and many were hurt and embarrassed by what they thought were the unflattering portraits Wolfe rendered of them. Wolfe's use of autobiography pushed to journalistic limits raises more questions about his fictional method.

Although Wolfe's rhetoric, his conception of structure, and the autobiographical element within his work have been discussed as weaknesses, these three elements can also be cited as the strengths of his writing. For example, it is true there is ample evidence to support De Voto's claim that Wolfe's rhetoric is often artificially heightened, but at the same time, one of his most compelling attributes is his ability to depict something as insignificant as a "ham-on-rye" so clearly that readers may suddenly find themselves hungry. More to the point, however, are passages such as the Laura James sections of *Look Homeward, Angel*, where Wolfe manages to capture as well as any writer what it means to be young and in love. There are also numerous passages within his other novels that stand as some of the most poetic set pieces to be found in prose. In large measure, Wolfe is still read today because of the magnificence of his style, however extravagant it may be at times.

Wolfe held to an organic theory of art, one in which content dictates form. He was constantly searching for new ways to communicate experience; in this sense, the criticism directed at him for being a "formless" writer may in some ways be unfair. Certainly there is no doubt that in his attempts to depart from traditional formats he sometimes lost control of his material—*Of Time and the River*, for example, is marred by this flaw. On the other hand, he did manage to find an effective structure in "The Web of Earth," his lengthy story written under the influence of James Joyce. The entire work is filtered through the consciousness of an old woman engaged in reminiscence, and it is the finest example of artistic unity in Wolfe's work. In *Look Homeward, Angel*, Wolfe modified a traditional novelistic form, the *Bildungsroman* (the story of a youth initiated by experience into maturity), organizing the novel not around a unified sequence of events but instead around a series of sense impressions. In this way, the loose structure serves to complement the rhapsodic style. The result is a powerful rendering of the book's central theme— that of an artistic youth lost and in search of self-knowledge and self-definition.

As for the contention that Wolfe is too highly autobiographical, that his writing too often approaches mere reportage, there can be no denying that on occasion, he is guilty as charged. In most instances, however, he was by no means a mere reporter of events. His fiction is memorable because he was such an apt interpreter of human beings and everyday experiences. He was able to synthesize experience into art; he himself claimed that everything in a work of art is changed, that nothing is a literal representation of actual experience. Whether he always achieved this transmutation, it can safely be said that Wolfe is still read today because his novels stand as a testimony to human experience artistically rendered from a unique and personal vision.

LOOK HOMEWARD, ANGEL

Look Homeward, Angel, Wolfe's first and most significant novel, made use of extensive autobiographical material. In many ways, it is the story of his own life, the life of his family, his neighbors, and the region in which he lived. For those who know some-

thing of Wolfe's background, there are unmistakable connections between the fictional characters in *Look Homeward, Angel* and the real people among whom Wolfe grew up in Asheville, North Carolina. After the novel's publication, many from his hometown— and indeed many in his own family—were angered by what they took to be unflattering depictions of themselves in the novel. Wolfe's own account of the reaction to his novel can be found in *The Story of a Novel*, wherein he describes the uproar in Asheville and provides his own defense of his fictional method. Essentially, Wolfe believed that the people he described, whatever their faults, were magnificent. As magnificent as he thought his characters were, however, he often described them (no doubt truthfully) with all their faults made highly visible.

The ethics of his method can be questioned when one considers how it must have been to have lived in Asheville at the time the novel was published, to have opened its pages and to have found the characters so thinly fictionalized that their real counterparts could be easily identified. The ethical issue is not so much whether Wolfe was accurate in his depictions of the whole range of humanity he described, but rather how one would feel if he were identified as the model for the town drunk or as the counterpart of the unscrupulous businessman. It did not take long for the people of Asheville to start pointing fingers at one another after figuring out who was who in the novel. Perhaps with some justification, all fingers eventually pointed toward Wolfe himself; the controversy over what he had done to his town and the people in it was so pronounced that he was unable to return to Asheville until seven years after the publication of *Look Homeward, Angel*.

Wolfe departed from the development of a traditional plot in *Look Homeward, Angel* and instead made use of impressionistic realism to tie events and characters together. The narrator moves in and out of the consciousness of the principal characters, giving readers impressions of their inner feelings and motivations. As much as anything else, *Look Homeward, Angel* is the story of a quest, a search for self-knowledge and for lasting human interaction. The subtitle of the novel is *A Story of the Buried Life*, and much of what Wolfe depicts concerns itself with the inner lives of the characters in the novel—what they really think and feel as well as how isolated and alienated they are from one another. In this sense, the novel explores the relationship of time, change, and death as elements which will always frustrate the human desire for happiness and fulfillment.

Look Homeward, Angel was initially entitled *O Lost* and then *Alone, Alone*. The title on which Wolfe finally settled comes from "Lycidas," John Milton's poem in which the archangel Michael is asked to look back toward England to mourn a young man's death and all the unfulfilled potential it signifies. Eugene Gant, is, like most of Wolfe's protagonists, the isolated and sensitive artist in search of meaning and companionship in a hostile world. Given this theme, it is ironic that some of Wolfe's least effective passages are the results of his attempts to describe Eugene's feelings of loneliness and despair. In such segments (which recur in almost all of Wolfe's works), he often lapses into contrived language; rather than arising from natural consequences or from the interplay between one character and another, feelings seem forced by authorial intervention. On the other hand, the novel does contain some of his finest writing, especially when he describes people, places, and things with visionary intensity.

Look Homeward, Angel covers the first twenty years of Eugene Gant's life—his adolescence, his four years at the private school of Margaret Leonard, and his four years at the university. A pattern of potential fulfillment destroyed by frustration is personified in Eugene's parents, Eliza and Oliver, who are modeled after Wolfe's own mother and father. Oliver Gant is a stonecutter who passionately desires to create something beautiful, to carve an angel's head. He is an unfulfilled artist, a man of intense vitality who desires a full and sensuous life. His intensity, his capacity for life, is checked by his wife, Eliza, who is his antithesis: parsimonious, cold, and materialistic. This pattern of frustrated potential recurs throughout the novel. In one example, after spending his first year at the university and losing his innocence in a brothel, Eugene returns home to spend the summer at Dixieland, his mother's boardinghouse. There he

meets and falls in love with Laura James (based on his own first love, Clara Paul). In his descriptions of the young, passionate love that develops between them, Wolfe's prose becomes a lyrical celebration that turns to tragic frustration as Eugene learns that Laura is engaged to marry another young man back home, that she will never be a part of his life again. Thus, potential (in this example, physical and spiritual union between Eugene and Laura) is checked by reality (separation and isolation). This pattern manifests itself in varying ways throughout the novel. The story of a youth coming of age by initiation into experience, *Look Homeward, Angel* is a comprehensive account of the inner life of a sensitive and artistic youth.

With the publication of *Look Homeward, Angel*, Wolfe was thrust (not unwillingly) into the limelight as a legend, a novelist who demonstrated enormous potential. His success was spectacular, but because he was a driven artist (much like his fictional counterpart, Eugene Gant), his initial success created a good many subsequent problems. He immediately felt the burden to surpass his first effort with an even better second novel. At the same time, he ran into difficulty giving form to his expansive ideas (a problem with which he would grapple for the remainder of his life). During this same period, he also began leading a turbulent private life. He was involved with Aline Bernstein (the "A. B." to whom *Look Homeward, Angel* is dedicated), and their relationship—as tempestuous as any could conceivably be—would figure heavily in the remainder of his life and work.

OF TIME AND THE RIVER

Composed of eight sections, each of which is named after some epic or mythic figure, *Of Time and the River* exceeds nine hundred pages in length and spans two continents, continuing the story of Thomas Wolfe as personified in the character of Eugene Gant. Wolfe continues the story with Eugene's departure from Altamont for study at Harvard. He stated his ambitious theme for *Of Time and the River* in *The Story of a Novel*; his central idea was to depict the search for a father, not only in a literal but also in a figurative sense. While trying to exemplify his theme, Wolfe also struggled to form *Of Time and the River* out of the vast amount of manuscript he had written (a detailed discussion of that struggle is related in *The Story of a Novel*). The struggle reached its peak when his editor, Maxwell Perkins, sent the novel to press without Wolfe's knowledge. In one of his letters to Perkins, Wolfe claimed that another six months' work would have allowed him to complete the necessary revisions that would have made the book less episodic. There can be no doubt that had Wolfe written *Of Time and the River* without Perkins's influence, it would have been a very different novel—perhaps a better one than it is. As it stands, it is, as Wolfe himself noted, episodic; its parts are not always aligned to form a unified plot. Even so, there are fine passages throughout that more than compensate for its ponderous pace and meandering plot. In *The Story of a Novel*, Wolfe describes how he wrote one scene that ran to eighty thousand words (about two hundred pages). He was attempting to capture "the full flood and fabric" of four people simply talking to one another for four continuous hours. This scene, as good as he thought it was, eventually was cut, but it illustrates the massive amount of writing he did for the novel as well as the extensive amount of cutting he did to get it into publishable form.

Perhaps the novel's most magnificent scene is that which describes the death of Eugene's father, who has been slowly dying of cancer. Gant, the paternal figure whose presence was so unforgettable in *Look Homeward, Angel*, is now old and enfeebled. His death, which comes in a final moment of tranquillity, stands in stark contrast to his life, which was lived with violent gestures and howling protests. Often drunk, sometimes violent, he was a hard man to live with, but his death comes as a reminder that life lived intensely—however excessively—is life worth living. The death of his wife, Eliza, would not begin to elicit the intensity of emotion aroused by his final moments, for she stands as a testimony to all that opposes the force and fury of his life.

Other memorable scenes in the novel include those that take place in Boston with Eugene's uncle, Bascom Pentland. Uncle Bascom and his demented wife are two of the more finely drawn eccentrics in the novel. These segments as well as others involving

Eugene's dreams to become a playwright, his time spent as an English instructor at a city university in New York, and his eventual travel to Europe, all contribute to Wolfe's attempt to describe the vast array of people, places, and things unique to the American experience.

While working out his central theme of a search for a father, Wolfe developed a three-part vision of time: time present, time past, and time eternal. The first, time present, is the time in which the actual events in the novel take place, the time of reality. The second, time past, represents all of the accumulated experience that affects time present. The third, time eternal, stands for the lasting time of oceans, forests, and rivers, of things that form the permanent backdrop for people's experiences. These three levels of time allow Wolfe to contrast, in a vast and symbolic scale, the relationship of past, present, and eternal experience with the experience of Eugene Gant. The result is an intensely personal search for meaning, an attempt to reconcile opposites, to find something lasting and meaningful.

Throughout the novel, a scene that takes place in the present may be linked with past scenes and eternal scenes. In this way, all three levels of time are united. For example, a train ride taking place in present time provides Eugene with the opportunity to recall the travelers of earlier days, their epic searching, their longing for discovery, for movement. During the same segment, Eugene speculates that other people in the future (eternal time) will also travel the earth in search of one another. The novel frequently develops itself in this way, and it is these segments which give the novel its mysterious, almost haunting, quality. At the same time, however, these same passages become repetitious (if not tedious), and illustrate once again the lack of restraint so evident throughout Wolfe's work. In contrast to these overwritten segments are a good many specific characterizations as well as a variety of satiric passages aimed at mediocre people, middle-class values, and intellectual pretenders. This is a vast and comprehensive book that ends when Eugene sets sail back to the United States. Aboard ship he meets Esther Jack (Aline Bernstein), who, although certainly not the father for whom he is searching, is nevertheless someone who can help him transcend the tormented youth he has endured to this point in his life.

Both *The Web and the Rock* and *You Can't Go Home Again* were put together by Edward Aswell, Wolfe's editor at Harper's, and published posthumously as novels. It was not until 1962, when Richard S. Kennedy published *The Window of Memory: The Literary Career of Thomas Wolfe*, that the extent of Aswell's influence on the two novels became fully known. Just before his death, Wolfe left a large packing crate of manuscript with Aswell. From that collection of manuscript, it was generally assumed that Aswell found two separate narratives, which he then published as the two posthumous novels. Surprisingly, however, Professor Kennedy discovered, after an extensive study of Wolfe's papers and manuscripts at Harvard University, that Aswell constructed *The Web and the Rock* and *You Can't Go Home Again* from what was a massive—but fragmentary—amount of manuscript that Wolfe apparently intended to condense into a single narrative. Had Wolfe lived, he most certainly would not have published the two novels as Aswell published them. In a very real way, they are as much the product of Aswell's editorializing as they are a product of Wolfe's imagination. Even so, the two novels represent a significant part of Wolfe's creative output, and analysis of them can help put his entire achievement into a clearer perspective.

THE WEB AND THE ROCK

Wolfe claimed that he was turning away from the books he had previously written, that *The Web and the Rock* would be his most "objective" work to date. It should be noted that at that time, Wolfe had become particularly sensitive about the criticism he had received from De Voto and others concerning his alleged inability to exert artistic control over his material. As a result, not only did he claim his new novel to be objective, but also he abandoned his previous protagonist, Eugene Gant, in favor of a new one, George "Monk" Webber. The change was more in name than in substance, however, for Webber, like Eugene Gant, bears a close resemblance to Wolfe himself. Indeed, *The Web and the Rock* is quite similar to Wolfe's earlier works: Its first half parallels

Look Homeward, Angel, while its second half stands as a sequel to *Of Time and the River*.

One of the strongest chapters in the novel is enlightening insofar as it illustrates how Wolfe continually reshaped past material. "The Child by Tiger" was first published in 1937 as a short story, but in the eighth chapter of *The Web and the Rock*, Wolfe reworks the story with changes in character and point of view. It is a moving story about the nature of good and evil, innocence and experience. Dick Prosser, a black man of ability and potential, is the object of the racial prejudice that was so pronounced in the South during the early part of the twentieth century. He is a man who befriends several young white boys; he teaches them how to throw a football, how to box, and how to make a fire. In short, he becomes a kindly father-figure who initiates them into experience. There is, however, another side to Prosser. Driven to the point of madness by prejudicial treatment, by his own apocalyptic brand of religion, and by his involvement with a woman, he goes on a shooting spree one night, killing blacks and whites alike. Eventually shot by the mob formed to hunt him down, his bullet-riddled body is hung up for display in the window of the undertaker's parlor. In the course of these events, the young men who were Prosser's friends are initiated into a world full of violence and death. For the first time in their lives, they experience profound loss, and they witness evil as it is personified in the bloodthirsty mob. Woven within the story are stanzas from William Blake's poem "The Tyger," from which the chapter title is derived.

In what makes up the second half of the novel, Wolfe deals with his own experiences in New York City. He explores his relationship with Bernstein, depicting her as a sophisticated mistress and himself as a brilliant but egocentric genius. Their relationship is described in detail—from their love-making and eating to their quarrels and reconciliations. These segments are remarkable for their candor and intriguing because of the insight they provide into the tempestuous relationship between the two. Webber's past experiences, the environment in which he was reared, and his ancestry symbolically form the web in which he is snared, and, as Esther Jack becomes a part of that web, he escapes to Germany. His search for the rock, the strength and beauty of vision that is represented by the father-figure for whom he longs, is interrupted by his realization at the end of the novel that "you can't go home again." In short, he knows that he must look to the future to escape the past.

YOU CAN'T GO HOME AGAIN

Continuing the chronicle of George Webber's life and artistic development, *You Can't Go Home Again* metaphorically develops the theme that Webber cannot go "home," cannot return to past places, old ideas, and former experiences because time and change have corrupted them. In this sense, "home" is an idealized vision of the United States as it appeared to George in his youth. These youthful visions come into abrupt contact with reality, and the resulting clash allows Wolfe to explore the very fabric of American society.

The novel begins approximately six months after *The Web and the Rock* ends. Webber has returned home to the United States, and, against his better judgment, he decides to resume his relationship with Esther Jack. He also resumes work on his novel *Home to Our Mountains (Look Homeward, Angel)* and finds a publisher, James Rodney & Co. (Scribner's), as well as a sympathetic editor and father-figure, Foxhall Edwards (Maxwell Perkins). Before his book is published, however, he returns home for the first time in years to attend the funeral of his Aunt Maw. Home in this novel is Libya Hill (like the Altamont of *Look Homeward, Angel*, the locale still represents Asheville, North Carolina). On the train trip home, he meets his childhood friend Nebraska Crane, a one-time big-league baseball star. Crane, a Cherokee Indian, is now satisfied to lead the simple life of a family man and part-time tobacco farmer, standing in contrast to Webber, whose intellectual drive and literary ambition make him a driven "city" man.

Also on the train is Judge Rumford Bland, a blind syphilitic whose corruption serves to symbolize the corruption in Libya Hill toward which Webber is traveling. Upon his arrival, Webber finds that his quiet boyhood town has become crazed from a land-boom mentality that has everyone making huge paper

fortunes in real estate (these events parallel those immediately preceding the Depression). Thus, his idealized expectations of home are shattered by the corruption and madness running rampant throughout Libya Hill.

After the publication of his novel, Webber receives abusive letters from the residents of Libya Hill. Typically, Wolfe incorporated his own experiences into his fiction. In this instance, he drew upon his unpleasant memories of what happened after he published *Look Homeward, Angel*. An entire book in the novel ("The World That Jack Built") is devoted to the wealthy lives of Esther and Frederick Jack (the Bernsteins). Writing about his own breakup with Aline Bernstein, Wolfe describes Webber's move to Brooklyn and the end of his relationship with Esther Jack. In Brooklyn, Webber learns to love the low-life characters who inhabit the streets—the prostitutes, the derelicts, and the petty criminals—for they are very much a part of the American experience. To ignore them—or worse yet, to explain them away somehow—would be to deny the underbelly of America that Webber (and Wolfe) found so compelling.

After his years in Brooklyn (with scenes devoted to his relationship with Foxhall Edwards, his editor), Webber tires of New York and sails for Europe. In Germany, he is welcomed with the fame and notoriety he has sought for so long, but he also witnesses the darker side of Nazi Germany. The novel is the story of one man's pilgrimage, a search for a faith that will endure within a society so corrupt that each individual is destroyed by it. *You Can't Go Home Again* is not an entirely cynical book, however, for it concludes with a sense of hope and faith in the future.

Throughout his novels, Wolfe explored isolation, death, and the changes wrought by time—themes that exemplify his interest in the darker elements of life. In his attempts to capture the essence of a moment, he often overlooked the artistic demands that the novel imposes upon any writer. He was not a craftsman of the novel because he often sacrificed form, unity, and coherence to capture experience. His reputation is linked directly to his ambitious attempts to say it all, and *Look Homeward, Angel*, although only the beginning of the story Wolfe desired to tell, stands as his most satisfying and fully realized work.

Philip A. Luther

OTHER MAJOR WORKS

SHORT FICTION: *From Death to Morning*, 1935; *The Hills Beyond*, 1941; *The Complete Short Stories of Thomas Wolfe*, 1987.

PLAYS: *Welcome to Our City*, pr. 1923 (published only in Germany as *Willkommen in Altamont*); *The Mountains*, pb. 1940; *Mannerhouse*, pb. 1948.

POETRY: *The Face of a Nation: Poetical Passages from the Writings of Thomas Wolfe*, 1939; *A Stone, a Leaf, a Door: Poems by Thomas Wolfe*, 1945.

NONFICTION: *The Story of a Novel*, 1936; *Thomas Wolfe's Letters to His Mother*, 1943; *The Portable Thomas Wolfe*, 1946; *The Letters of Thomas Wolfe*, 1956; *The Notebooks of Thomas Wolfe*, 1970; *The Thomas Wolfe Reader*, 1982; *Beyond Love and Loyalty: The Letters of Thomas Wolfe and Elizabeth Nowell*, 1983; *My Other Loneliness: Letters of Thomas Wolfe and Aline Bernstein*, 1983.

BIBLIOGRAPHY

Bassett, John Earl. *Thomas Wolfe: An Annotated Critical Bibliography*. Lanham, Md.: Scarecrow Press, 1996. A helpful tool for the student of Wolfe. Indexed.

Bloom, Harold, ed. *Thomas Wolfe*. New York: Chelsea House, 1987. Several essays are devoted to *Look Homeward, Angel*, but Wolfe's other novels are covered as well, with an introduction, chronology, and bibliography.

Donald, David Herbert. *Look Homeward*. Boston: Little, Brown, 1987. Donald's fine late biography stresses Wolfe's accomplishment as a social historian and his novels as "a barometer of American culture." Like others, Donald admits the presence of much bad writing but confesses to responding enthusiastically to the good. Makes full use of Wolfe's letters to his mistress, Aline Bernstein.

Evans, Elizabeth. *Thomas Wolfe*. New York: Frederick Ungar, 1984. This quarto volume provides an excellent shorter introduction to Wolfe for both the beginning and the advanced student. Economical and accurate, it is keyed clearly to Wolfe scholarship and is rich in unpretentious literary allusion. Though Evans is cautious in her admiration of Wolfe's fiction, she is appreciative of it as well. Contains a chronology and a good short bibliography.

Holman, C. Hugh. *The World of Thomas Wolfe*. New York: Charles Scribner's Sons, 1962. An older text, an example of the "controlled research" concept popular in the 1960's, this book is specifically designed for high school and college students. A good cross section of Wolfe criticism is offered, with practical information for further study. Topics for library research and term papers are suggested.

Idol, John Lane. *A Thomas Wolfe Companion*. New York: Greenwood Press, 1987. Chapters on Wolfe's ideas, major themes, editors, and critics. Also a glossary of characters and places, a genealogical chart, collections of Wolfe material, and various organizations devoted to his study. An annotated bibliography and chronology make this a highly useful resource.

Johnston, Carol Ingalls. *Of Time and the Artist: Thomas Wolfe, His Novels, and the Critics*. Columbia, S.C.: Camden House, 1996. Looks at Wolfe's autobiographical fiction and the critical response to it.

Kennedy, Richard S. *The Window of Memory*. Chapel Hill: University of North Carolina Press, 1962. Remains indispensable to the study of Wolfe; objective, scholarly, and analytic, it melds the work and the man into an artistic synthesis. Particularly valuable as a study of the creative process.

Phillipson, John S., ed. *Critical Essays on Thomas Wolfe*. Boston: G. K. Hall, 1986. Essays on each of Wolfe's major novels, stories, and plays as well as overviews of his career. Includes an introduction but no bibliography.

Rubin, Louis D., Jr., ed. *Thomas Wolfe: A Collection of Critical Essays*. Englewood Cliffs, N.J.: Prentice-Hall, 1973. A collection, with an introduction by Rubin, of a dozen stimulating essays by a variety of critics, scholars, and writers ranging from the impressionistic—a mode Wolfe inevitably inspires—to the scholarly. Contains the notorious Bernard De Voto review (1936) of *The Story of a Novel* entitled "Genius Is Not Enough."

TOM WOLFE

Born: Richmond, Virginia; March 2,1931

PRINCIPAL LONG FICTION

The Bonfire of the Vanities, 1987
A Man in Full, 1998

OTHER LITERARY FORMS

Tom Wolfe became known as one of the most original and influential of the New Journalists who came to popular attention during the mid-1960's. His collections of essays and original drawings on contemporary American lifestyle include *The Pump House Gang* (1968), *Radical Chic and Mau-Mauing the Flak Catchers* (1970), and *Mauve Gloves and Madmen, Clutter and Vine, and Other Stories, Sketches, and Essays* (1976). In these and other works, Wolfe skewered the foibles of a period he named "the me decade." He addressed what he saw as the false pretensions and theory-driven impulses of modern art in *The Painted Word* (1975) and the similar hoaxing of the general public by architects in *From Bauhaus to Our House* (1981).

Prior to his venture into long fiction, Wolfe's most extensive and successful work was *The Right Stuff* (1979), a lengthy, well-researched, and totally engrossing study of the United States manned space effort from its beginning through the end of the original Mercury program. The book was widely recognized for its incisive and penetrating exploration of the unique worldview of test pilots and astronauts, and it helped explain to the reader the almost inexpressible concept of "the right stuff."

ACHIEVEMENTS

During his career, although he was often attacked by the literary establishment, Tom Wolfe became one of the most recognized and honored of American writers. In 1973, he received the Frank Luther Mott Award for research in journalism, and in 1977 he was named Virginia Laureate for Literature. After the publication of *The Right Stuff* he was widely recognized, winning the Award in Excellence in Literature from the American Institute of Arts and Letters, the Columbia Journalism Award, and the American Book Award. In 1986 he was given the Washington Irving Medal for Literary Excellence.

An even more important mark of Wolfe's achievement, however, was the fact that he was largely credited for an entire literary movement, New Journalism, which was established during the 1960's and 1970's and which influenced not only nonfiction writing but also fiction itself, as Wolfe's own novels were to demonstrate.

BIOGRAPHY

Born and raised in Richmond, Virginia, Tom Wolfe enjoyed a childhood that exposed him to the world of the arts, especially literature. After graduating from Washington and Lee University, he enrolled at Yale University, where he majored in American studies. Before completing his dissertation, but after finishing his course work, he left Yale to work at the Springfield *Union* newspaper, where he began as a city hall reporter. He received his doctorate from Yale in 1957.

In 1959, Wolfe took a position with the Washington *Post*, then moved on to the New York *Herald-Tribune* in 1962. At the *Herald-Tribune*, widely recognized as one of the most literate and best written newspapers in the nation, Wolfe was on the staff of the Sunday magazine supplement, *New York*, where he quickly established a reputation as one of the finest reporters, with a style that was innovative, energetic, and unique. In 1965 Wolfe angered the literary establishment with a scathing, accurate, and enormously funny dissection of the sacrosanct *New Yorker* magazine.

During these years Wolfe, along with such writers as Norman Mailer, Truman Capote, and Hunter S. Thompson, was establishing what became known as New Journalism, a genre which blurred or even erased the barriers between the reporter and the story, and which reveled in subjective and highly idiosyncratic styles. Wolfe's *The Kandy-Kolored Tangerine-Flake Streamline Baby* (1965) was a collection of articles chronicling the youth culture of the mid-1960's. It was followed by *The Electric Kool-Aid Acid Test* (1968), his in-depth study of author Ken Kesey and his drug-indulging band of Merry Pranksters. In 1979 Wolfe published the definitive volume of New Journalism, *The Right Stuff*, a history of the formative years of the United States space program.

In 1984, Wolfe embarked on a daring and risky adventure, writing a novel to be published in successive issues of *Rolling Stone* magazine. Much as English writers Charles Dickens and William Makepeace Thackeray had done, Wolfe committed himself to producing multiple chapters on a tight deadline. The first installment of *The Bonfire of the Vanities* first appeared in *Rolling Stone* in July, 1984; the twenty-seventh and final installment appeared almost exactly one year later. Wolfe subsequently substantially revised the work, which was published in hardcover in 1987 and became a best-seller which also won great critical acclaim. In 1990 it was made into a unsuccessful and greatly criticized motion picture.

Following *The Bonfire of the Vanities*, Wolfe returned to journalism for almost a decade. It was not until 1998 that he again turned to fiction, publishing *A Man in Full*, about Atlanta real-estate entrepreneur Charlie Croker. Like *The Bonfire of the Vanities*, the novel was embraced by critics and the reading public; it too became a best-seller and further confirmed Wolfe's ability to write successfully, even brilliantly, in both nonfictional and fictional genres.

ANALYSIS

When, after a lengthy and successful career in journalism, Tom Wolfe turned to long fiction, his novels were grounded in the social realism and satire of writers such as Dickens, Thackeray, and Honoré de Balzac and filled with the sharp observations of class and caste characteristic of his nonfiction pieces. His style was unique in American literature.

THE BONFIRE OF THE VANITIES

The Bonfire of the Vanities is satire in its clearest and most uncompromising sense, an expression of moral nausea made bearable only by the presence of sharp, mordant humor. Its title and much of its theme come from two major sources. The first is the career of the Italian reforming cleric Girolamo Savonarola (1452-1498), who for a brief time convinced the citizens of Florence to destroy their luxury goods in a literal bonfire of the vanities. After the initial exuberance wore off, the Florentines decided to burn Savonarola instead. The second source is Thackeray's novel *Vanity Fair* (1847-1848), which satirized the excesses of society in early nineteenth century England.

The plot of the novel is relatively simple: Sherman McCoy, a bond trader on Wall Street and self-

(Nancy Crampton)

proclaimed "master of the universe" for his financial dealings, is indulging in an adulterous affair with Maria Ruskin, wife of a wealthy financier. One evening, as Sherman is returning Maria from the airport in his Mercedes, he goes astray and ends up in the unfamiliar and frightening confines of the Bronx. Fleeing what appears to be a bungled highway robbery attempt, Maria, who is driving, accidentally runs into a young black man, Henry Lamb.

When Henry Lamb ends up with a concussion in the hospital, activist Reverend Bacon mobilizes the black community to force Bronx district attorney Abraham Weiss and his assistant Larry Kramer into action. The police find evidence that might link Sherman to the crime, and British tabloid journalist Peter Fallow writes a series of articles about the incident, which further inflames the city. Sherman is indicted, and during the trial he and Maria turn against each other. Her crucial evidence is disallowed on a technicality, and Sherman's indictment is dismissed, resulting in a near riot. In a brief, ironic epilogue cast a year later, many of the major characters have fallen, through divorce, disgrace, or defeat in reelection campaigns. Only Sherman remains, still a defendant, as well as Reverend Bacon, the manipulator of protests and protesters.

As befits a novel filled with the vanities of this world, the characters in *The Bonfire of the Vanities* are defined by their possessions. The book is a lovingly precise catalogue of clothes, shoes, furniture, and accessories, all of which claim to derive genuine value from innate qualities such as craftsmanship or artistry but are worshipped because of their expense. More than that, the vanities are appropriately relative: Sherman McCoy's $1.6 million apartment is juxtaposed with the $750 rent-controlled love nest which assistant district attorney Kramer takes over from Maria for his own mistress. The antics of Sherman's supposed friends as they try to make their way in the hive of society are no less ridiculous than the efforts of Abraham Weiss to remain district attorney.

The Bonfire of the Vanities falters when it approaches the terrain and the people so alien to its hero Sherman McCoy—the Bronx and its African American population, most of them poor, many of them victimized by crime, some of them criminals themselves. Although Wolfe's ear for speech and nuance is unrivaled, he is less certain about the other aspects of the lives of these characters, more cautious and ambivalent about entering into their minds and psyches. The Reverend Bacon is given minimal treatment, pictured as an accomplished, even sophisticated, shake-down artist skilled at piercing the armor of the white establishment, whether through guilt, fear, or power politics. It is a portrait accurate enough to be satirically truthful, but so broad as to be uncomfortably close to stereotype. Roland Auburn, a black youth involved in the aborted robbery attempt, is defined as a man who can arrange for endless deliveries of new white sneakers while imprisoned in the New York City criminal justice system. Beyond them, the black characters in *The Bonfire of the Vanities* are "extras" in the crowds during Reverend Bacon's demonstrations.

Still, the novel pulsates with the energy, vigor, and vulgarisms of New York City in the latter half of the twentieth century. Sherman McCoy and his fellow characters may not be up to anything essentially worthwhile in the long-range scheme of things (always a consideration of the satirist) and they are certainly deeply flawed human beings, but they are as destructive as the followers of Savonarola and as active as the puppets Thackeray created.

A MAN IN FULL

An acidly etched survey of the influences of race and wealth, caste and class on life in the new South, *A Man in Full* is set in the South's unofficial capital, Atlanta, Georgia. This is the city of Charlie Croker, who came roaring out of southwestern Georgia to achieve fame playing both offense and defense as Georgia Tech's "Sixty Minute Man" to become one of Atlanta's most successful and well-known real-estate developers. His latest creation, Croker Concourse, gleams proudly northeast of the central city, a symbol of his triumph, but already bank loan officers are demanding that Charlie restructure his company and sell off executive toys such as his jets, and they even cast coldly calculating eyes on his beloved plantation, Turpmtine.

Atlanta lawyer Roger White II (dubbed Roger Too White by his fraternity brother Wes Jordan, now Atlanta's mayor) is asked to secure Charlie Croker's public support of Fareek "The Cannon" Fanon, a star football player at Georgia Tech accused (although neither officially nor publicly) of date rape by the daughter of one of Atlanta's most influential businessmen. In exchange, Roger White can help Charlie Croker by having the banks ease their demands.

In the meantime, Conrad Hensley, a warehouse worker in California for Croker Global Foods, is laid off as part of a drive to cut costs for Charlie's far-flung companies. Before long, in a series of misadventures, Conrad sits in a prison cell, his only diversion a volume of Epictetus, the Stoic philosopher. He begins to read and then to understand. Delivered from prison by an earthquake, Conrad makes his way to Atlanta, where he meets and befriends Charlie Croker and imparts the teachings of Epictetus. At the news conference during which he is expected to support Fanon, Charlie turns away from the banks, black politicians, and the white power structure to reclaim his own integrity. It is when he renounces those who had a claim on his soul that Charlie Croker truly becomes "a man in full."

As Wolfe glaringly exposed New York City in *The Bonfire of the Vanities*, he goes after Atlanta in *A Man in Full*. The city's acclaimed economic strength, like Charlie Croker's own empire, is an illusion. The towers downtown are deserted when work ends as their inhabitants begin the longest and worst commute in the United States, leaving the inner city 75 percent African American, creating a division that is as fatal as it is fatally ignored. Within the two communities, black and white, there are further divisions, highlighted by degrees of color, levels of wealth, and shades of accents and dialect—all of which, once again, Wolfe captures with a mix of confidence and exuberance.

Michael Witkoski

OTHER MAJOR WORKS

NONFICTION: *The Kandy-Kolored Tangerine-Flake Streamline Baby*, 1965; *The Pump House Gang*, 1968; *The Electric Kool-Aid Acid Test*, 1968; *Radical Chic and Mau-Mauing the Flak Catchers*, 1970; *The New Journalism*, 1973; *The Painted Word*, 1975; *Mauve Gloves and Madmen, Clutter and Vine, and Other Stories, Sketches, and Essays*, 1976; *The Right Stuff*, 1979; *In Our Time*, 1980; *From Bauhaus to Our House*, 1981; *The Purple Decades: A Reader*, 1982.

BIBLIOGRAPHY

McKeen, William. *Tom Wolfe*. New York: Twayne, 1995. A volume in Twayne's United States Authors series, this book provides students and general readers with an introduction to Wolfe's life and career. Especially good in discussing Wolfe's career as a practicing journalist, including his articles, such as his piece on *The New Yorker* which so outraged traditionalists.

Salamon, Julie. *The Devil's Candy: "The Bonfire of the Vanities" Goes to Hollywood*. Boston: Houghton Mifflin, 1991. Although primarily about the making of the film version of Wolfe's novel, this study helps the reader better understand and appreciate the many artistic nuances and insights in Wolfe's carefully layered work, which were lost in its translation to the big screen.

Scura, Dorothy, ed. *Conversations with Tom Wolfe*. Jackson: University Press of Mississippi, 1990. A collection of essays about Wolfe and interviews with Wolfe that survey the range and impact of his writing and explain how he became the most important and influential literary journalist of his time.

Shomette, Doug, ed. *The Critical Response to Tom Wolfe*. Westport, Conn.: Greenwood Press, 1992. Contains a variety of critical responses to Wolfe's writings over the years, with a section devoted to the early responses and criticisms of *The Bonfire of the Vanities*.

VIRGINIA WOOLF

Born: London, England; January 25, 1882
Died: Rodmell, Sussex, England; March 28, 1941

(Courtesy D.C. Public Library)

PRINCIPAL LONG FICTION

The Voyage Out, 1915
Night and Day, 1919
Jacob's Room, 1922
Mrs. Dalloway, 1925
To the Lighthouse, 1927
Orlando: A Biography, 1928
The Waves, 1931
Flush: A Biography, 1933
The Years, 1937
Between the Acts, 1941

OTHER LITERARY FORMS

To say that Virginia Woolf lived to write is no exaggeration. Her output was both prodigious and var-

ied; counting her posthumously published works, it fills more than forty volumes. Beyond her novels her fiction encompasses several short-story collections. As a writer of nonfiction, Woolf was similarly prolific, her book-length works including *Roger Fry: A Biography* (1940) and two influential feminist statements, *A Room of One's Own* (1929) and *Three Guineas* (1938). Throughout her life, Woolf also produced criticism and reviews; the best-known collections are *The Common Reader: First Series* (1925) and *The Common Reader: Second Series* (1932). In 1966 and 1967, the four volumes of *Collected Essays* were published. Additional books of essays, reviews, and sketches continue to appear, most notably the illuminating selection of autobiographical materials, *Moments of Being* (1976). Her letters—3,800 of them survive—are available in six volumes; when publication was completed, her diaries stood at five. Another collection, of Woolf's essays, also proved a massive, multivolume undertaking.

ACHIEVEMENTS

From the appearance of her first novel in 1915, Virginia Woolf's work was received with respect—an important point, since she was extremely sensitive to criticism. Descendant of a distinguished literary family, member of the avant-garde Bloomsbury Group, herself an experienced critic and reviewer, she was taken seriously as an artist. Nevertheless, her early works were not financially successful; she was forty before she earned a living from her writing. From the start, the rather narrow territory of her novels precluded broad popularity, peopled as they were with sophisticated, sexually reserved, upper-middle-class characters, finely attuned to their sensibilities and relatively insulated from the demands of mundane existence. When in *Jacob's Room* she first abandoned the conventional novel to experiment with the interior monologues and lyrical poetic devices which characterize her mature method, she also began to develop a reputation as a "difficult" or "high-brow" writer, though undeniably an important one. Not until the brilliant fantasy *Orlando* was published did she enjoy a definite commercial success. Thereafter, she received both critical and popular acclaim; *The Years* was even a bona fide best-seller.

During the 1930's, Woolf became the subject of critical essays and two book-length studies; some of her works were translated into French. At the same time, however, her novels began to be judged as irrelevant to a world beset by growing economic and political chaos. At her death in 1941, she was widely regarded as a pioneer of modernism but also reviewed by many as the effete, melancholic "invalid priestess of Bloomsbury," a stereotype her friend and fellow novelist E. M. Forster dismissed at the time as wholly inaccurate; she was, he insisted, "tough, sensitive but tough."

Over the next twenty-five years, respectful attention to Woolf's work continued, but in the late 1960's, critical interest accelerated dramatically and has remained strong. Two reasons for this renewed notice seem particularly apparent. First, Woolf's feminist essays *A Room of One's Own* and *Three Guineas* became rallying documents in the growing women's movement; readers who might not otherwise have discovered her novels were drawn to them via her nonfiction and tended to read them primarily as validations of her feminist thinking. Second, with the appearance of her husband Leonard Woolf's five-volume autobiography from 1965-1969, her nephew Quentin Bell's definitive two-volume biography of her in 1972, and the full-scale editions of her own diaries and letters commencing in the mid-1970's, Woolf's life has become one of the most thoroughly documented of any modern author. Marked by intellectual and sexual unconventionality, madness, and suicide, it is for today's readers also one of the most fascinating; the steady demand for memoirs, reminiscences, and photograph collections relating to her has generated what is sometimes disparagingly labeled "the Virginia Woolf industry." At its worst, such insatiable curiosity is morbidly voyeuristic, distracting from and trivializing Woolf's achievement; on a more responsible level, it has led to serious, provocative reevaluations of the political and especially the feminist elements in her work, as well as to redefinitions of her role as an artist.

BIOGRAPHY

Daughter of the eminent editor and critic Sir Leslie Stephen and Julia Jackson Duckworth, both of whom had been previously widowed, Virginia Woolf was born in 1882 into a solidly late Victorian intellectual and social milieu. Her father's first wife had been William Makepeace Thackeray's daughter; James Russell Lowell was her godfather; visitors to the Stephens' London household included Henry James, George Meredith, and Thomas Hardy. From childhood on, she had access to her father's superb library, benefitting from his guidance and commentary on her rigorous, precocious reading. Nevertheless, unlike her brothers, she did not receive a formal university education, a lack she always regretted and that partly explains the anger in *Three Guineas*, where she proposes a "university of outsiders." (Throughout her life she declined all academic honors.)

In 1895, when Woolf was thirteen, her mother, just past fifty, suddenly died. Altruistic, self-sacrificing, totally devoted to her demanding husband and large family, the beautiful Julia Stephen fulfilled the Victorian ideal of womanhood and exhausted herself doing so; her daughter would movingly eulogize her as Mrs. Ramsay in *To the Lighthouse*. The loss devastated Woolf, who experienced at that time the first of four major mental breakdowns in her life, the last of which would end in death.

Leslie Stephen, twenty years his wife's senior and thus sanguinely expecting her to pilot him comfortably through old age, was devastated in another way. Retreating histrionically into self-pitying but deeply felt grief, like that of his fictional counterpart, Mr. Ramsay, he transferred his intense demands for sympathetic attention to a succession of what could only seem to him achingly inadequate substitutes for his dead wife: first, his stepdaughter Stella Duckworth, who herself died suddenly in 1897, then, Virginia's older sister Vanessa. The traditional feminine role would eventually have befallen Virginia had Leslie Stephen not died in 1904. Writing in her 1928 diary on what would have been her father's ninety-sixth birthday, Woolf reflects that, had he lived, "His life would have entirely ended mine. . . . No writing, no books;—inconceivable."

On her father's death, Woolf sustained her second incapacitating breakdown. Yet she also gained, as her diary suggests, something crucial: freedom, which took an immediate and, to her parents' staid friends and relatives, shocking form. Virginia, Vanessa, and their brothers Thoby and Adrian abandoned the Stephen house in respectable Kensington to set up a home in the seedy bohemian district of London known as Bloomsbury. There, on Thursday evenings, a coterie of Thoby Stephen's Cambridge University friends regularly gathered to talk in an atmosphere of free thought, avant-garde art, and sexual tolerance, forming the nucleus of what came to be called the Bloomsbury Group. At various stages in its evolution over the next decade, the group included such luminaries as biographer Lytton Strachey, novelist E. M. Forster, art critic Roger Fry, and economist John Maynard Keynes. In 1911, they were joined by another of Thoby's Cambridge friends, a colonial official just returned from seven years in Ceylon, Leonard Woolf; Virginia Stephen married him the following year. Scarcely twelve months after the wedding, Virginia Woolf's third severe breakdown began, marked by a suicide attempt; her recovery took almost two years.

The causes of Woolf's madness have been much debated and the treatment she was prescribed—bed rest, milk, withdrawal of intellectual stimulation—much disputed, especially since she apparently never received psychoanalytic help, even though the Hogarth Press, founded by the Woolfs in 1917, was one of Sigmund Freud's earliest English publishers. A history of insanity ran in the Stephen family; if Virginia were afflicted with a hereditary nervous condition, it was thought, then, that must be accepted as unalterable. On the other hand, the timing of these three breakdowns prompts speculation about more subtle causes. About her parents' deaths she evidently felt strong guilt; of *To the Lighthouse*, the fictionalized account of her parents' relationship, she would later say, "I was obsessed by them both, unhealthily; and writing of them was a necessary act." Marriage was for her a deliberately sought yet disturbing commitment, representing a potential loss of autonomy and a retreat into what her would-be novelist Terence Hewet envisions in *The Voyage Out* as a walled-up, firelit room. She found her own marriage sexually disappointing, perhaps in part because she had been molested as both a child and a young woman by her two Duckworth stepbrothers.

In the late twentieth century, feminist scholars especially argued as a cause of Woolf's madness the burden of being a greatly talented woman in a world hostile to feminine achievement, a situation Woolf strikingly depicts in *A Room of One's Own* as the plight of William Shakespeare's hypothetical sister. Indeed, the young Virginia Stephen might plunder her father's library all day, but by teatime she was expected to don the role of deferential Victorian female in a rigidly patriarchal household. Yet once she settled in Bloomsbury, she enjoyed unconventional independence and received much sympathetic encouragement of her gifts, most of all from her husband.

Leonard Woolf, himself a professional writer and literary editor, connected her madness directly with her genius, saying that she concentrated more intensely on her work than any writer he had ever known. Her books passed through long, difficult gestations; her sanity was always most vulnerable immediately after a novel was finished. Expanding on his belief that the imagination in his wife's books and the delusions of her breakdowns "all came from the same place in her mind," some critics go so far as to claim her madness as the very source of her art, permitting her to make mystical descents into inner space from which she returned with sharpened perception.

It is significant, certainly, that although Woolf's first publication, an unsigned article for *The Guardian*, appeared just two months after her 1904 move to Bloomsbury, her first novel, over which she labored for seven years, was only completed shortly after her marriage; her breakdown occurred three months after its acceptance for publication. Very early, therefore, Leonard Woolf learned to keep a daily record of his wife's health; throughout their life together, he would be alert for those signs of fatigue or erratic behavior that signaled approaching danger and the need for her customary rest cure. Rational, efficient, uncomplaining, Leonard Woolf has been condemned by some disaffected scholars as a pseudosaintly nurse who benignly badgered his patient into crippling dependency. The compelling argument against this extreme interpretation is Virginia Woolf's astonishing productivity after she recovered from her third illness. Although there were certainly periods of instability and near disaster, the following twenty-five years were immensely fruitful as she discarded traditional fiction to move toward realizing her unique vision, all the while functioning actively and diversely as a fine critic, too.

After Woolf's ninth novel, *The Years*, was finished in 1936, however, she came closer to mental collapse than she had been at any time since 1913. Meanwhile, a larger pattern of breakdown was developing in the world around her as World War II became inevitable. Working at her Sussex home on her last book, *Between the Acts*, she could hear the Battle of Britain being fought over her head; her London house was severely damaged in the Blitz. Yet strangely, that novel was her easiest to write; Leonard Woolf, ever watchful, was struck by her tranquility during this period. The gradual symptoms of warning were absent this time; when her depression began, he would recall, it struck her "like a sudden blow." She began to hear voices and knew what was coming. On February 26, 1941, she finished *Between the Acts*. Four weeks later, she went out for one of her usual walks across the Sussex downs, placed a heavy stone in her pocket, and stepped into the River Ouse. Within minutes Leonard Woolf arrived at its banks to find her walking stick and hat lying there. Her body was recovered three weeks later.

ANALYSIS

In one of her most famous pronouncements on the nature of fiction—as a practicing critic, she had much to say on the subject—Virginia Woolf insists that "life is not a series of gig lamps symmetrically arranged; but a luminous halo, a semi-transparent envelope surrounding us from the beginning of consciousness to the end." In an ordinary day, she argues, "thousands of ideas" course through the human brain; "thousands of emotions" meet, collide, and disappear

"in astonishing disorder." Amid this hectic interior flux, the trivial and the vital, the past and the present, are constantly interacting; there is endless tension between the multitude of ideas and emotions rushing through one's consciousness and the numerous impressions scoring on it from the external world. Thus, even personal identity becomes evanescent, continually reordering itself as "the atoms of experience . . . fall upon the mind." It follows, then, that human beings must have great difficulty communicating with one another, for of this welter of perceptions that define individual personality, only a tiny fraction can ever be externalized in word or gesture. Yet, despite—in fact, because of—their frightening isolation as unknowable entities, people yearn to unite both with one another and with some larger pattern of order hidden behind the flux, to experience time standing still momentarily, to see matches struck that briefly illuminate the darkness.

Given the complex phenomenon of human subjectivity, Woolf asks, "Is it not the task of the novelist to convey this varying, this unknown and uncircumscribed spirit . . . with as little mixture of the alien and external as possible?" The conventional novel form is plainly inadequate for such a purpose, she maintains. Dealing sequentially with a logical set of completed past actions that occur in a coherent, densely detailed physical and social environment, presided over by an omniscient narrator interpreting the significance of it all, the traditional novel trims and shapes experience into a rational but falsified pattern. "Is life like this?" Woolf demands rhetorically. "Must novels be like this?"

In Woolf's first two books, nevertheless, she attempted to work within conventional modes, discovering empirically that they could not convey her vision. Although in recent years some critics have defended *The Voyage Out* and *Night and Day* as artistically satisfying in their own right, both novels have generally been considered interesting mainly for what they foreshadow of Woolf's later preoccupations and techniques.

THE VOYAGE OUT

The Voyage Out is the story of Rachel Vinrace, a naïve and talented twenty-four-year-old amateur pianist who sails from England to a small resort on the South American coast, where she vacations with relatives. There, she meets a fledgling novelist, Terence Hewet; on a pleasure expedition up a jungle river, they declare their love. Shortly thereafter, Rachel falls ill with a fever and dies. The novel's exotic locale, large cast of minor characters, elaborate scenes of social comedy, and excessive length are all atypical of Woolf's mature work. Already, however, many of her later concerns are largely emerging. The resonance of the title itself anticipates Woolf's poetic symbolism; the "voyage out" can be the literal trip across the Atlantic or up the South American river, but it also suggests the progression from innocence to experience, from life to death, which she later depicts using similar water imagery. Her concern with premature death and how survivors come to terms with it prefigures *Jacob's Room, Mrs. Dalloway, To the Lighthouse*, and *The Waves*. Most significant is her portrayal of a world in which characters are forever striving to overcome their isolation from one another. The ship on which Rachel "voyages out" is labeled by Woolf an "emblem of the loneliness of human life." Terence, Rachel's lover, might be describing his creator's own frustration when he says he is trying "to write a novel about Silence, the things people don't say. But the difficulty is immense."

Yet moments of unity amid seemingly unconquerable disorder do occur. On a communal level, one such transformation happens at a ball being held to celebrate the engagement of two English guests at the resort's small hotel. When the musicians go home, Rachel appropriates the piano and plays Mozart, hunting songs, and hymn tunes as the guests gradually resume dancing, each in a newly expressive, uninhibited way, eventually to join hands in a gigantic round dance. When the circle breaks and each member spins away to become individual once more, Rachel modulates to Bach; her weary yet exhilarated listeners sit quietly and allow themselves to be soothed by the serene complexity of the music. As dawn breaks outside and Rachel plays on, they envision "themselves and their lives, and the whole of human life advancing nobly under the direction of the music." They

have transcended their single identities temporarily to gain a privileged glimpse of some larger pattern beyond themselves.

If Rachel through her art briefly transforms the lives of a small community, she herself privately discerns fleeting stability through her growing love for Terence. Yet even love is insufficient; although in the couple's newfound sense of union "divisions disappeared," Terence feels that Rachel seems able "to pass away to unknown places where she had no need of him." In the elegiac closing scenes of illness (which Woolf reworked many times and which are the most original as well as moving part of the novel), Rachel "descends into another world"; she is "curled up at the bottom of the sea." Terence, sitting by her bedside, senses that "they seemed to be thinking together; he seemed to be Rachel as well as himself." When she ceases breathing, he experiences "an immense feeling of peace," a "complete union" with her that shatters when he notices an ordinary table covered with crockery and realizes in horror that in this world he will never see Rachel again. For her, stability has been achieved; for him, the isolating flux has resumed.

Night and Day

Looking back on *The Voyage Out*, Woolf could see, she said, why readers found it "a more gallant and inspiring spectacle" than her next and least known book *Night and Day*. This second novel is usually regarded as her most traditional in form and subject—in its social satire, her obeisance to Jane Austen. Its dancelike plot, however, in which mismatched young couples eventually find their true loves, suggests the magical atmosphere of William Shakespeare's romantic comedies as well. References to Shakespeare abound in the book; for example, the delightfully eccentric Mrs. Hilbery characterizes herself as one of his wise fools, and when at the end she presides over the repatterning of the couples in London, she has just arrived from a pilgrimage to Stratford-upon-Avon. Coincidentally, *Night and Day* is the most conventionally dramatic of Woolf's novels, full of dialogue, exits and entrances; characters are constantly taking omnibuses and taxis across London from one contrived scene to the next.

Like *The Voyage Out, Night and Day* does point to Woolf's enduring preoccupations. It is, too, a novel depicting movement from innocence to maturity and escape from the conventional world through the liberating influence of love. Ralph Denham, a London solicitor from a large, vulgar, middle-class family living in suburban Highgate, would prefer to move to a Norfolk cottage and write. Katharine Hilbery measures out her days serving tea in her wealthy family's beautiful Chelsea home and helping her disorganized mother produce a biography of their forebear, a great nineteenth century poet. Her secret passions, however, are mathematics and astronomy. These seeming opposites, Ralph and Katharine, are alike in that both retreat at night to their rooms to pursue their private visions. The entire novel is concerned with such dualities—public selves and private selves, activity and contemplation, fact and imagination; but Woolf also depicts the unity that Ralph and Katharine can achieve, notwithstanding the social and intellectual barriers separating them. At the end, as the couple leaves Katharine's elegant but constraining home to walk in the open night air, "they lapsed gently into silence, travelling the dark paths side by side towards something discerned in the distance which gradually possessed them both."

The sustained passages of subtle interior analysis by which Woolf charts the couple's growing realization of their need for each other define her real area of fictional interest, but they are hemmed in by a tediously constrictive traditional structure. Except for her late novel, *The Years*, also comparatively orthodox in form, her first two books took the longest to finish and underwent the most extensive revisions, undoubtedly because she was writing against her grain. Nevertheless, they represented a necessary apprenticeship; as she would later remark of *Night and Day*, "You must put it all in before you can leave out."

JACOB'S ROOM

Woolf dared to leave out a great deal in the short experimental novel she wrote next. Described in conventional terms, *Jacob's Room* is a *Bildungsroman* or "novel of formation" tracing its hero's development from childhood to maturity: Jacob Flanders is first

portrayed as a small boy studying a tide pool on a Cornish beach; at twenty-six, he dies fighting in World War I. In structure, style, and tone, however, *Jacob's Room* defies such labeling. It does not move in steady chronological fashion but in irregular leaps. Of the fourteen chapters, two cover Jacob's childhood, two, his college years at Cambridge, the remainder, his life as a young adult working in London and traveling abroad. In length, and hence in the complexity with which various periods of Jacob's existence are treated, the chapters range from one to twenty-eight pages. They vary, that is, as the process of growth itself does.

Individual chapters are likewise discontinuous in structure, broken into irregular segments that convey multiple, often simultaneous perspectives. The ten-page chapter 8, for example, opens with Jacob's slamming the door of his London room as he starts for work in the morning; he is then glimpsed at his office desk. Meanwhile, on a table back in his room lies his mother's unopened letter to him, placed there the previous night by his lover, Florinda; its contents and Mrs. Flanders herself are evoked. The narrator then discourses on the significance of letter-writing. Jacob is next seen leaving work for the day; in Greek Street, he spies Florinda on another man's arm. At eight o'clock, Rose Shaw, a guest at a party Jacob attended several nights earlier, walks through Holburn, meditating bitterly on the ironies of love and death. The narrator sketches London by lamplight. Then, Jacob is back in his room reading by the fire a newspaper account of the Prime Minister's speech on Home Rule; the night is very cold. The narrator abruptly shifts perspective from congested London to the open countryside, describing the snow that has been accumulating since mid-afternoon; an old shepherd crossing a field hears a distant clock strike. Back in London, Jacob also hears the hour chiming, rakes out his fire, and goes to bed. There is no story here in any conventional sense, no action being furthered; in the entire ten pages, only one sentence is direct dialogue. What Woolf delineates is the *texture* of an ordinary day in the life of Jacob and the world in which he exists. Clock time moves the chapter forward, while spatially the chapter radiates outward from the small area Jacob occupies. Simultaneously, in the brief reference to the Prime Minister, Woolf suggests the larger procession of modern history that will inexorably sweep Jacob to premature death.

Such indirection and understatement characterize the whole novel: "It is no use trying to sum people up," the narrator laments. "One must follow hints." Thus, Jacob is described mainly from the outside, defined through the impressions he makes on others, from a hotel chambermaid to a Cambridge don, and by his surroundings and possessions. Even his death is conveyed obliquely: Mrs. Flanders, half asleep in her Yorkshire house, hears "dull sounds"; it cannot be guns, she thinks, it must be the sea. On the next page, she stands in her dead son's London room, holding a pair of Jacob's old shoes and asking his friend pathetically, "What am I to do with these, Mr. Bonamy?" The novel ends.

To construct Jacob's ultimately unknowable biography out of such fragments, Woolf evolves not only a new structure but a new style. Long, fluid sentences contain precise physical details juxtaposed with metaphysical speculations on the evanescence of life and the impossibility of understanding another person. Lyrical descriptions of nature—waves, moths, falling snow, birds rising and settling—are interspersed to suggest life's beauty and fragility. Images and phrases recur as unifying motifs: Jacob is repeatedly associated with Greek literature and myth and spends his last fulfilling days visiting the Parthenon. Most important, Woolf begins to move freely in and out of her characters' minds to capture the flow of sense impressions mingling with memory, emotion, and random association, experimenting with that narrative method conveniently if imprecisely labeled "stream of consciousness."

Jacob's Room is not a mature work, especially with its intrusive narrator, who can be excessively chatty, archly pedantic, and sententious. Woolf protests the difficulties of her task ("In short, the observer is choked with observations") and cannot quite follow the logic of her new method; after an essay-like passage on the necessity of illusion, for example, she awkwardly concludes, "Jacob, no doubt,

thought something in this fashion. . . ." Even the lovely passages of poetic description at times seem self-indulgent. The book definitely shows its seams. Woolf's rejection of traditional novel structure, however, and her efforts to eliminate "the alien and the external" make *Jacob's Room* a dazzling advance in her ability to embody her philosophic vision: "Life is but a procession of shadows, and God knows why it is that we embrace them so eagerly, and see them depart with such anguish, being shadows."

MRS. DALLOWAY

Within three years, Woolf had resolved her technical problems superbly in *Mrs. Dalloway*. The intruding narrator vanishes; though the freedom with which point of view shifts among characters and settings clearly posits an omniscient intelligence, the narrator's observations are now subtly integrated with the thoughts of her characters, and the transitions between scenes flow organically. Woolf's subject is also better suited to her method: Whereas *Jacob's Room* is a story of youthful potential tragically cut off, *Mrs. Dalloway* is a novel of middle age, about what people have become as the result of choices made, opportunities seized or refused. Jacob Flanders had but a brief past; the characters in *Mrs. Dalloway* must come to terms with theirs, sifting and valuing the memories that course through their minds.

The book covers one June day in the life of Clarissa Dalloway, fifty-two years old, an accomplished London political hostess and wife of a Member of Parliament. A recent serious illness from which she is still recovering has made her freshly appreciate the wonder of life as she prepares for the party she will give that evening. Peter Walsh, once desperately in love with her, arrives from India, where he has had an undistinguished career; he calls on her and is invited to the party, at which another friend from the past, Sally Seton, formerly a romantic and now the conventional wife of a Manchester industrialist, will also unexpectedly appear. Running parallel with Clarissa's day is that of the mad Septimus Warren Smith, a surviving Jacob Flanders, shell-shocked in the war; his suicide in the late afternoon delays the arrival of another of Clarissa's guests, the eminent nerve specialist Sir William Bradshaw. Learning of this stranger's death, Clarissa must confront the inevitability of her own.

Mrs. Dalloway is also, then, a novel about time itself (its working title at one point was *The Hours*). Instead of using chapters or other formal sectioning, Woolf structures the book by counterpointing clock time, signaled by the obtrusive hourly tolling of Big Ben, against the subjective flow of time in her characters' minds as they recover the past and envision the future. Not only does she move backward and forward in time, however; she also creates an effect of simultaneity that is especially crucial in linking Septimus's story with Clarissa's. Thus, when Clarissa Dalloway, buying flowers that morning in a Bond Street shop, hears "a pistol shot" outside and emerges to see a large, official automobile that has backfired, Septimus is standing in the crowd blocked by the car and likewise reacting to this "violent explosion" ("The world has raised its whip; where will it descend?"). Later, when Septimus's frightened young Italian wife Rezia guides him to Regents Park to calm him before their appointment with Bradshaw, he has a terrifying hallucination of his dead friend Evans, killed just before the Armistice; Peter Walsh, passing their bench, wonders, "What awful fix had they got themselves in to look so desperate as that on a fine summer morning?" This atmosphere of intensely populated time and space, of many anonymous lives intersecting briefly, of the world resonating with unwritten novels, comic and tragic, accounts in part for the richly poignant texture of nearly all Woolf's mature work.

In her early thinking about *Mrs. Dalloway*, Virginia Woolf wanted to show a "world seen by the sane and the insane, side by side." Although the novel definitely focuses on Clarissa, Septimus functions as a kind of double, representing her own responses to life carried to an untenable extreme. Both find great terror in life and also great joy; both want to withdraw from life into blissful isolation, yet both want to reach out to merge with others. Clarissa's friends, and indeed she herself, sense a "coldness" about her, "an impenetrability"; both Peter and Sally believe she chose safety rather than adventure by marrying the unimaginative, responsible Richard

Dalloway. The quiet attic room where she now convalesces is described as a tower into which she retreats nunlike to a virginal narrow bed. Yet Clarissa also loves "life; London; this moment of June"—and her parties. Though some critics condemn her partygiving as shallow, trivial, even corrupt (Peter Walsh could make her wince as a girl by predicting that she would become "the perfect hostess"), Clarissa considers her parties a form of creativity, "an offering," "her gift" of bringing people together. For Septimus, the war has destroyed his capacity to feel; in his aloneness and withdrawal, he finds "an isolation full of sublimity; a freedom which the attached can never know"—he can elude "human nature," "the repulsive brute, with the blood-red nostrils." Yet just watching leaves quivering is for him "an exquisite joy"; he feels them "connected by millions of fibres with his own body" and wants to reveal this unity to the world because "communication is health; communication is happiness."

Desperate because of his suicide threats, Septimus's wife takes him to see Sir William Bradshaw. At the center of the novel, in one of the most bitter scenes in all of Woolf's writing (certainly one with strong autobiographical overtones), is Septimus's confrontation with this "priest of science," this man of "lightning skill" and "almost infallible accuracy" who "never spoke of 'madness'; he called it not having a sense of proportion." Within three minutes, he has discreetly recorded his diagnosis on a pink card ("a case of complete breakdown . . . with every symptom in an advanced stage"); Septimus will be sent to a beautiful house in the country where he will be taught to rest, to regain proportion. Rezia, agonized, understands that she has been failed by this obtuse, complacently cruel man whom Woolf symbolically connects with a larger system that prospers on intolerance and sends its best young men to fight futile wars. Septimus's suicide at this point becomes inevitable.

The two stories fuse when Bradshaw appears at the party. Learning of the reason for his lateness, Clarissa, deeply shaken, withdraws to a small side room, not unlike her attic tower, where she accurately imagines Septimus's suicide: "He had thrown himself from a window. Up had flashed the ground; through him, blundering, bruising, went the rusty spikes. . . . So she saw it." She also intuits the immediate cause: Bradshaw is "capable of some indescribable outrage—forcing your soul, that was it"; seeing him, this young man must have said to himself, "they make life intolerable, men like that." Thus, she sees, "death was defiance," a means to preserve one's center from being violated, but "death was an attempt to communicate," and in death, Septimus's message that all life is connected is heard by one unlikely person, Clarissa Dalloway. Reviewing her own past as she has reconstructed it this day, and forced anew to acknowledge her own mortality, she realizes that "he had made her feel the beauty." Spiritually regenerated, she returns to her party "to kindle and illuminate" life.

TO THE LIGHTHOUSE

In her most moving, complexly affirmative novel, *To the Lighthouse*, Woolf portrays another woman whose creativity lies in uniting people, Mrs. Ramsay. For this luminous evocation of her own parents' marriage, Woolf drew on memories of her girlhood summers at St. Ives, Cornwall (here transposed to an island in the Hebrides), to focus on her perennial themes, the difficulties and joys of human communication, especially as frustrated by time and death.

The plot is absurdly simple: An expedition to a lighthouse is postponed, then completed a decade later. Woolf's mastery, however, of the interior monologue in this novel makes such a fragile plot line quite sufficient; the real "story" of *To the Lighthouse* is the reader's gradually increasing intimacy with its characters' richly depicted inner lives; the reader's understanding expands in concert with the characters' own growing insights.

Woolf again devises an experimental structure for her work, this time of three unequal parts. Approximately the first half of the novel, entitled "The Window," occurs during a single day at the seaside home occupied by an eminent philosopher, Mr. Ramsay, his wife, and a melange of children, guests, and servants, including Lily Briscoe, an amateur painter in her thirties, unmarried. Mrs. Ramsay's is the dominant consciousness in this section. A short, exquisitely beauti-

ful center section, "Time Passes," pictures the house succumbing to time during the family's ten-year absence and then being rescued from decay by two old women for the Ramsays' repossession. Periodically interrupting this natural flow of time are terse, bracketed, clock-time announcements like news bulletins, telling of the deaths of Mrs. Ramsay, the eldest son Andrew (in World War I), and the eldest daughter Prue (of childbirth complications). The final third, "The Lighthouse," also covers one day; the diminished family and several former guests having returned, the lighthouse expedition can now be completed. This section is centered almost entirely in Lily Briscoe's consciousness.

Because Mr. and Mrs. Ramsay are both strong personalities, they are sometimes interpreted too simply. Particularly in some readings by feminist critics, Mr. Ramsay is seen as an insufferable patriarch, arrogantly rational in his work but almost infantile emotionally, while Mrs. Ramsay is a Victorian Earth Mother, not only submitting unquestioningly to her husband's and children's excessive demands but actively trying to impose on all the other female characters her unliberated way of life. Such readings are sound to some extent, but they undervalue the vivid way that Woolf captures in the couple's monologues the conflicting mixture of motives and needs that characterize human beings of either sex. For example, Mrs. Ramsay is infuriated that her husband blights their youngest son James's anticipation of the lighthouse visit by announcing that it will storm tomorrow, yet his unflinching pursuit of truth is also something she most admires in him. Mr. Ramsay finds his wife's irrational habit of exaggeration maddening, but as she sits alone in a reverie, he respects her integrity and will not interrupt, "though it hurt him that she should look so distant, and he could not reach her, he could do nothing to help her." Lily, a shrewd observer who simultaneously adores and resists Mrs. Ramsay, perceives that "it would be a mistake . . . to simplify their relationship."

Amid these typical contradictions and mundane demands, however, "little daily miracles" may be achieved. One of Woolf's finest scenes, Mrs. Ramsay's dinner, provides a paradigm (though a summary can scarcely convey the richness of these forty pages). As she mechanically seats her guests at the huge table, Mrs. Ramsay glimpses her husband at the other end, "all in a heap, frowning": "She could not understand how she had ever felt any emotion of affection for him." Gloomily, she perceives that not just the two of them but everyone is separate and out of sorts. For example, Charles Tansley, Mr. Ramsay's disciple, who feels the whole family despises him, fidgets angrily; Lily, annoyed that Tansley is always telling her "women can't paint," purposely tries to irritate him; William Bankes would rather be home dining alone and fears that Mrs. Ramsay will read his mind. They all sense that "something [is] lacking"—they are divided from one another, sunk in their "treacherous" thoughts. Mrs. Ramsay wearily recognizes that "the whole of the effort of merging and flowing and creating rested on her."

She instructs two of her children to light the candles and set them around a beautiful fruit centerpiece that her daughter Rose has arranged for the table. This is Mrs. Ramsay's first stroke of artistry; the candles and fruit compose the table and the faces around it into an island, a sheltering haven: "Here, inside the room, seemed to be order and dry land; there, outside, a reflection in which things wavered and vanished, waterily." All the guests feel this change and have a sudden sense of making "common cause against that fluidity out there." Then the maid brings in a great steaming dish of *boeuf en daube* that even the finicky widower Bankes considers "a triumph." As the guests relish the succulent food and their camaraderie grows, Mrs. Ramsay, serving the last helpings from the depths of the pot, experiences a moment of perfect insight: "There it was, all around them. It partook . . . of eternity." She affirms to herself that "there is a coherence in things, a stability; something, she meant, that is immune from change, and shines out . . . in the face of the flowing, the fleeting." As is true of so much of Woolf's sparse dialogue, the ordinary words Mrs. Ramsay then speaks aloud can be read both literally and symbolically: "Yes, there is plenty for everybody." As the dinner ends and she passes out of the room triumphantly— the inscrutable poet Augustus Carmichael, who usu-

ally resists her magic, actually bows in homage—she looks back on the scene and sees that "it had become, she knew . . . already the past."

The burden of the past and the coming to terms with it are the focus of part 3. Just as "a sort of disintegration" sets in as soon as Mrs. Ramsay sweeps out of the dining room, so her death has left a larger kind of wreckage. Without her unifying artistry, all is disorder, as it was at the beginning of the dinner. In a gesture of belated atonement for quarreling with his wife over the original lighthouse trip, the melodramatically despairing Mr. Ramsay insists on making the expedition now with his children James and Cam, although both hate his tyranny and neither wants to go. As they set out, Lily remains behind to paint. Surely mirroring the creative anxiety of Woolf herself, she feels "a painful but exciting ecstasy" before her blank canvas, knowing how ideas that seem simple become "in practice immediately complex." As she starts making rhythmic strokes across the canvas, she loses "consciousness of outer things" and begins to meditate on the past, from which she gradually retrieves a vision of Mrs. Ramsay that will permit her to reconstruct and complete the painting she left unfinished a decade ago, one in which Mrs. Ramsay would have been, and will become again, a triangular shadow on a step (symbolically echoing the invisible "wedge-shaped core of darkness" to which Mrs. Ramsay feels herself shrinking during her moments of reverie). Through the unexpectedly intense pain of recalling her, Lily also comprehends Mrs. Ramsay's significance, her ability "to make the moment something permanent," as art does, to strike "this eternal passing and flowing . . . into stability." Mrs. Ramsay is able to make "life stand still here."

Meanwhile, Mr. Ramsay and his children are also voyaging into the past; Cam, dreamily drifting her hand in the water, begins, as her mother did, to see her father as bravely pursuing truth like a tragic hero. James bitterly relives the childhood scene when his father thoughtlessly dashed his hopes for the lighthouse visit, but as they near the lighthouse in the present and Mr. Ramsay offers his son rare praise, James too is reconciled. When they land, Mr. Ramsay himself, standing in the bow "very straight and tall," springs "lightly like a young man . . . on to the rock," renewed. Simultaneously, though the boat has long since disappeared from her sight and even the lighthouse itself seems blurred, Lily intuits that they have reached their goal and she completes her painting. All of them have reclaimed Mrs. Ramsay from death, and she has unified them; memory can defeat time. "Yes," Lily thinks, "I have had my vision." Clearly, Woolf had achieved hers too and transmuted the materials of a painful past into this radiant novel.

Although Woolf denied intending any specific symbolism for the lighthouse, it resonates with almost infinite possibilities, both within the book and in a larger way as an emblem of her work. Like the candles at the dinner party, it can be a symbol of safety and stability amid darkness and watery flux, its beams those rhythmically occurring moments of illumination that sustain Mrs. Ramsay and by extension everyone. Perhaps, however, it can also serve as a metaphor for human beings themselves as Woolf portrays them. The lighthouse signifies what can be objectively perceived of an individual—in Mrs. Ramsay's words, "our apparitions, the things you know us by"; but it also signals invisible, possibly tragic depths, for, as Mrs. Ramsay knew, "beneath it is all dark, it is all spreading, it is unfathomably deep."

THE WAVES

In *The Waves*, widely considered her masterpiece, Woolf most resolutely overcomes the limits of the traditional novel. Entirely unique in form, *The Waves* cannot perhaps be called a novel at all; Woolf herself first projected a work of "prose yet poetry; a novel and a play." The book is a series of grouped soliloquies in varying combinations spoken by six friends, three men and three women, at successive stages in their lives from childhood to late middle age. Each grouping is preceded by a brief, lyrical "interlude" (Woolf's own term), set off in italic type, that describes an empty house by the sea as the sun moves across the sky in a single day.

The texture of these soliloquies is extremely difficult to convey; the term "soliloquy," in fact, is merely a critical convenience. Although each is introduced in the same straightforward way ("Neville said," "Jinny said"), they obviously are unspoken, repre-

senting each character's private vision. Their style is also unvarying—solemn, formal, almost stilted, like that of choral figures. The author has deliberately translated into a rigorously neutral, dignified idiom the conscious and subconscious reality her characters perceive but cannot articulate on their own. This method represents Woolf's most ambitious attempt to capture the unfathomable depths of separate human personalities which defy communication in ordinary life—and in ordinary novels. The abstraction of the device, however, especially in combination with the flow of cosmic time in the interludes, shows that she is also concerned with depicting a universal pattern which transcends mere individuals. Thus, once more Woolf treats her theme of human beings' attempts to overcome their isolation and to become part of a larger stabilizing pattern; this time, however, the theme is embodied in the very form of her work.

It would be inaccurate, though, to say that the characters exist only as symbols. Each has definable qualities and unique imagery; Susan, as an example, farm-bred and almost belligerently maternal, speaks in elemental images of wood smoke, grassy paths, flowers thick with pollen. Further, the characters often evoke one another's imagery; the other figures, for example, even in maturity picture the fearful, solitary Rhoda as a child rocking white petals in a brown basin of water. They are linked by intricately woven threads of common experience, above all by their shared admiration for a shadowy seventh character, Percival. Their gathering with him at a farewell dinner before he embarks on a career in India is one of the few actual events recorded in the soliloquies and also becomes one of those miraculous moments of unity comparable to that achieved by Mrs. Ramsay for her dinner guests; as they rise to leave the restaurant, all the characters are thinking as Louis does: "We pray, holding in our hands this common feeling, 'Do not move, do not let the swing-door cut to pieces this thing that we have made, that globes itself here. . . .' " Such union, however, is cruelly impermanent; two pages later, a telegram announces Percival's death in a riding accident. Bernard, trying to make sense of this absurdity, echoes the imagery of encircling unity that characterized their thoughts at the dinner: "Ideas break a thousand times for once that they globe themselves entire."

It is Bernard—identified, significantly, throughout the book as a storyteller—who is given the long final section of *The Waves* in which "to sum up," becoming perhaps a surrogate for the author herself. (As a young man at school, worrying out "my novel," he discovers how "stories that follow people into their private rooms are difficult.") It is he who recognizes that "I am not one person; I am many people," part of his friends as they are part of him, all of them incomplete in themselves; he is "a man without a self." Yet it is also he who on the novel's final page, using the wave imagery of the universalizing interludes, passionately asserts his individuality: "Against you I will fling myself, unvanquished and unyielding, O Death!" Life, however obdurate and fragmented, must be affirmed.

The Waves is without doubt Woolf's most demanding and original novel, her most daring experiment in eliminating the alien and the external. When she vowed to cast out "all waste, deadness, and superfluity," however, she also ascetically renounced some of her greatest strengths as a novelist: her wit and humor, her delight in the daily beauty, variety, and muddle of material existence. This "abstract mystical eyeless book," as she at one point envisioned it, is a work to admire greatly, but not to love.

The six years following *The Waves* were a difficult period for Woolf both personally and artistically. Deeply depressed by the deaths of Lytton Strachey and Roger Fry, two of her oldest, most respected friends, she was at work on an "essay-novel," as she first conceived of it, which despite her initial enthusiasm became her most painfully frustrating effort—even though it proved, ironically, to be her greatest commercial success.

THE YEARS

In *The Years*, Woolf returned to the conventional novel that she had rejected after *Night and Day*; she planned "to take in everything" and found herself "infinitely delighting in facts for a change." Whereas *The Waves* had represented the extreme of leaving out, *The Years* suggests the opposite one of almost indiscriminate putting in. Its very subject, a history of the Pargiter clan spanning fifty years and three generations, links it with the diffuse family sagas of John Galsworthy and Arnold Bennett, whose books Woolf was expressly deriding when she demanded, "Must novels be like this?"

Nevertheless, *The Years* is more original than it may appear; Woolf made fresh use of her experimental methods in her effort to reanimate traditional form. The novel contains eleven unequal segments, each standing for a year; the longest ones, the opening "1880" section and the closing "Present Day" (the 1930's), anchor the book; the nine intermediate sections cover the years between 1891 and 1918. Echoing *The Waves*, Woolf begins each chapter with a short panoramic passage describing both London and the countryside. Within the chapters, instead of continuous narrative, there are collections of vignettes, somewhat reminiscent of *Jacob's Room*, depicting various Pargiters going about their daily lives. Running parallel with the family's history are larger historical events, including Edward VII's death, the suffrage movement, the Irish troubles, and especially World War I. These events are usually treated indirectly, however; for example, the "1917" section takes place mainly in a cellar to which the characters have retreated, dinner plates in hand, during an air raid. It is here that Eleanor Pargiter asks, setting a theme that suffuses the rest of the novel, "When shall we live adventurously, wholly, not like cripples in a cave?"

The most pervasive effect of the war is felt in the lengthy "Present Day" segment, which culminates in a family reunion, where the youngest generation of Pargiters, Peggy and North, are lonely, cynical, and misanthropic, and their faltering elders are compromised either by complacency or failed hopes. Symbolically, Delia Pargiter gives the party in a rented office, not a home, underscoring the uprooting caused by the war. Yet the balancing "1880" section is almost equally dreary: The Pargiters' solid Victorian house shelters a chronically ailing mother whose children wish she would die, a father whose vulgar mistress greets him in hair curlers and frets over her dog's eczema, and a young daughter traumatized by an exhibitionist in the street outside. One oppressive way of life seems only to have been superseded by another, albeit a more universally menacing one.

The overall imagery of the novel is likewise unlovely: Children recall being scrubbed with slimy washcloths; a revolting dinner of underdone mutton served by Sara Pargiter includes a bowl of rotting, flyblown fruit, grotesquely parodying Mrs. Ramsay's *boeuf en daube* and Rose's centerpiece; London is populated with deformed violet-sellers and old men eating cold sausages on buses. Communication in such a world is even more difficult than in Woolf's earlier books; the dialogue throughout is full of incomplete sentences, and a central vignette in the "Present Day" section turns on one guest's abortive efforts to deliver a speech toasting the human race.

Despite these circumstances, the characters still grope toward some kind of transforming unity; Eleanor, the eldest surviving Pargiter and the most sympathetic character in the novel, comes closest to achieving such vision on the scale that Lily Briscoe and Clarissa Dalloway do. At the reunion, looking back over her life, she wonders if there is "a pattern; a theme recurring like music . . . momentarily perceptible?" Casting about her, trying to connect with her relatives and friends but dozing in the process, she suddenly wakes, proclaiming that "it's been a perpetual discovery, my life. A miracle." Answering by implication her question posed fifteen years earlier during the air raid, she perceives that "we're only just beginning . . . to understand, here and there." That prospect is enough, however; she wants "to enclose the present moment . . . to fill it fuller and fuller, with the past, the present and the future, until it shone, whole, bright, deep with understanding."

Even this glowing dream of eventual unity is muted, though, when one recalls how Eleanor's embittered niece Peggy half pities, half admires her as a person who "still believed with passion . . . in the things man had destroyed," and how her nephew North, a captain in the trenches of World War I, thinks, "We cannot help each other, we are all deformed." It is difficult not to read the final lines of this profoundly somber novel ironically: "The sun had risen, and the sky above the houses wore an air of extraordinary beauty, simplicity and peace."

BETWEEN THE ACTS

Woolf's final work, *Between the Acts*, also deals with individual lives unfolding against the screen of history, but her vision and the methods by which she conveys it are more inventive, complex, and successful than in *The Years*. Covering the space of a single day in June, 1939, as world war threatens on the Continent, *Between the Acts* depicts the events surrounding a village pageant about the history of England, performed on the grounds of Pointz Hall, a country house occupied by the unhappily married Giles and Isa Oliver. The Olivers' story frames the presentation of the pageant, scenes of which are directly reproduced in the novel and alternate with glimpses of the audience's lives during the intervals between the acts. The novel's title is hence richly metaphorical: The acts of the drama itself are bracketed by the scenes of real life, which in turn can be viewed as brief episodes in the long pageant of human history. Equally ambiguous, then, is the meaning of "parts," connoting clearly defined roles within a drama but also the fragmentation and incompleteness of the individuals who play them, that pervasive theme in Woolf's work.

In *The Years*, Woolf had focused on the personal histories of her characters; history in the larger sense made itself felt as it impinged on private lives. This emphasis is reversed in *Between the Acts*. Though the novel has interesting characters, Woolf provides scant information about their backgrounds, nor does she plumb individual memory in her usual manner. Instead, the characters possess a national, cultural, *communal* past—finally that of the whole human race from the Stone Age to the present. That Woolf intends her characters to be seen as part of this universal progression is clear from myriad references in the early pages to historical time. For example, from the air, the "scars" made by the Britons and the Romans can be seen around the village as can the Elizabethan manor house; graves in the churchyard attest that Mrs. Haines's family has lived in the area "for many centuries," whereas the Oliver family has inhabited Pointz Hall for "only something over a hundred and twenty years"; Lucy Swithin, Giles's endearing aunt, enjoys reading about history and imagining Piccadilly when it was a rhododendron forest populated by mastodons, "from whom, presumably, she thought . . . we descend."

The pageant itself, therefore, functions in the novel as more than simply a church fund-raising ritual, the product of well-meaning but hapless amateurs (though it exists amusingly on that level too). It is a heroic attempt by its author-director, the formidable Miss La Trobe, to make people see themselves playing parts in the continuum of British history. Thus, the audience has an integral role that blurs the lines "between the acts"; "Our part," says Giles's father, Bartholomew, "is to be the audience. And a very important part too." Their increasing interest in the pageant as they return from the successive intermissions signals their growing sense of a shared past and hence of an identity that both binds and transcends them as individuals.

The scenes of the pageant proceed from bathos to unnerving profundity. The first player, a small girl in pink, announces, "England am I," then promptly forgets her lines, while the wind blows away half the words of the singers behind her. Queen Elizabeth, splendidly decorated with six-penny brooches and a cape made of silvery scouring pads, turns out to be Mrs. Clark, the village tobacconist; the combined applause and laughter of delighted recognition muffle her opening speech. As the pageant progresses from a wicked though overlong parody of Restoration comedy to a satiric scene at a Victorian picnic, however, the audience becomes more reflective; the past is now close enough to be familiar, triggering their own memories and priming them for the last scene, Miss La Trobe's inspired experiment in expressionism, "The Present Time. Ourselves." The uncomprehending audience fidgets as the stage remains empty, refusing to understand that they are supposed to contemplate their own significance. "Reality too strong," Miss La Trobe mutters angrily from behind the bushes, "Curse 'em!" Then, "sudden and universal," a summer shower fortuitously begins. "Down it rained like all the people in the world weeping." Nature has provided the bridge of meaning Miss La Trobe required. As the rain ends, all the players from all the periods reappear, still in costume and declaiming fragments of their parts while flashing mirrors in the faces of the discomfited audience. An offstage voice asks how civilization is "to be built by orts, scraps and fragments like ourselves," then dies away.

The Reverend Streatfield, disconcerted like the rest of the audience, is assigned the embarrassing role of summing up the play's meaning. Tentatively, self-consciously, he ventures, "To me at least it was indicated that we are members of one another. . . . We act different parts; but are the same. . . . Surely, we should unite?" Then he abruptly shifts into a fund-raising appeal that is drowned out by a formation of war planes passing overhead. As the audience departs, a gramophone plays a valedictory: "Dispersed are we; we who have come together. But let us retain whatever made that harmony." The audience responds, thinking "There is joy, sweet joy, in company."

The qualified optimism of the pageant's close, however, is darkened by the bleak, perhaps apocalyptic postscript of the framing story. After the group disperses, the characters resume their usual roles. Lucy Swithin, identified earlier as a "unifier," experiences a typically Woolfian epiphany as she gazes on a fishpond, glimpsing the silver of the great carp below the surface and "seeing in that vision beauty, power and glory in ourselves." Her staunchly rational brother Bartholomew, a "separatist," goes into the house. Miss La Trobe, convinced that she has failed again, heads for the local pub to drink alone and plan her next play; it will be set at midnight with two figures half hidden by a rock as the curtain rises. "What would the first words be?"

It is the disaffected Giles and Isa, loving and hating each other, who begin the new play. In a remarkable ending, Woolf portrays the couple sitting silently in the dark before going to bed: "Before they slept, they must fight; after they had fought they would embrace." From that embrace, they may create another life, but "first they must fight, as the dog fox fights the vixen, in the heart of darkness, in the fields of night." The "great hooded chairs" in which they sit grow enormous, like Miss La Trobe's rock. The house fades, no longer sheltering them; they are like "dwellers in caves," watching "from some high place." The last lines of the novel are, "Then the curtain rose. They spoke."

This indeterminate conclusion implies that love and hate are elemental and reciprocal, and that such oppositions on a personal level are also the polarities that drive human history. Does Woolf read, then, in the gathering European storm, a cataclysm that will bring the pageant of history full circle, back to the primitive stage of prehistory? Or, like W. B. Yeats in "The Second Coming," does she envision a new cycle even more terrifying than the old? Or, as the faithful Lucy Swithin does, perhaps she hopes that *"all* is harmony could we hear it. And we shall."

Eight years earlier, Virginia Woolf wrote in her diary, "I think the effort to live in two spheres: the novel; and life; is a strain." Miss La Trobe, a crude alter ego for the author, is obsessed by failure but always driven to create anew because "a vision imparted was relief from agony . . . for one moment." In her brilliant experimental attempts to impart her own view of fragmented human beings achieving momentary harmony, discovering unity and stability behind the flux of daily life, Woolf repeatedly endured such anguish, but after *Between the Acts* was done, the strain of beginning again was too great. Perhaps the questions Virginia Woolf posed in this final haunting novel, published posthumously and unrevised, were answered for her in death.

Kristine Ottesen Garrigan

OTHER MAJOR WORKS

SHORT FICTION: *Monday or Tuesday*, 1921; *A Haunted House and Other Short Stories*, 1943; *Mrs. Dalloway's Party*, 1973 (Stella McNichol, editor); *The Complete Shorter Fiction of Virginia Woolf*, 1985.

NONFICTION: *The Common Reader: First Series*, 1925; *A Room of One's Own*, 1929; *The Common Reader: Second Series*, 1932; *Three Guineas*, 1938; *Roger Fry: A Biography*, 1940; *The Death of the Moth and Other Essays*, 1942; *The Moment and Other Essays*, 1947; *The Captain's Death Bed and Other Essays*, 1950; *A Writer's Diary*, 1953; *Granite and Rainbow*, 1958; *Contemporary Writers*, 1965; *Collected Essays, Volumes 1-2*, 1966; *Collected Essays, Volumes 3-4*, 1967; *The London Scene: Five Essays*, 1975; *The Flight of the Mind: The Letters of*

Virginia Woolf, Vol. I, 1888-1912, 1975 (pb. in U.S. as *The Letters of Virginia Woolf, Vol. I: 1888-1912*, 1975; Nigel Nicolson, editor); *The Question of Things Happening: The Letters of Virginia Woolf, Vol. II, 1912-1922*, 1976 (pb. in U.S. as *The Letters of Virginia Woolf, Vol. II: 1912-1922*, 1976; Nicolson, editor); *Moments of Being*, 1976 (Jeanne Schulkind, editor); *Books and Portraits*, 1977; *The Diary of Virginia Woolf*, 1977-1984 (5 volumes; Anne Olivier Bell, editor); *A Change of Perspective: The Letters of Virginia Woolf, Vol. III, 1923-1928*, 1977 (pb. in U.S. as *The Letters of Virginia Woolf, Vol. III: 1923-1928*, 1978; Nicolson, editor); *A Reflection of the Other Person: The Letters of Virginia Woolf, Vol. IV, 1929-1931*, 1978 (published in U.S. as *The Letters of Virginia Woolf, Vol. IV: 1929-1931*, 1979; Nicolson, editor); *The Sickle Side of the Moon: The Letters of Virginia Woolf, Vol. V, 1932-1935*, 1979 (pb. in U.S. as *The Letters of Virginia Woolf, Vol. V: 1932-1935*, 1979; Nicolson, editor); *Leave the Letters Til We're Dead: The Letters of Virginia Woolf, Vol. VI, 1936-1941*, 1980 (Nicolson, editor); *The Essays of Virginia Woolf*, 1987-1994 (4 volumes).

BIBLIOGRAPHY

Abel, Elizabeth. *Virginia Woolf and the Fictions of Psychoanalysis*. Chicago: University of Chicago Press, 1989. With a focus upon symbolism and stylistic devices, this book comprehensively delineates the psychoanalytic connections between Woolf's fiction and Sigmund Freud's and Melanie Klein's theories. Sometimes difficult to follow, however, given Abel's reliance on excellent but extensive endnotes.

Baldwin, Dean R. *Virginia Woolf: A Study of the Short Fiction*. Boston: Twayne, 1989. Baldwin's lucid parallels between Woolf's life experiences and her innovative short-story techniques contribute significantly to an understanding of both the author and her creative process. The book also presents the opportunity for a comparative critical study by furnishing a collection of additional points of view in the final section. A chronology, a bibliography, and an index supplement the work.

Beja, Morris. *Critical Essays on Virginia Woolf*. Boston: G. K. Hall, 1985. In an excellent composite of literary analyses, Beja directs attention to both reviews and critical essays on Woolf's writings in order to demonstrate her universal and ageless appeal. Several critical disciplines are represented. Includes essay endnotes and an index.

Dowling, David. *Mrs. Dalloway: Mapping Streams of Consciousness*. Boston: Twayne, 1991. Divided into sections on literary and historical context and interpretations of the novel. Dowling explores the world of Bloomsbury, war, and modernism; the critical reception of the novel and how it was composed; Woolf's style, theory of fiction, handling of stream of consciousness, structure, characters, and themes. Includes a chronology and concordance to the novel.

Ginsberg, Elaine K., and L. M. Gottlieb, eds. *Virginia Woolf: Centennial Essays*. Troy, N.Y.: Whitston, 1983. Sixteen papers cover, among other topics, Woolf's style, gender consciousness, and feminist inclinations. Style, approach, and interpretation vary widely by presenter, and the text as a whole requires some familiarity with Woolf's writings. Notes on contributors, endnotes following each paper, and an index are provided.

Heilbrun, Carolyn G. *Women's Lives: The View from the Threshold*. Toronto: University of Toronto Press, 1999. This volume discusses George Eliot, Woolf, Willa Cather, and Harriet Beecher Stowe. Focuses on the female view and feminism in literature.

Lee, Hermione. *Virginia Woolf*. New York: Knopf, 1997. The most complete biography of Woolf so far, drawing on the latest scholarship and on primary sources. Includes family tree, notes, and bibliography.

Warner, Eric, ed. *Virginia Woolf: A Centenary Perspective*. New York: St. Martin's Press, 1984. With a nonpartisan approach, this text offers seven papers and two panel discussions from Fitzwilliam College's Virginia Woolf Centenary Conference in Cambridge, England. Notes at the end of each presentation, notes on the contributors, and an index are provided.

HERMAN WOUK

Born: New York, New York; May 27, 1915

PRINCIPAL LONG FICTION
Aurora Dawn, 1947
The City Boy, 1948
The Caine Mutiny, 1951
Marjorie Morningstar, 1955
Slattery's Hurricane, 1956
Youngblood Hawke, 1962
Don't Stop the Carnival, 1965
The Lomokome Papers, 1968
The Winds of War, 1971
War and Remembrance, 1978
Inside, Outside, 1985
The Hope, 1993
The Glory, 1994

OTHER LITERARY FORMS
Herman Wouk wrote several plays; the first, *The Traitor*, was produced on Broadway in 1949 and was published by Samuel French the same year. His most successful theatrical work, *The Caine Mutiny Court-Martial* (based upon the novel published in 1951), appeared on Broadway in 1954 and was published by Doubleday the same year. *Nature's Way* was produced on Broadway in 1957 and was published by Doubleday the following year. Eric Bentley, speaking of *The Caine Mutiny Court-Martial*, said that Wouk showed a gift for crisp dialogue that no other regular writer for the American theater could rival. The musical *Don't Stop the Carnival*, a collaboration with pop musician Jimmy Buffett, was produced in 1998. Wouk collaborated with Richard Murphy in writing the screenplay for *Slattery's Hurricane* (1949). Wouk also wrote teleplays, for *The Winds of War* (1983) and *War and Remembrance* (1988). *This Is My God*, which Wouk first published in 1959 and followed with a revised edition in 1973, is a description and explanation of Orthodox Judaism, especially as it is practiced in America. The volume was a Reader's Digest Condensed Book Club selection and an alternate selection for the Book-of-the-Month Club in 1959.

ACHIEVEMENTS

It is a peculiarity of American criticism to deni-
grate popular success in literature. Almost from the
outset of his career, Wouk was a very popular writer;
putting aside prejudicial presuppositions, this can be
acknowledged as a genuine achievement, for Wouk
did not attain his popular status by catering to the
baser tastes of his readers. Beginning with *The Caine
Mutiny*, his books appeared regularly on best-seller
lists. Several of his titles were selections of major
book clubs. Wouk was awarded the Pulitzer Prize for
Fiction in 1952 for *The Caine Mutiny*. That same
year, Columbia University presented him the Medal
of Excellence, an honor extended to distinguished
alumni. Several universities awarded him honorary
doctoral degrees.

Wouk might be described as a traditional novelist,
in that his writing does not reflect the experimental
qualities that are to be found in so much twentieth
century American fiction. Like John Updike, he gives
primacy of place to the narrative element in fiction;
he brings to the novel his own peculiar brand of
rough-hewn vigor. At a time when conventional wisdom judged it bad form for a novelist to take a clear
stand on moral issues—as if ambiguity itself were a
virtue—Wouk consistently declared his moral position in his writings. This was not always to the benefit of his fiction, but by and large, his novels are
stronger for his conviction that literary art does not
subsist in a vacuum but is part of a larger moral universe.

BIOGRAPHY

Herman Wouk was born in New York City on
May 27, 1915, the son of Abraham Isaac and Esther
(Levine) Wouk. Wouk's father, an industrialist in the

(National Archives)

power laundry field, started out as an immigrant laundry worker earning three dollars a week. Wouk was educated at Townsend Harris Hall and at Columbia University, where he was graduated with honors in 1934. While at Columbia, he studied philosophy and comparative literature and was editor of the *Columbia Jester*. From 1934 to 1935 he worked as a gag writer for radio comedians, and from 1936 to 1941, he was a scriptwriter for Fred Allen. In 1941, Wouk moved to Washington, D.C., following his appointment to the United States Treasury Department as a dollar-a-year man; his job was to write and produce radio shows to sell war bonds. He left this work to join the Navy. After completing Officer Candidate School, he was commissioned an ensign and assigned to mine sweeper duty in the Pacific fleet. He served in the Navy from 1942 to 1945, first aboard the U.S.S. *Zane* and then aboard the destroyer-mine-sweeper U.S.S. *Southard*; eventually he was to be promoted to the position of Executive Officer of that ship. He was decorated with four campaign stars during the war, and received a Unit Citation as well. When Wouk was processed out of the Navy in 1945, he held the rank of lieutenant. Wouk married Betty Sarah Brown in December, 1945. They had three sons, Abraham Isaac (who died before reaching his fifth birthday), Nathaniel, and Joseph.

Wouk began his career as a serious writer while he was in the Navy; before his release from the service, he had completed a good portion of his first novel. That novel, *Aurora Dawn*, was published by Simon and Schuster in 1947. The following year, his second novel, *The City Boy*, was published. Neither of these works gained a great deal of attention for Wouk, but with the publication of *The Caine Mutiny* in 1951 (awarded the Pulitzer Prize the following year), he was quickly established as a writer of consequence. His play, *The Caine Mutiny Court-Martial*, began its successful run on Broadway in 1954. *Marjorie Morningstar* appeared in 1955 and his nonfiction work on Jewish culture and religion, *This Is My God*, in 1959. The 1960's saw the publication of *Youngblood Hawke* and *Don't Stop the Carnival*. Wouk's sprawling two-volume fictional account of World War II, which he began writing in 1962, was

published in the 1970's; the first volume, *The Winds of War*, appeared in 1971, and the second, *War and Remembrance*, in 1978. Wouk wrote the teleplay for the eighteen-hour television film based on *The Winds of War*, which was broadcast during the week of February 6-13, 1983. He was coauthor of the teleplay for the television adaptation of *War and Remembrance*, which appeared in 1988.

Unlike many contemporary popular novelists, Wouk shunned the public spotlight throughout his career. Though the Wouks spent more than a decade after they were married in New York, they moved to the Virgin Islands in 1958, partly so that Wouk could find a place to write free of interruptions. In 1964, the family moved to Georgetown, a Washington, D.C., suburb, so that he could be closer to archival materials he needed to consult in order to write *The Winds of War* and *War and Remembrance*. During the next three decades, Wouk divided his time between his home in the nation's capital and one in Palm Springs, California, occasionally appearing at public events to accept awards or participate in fund-raising or religious events. In 1995, Wouk entered into an agreement with popular singer Jimmy Buffett to write the book for a musical based on *Don't Stop the Carnival*. Featuring a number of Caribbean songs composed by Buffett, the musical opened in Florida in 1997 and moved to Broadway in 1998.

Wouk's great popular success enabled him to devote his full time to his craft, but on occasion he took academic or semiacademic positions. From 1953 to 1957, he was a visiting professor of English at Yeshiva University, and during 1973-1974, he was scholar-in-residence at the Aspen Institute for Humanistic Studies. A member of the Authors Guild and the Dramatists Guild, he served on the board of directors for institutions and organizations such as the College of the Virgin Islands, the Washington National Symphony, and Kennedy Center Productions.

ANALYSIS

Herman Wouk is a novelist in the tradition of the great English novelists of the nineteenth century; he is also a spiritual descendant of such American writers as James Fenimore Cooper, William Dean Howells, Theodore Dreiser, and James T. Farrell. What he has in common with these writers is narrative prowess, a commitment to realism, and a lively moral consciousness. Furthermore, like these writers, Wouk addresses himself to the population at large. Since World War II, there has been detectable in American fiction a distinction between writers who seem to be inclined to write primarily for other writers or for academic critics, and those inclined to write for a general audience. That Wouk is numbered among the latter would appear to be traceable to a definite decision on his part. His first novel, *Aurora Dawn*, has the flavor of the experimental fiction that began to proliferate in the postwar period. If one were to have speculated in 1946 upon the course that Wouk's literary career was going to take, it would have been a safe guess to say that he would probably continue down the road of experimentation, that he would become more and more concerned with language as an end in itself, and that eventually, he would be writing books destined to be read only in upper-division English courses in universities. This was not what happened, however; in his second novel, *The City Boy*, Wouk followed a conventional narrative pattern and told his story in language which was not constantly calling attention to itself.

In *Aurora Dawn* and *The City Boy*, Wouk was still stretching his muscles and attempting to find his proper level as a writer. He came into his own with *The Caine Mutiny*. In that novel, and in every novel that followed for the next four decades, there is the presence of a central theme, treated in various ways and from varying perspectives. The theme is the conflict between traditional values and a modern consciousness which is either indifferent to those values or flatly antipathetic toward them. The conflict is not treated in abstract terms, but in terms of individuals who are caught up in it, and how the individual fares is in great part determined by the side with which he chooses to ally himself.

AURORA DAWN

Wouk's first novel, *Aurora Dawn*, which he began while serving as an officer in the Navy, is an effort at satire. The butt of the satire is the advertising industry and, more generally, the foolishness of anyone in

business whose ethical consciousness is dimmed by avarice. The moral of the story is explicit: Greed is the root of all evil. Andrew Reale, the novel's young protagonist, is bright, energetic, and imaginative, but until he undergoes a conversion at novel's end, his primary concern is getting ahead. He wants to be successful above all else, and to him, success means money. In his scramble to get to the top as quickly as possible, his myopia becomes acute and his values are severely twisted. He is willing to make compromises where compromises should not be made. A connection is intimated between Reale's moral weakness and his failure to continue to adhere to the religious principles according to which he was reared, a recurring theme in Wouk's fiction.

Reale's obsessive pursuit of success leads him to jilt his fiancée, the beautiful and innocent Laura Beaton, so that he can take up with the beautiful but frivolous Carol Marquis, daughter of the despicable but very rich Talmadge Marquis. It leads him to be crassly manipulative in his dealings with the Reverend Calvin Stanfield, who is simple, straightforward, and a good man. Finally, it leads him, in a move of pure expediency, to quit an employer who has been generous with him so that he can join forces with Talmadge Marquis. All Reale's machinations, however, are to no avail. The hastily courted Carol Marquis runs off with an eccentric painter, and Laura Beaton, brokenhearted at Reale's rejection of her, marries an older man. In the end, Reale gets better than he deserves. His thwarted attempt to blackmail Father Stanfield proves to be the occasion of a conversion experience for him. He suddenly sees the wickedness of his ways and decides to alter his course. Laura Beaton is miraculously released from her unconsummated marriage, so that Reale is able to get the woman of his dreams after all. Fleeing the wicked city, the bride and groom go off to live together in New Mexico.

The novel is not realistic and cannot be judged according to the criterion of verisimilitude. It is a light, playful work in which humor plays an important part. Despite several brilliant passages, however, the novel does not come across as successful satire, and that would seem to be attributable to the fact that Wouk is vacillating and hesitant in what he wants to say. What he takes with one hand, he gives back with the other. The novel is clever, in both good and bad senses. While its language is often lively, it can as well be pretentious and self-conscious at times. The anachronistic devices of addressing the reader directly, inserting explicit authorial commentary on the action, and interspersing the narrative with short philosophical asides do not always work to maximize the effect. The humor of the novel is capable of being right on the mark, but for the most part it is a bit forced; Wouk, the radio gagman, is too much in evidence. The flaws to be found in *Aurora Dawn* are flaws which are not uncommon in a first novel. Despite its weaknesses, however, already in evidence in this work are the two traits that have subsequently become the chief strengths of Wouk's fiction: a vigorous talent for narrative and a lively sensitivity to moral issues.

THE CITY BOY

Perhaps the most striking thing about Wouk's second novel, *The City Boy*, is that, stylistically, it represents a marked departure from the standards he had established in his first novel. The language of the work does not call attention to itself; it is clear, straightforward, and unpretentious. The novel is humorous in tone, and its plot structure is loose. It revolves around the adventures—most of which take place in an upstate summer camp—of a New York City boy, Herbie Bookbinder. John P. Marquand's comparison of this novel with Mark Twain's *The Adventures of Tom Sawyer* (1876) is well-founded. In many respects, Herbie is an urban version of the scamp from the Midwestern frontier. He is a bright and enterprising lad, and if he is mischievous at times, it is seldom with malice. Much of what he does is calculated to impress Lucille Glass, the object of his single-minded puppy love. Herbie is unlike Tom Sawyer in that he is an outsider as far as other boys are concerned, largely because of his poor athletic skills and his penchant for things intellectual. A goodly number of Herbie's efforts in the novel are given over to his attempts to gain the status of a regular guy. He succeeds, finally, and as a result is welcomed into the full fellowship of his peers. *The City Boy* is a light novel—in some respects a boy's

book—but in it, Wouk's moral consciousness is manifested by his underscoring the difference between good and evil in the actions of the characters.

THE CAINE MUTINY

The Caine Mutiny is Wouk's best novel, the work on which his reputation rests. The novel takes place against the backdrop of war, but it cannot be regarded as a "war story" in any simplistic sense. It is a story about the subtle and complicated relationships that exist among men who are part of the enclosed world that constitutes the military establishment. One of its central themes concerns the matter of authority—how it is exercised within a military context, and how it is abused. The novel explores the manner in which various personality types act and react within a hierarchical, authoritarian structure. In addition, it examines the ways in which the lives of those caught up in the trauma of war are altered, sometimes profoundly. Other themes which the novel treats are loyalty and disloyalty, patriotism, doers versus sayers, personal integrity, and the process by which young men are tested in stressful situations.

The Caine Mutiny can easily be misread. One might conclude that its chief concern is the everlasting battle between despotism and democracy, that Captain Queeg therefore is clearly the villain of the piece, and that its heroes are Lieutenant Maryk, Willie Keith, Tom Keefer, and the others who were involved in the mutiny. It is not that simple. If it were, *The Caine Mutiny* would be little more than a melodrama. Captain Queeg is not a hero, but neither is he a diabolical type. He is a sorry human being; he has serious personal problems (his eccentricity is not amusing—he is, in fact, a sick man); and, perhaps most serious, given his status as a commanding officer, he is incompetent professionally. For all that, he is consistent in trying to do his job to the best of his ability. Queeg's problem is that he is a man who is in over his head; he can at times scarcely cope with situations which are his duty to control. The circumstances surrounding the event which lead to the mutiny are sufficiently ambiguous as to render doubtful the claim of the mutineers that, had they not relieved Queeg of command when they did, the ship would have been lost.

Wouk's assessment of the situation seems to be communicated most directly through the character of Lieutenant Greenwald, the young aviator-lawyer who defends Maryk at the court-martial. Greenwald is not sympathetic with the mutineers, but he decides to defend Maryk because he respects the Executive Officer's personal integrity and because he is convinced that Maryk, in assuming command of the *Caine* during the typhoon, was acting in good faith. Greenwald succeeds in having Maryk acquitted of the charge of mutiny, mainly by drawing out of Queeg in the courtroom telltale signs of his emotional instability, but he takes no joy in his victory. After the trial, he puts the damper on the victory celebration being staged by the *Caine*'s officers when he gives them a stinging tonguelashing. His ire is directed particularly at Tom Keefer, whom he perceives correctly as being the chief instigator of the mutiny, but one who refused, when the matter came to a head, to put himself on the line. Greenwald's position seems to be that, while the *Caine*'s officers are legally innocent, they are morally guilty. However sophisticated a rationale they might provide for their actions, what was at the bottom of those actions, in his view, was disloyalty, and disloyalty, for a military officer, is an unforgivable sin. One might say that the trial does not prove either clear-cut guilt or innocence. If anything, it demonstrates the complexity and ambiguity of all human situations. Greenwald's position is that, given the ambiguity, it is always better not to second-guess legitimately constituted authority. It is the chief responsibility of the naval officer to do his duty through thick and thin.

If there is a clear villain in *The Caine Mutiny*, Tom Keefer would appear to be the most likely candidate for the role. Keefer is, in many respects, a preeminently modern man. He is committed to what he presumably regards as the absolute truths of Freudian psychology, which he employs in a reductionist way, as weapons against those who do not share his worldview. He is in the Navy, but not of it, and, in fact, he rather enjoys and exploits his position as an iconoclastic outsider. He maintains an attitude of supercilious superiority toward people such as Queeg, and toward everything that the Navy represents. His view is narrow, restricted by the dictates of his overriding egotism. Keefer is a carping critic of the Navy, but he does not hesitate to take selfish advantage of what the Navy can offer him at every turn. His hypocrisy allows him to talk a big game, but when the pressure is on and when circumstances call for words to be translated into action, he invariably backs off. Perhaps the most damning thing that could be said of Keefer is that he is a coward, as he demonstrates when he is captain of the *Caine* and precipitously abandons ship. By the novel's end, however, Keefer seem to have arrived at a degree of self-awareness which hitherto had eluded him; he confesses to Willie Keith, who succeeds him as commanding officer, that Keith is a better man than he. He is right.

Willie Keith is the central character of the novel; his moral education is the real subject of *The Caine Mutiny*. Willie is an aristocratic rich kid from New York who comes to learn, among other things, the value of democracy. His relationship with Maria Minotti, alias May Wynn, can be interpreted in this way. The bulk of Keith's education, however, takes place in the Navy. When he first comes aboard the *Caine*, he is very much under the influence of Tom Keefer, and he accepts Keefer's cynical interpretation of things as the correct one. Eventually, Keith realizes that the Navy, though imperfect, is not a bad organization. What is more, given the realities of the modern world, it is a necessary organization. Unlike Keefer, Keith is prepared to acknowledge that the Navy in World War II is contributing toward the preservation of the way of life into which both men have been born and to which they are devoted, and that, excepting a total transformation of human nature, navies will probably always be needed to ensure the protection of people's freedom. Keith is not changed into a mindless patriot and militarist, but his criticism of the Navy and its personnel becomes more discriminate, more intelligent, more responsible. He learns to judge matters according to criteria which are not self-centered, and develops an appreciation for the larger scheme of things. He takes pride in his work, and as he rises in rank, his conscientiousness increases; he tries to be the best officer he can.

The world of the Navy, in *The Caine Mutiny*, is in certain respects a microcosm of the world at large. It is beset by all sorts of problems, but there is no perfect alternative somewhere to which one might flee. A person's maturity is measured by his or her ability to establish standards of excellence and to work assiduously to achieve them in spite of various limitations, sometimes severe—limitations in him- or herself, in others, and in the situation.

MARJORIE MORNINGSTAR

On the surface, Wouk's fourth novel, *Marjorie Morningstar*, would seem to lead nowhere. It is the story of a young Jewish woman, the daughter of immigrants established comfortably in the middle class of New York, who has been sufficiently Americanized as to have for her chief ambition the desire to become a famous actress, a star. Marjorie Morningstar (née Morgenstern) is a beautiful woman whose theatrical talent, while not scintillating, is probably sufficient to underwrite the realization of her dream, given a lucky break here and there. She is willing to make the sacrifices, within certain bounds, and to invest the hard work that the ascent to stardom inevitably entails. If Marjorie is determined about anything, it is that she is not going to allow herself to lapse into the staid, conventional life that is the destiny of the vast majority of nice, middle-class Jewish girls. She is going to be different; she is going to break out of the mold. After several fruitless efforts to break into the theater and to make it big, after a sequence of adventures with an assortment of men, chiefly with Noel Airman, she ends up doing what she vowed she would never do. She marries a Jew, a successful lawyer by the name of Milton Schwartz, and she retires to a plush suburb to live the most conventional of conventional lives. The novel, then, would seem to end on an almost laughably anticlimactic note, but only if one fails to perceive the kind of statement that it is attempting to make.

If *The Caine Mutiny* delineates the education of Willie Keith, the education of Marjorie Morningstar is the primary concern of the novel that bears her name. If Marjorie comes full circle, as it were, and ends by embracing the conventional, it is because she discovers that the conventional is worthy of being embraced, the conventional not only as representing middle-class morality, but also, and much more important, as embodying traditional cultural and religious values. The glamorous life to which Marjorie aspired, whether or not she was always fully conscious of the fact, was a life that repudiated traditional values. As a teenager and young woman, she fought her own tradition, particularly as manifested in the Jewish religion; she looked upon it as crude and superstitious, a carry-over from humankind's primitive past. This tradition, however, was more deeply embedded in her, was more integral a part of her identity than she was willing to admit, and throughout her various experiences it guided her actions more than she knew.

Marjorie's failure to realize her dream of becoming a star actually represents the triumph of her better, truer self. Her concern shifts from thin, superficial values to those with substance and depth. The drama of her quest for self-realization is played out principally around her long and erratic affair with Noel Airman. When she first meets Airman, who is some ten years her senior, she is scarcely more than a girl, and she is completely enamored of him. He is handsome, intelligent, urbane, and witty, a talented composer of popular songs who shows promise of becoming a success in the theater. Noel represents much of what she wants to become, and all of what she has decided is most valuable in life, which is emphasized by the fact that she throws decorum to the winds and pursues him actively. When she finally catches him, however, she realizes that she does not really want him. The man who was once her ideal, her hero, the man whom she wanted to marry more than anyone else, is at last perceived, albeit faintly, as a god with clay feet.

Who is this Noel Airman? He is Saul Ehrmann, a man who has actively repudiated his Jewish identity and its associated traditions, but who has failed to come up with a viable substitute for either. He is a rootless vagabond, a shameless Casanova, a man who eschews commitment as a matter of principle, and who tries hard to make a profession of cynicism. It would be wrong, however, to think of him entirely in negative terms. He is not a character lacking in complexity, and he is not devoid of critical self-knowledge, which at times can be acute and penetrating. Still, this self-awareness serves only to accentuate the pathetic quality of the man, for in the final analysis, he is impotent to act upon his better impulses. He does not have the moral stamina to follow through, and this is so, Wouk implies, precisely because he has cut himself off from his tradition.

The fact that Marjorie arrives at a new state of consciousness which allows her to see Airman for what he is, and accordingly to reject him, is attributable in part to her brief but fateful acquaintance with Michael Eden. Eden, like Airman, is a Jew, but, unlike Airman, he is not in flight from the fact. He is a strong, taciturn man whose personal sufferings have led him to dedicate himself to a melancholy but determined altruism. He is involved in the very risky business of rescuing Jews from Nazi Germany. Here is a man who is every bit as bright and talented as Airman but who has what Airman lacks—integrity and a sense of purpose in life. Although it is not Marjorie's destiny to marry Eden, meeting him has the effect of altering her perception of Airman. Milton Schwartz, the man she marries, has in common with Eden a fundamental decency.

YOUNGBLOOD HAWKE

Wouk's sixth novel, *Youngblood Hawke*, based to some extent on the life of Thomas Wolfe, could be the story of many a young American writer of the twentieth century, and for that reason, the novel, besides its intrinsic worth as a work of fiction, has considerable value as a historical document. The story of Arthur Youngblood Hawke is a success story, but it is a story of failure as well. Indeed, Hawke's case is in many respects a tragic one. Hawke is a lanky, down-home Kentuckian who, after being released from the Navy at the end of World War II, moves to New York to conquer the city and the country, by his pen. He comes to his task with a spotty education, with an explosive imagination, and with a seemingly boundless store of energy. Writing is his life, and his engagement in it is passionate. There is much about Hawke which smacks of the all-American boy. He is crude and unpolished, but straightforward and gentle in his dealings with people—except with those who de-

serve otherwise. He is an honest man, in his way, and an assiduous worker. He wants to be a success as a writer. He wants to become a millionaire, not so that he can give up writing but so that, freed from financial worries, he can devote himself to it without distractions. Hawke is in the mold of the rustic innocent who has long played a part in American literature.

His early success works against him in the long run. His first novel, though receiving rough treatment at the hands of the critics, gains a large popular audience; his second novel wins the Pulitzer Prize and increasing respect from the critics. He is associated with a solid, respectable publishing house whose head values his work, has faith in his future, and is willing to be very generous in making contractual arrangements with him. Hawke's obsessional longing for financial independence, however, prompts him to break ties with his publisher and begin publishing his own books; he also makes some risky investments. His luck turns, and in a matter of months he finds himself on the threshold of bankruptcy. He determines that he is going to write his way out of his debts; leaving behind the plush life that he enjoyed only too briefly in New York, he returns to Kentucky, and there, living in a cabin in the woods, he works furiously to complete what proves to be his final novel. In fact, he overworks, devoting himself not only to the novel but also, earlier, to a theatrical production which he hopes will strike it rich. The strain brought about by his frenetic activities exacerbates an old head injury, and, after a wild chase to South America made in a state of delirium, he ends up back in New York. He is hospitalized there and dies at the age of thirty-three.

As Youngblood Hawke lies dying, his vaguely addressed prayer is that he might be given more time so that he can work. Everything that he has done he considers as only preparatory exercises to his great multivolume *Comedy*. That his magnum opus was never written is not simply attributable to the fact that Hawke showed poor business sense or that he was careless of his health. There is evidence in the novel to warrant the conclusion that Hawke's failure to fulfill his chief artistic ambition amounts to an exacting payment he has had to make for his sins. There have been two principal women in his life, but, by his own admission, there should have been only one. In the beginning of the novel, before he bursts upon the American literary scene, he meets a young editor, Jeanne Green, who subsequently becomes for him what Maxwell Perkins was for Thomas Wolfe. Jeanne, besides being a very talented editor, is, like Hawke, essentially a small-town person. She is simple, unpretentious, genuine. Hawke falls in love with Jeanne almost immediately—his better self tells him that this is the woman in his life, the woman he should marry—but he becomes involved in a torrid affair with a wealthy, sophisticated, fundamentally selfish New Yorker, Frieda Winters. Frieda is older than he; she is married, has three children, and is no stranger to adulterous affairs. Hawke is honest enough with himself to admit that he is involved in adultery; the reader is told that he hates both the word and the fact. He does not have the moral courage, however, to extricate himself from the affair—not until, as it turns out, it is too late. His relationship with Frieda proves to be an enervating experience; if it does not exactly destroy him, it contributes substantially toward his destruction.

What allowed Hawke to become involved in an affair which he knew to be wrong? One explanation is that he failed to be true to the basic religious principles which he had been taught as a boy but which in his impetuous youth he attempted to reject. Unlike Marjorie Morningstar, whose roots in a religious tradition were sufficiently deep and tenacious to carry her through the hard times, Hawke succumbs to the facile moral standards of a secularized society.

DON'T STOP THE CARNIVAL

Wouk's next novel, *Don't Stop the Carnival*, is the weakest of his entire corpus. It is a comic novel and it would seem to have some kind of satiric intent, but the humor, instead of carrying the moral import of the tale, more often than not obstructs it. The work's humor is hampered by obtrusive, heavy-handed moralizing, and its seriousness is trivialized by a humor which too often degenerates into tedious slapstick. Most damaging for the novel is the fact that Wouk's narrative talent, which is his forte, serves him poorly here. The plot is too often based upon contrivance,

and in some instances blatant authorial manipulation is very much in evidence. Add to this fact that characterization is unconvincing, and the sum total is a generally undistinguished piece of fiction that holds the reader's attention only by an adamant act of will. It is not that the novel is completely lacking in substance, but the detectably substantive elements are not allowed to emerge fully. There is, for example, a statement being made about the haplessness of "liberal" types who are awash in a world that in many respects is the result of their own brand of thinking, but the message is befuddled by static of various kinds and one must strain to detect it.

THE WINDS OF WAR and WAR AND REMEMBRANCE

Wouk's impressive companion novels, *The Winds of War* and *War and Remembrance*, published in 1971 and 1978, respectively, are in effect a single, sustained work of fiction, and therefore can be discussed together. Wouk spent sixteen years in completing the work, and it seems likely that he regards it as his magnum opus. *The Winds of War* is focused primarily on the European theater, beginning with the German invasion of Czechoslovakia and Poland, putting special emphasis upon the latter. The Battle of Britain is also treated at close range. The book ends with the bombing of Pearl Harbor, the point at which *War and Remembrance* takes up the story. This book, while continuing to trace the course of events in Europe, especially those events having to do with the systematic extermination of the Jews by the Nazis, shifts attention to the Pacific theater and provides poignant descriptions of the major naval battles fought there. The book ends with the dropping of the atomic bombs and the Japanese acceptance of unconditional surrender. In these two massive volumes which constitute a single work, an ambitious fictional history of World War II, Wouk once again shows himself to be a master of narrative. This is not a mere chronicle of events; rather, major events of the war are given dramatic immediacy by the tactic of having one of the many key characters in the narrative involved in those events. One is even provided access to the Axis point of view through excerpts from the analytic histories of the German General Armin von Roon, interspersed throughout the work.

The key character in the work is Victor "Pug" Henry, a naval officer who has given thirty years of his life to military service. He is a staid, conservative man, a patriot but not a jingoist, dedicated to professional excellence and quietly guided by deeply embedded religious principles. Following his various adventures in Europe and in the Pacific, one is not only brought into direct contact with important historical personages but treated to his thoughtful reactions to them as well. Wouk is the type of artist who likes to paint on a large canvas, but the canvas he is covering in this work is of mammoth proportions. All the more remarkable, then, is the control he exercises here; nothing gets away from him. There is about this wide-ranging tour de force a satisfying unity and completeness. It is thickly peopled with a vast array of characters, and their attitudes toward the war run the full gamut from self-sacrificing heroism to cold-blooded murderousness.

One of the most interesting characters in the work is Aaron Jastrow, a Jewish-American, world-renowned scholar and former Yale professor who at the outbreak of the war is living in active retirement in Italy. In tracing the story of Aaron Jastrow, and that of his Polish cousin Berel, Wouk recounts in moving fashion the sickening circumstances of the infamous "final solution." Aaron himself was born in Poland and reared in a strict Orthodox tradition. As he reached young manhood, he put aside his religion and settled into a benevolent agnosticism. Accompanied by his niece Natalie, he is hounded by the Nazis throughout Europe for years, until he finally ends up in the land of his birth, in a death camp. His life is choked out in the gas chambers. He speaks to the reader directly through *A Jew's Journey*. What one learns from this document is that the most significant journey in the waning months of Jastrow's life is a spiritual one. His personal confrontation with the horrors of Nazism has the effect of returning him to the religion of his birth. When he comes to die, he is possessed of an inner peace his murderers could never know, and he represents a basic human dignity which they have chosen to abandon for themselves and to attempt to destroy in others.

The Winds of War and *War and Remembrance* are about a specific war, but they are about war in general as well. Wouk does not romanticize World War II, but he suggests that it was absolutely essential that the Allied forces emerge as victorious. It was an unspeakably grim yet nevertheless necessary struggle. The bombs that ended the war, however, changed the nature of war forever. If humankind were capable before Hiroshima and Nagasaki of arguing that all-out war, however cruel and crude, was a workable solution to human problems, that argument proved no longer tenable. World War II was perhaps the most gruesome war that human beings have ever inflicted upon themselves. Wouk's thesis is that wars in the future will not be avoided simply by proclaiming them to be unthinkable. One must think about them; one must think especially about the most gruesome of wars. Through memory, perhaps a pathway to peace can be found.

INSIDE, OUTSIDE

Herman Wouk's *Inside, Outside* appeared in 1985. *The Caine Mutiny* is by consensus Wouk's single best work of fiction, but *Inside, Outside* could arguably be offered as a legitimate contender for that honor. Here one finds all Wouk's considerable skill in operation: his commanding ability to create characters that live and breathe and convince, telling their interesting and interlocking stories within the context of a fictional world which, while complex, never degenerates into incoherence. Wouk's characters move and make their marks in a world that can be as confused and disorienting as that created by any other modern fictionist, but the core, the center, of Wouk's world, although subjected to great strain, always manages to hold; that is, although Wouk's characters live in an extremely difficult and demanding world, that world preserves its essential meaningfulness. Wouk does not burden himself with the absurd task of attempting to populate an absurd universe.

It is difficult to specify what makes for the peculiar success of this novel, but certainly at work is Wouk's uncanny ability—which is singularly devoid of self-advertising and therefore easy to overlook—to create what one might call fictional immediacy. Wouk can effect the magic of bringing into being a fictional world which more than half persuades the reader that it is not fictional at all. In other words, he is a maker of art.

Inside, Outside revolves around the life and times of one Israel David Goodkind. It is principally his story, and he tells it with verve. The novel is interestingly structured. The time frame of the narration is 1973. In that year, Goodkind, a successful New York lawyer, finds himself in the rather unusual position—given the fact that he has been a lifelong Democrat—of serving in Washington as a special assistant to President Richard M. Nixon. The job, though flattering in its way, is anything but exacting, and Goodkind begins to expend his considerable free time in writing; however, this activity is not simply an idle exercise with which to fill the gaps in his undemanding day. He takes his writing quite seriously, and he intends to produce something of real literary worth. He endeavors to fulfill an ambition he has harbored since his youth, but which thus far he has not managed to accomplish. He writes about his own life, which takes him back to the turn of the century and the stories of his parents, two Jewish emigrants from Russia. They both arrive in New York; there they meet and marry, and there their children, Israel and Lee, are born. The reader follows the entire course of Goodkind's life as he recounts its developments, its delays, its assorted dramatic and melodramatic reversals, with meticulous and loving detail. The reader is brought into the very center of Goodkind's world and discovers it to be a world which is at once intensely provincial and intensely cosmopolitan—the kind of combination which is possible perhaps only in New York City. It is a wide world, thickly populated with a rich variety of relatives and friends. The reader is given the opportunity to meet them all, and, with differing degrees of completeness, to come to know their stories, too.

Such is the main strand of the novel's narrative. Its secondary strand is no less compelling. Goodkind is interrupted periodically in his recounting of his past by the pressing events that take place around him in 1973 as he continues his writing project. Two significant historical events mark that time period. One is the Israeli-Egyptian War; the other is the res-ignation of President Nixon in the wake of the Watergate scandal. The first event takes place within the time frame of the novel, and Goodkind reports on it as he writes. The second event draws closer and closer, but the novel ends without the president's resignation having yet taken place. The Israeli-Egyptian War plays an important symbolic role in the narrative because one of the central themes of the novel is the situation of the Jew in the modern world.

The "inside" of the novel's title refers to the somewhat self-enclosed, clearly identifiable, but far from homogeneous world of Jewish religion and culture, whereas the "outside" refers to the world at large. Herman Wouk is something of an oddity among contemporary American novelists because of his open and unapologetic commitment to his religious convictions. This fact largely explains the decided and persistent moral tone of his fiction. One can find expressions, more or less strong, more or less developed, of his commitment to Judaism throughout his fiction, but in no other novel, it seems, does his religious faith play so central and integral a part than in *Inside, Outside*.

What Wouk gives the reader in this novel, along with much else, is a dynamic and dramatic picture of the manifold consciousness that constitutes late twentieth century Judaism. The picture he presents is intricate, complicated, and in some respects even contradictory. Wouk deals with the rich reality that is Judaism in a manner which is—variously—intensely objective and intensely subjective. He seems to leave nothing out of the picture; negative elements are treated with as much thoroughness as are positive elements. Nevertheless, Wouk does not treat the heart of his subject matter, the essential identity of Judaism, with anything but respect and reverence.

If by novel's end one cannot identify its protagonist as a typical modern Jew, that is only because one has come to understand that there is no such thing. I. David Goodkind is a representative modern Jew, but so are many who are quite different from him, and Goodkind himself is far from simple. On the one hand, Goodkind reflects the "inside" component of his world, but a distinct "outside" dimension to his personality exists as well. Both together, "inside" and "outside," make up who he is. Goodkind is a religious Jew who faithfully practices his religion. He is also a political Jew who sympathizes with the Zionist tradition and takes great patriotic pride in the state of Israel. At the same time, Goodkind is a thorough American. In a larger sense, he is an eminently modern man, one who, even in spite of himself at times, reflects the consciousness of the contemporary Western intellectual, with all the limitations peculiar to it. His judgments on the major issues that impinge upon his life have to them a ring of confident cosmopolitanism, which disguises their lack of substantial metaphysical foundations. For example, although he is in many respects exemplary for his perspicacity and sensitivity, he is obtuse in response to some of the clear signs of decadence in modern culture.

Mention might be made of the unorthodox manner in which the novel deals with the character of President Nixon. Wouk goes beyond the crude journalistic stereotypes to discover in Nixon not merely a caricature but a real human being. Finally, *Inside, Outside* is simultaneously a serious and a humorous work, and both of these faces complement each other, helping to bring each into greater relief. In some of his other novels, Wouk has demonstrated his facility in handling humor, but that skill is especially in evidence in *Inside, Outside.*

THE HOPE and THE GLORY

Unfortunately, Wouk was not able to sustain in his next two novels the high level of artistry he achieved in *Inside, Outside.* In *The Hope* and *The Glory* he continues to exploit his interest in Judaic issues, using the techniques that proved successful in *The Winds of War* and *War and Remembrance.* Though published separately, *The Hope* and *The Glory* are much like Wouk's two-volume romance about World War II; collectively they provide a portrait of the early years of the state of Israel, depicting the struggles of the Jewish people to establish a new independent country in their ancestral homeland.

The Hope is set in the years immediately following World War II, when a small but determined group of Zionist freedom fighters ousted the British from Palestine and declared the foundation of the new state of Israel. As he did in *The Winds of War* and *War and Remembrance*, Wouk creates a number of fictional characters whose lives intersect with the real-life heroes and heroines of the new Jewish nation. Wouk offers a vivid account of the 1948 War of Independence, focusing on the struggles of leaders such as David Ben-Gurion and Moshe Dayan to unite the disparate political and paramilitary groups in the region. The climax of the novel is the stunning victory of the Israelis over their Arab enemies in the Six-Day War of 1967. *The Glory* is a sequel, containing many of the same characters. In recounting the tale of the Jewish nation from 1967 to the announcement of the Camp David Peace Accords, Wouk has his fictional characters support the likes of Golda Meir and Menachem Begin.

Though with less success than he realized in his World War II novels, Wouk gives his narrative a sense of immediacy by concentrating his attention on the effects of the Israelis' struggle on the lives of common men and women. To accomplish this, he creates four families whose fortunes are intertwined not only with historical personages of note but also with each other: the Baraks, the Blumenthals, the Pasternaks, and the Luries. Among them are fighters, local politicians, businessmen, and even ambassadors who represent Israel in the United States and at the United Nations. Political issues are paralleled by small acts of love and vengeance, bringing a certain degree of humanity to the large historical canvas on which Wouk depicts the nation he loves.

Like most novels published by Wouk since the appearance of *The Caine Mutiny*, both *The Hope* and *The Glory* attracted a large readership, but neither received praise from critics. The negative critical reaction seems justified. While the historical accounts are accurate and presented with a strong sense of control, at least one reviewer found this extremely complex political subject treated with "only slightly more subtlety than a grade-school Thanksgiving pageant." Knowing that he would be open to criticism because of his strong partisan views, Wouk was careful to offer a note in *The Hope* that he worked hard not to present a caricature of the Arabs. Unfortunately, there is a general laxity in dealing with both major and minor Jewish figures. Instead of striving for complexity, Wouk often resorts to stereotypes that create heroes and villains more commonly found in melodrama or popular romances. His men are almost all superhuman, his women submissive handmaids. What could have been a wonderful final performance in a distinguished career as a popular novelist seems to have emerged as little more than a drifting away into contemporary cliché.

Despite his broad popular appeal, Wouk has generally not found favor with the critics, especially academic critics. The common response of the latter has been simply to ignore him. It is difficult to explain precisely why this is so. Perhaps Wouk's very popularity militates against him, as if there existed a necessary relationship between popularity and artistic worth: The more popular a writer, the poorer the quality of what he writes. Perhaps Wouk's traditionalist worldview and forthright advocacy of Judeo-Christian moral principles, to which many critics today are hostile, account in part for the critical neglect of his work.

In any case, Wouk deserves more critical attention than he has received. He is not the greatest among the many fine novelists to appear in the United States since World War II, but neither is he an inconsequential figure. His prose is solid and vigorous, eschewing precosity and self-indulgence. Writing with intelligence and sensitivity, he appeals neither to a small clique of literary aesthetes nor to the lowest common denominator of a general audience. His attitude toward fiction is that shared by all the major novelists of literary history; his fiction is not concerned with itself but with the world at large. His fiction does not attempt the irrelevant task of creating a moral universe from scratch, but accepts and responds to the moral universe which is already in place.

Dennis Q. McInerny,
updated by Laurence W. Mazzeno

OTHER MAJOR WORKS

PLAYS: *The Traitor*, pr., pb. 1949; *The Caine Mutiny Court-Martial*, pr., pb. 1954; *Nature's Way*, pr. 1957; *Don't Stop the Carnival*, pr. 1998 (musical, with Jimmy Buffett).

SCREENPLAY: *Slattery's Hurricane*, 1949 (with Richard Murphy).

TELEPLAYS: *The Winds of War*, 1983; *War and Remembrance*, 1988.

NONFICTION: *This Is My God*, 1959, 1973; *The Will to Live On: The Resurgence of Jewish Heritage*, 2000.

BIBLIOGRAPHY

Beichman, Arnold. *Herman Wouk: The Novelist as Social Historian*. New Brunswick, N.J.: Transaction Books, 1984. A lifelong friend of Wouk, Beichman offers a strident defense of the novelist against those who fault him for both his conservative political stance and his decision to stress narrative and action over complex characterization. Beichman attacks academic critics who demand that Wouk subscribe to the tenets of modernism. His critiques of individual novels are abbreviated and colored by his belief that Wouk is one of America's greatest novelists.

Mazzeno, Laurence W. *Herman Wouk*. New York: Twayne, 1994. Written for the U.S. Authors series, this volume offers a brief biographical sketch and analyses of the major novels through *Inside, Outside*. Mazzeno is generally sympathetic toward Wouk, finding his populism a strength in reaching a wide reading audience whom he wishes to influence on important social and moral issues. The book contains excerpts from hundreds of reviews of Wouk's fiction, providing a sense of the contemporary reaction to each of Wouk's major works.

Shapiro, Edward S. "The Jew as Patriot: Herman Wouk and American Jewish Identity." *American Jewish History* 84 (December, 1996): 333-351. Shapiro provides a retrospective review of Wouk's career, arguing persuasively that Wouk is concerned principally with defining American Jewish identity. He offers sympathetic and perceptive readings of *The Caine Mutiny*, *The Winds of War*, *War and Remembrance*, *The Hope*, and *The Glory*. Shapiro claims that Wouk tries in all his novels to expose parallels between the United States and Israel, thereby making it palatable to claim that being a good Jew in America is equivalent to being a good American.

RICHARD WRIGHT

Born: Natchez, Mississippi; September 4, 1908
Died: Paris, France; November 28, 1960

PRINCIPAL LONG FICTION
Native Son, 1940
The Outsider, 1953
Savage Holiday, 1954
The Long Dream, 1958
Lawd Today, 1963

OTHER LITERARY FORMS

In addition to his five novels, Richard Wright published collections of essays and short stories and two autobiographical volumes. Two collections of short stories, the early *Uncle Tom's Children* (1938, 1940) and the posthumously collected *Eight Men* (1961), represent some of Wright's finest fiction. Wright himself felt that the characters in *Uncle Tom's Children* were too easily pitied and that they elicited from readers a sympathy that was unlike the tough intellectual judgment he desired. Wright later wrote that his creation of Bigger Thomas in *Native Son* was an attempt to stiffen that portrayal so that readers could not leniently dismiss his characters with simple compassion, but would have to accept them as free, fully human adults, whose actions required assessment. Nevertheless, the stories of *Uncle Tom's Children* are carefully written, and the characters, though sometimes defeated, embody the kind of independence and intractability that Wright valued in his fiction.

Two stories from *Eight Men* reveal the themes to which Wright gave sustained development in his novels. In "The Man Who Was Almos' a Man," the main character learns that power means freedom, and although he first bungles his attempt to shoot a gun, his symbol of power, he lies to his family, keeps the gun, and at the conclusion of the story leaves home to grow into manhood elsewhere. In "The Man Who Lived Underground," the main character, nameless at first, is accused of a crime he did not commit. Fleeing underground to the sewers of the city, he becomes a

voyeur of life, seen now from a new perspective. The values that served him badly above ground do not serve him at all below. By the end of the story, he has come to understand that all men are guilty; his name is revealed, and with his new values, he ascends once more to accept responsibility for the crime. Since all men are guilty, it is less important to him that the crime is not his own than that he acknowledge freely that he shares in human guilt.

Even more important than these two collections is the first volume of Wright's autobiography, *Black Boy* (1945), which opens up a world of experience to the reader. It traces the first seventeen years of Wright's life—from his birth in Mississippi and the desertion of the family by his father, through years of displacement as he travels from one relative to another with his ill mother and religious grandmother. The early years find Wright, like his later protagonists, an outsider, cut off from family, from friends, from culture. He is as out of place among blacks as among whites, baffled by those blacks who play the roles whites expect of them, himself unable to dissimulate his feelings and thoughts.

Although the work is nonfiction, it is united by powerful metaphors: fire, hunger, and blindness. Wright's inner fire is mirrored throughout the work by actual fires; indeed, his first act is to set afire the curtains in his home. His physical hunger, a constant companion, is an image of his hunger for knowledge and connection, and his two jobs in optical factories suggest the blindness of society, a blindness given further representation in *Native Son*.

What Wright learns in *Black Boy* is the power of words. His early life is marked by physical violence: He witnesses murders and beatings, but it is the violence of words which offers liberation from his suffocating environment. Whether it is the profanity with which he shocks his grandmother, the literalness with which he takes his father's words, or the crude expressions with which he taunts Jewish shopkeepers, he discovers that words have a power which makes him an equal to those around him. When he feels unequal, as in his early school experiences, he is speechless. The culmination of this theme occurs when Wright acquires a library card and discovers through his readings in the American social critics of the early part of the twentieth century, such as H. L. Mencken and Sinclair Lewis, that he is not alone in his feelings and that there are others who share his alienation and discontent.

When Wright finally sees his father many years after his desertion, his hatred dissolves: He realizes that his father, trapped by his surroundings, with neither a cultural past nor an individual future, speaks a different language from his own, holds different thoughts, and is truly a victim and therefore not worthy even of his hatred. Wright's characters must never be victims, for as such they hold no interest. At the end of the book, he goes north, first to Memphis and, when that fails, north again to Chicago, pursuing the dream, having now the power of words to articulate it and to define himself.

The record of his years in Chicago is found in the posthumously published second autobiographical volume, *American Hunger* (written in 1944, published in 1977). Largely a record of his involvement and later disillusionment with the Communist Party, this book is interesting for its view of a later, mature Wright who is still struggling with institutions which would limit his freedom.

ACHIEVEMENTS

In his best work, Wright gives American literature its strongest statement of the existential theme of alienated people defining themselves. Wright's use of the black American as archetypal outsider gives his work a double edge. On the one hand, no American writer so carefully illuminates the black experience in America: The ambivalence of black feeling, the hypocrisies of the dominant culture, and the tension between them find concrete and original manifestation in Wright's work, a manifestation at once revealing and terrifying.

It is not only in his revelation of black life, however, that Wright's power lies, for as much as his writing is social and political, it is also personal and philosophical. The story of alien-

ated people is a universal one; because the concrete experiences of the outsider are so vividly rendered in Wright's fiction, his books have an immediate accessibility. Because they also reveal deeper patterns, they have further claims to attention. Much of Wright's later fiction seems self-conscious and studied, but it cannot diminish the greatness of his finest work.

BIOGRAPHY

Born in Mississippi of sharecropper parents, Richard Wright had a lonely and troubled childhood. His father deserted the family early, and after his mother suffered a stroke, Wright was forced at a young age to work to help support the family, which moved frequently from one relative to another. His portrayal of his mother is of a stern but loving parent, unable to contend with the stronger personality of his extremely

(Library of Congress)

religious grandmother. Wright's grandmother believed that all fiction was "the devil's lies"; her chief goal was to force Wright into a religious conversion, a goal in which she was singularly unsuccessful.

Wright moved from school to school, attempting to make friends and make his talents known. Though both tasks were difficult, he became valedictorian of his class. Even this accomplishment was spoiled when the principal insisted that Wright read a speech which the principal himself had written, and Wright refused. An uncle told Richard, "They're going to break you," and society, both black and white, seemed intent on doing so. Wright was determined to resist, not to be claimed by his environment as he felt so many blacks around him were.

Wright left Mississippi for Memphis, Tennessee, had little luck there, and—with money stolen from the film theater where he worked—moved to Chicago. When others stole, Wright disapproved—not for moral reasons, but because he felt stealing did not change the fundamental relationship of a person to his environment. When it offered a chance to change that environment, Wright accepted it.

In Chicago, Wright became involved with others who viewed the country as he did, first in a federal theater project and then with the Communist John Reed Club, which supported his writing until Wright's goals differed from their own. In 1937, he moved to New York City to become the editor of the *Daily Worker*. A year later, he published his first important work, *Uncle Tom's Children*, after which he won a Guggenheim Fellowship, which provided him with the time and funds to write *Native Son*. The novel was published to great acclaim and was followed by a second major work, *Black Boy*. Although his writing career was a success, Wright was arguing more frequently with the Communist party, with which he finally broke in 1944, and was becoming less optimistic about the hope of racial progress in the United States.

In 1946, Wright moved to France, where he spent the rest of his life. Although he wrote a great deal there, nothing in his later work, with the possible exception of *The Outsider*, approaches the strength of *Native Son* and *Black Boy*. The existentialism which

was always implicit in his work became the dominant theme, but—displaced from his native environment— Wright never again found a convincing dramatic situation in which to work out his preoccupations.

Wright died in France of a heart attack on November 28, 1960. After his death, three more works, *Eight Men, Lawd Today*, and *American Hunger*, were published.

ANALYSIS

Richard Wright's best work is always the story of one man's struggle to define himself and by so doing make himself free and responsible, fully human, a character worthy not of pity but of admiration and horror simultaneously. Typically, the character is an outsider, and Wright uses blackness as a representation of that alienation, though his characters are never as interested in defining their blackness as in defining their humanity. Although many characters in Wright's works are outsiders without being aware of their condition, Wright is never interested in them except as foils. Many of them avoid confronting themselves by fleeing to dreams; religion and liquor are two avoidance mechanisms for Wright's characters, narcotics that blind them to their surrounding world, to what they are and what they might be.

Even Wright's main characters must not think about that world too often: To let it touch them is to risk insanity or violence, and so his characters strive to keep the fire within in check, to keep the physical hunger satisfied. Thus, all of Wright's protagonists are initially trapped by desire and by fear—fear of what might happen to them, what they may do, if they risk venturing outside the confines of black life in America—and the desire to do so. The life outside may be glimpsed in films; Bigger Thomas, for example, goes to a film and watches contrasting and artificial views of black and white society. Yet as untruthful as both views are, they remind Bigger of a reality beyond his present situation. Desire is often symbolized by flight; Bigger, like other Wright characters, dreams of flying above the world, unchained from its limitations.

Most of Wright's stories and novels examine what happens when the protagonist's fear is mastered for a moment when desires are met. The manifestation of desire in Wright is almost always through violence (and it is here, perhaps, that he is most pessimistic, for other, more positive, manifestations of desire, such as love, can come only later, after the protagonists have violently acted out their longings). Violence is central to Wright's fiction, for as important as sex may be to his characters, power is much more so, and power is often achieved through violence; in Wright's world, beatings and murders are frequent acts—central and occasionally creative.

Once the character has acted, he finds himself trapped again in a new set of oppositions, for in acting, he has left the old sureties behind, has made himself free, and has begun to define and create himself. With that new freedom comes a new awareness of responsibility. He is without excuses, and that awareness is as terrifying as—though more liberating than—the fears he has previously known. Although Wright does not always elaborate on what may follow, the characters open up new possibilities for themselves. If one may create one's self by violence, perhaps, Wright sometimes suggests, there are other, less destructive ways as well.

Some of Wright's novels end on this note of optimism, the characters tragically happy: tragic because they have committed violent and repulsive acts, but happy because for the first time they have *chosen* to commit them; they have freed themselves from their constraints, and the future, however short it may be, lies open. Others end simply with tragedy, the destruction achieving no purpose, the characters attaining no illumination.

LAWD TODAY

Lawd Today, written before *Native Son*, but not published until after Wright's death, tells the story of Jake Jackson from his awakening on the morning of February 12, 1936, to that day's violent conclusion. Jackson is Wright's most inarticulate protagonist: He has a banal life, undefined dreams, and a vague sense of discontent which he is unable to explain. Violent and prejudiced, he speaks in clichés, a language as meaningless as his life.

Technically, the book incorporates a montage of radio broadcasts, newspaper articles, and religious and political pamphlets into the narration of Jake's day. Divided into three sections, *Lawd Today* opens with Jake's dream of running up an endless staircase after a disappearing voice. That dream gives way to the reality of his life: hunger, anger, and recrimination. Tricked by Jake into an abortion for which Jake still owes five hundred dollars and now claiming to have a tumor which will cost another five hundred dollars to remove, Jake's wife represents his entrapment. In the first section, "Commonplace," Jake reveals his brutish and trivial character: his anger at his wife, a jealousy and resentment that lead him to bait her so he can hit her, a mock battle straightening his hair, and a meeting with friends who work with him at the post office. As they play bridge to pass the time until work, Wright presents without comment their stupid, cliché-ridden conversation.

Section 2, "Squirrel Cage," shows the men at work. They are all alienated in meaningless, routine jobs, but Jake's position is the most desperate, for his wife has been to see his boss, and he is now threatened with the loss of his job. Falling deeper into debt by borrowing more money and making mistakes on the job, Jake is trapped by his work—despite his own protestations, as a self-proclaimed Republican and capitalist, that work is liberating. This section, too, ends with a long, rambling, and banal conversation among the men at work.

In the concluding section, "Rat's Alley," the men go to a brothel for a good time on some of Jake's borrowed money. There, Jake is robbed and then beaten for his threats of revenge. Finally, Jake stumbles homeward, his day nearing an end. The February weather, pleasant when the book began, has turned bad. All of Jake's frustration and anger finally erupt; he beats his wife, whom he finds kneeling asleep by the bed in an attitude of prayer. As they struggle, he throws objects through the window. She grabs a shard of broken glass and slashes him three times. The book ends with Jake lying in a drunken stupor, bleeding, while his wife is on her knees, also bleeding, praying for death. Outside, the wind blows mercilessly.

Although some of the experimentalism of *Lawd Today* seems artificial, and although the protagonist is too limited to sustain the reader's interest, this early work is powerful and economical. The situation, if not the character, is typical of Wright's work, and the reader understands Jake's violent frustration. *Lawd Today* has its flaws, but it foreshadows the strengths of Wright's best work and in its own right is a daring and fascinating novel.

Native Son

Along with *Black Boy, Native Son* is one of Wright's finest achievements: a brilliant portrayal of, as Wright put it, the way the environment provides the instrumentalities through which one expresses oneself and the way that self becomes whole despite the environment's conspiring to keep it divided.

The book parallels Theodore Dreiser's *An American Tragedy* (1925): Both are three-part novels in which there is a murder, in part accidental, in part willed; an attempted flight; and a long concluding trial, in both cases somewhat anticlimactic. Both novels are concerned with the interplay of environment and heredity, of fate and accident, and both have protagonists who rebel against the world which would hold them back.

In the first part of *Native Son*, Bigger Thomas is a black man cut off from family and peers. Superficially like his friends, he is in fact possessed of a different consciousness. To think about that consciousness is for him to risk insanity or violence, so Bigger endeavors to keep his fears and uncertainty at a preconscious level. On the day of the first section, however, he is required by the welfare agency to apply for a job as a menial at the home of the rich Dalton family. Mr. Dalton is a ghetto landlord who soothes his conscience by donating sums of money for recreational purposes. That it is a minuscule part of the money he is deriving from blacks is an irony he overlooks. Mrs. Dalton is blind, a fact that is necessary to the plot as well as being symbolic. Their daughter, Mary, is a member of the Communist Party, and from the moment she sees Bigger, who wants nothing more than to be left alone, she begins to enlist his support.

The first evening, Bigger is to drive Mary to a university class. In reality, she is going with Jan Erlone, her Communist boyfriend, to a party meeting. Afterward, they insist that Bigger take them to a bar in the black part of town. Jan and Mary are at this point satirized, for their attitudes toward blacks are as limited and stereotyped as any in the novel. Bigger does not want to be seen by his friends with whites, but that fact does not occur to Mary. After much drinking, Bigger must carry the drunken Mary to her bedroom. He puts her to bed, stands over her, attracted to the woman he sees. The door opens and Mrs. Dalton enters. When Mary makes drunken noises, Bigger becomes frightened that Mrs. Dalton will come close enough to discover him, so he puts a pillow over Mary's face to quiet her. By the time Mrs. Dalton leaves, Mary is dead.

Wright wanted to make Bigger a character it would be impossible to pity, and what follows is extremely grisly. Bigger tries to put Mary's body in the furnace and saws off her head to make her fit. However accidental Mary's death may appear to the reader, Bigger himself does not regard it as such. He has, he thinks, many times wanted to kill whites without ever having the opportunity to do so. This time there was the act without the desire, but rather than seeing himself as the victim of a chance occurrence, Bigger prefers to unite the earlier desire with the present act, to make himself whole by accepting responsibility for the killing. Indeed, he not only accepts the act but also determines to capitalize on it by sending a ransom note. Later, accused of raping Mary as well, an act he considered but did not commit, he reverses the process, accepting responsibility for this, too, even though here there was desire but no act. His only sign of conscience is that he cannot bring himself to shake the ashes in the furnace; this guilt is not redemptive, but his undoing, for, in an implausible scene in the Dalton basement, the room fills with smoke, the murder is revealed to newspaper reporters gathered there, and Bigger is forced to flee.

He runs with his girlfriend, Bessie Mears. She, like Bigger, has a hunger for sensation, which has initially attracted him to her. Now, however, as they flee together, she becomes a threat and a burden; huddled with her in an abandoned tenement, Bigger wants only to be rid of her. He picks up a brick and smashes her face, dumping her body down an air-shaft. His only regret is not that he has killed her, but that he has forgotten to remove their money from her body.

The rest of the plot moves quickly: Bigger is soon arrested, the trial is turned into a political farce, and Bigger is convicted and sentenced to death. In the last part of the novel, after Bigger's arrest, the implications of the action are developed, largely through Bigger's relations to other characters. Some of the characters are worthy only of contempt, particularly the district attorney, who, in an attempt at reelection, is turning the trial into political capital. Bigger's mother relies on religion. In a scene in the jail cell, she falls on her knees in apology before Mrs. Dalton and urges Bigger to pray, but toughness is Bigger's code. He is embarrassed by his mother's self-abasement, and although he agrees to pray simply to end his discomfort, his attitude toward religion is shown when he throws away a cross a minister has given him and throws a cup of coffee in a priest's face. In his view, they want only to avoid the world and to force him to accept guilt without responsibility.

Bigger learns from two characters. The first is Boris Max, the lawyer the Communist Party provides. Max listens to Bigger, and for the first time in his life, Bigger exposes his ideas and feelings to another human. Max's plea to the court is that, just as Bigger must accept responsibility for what he has done, so must the society around him understand its responsibility for what Bigger has become and, if the court chooses to execute Bigger, understand the consequences that must flow from that action. He does not argue—nor does Wright believe—that Bigger is a victim of injustice. There is no injustice, because that would presume a world in which Bigger could hope for justice, and such a world does not exist; more important, Bigger is not a victim, for he has chosen his own fate. Max argues rather that all men are entitled to happiness. Like all of Wright's protagonists, Bigger has earlier been torn between the poles of dread and ecstasy. His ecstasy, his happiness, comes from the meaningfulness he creates in his existence, a product of self-realization. Unhappily for Bigger, he realizes himself through murder: It was, he feels, his highest creative act.

If Max articulates the intellectual presentation of Wright's beliefs about Bigger, it is Jan, Mary's lover, who is its dramatic representation. He visits Bigger in his cell and, having at last understood the futility and paucity of his own stereotypes, admits to Bigger that he too shares in the responsibility for what has happened. He, too, addresses Bigger as a human being, but from the unique position of being the one who is alive to remind Bigger of the consequences of his actions, for Bigger learns that Jan has suffered loss through what he has done and that, while Bigger has created himself, he has also destroyed another.

Native Son ends with the failure of Max's appeals on Bigger's behalf. He comes to the cell to confront Bigger before his execution, and the novel closes with Bigger Thomas smiling at Max as the prison door clangs shut. He will die happy because he will die fulfilled, having, however terribly, created a self. *Native Son* is Wright's most powerful work, because his theme, universal in nature, is given its fullest and most evocative embodiment. In the characterization of Bigger, alienated man at his least abstract and most genuine, of Bigger's exactly rendered mind and milieu, and of Bigger's working out of his destiny, *Native Son* is Wright's masterpiece.

THE OUTSIDER

Wright's next novel, *The Outsider*, written in France and published thirteen years after *Native Son*, suffers from a surfeit of internal explanation and a failure to provide a setting as rich as that of *Native Son*. Still, its portrayal of Cross Damon and his struggle to define himself, while too self-conscious, adds new dimensions to Wright's myth.

As the novel opens, Damon is trapped by his life. His post-office job is unfulfilling, his wife is threatening, and his underage mistress is pregnant. He "desires desire," but there is no way for that desire to be completed. "A man creates himself," he has told his wife, but the self Damon has created is a nightmare. He broods, his brooding as close as he comes to religion. Another underground man, Damon gets his chance for new life on the subway. Thought dead after his identification papers are found near the mangled body of another, Damon gets a chance to create himself anew. He must invent, he thinks, not only his future, but also a past to fit with his present; this new opportunity brings with it a different and more potent sense of dread.

From the beginning of this new life, Damon is remarkably successful at the mechanics of creating a past. He easily obtains a birth certificate and a draft card. At a deeper level, however, he traps himself as surely as he has been trapped in his old life, so that his new one becomes a continuous act of bad faith. Even before he leaves Chicago, he hides in a brothel where he encounters a co-worker who recognizes him. Damon murders the man and throws his body out a window. The pattern of violence, so typical of Wright's characters, begins in earnest for Damon.

Taking a train to New York, Cross meets two people who will influence his new life, a black waiter who introduces him to the world of Communist politics in New York City, and Ely Houston, the district attorney, who is the most articulate person in the novel and the only one fully to understand Damon. Houston asks Damon why, when all blacks are outsiders, so few seem conscious of this fact. Wright suggests that being human is too much to be borne by people, that the struggle to define oneself is too difficult; the novel is a testament to that suggestion.

The Communist Party members, too, are outsiders, and there is nothing unified about their company. Each one that Damon meets is playing god, hoping to protect and extend his personal power. Their awareness of their motives varies, but they are a threat to Damon, and the action of the book is propelled by a series of murders: Damon himself wants to act like a god. Near the end of the book, Houston comes to understand that Damon is the killer, but—rather than indicting and punishing him legally—Houston allows him to go free, alone with his knowledge of what he is. Damon is horrified by his fate, but he is robbed of even that when he is killed by two Communist Party members who fear him.

The Outsider is both an extension and a modification of Wright's earlier views; it is far more pessimistic than *Native Son*, and the influence of the French existentialists is more pervasive. Like earlier Wright heroes, Damon is engaged in defining the world and himself. "The moment we act 'as if' it's true, then it's true," he thinks, because each person, in the absence of a god, is able to create the world and its truth. From Fyodor Dostoevski, Wright again borrows the notion of underground man and the idea that without a god, all is permitted. Yet as each man plays god, as each becomes criminal, policeman, judge, and executioner, there are no longer limits. People desire everything, and desire is described as a floating demon. People are jealous gods here—the worlds they create are petty, their jealousy destructive. Cross Damon is loved in the novel, but that love, unlike the love in *Native Son*, which is held up as potentially meaningful, is here without promise. Although he creates himself and his world in *The Outsider*, all that is made is violent and brutal, a world without redemption even in the act of self-realization.

At the end of the novel, Cross Damon dies, not with Bigger Thomas's smile, but with the knowledge that alone, people are nothing. Searching in his last moments of freedom for a clean, well-lighted place in which to rest before he confronts the world again, Cross finds only death. Before he dies, he admits his final act of bad faith: He has thought that he could create a world and be different from other men, that he could remain innocent. Like Joseph Conrad's Kurtz in *Heart of Darkness* (1902), Damon dies realizing the futility of that hope; having looked into his own heart of darkness, he dies with the word *horror* on his lips.

It is Wright's bleakest conclusion, the book his most relentless examination of the consequences of his own philosophy. If *The Outsider* lacks the narrative drive of *Native Son*, it remains a strongly conceived and troubling piece of fiction.

THE LONG DREAM

Wright's last novel, *The Long Dream*, despite some effective scenes, is one of his weakest. The story of Rex "Fishbelly" Tucker's growing up and coming to terms with his environment is a pale repetition of earlier themes. The first section describes Tucker's youth. His father, an undertaker, is the richest black man in town, but his money comes also from a brothel he runs on the side. Tucker admires his father's success while detesting his obsequiousness with whites. When, however, Fishbelly is arrested, he twice faints at the white world's threats. Having presented himself as a victim, he becomes one. Walking home after his father has arranged his freedom, Fishbelly sees an injured dog, which he puts out of its misery. Fishbelly then comes upon a white man, pinned to the ground with a car door on his body. When the white man calls out to Fishbelly, using the term "nigger," Fishbelly walks on, leaving the man to die.

In the second section, Fishbelly finds a woman, but she and forty-one others are burned to death in a fire at the bar. The rest of the novel is an unconvincing story of the police who want the return of the cancelled checks that Fishbelly's father has used to pay them off, the police's arranged murder of the father, the subsequent framing and imprisoning of Fishbelly for rape, and Fishbelly's keeping the checks for his future use. All of this is seriously contrived. At the end, Fishbelly is on a plane leaving for France, where his childhood friends are stationed in the army, which they describe as exciting. He is talking to an Italian whose father has come to America and found a dream, where Fishbelly himself has known only a nightmare. France, he dreams, will offer him what America has not.

In Fishbelly's attempt to understand himself and his environment, he is a typical Wright protagonist. He is weaker than Wright's usual characters, however, and that shallowness, coupled with an implausible plot, prevents Wright's last work of long fiction from succeeding.

Unlike many highly acclaimed books of the 1940's, *Native Son* and *Black Boy* have not dated. They are a lacerating challenge to contemporary readers and writers—a challenge to share the relentless integrity of Richard Wright's vision.

Howard Faulkner

OTHER MAJOR WORKS

SHORT FICTION: *Uncle Tom's Children*, 1938, 1940; *Eight Men*, 1961.

PLAY: *Native Son: The Biography of a Young American*, pr. 1941 (with Paul Green).

NONFICTION: *Twelve Million Black Voices*, 1941; *Black Boy*, 1945; *Black Power*, 1954; *The Color Cur-*
tain, 1956; *Pagan Spain*, 1957; *White Man, Listen!* 1957; *American Hunger*, 1977.

BIBLIOGRAPHY

Baldwin, James. *The Price of the Ticket: Collected Nonfiction, 1948-1985.* New York: St. Martin's Press/Marek, 1985. The essays "Everybody's Protest Novel" and "Alas, Poor Richard" provide important and provocative insights into Wright and his art.

Bloom, Harold, ed. *Richard Wright.* New York: Chelsea House, 1987. Essays on various aspects of Wright's work and career, with an introduction by Bloom.

Butler, Robert. *"Native Son": The Emergence of a New Black Hero.* Boston: Twayne, 1991. One of Twayne's Masterwork Studies, this is an accessible critical look at the seminal novel. Includes bibliographical references and an index.

Fabre, Michel. *The Unfinished Quest of Richard Wright.* Translated by Isabel Barzun. New York: William Morrow, 1973. The most important and authoritative biography of Wright available.

_____. *The World of Richard Wright.* Jackson: University Press of Mississippi, 1985. A collection of Fabre's essays on Wright. A valuable but not sustained full-length study.

Hakutani, Yoshinobu. *Richard Wright and Racial Discourse.* Columbia: University of Missouri Press, 1996. Chapters on *Lawd Today, Uncle Tom's Children, Native Son, The Outsider,* and *Black Boy,* as well as discussions of later fiction, black power, and Wright's handling of sexuality. Includes an introduction and a bibliography.

Kinnamon, Keneth, ed. *Critical Essays on Richard Wright's "Native Son."* New York: Twayne, 1997. Divided into sections of reviews, reprinted essays, and new essays. Includes discussions of Wright's handling of race, voice, tone, novelistic structure, the city, and literary influences. Index but no bibliography.

_____. *The Emergence of Richard Wright.* Urbana: University of Illinois Press, 1972. A study of Wright's background and development as a writer, up to the publication of *Native Son* in 1940.

Walker, Margaret. *Richard Wright: Daemonic Genius*. New York: Warner Books, 1988. A critically acclaimed study of Wright's life and work written by a respected novelist.

Webb, Constance. *Richard Wright: A Biography.* New York: Putnam, 1968. A well-written biography which remains useful.

Y

FRANK YERBY

Born: Augusta, Georgia; September 5, 1916
Died: Madrid, Spain; November 29, 1991

PRINCIPAL LONG FICTION

The Foxes of Harrow, 1946
The Vixens, 1947
The Golden Hawk, 1948
Pride's Castle, 1949
Floodtide, 1950
A Woman Called Fancy, 1951
The Saracen Blade, 1952
The Devil's Laughter, 1953
Bride of Liberty, 1954
Benton's Row, 1954
The Treasure of Pleasant Valley, 1955
Captain Rebel, 1956
Fairoaks, 1957
The Serpent and the Staff, 1958
Jarrett's Jade, 1959
Gillian, 1960
The Garfield Honor, 1961
Griffin's Way, 1962
The Old Gods Laugh: A Modern Romance, 1964
An Odor of Sanctity, 1965
Goat Song, 1968
Judas, My Brother, 1968
Speak Now: A Modern Novel, 1969
The Dahomean: An Historical Novel, 1971
The Girl from Storyville, 1972
The Voyage Unplanned, 1974
Tobias and the Angel, 1975
A Rose for Ana Maria, 1976
Hail the Conquering Hero, 1978
A Darkness at Ingraham's Crest, 1979
Western, 1982
Devilseed, 1984
McKenzie's Hundred, 1985

OTHER LITERARY FORMS

In addition to his novels, Frank Yerby wrote poetry and short stories that are often found in anthologies of black literature. One story, "Health Card," first published in *Harper's* magazine, won a special O. Henry Memorial Award in 1944.

ACHIEVEMENTS

Yerby wrote many best-selling historical novels over a long career beginning in the 1940's. Most of his best work, however, dates from the 1960's, after he had established himself as a prolific popular novelist. Yerby excelled at creating complicated, fast-moving plots that give vivid impressions of historical eras and periods. Often the novels contradict myths and stereotypes of the periods in question. Almost every novel, too, suggests the futility of finding real truth in the universal confusion of the human condition. While Yerby's protagonists are flawed, often by ruthlessness and infidelity, they are also character-

(Library of Congress)

3597

ized by a fierce sense of dignity based on the worth of a human life.

BIOGRAPHY

Frank Garvin Yerby, an African American novelist, was born in Augusta, Georgia, on September 5, 1916. He received a B.A. at Paine College in 1937 and a M.A. at Fisk College in 1938. Subsequently, he did graduate work in education at the University of Chicago.

From 1939 to 1941, Yerby taught English, first at Florida A&M and then at Southern University and Agricultural and Mechanical College. Married in 1941, he worked from 1941 to 1944 at the Ford Motor Company in Dearborn, Michigan, as a technician and then as an inspector at Fairchild Aircraft from 1944 to 1945. In 1944, he won an O. Henry Memorial Award for the short story "Health Card," a story that dealt sensitively with black issues. In 1945, he started work on a novel, *The Foxes of Harrow*, which he aimed to make a commercial success. Thereafter, Yerby wrote many similar melodramatic best-sellers. His books have sold millions of copies and have been translated into at least fourteen languages.

Divorced in the 1950's, Yerby moved to France and then to Spain, where he died in 1991. He had four children from his first marriage. His second wife was his researcher and general manager; some of his later novels give evidence of considerable research. He traveled widely, and sometimes his travels involved investigating locales of works in progress.

ANALYSIS

Frank Yerby was a best-selling author, and much of what he did has clear commercial appeal, a point on which Yerby made inconsistent remarks. His plots are intricate and involved, but in many of his novels, the characterizations are basically flat. His most-used era is that of the nineteenth century South, yet he wrote about many other places and times in his more than thirty novels. Occasionally, he set a novel in modern times. The superficial reader of best-sellers will find in Yerby's novels fast-paced narrative with appropriate amounts of violence and sex.

Yerby was more, however, than a mere best-selling writer. His short stories written early in his career show promise and develop radically different themes from those of his costume novels. In the 1960's, secure after many commercial successes, Yerby began to do his best work, dealing with larger issues of race and religion, which figure less prominently in his earlier novels. The characters in these later novels are no longer cardboard figures, while the backgrounds are as richly detailed and vividly recreated as ever. Yerby's historical novels must be evaluated within the context of that often unappreciated genre. His novels almost always show the conflict between two worlds or orders, as great historical novels do. Yerby rarely deals with actual historical figures but rather creates characters who have to deal with the essential conflicts of their eras. Often his novels, even the early ones, destroy widely held myths and stereotypes; Darwin Turner suggests that this revisionism might be Yerby's most significant contribution as a novelist. While extensive research is not evident in his early work, many of Yerby's later novels were thoroughly researched. Yerby was at his best in creating the color and movement of a particular era.

Yerby's typical protagonist is, in the words of his main character in *The Serpent and the Staff*, an *auslander* or outsider, excluded from the ruling social order. The protagonist experientially develops a philosophy that often approaches modern existentialism, an attitude that life has no answer but that people still must cope with the bleakness of human existence with both dignity and humanity. This pattern emerges in Yerby's first novel, *The Foxes of Harrow*, and is developed in three of his best novels: *Griffin's Way, An Odor of Sanctity*, and *The Dahomean*.

THE FOXES OF HARROW

The Foxes of Harrow, Yerby's first novel, is set in the South and covers the years from 1825 to just after the end of the Civil War. Superficially, it is a novel about a clever schemer who rises to own a plantation with a neoclassical mansion, Harrow, and who has marriages to beautiful white women and a liaison with a stunning mulatto. Much of the novel is composed of stock devices of pulp fiction, and Yerby himself said of *The Foxes of Harrow* that he set out to write a popular novel that would make him a lot of money, regardless of literary merit. Yerby added, however, that he became strangely involved with the writing of the novel and, despite himself, exceeded the ambitions of the pulp genre. Stephen Fox, the protagonist, is an outsider, originally shanty Irish. He is not merely the rogue that early reviewers took him for, whose success and eventual fall conform to a predictable pulp outline. Fox sees all values and ideals slip from him, so that at the end, he is a failure despite his humanity and perception. He is superior to the Southerners with whom he sympathetically deals. More than merely a novel of stock devices, *The Foxes of Harrow* is a story about the failure of a culture.

In the opening of the novel, Yerby's authorial voice establishes a pensive tone as he describes a visit to Harrow, now in ruins, in the twentieth century. Harrow is the symbol of a lost cause. Thus, for symbolic purposes, Harrow is cut off from the modern world. Bathed in moonlight, the ruins of Harrow have a decadent grandeur. The visitor feels driven from room to room and finally away from the house, never wanting to look back. The shortness of the opening, six brief paragraphs, makes the tone all the more striking, and the mood shifts quickly into the dialogue and description of the arrival of Stephen Fox in New Orleans in 1825.

Yerby was at his best in the novel in creating vivid images and scenes of the region during the forty or so years the novel spans. New Orleans appears as a lush feudalistic world where color is measured by degrees, given the novel's constant references to mulattos, quadroons, and octaroons, references which are historically true to the setting. New Orleans emerges as a backward society that refuses to drain the marshes where the mosquitoes carrying yellow fever breed and instead fires cannon to disperse the plague. The society also destroys the creativity of freed blacks. In one case, a thoroughly educated black returns from France and is killed for acting as if he were equal to whites. The most poignant scene occurs at the end of the novel, when the young heir to Harrow returns after the war to New Orleans to be confronted by a former slave of Harrow now in control. This former slave presents the heir's unknown half brother (by a beautiful mulatto) to his former master, who sees the image of his father as a young man—but the half brother is mentally retarded. As the scene concludes, Yerby deftly shows the social history of the next one hundred years of the South. The former slave, now the ruler, knows that power will again return to the whites but suggests that blacks and whites can live together and respect one another. The heir, a combination of the worst of his father's roguish tendencies and the excesses of New Orleans, emphatically denies that such equality and reconciliation between the races are possible.

Yerby was weakest in his creation of character in *The Foxes of Harrow*, for the characters are one-dimensional and move woodenly through a convoluted, overheated plot. Stephen Fox is the fox, the rogue set off from Southern society by his birth, whose goals are riches and the most beautiful woman in New Orleans, Odalie Arceneaux, a cold, haughty belle. Her sister Aurore is a foil to her, for she is warm and beautiful and in love with Stephen, who is too blind at first to see her love. As is common in pulp fiction, Odalie dies in childbirth, and Stephen then marries gentle Aurore, but only after having fathered a child by a beautiful mulatto when Odalie had spurned his strong sexual drives.

Underneath this claptrap, though, is an author working with social issues not to be found in the typical 1946 pulp novel. In one scene, a black woman recently inducted into slavery throws herself into the Mississippi rather than live in bondage. Old Calleen, a trusted slave at Harrow, later tells her grandson Inch (the son of the drowned slave) that someday, the rightness of their freedom will be made apparent. More significantly, in understated dialogue Stephen talks to his son Etienne about freeing slaves and says that the country must treat all people equally, including the blacks and the poorest whites. When his son dismisses the poor, white or black, Stephen uses history as a defense, mentioning the French Revolution, Haiti, and insurrectionist Nat Turner. It is in his sympathy and balance in treating social matters that Yerby's "moral mobility" appears, a phrase that a London *Times* writer used in reviewing a later Yerby novel.

GRIFFIN'S WAY

Griffin's Way was published in 1962, sixteen years after *The Foxes of Harrow*, and is a departure in some respects from Yerby's work up to that time. It treats the Mississippi of the 1870's unglamorously, highlighting squalor, inbreeding among whites, and the violence of the Klan in a manner more characteristic of William Faulkner than of the standard best-selling author. The novel shows the paralysis of humane white society after the war, a paralysis symbolized by the central hero's amnesia and invalid status.

Much of the novel debunks the grandeur and opulence of the old South, which Yerby himself had occasionally exploited in earlier novels. The ruined South appears first through the eyes of a Northerner, Candace Trevor, a New England minister's daughter married to a paralyzed Southerner and hired as a nurse for Paris Griffin as the novel opens. She despises the Southern "courtesy" to which women are subjected, dismisses the neoclassical architecture in the poorly constructed homes, and comments on how most planters lived in squalor even before the war. Unlike her father, she believes in a Darwinian theory of evolution and sees the darker forces in herself as part of the ape still remaining in people. Candace knows that to cure Paris of his amnesia she must find the key to it from Paris's oversexed wife Laurel. Ferreting out answers with the right leading questions, she discovers the tawdry, twisted story that led to Paris's amnesia and emotional paralysis. It is only her austere moral upbringing that allows her to control her love for Paris to use her knowledge to help him.

When Candace does cure him, Paris tries to return to his home, Griffin's Way, and to his wife Laurel, but while his cure is a rebirth, it does not allow a return. To begin with, he has returned to a world changed by the war, a world of political corruption and violence, a world that has regressed, so that even a sixty-mile trip, once possible in three hours, now involves an arduous three-day journey because the railroads remain unrepaired even five years after the war. Three years later, with the railroad rebuilt, Paris and Laurel visit Vicksburg, where Paris, despite his humanity, appears troubled by the apparent ascendancy of blacks. Yerby balances the situation by hav-

ing Paris also see the obvious corruption of the black superintendent of schools, who lives in the grand style of the old South on money intended for the schools. Paris is thus caught between two worlds: He rejects the Klan as apes but resents a black man wearing a suit as if he is accustomed to it. Even renewed, Paris still represents the paralysis of the humane white during the Reconstruction.

Yerby entitled the last third of the novel "Apocalypse," and this part has unresolved elements, unresolved on account of Yerby's honesty in dealing with his material. Paris watches the new world tumble around him, powerless to do anything. Black militants and white Klansmen fight all over the South, but Paris can only catalog the battles; he cannot change events. His moment of action does allow him to rescue Samson, a former slave, and Samson's wife by helping them escape to the North. He can do nothing to help his brother, his mulatto wife, and their children, who are burned in their house except for one daughter, who dies after being repeatedly raped, all of them victims of the Klan. He also helps a black minister escape, but only after the dynamiting of the minister's house, which killed a daughter. At his daughter's funeral, the minister delivers a stern sermon to the Klan members, who then threaten his life so that Paris must again help him. The Klan members finally back off from Paris's house when one accidentally shoots Laurel, still very much a symbol of Southern womanhood. The novel ends with dawn imagery, the night having been endured and the humane whites now waiting for the light of morning. Whether the whites threatened by the Klan can start anew is unclear. Given the implied parallel to modern events, Yerby seems to be saying that it is too soon to tell whether the twentieth century can rise above racial violence; nevertheless, the concluding imagery does suggest hope.

AN ODOR OF SANCTITY

In *An Odor of Sanctity*, Yerby is at his best as a historical novelist. It is a long, deftly paced novel which, while using many of the stock elements of Yerby's novels of the 1940's and 1950's, also deals intelligently with a religious theme. Once again, Yerby creates an outsider, Alaric Teudisson, as hero; he is set off by his odor of sanctity, a saintly force in him of which he is not fully aware for most of his life. Teudisson must deal with the complex culture of medieval Spain, a battleground for Christians, Moors, and numerous bands of marauding barbarians.

Like earlier Yerby protagonists, Teudisson is involved in many liaisons and several marriages. Teudisson is a striking blond of Visigoth extraction who, before the male hormones take effect, is so "beautiful" that at one point he is almost made a catamite. Thereafter, Teudisson has numerous sexual encounters, one unconsummated marriage, and finally a marriage to a woman who has been repeatedly raped by bandits, a marriage which shows Teudisson's magnanimity and one which also brings Teudisson genuine happiness and a family.

The religious motif of *An Odor of Sanctity* adds depth to what would otherwise be an entertaining but rather shallow melodrama. Despite himself, Alaric Teudisson becomes a saint by the end of the novel. As a man, Teudisson is handsome but scarred by battle, but as a boy, his beauty, so unlike the usual rough Goth face, led his mother and others to think he was marked for the priesthood. He turns from his religious impulses to lead a secular life, however, and while doing so, he finds his saintliness. In dealing with women, he shows a compassion and love that are the basis of his profound sexual appeal; at one point of seeming dissolution, he has numerous prostitutes loving him because he has talked to them and treated them as human beings and not merely as sex objects. Misused by a woman, he always responds with kindness. By the end of the novel, Teudisson becomes the arbiter between Moor and Christian factions when a certain group of fanatic Christians wants to destroy all tolerance for the predominant Moors. Throughout the novel, Teudisson has been a genuine ecumenist. At the end, Teudisson, doubting his saintly powers because he is unable to save his wife, willingly seeks crucifixion and thus enters sainthood and legend. In losing himself, he gains sainthood.

As in most of his novels, Yerby's greatest strength in *An Odor of Sanctity* is his re-creation of a time, a re-creation imbued with color and action. Again, a humane authorial voice speaks throughout the novel. The book shows that the diversity of medieval Spain is indeed its glory. While the Moorish culture encourages learning and recognizes Christ as a prophet, the contrasting Christian culture (except for Teudisson and a few Church fathers) is dark and intolerant. In showing the clash between these cultures, *An Odor of Sanctity* is first-rate historical fiction.

THE DAHOMEAN

If one of Yerby's novels is destined to last, it is *The Dahomean*, a novel unlike any of his others. It is a simple, moving tale of the life of a black man in hisAfrican culture before he was sold into slavery. Yerby neither idealizes nor sensationalizes his material but presents a story composed of love, envy, and hatred that reads as a legend, a story of characters and events drawn larger than life. The protagonist, Nyasanu, is like other Yerby protagonists because he is an alien or outsider: He is far less violent and far more handsome than most men of his society. Caught in the ugliness of the American slave system, he has the tragic quality of some of the great existentialist heroes.

Yerby begins the chronological narrative of Nyasanu as he is about to enter manhood, a passage marked by the painful ritual of circumcision. The early parts of the novel present such rituals in convincing detail. Yerby moves the reader from Nyasanu's initiation to an enemy's attempt to destroy his guardian tree to his wedding and the deflowering of his bride. In "A Note to the Reader," Yerby explains that the novel is based on research into the customs of the Dahomeans of the nineteenth century, but Yerby adds to his research his own respect of this African culture.

As Nyasanu moves through his period of manhood, Yerby depicts the society of the Dahomeans as a stage for the great primal emotions and forces of life. Nyasanu has encounters with numerous women, but his sexual experiences are never merely sensational, the stuff of popular fiction: Nyasanu has a reality which sets him apart from Yerby's typical protagonists. In addition to his sexual encounters, Nyasanu has the experience of real brotherhood, for his society expects each male to have his three closest friends identified in order. Battles with warring tribes give Nyasanu the chance to show bravery and also to distinguish himself as more sensitive to violence than the average Dahomean. In addition, Yerby shows the diversity of Dahomean society, which includes both male homosexuals and Amazonian warriors.

In a moving discussion with his number-one friend, Kpadunu, Nyasanu learns that the generations are all of one fabric. Each generation faces the same problems of love, the family, and death. The old priests, therefore, give answers based on the past to the young and the unsure, and—given the coherence of their society—the answers generally hold. Facing the problem of belief in the gods which these old priests try to inculcate in the young, Nyasanu realizes that their wisdom is not divine but experiential, that the past of his society answers the present needs. Ironically, his friend Kpadunu is trying to help Nyasanu rise above the control of priests by showing where their wisdom resides, yet he actually makes the skeptical Nyasanu believe more than he did, so that he must face the priestly prediction that his life will end in Dahomey but will begin again in another place.

Nyasanu does learn that he can count on the inexorability of fate and not the protection of the gods. In quick succession, he loses his friend Kpadunu, his wife in childbirth, and his father. He comes to see his heroism as mere foolishness in taking risks. Rather than listening to the gods, he simply faces life as chieftain and husband of Kpadunu's widow. Far more than the ritual of circumcision, his acceptance of life and his rejection of the illusion of divine protection mark Nyasanu's adulthood. When Nyasanu next appears in the novel, he is chieftain and has four wives. His life is successful until he is sold into slavery with the aid of his homosexual brother and rival.

The betrayal of Nyasanu has the archetypal pattern of tragedy, the hero fallen from great heights, undone by his own blindness in not facing the evil of his brother and his incestuous brother-in-law and by his pride in not following the past and living with his extended family in the same compound. He faces the guns of his attackers with his sword, only to be told to put his sword down, for in the modern era, swords are powerless against guns. First, he must watch the murder of his mother (the slavers see that she is too old to have children), the subsequent murder of all his children (the slavers know that they would die on the voyage across the Atlantic), and the subjugation of his wives, the rape of some and the suicide of one. His response is disassociation, a silence which lasts the rest of his life.

Like a classical tragedy, *The Dahomean* treats terrible despair in its conclusion but leads to an illumination, Nyasanu's enlightenment. He recognizes the evil of blacks selling blacks into American slavery, although they have no conception of the degradation of this foreign slavery, their domestic slavery being gentle and indulgent. Philosophically, Nyasanu faces the bleakness of life with the realization that there are no answers. Truth is only that there is no truth. Nyasanu acquits himself with honor; like a great tragic hero, he has his dignity, the dignity of silence in the face of the emptiness of the human condition.

Dennis Goldsberry

OTHER MAJOR WORK
SHORT FICTION: "Health Card," 1944.

BIBLIOGRAPHY

Bone, Robert A. *The Negro Novel in America*. Rev. ed. New Haven, Conn.: Yale University Press, 1965. A general survey of black novels. Bone dismisses Yerby as the "prince of pulpsters."

Hemenway, Robert, ed. *The Black Novelist*. Columbus, Ohio: Merrill, 1970. Darwin Turner comments on Yerby's "painful groping for meaning" behind a "soap-opera façade."

Klotman, Phyllis. "A Harrowing Experience: Frank Yerby's First Novel to Film." *College Language Association Journal* 31 (December, 1987): 210-222. Focuses on the changes made to Yerby's story when *The Foxes of Harrow* was adapted to the screen.

Mendelson, Phyllis Carmel, and Dedria Bryfonski, eds. *Contemporary Literary Criticism*. Vol 7. Detroit: Gale Research, 1977. Contains excerpts of positive criticism about Yerby's use of racial themes.

Metzger, Linda, and Deborah A. Straub, eds. *Contemporary Authors*. New Revision Series 16. Detroit: Gale Research, 1986. A sympathetic look at Yerby's work. Also contains an interview with the novelist.

Ryan, Bryan. *Major Twentieth-Century Authors*. Detroit: Gale Research, 1991. Contains a brief entry on Yerby.

AL YOUNG

Born: Ocean Springs, Mississippi; May 31, 1939

PRINCIPAL LONG FICTION

Snakes, 1970

Who Is Angelina?, 1975

Sitting Pretty, 1976

Ask Me Now, 1980

Seduction by Light, 1988

OTHER LITERARY FORMS

In addition to his fiction, Al Young has produced nonfiction and numerous volumes of poetry, the first being *Dancing* (1969). His twin themes are the American family and individual maturation. Early in the twentieth century, Ezra Pound warned modern poets that music separated from dance will atrophy, as will poetry separated from music. Accordingly, Young's love of the rhythms of life places music between poetry and dance. His second volume of poems is entitled *The Song Turning Back into Itself* (1971). Here, the singer of life confronts images of a Whitmanesque America less musical, choral perhaps, but certainly panoramic: The singer's song becomes the poet's vision. In *Geography of the Near Past* (1976) and *The Blues Don't Change: New and Selected Poems* (1982), the music and the dancing continue along Young's thematic lines of loving and growing. *The Blues Don't Change* incorporates musical rhythms and quotations from Chinese poets into a collection of poems designed to dance with "laughter in the blood." *Heaven: Collected Poems 1958-1988* (1988) presents a chronological time line of Young's works. *Straight No Chaser* (1994), not to be confused with the biography of Thelonius Monk with the same title (written by Leslie Gourse), is a tribute to the jazz great as well as homage to Young's love of music and his own musical career. *Conjugal Visits: And Other Poems in Verse and Prose* was published in 1996.

In 1981, Young published his autobiographical *Bodies and Soul: Musical Memoirs*, which makes use of specific pieces of music to provide continuity and to set the tone for related essays, each based on personal recollection. Several more books of a similar nature followed: *Kinds of Blue: Musical Memoirs* (1984), *Things Ain't What They Used to Be: Musical Memoirs* (1987), and *Drowning in a Sea of Love: Musical Memoirs* (1995). In 1989, he published a tribute to jazz musician Charles Mingus, *Mingus/ Mingus: Two Memoirs*, written with Janet Coleman.

Young's poetry, fiction, and essays have appeared in such publications as *Antaeus*, *Essence*, *Evergreen Review*, *Harper's*, *Journal of Black Poetry*, *The New York Times*, *The Paris Review*, *Rolling Stone*. His work is also represented in many major anthologies and books. Among them are *How Does a Poem Mean?* (1976, edited by John Ciardi and Miller Williams), *The Wedding Cake in the Middle of the Road: Twenty-three Variations on a Theme* (1992, edited by Susan Stamberg and George P. Garrett), *Moment's Notice: Jazz in Poetry and Prose* (1993, edited by Art Lange and Nathaniel Mackey), *Every Shut Eye Ain't Asleep: An Anthology of Poetry by African Americans Since 1945* (1994, edited by Michael S. Harper and Anthony Walton), *Listening to Ourselves: More Stories from "The Sound of Writing"* (1994, edited by Alan Cheuse and Caroline Marshall), and *Berkeley: A Literary Tribute* (1997). Young has also been translated into over a dozen languages.

Young has also written screenplays and scenarios for Laser Film Corporation and Stigwood Corporation in New York and for Verdon Productions, First Artists Ltd., and Universal Pictures in California.

ACHIEVEMENTS

During the mid-1960's, Young founded and edited *Loveletter*, an avant-garde review that has received awards from the National Arts Council. He was the West Coast editor of *Changes* and in 1975 was guest fiction editor of the *Iowa Review*. With Ishmael Reed, he founded and, for a time, edited the biennial anthology *Yardbird Reader* and *Quilt*, pioneering multicultural arts journals, and he was coeditor of *Yardbird Lives!* (1978).

A selection of Young's poems and an introductory essay are included in the 1979 anthology *Calafía: The California Poetry*. *Calafía* is a widely recognized project that examines the poetry of the West Coast, with recognition of a regional tradition extending back through the nineteenth century.

Young was a Wallace E. Stegner Fellow in 1966 and in 1969 was the recipient of the Joseph Henry Jackson Award for his first collection of poetry, *Dancing*. The California Association of Teachers of English selected Young to receive a special award in 1973. Young was a Guggenheim Fellow in 1974, has been a Fulbright Fellow, and received grants from the National Endowment for the Arts in 1968, 1969, and 1974. In 1980 he received the Pushcart Prize for poetry and, 1982 the Before Columbus Foundation Award.

BIOGRAPHY

Albert James Young, the son of Mary (Campbell) and Albert James Young, attended the University of Michigan from 1957 to 1961 before moving to the San Francisco Bay area in 1961. There he received his A.B. degree in Spanish from the University of California at Berkeley in 1969. He and his wife Arline June (Belch) were married in 1963 and have a son, Michael James Young.

Among various other jobs, Young's early career included an acting role in a television documentary about Archie Moore, a year as a disc jockey, and, prior to that, eight years as a professional jazz musician. His love of music deeply influences his writing, and music and musicians are often among its subjects.

Young taught writing at the San Francisco Museum of Art during the late 1960's and was linguistic consultant for the Berkeley Neighborhood Youth Corps. From 1969 to 1973, he held Stanford University's Edward H. Jones Lectureship in Creative Writing. He was the 1979 director of Associated Writing Programs, an organization of graduate university administrators, teachers, and students of creative writing, was writer-in-residence at the University of Washington from 1981 to 1982, and served as consultant to the New York writer's organization Poets & Writers in 1974 and 1975.

Young lectured at numerous universities in the United States and traveled extensively in Canada, Mexico, Portugal, Spain, and France. He has also had presentations of his work produced and broadcast by KQED-TV San Francisco and by the Pacifica Radio Network.

ANALYSIS

Al Young's concern for language, a concern that embraces both mistrust and love, is clearly evinced in his prose. His second novel, *Who Is Angelina?*, and his fourth, *Ask Me Now*, have third-person narrative personae who stand distractingly close to their author; they appear hesitant to act freely for want of purpose. Readers of the first and third novels, however, will quickly recognize Young's ability to render in his first-person narrative personae a vibrant male voice of new adulthood (*Snakes*), or sagacious middle age (*Sitting Pretty*).

The author's background as a professional musician enables him to use music descriptively as well as metaphorically; the reader shares the experience of making music and feeling music make life known. The music of language also affects Young's style. Sparingly, he alters standard syntax and diction, sometimes punctuation, in order to set the speech closer to its natural human tone. His objective is not merely to create contemporary dialect, but also to create an enduring contemporaneity, to offer rhythmically, as the poetmusician should, the nonverbal meanings that language can carry in its sounds. Young creates this quality of speech through narrative personae who speak softly or stridently, sometimes too literally, yet with voices constant and sincere.

Love, like a curse or a whimper, extends most intensely from the individual to those nearby. The contemporary American social dilemma is thereby represented in Young's prose just as it appears in his poetry: Each person must somehow maintain the unity, fidelity, and consistency love requires while grappling for the freedom and oneness that American mythology promises. Although *Snakes* and *Sitting Pretty* are more successful, all Young's novels contain graphic portrayals of mainstream urban America—middle-class people who try to be good at being themselves. They emote, they dream, and they reason. At worst, they stand too large on the page; at best, they find purpose to complement the dignity they feel. Whether he narrates with commentary from a third-person point of view, or with the immediacy of first-person sensory experience, Young confronts the problems of individuals growing into their individuality, and the qualities of life central to the congregate American family.

SNAKES

The narrative persona of Young's first novel, *Snakes*, is M. C. Moore, who recollects his youth and adolescence in the mature, seasoned voice of the novel's master of ceremonies. A novel of formation, *Snakes* is in the *Bildungsroman* tradition and is rendered in a tone of voice at once nostalgic and fatherly. Although he has only snapshots of his true parents by which to remember them, M. C. gradually finds their love implanted in his own initialed name, "so it sound[s] like you had some status," his first lover explains, "whether you did or not." For M. C., the process of learning who he is becomes the composition of his own music.

M. C. discovers music in his soul and he makes music the core of his world. He finds music everywhere, "in the streets, in the country, in people's voices," and "in the way they lead their lives." Providing counterpoint, M. C.'s grandmother Claude offers guidance and family history, and M. C. is her captive audience: "I could listen to Claude talk all day long, and did, many a time. Her voice was like music." The association expands as his views of love and music merge, and women ultimately become "lovable fields of musical energy."

While living with relatives in the South, M. C. learns at the age of ten that music will be his life. His Uncle Donald, a "night rambler" with a "talent for

getting hold of a dollar," turns their impoverished household into a "blind pig," or a Meridian, Mississippi, version of a speakeasy. During his first exposure to the amoral world of adults, M. C. meets Tull, an itinerant jazz pianist who in effect provides the novel's premise: "You'll get it if you keep at it. Listen, just take your time, one note a time over here with your right hand. Just take your time, that's all it is to playin' the piano or anything else. Take your time and work it on out." The impression lasts; M. C. goes on to structure his life around his love of music and his faith that music will help him grow.

Literature also has a formative effect on him. It is not literature as found in the classroom or in books—M. C. attends high school in body only, and barely earns his diploma—rather, literature personified in Shakes, his closest friend, whose name is short for Shakespeare. Shakes has a "greedy memory and a razor tongue." He is bright, musical, and funny: "You hip to Cyrano de Bergerac? Talk about a joker could talk some trash! Cyrano got everybody told! Didn't nobody be messin with Cyrano, ugly as he was."

Yet there is more to know about life than its music and its literature; such knowledge appears in the person of Champ, who exposes M. C. to contemporary jazz and the business hemisphere of that musical world. In his bemusing, self-sacrificial way, Champ also demonstrates his worsening drug addiction and the consequential brutalization of his sensibilities. "Poor Champ," M. C. soon observes while he learns to jam, to feel his music come alive inside himself and issue forth, "who wanted to play an instrument so badly, would stand around working his arms and fingers for hours sometimes, shaping the smoky air in the room into some imaginary saxophone. . . . We all wanted to get good."

The evil to which Champ submits himself opposes the good that he gives M. C.—music as growth and expression. M. C.'s band, "The Masters of Ceremony," discover in their art a meaning that transcends the music they produce, and although the group separates after one demo and some local gigs, M. C.'s early success provides him with a clearer view of the possibilities of his life and a deep sense of wonder. He emerges from his plain, ordinary background complete, communicative, and capable of more, having also achieved his own narrative voice, that husky, now masculine voice the reader has heard maturing since the story's outset. He boards the New York bus a musician, grown: "I don't feel free . . . but I don't feel trapped." Awkwardly, painfully, naturally, M. C. has learned to look for the subtle ironies that enrich both life and art. Ready at last for the rest of what he will be, the young adult takes with him his guitar, his music, and precious recordings of his song "Snakes," which throughout the novel parallels his experience of youth: "The tune sounded simple the first time you heard it, but it wasn't all that simple to play."

WHO IS ANGELINA?

While the narrative voice of *Snakes* provides contrast and consistency—a gradual merging of the maturing young man with his adult consciousness— the narrative voice of *Who Is Angelina?* accomplishes neither. Angelina is already grown, but her adult life has entered a phase of meaningless triviality. This she blames on the shifting cultural milieu of Berkeley, California. Life in Berkeley seems different now—dangerous—and the people's sense of freedom and fun, that community spirit of festivity, is gone. She uses the burglary of her apartment as the justification, and a friend's convenient cash as the means, to skip town—an act she considers the prerequisite for introspection. She flees not only her fictional problems but also her reader as well; a character with both brains and beauty who struggles with mere communal ennui is less than sympathetic. Moreover, even the reader who can overlook her escapist behavior needs to know more about her, and most of her background is provided through recollection and reminiscence. The novel's principal events—travel in Mexico, some romantic sex, an emergency trip home to Detroit, an encounter with a street thief—facilitate reflection by the viewpoint character, and the reader must simply accept her gradual appraisals. Dramatically, little takes place. Most of this novel is exposition; what little action there is consists of Angelina's consideration of an adaptation to what goes on around her.

The unifying thematic metaphor of *Who Is Angelina?* is the act of taking away: Angelina is robbed (her reaction is passive); her lover's mysteri-

ous occupation suggests more of the same; her father is robbed and nearly killed; a friend's purse is stolen (her reaction this time is spontaneous and violent). Eventually, Angelina's searching appears to reach some sort of resolution that makes her worthy of new self-esteem. Yet the reader can only observe, not participate in this search, because—unlike *Snakes*'s composer-narrator—Angelina does not experience within the narrative a process of growth.

Plainly, Angelina is a woman experiencing a crisis of self-identity during a series of events that propel her toward introspection. What she ultimately discovers within herself is a typical American complex of contradictions, such as the one she describes to a fellow traveler early in her journey, the contradiction Americans create by equating individuality with isolation: "Angelina explained that in America it's the individual who matters most and that she and her family, such as it was, lived at separate ends of what's called reality. She too was lonely and fed up with a kind of life she'd been leading."

Whether the narrator addresses the reader directly or through the medium of a letter to a former lover, the exposition continues: "Everyone nowadays is busy digging for roots. Well, I know them well and it doesn't make a damn bit of difference when it comes to making sense of who I am and why I make the kinds of mistakes I do. In the end, I've discovered, it all comes down to being in competition with yourself." At moments, Angelina's concern waxes angry and the culturally contemplative author intrudes: "I'm not so sure that all those chitlins, hamhocks, hog maws, pigsfeet, spareribs and cooking with lard— soulfood so-called—isn't contributing more toward bringing about black genocide, as the phrasemongers would have it, than Sickle Cell Anemia." An important discovery about herself does take place, however, and this is what her wandering is all about. The exploration has been a contemporary one that many young, single Americans never complete: "The truth was that, most of all, she loved open-hearted vulnerable strangers for whom she wasn't strictly obliged to feel anything."

In the end, Angelina also learns that she has been changing at the same time that her surroundings have

been changing. Because she has confused one process with another, separation followed by a reasser-
tion of self followed by a return to her point of departure appears to be cathartic. If so, the reader hopes
that she also learns that life is and continues to be a
process of change, some small part of which is subject to each individual's conscious control. Angelina's recognition of this consciousness is both the
special story and the ordinariness of Young's second
novel.

SITTING PRETTY

Sidney J. Prettymon, the narrative persona of *Sitting Pretty*, is streetwise, sardonic, and ironically
self-conscious. He establishes early a mock superstitious mentality—astronauts may mess up the moon
so that it can no longer be full—and verbalizes "the
integral aspects of [his] personal philosophy to be
cool." Prettymon is dangerously learned: "I cut this
article out of the *National Inquirer* that maintain how
you can succeed and develop yourself and trans-
formate your whole personality by the buildin' up
your vocabulary." His inborn sense of linguistic
sound combines comically with his interest in discovering associative meanings (*radical chic* connotes
to him the concubine of a politically motivated Arab
husband of many wives), but the best humor to be
found in *Sitting Pretty* is derived from Prettymon's
command of the text. The reader is at all times close
to Prettymon, and he exploits the closeness. Having
pondered his plot-situation at the story's outset, he
describes himself to himself as being "on the threshold of destiny, temptation, and fate." Turning aside,
he speaks directly to the reader: "Now, that's bad!
[good] Let me run through that one again so y'all can
savor it."

The narrative opens below the closing sentence of
Mark Twain's *The Adventures of Huckleberry Finn*
(1884); in many ways, Sidney J. Prettymon is a contemporary, self-possessed Jim. As Twain's narrative
control allowed him to elevate linguistic puns through
burlesque to high satirical levels, Young's narrative
is successful here by virtue of its consistently controlled authorial distance: "All I mean by imagination," Prettymon says, "is the way stuff look when you
pull back from it and give it some reflection room."

Prettymon as first-person narrative persona allows the
author to work most effectively; because his imagination provides Prettymon with overview, it allows him
to construct connotative ironies.

The incongruous coexistence of common insight
and aesthetic misinterpretation (Huck does not misinterpret aesthetic qualities; he misses them entirely)
works through sarcastic understatement: "Carpe
Diem, like they say in Latin. Save the day." The author's hand moves subtly, characterizing by mis-
quotation.

Like M. C.'s unknown parents, Prettymon has
given his son an inspirational name with which to
command respect—Aristotle: "He is a lawyer." Professionally successful, Aristotle is a son ungrateful
for his name, and workingclass Prettymon must
struggle to disguise his pride as resentment: "He go
around callin hisself A. Winfred Prettymon. I'm the
one give him his first name and that's his way of
gettin back at me. I wanted him to stand out and be
distinguished and be the bearer of a name that smack
of dignity." Telephoning his daughter, Prettymon
again creates linguistic pandemonium, quoting Ralph
Waldo Emerson in order to reinforce some fatherly
advice, then addressing the reader as the individualistic, pro-consumer Henry David Thoreau: "I hung up
fast, then taken the receiver back off the hook again
so the operator couldn't ring me back for that extra
ten cent. I ain't go nothing but the vastest contempt
for the Phone Company. Leeches and rascals! Need
to be investigated."

Sitting Pretty is Young's best novel in three ways:
consistency of viewpoint, ingenuity of the narrative-
persona, and control of the language. The last must
be perfect for an author to choose suggestive, convincing variations consistent with popular speech.
Young's rendering of black dialect for artistic purpose is found throughout his fiction, and it works effectively here. The novel's language is an uncon-
cealed treasure:

> What with all that racket and commotion and the drink
> I'd just taken, I was startin to feel randy—a term the
> Professor use, British word for horney—randy for my
> own private bottle of sweet wine. Got a job lines up

and just *know* Aristotle gon spring my Plymouth loose. Celebratin time! Time to do that quiet furlough down to Adamo's again.

Surprised, uniquely joyful, Sidney J. Prettymon rediscovers his treasure again and again.

ASK ME NOW

Whereas Young's first and third novels may be paired according to their points of view and the consistency of their narrative voices, *Ask Me Now*, Young's fourth novel, contains narrative weaknesses similar to those found in *Who Is Angelina?* Like Angelina, Woody Knight also finds himself in a world changing at a pace inconsistent with his own ability to change, a major source of frustration for this retired professional basketball player who has always depended upon the musical, built-in rhythms of his game. In life on the outside, it seems to Woody, the court lines keep shifting.

The sequence of events that brings crisis and reunion to Woody's middle-class family is, like the catalytic changes Angelina experiences, rather improbable. As the narrative opens, Woody is not trying to control the ball and the players in motion, but a double arm-load of groceries, rain, a raucous crowd in a shopping mall, the theft of his car, and his wife's winning of a sweepstakes raffle, all in the time it takes to report his loss to a security man who mistakes him for someone he is not. This complexity of absurd events may be American, middle-class normality, but the mid-life, change-related distance Woody discovers growing between himself and his wife (the prize she wins is a trip to Reno, America's emblematic city of the free and the damned), his children, and society becomes less believable as the plot progresses.

The kidnapping of his daughter by the street gang who stole his car and hid cocaine in one of its tires provides crisis and denouement, but at the cost of increasing the distance between Woody and the reader. Secondary characters quickly become contemporary types that provide color, not credibility, and a final chase scene produces climactic anger, not release. On Woody's mind as the final seconds tick away—the police and the mobsters in the mysterious limousine move aside—is the "elbow room" he valued so

highly on the court, the kind of elbow room Angelina sought in her flight to Mexico City. Although this moment contains a great burst of energy—Woody charging in to rescue his daughter, his family, and himself—the climax rings false: He finds and then abandons his daughter in order to pursue the criminal, whom the police ultimately must rescue from a murderous Woody. Despite rather than because of his heroics, all ends well. New insights are gained by all, including that minority of readers for whom the fiction maintains its illusion of reality.

The unbelievable crime and the stock family crisis notwithstanding, Young's control of language is complemented by the twin metaphors of basketball as dance and music as movement. Woody works the ball along the novel's narrative line with eloquence and style. If what he does and what others do to him are too pat, too contrived, his responses are genuine. Woody is a man both worthy of respect and capable of love. He proves himself. The crisis past, he finds himself renewed, as did Angelina, yet, for the reader, there remains at best an evanescent certainty that Woody's reaction to events, not himself, and his reaction to selected alternatives, not decisions, have brought resolution. Unlike the courageous M. C. and the umbrageous Prettymon, Woody is yet incompletely his own. His story ends, but his score remains tied with time remaining on the clock.

Young's main characters experience their passages with a fortitude that affects their worldviews. M. C. copes with the pressures of adolescence and street danger while Angelina seeks alternatives to her past; Prettymon nurtures his self-concept, and Woody deals clumsily with his mid-life crisis. Their stories inform their thoughts and expression. The music and love in their living are heard and felt; the reader wants to dance with them, to celebrate. "Celebratory" is a good word to describe Young's style. His major characters are able to seek and find better versions of themselves when they become able and willing to celebrate what they already are.

SEDUCTION BY LIGHT

For his fifth novel, Young again employs a first-person narrative persona, female and clairvoyant. Mamie Franklin is a woman in her forties, rich in impressions and experience. Having grown up in Mississippi an admirer of her namesake and imaginary tutor/yogi Benjamin Franklin, having made those feelings real through writing, having left home early to perform in the style of Dinah Washington with her husband's group, the Inklings, and having married and begotten her son Benjie out of wedlock, she lives now in Santa Monica with Burley, the man she loves and whose love is returned until—cataclysmically—Mamie's past and future upheave into the narrative present.

As in *Snakes* and the adventures of Sidney J. Prettymon, there is a running commentary on situation and circumstance along with a steady stream of verbal ironies and satiric asides. Mamie works part-time in Beverly Hills as a domestic for Mr. Chrysler and his French wife Danielle, who live in "a big stockbroker Tudor" graced with eucalyptus, or "Noxema trees." Mamie has the confidence of her employers, in fact their favor, as she drives her Honda Civic (nicknamed Sweepea) up the front driveway and strolls into the house. There she discovers a strange, unclothed woman with toes and fingernails painted black who looks like "a bleached-out, fuzzy-headed raccoon," and a Monopoly board, which compromises Mr. Chrysler ("that man loves to play Monopoly . . . with real money").

This kind of fun—the world according to Mamie Franklin—enlivens the novel's complication. Regarding the 1970's, that too-short period when black consciousness merged with African American professional development and economic opportunity, Mamie says, "[I]t mighta looked to the public like anything black was gonna make money . . . but that wasn't nothin but an illusion."

More than witty, these quips come from a woman who made her living as a performer during the 1950's, when the business of entertainment reinstituted racial segregation, and who now sees further deterioration in the filmmaking business: "This old brotherhood junk, funny stuff and jive everybody use to be talkin—all that went out the minute the money started gettin shaky." With a tonal admonition for more education, she observes that the film industry is being run by young white men who "started readin

Variety and *Billboard* when they were nine." For Mamie, age enables one to "ripen into know-how, or better yet, know-when." After all, she says, "The smarter you are, the harder you smart when you fall."

Throughout the novel, light and light imagery brighten the reader's way like the sunlit flowers of Alice Walker's *The Color Purple* (1982) or the moonlit landscapes of Nathaniel Hawthorne's tales. Mamie's vision captures both the brilliance and the business of the California landscape while nuances of Eastern philosophy energize her sensibility and evoke a mood of resolution. Such evocations occur in dreams or dreamlike experiences, such as the surreal state of shock following the reality of an earthquake or the emotional upheaval of sexual renewal. "It was all done with light," Mamie says of cinematic production and marketing. Like the girl she "use to be" watching a film at the Grand Lux Theatre, Mamie learns that "pretty much every last one of us out here [in California] gettin seduced." As girl and as mother, as woman and as lover, Mamie looks over her shoulder to see "nothin but light, not a thing but light quiverin and makin patterns on a screen."

Throughout her life, Mamie has had enlightening experiences. She recalls a vision of sunlight playing over a leaf, how the light "shimmered all around it; then the leaf sends out this invisible feeler [and] suck up the light around it, drink it up, sip on it like you would a glassa buttermilk." Similarly, when Mamie's housemate Burley returns in spirit, he describes his passage from life: "It was like this hole opened up in the middle of my forehead and the light started pourin into it."

Moreover, Mamie contemplates the textuality of her life by the light of her contemplations, suggesting that this affects the storyteller, too:

> Where do you begin when you start tellin your story and rememberin as you go along? Do you start with the source of light itself, the sun? Or do you start with what the sun touches, the moon? Or do you only deal with what the moonlight touches?

We must consider the light by which we live our lives, Mamie suggests, as we rewrite the texts of our lives:

It's actually possible in one lifetime to do so much and to get caught up in so many of your own illusions and lies and half lies until it can finally come down to sun versus moon versus moonlight.

Celebratory and down-to-earth, Young's novels glow with human warmth. In the mode of vernacular speech, *Seduction by Light* rings true with contemporary experience while transmuting everyday life into the light of love.

Joseph F. Battaglia,
updated by Daryl F. Mallett

OTHER MAJOR WORKS

POETRY: *Dancing*, 1969; *The Song Turning Back into Itself*, 1971; *Geography of the Near Past*, 1976; *The Blues Don't Change: New and Selected Poems*, 1982; *Heaven: Collected Poems 1958-1988*, 1988; *Straight No Chaser*, 1994; *Conjugal Visits: And Other Poems in Verse and Prose*, 1996.

NONFICTION: *Bodies and Soul: Musical Memoirs*, 1981; *Kinds of Blue: Musical Memoirs*, 1984; *Things Ain't What They Used to Be: Musical Memoirs*, 1987; *Mingus/Mingus: Two Memoirs*, 1989 (with Janet Coleman); *Drowning in a Sea of Love: Musical Memoirs*, 1995.

EDITED TEXTS: *Yardbird Lives!*, 1978 (with Ishmael Reed); *Calafía: The California Poetry*, 1978 (contributing editor; Ishmael Reed, director); *Changing All Those Changes*, 1976 (with James P. Girard); *Zeppelin Coming Down*, 1976 (with William Lawson); *Quilt*, 1981 (with Reed); *Quilt 2*, 1982 (with Reed); *Quilt 3*, 1983 (with Reed); *Quilt 4*, 1984 (with Reed); *Quilt 5*, 1986 (with Reed); *African American Literature: A Brief Introduction and Anthology*, 1996.

BIBLIOGRAPHY

Bell, Bernard W. *The Afro-American Novel and Its Tradition*. Amherst: University of Massachusetts Press, 1987. Bell compares African American writers and their works. Especially useful is his comparison of Young's *Snakes* to 1960's novels by Gordon Parks, Kristin Hunter, Rosa Gunn, Barry Beckham, and Louise Meriwether. Because Bell classifies these works as *Bildungsromane* in the European literary tradition, his analysis helps establish Young as a viable black-experience author in the United States and abroad.

Davis, Thadious M., and Trudier Harris, eds. *Dictionary of Literary Biography*. Vol. 33. In *Afro-American Fiction Writers After 1955*. Detroit: Gale Research, 1984. This reference provides a cursory glance at Young's career as a postmodernist writer on the American scene. The citation itself is brief yet helpful to place the author in the mainstream of contemporary writers of various ethnic backgrounds.

Draper, James P. *Black Literature Criticism: Excerpts from Criticism of the Most Significant Works of Black Authors over the Past Two Hundred Years*. Detroit: Gale Research, 1997. Contains a fifteen-page chapter on Young that includes criticism, interviews from 1976 to 1989, a short biography, and a bibliography.

Johnson, Charles. *Being and Race: Black Writers Since 1970*. Bloomington: Indiana University Press, 1988. Contains a thorough discussion of the common background of black American writers plus lengthy discussions of female and male viewpoint-writing, with philosophical references and a preface which establishes the text's postmodernist critical approach.

Kirkpatrick, D. L., ed. *Contemporary Novelists*. 4th ed. New York: St. Martin's Press, 1986. This compilation features a condensed biography of Young plus an extensive listing of the author's works through 1982. A useful guide to Young as an emerging American artist, this reference profiles him among novelists of various ethnic backgrounds.

Matney, William C., ed. *Who's Who Among Black Americans*. 5th ed. Lake Forest, Ill.: Educational Communications, 1988. A collection of interviews and personal profiles, this presentation of the author considers his manifold interests as a young African American writer. Those who know Young as poet, musician, screenwriter, editor, or teacher will find useful material regarding the manifold interests of the novelist.

Ostendorf, Berndt. *Black Literature in White America*. Totowa, N.J.: Barnes & Noble Books, 1982. Considers black writers' roots and the influence of music on their lives and art as both expression and performance. While the references to Young are brief and pertain to his poetry, the musical context of this presentation will be useful for those researching Young's concern for music in American culture and literature.

Shockley, Ann Allen, and Sue P. Chandler. *Living Black American Authors: A Bibliographical Directory*. New York: R. R. Bowker, 1973. Recognition of black writers was new during the early 1970's, especially in the overall context of American letters. This article contains extensive interpretive detail regarding Young's early works, his achievements other than writing fiction, and his personal values and insights.

(Jacques Robert, Editions Gallimard)

MARGUERITE YOURCENAR
Marguerite de Crayencour

Born: Brussels, Belgium; June 8, 1903
Died: Northeast Harbor, Maine; December 17, 1987

PRINCIPAL LONG FICTION

Alexis: Ou, Le Traité du vain combat, 1929 (*Alexis*, 1984)

La Nouvelle Eurydice, 1931

Denier du rêve, 1934 (*A Coin in Nine Hands*, 1982)

Le Coup de grâce, 1939 (*Coup de Grâce*, 1957)

Mémoires d'Hadrien, 1951 (*Memoirs of Hadrian*, 1954; also known as *Hadrian's Memoirs*)

L'Œuvre au noir, 1968 (*The Abyss*, 1976)

Anna, Soror . . . , 1981

Comme l'eau qui coule, 1982 (*Two Lives and a Dream*, 1987)

OTHER LITERARY FORMS

Marguerite Yourcenar, though best known as a novelist, wrote in virtually every other literary form

as well. Her first published work, *Le Jardin des chimères* (1921), was a poem about Icarus. It was followed by a collection of poems entitled *Les Dieux ne sont pas morts* (1922). Of these early works she did not speak highly. *Feux* (1936; *Fires*, 1981) is a collection of prose poems about love centered on such characters as Phaedra, Achilles, Antigone, Sappho, and Mary Magdalene, but shot through with images and allusions that reflect the modern world. *Les Charités d'Alcippe et autres poèmes* (1956; *The Alms of Alcippe*, 1982) is another verse collection. *Pindare* (1932) is a study of the Greek poet, another early work with which she later became dissatisfied. *Les Songes et les sorts* (1938) concerns the mythic aspects of dreams. The collection *Sous bénéfice d'inventaire* (1962; *The Dark Brain of Piranesi and Other Essays*, 1984) includes essays on such diverse subjects as the engravings of Piranesi, the château of Chenonceaux, Selma Lagerlöf, and Thomas Mann. *Mishima: Ou, La Vision du vide* (1980; *Mishima: A Vision of the Void*, 1986) is a study of the Japanese novelist. *La Mort conduit l'attelage* (1934) and

Nouvelles orientales (1938; *Oriental Tales*, 1985) are volumes of short stories. She also wrote many plays. She translated the poetry of Constantine Cavafy and Hortense Flexner; a volume of black spirituals, *Fleuve profond, sombre rivière* (1964); and a selection of Greek poetry, *La Couronne et la lyre* (1979). *Le Labyrinthe du monde*, a three-part chronicle of her forebears, comprises *Souvenirs pieux* (1974), *Archives du nord* (1977), and the unpublished "Quoi, l'éternité?" *Les Yeux ouverts: Entretiens avec Matthieu Galey* (1980; With Open Eyes: Conversations with Matthieu Galey, 1984) is a series of interviews in which she talks about her life, her values, and her work.

ACHIEVEMENTS

Yourcenar's greatest achievement is probably *Memoirs of Hadrian*, a novel in the form of a letter written by the Emperor shortly before his death. Like nearly all of her mature works, it had a long gestation period—more than a quarter of a century in fact. She destroyed some early versions of it, and between 1939 and 1948, she put it wholly aside. *The Abyss* is another novel with a long history. The original impulse goes back to the early 1920's, and the final version is a development of material from the first story in the 1934 collection *La Mort conduit l'attelage*. Such perfectionism is seldom rewarded with popular success, however respectful the critics may be. *Memoirs of Hadrian*, however, was not only very favorably reviewed (like most of her previous works) but also widely read by a large and enthusiastic public. It won the Prix Femina-Vacaresco. Yourcenar was awarded the Légion d'Honneur and the National Order of Merit. Other honors include membership in the Royal Academy of Belgium, the Prix Combat (1963), the Prix Femina for *The Abyss*, the Grand Prix National des Lettres (1974), and the Grand Prix de la Littérature de l'Académie Française (1977). In 1980, international attention was focused on her and her work when she was elected to the Académie Française, the first woman member in its history.

BIOGRAPHY

Marguerite Yourcenar was born Marguerite de Crayencour in Brussels in 1903. Her mother died a few days after Marguerite was born, and she was reared by her father, who supervised her education at home. They would read aloud to each other in French, English, Latin, and Greek. As a child, she lived sometimes at Mont Noir, the family home near Lille, and sometimes in Paris or the south of France. Her father took her to England in 1914, in flight from the Germans. A year later, they returned to Paris and then fled to the south of France.

In *Les Yeux ouverts*, Yourcenar says that she felt herself and her father to be contemporaries from the time she was about thirteen. He paid for the publication of her first book, *Le Jardin des chimères*, as a Christmas gift, and he helped her to invent the anagrammatic pseudonym which she later made her legal name. He died when she was in her midtwenties. His portrait is given at length in the second volume of her family chronicle, *Archives du nord*.

Yourcenar traveled extensively. She made her first visit to the United States during the winter and spring of 1937-1938. At the beginning of the war in 1939, she returned to the United States at the invitation of an American friend, Grace Frick, whom she had met in Paris two years earlier. Frick became Yourcenar's lifelong companion and her English translator. What was planned as a visit of six months became a permanent change of residence for Yourcenar. For a while she taught French and comparative literature part-time. She and Grace Frick (Yourcenar always referred to her by her full name) first visited Mount Desert Island in Maine in the early 1940's, and they eventually bought a house there. Grace Frick died of breast cancer in 1979.

Yourcenar became an American citizen in 1947. Among her many interests were an active concern for the environment. She contributed to a variety of organizations for reducing overpopulation and pollution and for saving whales, seals, trees—whatever is threatened with extinction by avaricious exploiters.

ANALYSIS

Some of Marguerite Yourcenar's novels have appeared in English, including *A Coin in Nine Hands, Coup de Grâce, Memoirs of Hadrian*, and *The Abyss*. *A Coin in Nine Hands*, first published in 1934 and extensively revised in 1959, takes place in Rome in 1933 and is thus unlike the other three novels in having (in its first version at least) a contemporary setting. It is also atypical in the number of its important characters. *Coup de Grâce* has only three major characters. *Memoirs of Hadrian* and *The Abyss* have large casts of secondary figures, but each is firmly centered on a single protagonist. *A Coin in Nine Hands*, in contrast, gives fairly full treatment to about a dozen characters, some of them only tenuously connected to one another. The looseness of structure that might have resulted is guarded by the concentration of the time scheme: Though the novel contains a certain amount of retrospective narrative (the past is always a concern for Yourcenar), the main action is confined to a period of about eighteen hours.

A COIN IN NINE HANDS

The English title refers to a unique structural feature of the novel, its tracing of the passage of a ten-lira piece from one character to another. The nine characters who handle the coin, and several others as well, are linked by a network of relationships, often casual or accidental, although none of them sees the whole pattern. The coin, though it is in itself of no great value to any of them and might seem a facile contrivance to a skeptical reader, in fact takes on considerable symbolic weight. In the afterword to the revised version of the novel, Yourcenar calls the coin "the symbol of contact between human beings each lost in his own passions and in his intrinsic solitude." The casual or mechanical nature of many of these contacts is obvious, and the coin, belonging to anybody and finally to nobody in particular, suggests the inability of the characters to form any real bonds with others. In *Les Yeux ouverts*, she offers another meaning for the coin, saying that it represents the external world, the State, all that is opposed to the intimate, secret lives of people. This meaning is also suggested by the title of the play that Yourcenar adapted from the novel in 1961, *Rendre à César*, an echo of Mark 12:17.

Any coin has two sides, and a symbolic coin may well be allowed several. Another meaning is suggested by the French title for the novel, *Denier du rêve*, literally "denarius of the dream." The coin is as-

sociated with the characters' dreams or illusions. The reader first sees the coin in the hand of Lina Chiari, a prostitute who received it from a man who has become a regular client since his wife deserted him. The narrator comments that although love cannot be bought, dreams can be, and adds, "The little money Paolo Farina gave Lina each week was used to create for him a welcome illusion; that is to say, perhaps the only thing in the world that does not deceive." Lina, after learning that she must have a mastectomy, uses the coin to buy a lipstick, makes up her face, and forces a smile that gradually becomes sincere: "Party to an illusion that saved her from horror, Lina Chiari was kept from despair by a thin layer of makeup." The storekeeper who sold her the lipstick buys votive candles to petition the Madonna for relief from his domestic problems, and the candles "maintain the fiction of a hope." The candle vendor, learning of the sale of her childhood home in Sicily, to which she has long dreamed of returning, buys coals to light a fire to asphyxiate herself. Marcella, the seller of the coals, passes the coin to her estranged husband as payment for a gun she stole from him, with which she plans to shoot Mussolini. Her husband is in good standing with the Fascists, and she hates herself for still feeling drawn to him in spite of his politics. The gesture of paying for the gun is intended to free her from any debt to him, to purchase an illusion of independence. He, in turn, uses the coin to buy flowers for a stranger to whom he has made love in a film theater, as if to mitigate the sordidness of the encounter. The flower vendor, uneasy at having been called a miser, proves to herself that the charge is untrue by passing the coin to a man that she takes for a beggar. He is in fact a famous painter, old and frightened by increasingly frequent attacks of angina. He throws the coin into the Trevi Fountain, like those tourists who hope to return, but thinking instead that he may soon see a quite different "Eternal City." Finally, under cover of darkness, a worker scoops up the coin with a handful of others and goes to a tavern to purchase a few hours of exaltation and oblivion in drink. Each character uses the coin to maintain a protective illusion or to soften the pain of a loss.

As the foregoing sketch indicates, death is a prominent theme in the novel. Lina thinks of her impending mastectomy as a death. The attempt on Mussolini's life is the novel's central event, and Marcella expects that even if she succeeds she will be killed. She is right. Her most important confederate, a dissident writer named Carlo Stevo, who has been deported to Lipari Island, has exerted a potent influence on her and on several other characters, too. Ironically, the reader learns halfway through the book that Stevo has been dead since before the story began. For Marcella the news is a blow, the more so since Stevo's captors seem to have succeeded in breaking his spirit before he died. His death increases the sense of the futility of Marcella's attempt.

The settings often reinforce the novel's emphasis on death. The darkness in Marcella's little bedroom is repeatedly mentioned. As she moves toward the place where she hopes to kill and knows she will be killed, the street becomes a "river of shades . . . carrying along in its waves inert, drowned corpses who thought they were alive." The film theater that is the setting of the immediately succeeding chapter is a "cave full of specters," a version of the underworld of classical myth. The films offer illusory reflections of real life so distorted that they suggest life's opposite. Moreover, the fact that Marcella has been killed is withheld until the end of this scene. Thus, the whole chapter draws together the themes of illusion and death.

The larger setting, the Eternal City itself, is rendered with remarkable economy. There are no extended descriptions or set pieces, yet the city is vividly evoked. Moreover, Yourcenar succeeds in giving it a kind of double identity. There is the Rome of 1933 and, opening out behind it, the long vista of its past, the Rome of history. The characters, too, transcend their particular historical moments through their connections with mythological figures. The 1959 version reduces the frequency of such mythical parallels, but they are still there, giving added dimension to the characterization. Marcella, moving toward her fatal encounter, is "like a Greek woman in Hades, like a Christian one in Dante's Inferno, carrying a burden as old as History itself." It is not a matter of detailed correspondences in the sequence of events or in the relationships among characters, as in, for example, James Joyce's *Ulysses* (1922). Rather, the mythological references arise out of particular situations and character traits. Moreover, a single character may be associated with several mythological figures and a single mythological figure with several different characters, so that the correspondences have the indefiniteness and flexibility of figures in dreams. Thus, Marcella is called Medusa, Judith, Martha, and Mary, and she resembles Electra as well (Mussolini had betrayed her father). The candle vendor sees her feeding pigeons and is reminded of a statue of Venus with her doves, but the candle vendor's sister, a film star, is also a Venus, and a Narcissus, too. A young friend of Marcella and Stevo is also Narcissus, and he is Thanatos and Hermes as well. There is something of Antigone in the candle vendor. The old flower seller is the Earth Mother, while the worker who takes the coins from the fountain is a kind of Dionysus.

These parallels would be merely empty gestures, however, if the characterization were not so rich and firm in realistic terms. The dozen or so major figures are all interesting and convincing, and there are a good number of secondary ones who are brought fully to life in the space of a few paragraphs. On the whole, the most effective characterizations are of women, and the women carry the story. The novel therefore takes a special place in the body of Yourcenar's work that is available in English, for (along with most of the prose poems in *Fires*) it constitutes an interesting counterbalance to her male-dominated novels. The men in *A Coin in Nine Hands* are often remarkable, but Marcella, Lina, the candle vendor, and the old flower seller are extraordinary.

COUP DE GRÂCE

Coup de Grâce appeared in 1939, only about twenty years after the time of the events it describes. Yet in spite of its modern setting, it is in a sense a historical novel. In her preface, Yourcenar cites dramatist Jean Racine's view that "remoteness in space . . . is almost the equivalent of distance in time." The story is set in Kurland during the Baltic civil wars in the years immediately following World War I, a place and an episode which drew little attention from the rest of Europe. Because of the remoteness of its setting, the novel required patient research and an effort of imaginative projection of a kind similar to that which later went into *Memoirs of Hadrian* and *The Abyss*, though *Coup de Grâce* was written in a matter of weeks, while the other two took years to reach their final forms.

The civil war makes a fitting background for this story of three people locked in a close and ultimately destructive relationship by feelings that—in two of them at least—oscillate unpredictably between love and repulsion. The story (which the author says she heard from "one of the best friends of the principal person concerned") is told in the first person by Erick von Lhomond, a soldier of fortune with a penchant for lost causes. He is a Prussian with some French and Baltic blood. His best friend, Conrad de Reval, is a Balt with some Russian ancestry. There is between them a physical similarity so close that they are often mistaken for brothers. Erick has chosen to limit his experiences with women to commerce with the least respectable of them; his strongest inclinations are homosexual. The circumstances of the narrative (Erick is telling his story to two auditors met by chance in a train station) preclude his dwelling on the nature of his bond with Conrad; in any case, homosexuality is not the main issue in the novel, and Conrad is the least important of the three main characters. The central conflict is between Erick and Conrad's sister, Sophie.

As a young officer, Erick joins a German volunteer corps supporting the White Russians against the Bolsheviks in Estonia and Kurland. Conrad turns up, and the two are posted to Kratovitsy, Conrad's family estate, which had been briefly occupied by the Reds. There Sophie falls in love with her brother's friend. The mixture of bloodlines in Erick and in Sophie suggests their conflicting emotions, and their relationship develops in a pattern of ironic oscillations that reflect the uncertainties of the political struggle.

Because Erick resembles her brother, Sophie's attraction to him seems to involve a kind of transference of an unconscious incestuous impulse. Sophie and Conrad also resemble each other, a fact that complicates Erick's response to the girl. When she confesses her love to Erick, he is stunned, but they

develop an intimacy "like that between victim and executioner"—a simile that foreshadows the novel's conclusion. His attitude toward her fluctuates between insolence and tenderness, and "when she began to mean more to me, I suppressed the tenderness." He comes to see her as an adversary whom, in a "show of bravado," he treats as a friend. In an attempt to arouse his jealousy, she turns to promiscuous relations with other soldiers. He remains indifferent to these activities as long as it is obvious to him that she has no pleasure in them.

The turning point in their relationship comes one night when Erick sees a light in Sophie's window during an air attack. He goes to her room and rebukes her for endangering the lives of everyone in the house, but then he himself leads her out onto the balcony. The language and imagery of this scene in which the two perversely court death is full of references to love and sexual consummation as well as to physical cruelty and death. They embrace, but then, in a characteristically abrupt reversal, Erick's "ecstasy changed into horror," and what Sophie sees in his expression makes her recoil, "covering her face with her upraised arm, like a child who is slapped."

In reaction, Sophie takes a new lover, Volkmar, and this time her choice upsets Erick. As Sophie's resentment of Erick begins to outweigh her love for him, his jealousy, ironically, increases. When she ostentatiously kisses Volkmar at a party, Erick slaps her in public, and the ground of their relationship shifts again, for she comes to his door later that night. For fear of waking Conrad, Erick does not admit her, but he finds himself considering marriage to her.

Volkmar tells Sophie of Erick's homosexuality, and she leaves Kratovitsy after a brief but painful confrontation with Erick. Her sympathies have long been with the Bolsheviks, and she sets out to join them, wearing men's clothing provided by the mother of the young man who had converted her to the Red side.

Erick conceals from Conrad his role in Sophie's departure. Conrad's love for his sister turns to hatred, and he begins to believe that she had long been spying on their band for the Reds. Yourcenar underlines this reversal with one of those paradoxes that are a feature of her gnomic style. Erick says that the brother and sister grew to be complete strangers "such as only two members of the same family can manage to become." In this novel, hatred grown out of love is the strongest kind, just as a civil war is often the bitterest of wars.

It is not long after Sophie's flight that Erick summarizes the political developments that are weakening the anti-Bolshevist cause and comments, "Europe was betraying us." The public events thus seem to reflect the personal situation. They are forced to abandon Kratovitsy. Erick is in command. Conrad is killed in a skirmish with some Cossack cavalry and is thus spared the next engagement, in which Erick's troop captures Sophie with a small band of Bolshevik soldiers. Neither side is taking prisoners. In a final interview, Sophie rejects with indifference Erick's efforts to find a way to save her. Here and in the final scene, the language and certain gestures repeat the love theme in inextricable conjunction with its opposite, as had been the case in the scene on the balcony. The next morning, after the other prisoners have been shot by the butcher from Kratovitsy, who now serves as executioner for the troop, Sophie's turn comes. She indicates to her former family servant that she wants Erick to pull the trigger. He does so. He interprets her request at first as conclusive proof of her love. "But I understood afterwards that she only wished to take revenge, leaving me prey to remorse." He remarks wryly, "One is always trapped, somehow, in dealings with women."

As he prepares to fire at Sophie, Erick says, "I clung to the thought that I had wanted to put an end to Conrad, and that this was the same thing." Conrad had lain dying all night in the cemetery where the Cossacks had attacked them, and Erick says that cowardice prevented his putting an end to his friend's agony. This cowardice, however, is clearly not fear for his own safety, for, at Conrad's request, Erick lights "one of those iron lanterns that they hang on the tombstones in that region," in spite of the risk of its drawing enemy fire.

Through the reference to the possibility that the lantern would draw enemy fire, which recalls the scene between Erick and Sophie on the balcony, and

through Erick's thinking of Conrad's death as he fires at Sophie, the link between the brother and the sister is reaffirmed, and it seems that the reader is to regard the terrible end of Sophie as another heroic death. She chooses her own fate and even appoints her executioner, thus gaining the upper hand over Erick, whom she at last forces to do her bidding. Her choice, moreover, raises him to the level of tragic heroism. Erick does not dwell on it (his personality, Yourcenar warns in the preface, often leads him "to offer the least favorable interpretation of his actions"); to administer the *coup de grâce* in this case surely requires as much courage as to request it. The ending, though grim, fully justifies the connotations of chivalric nobility carried by the novel's title.

MEMOIRS OF HADRIAN

Memoirs of Hadrian resembles *Coup de Grâce* in that it is a first-person monologue in which a character confronts his past. This is a device Yourcenar used often and favored, because, as she says in the preface to the earlier novel, it eliminates the author's point of view and puts the reader in immediate contact with a character looking directly at his own life. The monologue is here cast in the form of a letter from the dying Emperor to the young Marcus Aurelius. In *Les Yeux ouverts*, Yourcenar says that when she unexpectedly recovered a draft of the opening of the novel in 1948 (in a trunk that had been stored in Switzerland during the war), she found its tone, that of an intimate journal, inappropriate for the character. The Romans kept no journals in the contemporary sense of the term, so something rather more formal and organized was required. Her approach depends heavily on her ability to portray a voice actually speaking; in fact, in "Reflections on the Composition of *Memoirs of Hadrian*" (appended to later editions of the novel), she calls the book a "portrait of a voice."

In *Les Yeux ouverts*, Yourcenar remarks on a similarity between Hadrian and Erick. They are alike in being at once hard and tender, and alike, too, in their lucidity. Another obvious parallel is their bisexuality, though Erick's is actually something of a technicality: He is a misogynist who has had little pleasure in his relations with women. Hadrian's attitude toward women is more positive. As a young man, he had a string of mistresses whom he genuinely enjoyed, and his nonphysical relationship with Plotina, the wife of his predecessor Trajan, shows that his deeper friendships are not limited by considerations of gender. (Here, too, historical authenticity comes into play: Yourcenar notes in *Les Yeux ouverts* that exclusively homosexual individuals were rare in antiquity.) For Hadrian, however, as for Erick, the fully satisfying relationship is with one of his own sex—namely, the Bithynian youth Antinous. Just as Conrad may have died to save Erick's life, Antinous's suicide is a ritual offering which the youth believes will in some mystical way extend Hadrian's life. Hadrian's indirect responsibility for Antinous's death can be compared to Erick's more direct responsibility for Sophie's. Yourcenar has called Hadrian "a man who was *almost* wise." Hadrian fails in wisdom, by a growing insensitivity to the youth's feelings, as he comes to take him increasingly for granted. Antinous's suicide is a complex act. It is both a gift and a reproach, and Hadrian sees that he has been master of Antinous's destiny but that he "must leave to the boy the credit for his own death." Similarly, Erick credits Sophie "with the initiative for her death."

Memoirs of Hadrian, however, is a larger book in every sense than *Coup de Grâce*; the paradoxical link between love and hatred and the mysterious affinity between love and death make up only one of its themes. Antinous, whom Hadrian calls "that fair stranger who each loved one is," is only one of several characters who evoke in the Emperor an acute sense of the separateness of others. His friends Plotina and Attianus were present at the death of Trajan and may have been responsible for Hadrian's being named the successor. One of the few other witnesses, an enemy of Hadrian, died suddenly, shortly after Trajan did. Hadrian has never known for certain to what lengths his friends had to go in order to secure for him the imperial succession.

In addition to the impenetrable isolation in which the most fundamental parts of people's experience is wrapped, Hadrian is concerned at the start of the book with the shapelessness of his own life. By the end, however, one's strongest sense is not of shape-lessness but of a clearly defined arc, or—to use a figure the author herself invokes in *Les Yeux ouverts*—a pyramid. One follows Hadrian through the years of his education and his preparation for power, to the high point of public glory combined with personal happiness, thence to the loss of Antinous and a correspondingly important defeat in the public sphere—namely, the Jewish revolt under Simon Bar-Kochba. The phase of decline continues through the death of the brilliant and charming Lucius, whom he had adopted as his successor; the struggle for patience under the burden of failing health; and the difficult preparation for the attempt "to enter into death with open eyes." Without ever denying the considerable role of chance, the narrative succeeds in imposing a pattern on experience. Moreover, the Emperor overcomes to some extent the isolation of the individual self, for he takes the reader with him virtually as far as he himself can go in the contemplation of his past and in the experience of his approaching death. Indeed, it seems possible to say that the reader comes to know Hadrian better than Hadrian knew Antinous or Plotina.

The convincing characterization proceeds in part from an imaginative identification that Yourcenar has described in terms almost mystical, "a method akin to controlled delirium," as she says in "Reflections on the Composition of *Memoirs of Hadrian*." In *Les Yeux ouverts* (which takes its title from Hadrian's last words), she speaks of the necessity of cultivating an interior silence that enables her to hear what the characters have to say. She also mentions a letter from a university professor who had set his students the exercise of translating a page of the novel into Greek (the language in which the Emperor says he thought). Yourcenar decided to try to do the same and found that much of it went easily into Greek, but one or two phrases did not. The reason, she concluded, was that they were hers, not Hadrian's. In "Reflections on the Composition of *Memoirs of Hadrian*," speaking of the choice of a first-person narrative, she remarks, "Surely Hadrian could speak more forcibly and more subtly of his life than could I." She says, too, that at some moments it even occurred to her that the Emperor was lying. "In such cases I had to let him lie, like the rest of us." Through her method of intense contemplation, her characters take on an independent reality which she succeeds in conveying to her readers. Speaking in *Les Yeux ouverts* of the death of the central character in *The Abyss*, she says that she loved him too much to be willing to make him suffer greatly.

In spite of the semimystical terms in which Yourcenar discusses this contemplative preparation, it is firmly grounded in preparation of a different kind—long and painstaking historical research. Her bibliographic note attests the thoroughness and range of her reading of both primary and secondary sources, and professional historians have endorsed her scholarship. For her, the public and political aspects of Hadrian's life are at least as important as the private and philosophical. He was a man of action as well as of letters. She says in *Les Yeux ouverts* that she would not have seen the statesman if she had written the novel earlier, and in "Reflections on the Composition of *Memoirs of Hadrian*" she remarks, "The fact of having lived in a world which is toppling around us [during World War II] had taught me the importance of the Prince." With remarkable economy, the novel succeeds in conveying the extent of the Emperor's public achievements: his encouragement of trade, his interest in founding and rebuilding cities, his administrative reforms, his fostering of the culture of Greece, his reversal of the expansionist policies of Trajan in order to concentrate on a policy of stability within the existing frontiers of the already vast empire, his commitment to peace. In Hadrian, supreme political power was united with an incisive and disciplined intellect as well as with a highly developed artistic sense. The convincing presentation of all of his facets evidences Yourcenar's extraordinary gifts, and *Memoirs of Hadrian* is perhaps the most persuasive justification of the often maligned genre of the historical novel that the twentieth century has produced.

THE ABYSS

The Abyss is a third-person narrative with, for the most part, invented rather than historical characters (though the author's note validates many of the details of the story by citing parallels from the lives of real people). The hero is, like Hadrian, a man who

seeks to be useful. Zeno, a physician, identifies himself at one point with the words, "I take care of my fellow men." The novel is set in a time of unrelenting religious and political conflict, the mid-sixteenth century, and it is in every way a darker book. Its theme, as the epigraph to part 1 indicates, is freedom and people's ability to choose. In "Reflections on the Composition of *Memoirs of Hadrian*," Yourcenar says that in the second century "men could think and express themselves with full freedom," and Hadrian's position as Emperor made his own freedom all the greater. In Zeno's world, however, freedom is narrowly circumscribed. Zeno must plant obscure passages in his books to avoid being accused of heresy, and even with this precaution his writings are often suppressed. When he returns to Bruges, his birthplace, after half a lifetime of travels, he must conceal his true identity. Figurative and literal references to prisons and traps occur throughout the book. "Who would be so besotted," Zeno asks at the beginning of his travels, "as to die without having made at least the round of this, his prison?" He refers to the body as a prison, and he ends his life in an actual prison. On the eve of his death, he is offered the opportunity to save himself from the fire by recanting: He can win physical freedom at the price of his intellectual freedom. Having concealed a scalpel among the few personal belongings left to him, he has one last liberty of choice, but he realizes that he could be deprived of even this by a chance intrusion of his jailer or a priest. Only at the moment of his death does he finally feel free. He had once heard of a man burned at the stake at the end of a long chain which enabled him to run about in flames until he fell. "I have often reflected that that horror could serve as allegory for the plight of a man who is left *almost* free."

That is one of a large number of references to fire, which serves as the other of the book's two governing images. In an early scene in which Zeno is sitting by a hearth, the narrator calls him "the companion of the fire." Zeno has been a student of alchemy, and the many images of fire are directly or indirectly related to the use of that element in alchemical experiments. Transformations analogous to those at which alchemy aimed are everywhere stressed, though they tend to be baleful ones. The plague transforms its victims overnight. During a rainstorm in Innsbruck, air and water "turn the world into one vast, melancholy chaos." The human bowels perform an alchemy which proceeds constantly, in secret and independently of the conscious will. Life passes into corruption. Neither are these changes restricted to the physical level. Zeno learns that "ideas die, like men." John Calvin's doctrines are "rebellion transformed into law." The hidden meanings Zeno puts into his works "alter the whole." Knowledge and contemplation can be transmuted into power.

In alchemy lie the fumbling beginnings of modern chemistry. This search represents people's attempt to gain control over the processes of nature. In a long chapter at the center of the novel, a chapter whose importance is indicated by its having the same title as the novel itself, Zeno contemplates his past. He had turned away from alchemy, impatient with its encumbrance of arcane metaphors, to study "such sciences as are less imbedded in the stuff of dreams." Now, however, he finds that

> the two branches of the curve, the metaphysical and the pragmatic, were meeting; the *mors philosophica* had been accomplished: The operator, burned by the acids of his own research, had become both subject and object, the experiment that he had thought to confine within the limits of the laboratory had extended itself to every human experience.

Later in the novel, Zeno remarks that alchemy, like magic, postulates the unity of matter, and the chapter entitled "The Abyss" describes a kind of visionary insight into that unity. It is full of images of things and people merging and fusing, images of the breaking down of the boundaries of time and space. Zeno himself passes through the changes that turn water to mist and rain to snow, and he unites himself with the element of fire. Zeno's experience in this chapter reflects that phase of alchemical experiment called "the black work" (the novel's French title is *L'Œuvre au noir*). According to the author's note, this is the first and "most difficult phase of the alchemist's process, the separation and dissolution of substance." The term may be applied to both "daring experiments on

matter itself . . . [and to] trials of the mind in discarding all forms of routine and prejudice."

The kind of correspondence that the last quotation establishes between two different activities recurs in other forms throughout the book. The Renaissance concept of the relation between macrocosm and microcosm appears in Zeno's statement that mathematics, mechanics, and alchemy "apply to our study of the universe only those same truths which our bodies teach us; for in our bodies is repeated the structure of the Whole." The abyss through which Zeno passes is "both beyond the celestial sphere and within the human skull." Zeno bases his limited faith in astrology on the system of correspondences, and he calls the human heart a "fiery star palpitating in the dark of our bodies." He goes so far as to conceive of the possibility of roads in time like those in space.

Of the various areas of human experience in which transformations comparable to those of alchemy are seen to occur, two gradually assume special prominence in the pattern of the novel: religion and sex. They are linked to each other and to alchemy by a network of analogies and images. Zeno returns to Bruges in the company of the prior of a monastery of the Cordeliers, whom he met by chance in Paris. The two become friends, and the Prior gives the physician the use of a small building attached to the monastery, in which Zeno opens a dispensary for the poor. In one of their conversations, the Prior mentions an alchemical theory that Jesus Christ is the true Philosopher's Stone and that the *opus magnum* of the alchemists is equivalent to the transubstantiation of the bread and wine into the body and blood of Christ in the Mass. Zeno says that this shows merely "that the human mind has a certain bent," yet it is surely an important indication of the bent of the author's mind. Moreover, the link thus suggested is reinforced by the very fact of the friendship between the scientist and the churchman, a bond so strong that Zeno stays in Bruges longer than is safe because the Prior is dying and the physician will not abandon him. One night, Zeno hears footsteps hurrying toward his door. No one is there, but he goes to the Prior and finds him on the point of death. At the moment of his own death, Zeno again hears footsteps.

Yourcenar says in *Les Yeux ouverts* that they are those of the Prior.

A link between sex and religion is established early in the novel, in the powerful chapter describing the way the religious enthusiasm of the Anabaptists in Münster transformed itself into debauchery under the leadership of John of Leyden. More important are the events that lead to Zeno's arrest in Bruges. A young monk named Cyprian, who assists Zeno in the dispensary, tries to lure him to join in the clandestine meetings of several young monks with a girl of good family and her servant. Their orgies involve eating and drinking the consecrated bread and wine and addressing each other in the language of a heretical sect that Zeno thought had been suppressed years earlier. Zeno is arrested on false testimony obtained from Cyprian under torture. Though his judges do not credit Zeno's participation in the debauchery, his revelation of his true identity enables them to charge him with the authorship of heretical books. Zeno reflects more than once on the special severity which the Church reserves for sexual offenses, and, as one of Yourcenar's bisexuals, he is particularly struck by the fact that the punishment for homosexual activity is the same as that for heresy.

The triangle is completed by the figurative linking of sex with alchemy: "The abandoned underground room [in which the monks and the girls were accustomed to meet] was truly a magic chamber; the great flame of carnal desire had power to transmute everything, as did the fire of the alchemist's furnace."

The Abyss is a remarkable example of the kind of historical novel in which the past is clearly related to present realities. It reflects some of the most pressing problems of modern life. In Zeno's world, war rather than peace is the norm, oppressive institutions threaten personal liberties, and change has begun to proceed too rapidly to be readily integrated. The enormously wealthy banking families that have sprung up are "a greater danger to the established order of things than the infidel Turk, or the peasants in revolt"; they are effecting a radical shift in the basis of power. The problems of industrialization and automation are foreshadowed in the passages concerning certain mechanical looms, which in his youth Zeno helped to design and which, instead of easing the lot of the workers, facilitate their exploitation by the owners. Late in life, Zeno realizes that he shares in the guilt for human suffering: As "any other artificer would have done," he sold his formula for liquid fire to the Emir Noureddin. The passage points directly to the ethical problems of individual responsibility that are raised about modern scientific research. Zeno foresees the possibility that "some Phaeton could one day set fire to the earth of his own accord. . . . Who knows but what some baneful comet will emerge one day from our alembics?" His reference to "the stupid and ever-increasing primacy of sheer numbers" is a warning of the dangers of overpopulation. There is even a reference to the theory of relativity when Zeno imagines roads in time like those in space.

Most reviewers judged *The Abyss* a lesser achievement than *Memoirs of Hadrian*. Perhaps it is less accessible in some ways. The lack of a prominent love interest may disappoint some readers, and its vision is, without doubt, a dark and pessimistic one. The narrative line in the earlier novel is a fairly straightforward, chronological one, whereas *The Abyss* tends more toward a fragmented, elliptical, and discontinuous presentation, especially in the descriptions of Zeno's travels. An episode may at first be only sketched or alluded to, with the details filled in later. The sense of disunity that this may create for the hasty reader is exacerbated by the fact that several times in the novel the focus switches to experiences of other characters in which Zeno has little or no part. Such is the episode of the Anabaptists in Münster. The thematic relevance of that chapter, however, is not hard to see, and the same can be said for other scenes that might at first appear to be digressions. Throughout the novel, the author's vivid imagination is controlled by a coherent intelligence. On its own terms, *The Abyss* is a notable achievement, with aims and virtues different from those of *Memoirs of Hadrian*.

John Michael Walsh

OTHER MAJOR WORKS

SHORT FICTION: *La Mort conduit l'attelage*, 1934; *Nouvelles orientales*, 1938 (*Oriental Tales*, 1985).

PLAYS: *Électre: Ou, La Chute des masques*, pb. 1954 (*Electra: Or, The Fall of the Masks*, 1984); *Rendre à César*, pb. 1961 (*Render unto Caesar*, 1984); *Le Mystère d'Alceste*, pb. 1963; *Qui n'a pas son Minotaure?* pb. 1963 (*To Each His Minotaur*, 1984); *Théâtre*, pb. 1971 (partial trans. *Plays*, 1984).

POETRY: *Le Jardin des chimères*, 1921; *Les Dieux ne sont pas morts*, 1922; *Feux*, 1936 (*Fires*, 1981); *Les Charités d'Alcippe et autres poèmes*, 1956 (*The Alms of Alcippe*, 1982).

NONFICTION: *Pindare*, 1932; *Les Songes et les sorts*, 1938 (*Dreams and Destinies*, 1999); *Sous bénéfice d'inventaire*, 1962 (*The Dark Brain of Piranesi and Other Essays*, 1984); *Souvenirs pieux*, 1974; *Archives du Nord*, 1977; *Les Yeux ouverts: Entretiens avec Matthieu Galey*, 1980 (*With Open Eyes: Conversations with Matthieu Galey*, 1984); *Mishima: Ou, La Vision du vide*, 1980 (*Mishima: A Vision of the Void*, 1986); *Le Temps, ce grand sculpteur*, 1983 (*That Mighty Sculptor, Time*, 1988); *La Voix des choses*, 1987.

TRANSLATIONS: *Les Vagues*, 1937 (of Virginia Woolf's *The Waves*); *Ce que savait Maisie*, 1947 (of Henry James's *What Maisie Knew*); *Présentation critique de Constantin Cavafy*, 1958 (of Constantine Cavafy's poetry); *Fleuve profond, sombre rivière*, 1964 (spirituals); *Présentation critique d'Hortense Flexner*, 1969 (poetry); *La Couronne et la lyre*, 1979 (selection of Greek poetry); *Le Coin des "Amen,"* 1983 (James Baldwin); *Blues et gospels*, 1984.

MISCELLANEOUS: *Œuvres romanesques*, 1982.

BIBLIOGRAPHY

Farrell, C. Frederick, and Edith R. Farrell. *Marguerite Yourcenar in Counterpoint*. Lanham, Md.: University Press of America, 1983. An introductory study of Yourcenar's novels and essays, with a biographical note, chronology, and bibliography.

Frederick, Patricia E. *Mythic Symbolism and Cultural Anthropology in Three Early Works of Marguerite Yourcenar: "Nouvelles orientales," "Le Coup de grâce," "Comme l'eau qui Coule."* Lewiston: Edwin Mellen Press, 1995. Concentrates mainly on Yourcenar's short fiction, but the introduction and conclusion contain valuable insights into all of her writing. Includes notes and bibliography.

Horn, Pierre. *Marguerite Yourcenar*. Boston: Twayne, 1985. A reliable introductory study, with a biographical chapter, two chapters on *Memoirs of Hadrian*, a chapter on autobiographical works, and another on writing in other genres. Provides chronology, notes, and an annotated bibliography.

Howard, Joan E. *From Violence to Vision: Sacrifice in the Works of Marguerite Yourcenar*. Carbondale: Southern Illinois University Press, 1992. Chapters on all the major fictional works, with notes and bibliography.

Savignau, Josyane. *Marguerite Yourcenar: Inventing a Life*. Translated by John E. Howard. Chicago: University of Chicago Press, 1993. A very reliable and well annotated biography which also examines the significance of her contributions to litearture. Family tree, notes, and bibliography.

Shurr, Georgia Hooks. *Marguerite Yourcenar: A Reader's Guide*. Lanham, Md.: University Press of America, 1987. Two chapters on Yourcenar's experimental fiction, her fictional studies of politics, a chapter on *Memoirs of Hadrian*, and a chapter on women in Yourcenar's fiction. Includes a chronology, notes, a bibliography of books and articles about Yourcenar, and a bibliography of Yourcenar's works in English translation.

Z

ÉMILE ZOLA

Born: Paris, France; April 2, 1840
Died: Paris, France; September 28, 1902

PRINCIPAL LONG FICTION

La Confession de Claude, 1865 (*Claude's Confession*, 1882)

Le Vœu d'une morte, 1866 (*A Dead Woman's Wish*, 1902)

Les Mystères de Marseille, 1867 (*The Flower Girls of Marseilles*, 1888; also as *The Mysteries of Marseilles*, 1895)

Thérèse Raquin, 1867 (English translation, 1881)

Madeleine Férat, 1868 (English translation, 1880)

La Fortune des Rougon, 1871 (*The Rougon-Macquart Family*, 1879; also as *The Fortune of the Rougons*, 1886)

La Curée, 1872 (*The Rush for the Spoil*, 1886; also as *The Kill*, 1895)

Le Ventre de Paris, 1873 (*The Markets of Paris*, 1879; also as *Savage Paris*, 1955)

La Conquête de Plassans, 1874 (*The Conquest of Plassans*, 1887; also as *A Priest in the House*, 1957)

La Faute de l'abbé Mouret, 1875 (*Albine: Or, the Abbé's Temptation*, 1882; also as *Abbé Mouret's Transgression*, 1886)

Son Excellence Eugène Rougon, 1876 (*Clorinda: Or, The Rise and Reign of His Excellency Eugène Rougon*, 1880; also as *His Excellency*, 1897)

L'Assommoir, 1877 (English translation, 1879; also as *The Dram-Shop*, 1897)

Une Page d'amour, 1878 (*Hélène: A Love Episode*, 1878, also as *A Love Affair*, 1957)

Nana, 1880 (English translation, 1880)

Pot-Bouille, 1882 (*Piping Hot*, 1924)

Au bonheur des dames, 1883 (*The Bonheur des Dames*, 1883; also as *The Ladies' Paradise*, 1883)

La Joie de vivre, 1884 (*Life's Joys*, 1884; also as *Zest for Life*, 1955)

Germinal, 1885 (English translation, 1885)

L'Œuvre, 1886 (*His Masterpiece*, 1886; also as *The Masterpiece*, 1946)

La Terre, 1887 (*The Soil*, 1888; also as *Earth*, 1954)

Le Rêve, 1888 (*The Dream*, 1888)

La Bête humaine, 1890 (*Human Brutes*, 1890; also as *The Human Beast*, 1891)

L'Argent, 1891 (*Money*, 1891)

La Débâcle, 1892 (*The Downfall*, 1892)

Le Docteur Pascal, 1893 (*Doctor Pascal*, 1893; previous 20 novels [*La Fortune des Rougon* through *Docteur Pascal*] collectively known as *Les Rougon-Macquart* [*The Rougon-Macquart Family*])

Lourdes, 1894 (English translation, 1894)

Rome, 1896 (English translation, 1896)

Paris, 1898 (English translation, 1897, 1898 previous 3 novels collectively known as *Les Trois Villes*)

Fécondité, 1899 (*Fruitfulness*, 1900)

Travail, 1901 (*Work*, 1901)

Vérité, 1903 (*Truth*, 1903 previous 3 novels collectively known as *Les Quatre Evangiles*)

OTHER LITERARY FORMS

Émile Zola is remembered today chiefly as a prolific novelist and as the outspoken defender of Captain Alfred Dreyfus, who had been falsely sentenced for disclosing French military secrets to German authorities. This defense reached its apex in an open letter to the President of the French Republic. (Georges Clemenceau, editor of *L'Aurore*, the journal in which the letter appeared, entitled it "J'accuse.") Although the letter precipitated Zola's trial for libel and his exile to England, it helped bring about Dreyfus's pardon in 1899 and his ultimate exoneration in 1906. While Zola was praised as a man of courage and honesty for his role in the Dreyfus Affair, he had already gained national and international renown for his work as a novelist. His literary reputation rests solidly upon his fiction, especially upon the multivolume *The Rougon-Macquart Family.*

Zola had first intended, however, to be a poet. Having come under the influence of Alfred de Musset while a schoolboy, Zola wrote several poems, the most notable of which are the three parts of *L'Amoureuse Comédie* (written 1860; the loving comedy). When he showed his poetry to his employer, the publisher Louis Hachette, in 1862, Hachette advised Zola to turn to prose. As a result, Zola wrote his first book of short stories, *Contes à Ninon* (1864; *Stories for Ninon*, 1895), a mixture of highly Romantic tales in the style of Victor Hugo, a story of disillusionment that shares in the dark side of the Romantic tradition, and the satiric "Aventures du grand Sidoine et du petit Médéric," which takes a Voltairean look at the politics of the Second Empire at home and abroad. Some of the attitudes and themes of *Stories for Ninon* anticipate Zola's concerns in *The Rougon-Macquart Family.* This is even more the case with his *Nouveaux Contes à Ninon* (1874; more stories for Ninon), a collection containing several autobiographical pieces, *souvenirs*, and sketches of characters who would appear in one or more of his novels. In addition to these two collections for Ninon, Zola's contribution to the anthology of short fiction *Les Soirées de Médan* (1880), "L'Attaque du moulin" ("The Attack on the Mill"), ranks him as one of the nineteenth century's great storytellers. *Les Soirées de Médan* was inspired by an evening of reminiscing about the Franco-Prussian War and was named for Zola's country house; its publication is an important event in the history of French naturalism, and Zola's particular contribution marks a high point in the development of naturalistic fiction, a point he would surpass with his installment of *The Rougon-Macquart Family* for 1880, *Nana.*

Zola's defense of naturalism as a literary and dramatic theory and practice in several of his mature critical works, principally in *Le Roman expérimental* (1880; *The Experimen-*

tal Novel, 1893), *Les Romanciers naturalistes* (1881; *The Naturalist Novel*, 1964), and *Le Naturalisme au théâtre* (1881; *Naturalism on the Stage*, 1893), reveal him as a deft controversialist who advanced significantly beyond the prorealist posture of his first collection of essays, *Mes haines* (1866; *My Hates*, 1893). This earlier work, a collection of his journalistic efforts and addresses, provides an interesting view of the young Zola forming opinions and points of view that would surface later in his novels and in his criticism as he progressed from an advocate of realism to the leader of the naturalist movement.

Like his poetry, and unlike his criticism and fiction, Zola's dramatic efforts met with little or no success. *Thérèse Raquin* (1873; English translation, 1947), a dramatic presentation of his 1867 novel, was a short-lived failure. A much worse critical reception greeted his *Les Héritiers Rabourdin* (1874; *The Rabourdin*

(Library of Congress)

Heirs, 1893), a reception that united him with the fraternity of Gustave Flaubert, Edmond de Goncourt, Alphonse Daudet, and Ivan Turgenev, who met with Zola once a month in 1874 for a "Dinner of the Hissed Authors." After another of his plays, *Le Bouton de rose* (1878; the rosebud), was judged a complete failure, Zola wisely withdrew from the theater, although the theater greatly attracted him, figured prominently in his critical work, and formed the background against which he set *Nana*.

ACHIEVEMENTS

Hailed as "the French Charles Dickens" and, in the funeral eulogy delivered by Anatole France at the Montmartre cemetery, as "a moment of human conscience," Zola claims many achievements, the foremost of which are his place as a great master of French fiction and his campaign to defend Dreyfus. Zola spoke to the people of Paris about their lives, conditions, aspirations, dreams, and failures; he also spoke out, in their hearing, about the injustice perpetrated upon Dreyfus and the whitewash of injustice by officialdom—and he suffered self-imposed exile for his outspokenness. He achieved a kind of heroic status, then, by a prodigious literary output and by his courage and will to be heard as a citizen.

His passion for truth in the fictional representation of life is fundamental to his theory of realistic treatment that came to be called naturalism. Likewise, his passion for truth in the Dreyfus Affair led him to proclaim in *Le Figaro*, on November 25, 1897, "Truth is on the march, and nothing will stop it." His prediction proved correct; Dreyfus was pardoned in 1899.

Zola's principal achievement is in his advocacy and practice of naturalism. Zola argued for naturalism in the theater as well as in fiction, but while he superbly illustrated that theory in his novels, he did not succeed in doing so in his plays. Zola's dramatic achievement, in fact, lies more in the influence he exerted upon dramatists of his time than in his own work as a playwright. His short fiction is, like the novels, remarkable for its realism and naturalism, although some of the early stories clearly hark back to a fresher, possibly more innocent brand of Roman-

ticism than that for which he is famous. Indeed, realism and naturalism may be seen as hybrids, late flowerings of a decayed Romanticism.

Zola's essays, critiques, and reviews from the 1860's onward, in a wide variety of French journals and in the Russian *Vestnik Evropy*, form another dimension of his achievement as an accomplished chronicler of his own times, a keen observer and acute critic of society, a controversial literary theorist, and a political commentator of acuity and courage.

Largely in consequence of the controversial nature of his fiction, the charges of obscenity that attached to it, and the naturalistic portrayal of humanity, Zola never achieved the one honor to which he aspired, election to the Académie Française, for which he presented his name each year from 1890 on. He was elected president of the Société des Gens de Lettres in April, 1891, and was received into the Légion d'Honneur in 1888. The accounts of Zola's state funeral provide some of the most moving tributes to his achievement as a writer and as an individual. His cortege was greeted by the people of Pariswith cries of "Germinal!" and "Glory to Zola!" Anatole France's eulogy provoked great applause. Six years later, in June, 1908, Zola's ashes were removed from Montmartre in a formal public ceremony and placed in the Panthéon alongside the remains of Voltaire, Jean-Jacques Rousseau, and Hugo; this ceremony raised again the controversies surrounding the Dreyfus case and inflamed public opinion on both sides of the issue: As in life, so well beyond his death, Zola remained and still remains a figure of controversy, not only for his role in the Dreyfus Affair but also for the trenchancy of his writing. Zola had also seized the consciousness and imagination of the French in other ways, as Marc Bernard illustrates: During his lifetime, such articles as clay pipes, dinner plates, jewelry, pens, and statuettes bore the likenesses of his characters and of Zola himself, all of which added to the folklore of a living legend.

BIOGRAPHY

Born in Paris on April 2, 1840, Émile Zola was the only child of a French mother, Émilie-Aurélie

Aubert, and an Italian father, Francesco Zola. The Zolas moved to Aix-en-Provence, where Francesco was engaged to work on the muncipality's water supply system. Upon his father's premature death in 1847, Émile and his mother began a series of moves to ever less expensive housing, first in Aix and later in Paris. Zola's childhood friends from the Pension Notre-Dame and the Collège Bourbon, Philippe Solari, Marius Roux, Baptistin Baille, and Paul Cézanne, proved to be lifelong friends, and the countryside of Provence, in all its variety, remained in Zola's memory and consciousness long after he moved to Paris in 1858, appearing in many of his novels.

The move to Paris was a major turning point in Zola's life, and the transplantation from rustic Provence to the teeming streets of the city proved difficult. Having failed his *baccalauréat* examination in August and again in November of 1859, Zola appears to have lost interest in further attempts to earn the diploma and in further education, possibly in part because he lacked the money to continue his studies. The period from 1858 to 1862 is not a well-documented one in Zola's life, though some of his early poetry, short stories, and an unfinished play date from this period. The chronic poverty the Zolas faced prompted Émile to try his hand at clerking on the Paris docks in 1860. The same year, Zola had his first love affair, one that cured him, when it ended early in 1861 in disillusionment, of some of his Romanticism and brought him a poverty of a different sort. He finally secured a position with the publishing firm of Hachette in 1862 and was soon promoted to the advertising department by Louis Hachette, who also gave him the sound advice that he should pursue prose rather than poetry as his métier. While Zola was composing the last of his *Stories for Ninon*, his friend Paul Cézanne, the Impressionist painter, made several trips to Paris, taking Zola to see the famous Salon des Refusés of 1863 and introducing him to Gabrielle-Eléonore-Alexandrine Meley, who soon became Zola's mistress and, in 1870, his wife.

In the early 1860's, Zola also became a *chroniqueur* and literary critic for such publications as *Le Petit Journal*, *Le Courrier du monde*, and *Le Salut*

public of Lyons. Later in the decade, beginning in 1866, he wrote for *L'Événement illustré* and, subsequently, for a number of other journals, such as *La Revue contemporaine*, *Le Gaulois*, *La Tribune*, *Le Rappel*, *La Cloche*, and *Le Sémaphore de Marseille*. By the time he published the first novels of *The Rougon-Macquart Family*, in 1871, he had established himself not only as a controversial novelist but also as a critic and social commentator of acknowledged force and insight. In one of his more notable reviews, he defended a work many found indefensible, the Goncourt brothers' *Germinie Lacerteux* (1865), and praised its extreme realism in depicting the more depraved elements of human life with absolute honesty. This defense of realism and his emphasis on the validity of a writer's individual vision of life take on central roles in Zola's own practice as a novelist.

Zola's first novel, *Claude's Confession*, came under attack for its grim realism in the portrayal of poverty, the sordid side of bohemian life, and the disillusionment of a love affair that cannot succeed. Another early novel, *Thérèse Raquin*, is fully within the naturalistic mode; hailed by some as his early masterpiece, it brought him wide recognition as a serious novelist. *Madeleine Férat* added to his reputation as a forceful writer but fell short of the standard he had set in *Thérèse Raquin*. By the time *Thérèse Raquin* was published, Zola had resigned from Hachette and planned to live as a writer, proposing to write two novels a year to complete a series of ten novels that would incorporate the varied influences of heredity and environment upon his characters.

Embarked on this venture to write the natural and social history of a family under the Second Empire—a series that would extend to twenty novels over the next twenty-five years—Zola, however, did not confine himself to writing novels. Shortly after his marriage in 1870 to Alexandrine and the publication of the first serial installment of *The Fortune of the Rougons*, the Franco-Prussian War began (July 19, 1870), and Zola spoke out against the policies of Napoleon III to find himself charged with inciting others to civil disobedience. Although the events of 1870 resulted in the abandonment of the case against him, Zola's frank opposition to official policies and governmental injustice did not abate and would resurface in the 1890's. Zola left Paris for Marseilles in September, 1870; began a short-lived journal there with Marius Roux; served for a time as secretary to Glais-Bizoin, a member of the Government of National Defense at Bordeaux; and returned to Paris in time to witness and chronicle the Civil War of the Commune, which officially began on March 18, 1871.

With the publication of *The Fortune of the Rougons*, Zola's own fortune turned, and he became an even more controversial and respected force in Parisian literary circles. His own circle included Gustave Flaubert, Alphonse Daudet, Ivan Turgenev, Edmond de Goncourt, Paul Alexis, and Joris-Karl Huysmans, among others—writers who shaped the literary consciousness of the late nineteenth century in France and abroad. Zola's novelistic success in the 1870's reached its peak with his *succès de scandale, L'Assommoir*, a work that shocked the literary establishment with its intense, unrelieved portrayal of the working class. The volley of criticism aimed at Zola for what many mistakenly took to be his deliberate denunciation of the Parisian workers not only provoked controversy but also helped sales of the book. Zola received recognition as the author of a grim masterpiece and great financial rewards once Charpentier started paying him royalties; in all, about 91,000 copies were printed between 1877 and 1881. Zola's financial success allowed him to purchase a property at Médan, where he spent much of his time writing when he was not in Paris, turning out novel after novel until he surpassed *L'Assommoir* with what many consider to be his greatest work, *Germinal*.

In the late 1880's, Zola entered into the sort of relationship that is at the disillusioning center of much of his fiction and of which he had written with considerable distaste: In 1888, he took as his mistress a woman half his age whom his wife had employed as a seamstress, Jeanne Rozerot, with whom he had two children, Denise and Jacques. Zola's union with Rozerot lasted for the remaining fourteen years of his life, although he remained married to and continued

to live with Alexandrine, who, though furious when she discovered the affair, took legal action after Zola's death so that his children could bear his name. His liaison with Rozerot profoundly altered his life in many regards, generally for the better; it brought him, in addition to a happy, satisfying relationship and rejuvenation, renewed inspiration to complete the remaining four volumes of *The Rougon-Macquart Family*, to write the trilogy *Les Trois Villes*, and to write three of the projected "Four Gospels" of *Les Quatre Evangiles*. As Elliott Grant has written, Zola's association with Rozerot became "something fine and beautiful"; in fact, Rozerot became the model for feminine virtue and positive female qualities in Zola's later work.

A major event in Zola's public life was his intervention in the Dreyfus Affair, in which Captain Alfred Dreyfus was convicted by a court-martial on trumped-up charges of selling military information to the Germans and was sent to the infamous Devil's Island penal colony in the Caribbean. Zola became his advocate in a series of essays begun in November, 1897, that led to Zola's own trial for libel and his flight to England to avoid imprisonment. After eleven months, new evidence in the Dreyfus case made it appear likely that Zola could return to France; Dreyfus was pardoned in 1899 and, finally, rehabilitated in 1906. By the time of this last event, Zola was dead, asphyxiated by coal dust from a defective fireplace flue on September 28, 1902; some have suggested that the flue was blocked by anti-Dreyfusards bent upon assassinating Zola. All of Paris, including Dreyfus, mourned him in a public funeral on October 5; nearly six years later, his ashes were transferred to the Panthéon. Zola was survived by his wife and by Jeanne Rozerot and their children, one of whom, Denise Le Blond-Zola, wrote a biography of her father.

ANALYSIS

Émile Zola's novels, from first to last, may be justly characterized as representing his lifelong quest for truth and its exposition—the truth of human situations and circumstances, of social conditions and of the conventions of his society, of the innermost fears, desires, aspirations, horrors, depravities, and exultations of humanity. As the founder of the naturalist school, Zola attempted to apply the methods of natural science as they emerged in the mid-nineteenth century to the writing of fiction, regarding himself as an "experimental novelist" and "practical sociologist" who took into account both heredity and environment in presenting his characters. Among the notions he espoused and eclectically applied to his own writing were the determinist theories of the critic Hippolyte Taine, Charles Darwin's thoughts on natural selection and evolution, the hypotheses of Dr. Prosper Lucas on heredity, and many other contemporary ideas about physiology, psychology, and positivist philosophy gleaned from varied sources. His literary models, Honoré de Balzac, Flaubert, and Stendhal, predisposed him to write realistic fiction; his scientific studies disposed him to take realism one step further to its logical extension. From all of these studies, he formed a plan to write not the history of an individual but the history of an entire family under the Second Empire of Napoleon III—the scientific study of a family and the effects of his own age upon it, "its breakdown through the ravaging passions of the epoch, and the social and physical action of the environment." This plan is the basis for Zola's outstanding series of novels, *The Rougon-Macquart Family*.

CLAUDE'S CONFESSION

He had published three novels before he began this multivolume series, and these novels contain elements and concerns that would reappear in his later work; indeed, they form a prelude, however tentative, to *The Rougon-Macquart Family*. His first novel, *Claude's Confession*, is an autobiographical inner quest for the true meaning of experience, experience that is presented in the grim and somber tones of Zola's own life and that includes abject material poverty and an emotional poverty resulting from an improbable and impossible love affair that the critic Angus Wilson and others suggest was an attempt on Zola's part to reclaim a young prostitute. The next of these three novels, *Thérèse Raquin*, explores human motivation from the perspective of lust, murder, remorse, and suicide. Not unlike Flaubert's *Ma-*

dame Bovary (1857), *Thérèse Raquin* is a scientific study of the temperaments of persons dominated by "nerves and blood" (Zola's phrase), persons who wantonly satisfy their lust for each other, commit murder to that end, are haunted by the horror of their actions, and finally, with all fleshly desire dead between them, commit double suicide. *Madeleine Férat* is as bleak and as obsessed with sex as the first two novels, but it is much more artificially contrived than its predecessors and transgresses the bounds of probability as Zola attempts to illustrate a suspect physiological theory by hinging the novel's action on a series of unlikely coincidences.

THE FORTUNE OF THE ROUGONS

Zola's major novelistic enterprise, the fictive history of the Second Empire and of the Rougon-Macquart tribe, begins with Louis-Napoleon's *coup d'état* late in 1851 and with the ancestry and relations of the clan whose story Zola would unfold over the course of more than two decades. *The Fortune of the Rougons* is set in Plassans (Aix-en-Provence, Zola's boyhood home) and recounts both the defeat of Republican resistance to the coming Empire and the idyllic but tragically doomed love of Silvère and Miette against a background of the grasping, manipulative, and acquisitive actions of the Rougons and of the Bonapartists, who create an empire predicated upon the slaughter of the innocents. In Zola's second installment, naturalistic excess triumphs as Zola presents Aristide Rougon (who consented to the killing of Silvère in the first novel) as a money-mad speculator whose rush for the spoils in *The Kill* typifies the graft and corruption possible in the vast urban-renewal projects directed by Baron Haussmann in the late nineteenth century. Social corruption is at the novel's core, a corruption that permeates every level of society but that is fully developed in the lives of the great middle class, the bourgeoisie.

Another sort of corruption is the target of Zola's dual focus, the moral corruption that complements the speculative morass; in this case, it is the deliberate, premeditated, and shocking act of incest between Aristide Rougon's wife, Renée, and his son, Maxime. (In some of his descriptions, Zola appears to have been carried away by the voluptuousness of his own creation and truly exceeds the bounds of any possible convention or propriety as he debases the Phaedra theme and makes it utterly sordid.) Aristide, in need of Renée's signature and agreement, remains complaisant in the face of her incest, thus subordinating any possible moral consideration to a merely financial one.

SAVAGE PARIS

Savage Paris is, like its predecessors, a polemical sociopolitical inquiry into the war between the haves and the have-nots. Set in one of the new wonders of reconstructed Paris, Les Nouvelles Halles (today, Les Halles Centrales), the novel places the poor, the lower classes, the politically alienated on a symbolic food chain that puts them at the mercy of their natural predators, the rapacious middle class. While *Savage Paris* is a novel of considerable originality, it ranks well below *The Kill* and, although ample in its descriptive passages, is decidedly thin in respect to plot.

Three more novels followed the first three before Zola was to achieve recognition and success with *L'Assommoir: The Conquest of Plassans, Abbé Mouret's Transgression*, and *His Excellency*. In these novels, Zola applied his formulaic notions of heredity and environment to diverse situations. *The Conquest of Plassans* continues the examination of provincial France that the first novel had begun by presenting the political intrigues that turn Plassans from a Legitimist to a Bonapartist town and ecclesiastical intrigues that complement the political and show the priest, Faujas, undertaking other conquests. *Abbé Mouret's Transgression* explores the religious questions of the era; here, the conflict between nature and religion assumes mythic rather than naturalistic dimensions. *His Excellency* is Zola's contribution to the political novel in France, a genre Anthony Trollope perfected in England, and contains a biting satire on the Empire, the government, and its minions; it is also, on one level, a *roman à clef* in which the figures of Napoleon III's regime could find themselves unflatteringly portrayed. Taken together, then, the first six novels of *The Rougon-Macquart Family* represent a prodigious effort on Zola's part and form a fascinating group that brings before us many aspects of the Empire and many character types common to it.

As artistically successful as these works are, the popular success of which he dreamed and for which he labored continued to elude Zola until the publication in 1877 of *L'Assommoir*. In that novel, Zola presented the Parisian proletariat exactly as he saw it; indeed, *L'Assommoir* is virtually the first French novel to do so. The reactions of the mainstream critical community and of the general public were similar: outrage at the naturalistic, despair-ridden depiction of the working class with an honesty and frankness unparalleled by any previous work. Responses to the novel remain divided: Some deem the work a bitter and bleak indictment of the proletariat; others agree that Zola presents a bleak but sympathetic view of the workers. One may approach the novel on many levels: as an exposé of the pervasive, devastating, and debilitating power of drink, as a sociological study of the wearying Parisian working life, as a character study of the psychology of human frailty and weakness and of the small comforts that both relieve an otherwise barren existence and hasten its end. Death in all its brutal, naked force, resulting from exhaustion through work and poverty, is never far from the novel's characters; death is, in fact, a logical and predictable end to, almost a relief from, the already dehumanized existence that Gervaise Macquart and her husband, Coupeau, endure as their lot. The deaths of Gervaise and her husband reinforce in strikingly poignant ways the futility of their lives, their impossible aspirations and broken dreams, and the inexorable fate stemming from the irremediable condition of the poor.

L'ASSOMMOIR

One useful way of considering Zola's artistry in *L'Assommoir* is to reflect on the work's structure; another is to examine its symbolism; a third is to focus upon the highly wrought characters it contains. While exploring these three elements represents only a partial foray into this highly complex novel, it does provide some insight into Zola's intentions and achievement. Unlike several of his earlier works, *L'Assommoir* is not full of varied themes, multiple subplots, and a wide range of characters; rather, it has a single emphasis (on Gervaise), relatively few important characters, and a line of dramatic action that is classical in its simplicity. Gervaise's rising fortunes reach an apex when, through an initially fortunate marriage with Coupeau and the kindness of a shy admirer, she finds her hard work rewarded and becomes the proprietress of a small laundry business with employees of her own. Coupeau's literal fall from a high building (and his consequent inability to work) results in Gervaise's metaphoric fall, a downward journey that is entirely unrelieved and ends only as she achieves the oblivion of a death she surely sought. The turning point, Zola clearly and heavy-handedly points out, occurs one afternoon in the laundry, when Coupeau, having been encouraged in his self-indulgence by Gervaise, turns up drunk, falls over the mounds of clothes, and insists upon kissing her. That kiss marks the beginning of the couple's decline. Gradually, Gervaise yields to the temptation of drink in Colombe's Bar, where the still appears to be a living, monstrous thing that dispenses poison.

The still is one among many symbols heralding Gervaise's end; like it, other objects seem to assume lives of their own within the novel's pages. Zola uses the physical environment, for example, to signify the impact of the exterior landscape upon the interior landscape of his characters. From her first small apartment in Paris, to the laundry room where she works, to the bewildering surroundings of the Louvre, to the succession of buildings in which she lives while she is on her downward spiral, each worse than the last, the physical environment triumphs over Gervaise and modifies her perceptions of life and its meaning. Apart from the most obvious and powerful symbol in the work, the still, another symbol contends for notice: clothes. The heaps and mounds of clothes in the laundry rooms Gervaise inhabits, her unending task of cleaning them, and the disreputable state of her own attire after her fall combine to reinforce the fetid atmosphere of the novel and to form the impression that this atmosphere is inescapable.

Above all, at the core of the novel are Zola's characters. Gervaise's first lover, Lantier, abandons her and their two children as the novel opens, only to reappear and be invited by the sodden Coupeau to lodge with them. Lantier becomes a true *copain* for Coupeau, a drinking buddy whom Gervaise must also support by her hard work and who, predictably, becomes master of the house and, eventually, of Gervaise. Coupeau himself is a case study in frailty who succumbs to his first adversity, the fall, continues through a deterioration of will, and finally abandons himself to drinking away all of Gervaise's earnings and the scant resources their goods bring in from pawnbrokers. He ultimately suggests that Gervaise gain money to satisfy his addiction to alcohol and her own newly acquired drinking habit through prostitution. She has grown so slovenly and has so aged prematurely that no man will have her. Finally, one of the men she attempts to interest, the blacksmith Gouget, who had loaned her the money to set up her own laundry, takes pity on what she has become. She will eat his food but only out of animal instinct; she will neither stay with him nor seek to infect his life with hers.

The central character is Gervaise, whose fortunes form the locus of narration, whose history is the subject of the work, and through whose eyes we see most in the novel. As one example of the intractability of some of Zola's thinking about heredity and environment, she is doomed to the unhappiness he provides for her; as a character whose good intentions are subverted by fate and foiled by chance, she is the object of pity; as a representative of the working class whose best of many dwelling places is in a slum and whose social position can be altered only for the worse, she exists as an indictment of the ruling forces of the Second Empire, the great bourgeoisie, whose members simply ignored the plight of workers and the problems of those below their social level. It is not without significance that a character who receives minor but nevertheless important attention in *L'Assommoir*, Nana, would be the focal point of yet another novel in Zola's series and would provide him with another vehicle for raising similar issues concerning the gulf between the social classes.

NANA

If Zola astounded Paris with *L'Assommoir*, he outdid himself with a second masterpiece, *Nana*. A novel that Zola had planned to write for several years, *Nana* was greeted, like *L'Assommoir*, as a work of great obscenity, in this case for its candid treatment of what Zola termed *la vraie fille* (the true prostitute), who makes her life in the theater. Like the Goddess of Reason in earlier Republican days, Nana assumes a symbolic value in the novel, to become, as we first see her and as she develops, a Venus who not only offers the joy and excitement of sexual abandon but also exercises formidable destructive power, a femme fatale who brings ruin in her wake, ruin that involves the Empire's aristocrats and financiers. In some sense, this seductive and destructive offspring of Gervaise Macquart may represent the revenge of workers upon their oppressors. Nana's dual nature does, in many senses, mirror Zola's own ambivalent attitudes toward sexuality present in most of his works (certainly in the novels he wrote before his transforming affair with Jeanne Rozerot brought him joy without apparent remorse or destruction). Commenting on the mythic dimension of the novel, Flaubert was quick to point out the work's thorough grounding in the actual world of the Second Empire and characterized the work as Babylonian, something not unlike his own attempt to "fix a mirage" in *Salammbô* (1862), in this case a mirage that springs from and undercuts the hothouse world of the grisette.

The novel's mythic aspect is only one facet of this highly controversial study of the Second Empire's decadence. Nana herself assumes mythic proportions in the book's first chapter, as she emulates Venus rising from the sea with her tresses as her only veil. As she becomes Venus on-stage, so she becomes Venus off-stage, capturing the attention and wealth of Steiner the banker, Count Muffat, a chamberlain of the Second Empire, and several others. There are two sides to this Venus, however. She can please but she can also conquer. The destroying Venus is announced early in the novel, when, having captured the attention of all in Bordenave's theater with her considerable beauty, Nana smiles "the smile of a man-eater." This clearly signals that the major theme of the work, sex as personified in Nana, is not pleasurable but is, instead, compulsive, sordid, furtive, unsatisfying, and arid. To the extent that this is so, sex itself is mythologized and removed from truly human experience to an extrahuman, subhuman plane.

Like *L'Assommoir*, *Nana* has a simple architectural principle: The action consistently rises throughout the novel until immediately before its, and its heroine's, end. Although Gervaise's fall is a long, gradual, and painful one, Nana's is sudden; though fortuitous, it is quite credible. The principle at work, with some minor variation, is to show Nana's rise in relation to the characters present in the first chapter as they seduce or are seduced by her. One chief element the characters share is their dehumanization and reduction to a merely animal state by a Venus-turned-Circe. The most notable example of this transformation is Count Muffat, whose persistence in the face of Nana's rebuffs finally wins him the prize he so intently desires. The progress of Muffat's degradation is a simulacrum of the degradation of the Second Empire's officialdom, of which he is both member and symbol. At one point, Nana forces him into a naked romp in which he must pretend to be a bear, a horse, and a dog; she takes great delight in demeaning him and then of making fun of his unattractive nakedness. A final degradation occurs when Muffat discovers Nana in bed with his father-in-law, a marquis. Throughout the novel, Nana allows herself to be used by a variety of men and also uses them as an antidote to boredom, poverty, and a life in the streets. Zola characterizes her by using a variety of animal images ranging from the tigress man-eater of the first chapter to the horse named after her that wins the Grand Prix de Paris. All of these images reinforce the subhuman depiction of the denizens of Second-Empire Paris.

In the larger context of the Empire's history that Zola chronicles in *The Rougon-Macquart Family*, Nana becomes a symbol of the Empire's decline, her life ending as the government is about to crumble. She breathes her last as an ugly, scabrous smallpox victim in a squalid Parisian hospital while the first salvos of the Franco-Prussian War penetrate Paris. Zola is intent, in his skillful but sometimes too obvious use of myth and symbol, upon probing the frailty of his characters and upon relating that pervasive frailty to the decay and debilitating weakness of the much-hated Second Empire.

GERMINAL

L'Assommoir and *Nana* are universally acknowledged masterpieces upon which Zola's reputation as
a novelist of the first order rests. A third work, *Germinal*, is still, as it was in his own time, acknowledged to be Zola's supreme novelistic achievement
(some would add *Earth*, his novel of peasant life, as
his fourth major achievement in this series). *Germinal* is a brilliant, if depressing, depiction of a facet of
proletarian life quite different from that which he
portrayed in *L'Assommoir*. Zola set *Germinal* in the
mining town of Montsou, and in it he scrutinizes the
issues of the exploitation of workers, attempts at collective action on their part in a bitter strike not uncharacteristic of the era, and the inevitable destruction that awaits them in what becomes an epic class
struggle between labor and capital. Zola's is one
of the earliest and relatively few nineteenth century
novels that examines Marxist thought (embodied in
Étienne Lantier, a son of Gervaise Macquart) in more
than a superficial and partisan way. While he takes
great pains to present the arguments of the mine owners (who are absentee landlords) and of the mine's
manager, Zola is emotionally and intellectually on
the side of the workers. As in *Savage Paris*, Zola pits
the haves against the have-nots and presents their
personal dramas with heavy satire of the former
and great sympathy and sensitivity toward the latter,
a sympathy that informs all of his treatments of
working-class life.

Other important novels in *The Rougon-Macquart
Family* are *Earth*, a naturalistic paean to the love of
the land and the love of a woman; *The Human Beast*,
Zola's most pessimistic work, which treats the railroads and the judicial system while presenting raw
human passion; and *The Downfall*, the great war
novel he had planned for many years, in which he
succeeds in illustrating the utter confusion and horror
of war by fictionalizing the fall of Napoleon III at Se-
dan and the ensuing Civil War of the Commune.
When he finished *The Rougon-Macquart Family*
with *Doctor Pascal* in 1893, Zola had chronicled, in
an unsystematic way, the history of the Second Empire from its inglorious inception to its ignominious
demise and had developed an entire world populated by representatives of every class and segment of
French society. This panoramic epic of his own times
remains as an enduring literary monument to Zola's
genius and to his passionate quest for truth. He was
never to match, in his later fiction, the intensity and
literary worth of *The Rougon-Macquart Family*.

Zola's later works, *Les Trois Villes* and *Les Quatre
Evangiles*, while containing some brilliant writing
and some hard-hitting social criticism, on the whole
fail as novels because their propaganda for a Socialist
utopia overshadows the artistry Zola had brought to
bear upon the ethical, social, political, and philosophical concerns in *The Rougon-Macquart Family*.
As Wilson observes, Zola's happiness with Jeanne
Rozerot meant for him a gradual slipping away of his
fears and horrors and the consequent decline in the
need to sublimate their expression, and his physical
paternity "was undoubtedly the precursor of literary
sterility."

John J. Conlon

OTHER MAJOR WORKS

SHORT FICTION: *Contes à Ninon*, 1864 (*Stories for
Ninon*, 1895); *Esquisses parisiennes*, 1866; *Nouveaux Contes à Ninon*, 1874; *Le Capitaine Burle*,
1882 (*A Soldier's Honor and Other Stories*, 1888);
Naïs Micoulin, 1884; *Contes et nouvelles*, 1928; *Madame Sourdis*, 1929.

PLAYS: *Madeleine*, wr. 1865, pb. 1878; *Thérèse
Raquin*, pr., pb. 1873 (adaptation of his novel; English translation, 1947); *Les Héritiers Rabourdin*, pr.,
pb. 1874 (*The Rabourdin Heirs*, 1893); *Le Bouton de
rose*, pr., pb. 1878; *Théâtre*, pb. 1878; *Renée*, pr., pb.
1887 (adaptation of his novel *La Curée*); *Lazare*, wr.
1893, pb. 1921 (libretto; music by Alfred Bruneau);
Violaine la chevelue, wr. 1897, pb. 1921; *L'Ouragan*,
pr., pb. 1901 (libretto; music by Bruneau); *Sylvanire:
Ou, Paris en amour*, wr. 1902, pb. 1921 (libretto;
music by Robert Le Grand); *L'Enfant-Roi*, pr. 1905
(libretto; music by Bruneau); *Poèmes lyriques*, pb.
1921.

POETRY: *L'Amoureuse Comédie* (wr. 1860; in
Œuvres complètes).

NONFICTION: *Mes haines*, 1866 (*My Hates*, 1893);
Le Roman expérimental, 1880 (*The Experimental*

Novel, 1893); *Documents littéraires*, 1881; *Le Naturalisme au théâtre*, 1881 (*Naturalism on the Stage*,
1893); *Nos auteurs dramatiques*, 1881; *Les Romanciers naturalistes*, 1881 (*The Naturalist Novel*,
1964); *Une Campagne*, 1882; *The Experimental
Novel and Other Essays*, 1893 (includes *The Experimental Novel* and *Naturalism on the Stage*, better
known as *Naturalism in the Theater*); *Nouvell
Campagne*, 1897; *La Vérité en marche*, 1901.

MISCELLANEOUS: *Œuvres complètes*, 1966-1968
(15 volumes).

BIBLIOGRAPHY

Baguley, David, ed. *Critical Essays on Émile Zola*.
Boston: G. K. Hall, 1986. In a lengthy introductory essay, Baguley surveys the range of reaction to Zola's work. The volume itself reprints, in
chronological order, eighteen essays, starting with
an 1868 review of *Thérèse Raquin* entitled "Putrid
Literature." The nineteenth and twentieth essays
were specifically commissioned for this collection. When contrasted with the title of the first selection, that of the twentieth, "Zola: Poet of an
Age of World Destruction and Renewal," gives
some sense of how Zola's reputation has changed
over time. The volume also includes a checklist of
works by Zola, as well as a selected, annotated
bibliography of works about Zola for readers of
English.

Berg, William J., and Laurey K. Martin. *Émile Zola
Revisited*. New York: Twayne, 1992. Focusing on
The Rougon-Macquart Family, this book employs
textual analysis rather than biography to analyze
each of the twenty volumes in Zola's most widely
known series. Berg and Martin also use Zola's
own literary-scientific principles to organize their
study.

Brown, Frederick. *Zola: A Life*. New York: Farrar,
Straus & Giroux, 1995. Any reader who wants a
Zola biography as sweeping and comprehensive
as Zola's own narratives should start here. This
888-page life study includes seventy-six illustrations and a formidable list of sources. A helpful
chronology leads readers into the biographical narrative, which is, despite its length, very engaging.
There can be no last word in biographical studies,
but this book comes close to being definitive.

Hemmings, F. W. J. *The Life and Times of Émile
Zola*. New York: Scribner's, 1977. Venerable Zola
scholar Hemmings produced this short, copiously
illustrated life of Zola as a complement to his
other, more learned work on the great French naturalist. This book can serve as a good introduction
to the life and times of this most sociological of
writers. Hemmings is particularly good at describing how the cross-fertilization between naturalism
in literature and Impressionism in art manifested
itself in Zola's works.

Richardson, Joanna. *Zola*. New York: St. Martin's
Press, 1978. This short, well-written biography
moves along at a fast pace and does a fine job of
relating the details of Zola's life while maintaining
a strong narrative line. A postscript relates what
happened to the other major players in the writer's
life after he was gone. Decidedly non-academic,
Richardson's biography nonetheless includes a
substantial selected bibliography of works by and
about Zola written in French and English.